Encyclopedia of the

AMERICAN LEGISLATIVE SYSTEM

Encyclopedia of the

AMERICAN LEGISLATIVE SYSTEM

Studies of the Principal Structures, Processes, and Policies
of Congress and the State Legislatures
Since the Colonial Era

JOEL H. SILBEY

Editor in Chief

Volume II

CHARLES SCRIBNER'S SONS/NEW YORK
MAXWELL MACMILLAN CANADA/TORONTO
MAXWELL MACMILLAN INTERNATIONAL/NEW YORK OXFORD SINGAPORE SYDNEY

Charles Scribner's Sons   Maxwell Macmillan Canada, Inc.
Macmillan Publishing Company   1200 Eglinton Avenue East

866 Third Avenue   Suite 200
New York, New York 10022   Don Mills, Ontario M3C 3N1

Macmillan Publishing Company is part of the Maxwell Communication Group of
Companies.

Library of Congress Cataloging-in-Publication Data

Encyclopedia of the American legislative system / Joel H. Silbey,
    editor in chief.
        p.   cm.
    Includes bibliographical references.
    ISBN 0-684-19243-8 (set)—ISBN 0-684-19601-8 (vol. 1)—ISBN 0-684-19602-6
    (vol. 2)—ISBN 0-684-19600-X (vol. 3)
    1. Legislative bodies—United States—Encyclopedias. I. Silbey,
Joel H.
JF501.E53   1994
328.73'003—dc20   93-35874
                                                             CIP

1   3   5   7   9   11   13   15   17   19   V/C   20   18   16   14   12   10   8   6   4   2

PRINTED IN THE UNITED STATES OF AMERICA

The paper used in this publication meets the minimum requirements
of American National Standard for Information Sciences—Permanence
of Paper for Printed Library Materials. ANSI Z3948-1984. ∞™

CONTENTS

Volume II

CONTENTS

CONTENTS

Part III

LEGISLATIVE STRUCTURES AND PROCESSES

LEGISLATIVE STRUCTURE AND ITS EFFECTS

Melissa P. Collie

The purpose of this essay is to examine the impact of legislative structure on legislative operations and performance. This purpose presumes two basic questions: What is legislative structure, and what are its effects?

While these questions are easily put, the answers are more challenging to articulate. The challenge arises not from lack of interest in legislative structure nor from lack of intuition as to the possible effects. Since Woodrow Wilson wrote *Congressional Government* in the nineteenth century, scholars have recognized that an understanding of legislative structure is integral to the understanding of how the legislature functions internally, as well as externally in relation to other institutions of government and to the populace itself. Indeed, Wilson's particular insight was to suggest the relationship between the national legislature's internal structure and its operation in the political system as a whole. Moreover, intuition implies that structure makes a difference: Replace a king with a parliament, and the government's yield is likely to change. Whether applied to legislatures or governments themselves, the notion that structure matters is hardly radical and virtually synonymous with the American experience in constitutional democracy, one of the most eloquent testimonies to the presumption of structural effects still being James Madison's logic in *The Federalist,* nos. 46–51. Quite simply, the idea that the structure of an institution has an effect on how it operates and what it produces has always had a warmer reception than the idea that it does not.

What legislative structure is and how it relates to operations and performance is challenging to articulate; depending on the perspective one takes, there are either too many answers or none at all. More than a century after Wilson's work and despite nearly universal acceptance of the notion that legislative structure matters, research has produced surprisingly little consensus beyond the conclusion that it does. To take an example that skirts the problem of defining "structure"—a problem that is far from inconsequential—most scholars agree that a system of committees is a key structural feature of legislatures. Yet disagreements persist on such basic and compelling issues as why committees are important, which committees contribute to the legislative process, whether committees are healthy for the legislature and legislators alike, and whether the committee system itself retards the development of policy that is in the public interest.

Dissent notwithstanding, the time is especially propitious for taking stock of research on legislative structure. One reason is the enhanced attention that structural features of the legislature have received in recent years. According to many scholars, the postbehavioral era (since the mid-1960s) has already proved more hospitable than its predecessor to contemplating issues surrounding the impact of legislative structure. Indeed, postbehavioral inquiry has been represented in some quarters as being almost synonymous with the rediscovery of institutions and institutional analysis. A second reason is that the study of institutional structure has advanced primarily in terms of two quite different and complementary research perspectives, rational choice and organization theory. Like any conceptual framework, each has its strengths and limitations. But their collective impact has been to challenge with theoretical depth and clarity the conventional wisdom about the effect of structure on legislators and the legislature. A third reason is related to the growing interest among political scientists in examining institutional issues at the meeting point of history and politics. For legislative studies, this convergence has meant not only an enhanced sensitivity to the stability and change of legislative structure but also greater attention to its historical forms. While historical research on legislative structure remains overshadowed by theoretical treatments of contemporary institutional features, theoretical exercises must eventually confront the historical example. The likelihood of such exchange is greater now than ever. Taking stock is timely, then, because of the volume of research that has been generated, its theoretical depth and diversity, and, increasingly, its historical consciousness.

There has been no single inspiration behind the development of the scholarly literature generated by this new research on legislative structure. One major stimulus to the focus on structure that now characterizes legislative scholarship was undoubtedly the wave of reforms that occurred in the U.S. Congress during the early 1970s. While several of the most sweeping reforms that were proposed, such as an overhaul of the existing system of standing committees, were not adopted, the debate they generated among congressional members stirred scholars to reexamine traditional assumptions about the stability and effect of the existing structural arrangements within the national legislature.

More generally, however, the new literature has been part of a larger, multidisciplinary renaissance in institution-oriented research. As implied above, such research has been represented frequently as a repudiation of, or at least a most welcome corrective to, behavioralism's allegedly casual treatment of enduring institutional realities. Especially for legislative studies, the focus on structure is said (fortunately) to hark back to the prebehavioral era of studies that documented the formal status of structure and procedure.

While the new research owes something of its genesis to prebehavioral scholarship, too often the link between the two is overstated and its behavioral legacy understated. No doubt, one of the behavioral revolution's effects on legislative scholarship was to relegate the study of legislative structure and procedure to secondary status in favor of the examination of individual and group behavior. While legislative scholars were never wholly inclined to ignore such important structural aspects of legislative life as committees and party leaders, interest in their effects per se was incidental to understanding the roles and patterns of legislators' interactions. Especially influential examples of such research include Richard Fenno's *The Power of the Purse,* Donald Matthews's *U.S.*

Senators and Their World, and *The Legislative System* by John Wahlke, Heinz Eulau, William Buchanan, and LeRoy Ferguson. In addition, institutional structure was seldom explicitly identified as part of the explanation behind legislators' or parties' behavior. Instead, scholars typically looked to outside factors (such as electoral margins and constituency characteristics) to explain legislators' behavior, which occurred by analytic default in something akin to an institutional vacuum.

Yet recent analysis of legislative structure has probed more self-consciously into the causes and effects of institutional structure than its prebehavioral antecedent, which characteristically tended toward a historical, legalistic, and descriptive orientation. It also is less overtly concerned with articulating the normative implications of alternative forms of legislative structure, a tendency that also distinguishes it from prebehavioral research. These same characteristics that mark its departure from the prebehavioral mode of legislative scholarship reflect its connection to the behavioral paradigm. Testifying to its behavioral lineage, research objectives encompass explanation and prediction rather than merely legal and historical description. Likewise, analytic rigor is prized over normative persuasiveness. Indeed, the newest of the "new institutionalism" that now characterizes legislative studies is rooted in the twin goals of understanding how legislative structure affects the operation of the legislature and, in turn, understanding the factors that generate particular legislative structures. In sum, the recent study of legislative structure is better regarded as a marriage of prebehavioral and behavioral research than a celebration of one and a rejection of the other.

It is a marriage that has both sharpened and confused investigations of legislative structure. In the *Handbook of Legislative Research* (Gerhard Loewenberg, Samuel Patterson, and Malcolm Jewell), for example, one of the sixteen articles is devoted explicitly to research on legislative structure under the guise of examining "organizational attributes." Yet another eight focus on aspects of the legislature that many scholars deem structural in character, including committee selection and operation, party organization and leadership, and legislative staff. Additional articles deal with voting and the policymaking process, which are at least directly connected to the structural arrangement of the legislature and, at most, manifestations of it. Thus a consideration of structure penetrates most of the topics in this comprehensive series of articles on legislative research.

The organization of this handbook is a testimony to the difficulties of studying legislatures without addressing structure and of isolating structure from other characteristics of the legislature. The fact that scholars have long recognized the importance of legislative structure is not to say that they have established a definition or even common understanding of what constitutes legislative structure. While a legislative committee is undeniably a structural unit of the legislature, what of a seniority "rule" or ideological voting or deference to policy specialists or a budget timetable? The term *structure* has been adopted flexibly enough; it is not unusual to find, for example, references to the structure of voting or norms or decision-making. Complicating matters is the development of a new nomenclature in rational-choice research that avoids the word structure in favor of "institutions" or "institutional arrangements," even though they include elements of the legislature traditionally understood as structural.

In describing the ways scholars have thought about legislative structure and explored its effects, this essay highlights the concepts and points of dispute that characterize this body of research. It seeks also to identify the impediments to differentiating legislative structure as a phenomenon of analysis and to recognize contending positions on the impact of legislative structure.

In the next two sections, I consider successively how legislative structure is defined in organization theory and rational choice, noting the questions and issues each approach has addressed concerning the study of legislative structure. In each section, assessment of the approach focuses on a key problem that the approach presents for the study of legislative structure. A third section addresses three substantive topics that relate to legislative structure: institutional development, legislative policy-making, and the role of the legislature in American democracy. With regard to each topic, the contribution of organization theory and rational choice is evaluated.

At the outset, it should be noted that organization theory and rational choice are some-

times regarded as complementary, if not incompatible, approaches to the study of legislative (and nonlegislative) politics. This assessment is not surprising in light of the distinct research traditions in which they are rooted. The rational choice perspective has developed within a positivistic research tradition that encompasses mathematical models of social choice and game theory and frequently uses the methods and ideas of microeconomics. Organization theory is also positivistic, but its foundations are more sociologically oriented and tied to structural-functional analysis and the study of large and complex private bureaucracies. Part of my purpose is to pinpoint some of the common themes in the two approaches.

Before considering each perspective, two points are worth bearing in mind. First, neither of these perspectives has by design been developed with reference to a legislature, though some of the more recent work in the rational choice tradition attempts to model features of the U.S. Congress. This fact of importation has meant that "goodness of fit" issues are always a part of the dialogue that surrounds such research. It also means, however, that one assumes that legislatures can be extracted from their culture and tradition, which become irrelevant beyond the extent to which they can be assessed at a higher level of abstraction. Using an example from the rational choice perspective, it is assumed that legislative committee power in the parent chamber is equivalent when comparing legislatures, provided that identical institutional and behavioral assumptions apply regardless of the legislature in question. Likewise, from an organization theory perspective, it is expected that such structural features as the degree to which rules are codified and authority is decentralized can be explained in terms of key features of the environment external to the legislature regardless of the legislature in question.

A second point that deserves mention is that the bulk of work concerning structural features of legislatures is not explicitly phrased in terms of either perspective. Instead, the aim of research is to examine certain concrete structural features, such as the operation of conference committees, with equally concrete questions in mind. Too frequently the result is that theoretical insights, whether from rational choice or organization theory, elude empirical study, a circumstance that also negatively affects the evolution and refinement of theory.

ORGANIZATION THEORY AND LEGISLATIVE STRUCTURE

As Joseph Cooper and David Brady have argued in "Toward a Diachronic Analysis of Congress," one of the most important payoffs to examining legislatures from the perspective of organization theory is the possibility for comparative research. Though their concern is with research on the Congress in different time periods, the point holds for cross-sectional analysis of legislatures as well. That is, by defining legislative structure in more abstract terms at an institutional level, the analyst is in a position to compare and contrast the structural dimensions of legislatures and their relationships to one another and to other nonstructural features of legislatures over time and across legislatures. Organization theory's level of abstraction encourages the analyst to consider the conjunction (or disjunction) of concrete aspects of structure, such as the party system and the committee system, in light of how they contribute to the distribution of power or functional responsibility.

The theoretical import of adopting the approach of organization theory is that such a conceptualization of legislative structure better enables us to come to some understanding of why structures persist or change as well as what their impact in the legislature is. It is a perspective, for example, that invites us to consider not only why legislatures (relative to other institutional forms) have a low tolerance for hierarchy but also why the tolerance for hierarchy differs among legislatures and at various times. A case in point is the U.S. Congress, whose history reflects considerable change over time in the degree to which power has been centralized.

Nonetheless, there have been doubts expressed about the feasibility and analytic tenability of adopting the concepts and insights of organization theory for the purpose of understanding legislative structure. One observation has been that structural changes (such as changes in formal rules) are not necessarily as-

sociated with intended improvements in legislative performance. A variant of this position is that a legislator's preferences exert a more powerful effect than structural components on what happens in the legislature. Another variant is that elections, both as a motivating force among legislators and a personnel selection device for the institution, are more important to the operation of the legislature than structure. A second observation has been that the insights of organization theory, most of which have been derived from analysis of private bureaucracies (that is, private businesses), are hardly applicable to such an institution as a legislature.

Neither of these reservations is as troubling as it might initially appear. To conclude that structural reforms do not always yield the intended consequence is not to conclude that structure has no impact. Even circumstances that suggest that a structural reform has no impact at all do not necessarily undermine the need for structural inquiry. Indeed, such circumstances may imply more about the limitations of our understanding of how structure informs the legislature than about the irrelevance of the legislature's structure. Likewise, to argue that legislators' preferences have a substantial and independent impact on legislative outcomes is not to deny that structure has an impact as well. Indeed, the very fact that all legislators are unlikely to agree on policy ends, not to mention means, suggests that structure can have a profound impact insofar as it introduces (or precludes) forms of bias in collective decision-making. The same may be said for the impact of elections as either a motivating force or a selection mechanism. Whether elections motivate legislators' policy positions or encourage them to favor some policy positions over others, the point is that policy positions are channeled through the legislative structure; collective decisions do not materialize from thin air.

Finally, with regard to organization theory's "goodness of fit" in legislative analysis, the legislature is but one form of institution that may be compared in many ways with other forms of institutions. The fact that a legislature is different from other institutions in certain aspects hardly implies that comparison is fruitless. Such comparison may in fact enhance analytic sensitivity to the strength and rigor of presuppositions and assumptions about how institutional features and performance interact. Indeed, the differences between a legislature and a private bureaucracy are likely to enrich the modelling of organizations instead of rendering the application of such models useless.

Research Issues and Answers

In the language of organization theory, structure is usually understood as the network of relatively durable and formally sanctioned organizational arrangements and relationships. In the early twentieth century German sociologist Max Weber proposed that elements of structure typically include the distribution of authority, interunit communications, functional specialization, and the formal specification of rules and procedures. According to Pradip Khandwalla in *The Design of Organizations,* the distinctive characteristics of each element of organizational structure include the formally sanctioned nature of the relationship, its intended durability, and its use as an administrative instrument for achieving organizational purpose.

Research that has adopted organization theory has strayed to varying degrees from such a standard for distinguishing structure. In general, however, these three characteristics—formality, durability, and instrumentality—are frequently an explicit or implicit part of the definition of structure in the legislative context.

In "Organizational Attributes of Legislative Institutions," by Ronald Hedlund, for example, formality plays a prominent role in defining the structural aspects of legislatures, aspects he maintains are differentiated from other organizational characteristics, including personnel, technology, task, and environment. According to Hedlund, however, structural components of a legislature include its formal features, which are frequently documented, and also rules and procedures, arrangements of power and influence, and the institution's physical setting and history.

In perhaps the most comprehensive statement of how organization theory can inform the study of legislatures, Joseph Cooper's "Congress in Organizational Perspective" cites two forms of legislative structure: an instrumental (or task) structure, which develops in order to produce outputs, and a social structure, which arises around and complements (sometimes displacing functions of) the task structure. Each is supported by a distinct and complementary set of norms. In a later article, "Organization and Innovation in the House of Representatives," Cooper discusses five structural characteristics of the House during the 1970s: a high degree of organizational elaboration and variation, a limited but complex division of task or functional responsibilities, a limited degree of specialized expertise, extensive but irregular formalism, and a limited centralization of power. In other words, the House was divided into a variety of subunits (parties, committees, caucuses, for example), had various but interrelated objectives (including policymaking, oversight, constituency service, representation, and education), was composed of generalists rather than specialists, was governed by an extensive set of rules that still left considerable room for bargaining and negotiation, and had no leader with sufficient power to control the operations or outcomes associated with any of the House's main objectives.

These examples of research reflect several considerations that accompany the adoption of an organization theoretic approach to defining structure within the legislature. First, they indicate the effort to transcend the concrete, mundane, and even familiar ways of conceptualizing legislative structure, i.e., in such terms as committees, party leadership, or written rules. Second, they show that the definition of structure varies with researchers (and studies). Third, they assume that legislative structure may be defined and examined at an institutional level of analysis. This last point hardly seems insightful: At what other level of analysis could legislative structure be defined? But it is important because, as I will discuss, the institutional level is in organization theory the path to explanation and prediction. That is, organization theory looks to institutional, as opposed to individual, sources for structural change and effects.

With such a working (albeit variable) definition of legislative structure, organization theory has been used to examine a number of research questions. But the central preoccupation of most such legislative studies has been to study the relationships of the environment in which the legislature exists, dimensions of legislative structure, and legislative performance.

One of the early and now classic examples of such an application is Nelson Polsby's account of "The Institutionalization of the U.S. House of Representatives" (1968). For Polsby, the "institutionalization" of the House, as one example of democratic, political organizations, occurred at the point when its activity became specialized (i.e., in politics) and it achieved the means for representing diverse viewpoints but legitimating and containing conflict. The bulk of Polsby's analysis was devoted to an examination of the House in terms of three characteristics of the institutionalized legislature: its boundedness, or the degree to which it is set apart from its environment; its internal complexity, which includes such factors as role definition and recruitment, division of labor and specialization, and functional specificity, among others; and the use of universalistic as opposed to particularistic criteria and automatic, or rule-based, methods of operation. With these theoretical guidelines, Polsby documented the establishment of boundaries mainly in terms of changing House careers; the growth of internal complexity mainly in terms of changes that took place in committees, the party leadership, and legislative staff and aid; and the primacy of universalistic criteria and automated decision-making mainly in terms of the entrenchment of seniority rule.

Besides the obvious contribution of expanding the historical profile of the House, Polsby's contribution was twofold and characteristic of the major strengths and preoccupations of later organization theoretic analyses. First, he suggested that a set of organizational attributes—most of which were structural—is not coincidentally present at the same time, which is to imply that institutions evolve in nonrandom ways. Second, not surprisingly, he focused attention on identifying the causes and consequences of the institutional profile that he had uncovered. While Polsby's central concern was with distinguishing the institutionalized House, and his treatment of causes and consequences was thus limited, the questions of why institutional change occurs and what effects it has have nowhere been more explicitly stated.

Since Polsby's article appeared in 1968, a number of studies have employed the ideas of organization theory to explain structural change and its effects. Examples include Roger Davidson and Walter Oleszek's study of congressional reform during the 1970s, Ronald Hedlund and colleagues' work on various aspects of structural innovation and legislative performance, and Steven Smith and Christopher Deering's work on committee change. But as a collection, the works of Joseph Cooper remain the most sophisticated and elaborate statements of the theoretical and empirical implications of organization theory for the understanding of legislatures in general and Congress in particular.

The recurrent theme in Cooper's research has been to pinpoint the impact of environmental constraints and stimuli on the structure of Congress and, in turn, the bearing both environment and structure have on congressional performance. A number of key insights have followed. One is that the environment of Congress can be thought of in terms of two broadly defined sets of values—democracy and separation of powers—that determine the two most important sets of expectations to which the Congress conforms, those of the electorate and of the executive branch. These expectations shape the role Congress legitimately plays in the legislative system and serve as the primary sources of demands. A second insight is that Congress adjusts itself structurally to meet changes in its environment, but the environment also acts as a constraint on the direction and magnitude of structural change.

In the first instance, gaps between environmental expectations and legislative output may result in organizational strain or, in acute cases, stress, thus stimulating the need for structural adjustment. In the second case, adherence to democratic values and separation of powers limits Congress's ability to adjust its bases of individual motivation, division of labor, or integration so as to meet or relieve the conditions of strain and stress in which it exists. Following from the presumption that structural change can alter institutional performance, a third point is that performance needs to be considered not only in terms of how much the legislature produces but also in terms of what the legislature does. In other words, to specify structural effect requires attention not only to the absolute quantities of laws passed, constituent services provided, or agencies overseen but also to the nature of Congress's role within the system. Thus, organization theory supplies a justification and basis for bridging system-conscious evaluations of legislative performance (a classic example being Samuel Huntingdon's indictment of the national legislature at mid-century) and more specific analyses of various legislative capacities, such as those for lawmaking and oversight.

Several implications deserve mention. At least within the constraints imposed by Congress's environment, no one form of legislative structure is superior to another. The structural profile represents adjustments to changing aspects of Congress's environment, which have either a bureaucratic or an electoral impulse. A second implication, indeed, is that structural change can have both an electoral and a bureaucratic impulse, that the structural character of Congress shifts as a function not only of the electoral environment with which career-minded incumbents must cope but also of the bureaucratic and executive/political environment within which legislators work. A third implication is that different structural profiles are associated with different capacities for production and mixes of products. This last point explicitly opens a path for research exploring connections between different structural arrangements and different institutional tolerances for constituency service, lawmaking, and oversight.

Assessment

Despite its contributions to the study of legislative structure, organization theory is not without its shortcomings and ambiguities. For the most part, it has failed to generate an impressive array of testable hypotheses. The gap between its use as a conceptual apparatus and its use in practical application is wide indeed. Furthermore, its use in explaining aspects of institutional differences and change has been limited. Thus its central potential strength, that of a framework for comparative and longitudinal analysis, has been largely unexploited. This failing may be due to the level of abstraction associated with organization theory. But an equally important (and probably related) reason is that organization theory itself has not yielded sufficiently precise hypotheses about the interrelationships among environment, structure, and performance in the legislative context.

The consequence is that organization theory has been fruitfully adopted to describe and explain only certain structural features of the legislature. Cooper and Brady (1981) used it to relate the operation of political parties in the electorate to changes in the authority vested in the party leadership in the House during the twentieth century. Collie and Cooper (1989) discussed the historic use of multiple reference in current Congresses. Cooper and Young (1988) studied bill introduction in the Congress during the nineteenth century. That organization theory has provided a compelling explanation for these changes in procedure and leadership is a substantial contribution on its own. Nevertheless, more comprehensive changes in the institutional profile of Congress have yet to be assessed in light of organization theory.

Its potential in this regard is limited by a set of problems that stem from how legislative structure itself is defined in organization theory. The problems become all the more vexing in light of the central questions organization theory poses for the study of legislative structure, namely, what creates legislative structure and what are its effects?

To understand the nature of these problems, we must first underscore some assumptions in organization theory with regard to organizational structure. The first assumption is that the organization does not reduce to organizational structure, in other words, that organizations are greater than or separable from their structure. The second and related assumption is that structure is but one feature of an organization; otherwise, the organization cannot be distinguished from its structure. The third assumption is that structure is a key but not the only determinant of organizational performance. Taken together, these assumptions mean that organizational performance may be a function of both structural and nonstructural features of the organization and, less obviously, that structural features may have an impact on nonstructural features of the organization and vice versa. Taking into account an environmental role means that environmental conditions may directly affect the structural and nonstructural features of the organization and thus exert an indirect effect on organizational performance in addition to any direct effect they may have.

Whether the purpose is to understand the cause or the effect of different forms of legislative structure, the analytic consequence of these presumptions is that structure must be distinguishable from other legislative features. The two most obvious (and troublesome) features are process and behavior. Is structure in organization theory distinct from process and behavior? Consider the question first in light of the definitions of legislative structure presented earlier.

For Hedlund, structure covers the formal arrangements of power and influence and also rules and procedures. Assuming for the moment that structure means only those arrangements and rules that are formally codified, we can say that his definition includes committees and party caucuses as well as the rules associated with bill referral and any rule that serves as an aggregative mechanism, such as a majority rule. Note, parenthetically, that all these arrangements meet the criteria for distinguishing structure: they are formal, durable, and used to advance institutional goals.

When formal structure is defined in such a way, it appears fully determinative of, if not equal to, formal process; some elements of structure, such as committees, establish units of authority that other elements of structure, such as referral and majority rules, relate. In short, "process" becomes either structure itself or "structure in motion." The problem is that scholars have for some time had a broader understanding of process, which is implicit in their conclusion that the formal structure of an institution is not fully determinative of process. This conclusion has, in turn, inspired considerable investigation into the importance of *informal* structure. But when the criterion of formality is relaxed (as it frequently is in this research and also in Hedlund's framework), any distinction between structure and process becomes ever more blurred. For example, is senatorial courtesy an element of legislative structure? What of the seniority rule? What of committee chairs' powers, which were unwritten during the 1950s and 1960s, or the negotiation and bargaining that accompanies virtually every effort to make new laws?

It is a theoretical tangle that surfaces even when a distinction between structure and process is explicitly made, as in Cooper's works. In "Organization and Innovation in the House of Representatives," for example, he cites, along with the House's structural features, several characteristics of operations or process, including turbulence and uncertainty; dependence on external sources of information and influence; emphasis on sufficiency, not efficiency; pervasive politicalization, and high participation costs and rewards. In other words, House operations were usually chaotic, very dependent on presidential and bureaucratic input, full of redundancies, and associated with politically rather than technically determined outcomes. The fact that he defines the characteristics of both structure and process implies that he does not regard the two as interchangeable. Yet he defines no organization theoretic basis for distinguishing the two. As a consequence, one is left to wonder, for example, why the "degree to which processes are ordered or standardized by set procedures" is considered a dimension of structure rather than process.

Even retaining the criterion of formality, still another problem is that process becomes indistinguishable from behavior. This circumstance persists unless we are willing to treat process as a structurally induced sequence of actions and behavior as a nonstructurally induced sequence of actions. This choice, in effect, relegates behavior to the status of residual.

The distinction between structure and behavior is at least as murky as that between structure and process. While Hedlund maintains that the structure of the legislature provides the context for members' behavior, a position that suggests that he distinguishes between structure and behavior, he fails to specify with sufficient clarity where structure ends and behavior begins. For example, rules and procedures, which he treats as a structural feature of the legislature, include prescriptions for both formal and informal behavior.

Cooper's distinction between structure and behavior is likewise difficult to discern. As already noted, in "Congress in Organizational Perspective" he presents both an instrumental and a social component to organizational structure, the latter being intimately associated, if not synonymous, with the organization's group life. With such a working conception of structure, what constitutes behavior is difficult to establish. The problem is compounded when structure is differentiated from process, as in "Organization and Innovation." For example,

Cooper uses as testimony to the pervasiveness of politics in House operations the degree to which parties and policy coalitions exploit policy positions for electoral advantage and their reluctance to participate in policy analysis. The analytical dilemma is that when structure and process are distinguished in this way and explicated, behavior is lost as a separate factor.

These applications of organization theory to the legislature suggest that the blurring of structure, process, and behavior may be linked to relaxing the criterion of formality as a defining characteristic of organizational structure. Let us take formality to mean codification, that is, documentation in some form in the legislature's governing rules. If the concept of legislative structure is so restricted, elements of structure may still, but not necessarily, include the degree to which legislative subunits are elaborated, the arrangement of tasks or functional responsibilities, the manner in which authority is distributed, and the degree to which power is centralized. Whether these features constitute structure is contingent on their formal specification. Confining the definition of structure to codification is not to imply that the institution is merely the set of codified rules. A legislature cannot be reduced to a set of formal rules any more than a house can be reduced to a set of blueprints. Yet institutions with different sets of formal rules are unlikely to operate similarly, just as houses built from different blueprints are unlikely to look the same.

One obvious problem with such a restricted definition of legislative structure is that seemingly structural elements of the legislature (the most profound example being the legislative parties) may not be deemed a structural feature. This problem only becomes more perplexing in light of the fact that these seemingly structural entities (as outlined here) may, as I have described, generate their own structure. For example, congressional parties are not mentioned in the governing rules of the House and Senate, but they form caucuses that then codify rules of operation.

Retaining formality as a criterion for distinguishing structure is thus not without its costs. The relevant question, however, is not whether maintaining this criterion is analytically cost-free but whether it is a better choice than eliminating it. Based on our discussion, the cost of eliminating it is that distinctions among structure, process, and behavior, which are tenuous already, would be virtually impossible to identify. The more fundamental question is whether these distinctions aid our understanding.

In light of the questions organization theory poses, it would seem that the payoffs of making these distinctions are sufficiently attractive to merit consideration. Without a structure-process-behavior distinction, everything collapses into structure. There are several related consequences. First, it becomes conceptually difficult to isolate institutional structure from the institution itself. The institution becomes synonymous with its structural profile. Second, we cannot readily find institutional sources of institutional change. That is, while some institutional change is inspired by varying environmental conditions, other institutional change is as inspired by changing internal conditions. Third, mixing up structure with process and behavior reduces the potential for specifying environmental and institutional sources of institutional change and leads to the overestimation of an environmental impact on structural change and the overestimation of a structural impact on institutional performance.

One example of how structural change can beget institutional change is the use of "multiple referral," a procedure first adopted in the 1970s for referring bills to more than single committees. Its adoption can be reasonably portrayed as an example of structural change. Among its consequences has been the enhancement of the power of party leaders because of the need for brokerage among committees managing the same legislation. It has also led to the enhancement of the power of committee chairs as representatives and managers of their committees' impact in the brokerage process. As Collie and Cooper have argued, while a preference for multiple referral among members of Congress and the procedure's institutional justification are tied to changed environmental circumstances, the enhancement of party and committee leaders' power is less directly tied to environmental conditions than to the challenge for coordination and integration that multiple referral itself presents. Without demarcating structural and nonstructural characteristics of the legislature, however, organization theory in its present form would lead us to assign an environmental cause (or possibly a personal one—party and committee leaders are more assertive personalities these days) to the enhanced power of legislators.

Another example is the adoption of the Budget and Impoundment Control Act of 1974. This act created new budget committees in the House and the Senate and prescribed a new budget process. Thus it can be also regarded as an example of structural change. Scholars have for some time agreed on two basic points: first, that the congressional budget process after the act's passage has been different from the budget process before its passage and, second, that the budget process has never worked in the way the act prescribed. Was this structural change fully determinative of post-1974 budgetary politics in the Congress? Hardly. Did this structural change have an impact, independent of environmental conditions, on budgetary politics in Congress? Absolutely.

In sum, organization theory and the presumptions leading from it suggest the following model of legislative performance. Environmental conditions may directly affect the structural and nonstructural features of the legislature and directly affect performance. Their effects on performance may be indirect as well, through their impact on structural and nonstructural legislative characteristics. The structural and nonstructural features of the legislature may directly affect each other and both may have a direct effect on performance. This is not the model, however, that is evident in organization theory analyses of the legislature, which tend to focus primarily on the connection between environmental conditions and structural change and between structural change and legislative performance. If we are to understand the sources of structural change as well as its impact on legislative performance, we must acknowledge that these more subtle connections are theoretically worth examining. The point is not to dismiss the theoretical insights organization theory supplies but to elaborate them more straightforwardly in analyses of structure and its effects.

RATIONAL CHOICE AND LEGISLATIVE STRUCTURE

The study of structural effect has received major emphasis during the past decade in rational choice work concerning legislatures. But just as the use of organization theory to inform the study of legislative structure has generated criticism, so too has the use of rational choice. In his major reformulation of the conventional rational choice approach to portraying the legislative scenario, *Information and Legislative Organization,* Keith Krehbiel notes three objections commonly leveled against such studies: first, that the focus of research has been so far removed from real world political problems as to be irrelevant; second, that the work is not accessible to the larger scholarly community because of its mathematical orientation, and third, that those who conduct such research don't know much about politics.

While the third objection may be weak, reservations associated with the first two have the ring of truth. The focus of rational choice literature that has seemed most relevant to legislative research, such as on the formation and size of coalitions as well as collective decisions on policy choice, has often appeared remote indeed from the observed world of legislative coalitions and policy formation. For example, minimum winning coalitions and global cycling over policy alternatives, two primary theoretical results associated with rational choice, have happened so rarely in American legislative history as to be arguably deemed nonexistent. A major variant of this objection has been the unreasonableness of certain assumptions, such as fixed preferences and perfect knowledge of the costs and benefits associated with different policies, that traditionally have characterized these models. Nor is there doubt that the (ever more sophisticated) mathematical cast to virtually all of rational choice renders it challenging, if not impenetrable, to many legislative scholars.

To some extent, such reservations are more easily leveled against the rational choice research of twenty years ago. There has been real effort to increase the extent to which models comport with reality, an effort that has become synonymous with a school of "new institutionalism" and has involved relaxing some of the more controversial assumptions associated with the models. In addition, there has been greater effort to relate, if not translate, theoretical results to the political world. Still, even the initial and considerable investment in the seemingly arcane matter of global cycling, which can mean roughly a collective inability to select a policy alternative by majority vote, has, as I shall discuss, profound implications for the study of institutional structure, the main one being that the continuity or stability of policy choice cannot be explained solely in terms of individual preferences. In any case, the lack of verisimilitude between the theoretical results on coalition size and cycling and the real world of coalition formation and policy selection is hardly a sufficient reason to dismiss the whole of this type of theoretical work. Indeed, to dismiss such insights is tantamount to dismissing research on the effects of gravity because we don't observe vacuums. Finally, it is important to note that a new generation of scholars has become increasingly fluent in the language of rational choice. Thus the larger scholarly community has become more attentive to the arguments of rational choice.

But the bottom line response to criticisms of the application of rational choice theory to issues in legislative research is that rational choice theorists are now more than ever examining issues at the center of legislative research—bargaining, specialization, leadership, policy selection, and, most significantly for our present purposes, structural development and effect—in short, the same issues that legislative scholars have always found fascinating. And they are examining these issues with a precision at the individual level that has often been lacking in more traditional qualitative and quantitative genres of research. To put the matter in a slightly different way, the important point about rational choice work is not that it is right (about the empirical world) but that it is relevant (to our understanding of it).

Research Issues and Answers

To understand the questions regarding legislative structure posed in this framework, some background is needed. All models in rational choice seek to describe or explain the collective choice emerging from a set of individual decision makers. These models contain assumptions and definitions regarding the choices before legislators and their preferences, behavior, and access to information. They also have been structure-oriented from the outset, though they are seldom represented in this way. Indeed, the most important stimu-lus for the new generation of structurally sensitive models was one that itself was, in part, structurally induced.

This stimulus was a theoretical result of a model of collective decision-making that had elements of some very standard circumstances characterizing the typical legislature. It assumed an odd number of legislators in the legislature, each of whom has an equal vote. It also assumed that legislators face more than two policy choices, disagree on the superiority of any single choice as well as on the relationship of one choice to another (which equates with multidimensionality or non-single-peakedness), and, as individuals, have preferences of a transitive order over these choices. It also assumed all legislators vote sincerely, that is, for the choice that they most prefer. Finally, it defined the winner as the alternative that beat the others in a series of paired comparisons under majority rule. In sum, the model incorporated assumptions about the nature of choices (that at least three exist), preferences (that they are heterogeneous in the collective and that individuals' choices are transitive), behavior (that voting is sincere), and legislative structure (that a majority rule and a "one person, one vote" rule apply).

The central theoretical result associated with this model is disequilibrium, meaning that no single choice prevails. The standard interpretation is that the collective body of decision makers, which could very well be a lawmaking body such as a legislature, is unable by majority vote to select a policy without resorting to additional rules, such as the use of a dictator or predetermined orders of voting. Variations of this result were presented in several major books and journals, including those of Arrow (1951), Black and Newing (1951), and McKelvey (1976), whose work ultimately and disturbingly implied that majority preference was no match for a legislator who could arrange the sequence of votes and who, presumably, would arrange them in such a way as to achieve the policy decision he or she most preferred.

Discussing the implications of this result, most scholars have spoken in terms of the fragility of majority preference as a determinant of policy choice when collective decisions are in order. It is a fragility that became associated with a "chaotic," "unpredictable," and "unstable" portrayal of decision-making in such scenarios. It is equally important to note, however, that the chaos was as much driven by the character of structure—that is, the relevance of a majority rule—as by the nature of preferences and that relief appeared initially in the form of an alternative structural arrangement, that is, the use of a "dictator" with the power to arrange votes.

Despite the structural cast of the result itself and of its solution, the first direction rational choice theorists turned to investigate the conditions for equilibrium was to the nature of decision makers' preferences. Theoretical results showed that only extremely unlikely conditions in individual preferences precluded disequilibrium. One scenario was perfect unanimity, where all decision makers most preferred the same alternative. Another scenario was unidimensionality, where all decision makers evaluated the choices in terms of one issue (Black, 1958). Such a condition occurs when all legislators view programs in terms of expense only. Thus everyone agrees on where the alternatives fall on a cost continuum, and everyone votes on the basis of cost alone, though some prefer to spend more than others. The last condition was near perfect symmetry, where all decision makers' preferences canceled each other until the last decision maker's preference (in the odd-numbered body) prevailed (Plott, 1967). These scenarios exhausted the "preference driven" possibilities of equilibrium in institutions where a majority rule decides winners and because of their exceptional nature, cemented the conclusion that majority-rule equilibrium almost never exists.

The result, then, was a function of the interaction between a set of institutional rules and a set of preferences in a decision-making body where no one individual controls the decision-making process. Its importance derived from its realistic representation of the heterogeneity of individual preferences and the challenge it presented for the use of majority rule as a method for settling disputes over the common good. Given that virtually all legislatures incorporate a majority rule that governs collective decision-making, the result appeared especially relevant to legislative research.

Scholars interpreted the implications of this result in several ways. One interpretation was that collective decisions are inherently unpredictable and inexplicable. This interpretation drove the effort to distinguish the forms of preference-driven equilibrium, which then appeared to confirm it. A second interpretation was that the political world, and especially that associated with democracies in light of their celebration of collective decision-making, is inherently in a state of flux. This means either that all collective decisions are subject to amendment or that no decision is or can be protected or lasting. This interpretation seemed to be especially relevant to institutions, such as legislatures, that establish policies based on majority rule. A third and more sanguine interpretation was that collective decisions were explicable and even predictable, but that scholars had been looking in the wrong place to understand the sources. This latter interpretation was the main inspiration behind the generation of structurally induced equilibrium models of collective decision-making.

These models arose generally in response to the failure of explorations into different distributions of preferences to avert the problem of disequilibrium and specifically in response to a question posed by Gordon Tullock in a 1970 article, "Why So Much Stability?" The thrust of his argument was that real legislatures exhibit none of the traits that are consistent with the disequilibrium cited in the theoretical world, notably, constantly shifting majorities, endless cycling over alternative policies, or policy reversals. Tullock's answer was to look toward vote trading and logrolling. A second answer was to attempt a fuller *structural* description of institutions that employ a majority rule.

The notion in this wave of studies was that institutional, or structural, constraints play a part in real-world institutions of collective choice and, relatedly, that a majority rule is but one of their common structural features. Two of the most influential statements in political science concerning the impact of structural features are the articles by Kenneth Shepsle (1979) and, later, Shepsle and Barry Weingast (1981). The thrust of both works was that the disequilibrium hitherto synonymous with decision making in theoretical majority-rule scenarios could be arrested—indeed, they suggested that it is arrested in the real world—by typical structural features of such institutions, such features as a system of committees assigned particular jurisdictions with certain "rights" to propose or stifle policies for review by the majority. With further structural elaboration incorporated in the model and individual preferences held constant, the interaction between individuals' preferences and institutional structure yielded an equilibrium, hence the term "structure induced" equilibrium.

Strictly in terms of rational choice theory, these models and their successors defined a central structural effect—namely, equilibrium—when before there was none. More broadly, they also represented the beginning of a novel and major effort to understand precisely the effects of different institutional structures, given different behavioral assumptions and different levels of information available to individual decision makers. As Keith Krehbiel (1988) has underscored in his excellent review of social choice and game theory models, the work has evolved under the presumption that "institutions matter" where an "institution," which can be equated with an institutional structure, is understood to be a more or less durable constraint on behavior and ranges from the very durable, an example being a standing committee and its jurisdiction, to the not so durable, such as a special rule relevant to consideration of a specific policy choice.

For the most part, these efforts have meant relaxing the relatively strict assumptions, including those pertaining to institutional structure, articulated in the original models. Whereas the first generation of models was based on unidimensional and nonoverlapping committee jurisdictions, perfect information about policy preferences and consequences, and particular (germane and closed) rules governing amendments, the second generation of models has considered multidimensional jurisdictions, imperfect information, and a more varied set of rules governing the consideration of amendments.

At least three major avenues of research related to institutional structure have emerged. One has concerned relations between committees and the parent chamber, exemplified by the work of Denzau and Mackay (1983) and Krehbiel, Shepsle, and Weingast (1987). In most cases, the motivating question has been whether (and under what assumptions) committees are able to exert negative or positive power over a legislative majority's preference, negative power being a committee's ability to keep a legislative majority from changing the status quo and positive power being its ability to change the status quo over the legislative majority's objection. A second focus of research has concerned incorporating uncertainty, or less-than-perfect information, into the legislator's decision-making. Uncertainty is usually characterized as a lack of knowledge either about other legislators' policy preferences or about the policy consequences of proposals. Represented by the work of Austin-Smith and Riker (1987), Gilligan and Krehbiel (1988), and Enelow and Hinich (1983), such studies have examined the effects of legislators' asymmetric or limited information on their voting and the impact of the specialization embodied in the committee system on collective decisions. A third area of focus has been the investigation of different agendas, understood as the arrangement or ordering of votes on different alternatives, and the power of agenda-setters, understood as the legislator(s) who make these arrangements. The key question here has often been whether those who set agendas can control absolutely or partly the final outcome, thus refining the notion of a structural impetus to the legislative choice. Examples of such studies are the work of Banks (1985), Riker (1982), and Ordeshook and Schwartz (1987).

Many of the analyses mentioned have delved into all three areas of research. For example, Denzau and Mackay's work examines committee power vis-à-vis the parent chamber under different assumptions concerning the committee's information on the majority's preference. In addition, rational choice scholars have begun to think in terms of not only the selection of policies in majority-rule institutions but also the selection of structures and procedures in such institutions. Gilligan and Krehbiel (1990), for example, assess why a legislative majority selects a procedure that subverts or limits its ability to decide the final outcome.

In sum, the direction of more recent work in rational choice has been toward theoretical scenarios that bear more resemblance to actual legislatures on several counts. One is the incorporation of legislative subunits, such as committees, and the rules that govern their decision-making and connection to the parent chamber. A second is the investigation of the effects of information or uncertainty with respect to legislators' own behavior and decision-making at different stages of lawmaking. And a third is the ever more realistic consideration of how the distribution of power, derived from the authority to establish agendas, can effect collective decisions of one sort rather than another.

Assessment

Perhaps the most salient impact of the structure-induced modeling effort on legislative scholarship has been that it has opened up the field of rational choice to bigger questions regarding institutional design. This new structure-oriented research agenda, however, has produced results and conclusions that depart from the previous preference-oriented agenda in more than just its discovery of the relevance of institutional structure. That is to say, previous research, which explored the conditions for preference-driven equilibrium, arrived at the same basic conclusion: preference-driven equilibrium should be rare, given the exceptional shape preferences need to assume for equilibrium to exist. In contrast to the consensus on this conclusion, fundamental dissent characterizes the literature on institutional effects in the newer structure-oriented literature. The broadening of research, with its keener investigation of institutional effect and its consideration of larger issues, has brought disagreements on the rationale behind the establishment of institutional structure, its effects on legislative performance, and, indeed, even which institutional structures matter. A consideration of several major statements on institutional structure, each adopting a rational choice perspective, illustrates the point.

Though not expressed technically in terms of rational choice but primarily informed by it, the first major effort to assess the relationship between individual preferences and institutional structure was David Mayhew's *Congress: The Electoral Connection* (1974). Now a classic, it sought to describe the implications of a Congress (and, implicitly, any legislature) populated by single-minded seekers of reelection for individual legislators' behavior, legislative structure, and public policy-making. Identifying three primary institutional structures—member offices, the committee system, and the party system—Mayhew's conclusions regarding the latter two provide especially interesting benchmarks from which to evaluate later research.

From his perspective, the establishment of the committee system was an outgrowth of seeking reelection and provided members with platforms or arenas to take positions on certain issues, claim credit for policy-making, and, in the best of circumstances, direct particularized benefits to their districts, all three being activities that Mayhew argued were electorally useful. The congressional party system, envisioned primarily in terms of the roles its leaders choose to play, also serves reelection purposes, though somewhat less directly. That is, leaders choose to broker interests rather than act as whips or leaders of party positions and to assume the burden of institutional maintenance, which entails attention to matters that reelection-minded legislators opportunistically prefer to ignore. The effect is to free individual legislators to do and say what they needed for reelection while maintaining (in however crippled a form) the institution in which they wish to serve. Mayhew also singled out several dimensions of legislative performance—such as delay and inaction, particularistic and symbolic policymaking, and servicing of the organized—which he tied most directly to the inspiration of the electoral incentive itself rather than the structural arrangement stemming from it. Thus, for Mayhew, the committee system and the party system were engendered by electoral ambition and entirely compatible with it, the one system for what it did and the other system for what it left undone. Still, he attributed at most an indirect effect on legislative performance to these dual institutional features.

In "The Industrial Organization of Congress," Barry Weingast and William Marshall (1988) consider committees in the legislature from the more general standpoint of why legislatures find committee systems to be attractive structural arrangements in the first place. They arrive at a distinct perspective on the rationale behind the committee system. They, too, assume an electorally motivated legislator but, more important, one who seeks the support of the "politically responsive" set of interests in his or her district, these interests being non-uniformly distributed across districts. Insofar as a majority rule precludes any single legislator from effectively providing such supporters with the benefits they demand, legislators must cooperate to some extent (to form majorities) but always face the temptation to renege on bargains struck once their constituencies' policies or benefits have been secured.

For Weingast and Marshall, the committee system emerges as a structural arrangement that ensures "gains from trade" or, alternatively, protects against opportunistic behavior, by carving the policy agenda into committee jurisdictions and giving committees "property rights" over policy changes in their jurisdictions. In that responsive interests are not uniformly distributed across districts, legislators make sure they are selected with the property rights they favor. The effect is to bias committee membership and, in turn, committee policy alternatives toward serving particular interests; legislative policy-making thus is generally characterized as particularistic. The committee system is not viewed as an institutional solution to reelection per se; rather it is an institution that enforces cooperation. While Weingast and Marshall have in mind reelection-seeking legislators, their perspective on the committee system is not dependent on such an assumption, as is Mayhew's, but is instead dependent on legislators' pursuit of district interest groups' approval. Their perspective differs from Mayhew's, however, on two additional important counts. First, they see no role in the legislature for the congressional party system; one of their assumptions is that the party system places no constraints on individual behavior. Second, they see legislative structure—that is, the committee system—as designed exclusively to secure particularized policy, such policy-making implicitly being the only dimension of legislative performance compatible with the model, and as exerting a direct rather than an indirect impact on legislative performance.

Like Weingast and Marshall, Keith Krehbiel also examines how legislatures are organized and why. The two mainstays of Krehbiel's analysis in *Information and Legislative Organization* are the "Majoritarian" postulate, defining the relevance of a majority rule for collective decisions, and the "Uncertainty" postulate, defining legislators' uncertainty regarding the connection between policy choices and policy consequences. In contrasting the compatibility of the postulates with distributive models of legislative organization (such as Weingast's and Marshall's) and with his own information-based model of legislative organization, he develops a justification for a legislative committee system that proceeds from institutional need and legislators' incentives for acquiring expertise (meaning knowledge about the relationship between policy choices and policy consequences) in specific policy areas. Arguing that all legislators benefit from better information regarding the connection between policy choices and their consequences, Krehbiel establishes and empirically examines several propositions that explain the development of a standing committee system, the acquisition of expertise within committees, and the use of committee expertise by majorities in the parent chamber. The structural design of the legislature becomes one that encourages committees to share their expertise with the parent chamber but reduces their ability to bias policy, from a distributional angle, in their favor and over majority objection. Not surprisingly, legislative performance assumes two standards, a distributional one connected to particularistic policy-making and an informational one connected to the development and sharing of expertise. Both are directly affected by the institutional arrangement.

Krehbiel's analysis of legislative structure thus differs from Mayhew's and Weingast and Marshall's on several counts. Unlike Mayhew, he does not treat the reelection incentive as the primary factor behind the committee system. Unlike Weingast and Marshall, he does not view the committee system as a structure designed to distribute particularistic benefits to responsive interests, nor does he see policy as biased necessarily in favor of committee members' preferences. Perhaps most important, committees (under certain institutional arrangements) enhance rather than thwart majorities' determination of policy in their interest.

While the Weingast and Marshall and Krehbiel theories of legislative structure give different rationales for the committee structure and assign different implications to it, they both emphasize its primacy in the structural profile of the legislature. This primacy is explicit in Weingast's and Marshall's research; as already noted, they model a legislature in which party does not constrain member behavior. It is implicit in Krehbiel's work in that his research concerns the organization of the legislature but focuses on committees and the procedural constraints on committee behavior. Thus the key relation in both theories is between committees and chamber majorities in a nonpartisan legislature.

Such a representation of the structural arrangement of the Congress is strictly incompatible with that developed in Roderick Kiewiet's and Mathew McCubbins's *The Logic of Delegation* (1991), which is also heavily informed by a rational choice perspective. They present the legislative party as the key structural feature of the Congress. Indeed, chamber majorities are for them party majorities, which, they argue, constrain committee action and determine final policy.

In contrast to Mayhew, the electoral motivation relevant to structure is legislators' vested interest in preserving an electorally meaningful distinction between the parties. In contrast to the views expressed by Weingast and Marshall and Krehbiel, legislative parties act as a singularly important constraint on member behavior and committee behavior. Kiewiet's and McCubbins's argument is, in fact, grounded on their position that the committee system itself is but testimony to the congressional majority party's basically efficient delegation of power to institutional subunits of itself, namely, committees. Furthermore, they argue that committees have sufficient incentives to yield policy that agrees with the party's program. Thus, committees do not traffic in particularized policy producing, as Weingast and Marshall suppose. Nor are they convinced via institutional procedures to share information, as Krehbiel argues. Instead, committees prepare policy choices that are in the majority party's interest; they do so because of the set of institutional sanctions and prerogatives available to the party to discipline its committee members and, ultimately, to alter committee products on the floor. Finally, performance becomes not the provision of particularized benefits nor the efficient use of expertise but the successful enactment of majority party policy.

As a set, these four studies share a number of features. They each recognize a role for electoral ambition and see electoral politics as bearing on the structural arrangement and the performance of the legislature. They each recognize the importance of institutional structure and especially of the committee system and the procedures relating committees to the larger body. They each recognize that legislators' interests are diverse and often conflicting. At the same time, they come to a remarkably diverse array of conclusions regarding institutional structure. The importance of the party system ranges from insignificant (Weingast and Marshall and Krehbiel) to moderately significant (Mayhew) to fundamental (Kiewiet and McCubbins). The committee system functions primarily to satisfy electoral ambition (Mayhew), enforce cooperation (Weingast and Marshall), develop and share expertise (Krehbiel), and fashion party policy (Kiewiet and McCubbins). Legislative performance is multidimensional and determined primarily by reelection interests (Mayhew), or it is nothing more than nonpartisan particularistic policy-making and directly tied to the committee system (Weingast and Marshall), or it is policy- and information-related but nonpartisan and directly tied to the committee system (Krehbiel), or it is policy-making of a partisan and not necessarily particularistic nature and directly tied to the party system (Kiewiet and McCubbins).

Thus the key problem in rational choice research concerning structure and its impact is the lack of consensus on questions regarding which legislative structures matter and why. As our discussion implies, answers to both questions are also tied to different perspectives of legislative performance and its relation to legislative structure. In short, rational choice appears to supply a single answer to the question, What is legislative structure? That answer can be expressed positively as a "durable constraint" on behavior or negatively as whatever is not preferences, not behavior, and not choice. Regarding the effects of legislative structure, there are different answers depending on whom is asked.

In identifying this disagreement as the

most critical feature of recent work in rational choice research on legislative structure, I suggest that the problem of differentiating structure from process and behavior is less troublesome than it is for organization theory. In rational choice work, process, as separate from structure, is rarely contemplated. It is possible, extrapolating from extant work, to suppose that process could be thought of as the set of institutions that affect the collective decision or, in sequential games, as the individual's strategy of decision-making when presented with certain structural constraints, for example, agendas. In the former case, structure equates with process and in the latter process equates with behavior.

The more fundamental problem is with the definition of structure itself. Specifically, what forms of institutional regularities are to be regarded as "durable constraints on behavior" and thus structural? For the most part, work in rational choice has adopted a fairly restrictive definition of behavior—as either sincere or strategic voting—and treated select institutions—such as committees—as exogenous; behavior that cannot be regarded as sincere or strategic is either dismissed or treated as structure. Yet individual analyses are buttressed by other regularities or constraints that appear as important to outcomes as the institutions under consideration. So, for example, Weingast's and Marshall's conclusions about the relationship between policy-making and the committee system are as dependent on the tendency of legislators to contrive to get on specific committees as they are on the establishment of committee jurisdictions; the latter they regard as an institution, but the former they do not.

Thus, as with organization theory, ambiguities regarding the definition of structure plague analysis. The effect in rational choice work, however, is to mask the number and complexity of assumptions that are necessary to sustain conclusions. Put another way, these models of parsimony are far less parsimonious than modelers imply.

THE STATE OF THEORY

Considered in tandem, organization theory and rational choice perspectives supply an important message about understanding legislative structure and its impact. The key insight of organization theory is that institutions embody function and purpose that transcend individuals and, for this reason, can and ought to be studied on their own terms. Thus, its central contribution to legislative scholarship has been to encourage thinking at an institutional level and in terms of institutional interests. In contrast, the central contribution of rational choice theory has been to confront squarely and precisely some of the perplexities of the relationship between individual interests and collective decisions. Complementing the institutional orientation of organization theory, it is a perspective that demands a justification of phenomena in terms of the individual, as opposed to the institution. The message, then, is that legislative structure, its causes, and its effects must be reconciled at the individual *and* the institutional level. To exploit the analytic possibilities of the one at the expense of the other is to invite misrepresentation of both.

Our discussion of organization theory and rational choice leads to several observations about the theoretical vision of legislative structure that each perspective incorporates. First and fundamentally, both perspectives regard legislative structure, in some form, as important. Organization theory analyses imply that all legislative structure is important but are less clear about what is not legislative structure. Rational choice analyses conclude that only the legislative structure that is important should be considered but differ on which legislative structures are important. Second, neither perspective differentiates between structure and process, at least very well. Organization theory appears to accommodate some distinction, but the distinction is not defined in any rigorous fashion. Rational choice theory makes no distinction at all, nor is there much written about the need to do so. Third, neither perspective achieves much distinction between structure and behavior. In organization theory, structure becomes indistinguishable from behavior that is formally sanctioned and indistinguishable from all behavior once the criterion of formality is relaxed. Rational choice manages the distinction between structure and behavior by eliminating from consideration all behavior that is not reducible to the individual legislator.

Thus, one question is whether any gains are to be made by maintaining distinctions among structure, process, and behavior. The fact that two major theoretical perspectives do not maintain such distinctions may indeed mean that the distinctions are not worth maintaining. Another possibility is that neither perspective has the conceptual framework to do so.

The fact of the matter is, however, that fundamental irresolution characterizes the study of legislative structure and its effects. This irresolution is not merely in evidence among studies explicitly informed by organization theory and rational choice; it pervades other analyses where connections to either research perspective are more limited. Taking research on the Congress as exemplary, consider recent contributions on the questions of institutional development, policy-making, and control of the executive branch.

In *The Transformation of the U.S. Senate,* Barbara Sinclair presents an analysis of how and why the upper chamber has metamorphosed into a more open, media-oriented, egalitarian arena of conflict where the stars are senators who are activists in many policy areas and where the norms that characterized the Senate of three decades ago—specialization, legislative work, reciprocity, institutional respect, apprenticeship—are substantially different if not defunct. Two factors, according to her argument, are behind the change, the first being an infusion of new members during the 1950s and 1960s and the second being a more dynamic, diversified, and aggressive Washington policy community.

Sinclair's point is that the Senate of today is a basically different institution and its membership a basically different membership from the Senate of the 1950s, and she is far from alone in her assessment. The challenge her analysis raises for the study of institutional structure is that this transformation that she argues has taken place was only marginally related to any change in institutional structure, that is, unless institutional structure is thought to include all significant aspects of legislative behavior and process, in which case we have the tautological assertion that structural change begets itself.

Now consider Douglas Arnold's argument on congressional policy-making in *The Logic of Congressional Action.* His objective is to explain the factors behind congressional policy-making and, specifically, the conditions that lead to policy that is nonparticularistic, or in the general interest. Arnold rests his claims mainly on a respecification of the electoral connection to and incentive for the two types of public policy. Arguing that legislators estimate existing and potential voter preferences on policy alternatives, he maintains that legislators cast their votes to avoid electoral penalties from attentive and potentially attentive voters. Coalition leaders, who are not necessarily party leaders or committee leaders, then seek to effect whichever preferences most favorably bear on the policy outcome they seek to achieve. They do so through strategies of persuasion, which are mainly forms of rhetorical packaging, procedural strategies, and policy modification strategies.

While Arnold mentions the impact of committees and views the use of procedure as one of several coalition-building tools, his argument is far more dependent on explicating the relationship between legislators and voters as the central inspiration behind congressional policy-making. Moreover, this relationship and its exploitation by coalition leaders is the central reason behind whether Congress makes policy in the general interest as opposed to currying special interests. Thus, the challenge Arnold's argument presents to the study of legislative structure is how so fundamental a legislative activity—policy-making in the nation's interest, or not—can occur largely without any but a marginal structural effect.

Finally, consider Arthur Maass's argument in *Congress and the Common Good* regarding legislative control of the executive branch. According to Maass, the primary guarantee of Congress's ability to control the executive branch, an ability that he regards as the national legislature's central contribution to policy-making in the general interest, exists in the structural arrangements—and the behavior that they inspire—that connect committees to the parent chamber and the parent chamber to the executive branch. His argument finds a role for party leaders, committee leaders, and members; the committee assignment process; and authorization and appropriation procedures, to mention just some of the structural permutations the analysis takes.

The unanswered question in Maass's work is whether an institutional arrangement that differs from the one he investigates, which largely reflects the House during the late 1970s, harbors the same results for legislative performance that he assigns to this one. If Maass's conclusion is that all structure matters, the challenge for other students of legislative structure (not to mention the Senate) is to discern the effects of alternative institutional arrangements. The larger point, however, is that in marked contrast to Sinclair's analysis of institutional development and Arnold's analysis of congressional policy-making, Maass's analysis of congressional control asserts a fundamental structural effect.

We have in the research of Sinclair, Arnold, and Maass a collection of ideas, some more explicit than others, regarding the nature of legislative structure and its effects that are not easily reconciled. Nor is it entirely clear how organization theory or rational choice might address the disjunctures.

From an organization theory standpoint, for example, one way to evaluate the Senate's transformation is to view it as an example that proves the point. That is, changed environmental circumstances that were reflected in the evolving character of the Washington policy community and behind the infusion of new members led to a change in significant operational characteristics of the body. Such an interpretation, however, appears merely to dress up Sinclair's conclusions without resolving a question her research implies, which is whether an institutional structure, as embodied in the virtually unchanged committee and party systems, that tolerates the operation of the "old" Senate and the "new" Senate has much impact at all on legislative operations or performance.

Arthur Maass's conclusions regarding the importance of institutional structure are in keeping with the general conclusion in rational choice work that structure matters. Yet they are at variance with the conclusions regarding

structure and policymaking in each of the four analyses discussed earlier. For Maass, structure does not merely service reelection quests (as Mayhew has it), does not yield particularistic policy (as Weingast and Marshall say), is not defined merely in terms of committee/chamber relationships (as Krehbiel contends), and is not designed necessarily to promote the majority party's policy program (as Kiewiet and McCubbins assert).

Perhaps most at odds with both organization theory and rational choice work on legislative structure is Arnold's perspective of policymaking. Arnold's work is basically an argument for the insignificance of institutional structure. The primary inspiration for members' policy positions is constituency-based, whether the relevant constituents are attentive or inattentive at the time, and the primary stimulus behind policymaking itself is the emergence of a coalition leader who successfully manipulates attentiveness in these electorates. Thus the only institutional structure that is apparently of crucial importance is a majority rule that necessitates coalition-building.

Overall, the literature on legislative structure is perhaps even more diverse and inconclusive than I initially portrayed it. Studies of legislative structure that are informed by organization theory or rational choice converge on the conclusion that structure matters, even while they diverge on the definition of structure and which elements of it make a key difference in how the legislature operates or what it produces. Once we consider research not no vested in either perspective, however, we must also entertain the question of whether legislative structure has the importance organization theory and rational choice theory both contend it has.

BIBLIOGRAPHY

Congress and Other Legislatures—General
See R. DOUGLAS ARNOLD, *The Logic of Congressional Action* (New Haven, Conn., 1990); ROY P. FAIRFIELD, *The Federalist Papers* (Baltimore, 1981); RICHARD F. FENNO, JR., *The Power of the Purse* (Boston, 1966); SAMUEL P. HUNTINGDON, "Congressional Responses to the Twentieth Century," in DAVID B. TRUMAN, ed., *The Congress and America's Future*, 2d ed. (1973); GERHARD LOWENBERG, SAMUEL C. PATTERSON, and MALCOLM E. JEWELL, *Handbook of Legislative Research* (Cambridge, Mass., 1985); ARTHUR MAASS, *Congress and the Common Good* (New York, 1983); DONALD MATTHEWS, *U.S. Senators and Their World* (Chapel Hill, N.C., 1960); BARBARA SINCLAIR, *The Transformation of the U.S. Senate*

(Baltimore, 1989); JOHN WAHLKE, HEINZ EULAU, WILLIAM BUCHANAN, and LE ROY FERGUSON, *The Legislative System* (New York, 1962); and WOODROW WILSON, *Congressional Government* (Boston and New York, 1885).

Organization Theory—General
See PRADIP N. KHANDWALLA, *The Design of Organizations*, (New York, 1977).

Legislative Structure: Organization Theory Perspectives
See MELISSA P. COLLIE and JOSEPH COOPER, "Multiple Referral and the 'New' Committee System in the House of Representatives," in LAWRENCE C. DODD and BRUCE I. OPPENHEIMER, eds., *Congress Reconsidered*, 4th ed. (Washington, D.C. 1989); JOSEPH COOPER, "Assessing Legislative Performance: A Reply to the Critics of Congress," *Congress and the Presidency* 13 (1986); COOPER, "Organization and Innovation in the House of Representatives," in JOSEPH COOPER and G. CALVIN MCKENZIE, eds., *The House at Work* (1981); COOPER, "Congress in Organizational Perspective," in LAWRENCE C. DODD and BRUCE I. OPPENHEIMER, eds., *Congress Reconsidered* (1977); COOPER and DAVID W. BRADY, "Toward a Diachronic Analysis of Congress," *American Political Science Review* 75:4 (1981); COOPER and DAVID W. BRADY, "Institutional Context and Leadership Style: The House from Cannon to Rayburn," *American Political Science Review* 75 (1981); JOSEPH COOPER and CHERYL D. YOUNG, "Bill Introduction in the Nineteenth Century: A Study of Institutional Change," *Legislative Studies Quarterly* 14 (1989); ROGER DAVIDSON and WALTER OLESZEK, "Adaptation and Consolidation: Structural Innovation in the U.S. House of Representatives," *Legislative Studies Quarterly* 1 (February 1976); RONALD D. HEDLUND, "Organizational Attributes of Legislative Institutions: Structure, Rules, Norms, Resources," in GERHARD LOEWENBERG, SAMUEL C. PATTERSON, and MALCOLM E. JEWELL, eds., *Handbook of Legislative Research* (Cambridge, Mass., 1985); RONALD D. HEDLUND and KEITH HAMM, "Institutional Innovation and Performance Effectiveness in Public Policy Making," in LEROY RIESELBACH, ed., *Legislative Reform* (Lexington, Mass., 1978); NELSON POLSBY, "The Institutionalization of the U.S. House of Representatives," *American Political Science Review* 62 (March 1968); and STEVEN SMITH and CHRISTOPHER DEERING, *Committees in Congress* (Washington, D.C., 1984).

Rational Choice Theory—General
KENNETH J. ARROW, *Social Choice and Individual Values* (1951); DUNCAN BLACK, *The Theory of Committees and Elections* (Cambridge, Mass., 1958); DUNCAN BLACK and R. A. NEWING, *Committee Decisions with Complementary Valuation* (London, 1951); McKELVEY, RICHARD D., "Intransitivities in Multidimensional Voting Models and Some Implications for Agenda Control," *Journal of Economic Theory* 12 (June 1976); CHARLES PLOTT, "A Notion of Equilibrium and Its Possibility under Majority Rule," *American Economic Review* 57 (1967); WILLIAM RIKER, *Liberalism against Populism* (New York, 1982); and GORDON TULLOCK, "Why So Much Stabililty?" *Public Choice* 37 (1981).

Legislative Structure: Rational Choice Perspectives
See DAVID AUSTIN-SMITH and WILLIAM RIKER, "Asymmetric Information and the Coherence of Legislation," *American Political Science Review* 81 (1987); JEFFREY BANKS, "Sophisticated Voting Outcomes and Agenda Control," *Social Choice and Welfare* 1 (1985); MELISSA P. COLLIE and JOSEPH COOPER, "Multiple Referral and the 'New' Committee System in the House of Representatives," in LAWRENCE C. DODD and BRUCE I. OPPENHEIMER, eds., *Congress Reconsidered*, 4th ed. (Washington, D.C., 1989); ARTHUR T. DENZAU and ROBERT J. MACKAY, "Gatekeeping and Monopoly Power of Committees: An Analysis of Sincere and Sophisticated Behavior," *American Journal of Political Science* 27 (November 1983); JAMES M. ENELOW and MELVIN J. HINICH, "Voting One Issue at a Time: The Question of Voter Forecasts" *American Political Science Review* 77 (1983); THOMAS W. GILLIGAN and KEITH KREHBIEL, "Organization of Informative Committees by a Rational Legislature," *American Journal of Political Science* 34 (1990); D. RODERICK KIEWIET and MATHEW D. MCCUBBINS, *The Logic of Delegation* (Chicago, 1991); KEITH KREHBIEL, *Information and Legislative Organization* (Ann Arbor, Mich., 1991); KREHBIEL, "Spatial Models of Legislative Choice," *Legislative Studies Quarterly* 13 (August 1988); KEITH KREHBIEL, KENNETH A. SHEPSLE, and BARRY R. WEINGAST, "Why Are Congressional Committees Powerful?" *American Political Science Review*, 81 (1987); and DAVID MAYHEW, *Congress, The Electoral Connection* (New Haven, Conn., 1974).

LEGISLATIVE NORMS

Heinz Eulau

The members of legislative institutions are bound by rules and regulations that prescribe permissible or proscribe impermissible personal and interpersonal conduct. These rules and regulations are unlikely to cover all behavioral possibilities. This leaves to the individual legislator an area of wide scope and unbounded discretion that, even if he or she is exceptionally prudent, wise, or moral, would produce a high level of unpredictability in interpersonal relations among an institution's members and might even undermine the effectiveness of the institution itself. However, in legislative (as in other) institutions an informal, unwritten, and, to an extent, even unspoken understanding develops of what is proper and improper conduct. These normative understandings orient and channel otherwise discretionary personal and/or interpersonal behavior in a socially mandated direction and call for expressions of approval or disapproval on the part of group members.

Legislatures are especially fertile soil for the emergence and development of informal norms because, on a continuum of control and discretion, they stand somewhere between highly hierarchized institutions like an army or bureaucracy, on the one hand, and voluntary organizations, on the other hand. This is a result of the unique origin of their membership: unlike soldiers or civil servants, or unlike "joiners" of voluntary groups, legislators are both responsible to constituencies, at whose pleasure they serve, and obligated to abide by the institution's formal rules and informal understandings. This duality of condition makes the legislator's job probationary but also collegial, facilitating the emergence of norms potentially conducive to success in an otherwise volatile situation. A legislature is thus a "community of fate" and not simply an aggregate that can be assembled or disassembled at will; it is a collectivity of persons with similar experiences that, over time, comes to have a life of its own.

The legislature's originating and constitutive character is thus conducive to the emergence and development of normative and regulative principles that can be located at various points on a continuum of formality. At one end are enacted, or positive, rules of varying duration that are always subject to instant reform through amendment or new rules of a formal nature. Somewhere along the continuum are principles of an exemplary or prototypical nature well captured in the concept of precedents, representing "a blend of the formal and informal," governing procedures not explicitly covered by rules but often codified in volumes prepared by a legislature's parliamentarians (Oleszek, pp. 11–12). At the other end of the continuum are those informal norms that, in legislative settings, have also been called "rules of the game" or "folkways."

The systematic study of informal norms is one of the more neglected areas of legislative research. After a propitious beginning in the 1950s and some experimental development in the 1960s and early 1970s, the study of norms guiding interpersonal and intergroup relations in legislatures has entered a state of atrophy if not entropy. With one or two exceptions (notably Schneier and Sinclair; see bibliography), there has been no significant new research reported in published form since about 1980. The study of legislative norms thus remains in the "natural history" stage of scientific development in which discovery or, better, *un*covery is the dominant mode of procedure.

THE PROBLEM OF DEFINITION

Contrary to impression, there is no "standard definition" of the concept of *norm*, especially as it might be used in legislative settings. As will appear later on, even a minimal definition implicates a host of difficulties in theoretical and operational research. "Most commonly," according to an authoritative source, "the concept [of rules of the game, or norms] denotes widely shared beliefs about how the government, or various categories of political actors, ought to behave" (Matthews, 1968, p. 571). More often than not, however, the research literature includes definitions beset by fallacies that make for conceptual ambiguity and operational instability, due to inclusion in the definition of (1) some teleological "rationale" for the existence of a norm; or (2) a linkage between a norm and sanctions.

Paradoxically, the first fallacy appears in the two mutually exclusive orientations of structural functionalism and purposive individualism. "In any group," according to one structural-functional definition, "there exist certain norms of behavior which structure the interactions of the individuals in that group so as to enable it to achieve its purposive goals and/or maintain its viability" (Kornberg, p. 261). According to a typical purposive-individualistic definition, "The existence of norms implies that the institution or its members collectively benefit from the behavior prescribed by those norms and therefore have an interest in promoting that behavior" (Sinclair, p. 14).

In both of these definitions, norms are presumed to perform functions for the institution or provide benefits for its members that encourage appropriate behavior or discourage inappropriate behavior. Both definitions are essentially teleological: they presume what is yet to be empirically demonstrated—that legislative norms do in fact have the consequences that are stipulated in the definitions.

The second fallacy, including the issue of sanctions in a norm's definition, is evident in these two recent examples:

> A system of norms implies a system of enforcement. If the concept of legislative norms is to be useful, it must be shown that something different happens to those who observe and flaunt them. (Schneier, p. 129)

> . . . both generally and in the congressional literature, the concept of norm implies shared expectations of desirable behavior and en-

forcement mechanisms for deviance (Rohde, 1988, p. 140)

Making enforcement (sanctions, punishment, etc.) part of the definition of norms leads to fallacious inferences about their existence. "A norm exists . . . to the extent that individuals usually act in a certain way and are often punished when seen not to be acting in this way" (Axelrod, p. 1097).

An attempt has been made to distinguish between prescriptive norms that are sanctioned and those that are unsanctioned. First, norms not including a threat of explicit or implicit sanctions for nonconformity are said to be in the nature of strategic advice—"lessons from experience, or rules of thumb, as are commonly received by newcomers from experienced members." Second, norms associated with sanctions for nonconformity are in the nature of regulations "enforced by other members, such as party and committee leaders" (Smith, p. 131). Bringing different terms into the definition of norms does not clarify but tends to further confuse an already murky problem.

Toward a Proper Definition

A definition that can serve both the conceptual and operational needs of research does not require elaborations of the kind that have been reviewed. The definition only has to stipulate that some norms, however called, may only be rather inconsequential maxims of minimal orienting or directive power, while other norms may well be strict prescriptions or proscriptions that leave little or no behavioral leeway. A definition of this sort was proposed in connection with an empirical research study: "Legislative norms describe expectations which more or less effectively define the boundaries of appropriate conduct for the members of the legislature" (Hebert and McLemore, p. 506). This linear conception of what norms conceived as expectations do avoids the fallacies of linking the definition of a norm with the twin problems of false causal attribution (teleology) and sanctions to enforce conformity. The effectiveness of norms lies in their more or less setting boundaries for what is thought to be proper legislative conduct. As the boundaries may vary from situation to situation and from norm to norm, the definition does not lead to premature judgments about whether a particular act has or has not been conformist or about the act's differential consequences in case of more or less nonconformity—that is, how much it will be punished, or whether it will be punished at all.

In reviewing the research that has been done on legislative norms, a "stages of development" approach seems to be the most convenient way to proceed. It is also the most informative because the four decades of research on legislative norms covered here coincided with four decades of sometimes slow and sometimes fast but, over the period as a whole, considerable change in the "life histories" of the respective legislatures—notably the Senate of the United States and the House of Representatives, and to a lesser (and much less documented) extent American state and foreign legislatures. There is an interchange between events in the "real world" of politics and the moods in which observers of these events approach their research—in the choice of topics, theories and methods. This was clearly the case in the study of legislative norms.

A TIME OF EXPLORATION, 1950–1965

Precursor: David Truman

No review of writing and research on legislative norms can ignore the seminal and significant theoretical contribution made by David B. Truman in *The Governmental Process*, published in 1951. It was Truman who introduced the term "rules of the game" into discourse about politics in general and legislative behavior in particular.

In some respects, Truman's book was not a product of the late 1940s or early 1950s when, after a long and victorious war, the nation groped for stability and a new normalcy. It was a product of the revolt against the legal and institutional formalism in political science that had its roots in the pre–World War I Progressive movement and had been revived with the New Deal which, perhaps more than any prior era in American history, was characterized by a politics of interests. Truman's understanding of the legislature's "group life" was truly revolutionary:

Such a body is not properly conceived of as a collection of individual men, unorganized and without internal cohesion. Nor is it any better accounted for exclusively in terms of the formal, legal structure of the legislature. A legislative body has its own group life, sometimes as a unit, perhaps more often as a collection of subgroups or cliques. It has its own operating structure, which may approximate or differ sharply from the formal organization of the chamber. When a man first joins such a body, he enters a new group. Like others, it has its standards and conventions, its largely unwritten system of obligations and privileges. (pp. 343–344)

Words, phrases and sentences of this sort were something new in thinking about legislatures, even though Truman had almost no empirical research to draw on to warrant a behavioral diagnosis of the legislature and its norms. Truman conceived of norms not as absolute prescriptions that, if not followed, are invariably sanctioned but as "the approximate limits within which his [the legislator's] discretionary behavior may take place" (Truman, pp. 348–349). This view is very different from the restrictive view that sees norms only as constraints on behavior and not as channels for creative endeavor.

Explorers: Huitt, Matthews, Wahlke

The mood of the 1950s, when the pioneer studies on legislative norms were done, was conservative in the old (Burkean) sense. Research interest centered in the problems of consensus and stability rather than reform or change—in how political institutions maintained themselves and in how their maintenance could satisfy human needs. Norms were interpreted as contributing to stability and regularity at the institutional levels of politics by prescribing or proscribing how individual legislators or, indirectly, subinstitutional units should conduct themselves vis-à-vis each other.

Three names constitute an invisible college of researchers who, during the 1950s, concerned themselves with legislative norms— Ralph K. Huitt, Donald R. Matthews, and John C. Wahlke. Their work had considerable influence on later writing and research, though in quite different ways.

Ralph Huitt Huitt was the first to publish his work. Published in 1954, his study of a legislative committee was based on materials from the 1946 hearings on price control before the U.S. Senate Committee on Banking and Currency. This work and his other studies came to be much admired and quoted but not really followed up in later research, probably for three reasons. First, two of the studies (1954 and 1957) had been based on qualitative, literary content analyses of documents—a mode of research soon to be out of fashion (but, for a revival, see Baker, 1985). Second, the study of the role of the "outsider" as a person not conforming to norms was largely based on an unusual opportunity for participant observation that Huitt had as Senator Proxmire's legislative assistant during the senator's first year in the chamber. Third, despite his aspiration to be "theoretical" about his observations of Senate life and his drawing on some behavioral concepts useful for this purpose, the theory was underdeveloped and left incomplete.

Donald Matthews Matthews's article on the "folkways" of the Senate—introducing a new term for legislative norms—was published in 1959, though most of his interviews were conducted between January and September of 1956, with a few follow-up interviews in 1958. Matthews did not indicate why he chose the term "folkways" to characterize the legislative norms he was uncovering in his study of the Senate. Like rules of the game, and perhaps even more so, the concept of folkways refers to things that seem permanent and immutable. There is no reference to the conservative turn-of-the-century sociologist William Graham Sumner whose treatise entitled *Folkways* (1906) had a pervasive influence on social analysis into the 1930s and 1940s. The book's subtitle, "A Study of the Sociological Importance of Usages, Manners, Customs, Mores, and Morals," suggests that Sumner's concept of folkways was considerably broader than the concept of informal norms in current usage. It is impossible to say whether Matthews thought of them in Sumner's severe sense as mores or in some more attenuated sense as conventions. He initially defined them as "unwritten but generally accepted and informally enforced norms of conduct in the chamber" (Matthews, 1959, p. 1064).

Matthews noted that the kind of questions he was asking about the folkways were "difficult questions for an outsider [i.e., himself] to

analyze. Only those who have served in the Senate, and perhaps not even all of them, are likely to grasp the folkways in all their complexity" (Matthews, 1959, p. 1065). Nevertheless, his uncovering and formulation of legislative norms in the Senate has served as a point of reference in most later research and writing. So authoritative was his treatment that the six categories into which he had sorted the folkways (apprenticeship, legislative work, specialization, courtesy, reciprocity, and institutional patriotism) came to have an almost canonical quality and impact. His categories appear and reappear in the literature with monotonous regularity, first as almost self-evident truths, later as guideposts to record change (as in Rohde et al., and Sinclair; see bibliography). In the beginning they even seemed to have had the effect of discouraging further inquiry or testing of Matthews's propositions about their origins and possible consequences. Later writers, eager to make a "contribution" of their own without doing the necessary fieldwork, tended to rephrase, expand, or embellish Matthews's norms and, thereby, change some of their meanings. When, in due time, one or another of the norms was found to be obsolete, fading, or changing, the news was treated as a great discovery of the mutability of norms. Alas, counter to impression, Matthews himself had never assumed immutability. "It would be a mistake to assume that the folkways of the Senate are unchangeable," he concluded, and he gave a number of reasons for thinking so (1959, pp. 1088–1089).

John Wahlke Wahlke's chapter on "Rules of the Game" was published in *The Legislative System* in 1962, but the research involving interviews with 474 legislators in four American state legislatures was designed during the period 1955–1956 and conducted, after several pretests, from January to June 1957. The theoretical framework guiding the research on and analysis of norms was inspired, at the level of the institution, by sociological concepts and, at the individual level, by an adaptation of the social-psychological theories of the self-other relationship. The following quotation, from the conclusion, conveys something of the work's flavor:

> Rules of the game are not pious platitudes about good behavior. They are rules enforceable by clearly recognized sanctions

which all members have in their power to impose on errant members. Their observance would nonetheless seem to be obtained not primarily through members' fear of such punishment but through their general acceptance of the functional utility of the rules for enabling the group to do what a legislature is expected to do. (p. 168)

Wahlke coded forty-two different categoric types of response about rules of the game which, in turn, were placed into five functional categories—rules primarily promoting group cohesion and solidarity, rules primarily promoting predictability of legislative behavior, rules primarily channeling and restraining conflict, rules primarily expediting legislative business, and rules primarily giving tactical advantages to individual members. A residual category included "desirable personal qualities" cited as rules by some respondents.

Unlike Huitt's and Matthews's ethnographic field procedures, Wahlke's research was from the beginning designed in the mode of systematic survey research, making it possible and easy to adopt the procedures in other research settings. It had not been quite clear just what questions Matthews had asked of his interviewees; Wahlke's four-state project was the first to formulate precise, open-ended, and separate questions about norms and sanctions.

Exponent: Richard Fenno

The theoretical orientation prevalent in the late 1950s and 1960s was best expressed in Richard Fenno's work on the politics of the appropriations process in Congress (Fenno, 1962, 1966). As David Mayhew pointed out years later, about the time when there was a shift in theoretical orientation in which Fenno himself was a leading spirit, "it is fair to say that legislative research in the 1950s and 1960s had a dominant sociological tone to it. The literature abounded in terms like *role, norm, system*, and *socialization*" (Mayhew, p. 1). Fenno's works were studded with references to the work of sociologists and social psychologists whose writings he evidently found useful.

Fenno appears as the consummate exponent of the new behavioral political science in the study of legislative institutions, combining relevant theoretical notions and flexible methods with a vision of the problems whose solu-

tion was of interest to him. Actually, his immediate interest was not in legislative norms as such but in the structural problem of a legislative committee's integration; as he pointed out, "a concomitant of integration is the existence of a fairly consistent set of norms, widely agreed upon and widely followed by the members" (1962, p. 310). If, he suggested, "a committee has developed . . . a number of norms to foster integration, repeated and concentrated exposure to them increases the likelihood that they will be understood, accepted and followed" (1962, p. 313).

Some of the norms Fenno described for the House of Representatives were not unlike those that Huitt and Matthews had uncovered in the Senate, but a major stride was a shift from the previous emphasis on norms guiding legislators as individuals to the discovery that norms guided institutionalized groups of individuals like legislative subcommittees. For instance, the three norms of specialization, reciprocity, and subcommittee unity appear as properties of all the subcommittees in the House Appropriations Committee. A norm called "minimal partisanship" was to be observed by the members of "both party contingents" (1962, p. 317). Although not explicitly articulated by Fenno himself, careful reading suggests that legislative norms can and do occur on three levels: norms guiding person-to-person relations, person-to-group and/or group-to-person relations, and group-to-group relations. This complexity had *not* been noted, described, or explained in the prior work on norms, nor has it been much noted since, perhaps partly because Fenno's theoretical orientation gradually shifted from the functionalism of the 1960s to a more—for lack of a better word—"purposive-individualistic" type of approach in the 1970s.

A TIME OF EXPERIMENTATION, 1965–1980

Scientific research does not follow the arbitrary fault lines of years or decades. A temporal classification may be at odds with a generic classification that might be more desirable. For this reason, Fenno's (1973) revision of his view on norms and a study of change in Senate norms by Rohde, Ornstein, and Peabody (1973, 1985), both first reported in 1973, will be treated in the next section. On the other hand, included here is at least one major piece of research not reported until the late 1980s, though the research had been conducted in the mid-1970s (Loewenberg and Mans).

It is convenient to treat 1965 as a first cutting point for two reasons. First, the world of politics was changing: the quiescent years of the 1950s were followed by a decade of unrest at home, an unpopular war abroad and, in the 1970s, institutional reform in the U.S. Congress. These events shattered the static structural-functional and systems-oriented modes of thinking about norms. Second, the world of political science was changing: the arrival of a cadre of young scholars, well trained in new research methods, coincided with the diffusion of digital computing. However, counter to what one might have expected after the hopeful beginnings of the 1950s, the new era was not one of great advance in the study of legislative norms. Except for Fenno's 1973 revision of the functional interpretation of norms in a comparative study of congressional committees, there was little theoretical development.

There was also comparatively (compared to other topics in legislative studies) little empirical research on norms. Studies of norm learning in the House (Asher, 1973) and of change in Senate norms (Rohde, Ornstein, and Peabody, 1973, 1985) were the only major projects in the congressional field. There was some interest in the problem of conformity and deviance (Swanson, 1969). Among the particular norms uncovered in the pioneer period, only apprenticeship was given more than casual attention (Price and Bell, 1970; Bell and Price, 1975; Bullock, 1970; Asher, 1973, 1974, 1975). The period's end saw the publication of two books on the Senate. One was a study by an English historian who, in the mode of the traditional historian, traced the impact of the liberals on the Senate between 1959 and 1972, giving glimpses of how they despaired of and/or came to terms with Matthews's six folkways (Foley, 1980). A lively book, by Ross Baker (1980), dealt primarily with the informal relations of friendship and enmity in the Senate rather than norms in particular. What Baker called "institutional kinship"—involving trust, diligence, and mutual understanding in pairs of senators—helped the Senate to function, he

found, even though the "old norms" seemed to have changed since the 1950s.

The years from 1965 to 1980 were more a time of experimentation with research instruments (especially the kinds of questions asked in surveys, problems of participant observation, statistical analysis of roll calls, etc.) and designs than of testing substantive hypotheses. The first studies were designed to replicate earlier work and, through comparison, discover similarities and differences in norms and norm structures. In this endeavor, Wahlke's explicit research design and instrumentation were more easily adoptable or adaptable than the more ethnographic approaches of Huitt, Matthews, or Fenno. His structured, open-ended questions were replicated with some success (but sometimes without credit) in the United States and abroad (Kornberg, 1964, 1971; Price and Bell, 1970; Agor, 1971), though not in the Congress.

Most significant was the effort to transform Wahlke's open-ended questions into specific closed ones to make the study of norms more amenable to quantitative analysis. Except for Asher (1973), all of this work was in the field of state politics. Instrument construction, conceptualization, and analysis turned out to be highly interdependent: even though the intention may only have been to close up a set of questions, it sometimes involved the use of words that differed from one study to another. This would so change meanings that it also inadvertently entailed conceptual revision and raised the twin issues of a norm's existence and knowledge about its existence.

The Ontological Problem

The ontological problem—whether norms exist independent of the articulations, beliefs, or cognitions of particular persons—actually arose out of the critique of the open-ended approach to the uncovering of legislative norms. This approach had not considered the number of respondents who articulated one or another norm important, for it was assumed that, whatever the number, the norms were "generally accepted and understood by *all* members" (Wahlke, 1962, p. 143; emphasis added). The resultant overinterpretation of the data was easy to challenge. "Rather than establishing the existence of legislative norms," it was pointed out, "their study would seem to suggest the absence of norms in the four states studied if 'statistical commonality' is a criterion which must be applied" (Hebert and McLemore, p. 510). This critique was clearly at odds with the structural view that norms are "organizational attributes" of the legislature that exist independently of the particular persons serving at a given moment (Wahlke, 1966, p. 127; Loewenberg and Patterson, p. 20).

It is interesting that in response to an open-ended question relatively few respondents articulate any specific norm. One obvious answer would surely have to be that not every norm, not even an important one, comes to mind at the very moment when the question is asked. Another answer has been that "for the most part, this problem arises because respondents have limited time and few incentives to answer open-ended questions, whether these are posed in a mail survey or a personal interview" (Bernick and Wiggins, p. 192). More controversial is the answer that some norms have been so deeply internalized and are so frequently acted out in behavior that legislators are actually incapable of articulating them (Loewenberg and Mans, p. 158). Finally, a rather conspiratorial answer has been suggested by Kornberg who had found, in response to an open question, that "a considerable proportion" of his respondents were "not aware" of rules inside or outside the Canadian House. The reason for this "may have been a suspicion . . . that such rules might be perceived as being underhanded, or operating to the advantage of some members" and therefore not be acknowledged (p. 265). Two later critics suggested that the open question asking respondents what the norms are carries the assumption that norms "do exist," and that the question thus "prejudices respondents who might otherwise deny that assumption" (Carroll and English, p. 307). However, their substitute, asking directly whether norms "exist," is at best naive and even less likely to validate the existence of norms.

The Epistemological Problem

The heuristic activity of uncovering a norm must thus be distinguished from confirming the validity and reliability of its identification. A closed question can do this only after a norm has been identified. However, normative opin-

ions or attitudes about proper personal or interpersonal behavior in legislative settings can be solicited in various ways. Differently constructed questions create much ambiguity and scientific havoc. A typical forced-choice questionnaire confronts the respondent with items that imply some "do" (like "standing by your commitments even though you had a change of heart") or some "don't" (like "concealing the real purpose of a bill to assure its passage"). The respondent is asked to indicate his feeling in the matter on some linear scale. In the research reviewed here, some of the items were the same from one study to another, some were different. More disturbing is the fact that different investigators provided for different response categories. Some asked whether the behavior described in the items is "desirable" (Hebert and McLemore, p. 513; Bernick and Wiggins, p. 192); "approved" (Kirkpatrick and McLemore, p. 689); "acceptable" (Loewenberg and Mans, p. 160); "expected" or "acceptable" (Hedlund and Wiggins, p. 33); or "important" (Asher, 1973, p. 501; Loomis, 1984, p. 195).

Each of these wordings taps quite different aspects of the "norms problem." Asking about the acceptability of an act is to ask about the respondent's sense of permissiveness or tolerance. By way of contrast, the question whether the respondent approves an act is said to tap an "affective dimension" that "refers to the manner in which legislators are affectively oriented toward particular types of behavior or patterns of behavior in the legislature." Approval is then translated into "liking," disapproval into "disliking" (Kirkpatrick and McLemore, p. 686). The evident confusion is compounded when set side by side with the question about the desirability of an act. A not unreasonable interpretation of the question would be that it elicits preferences for some norms as against other norms. But this is not the interpretation given. Rather, the responses in this case are said to answer the question of "what norms are actually present." (Bernick and Wiggins, p. 193).

The question about a norm's importance is of a somewhat different order. The respondent is not asked about his or her sense of tolerance or intolerance, acceptance or nonacceptance, approval or disapproval, or some degree of preference for some kind of behavior. In fact, none of the fixed-choice questions ask about norms but about behavioral acts that, when tolerated, accepted, approved, or preferred by some specified number of respondents, are declared to be norms by the investigator! The issue of whether a presumed norm with a high score is any "more of a norm" than a norm with a low score is left in limbo. And it is this issue that the question about a norm's importance addresses. Like the research using the open-ended format, the question about a specified norm's importance takes the existence of the norm for granted and simply seeks to determine how, in the respondent's judgment, one norm's importance compares with another's. Even if the average assessment of a norm's importance is very low, this does not mean that the norm does not "exist" in the legislature.

The Search for Consensus

The quandaries of quantitative analysis are symptomatic of a misguided cognitive operationalism. A good example is Asher's specification that "once we have found marked disagreement with certain items thought to be legislative norms, then by definition these items no longer are norms" (Asher, 1973, p. 501, n.8). Faulting the method and findings of the open-ended approach, one research team complained that "little precision has been achieved in identifying specific norms.... Unfortunately, they [Wahlke and associates] did not find consensus or near-consensus on specific items" (Hebert and McLemore, p. 509). Precisely measured consensus is made into a defining property of an informal norm.

There seem to have been three sources leading (and, in effect, misleading) to the search for consensus. One source was Wahlke's empirically unsupported proposition that legislative norms are "generally accepted and understood by *all* members" of a legislature (Wahlke et al., 1962, p. 145; emphasis added). The second source was the consensual views of small groups, articulated by sociologists and social psychologists who influenced the study of legislative norms. There is really no reason to expect that what is true in small groups of 5 or 9 or even 15 persons will be true in large legislative assemblies with their intricate processes and complex politics. The third source probably was the very common but untenable assumption of earlier political thought (Prothro and Grigg, 1960; McClosky, 1964) that a de-

mocracy, to be an effective and viable governing system, requires a consensus on certain fundamental values.

Against this background, combined with the emphasis on technique and quantification, it becomes understandable how and why "statistical commonality" seemed essential as a criterion for defining a norm. Statistical commonality "must be evident on any given expectation if it is to be regarded as a norm.... The major criterion is suggested by the norm concept itself—norms must unambiguously prescribe or proscribe behavior" (Hebert and McLemore, p. 515). The assertion that norms must be unambiguous has no theoretical foundation whatever but adds a new wrinkle to an already complex ontological problem. Its only justification seems to be that it is designed to make plausible the criteria to be used in determining whether a questionnaire item stands for a norm in the "real world." This operational definition specifies that 50 percent of the respondents be clustered near one or the other end of a scale, that no clustering occur near the scale's midpoint, and that the distribution of responses be unimodal (bimodality implying the existence of subgroups).

There is of course nothing wrong with greater precision in measurement in order to make norms usable variables in a fully identified causal system. What is wrong is the implication that there cannot exist ambiguous or even opposing norms among legislators and that these ambiguous or opposed norms cannot attenuate whatever ambivalent or negative reactions to one or another norm might be expected in the conflict situation. But considerations of this sort cannot be resolved in single-chamber studies of norms; they require a comparative design and comparative analysis.

Comparative Studies

In an exceptionally important article that goes well beyond the confines of the topic of norms (and therefore cannot be adequately treated here) but is highly germane, Nelson Polsby called for "appropriate tests" of his theory of structural institutionalization. "The best test of the hypothesis, to be sure," he averred, "remains the cross-sectional one," and he suggests that this test should compare "contemporary legislatures that vary with respect to boundary-maintenance, internal complexity, and universalistic-automated internal decision-making." Comparison of American state legislatures that differ in structural institutionalization, Polsby suggested, "may also be found to vary concomitantly with respect to the application of the norms of professional legislative life" (Polsby, p. 168). After forty years of research, one can cite only two genuinely comparative studies of norms in American state legislatures (Wahlke et al.; Bernick and Wiggins) and one comparative study abroad.

Although the research literature through the 1960s and 1970s occasionally referred to a "norm structure," no such structure was in fact ever identified. An attempt to discover a structure of norms was made in connection with a study in the British House of Commons, using interview data from 1971 and 1972 but not published until 1983 (Crowe). The study did not really identify norms but used the attitudes of members of Parliament (MPs) on breaches of party discipline to make inferences about a norm structure. Given its limited topic, its one-country locus, and prior knowledge, the study was almost ordained to find both "consensus" and "structure." But in referring at times to American studies, the article seeks to minimize any number of analytical and interpretative difficulties in this single and highly atypical case by arguing that "the set of norms found in a particular legislature defines its character as an institution, serves to distinguish it from the outside world and from other elective assemblies, and also helps it to function effectively" (p. 908). This may well be so, but no conclusions concerning this "distinction" can be drawn without genuine comparison (in contrast to Crowe's intuitive juxtaposition).

It is in this context that a study of three European parliaments by Loewenberg and Mans (1988) obtains its significance. This sophisticated quantitative and theoretically eclectic study of legislative norms in countries as different as Belgium, Italy, and Switzerland is notable on three grounds. First, it rejected the most similar system design as a basis for comparison because it produces "overdetermined explanations of cross-national variation (p. 155). The same can of course be said of all single-legislature studies that presume that their findings are generalizable. Second, it is of particular interest that Loewenberg and Mans

emphatically rejected the consensus theory of norms. As they put it, norms can appear in many different patterns, "including differing perceptions of norms among members of different groups within parliament." They also pointed out that it is a mistake to hold that consensually held norms "permit no explanation. Variance can, after all, exist across chambers even if it is slight within them" (p. 157). Third, these investigators were extraordinarily sensitive to the level-of-analysis problem, recognizing that "norm perceptions are the properties of individual MPs, but patterns of norm perceptions are properties of legislative institutions" (p. 165).

Loewenberg and Mans dealt only with norms concerning relationships between members and leaders, and norms governing personal relationships. After subjecting the data to factor analysis and multiple analysis of covariance, two groups of norms were identified— "norms of parliamentary courtesy" and "norms of parliamentary party loyalty." These norms appeared in all three parliaments. The most significant finding was that the perceptions of individual persons "vary not so much by their individual backgrounds or political attitudes as by their parliamentary status, their party membership, and the institution in which they serve." The distribution of these perceptions "produces compositional consequences for parliaments." Any given parliament is distinguished by "a pattern of norm perceptions rather than by a consensus on norms among all its members." It is a mistake, Loewenberg and Mans emphasized, "to define norms as standards shared by all members" (pp. 175–176).

It is fitting to conclude this section on "a time of experimentation" with Loewenberg and Mans's comparative study which, although published long after the fieldwork had been completed, probably represents the best that theoretically and methodologically oriented research produced between 1965 and 1980.

A TIME OF EXPLANATION: 1980–1990

A new period, which began in the mid-1970s but bloomed in the 1980s, can be characterized by its theoretical preoccupations. The rather static structural-functional approach had failed to explain satisfactorily the emergence and evolution of legislative norms. Two distinct but related strains of theory can be distinguished—"rational individualism" and "purposive individualism." Theorizing about norms in the mode of rational individualism is only marginally related to the familiar conceptions and interpretations of legislative norms. Its importance in connection with the study of norms lies in its influence on the theoretical formulations of the more empirically-based purposive individualism.

Rational Individualism

The major substantive interest of the theorists in the essentially social choice tradition is to give rational explanations for the frequent appearance of unanimous or near-unanimous coalitions in legislative voting involving "distributive bills"—bills that allocate benefits to particular constituencies (states or districts) while diffusing costs through general taxation. These theorists speak of the tendency toward unanimity as "universalism" and, in addition, christen it a "norm." This is rather unfortunate, for two reasons. First, in the standard terminology of legislative scholarship, the notion of universalism refers to informal norms and/or practices that, over time, have come to be institutionalized (i.e., become more automatic and less discretionary), like the seniority system of selecting committee chairs in the Congress (Polsby, 1968, 1969) or question time in the British House of Commons (Hibbing). Institutionalized norms are not whimsical expressions of self-interested individuals. Second, the rational models have built-in biases against normative explanations of behavior. As Krehbiel has candidly noted, "distributive theorists, especially of the formal genre, instinctively object to the use of the term *norm* when users casually presume that a norm somehow explains a pattern of behavior or type of legislative outcome" (Krehbiel, p. 49).

There is a great deal of ambiguity in the use of terms like *universalism* or *reciprocity*. Polsby's notion of universalism as an aspect of institutionalization (p. 145) was extended to policies (rather than structural phenomena) by David Mayhew who, noting the ease with which distributive bills passed through Congress, spoke of a "policy of universalism." More specifically, Mayhew elaborated, "every member, regardless of party or seniority, has a right to his share of the benefits" (Mayhew, p. 88). When Mayhew's anecdotal approach became formalized in the works of researchers called "rational individualists," universalism came to be used in quite diverse and ambiguous ways—sometimes being referred to as a "norm," sometimes as a "practice," sometimes as an "agreement," and sometimes as a "preference."

The interest of rational-choice policy analysts in universalism was occasioned by two interrelated puzzles in the behavior of legislatures (at least in American government). A long-recognized puzzle was the inordinate frequency of unanimity or near-unanimity even in legislative situations where conflict should be expected (Eulau, 1963, 1986). The other puzzle was that this unanimity was at odds with the prediction that in the absence of uncertainty winning coalitions would be of minimal size (Riker, 1962).

Barry Weingast seems to have been the first to use the expression "universalism norm" in connection with research that tries to explain these two puzzles, unanimity and the absence of a minimum winning coalition in distributive policy making (Weingast, pp. 245–246). To judge from the context, Weingast refers to "norm" as something that is "normal" in its behavioral rather than prescriptive sense. He subsequently avers that this perspective has wider applicability: it suggests a rationale for such other features of Congress as "the existence of various 'norms,' 'roles,' and 'expectations.'" These features, he continued, "are interpreted as the informal rules or institutions of the legislatures," and they are "chosen" to "further the interests of legislators" (p. 246). Weingast's technical model, designed to explain the existence of universalism, is more concerned with practices than with norms.

Weingast also distinguishes between universalism and reciprocity. "This distinction is made," he emphasizes, "because the phenomena and their rationales are different" (p. 246, n.1). One reason for this distinction might be that whereas universalism appears not to be a norm in the prescriptive sense, reciprocity seems to be. Weingast, however, offers no elaboration of his reasons for making the distinction.

In his 1981 study, Morris Fiorina at least initially retained the idea that universalism is defined by behavior but gives reciprocity a clearly normative definition as "the expectation that concerned or otherwise involved minorities should have their way" (p. 198). He then makes the enigmatic statement that "exactly what universalism and reciprocity are is less certain." He finally obfuscates the two terms' empirical properties: "For the moment let us characterize universalism and reciprocity as 'practices' or 'arrangements'; these terms fall somewhere between 'norms' and 'agreements'" (p. 199). He also speaks of "the newer conception of universalism and reciprocity (more or less conscious agreements) . . ." Both are "voluntary (if tacit) agreements by legislators whose primary goal is to remain legislators" (p. 203).

Shepsle and Weingast, generalizing and extending the results of the previous models to pork barrel legislation (i.e., economically inefficient projects), show very much the same conceptual conflation. In the very first sentence of their 1981 study they inform us that it is their purpose "to establish some general conditions under which rational legislators institute and maintain the norm of universalism in the realm of distributive politics. This practice . . . is characterized by legislative support coalitions well in excess of minimal winning size . . ." (p. 96). The model to explain the practice of universalism is said to provide "a general condition which insures that rational legislators prefer it to a pure majority-rule system, on the one hand, and to the constitutional abolition of the pork barrel on the other" (p. 98). The question to be raised and answered thus turns on the source of this unique preference.

The distinction between universalism and reciprocity is jettisoned with the assertion that "reciprocity across committees and policy jurisdictions is universalism as manifested in a structurally differentiated legislature" (p. 110). The symbiosis of reciprocity and universalism is accomplished by lifting the veil of ignorance (i.e., uncertainty about majority-rule outcomes) previously assumed to make for universalism. Congressmen have in fact a good deal of knowledge about which committees have influence in policy domains that are likely to benefit their own districts; and as the districts are diverse, members of Congress seek membership on committees likely to benefit their districts. As a result, "reciprocity replaces universalism as legislative 'insurance' [against defeat] in this context" (p. 110).

An interesting modification of the previous models for research is a model of a noncooperative game by Niou and Ordeshook that allows for constituents who can vote either for representatives advocating efficient programs (i.e., who are opposed to universalism) or for representatives who promise benefits of interest to them (i.e., who subscribe to universalism). By implication, constituents would be foolish to vote for a representative opposed to universalism. The notion that legislators might engage in universalistic practices either because they acknowledge equity and fairness as proper standards of behavior or because such concerns are expectations shared by constituents is not within the scope of rational-individualistic research.

The concept of a "universalism norm" as used by the rational-choice theorists is generally sloppy. The sloppiness is not excused by Krehbiel's explanation that "a norm is a phenomenon in need of a theoretical explanation." What Krehbiel seems to mean by a "theoretical explanation" is not clear. He simply asserts that the "interesting question" is: "Why, or under what conditions, is it rational for individuals to conform to a norm?" (Krehbiel, 1991, p. 49). This question once again confuses explanation of a norm's existence and explanation of conformity to the norm.

Krehbiel, in his 1986 study, proposes to "reconsider norms from a rational-choice perspective in a narrowly defined setting." His point of departure is the empirical observation that U.S. senators can kill legislation by objecting to a request for unanimous consent. Yet, he notes that "instances of this seemingly effortless obstruction are rare" (p. 542). Krehbiel argues that "the conventional sociological notion of norms" requires reformulation in order to explain satisfactorily why legislators agree to unanimous-consent requests, on two grounds. First, the conventional explanation "would be virtually tautologous:" senators consent because it is appropriate to do so; "yet, in reverse, consent is regarded as a norm precisely because senators conform to the appropriate standard" (p. 543). The charge of tautology is misplaced: a proper formulation cannot derive the existence of a norm from a presumed behavioral conformity to its prescriptions.

More revealing of the error involved is Krehbiel's second reason for reformulation. He argues that norms as conventionally defined "are not useful for deriving testable hypotheses: they define appropriate behavior in a group but are silent on the questions of when and why individual deviations occur." But "the mere existence of norms as standards of conduct cannot account for variation" (p. 543).

Krehbiel asserts that this "newer, modified perspective on norms focuses on strategies of individuals rather than on rules or standards of groups." Then, distorting the sociological view, he continues that "this strategic perspective is not inconsistent with the preceding conventional perspective of norms as patterns of behavior." These patterns, "while typically described as attributes of groups, are nevertheless products of individual self-interested decisions" (p. 543). This is not a "reformulation" at all but an altogether different undertaking. Krehbiel's is a behavioral model of conformity or deviance, not a model of normative influence. "To reiterate," he concludes, "norms are not merely collective and regular standards of conduct; more specifically, they are products of individual and variable strategic decisions. Congressmen have reasons for choosing to conform to norms and neither more nor less selfish reasons for choosing to deviate" (p. 562). Here Krehbiel first admits that norms are "collective" phenomena (and they are not "merely" so); but then he makes them "products" of strategic individual decisions.

More recently and within the rational-choice community, David Baron and John Ferejohn, while conceding the possibility of universalistic outcomes in legislatures with "a few internally homogeneous blocks that can act in a concerted manner," have come to the rescue of the minimum winning coalition as a function of bargaining under specified structural conditions (Baron and Ferejohn, p. 1200; also Baron, 1989, 1991).

For an understanding of personal or interpersonal norms in real-world, as opposed to theoretical, legislatures, the rational-individualistic models offer less than meets the eye. Melissa Collie, in a brilliant *Legislative Studies Quarterly* essay reviewing the models, challenges the universality of universalism as postulated in these models and raises a number of searching questions about the empirical foundations of the formal models (see also Collie, "Universalism and the Parties in the U.S. House of Representatives, 1921–1980").

Purposive Individualism

The realization that some of the legislature's informal norms advantage certain individuals has always been part of thinking about them. It is really only a small step of translation that those advantaged by a norm also benefit from it and have an interest in the norm's maintenance because it serves their goals or purposes. Purposive individualism is rational individualism minus its bias that all "interest" is "self-interested."

Fenno's Metamorphosis Nobody's work better reveals the transition from structural-functionalism to a purposive individualism than Fenno's (1973) study of committees. As its title made clear, this was a study of individuals in committees as much as a study of committees. Not that Fenno altogether abandoned the macro-systemic approach, but finding that committees' behavioral patterns differ a great deal, it was plausible for Fenno, in the context of the emergent individualistic *zeitgeist*, to seek the cause of these different emphases in the different goals that individual congressmen hope to achieve by seeking membership in one committee or another. Personal goals like increasing one's influence in the legislature, making good public policy, and getting reelected, as well as the necessity of adapting to environmental constraints, shape the committee members' and, therefore, the committees' decision-making norms or premises. For instance, "the elaborate system of norms to insure subcommittee autonomy and influence" in the U.S. House Appropriations Committee (whose individual members' goal presumably is influence) was absent from the Interior Committee where "specialization is primarily the result of each member's constituency-based interest" (Fenno, 1973, pp. 98–99).

There are two problems with this mode of theorizing: (1) it may involve the "individualistic fallacy" by making inferences from individual members' to the committee's premises and/or interests; and (2) there is, at times, in this revised theory of committees, a conflation of norm in the descriptive sense of actual modal behavior, of norm in the prescriptive or traditional normative sense, and of certain other terms such as *strategic premise* or *decision rule.*

Matthews Revisited   Also to the rubric of purposive individualism belongs the first interview study of U.S. senators since Matthews's (conducted by Rohde, Ornstein, and Peabody in 1973–1974, reported in 1974, but not published until 1985). On the empirical side, this study did not transcend Matthews's categories or findings. Of course, some of Matthews's six folkways had probably changed in some way, as one might have expected, but the critical point to be made is that these researchers did not discover or uncover anything startlingly new. Done in the tradition of the semistructured interview with open-ended questions, the study is disappointing. The internal evidence is overwhelming that the investigators' casual mode of interviewing and ad-hoc observations made their interpretations rather indeterminate.

One contribution of the study seems to have been, in the spirit of the new times, a classification of Matthews's folkways into two bundles called "general-benefit norms" and "limited-benefit norms." As to general-benefit norms, including legislative work, courtesy, reciprocity and institutional patriotism, "in the long run, adherence to this type of norm benefits all members" (pp. 149–150). By way of contrast, a limited-benefit norm, like apprenticeship or specialization, "gives an advantage primarily or solely to a group of members who occupy certain positions, hold a common belief, or pursue certain goals" (pp. 151–152).

The classification was needed to explain presumably observed change. The study's twin hypotheses, applied to change in each of Matthews's old norms, are: (1) general-benefit norms will not change if the benefits to be had from the norm do not change; and (2) limited-benefit norms will change or even disappear if there is a shift in power from those who benefited from a norm to those who did not. These hypotheses about change are really nontestable: those who do observe a norm will benefit (because it helps them to achieve a goal), and those who do not observe it will also benefit (because noncompliance will help them to achieve a goal).

Of the same theoretical genre but much more systematic and informative is some work on norm socialization and related topics in the

U.S. House by Burdett Loomis and Jeff Fishel (1981; see also Loomis, 1984, 1988). The study is principally based on questionnaires and interviews with Democratic members first elected in 1974 and earlier research from the 1960s. One of the study's arguments is that "a focus on change and continuity in the informal normative structure of the House is one of the best ways of understanding and anticipating the limits, as well as the possibilities, of institutional transformation" (Loomis and Fishel, pp. 82–83). Once again, however, the study does not transcend Matthews's six norms.

Finding that "of the six norms under consideration, seniority and apprenticeship were viewed as the least important," Loomis and Fishel speculate that "changes in both the caucus rules and member incentives [between 1964 and 1974] created a more responsive environment for new members, undercutting the limited benefit components of the apprenticeship and seniority norms" (p. 85). How one might sort out these components of the two norms from others is left hanging. When measured in terms of their relative "importance," while only 19 percent of the respondents thought apprenticeship "very important," 56 percent still thought it "somewhat important," and 25 percent opted for "not very important." It is of course impossible to say what these nominal scale points may mean to different respondents. And comparison between the data with data from the 1960s (Fishel, 1973; Asher, 1973) presented "large problems of comparability" due to different question wordings (Loomis and Fishel, p. 86, Table 1).

How Much Change? Sinclair and Schneier

Renewed empirical concern with norms can be found in two studies of the late 1980s, one by Barbara Sinclair (1989) in the context of the first systematic and admirable effort since Matthews to explain the workings of the U.S. Senate as a whole; the other in a self-standing study of norms alone in both the House and the Senate by Edward Schneier (1988). However, what Sinclair and Schneier both report are not changes in norms but changes in behavior perhaps related to norms. In both studies the "hard," over time data are time series concerning such floor activities as amendments, quorum calls or extended debate going back to the 1950s. The two studies differ in two respects: first, Schneier is much more cautious than Sinclair in the inferences he makes from the data, concluding that the classical norms may be less moribund than Sinclair considers them to be; and second, while Sinclair is committed to a theory of purposive individualism, Schneier sees norms in terms of their function in the social system of the legislature's internal power relations. It is too early to say whether his study augurs a return to functionalism.

Information about aggregate, long-term trends in behavior can only be used to assess the degree to which a presumed norm is practiced; it cannot be used to determine whether a norm exists or has changed, for two reasons: (1) there is no agreed-on criterion for inferring the existence of a norm from a behavior pattern; and (2) even if a criterion were available, it could not be used, because psychological states, such as normative expectations regarding how persons ought to behave, are likely to be fallacious when inferred from behavior.

In addition to the documentary data, Sinclair's study is also based on interviews with senatorial staffers. However, she did not ask them about Senate norms directly but about their senators' "current and recent activities" (Sinclair, p. 91). Knowing about a senator's activities does not permit inferences about their normative views. Norm-related expectations are highly personal and may or may not be "acted out." Even if Sinclair had asked about norms directly, it is doubtful that staffers' responses to open-ended questions in the mid-1980s are comparable to senators' own responses in the mid-1950s. One person, no matter how close to another, is a poor informant on how that other person "feels" about something like a norm. Given these problems, Sinclair's conclusions are suspect: "Both in terms of expectations and behavior, the norms of apprenticeship, specialization, and legislative work are defunct; reciprocity and institutional patriotism have undergone major changes; courtesy is still a senate norm but is more frequently breached in practice. In sum, both expectations and behavior have changed" (p. 101). These unreserved conclusions about changes in the folkways of the Senate are not warranted by the data. Moreover, the theory is not about norms as such but about conformity to them.

For Sinclair the existence of norms implies that "the institution or its members collectively benefit from the behavior prescribed by those norms." But being obligatory, "abiding by norms involves some cost to the individual. If the payoff for norm-abiding behavior were intrinsically high—if it were the best way for a member to advance his or her goals—the development of a social rule obligating members to so behave would have been unnecessary" (p. 14).

In this connection, Sinclair argues that "the prisoner's dilemma provides a good model for norm abidance" (p. 14). But the PD game is not really relevant to the theoretical reasoning about obligations implied by the existence of norms. Obligations have sources other than the mutually rewarding or punishing expectations and/or behavior postulated by the PD game. Obligations are often entered regardless of cost precisely because they cannot be given a price tag. Sinclair is quite aware of the dilemma she created for herself: "The prisoner's dilemma is a good model for norm abidance only as long as senators as individuals receive a benefit when all abide by the norms. Any contribution to institutional functioning would simply be a byproduct" (p. 15).

In trying to explain the changes in Senate norms that she claims to have observed, Sinclair rejects the simple hypothesis that they were due to the arrival, in the late 1950s and early 1960s, of a new group of liberal senators who, disadvantaged by the norms, refused to conform to them. Rather, she attributes them to senators' "reactions to later changes in the external environment," which she calls "the Washington policy system" and which "is characterized by a much larger and greater diversity of significant actors, by more fluid and less predictable lines of conflict, and, consequently, by a much more intense struggle to gain space on the agenda" (p. 5). In such an environment the functions of norms in the legislative process, as described by Matthews, are no longer viable. If an institution distributes resources by adopting certain "rules," Sinclair suggests in a theoretically pregnant comment, it conditions their use through "norms."

Sinclair is a kind of prisoner on the three islands of theory she seeks to bridge—something from a theory of obligation, something from cost-benefit theory, and something from game theory. As a result, she does not really take an empirically "fresh look" at norms but apparently assumes that (1) Matthews's six norms alone are germane, whether continuing, declining, or disappearing; and (2) that no other or new norms could be uncovered. Sinclair speaks of a "new style . . . predicated upon high rates of activity in multiple arenas and across a broad range of issues" (p. 101). What norms give credence and/or support to the new patterns of senatorial conduct remains to be investigated.

Schneier does not deny that changes in apparently norm-related behavioral patterns have occurred in the Congress since the 1950s or 1960s. However, he suggests "that the basic 'folkways' of the House and Senate—despite dramatic changes in both the demand environment and formal rules in both institutions—have been remarkably durable, and that conformity to these norms remains an important paving stone in the road to institutional power" (p. 117). His retrospective view on the Senate of Matthews's time is also considerably more circumspect than the view of those who either hold an ideal-typical image of the past or infer more change in norms than has actually taken place. Neither were the norms of the 1950s as well defined nor was there as much conformity to them as later assumed.

After reviewing what the data told him about apprenticeship, specialization, institutional loyalty, reciprocity, and deviance, Schneier notes

> that [although] there are reasons for the folkways to fade in salience does not mean that they did. Indeed the persistence of the basic norms—including apprenticeship—is clear, and the distinction between Matthews' "man of Accommodation" and Huitt's Outsider is as viable as it was a quarter of a century ago. That the norms are less manifest and the "inner club" larger and less institutionalized is not to gainsay the continuing viability of both. (p. 132)

In his conclusion, Schneier asserts that "interview-based studies of legislative norms are likely to record widely divergent points of view that may even reveal as much about the questions as the responses" (p. 134). He therefore places his trust in the "behavioral evidence" even though it is "circumstantial." Even in regard to apprenticeship "whose premature obituary has been most widely published," the data show that "important junior/senior distinctions remain. The 1960–1961 cohort of junior senators was as active and as successful on the Senate floor as their 1980–1981 counterparts. Even in the increasingly egalitarian House not one of the legislatively-active junior representatives was subsequently appointed to a prestige committee, while twelve who refrained from floor amendments were" (p. 134). Taking issue with individualistic interpretations, Schneier writes: "Unless one argues that the observed differences between junior and senior members reflect not a system of norms but a realistic aggregation of individual choices—that most freshmen don't want major legislative responsibilities—then there must be some sort of signalling process taking place" (p. 134). Schneier concludes that "the question in part is one of whether the importance of norms is better measured in terms of universality or power relations." As an "obligatory standard" apprenticeship "is no longer an important norm in the House (if it ever was). But insofar as norm observance is seen "as conduct conducive to the attainment of institutional influence, it [apprenticeship] is very much a norm" (p. 135).

That Schneier and Sinclair can come to so dissimilar conclusions based on similar data sets attests to the danger of making inferences about norms from aggregate behavioral data, even time-series distributions. Both also practically redefine norms by not treating them as prescriptive expectations, an obvious criticism made by Rohde (1988) of Schneier's study that can also be extended to Sinclair's analysis.

CONCLUSION

The study of legislative norms in the early 1990s is in a state of suspension. With some mode of individualism dominating theoretical work and playing havoc with the concept of legislative norms, and with most empirical research depending on documentary information and aggregate data to study behavior, there is little progress being made in direct research on norms as social phenomena at either the individual or group levels of analysis, by way of systematic interviewing or by way of *in situ* observations. Finally, the study of norms has become highly parochial. The topic is dominated by studies of and references to the American Congress. Yet, the field remains a rich, largely unexplored mine for new investigations. In particular, research is needed that will theoretically and empirically disentangle the issues of a norm's existence, conformity to the norm, and sanctions.

BIBLIOGRAPHY

General Studies

For general works on legislative norms see HERBERT ASHER, "The Learning of Legislative Norms," *American Political Science Review* 67 (1973); and his "Committees and the Norm of Specialization," *Annals of the American Academy of Political and Social Science* 411 (1974); ROBERT AXELROD, "An Evolutionary Approach to Norms," *American Political Science Review* 80 (1986); DAVID P. BARON, "A Noncooperative Theory of Legislative Coalitions," *American Journal of Political Science* 33 (1989) and with JOHN A. FEREJOHN, "Bargaining in Legislatures," *American Political Science Review* 83 (1989); and BARON, "Majoritarian Incentives, Pork Barrel Programs, and Procedural Control," *American Journal of Political Science* 35 (1991); CHARLES G. BELL and CHARLES M. PRICE, *The First Term: A Study of Legislative Socialization* (Beverley Hills, Calif., 1975); MELISSA P. COLLIE, "The Legislature and Distributive Policy Making in Formal Perspective," *Legislative Studies Quarterly* 13 (1988); HEINZ EULAU, "Logics of Rationality in Unanimous Decision Making," *Politics, Self, and Society: A Theme and Variations* (Cambridge, Mass., 1986; first published in 1963); RICHARD F. FENNO, JR., *The Power of the Purse: Appropriations Politics in Congress* (1966); and his *Congressmen in Committees* (Boston, 1973); MORRIS FIORINA, "Universalism, Reciprocity, and Distributive Policy-Making in Majority Rule Institutions," JOHN P. CRECINE, ed., *Research in Public Policy and Management*, vol. 1 (Greenwich, Conn., 1981); F. TED HEBERT and LELAN E. McLEMORE, "Character and Structure of Legislative Norms: Operationalizing the Norm Concept in the Legislative Setting," *American Journal of Political Science* 17 (1973); RALPH K. HUITT, "The Congressional Committee: A Case Study," *American Political Science Review* 48 (1954); SAMUEL A. KIRKPATRICK and LELAN McLEMORE, "Perceptual and Affective Components of Legislative Norms: A Social-Psychological Analysis of Congruity," *Journal of Politics* 39 (1977); KEITH KREHBIEL, *Information and Legislative Organization* (Ann Arbor, Mich., 1991); BURDETT A. LOOMIS, *The New American Politician: Elected Entrepreneurs and the Changing Style of Political Life* (New York, 1988); and with JEFF FISHEL, "New Members in a Changing Congress: Norms, Actions, and Satisfaction," *Congressional Studies* 8 (1981); HERBERT McCLOSKY, "Consensus and Ideology in American Politics," *American Political Science Review* 58 (1964); DONALD R. MATTHEWS, "Rules of the Game," in D. E. SILL, ed., *International Encyclopedia of the Social Sciences*, vol. 13 (New York, 1968); DAVID R. MAYHEW, *Congress: The Electoral Connection* (New Haven, Conn., 1974); EMERSON M. S. NIOU and PETER C. ORDESHOOK, "Universalism in Congress," *American Journal of Political Science* 29 (1985); WALTER J. OLESZEK, *Congressional Procedure and the Policy Process* (Washington, D.C., 1978); CHARLES M. PRICE and CHARLES G. BELL, "The Rules of the Game: Political Fact or Academic Fancy?" *Journal of Politics* 32 (1970); JAMES W. PROTHRO and CHARLES M. GRIGG, "Fundamental Principles of Democracy: Bases of Agreement and Disagreement," *Journal of Politics* 22 (1960); WILLIAM H. RIKER, *The Theory of Political Coalitions* (New Haven, Conn., 1962); DAVID W. ROHDE, "Studying Congressional Norms: Concepts and Evidence," *Congress and the Presidency* 15 (1988); EDWARD V. SCHNEIER, "Norms and Folkways in Congress: How Much Has Actually Changed?" *Congress and the Presidency* 15 (1988); KENNETH A. SHEPSLE and BARRY R. WEINGAST, "Political Preferences for the Pork Barrel: A Generalization," *American Journal of Political Science* 25 (1981); STEVEN S. SMITH, *Call to Order: Floor Politics in the House and Senate* (Washington, D.C., 1989); DAVID B. TRUMAN, *The Governmental Process: Political Interests and Public Opinion* (New

York, 1951); JOHN C. WAHLKE, HEINZ EULAU, WILLIAM BUCHANAN, and LEROY C. FERGUSON, *The Legislative System: Explorations in Legislative Behavior* (New York, 1962); and BARRY R. WEINGAST, "A Rational Choice Perspective on Congressional Norms," *American Journal of Political Science* 23 (1979).

Comparative Studies
EDWARD W. CROWE, "Consensus and Structure in Legislative Norms: Party Discipline in the House of Commons," *Journal of Politics* 45 (1983); GERHARD LOEWENBERG and SAMUEL C. PATTERSON, *Comparing Legislatures* (Boston, 1979); JOHN R. HIBBING, "Legislative Institutionalization with Illustrations from the British House of Commons," *American Journal of Political Science* 32 (1988); ALLAN KORNBERG, "The Rules of the Game in the Canadian House of Commons," in H. HIRSCH and M. DONALD HANCOCK, eds., *Comparative Legislative Systems* (New York, 1971; first published in 1964); and GERHARD LOEWENBERG and THOMAS C. MANS, "Individual and Structural Influences on the Perception of Legislative Norms in Three European Parliaments," *American Journal of Political Science* 32 (1988).

House Studies
HERBERT ASHER, "The Changing Status of the Freshman Representative," in N. J. ORNSTEIN, ed., *Congress in Change: Evolution and Reform* (1975); ROSS K. BAKER, "Party and Institutional Sanctions in the U.S. House: The Case of Congressman Gramm," *Legislative Studies Quarterly* 10 (1985); CHARLES S. BULLOCK III, "Apprenticeship and Committee Assignments in the House of Representatives," *Journal of Politics* 32 (1970); MELISSA P. COLLIE, "Universalism and the Parties in the U.S. House of Representatives, 1921–1980," *American Journal of Political Science* 32 (1988); RICHARD F. FENNO, JR., "The House Appropriations Committee as a Political System: The Problem of Integration," *American Political Science Review* 56 (1962); RONALD D. HEDLUND, and CHARLES W. WIGGINS, "Legislative Politics in Iowa," in S. C. PATTERSON, ed., *Midwest Legislative Politics* Iowa City, Iowa, (1967); BURDETT A. LOOMIS, "Congressional Careers and Party Leadership in the Contemporary House of Representatives," *American Journal of Political Science* 28 (1984); SAMUEL C. PATTERSON, "The Role of the Deviant in the State Legislative System: The Wisconsin

Assembly," *Western Political Quarterly* 14 (1961); and NELSON W. POLSBY, "The Institutionalization of the U.S. House of Representatives," *American Political Science Review* 62 (1968).

Senate Studies
WESTON H. AGOR, "Senate: Integrative Role in Chile's Political Development," in H. HIRSCH and M. D. HANCOCK, eds., *Comparative Legislative Systems* (New York, 1971; first published in 1964); ROSS K. BAKER, *Friend and Foe in the U.S. Senate* (New York, 1980); MICHAEL FOLEY, *The New Senate: The Senate Liberals and Institutional Change, 1959–1972* (New Haven, Conn., 1980); RALPH K. HUITT, "The Morse Committee Assignment Controversy: A Study in Senate Norms," *American Political Science Review* 51 (1957) and his, "The Outsider in the Senate: An Alternative Role," *American Political Science Review* 55 (1961); ROBERT G. LEHNEN, "Behavior on the Senate Floor: An Analysis of the Debate in the U.S. Senate," *Midwest Journal of Political Science* 11 (1967); DONALD R. MATTHEWS, "The Folkways of the United States Senate: Conformity to Group Norms and Legislative Effectiveness," *American Political Science Review* 53 (1959) and his *U.S. Senators and Their World* (Westport, Conn., 1960); DAVID ROHDE, NORMAN J. ORNSTEIN and ROBERT L. PEABODY, "Political Change and Legislative Norms in the U.S. Senate, 1957–1974," in G. R. PARKER, ed., *Studies of Congress* (Washington, D.C., 1985); BARBARA SINCLAIR, *The Transformation of the U.S. Senate* and (Baltimore, 1989); WAYNE R. SWANSON, "Committee Assignments and the Nonconformist Legislator: Democrats in the U.S. Senate," *Midwest Journal of Political Science* 13 (1969).

State Legislative Studies
E. LEE BERNICK and CHARLES W. WIGGINS, "Legislative Norms in Eleven States," *Legislative Studies Quarterly* 8 (1983); JOHN J. CARROLL and ARTHUR ENGLISH, "'Rules of the Game' in Ephemeral Institutions: U.S. State Constitutional Conventions," *Legislative Studies Quarterly* 6 (1981); NELSON W. POLSBY, MIRIAM GALLAHER, and BARRY S. RUNDQUIST, "The Growth of the Seniority System in the U.S. House of Representatives," *American Political Science Review* 63 (1969); and JOHN C. WAHLKE, "Organization and Procedure," in ALEXANDER HEARD, ed., *State Legislatures in American Politics* (New York, 1966).

EXECUTIVE LEADERSHIP AND PARTY ORGANIZATION IN CONGRESS

Barbara Sinclair

For the U.S. Congress to perform its core function of lawmaking adequately, a number of component tasks must be satisfactorily carried out. Agenda setting is for all legislatures a key prerequisite to lawmaking; among the countless problems, issues, and policy proposals that someone in society would like the legislature to deal with, a manageable subset must be selected for serious consideration. The construction of legislative majorities, that is, the support of a majority of members of Congress for legislation, is another integral task and one that is often problematic in the U.S. political system, where numerical party majorities in Congress do not automatically translate into policy majorities.

The constitutional separation of powers among the legislature, the executive, and the judiciary, and the relatively weak and decentralized party system fostered by the Constitution create ambiguity about where responsibility for agenda setting and the construction of legislative majorities lies. Executive power is vested in the president, who is also the leader of his party. However, as head of a separate branch of government, the president has no legal authority over the congressional agenda or the internal legislative process. He may even face a legislature controlled by the opposition party. The central leaders in Congress are party leaders. While the institutional and political resources that majority-party leaders possess have varied widely over time, congressional party leaders have seldom had more than a peripheral effect on members' election and reelection. Their ability to construct legislative majorities has, consequently, often been problematic.

The varying roles of president and congressional majority-party leadership in agenda setting and constructing legislative majorities and the factors that determine those roles are the subject of this essay. The focus will be on current roles but understanding those requires tracing the development of and changes in roles over time. The relationship between the president and the congressional majority-party leadership—whether cooperative or conflictual—is given special attention.

THE INSTITUTIONALIZED PRESIDENCY IN THE LEGISLATIVE PROCESS

The public and political elites alike expect the president to play a central role in agenda setting and the construction of legislative majorities. Yet his constitutional authority in the legislative realm is meager; the only unequivocal legislative power granted to the president by the Constitution is the veto, that is, the right to veto legislation and thus require a two-thirds majority approval of both houses for that legislation to become law.

The president's unparalleled visibility and media access are essential to his agenda-setting role and important to his ability to affect the outcome of legislation. As the most visible person by far in the American political system, the president is more capable than anyone else of focusing attention upon an issue or problem and building pressure for legislative action.

The president's legislative role has become highly institutionalized. He is expected to present an annual legislative program to Congress. Although the president can and does send Congress numerous messages requesting legislation throughout the year, the State of the Union address delivered early in the year has become the premier occasion for the president to outline his agenda for the coming year.

Newly elected presidents usually do not give a State of the Union address yet nonetheless find an occasion to address a joint session of Congress in the first months of their term; that speech, along with the inaugural address, serves the same purpose. In addition, presidents are legally required to submit an annual budget to Congress, accompanied by a budget message. The budget is a statement of the president's policy priorities and, as such, a mechanism through which the president attempts to set the agenda for Congress.

All White Houses in the mid-1960s have included a domestic-policy office with a sizable staff (varying between about thirty and eighty since the 1970s). In some administrations the office has been the primary locus of policy development; in others, its function has mainly been the coordination of major policy initiatives for the president. However a president chooses to use this staff, its existence gives him significant capacity to develop a domestic program independent of the departments and agencies.

The Office of Management and Budget (OMB), with a staff in the hundreds headed by approximately two dozen high-ranking political appointees, also functions as a policy arm of the president. The OMB prepares the president's budget, adjusting agency and department requests to conform with his preferences; it must approve all agency and department requests for legislation, again checking for conformity with the president's program (a process called central clearance); and it provides technical analyses (cost estimates, for example) of policy proposals from other sources that a president may be considering for inclusion in his program (it can also provide such analysis for proposals offered by the president's congressional opponents). In recent years the domination of the political agenda by budget issues has increased the centrality of the OMB and its director in the policy process.

The president's program is, of course, a political document. Some of its components are chosen to appeal to important constituencies within his party and to groups that he is attempting to attract; others are responses to pressing problems or crises that threaten political damage if left unaddressed. The sources of the ideas and the specific policy proposals are also manifold; presidents draw on their policy advisers and on ideas emerging from executive-branch bureaucracy, but also on proposals advocated by interest groups, by independent experts, and often by members of Congress. Because the president is central to the agenda-setting process, other groups vie to have their initiatives included in his program. Thus, many of the items in the program will have some previous congressional history and a core group of strong supporters who advocated the proposal before the president adopted it.

Although Congress expects the president to submit a program to it and at least some of the items in that program will be of congressional parentage, presidents can seldom expect congressional enactment of their program without effort or trouble. The opposition party may control the Congress and, even if control is united, U.S. parties' relatively weak and non-ideological character means that the president cannot necessarily count upon support from every member of his own party. Consequently, presidents must sell their program to the Congress by winning the support of a majority of its members for each component.

Toward that end of executive persuasion, the veto is an important though blunt tool. Given the two-thirds majority in each chamber required to override it, the veto makes it possible—if not always politically advisable—for a president to kill most of the legislation he strongly opposes. It also gives him a bargaining tool: the president can extract changes in the substance of legislation in return for a promise not to veto.

Just as Congress expects the president to propose a political program, it expects his department and agency officials to appear before congressional committees to defend its components. A congressional liaison staff in the White House functions as the president's own lobbyists, selling his program directly, coordinating the lobbying activities of agency and departmental liaison staff, and doing favors for members of Congress with the intention of putting them in the president's debt.

The Office of Public Liaison is a point of access for interest groups seeking to influence the administration. In addition, it mobilizes interest groups supporting presidential policies. Depending upon the priority of the issue, the office's activities vary from arranging briefings for group representatives and community leaders to orchestrating massive campaigns of group pressure on Congress.

The White House communications operation has become increasingly large and sophisticated. By the 1980s more than one-third of White House staffers were engaged in public-relations activities of one sort or another. The effort to sell the president and his programs is highly differentiated and targeted, extending far beyond the television networks and the national press to local and specialized media.

This formidable array of administrative and staff resources available to the president for influencing the legislative process does not, however, fully compensate for the president's lack of legal authority. His ability to influence legislative outcomes depends heavily on the state of key political circumstances over which he has at best only partial control. Whether his party controls one or both houses of Congress, and the size and cohesion of each party's contingents, are the most critical of the political factors determining presidential legislative success.

THE CONGRESSIONAL PARTIES: ORGANIZATION AND LEADERSHIP

Majority status in Congress is critical because the majority party of a chamber organizes it. Organizational control brings with it considerable control over the legislative agenda, especially in the House. To be sure, congressional parties are not highly cohesive: on questions of policy and even of process, such as the character of special rules discussed below, members of a party seldom all vote together. Organizational control does not translate automatically into policy control or even always into procedural control. Yet, while intraparty agreement on policy is far from perfect, members of a party tend to share policy preferences; certainly the ideological homogeneity within each party is considerably greater than across the parties.

The House of Representatives

Only a bare majority is necessary to organize either chamber because straight party-line votes determine control in the modern Congress. The Speaker of the House, the only officer of that chamber mentioned in the Constitution, is its presiding officer and formally is elected by its entire membership, though on a straight party-line vote. Chosen by the majority-party's membership, he or she is that party's leader. Although the Speaker's powers have changed over time, being both the leader of the majority party and the presiding officer in a chamber with complex and constraining rules provides the Speaker with the potential for a position of considerable influence. Both political factors, such as the extent of cohesion within the party and the size of its majority, and institutional factors, such as the powers conferred on him by party and chamber rules, affect the extent to which that potential is realized. Currently, both sets of factors are conducive to a relatively strong speakership. Party cohesion is not, however, so high—nor has it been for more than a half century—that majorities simply materialize around policies; they must be constructed issue by issue.

Relatively elaborate forms of organization have developed in both chambers, especially in the much larger House. There, the two parties are organized somewhat differently. As Democrats have been the House's majority party since 1955, their organization and procedure will be emphasized. Traditionally, the core leadership in the House consisted, in addition to the Speaker, of the majority leader and the four chief deputy whips, all of whom are elected by the Democratic Caucus, the organization of all House Democrats. Increasingly, the chief deputy whip, who is chosen by the three top leaders mentioned above, and the caucus chair and vice chair, who are elected by the caucus, are a part of the inner circle.

The majority party, through its leaders and the caucus, plays the major role in organizing the House. For example, the assignment of members to the standing committees that do the bulk of the legislative work is carried out through the parties. All committees are chaired by majority-party members, and the majority party holds a majority of the seats on all committees.

The assignment of members to committees and the nomination of committee chairs are carried out by the Steering and Policy Committee. The Speaker chairs that committee and appoints ten of its thirty-six members. Nine other core leaders are ex officio members (that is, members by virtue of their office). The chairs of the Appropriations, Ways and Means, and Rules and Budget committees also sit on the committee ex officio, and a number of members elected by regional groupings of Democratic representatives round out the Steering and Policy Committee's membership.

Committee-assignment decisions are important to members' careers and to public policy. Most of the time that members devote to legislative matters is spent in committee; a member's chance of influencing policy in any given area is much greater if he or she sits on the appropriate committee; committees have disproportionate influence upon policy in their area of control. Consequently, the assignment process can be used to do favors for members, shape the composition of committees, or both. Party loyalty is a significant criterion—though not the only one—in the appointment of members to key committees such as Ways and Means (the tax-writing committee), Budget (the committee that drafts the budget resolution setting the framework for spending decisions), and Appropriations (which makes spending decisions), according to members of the Steering and Policy Committee. On other committees, especially those for which there is little competition, the rule of thumb is to give Democrats what they request.

The assignment process thus gives the party influence, but not control, over committee composition and consequently some impact upon policy. Minority-party committee members are chosen by that party and, on most committees, once a member receives an assignment, he or she is entitled to hold it as long as he or she remains in the chamber.

The Steering and Policy Committee nominates committee chairs, almost always based on who has served on a committee the longest. These nominations must be approved by a majority vote of the party on a secret ballot in the Democratic Caucus. Subcommittee chairs of the Appropriations and Ways and Means committees must also receive caucus approval. As a result, committee chairs and the subcommittee chairs of these particularly important committees have a powerful incentive to be responsive to strongly held majority sentiments.

The caucus is available to members for the expression of such sentiments. The caucus meets monthly, and a petition signed by fifty members triggers a special meeting. The frequency of unprescribed meetings varies, depending on whether an appreciable number of members feel the need for a forum to discuss a particular, usually highly contentious, issue. Although the caucus seldom passes resolutions instructing committees, the debate often serves to send a strong message to committee and party leaders.

The committee-assignment process, in the majority of cases, produces party committee contingents, or party's membership on committee, that are reasonably representative of the party membership. The need for caucus approval serves to keep committee chairs responsive to party sentiment, and the availability of the caucus as a forum to which committees are accountable means that Democratic committee contingents can ignore strongly held caucus sentiments only at their peril. The help the party leadership can give a committee in passing its legislation on the floor further heightens the committee's responsiveness to the leadership and the party majority. Committees are not under continuous, tight party control. When few majority-party members outside the committee have strong preferences on a matter at issue, or when the party membership is split, the committee has great discretion; these circumstances are in fact the norm. However, on the relatively few bills in each Congress on which a strong and relatively united majority-party sentiment exists, committee discretion is limited. The majority party has the tools for bringing a recalcitrant committee to heel.

Democratic Caucus rules give the Speaker sole authority to nominate its Democratic members, subject only to Caucus ratification. The Rules Committee reports out special rules that allow specified bills to be considered out of order and govern the conditions under which that legislation is debated and amended. In that almost all important and controversial legislation reaches the floor of the House by way of a special rule, control of the Rules Committee is a prerequisite to control of the floor agenda. Caucus rules make clear that the Speaker nominates Democratic Rules Committee members anew at the beginning of each Congress, and that he or she is not obligated to renominate sitting members. Consequently, the Rules Committee has become an arm of the House leadership, giving the Speaker true control over the floor schedule.

Special rules structure floor choices by allowing or barring amendments generally or specifically, waiving points of order, and making other determinations about floor consideration of bills. The leadership can and does get involved in the design of special rules, structuring them to advantage the party position, often by protecting Democratic committee contingents' legislation from having to face large numbers of Republican amendments on the floor.

A special rule must be approved by a majority on the floor; thus their use by the Democratic leadership depends upon the acquiescence of a majority of the whole House. The leadership needs the support of a large proportion of its own membership when a rule is controversial (when it bans amendments the minority wants to offer, for example). Occasionally the leadership miscalculates and a rule is voted down. The defeat of a rule is not, however, sufficient to turn control of floor consideration of the legislation over to the minority. If a rule is defeated, the majority leadership can try again with a revised rule. For the minority to wrest control from the majority, it must defeat the previous question (a motion to cease debate and force a vote on the issue at hand) on the rule. On this usually obscure procedural vote, party loyalty is expected and the minority almost never prevails. House and Democratic party rules thus provide a firm basis for majority-party control of the floor agenda.

Multiple referral of legislation (to more than one committee) and more frequent use of omnibus legislative vehicles (bills encompassing many issues that are sometimes unrelated) have increased the party leaders' involvement in the legislative process at the prefloor stage. Because of the number of committees and the number and magnitude of issues often involved in such legislation, the Speaker and, at his designation, other leaders often act as brokers between committees and intrafactions and as coalition builders attempting to shape legislation that will pass on the floor.

The division of labor among the core leadership of the House depends ultimately on the Speaker, but certain elements of this responsibility have become institutionalized, so that other members of the leadership regularly perform specific duties. The majority leader does the day-to-day floor scheduling, a task that involves working with committee leaders to ensure a smooth flow of legislation, the meeting of deadlines and for members' convenience, as

much predictability as possible. Although scheduling decisions involving political strategy are made by the leadership group in concert, the Speaker retains ultimate control.

In recognition of the parties' stake in the Budget Committee's decisions, two special committee slots, one for the majority and one for the minority, are provided. The majority leader holds that position for the Democrats.

The majority whip, elected by the majority party's caucus, oversees the whip system, which collects information on members' voting intentions and attempts to ensure that that there are enough votes to pass key legislation. Both as a staff operation geared to providing services to members and as a member organization, the whip system is large and elaborate. A variety of information is produced and disseminated to all Democratic members of which the most important are the weekly floor schedule and a whip advisory summarizing each major bill scheduled for floor consideration. The whip system in the 102d Congress (1991–1993) consisted of the whip, 3 chief deputy whips, 15 deputy whips, 3 task-force chairmen, 62 at-large whips, and 18 regionally elected zone whips. All but the latter are leadership appointees. Weekly whip meetings attended by all of the top leaders serve as an important forum for the exchange of information between leaders and members.

The whip system's core task is vote mobilization. On important legislation, a whip count to ascertain the level of support among Democrats is conducted. Shortly before the leadership brings the legislation to the floor, regional whips ask the members in their zones how they intend to vote. If the count indicates insufficient support because of a large number of opposing or undecided votes, a task force is formed. All the whips and supporting Democratic members of the committee from which the bill originated are invited to take part. Working from the initial count, the task force, distributes the names of all Democrats not listed as supporting the party position among its members. The members' task is to talk to those Democrats, find out how they intend to vote, and persuade a number sufficient for victory to support the party position.

During the 100th, 101st, and 102d Congresses, task forces functioned in about seventy instances, and about 60 percent of House Democrats served on one or more task forces during the 100th Congress. The task-force device and the large whip system of which it is a part enable the party leadership to mount frequent and extensive vote-mobilization efforts. Task forces also provide members with opportunities to participate broadly in the legislative process—opportunities especially attractive to junior members who do not yet chair a subcommittee. In this way, task forces channel members' energies into efforts that help the party.

The House majority-party leadership possesses sufficient institutional and organizational resources to control the floor agenda and to play a highly active role in efforts to construct legislative majorities. Political factors—especially, but not only, the size and cohesiveness of its majority—influence its success. The majority leadership seldom loses formal control over the House floor, but political pressures sometimes force it to consider measures and issues that it would prefer to keep off the agenda. The House leadership's coalition-building efforts ultimately depend on persuasion; members must be convinced that supporting the party position is in their own interest, that doing so at least will not retard their election and policy goals. For leaders to be able to so persuade members on a regular basis requires that the party membership be ideologically homogeneous to a reasonable degree.

The minority-party organization in the House generally parallels the majority organization. Without access to the institutional mechanisms of control, however, the minority leadership is much weaker than its majority counterpart. The minority party—the Republicans since 1955—elects a leader, a whip, and several other officers who head a variety of party committees. The whip oversees a whip system that is extensive, though not so inclusive as the Democrats'.

Committees vary widely in the extent to which decision-making is partisan. On some committees and regarding some legislation, bipartisanship prevails, and in such cases, the Democratic committee or subcommittee chair consults his or her minority counterpart about floor-scheduling decisions, often working closely with him or her on the floor. However, on legislation that elicits a split along party lines, the minority has no say on scheduling. The majority leadership may consult the minority leaders out of courtesy and informs them of the decisions it makes, but the power to make the decisions and the strategic advantages that such power entails rest with the majority. Only under special circumstances can the minority wrest control from the majority. To persuade enough majority members to defect on the key vote usually requires making highly visible the vote on the previous question on the rule, a complex procedural vote of the sort that is usually obscure and elicits party-line voting. This the House minority party is unlikely to be able to do on its own.

In building successful coalitions around legislation in competition with the majority party, the minority is disadvantaged by its smaller numbers and by the majority's control over the conditions of floor debate. Nevertheless, most legislation is considered under conditions that give the minority some opportunity to offer amendments (either directly or through a motion to refer it back to the committee with instructions). This opportunity can sometimes be used to bring up issues and alternatives the majority would rather not consider, which can in effect influence the agenda. Furthermore, because policy decisions have intrinsically higher visibility than decisions on process, majority-party members may be less inclined to vote along party lines and, thus, the minority has a better chance of floor victory on amendments and other substantive floor decisions than on procedural votes. Much depends upon the political context—the character of the issue and, of course, the ideological homogeneity of both majority and minority. However, because the House is institutionally a majority-rule chamber, the minority can exert influence only when the majority is split.

The Senate

The Senate, in contrast, is not a majority-rule institution; control of the floor agenda is less firmly in the hands of the majority party, and all stages of the legislative process are more open to influence from individual senators, whether they are from the majority or the minority.

In the Senate, too, the parties organize the chamber. Each party elects both a floor leader and a whip from among its membership. Senators receive their committee assignments from party committees.

The Senate majority leader is the leader of the majority party in the Senate, but unlike the Speaker he is not the chamber's presiding officer. In any event, the presiding officer of the Senate has much less discretion than his House counterpart. The only important resource that the Senate rules give to the majority leader to aid him with his core tasks of scheduling legislation and floor leadership is the right to be recognized first when a number of senators are seeking recognition on the Senate floor.

Senate rules give the majority-party leadership few special resources, but they bestow great powers on rank-and-file senators. In most cases, any senator can offer an unlimited number of amendments, even those not germane to the central issue of a piece of legislation on the Senate floor. A senator can hold the Senate floor indefinitely unless cloture is invoked; and cloture requires an extraordinary majority of votes. In the U.S. Senate, sixty votes, or a three-fifths majority, are needed to invoke cloture and terminate debate.

A single senator can disrupt the work of the Senate by, for example, exercising his right of unlimited debate or objecting to the unanimous-consent requests through which the Senate does most of its work. Clearly, a partisan minority of any size can bring legislative activity to a standstill. The Senate necessarily operates in a more bipartisan fashion than does the House. As the majority leader makes decisions on the scheduling of legislation for debate on the floor, he confers on an almost continuous basis with the minority leader and in fact touches base with all interested senators. In the negotiation of unanimous-consent agreements, which the Senate often uses to set the ground rules for the consideration of legislation on the floor, the majority leader must obtain the assent not only of the minority leadership but of all interested senators. An objection from any one senator would kill such an agreement.

Control of the Senate, even by a narrow margin, brings important advantages. The right of first recognition gives the majority leadership more influence on the floor agenda than the minority. Committee chairs exercise considerable control over their committee's agenda and all are majority-party members. However, because the institutional tools of control are considerably weaker than in the House, policy control depends more heavily on the size and cohesiveness of the majority party. Furthermore, a simple majority is often not enough to pass legislation.

PRESIDENTIAL-CONGRESSIONAL RELATIONS

The president and the majority-party leaderships in the two chambers each have considerable though varied resources for influencing the legislative process. Quite clearly the result of the application of these resources to the legislative process depends heavily upon whether these three political actors work together or in opposition. The likelihood of cooperation rather than conflict relates strongly to the pattern of partisan control. When the same party controls the presidency and both houses of Congress, cooperation is the norm; divided control does not necessarily breed conflict on every important piece of legislation, but conflicting electoral and policy goals usually limit the opportunities for cooperation.

When the presidency and the Congress are controlled by the same party, the majority-party leaders of House and Senate usually operate as the president's legislative lieutenants. Because they are elected by their fellow partisans in their chamber, the congressional leaders owe their first loyalty to their own members and occasionally a conflict with the president arises. Most of the time, however, the congressional leaders perceive presidential legislative success as being in their own best interest because the president is leader of their party. Whether enough of their members perceive presidential legislative success to be in their own best interest to constitute a chamber majority is, of course, a critical variable. Given the character of U.S. parties, members may disagree with some of the legislative aims of a president of their own party but are much more likely to support him than are members of the other party.

When control is united the president, through the majority-party leadership and usually also the committee leadership, has access to the institutional levers of control. As his fellow partisans chair and hold a majority of seats on all the committees, priority consideration of the president's program in committee is usually unproblematic. The party leaders can use their control over floor scheduling to the president's bills' advantage. Vote mobilization can be a cooperative effort, with executive-branch liaison staff working in concert with the congressional party's internal operation.

Whether control is united or divided, modern presidents meet regularly with the congressional leaders of their party and work with and through them to influence the legislative process. When his party controls the Congress, the president's party leaders can do a great deal to further his legislative aims. When the opposition controls Congress, however, the president's party leaders can give him much less help, especially in the House. To pass his program, the president must deal with the majority.

The nature of the relationship between a president of one party and a congressional majority of the other depends on the extent to which the policy preferences of the president and those of the congressional majority coincide or conflict, and on the resources each has to impose its own preferences. Even when the ideological distance between president and congressional majority is considerable and the president's stock of political resources is meager, the widespread expectation that the president's program sets the agenda limits the congressional majority's ability to deny him agenda space. Nevertheless, the extent of presidential dominance of agenda setting, as well as his and the congressional party leadership's success at coalition building, depends on a variety of political factors. After a discussion of the historical development of current structures and roles, those determinants will be assessed.

CONGRESSIONAL ASCENDANCY: THE NINETEENTH AND EARLY TWENTIETH CENTURIES

The constitutional stipulation that the president "shall from time to time give to the Congress information of the state of the Union, and recommend to their consideration such measures as he shall judge necessary and expedient" (Article II, Section 3) is now generally cited as the basis for an extensive presidential role in agenda setting. In the nineteenth century, how-ever, few presidents had clearly stated legislative goals, much less a true legislative program. Widespread belief in the separation of powers, weak and factionalized parties during much of the pre–Civil War period, and the restricted sphere of federal government action all served to limit presidential involvement in the legislative process. Instances of presidential leadership confirm the importance of the latter two factors. In the first decade of the nineteenth century, the Democratic-Republican party was strong and cohesive, and President Thomas Jefferson's successful leadership of Congress was based on his being the acknowledged leader of the party. The 1800 election (called, indicatively, the Revolution of 1800) was a party triumph that both the newly elected president and his fellow partisans in Congress perceived as carrying a mandate. Abraham Lincoln's active role in the 1860s in proposing specific legislation and working for its adoption was a response to, and was justified by, the crisis of civil war.

In this period, however, presidential leadership was the exception, not the rule. "During at least part of the nineteenth century the congressional leaders of the majority party defined the chief legislative needs for the country," Randall Ripley writes. "Only occasionally were they confronted with a President who had any clearly conceived and articulated legislative goals" (p. 4).

By the late nineteenth century a strong centralized party leadership had emerged in both chambers of Congress. Over the course of the post–Civil War period, in response to a burgeoning workload and minority-party obstructionism, Speakers of the House developed means of controlling the flow of legislation to and on the House floor. The Rules Committee, which the Speaker chaired, began to report special orders (rules) providing for the consideration of a particular bill, thereby allowing the Speaker to bring up for floor consideration bills difficult to reach in the regular order. Through a series of rulings and rules changes, most notably the Reed Rules established in 1890, the Speaker severely curtailed the minority's ability to delay and obstruct and enhanced the presiding officer's control over the flow of business on the floor. When combined with the Speaker's power to appoint chairs and members of committees, this enhanced control over the floor agenda made the speakership truly powerful institutionally.

During the same period, a strong centralized leadership also emerged in the Senate, with the consolidation of power in the hands of a group of Republican committee chairmen led by Nelson Aldrich of Rhode Island and William Allison of Iowa. However, in the much smaller chamber, this new distribution of influence did not become institutionalized; neither significant rules changes nor even the establishment of formalized party-leadership positions marked the era.

The strong party system of the post–Civil War period made the development of strong centralized congressional leadership possible and also shaped its exercise. Vigorous parties with distinctive constituency bases, which commanded the loyalty of most voters and played an important role in the recruitment and election of candidates, produced a congressional majority-party membership that was substantially like-minded in terms of the legislation members desired to satisfy their electoral and policy goals. Consequently, such members were willing, in the case of the House, to give their leaders very substantial new powers in order to allow them to overcome minority obstructionism and satisfy their members' legislative goals. In both houses, members were willing to allow their leaders to exercise strong, directive leadership because leaders did so, generally, in furtherance of their members' goals.

Commanding an unprecedented combination of political and institutional resources, congressional leaders from approximately 1890 to 1910, the Speaker particularly, were the premier legislative leaders. They determined the legislative agenda and saw to its enactment. To a much greater extent than either before or since, the majority party was sufficiently cohesive that legislative majorities did not have to be constructed but simply mobilized.

In 1910–1911 the Speaker of the House, Joseph G. Cannon, was stripped of much of his institutional power by a coalition of Republican and Democratic insurgents, and his capacity for legislative leadership was severely weakened. The power to make committee and chairmanship assignments was taken from the Speaker,

and he was removed from the Rules Committee. By about 1920 seniority on the committee had become the sole criterion for the attainment of committee chairmanships, which consequently became independent positions of power. In the Senate also, strong central leadership gave way to a much more decentralized distribution of influence, in which committees and chairs enjoyed considerable autonomy.

These changes in the internal distribution of influence in the two chambers are largely explainable as consequences of changes in the party system. As the party system weakened, the costs to members of Congress of such highly centralized internal leadership began to outweigh the benefits. Thus the Progressive Republicans combined with the minority Democrats in the 1910 revolt against Speaker Cannon because his leadership thwarted rather than advanced their electoral and policy goals, which were at odds with those of the regular Republicans.

Even before this reduction in the central congressional party leadership's capacity for legislative leadership, some expansion in the president's role appears to have occurred. President William McKinley (1897–1901), a product of the Congress and very popular with congressional Republicans, cooperated with the congressional leadership. Theodore Roosevelt's interpretation of the role of the president was a highly aggressive one by nineteenth-century standards; he had a program that he forcefully advocated to Congress during his presidency (1901–1909). He pursued his legislative aims vigorously, but usually in cooperation with the congressional leaders, who regarded themselves as at least the president's equal in determining party legislative positions. Roosevelt did not, for example, send draft legislation to Congress, fearing that would be seen as overstepping accepted bounds and would only irritate Congress. Woodrow Wilson (1913–1921) advocated an aggressive legislative role for the president and the circumstances of his election made it possible for him to act in that way as president. The first Democratic president elected in two decades, having run upon a reform platform and coming in with a much enlarged House majority and a new Senate majority, Wilson and congressional Democrats perceived themselves as possessing a mandate. Wilson worked very closely with the Democratic congressional leadership, but more clearly than was the case with Roosevelt, Cannon, and Aldrich, the president was the leader; he was the primary agenda setter and was intimately involved in determining legislative strategy, tactics, and substance. Wilson presented his legislative recommendations in person to a joint session of Congress, the first president in over a hundred years to do so. Details of Wilson's New Freedom legislation were worked out at meetings between administration officials and Democratic members of Congress; during World War I, draft legislation was often sent from the administration to Congress.

The Republican presidents of the 1920s were much less legislatively active; Warren G. Harding (1921–1923), Calvin Coolidge (1923–1929), and Herbert Hoover (1929–1933) advocated a retreat from the aggressive role Wilson had played and none wanted much legislation. Yet even they continued some elements of the more activist role. Thus Harding continued Wilson's practice of delivering the State of the Union address and other important messages personally before joint sessions of Congress. Hoover did propose, though belatedly, a modest program to deal with the Great Depression.

ROOSEVELT AND THE BEGINNINGS OF THE MODERN LEGISLATIVE PRESIDENCY

Victorious Democrats interpreted the 1932 elections as carrying a mandate for vigorous governmental action to combat the depression. A presidential landslide, huge new majorities in both chambers, and the magnitude of the economic crisis provided the conditions for a major expansion in the presidential role.

Franklin Roosevelt (1933–1945) set the agenda for the Congress from the beginning of his presidency. The "first hundred days," the emergency special session of Congress called by Roosevelt immediately upon taking office, was devoted to considering and passing emergency measures recommended and mostly drafted by the president and his aides. Roosevelt continued his activism, and between 1934 and 1936 a large body of innovative legislation, much of it designed in the executive branch, passed at his behest. In a pattern that was to

become typical, the components of Roosevelt's legislative agenda were diverse in origin: some had long been advocated by Democratic members of Congress, some came from interest groups, others from academia. Yet even when the president was less than enthusiastic and embraced the legislation only at the penultimate stage, he received the credit (or the blame).

Roosevelt worked closely with the congressional party leaders and with the committee chairmen who would consider his legislation. He regarded the Democratic party leaders in Congress as his lieutenants, as did they themselves. They saw their primary function as passing the president's program and judged their success as party leaders on that basis. At the beginning of Roosevelt's presidency, the House Democratic leadership set up a whip system to aid it in the passage of the president's program. The states were divided into fifteen zones and an assistant whip chosen for each. Roosevelt also used various personal agents to lobby for his legislation on the Hill.

Roosevelt did not, however, rely only on such insider strategies for selling his program. Exploiting new opportunities, Roosevelt spoke to the public directly via radio and also reached people via newsreels and newspapers.

The first Roosevelt was the first president to take advantage of the mass circulation press that developed in the post–Civil War era to reach the public in a more direct and personalized way than previously possible. Defining the White House as a "bully pulpit," he dramatized himself and the issues he cared about, thus providing good copy to the press. He made himself accessible to reporters and, in return, received extensive coverage. Wilson, who in 1908 wrote that the president "has no means of compelling Congress except through public opinion," firmly believed a president could lead by influencing the public. "He can dominate his party by being spokesman for the real sentiment and purpose of the country, by giving direction to opinion, by giving the country at once the information and the statements of policy which will enable it to form its judgments alike of parties and of men," he asserted (*Constitutional Government in the United States*, pp. 68, 70–71). When he became president, Wilson combined public appeals with insider strategies and, like Theodore Roosevelt, maintained a high presidential profile. Presidential press conferences had begun on a regular but informal basis during the elder Roosevelt's administration and became scheduled events during Wilson's.

The president's dominance in media coverage of government and his centrality in the public's conception of the governmental process seem to stem from the presidency of Franklin Roosevelt. The depression and then World War II focused public attention on the national government; Roosevelt's extraordinary gifts as a communicator as well as his legislative and executive leadership made him personally the focal point of that attention.

By the time of Roosevelt's death in 1945, the federal government and the presidency had been transformed. The post–New Deal, post–World War II federal government was much larger and more extensively involved in the economy and the society than the government of 1933. With the expansion in the government's role had come a change in citizens' expectations; a return to the status quo ante was never a possibility. Citizens' expectations of the president's role had also changed fundamentally. Roosevelt's activist leadership in the legislative realm over such a long period of time set a standard by which subsequent presidents would be judged. In the past, activist presidencies had often been followed by a return to a much more modest presidential role. Popular expectations and the dictates of the government's expanded role now foreclosed such a retreat.

Many of the activities Roosevelt engaged in and the techniques he employed were unprecedented only in frequency and not in kind. Like earlier activist presidents, Roosevelt influenced the legislative process through a variety of informal and often ad hoc means. In addition, however, several organizational developments during his tenure contained the core of what is now known as the institutionalized presidency. In 1939 the Executive Office of the President (EOP) was created; under the authorizing legislation, the president was provided with increased staff help that previously had been meager. Since that time, presidents have increasingly relied on these officially designated but personal aides, rather than on cabinet secretaries or unofficial advisers, for carrying out their legislative responsibilities.

Concerned about federal budget deficits, Congress in 1921 passed the Budget and Accounting Act, which gave the president the responsibility of submitting an annual executive budget to Congress; the Bureau of the Budget (BOB) was set up, by the above act, to provide staff help. The act gave the president the tools to make the budget his own, a statement of his priorities; previously each department or agency had submitted its requests directly to Congress. Roosevelt also used the BOB to screen all legislative proposals from the departments and agencies for conformity with the president's program and to review all bills passed by Congress and recommend whether the president should sign or veto. The movement of the BOB from the Treasury Department to the EOP in 1939 signaled a recognition that the BOB had become an essential and central arm of the presidency.

PRESIDENT AS CHIEF LEGISLATOR

By Dwight Eisenhower's election in 1952, both citizens and politicians expected the president to set the legislative agenda. The central congressional leaders were expected to act as the president's lieutenants, using their institutional and political resources to pass the president's program. They, in turn, expected aid from the president in the process of building majorities.

These expectations had, however, developed during a long period in which the Democratic party controlled both Congress and the presidency. Even so, by the end of World War II, congressional concern about a shift of power from Congress to the presidency was widespread. The 1946 Legislative Reorganization Act was one response. An attempt to increase congressional capabilities for dealing with the more complex problems facing the federal government, it expanded staff resources and realigned committee jurisdictions but accomplished little else. Its effort to institute a more coherent budgetary process in Congress proved a failure from the start.

The negative response to Eisenhower's failure to present Congress with a legislative program in 1953 indicated that the president's agenda-setting role was no longer discretionary. Criticized by Republicans and Democrats alike, Eisenhower thereafter followed the lead set by Truman and submitted an annual legislative program. Compared to that of the Democratic presidents that preceded and succeeded him, Eisenhower's agenda, especially in the domestic area, was quite modest. His views of the proper legislative role of the president harkened back to a previous era and his notions of good public policy more often dictated governmental restraint than activism. Nevertheless, it was Eisenhower who in 1953 set up the first organized congressional liaison unit in the White House. The office's function, then as now, was to aid in the constructing of legislative majorities for the president's program. Its operation during the 1950s tended to be low-key and generally bipartisan.

The 1952 elections brought in a Republican Congress but in 1954, Democrats regained control of both houses and retained their majorities throughout the Eisenhower presidency. The congressional Democratic party leadership was, however, not well positioned to challenge the president's expanded legislative role even had it wanted to. Margins of control were narrow in both houses, and the Democratic membership was ideologically split. In both chambers, liberals, mostly from the North, wanted their leaders to pursue an activist policy role, advocating and attempting to enact an innovative domestic agenda. The large southern segment of the party was mostly conservative and in many areas of domestic policy, found Eisenhower's proposals more congenial than those of their liberal party colleagues.

Furthermore, the leaders' institutional resources were meager. Committees were autonomous and committee chairmen, powerful. Southern conservatives held many of these positions of independent influence. In the House, the Rules Committee was controlled by a bipartisan conservative coalition; consequently the Speaker's control over the floor schedule was only partial.

Eisenhower's relatively inassertive performance of the expanded presidential role, as well as the Democratic leadership's politically and institutionally weak position, resulted in a mixture of cooperation, compromise, and only occasional major battles. Both attempted to pick their spots for all-out conflict carefully, avoiding fights they thought they would lose. The lack of any great public demand for action made such a cautious approach feasible. The result was a relatively lackluster legislative record, certainly few landmark policy departures, yet little public perception of a conflict-ridden government unable to function effectively.

When the 1960 election of John Kennedy to the presidency reestablished united control, circumstances were conducive to a maximal presidential role in the legislative process. The common understanding of how American government did and should work, as disseminated by scholars, pundits, and practicing politicians, emphasized the president as the source of energy and ideas; the oft-repeated saying "the president proposes, the Congress disposes" captures the generally accepted expectation. Since the 1930s the presidency had steadily increased its capacity to play a lead role in the legislative process and continued to do so during the 1950s. Congress, in contrast, had done relatively little to make its individual members, its committees, or its party leaders more capable.

Presidents Kennedy (1961–1963) and Lyndon Johnson (1963–1969) were the primary agenda setters for the Democratic-controlled Congresses of the 1960s. Both strong believers in an activist presidency, they found in the White House staff and the Bureau of the Budget mechanisms that could be used and refined to enhance the president's capacity to play an active legislative role. The creation of an annual presidential legislative package was, in the Truman and Eisenhower administrations, still closely linked to the BOB's legislative-clearance operation in which proposals from the departments and agencies were screened for conformity with the president's objectives. Kennedy and Johnson opened this programming process up to get ideas from outside the government, using task forces as one device for that purpose. The White House staff coordinated and synthesized these efforts in which often-large numbers of people were involved. In 1965 a separate domestic-policy staff was established in the White House to systematize the development of the president's program. The technical support staff provided by the BOB was vital to administrations emphasizing new policy initiatives, enabling them to engage in dispassionate analyses of policy alternatives.

Congress had altered its mode of operation and enhanced its capacity for legislative initiative only marginally since the 1930s. Staff resources had increased but remained relatively meager through the late 1960s, especially in the House; support services were marginal and computer capacity was lacking. Budgetary decision-making was highly decentralized, and no coordination mechanism existed. Central party leaders saw themselves as the president's lieutenants and their job as passing his programs; their resources for constructing legislative majorities were so meager that they relied heavily on White House help.

The White House congressional-liaison operation expanded in function during the Kennedy-Johnson years. The job of the more active, assertive staff was to sell the president's program on Capitol Hill. To that end, the staff was deeply involved in the planning and implementation of legislative tactics. Indicative of the internal party leadership's restricted capacity to influence legislative outcomes and the deep involvement of the White House in internal congressional matters was the fight early in 1961 to enlarge the Rules Committee. The battle was precipitated by conservative control of the Rules Committee and the Speaker's consequent inability to assure that Kennedy's program would even receive floor consideration. The president's liaison staff was integrally involved, doing a head count and appealing to the undecided. According to some accounts, the White House took the lead in orchestrating the effort. Throughout the Kennedy-Johnson years, the liaison staff routinely took head counts on presidential-priority legislation and played a central role in persuading the undecided.

During the 1960s, then, the presidency assumed the preeminent role in agenda setting and the construction of legislative majorities. To be sure, much of the president's agenda had its legislative origins in the Congress of the 1950s, when liberals publicized and built support for a broad range of domestic-policy initiatives. The willingness of Congress to follow the president's lead, especially after Johnson's 1964 landslide election victory, was due in good part to liberals' ideological commitment to the passage of programs they had long advocated. Furthermore, even highly assertive presidential involvement in the legislative process has by no means guaranteed the president legislative success. Even Roosevelt and Johnson, who in the wake of landslide elections enjoyed

periods of great legislative triumph, eventually found themselves stymied on the Hill. The Congress never lost its capacity to say "no" to presidents.

Nevertheless, by the late 1960s the president seemed ascendant and Congress appeared incapable of playing a sustained positive role. Congressional concern about this state of affairs began to rise during the latter part of the Johnson presidency, as policy toward Vietnam became controversial, coming to a head during the Nixon presidency in response to his assertion of unprecedented presidential power.

CONGRESSIONAL RESURGENCE

During the 1970s, Congress transformed itself. Concern about the shifting balance of power between the president and Congress was one, but by no means the only, motivating force behind the transformation. The consequences of the changes for Congress's legislative capacity were complex.

The expansion of both personal and committee staffs that had begun with the 1946 Reorganization Act accelerated greatly during the 1970s, making members of Congress much less dependent upon the Executive for information and greatly enhancing members' and committees' independent legislative capabilities. Support services were expanded and strengthened. The Congressional Research Service (CRS) and the General Accounting Office (GAO) were upgraded, and the Congressional Budget Office (CBO) and Office of Technology Assessment (OTA) were created. These bodies collectively provide Congress with information, analyses, policy options, and specialized expertise. As a result, Congress gained access to expertise that was independent of the executive in a range of key areas. The Budget and Impoundment Control Act of 1974, which created the CBO, limited the power of presidents to impound—or refuse to spend—funds appropriated by Congress, a power many presidents had occasionally exercised that Nixon had attempted to expand. More important, the act set up a mechanism by which Congress can make decisions about the overall level of spending, taxes, and the deficit as well as about spending priorities. This enabled Congress to challenge the president's recommendation in a comprehensive rather than a piecemeal manner.

In the House, though not the Senate, majority Democrats gave their party leadership enhanced resources. The task of assigning members to committees was shifted from Democrats on Ways and Means, who had performed it since the revolt against Speaker Cannon in 1910, to a new Steering and Policy Committee. As the Speaker was made chair of the committee and given the power to appoint eight of its members, his ability to influence committee assignments and consequently the composition of committees was greatly augmented. When the House in the mid-1970s adopted multiple referral, wherein legislation may be referred to more than one committee, the Speaker was given new powers over bill referral. By the late 1970s the Speaker had acquired the power to set a deadline for when a committee must report out legislation, a power routinely used when legislation is sequentially referred to several committees. Most important of all the leadership-strengthening rules changes was the new procedure for choosing Democratic members of the Rules Committee. The Speaker was given the power to nominate all Democratic members of Rules subject only to ratification by the Democratic Caucus and thereby gained true control of the legislative floor schedule.

Although House Democrats enhanced their leaders' resources, during the 1970s those members only occasionally acted in such a way as to make effective central leadership possible. Disgruntlement with policy and concerns about the role of Congress vis-à-vis the executive fueled the reform movement, but so did dissatisfaction about the restricted opportunities for rank-and-file participation. Reducing the power of the committee chairs and increasing opportunities for rank-and-file participation in committee and on the floor were major thrusts of the reforms. Having multiplied opportunities and incentives for participation by spreading around subcommittee chairmanship, democratizing internal committee procedures, and altering the floor amendment process, members were loath to show sufficient restraint in the use of these opportunities to make effective leadership possible. In the Senate, also, altered rules and norms and an expansion of staff resources increased individual senators' opportunities to participate in the legislative process.

Senators' taking advantage of these opportunities led to an explosion of floor amendments and filibusters, wherein members would block action on legislation through prolonged debate. In both chambers the ideological heterogeneity of the Democratic membership further restricted the party leadership's, as well as President Carter's, ability to exert policy leadership.

In the House, the party leadership responded to the uncertainty spawned by increased participation by expanding the whip system and by making some use of its new control over rules to structure floor choices. The whip system, largely unchanged since the 1930s, was enlarged with the addition of leadership-appointed whips. The leadership's ability to do frequent and accurate counts, a necessity given the uncertainty, was enhanced by the increased number and political reliability of whips.

In the politically adverse climate of the 1980s, with a conservative confrontational president and, for much of the decade, a Senate also controlled by the Republicans, House Democrats turned to their party leaders for legislative aid and allowed them to make much more aggressive use of the resources granted them in the 1970s. With the acquiescence of their increasingly ideologically homogeneous membership, the Democratic party leadership, from 1983 on, maintained tight control over the floor and used rules to control the amending process and protect Democratic bills on the floor. The whip operation was further refined and employed routinely to mobilize floor votes. Outreach to interest groups became more aggressive and more routinized, and their integral involvement in the leadership's efforts became frequent.

Also in response to members' expectations, the majority leaders in the House and, after Democrats retook the Senate in the 1986 election, those in the Senate as well, increased their efforts to counter the president in the media. Ronald Reagan (1981–1989) effectively used the president's great access to the media to shape the political agenda and to sell a highly negative image of the Democratic party. Unable to counter this threat to their policy and electoral goals individually, congressional Democrats expected their party leaders to take on the task. Although their media access is much less than that of the president, the congressional majority leaders can nevertheless command considerable media attention. In the 1980s they increasingly used their role as spokesmen to focus attention on Democratic policy priorities. During the 100th Congress, the last of the Reagan presidency, the House Speaker laid out an ambitious legislative agenda, all of whose elements were enacted.

Over time, then, both the president and the congressional majority party have increased their capacity to influence the legislative process. Based on inadequate legal authority, in the case of the presidency, and on a decentralized, intrinsically weak party system, in the case of the majority-party leadership, this capacity does not assure control, even when president and congressional majority are fellow partisans. Control depends, in addition, on the state of key political factors.

POLITICAL DETERMINANTS OF ROLE PERFORMANCE AND SUCCESS

The president is clearly the single most prominent agenda setter. Public expectations that he play that role and his high visibility assure that the president's program will receive some congressional attention. Even when opposition-party congressional leaders firmly control access to the floor agenda, political considerations militate against their simply shutting out the president.

Although central in the agenda-setting process, the president has never exercised a monopoly and in the contemporary period, seems to be experiencing increasing competition from the congressional majority party when control is divided. There have always been policy entrepreneurs inside and outside government seeking to place items on the agenda. The president's program is largely made up of items that others, often including members of Congress, have long promoted. The congressional reforms of the late 1960s and 1970s promoted individual policy entrepreneurship. But by the mid-1980s, congressional Democrats began to realize that individual entrepreneurship was no match for the president, especially in an era of big deficits. As divided control came to seem the norm, rather than extraordinary and temporary, Democrats

began to believe that only by collective action could they challenge an opposition party president's dominance of the agenda, and they began to expect their leadership to play a more active agenda-setting role. The party leadership has responded, though it remains at a severe disadvantage vis-à-vis the president; the party leaders' access to the media is less, and in the public's view, their position does not lend them any special legitimacy for agenda setting. The party leaders' control over the congressional floor agenda and their ability to advantage items they favor in the legislative process compensate for these disadvantages, but only partially.

Although modern presidents are assured of some agenda-setting role, the extent to which they can dominate the agenda depends on political circumstances. Electoral resources are critical. Presidents tend to be more dominant if their party controls the Congress than if the opposition party does. They also tend to be more dominant early in their term because members of Congress believe the public wants a new president to be given a chance. If the election is interpreted by the political community as carrying a mandate, that effect is greatly heightened. That is, if members of Congress believe their constituents want them to support the president's policy departures and that they risk defeat if they oppose the president, his program is assured of priority consideration, even by a Congress controlled by the opposition party.

Later in a president's term, and when his popularity is lower, his ability to dominate the agenda declines. The president remains a significant figure, but his proposals are not given the same priority, and competition from other sources increases. In part, this results from presidencies running out of new proposals; after a few years, the various elements of the initial program have either been enacted or shown themselves to lack the political support necessary for passage. In addition, policy opponents, especially but not exclusively those of the opposition party, perceive less political cost to giving their own proposals priority over the president's.

Both the president and the congressional majority-party leadership are expected to engage in the construction of legislative majorities. Whether they work together or in opposition strongly affects the character of coalition-building efforts and the likelihood of success. The extent to which the president's policy preferences and those of the congressional majority coincide or conflict, and the resources each has to impose its own preferences, determine the balance between cooperation and conflict. Policy preferences are much more likely to coincide when the president and the congressional majority are of the same party, so united control is more likely than divided control to lead to cooperation. Nevertheless, given the character of American political parties, united control is no guarantee of policy agreement across the branches.

The cohesiveness of a congressional party is largely, though not exclusively, determined by external factors. It is, to a large extent, a function of the homogeneity or heterogeneity of members' constituencies, which neither president nor congressional party leaders can significantly influence. The issues on the agenda also make a difference; a party's membership is likely to be more cohesive on some issues than on others. Leaders, especially the president, can and do influence the agenda but cannot control it; external events—a recession or a foreign crisis, for example—often force issues onto the agenda. In attempting to build winning coalitions, leaders thus operate at the margins. When his congressional party is badly split on the major issues of the day, a president can do little to engineer legislative success even if the party's numerical majority is large, as Jimmy Carter learned. Presidential favors—appointments for political allies or constituents, help with a district project, or attendance at a fund-raiser—can pick up a handful of votes but cannot be the basis for the construction of winning coalitions.

The problematic cohesiveness of U.S. parties does mean that a president facing a Congress controlled by the other party is not doomed to total futility. Some segment of the opposition party may be closer in policy preferences to him than to the majority of its party colleagues. Thus, a president may be able to pick up enough defectors from the opposition to construct a majority; Republican presidents from Eisenhower through Bush have attempted to lure the more conservative southern Democrats into their camp, often with success. Fur-

thermore, the ideological distance between the president and the center of gravity of the majority party has varied and has sometimes been small enough to encourage considerable cooperation. For example, although such estimates cannot be made with precision, Eisenhower and the congressional Democratic party of the 1950s certainly were closer in policy preferences than Reagan and the congressional Democratic party of the 1980s; consequently, cooperation was more frequent. Even when that ideological distance is large, a considerable amount of cooperation usually does occur, forced by the necessity of keeping the government running and usually also by a consensus on large parts of current government policy.

Nevertheless, policy agreement tends to be considerably greater within than across parties; consequently, when members of the president's party make up the congressional majority, they and the president will often agree at least on the general thrust of policy. Furthermore, the members of his party have an interest in the president's success that transcends any specific legislative battle. Because many such members believe a strong president will be able to help them attain some of their goals, they may be willing to support the president even when their policy preferences on that particular issue do not coincide with his.

In contrast, when control is divided, members of the congressional majority party are likely to see a strong successful president as a threat to their future goal advancement. As they are less likely to agree with him on policy, an increase in his legislative effectiveness may threaten their policy goals. Their electoral goals are diametrically opposed to his; the president wants his party to hold the White House and increase its congressional representation until it attains control. To the extent that the president's legislative success advances his party's electoral success, contributing to that success is costly for members of the other party.

For the president to elicit support from members of the opposition party beyond that based purely on policy agreement, such members must be persuaded that the costs of opposing the president are higher than the costs of supporting him. The most likely basis for doing so is via a threat to the member's personal reelection chances. Circumstances that make that threat credible provide a president with significant resources for influencing Congress. Thus, presidents can convert into support a perception that an election carried a mandate for him and his program, as Reagan did in 1981. High presidential popularity can sometimes be translated into policy support but seemingly only if members read that popularity as resting, at least in part, on constituents' support for the president's policy proposals. Crises seem to offer presidents their best opportunities for increasing their popularity and converting it into policy support.

While skill in the use of resources undoubtedly affects a president's success at building legislative majorities for his programs, success seems to depend much more heavily on the stock of resources a president possesses and the opportunities circumstance presents. The president has little control over either. Similarly, congressional party leaders' success at coalition building depends on factors over which they have very limited control. The size and cohesion of party contingents, whether the president is of the same party and his resources are much more important determinants of congressional leaders' success than is their skill.

When control of Congress and the presidency is divided, as it has frequently been in the post–World War II period, neither the president nor the congressional majority party may possess resources sufficient for the building of winning coalitions in opposition to the other on a regular basis. Yet the Constitution establishes a relationship of mutual dependence between president and Congress. The president is dependent on Congress not just for new programs but also for money to carry out existing programs. Unless the majority party can muster a two-thirds vote in each chamber, it depends on the president's assent for the enactment of legislation it favors. If neither has the resources to impose its will on the other, and if their policy preferences are significantly in conflict, policy stalemate is a likely outcome.

In the 1980s, policy differences between the parties grew in the context of huge budget deficits. After 1982 the majority Democrats became increasingly cohesive, and stalemate, even on legislation necessary to keep the government functioning, became a real threat. This would have posed immense electoral risks for both the president and the congressional majority party and in response, new processes for reaching agreement were developed. Omnibus legislative vehicles such as continuing (appropriations) resolutions were frequently used to bundle hard decisions. Top-level negotiations between the president or his principal advisers and the congressional majority-party leadership (often called summits) became increasingly common. Although they helped to avoid total stalemate, these new processes seem unlikely to offer a means of surmounting the basic problems of policy-making created by divided government. Rank-and-file members of Congress oppose their use as anything but a last resort because they severely centralize decision-making, thus reducing the role of most members. More important, their use for positive policy-making in noncrisis circumstances is limited by the parties' conflicting policy and electoral goals. Even in crisis circumstances where no agreement carries unacceptably high electoral and policy costs, the results tend to be lowest-common-denominator compromises, not bold policy departures. Despite two hundred years of evolution and change, overcoming the structural barriers to bold policy-making erected by the Constitution still requires either a coincidence of policy preferences across the branches, which single-party control makes more likely but does not guarantee, or an unusual concentration of political resources in one branch.

BIBLIOGRAPHY

JAMES L. SUNDQUIST, *The Decline and Resurgence of Congress* (Washington, D.C., 1981), traces the changing relationship between president and Congress, with special attention to the post-1933 period. More detailed information on earlier periods can be found in W. E.

BINKLEY, *The Powers of the President: Problems of American Democracy* (New York, 1937).

Presidential Leadership

Broad treatments of presidential leadership include RICHARD NEUSTADT, *Presidential Power: The Politics of Leadership from FDR to Carter* (New York, 1980), and FRED I. GREENSTEIN, ed., *Leadership in the Modern Presidency* (Cambridge, Mass., 1988). The discussion of presidential leadership in WOODROW WILSON, *Constitutional Government in the United States* (New York, 1908), is interesting both intrinsically and because the author later became president.

Presidential-Legislative Relations

Works that analyze the president's role and success in the legislative process include STEPHEN J. WAYNE, *The Legislative Presidency* (New York, 1978); PAUL C. LIGHT, *The President's Agenda: Domestic Policy Choice from Kennedy to Carter (with Notes on Ronald Reagan)* (Baltimore, 1983); GEORGE C. EDWARDS III, *At the Margins: Presidential Leadership of Congress* (New Haven, Conn., 1989); JON R. BOND and RICHARD FLEISHER, *The President in the Legislative Arena* (Chicago, 1990); and MARK A. PETERSON, *Legislating Together: The White House and Capitol Hill from Eisenhower to Reagan* (Cambridge, Mass., 1990).

Congressional Party Leadership

Congressional party leadership, its development, exercise, and the factors that influence it are treated in RANDALL B. RIPLEY, *Majority Party Leadership in Congress* (Boston, 1969); CHARLES O. JONES, *The Minority Party in Congress* (Boston, 1970); BARBARA SINCLAIR, *Majority Leadership in the U.S. House* (Baltimore, 1983); JOSEPH COOPER and DAVID W. BRADY, "Institutional Context and Leadership Style: The House from Cannon to Rayburn," *American Political Science Review* 75 (October 1981): 411–425, and BARBARA SINCLAIR, "Strong Party Leadership in a Weak Party Era: The Evolution of Party Leadership in the Modern House," in RONALD PETERS and ALLEN HERTZKE, eds., *The Atomistic Congress* (Armonk, N.Y., 1992), pp. 259–292.

SEE ALSO Legislative-Executive Relations AND The Role of Congressional Parties.

EXECUTIVE LEADERSHIP AND PARTY ORGANIZATION IN STATE LEGISLATURES

Sarah McCally Morehouse

The governor is the chief policymaker in the state political system and must build a political coalition to make policy responsive to a state's needs. The success of the governor as chief policymaker is largely determined by the alliance between the legislative party and the governor's party. The legislature is a partner in the policy-making process, and the partnership depends upon the type of party that operates in the state, both inside and outside the legislature. The importance of understanding the relationship between the governor and the legislature can hardly be exaggerated. State governments are now called on to meet a larger share of the nation's social needs, with the federal government cutting back on most social programs and with local governments limited by their dependence on the unpopular property tax.

The "new federalism"—the redirection of responsibility for education, welfare, and health to the states and the withdrawal of federal funds for these programs—has made a significant impact on the delivery of services to the nation's disadvantaged. This change in direction has resulted in political struggles at the state level as the groups served battle to keep valued programs from annihilation or underfunding. The ability of the governor and the party coalition to meet these demands to maintain such services is crucial to the future of federalism.

The Governor and the Electoral Party

A governor is both head of a party and head of the state government. To obtain the governorship, a candidate must campaign for both the party nomination and the electorate's approval. A candidate's success as a party leader is vital to success as a governor, for he or she must convince legislators and administrators to support gubernatorial programs. Because of the importance of governors and their policies to the health and welfare of the people of each state, the office is eagerly sought. In only a handful of states does the weaker party draft a sure loser and the stronger party nominate a sure winner. In all but five states competition for the office is keen. A governor must deliver on his promises to the people or he will have little chance for future election and political advancement.

To deliver on his or her promises, a governor must deal in the politics of personalities and issues. He must put together a coalition large enough to ensure the nomination of his party. The coalition must convince the legislators of his party that he is a strong candidate who can also help the legislators advance. Legislators also aspire to reelection. In some states, a gubernatorial candidate has a party leadership corps that will back the candidate and provide services and money. In other states, the candidate must put together an organization to win the primary and general elections.

There is a tendency for competitive parties to be unified in the nominating process. The uniquely American "direct primary" form of nomination exists in all states, although it takes different forms. In about one-third of the states, laws or informal rules authorize the parties to make pre-primary endorsements as a way of increasing party control over the nomination or of guiding voters in the primary toward choosing a party-endorsed candidate. In eight of these states, there are legal provisions for party conventions or committees to make endorsements for the primary. In another eight, endorsements are by party rule, and again the endorsing is done in party conventions or committees. States with strong parties are most likely to have pre-primary endorsing procedures. Conventions are gatherings of a thousand or so party leaders, legislators, mayors, county officials, and other party activists. They are united in wanting a winner for governor, a leader who can provide for the people of the state as well as their own personal ambitions. Usually, but not always, such endorsed candidates win in the following primary. Hence, they go into office with a coalition that includes legislators upon whom the governor can count for support.

In most states, the direct primary is the point of decision. Candidates raise a war chest, get themselves on the primary ballot, and campaign for the nomination; here party leaders can back their favored candidates, but they cannot deliver the money and support typically given the endorsee in convention states. In these situations, the candidate has to develop a personal organization and try for early money in order to beat off other contenders. V. O. Key predicted that the primary would ignite and reflect the factionalism within the party. Certainly the direct primary offers a battleground for contending factions, particularly when a newcomer for the nomination wishes to seize the party banner. This struggle for the nomination carries over into the governing process and affects the ability of the governor and the legislature to unite on a program. It takes coalitions to pass programs.

If the gubernatorial candidate who won a handsome percentage of the primary vote invariably won over the candidate whose party was weak and divided, the political process would accord with political theory. A governor and a united party could fulfill election promises, motivated by the need to face the electorate in the next election with accomplishments to their credit. Unfortunately this hypothesis falls by the wayside when the results are examined. Figure 1 shows the distribution of all gubernatorial primary elections won by incumbents and nonincumbents from both parties according to their primary percentage for the period 1976–1990. The nonincumbent records for both parties indicate that many times elections are won by gubernatorial candidates who have not taken their parties by storm. Of the seventy-seven contests in which a nonincumbent Democrat was running, only 12 percent

Figure 1.

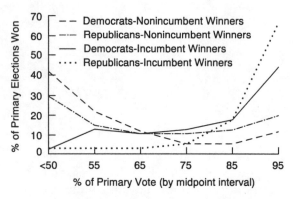

Primary record of winning gubernatorial candidates, 1976–1990, showing the distribution of 212 gubernatorial primary elections won by Republican and Democratic governors according to their percentage of the primary vote.

Source: Richard Scamon, ed., *America Votes*, appropriate volumes.

were won by candidates who had consolidated party backing (more than 80 percent of the primary vote). For the forty-six Republican nonincumbents, the figure is 20 percent. Well over 75 percent of the time, each party sends green governors into the statehouse with less than 80 percent of the party's backing. The results also show each incumbent governor has a great opportunity to consolidate his party. More than 70 percent of the time the party unites to deliver the nomination.

One would expect that if a party is unified, it would provide money and services to its candidate in the primary and general elections. Campaigns are tremendously expensive today and gubernatorial candidates must raise several millions of dollars to compete. The increased costs arise from changes in campaign methods since the early 1970s, including expanded use of polling, television advertising, campaign management consultants, and direct mailings. In 1986 the average cost of a gubernatorial election was $7.369 million, but five states witnessed a great deal more spending than that, particularly Texas, where the race cost $34.6 million and the incumbent was defeated. A 1990 study by Sarah McCally Morehouse demonstrates that candidates with strong party support spend less money on the nominating race than candidates who must battle in a direct primary. Another study indicates that gubernatorial candidates backed by strong parties are likely to have greater success in gubernatorial elections (Cotter, et al.). But what about candidates in states where the parties are rent by factions and there is no party support? Figure 1 provides evidence that many of them win the election. They must seek campaign support from those willing to give it, special-interest groups in particular. When it comes to proposing programs, coalition building will be difficult among the many independently elected prima donnas within such a party, each of whom will incur some measure of obligation to an outside group. The new governor will face a legislature in which sit remnants of the factions that opposed him in the primary contest. In such cases, the governor must put together a coalition for policy-making.

Incumbents have more cohesive party backing, as Figure 1 shows. Their respective parties unite behind them 70 percent of the time, and thus incumbents are likely to run again (only one state prohibits the governor from seeking a second consecutive term). Between 1977 and 1990, 79 percent of the incumbents who could run again did so, and of those who ran, 75 percent were successful. Incumbents are better known than their opponents, and voters feel more comfortable returning an officeholder than a challenger. Incumbents can almost always win a party nomination, and in endorsing states, it is rare for the governor to be denied party endorsement if he chooses to run. Upon reelection, the governor can face the legislature knowing that out there, in that sea of faces, there are friends and allies made over the past four years.

The Governor and the Legislative Party

Most scholars who study the links between the governor and the legislature agree that the factions that contend during the process of nominating the governor are represented in the governing process. A governor who has been successful in building a party coalition to support him or her in the primary and election can count on its help in governing. The governor's faction, if it is large enough, can be expected to produce the votes needed to pass legislation. A governor, hamstrung by factions, cannot hope to govern effectively. Governing parties need internal cohesion in order to pass programs to which they are committed.

If the governor's party is cohesive and loyal to his program, it makes a great difference whether or not it holds a majority in both houses of the legislature. It is reasonable to hypothesize that a governor whose party controls the legislature will have more success in obtaining passage of legislation than one who faces a majority-opposition party. Many advantages accrue to a governor who is backed by a majority. The speaker of the house, the president pro tem of the senate, majority leaders, and chairs and majorities of committees are all from the majority party. This gives the governor a degree of control over legislation that he or she does not have with a minority. However, when that majority becomes too large, the governor has trouble in obtaining enough votes for passage of legislation. Apparently an oversized majority breeds factionalism, which the governor cannot control. Governors have a finite amount of resources. They must calculate at the margins and not expend more rewards or punishments than necessary to gain support for their projects. Minority-party governors can buy high support from their party members. However, they must also bargain with the opposition for votes and use some of their supply of payoffs. The power split between the two branches of government and how this impacts on the policy-making process will be discussed in a later section.

The discussion of the governor here will include his role as policy leader in terms of developing a legislative program and the formal and informal resources he uses to persuade the legislators to support the program. There is no guarantee, of course, that a governor imbued with formal and political powers will use them to best advantage. If a governor's party is split into warring factions, it will be exceedingly difficult to govern, in spite of a well-equipped executive branch.

THE GOVERNOR AS POLICY LEADER

A governor develops policy during the course of an electoral campaign. The candidate explains it to the people of the state in the form of election speeches and then develops these ideas into an administrative program upon attaining office. A governor can claim a mandate from the voters for his or her policies, although proving this assertion is nearly impossible.

State constitutions provide for the initiation of policy by governors. Article V, Section I, of the New Jersey constitution states that "the Governor shall ... recommend such measures as he may deem desirable." This is a statement of expectation that the governor will present to the legislature a program for its enactment. How does the governor craft a legislative program, and from where does it spring? The political circumstances dictate the conditions under which the governor fashions the issues into a set of administration bills introduced by party leaders into the legislature. For example, in the five southern states of Alabama, Arkansas, Georgia, Louisiana, and Mississippi, where the Democratic party dominates the elections for governor and the state legislature, the governor has the freedom to form a platform because the party itself has no platform except those of the individual members of the party who are running for office. In the primary contest, the platforms of the candidates for governorship (and, in fact, all other administrative and elected offices), represent the views of the candidates and may be quite dissimilar. As a result, when the primary is over, the platforms of the winning gubernatorial candidate, the other elective candidates, and those of the legislators are not necessarily related (Ransone). The party itself has no platform in the primary, of course, because it cannot impose one on such a diverse assortment of hopefuls, and in the general election, each must calculate the odds of winning approval of his or her own program. The governor may not put forth ambitious programs that are sure to be defeated, because defeat is not the mark of a successful politician, and the governor wants to make a good record. This record he or she must make alone. There is no party organization, no support for the governor's efforts.

In the approximately twenty modified one-party states, be they Republican or Democratic, the governor is in much the same position, since he or she is actually elected in the primary and has created the platform while campaigning. If the weaker party has shown signs of strength, the candidate may alter the platform to conform to collective party wisdom. This collective judgment may be that of the state chair, the state senators, and the party committee. At any rate, if the party feels challenged in any way, the individual candidate in the modified one-party state may have to yield slightly in the interests of winning.

In a two-party state, a potential governor heads the state ticket, and the others who run on it, such as state legislators, campaign on the same platform. This does not always work out in practice, since many legislators, as well as governors, must build electoral organizations independent of each other. Most platforms of the state's governing party originate in draft form in the incumbent governor's office. Once adopted by a state convention, the platform for a party provides the party leaders and candidates a convenient source for political positions on issues.

The Governor's Program

The governor of every state goes into office with a platform that has been crafted by the governor and his or her advisers. The platform reflects enough of the governor's major policies so that it can be used as a basis for the legislative program. When a newly elected governor takes office, particularly when this represents a change of party, he or she is generally forced by lack of time to have most of the program prepared by members of the transition staff who are outside the government. The first opportunity for the governor to articulate a program comes in the inaugural address. It will lay out themes and hopes for the future and will be monitored by the legislators as a sign of things to come.

When the governor has been in office for a while, many of the program measures will be the products of the departments under his supervision. The preparation of legislation is also influenced—or even prepared—by pressure groups. Out of this mixture of the governor's desires, the party platform, the work of the governor's staff, pressure from special-interest groups, and legislation prepared by the governor's department heads come the major pieces of the governor's program.

Every year the governor presents a "state of the state" address to a joint session of the legislative houses. In it, the governor outlines the substance of the programs he or she wants passed for the session. This is translated into administration bills, which are usually introduced by the governor's party leaders or by legislators whom the governor may specify. A survey of forty-seven state-of-the-state speeches given in the spring of 1990 indicated that jobs and economic development were the leading policy topics, accounting for about one-fourth of the policy references. Table 1 gives a summary of all references. The researchers discovered that there was an interesting correlation between the governor's and legislature's relationship and an emphasis on budget and taxes. The weaker the governor's formal powers and the stronger the legislature's capabilities, the more emphasis was placed on money matters. Consistent with this, governors who faced opposition majorities in both houses also gave most attention to that topic. At a time when many states were suffering from recession, revenue questions were most difficult for governors to deal with. Apparently, if the governor was in a strong position with respect to the legislature, he or she did not mention revenue questions, but when the legislature was professionalized and in the hands of the opposition party, the governor had no choice but to focus on those issues and attempt to place some of the blame for past failure or future inaction upon its members (Monroe, Kiser, and Walesby).

Whether or not the governor emphasizes the budget and taxes in the state-of-the-state address, in most states he or she is required to play a legislative role in budget-making. The governor has the initial responsibility for pre-

Table 1
POLICY TOPICS REFERENCED IN GOVERNORS' STATE-OF-THE-STATE ADDRESSES, 1990

Policy Topic	Percent of References
Jobs and economy	24
Budget and taxes	10
Education	17
Environment	13
Family issues	6
Drugs and crime	17
Social welfare	9
State government, other	4

Source: Adapted from Monroe, Kiser, and Walesby, "Comparing the State of the States" (1991).

paring the budget and in most places is expected to submit an executive budget bill. This power can be used to put dollar figures on many of the policies that the governor wants to see enacted. The governor ordinarily delivers the highlights of the budget to the legislature in a special message. This is an important media event for the legislators and the public.

In the past when the governor and both legislative houses were controlled by the same party, the budget was rubber-stamped. Even when the governor faced opposition in one or both legislative houses, the budget-making potential within the legislature was weak, for the committees that were supposed to review the budget had insufficient staff to challenge the document, and it usually received bipartisan support. According to Jewell and Miller (p. 131), "one of the most consistent and most important trends over the last twenty years in American state legislatures has been the growing scrutiny of the executive budget and increasing influence over budgetary decisions." A committee on appropriations or on appropriations and revenue plays the major role in reviewing the budget. The writers trace this development in Kentucky from 1966, when Governor Edward "Ned" Breathitt's budget was passed by both houses ten days after it was submitted, to the rejection of Governor Martha Layne Collins's 1984 tax package by the legislature on 19 March after two months of hearings. Following this, the appropriations committees of both houses of the legislature assumed responsibility for writing a new budget.

The increasing probability that one or both houses of a state legislature will be in the hands of a party opposed to the governor, along with the growing professionalism of the legislative budgetary process, means that the days of rubber-stamping are over. The trend in 1991 appeared to be a deadlock between the governor and the legislature in many of the larger states hardest hit by the recession. Connecticut, California, Illinois, Maine, Pennsylvania, and Texas struggled to reach an agreement between budget cuts and tax increases long past the 30 June deadline. In these situations, governors have to use all of their powers, both informal and formal, to help forge an agreement. These powers will be discussed in the following sections.

THE GOVERNOR'S FORMAL POWERS

In 1987 the National Governors' Association analyzed the changes in the formal powers of the fifty state governors over twenty years. It found that governors have proven to be vital and strong leaders in many areas, despite institutional shortcomings that may hamper their success. Conversely, some governors have failed to provide strong leadership to their states even where formal provisions indicate an authoritative base. Political scientists have been making a comparative study of the power of state governors since 1965 when Joseph Schlesinger developed the first index, and most indices since then have used or modified his components (Mueller; Dometrius). The index for each state is a sum of its values on each component. States can then be ranked and compared. The components of the index have traditionally included tenure, appointment, and budget and veto powers. But there has been little agreement on the value of the index in explaining why one governor is more successful with the budget, taxes, or educational initiatives than another. The National Governors' Association added two additional powers to the index: the legislature's power to change and amend the budget submitted by the governor and the degree to which the governor's political party has control over the state legislature. This last variable stands out as being totally different from the others in that it is not an administrative tool but a result of the electoral process. Its inclusion in the index results in an unwieldy combination of electoral and administrative power.

Tenure in Office   The turnover in the office of the governor has traditionally been high. This is a product of two factors: the constitutional limits on the term of office and the inadequacy of revenues to meet the demands of the people. More recently, governors have been spending more time in office, in part because of an increase in the number of states adopting four-year terms and permitting the incumbent to run for reelection. In 1992 forty-seven states had four-year terms for the governor, compared to thirty-four in 1960. Only New Hampshire, Rhode Island, and Vermont consider it necessary to submit the governor to public approval every two years. The increase in the gubernatorial term means that in forty-seven states governors can count on a respectable time to prove themselves. If they decide to increase taxation to pay for burgeoning education and medicare services, they can do so in the first two years of the term and hope the results will appear before they come up for reelection. Fifty percent of the governors can expect to serve for more than four years.

Appointive Power   The assumption underlying the appointment power as measured by the National Governors' Association is that governors who can appoint officials without confirmation by any other authority are more powerful than those who must have either or both houses of the legislature confirm an appointment. Governors with the least power are those in states that provide for public election of statewide officials, such as the commissioner of agriculture in Kentucky and the superintendent of public instruction in California. Governors whose power to appoint is unrestricted by popular election or by the requirement of legislative confirmation will be in a better position to influence the direction of policies and programs within their administrations. Governors use the appointment process as a major vehicle for developing relationships with political and special-interest groups and the legislature. Promises of appointments to high-level executive positions and to the state judiciary are often dangled in front of recalcitrant legislators. Since 1965, the governors have gained more appointment power in the areas of corrections, welfare, highways, health, and public utilities, but gained little appointive power in education. The governors of Massachusetts, Indiana, and Tennessee have strong appointive powers. Those with weak powers govern in Texas, Georgia, Mississippi, South Carolina, and Oklahoma (Beyle, 1990). There are few empirical bases for the assumption that the governor's appointing power really helps to get bills through the legislature. The only supporting evidence is Sharkansky's study on the impact of the governor versus the department heads with respect to the budget. This study shows that in states where governors have broad appointing power, they have more control over the budget process than in those states where there are a number of elected officials who may compete with them.

Budgetary Power   There are two more weapons in the arsenal of the governor's formal powers that are widely recognized as powerful ammunition if used with skill. The first is the power of the purse, which the governor shares with the legislature, but over the years, the responsibility for preparing the budget has become the governor's. In 1970 thirty-five states gave the governor full responsibility over the budget, and by 1990 the number had grown to forty-four; five others do not limit the governor's responsibility for budget-making by much (Beyle, 1990). Since forty-nine out of fifty states have professionalized the process, this component of the gubernatorial powers index offers little in measuring differences among them. Apparently in most states, the budget is seen as a major expression of gubernatorial policy and as an important means of administrative control. The budget officer, appointed by the governor, must be able to prepare a budget that is an accurate expression of the governor's proposed program. In most states, the governor does appoint the budget director, usually with confirmation by one or both houses.

While the states have been giving their governors impressive budgetary powers, they have also been increasing their legislatures' ability to change those recommendations. Forty-three states give their legislatures unlimited power to change the executive budget (Beyle, 1990). The number of states granting this power increased by four between 1965 and 1992, possibly a reflection of the same trend on the national level, as embodied in the Budget and Impoundment Control Act of 1974. In addition, legislatures have been giving themselves the capability to review and react. Specialized fiscal staff agencies, computerized fiscal information systems, and the establishment of revenue-estimating capability have all contributed to enhancing the legislatures' performance on the budget. Legislatures can add to, subtract from, or eliminate funds, programs, and projects as a result of their review. The new budget process is marked by intense scrutiny, bargaining, and sharing of power. This is the case in almost all states, even those in which the same party controls the executive and legislative branches. New York State offers an example of skilled negotiations, with Governor Mario Cuomo proposing a budget in 1989 that slashed state programs severely so that the legislature could make increases and still keep within his spending goals. The governor prevailed on the overall rate of spending, but the legislature decided where to add and where to cut (Rosenthal, 1990).

Veto Power   At the other end of the legislative process is the power to veto bills passed by the legislature. This is a potentially powerful weapon. It is a means by which the governor can prevent administrators from going over his head and getting support from the legislature. By vetoing particular items in a bill, a governor can keep the budget within the chosen spending confines. In thirty-eight states, the governor has the item veto, which can only be overturned by three-fifths of those elected or two-thirds present. Practically speaking, this means that the governor need persuade only a small percentage of gubernatorial party members to oppose a potential veto override. Because most legislators know that it is almost impossible to overturn a veto unless the governor's party is hostile and divided or unless it commands less than one-third of the legislature (as in the case of Republican governor Guy Hunt of Alabama [1987–1993]), the threat of a veto is effective.

Fifteen states give the governor additional leverage by means of "executive amendment," whereby the governor can return a vetoed bill to the legislature with suggested amendments. In Illinois the governor can return a bill with specific recommendations for changes and language to amend the bill. If the legislature accepts the revisions by a majority vote in each house, the governor certifies the bill and it becomes law as amended. If the governor does not sign it, the bill is returned as a vetoed bill requiring a three-fifths vote in each house to override (Van Der Slik and Redfield).

Calling Special Sessions   In all states, the governor has the power to call special sessions. In twenty states, this power resides with the governor alone, and in thirteen states, only the governor may determine the subject matter of such a session. The governor can use the special session as a threat to the legislature to complete its work before the constitutional adjournment date. He can also call the special session to get the people of the state to become aware of the immediacy of a financial crisis and the gubernatorial program to cope with it. The legislators are then in the position of going along with the proposals of the governor or taking the consequences, which can be serious if the electorate is really alarmed.

The effectiveness of most of the powers listed above depends on the skill of the governor. A governor at odds with legislative leaders will find that many of these powers will fade. The real energy that drives the cooperation between the governor and the legislature is the political coalition of which they are both part. It takes such a coalition to bring to fruition the hopes embodied in the governor's program.

THE GOVERNOR'S POLITICAL RESOURCES

All governors have resources at their disposal, but their skill in using them marks the difference between successful and unsuccessful governors. A governor who has built up a good-sized coalition within the party can expect to have a nucleus of support. There is already a group whose members worked for the campaign and shared the fruits of victory. Friendships, loyalty, psychological rewards—all have a part to play in the legislative coalition. Here are discussed some of the resources at the disposal of the governor.

Appointment Powers

From the perspective of the legislator, appointments to high administrative positions count for less than the more modest appointments to the Commission on Aging, the Commission on Fair Employment Practices, and others of an advisory or regulatory nature. These are the rewards the legislators want to secure for their constituents and contributors to their campaigns. Most of the positions are unpaid, but they confer status on the recipient, who credits the legislator with making the arrangements. In turn, this provides the governor with a reward system that keeps legislators supportive.

While there are many fewer traditional patronage jobs because of the establishment of civil-service systems, governors use the jobs they have as skillfully as possible. Party workers, campaign contributors, and legislative constituents can be rewarded and turned into future supporters.

Patronage The number of projects for bestowal by governors differs from state to state. Jobs, contracts, and favors are not put at the governor's disposal the way they used to be, but they can still be used for maximum advantage. Rosenthal (1990) gives as an example the creation by Governor James R. Thompson of Illinois of a "Build Illinois" program that blended economic development policy with "pork" (special projects located in legislative districts to benefit the constituents). Thompson adopted projects selected by legislators for his plan, and agreed that about one-fifth of the funding for the program would be given to the legislature for allocation. The total was divided among the four party caucuses, giving the legislative leaders the power to allocate the pork to the most deserving.

Social Recognition

Legislators are used to receptions given by lobbyists, but receptions at the governor's mansion are special occasions. Breakfast with the leaders or even a late-night session at the governor's dining-room table to hammer out the budget gives the impression that the governor is a human being in need of support. Governor Nelson A. Rockefeller of New York invited legislators to his estate at Pocantico to tour the grounds, enjoy the view, and partake of a sumptuous repast. They were more likely to stay on good terms with the governor when it came to needed support.

Publicity The governor, unlike the legislator, has guaranteed access to newspapers, radio, and television. The governor has repeated opportunities to speak and to capture the headlines and to appeal to public sentiment as a way of focusing public attention to the legislative program. Many governors use weekly or biweekly radio or television programs to explain to the people the major issues before the legislature and their own positions. Added to these means of direct access to the citizen are the daily press conferences held by most governors. No single legislator or group of legislators can hope to command the audience that the governor can, largely and simply because of his or her position. The skill and imagination with which governors use these techniques and opportunities varies widely. Television was essential to building what Paul West describes as a love affair between Governor Thomas H. Kean of New Jersey and the voters. Kean's first step was to preside over a series of televised town meetings in each of the state's twenty-one counties. Since New Jersey has no commercial television station, Kean relied on cable television. He also began hosting a regular television show. Eventually Kean's patrician voice became almost as recognizable as his face. A set of television commercials featuring the governor and celebrities such as Bill Cosby and Brooke Shields urged vacationers to see their state. His heightened personal popularity enabled him to build support in the legislature.

Promise of Campaign Support

Governors head the ticket on which the legislators campaign for election, and legislators hope the governor's coattails will help them win. While most of them have to run independent campaigns, there is a bond that develops from standing under the same political umbrella. If governors have a strong interest in party coalition building, they will involve themselves in legislative elections. They will probably not get involved in a legislative primary unless a particularly strong supporter is fighting for his or her life against a challenger, in which case the governor may endorse the legislator and see that money goes into the fight. It is much more likely that governors will become involved in legislators' elections. Most of the party's candidates are incumbents and believe the governor should come into their district for a testimonial dinner or a birthday party and put in a good word for their record. According to a National Governors' Association survey, it was generally agreed that governors should campaign for the whole ticket, and half the respondents felt that the governors should campaign for their party's legislative candidates (Rosenthal, 1990).

A governor faced with a minority in the legislature may want to help in some races in which challengers from the party are making an attempt to unseat opponents. If the governor, through the party organization, sees that money and support are provided in such a race, a potential legislator will feel a special debt to the executive. To summarize, the support of the governor in an election campaign can be a powerful stimulus to a legislator. Generally, legislators hope their gubernatorial candidate will give them a plank upon which to campaign. The legislator in the governor's party has a personal stake in the governor's success.

THE LEGISLATURE AS PARTNER OR RIVAL

The discussion of the governor's role in policymaking has emphasized the governor as party leader both inside and outside the legislature. The major theme is that the coalitions formed by the governor in the electoral process carry over into the legislative process and affect his or her ability to obtain legislative support. Formal powers of the governor also affect his or her strength to see the program through the legislature. The overriding consideration is the skill with which the governor makes use of these resources. A governor with a strong electoral coalition can get support.

This support, however, is not in any sense automatic. It is a partnership when it works and a rivalry when it does not. The ingredients for either condition exist in most legislatures today. Because the legislatures have become powerful decision-making centers since the 1960s, they are insisting on the right to examine, review, and analyze executive legislation. They used to be malapportioned, high-turnover, part-time bodies. Now they have become professional and capable, and offer attractive careers. The frequency and length of sessions have increased. Compensation was raised, professional and support staff were added, the physical setting was enhanced, and access to electronic technology for such tasks as bill retrieval, redistricting, and economic forecasting was provided for. Hence, the governor dwells with an independent power center under the capitol dome, one that can offer independent analyses, independent predictions, and independent action. Cooperation is necessary to best serve the citizens, but it is cooperation between two formidable actors, and the powers and strategies that used to bring coordination are changing.

Support staffs and high technology do not equal representation, however. Political parties still matter: legislators run for office under party banners, and legislatures are organized according to party strength. The party needs electoral votes to stay in business, and the legislators make promises to get votes—promises that must be kept if the legislator wants to be returned in the next election. It is vital for the party organization that its members perform in accordance with the needs of the people if the organization is to be nourished by electoral success. Thus, there is a symbiotic relationship between the needs of the legislator to be re-elected and the need of the legislative party organization to maintain itself. The ability of the party leaders to garner support from the legislators depends on the rewards the party can offer them for their loyalty. The conditions under which the legislator supports the party versus the pressure groups or the constituency is related to the political ambition of the legislator and the way the party can further that ambition. Thus, strong parties, both within and without the legislature, can be of great aid to legislators seeking election.

The Legislator's Party Ambitions

Whether the political party can help the legislator advance is related to the type of district he or she represents. Tidmarch, Lonergan, and Sciortino report that a majority of districts in state legislatures are safe for one party or the other and that marginal seats are on the wane. However, in a majority of the states, at least 20 percent of the legislative districts are won by less than 55 percent of the vote. It is commonly believed that legislators from competitive districts will tend to represent their districts before the interests of their legislative party, because they must please their districts if they want to be reelected. It is precisely those competitive districts which are of interest to legislative leaders, particularly in legislatures where the party balance is close. These districts are the ones that can win or lose majorities. However, legislators from comfortably one-party districts do not need the support of a state party for election. If they want to advance within the legislative hierarchy, however, they must please their leaders who control committee assignments and political positions. Since the early 1970s a high percentage of incumbents have sought reelection. In 1986 ten out of fourteen states had at least one chamber in which 80 percent of its members sought reelection. The rate at which incumbents seek reelection has not changed, nor has their success rate. On average, well over 90 percent of the incumbents win. What has changed, however, is the margin by which incumbents win. This has increased dramatically (Jewell and Breaux). Incumbents now win by about 75 percent on average, up from about two-thirds (Garand). The

high degree of incumbency and the increasing margins by which legislators win indicate that they may be independent of political parties as electoral organizations. However, their advancement within the legislature depends upon the party leadership.

Some hypotheses emerge from this discussion: (1) Legislators have ambitions for advancement that are related to the political opportunity structure in their districts and in the state. (2) If legislators see their chance for advancement bound up with the record of the party, they will support their party program and thus will support the governor's program if their party has the governorship. (3) If legislators are from atypical districts and from a faction opposing the governor, they will support district or interest-group needs over those of the party. Thus it is important to consider the conditions under which legislators run for office, notably their dependence on, or independence of, the local party, the legislative party, and the state party.

Party Nominations in the Legislative Districts

Because state legislative office is the most common starting point in the political career of elected officials, it is important to know just what motivates candidates to seek this first stepping-stone. Relevant to this decision are the degree of competitiveness in the district, the type of primary, and the incumbent. It is not wise politically to run in a district held by an incumbent who has been increasing the percentage of the vote since first winning office. Better to look for a competitive district and settle there. Since, in most states, only about 20 percent of the districts are competitive, the selection is limited. Most incumbents win, but 10 percent of them lose, so a particularly intrepid challenger might be willing to beard an incumbent, especially if there was some evident weakness. In most districts, candidates are self-starters, deciding to run on their own and organizing the effort by themselves. In states where the parties are strong, such as Connecticut and Pennsylvania, party leaders at the state or local level may recruit candidates for the nomination.

The rules that govern primaries determine the way the game is played. State nominating systems differ from each other in important ways. Restrictive systems, such as Connecticut's party convention or Pennsylvania's closed primary, limit public participation to those who are registered party members, strengthen a party's control over nominations, and increase the power of politicians. This type of system tends to breed professional, career-oriented politicians who are linked to the parties. The use of pre-primary endorsements and organizational help usually means that a united party can see to it that its preferred nominees are selected. Connecticut, Pennsylvania, Ohio, Indiana, Minnesota, and Colorado are examples of states where local parties endorse and work for candidates in legislative primaries. Public endorsements are provided by law in Colorado and Connecticut and by party rules in Minnesota. Studies have shown that where parties endorse, competition in the primaries is low (Grau; Kunkel).

If the nominating system is open, as it is in most states, the electoral conflict is broadened and expands the range of participating groups. Hence, the party leader's control over recruitment is reduced. Influence is more widespread and the outcome's predictability decreases as competition in the primary increases.

When incumbents seek reelection (which occurs 80 percent of the time), they are less likely to have opposition in the primary; only 30 percent are challenged. When combined with the fact that only 3 percent of them lose the primary contest, one concludes that there are not as many openings available for legislative aspirants as might be assumed (Grau). The picture emerges of legislative nominations going primarily to those who have already served and to self-starters who organize their own campaign. This does not indicate that legislative party leaders will have much influence over such a pool of political independents.

Legislative Party Funding

According to Malcolm Jewell and David Olson, many legislative candidates, whether incumbents or challengers, are on their own during the campaign. They receive little assistance from the state party organization, which concentrates on statewide races, or from local organizations, which give priority to races for mayor or sheriff. With the exception of candidates in the sixteen states that endorse candidates and hence have a stake in their success and those in a few southern Republican parties that have been recruiting candidates for election (Aistrup), legislative candidates have usually run on their own. However, legislative party leaders are increasingly taking an interest in elections. Legislative candidates from marginal districts are of great concern to political leaders, for it is within the marginal districts in closely competitive legislatures that legislative majorities are won or lost. It is ironic that as legislative parties are becoming more competitive, legislative districts are becoming less, thus, the number of competitive districts that can make or break a majority is continually decreasing. Coupled with this, the cost of seriously contested legislative campaigns is escalating and candidates need help. This help can come from the parties or from political action committees (PACs), and the latter could turn the candidates away from party loyalty.

Many studies have documented the dramatic increase in campaign spending for state legislative seats. The curve in state electoral spending has matched that of congressional spending. In California the cost of a campaign for the state's lower house in 1980 was $310,570; four years later it was $384,406. In Florida for the same two periods the costs were $36,000 and $63,000, respectively (Sorauf). In frugal Connecticut, costs between 1984 and 1986 rose from $5,786 to $8,288. The value of making dollar comparisons like this when the district populations are not compared is meaningless. California house districts averaged 296,101 people; those in Connecticut averaged 20,000. However, the trend is obvious: elections are more costly every time. Ruth Jones reports that the costs of legislative campaigns seem to have increased more rapidly and more sharply than most other campaigns. Between 1978 and 1980 the average cost of a legislative seat doubled or tripled in almost every state for which there are records. These figures generally lump together the amounts spent on primaries and general elections and thereby obscure the importance of money spent on primaries. Several reports that do separate the spending on each indicate that candidates report greater expenditures on primaries than on general elections.

Couple this with what is already known

about incumbents—that they win more than 90 percent of the time—and one begins to see the futility of running against them. Furthermore, it is easy for incumbents to raise money. According to Sorauf, the dominance of incumbents in California is related very directly to PAC expenditures in the state. In 1986 PACs and businesses accounted for more than 80 percent of the receipts of incumbents in the assembly and about one-third of the much smaller sums their challengers received. In Connecticut, PACs have given three times more money to incumbents than to challengers.

Legislative leaders and legislative caucuses have viewed the increasing costs of campaigns with concern. Candidates, incumbents as well as challengers and open-seat candidates, would turn to interest groups and PACs for money— groups that have pressured for single issues often at variance with the party program. If this continues, legislators, who are independent enough at best, would be enticed further away from the party fold. Party leaders reason that raising funds to help incumbents and challengers who both face close races would accomplish two objectives: it would make legislators more likely to cooperate with the party leaders and would help build or maintain a majority in the legislature. In addition, funding party members in open races would bring loyalty and gratitude on the part of the newly elected.

With these concerns and strategies on the part of the legislative parties, it is not surprising that the years since the early 1980s have seen the growth of legislative campaign committees to implement the strategies. These committees are of two types: legislative party caucus committees and party leadership committees. The former are established by the party caucuses in each legislative chamber, which can determine the rules for their operation and allocation of funds. The leadership committees are established by individual party leaders who have total discretion to determine how the funds will be distributed. According to Alan Rosenthal, professor of political science at Rutgers University and a leading expert on state legislatures, leadership giving to legislative candidates began in California in the 1960s when Jesse Unrah, Democratic speaker of the assembly, had money left over from his own campaigns and bestowed it upon his party's needy candidates.

A careful study of caucus and leadership committees was made in eight states, and a number of common characteristics were found. The caucus committees receive funds from both individuals and PACs and often from individual legislators as well as from state, national, and local party organizations. In terms of PAC-giving, business PACs were more likely to give to Republican caucus committees, and labor was more likely to give to Democratic caucus committees. Speaker Tom Loftus of Wisconsin said, "A utility PAC gives the committee I head $100. Part of what I give to a candidate comes from that $100. The candidate may believe in state ownership of utilities. I don't care, nor do the other members of the ADCC care. Our only test is that our candidate is in a winnable seat and he or she is breathing, and those two requirements are in order of importance" (p. 109).

Most caucus committees distribute funds disproportionately to candidates in close races, and most committees give priority to nonincumbent candidates. Because leaders dominate the decision-making in some caucus committees, the differences between the two types of operations may not be pronounced. Leadership campaign committees, however, are less likely to support nonincumbent candidates (Gierzynski and Jewell). This may be a reflection of leadership's desire to obtain loyalty for party programs and the need to be reasonably sure that the candidates they support will return.

The relationship between the state party committee and the caucus committees is vital to understanding the ability of the party to govern. The governor *is* state party leader and must build a coalition which includes the legislative party as well. If there is no cooperation between the two, the coalition will be impossible to achieve. According to Gierzynski and Jewell, caucus campaign committees indicate that the state party organization has no control over the committees' operation. However, some state committees said that there is cooperation between the two and that the legislative party committees use state party resources, such as mail privileges or phone banks. Time will tell whether these two party organizations will cooperate or operate independently of each other. The political party is supposed to merge the separate branches of government;

only to the extent that these new legislative committees cooperate with the state party can this be accomplished.

This section started with the hypothesis that the pattern of competition in a legislator's district would affect his relationship with the state party. If the legislator needs its help to win, he will support its leaders and program. If the election campaign was aided by a rival faction or by interest groups and not by the party, the legislator owes it little allegiance. However, a legislator from a noncompetitive district may face a primary and need the support of the party, and legislative caucus committees occasionally enter these races. The party is of major importance in legislative elections and can extract loyalty from those legislators it has aided in the process of the campaign.

The Party in the Legislature

Following the elections of 1990, the Republican party had legislative majorities in twenty-three state chambers and the Democrats claimed majorities in seventy-three. Two legislatures had ties and contemplated some way of breaking the deadlock. For the ninety-six partisan bodies, the majority leaders prepared to make the crucial decisions about party membership on committees, the party ratio, appointment of chairs, the rules, and settling the chamber down to its jobs. If the governor's party is in a minority, it must deal with the majority leaders in order to pass the governor's program bills.

Party Leadership

The speaker of the lower house is clearly the most powerful figure in that branch, elected by the membership and representing whatever party or faction has a majority. In most cases, the speaker of the house is granted broad powers to appoint members to committees and to preside over the operation of the chamber.

Traditionally the lieutenant governor presided over the senate. However, as state parties became more competitive and the possibility increased of having a minority-party lieutenant governor in the senate chair, the legislative powers of the lieutenant governor were considerably curtailed. Many of them are no longer allowed to preside. There are forty-two states that elect a lieutenant governor; in twenty-eight

of these that official presides over the senate. In the remaining twenty-two states the presiding officer is elected by members of the senate (including Tennessee, where the presiding officer is elected and is called lieutenant governor). Where the lieutenant governor presides over the senate, power is shared with an elected president pro tem.

When the legislative party is strong, the speaker of the house and the senate's presiding officer are in fact chosen by the majority party caucus as its first order of business at the start of the session. Though the minority party nominates its own candidates for these posts, this is a time when party lines remain firm and the majority candidate wins. Based on a survey of legislative staff members in 44 states, Rosenthal (1984, p. 24) concluded that in 29 senates and 30 houses, the presiding officer is invariably chosen by the majority party. He also discovered that there are 7 senates and 5 houses (mostly southern) that are often organized by a bipartisan coalition, and another 8 senates and 8 houses where it sometimes happens.

In moderate-strong party states such as Rhode Island, Pennsylvania, Wisconsin, New York, and Connecticut, advancement from party whip to floor leader to speaker for one or both parties, is the norm. In other states such as Illinois, Iowa, and Montana, the speaker and floor leaders have been chosen more often from among committee chairs or members of the judiciary or appropriations committees. In one-party states, the house and senate leaders are invariably from the governor's party, but they are not necessarily from the governor's faction. The selection of party floor leaders, assistant leaders, or whips is usually done within the party caucus, but there are eight houses and five senates where the majority leader is picked by the presiding officer.

There are few legislatures where speakers or senate presidents serve only one term. At one extreme are a few legislatures that regularly elect a new presiding officer every two years; at the other extreme, a few legislatures return the leaders for as many as 6 two-year terms. Speakers are reelected more frequently now. While party turnover, of course, accounts for much of the turnover in speakers, the professionalism of the legislature—and with it increased compensation—may affect speaker stability. Many of the states where leaders have recently broken precedent by seeking second or third terms are in the South. One reason for change may be that most southern states now permit their governors to serve a second consecutive four-year term; thus, this also puts the lid on the speaker's notions for advancement and makes him wait longer to run for higher office (Jewell and Patterson, 1986, p. 119).

Party Caucus

Most legislatures use the party caucus as a way of building cohesion. Political party caucuses play some role in the legislative process in forty-three states. In the remaining seven, the caucus meets at the start of a legislative session to choose legislative leaders (Nebraska, Alabama, Arkansas, Florida, Mississippi, Maryland, and New Hampshire) (Jewell and Olson, 1988, p. 236). The importance of the party caucus for party cohesion is impressive. Caucuses are most important in the majority party or the minority party that controls the governorship.

Cohesion is built in different ways. In general most legislators have run their own campaigns, although they may have received caucus money in the process. They have a working staff, respectable salaries, and modern technology; legislators can't be herded along. Diplomacy and skill are needed to deal with them. They are professionals and hope to advance politically; however, the party leaders have control over the avenues of advancement. They interact with the governor and can recommend that good things happen to the legislator's constituents. A caucus, therefore, is a way of unifying many ambitions into a cohesive effort; one that will, hopefully, benefit the state and its citizens.

Thus, the manner in which caucuses operate depends to a great extent upon the strength of the party and its leaders and the expectations of the legislators. There are six categories of caucuses ranging from those that are found in strong party states to those that function in their weak sister states (Jewell and Olson, 1988). The first example is the strong caucus in which major pieces of legislation are discussed and voted upon; the votes are binding on the members. Because caucuses are held in secret in some states, the number of examples of such strong party caucuses is unknown. The majority party in Colorado takes binding votes on the budget bill which is then passed on the floor in the exact form that it has passed the caucus. The second type of caucus is also found in strong-party states and is used by strong leaders to obtain cohesion for the floor vote. Caucus votes are not binding, but both leaders and legislators are aware of the commitments made in such a meeting and are expected to hold to them. Both political parties in Pennsylvania use such caucuses. The third type of caucus, also found in states where parties are significant as organizations, but perhaps not quite as strong as those mentioned above, is the one that arrives at a consensual type of party cohesion. This type of caucus occurs in legislatures where a close balance exists between the parties so that it becomes necessary to unite the party of the governor, in particular, to pass administration bills (Jewell and Olson). In this case, the governor could have a close majority or a close minority in the chamber. The caucus meets regularly, discusses the issues, and takes *straw*, or unofficial, votes. The members are not bound, but they may sense the urgency to maintain cohesion if the governor's program is to be passed.

The next class of caucuses occur primarily within legislatures where party balance is uneven. A large majority party, usually composed of factions or groups that are difficult to unite, meets to discuss policy issues and to inform the members. Even in legislatures where the Democrats outnumber the Republicans two to one, as in Kentucky, the leadership withdraws a piece of legislation following discussion if it appears that there are not enough Democrats to pass the bill (Jewell and Olson, 1988). The caucus is designed to give the leadership a strategy and encourage the members to "think party" not faction. Caucuses which are meetings to keep the members informed are usually held within the minority party in large majority chambers. Party action is not key, here, because there is little that can be done by the party to change the floor vote. Caucus members develop a set of expectations about the use of such meetings, which may be important when the party finds itself with a governor. The last caucus functions largely because the members of a party want to exert more power over policy-making and appointments. This indicates a party with divisions that the leadership has not or cannot control. Again, this type of caucus could become more of a policy-making body if cohesion became more crucial.

Organization of Committees

The assignment of legislators to committees and the selection of committee chairs are controlled by house speakers and senate presidents. Wayne Francis considers the degree to which the party leaders use this assignment process to build legislative party cohesion. He believes that the leadership (usually the speaker or the president but also a "committee on committees" in many cases) does not necessarily assign an inner group of key members to important committees and chairmanships, but instead tries to honor as many members' requests for chair appointments and committee assignments as possible. This often results in committee autonomy; however, the leaders do not see this as detrimental to their leadership agenda as long as they can get their way on major party issues, such as fiscal policy (Francis, 38). Apparently there is great variation among the states in the balance between party-oriented decision-making and committee dominance. In states with strong party systems, the leaders probably make committee assignments based on party loyalty and expect the committees' agendas to conform to the party leadership's agenda. In other states, committees are dominant and no appreciable party influence is noticeable. These conditions occur in states with a long tradition of one-party dominance.

Francis believes that party leaders accommodate members by making committee assignments that pass out many favors at the beginning of the legislative session; however, coalition favoritism is probably more evident in committee chairmanships. The most significant committees such as "appropriations" and "ways and means" are chaired by coalition supporters who will work to promote party policy. The assignment of members to committees based on their communities of interest—agriculture, education, health, hospitals, banking, insurance—probably is a function of the new professionalization of the legislative process. This accommodation of member interest is part of this professionalization, and is probably key to legislator party loyalty.

THE PARTY AND POLICY-MAKING

In states where parties are strong, both the governor and the legislators represent a common program commitment. The governor as party head proposes legislation to fulfill that program and works to obtain enough votes to ensure its passage. In various states, it is possible to measure the extent to which this happens. A legislator's party-voting loyalty can be determined by analyzing roll-call votes, which are an essential part of reaching decisions on bills. The political party is the most important cue-giving mechanism for determining how legislators will vote. The degree of partisanship may vary from issue to issue, but if the political party does not organize the legislature, as in some one-party states, there is no voting cue or structure for voting behavior (LeLoup, 1976).

The package of bills a governor presents to the legislature as his policy program is the most important and, hence, the most controversial. Those researchers who study those issues that are most likely to divide the legislature along party lines usually agree that three categories are most likely to cause conflict: (1) those in the administration's program; (2) social and economic issues that can divide the parties along liberal-conservative lines and in which major interest groups have taken a stand; and (3) issues involving either the special interest of a state, such as reorganization and administration of state government, or the special interests of legislative parties such as the election of a speaker or adoption of legislative rules.

Party Control of the Legislature

The constitutional separation of powers between the executive and legislative branches of government is expected to be softened by the synthesizing effects of a political party. The ability to capture both executive and legislative branches is the minimum condition essential for parties to perform their supposed function of meshing the independent organs of government. Table 2 indicates how many states in the last fourteen years have enjoyed this condition and also reveals that half or more of the states at any one time do not have the meshing of executive and legislative branches under a party umbrella. This may be a function of the increasing competitiveness of state parties on the gubernatorial level.

Most states can elect a governor from either party. Also, as previously discussed, incumbents can be reelected more than 90 percent of the time in state legislatures, so whatever the traditional partisan division of a legislature, it is likely to stay that way for some time. This is particularly noticeable in the South where the Republican party can elect governors but not legislative majorities. Also, Democrats have made gains in formerly Republican states like Vermont and Indiana. For example, after the election of 1990, power was divided in twenty-eight states. In only eighteen states did the Democrats control both the governorship and the two houses of the state legislature; the Republicans had unified control in only three. Of the twenty-eight states in which power was divided between the legislature and the governor, twelve had at least one house controlled by the governor's party. In sixteen, then, the governor faced a legislative branch that was held by the opposition party.

If the governor's party controls the legislature, success in obtaining the passage of his program will be increased because the legislative leaders and committee chairs are from the party. While a legislative majority can work to the advantage of a governor, the percentage of seats a governor's party holds in the legislature also is a predictor of the legislators' support.

Governors calculate closely and do not dispense more rewards or punishments than is necessary to gain support for their projects. Governors can handle modest majorities in their legislatures. But, when the governor's party has an overwhelming majority, coalitions form against him that cannot be assuaged with the traditional stock of rewards and punishments.

Minority-party governors can expect high support from their party members; however, they must bargain with the opposition for some votes. The strategy of dealing with the opposition to win enough votes to pass legislation has been a common phenomenon in the 1990s. A governor in a strong position within the minority party can convince both his minority members and, when necessary, some of the majority to support the program.

Party Voting

Table 3 presents party support and opposition to the governor's program in eighteen state legislatures in 1971. The states are categorized according to their degree of interparty competition based on an index introduced by Austin Ranney. This index combines competition for the governorship, the senate, and the house and is appropriate because it provides an overall measure of the strength of the political party in both legislative and executive branches (Ranney, 1976, p. 87). Since most political scientists concur that a state's level of interparty competition is strongly related to the organization and activities of its political parties, this provides an acceptable sampling frame for selecting states (Patterson and Caldeira).

Table 2

PARTY CONTROL OF STATE LEGISLATURES AND GOVERNORSHIPS, 1976–1990

	1976	1978	1980	1982	1984	1986	1988	1990
Democratic*	29	21	17	26	19	14	15	18
Republican*	1	5	6	3	4	6	4	3
Mixed	19(13)	23(17)	25(19)	20(17)	26(16)	29(18)	30(12)	28(16)

*Includes tied chambers.
Some legislative elections fall in the odd year following the date given (KY, LA, MI, NJ, VA).
The numbers in parentheses indicate the number of states in which both houses of the legislature are held by the party opposed to the governor.

Source: Council of State Governments, *The Book of the States* (1976–1977, 1978–1979, 1980–1981, 1982–1983, 1984–1985, 1986–1987, 1988–1989).

Table 3
THE GOVERNOR'S PROGRAM:
PARTY SUPPORT AND OPPOSITION

State[a]	House		Senate	
	Average Index of Support[b]	Average Index of Opposition[c]	Average Index of Support[b]	Average Index of Opposition[c]
One-Party Democratic				
D.-Ark.	58.8		59.7	
D.-Miss.	58.9		67.5	
Average	58.9		63.6	
Modified One-Party				
R.-N.H.	58.7	67.9	72.2	55.0
R.-Wyo.	79.2	32.8	75.5	26.3
D.-N.C.	61.2	70.8	66.7	55.4
D.-Ky.	77.3	55.2	86.3	56.3
Average	69.1	56.7	75.2	48.3
Two-Party				
**R.-Mass.	69.1	57.2	72.1	50.1
D.-R.I.	74.9	86.5	77.9	57.7
*R.-Wash.	75.2	29.2	67.0	43.7
*R.-Ill.	80.0	41.0	83.1	52.2
*D.-Mont.	81.1	36.0	85.4	45.9
*D.-Nev.	82.4	52.4	81.3	33.0
**D.-Ohio	83.5	62.3	78.4	65.5
R.-N.Y.	84.0	50.7	91.0	58.0
D.-Pa.	87.7	65.7	89.6	66.1
**R.-Calif.	88.7	65.7	81.0	59.0
*D.-Wis.	88.7	76.0	93.6	70.6
R.-Colo.	91.3	78.8	89.5	82.4
Average	82.2	58.5	82.5	57.0

[a]Ranney's Index of Competitiveness (Ranney, 1976, p. 87)
According to party affiliation of Governor, 1971
[b]Index of Support—Governor's party votes cast for governor
for one bill   Total party votes
[c]Index of Opposition—Opposition party votes cast against governor
for one bill   Total party votes
[b,c]The Average Index is the arithmetic mean of the indices derived for the various votes on the governor's program bills.
*/**Divided control: One (*) or both (**) houses in the hands of the opposite party, 1971.

Source: Compiled by author.

Table 3 gives the average index of support for the bills in the governor's program by the members of his party and the average index of opposition to the bills in the program by the members of the opposition party in the house and senate (Morehouse, 1981, p. 295). The index of support reveals how loyal a governor's party was when voting on the bills in the governor's program. The index of opposition indicates how loyally the opposition party closed ranks against the bills in the governor's program. The index of support reveals that the average party support for a governor is higher in competitive states than in one-party or modified one-party states. The average index of support climbs to a high of eighty-two in competitive states for the governors' parties in both the house and the senate; this is considerably higher than the corresponding measure for Congress.

The index of support for the governor's program is low in states that are completely dominated by the Democratic party, indicating that the governor has a difficult time obtaining votes from members of his or her legislative contingent. The governor has no dependable cohesive faction to support the policy program. In modified one-party states, be they Democratic or Republican, the average support for the governor is approximately midway between the one-party and the two-party states, indicating that even a small legislative opposition party can bring increased voting support for the governor.

Governors in competitive states must get every party vote that they can garner to hold the line against the opposing party. In these states, the governor's party is likely to have a narrow majority or minority and therefore it must provide a loyal voting group. While the mean index of support for the dozen two-party senates and houses is 82, the mean opposition score is 58. This indicates that there is opportunity for the governor's party to bargain for votes, perhaps with various promises of rewards and favors for constituents in the legislators' districts.

THE GOVERNOR AND THE LEGISLATIVE PARTY

The governor is the chief policymaker and chief party leader in the state. His ability to lead his party to victory in the general election and then to build a coalition to pass the party program in the legislature is dependent upon the factional structure of the party and how successful he is in forging it into a united effort. To accomplish this, the governor has certain informal and formal powers to persuade party members to join the coalition. He now must work with a professionalized legislature in which legislators enjoy higher pay, more staff, and high technology to help them evaluate and to act on policies. The legislative party leaders must also deal with this increased independence on the part of the legislators and gain their support by offering money and services to aid their reelection.

Legislators who are helped by their party owe it allegiance after they are elected; party leaders expect loyalty from those they helped recruit and elect. Since state legislative leaders are much more powerful than leaders in the U.S. House and Senate in controlling committee assignments and selecting committee chairmen, they have additional tools to enforce loyalty. This loyalty is garnered to pass the governor's program—the most important and controversial legislation in the session. Especially if the governor's party is a minority within the legislature, minority leaders need to support the program because they can provide the base from which to add additional votes.

Legislatures are becoming independent power centers. A governor must deal with them as such and use his powers with skill. He can command the attention of the state, and the legislature, composed of a hundred or so legislators, cannot compete with the chief party leader and policymaker. The legislature has the resources to check and to bargain, however, and hopefully both partners have the will to serve the people.

EXECUTIVE LEADERSHIP IN STATE LEGISLATURES

BIBLIOGRAPHY

The Governor as Political Leader

Interest in state political parties and in elections for governor as the most prominent political leader began with the works of V. O. KEY in the 1950's; among them *American State Politics: An Introduction* (New York, 1956). It was Key's theory that competitive politics produced cohesion within parties and that governors with cohesive parties could better serve the citizen's interests. Despite current notions that parties are no longer effective, many writers continue to test and verify Key's theories; among them are THAD BEYLE, "From Governor to Governor," in CARL E. VAN HORN, ed., *The State of the States* (Washington, D.C., 1989); CORNELIUS P. POTTER, JAMES L. GIBSON, JOHN F. BIBBY, and ROBERT HUCKSHORN, *Party Organizations in American Politics* (New York, 1984); MALCOLM E. JEWELL and DAVID OLSON, *Political Parties and Elections in American States* 3rd ed. (Pacific Grove, Calif., 1988); SARAH MCCALLY MOREHOUSE, "Money Versus Party Effort: Nominating for Governor," *American Journal of Political Science* 34 (August 1990); SAMUEL C. PATTERSON and GREGORY A. CALDEIRA, "The Etiology of Partisan Competition," *American Political Science Review* 78 (September 1984); and AUSTIN RANNEY, "Parties in State Politics," in HERBERT JACOBS and KENNETH VINES, eds., *Politics in the American States: A Comparative Analysis*, 3d ed. (Boston, 1976).

The Governor as Policy Leader

The success of the governor as chief policy-maker is largely determined by the alliance between the legislative party and the governor's party. This alliance depends on the type of party that operates in the state, both inside and outside the legislature. The political scientists listed below address this relationship: THAD L. BEYLE, "Governors," in VIRGINIA GRAY, HERBERT JACOB, and ROBERT ALBRITTON, eds., *Politics in the American States: A Comparative Analysis*, 5th ed. (Glenview, Ill., 1990); NELSON C. DOMETRIUS, "Changing Gubernatorial Power: The Measure vs. Reality," *Western Political Quarterly* 40 (June 1987); KEITH J. MUELLER, "Explaining Variation and Change in Gubernatorial Powers," *Western Political Quarterly* 38 (September 1985); NATIONAL GOVERNORS' ASSO- CIATION, *The Institutionalized Powers of the Governorship: 1965–1985* (Washington, D.C., 1987); IRA SHARKANSKY, "Agency Requests, Gubernatorial Support and Budget Success in State Legislatures," *American Political Science Review* 62 (December, 1968); JACK R. VAN DER SLIK and KENT D. REDFIELD, *Lawmaking in Illinois: Legislative Politics, People and Process* (Springfield, Ill., 1986); and PAUL WEST, "They're Everywhere! For Today's Governors Life Is a Never-ending Campaign," *Governing* 3 (March 1990).

Legislative Elections

Governors need legislators loyal to their programs. Loyalty depends upon many things, among them the ability of the governor and the political party to help the legislator win elections. This is related to the type of district the legislator represents. Much research has been done on the cost and conditions of legislative elections. DONALD A. GROSS, "Governors and Policy-making: Theoretical Concerns and Analytic Appoaches," *Policy Studies Journal* 17 (Summer 1989); MALCOLM JEWELL and PENNY M. MILLER, *The Kentucky Legislature: Two Decades of Change* (Lexington, Ky., 1988); ALAN D. MONROE, GEORGE C. KISER, and ANTHONY J. WALESBY, "Comparing the State of the States," presented at the annual meeting of the Midwest Political Science Association, Chicago (1991); COLEMAN RANSONE, JR., *The American Governorship* (Westport, Conn., 1982); and ALAN ROSENTHAL, *Governors and Legislatures: Contending Powers* (Washington D.C., 1990).

The Governors' Formal and Informal Powers

Political scientists have been making a comparative study of the legal powers of governors since the 1960s. They have developed an index for comparative purposes made up of several components including tenure, appointment, budget, and veto powers. There has been little agreement on the value of the index in explaining why one governor is more successful than another. Some political scientists believe that informal powers and the skill with which the governor makes use of them are more important than the formal powers. Among those who have contributed to this ongoing discussion are JOSEPH A. AISTRUP, "Republican Contestation of U.S. State Senate Elections in the South," *Legislative Studies Quarterly* 15 (May 1990); JAMES C. GARAND, "Electoral Marginality in State Legislative Elections, 1968–1986," *Legislative Studies Quarterly* 16 (February 1991); CRAIG GRAU, "Competition in State Legislative Primaries," *Legislative Studies Quarterly* 6 (February 1981); ANTHONY GIERZYNSKI and MALCOLM JEWELL, *Legislative Party and Leadership Campaign Finance Committees: An Analysis of Resource Allocation*, presented at the annual meeting of the American Political Science Association, Atlanta (1989); MALCOLM E. JEWELL and DAVID BREAUX, "The Incumbency in State Legislative Elections," *Legislative Studies Quarterly* 13 (November 1988); RUTH S. JONES, "Financing State Elections," in MICHAEL J. MALBIN, ed., *Money and Politics in the United States: Financing Elections in the 1980s* (Chatham, N.J., 1984); JOSEPH A. KUNKEL III, "Party Endorsement and Incumbency in Minnesota Legislative Nominations," *Legislative Studies Quarterly* 13 (New York, 1988); TOM LOFTUS, "The New Political Parties in State Legislatures," *State Government* 58 (Fall 1985); FRANK J. SORAUF, *Money in American Elections* (Glenview, Ill., 1988); and CHARLES TIDMARCH, EDWARD LONERGAN, and JOHN SCIORTINO, "Interparty Competition in the U.S. States: Legislative Elections, 1970–1978," *Legislative Studies Quarterly* 11 (August 1986).

Legislative Party Organization

The political party can explain legislative party loyalty more than any other factor. How the legislative leaders are selected and how they organize the legislature for maximum policy loyalty are considered by the following political scientists: WAYNE L. FRANCIS, *The Legislative Committee Game: A Comparative Analysis of Fifty States* (Columbus, Ohio, 1989); MALCOLM E. JEWELL and SAMUEL C. PATTERSON, *The Legislative Process in the United States* 4th ed. (New York, 1986); LANCE T. LELOUP, "Policy, Party, and Voting in U.S. State Legislatures: A Test of the Content-Process Linkage," *Legislative Studies Quarterly* 1 (May 1976); and ALAN ROSENTHAL, "Dimensions of Partisanship: Exploring Legislative Parties in the States," unpublished manuscript (1984).

SEE ALSO Budget Procedures and Executive Review in State Legislatures; Committees in State Legislatures; Elections to the State Legislatures; PACs and Congressional Decisions; Political Parties in State Legislatures; Reform in State Legislatures; **AND** State Legislatures in the Twentieth Century.

THE CONGRESSIONAL COMMITTEE SYSTEM

Steven S. Smith

Committees, along with bicameralism and political parties, are the central organizational features of the U.S. Congress. Their prominence within Congress and in national policymaking has led scholars to give them a great deal of attention. Studies have been conducted on committee origins and development, legislator assignments to committee, committee floor success and voting behavior, intracommittee voting behavior, committee reform, committee decision-making styles, individual committees, and conference committees. Attention has also been given to the ebb and flow of committee power, and to the formal modeling of the place of committees in the legislative game.

This essay does not attempt to review the research on congressional committees systematically. Instead this essay, drawing heavily from Steven S. Smith and Christopher J. Deering's study *Committees in Congress* (2d ed., 1990), focuses on the historical development of the committee system, the place of the committee system in the decision-making process of the modern U.S. House of Representatives and Senate, and developments affecting the structure and power of committees. It begins with a brief overview of the modern committee system.

ORGANIZATION OF THE MODERN COMMITTEE SYSTEM

The U.S. Constitution makes no provision for committees, except to allow each house to devise its own rules to govern procedure (Article I, Section 5). House Rules 10 and 11 and Senate Rules 24 through 28 identify the standing committees, specify their jurisdictions, and prescribe certain features of committee procedure and organization. Each chamber can change its rules, and the two chambers have adopted rules that differ in important ways.

Chamber rules are not the only source of committee structure and procedure. Statutes can provide for the creation of committees and procedures related to their activities. Rules adopted by party caucuses may affect committee procedure and organization, govern appointments to committees, and limit the power of committee and subcommittee chairs. Informal practices also regulate committee powers, organization, and procedures.

Committees have two formal functions: (1) the collecting of information through hearings and investigations, and (2) the drafting and reporting of legislation. Committees are the primary means whereby the testimony of representatives of the executive branch, organized interest groups, and the general public may be formally received. Committees undertake most congressional investigations of administrative agencies and practices, and of official misconduct. The vast majority of legislation introduced by members of Congress is routinely referred to the committee or committees of appropriate jurisdiction. And most of the details of legislation are scrutinized or written in committee meetings.

The House and Senate have developed various types of committees to perform these informational and legislative functions. All committees may hold hearings and investigate policy problems falling within their jurisdictions. Not all committees have the right to receive and report legislation and not all committees are considered to be standing or permanent committees.

Standing committees have legislative authority and permanent status. Their legislative jurisdiction is specified in chamber rules and precedents, and they may write and report legislation on any matter within their jurisdictions.

In the case of the House, which must approve its rules at the start of each Congress, the jurisdictions of standing committees are routinely reapproved every two years. The rules articulating the jurisdictions and regulating the behavior of standing committees may be changed, of course, as they have been on occasion, but for the standing committees the burden is on proponents of change to gain support for amendments to the rules. Table 1 lists the standing committees of the 101st Congress (1989–1991).

Ad hoc committees may be created and appointed to design and report legislation, but they are temporary and often dissolve upon reporting legislation or at a specified date. Since 1975 the Speaker of the House has been permitted to appoint an ad hoc committee, with House approval, but this authority has been used on only a few occasions.

Conference committees are also temporary and have legislative responsibilities. They are appointed to resolve the differences between House and Senate versions of legislation. The Constitution requires that legislation be approved by both houses in identical form before it is sent to the president. For important, complex legislation, the task of resolving differences is often difficult and time consuming. While there are other ways to resolve interchamber differences, conference committees are named for most important legislation. Conference committees have wide but not unlimited discretion to redesign legislation in their efforts to gain House and Senate approval. When a majority of House conferees and a majority of Senate conferees agree, a conference committee issues a report that must be approved by both houses. Conference committees dissolve as soon as one house takes an action on the conference report.

Joint committees are permanent but lack legislative authority. Comprised of members from both houses, with the chairmanships rotating between members of the two houses, these committees conduct investigations, issue the results of studies, and may recommend legislative action. But bills are not referred to them and they cannot report legislation di-

Table 1
STANDING COMMITTEES OF THE 101st CONGRESS, 1989–1991

House Committees	Size	Senate Committees	Size
Agriculture	45	Agriculture, Nutrition, and Forestry	19
Appropriations	57	Appropriations	29
Armed Services	52	Armed Services	20
Banking, Finance, and Urban Affairs	51	Banking, Housing, and Urban Affairs	21
Budget	35	Budget	23
District of Columbia	11	Commerce, Science, and Transportation	20
Education and Labor	34	Energy and Natural Resources	19
Energy and Commerce	43	Environment and Public Works	16
Foreign Affairs	43	Finance	20
Government Operations	39	Foreign Relations	19
House Administration	21	Governmental Affairs	14
Interior and Insular Affairs	37	Judiciary	14
Judiciary	35	Labor and Human Resources	16
Merchant Marine and Fisheries	43	Rules and Administration	16
Post Office and Civil Service	23	Small Business	19
Public Works and Transportation	50	Veterans' Affairs	11
Rules	13		
Science, Space, and Technology	49		
Small Business	44		
Standards of Official Conduct	12		
Veterans' Affairs	34		
Ways and Means	36		

Source: "Committees of the 101st Congress," *Congressional Quarterly Special Report*, May 6, 1989.

rectly to the floor. The Joint Economic and Joint Taxation committees house sizable staffs and conduct newsworthy hearings from time to time. The Library and Printing committees perform the more ministerial duties of overseeing the operations of the Library of Congress and the Government Printing Office.

Select or *special committees* are, in principle, temporary committees without legislative authority. They may be used to study problems falling within the jurisdiction of several standing committees, to symbolize Congress's commitment to key constituency groups, or simply to reward particular legislators. Select committees have been used for prominent investigations—the Senate's 1973 Watergate committee and the 1987 House and Senate select committees on the Iran-contra affair are examples. Major reforms of congressional rules and organization have originated in select committees. Unfortunately, committee nomenclature can be misleading. For example, without eliminating the word *select* from their names, the House and Senate have made their intelligence committees permanent and granted them the power to report legislation.

Of all of the above, the committees of greatest interest are the standing committees. In the modern Congress, standing committees originate most legislation, and their members manage the legislation on the floor and dominate conference committees. It is the development, as well as the power, of standing committees in the two chambers that is the subject of this essay.

THE DEVELOPMENT OF THE COMMITTEE SYSTEM

The decision-making process of the House and Senate represents an interaction of committees, parties, and the parent chambers. The relationship between the three varies from time to time, as does the relative importance of each in shaping public policy. Committees have been used since Congress's first session in 1789, but their functions and influence have changed as the chambers, parties, and their political environment have evolved. This section traces the development of the House and Senate committee system, beginning with general propositions about the power of committees.

Basic Propositions About Committee Power

On a hypothetical basis, one can devise three models of committee power vis-à-vis congressional decision-making: the autonomous committees model, the party-dominated committees model, and the chamber-dominated committees model. The models highlight the advantages and disadvantages of the modern committee system and provide a basis for specifying the conditions that shape the role of committees.

In the *autonomous committees model,* members of each committee determine policy within their jurisdiction, irrespective of the policy preferences of the parent chamber and parties. That is, committees have monopoly control over both setting the agenda for their parent chamber and making policy choices.

In the *party-dominated committees model,* committee members are agents of their parties. The parties have the capacity to shape the composition and policy outlook of their committee contingents because they control appointments to committees. Committee members take direction from their party leaders on what issues to consider and what policy choices to make. Noncompliant committee members are replaced with compliant members or their legislative proposals are ignored.

In the *chamber-dominated committees model,* committee members are agents of their parent chambers. Committees are created to meet the needs of the chamber for a division of labor, the development of expertise, the acquisition of information, and the organization of a supporting staff. Committees must obtain majority support on the floor for their legislation and so must anticipate floor reactions to their recommendations.

Each of the three models has attractive features. A system dominated by autonomous committees allows Congress to manage a large work load by providing a division of labor, and encourages the development of expertise among committee members, who know that their work will be respected and approved by others. A party-dominated system allows for the emergence of strong party leadership, which can supervise the development of coherent, timely policy, and makes it possible to hold a party accountable for congressional decisions.

A chamber-dominated system seems quite democratic because it preserves the equality of all members, regardless of their committee assignments or party affiliation, and allows all members to have an active voice in important decisions.

The fit of these models to actual House and Senate practices has varied over time in response to several sets of factors: the character of Congress's policy agenda, the distribution of policy preferences, and the institutional context. The effects of these factors can be summarized in the propositions below.

Policy Agenda   This proposition asserts that the more numerous and separable the issues the greater their recurrence, and the less salient they are, the more Congress relies on committees to make policy choices. Large agendas require a division of labor to handle the work load, and a system of powerful committees provides such a division of labor. If the issues are quite separable into distinct categories, then a system of committees with distinct jurisdictions works well. Furthermore, if issues recur frequently, then fixing committee jurisdictions can be done without concern that some committees will become superfluous over time. Moreover, if most issues concern only a few members, committees can make decisions without serious challenge on the floor.

Throughout its history, Congress's growing policy agenda has produced a nearly continuous elaboration of its committee systems, which provide the basic means for dividing labor and increasing Congress's capacity to process legislation. Often, new issues have been sufficiently distinctive to allow the assignment of jurisdiction for a new issue to a single committee in each house. But frequently, particularly with the increasing integration of national and international society in the twentieth century, new issues have not fallen neatly within established jurisdictions, creating conflict among committees, sometimes producing slow and incoherent policy-making, and generating interest in reform.

Policy Preferences   This proposition states that the more salient the issues and the more cohesive the majority party, the more Congress relies on the majority party to make policy choices. To the extent that the majority party lacks cohesiveness, Congress relies on the chamber floors to make policy choices.

When members take an active interest in policy decisions, they will not tolerate autonomous committees that do not share their policy views. If members' policy preferences exhibit a partisan alignment leading to majority-party cohesiveness, the majority party will have both the incentive and the capacity to control committees. Central party leaders will be encouraged to see that committees either have little influence over outcomes or are stacked with friendly members. If issues are salient to most members, preferences are not aligned by party, and the majority party lacks sufficient cohesiveness, then coalitions cutting across the parties—perhaps different coalitions on different issues—may assert themselves on the floor and determine policy outcomes.

Historically, the partisanship of policy alignments has been uneven. Highly partisan alignments have followed dramatic shifts in the coalitions supporting the two major parties, shifts that have been labeled "realignments." The timing of realignments in the Civil War years, the 1890s, and the 1930s gives congressional partisanship a cyclical cast that contrasts sharply with the more monotonic (that is, moving in only one direction) increases in the size and complexity of the congressional agenda. Thus, a pattern of periodically centralized party leadership appears to overlay a more linear pattern toward more elaborate committee systems.

Institutional Context   The final proposition asserts that the more chamber rules and practices preserve the right of individual members to debate and offer amendments at will on the floor, the less autonomy committee members and party leaders will have. The House and Senate are very different institutions. There is greater need for a strong presiding officer and for observance of formal rules in the larger, more unwieldy House. In the Senate there is greater tolerance of individual initiative and greater resistance to committee- or party-imposed policy choices. That tolerance is represented in the rules of the Senate that protect the individual senator's right to offer amendments on any subject and conduct extended debate. Such rules preserve the bargaining leverage that individual senators have when dealing with committee and party leaders.

The critical feature of past procedural and structural choices is that they limit the range of feasible institutional arrangements for the future. Neither house has the time or capacity to reconstitute its decision-making processes completely. Elaboration of existing procedures and structures is the common response to new demands. Differences in existing institutional arrangements in the House and Senate are likely to cause different responses to similar changes in issue agendas and policy alignments. In general, the autonomous and party-dominated committee models generally fit the House better than the Senate.

A Brief History of the Committee Systems

The organization of Congress has proven to be quite dynamic. At times, committees have been subservient to parties and at other times have exhibited remarkable autonomy. Even their position in the sequence of the legislative process has varied widely. And House and Senate committees frequently have differed greatly in their legislative functions and power.

Members of the first Congresses were influenced by their experiences in the Continental Congress or in their colonial and state legislatures. They devised mechanisms allowing for the full expression of the will of congressional majorities while maintaining the equality of all legislators. They preferred that each chamber, as a whole, determined general policy through discussion prior to entrusting a subgroup of the membership with the responsibility to devise detailed legislation. Because legislators feared that committees with substantial policy discretion and permanence might distort the will of the majority, House committees of the first eight or nine Congresses usually took the form of special or select committees that dissolved upon the completion of their tasks. While the chamber-dominated committees model clearly fit these early years, the House began to develop the foundations of a standing-committee system as well. By 1810 the House had created ten standing committees in routine policy areas and in other recurrent, complex policy areas requiring regular investigation. The practice of referring legislation to a select committee gradually declined thereafter.

In its formative years the Senate used select committees exclusively for legislative matters, creating only four standing committees to deal with internal housekeeping affairs. A smaller membership, greater flexibility in floor procedure, and a much lighter work load—with the Senate always waiting for the House to act first on legislation—permitted the Senate to use select committees in a wider variety of ways than did the House, while still maintaining full chamber control over legislation. But beginning in 1806 the Senate adopted the practice of referring to a committee all matters relating to the subject for which the committee had been created, creating implicit jurisdictions for select committees.

In the fifty-year period prior to the Civil War, the standing-committee systems of both houses became institutional fixtures. Both houses of Congress began to rely on standing committees, regularly adding to their number. In the House, the number of standing committees increased from ten to twenty-eight between 1810 and 1825 and to thirty-nine by the beginning of the Civil War. The Senate established its first significant standing committees in 1816, when it created twelve. It had added ten more by the onset of the Civil War.

The expansion of the standing-committee system had roots in both chamber and party needs. A growing work load and regularized congressional interaction with an increasing number of executive departments combined to induce committee growth. And the House began to outgrow a floor-centered decision-making process. The House grew from 64 members in 1789 to 241 in 1833, making open-ended floor debate chaotic.

Partisan considerations were important in the House. Henry Clay (R.-Ky.), who assumed the speakership in 1811 and served for six nonconsecutive terms over the next fifteen years, transformed the speakership into a position of policy leadership and increased the partisan significance of committee activity. Rather than allowing the full House to conduct a preliminary debate, Clay preferred to have a reliable group of friendly committee members write legislation. The Speaker's control of committee appointments made this possible. During Clay's era, two procedural changes transformed the committee's place in the sequence of House decision-making, further enhancing its value to the Speaker. First, the practice of allowing standing committees to report at their own discretion was codified into the rules of the House in 1822 for a few committees. Second, by the end of the 1820s first referral of legislation to a committee became the norm, bypassing preliminary floor debate. Empowered standing committees under Clay's control approximated the party-dominated committees model.

By the late 1830s, after Clay had left the House, all House committees could introduce new legislation and report it to the floor at will. Preliminary debate by the House came to be viewed as a useless procedure, and the participation of the full membership soon was reserved for review of committee recommendations. With these changes, House standing committees gained a critical role in proposing legislation and assumed a regular role in the consideration of virtually all legislation.

Pressures for change in the Senate's committee system were not so great as they were in the House of Representatives. The Senate could manage its legislative agenda in serial fashion by waiting for the House to act first, lessening the need for an elaborate committee system. Moreover, the Senate did not grow in size so quickly as the House. In 1835 the Senate had only forty-eight members, fewer members than the House had during the First Congress. And, in sharp contrast to the House, the development of party activity in the Senate had the effect of de-emphasizing committee decisions. Factionalism led senators and their weak party leaders to distrust committees and avoid referral to unfriendly ones. As a result, the Senate's standing committees, with one or two important exceptions, played a relatively insignificant role in the legislative process prior to the Civil War, the Senate retaining a floor-centered process.

In the half century following the Civil War, the role of committees was strongly influenced by issues associated with the dramatic growth in the size of the nation, further development of American political parties, and the increasing careerism of members. Both houses demonstrated a strong tendency to respond to these issues by creating new committees, rather than by enlarging or reorganizing existing committee jurisdictions. Party leaders often took the opportunity to appoint friendly members to a new committee with jurisdiction over an important issue. And committee chairs, who acquired offices and clerks with their chairmanships, resisted efforts to eliminate committees. By 1918 the House had acquired nearly sixty committees and the Senate had seventy-four. About half of them had no legislative or investigative business.

The most important jurisdictional changes during the late 1880s concerned money matters. The House Ways and Means and Senate Finance committees' expenditure and revenue-raising responsibilities increased dramatically during the Civil War. Concern about their power led both houses to create separate appropriations committees in the mid-1860s. Factional and intercommittee antagonisms later led to a further distribution of appropriations authority to several other committees of the House and the Senate. By 1900 the unified control over government financial matters originally invested in the Ways and Means and Finance committees had been distributed among nearly twenty committees.

These structural developments did not lead to a more "decentralized" Congress. One might be inclined to think that they did, particularly in the House, which in 1880 adopted a rule requiring legislation to be referred to committee. In response to the stabilization of the two-party system and the cohesiveness of the majority-party Republicans in the late 1800s, majority-party leaders of both houses used the established committee systems as tools for asserting control over policy choices. In the House, the period between the Civil War and 1910 brought a series of activist Speakers who aggressively used committee appointments to stack important committees with friendly members and to take advantage of a new bill-referral power to send legislation to friendly committees. These Speakers also ruled that a petition to discharge a bill from a committee was not a privileged motion; asserted the power to recognize members seeking to speak on the floor; transformed the Rules Committee into a standing committee chaired by the Speaker; and gave the Rules Committee the authority to report resolutions that set the floor agenda. With these powers, the Speaker gained the ability to grant a right-of-way to certain legislation and to block other legislation. The 1890s represented the zenith of the party-dominated committees model in the House.

Senate organization in the years following the Civil War was dictated by Republicans who controlled that chamber for all but two Congresses between 1860 and 1913. The Republicans emerged from the war with no party leader or faction capable of controlling the Senate. Relatively independent committees and committee chairs became the leading force in Senate deliberations. By the late 1890s, however, elections had made the Senate Republican party a smaller and more homogeneous group, and a coterie of like-minded Republicans had ascended to leadership positions. This group controlled the party's Committee on Committees, which made committee assignments, and the Steering Committee, which controlled floor scheduling. These developments made Senate committees agents of a small set of party leaders.

Despite the party leaders' control over committee assignments in the House and Senate in the late 1800s, their discretion became constrained by the emerging norms of seniority and property rights—unwritten rules that gave committee chairmanships to members with the longest continuous service on each committee and allowed members to remain on a committee for as long as they wished. The norms took hold earlier in the Senate than in the House. This was due, at least in part, to the fact that the House had developed a regular appointment procedure at an early date, while assignments had been subject to great controversy in the Senate in almost every Congress up to the Civil War. Seniority and routine reappointment provided for a process that minimized conflict among senators. These norms were also consistent with the developing careerism prevalent in the Senate, which increased the salience of issues that affected members' electoral prospects and made rank-and-file members more concerned about their long-range committee responsibilities and power and less willing to depend on the whims of party leaders. Thus, even by the 1870s, seniority had become the standard guide for making Senate committee assignments and chair selections.

The seniority and property-rights norms suffered a setback in the House during the first decade of the twentieth century. Republican Speaker Joseph G. Cannon (R.-Ill.) used his appointment authority, control of the Rules Committee, and recognition powers to block the legislative efforts of Progressives within his own party. The subsequent revolt against Cannon by Republican insurgents and opposition Democrats produced a lasting change in the composition of the Rules Committee. New House rules prohibited the Speaker from membership on Rules, expanded the size of the committee, and stripped away the Speaker's power to appoint the committee's members.

The Democrats instituted major changes in their committee-assignment procedures after they gained control of the House in the 1910 elections. They transferred assignment authority for their caucus from the Speaker to the Democratic members of the Committee on Ways and Means. Because the majority leader typically chaired Ways and Means, the power remained in the leadership's hands, although not in the hands of the Speaker. Democratic leaders also used the temporarily cohesive party caucus, the so-called King Caucus, to bind party members to policy positions. But the caucus's cohesiveness began to wane in 1916, reducing the power of its leadership and forcing the observance of seniority in committee assignments. House Republicans continued to allow their party leaders to make committee assignments for them until they created a separate Committee on Committees in 1917.

The 1915–1920 period also witnessed disenchantment with the structure and operation of the congressional committee system. The fact that such a bloated, incoherent system had not created complete chaos much earlier is testimony to the strength of party rule. With declining leadership power, the fragmented, overlapping jurisdictional structure of the committee system was less tolerable. In 1920 the Republican Senate eliminated forty-one inactive standing committees, a move tolerated by senators because of the nearly simultaneous expansion of personal staff assistance and office space. Moreover, in anticipation of an improved executive-branch budgeting system, implemented in 1921, the House restored its Appropriations Committee's jurisdiction in June 1920. The Senate followed suit in 1922.

The Republican years of the 1920s resulted in a substantial weakening of the links between party leaders and committees. As a result of Republican reforms, the majority leader no longer chaired a major committee, chairs of major committees could not serve on the party's Steering Committee, and no committee chair could sit on the Rules Committee. Democrats adopted similar practices. Both House parties earmarked certain major committees—Appropriations, Rules, and Ways and Means—as exclusive by prohibiting members of those committees from gaining membership on other committees (although Republicans occasionally granted exemptions). And both parties rigorously began to apply the seniority and property-rights norms in committee appointments. These changes formally divorced the leadership from the committee system, allowing committee chairs to become independent powers within the jurisdiction of their committees and moving the House closer to the autonomous committees model.

Increasing committee autonomy was most evident in the case of the House Rules Committee. In the 1920s the Rules Committee retained all of its vital functions in setting the floor agenda and gained even greater independence with uniform application of the seniority and property-rights norms. The committee often refused to report a resolution allowing important legislation to be considered on the floor and sometimes held legislation hostage until a legislative committee made changes demanded by Rules members. The Rules Committee chair even refused to report resolutions adopted by the committee itself. During most of the 1920s and 1930s, the Rules Committee cooperated with the majority-party leadership, so its decisions were not so arbitrary and self-serving as they sometimes appeared. Beginning in late 1937, however, a coalition of conservative majority-party Democrats and minority Republicans used the committee to block President Franklin D. Roosevelt's programs and to pave the way for conservative legislation.

As a result of Republican ability to win nonsouthern seats during the 1920s, southern Democrats were able to gain seniority and access to prestigious committees in disproportionate numbers. When the Democrats took control of the House in 1931 and the Senate in 1933, southerners acquired far more than half of the committee chairmanships, much more than their proportion of the party. President Roosevelt and party leaders were able to keep the chairs in line during his first term, but conservative chairs, especially the southerners, began to challenge Roosevelt's program in his second term. This factional split within the Democratic party marked not only the origin of the conservative coalition in Congress, but also the beginning of a long period marked by more autonomous committees led by independent chairs willing to oppose leaders of their own party.

A confluence of pressures for committee-system reform had developed by the 1940s, resulting in the Legislative Reorganization Act of 1946. The power of conservative committee chairs distressed liberals, but most members shared concerns about the increasing size and power of the executive branch during the New Deal and World War II. Critics noted that the large number of committees and their overlapping jurisdictions were responsible for unequal distributions of work and participation among members, caused difficulties in coordination between the House and the Senate, and made oversight of executive agencies difficult. Committees also lacked staff assistance to conduct studies of policy problems and executive-branch activities.

The 1946 act reduced the number of standing committees to nineteen in the House and fifteen in the Senate by consolidating the jurisdictions of several groups of committees. The standing committees in each house were made nearly equal in size, and the number of committee assignments was reduced to one for most House members and two for most senators. Though provisions dealing with regular committee meetings, proxy voting, and committee reports constrained chairs in some ways, they were the clear winners. Most chairs benefited from greatly expanded committee jurisdictions and the addition of more committee staff, whom they would direct. Chairs continued to control their committees' agendas, subcommittee appointments, the referral of legislation to subcommittees, the management of committee legislation on the floor, and conference delegations.

The autonomous committees model had seemed to fit both chambers for the next fifteen years. Democrats controlled both houses in all but two Congresses and during most of the period were led by two skillful Texans, Lyndon B. Johnson in the Senate and Sam Rayburn in the House. During this period, only one new committee, with jurisdiction over aeronautics and space, was added in each chamber. Committee chairs exhibited great longevity. More than 60 percent of those serving between 1947 and 1964 held their positions for more than five years, including approximately two dozen who served more than a decade in their positions. And, by virtue of conservatives' seniority, chairs were disproportionately conservative. They, along with most Republicans, constituted a conservative coalition that used committees to block legislation favored by congressional and administration liberals.

A set of strong, informal norms seemed to govern individual behavior in the 1940s and 1950s. Two norms directly affected committees. First, members were expected to specialize in matters that came before their committees. Second, new members were expected to serve an apprenticeship period during which they listened and learned from senior members and refrained from active participation in committee or floor deliberations. These norms emphasized the development of expertise in the affairs of one's own committee and deference to the assumed expertise of other committees. The collective justification for these norms was that the development of, and deference to, expertise would promote high-quality legislation. By the mid-1960s new cohorts of members, particularly liberals, proved unwilling to serve apprenticeships and defer to conservative committee chairs. Many members began to demand major reforms in congressional operations. A series of reforms was enacted during the 1965–1975 period.

A five-year effort yielded the Legislative Reorganization Act of 1970. It required committees to make public all recorded votes, limited proxy votes, allowed a majority of members to call meetings, and encouraged committees to hold open hearings and meetings. House floor procedure also was affected—primarily by permitting recorded teller votes during the amending process and by authorizing (rather than requiring) the use of electronic voting. These changes made it more difficult for House and Senate committee chairs to camouflage their power in legislative jargon and hide their domination behind closed doors.

After the 1970 act was implemented, House liberals succeeded in adding party rules that further democratized decision-making processes within committees. Democrats limited their members to holding one legislative subcommittee chair, meaning that full committee

chairs no longer could chair several subcommittees. Subcommittee chairs were allowed to select one professional staff member for their respective subcommittees—subject to approval by their full committee caucus. The new rules called for the party to hold separate votes on each committee chairmanship, with a secret ballot to be provided on the demand of 20 percent of the caucus (House Republicans adopted a similar rule). A Steering and Policy Committee, chaired by the Speaker and composed of other party leaders, leadership appointees, and elected members, was created within the caucus to make Democratic committee assignments, taking that responsibility away from the Democratic members of the Committee on Ways and Means. And the Democrats adopted a "Subcommittee Bill of Rights" that included guaranteed referral of legislation to subcommittee, stripped full committee chairs of their power to appoint subcommittees single-handedly, and guaranteed fixed jurisdictions for subcommittees.

A subsequent effort to alter more dramatically the number and jurisdictions of House standing committees failed. However, in 1974 the House did provide for the referral legislation to multiple committees, directed committees with fifteen or more members to establish at least four subcommittees (a rule aimed at Ways and Means), increased committee-staff sizes, guaranteed one-third of House committee staffs to the minority party, and banned proxy voting in committee. The Democrats also required subcommittee chairs of the Appropriations Committee to stand for caucus election and granted the Speaker the responsibility to nominate Democratic members of the Rules Committee.

The Senate never adopted rules to create independent subcommittees, but it did accept a modest realignment of committee jurisdictions. Almost all of the Senate's select and special committees were abolished, and the District of Columbia, Post Office, and Government Operations committees were consolidated into a single committee. Wholesale jurisdictional changes, involving energy, the environment, science and technology, human resources, and government affairs, were achieved. Limits were placed on the number of assignments (three committees and eight subcommittees) and the number of chairs (four committees and subcommittees in the Ninety-fifth and three in the Ninety-sixth Congresses) that senators could hold. The reforms also expanded minority staffing.

THE MODERN COMMITTEE SYSTEM

This brief historical account makes plain that both partisan and nonpartisan motives have figured prominently in the development of the committee systems in both the House and Senate. The burden of an expanding and increasingly complex work load frequently stimulated each house to elaborate its system of standing committees. Parties sometimes bolstered the power of standing committees in order to expand their own control over policy outcomes, only to find later that committees could use their institutional position to ignore weakened parties. And procedural choices had consequences that had not been fully anticipated. The modern committee systems of the two houses, reflecting somewhat different histories of political alignments and procedural choices, are the product of this evolutionary process.

The Legislative Power of Modern Committees

Committees have no power that is not expressly or implicitly granted to them by the parent chambers and political parties. Their continued existence and parliamentary privileges depend on the sufferance of both. While the parent chambers go through the motions of approving committee assignments, it is the parties that construct the committee lists that are routinely ratified by the chambers. This function gives the parties a source of leverage with committee members and allows the parties to regulate the behavior of committee members through formal and informal rules. In the main, committees must function in a procedural fashion and with a substantive effect consistent with the interests of their parent chambers and parties.

Nevertheless, committees exercise real power in the modern Congress. Their power stems in part from the indifference of the two parties and most members to the details of legislation. Parties and their leaders focus on the few issues each year that are likely to effect party reputation and electoral prospects. The average member does not and could not take an interest in the details of most of the legislation that is considered on the floor. Party and member indifference varies from committee to committee, as well as over time, but it is a common circumstance for the vast majority of measures that Congress processes.

When members are not indifferent, committees still have advantages that give their members disproportionate influence over policy outcomes. If committees abuse their advantages, it is often difficult to mount credible challenges to their power. Threats to strip a committee of jurisdiction, funding, or parliamentary privileges, or to retract members' committee assignments, usually are not credible, if for no other reason than that such actions might set precedents that members of other committees would not like to have established. In this way an implicit, self-enforcing pact among members underpins committee power. The most practical means for keeping committees in check is to reject their policy recommendations.

It is convenient to consider two forms of committee power. *Negative power* is the ability of committees to block legislation favored by others; *positive power* is the ability of committees to gain the approval of legislation opposed by others. On both counts, committees have substantial advantages over rank-and-file members of the parent chambers and parties. Indeed, modern congressional committees have sources of negative and positive power that committees lack in most other national legislatures.

Negative power rests on committees' ability to control newly introduced legislation and obstruct alternative routes to the floor. This is accomplished more effectively in House rules than in Senate rules.

In the House, such "gatekeeping" power is supported by rules that give committees near-monopoly control over newly introduced legislation and make it very difficult to circumvent committees. House Rule 10 requires that all legislation relating to a committee's jurisdiction be referred to that committee, a rule that has been in place since 1880. Prior to 1974 this meant that the single committee with the most relevant jurisdiction received the referral. Beginning in 1974, the rule provides for multiple referral by granting to the Speaker authority to refer legislation to each committee with relevant jurisdiction. Monopoly control by single committees was broken by the new rule, but the practice of referring legislation to committee remains in place. Short-circuiting the bill-referral rule and bringing legislation directly to the floor requires that either the rules be suspended by a two-thirds vote or a resolution from the Rules Committee be approved by majority vote.

House committees, like their Senate counterparts, are free to act in any way they see fit on most legislation that is referred to them. They may simply refuse to act, hold hearings but take no legislative action, amend the legislation in some way, or accept the legislation without change. And they may write their own legislation. They may vote to report legislation with a recommendation that it pass, with no recommendation, or with a recommendation that it be rejected. These options give congressional committees what Nelson W. Polsby termed a "transformative" character, in contrast to committees in other systems that serve only as arenas for holding hearings and debating legislation and lack the ability to alter the content of legislation.

Circumventing House committees is difficult but not impossible under current rules. The House operates under a germaneness rule that requires a floor amendment to be relevant to the section of the bill or resolution it seeks to modify. Thus, it is difficult to bring to the floor as an amendment a policy proposal whose subject has not been addressed in legislation reported by a committee. The germaneness rule can be waived, but only if the Rules Committee approves a resolution (a special rule) waiving the rule, and if the resolution is approved by a majority on the House floor.

House rules provide other means for bringing legislation to the floor. At certain times members may move to suspend the rules to consider a measure blocked by a committee. But this route is usually infeasible because it requires recognition by the Speaker to make the motion and two-thirds support from the House. Alternatively, members may seek to discharge a measure from committee by gaining the signatures of 218 members (a simple majority) on a discharge petition. But many members are hesitant to encourage the use of discharge petitions because doing so threatens the power of their own committees. The political pressure to sign petitions is minimal because the names of signatories are not disclosed until 218 signatures are acquired. A final alternative is to gain a special rule from the Rules Committee to discharge a measure from committee, but this route requires Rules Committee support and majority support in the House for the special rule. All of these means for circumventing committees have been used from time to time, though infrequently, and the threat of their use has occasionally stimulated committees to act in accordance with the floor majority's preferences.

The blocking power of House committees is further enhanced by their domination of conference committees. House-Senate differences on complex legislation are usually resolved in conference; conferees usually are named from the membership of the committees that originated the legislation. The power of these conferees rests in their wide latitude in negotiating with the Senate conferees and in a rule that prohibits amendments to the conference report. The House must accept or reject the entire report in most circumstances. This process gives conferees substantial discretion in designing the final form of legislation so long as they can gain the support of the Senate conferees and majority support in both houses.

The situation in the Senate is very different. While measures are routinely referred to Senate committees upon introduction, it is easy to object to a referral and keep a measure on the calendar for floor consideration. Furthermore, the Senate lacks a germaneness rule for most measures, making it possible for senators to circumvent committees by offering whole bills as amendments to unrelated legislation. Senators often are hesitant to support efforts to bypass a committee in this way, but it is a procedural route that is used much more frequently than the more complicated procedures for circumventing committees in the House. And most conference reports are subject to filibusters in the Senate, giving Senate minorities a source of bargaining leverage with conferees that does not exist in the House. In sum, the Senate's rules combine to create only very weak blocking power for its committees.

Most positive power, it seems fair to say, results from general disinterest in the issues addressed in much legislation. But committees do have ways to gain the support of members who might not otherwise support committee legislation. By threatening to use their blocking power, for example, committees may gain bargaining leverage with members who want something from them. And committees may force their chambers to enact certain policy positions by giving them ultimatums in the form of conference reports.

Yet committees cannot circumvent the floors of their parent chambers and must depend on majority support for their policy proposals. Successful promotion of committee proposals often rests on extraprocedural resources that can be used in efforts to persuade members of the wisdom of committee measures. And committees have advantages here, too. Most important, committees gain a tactical edge over most opponents through their advantages in political and policy information. By virtue of sitting through hearings and having previous experience with most issues before their committees, committee members usually are better informed than other members about the political and policy implications of committee recommendations. Committees' large expert staffs and their extensive network of allies in the executive branch and the interest-group community further enhance their informational advantage over competitors.

The Investigative Power of Modern Committees

Central to the legislative power of committees and vital to the institutional power of Congress is the ability of committees to monitor or investigate the activities of the executive and judicial branches, as well as private activity that is or might be the subject of public policy. Congress's power to compel cooperation with its investigations, courts have ruled, is implicit in its constitutional functions of legislating and appropriating funds. Without broad powers to investigate and compel cooperation, Congress would not be able to set public policy knowledgeably or authorize the use of public moneys. The subject of monitoring and investigations usually is narrowed to the subtopic of legislative oversight of the executive branch. This is convenient because oversight of the executive branch is an officially assigned function

of congressional committees in the modern Congress. Beginning with the Legislative Reorganization Act of 1946, committees have been assigned the duty to maintain "continuous watchfulness" over executive-branch activities within their jurisdictions.

Because the subject of oversight is addressed elsewhere in William West's essay in this volume, it will suffice to emphasize two points about it here. First, oversight opportunities often enhance members' interest in particular committees. Two committees, House Government Operations and Senate Governmental Affairs, attract members primarily because they have government-wide oversight responsibilities that allow their members to participate in hearings and investigations of nearly all policy fields. Others, such as the commerce committees, have very broad jurisdictions that permit them wide oversight opportunities. Such opportunities give members a chance to attract the attention of the media and their constituents, to be associated with issues that do not have immediate implications for new legislation, and to be seen as opposing mismanagement and the misuse of taxpayers' dollars.

Second, oversight appears to have become an increasingly important part of committee activity. According to one count, the number of days of oversight hearings conducted by House and Senate committees increased from 159 in 1963 to 290 in 1973 and to 587 in 1983. These totals represent a change from less than 10 percent of committee meetings and hearings devoted to oversight to more than 25 percent devoted to oversight. The surge in the 1970s appears to be the product of several factors: the independence of subcommittee chairs to pursue oversight, the expanded capacity to conduct oversight activities associated with larger staffs, the frequency of split party control of Congress and the White House, and a generally more assertive Congress.

Committee Assignments in the Modern Congress

A committee's power makes its composition important. The assignment of members to committees is a subject of great interest to members at the start of each Congress when new freshman members are named to committees and nonfreshmen may attempt to transfer from one committee to another. Nonfreshmen who do not seek to transfer are routinely reappointed to their committees, following the property-rights norm.

The majority party in each chamber holds a majority of the seats on most committees, roughly in proportion to its size in the chamber as a whole. The exceptions are the House Appropriations, Budget, Rules, and Ways and Means committees, which are particularly important committees on which House Democrats have reserved a larger than proportionate number of seats for themselves, and the House and Senate ethics committees, on which there is an equal number of majority- and minority-party members. The specific size of committees is negotiated by majority- and minority-party leaders, with the majority leaders having the upper hand because of their ability to win a vote for the resolutions providing for committee sizes. Vacancies are created by retiring, defeated, or transferring members, and by increasing the size of committees. Committee sizes have grown to accommodate members' requests for desirable assignments.

Each of the majority and minority parties in both houses has its own committee on committees. These party committees are chaired by party leaders, although the degree to which party leaders dominate their proceedings varies. Assignment decisions are constrained by the availability of vacancies, the number of members competing for assignments, and certain rules on the number and type of assignments each member may hold, to which exemptions are frequently granted. Only for Senate Republicans is seniority a decisive consideration in choosing among competitors for coveted assignments. The other parties consider seniority among many other factors, such as party loyalty, electoral needs, and geographic balance, in making assignment decisions. However, since the 1950s both Senate parties have observed a practice of granting every senator a seat on one of the top four committees before any senator gets two such seats.

Distinct patterns are observable in members' requests for assignment to particular committees and party committees' assignment decisions. Committees' appeal to members and importance to parties varies widely, both across committees and over time, in response to variation in committee jurisdiction, active policy agendas, and political environments. The money committees (House Appropriations, Budget, and Ways and Means; Senate Appropriations and Finance) and certain other committees with large and important jurisdictions (for example, House Energy and Commerce and Senate Armed Services) have wide appeal and are considered vital to the policy interests of the parties. There is intense competition for assignments to these committees, and party leaders exercise care in making appointments to them. Other committees attract only the few members whose constituencies are most affected by policy under their jurisdictions. Party leaders have little interest in these committees and seek to accommodate members requesting appointment to them.

Scholars have ranked committees according to their attractiveness, as indicated by the balance of transfers to and transfers from each committee. Table 2 lists House committees according to their attractiveness to members (similar ratings are not available for the Senate). The table also indicates what research shows to be the distinctive political motivation for seeking assignment to each committee. The table demonstrates that committees noted for their influence within the House are the most attractive committees. Committees with jurisdictions in which members have personal policy interests tend to be more attractive than committees that draw members because of their relevance to particular types of constituencies. A few committees attract the interest of virtually no members because of their limited jurisdiction or focus on housekeeping matters.

The assignments to the House Committee on Rules deserve special notice. The Rules Committee's primary regular function is to consider, devise, and report "special rules"—resolutions that provide for the floor consideration of measures, usually reported by other committees, that would otherwise not receive timely consideration under the standing rules. The twentieth century has witnessed great swings in the independence of the committee in performing this function. In the 1960s and early 1970s, the independence of Rules Committee members continued to be a concern, ultimately leading Democrats to transfer the appointment power for Rules back to the Speaker, subject to caucus approval, when they

Table 2

HOUSE COMMITTEES RANKED BY ATTRACTIVENESS, WITH MEMBER GOALS

Attractiveness Ranking	Member Goals
1. Ways and Means	prestige/influence
2. Appropriations	prestige/influence
3. Rules	prestige/influence
4. Energy and Commerce	policy
5. Armed Services	constituency
6. Foreign Affairs	policy
7. Budget	prestige/influence
8. Interior and Insular Affairs	constituency
9. Banking, Finance, and Urban Affairs	policy
10. Agriculture	constituency
11. Education and Labor	policy
12. Government Operations	policy
13. Small Business	constituency
14. Science, Space and Technology	constituency
15. Merchant Marine and Fisheries	constituency
16. Post Office and Civil Service	constituency
17. Judiciary	policy
18. Veterans' Affairs	constituency
19. Public Works and Transportation	constituency

Note: Three committees are not included: the District of Columbia and House Administration committees attract very few members; members generally do not take the initiative to request seats on Standards of Official Conduct but rather are solicited by party leaders.

Source: The attractiveness rating is an updated transfer ratio for the Ninty-fifth to the Ninety-ninth Congresses, as reported in Michael C. Munger, "Allocation of Desirable Committee Assignments: Extended Queues Versus Committee Expansion," *American Journal of Political Science* 32 (May 1988): 325; member goals are based on freshmen's motives for committee requests in the 100th and 101st Congresses, as reported in Steven S. Smith and Christopher J. Deering, *Committees in Congress*, 2d ed. (Washington, D.C., 1990), Chapter 3.

organized after the 1974 elections. Republicans also have since given to their leader the responsibility for making assignments to the Rules Committee. Rules Committee members are now clearly agents of their party leadership. They retain substantial independence when they design special rules for routine legislation of little interest to their parties, but special rules for major legislation are subject to close consultation or even specific direction from the Speaker.

Committee Leadership in the Modern Congress

Both the majority party and minority party designate a formal leader for each committee and subcommittee. The majority party names the chair of all committees and subcommittees and the minority party appoints a ranking minority member for every committee and subcommittee. The seniority norm dictates that the member with the longest continuous service on the committee serve as chair, although there are limitations on the number and type of chairs a member may hold. Subcommittee chairs and ranking minority members are chosen, in most cases, on the basis of committee seniority as well. Accruing seniority toward leadership posts is one reason members are reluctant to transfer to other committees, where they must start at the bottom of the seniority ladder.

Since the 1970s the seniority norm was checked in both houses by new party rules that require a secret-ballot election of full committee chairs and ranking minority members.

House Democrats led the way by requiring that all committee chairs and the chairs of the Appropriations Committee subcommittees stand for election in the Democratic caucus at the start of each Congress. Three full committee chairs were deposed in 1975, another was defeated in 1985, two were defeated in 1990, and an Appropriations subcommittee chair was replaced in 1977.

Subcommittee chairs traditionally were appointed by the full committee chair of each committee, giving full committee chairs the opportunity to manipulate subcommittee activity. That procedure was also transformed into a more egalitarian one in the 1970s. House Democrats require that committee Democrats bid for subcommittee chairmanships in order of seniority and that their choices be ratified by a majority vote of the party members on the committee. While seniority generally is observed, this procedure gives party members on a committee the right to reject the most senior member and elect someone else, as has happened more than a dozen times since the mid-1970s. House Republicans leave the appointment process to each committee's ranking minority member, but in practice Republicans also select most of their subcommittee ranking members by seniority on the committee. Both Senate parties also allow committee members to select their subcommittee chairmanships or ranking positions in order of seniority.

Restrictions on chairmanships were developed in the 1970s to spread the chairmanships among more members. The rules of the House Democratic caucus limits members to one full committee and one subcommittee chairmanship. Full committee chairs may chair only one subcommittee, and that must be on the committee they chair. This rule, along with the increasing number of subcommittees, greatly increased the number of members holding subcommittee chairs—more than half of the House Democrats now hold a subcommittee chair, up from one quarter in 1955. Senate rules merely prohibit any member from holding more than one chair on each committee on which he or she serves. Because most senators are limited to three standing committee assignments, they can have up to three subcommittee chairmanships, in addition to a full committee chairmanship of one of those standing committees. Nearly all majority party members hold at least one subcommittee chairmanship today and over half of the majority party Democrats hold two or three subcommittee chairs.

The most powerful member on most committees is the full committee chair. The chair exercises considerable control over the agenda of the committee, schedules meetings and hearings of the full committee and influences the scheduling of subcommittees' meetings and hearings, benefits from years of experience in dealing with the policy problems and constituencies of the committee, normally names conferees, controls the committee budget, supervises a sizable full committee staff, and often serves as a spokesperson for his committee and party on issues that fall under the committee jurisdiction. Consequently, the support of the full committee chair can be critical to sponsors and opponents of bills. That is as true in the 1990s as it was in the 1950s and 1960s.

Nevertheless, compared with their predecessors of the 1950s and 1960s, committee chairs are more accountable to their party colleagues and face more effective competition for control over policy choices. This is due in part to changes in the formal rules limiting chairs' discretion on a variety of procedural matters, particularly in the House, and in part to the acquisition of resources by other members who may not share the policy views of chairs.

The House and the House Democratic caucus adopted rules in the 1970s to reduce the influence of full committee chairs over the decisions of their committees. Chairs were required to stand for election by the Democratic caucus at the start of each Congress, subcommittees were required on committees with fifteen or more members and were empowered with written jurisdictions and staffs; proxy voting was restricted; the minority party contingents on committees were guaranteed staff; committees were required to open their meetings to the public unless a majority of committee members agreed to close them; a procedure for committee majorities to call meetings was created so the chairs could no longer refuse to hold meetings; and chairs were required to report to the floor promptly legislation that had been approved by their committees. The ability of full committee chairs to delay the referral of legislation to the proper subcommittee or to delay the reporting of committee-approved legislation to the floor was curtailed. And House Democrats adopted a self-selection procedure for subcommittee assignments so that full committee chairs could no longer stack important subcommittees with their supporters. In both houses, committee meetings were required to be held in public sessions, except by a recorded majority vote of the committee, making all committee members, including chairs, more accountable to outside colleagues and constituents.

Like the House, the Senate adopted rules providing guidelines for the conduct of committee meetings, hearings, and voting, and requiring committees to publish additional rules governing committee procedure. But unlike the House, Senate chamber and party rules do not specify internal committee organization in any detail and are silent on the functions of subcommittees. Compared with the rules of House committees, most Senate committee rules are very brief, usually not even mentioning the structure, jurisdictions, or functions of subcommittees. In most cases, the full committee chair is assumed to have great discretion, although even that is left unstated. The referral of legislation to subcommittees, the discharge of legislation from subcommittees, and the distribution of labor between the full committee and subcommittees remain under the formal control of nearly all Senate full committee chairs. Thus, Senate chairs are granted more discretion in designing the internal decision-making processes of their committees than House chairs, and Senate subcommittee chairs enjoy less autonomy than their House counterparts.

It is in the House, then, that the ability of full committee chairs to control committee decisions by procedural means has declined the most. Even the ability to keep issues off the agenda was undermined by the empowerment of subcommittees. House committee chairs must be responsive to the demands of the Democratic caucus or risk losing their chairmanships in the future and must tolerate independent subcommittees with professional staffs. Senate chairs enjoy greater freedom in the internal affairs of their committees, but must tolerate and anticipate more frequent and successful efforts to circumvent their committees altogether. In both houses, however, a majority of committee members may call and set the agenda for committee meetings if chairs refuse to do so on their own authority.

Subcommittees in the Modern Congress

Subcommittees became more important on many committees after the Legislative Reorganization Act of 1946 consolidated committee jurisdictions and reduced the number of standing committees in both chambers. The number of subcommittees grew after World War II and continued into the 1970s as individual committees responded to changes in the policy problems they faced and to demands from members for their own subcommittees. By the early 1990s there were more than 130 House subcommittees and more than 90 Senate subcommittees. Of the committees with authority to report legislation, only the House Budget and Standards of Official Conduct committees and the Senate Budget, Rules and Administration, Ethics, Indian Affairs, and Veterans' Affairs committees lack standing subcommittees.

In the House, the resistance of some full committee chairs to efforts to create legislative subcommittees was eventually overcome by the 1974 rule that requires that "each standing committee . . . , except the Committee on the Budget, that has more than twenty members shall establish at least four subcommittees." Later, problems associated with the growth in the number of House subcommittees—jurisdictional squabbles between subcommittees, scheduling difficulties, and the burden of subcommittee hearings on executive officials—led the Democratic caucus to limit the number of subcommittees. A 1981 caucus rule limits large committees (those with at least thirty-five members) to eight subcommittees, with the exception of Appropriations, and small committees were limited to six subcommittees.

Neither the Senate nor the Senate parties have a formal rule on the number of subcommittees any committee may have, although limits on the number of subcommittee assignments that individual senators may hold effectively curtail the number of subcommittees that can be created. The stricter enforcement of limits on subcommittee assignments in 1985 led five committees to eliminate one or more subcommittees after a few senators were forced to give up one of their subcommittee chairmanships. On other committees, enforcement of the rule meant there were not enough members able and willing to take subcommittee assignments, forcing the abolition of some subcommittees. A total of ten Senate committees either chose or were compelled to eliminate at least one subcommittee that year.

Subcommittees have gained great importance in committee decision-making in the House. As noted above, the House adopted rules in the early 1970s that substantially weakened the ability of full committee chairs to control subcommittees. The net result is that decision-making processes within House committees are now more decentralized than they were in the 1950s and 1960s. Most legislation originates in subcommittee, the vast majority of hearings are held in subcommittees, about half of all committee staff is allocated to subcommittees, and subcommittee chairs usually serve as the floor managers for legislation originating in their subcommittees. The pattern in the House has led some observers to label House decision-making "subcommittee government."

The empowerment of House subcommittees greatly increased the importance of subcommittee chairs. One indication of the importance of subcommittee chairs is that several House members in line for a chairmanship by virtue of seniority have been rejected by committee colleagues in favor of competitors. The few systematic studies of intracommittee decision-making since the reforms of the 1970s indicate that subcommittee chairs, full committee chairs, and ranking minority members are the most influential members of their committees. Because of their limited jurisdiction, most subcommittee chairs are not so powerful as many full chairs were in the 1950s and 1960s, but their independence of action makes them central players on most legislation.

In the Senate, subcommittee-appointment practices are much like those of the House. Committee rules often mandate a process guaranteeing members a first (or second) subcommittee choice before any other member receives a second (or third) choice, and all party contingents operate that way even in the absence of a formal rule. Consequently, committee members are no longer dependent on the full committee chair for desirable subcommittee assignments.

But the lack of formal rules empowering subcommittees in the Senate has produced great variation among committees in their reliance on subcommittees. Several Senate committees hold very few hearings in subcommittee and only a few Senate committees use subcommittees to write legislation. The label "subcommittee government," therefore, does not fit decision-making processes in most Senate committees.

In addition to their standing subcommittees, committees occasionally create other subunits. Most but not all committees allow their chairs to create an ad hoc subcommittee to handle matters that fall in the jurisdiction of more than one subcommittee. Unfortunately, there is no reliable record of the frequency with which such ad hoc arrangements are employed, but the relative ease of altering subcommittee jurisdictions keeps the number very small. Committee rules generally imply that the ad hoc subcommittees dissolve upon completing action on the specific matters assigned to them.

Committee Staff in the Modern Congress

Committee staffs exhibited nearly monotonic increases in size between 1946 and the early 1980s. The 1946 Legislative Reorganization Act granted each standing committee authority to hire four professional staff assistants and six clerical aides, and the 1970 act increased to six the number of professional assistants each committee could hire. In 1974 the House increased the number to eighteen professional assistants and twelve clerical aides. Minority-party control of at least two professional staff assistants on each committee was guaranteed by the 1970 act, and both chambers later adopted rules guaranteeing even larger staffs to the minority party. The House now gives the minority party control over one-third of professional and clerical staffs, and the Senate requires that staff be allocated to the minority party in proportion to the number of minority-party members on each committee. Since the early 1980s budget constraints have caused many committees to reduce staff sizes somewhat and little overall growth has occurred.

The importance of staffing for committee power has been noted. Staffing also has altered the distribution of power within committees. In rules adopted in the early 1970s, the House guaranteed that both the chair and the ranking minority member of each standing subcommittee may appoint at least one staff member. Unless authorization for additional staff is obtained from the House, subcommittee staff come out of the allocation guaranteed to the full committee; this directly reduces the number of staff under the control of the full committee chairs and ranking minority members. This rule dramatically altered staffing patterns in House committees. Between 1969 and 1985 the percentage of all committee staff that is assigned to subcommittees grew from about 23 to almost 46. Some House subcommittee staffs have grown quite large, fifteen to twenty aides in a few cases, far beyond the minimum required by House rules.

In the Senate, where no rule guaranteeing subcommittee staff was adopted, subcommittee staff has maintained a level of about 40 percent of all committee staff. Indeed, while the total number of House committee staff more than tripled between 1969 and 1979, due primarily to the expansion of subcommittee staffs, Senate committee staff grew by only 80 percent or so.

House committees, operating under requirements that committee staff be shared with subcommittees and the minority, now have very similar distributions of staff between full committee and subcommittees. But there are still cases, most notably Ways and Means, where the full committee chair, through the senior full committee staff, exercises substantial control over at least the majority-party staff of the committee and subcommittees. Senate committees, because they are not constrained by chamber or party rules requiring separate subcommittee staffs, continue to vary widely in the manner in which they staff subcommittee activities.

Committee Decentralization in the Modern Congress

The extent of decentralization in the decision-making processes of House and Senate committees is indicated in an index of "subcommittee orientation." The index is the mean of the following measures: (1) the percentage of measures considered on the floor that are managed by a subcommittee chair; (2) the percentage of measures reported to the floor that were referred to a subcommittee or on which a subcommittee hearing was held; (3) the percentage of meetings (primarily markups) that were subcommittee meetings; and (4) the percentage of staff specifically allocated to subcommittees. The higher the index score, the more the committee relies on subcommittees. The higher the reliance on subcommittees, the more decentralized the committee's decision-making process is said to be.

Table 3 lists House and Senate committees according to the degree of decentralization that was found in the 100th Congress (1987–1988). House committees were more decentralized than Senate committees. House committees had an average subcommittee orientation of 47 percent in 1969–1971, 62 percent in 1979–1981, and 57 percent in 1987–1989. In contrast, the respective levels for the Senate were 26 percent, 25 percent, and 20 percent. Relative to their positions in the late 1960s, all but one of the fourteen House committees examined became more subcommittee-oriented by the late 1970s. House Appropriations remained highly subcommittee-oriented. Budget has not adopted legislative subcommittees. And Rules conducts all of its business on its most important responsibility, writing special rules, at full committee. In sharp contrast, eight of the twelve Senate committees for which complete data are available became less subcommittee-oriented during the 1970s.

Table 3 demonstrates that "subcommittee government" is a more appropriate description of the internal decision-making processes of House committees than of Senate committees. House subcommittees have developed a more thoroughly institutionalized role. This role is established not only in the rules of the House and Democratic caucus, but also in the interests of individual representatives. Representatives with sufficient seniority to chair a subcommittee ordinarily chair only one. That chairmanship gives them additional staff, control over hearings on matters under their subcommittee's jurisdiction, and the power to initiate or block legislation in the absence of actions by the full committee.

In contrast, a typical majority-party senator

Table 3
HOUSE AND SENATE COMMITTEES OF THE 100th CONGRESS,
1987–1988
Ranked by Subcommittee Orientation (Most to Least Decentralized)

1. House Energy and Commerce
2. House Science, Space, and Technology
3. House Judiciary
4. House Banking, Finance, and Urban Affairs
5. House Government Operations
6. House Interior and Insular Affairs
7. House Public Works and Transportation
8. House Education and Labor
9. House Agriculture
10. House Merchant Marine and Fisheries
11. House Foreign Affairs
12. House Armed Services
13. House Veterans' Affairs
14. Senate Judiciary
15. Senate Commerce, Science, and Transportation
16. House Small Business
17. Senate Governmental Affairs
18. Senate Environment and Public Works
19. House Ways and Means
20. Senate Labor and Human Resources
21. Senate Energy and Natural Resources
22. Senate Banking, Housing, and Urban Affairs
23. Senate Armed Services
24. Senate Agriculture, Nutrition, and Forestry
25. Senate Finance
26. Senate Rules and Administration
27. Senate Foreign Relations
28. Senate Small Business
30. Senate Veterans' Affairs
30. House Budget
30. Senate Budget

Note: Data not available for House Appropriations, House Rules, and Senate Appropriations. Table excludes three minor House committees: House Administration, Standards of Official Conduct, and District of Columbia.

Source: Adapted from Steven S. Smith and Christopher T. Deering, *Committees in Congress* (1990), pp. 157–158.

chairs two or three subcommittees. A senator is not very dependent on any one subcommittee or subcommittee chairmanship for his or her legislative livelihood. The tremendous demands on senators' time make them less likely to insist that their subcommittees be active, effective decision-making units. As a result, the importance of Senate subcommittees is more variable. On several Senate committees, subcommittees play no formal role in writing legislation. And since the 1980s, reliance on subcommittees has declined in the Senate. Rather than developing a central role in policy-making, Senate subcommittees have proven to be a component of a very individualistic decision-making process.

DEVELOPMENTS IN THE CONGRESSIONAL COMMITTEE SYSTEM

Committee power has come under attack since the 1970s. While committees continue to draft the details of nearly all legislation, and their members remain central players in nearly all congressional policy decisions, they no longer operate as autonomously as they once did. Change has been most dramatic in the House of Representatives, where committees traditionally dominated policy-making more completely than they did in the Senate. But both houses have become less committee-centered.

Changing Issues and Alignments

Changes in both the policy agenda and political alignments have led to a decline in committee autonomy. Many new issues appeared on Congress's agenda in the 1960s and 1970s. Energy, the environment, consumer protection, civil rights, and many other topics emerged, creating new demands for congressional action. Many of the issues, like energy and the environment, were interconnected and fell under the jurisdiction of several committees. And the agenda became less predictable and recurrent. Issues died and new ones were born in more rapid succession.

More members, particularly recently elected ones, insisted on having a voice in decisions concerning the wide range of new issues before Congress. Many sought comprehensive policies that required the coordination of action by several committees. But the established system of fairly autonomous committees presented obstacles. Committees found themselves in conflict with one another, and outsiders resented the resistance of some committees to act on new issues.

Conditions changed in the 1980s, when concern about the federal budget deficit began to dominate policy-making. Most other domestic-policy issues were set aside or reinterpreted in terms of their budget consequences. The agenda contracted and the remaining issues, all seen as connected to fiscal policy, concerned almost all members.

While the agenda fluctuated, the political alignments among members shifted. In the 1970s, fights over how and where to expand the role of the federal government continued to divide congressional Democrats. Liberal, largely northern Democrats generally favored an expanded federal role and were opposed by much more conservative southern Democrats. Republicans experienced similar divisions within their ranks. Because of electoral changes and a new agenda, the party coalitions proved far more cohesive in the 1980s. In many southern states, conservative Republicans were elected in place of conservative Democrats. The remaining southern Democrats in Congress were more supportive of their party leaders and the new southern Republicans proved highly partisan, making both parties more homogeneous. In addition, after 1981 Democrats from all regions supported most of the domestic programs, creating greater cohesion in their party.

The changes in the policy agenda and political alignments activated non–committee members and party leaders and produced less autonomous committees. Declining committee autonomy is evident in several specific developments: (1) expanded floor activity; (2) the revitalization of the party caucus; (3) multiple referral of legislation in the House; (4) changing conference practices; and (5) modified budget procedures.

Expanded Floor Activity

Weakening committee autonomy and the demise of the committee-deference norm are reflected in the record of floor amending activity since the mid-1950s. In terms of the absolute number of floor amendments, the number of amendments per measure, and the proportion of measures amended on the floor, floor amending activity increased in both chambers during the 1950s and 1960s and surged upward in the 1970s. In the Senate, the number of floor amendments nearly tripled between the mid-1950s and late 1970s, with most of the increase occurring in the 1960s. House floor amendments more than quadrupled in number between the mid-1950s and late 1970s, with most of the increase occurring in the early 1970s. The surge in House-floor amending activity in the early 1970s is associated with the adoption of recorded, electronic voting. Previously, recorded votes were not possible on most amendments, which made it difficult to bring public pressure to bear and enhanced the influence of powerful insiders, particularly committee chairs.

Floor-amending activity was perceived to be a more serious problem in the House, where committee autonomy had been stronger than in the Senate, so stronger reactions occurred in the House. House committees, with the help of the Speaker, countered by frequently seeking to suspend the rules to pass legislation. The rule providing for a motion to suspend the rules limits debate to forty minutes, bars amendments, and requires a two-thirds vote to adopt (simultaneously) the motion and measure. The procedure was designed to expedite the consideration of minor legislation. By expanding the number of days on which suspension motions are in order and coordinating committee and leadership plans, the Democrats increased the number of measures passed under suspension from fewer than a total of two hundred between 1967 and 1972 to more than four hundred in three of the four Congresses between 1977 and 1984. But a by-product of this development was greater discretion for the Speaker, whose recognition on the floor is required in order to offer a suspension motion.

The requirement of a two-thirds vote made suspension of the rules useless for major legislation, however. Starting in late 1979, the House majority-party leadership and the Rules Committee began to employ special rules more frequently to restrict floor amendments in some way. Special rules are necessary for most major legislation and so offer a regular opportunity for the Rules Committee to bar amendments, order the consideration of amendments, or even allow amendments that otherwise would violate the rules of the House. They also give the Speaker, who effectively controls the Democratic contingent on the Rules Committee, an opportunity to structure floor consideration of legislation in a manner that meets the needs of the party and of the standing committees that the party controls.

The change in the content of special rules in the 1980s was quite dramatic. Between the 1975 and 1976 and 1981 and 1982 sessions, the percentage of special rules that restricted amendments in some way increased from 15.7 to 28.8, and to 44.6 in 1985–1986. In 1985–

1986, 65 percent of House floor amendments were offered under special rules that limited or structured amending activity in some way, up from slightly more than 13 percent in 1979–1980.

The innovations in special rules were, in most instances, the fruit of a partnership between the majority-party leadership, Rules Committee Democrats, and the committee originating the legislation. Majority leaders and the Rules Committee often cared most about an orderly, efficient, and predictable consideration of legislation, while committee leaders sought to reduce uncertainty about the timing, sources, and content of unfriendly amendments to their bills. To a large degree, restrictive rules helped House committees regain some of the autonomy they had lost during the 1970s.

Nevertheless, on numerous important measures majority-party leaders design a rule to suit party needs, even when party needs are inconsistent with committee interests. Prominent bills that involve conflict between two or more committees also are particularly apt to draw the majority-party leadership into the process of designing a special rule. By employing a special rule to protect some provisions from amendment, order amendments, and authorize amendments that might otherwise violate House rules, the Speaker is in a position to enforce prefloor compromises and to minimize damage in cases where it is not possible to resolve conflict informally before the bill reaches the floor. Such cases create new opportunities for the leadership to influence the outcomes, and thus reduce committee autonomy, by controlling an important procedural tool.

In contrast to the House, no Senate strategy to control floor amending activity and enhance the autonomy of the committees has emerged. To the contrary, efforts to make it easier to block nongermane amendments, which make it possible to circumvent committees, and to prevent unlimited debate, which gives individual senators substantial blocking power, have failed. Adjustments in the cloture rule have made it marginally easier to limit debate and impose a germaneness requirement on remaining amendments, but cloture still requires an extraordinary majority (three-fifths of all senators) that limits its utility as a tool for managing the floor. In only two areas, budget measures and certain trade agreements, has the Senate moved to limit debate and amendments. In general, therefore, there is no way for a majority of senators to insulate committee bills from unfriendly or nongermane amendments whose sponsors are committed to offering them.

Revitalization of the Party Caucus

Parties continue to exercise less control over standing committees and policy-making than they did at the turn of the twentieth century, but they have become much more important since the mid-1970s. Committees of the 1980s and early 1990s are less independent of party leaders, and leaders are more assertive in prodding committees to act.

The single most prominent source of declining congressional-committee autonomy was the revitalization of the House Democratic caucus in the late 1960s and its subsequent activism, particularly in the 1980s. The Democratic caucus was an engine for the reform of committee procedures in the 1970s and it has become a forum for frequent policy debates, occasionally serving as a platform for criticizing the actions of committee leaders.

The most direct assault on committee autonomy by the House Democratic caucus concerned the committee-assignment process. The relationship between standing committees and the majority party was transformed by two key changes, both implemented in 1975: the shift of committee-assignment authority to the Steering and Policy Committee, chaired by the Speaker, and the requirement that committee chairs and subcommittee chairs for Appropriations stand for election in the Democratic caucus. Democrats now had to lobby the leadership directly for coveted committee assignments, and committee chairs were forced to pay closer attention to the preferences of the party rank and file.

The most conspicuous winner was the Speaker, who regained more direct influence over committee assignments and could play an important role in the election of committee chairs. Full committee chairs were the clear losers. Since the mid-1970s, successful challenges to six full committee chairs and one Appropriations subcommittee chair, along with threats to unseat others, have compelled committee leaders to heed the preferences of the Democratic caucus.

House Democrats also have effectively transferred policy and strategy responsibilities to party organs for many issues. Task forces, which include members without a related committee assignment, and other party committees occasionally have been more important than standing committees in setting the floor agenda and shaping party tactics. Participation in caucus activities is now so widespread and affects so many important issues, that its effects are difficult to isolate and measure. The important point is that their party has provided rank-and-file Democrats avenues of influence through the party that did not exist in the early 1970s.

In the Senate, Majority Leader George Mitchell (D.-Maine) rejuvenated the role of Democratic party organs after gaining his post in 1989. Under his predecessor, Robert Byrd (D.-W.Va.), the Democratic party conference and its committees met infrequently or not at all and had little role in policy-making. Byrd preferred to work directly with committee chairs and bill managers. In contrast, Mitchell encouraged the new party leaders to be active in setting a direction for the Senate on important issues and called more regular meetings of the party conference. Nevertheless, Senate Democrats, like House and Senate Republicans, impose no formal rules on committee operations and have not changed their committee assignment procedures in material ways.

Multiple Referral in the House

In 1974 the Speaker of the House was granted the authority to send legislation to committees jointly, sequentially, or by splitting it into parts. Before 1974 the Speaker was required to assign legislation to the single committee that had predominant jurisdiction over a bill, a practice that guaranteed monopoly referral rights to a single committee in each policy area. Under the existing rule, the Speaker is encouraged to recognize overlapping jurisdictions and the desirability of coordinating the decisions of committees on complex issues. In fact, in recent Congresses, about one quarter of the work load for the average House committee is multiply referred legislation. By the 1980s almost one in five bills important enough to warrant a special rule originated in two or more committees. In the Senate, multiple referral has always been possible but remains far less common than in the House, perhaps because it is so easy for committees to protect their jurisdictional interests by seeking to amend legislation on the floor.

Multiple referral has several important implications for committee autonomy in the House. First, committee autonomy is replaced by committee interdependence. The multiple-referral rule has encouraged committees to stake jurisdictional claims on a wide variety of issues and almost guarantees that conflicts between committees will arise with some frequency. Since the mid-1970s many committees have developed informal understandings about areas of shared jurisdiction that reduce open conflict, but these arrangements represent perforations in the autonomy of those committees that once enjoyed sole jurisdiction over those issue areas.

Second, conflict between two or more committees creates opportunities for others to exercise greater influence on policy outcomes. Sometimes that conflict spills onto the House floor, where votes on a series of amendments may impose a resolution on the contesting committees. And party leaders may be encouraged to intercede between committees in order to avoid open conflict on the floor between fellow partisans of different committees. Committees have recognized, however, that they may be better off resolving their differences before the legislation goes to the floor. The Rules Committee has encouraged such prefloor compromises by granting special rules limiting floor amendments and by allowing a compromise version to be taken to the floor as a substitute for the competing committee proposals. The process often involves compromises of committee positions that might not otherwise have been made.

Finally, and perhaps most important, the multiple-referral rule and associated practices substantially strengthen the Speaker's influence on committee decisions. The Speaker determines, without appeal, the original referral of legislation to multiple committees and may rerefer a measure after it has been amended by a committee so as to affect another committee's jurisdiction. The Speaker may also set deadlines on committee decisions when legislation is subject to multiple referral. In designing such arrangements, the Speaker is in a position to favor some committees, speed or delay committee action for strategic purposes, and send strong signals about his own policy preferences. Thus, when multiple referral is a possibility, committees are much less independent of the majority-party leadership, and much less autonomous than they were before multiple referral was permitted and exploited.

Committees in Conference

The ability of committees to control conference negotiations on behalf of their chambers has long been a vital source of power. In the House of the 1970s and 1980s, challenges to committee autonomy were accompanied by challenges to committee monopolies over appointments to conference delegations. New rules were adopted in 1975 and 1977 imploring the Speaker to appoint delegations that represented House preferences, to include members who sponsored major components of legislation, and to require conferences to hold their meetings in public sessions. The rules were targeted at senior committee members who had dominated conferences for decades.

In fact, committee outsiders have been appointed to House delegations with some frequency since the mid-1970s, much to the consternation of many committee members. During the 1980s, efforts were made to circumscribe the jurisdiction of outsiders by limiting the subjects on which they are entitled to vote. The pattern was similar to that observed in House floor amending activity: Committee autonomy was reduced but committees then invented means to limit their losses.

The Budget Process

The imposition of enforceable constraints on committee decisions or the adoption of affirmative-policy directives to committees in advance of committee action would greatly alter the sequence of legislative process and reduce committee power. The adoption of the Congressional Budget and Impoundment Control Act in 1974 created the possibility of rearranging the normal sequence and placing the initiative for policy change in the hands of members not serving on the committees of relevant jurisdiction. That threat was realized in the 1980s when budget deficits became very large. Several times major changes in policy and process were enacted to implement agreements negotiated by central party and budget leaders. Committee leaders often objected and occasionally resisted changes that put their power in jeopardy, but party leaders generally were able to muster floor majorities to impose new constraints on committees.

Reconciliation procedures and enforcement rules constitute the deepest encroachment on committee autonomy. Reconciliation instructions adopted in budget resolutions compelled authorizing committees to report legislation that achieved specified savings in programs under their jurisdictions. Committees were forced to accept changes in programs under their jurisdictions that they otherwise would not have reported. But committees also exploited reconciliation to incorporate non-budget items. Because reconciliation measures are seen as "must-pass" bills, are generally protected from floor amendments in the House, and are subject to a germaneness restriction for amendments and time limits in the Senate, they provide a ready means of insulating some pet legislation from attack. In response, the House and Senate have adopted enforcement mechanisms that limit committee discretion in composing reconciliation legislation. The net effect of reconciliation politics has been a shrinkage in the autonomy of committees.

The House and Senate appropriations committees have been subject to limits as well. By the end of the 1980s, a process for setting binding limits on the size of each appropriations bill had been established. Efforts by some appropriators to camouflage spending have been rejected by budget leaders who carefully scrutinize the allocation decisions within the two appropriations committees. The committees used the spending limits to their advantage on the floor as a way of repelling limit-breaking amendments. But in the early 1990s the limits on appropriations committees remained in place and represented a genuine new restriction on committee discretion.

CONCLUSION

The congressional committee system is integral to the remarkably complex congressional decision-making process. For most of the twentieth century, the basic structure of the committee system has remained stable, but the functions committees play in policy-making have changed. The degree to which the congressional decision-making process is committee-centered, party-centered, or floor-centered has varied widely between the two houses and over time. The particular mix exhibited in either chamber appears to result from the nature of the issues confronting each house and its members, the alignment of policy preferences, and past choices that limit the range of feasible institutional arrangements.

Certain features of the committee system will continue to make fairly strong committees attractive to members. The ability to respond to constituency demands, to house sizable staffs, to publicize favorite issues and policy proposals, and to exercise substantial influence in a policy field will motivate individual members to object to efforts to limit committee independence. But the ability of committees to control policy outcomes—their policy-making autonomy—is likely to vary as conditions vary. Stability is no more likely to be characteristic of the committee system of the future than that of the past.

BIBLIOGRAPHY

Committee System Dynamics
A general work from which most of the material for this essay is drawn is STEVEN S. SMITH and CHRISTOPHER J. DEERING, *Committees in Congress*, 2d ed. (Washington, D.C., 1990). See also RICHARD F. FENNO, JR., *Congressmen in Committees* (Boston, 1973); GEORGE GOODWIN, *The Little Legislatures: Committees of Congress* (Amherst, Mass., 1970); RALPH K. HUITT, "The Congressional Committee: A Case Study," *American Political Science Review* 48 (June 1954); CHARLES O. JONES, "Representa-

tion in Congress: The Case of the House Agriculture Committee," *American Political Science Review* 55 (June 1961); JOHN D. LEES, *The Committee System of the United States Congress* (New York, 1967); WILLIAM L. MORROW, *Congressional Committees* (New York, 1969); and DAVID E. PRICE, *Who Makes the Laws? Creativity and Power in Senate Committees* (Cambridge, Mass., 1972).

For a review of the research on congressional committees and a good bibliography, see HEINZ EULAU, "Committee Selection" and HEINZ EULAU and VERA MCCLUGGAGE, "Standing Committees in Legislatures," in GERHARD LOEWENBERG, SAMUEL C. PATTERSON, and MALCOLM E. JEWELL, eds., *Handbook of Legislative Research* (Cambridge, Mass., 1985).

Committee System Development

Historical studies of the congressional-committee system can be found in MICHAEL ABRAM and JOSEPH COOPER, "The Rise of Seniority in the House of Representatives," *Polity* 1 (Fall 1968); DEALVA STANWOOD ALEXANDER, *History and Procedure of the House of Representatives* (Boston, 1916); HERBERT B. ASHER, "The Learning of Legislative Norms," *American Political Science Review* 67 (June 1973); DAVID W. BRADY, *Critical Elections and Congressional Policy Making* (Stanford, Calif., 1988); JOSEPH COOPER, "Congress and Its Committees" (Ph.D. diss., Harvard University, 1960); JOSEPH COOPER, *The Origins of the Standing Committees and the Development of the Modern House* (Houston, Tex., 1970); JOSEPH COOPER and CHERYL D. YOUNG, "Bill Introduction in the Nineteenth Century: A Study of Institutional Change," *Legislative Studies Quarterly* 14 (February 1989); ROGER H. DAVIDSON and WALTER J. OLESZEK, *Congress Against Itself* (Bloomington, Ind., 1977); RICHARD F. FENNO, JR., *The Power of the Purse: Appropriations Politics in Congress* (Boston, 1966); MARY P. FOLLETT, *The Speaker of the House of Representatives* (New York, 1974); BURTON L. FRENCH, "Sub-committees of Congress," *American Political Science Review* 9 (February 1915); GEORGE B. GALLOWAY, *The History of the House of Representatives*, 2d ed. (New York, 1976); GERALD GAMM and KENNETH SHEPSLE, "Emergence of Legislative Institutions: Standing Committees in the House and Senate, 1810–1825," *Legislative Studies Quarterly* 14 (February 1989); RALPH V. HARLOW, *The History of Legislative Methods in the Period Before 1825* (New Haven, Conn., 1917); PAUL D. HASBROUCK, *Party Government in the House of Representatives* (New York, 1927); BARBARA HINCKLEY, *The Seniority System in Congress* (Bloomington, Ind., 1971); RALPH K. HUITT, "The Morse Committee Assignment Controversy: A Study in Senate Norms," *American Political Science Review* 51 (June 1957); RALPH K. HUITT, "The Outsider in the Senate: An Alternative Role," *American Political Science Review* 55 (September 1961); WALTER KRAVITZ, "Evolution of the Senate's Committee System," *Annals of the American Academy of Political and Social Science* 411 (January 1974); DONALD R. MATTHEWS, *U.S. Senators and Their World* (Chapel Hill, N.C., 1960); LAUROS G. MCCONACHIE, *Congressional Committees: A Study of the Origin and Development of Our National and Local Legislative Methods* (New York and Boston, 1898); NELSON W. POLSBY, "The Institutionalization of the U.S. House of Representatives," *American Political Science Review* 62 (March 1968); NELSON W. POLSBY, MIRIAM GALLAHER, and BARRY SPENCER RUNDQUIST, "The Growth of the Seniority System in the U.S. House of Representatives," *American Political Science Review* 63 (September 1969); LEROY N. RIESELBACH, *Congressional Reform* (Washington, D.C., 1986); RANDALL B. RIPLEY, *Power in the Senate* (New York, 1969); GEORGE L. ROBINSON, "The Development of the Senate Committee System," (Ph.D. diss., New York University, 1954); DAVID W. ROHDE, NORMAN J. ORNSTEIN, and ROBERT L. PEABODY, "Political Change and Legislative Norms in the U.S. Senate, 1957–1974," in GLENN R. PARKER, ed., *Studies of Congress* (Washington, D.C., 1985); DAVID J. ROTHMAN, *Politics and Power: The United States Senate 1869–1901* (Cambridge, Mass., 1966); THOMAS W. SKLADONY, "The House Goes to Work: Select and Standing Committees in the U.S. House of Representatives, 1789–1828," *Congress and the Presidency* 12 (Autumn 1985); and WOODROW WILSON, *Congressional Government* (Boston, 1885).

The Modern Committee System

For studies on the legislative power of modern committees, see GARY W. COX and MATHEW D. MCCUBBINS, *Parties and Committees in the U.S. House of Representatives* (forthcoming); LEWIS A. FROMAN, JR., *The Congressional Process:*

Strategies, Rules, and Procedures (Boston, 1967); KEITH KREHBIEL, *Information and Legislative Organization* (Ann Arbor, Mich., 1990); KEITH KREHBIEL, KENNETH A. SHEPSLE, and BARRY R. WEINGAST, "Why Are Congressional Committees Powerful?" *American Political Science Review* 81 (September 1987); NELSON W. POLSBY, "Legislatures," *Handbook of Political Science* (Reading, Mass., 1975); KENNETH SHEPSLE and BARRY WEINGAST, "The Institutional Foundations of Committee Power," *American Political Science Review* 81 (March 1987); STEVEN S. SMITH, "An Essay on Sequence, Position, Goals, and Committee Power," *Legislative Studies Quarterly* 13 (May 1988); BARRY WEINGAST, "A Rational Choice Perspective on Congressional Norms," *American Political Science Review* 23 (May 1979); BARRY R. WEINGAST, "Floor Behavior in the U.S. Congress: Committee Power Under the Open Rule," *American Political Science Review* 83 (September 1989).

Committee investigative power is the subject of JOEL D. ABERBACH, "The Congressional Committee Intelligence System: Information, Oversight, and Change," *Congress and the Presidency* 14 (Spring 1987); JOEL D. ABERBACH, *Keeping a Watchful Eye: The Politics of Congressional Oversight* (Washington, D.C., 1990); JOHN F. BIBBY, "Committee Characteristics and Legislative Oversight of Administration," *Midwest Journal of Political Science* 10 (February 1966); and LAWRENCE C. DODD and RICHARD L. SCHOTT, *Congress and the Administrative State* (New York, 1979).

For information on committee assignments, see KENNETH A. SHEPSLE, *The Giant Jigsaw Puzzle: Democratic Committee Assignments in the Modern House* (Chicago, 1978); STEVEN S. SMITH and BRUCE A. RAY, "The Impact of Congressional Reform: House Democratic Committee Assignments," *Congress and the Presidency* 10 (Autumn 1983); and STEVEN S. SMITH and CHRISTOPHER J. DEERING, *Committees in Congress* (Washington, D.C., 1990).

Committee leadership is the focus of C. LAWRENCE EVANS, *Influence in Senate Committees* (Ph.D. diss., University of Rochester, 1987); LAWRENCE EVANS and RICHARD L. HALL, "The Power of Subcommittees," *Journal of Politics* (forthcoming); RICHARD L. HALL, "Participation and Purpose in Committee Decision Making," *American Political Science Review* 81 (March 1987); JOHN F. MANLEY, "Wilbur D. Mills: A Study in Congressional Influence," *American Political Science Review* 63 (June 1969); JOHN F. MANLEY, *The Politics of Finance: The House Committee on Ways and Means* (Boston, 1970); RANDALL STRAHAN, *New Ways and Means: Reform and Change in a Congressional Committee* (Chapel Hill, N.C., 1990); and JOSEPH K. UNEKIS and LEROY N. RIESELBACH, "Congressional Committee Leadership, 1971–1978," *Journal of Politics* 40 (1983).

Subcommittees are the subject of ROGER H. DAVIDSON, "Subcommittee Government: New Channels for Policy Making," in THOMAS E. MANN and NORMAN J. ORNSTEIN, eds., *The New Congress* (Washington, D.C., 1981); STEVEN HAEBERLE, "The Institutionalization of the Subcommittee in the United States House of Representatives," *Journal of Politics* 40 (November 1978); CHARLES O. JONES, "The Role of the Congressional Subcommittee," *Midwest Journal of Political Science* 6 (November 1962); and NORMAN J. ORNSTEIN and DAVID W. ROHDE, "Shifting Forces, Changing Rules and Political Outcomes: The Impact of Congressional Change on Four House Committees," in ROBERT L. PEABODY and NELSON W. POLSBY, eds., *New Perspectives on the House of Representatives*, 3d ed. (Chicago, 1977).

For information on committee staff, see DAVID W. BRADY, "Personnel Management in the House," in JOSEPH COOPER and G. CALVIN MACKENZIE, eds., *The House at Work* (Austin, Tex., 1981); HARRISON W. FOX, JR., and SUSAN WEBB HAMMOND, *Congressional Staffs: The Invisible Force in American Lawmaking* (New York, 1977); GLADYS M. KAMMERER, *The Staffing of the Committees of Congress* (Lexington, Ky., 1949); KENNETH T. KOFMEHL, *Professional Staffs of Congress* (West Lafayette, Ind., 1962); MICHAEL J. MALBIN, *Unelected Representatives: Congressional Staff and the Future of Representative Government* (New York, 1980); DAVID E. PRICE, "Professionals and 'Entrepreneurs': Staff Orientations and Policy Making on Three Senate Committees," *Journal of Politics* 33 (May 1971); and ROBERT H. SALISBURY and KENNETH A. SHEPSLE, "Congressional Staff Turnover and the Ties-That-Bind," *American Political Science Review* 75 (June 1981).

Developing Issues

For the effect of party alignments on congressional decision-making, see DAVID W. ROHDE,

"Democratic Party Leadership, Agenda Control, and the Resurgence of Partisanship in the House," paper prepared for the annual meeting of the American Political Science Association, Atlanta, 1989; and BARBARA SINCLAIR, "The Changing Role of Party and Party Leadership in the U.S. House," paper presented at the annual meeting of the American Political Science Association, Atlanta, 1989.

For developments in floor activity, see STANLEY BACH and STEVEN S. SMITH, *Managing Uncertainty in the House of Representatives: Adaptation and Innovation in Special Rules* (Washington, D.C., 1988); BARBARA SINCLAIR, *The Transformation of the U.S. Senate* (Baltimore, Md., 1989); and STEVEN S. SMITH, *Call to Order: Floor Politics in the House and Senate* (Washington, D.C., 1989).

The influence of party caucuses on the committee process can be found in ROGER H. DAVIDSON, "The New Centralization in Congress," *The Review of Politics* 49 (Summer 1988); BARBARA SINCLAIR, "House Majority Leadership in the Late 1980s," in LAWRENCE C. DODD and BRUCE I. OPPENHEIMER, eds., *Congress Reconsidered,* 4th ed. (Washington, D.C., 1989); BARBARA SINCLAIR, *Majority Leadership in the U.S. House* (Baltimore, Md., 1983); and DON WOLFENSBERGER, "The Role of Party Caucuses in the U.S. House of Representatives: An Historical Perspective," paper prepared for the annual meeting of the American Political Science Association, 1988.

Studies on multiple referral include ROGER H. DAVIDSON, WALTER J. OLESZEK, and THOMAS KEPHART, "One Bill, Many Committees: Multiple Referrals in the U.S. House of Representatives," *Legislative Studies Quarterly* 13 (February 1988); and MELISSA P. COLLIE and JOSEPH COOPER, "Multiple Referral and the 'New' Committee System in the House of Representatives," in LAWRENCE C. DODD and BRUCE I. OPPENHEIMER, eds., *Congress Reconsidered,* 4th ed. (Washington, D.C., 1989).

For information on congressional conferences, see LAWRENCE D. LONGLEY and WALTER J. OLESZEK, *Bicameral Politics: Conference Committees in Congress* (New Haven, Conn., 1989); and STEVEN S. SMITH, *Call to Order: Floor Politics in the House and Senate* (Washington, D.C., 1989).

On developments stemming from the budget process, see JOHN W. ELLWOOD, "The Politics of the Enactment and Implementation of Gramm-Rudman-Hollings: Why Congress Cannot Address the Deficit Dilemma," *Harvard Journal on Legislation* 25 (Summer 1988); LOUIS FISHER, "The Budget Act of 1974: Reflections After Ten Years," paper presented at the annual meeting of the Midwest Political Science Association, 1985; ALLEN SCHICK, *Congress and Money: Budgeting, Spending, and Taxing* (Washington, D.C., 1980); ALLEN SCHICK, "The Whole and the Parts: Piecemeal and Integrated Approaches to Congressional Budgeting," report prepared for the Task Force on the Budget Process, Committee on the Budget, U.S. House of Representatives, Serial No. CP-3 (Washington, D.C., 1987); and JOSEPH WHITE, *The Functions and Power of the House Appropriations Committee* (Ph.D. diss., University of California, Berkeley and Los Angeles, 1989).

SEE ALSO Committee Selection in Congress; Congressional Oversight; The Congressional Budget Process and Federal Budget Deficit; The House Committee on Ways and Means; The Role of Congressional Parties; AND The Rules Committee: The House Traffic Cop.

COMMITTEES IN STATE LEGISLATURES

Keith E. Hamm
Ronald D. Hedlund

From their beginnings, American state legislatures have used committees as organizational devices that allow for the distribution of work load among members (division of labor) while permitting the focus of attention on a narrow range of issues (specialization) and advancing the development of detailed knowledge about a topic (expertise development). Utilization of these devices has permitted the collective decision-making nature of a legislative body to be maintained amid the transformation from a slow-paced, relatively unified eighteenth-century agrarian political society to a fast-paced, diverse urban society of the twentieth century. Legislatures have been able to meet emerging demands in the presence of changing expectations by adapting parts of the committee process while maintaining its basic structure and purpose. Consequently, understanding the basic components of a committee system is important for understanding the nature of the legislative system in the fifty states. This essay focuses attention on five major topics: (1) the role that committees play in decision-making relative to that of legislative leaders and political parties; (2) the extent to which committees perform the function of specialization; (3) committee personnel, both members and staff; (4) the extent to which committees are influenced by legislative actors and by nonlegislative groups; and (5) committee-system performance. The conclusion will comment on the nature of state legislative committees in the 1990s.

This examination relies on findings from studies of state legislative committee systems, as well as on four sets of original data. The first set of data is an eighteen-state questionnaire study of legislator perceptions. The questionnaire was mailed to members in thirty-six legislative chambers and covers the period 1971–1986. This project began in 1975, when questionnaires were mailed to all members of the Iowa and Wisconsin legislatures asking for their impressions as to how their legislative chamber worked for the existing two-year session. From 1979 through 1986 this effort was extended to include an additional sixteen states. In addition, through written prompts describing key elements, legislators were asked to recall sessions as early as 1971 and to offer their impressions. Questions covered an array of topics including: (1) the importance of committees in decision-making; (2) the functioning of committees; (3) the availability and competence of staff; and (4) the issue of who influences committees. Two follow-up questionnaires augmented legislator responses. All told, 4,630 legislators responded. The proportion of members responding varied considerably, from a low of zero (0) for a few chambers asked to recall efforts in the early 1970s to a high of 74 percent for the Iowa state senators in 1977–1978.

The second set of data, an eighteen-state study of legislative operations, focuses on a variety of rules and procedures utilized by legislators in thirty-six chambers covering the period 1971–1986. Topics covered include rules governing creation and operation of standing committees and committee assignments. The third set of data focuses on the degree of carryover, experience, and constancy of committee membership in the thirty-six chambers in our eighteen-state study of legislative operations for the period 1971–1986. Finally, the fourth set of data presents the results of legislators' requests for assignment to committee positions in five chambers.

LEGISLATIVE STRUCTURES AND PROCESSES

I. THE ROLE OF COMMITTEES IN DECISION MAKING

One concern among political scientists and legislative observers centers on where important decisions are made regarding the content of legislation. Any analysis of the legislative process in the U.S. confirms the existence of many different locales or points of decision-making, each of which influences legislation profoundly. In describing legislative decision-making, several authors, including Malcolm E. Jewell, Samuel C. Patterson, William J. Keefe, and Morris S. Ogul note its fragmented and decentralized nature. A review of previous research reveals that the most frequently discussed groups and individuals who impact legislative decisions are legislative committees/subcommittees, legislative leaders, the governor, administrative agencies, floor debate, interest groups, and constituents. Much attention has been given to evaluating the roles played by these groups and individuals regarding specific bills and legislation in general. The initial question asked in this essay regarding committees/subcommittees relates to an evaluation of their role in state legislative decision-making.

Wayne L. Francis, using questionnaire data from the early 1980s, tried to determine the importance of committees relative to political parties and leadership in state legislative chambers. Committees were considered important in the decision-making process in eighty-one of the ninety-nine state legislative chambers. Committees were seen by majority-party respondents to be the only center of decision-making in fifteen chambers. They were perceived to share power with the leadership in twenty-nine chambers, with the party caucus in sixteen, and with both in an additional twenty-one chambers. While committees are not always seen as the only focal point in the state legislative process, according to Francis's study they are perceived as significant in most state legislatures.

Our eighteen-state questionnaire study of legislator perceptions offers insight for eight sessions in thirty-six state legislative chambers. One questionnaire item requested that respondents select up to three groups or individuals who had the most significant impact on the decisions made during each specific session of their legislative chamber. Choices included party caucuses, the chamber floor, regular committee meetings, prelegislative sessions, the governor's office, and policy committee meetings. Write-in responses were permitted, and many respondents listed the presiding officer and leadership among their three choices. Table 1 illustrates the high degree of importance given to committees in state legislative decision-making by legislators responding to this question.

Out of eight possibilities, "regular committee meetings" were selected most frequently as one of the three places where most significant decisions were made during these eight sessions in the eighteen states: approximately two out of every three respondents selected committees as one of their three choices. This is the most frequently selected locus for decision-making out of 256 state-chamber-session combinations (either ranked number 1 or tied for that rank in 145; 57 percent), and among the top three ranked choices for 244 cases (95 percent). Least-frequently selected were party caucuses and the chamber floor.

Additional insight about the endurance of this perceived importance for committees is available by comparing rankings and percentages across time (1971–1980 and 1981–1986). Four patterns are observed among the eighteen states summarized in Table 1. The vast majority of chambers have a pattern in which regular committee meetings are of uniformly high importance—always being ranked in the top three and always being selected by more than 50 percent of the legislators as a key decision-making center (i.e., both chambers in Florida, Georgia, Maine, Nevada, North Carolina, North Dakota, South Dakota, Washington, and West Virginia, as well as the state senates of Arizona, Ohio, and Tennessee, and the state houses of Massachusetts and Texas). The same pattern holds in the Iowa Senate and Wisconsin Assembly, although data are available for the 1981–1986 period only. Thus, in twenty-five of thirty-six chambers, regular committee meetings were consistently selected as an important place for significant decision-making activity.

The second most prevalent pattern is where committees are generally, but not always, important—being selected by 50 percent or more of the respondents and having a mean rank between one and three for all but one session across the eight sessions studied (both

Table 1
SELECTION OF COMMITTEE (AS 1ST, 2D, OR 3D CHOICE) AS PLACE WHERE MOST IMPORTANT LEGISLATIVE DECISIONS ARE MADE BY SESSION, CHAMBER, AND STATE (ENTRIES ARE PERCENT[a] OF RESPONDENTS SELECTING CAUCUS AND RANK OF THIS PERCENT, 1–8).

| | | 1971–1980 (5 Sessions) | | | | | 1981–1986 (3 Sessions) | | | | |
| | | Percent | | Rank | | | Percent | | Rank | | |
State	Cham	Mean	Range	Mean	Range	# Sessions Top 3	Mean	Range	Mean	Range	# Sessions Top 3
Ariz.	S	91%	80–100%	1.5	1–2	4*	87	84–91%	1.7	1–2	3
	H	33	0–61	4	2–8	3	76	70–79	1.3	1–2	3
Calif.	S	70	0–100	3	1–8	3**	64	31–100	3.0	1–5	2
	A	19	0–58	6.3	3–8	1**	39	22–58	4.0	3–5	1
Fla.	S	89	57–100	1.5	1–3	4*	89	76–100	1.0	1	3
	H	93	76–100	1	1	5	74	56–88	1.0	1	3
Ga.	S	88	50–100	1.3	1–2	4*	76	73–81	1.0	1	3
	H	80	76–89	1.0	1	5	76	73–78	1.0	1	3
Iowa	S	NA	NA	NA	NA	NA	69	66–73	2.0	2	3
	H	NA	NA	NA	NA	NA	44	38–50	3.0	3	3
Mass.	S	70	41–100	2.4	1–4	4	74	40–100	2.0	1–4	2
	H	75	52–92	1.6	1–2	5	85	81–91	1.0	1	3
Maine	S	92	67–100	1.6	1–3	5	81	59–100	1.7	1–2	3
	H	72	51–87	2.2	1–3	5	78	73–82	1.0	1	3
Nev.	S	88	50–100	1.3	1–2	4*	100	100	1.0	1	3
	A	91	73–100	1.2	1–2	5	88	80–93	1.0	1	3
N.C.	S	97	85–100	1.0	1	5	78	68–96	1.3	1–2	3
	H	90	80–100	1.0	1	5	83	77–89	1.0	1	3
N.Dak.	S	88	78–100	1.8	1–3	5	91	84–96	1.7	1–2	3
	H	83	68–100	1.6	1–2	5	82	73–90	1.7	1–2	3
Ohio	S	92	67–100	1.3	1–2	4*	74	54–89	2.3	2–3	3
	H	70	50–80	1.5	1–2	5	66	44–78	1.7	1–3	3
Pa.	S	80	53–100	1.6	1–2	5	62	39–93	2.3	2–3	3
	H	61	45–78	2.6	1–4	5	64	61–68	1.7	1–2	3
S.Dak.	S	82	55–100	1.6	1–2	5	73	70–76	2.7	2–3	3
	H	95	83–100	1.2	1–2	5	73	72–74	2.3	2–3	3
Tenn.	S	100	100	1.0	1	5	94	83–100	1.3	1–2	3
	H	86	43–100	1.4	1–3	5	96	91–100	1.0	1	3
Tex.	S	62	0–100	3.3	1–8	1**	88	80–100	1.0	1	3
	H	80	67–94	1.2	1–2	5	87	77–95	1.0	1	3
Wash.	S	92	69–100	1.3	1–2	4*	65	60–74	2.0	2	3
	A	72	60–82	2.0	2	5	74	66–79	2.0	2	3
W.Va.	S	87	71–100	1.8	1–3	5	93	88–100	1.3	1–2	3
	H	79	59–100	1.4	1–3	5	82	78–90	1.0	1	3
Wis.	S	NA	NA	NA	NA	NA	60	49–81	2.7	2–4	2
	H	NA	NA	NA	NA	NA	56	51–64	3.0	3	3

[a]Percents are from a weighted analysis to assure proper party balance in responses.
*Indicates data is available for only 4 two-year sessions.
**Indicates data is available for only 3 two-year sessions.
NA – Question not asked for this set of respondents.

chambers in Pennsylvania as well as the Ohio House, the Tennessee House, and the Texas Senate). The Wisconsin Senate also fits this pattern, although data exist for only three sessions, 1981–1986. Cases falling in this second pattern continue to indicate a high level of importance given to committees.

The third group contains a more mixed evaluation. Here, committees are neither all-important nor consistently unimportant. Instead, the evaluation has varied across the sessions. Included here are the California Senate, Massachusetts Senate, and the Arizona House. The Iowa House presents a more complicated picture. Here, we only have data for the 1981–1986 period. While committees are ranked third overall in each two-year session, less than 51 percent of the membership see them as being key decision-making points.

In the fourth pattern, committees are not perceived to be important in the decision-making process. The mean ranking is three or greater and, in a majority of the sessions, less than 50 percent of the respondents chose the committee as a key decision-making locus. The only chamber in which committees were perceived to be this weak is the California Assembly.

Trends in two chambers are worth noting in that they point to the potential for change in the importance of committees across time. The Arizona House is an interesting case. In the early 1970s committees were not rated as important. During the 1980s, however, they assumed a greater prominence, always being ranked first or second in terms of importance. On the other hand, while pre-1980s committees have always been ranked among the top three in the Pennsylvania Senate, there is a discernible trend for committees to be less highly evaluated in the mid-1980s than in the mid-1970s.

Consequently, during the 1971–1986 period, state legislators from these eighteen states generally gave high rankings to committees when evaluating the importance of alternative loci for decision-making. While there are some differences in terms of state, chamber, and session, overall, committees are more highly ranked than leadership, the governor's office, the chamber floor, prelegislative sessions, or party caucuses. This indicates to us that legislative committees at the state level are important centers for decision-making on the content of bills and on the nature of public policy.

II. COMMITTEES AND SPECIALIZATION

Political scientists are virtually unanimous in asserting that understanding specialization in American legislatures depends in large part on focusing research attention on legislative committees. The assumption typically made is that committees make a difference in the policy-making process at both the state and national legislative levels and that much of this impact is due to the specialization realized because of committees and subcommittees. From a generalized legislative organization perspective, Wayne Francis and James Riddlesperger noted that committees are the primary means used by legislative bodies to respond in a measured and reasonable way to the increasing number and range of emerging policy needs and demands in states. This perspective clearly affirms a belief that legislative committees serve as important organizational subunits that review, revise, and structure policy decision-making. Further, committees become a means whereby legislative organizations can process the large number and range of legislative proposals coming before a state legislature in any two-year session. Finally, and most importantly, committees are viewed as a device for accomplishing the review functions for a range of proposals because they provide for a division of labor and specialization of tasks.

In order to evaluate specialization via committees, the researcher must be sensitive to the unit (level) of analysis. As it relates to legislative committees, Heinz Eulau and Vera McCluggage advocate an explicit recognition that both organizational- and individual-level investigations are necessary to an understanding of organizational specialization via legislative committees. In keeping with this perspective, they provide a multilevel conceptual definition that emphasizes organizational specialization via committees in terms of three subject units (levels) of action: (1) the legislative chamber of which committees are a part; (2) the committee units themselves; and (3) the individual legislators comprising committees. Below, we apply their conceptualization to analyze state-level committee systems.

CHAMBER PERSPECTIVE ON COMMITTEE SPECIALIZATION

In analyzing state legislative committees at the chamber level, we are not referring to those situations in which the entire legislature sits as the committee of the whole. Likewise, we are not concerned with the structure or actions of any single committee, nor with its membership. Instead, we wish to assess the level of organizational specialization at the legislative-chamber level by concentrating on the attributes of committee systems. Specifically, the focus is on four legislative-level traits: (1) permanence of committees in the legislature; (2) chamber versus joint committees; (3) number of standing committees and subcommittees; and (4) total number of committee positions.

Permanence of Committees in the Legislative Chamber

Committees have been an enduring feature of American legislative bodies since their first appearance in colonial assemblies, the predecessor institution for most of our current state legislatures. Within state legislative chambers, a core of committees has existed with only minor changes in jurisdiction over numerous two-year sessions. Basic state-policy responsibilities have been represented by some type of committee for decades. Examples include finance (appropriations, revenue, ways and means), education (formerly schools), business (commerce), and local government (urban problems, cities and towns, counties). While names change and minor modifications in topic jurisdictions are noted, these committees exist from session to session and provide continuity to the legislative process.

Specific concerns may result in the creation of a committee for a session that will focus attention on that topic until legislation is passed. The typical pattern has been for state legislatures, through the leadership, to create new committees to deal with this legislation or to add that responsibility to an existing committee by a change in jurisdiction. Thus, in the 1970s and 1980s, energy and environmental

concerns led to the creation of state legislative committees specializing in these topics. Similarly, the decline of the manufacturing base of some states led to the creation of economic or business development committees in the late 1980s.

The existence of committee permanence provides for continuity and the development of expertise on topics coming before legislative chambers. Add to this the tendency for many legislators to remain on the same committee across sessions, and additional permanence is built in. This results in policy-making that tends to recognize previous decisions and approaches so that it is cumulative in nature, with current decisions being based on and reflecting those earlier decisions. As a consequence, radical changes of direction in a state's policies and approaches are rare.

Standing Versus Ad Hoc Committees In evaluating committee systems, a crucial distinction must be made between standing and ad hoc committees. For our purposes, the distinction is between those committees that exist for the life of the particular legislative session, typically for two years, versus those instances in which a group of legislators are brought together to scrutinize one bill or one specific issue and then disband. The assumption is that organizational specialization is enhanced when legislatures have a greater preponderance of the longer-standing committees, although it may be the case that there is a mixture of the two types at any point in time. As we shall show, the trend in American state legislatures from their foundings has been to proceed from a proclivity to employ ad hoc committees to a preference, if not a need, for more-permanent committees.

A committee system having a key responsibility for the shaping and screening of legislation developed among the state legislatures during the eighteenth century, but not at a uniform rate. One cause for greater dependence on standing committees was the need for a system that would sift and sort the increasing legislative work load that emerged after individual members began to introduce their own legislative proposals. The organizational advantage in relying on these committees was that the committee of the whole's calendar remained manageable. The uneven development of a standing committee system extended in some cases into the middle of the nineteenth century. For example, in Georgia, at least through the early 1860s, most bills were not referred to standing committees; instead, an ad hoc committee of three or four members, with the legislator who proposed the legislation serving as chairperson, was given responsibility for shaping the legislation. Even if legislation was referred to committees, there are indications that the rise in the number of first-term members during the first half of the eighteenth century worked against the development of committee expertise. In the New York Assembly, for example, committees may have gathered information, but they did not switch the locus of decision-making from the committee of the whole.

From the 1870s to the early part of the twentieth century, the standing committee system in several states exploded. The number of committees increased dramatically, the total number of committee positions proliferated, and the number of assignments per member increased significantly. Several explanations have been offered for this rapid transformation: increased work load, legislators' preferences for committee chairs, and legislative leaders' need for patronage. Still, it is very likely that these committees did not provide a high level of performance in terms of screening and shaping legislation. The lack of time to make decisions, information, and expertise all worked against an effective committee system. At the same time, the reliance on select committees during the legislative session never abated entirely. The extent to which these specialized committees were used appears to have varied from state to state, although no precise figures have been documented. In any event, by the turn of the twentieth century, the standing committee system seems to have taken hold in all state legislatures.

Standing Committees and the Interim Period   At the outset we suggested that standing committees existed at least for a given legislative session, whatever its length. Therefore, in legislatures that meet on basically a year-round basis, standing committees operate continuously, with staff and members forming a work group that interacts throughout the legislative session.

Another aspect of permanence, however, involves the activities of committees in those legislatures that are not in continuous session.

Among these legislatures, the issue is whether standing committees continue to operate in the interim or whether the activities are carried out by specially created ad hoc committees. The expectation is that organizational specialization is enhanced if the standing committee system operates during the interim, although by the late 1960s this was an option selected by only a minority of state legislatures. In the late 1980s, standing committees operated year-round in some capacity in a majority of the state legislative chambers, although in slightly less than 40 percent of these bodies no authorization exists for them to operate in the interim.

Chamber Versus Joint Committees

In designing a permanent committee system, the issue of formal organization must be settled. Two general models are provided. In the traditional system each chamber of a bicameral legislature appoints its own committees, with membership limited to just those legislators serving in the particular chamber. This chamber-specific model is often assumed when committee organization is discussed. However, another option is the joint-committee system. In its purest form, all committees would be composed of members from both chambers, although not necessarily with the same number of members from each. Committee hearings would involve committee members from both the upper and lower chambers. For example, a joint appropriations committee would issue one appropriations bill that would be referred to both chambers simultaneously, rather than having an appropriations committee in each chamber file its separate bill with its own chamber.

The development of joint committees in American state legislatures is difficult to trace. However, an intriguing finding is that in examinations of legislatures done in the late 1920s, late 1940s, and late 1980s, all but a handful of states (Alabama and Ohio are examples) were shown to have used joint committees, even if for just one issue for one of these sessions. C. I. Winslow, writing in 1931, argued that at least one joint committee existed in twenty-one state legislatures. In three states—Massachusetts, Maine, and Connecticut—the joint-committee system prevailed, although there were a few chamber-specific committees in each chamber in the three states. These three state legislatures have maintained this pattern through the present day. A substantial number of joint committees existed in New Jersey, North Dakota, and Rhode Island. During the late 1940s, more than a majority (twenty-seven) of state legislatures had at least one joint committee. In the late 1980s, joint committees were used by twenty-nine state legislatures, with extensive use in California, Kansas, Maryland, Mississippi, New York, Rhode Island, Utah, and Wisconsin. At this point, we can only speculate as to the reasons for the tendency to use this nontraditional form of organization.

Number of Standing Committees and Subcommittees

A major function of the committee system is to create an efficient division of labor. Organizational theorists argue that organizational specialization can be indicated by the number of subunits within an organization. Obviously, given the abundant number of bills that each state legislature must consider, members sitting as a committee of the whole legislature will be inefficient. At the same time, however, creating an ad hoc committee for each bill is also inefficient. With this latter arrangement, a major advantage of a committee system—the opportunity to bundle together proposed legislation dealing with similar topics—is lost. Current practice calls for the establishment of a limited number of standing committees with jurisdictions specified according to their names. This arrangement permits legislators and their leaders to determine what array of committee jurisdictions, and consequently specializations, they will have for considering legislation. A key question is whether changes in the number of committees in state legislatures over time represent an increase or decrease in specialization.

Several state legislative scholars suggest that reductions in the number of state legislative committees during the past several years have actually increased specialization. Alan Rosenthal, for example, has argued that fewer committees enhance the rational division of labor and help produce improved performance levels. Malcolm E. Jewell and Samuel C. Patterson have added that the elimination of committees at the state legislative level has

helped to balance the work load among committees and to eliminate a multitude of minor committees that handled little or no legislation. Thus, a reduction in the number of committees is seen as producing positive benefits for the legislative organization.

Unfortunately, our knowledge about the changes in the number of committees in state legislatures that occurred during the late nineteenth and early twentieth centuries is incomplete, as few empirical studies exist that focus on this topic. However, Paul S. Reinsch, writing in 1907 in *American Legislatures and Legislative Methods,* observed that "it is a notable fact that during the past few decades both the number of committees and the average of membership have increased rapidly" (p. 163).

Data is available for the 1917 legislative session in all forty-eight states. During that session, the mean number of standing committees in state senates was slightly greater than thirty-one, with the range being between five in the Wisconsin Senate and sixty-two in the Michigan Senate. In the lower houses, the mean was about forty committees, with the range between fourteen in Rhode Island and sixty-five in Kentucky. Little overall change occurred during the next decade or more. For example, during the 1929 session the average number of committees in state senates was 32.3, and in the lower houses it was 39.2. By 1950, twenty-one years later, the averages had dropped slightly to 31.0 in the state senates and 36.7 in the state houses.

Somewhat unexpectedly, the major change during this roughly seventy-year period occurred between the 1949 and 1969 legislative sessions; in both the senates and houses the number of committees decreased significantly. In the 1969 session, the mean number of committees dropped to slightly below twenty in the senates and twenty-three in the state houses. The maximum number of committees fell from sixty-six to forty-five and from seventy-two to fifty-one in the state senates and state houses, respectively.

The surprising finding, in light of a substantial amount of political science writing, is that little overall change occurs when the mean number of total committees for the 1969 and 1989 legislative sessions are compared. Decreases are noticed in both chambers, but they are extremely small. How is this finding to be reconciled with several reports of major changes in the committee system during this period? Two plausible explanations may account for the differences. First, the major reduction in the number of standing committees in some legislatures occurred in the late 1960s, perhaps even in the 1969 session. Second, another set of legislatures initially reduced the number of standing committees in the early 1970s only to have them increase over time such that by 1989, it appeared that little or no change had occurred over the twenty-year period.

This latter point can be understood better if we examine changes in the number of committees from session to session over a long period of time. An example underscores the magnitude of this change and helps to explain the contradictory findings regarding changes in organizational specialization from 1969 to 1989. In 1969 in the Texas House, there were forty-five standing committees, while in 1989 there were thirty-six, approximately a 20-percent decrease. However, during this same twenty-year period, the highest number of committees was forty-six in 1971–1972 and the lowest number twenty-two in the 1973–1974 session. After reaching this nadir, the number of standing committees began a slow ascent, although no linear monotonic pattern is evident. Therefore, while the observer of the committee system in the early 1970s may conclude that a significant increase in organizational specialization occurred because the number of committees decreased by approximately 52 percent, those who examine the end points of 1969 and 1989 may respond by saying that the increase in specialization was not all that significant. A more in-depth analysis by the authors, conducted in 1992, documents the magnitude of change between the 1929 and 1989 sessions. The number of committees decreased in eighty-eight of the ninety-seven legislative chambers, with there being a mean decrease of 15.3 committees in the state senates and 17.6 in the state houses. Stated differently, in seventy-two chambers there was a decrease of at least ten committees, and in thirty-seven of these there were at least twenty fewer committees in 1989 than in 1929.

Another device sometimes used to produce specialization in legislatures has been the institutionalization of a more elaborate system of subcommittees. The implications of this trend in terms of heightened specialization, decentralization, and access to decision-making has been documented at the congressional level; however, very little is known about this trend among the states. Different estimates exist on the frequency with which subcommittees are used. Employing survey data, Francis and Riddlesperger estimated that subcommittees were used in about two-thirds of the chambers, being more prevalent in the lower chambers than in the state senates. In a 1988 survey by the American Society of Legislative Clerks and Secretaries, subcommittees were listed as being used in fifty-one state legislative chambers: twenty-two state senates and twenty-nine state houses. Ronald D. Hedlund, Diane Powers, and Ronald H. Lingren, relying on official state legislative publications, demonstrated an increase in subcommittee use among their sample of thirty-six chambers from 1971 to 1986 (not counting ad hoc and nonlisted subcommittees). Where are subcommittees most likely to be utilized? Research indicates that frequency of subcommittee use and committee reliance upon subcommittee reports is at least partially a function of the average committee size: the larger the committee size, the greater subcommittees are used and their reports relied upon.

Total Number of Committee Positions

A final component of organizational specialization is the total number of committee positions. Here, most state legislative leaders have historically had a fair amount of discretion. Expansion and contraction of the total number of positions was a tool leaders could use to structure the committee system to their liking. Given this potential for altering the makeup of the committee system, one relevant research question is, Does the absolute number of committee positions vary significantly over time? To answer this question, we collected two sets of data. The first set consists of the total number of committee positions in the 1929 and 1989 sessions for all legislative chambers. The second set consists of the total number of committee positions for every two-year period from 1971 to 1986 for the senates and houses in eighteen state legislatures.

The most general observation that can be made from comparing 1929 and 1989 data is that the total number of committee positions in state legislatures has declined precipitously. As Hamm and Hedlund found, the mean number of positions has fallen in the state senates from 275 to 163 (41 percent), while in the state houses the drop has been from 505 to 321 (36 percent). The largest contraction was an incredible 1,289 positions in the Georgia House, while in the state senates the largest decline was 689 positions in the Georgia Senate. More than 200 positions were lost in twenty-seven chambers. This trend, however, was not uniform. While decreases occurred in seventy-nine chambers, the total number of committee positions increased in sixteen chambers, with the largest increase being 240 in the New York House.

With all of this change over time, is there any relationship in the number of positions between the two time periods? The answer is yes, with a modestly strong correlation coefficient of .655. In addition, for both time periods, the larger the chamber, the greater the number of committee positions (r=.537 in 1929 and .662 in 1989). Measuring change over a sixty-year time period, however, does not capture the degree of change that may occur in the short term. Thus, to understand how stable the number of committee positions are from session to session, we analyzed the results for thirty-six chambers over a sixteen-year period, 1971 to 1986. Two points deserve special mention. First, the major contractions in committee positions occurred during the early years of the time period under study. That is, ten of the fifteen major contractions in the state senates and six of eight major contractions in the lower houses occurred in the 1971–1976 period. By contrast, only about 18 percent of the major expansions took place during the same time period. The major reductions in the number of committee positions may be tied to the remnants of reform in the number of committees discussed earlier.

A second trend is specific to chamber, rather than to time. In five chambers the changes in the total number of committee positions exceeded 10 percent, be it positive or negative, for at least four of the seven intersession comparisons. Most unstable in this regard was the Florida legislature, where in a total of ten out of fourteen comparisons, the changes are major.

While it is unclear what factors account for the change in the total number of committee positions between 1927 and 1989, there is some indication as to the key variables involved in short-term change (i.e., between consecutive legislative sessions). Several studies attempt to answer this question for the U.S. Congress, but only one study on this topic exists at the state level. In that study, published in the May 1990 issue of *Legislative Studies Quarterly,* Keith Hamm and Ronald Hedlund found that when the continuing membership on committees is low, when the leadership has more control over committee appointments, and when the committee system is perceived to be less important for legislative decision-making, greater change is observed in the number of committee positions. In other words, "significant change takes place where the committee system least approximates the congressional model" (pp. 217–218).

COMMITTEE PERSPECTIVE ON SPECIALIZATION

Specialization may also be evaluated at the committee level. Two of the most important indicators of committee specialization at this level are the diversity of issues handled and the size of the committee.

Committee Jurisdiction and Diversity of Issues Handled

A key aspect of committee specialization is the nature of the committee's purview. The diversity of topics covered by a committee has important implications for the operation of that committee. To the degree that a broad range of topics come under a committee's purview, specialization of decision-making of that committee may be retarded. An extreme example highlights this potential problem: Suppose that a committee system is composed of five committees designated A, B, C, D, and E. Also, assume that bills are randomly assigned to each committee. What would be the consequences of this system? Two major shortcomings would be the lack of subject-matter expertise and the lack of related proposals being assigned to the same committee.

In an attempt to address this issue, we have classified each legislative chamber in terms of the extent to which the jurisdictions of committees are formalized in the chamber rules. While this delineation of the subject matter to be considered by each committee is no guarantee of the scope of issues considered, the assumption is that the probability of a broader range of issues coming before a committee are greater in chambers without this type of rule.

In the late 1980s and early 1990s, roughly 35 percent of the state senates and 35 percent of the state houses had explicit jurisdictions for all of the committees; in another 9 percent of the chambers, jurisdictions were outlined for some of the committees. No attempt has been made, however, to see if a subject is considered to be the responsibility of more than one committee; whether, for instance, two committees have jurisdictions over the environment or natural resources. The formal rules appear to provide at least some semblance of jurisdictions in a substantial number of state legislatures.

Leaders in state legislatures appear to alter the jurisdictions of committees more frequently than in the U.S. Congress. Thus the highway committee may have its jurisdiction expanded and be renamed the transportation committee. Or the agriculture and environment committee may be split into two separate committees, one focusing on agriculture and the other on the environment. It is difficult to pinpoint the exact amount of jurisdictional change without substantial in-depth analysis of each legislative session. For the purposes of this essay, our approach is to assume that jurisdictions are tied to committee names and to compare the similarity in committee names between two consecutive sessions. For example, if there were fifteen committees in session one and twenty-five committees in session two, and the names of ten committees in session two were the same as in session one, then the similar jurisdiction score would be 66.7 percent (i.e., 10/15). Using this procedure we examined the degree of committee-name similarity for the years 1971–1972 and 1985–1986 for thirty-six state legislative chambers. [The number of cases for both the senate and the house (N=126) is obtained by multiplying the number of intersession comparisons per chamber

(i.e., 7) times the number of chambers (eighteen senates and houses).]

As illustrated in Table 2, the extent of jurisdiction continuity varies significantly. On the stable side, roughly two-fifths of the committees in the state senates and houses experience no change in name from session to session. At the other extreme, four state senates and one state house have less than 50 percent committee-name similarity.

Changes in the legislature's external environment often cause the committee systems to adjust to the emergence of new issues, or to heighten their interest in an existing policy area. Insight into this process can be gained by examining how state legislatures deal with one of the more enduring issues, education. Given the importance and cost of education policy at the state level, it was believed that each of the ninety-nine legislative chambers would have created a standing committee to deal with the various bills dealing with education policy. In fact, the various aspects of education policy are so diverse that it seemed likely that states would have created two separate committees, one for kindergarten through twelfth grade and the other for higher education. The overall distributions of the ninety-nine state legislative chambers for two different legislative sessions during the 1970s and 1980s are shown in Table 3.

An initial observation shows that tremendous differences existed among these legisla-

Table 2

PERCENT OF COMMITTEE NAMES CARRIED OVER FROM ONE SESSION TO THE NEXT IN 18 STATE SENATES AND 18 STATE HOUSES (1971–1986)

Percent Committees with Same Name	Percent in Chamber	
	Senate	House
100.0	42.9	38.1
90.0–99.9	14.3	35.7
80.0–89.9	19.8	15.1
70.0–79.9	6.3	4.0
60.0–69.9	4.8	2.4
50.0–59.9	7.1	4.0
0.0–49.9	4.8	.8
TOTAL PERCENT	100.0	100.1
NUMBER OF CASES	126	126

Table 3

COMMITTEES DEALING WITH EDUCATION POLICY IN STATE
LEGISLATIVE CHAMBERS (1977–1978 AND 1985–1986)*

Type of Committee(s) with Education Policy	Years	
	1977–1978**	1985–1986***
	Percentage	
I. No education-related committee listed	2.0%	3.0%
II. Single committee with shared policy jurisdiction (e.g., Health, Education, and Welfare)	10.1	11.1
III. Single education committee	61.6	58.6
IV. Single joint education committee for house and senate chambers****	6.1	6.1
V. Two education committees— "education" committee and second education-related committee	0.0	1.0
VI. Two committees—education committee and shared jurisdiction committee (e.g., higher education and regulated professions)	0.0	2.0
VII. Two education committees—K–12 committee and higher education committee	20.2	17.1
VIII. Three education committees—K–12 committee, higher education committee, and "other" education committee (i.e., select school-reorganization committee)	0.0	1.0
	100.0	100.0
	N=99	N=99

*Appropriations committees are excluded.

**Information on committees in 1977–1978 is taken from the National Conference of State Legislatures's *Directory of State Legislative Leaders and Committee Assignments*.

***Information for 1985–1986 is taken from Council of State Governments's *State Legislative Leadership, Committees, and Staff, 1985–1986*.

****In Connecticut, Maine, and Massachusetts, there is a single joint education committee. These committees have been counted twice, once for each chamber.

tures as to how education policy was parceled out among committees. As expected, more than a simple majority of the chambers assigned a single committee exclusive responsibility for education policy. Most of these committees were chamber specific, but in three legislatures (or six chambers) a joint committee, composed of members from both the house and senate, performed this task. In roughly 20 percent of the five chambers, specialization had developed to the point that there were two identifiable, but nonoverlapping education committees. The surprising finding is that in roughly one out of eight legislative chambers during the late 1970s, educa-

tion was not given its own exclusive niche within the committee system. In some cases, the shared jurisdiction was logical, as when health, education, and welfare were all under one committee's jurisdiction. At other times, the configuration of subject matter made it difficult to see how specialization was being advanced, as in the example of education and cultural resources or higher education and regulated professions. Finally, the most unexpected finding is that in a few state legislative chambers we could find no evidence of the listing of an education-related committee, even with shared jurisdiction.

How did state legislatures respond in the

early 1980s as the issue of education became even more prominently discussed in the media and several critical reports were issued on the underwhelming performance of the schools? As the results presented in Table 3 indicate, at least in the aggregate, relative stability prevailed between 1977–1978 and 1985–1986. A chamber-by-chamber analysis indicates that changes in committee names occurred in chambers, although no obvious pattern of increased specialization is evident.

A more in-depth, session-by-session analysis from 1971 through 1985 for thirty-two legislative chambers suggests that significant variation exists among the chambers on this point. Roughly 62 percent of the chambers evidenced no change in committee jurisdiction over the eight sessions examined. On the other hand, three chambers experienced one realignment of education policy jurisdictions, six undertook change on two different occasions, and three chambers instituted at least three significant changes in committee responsibility. The most extreme case was the Wisconsin Senate, which changed the jurisdiction for education policy at the beginning of each session throughout the sixteen-year period.

In summary, the degree of specialization by individual committees does vary, although it is not as if change occurs for every committee for each session. Rather, the main observation is that the extent of change varies widely across legislative chambers. Future research will have to determine exactly why these varying rates of change occur.

Committee Size

Is there an optimal size for committees? Survey research by Wayne L. Francis (in *The Legislative Committee Game,* 1989) indicates that legislators adjust the optimal size based upon two major criteria. Specifically,

> the optimality estimate in large chambers is about *eleven,* whereas it is closer to seven in smaller chambers.... In large chambers that experience high subcommittee use the optimal committee size estimate moves upward to *between twelve and thirteen*—as opposed to approximately *nine* where there is low subcommittee use. In small chambers (80 or less), however, the use of subcommittees seems to make very little difference in the response patterns. (pp. 114–115)

Significant differences existed in the size of committees in state legislatures during the late nineteenth and early twentieth centuries. For example, the Michigan Senate and House had the fewest number of members per committee, with 3.5 and 4.5 members, respectively. At the other extreme was the Pennsylvania House, with an average of twenty-five members per committee. During the late nineteenth century the size of standing committees tended to increase in more than a majority of the states. Speculating on the reason for the tendency to enlarge committees, Paul S. Reinsch notes that it was partly driven by members' desires to have influence and visibility within the institution. Perhaps more importantly, the increase was strongest in states that had strong political party organizations. Not only did the enlargement of the committees permit leaders to reward their followers, but it also contributed to a fairly inefficient system, which Reinsch felt rebounded to the advantage of the party leaders. In the first decades of the twentieth century, numerous commentators deplored the excessive size of state legislative committees.

To the extent that committees increase in size, the difficulties of deliberation and decision-making may begin to approach those associated with the large size of the parent chamber, resulting in reduced levels of specialization. Three issues regarding committee size will be investigated below: (1) the relevance of optimal committee size; (2) trends over time; and (3) variables accounting for chamber differences.

How do we evaluate whether committees were too large to effectively perform their tasks? One approach is to apply the optimal committee sizes suggested by Francis. Winslow, in his comprehensive 1931 study, found that the average size of committees in state houses was 12.8 members. However, assuming that subcommittee use was fairly undeveloped in this period, the optimal size of the committees should have been approximately nine members. If some variation around this optimal size is permitted, such that the optimal size is eight to ten, using this criterion, only seven state houses were optimally arranged. The critics' contention that the committees had too many members is substantiated in twenty-nine of the lower chambers, with Georgia having the most egregious system with an average of 35.3

members per committee. An overlooked point by some commentators during this period, however, is the fact that in twelve chambers there were fewer members than the estimated optimal number, with the lowest number being 4.7 members in the Nevada House.

In the state senates, the average size of committees per chamber was approximately 8.6 members, which is somewhat larger than the Francis optimal size of seven in smaller chambers. If some variation around the optimal mean is permitted such that the optimal size is now six to eight members, then sixteen state senates had a mean committee size that fell within the relaxed optimal range. The interesting finding is that there were almost as many chambers in which committees were below the optimal range (N=14) as those that were above it (N=18), although a few of the latter were extreme outliers (e.g., the fifty-one-person Illinois senate had an average of twenty-three members per committee).

If Francis's optimal-size criteria are used for the 1989 legislative session, the assumption that the size of committees has decreased over time is not confirmed. In the state senates, only twelve chambers had the mean optimal size, a decrease from sixteen in 1929, while twenty-nine sessions were over the optimal number, a substantial increase from eighteen in 1929. In the state houses, the trend was the same. In 1989 there was an average of between eight and ten members per committee in only five chambers, while the mean was in excess of ten in forty chambers, up from twenty-nine in 1929. In fact, average committee size increased in sixty-nine chambers while falling in just twenty-six. Committee size increased by one or more members in fifty-four chambers, while decreasing by one or more in fifteen chambers. Thus, not all elements of committee systems move in the same direction over time. While there were fewer committees and fewer total committee positions in 1989 relative to 1929, the average size of state legislative committees actually increased in a majority of chambers over time.

What accounts for this upward movement? Perhaps part of the increase is due to an increase in the use of subcommittees in large chambers, which in turn raises the optimal size for the committee. If the optimal size is treated as between eleven and fourteen, then we have twenty-eight chambers with a mean committee size above the upperbound of the optimal level, or about the same number that exceeded the nonsubcommittee use optimal value in 1929. At best, then, the distribution of chambers relative to an optimal committee size has not improved over a sixty-year period.

The variations in the size of legislative committees in the late 1980s appear to be, in part, a function of chamber size and type of chamber, as Hedlund and Hamm report. The larger the chamber, the larger the average size of the committees. Also, even when controlling for a series of factors including chamber size, lower houses of the legislatures have a larger average size than do state senates.

LEGISLATOR PERSPECTIVE ON SPECIALIZATION

The level of specialization displayed by committees is obviously tied to the individual legislators who comprise these small decision-making bodies. The legislative organization and the committees may be structured to facilitate specialization, but without the activity of the committee members, the outcomes may be less than expected. Four indicators are used to evaluate the extent that members specialize in their committee activities: (1) number of committee assignments; (2) continuity of committee membership; (3) time spent in committee activities; and (4) legislators' subjective evaluations of committee specialization.

Number of Committee Assignments

A common lament during the first part of the twentieth century was that state legislators had too many committee assignments, although examples were often cited in which the number of assignments was sufficiently small to permit careful consideration of legislation. To our knowledge, Winslow provided the first comprehensive collection of data on the average number of committee assignments per member. His analysis indicated that state senators were assigned to an average of 7.6 committees, whereas members of the lower houses were given assignments to 4.5 committees. Three general observations emerge from an examination of Winslow's data.

First, state senators were assigned to more committees than their colleagues in the lower chamber in forty-four of the forty-eight state legislatures. Second, significant variability existed within each type of chamber. For example, in the state senates, the range was from a low of 1.5 in Wisconsin to an incredibly high 18.5 positions per member in Illinois. In the lower houses the boundaries were from a low of 1.3 in New Hampshire to a high of 9.2 positions in Tennessee. The magnitude of this disparity can be seen in the number of chambers in which members were at the extremes in terms of specialization. For example, if we arbitrarily assume that specialization would be enhanced best if members had two or fewer appointments, then legislators in six lower houses and only one senate chamber were at this level in 1929. On the other hand, if we assume that members drop to a minimal level of specialization once they reach seven appointments, then a striking difference emerges when the two houses are contrasted: in only six lower house chambers did members serve on this number of committees, while this situation existed in twenty-four state senates, with legislators having ten or more appointments in seven of these states during the 1929 session. In approximately the next twenty-five years, the mean of the averages for the state senates had decreased to 6.09, while in the state houses little overall movement was evident, with a mean of 4.4 appointments as found in Belle Zeller's analysis. During the peak of the state legislative reform movement in the late 1960s and early 1970s, an often-stated argument was that state legislatures had too many committee assignments. In fact, the Citizen's Conference on State Legislatures indicated that this problem existed in more than a majority (i.e., twenty-eight) of the fifty state legislatures. Rosenthal, writing in 1974, pointed out that extreme cases existed in which members had an average of ten assignments, but cautioned that this was not the norm. Rather, he contended that in most legislatures the typical legislator was assigned to between two and five committees.

By 1989 the number of assignments per member dropped to 4.02 in the state senates and 3.00 in the state houses. More importantly, legislators reached a minimal level of specialization with seven or more appointments in only two senate chambers, a decrease from a total of thirty chambers in 1929. On the other hand, there was a doubling to thirteen (ten houses and three senates) in the number of chambers in which legislators had two or fewer appointments.

In summary, during the sixty-year period we have examined, increased legislator specialization through fewer committee assignments has been the norm. The average number of committee assignments per member decreased in eighty chambers while increasing in only fifteen. On average, members lost 3.04 assignments in the state senates and 1.54 in the state houses. The largest reductions in committee assignments were 14.3 per member in the Georgia Senate and 7.2 in the Tennessee House.

Continuity of Committee Membership

Unlike Congress, relatively few state legislative chambers require the strict use of seniority in making committee appointments. Consequently, members of state legislative committees appear to be able to move from committee to committee with fewer prohibitions and organizational constraints than are found in Congress. Such nonuse of seniority in making committee appointments could foster member turnover and diminish stability in committee membership. Substantial movement of members across committees could also affect subject-matter continuity. According to Malcolm Jewell, if such movement is sizable, it could impair the development of specialization, since familiarity with a subject-matter area and with prior legislation on a topic are associated with extended service on a committee.

Our eighteen-state study of legislative operations provides data on committee-to-committee movement of members across eight legislative sessions and documents the actual frequency of member reappointment when reappointment to a committee is not required by the rules. These data provide further insight regarding the development of specialization on committees, called here "continuity of committee membership," through members remaining on a comparable committee across time (a comparable committee is defined as one with exactly the same or very similar title for two consecutive two-year sessions). Committee continuity is represented in the following measures: (1) carryover, (2) legislative service, and (3) constancy.

Committee carryover is the proportion of members on a committee in one session who also served on the comparable committee in the previous session. This represents a simple indicator of committee members with previous experience on that committee. The greater the proportion of members serving on a committee in the later session who also served on the committee in the former session, the greater the amount of carryover, the higher (or closer to) the measure, and the greater the potential for developing expertise and specialization.

The second measure of committee continuity—legislative service—reflects the level of prior legislative experience held by committee members. This measure represents the proportion of legislators on a committee who served as members of that chamber in the previous session. As such, this measure represents the presence of veteran legislators on a committee.

While carryover is a useful concept that indicates committee continuity, it does not reflect an important factor—the nonreturn of committee members to the legislature. This third measure—constancy—is defined as the proportion of *reelected* committee members (again from a comparable committee) from the first session who return and choose to serve on the same committee in the second session. This measure reflects committee continuity but is also sensitive to the reelection patterns found in a legislative chamber where carryover is not.

The differences among these three measures of committee continuity rest in what one considers a distinguishing characteristic for continuity. Carryover identifies *prior experience on a comparable committee* as the feature necessary for continuity. Thus, in those legislatures in which membership on a chamber organization committee is defined according to positions (i.e., the presiding officer, majority leader, assistant majority leader, minority leader, and assistant minority leader) and in which these leaders remain the same over two sessions, there would be a high level of carryover (1.00) for that committee. Legislative experience, on the other hand, stresses the importance of prior legislative experience for high levels of continuity. In this case, very

technical committees like pensions and retirement to which legislators with prior experience in the chamber, but not necessarily that specific committee, are likely to be appointed would have high levels of legislative experience. The third continuity measure—constancy—recognizes that the nonreturn of members may affect the score and thus evaluates committee continuity in terms of members returning to a committee of those reelected to the chamber. Thus, in years of high legislative turnover at the state level, such as 1964, the constancy indicator would measure committee continuity for comparable committees in terms of those reelected and "eligible" for reappointment.

The levels attained for these three measures, illustrated in Table 4, provide a basis for estimating the development of stability on state legislative committees. They also permit an evaluation of committee continuity and potential for specialization. Table 4 presents the distribution of proportions, grouped into twelve categories, for these three continuity measures.

These data were collected for the eighteen states from seven pairs of consecutive legislative sessions from 1971 to 1986, based on 76,435 committee seats for 4,059 standing committees. The mean values for each of these scores based on type of chamber committee (senate, house, or joint) indicate relatively high levels for all three continuity measures (a mean proportion of less than 0.5 indicates that less than half of all the chamber's committees met requirements for that continuity measure for the seven paired sessions). In only two instances, carryover for house and joint committees, are the means less than 0.5, while in four instances they exceed 0.7. These values reflect the relatively high levels of committee continuity achieved in these eighteen states for the 1971–1986 period.

Also illustrated in Table 4 are similarities across the three types of committees—senate, house, and joint. For example, the three lowest mean scores all occur for carryover, while the highest all occur for experience. In contrast, all three types of continuity are lowest for the house and highest for the senate. These patterns reflect both the degree to which these three indicators of committee continuity are differentiated from one another and consistencies within chambers.

Table 4

DISTRIBUTION OF CARRYOVER, EXPERIENCE, AND CONSTANCY SCORES FOR ALL COMMITTEES IN THE 18 STATES, 1971–1986, BY CHAMBER

(percent of committees by column)

Proportion of Continuity	Percent Carryover			Percent Experience[a]			Percent Constancy		
	Sen.	House	Joint	Sen.	House	Joint	Sen.	House	Joint
0.00	1	2	–[b]	0	–	0	1	2	–
0.01–0.10	1	1	1	–	–	0	–	–	1
0.11–0.20	2	6	4	0	1	0	1	2	–
0.21–0.30	8	12	9	1	1	1	3	5	4
0.31–0.40	8	17	18	3	3	4	4	6	5
0.41–0.50	11	19	14	5	6	3	5	9	10
0.51–0.60	16	18	23	11	13	8	13	16	15
0.61–0.70	16	14	18	14	19	23	18	16	20
0.71–0.80	14	6	8	18	19	18	13	16	16
0.81–0.90	13	4	3	24	17	22	19	14	19
0.91–0.99	4	–	1	6	7	11	5	6	5
1.00	6	1	1	18	14	11	18	8	5
TOTAL	100	100	100	100	100	100	100	100	100
N =	1545	2197	317	1794	2455	340	1545	2197	317
MEAN	.595	.455	.497	.755	.725	.753	.707	.634	.654
STAND. DEV.	.233	.195	.187	.186	.188	.168	.227	.235	.201

[a]This measure did not require that committees have the same name in order for the calculations to be made. Therefore, data for this variable include all committees, not just comparable committees.
[b]A hyphen (–) indicates less than 0.5 percent in this category.

Considering the distribution of responses by chamber reveals that 18 percent of the committees in state senate chambers have 100 percent of their members with prior experience in that chamber. This compares with 14 percent for house/assembly and 11 percent for joint committees. While some of the committees with high experience scores are procedural in nature, and thus dominated by leaders, most are not. Many committees, regardless of chamber, have members with prior chamber experience on them.

Turning to constancy and carryover, fewer committees have the high 100-percent levels exhibited in prior experience. However, although the proportion of committees having high levels of carryover are smaller than for experience or constancy, these levels do indicate an impressive amount of across-time continuity in state committees. In only a relatively few instances are there committees with less than 20 percent of the same membership from the previous session. Thus, data representing three different measures indicate that there are high levels of continuity for committee membership among these eighteen states, and this has occurred without the existence of written requirements compelling reappointment. These findings argue strongly for the potential development of expertise and specialization among state legislative committees.

Time Spent on Committee Work

An argument could be made that reduction in the number of committee assignments and an increase in continuity of membership are preconditions for legislator specialization in committees. Another key component, however, involves the commitment legislators make to the process of committee deliberations. If legislators fail to attend committee meetings, or appear only for a few "visible" issues, then the level of specialization has not been necessarily enhanced. While it is possible to identify certain behavioral measures of participation in committees in the U.S. Congress, a similar feat for the multitude of state legislatures is beyond the scope of most state legislative scholars. However, simple counting measures of committee activity are available for single legislatures such as Connecticut in 1959.

A more reasonable approach is to identify the mean amount of time members spend in committee relative to their other legislative obligations. As with most attempts to understand changes in state legislative committee systems, a dearth of information exists even as late as the 1970s. Francis and Riddlesperger, using questionnaire data, identified the amount of time members spent on committee activities in the early 1980s. In that period, members averaged more than six hours per day on committee work in the Hawaii, Maryland, Nevada, Oregon, and Washington legislatures. At the other end of the spectrum, they report that legislators in the Delaware House and Senate spent less than two hours daily on committee work. What accounts for this relatively large difference? As expected, in legislatures in which committees were an important part of the decision-making process, members spent a greater amount of time in committee activity, although this factor does not account for even a majority of the variation among the states.

Even though committees are important in the legislative process, and even though committee members spend more time in committees, are they perceived by legislators to be the specialized bodies often described by legislative scholars? In the following section, we focus on legislator perceptions to answer this question. In succeeding sections we utilize legislator perceptions to address a variety of other issues related to committee systems.

Subjective Evaluation of Specialization

Another method for assessing specialization and expertise in the committee system is the analysis of member evaluations—in this case, those that were prompted by our eighteen-state questionnaire of legislator perceptions. The instructions asked respondents to indicate how well each of a series of statements described how committees worked during that session of their chamber (legislators used an eleven-point numerical scale to respond). Each extreme and the midpoint on the eleven-point scale were identified using descriptive phrases (e.g., 0 = "to a very little extent"; 5 = "to some extent";

and 10 = "to a very great extent"). In this paper, we focus on legislator responses to the statement, "Committee and subcommittee members generally were experts on the bills handled by their committees."

As shown in Table 5, the aggregated response patterns suggest that in general, committee members are perceived to be somewhat expert on the legislation they considered, but nowhere near the level of specialization often ascribed to members of the U.S. Congress. For 50 percent of the 276 sessions, the mean evaluation was below the midpoint, with less favorable evaluations occurring more frequently for the lower houses (56 versus 43 percent, respectively). At the same time, members were judged to be at the extreme ends of the expertise continuum infrequently. In only thirteen sessions did the mean score indicate very low levels of perceived expertise (below 3.0), and in only nine sessions were committee members judged to be highly expert in their field (above 7.0). Somewhat unexpectedly, all but two of these extreme evaluations occurred during the 1971–1977 period. Since then, the expertise level of members has been shown to be somewhere in the broad middle of the spectrum. Comparing the thirty-six chambers over the sixteen-year period, committee members were considered to have the highest level of expertise in the Iowa senate, while the lowest levels were found for both chambers in Texas, the Arizona state house, and the Tennessee state senate.

Summary

What are our conclusions regarding the level of specialization in state legislative committee systems? When examined from three perspectives (i.e., chamber, committee, and legislator), we believe that the following statements are justified.

From the chamber perspective, all state legislatures have an operating committee system with the preponderance of work done in permanent, not ad hoc, committees. The number of committees per chamber has declined significantly since the late 1920s, with the bulk of this decrease occurring during the late 1960s and early 1970s, in part as a consequence of the state legislative reform movement that swept the country. In addition, the total num-

Table 5
EVALUATION OF COMMITTEE MEMBERS AND COMMITTEE STAFF

State	Cham	Number of Sessions with Data	Committee-Member Experts on Bills in Committee[a]			Knowledgeable Staff Available to Committee[b]		
			Session Mean	Range	Number of Sessions >7.0	Session Mean	Range	Number of Sessions >7.0
Ariz.	S	7	4.07	1.00–7.00	0	7.94	7.00–9.24	7
	H	8	3.81	2.25–4.75	0	6.91	5.55–8.53	3
Calif.	S	7	4.91	3.00–7.02	2	8.95	7.50–10.0	7
	H	6	4.68	3.88–5.37	0	8.37	7.23–10.0	6
Fla.	S	7	5.53	3.00–10.0	1	9.01	8.00–10.0	7
	H	8	4.59	2.56–5.28	0	8.27	6.69–9.12	7
Ga.	S	7	5.50	4.73–7.00	1	6.43	0.00–9.55	8
	H	8	5.24	3.63–6.00	0	6.55	4.26–7.53	3
Iowa	S	8	6.12	5.01–6.94	0	6.73	4.97–8.75	3
	H	8	5.58	4.55–6.20	0	7.16	5.06–8.61	5
Maine	S	8	5.31	4.64–6.44	0	6.38	2.00–8.73	4
	H	8	4.46	3.14–5.38	0	7.21	4.02–8.56	6
Mass.	S	8	5.41	1.50–8.00	3	7.08	4.00–9.30	4
	H	8	5.51	4.07–6.41	0	7.96	7.40–8.73	8
Nev.	S	7	5.33	3.50–6.50	0	7.09	5.50–9.00	3
	H	8	4.84	3.33–8.00	1	6.44	3.79–8.28	3
N.C.	S	8	4.75	2.00–5.90	0	8.37	7.90–9.08	8
	H	8	4.61	3.86–5.30	0	7.38	3.95–9.00	6
N.Dak.	S	8	5.30	4.51–6.27	0	7.55	5.88–8.21	6
	H	8	4.89	4.00–5.40	0	8.16	7.18–8.64	8
Ohio	S	7	5.79	3.20–10.0	1	7.97	6.97–10.0	6
	H	8	4.89	3.89–5.42	0	8.00	7.41–9.20	8
Pa.	S	8	4.31	2.00–5.42	0	7.21	6.00–9.50	4
	H	8	4.81	3.35–6.12	0	7.49	5.96–7.87	7
S.Dak.	S	8	4.60	3.66–5.90	0	7.35	6.85–8.45	7
	H	8	5.41	4.11–6.27	0	7.80	6.90–8.47	7
Tenn.	S	8	4.08	3.36–5.00	0	6.07	1.00–7.48	2
	H	8	5.20	4.19–6.18	0	7.27	6.28–8.22	5
Tex.	S	6	3.32	0.00–4.54	0	8.07	7.32–10.0	6
	H	8	3.95	2.33–4.74	0	6.47	5.33–7.00	1
Wash.	S	6	5.40	4.62–6.26	0	8.51	7.92–9.50	6
	H	8	4.70	3.97–5.07	0	7.55	6.03–8.53	5
W.Va.	S	8	5.12	4.00–6.00	0	7.61	7.00–8.68	8
	H	8	4.77	4.02–5.72	0	6.94	6.25–8.00	3
Wis.	S	8	5.22	4.69–5.65	0	7.62	5.49–8.60	7
	H	8	5.25	4.52–5.94	0	7.54	5.89–8.55	6
TOTALS								
SENATE		134	5.01	0.00–10.0	8 (6.0%)	7.51	0.00–10.0	100 (74.6%)
HOUSE		142	4.83	2.25–8.00	1 (0.7%)	7.40	3.79–10.0	97 (68.3%)

[a]Legislators responded to statement, "Committee and subcommittee members generally were experts on the bills handled by their committees."

[b]Legislators responded to statement, "Knowledgeable legislative staff was available to help committees and subcommittees prepare and revise legislation."

ber of committee positions has also undergone a significant decline.

From the committee perspective, the most unexpected finding is that the average size of committees in most state legislative chambers has actually increased since the 1920s. The initial expectation had been that the various elements of the committee system underwent change in the same direction. Thus, if the number of committees, the number of total committee positions, and the number of assignments per member decreased, then the size of committees would also decrease.

From the perspective of the individual legislator, the general conclusion is that individual committee specialization is at a reasonable level. The number of committee assignments per member has decreased over time. The various aspects of committee continuity are at fairly modest levels. Committee members spend a considerable amount of each legislative day on committee work in a number of legislatures. Legislators judge committee members to be somewhat expert on the bills dealt with by their committees, although they are in no way considered to have the highest level of specialization.

III. COMMITTEE PERSONNEL: MEMBERS AND STAFF

Appointments to Committees

In more than two-thirds of the ninety-nine state legislative chambers, the committee chair and majority-party committee members are appointed by the presiding officer or another leader. In roughly one-half of these ninety-nine chambers, minority-party members on the committee are recommended by the minority-party leader. Given the importance of committee assignments to a legislator's career and the legislature's operations, substantial consideration is given to this process at the beginning of a legislative session. Typically, leaders responsible for appointing members to committees obtain requests from members either in writing or in personal meetings. Considerable attention is given by members to persuading the appointing authority to comply with member requests, particularly among first-term members and those seeking to move to more-important,

sought-after committee posts. At the same time, leaders seek to accommodate member requests, thereby building support and potential voting coalitions in committees and on the floor. A member satisfied with his/her committee appointments is more likely to support the leadership in procedural and policy matters; therefore, some minimal accommodation for a maximum number of members is frequently a strategy used by the leader when appointing members to committees.

Accommodation may also be advanced when appointing authorities adjust committee size, create more committees, and adjust committee jurisdictions via title changes. The availability of member request data for Democrats from five sessions of the Wisconsin Assembly, two sessions of the Iowa House, and one session each of the Maine House, Wisconsin Senate, and Pennsylvania House, and for Republicans from three sessions of the Wisconsin Assembly and one session of the Maine House provide a unique insight into the outcome of leader efforts to meet member expectations for committee assignments. Table 6 summarizes, for these fourteen cases, the success of members in obtaining their requested committee assignments.

These data clearly show that members enjoy great success in obtaining their committee requests. The generally lower percentages for Maine, Iowa, and Pennsylvania reflect the fact that legislators in these states made a larger number of requests for a smaller number of committee assignments. The very small percentage of members receiving none of their requests confirms that accommodation is taking place in the committee assignment process. All respondents were assigned to at least one of their requested committees in six of the fourteen cases. Only among Maine Republicans did more than 10 percent of the requestors receive none of their requested assignments. If the criteria are raised to require members to receive at least 50 percent of their requested assignments, the argument for accommodation still holds. A majority of members did not meet this criteria in only three cases—both parties in the Maine House and Democrats in the Pennsylvania Assembly. The major reason for the higher percentages for these three groups is the greater ratio of requests to possible assignments associated with the assignment process

Table 6

PERCENT OF STANDING COMMITTEE REQUESTS RECEIVED BY LEGISLATORS OF THOSE REQUESTED, BY STATE, CHAMBER, SESSION, AND POLITICAL PARTY (PERCENT BY ROW)

State/Chamber/ Session/Party	Percent	Requests	Received		Total %	N	Overall% Received
	0%	1–49%	50–99%	100%			
Wisconsin Assembly							
1975–76 Democrats	1.8	12.5	46.5	39.3	100.1	56	64.8
1979–80 Democrats	0.0	10.6	55.1	34.5	99.9	58	67.0
1981–82 Democrats	3.5	15.8	45.6	35.1	100.0	57	65.5
1983–84 Republicans[a]	0.0	38.4	38.5	23.1	100.0	39	50.3
1985–86 Democrats	6.5	10.9	52.2	30.4	100.0	46	63.5
1985–86 Republicans[a]	0.0	48.8	41.9	9.3	100.0	43	45.5
1987–88 Democrats	3.8	15.4	53.8	26.9	99.9	52	63.2
1987–88 Republicans[a]	0.0	28.9	52.7	18.4	100.0	38	53.3
Wisconsin Senate							
1987–88 Democrats	7.7	7.7	30.8	53.8	100.0	13	77.5
Iowa House							
1985–86 Democrats	0.0	39.0	61.0	0.0	100.0	59	48.0
1987–88 Democrats	0.0	37.5	62.5	0.0	100.0	56	48.0
Maine House							
1987–88 Democrats	6.7	45.3	22.7	25.3	100.0	75	39.4
1987–88 Republicans[a]	13.3	60.0	13.3	13.3	99.9	15	39.4
Pennsylvania House							
1987–88 Democrats[b]	1.6	71.9	12.5	14.4	100.1	64	39.7

[a]This was the minority party in this session.
[b]Since Democratic members of the Pennsylvania House were asked by their leaders to rank order their preferences for twenty-one committees, only the first nine listed were included in these calculations.

itself. The nature of this effect is confirmed when one looks (not shown in table) at the percentages for members receiving their first requested committee in these three cases—72 percent for Maine House Democrats, 60 percent for Maine House Republicans, and 64 percent for Pennsylvania House Democrats. From this evidence we conclude that leaders do succeed in accommodating member committee requests.

A related question concerns what individual-level factors appear to explain success best in obtaining one's committee requests. Among experienced members, requesting the same committee assignments one had in the previous session is the best predictor of success. Next most important for all legislators were factors related to one's choice strategy—the number of requests made and requests for appointments to a particular committee in great de-

mand. Of considerably less importance were factors related to one's background and to the margin of one's electoral victory (some slight gender effects were noted in a few instances and wide election margins were associated with higher success in two cases). Cross-state differences in a legislator's success in obtaining committee requests suggest variation due to unique factors—perhaps leadership goals and behavior.

Staff

Several early studies pointed out the lack of basic staff in most state legislatures, but in the intervening years since those observations were made, staffing patterns have changed considerably. The major source of information regarding staff in the fifty states has been the National Conference of State Legislatures. This organization has conducted at least two major studies of staff, authored by Lucinda Simon in 1979 and by Brian Weberg and Beth Bazar in 1988, respectively.

Using data from these studies, Hamm and Hedlund found tremendous variations exist between the state with the largest staff (New York, with 4,157) and that with the smallest staff (Vermont, with 71). The ten states with the largest staff in 1988 (New York, California, Pennsylvania, Texas, Florida, Michigan, Illinois, Washington, Minnesota, and Oregon) had 53 percent of all state legislative staff, an average ratio of 10.7 staff for every legislator. The ten states with the smallest staff (Vermont, South Dakota, Wyoming, New Hampshire, Idaho, Delaware, Maine, Utah, North Dakota, and Nevada) had just 4.7 percent of the total staff and just 1.3 staff persons per legislator.

Several general trends occurred during the decade of the 1980s. In the 1979 study, "more than 16,000 year-round professional, clerical, and administrative staff" and 9,000 session-only staff were employed in the ninety-nine legislative chambers. Between 1979 and 1988, total staff increased by 24 percent as state legislatures moved away from hiring session-only staff, as Brian Weberg's 1988 study revealed. As Weberg notes, while session-only staff represented 37 percent of total staff in 1979, by 1988 this figure had fallen to just 26 percent. Second, full-time professional staff represented 85 percent of the change during the nine-year period. Of the 33,396 total staff in 1988, professional staff comprised 45 percent: 91.5 percent of them were full-time employees, while only 58.8 percent of the support staff had such status. In summary, some state legislatures appear to be following the path of the U.S. Congress with an emphasis on full-time staff, several of whom are professional staffers, while in some state legislatures there is a skeletal staff, with very few full-time professional staffers available.

In terms of committee staffing, in 1979 professional staff were assigned to all committees in fifty-five chambers, to some committees in twenty-six chambers, to just money committees in ten chambers, and not to any committees in eight chambers. By 1988, in all ninety-nine chambers, professional staff were available to at least one committee, even if only on a pooled basis. More important, all committees were professionally staffed in seventy-one chambers, including all of the most professional legislatures.

The eighteen-state questionnaire study of legislator perceptions provides further insight regarding committee staffing. In the question sequence on committees, legislative respondents were asked about the extent to which knowledgeable staff were available in their chamber to help prepare and revise legislation. Respondents were asked to evaluate the level of staffing on an eleven-point scale, ranging from zero (0) ("to a very little extent") to ten (10) ("to a very great extent"), with five (5) being the midpoint ("to some extent"). Only 9 percent of all respondents across this eight-session period rated committee staff in the lowest five numerical response categories, indicating relative inadequate staffing patterns. Conversely, 64 percent ranked committee staff adequacy in the top three categories. Aggregating to the chamber level, only 11 of the 276 session means fall below the midpoint of 5.0. As expected, these very low values all occurred in the early 1970s before staffing was upgraded in several legislatures (see Table 5).

Legislators were most likely to feel that knowledgeable staff were available to help committees with legislation in the California, Florida, Washington, North Carolina, and Texas senates, along with the California Assembly and North Dakota House. The lowest evaluative scores were registered in the Tennessee Senate and Texas House, but even these chambers were at least one category above the midpoint. In summary, committee staffing seems to be considered adequate by a substantial majority of the state legislators.

IV. WHO INFLUENCES COMMITTEES

State legislative committees do not operate in a vacuum. Interested political participants testify at committee hearings, submit reports, mobilize constituents, and engage in a variety of other activities in order to affect the decisions committees make. In this section the focus will be on the influence of these "outside" sources and "inside" sources such as the "inside" party leadership.

One potential source of influence is party leadership. As mentioned earlier, the leadership appoints the chair and majority-party members of committees in more than two-thirds of the state legislative chambers. Another potential source of power for the leaders is in the assignment of bills to committees. Here, in more than three-fourths of the legislatures, the presiding officer or another designated leader is responsible for referring proposed legislation to the various committees. In addition, party leaders exercise some involvement in "shepherding" legislation through the legislative process after the committee is finished, and in assisting members in a wide variety of ways. Presumably, because of these powers and actions, legislative leaders have some ongoing influence over committee work during the legislative session.

Another contention is that committees are influenced by nonlegislative forces such as outside experts and groups. Sometimes this process is conceptualized as a direct two-stage model of the flow of information in which the outside agencies and groups contact specialist legislators, typically on the committee, who in turn influence nonspecialist legislators in the chamber. The three-stage model suggests that the outside forces utilize committee staff as a conduit for transmitting requests to the specialist legislators. The more professional legislatures, such as that of California, are more likely to be the site for this more complex flow of information as demonstrated by Sabatier and Whiteman.

Another conceptualization involving interest groups, along with legislative committees and executive bureaus, is the subgovernment model. Committee members are thought to share values and perhaps even preferences for specific policy proposals of these "insider" groups and agencies because of occupational or constituency similarities, or membership in similar associations. In part, for this reason, committees are seen as reflecting the preferences of these insider interest groups and agencies when deciding the fate of legislation. A study of six Colorado committees found that those groups or agencies thought to be insiders in the subgovernment model are more likely to prevail against outsiders in conflictual contests over legislation. Committee members, however, do not simply adopt the perspective of the insiders all of the time; sometimes they require compromises or even defeat legislation requested by the insiders.

In the eighteen-state study of legislators' perceptions, we measured the amount of influence by focusing on legislators' responses to three statements: (1) "Committees and subcommittees were very independent from party leaders"; (2) "A number of independent, outside experts helped committees and subcommittees prepare and revise legislation"; and (3) "Committees and subcommittees were influenced in what they recommended by various nonlegislative groups." Respondents used the standard eleven-point scale, anchored on one end by "to a very little extent" and on the other by "to a very great extent."

The results presented in Table 7 indicate that legislators view nonlegislative groups as having the greatest impact. (Some difficulty may exist in interpreting Table 7, since the question about party leaders refers to independence, while the one about nonlegislative groups refers to influence. Also, the reader should keep in mind that the lower the score for the party leader question, the greater the perceived impact of party leaders.) For example, at the chamber level, legislators rated interest-group influence at at least a mean of 5.0 in 95.7 percent of the sessions, while the corresponding percentage for outside experts was 70.6 percent. In 66 percent of the sessions, committees were rated at below the midpoint in terms of their being independent from party leaders. Measured by a mean score greater than 7.0, interest groups had significant influence in slightly more than 20 percent of the sessions, while outside experts had the greatest impact in about 9 percent of the sessions. Party leaders had their greatest impact, indicated by a mean score of less than 3.0, in about 14 percent of the sessions. In addition, none of the three external agents were unimportant in any significant number of legislative sessions. Interest groups were seen as being of lesser importance in just 3 of 256 sessions; outside experts were used infrequently in just 9 of 276 sessions; and committees were very independent from political party leadership in only 22 of the sessions. In other words, interest groups, outsider experts, and party leadership typically play at least a moderate role in the activities of state legislative committees.

Turning to an individual chamber analysis, interest groups have a mean evaluation over the eight sessions of at least 5.0 (i.e., midpoint) in all thirty-six chambers. Yet it would be a mis-

Table 7
EXTENT TO WHICH COMMITTEES ARE INFLUENCED BY PARTY LEADERS, NONLEGISLATORS, AND OUTSIDE EXPERTS (1971–1986)

State	Cham	Number of Sessions with Data	Committees & Subcommittees Independent of Party[a] Session Mean	Range	Number of Sessions >7.0	Committees & Subcommittees Influenced by Nonlegislators[b] Session Mean	Range	Number of Sessions >7.0	Committees & Subcommittees Helped by Independent Outside Experts[c] Session Mean	Range	Number of Sessions >7.0
Ariz.	S	7	5.04	2.00–6.80	0	6.66	5.26–7.42	3	6.38	5.35–9.00	1
	H	8	3.83	2.65–4.97	0	6.95	6.42–8.00	3	6.12	5.34–7.00	1
Calif.	S	7	6.45	4.00–9.00	3	6.60	3.00–10.0	3	6.46	5.00–8.00	3
	H	6	3.59	2.92–4.81	0	6.56	5.00–7.71	2	6.84	5.19–10.0	1
Fla.	S	7	5.07	0.00–9.00	2	6.48	3.00–8.00	3	5.38	2.00–7.10	2
	H	8	3.40	2.58–4.05	0	6.71	5.86–8.79	1	6.14	4.44–6.93	0
Ga.	S	7	7.07	4.67–9.28	5	5.75	4.43–7.00	1	5.53	5.00–7.42	1
	H	8	5.05	4.31–5.89	0	5.28	4.06–5.63	0	4.88	2.77–5.75	0
Iowa	S	8	4.75	4.03–5.66	0	6.32	5.63–7.04	1	5.84	4.57–6.80	0
	H	8	3.99	2.87–4.99	0	6.07	5.79–6.23	0	5.98	5.50–7.11	1
Maine	S	8	4.72	2.00–6.32	0	6.28	5.16–7.09	2	4.82	2.83–5.98	0
	H	8	4.70	3.97–5.06	0	5.70	4.83–6.61	0	5.16	4.27–6.10	0
Mass.	S	8	4.15	1.00–5.45	0	6.76	5.65–8.00	3	4.78	3.00–8.67	1
	H	8	2.95	1.84–4.47	0	5.57	4.76–6.09	0	4.86	3.47–5.63	0
Nev.	S	7	6.31	4.00–8.00	2	6.05	3.00–7.71	3	5.23	4.10–6.50	0
	H	8	5.43	3.33–7.51	1	7.17	6.57–7.79	6	5.93	4.52–7.00	1
N.C.	S	8	5.35	3.55–7.00	1	5.85	4.85–7.00	1	5.26	1.65–8.00	1
	H	8	4.45	2.79–7.57	1	6.12	5.25–7.14	1	5.94	4.96–7.00	1
N.Dak.	S	8	4.04	2.63–4.73	0	5.76	4.37–7.53	1	4.94	3.73–6.99	0
	H	8	4.26	3.42–5.03	0	5.88	3.85–6.59	0	4.60	2.20–5.77	0
Ohio	S	7	4.34	1.99–8.00	1	6.57	4.00–8.00	3	5.21	2.00–7.43	1
	H	8	2.93	2.18–4.00	0	6.51	5.80–7.13	2	6.05	4.00–6.95	0
Pa.	S	8	3.67	3.04–4.51	0	6.93	5.06–10.0	4	5.50	4.08–7.00	1
	H	8	3.34	1.29–4.39	0	5.65	3.38–7.26	1	5.32	4.04–6.89	0
S.Dak.	S	8	4.46	2.93–5.90	0	6.06	5.36–6.65	0	5.04	2.69–6.32	0
	H	8	3.89	2.25–4.58	0	6.01	5.20–7.03	1	5.22	4.04–6.29	0
Tenn.	S	8	4.81	3.63–6.27	0	6.19	5.07–9.00	1	4.58	3.59–8.00	1
	H	8	3.39	1.44–4.56	0	6.34	5.46–7.79	1	4.70	3.70–5.62	0
Tex.	S	6	7.63	5.00–10.0	5	7.13	6.25–10.0	2	7.64	6.63–10.0	2
	H	8	6.98	3.67–9.33	4	6.77	6.18–7.67	2	5.58	4.52–6.60	0
Wash.	S	6	4.31	2.71–6.26	0	6.37	4.00–7.30	3	5.78	4.00–7.12	1
	A	8	3.32	1.35–4.89	0	6.82	6.01–7.67	1	5.52	4.55–6.82	0
W.Va.	S	8	6.02	4.00–7.02	1	6.66	6.00–8.00	2	5.98	4.67–7.13	2
	H	8	4.02	3.60–4.46	0	6.36	5.45–6.91	0	5.29	7.09–6.57	0
Wis.	S	8	6.00	4.46–7.70	2	6.68	6.24–7.36	1	5.95	4.93–7.28	2
	H	8	4.73	4.22–5.74	0	6.50	6.17–6.84	0	5.61	4.57–6.32	0
TOTALS											
SENATE		134	5.19	0.00–10.0	22 (17.7%)	6.38	3.00–10.0	37 (29.8%)	5.53	1.65–10.0	19 (15.3%)
HOUSE		142	4.13	1.29–9.33	6 (4.5%)	6.27	3.38–8.79	21 (15.9%)	5.52	2.20–10.0	5 (3.8%)

[a]Legislators responded to statement, "Committee and subcommittee members generally were experts on the bills handled by their committees."

[b]Legislators responded to statement, "Knowledgeable legislative staff was available to help committees and subcommittees prepare and revise legislation."

[c]Legislators responded to statement, "A number of independent, outside experts helped committees and subcommittees prepare and revise legislation."

take to view interest groups as having the same impact on committees in all chambers. Legislators evaluate committees as having a significant impact, with a mean score greater than 7.0 for two or more sessions, in just eighteen chambers. In the other eighteen chambers, interest groups have moderate influence. The highest overall-perceived impact is in the Nevada Assembly, the Texas, Massachusetts, and Florida senates, and the Arizona, Pennsylvania, Florida, and Washington houses. The lowest impact is registered in the Georgia House. The lowest perceived use of outside experts was found for both chambers in Tennessee and North Dakota. More extensive reliance on outside experts was found for the Texas Senate, the Florida and Ohio houses, and both chambers in California and Arizona.

For party leadership, chamber differences between the high- and low-independence groupings existed for sixteen of the eighteen states—the senates were always perceived to have higher levels of committee independence from party leaders than were the houses/assemblies. Extending the analysis, it is evident that in fifteen houses the overall mean respondent evaluation is less than the midpoint for more than one-half of the sessions, while this pattern holds in only seven senates. The seven chambers with the lowest committee-independence scores are all the lower houses in Ohio, Massachusetts, Washington, Tennessee, Pennsylvania, Florida, and California. The major factor accounting for this finding may be that the legislative leaders in the lower houses are more likely to appoint members to the committees than are the leaders in the senates.

The argument could be made that in chambers in which the committees were not independent from the party leadership, the nonlegislative groups would have lower levels of perceived influence. We tested this idea by simply correlating the scores for these two variables for each session. The results are surprising. At least in terms of legislators' perceptions, there is no relationship between committee independence from party leadership and the influence of nonlegislative groups. Even if the analysis is confined to just the 1980s, no discernible relationship can be uncovered. While it may be that the power of political parties and interest groups are inversely related in the state political process, we find no similar

relationship in terms of committee decision-making.

V. COMMITTEE SYSTEM PERFORMANCE

Case studies of bills, legislator (and observer) comments, and general legislative studies reinforce the assumption that committees do in fact affect legislation. Rosenthal suggests in *Legislative Performance in the States* (1974) that the committees' role in the lawmaking function can be evaluated on five dimensions: referral, shaping, screening, chamber acceptance, and development of legislation. The first four dimensions will be examined below.

Referral

Committees cannot be substantially engaged in the lawmaking process unless they have legislation referred to them for consideration. The by-passing of standing committees when bills are sent to an ad hoc, one-bill committee or directly to the floor, obviously negates the entire rationale for a standing-committee system. No specific figures exist to indicate the percent of bills and resolutions referred to committee in any one session for all ninety-nine chambers, although our impression is that it is rare for more than a small percentage of the proposals to bypass the standing-committee system.

Shaping

The shaping of legislation refers to the extent to which committees shape or modify proposed legislation that has been referred to them. The proposed changes could be an amendment to one section of the bill or a total rewriting of the proposed legislation. Rosenthal in *Legislative Performance in the States* makes the basic assumption that "a committee system performs less well if it makes changes in proportionately few of the bills it proposes for passage on the floor" (p. 28). Impressions are that the amount of legislative shaping by committee has increased since the 1970s, specifically after changes were made in the structure of several committee systems.

The role of committees in shaping legislation was addressed by several items in the eighteen-state questionnaire study of legislator perceptions. We asked legislators to rate the extent to which committees and subcommittees changed most bills referred to them. Legislators rated the committees using the eleven-point scale described previously. Aggregating the responses to the chamber level reveals that for 255 of the 276 sessions studied, the chamber mean did not fall below the midpoint. Committees are thus perceived to be an important mechanism for changing proposed legislation.

An examination of Table 8 demonstrates the relatively similar evaluations provided by legislators in the two chambers of a state legislature. Rarely do the overall evaluations of the committees in the two chambers differ radically. Respondents, however, did not provide uniform evaluations of committees. In terms of the frequency with which they changed legislation, committees had the most consistently high ratings in the West Virginia and Ohio senates and in the Arizona, Florida, and Ohio houses. The lowest session mean values were found for both chambers in Massachusetts, Tennessee, North Dakota, and Pennsylvania, along with the California Senate.

Regarding across-time trends for the eighteen states, there are no uniform or linear patterns of increasing or decreasing levels of activities in changing bills referred to the committee. Rather, some states and chambers tend to increase over time (e.g., the North Dakota Senate), others decrease (the California House), some remain fairly stable (the Arizona House), and still others fluctuate widely (the California Senate).

Screening

Screening of legislation refers to the committees' behavior in exercising their prerogative to accept or reject proposed legislation. The basic assumption, according to Rosenthal, is that "if committees report a high percentage of bills favorably, the likelihood is that they are not really in control of the screening of legislation" (*Legislative Performance in the States*, p. 24). Differences exist among the state legislatures in whether committees have the authority to kill a bill in committee or even to simply let it die there without taking any action. In the majority of the states, committees have this power,

although it is possible that a petition signed by a majority or more of the chamber membership may force the legislation to the floor. On the other hand, in a few state legislatures (such as North Dakota), committees must report all proposed legislation referred to them back to the full chamber with a recommendation that the bill pass or not pass. At present, no study exists that provides quantitative information on the exact percentage of legislation that committees in the ninety-nine state legislative chambers screen.

In one item of the eighteen-state questionnaire study of legislator perceptions, respondents rated the degree to which committees and subcommittees recommended passage on most of the bills they reported out (using the eleven-point scale). An examination of the mean scores presented in Table 8 reveals that overall legislators perceive committees as positively recommending most bills they report out. Chamber differences do exist, however. Respondents in both chambers in Massachusetts and Maine, and the North Dakota and Wisconsin senates tended to perceive committees endorsing legislation at substantially lower levels. Higher levels occurred for both chambers of West Virginia and Washington, plus the Ohio, Nevada, and Texas senates.

Chamber Acceptance

The ultimate test of a committee's power is the degree to which its recommendations are followed during debate and in voting when the bills come before the entire chamber. Rosenthal states that "committees must not only make choices, they must also persuade their parent chamber to adopt the choices they have made" (*Legislative Performance in the States*, p. 28). Committees may be very diligent in their responsibilities to screen or shape legislation, but if their recommendations are frequently overturned or ignored by the legislature, their influence cannot be judged as significant. In this process, however, the chamber membership must not only agree to pass bills or resolutions supported by the committee, but committees must also prevail in having their amendments adopted and in limiting the acceptance of modifications they oppose. Committees in Oregon have probably the greatest formal opportunity to prevail in this regard be-

Table 8
EVALUATION OF COMMITTEE PERFORMANCE

State	Cham	Number of Sessions with Data	Committees Changed Most Bills[a]			Committees Recommended Passage of Most Bills[b]			Committees' Recommendations Were Followed[c]		
			Session Mean	Range	Number of Sessions >7.0	Session Mean	Range	Number of Sessions >7.0	Session Mean	Range	Number of Sessions >7.0
Ariz.	S	7	7.40	6.24–9.00	5	8.47	7.50–10.0	7	7.70	6.81–8.71	6
	H	8	7.50	7.12–7.70	8	7.88	6.00–10.0	7	6.99	5.00–8.00	5
Calif.	S	7	5.60	3.00–8.00	2	8.19	6.50–9.00	6	7.15	5.00–9.00	5
	H	6	7.31	4.96–9.29	3	7.34	6.63–9.00	5	8.07	7.24–9.00	6
Fla.	S	7	6.21	5.00–10.0	1	6.37	5.00–8.00	3	7.04	5.00–8.00	4
	H	8	7.54	6.28–9.36	6	6.95	5.12–8.10	3	7.38	6.60–8.72	6
Ga.	S	7	6.51	3.50–7.73	3	8.62	7.67–9.91	7	8.08	7.41–9.82	6
	H	8	6.30	4.95–7.09	1	7.54	6.67–8.17	7	7.63	6.50–8.25	7
Iowa	S	8	6.28	4.96–7.09	1	6.55	4.44–8.92	3	7.11	6.32–7.90	4
	H	8	6.69	5.49–7.40	2	6.35	4.47–9.00	3	7.28	6.55–7.81	6
Maine	S	8	7.37	6.40–8.05	5	5.05	4.40–5.74	0	7.70	7.00–7.94	8
	H	8	6.56	4.45–7.46	3	5.76	5.25–6.33	0	7.34	6.94–7.75	6
Mass.	S	8	5.55	3.10–9.00	1	3.69	1.00–5.67	0	7.59	6.00–8.67	6
	H	8	5.37	4.53–7.20	1	4.03	2.81–5.59	0	7.99	7.29–9.04	8
Nev.	S	7	7.25	6.00–8.80	4	8.40	5.50–9.50	6	8.33	7.00–9.00	7
	H	8	7.14	5.00–8.57	5	8.64	7.77–9.31	8	7.94	8.00–8.84	8
N.C.	S	8	7.45	6.08–9.00	5	8.09	7.00–9.00	8	8.34	7.69–9.00	8
	H	8	6.85	6.29–7.71	2	6.99	6.19–7.85	4	7.50	7.00–8.04	8
N.Dak.	S	8	6.02	4.86–7.17	1	6.63	6.08–7.65	2	8.00	7.53–8.77	8
	H	8	5.93	4.40–7.02	1	5.85	5.40–6.72	0	7.62	7.25–8.60	8
Ohio	S	7	8.21	7.00–10.0	7	8.98	8.05–10.0	7	7.79	4.64–9.00	6
	H	8	7.71	6.36–8.50	7	8.45	6.20–9.19	7	7.80	7.20–8.50	8
Pa.	S	8	6.08	4.93–9.00	2	8.35	5.50–10.0	7	6.74	4.96–8.00	4
	H	8	5.97	5.05–7.21	1	7.84	7.56–8.09	8	6.40	5.07–7.44	2
S.Dak.	S	8	6.55	6.03–8.00	1	8.01	7.31–8.71	8	7.11	6.55–7.65	5
	H	8	7.07	6.25–8.23	3	7.55	6.81–8.67	7	7.02	6.46–7.74	4
Tenn.	S	8	5.21	4.00–6.19	0	8.39	7.41–9.00	8	7.03	5.00–8.43	5
	H	8	5.83	3.87–7.44	1	7.85	7.14–8.70	8	7.44	6.67–8.00	7
Tex.	S	6	6.44	5.00–10.0	1	8.70	8.00–9.50	6	7.20	5.00–8.00	4
	H	8	6.29	5.00–6.93	0	8.19	7.59–9.04	6	7.31	5.60–8.09	6
Wash.	S	6	7.02	4.50–8.29	4	8.52	8.00–9.18	6	7.02	5.50–9.00	3
	A	8	7.31	6.34–7.82	6	8.70	8.41–9.00	8	7.02	6.39–7.76	5
W.Va.	S	8	7.95	6.29–10.0	6	9.28	8.78–10.0	8	7.78	6.12–8.68	6
	H	8	7.07	5.64–7.94	5	8.75	8.10–9.10	8	7.50	6.80–7.93	6
Wis.	S	8	6.22	5.41–7.25	1	6.18	4.54–8.51	3	6.96	5.97–7.74	4
	H	8	6.57	5.55–7.71	2	5.73	3.31–8.37	3	6.60	6.22–7.15	2
TOTALS											
SENATE		134	6.61	3.00–10.0	50 (37.3%)	7.52	1.00–10.0	95 (70.9%)	7.48	4.64–9.82	99 (73.9%)
HOUSE		142	6.71	3.87–9.36	56 (39.4%)	7.24	2.81–10.0	94 (66.2%)	7.37	5.00–9.04	108 (76.1%)

[a]Legislators responded to statement, "Committees and subcommittees changed most bills which were sent to them."
[b]Legislators responded to statement, "Committees and subcommittees recommended passage for most bills which were sent to them."
[c]Legislators responded to statement, "Committee and subcommittee recommendations on bills were generally followed."

cause any floor amendment must be adopted with unanimous consent, unless the rules are suspended. At this point, bills are often rereferred to committee to permit the members to discuss and perhaps compromise on the changes. At the other end of the spectrum, committees in North Dakota must report back all legislation referred to them, including those they unanimously oppose. Committees in the remaining state legislatures fall somewhere in between the ends of this continuum in terms of formal ability to have their recommendations followed. Unfortunately, no political science study has tried to examine the extent to which committee recommendations are followed by examining decisions made on the floor in all ninety-nine chambers, although several chambers at a time have been examined by Hamm and Moncrief.

In order to gauge the level of committee performance in this area, legislators in the eighteen-state questionnaire study were asked their perceptions concerning the degree to which committee and subcommittee recommendations were followed by the chamber membership. Using the eleven-point scale, responses aggregated to the chamber level indicate that there was relative agreement that committee recommendations generally were being followed in the legislative process (see Table 8). In only one session in the Ohio and Pennsylvania senates did the legislators rank the level of support for committee decisions at or below the midpoint. By far the most prevalent pattern was to evaluate the committee recommendation as being generally if not always followed, with the mean score being greater than 7.0 in about 75 percent of the house and senate sessions. The highest mean level of committee influence perceptions occurred in the California House and in the Georgia, Nevada, North Carolina, and North Dakota senates. In no chamber were the evaluations generally low.

Are the various dimensions of committee performance related? The working hypothesis is that the more committees shape and screen legislation, the more likely they are to have their recommendations accepted by the entire chamber. To test this hypothesis, we correlated the mean session scores for the various perceived performance measures. The results (not shown in Table 8) indicate that the higher the level of perceived shaping of legislation, the

higher the perceived acceptance of committee recommendations in both the senates and houses. On the other hand, there is no relationship between the perceived level of percent of bills reported out with positive recommendations and the perceived level of floor acceptance. That is, there is no significant relationship between the perceived propensity for committees to recommend passage of bills they report out and the chamber's subsequent following of the committee recommendations.

In summary, from the eighteen-state legislator-perception questionnaire data, we can conclude that committees are seen as an important mechanism for changing proposed legislation; they generally report out bills with a positive recommendation; and the chamber generally accepts committee recommendations. While state legislative committees may not be seen as having the same level of importance attached to committees in the U.S. Congress, it is clear that legislators evaluate them as performing at an adequate level. They contribute, in some cases significantly, to the lawmaking process.

CONCLUSION

Analysts do not foresee any erosion or weakening of the committee system at the state legislative level; in fact, legislative critics as well as reformers generally cite the committee system as a primary means of improving the performance of legislative bodies as well as of legislators themselves. The demise of state legislative committees thus appears contradictory to trends evidenced in the last decade of the twentieth century. It is indeed doubtful whether a representative body, comprised largely of generalists charged with collective decision-making on a broad range of specialized topics, could continue their policy-making *without* an organizational mechanism that fosters and develops division of labor, specialization, and expertise development. For the foreseeable future, then, we expect to see committee systems continue to thrive at the state governmental level and to be an important locus for decision-making.

If the movement for term limitation continues and success in restricting the amount of time a state legislator can serve is observed, the role of committees will take on increasing importance. For example, in developing and fostering specialization and an institutional memory for decision-making, committees will become even more important. Under these conditions, a "fast track" for a legislator displaying his or her effectiveness through committee activities will become more critical. The imposition of term limits at the state legislative level will only increase the importance of committees.

Because of the increasingly technical nature of the decisions being required of state legislatures, we expect committees to continue as primary devices for specialization. This probably will *not* take the form of a proliferation in the number of standing and ad hoc committees (any increase or decrease in the number of committees is likely to be short term); rather, it can be expected that more state legislatures will continue experimenting with subcommittees as the primary means of achieving added specialization, permitting committee systems to remain relatively stable. We do not, however, expect the development of subcommittees to parallel that found in Congress. Subject matter specialization by committees is most likely to take place through subcommittee development. This development of subcommittees will mute concern about the size of committees.

Legislators will continue to have conflicting strategies regarding the number of committee positions they will hold during any two-year session; but the movement will be toward holding positions on a fewer number of committees. Much of this will be necessitated by the growth of subcommittees at the committee level. This trend will enhance member specialization and may result in a heightened calculus about the impact of committee assignments on reelection prospects. Members will also see committees and subject matter specialization increasingly as the means to demonstrate their overall legislative effectiveness for voters. All of this will increase member attention to committee work strategies and how this "plays" to their constituents. Legislators will face increasing pressure to concentrate their efforts in a fewer number of committee appointments and will place increasing emphasis on how their committee work affects reelection.

The pressure on the committee-appointment process to accommodate member requests will increase. Whether the appointment is by the presiding officer, a small select group, or the entire chamber, the increasing relationship of committee work to reelection will force legislatures to maximize accommodation. This trend will continue to confront the necessity for members being appointed to a variety of committees. Accommodating members' appointment requests will continue to provide stress at the state legislative level with only a few states choosing to resolve the dilemma by altering drastically the committee system itself.

We see little *further erosion* of staffing for state-committee systems that now have professional staffs. In spite of increasing public pressure for "trimmed down" legislatures, a return to legislative dependence on lobbyists and bureaucrats for information and recommendations on policy issues seems remote. While the growth of state legislative committee staffs observed in the 1970s is not likely to be repeated, committees and subcommittees will continue to require the vital supportive and independent information provided by legislative committee staffs. Staffs for state legislative committees will continue with only marginal increase or decrease.

The future for committees under an expanding work load and enhanced public expectations regarding legislative effectiveness seems very promising. Committees should undoubtedly experience continuing enhancement of their role in decision-making and in the operations of state legislatures.

BIBLIOGRAPHY

Early Studies
For a glimpse as to how state legislatures operated at the beginning of the twentieth century, we suggest starting with PAUL S. REINSCH, *American Legislatures and Legislative Methods* (New York, 1907). Two later volumes worth pursuing include H.W. DODDS, *Procedures in State Legislatures* (Philadelphia, 1918) and

COMMITTEES IN STATE LEGISLATURES

ROBERT LUCE, *Legislative Procedure: Parliamentary Practices and the Course of Business in the Framing of Statutes* (Boston, 1922). Significant information about state legislatures in the early 1950s is contained in BELLE ZELLER, ed., *American State Legislatures* (New York, 1954). A somewhat later but insightful piece is DUANE LOCKARD, "The State Legislator," in ALEXANDER HEARD, ed., *State Legislatures in American Politics* (Englewood Cliffs, N.J., 1966). An excellent book-length study of state legislators is JAMES DAVID BARBER, *The Lawmakers* (New Haven, Conn., 1965).

Early systematic studies of state legislative committees are difficult to find. Three articles worth mentioning are C. LYSLE SMITH, "The Committee System in State Legislatures," *American Political Science Review* 12 (November 1918); C. I. WINSLOW, *State Legislative Committees: A Study in Procedures* (Baltimore, 1931); and HENRY W. LEWIS, *Law and Administration: Legislative Committees in North Carolina* (Chapel Hill, N.C., 1966). Of the three, Winslow's is the most informative and provides a wealth of information for the person who is interested in the operation of state legislative committees more than seventy-five years ago.

Research from the Past Twenty-five Years

Background information about state legislatures can be found in several books, including MALCOLM E. JEWELL and SAMUEL C. PATTERSON, *The Legislative Process in the United States,* 4th ed. (New York, 1986) and WILLIAM J. KEEFE and MORRIS S. OGUL, *The American Legislative Process: Congress and the States,* 6th ed. (Englewood Cliffs, N.J., 1985). To understand the changes state legislatures have undergone during the past few decades, we suggest examining CITIZEN'S CONFERENCE ON STATE LEGISLATURES, *State Legislatures: An Evaluation of Their Effectiveness* (New York, 1971). To see how the various legislatures have changed, the authors of this chapter conducted research from 1971–1986 in thirty-six chambers and reported our results in KEITH E. HAMM and RONALD D. HEDLUND, "Legislative Professionalization and the State Policy-making Process," a paper presented at the annual meeting of the American Political Science Association, 1990. Specific descriptive information about legislatures at the end of the 1980s can be found in *Inside the Legislative Process: A Comprehensive Survey of the American Society of Legislative Clerks and Secretaries* (Denver, 1988), published by the AMERICAN SOCIETY OF LEGISLATIVE CLERKS IN CONJUNCTION WITH THE NATIONAL CONFERENCE OF STATE LEGISLATURES.

For those wishing to study committees, HEINZ EULAU and VERA McCLUGGAGE, "Standing Committees in Legislatures," in *Handbook of Legislative Research* (Cambridge, Mass., 1985) is required reading, as is HEINZ EULAU, "On Units of Analysis," in *Micro-Macro Political Analysis: Accents of Inquiry* (Chicago, 1969).

Studies of the U.S. Congress have often been used to inform scholars about the possible workings of state legislative committees. While a plethora of research exists, we would suggest examining two classics: RICHARD F. FENNO, *Congressmen in Committees* (Boston, 1973) and KENNETH A. SHEPSLE, *The Giant Jigsaw Puzzle: Democratic Committee Assignments in the Modern House* (Chicago, 1978).

While somewhat dated, MALCOLM SHAW, "Conclusion," in *Committees in Legislatures: A Comparative Analysis,* JOHN D. LEES and MALCOLM SHAW, eds. (Durham, N.C., 1979) is worth the time in order to understand the differences between committees in the U.S. Congress and in other countries.

Professional political science articles about congressional committees most germane to the material contained in this chapter include, but are not limited to, BRUCE A. RAY and STEVEN S. SMITH, "Committee Size in the U.S. Congress," *Legislative Studies Quarterly* 9 (1984); MICHAEL C. MUNGER, "Allocation of Desirable Committee Assignments: Extended Queues versus Committee Expansion," *American Journal of Political Science* 32 (May 1988); DAVID WHITEMAN, "A Theory of Congressional Organization: Committee Size in the U.S. House of Representatives," *American Politics Quarterly* 11 (January 1983); and RICHARD L. HALL, "Participation and Purpose in Committee Decision Making," *American Political Science Review* (March 1987).

Studies about the development of committee systems in the U.S. state legislatures include DONALD A. DEBATS, "An Uncertain Arena: The Georgia House of Representatives, 1808–1861," *The Journal of Southern History* 56 (August 1990); L. RAY GUNN, "The New York State Legislature: A Developmental Perspective: 1777–1846," *Social Science History* 4 (August

1980); KEITH E. HAMM, "The Evolution of State Legislative Education Committees: Independent Sources of Power or Part of 'Cozy Triangles'?," a paper presented at the annual meeting of the American Education Research Association, 1989; KEITH E. HAMM and RONALD D. HEDLUND, "Accounting for Change in the Number of State Legislative Committee Positions: Evidence from 36 State Legislative Chambers (1971–1986)," a paper presented at the 1988 annual meeting of the American Political Science Association; KEITH E. HAMM and RONALD D. HEDLUND, "Accounting for Change in the Number of State Legislative Committee Positions," *Legislative Studies Quarterly* 15 (May 1990); and RONALD D. HEDLUND, "Explaining Cross-section Committee Membership Trends: Evidence from 18 State Legislatures," a paper presented at the annual meeting of the American Political Science Association, 1989.

Studies of the committee-assignment process and the composition of committees can be found in several articles and papers written by the authors of this chapter. Included are three pieces by RONALD D. HEDLUND: "Entering the Committee System: State Committee Assignments," *Western Political Quarterly* 42 (December 1989); "Accommodating Member Requests in Committee Assignments: Individual Level Explanations," a paper presented at the annual meeting of the Western Political Science Association, 1990; and "Accommodating Member Requests in Committee Assignments: Individual Level Explanations," in *Changing Patterns in State Legislative Careers*, GARY MONCRIEF and JOEL THOMPSON, eds. (Ann Arbor, Mich., 1992). The two authors of this chapter collaborated on one relevant piece: KEITH E. HAMM and RONALD D. HEDLUND, "Occupational Interests and State Legislative Committees," a paper presented at the meeting of the Midwest Political Science Association, 1989. The impact of committee assignments for electoral purposes is explored in RONALD D. HEDLUND and SAMUEL C. PATTERSON, "The Electoral Antecedents of State Legislative Committee Assignments," *Legislative Studies Quarterly* 17 (November 1992).

Viewing committees as specialized aspects of legislatures is explored in RONALD D. HEDLUND, DIANE POWERS, and RONALD H. LINGREN, "Organizational Specialization and Legislative Committees in 18 States," a paper presented at the annual meeting of the Southwestern Social Science Association, 1986; and HAMM and HEDLUND, "The Evolution of Specialization in State Legislative Committee Systems: A Multi-Level Exploration," a paper presented at the annual meeting of the Midwest Political Science Association, 1992. For those who wish to have a better grounding in organizational theory in order to understand some of this literature, we would suggest L. PETER JENNERGEN, "Decentralization in Organizations," and DONALD GERWIN, "Relationships Between Structure and Technology," both in PAUL C. NYSTROM and WILLIAM H. Starbuck, eds., *Handbook of Organizational Design,* vol. 2 (Oxford, 1981).

The impact of committees in terms of shaping and screening legislation is addressed in several studies, including two by ALAN ROSENTHAL: "Legislative Committee Systems: An Exploratory Analysis," *Western Political Quarterly* 26 (June 1973) and *Legislative Performance in the States* (New York, 1974). Other works focusing on committee performance include KEITH E. HAMM and GARY MONCRIEF, "Effects of Structural Change in Legislative Committee Systems on Their Performance in U.S. States," *Legislative Studies Quarterly* 7 (August 1982) and KEITH E. HAMM, "Committee Success on the State Legislative Floor: The Relative Impact of Legislative Rules and Committee Attributes," a paper presented at annual meeting of the Midwest Political Science Association, 1985.

Using a more public choice approach, WAYNE L. FRANCIS has studied numerous aspects of committee activity. Relevant publications of his include "Legislative Committee Systems: Optimal Committee Size and the Costs of Decision Making," *Journal of Politics* 44 (August 1982); *The Legislative Committee Game: A Comparative Analysis of Fifty States* (Columbus, Ohio, 1989); and "U.S. State Legislative Committees: Structure, Procedural Efficiency and Party Control," *Legislative Studies Quarterly* 7 (November 1982), which was coauthored with JAMES W. RIDDLESPERGER.

For those who want to read and understand staffing patterns in state legislatures, we recommend LUCINDA SIMON, *A Legislator's Guide to Staffing Patterns* (Denver, 1979); BRIAN WEBERG, "Changes in Legislative Staff,"

Journal of State Government 61 (November/December 1988); and BRIAN WEBERG and BETH BAZAR, *Legislative Staff Services: 50 State Profiles 1988* (Denver, 1988). The relationship between staffing patterns and information flow is nicely laid out in PAUL SABATIER and DAVID WHITEMAN, "Legislative Decision Making and Substantive Policy Information: Models of Information Flow," *Legislative Studies Quarterly* (August 1985).

If you wish to see data about committees, then editions of *The Book of the States* (Lexington, Ky., 1970), which are published by COUNCIL OF STATE GOVERNMENTS, serve as a starting point. Those interested in information about number, size, and membership of state legislative committees could consult STATE NET and CALIFORNIA JOURNAL, *50-State Legislative Directory, 1989–1990, Committees* (Sacramento, Calif., 1989).

LEGISLATING: FLOOR AND CONFERENCE PROCEDURES IN CONGRESS

Stanley Bach

The results of the legislative process in the U.S. Congress reflect, among other things, the recommendations of its standing committees, the activities of its party leaders, the initiatives and reactions of its individual members, and the collective preferences of its two houses. The arenas in which these influences come together to be weighed and to shape the domestic and international policies of the United States are the chambers, or "floors," of the House of Representatives and the Senate. Sometimes tumultuous and sometimes routine, it was the floor proceedings of Congress that Alexander Hamilton was supposed to have been observing when he commented, "Here, sir, the people govern."

How the people govern through their elected representatives and senators as they debate and vote on the floor depends on the procedures by which the members of each house choose to govern themselves. Because collective decisions in Congress are made by large bodies of strong-willed men and women, who advocate disparate visions of the proper means and ends of government and who represent diverse and often conflicting constituency interests, each house must have rules to organize members' conflicts and help them achieve peaceful and widely acceptable resolutions. When it is too much to expect all members to be satisfied with the policies Congress approves, it becomes even more important that members be satisfied with how those policy decisions are made.

For this purpose, the Constitution makes Congress largely responsible for governing itself. Each house is empowered to adopt its own rules of proceedings and to do so without the approval of the other, without the involvement of the president, and in practice, without the likelihood of review by the Supreme Court.

The Constitution does impose a few procedural requirements but also leaves each house with considerable latitude in deciding how it intends to interpret and enforce them. For example, Article I requires that votes in the House or Senate on overriding presidential vetoes shall be "determined by yeas and nays," so that all members participating in the roll-call vote are publicly and individually accountable to their constituents. Yet the Constitution does not prescribe when these votes shall occur or even that they must occur at all. As each house decides such matters for itself, therefore, its members remain in almost total control of how they conduct their business.

The House and Senate exercise this control through the rules they adopt, the precedents they establish, and the less binding but equally important practices and customs they follow. The standing rules of the Senate enjoy more formal permanence than those of the House. Because two-thirds of the Senate's membership continues from one two-year Congress to the next, the Senate considers itself a continuing body; its rules remain in force from year to year and from Congress to Congress until the Senate decides to change them. Because the House is formally reconstituted every two years, by contrast, it adopts its rules anew at the beginning of each Congress. In practice, however, the legislative rules of both houses have been marked by an impressive degree of stability. Some of the more arcane terms and forms of the legislative process can be traced back to the eighteenth-century Continental Congress and beyond. But the House and Senate have also demonstrated the capacity to make changes, usually of an adaptive and incremental kind, in their procedures when old ways prove inadequate for coping with new demands. It is precisely because of this adaptive and incremental process of change that Congress's procedures can seem so complicated; their uses, effects, and interrelationships reflect institutional history as much as organizational logic.

One reason why so many characteristics and elements of congressional procedures have endured for so long is the flexibility that the House and Senate enjoy in applying and enforcing them. The authority of each house to make its rules is a power it can exercise at any time; it is always free to amend or repeal any of its rules permanently and to do so at any time and by whatever procedures it has established for that purpose. Moreover, each house may amend or repeal a rule temporarily by voting to waive or suspend it or simply by deciding to ignore it. With the exception of the few constitutional requirements that govern congressional action, the House or Senate may insist on enforcing a rule today, when the circumstances of the moment make strict compliance useful, but agree to set that same rule aside tomorrow, when different circumstances make a different procedural approach preferable. Furthermore, the two houses retain this discretion in enforcing their rules regardless of how the rules have been created. Even when a particular legislative procedure has been created by law—as by the Congressional Budget Act, for example—either house retains the unilateral authority to amend, repeal, suspend, or waive any such rule-making provision of law so long as it affects only that house's internal organization and procedures.

In examining how each house makes its own legislative decisions, and then how the two houses resolve their differences on a bill, it is important to understand what their formal rules permit, require, and prohibit. It is equally important, however, to understand how and when these rules are most likely to be adjusted or waived as the House and Senate go about their daily business.

DEBATE RULES AND THEIR CONSEQUENCES

The legislative process in Congress involves complicated and interrelated rules and practices. The best way to begin unraveling these complexities is by examining the procedures of the House and Senate that govern floor debate. These procedures are important in their own right. Legislatures are supposed to be deliberative bodies; assemblies that approve policies without the benefit of adequate and informed debate are properly derided as rubber-stamp bodies that merely ratify decisions made elsewhere. Simply calling a collection of people a legislature does not make it so. But there are two additional reasons for studying the debate rules of the House and Senate. First, these rules shape many of the other formal and informal ways of doing business that characterize each house. Second, these rules exemplify the profound differences that separate the House and the Senate and their respective approaches to meeting their legislative responsibilities under the Constitution.

In the House

Just as a legislature's procedures embody an implicit balance between its need to deliberate and its duty to decide, so too do they reflect an equally important balance between minority rights and majority powers. Throughout its history, the House of Representatives has given greater weight to ensuring the majority's power to act. The size of the House's membership and the changing lines that define its members' districts have been among the factors leading the House toward a largely majoritarian and even mechanistic approach to legislative decision-making. Implicit in the House's procedures is the position that the minority deserves to be heard, but ultimately the preferences of the majority must prevail; that is the essence of democratic government. To this end, the majority must be able to do more than merely decide what choices will be made; it must also be able actually to make those choices. A majority that cannot control its schedule cannot control the policy outcomes of the legislative process.

The House's debate rules promote control of the floor schedule by any partisan or bipartisan majority, so long as it is unified and committed to its goal. These procedures impose pervasive limits on individual participation in floor debate. At no time do House rules permit any representative to speak for more than one hour, even at the end of the day when there is no legislative business being transacted, without the unanimous consent of his or her colleagues on the floor. Usually, the length of individual speeches is more severely limited. During debates on amendments, for example, each speech is typically limited to only five minutes. Such restrictions on individual debate are justified by the sheer size of the House and by members' preference for distributing opportunities to speak even if the result is often too disjointed to satisfy strict notions of what constitutes true debate or deliberation.

In addition, the House's standing rules impose some comparably rigorous controls on collective debate. For example, many bills and resolutions are considered under a set of procedures known as "suspension of the rules" (discussed more fully below), under which each measure can be debated by the entire House for no more than forty minutes. More important, it is almost always within the power of a simple majority of representatives to end debate on any bill after no more than one hour and on any amendment after no more than ten minutes. This power is essential to majority control of the House. Whether such control is exercised by a relatively unified majority party or by a cross-party majority such as a conservative coalition of Republicans and southern Democrats, that majority can control the legislative schedule by controlling the length of debates. A voting majority on the House floor can generally act as it chooses, when it chooses. Minority filibusters in the House are impossible.

In the Senate

The yards of corridor separating the House and Senate chambers are nothing as compared with the procedural gulf that separates the two houses of Congress. Not only are filibusters possible in the Senate, the fear of filibustering pervades the institution and its ways of doing business. There are no effective individual limits or majority controls on Senate floor debate. It is true that a simple majority of senators can end the debate on an amendment by voting to "lay it on the table" (or more simply, to "table it"). To table an amendment, however, is to reject it permanently; once something is tabled in the Senate, it can be taken from the table only by unanimous consent. Neither this motion nor any other can be used by a simple ma-

jority to bring the Senate to the point of taking some affirmative action. The Senate cannot vote on a bill or amendment so long as any senator seeks recognition to speak on it. The presiding officer must give the floor to any senator who seeks it, and the Senate's standing rules normally permit a senator who has been recognized and controls the floor to continue speaking for as long as he or she wishes or is physically able to continue.

To filibuster is to take advantage of the Senate's debate rules by prolonging a debate indefinitely until the majority agrees to compromise or even to withdraw the bill or amendment from consideration. Almost any bill, amendment, or motion that senators can debate is subject to a filibuster. To end a filibuster the Senate must vote to limit debate by invoking cloture under its Rule XXII. This requires that a group of senators sign a cloture motion; not until two days later does the Senate act on the motion, and then it requires the votes of at least sixty senators (three-fifths of the senators duly chosen and sworn). If the question being debated would change the Senate's standing rules, cloture requires the support of at least two-thirds of the senators present and voting. Then, even if and when cloture is invoked, the Senate can continue to consider the question at issue for as much as thirty more hours, during which time each senator is generally limited to one hour for debate. In short, the only procedure under Senate rules for forcing the Senate to a vote on adopting or rejecting a bill or amendment requires a super-majority and does not end the debate immediately or even soon.

The danger of a filibuster in the Senate is almost omnipresent. As a result, much of what occurs on the floor takes place precisely in order to guard against filibusters. Most important to this purpose, the Senate relies heavily on unanimous consent agreements by which all interested senators reach a consensus on the procedures they will follow in addressing a certain measure or issue. The negotiations leading to a unanimous consent agreement can be difficult and time-consuming, but if successful, they do guarantee against a filibuster by imposing effective time limits on debate. A senator who objects to such a proposed agreement implicitly or explicitly threatens to filibuster. Such a threat can be as effective as the act itself in delaying floor action on a bill or in stimulating negotiations that will satisfy opposing senators to the point that they will not make good their threat to engage in "extended debate."

Filibusters may be inconvenient, frustrating, and sometimes even embarrassing for the Senate. Nonetheless, they are a legitimate exercise of the rights that the Senate's rules preserve for its members. As a protection of individual and minority rights, filibusters exemplify the contrast between the Senate's approach to the legislative process and that of the House. In effect, Senate procedures take account not only of the number of senators who oppose a proposition, but also the intensity of their opposition. Quite deliberately, the Senate puts a casual majority at a disadvantage when it confronts a committed minority. Such emphasis on minority prerogatives has always been more practical in the relatively small Senate. During the first years under the Constitution, when there were many fewer states and when the Senate was first developing the principles of its procedures, there were hardly two dozen senators present at any time. Moreover, those senators represented states that had distinct histories and identities and that were not prepared to have their interests buried under the sheer weight of majority preferences. From the perspective of the Senate, therefore, sound national policy has never been merely whatever a majority of the moment is prepared to support. Instead, a legislative decision that is to have lasting value must embody compromises and accommodations among the various regional and other interests that minorities within the Senate protect and promote.

FROM COMMITTEE TO THE FLOOR

One reason why the House and Senate created their systems of standing committees was that there was not sufficient time for the full membership of either house to learn enough about all the legislation its members proposed. A division of labor among what is today roughly twenty committees in each house has enabled Congress to develop its own internal expertise and institutional memory. It has also created a potential bottleneck when the various committees all have legislation they wish to bring up on the floor for debate and passage as soon as

possible. It never was truly practical for either house to consider bills on the floor in the order in which the standing committees reported them. More discriminating procedures were required in the House. Over the years, therefore, the House developed an elaborate system of priorities and procedures that now govern how legislative proposals move from committee to the floor. In the Senate, members continue to rely for this purpose on consultations and negotiations to construct the daily order of business and the longer-term floor agenda.

In the House

When House committees report bills and resolutions with favorable recommendations for passage, they are placed on one of two lists known as the Union and House calendars. In general, measures that would raise or spend money, directly or indirectly, are assigned to the Union Calendar; all others go on the House Calendar. The procedures that determine which measures are taken from which calendar at what times for floor consideration turn on the concept of "privileged business." To say that a bill or resolution is privileged is to say that it may be called up for floor action at any time there is no other motion or measure being considered. If a measure does not become privileged, or if it is not brought to the floor under some privileged procedure, it can wither and die on the House or Union calendar, even though it has been reviewed and approved by one or more of the standing committees.

House rules make certain kinds of measures privileged because of their nature and purpose. For example, appropriations bills and resolutions relating to the rules of the House and the behavior of its members are considered so central to the constitutional functioning of the House, that they enjoy priority access to the floor. Other standing rules make certain kinds of business privileged for floor action on certain days of each month; special days are set aside, for example, for the House to act on private bills affecting specific individuals and entities (such as people with special immigration problems) and bills concerning the District of Columbia. These bills are usually not very controversial, nor are most bills considered as part of "motions to suspend the rules," which are privileged for consideration on Mondays and Tuesdays. Still other days of the month are set aside for the rare instances in which a majority of representatives want to discharge a House committee from further consideration of a measure and bring it directly to the floor for debate and passage.

There remain, however, most of the important and controversial bills that are not inherently privileged and that cannot reach the floor on any of these special days. With the possible exception of privileged appropriations bills, therefore, virtually all of the most significant legislation the House considers each year reaches the floor only with the assistance of the House Rules Committee. This committee has jurisdiction over proposals to change the House's rules, just as other committees have jurisdiction over legislative proposals on other subjects. In addition, the Rules Committee has authority to report privileged resolutions to affect the order of business on the House floor. Each of these privileged resolutions is commonly called a "rule" or "special rule," and it usually proposes to bring a certain bill to the floor so that members can debate it, act on proposed amendments to it, and then vote on whether to pass it. After the Rules Committee reports a special rule for a bill, the House first must debate and adopt that resolution before it can take up the bill to which the resolution refers. In other words, once the House adopts a special rule for a bill, that bill becomes privileged for floor consideration.

Control over the floor schedule is probably the single most important source of influence that the Speaker of the House enjoys and shares with the other members of the majority party leadership. One way in which the Speaker controls the flow of business is through the public and formal exercise of the power of recognition of members on the floor. The Speaker can often control the order of business by permitting one piece of privileged business to be called up in preference to another. More important, though, is the agenda control that majority party leaders exercise through the Rules Committee. Whereas the party ratio on most committees is roughly proportional to the party ratio in the House as a whole, the Democrats on Rules enjoy the advantage of a two-to-one-plus-one party ratio on their committee. In addition, whereas Democrats are

chosen for most committee assignments by the party's Steering and Policy Committee, the Speaker has sole authority to nominate and renominate the Democrats on Rules. (The Republican leader enjoys corresponding authority over Rules Republicans.)

Consequently, the Rules Committee is a generally dependable ally of the majority-party leadership. This has not always been the case; for most of the period from the mid-1930s through the early 1960s, the committee was populated by a conservative coalition that could stymie the Speaker's legislative plans. Today, however, when the Rules Committee acts as "traffic cop," deciding if and when individual bills should reach the House floor, it does so in close cooperation with the Speaker and the majority leader. The Speaker also has firm and personal control over what measures reach the floor under motions to suspend the rules; these motions can be made only with the Speaker's approval. In these two primary ways, therefore, the House's procedures for bringing important bills from the two calendars to the floor are available for the majority party, acting through its leaders, to use in support of its legislative and political goals.

In the Senate

In the Senate the movement of bills from committee to the floor is in some ways simpler and in others more complicated than in the House. The Senate distinguishes between its legislative and executive business (the latter being its constitutional role in confirming nominations and approving treaties) but has essentially only one calendar for bills and resolutions that are not in the custody of its committee system. Once placed on this calendar, all measures are equally eligible to be called up on the Senate floor. The Senate does not rely on any elaborate system of privileged business as the House does. Instead, Senate rules provide that any senator may make the simple motion that the Senate proceed to the consideration of a specific bill or resolution then listed on its legislative calendar. As is so often the case in the Senate, however, the process can actually be more difficult because this "motion to proceed," as it is often called, is usually debatable. This means that measures are typically subject to two potential filibusters on the Senate floor.

There may be a filibuster on the motion to proceed to the consideration of the measure even before the beginning of the filibuster on the measure itself, and each can require the Senate to invoke the time-consuming cloture process in order to break it.

Under these circumstances, the Senate prefers to set its floor schedule by unanimous consent rather than by use of this debatable motion. If a senator refuses to agree to a unanimous consent request to take up a bill, he or she is raising the threat of a dual filibuster. Especially when time is short, as when the end of the fiscal year, the end of the session, or some other deadline approaches, the threat is a potent one. When confronted with two bills of relatively equal importance, senators are naturally inclined to favor consideration of the measure that can be called up and considered with the fewest delays or other procedural complications. Thus, the threat to filibuster a motion to proceed can sometimes be enough to prevent it from being made, at least until attempts at negotiation have been exhausted.

One way in which a senator exercises this leverage is by placing a "hold" on a bill. A hold is a request that no attempt be made to call up a particular bill, at least until the senator placing the hold has been consulted. In effect, a hold is an announcement that at least one senator will object to bringing up a particular bill by unanimous consent and may, if necessary, filibuster a motion to proceed to its consideration. By honoring a senator's hold, the Senate makes it unnecessary for that member to remain on the floor in person in order to protect his or her rights and interests. A hold also informs all senators that the bill at issue could lead the Senate into the kind of procedural morass that filibusters so often create.

Faced with such potential complications, the Senate has given its majority leader both the responsibility and the authority to propose which bills and resolutions it should consider and when. Although the Senate's rules permit all senators to make motions to proceed, in practice only the majority leader or his designee does so. All other senators voluntarily relinquish an important procedural right so as to promote some order in the conduct of Senate business. It is the majority leader, negotiating with and through the minority leader and consulting with the leaders of the committee of jurisdiction and all other interested senators, who attempts to secure unanimous consent for the Senate to take up each major bill that one of its committees has approved. And when these attempts prove unsuccessful, it is the majority leader who must decide whether the bill is sufficiently important and timely to risk embroiling the Senate in a filibuster or whether its consideration should be put aside until some later, possibly more propitious, time.

There are two other respects in which Senate and House procedures differ that have important consequences for the relationship between committees and the floor. One has to do with committee monopoly control over bills; the other concerns committee monopoly control over proposals.

In the House, each bill and resolution is referred to at least one committee. The Speaker may refer a measure, concurrently or sequentially, to two or more committees if it touches on each committee's jurisdiction. Alternatively, a bill may be referred to one committee after having been been reported by another.

If the committee (or committees) fails to act favorably on the measure, it is likely to die in the committee's file cabinets when the Congress adjourns sine die to mark the end of its second session. The House's rules do contain a discharge procedure by which a majority of the House can vote to take a bill away from the committee to which it was referred and bring it directly to the floor for debate and a vote on passage. However, this procedure is rarely used successfully. First, its use is a direct challenge to the authority of one committee and an indirect threat to the power of all committees. Second, representatives are sometimes content to have a committee refuse to act on a measure that they would have to support if it were to reach the floor.

In the Senate each bill or resolution is referred to the standing committee with jurisdiction over the "subject matter which predominates" in the measure. As in the House, measures may be referred to two or more Senate committees, but multiple referrals in the Senate are arranged in almost all cases by unanimous consent agreements approved on the Senate floor. Unlike the House, the Senate has no discharge rule, making it almost impossible to take a measure away from the committee (or committees) to which it was referred.

Senate Rule XIV, however, enables senators to protect themselves from committee inaction by introducing a bill and bypassing the Senate committee system altogether. A senator can have his or her bill placed directly on the Senate's legislative calendar, just as if it had been referred to and reported from committee. This process involves several steps and may require days or even weeks to complete, but it can be invoked by any senator as a matter of right. No such opportunity exists in the House. As a result, Senate committees cannot exercise so conclusive a veto power over legislation as can their House counterparts.

A Senate committee can almost always kill a bill through inaction. Yet this power is of limited value because any senator can introduce another bill with precisely the same text and have it placed directly on the legislative calendar. Of course, members of the committee of jurisdiction can, and very well may, object to a unanimous consent request to bring that bill from the calendar to the floor, but the site of the struggle will then have shifted from the stronghold of the committee's meeting room to the Senate chamber, where it is more exposed and vulnerable.

Of even greater importance is that the House is governed by the requirement that an amendment be germane to the text it proposes to amend; the Senate is not. Every amendment that representatives offer must satisfy this requirement. Germaneness is akin to relevance and pertinence but it is a much more complex concept. More significant than its technical meaning is the general principle embodied by this requirement: that the House should not confront unexpected legislative proposals in the form of amendments that are unrelated to the bill under consideration. In the process, the germaneness requirement also strengthens the hand of each House committee, because it is very difficult for a proposal to reach the House floor unless a committee reports it as part of a bill or unless the committee reports a related bill to which the proposal could be a germane floor amendment.

In the Senate, however, a germaneness requirement is more the exception than the rule. Amendments must be germane when proposed to appropriations and budget measures and when offered under cloture. At virtually all other times, senators may offer amendments on whatever subjects they like to whatever measures they choose, unless the Senate agrees by unanimous consent to require that amendments to a particular bill must be germane. This lack of a generally applicable germaneness requirement has profound importance for the Senate. First, nongermane amendments undermine committee power far more than does the ability of senators to place measures directly on the calendar. Senate committees may be able to control the fate of measures, but they cannot control the fate of proposals. Any senator who is truly determined to force an issue to the Senate floor can generally compel the Senate to debate it and vote on it within a matter of days or weeks, no matter how much the committee of jurisdiction may oppose its consideration.

Second, the ability of senators to offer nongermane amendments makes the Senate a much more unpredictable arena than it otherwise would be. Unless the Senate has invoked cloture or decided by unanimous consent that all amendments to a bill must be germane, senators can never be absolutely sure what issues may arise during debate on the bill they are considering. The majority leader may call up a bill by unanimous consent, believing that the Senate can pass it quickly, without extended debate or unexpected complications. The committee that reported the bill may have no reason to believe otherwise. Yet there is always the possibility that a senator may choose that bill and that day to offer a nongermane amendment that is far more controversial than the bill itself. The result may be an unanticipated filibuster by the amendment's opponents, floor sessions that stretch unexpectedly into the night, and disrupted schedules for the Senate, its members, their staffs, and their families. On the other hand, senators' ability to offer nongermane amendments remains an important and cherished protection against committee vetoes, for themselves and for those whose interests and causes they support, which their House colleagues do not enjoy.

THE PROCESS OF CONSIDERATION

Whatever the merits of Woodrow Wilson's still-famous 1885 study, *Congressional Government,* may be, he has burdened succeeding generations with his exaggerated contention that congressional floor sessions are only the House and Senate "on public exhibition," compared with Congress "at work" in its committee rooms. Even if this characterization was true toward the end of the nineteenth century, it does not accurately depict Congress in the closing decades of the twentieth century. The process of consideration on the House and Senate floor does matter, both in the obvious sense that every bill must survive floor votes in both houses before it can become law and in the sense that what happens to legislation on the floor is often more than a routine formality. The recommendations of House and Senate committees continue to shape the outcomes of the legislative process, but they do not wholly determine them. It is on the floor that most members have their best or only opportunity to shape most public policies through amendments and votes on legislation that has not emerged from the committees on which they sit. The floor stage of the legislative process is frequently uneventful, but it is precisely when the policy stakes are greatest that the floor can become most important as an arena for making law.

In the House

The House has more than one set of procedures that it can use to govern floor consideration of measures; its choice generally depends on the nature of each bill and how important, controversial, and expensive it is. Three sets of procedures are most important. First is the underlying set of rules that apply "in the House" and that are too inflexible and ill suited for most contested legislation. Second, there are the rules that apply in what is known as "the Committee of the Whole," a device the House uses precisely because of its procedural flexibility and adaptability. Finally, there is a set of procedures known collectively as "suspension of the rules," which offers a convenient way for the House to dispose of relatively noncontroversial legislation.

The House's standing rules provide that, in theory at least, when a bill is being considered "in the House," each representative may speak for one hour on the bill and for an additional hour on each debatable amendment or motion

that is proposed during that bill's consideration. In a body of 435 members, relying on this one-hour rule would obviously be wholly impractical. And so the House actually considers relatively few measures "in the House" under this rule. Furthermore, there is a radical difference between the one-hour rule in theory and in practice. Instead of permitting one hour of debate per member on each debatable question, the practical effect of invoking the one-hour rule almost always is to limit the entire time the House considers a bill on the floor to not more than a total of one hour.

The reason lies in the motion to order the previous question. By the end of the first hour for debate, an hour that is always controlled by the bill's majority floor manager—typically the chair of the committee or subcommittee that reported it—that member invariably moves the previous question. This nondebatable motion proposes that the House vote on passing the bill without further debate and without consideration of any floor amendments. If the motion is adopted, the House then proceeds to the vote on final passage with little if any opportunity for further deliberation. In fact, the House rarely rejects the previous question, for at least two reasons. First, majority party and committee leaders avoid calling up bills under the one-hour rule if most members want to debate them at greater length and to amend them. Second, the vote on ordering the previous question is often characterized as a procedural vote on which party leaders believe that their fellow partisans can and should support the party position.

In a sense, the vote on ordering the previous question is a procedural vote, but it can have direct and important policy consequences. If anyone wishes to offer an amendment to a bill being considered "in the House," that member must first persuade a majority to reject the motion for the previous question. If this motion fails, the member can seek recognition for an hour during which he or she can propose an amendment. In other words, a vote against ordering the previous question is a vote to consider the amendment; conversely, a vote for ordering the previous question is a vote against considering any and all amendments to the measure. House members understand the meaning and effect of the previous question, of course, but it is difficult to focus public interest and understanding on something so seemingly arcane as a vote to "order the previous question."

These procedures clearly are not well designed for considering bills that many members wish to debate and that some are determined to amend. Such bills—relatively few in number but of great importance—are usually considered instead in the Committee of the Whole House on the State of the Union or, more simply, the Committee of the Whole. For most purposes, the Committee of the Whole is indistinguishable from the House: every representative serves on this committee, and it meets on the House floor. However, the Speaker does not preside over the Committee of the Whole but, rather, appoints a chairman who presides during the committee's deliberations on a particular bill. More important, the debate on amendments in the Committee of the Whole is governed not by the one-hour rule but by the much more flexible and accommodating five-minute rule. The House's rules require that all measures on the Union Calendar, which include authorization, appropriation, and tax bills, are to be considered in the Committee of the Whole. In practice, virtually all major bills are so considered, even those on the House Calendar.

Measures considered in the Committee of the Whole actually go through a four-stage process of floor consideration. The first stage involves only the transformation of the House into the Committee of the Whole. The Speaker announces this transformation at a time arranged with other party and committee leaders and under the authority previously granted the Speaker by a special rule that the Rules Committee has already reported and the House has adopted.

Once in the Committee of the Whole, the second stage of consideration is a period of one or more hours for general debate. This time is typically divided and controlled by the senior Democratic and Republican members of the committee (or committees) that have reported the bill. These representatives use the time to discuss the bill—its purposes and provisions, strengths and weaknesses—and yield parts of their time to other members who wish to speak. This is exclusively a time for debate;

no amendments or other motions are in order. At the end of this general debate, the committee may move on to the third stage of the process, which is the amending process, but it is not required to do so. At any time, the committee may vote to "rise" and transform itself back into the House, with the expectation of again resolving into the Committee of the Whole at some future time or day to resume action on the bill.

The amendment process in the Committee of the Whole sometimes becomes complicated, but its essential characteristics can be summarized briefly. The process is usually a systematic one: amendments are offered to each section or title of a bill in turn. If a standing committee has proposed amendments to the bill, its amendments are the first to be considered as each part of the bill is read or identified. When an amendment is proposed, a House clerk is required to read it for the information of members, but this reading is usually waived by unanimous consent. More often than not, a representative will inform a bill's floor managers and other interested members about his or her amendment; it usually proves more productive to try to reach agreement on amendments in advance than to offer them by surprise.

In recognizing members to offer and debate amendments, the chairman of the Committee of the Whole is guided by customs and practices that are well established and accepted, though not formally binding. The chairman gives preference in recognition to members who serve on the standing committee that has studied and reported the bill on which the Committee of the Whole is acting. The chairman generally recognizes standing-committee members in order of seniority and usually alternates between Democrats and Republicans. The reason for these practices is a straightforward one: committee members, and especially senior members, are presumed to be better informed about the bill than their noncommittee colleagues. However, these priorities guide the chair only when two or more members want to propose amendments at the same time. Representatives must assert their own interests by asking for recognition at the appropriate time to offer an amendment, just as they must protect their rights against defective amendments by making a point of order against such an amendment (as being nongermane, for example) before debate on it begins.

When an amendment is offered, its sponsor is allotted five minutes to explain and defend it. Another member may then claim five minutes to oppose the amendment. Other members who wish to speak gain recognition for five minutes each by offering "pro forma amendments." Such an amendment typically proposes to "strike the last word" from the pending amendment or section of the bill. In contemporary practice, this has no procedural significance other than as a device to secure five minutes for debate. Thus, each member could speak for five minutes on each amendment. At any time after the first ten minutes of debate on an amendment, however, the committee can decide by simple-majority vote to bring an end to debate on that amendment or even on the pending section of the bill and all amendments to it. Once again, a majority of the House retains control over the pace and flow of legislative business on the floor.

Before the Committee of the Whole votes on an amendment, members may offer amendments to it. An amendment to a bill itself is a first-degree amendment; an amendment to a first-degree amendment is a second-degree amendment. There are also two kinds of amendments to amendments. A perfecting amendment proposes to change only part of a first-degree amendment—for example, it may change a dollar amount in a first-degree amendment or add an additional provision to it. By contrast, a substitute amendment proposes a complete alternative to whatever change in the bill the first-degree amendment would make. After an amendment has been proposed to some part of a bill, one member can offer a second-degree perfecting amendment to the first-degree amendment, and another can offer a substitute for the same amendment. House rules also allow an amendment to the substitute.

There is a reasonable explanation for permitting such a complicated situation to develop. When members offer a first-degree amendment and a substitute for it, they are presenting the committee with two different alternatives for a certain provision in the bill itself. The House's procedures permit amendments

to perfect—presumably to improve—both alternatives before members decide whether either of them is preferable to what is already in the bill. Therefore, members first vote on any perfecting amendments to the first-degree amendment. Second, they vote on any perfecting amendments to the substitute for the first-degree amendment. Third, they choose between the two alternatives (perhaps now amended) by voting for or against the substitute. Finally, the Committee of the Whole completes the series of votes by voting on the first-degree amendment, however it may have been amended either by perfecting amendments or by a substitute amendment.

These amending rules give members a chance to consider several different positions on the same issue before having to choose among them. As a general rule, once a provision in a bill has been amended, it cannot be amended again. This makes it important for members to be prepared to offer their own proposals as second-degree perfecting amendments or substitute amendments, depending on how the procedural situation develops in the Committee of the Whole. Members also use the House's amending procedures in attempts to give themselves tactical advantages. For example, a member who wants to be sure that there is a vote on his or her amendment may try to offer it as a second-degree perfecting amendment because no amendments to such an amendment are in order. In general, representatives who have mastered the procedural opportunities that are available in the Committee of the Whole have a valuable potential advantage: they can use these opportunities to define issues and arrange choices in ways they think will increase their chances of winning.

When the Committee of the Whole has disposed of the last amendment to the last part of the bill, it "rises" (transforms itself back into the House) and reports the bill to the House with the amendments it has approved. The committee never votes on the bill as a whole, nor does it actually change the text of the bill. Instead, it makes recommendations about amendments, recommendations that the House almost always accepts. During the fourth and final stage of consideration, the House usually agrees to all the committee's proposed amendments with a single vote, but any member can single out any of them for a separate vote.

There is one last opportunity for a minority-party member to amend a bill. This takes the form of a motion to recommit the bill back to a standing committee, but usually with instructions that the committee immediately return the bill to the House floor with a specific amendment. In fact, members actually base their votes on their support or lack of support for the amendment included in the motion. This procedure originated at a time when votes on amendments in the Committee of the Whole could not be publicly recorded, so recommitting with instructions developed as a means to enable the minority party to have a roll-call vote in the House on its position on a bill. For the same reason, recommittal motions tend to divide the House largely along party lines.

Finally, the House votes on whether to pass the bill, with whatever changes that have been made during the floor-amending process. It is relatively unusual for the House actually to defeat a bill after it has completed this entire four-stage process of consideration. The vote on final passage is not only important, of course, it is absolutely necessary. But the likelihood of passage also emphasizes the importance of the legislation that the House's standing committees send to the floor and the changes that are made in the legislation.

The amendment process in the Committee of the Whole can justly be considered the most important stage of House floor action on the most important legislation that the House considers during each Congress. Yet only about 10 percent of the measures the House passes each year are considered in the Committee of the Whole. By contrast, more than one-third of the floor agenda in the contemporary House is considered under a different and far more restrictive set of procedures known as suspension of the rules. A procedure that began in the early nineteenth century as a way for the House to waive individual rules gradually evolved into a way to make bills privileged for floor action, and then into a set of procedures that also govern how these bills are actually considered.

In brief, House rules permit the Speaker, on Mondays and Tuesdays and during the closing days of each session, to recognize members to move to suspend the rules and pass individual bills (or take other legislative actions). No representative has a right to make such a motion; the Speaker has the right to permit a member to do so. Once the motion is made, usually by a committee or subcommittee chairman, the House proceeds to debate the bill to which it refers for a total of no more than forty minutes, during which time no floor amendments are in order. In effect, the House must accept or reject the bill as it is brought to the floor, most often at the direction of the committee of jurisdiction. However, the House will not pass a bill under such procedural constraints by simple-majority vote. Instead, passage requires the support of two-thirds of the members present and voting. If this majority is not achieved, the bill may be considered again, at some later time, under procedures that permit more debate and some opportunity for floor amendments.

In the Senate

Like the Senate's formal procedures for bringing bills from committee to the floor, its rules governing floor procedure are less numerous and complex than those of the House; but again, the actual legislative process on the Senate floor can be more difficult and complicated because of the leverage that senators derive from their right to filibuster. Unlike the House, the Senate's standing rules contain only one set of formal procedures for floor action on bills and resolutions. The Senate no longer uses the device of the Committee of the Whole, and it very rarely votes to suspend its rules and then only to escape from the constraints of specific procedural prohibitions. One reason that senators do not vote very often on motions to suspend any of their rules is that they do not insist on uniformly strict enforcement of many of these rules during routine consideration of legislation. But the more important and controversial the bill, the more likely are senators to insist that informality give way to strict compliance with their formal procedures.

The Senate's floor consideration of a major bill typically begins with speeches by the majority and minority floor managers, other members of the committee of jurisdiction, and perhaps other interested senators. This is a matter of custom that is neither protected nor required by Senate rules. After these speeches, the Senate first considers committee amendments to the bill, as does the House in its deliberations. Senators can amend these amendments, but they cannot offer their own unrelated amendments to the bill until after the Senate has disposed of all committee amendments.

Frequently, in fact, a single committee amendment dominates the Senate's attention for the entire time it is considering a bill. A Senate committee often reports a bill or resolution with one amendment that proposes an entirely different text for the measure. Such a complete substitute, as it is usually called in the Senate, proposes to replace everything after a bill's enacting clause (or a resolution's resolving clause), which always precedes the measure's substantive legislative provisions. Under these circumstances, senators direct virtually all of their amendments to the committee substitute, under the reasonable assumption that the Senate will eventually approve it, however it may have been amended by that time. Once the Senate agrees to the committee substitute, no additional amendments to the bill are in order. The Senate, like the House, prohibits amendments that only propose to amend language that already has been amended. Because a committee substitute replaces every word in a bill's text, adopting the substitute necessarily ends the amending process.

Whether senators direct their amendments to a bill itself or to a proposed committee substitute, they may offer their amendments in whatever order they like. Neither bills nor committee substitutes are read for amendment, section by section or title by title; they are open to amendment at any point. As a result, successive amendments may move senators' attention back and forth through a bill. The majority and minority leaders do receive priority over other senators when they seek recognition; to a somewhat lesser extent, so do the bill's floor managers. At all other times, however, the presiding officer is required to recognize any senator who seeks the floor when no one else controls it. Moreover, the presiding officer may not direct the Senate to vote on the bill or any amendment to it so long as there is a senator who wants to be recognized.

As a result, the pace of Senate floor consideration is often more desultory than in the House and is also subject to frequent stops and starts. When there is no senator on the floor who wishes to speak or offer an amendment, some senator usually will "suggest the absence of a quorum," which in the Senate is a way of temporarily suspending floor activity while senators engage in informal negotiations on or off the floor or until another senator comes to the floor with a statement to make or an amendment to propose. In short, the Senate's normal rules do not require its members to accommodate themselves to the pace of floor deliberations, as in the House. More often than not, the Senate accommodates itself to the convenience of its members.

As in the House, the process of floor consideration is usually fairly simple. A senator will offer an amendment and ask unanimous consent that it not be read in full. He or she will then be recognized to make a statement in support of the amendment. Unlike the House, however, the Senate has no five-minute rule or any other rule that limits how much time may be consumed by this or any other speech on an amendment. After other senators speak for or against the amendment, the Senate eventually will act on it, either by a direct "up or down" vote on the amendment itself or by a vote on a motion to table the amendment. If the amendment is tabled, it is rejected; if the motion to table is defeated, the Senate can resume debate on the amendment. The tabling motion having revealed senators' preferences, however, the amendment itself is often adopted shortly thereafter.

Again, as in the House, amendments to bills (first-degree amendments) are subject to second-degree amendments. The Senate's amendment procedures, however, can become even more elaborate and complicated than those of the House. Senators may be able to offer second-degree perfecting amendments, second-degree substitute amendments, and even amendments to the same part of the text that the first-degree amendment proposes to change. The amendments that senators can actually offer depend primarily on whether the first-degree amendment proposes only to insert some additional provision into the bill, proposes instead only to strike some provision from the bill, or proposes both to strike out a provision and to replace it with a different version.

A full explanation of the details and complexities of this amending process is beyond the scope of this essay. Suffice it to say that depending on the circumstances, senators can offer as many as three, five, or even seven or more floor amendments before any votes must take place. And when a committee proposes a complete substitute for the text of a bill, senators can offer some amendments to both versions. Only when senators have no more speeches to make, and only when they have no more amendments to offer or when the bill has been totally amended by a substitute, will the Senate vote on passing it.

Floor situations involving multiple amendments on the same subject are quite unusual. However, senators may use the amending rules in attempts to gain some procedural advantage. For example, a senator may want to amend a colleague's amendment before the vote on it takes place. To achieve similar purposes, senators also may offer motions to recommit bills to committee with instructions. Like similar motions in the House, recommittal motions with instructions are actually attempts at amendment. In the Senate, however, they are in order at any time during a bill's consideration, even while another amendment and various amendments to it are pending.

It bears repeating that the Senate's standing rules do not require floor amendments to be germane to the measure under consideration unless it is an appropriation or budget measure, or unless the Senate is operating under cloture. Moreover, every floor amendment is debatable, as are recommittal motions and certain other motions. This means that a filibuster is always a possibility whenever a minority of senators intensely opposes an amendment that most of their colleagues are prepared to adopt. In fact, as striking as the procedural prerogatives that senators enjoy is the self-restraint that they exercise in refraining from filibustering the many bills and amendments each of them opposes.

Senators recognize that constant filibustering would severely damage the Senate as an institution—both its reputation as well as its ability to function. All senators also have their own legislative goals that they want to achieve and for which they need the support of their colleagues. The senator who filibusters today can be the victim of a filibuster tomorrow; in this sense, self-restraint is in every senator's long-term interest. In addition, senators appreciate that there exists a line, even if no one can describe it precisely, between senators' legitimate use of their procedural powers and their abuse of these powers in ways that seriously inconvenience their colleagues or prevent the Senate from working. No senator approaches this line without giving careful thought to the consequences of crossing it.

Nonetheless, the option of filibustering remains when the costs of compromise and comity become too high. To guard against this possibility and to lend greater order and predictability to its floor proceedings, the Senate often agrees to supplant many of its standing rules in favor of unanimous consent agreements that sometimes resemble the resolutions known as "special rules" that the Rules Committee proposes in the House.

SPECIAL RULES AND TIME AGREEMENTS

To reiterate, the standing rules of both the House and the Senate give each house some valuable flexibility in deciding how it will address legislation on the floor. The House has several alternative sets of floor procedures available to it, especially suspension motions that limit debate and preclude floor amendments, in contrast to the more elaborate and multistage process involving the Committee of the Whole. Similarly, the Senate may proceed in a relaxed fashion under its conventional rules that permit virtually unlimited debate and nongermane amendments, or it may invoke cloture which, among other restrictions, imposes severe debate limitations and a germaneness requirement that senators dutifully enforce.

In addition, each house has also developed distinctive, though in some ways analogous, procedural devices that enable it to adjust its floor procedures to the challenges and dangers posed by the individual bills it considers.

In the House

When the House Rules Committee proposes a special rule to the House, it does more than recommend that a certain bill be brought to the floor. It also recommends how the House should consider that bill: whether it should be considered in the House or in the Committee of the Whole, and under precisely what terms and conditions. The variety of the provisions contained in these resolutions is limited only by the creativity of Rules Committee members, the procedural problems they try to anticipate, and the willingness of the House to accept their recommendations. However, there is a basic form of special rule that all representatives recognize. This typical rule provides for considering a bill in the Committee of the Whole. The resolution also specifies the length of general debate and how the control of that time is to be divided among the leaders of the committee or committees of jurisdiction. Such a special rule also includes standard and predictable provisions to expedite the final stage of consideration that takes place in the House, after the Committee of the Whole has voted on all amendments and recommended certain of them to the House.

In addition, the most important and controversial provisions of special rules affect the opportunities for members to offer amendments to a bill in the Committee of the Whole. Some resolutions merely state that a measure is to be read for amendment under the five-minute rule. This is an "open rule," in that it leaves the bill fully open to all amendments that are otherwise in order—for example, germane amendments that are properly drafted and that do not violate any requirement or prohibition of Congress's increasingly complicated budget rules.

At the other extreme, the Rules Committee occasionally reports a "closed rule," proposing to prohibit all floor amendments to the bill it would bring to the floor for consideration. In other words, the committee asks members to accept or reject a bill as it is brought to the floor and to relinquish voluntarily all opportunities to change it by amendment. Not surprisingly, the House does not engage in such self-denial very often or very happily. Still, it does so from time to time, especially when confronted with particularly complex and finely tuned legislative con-structions that could collapse under the pressure of tempting floor amendments. During the 1950s and 1960s, for example, the House often considered tax bills under closed rules on the grounds that tax law was too technical to be written on the floor and that floor amendments could easily destroy the delicate political and policy balances that the Ways and Means Committee had constructed.

By the end of the 1980s, closed rules had become much more unusual, both because representatives were less willing to forgo their amendment rights and because the Rules Committee had developed various kinds of special rules that restrict floor amendments without precluding them completely. Such rules may prohibit amendments on certain subjects or amendments to specific sections of a bill. More often, though, "restrictive rules" prohibit all floor amendments except those specifically listed by the Rules Committee in its resolution or in the accompanying report. Such a rule may also specify how long members may debate each amendment and whether they will be allowed to offer second-degree amendments to it. Under these restrictive rules, the only policy choices that members can make during the amending process in the Committee of the Whole are those which the Rules Committee has enumerated.

It is important to emphasize that the Rules Committee only makes recommendations to the House; if the House considers a bill under a closed or restrictive rule, it is only because a majority of members voted to do so. But the Rules Committee is adept at crafting sets of procedural ground rules that a majority will accept, and majority party leaders expect their fellow partisans to support the committee's resolutions, which typically reflect the leadership's policy preferences and strategic decisions. From time to time the House will reject a special rule, leaving it to the committee to return to the floor with a more acceptable set of procedures. However, it has proven extraordinarily difficult to amend one of the committee's resolutions on the floor.

These resolutions are considered "in the House," under the one-hour rule. Therefore, the House first must reject the motion to order the previous question on a special rule before any member can propose a floor amendment to it. The motion to order the previous question proposes to end the debate on a bill or resolution and preclude any amendments to it. So when representatives find that one of the committee's proposed resolutions would prevent them from offering an important amendment to a major bill, the key decision for them becomes this vote on the previous question. If a majority of the House votes to order the previous question, the rule cannot be amended to permit consideration of their amendment to the bill. In such cases, therefore, the House may actually settle the most important issue about a bill when it decides an ostensibly procedural question even before it begins debate on the bill itself.

In the Senate

The Senate also can develop sets of procedural ground rules that are individually designed for specific bills. Typical of the differences between the two houses, however, is that the House adopts its special rules by simple-majority vote whereas the Senate relies on unanimous consent agreements.

Senators ask and receive unanimous consent from their colleagues every day for a variety of purposes, many of them routine and predictable, such as to dispense with the reading of amendments, to insert statements into the *Congressional Record,* or to call off a quorum call before it is completed. In addition, though, they often negotiate far more complex procedural agreements that govern floor action on a bill they are considering or are about to consider. Because the primary purpose and effect of these complex agreements is to preclude the possibility of a filibuster by limiting debate time, they are known as "time agreements."

It is even more difficult to generalize about time agreements in the Senate than about special rules in the House because there are so many variations that the Senate has developed to address the political and procedural problems it can confront. Nonetheless, there is a form of time agreement that is familiar to all senators and on which variations and permutations are often built. Such an agreement imposes a time limit (often one hour) for debating each first-degree amendment, an even more stringent limit for debating each second-degree amendment or any other debatable

question that may arise, and an additional time limit for debate on the bill as a whole. Furthermore, such an agreement generally requires that all amendments to the bill must be germane. Senators are unlikely to give up their right to filibuster a bill without this assurance that their colleagues cannot offer any unexpected and controversial nongermane amendments to it.

Time agreements create procedural conditions on the Senate floor that are radically different from those created by its standing rules. Unlimited opportunities for debate by all senators give way to limited debate times controlled by a handful of senators. The result is a Senate that is much more orderly, controlled, and efficient than its regular procedures require it to be. At the same time, these are voluntary agreements among all interested senators. A time agreement may not be imposed by majority vote or even by a two-thirds vote. It is a unanimous-consent agreement that any senator can block simply by objecting when it is proposed on the floor.

The requirement for unanimity naturally makes time agreements difficult to arrange. The negotiations, in which the party leaders usually play a pivotal role, typically start before the Senate begins consideration of the bill at issue, but they may not be concluded successfully, if at all, until the bill has been on the floor for hours or even days. These negotiations frequently occur off the floor, so that senators can discuss alternatives more informally and confidentially. This helps explain why Senate floor proceedings can seem disjointed and unfocused; often the most serious legislative work is being pursued elsewhere as senators attempt to negotiate a procedural treaty.

Senators are inclined to endorse time agreements whenever they can, just as they are inclined not to filibuster. However, each of them has leverage that he or she can exert effectively. A senator may ask for additional time to debate an amendment or insist on offering one or more nongermane amendments. Time agreements often contain such special exceptions; they are included because they are needed to satisfy individual senators who otherwise might object. Even then, negotiations sometimes fail, leaving the majority leader with the choice of holding the bill from the floor, at least temporarily, or calling it up anyway, hoping that a filibuster will not materialize or that senators will eventually become more amenable to an agreement. In such cases, the Senate may reach partial unanimous consent agreements governing debate on a single amendment or a series of amendments, perhaps leading ultimately to an agreement that lists all the remaining amendments that senators will be allowed to offer to the bill. However the negotiations proceed, though, they are always shaped by the recognition that all senators possess a de facto veto power that any of them can exercise if convinced that his or her rights and interests are not being adequately protected.

REACHING BICAMERAL AGREEMENTS

The House and Senate have always jealously guarded their institutional autonomy against intrusions by each other as well as by the president. There is only informal coordination between the two houses in planning their legislative agendas, and members of each are discouraged from even referring in debate to what has happened on the other side of the Capitol building. Still, the House and Senate must eventually reach agreement on legislation before it can be presented to the president for signature or veto. The process of reaching bicameral agreement is usually uneventful. On occasion, however, House-Senate negotiations can seem as difficult and prolonged as international-treaty negotiations. In 1962, for example, the federal government almost stopped functioning when the chairmen of the House and Senate Appropriations Committees could not agree on where to meet and on who would chair their meetings.

For the legislative process to reach completion, both houses at some point must pass the same bill. It is not sufficient for each house to pass its own bill on the same subject. Only one bill can become law, and it requires approval by both the House and the Senate. Sooner or later, one house must take up a bill already passed by the other and pass it as well, perhaps after amending it in various ways. The House or Senate often devotes most of its time and energy on the floor to one of its own bills before finally amending and passing a bill from the other house on the same subject. If the House passes its bill before the Senate acts, for

example, the Senate may still debate and amend a bill that one of its own committees has reported. Ultimately, however, the Senate is likely to pass the House bill instead, after amending it to replace the House's text with the amended text from the Senate's bill. If the Senate acts first, alternatively, the House often passes its own bill and then also passes the Senate bill after having substituted the text of its bill for the Senate-approved text. In any event, the result is either a House bill that the Senate also has passed, but with one or more amendments, or a Senate bill that the House has also passed, again with one or more amendments. Before the legislative process is complete, the two houses must then agree on how best to dispose of these amendments.

Before and During Conference

One approach to reaching agreement is for the House and Senate to rely on a formal and public exchange of amendments and messages. Each house acts in turn, conveying positions and proposals to the other until agreement is reached. Under precedents that are essentially the same in both houses, each house has one opportunity to amend amendments from the other. Thus, in the case of a House bill that the Senate has passed with amendments, the House may amend the Senate amendments and the Senate then may amend those House amendments to the Senate amendments. A preferable procedure is, of course, for either house simply to accept (concur in) the amendments from the other, or for the interested representatives and senators to conduct informal negotiations resulting in compromises that are then embodied in amendments between the houses. If the House and Senate succeed in reaching agreement in this way, the final version of the bill on which both have agreed is printed (or "enrolled") and presented to the president. In fact, most of the bills that become law during each Congress involve no House-Senate differences at all or differences that are successfully resolved through this process of amendments between the two houses.

For the most important and complex bills, however, this process is too formal and inflexible to be effective. What is needed instead is a forum in which the disagreements between the House and Senate can be negotiated, which is precisely the purpose of a conference committee.

At any stage in the process of exchanging amendments and messages, either house can disagree to the other house's position or insist on its own position, and can propose that a conference committee be established to recommend a way to resolve their disagreements. In the House, the Speaker appoints all conference committee members. Most are drawn from the standing committee (or committees) that originally reported the House version of the bill, so the Speaker usually gives great weight to the committee leaders' recommendations. In the Senate the presiding officer is empowered to make the formal appointments, but the actual selections emerge from consultations among party and committee leaders. In both houses members can move to instruct their conferees to adhere to certain positions; however, any such instructions are only advisory, not binding. Neither house binds its conferees in advance because doing so would limit their negotiating ability and make the negotiating process more difficult.

For much the same reason neither house burdens its conferees (or managers, as they also are called) with elaborate procedures for conducting their negotiations. There must be at least one formal meeting of each conference, and this meeting must be open to the public unless the conferees follow the procedures required to hold it behind closed doors—usually to protect national security information. In all other respects the conferees are free to proceed as they think best. They select their own conference committee chairman and decide on whatever procedural rules they find necessary. Some conferences involve the formal exchange of proposals between delegations; others are much more informal discussions out of which an agreement emerges. In fact, staff members usually engage in thorough preliminary negotiations, isolating the most difficult issues that the conferees themselves must resolve. In the case of omnibus bills containing provisions on several related subjects, conference delegations frequently include members from several standing committees of each house, and the conference committee often divides informally into subconferences on discrete aspects of the bill.

There are significant limitations on the authority of conferees; these flow from the purpose of the conference committee, which is to resolve matters on which the two houses have disagreed. The conferees are to address only matters that are in disagreement. They should not change provisions that both houses have approved nor should they add provisions that neither house has approved. Furthermore, the conferees are to reach agreements that fall within the "scope of the differences" between the House and Senate positions; conference agreements are supposed to be compromises, not positions that are more extreme than the initial position of either house. When the House and Senate disagreements are measurable—when they disagree over appropriations levels, for example—these limitations are fairly easy to enforce. Very often, however, conferees are presented with entirely different House and Senate versions of the same bill. In these cases, the conference committee is empowered to draft still another version of the bill. This is to be a compromise between the versions the House and Senate have passed, but here conferees inevitably have more latitude than when they are presented with discrete disagreements over dollar amounts.

After Conference

A conference has reached a successful conclusion when a majority of the House managers and a majority of Senate managers sign two documents. One is the conference report itself, which presents the legislative language on which the conferees have agreed; the other is the joint explanatory statement (or statement of managers) that, much like a standing committee report, explains the conferees' intentions. The documents must be acceptable to a majority of each house's delegation. Consequently, any formal voting in conference committees takes place within each delegation. For this reason, there is no need for the House and Senate to appoint the same number of conferees; each house has a single vote in conference, no matter how many members it has appointed to the conference committee.

The conference report is privileged for House floor action. It is considered "in the House," under the one-hour rule, so debate rarely extends beyond the end of the first hour when the previous question is ordered. In the

Senate, the conference report may be called up by a nondebatable motion, but the report itself is debatable and therefore subject to a filibuster. The conference report is not amendable in either house. It is offered as a negotiated settlement of a series of House-Senate disagreements, and each house accepts or rejects the proposed settlement as a package. The House does have a procedure by which it can vote to remove a nongermane Senate amendment from a conference report, rather than having to accept or reject it as part of the report. But taking anything out of a conference report is like puncturing a balloon. So the House usually proposes to save the procedural situation by asking the Senate to accept the remainder of the conferees' agreement as an amendment between the houses.

If both houses do accept the conference report, the bill as amended by the terms of the report is reprinted and sent to the president for approval or disapproval. If either house fails to adopt it—if the report is defeated on a vote or if a point of order is upheld against it (because the conferees violated their authority in some way, for example)—the bill may die, but its death is not inevitable. The House and Senate may agree to a new conference, or they may try to reach agreement by resorting once again to an exchange of amendments and messages between the houses.

Sometimes the House and Senate managers fail to reach agreement on one or more of the amendments submitted to their conference committee. Then they submit a partial conference report that is accompanied by the amendments that are reported from conference as remaining in disagreement. After agreeing to the report itself, each house acts on the various amendments in disagreement. In the case of a Senate amendment in disagreement, for instance, the House may insist on disagreeing to it, but it is more likely to recede from its disagreement and either accept or amend the Senate amendment. Conferees also report amendments in what is called "technical" disagreement when their proposed compromises on those amendments cannot be included in the conference report itself without subjecting it to a point of order. In either event, to complete the legislative process the House and Senate must reach full agreement on each and every amendment on which they had disagreed.

CONCLUSION

The legislative procedures of the House and Senate are not merely the neutral mechanics of the lawmaking process; they can have important and sometimes decisive policy consequences. If a special rule prohibits the offering of certain amendments to a bill in the Committee of the Whole, those are policy options that the House has no opportunity to endorse. If the supporters of a bill in the Senate cannot attract the sixty votes needed to invoke cloture, that bill is likely to succumb to the filibuster and never reach a vote on final passage. Control of policy in Congress is impossible without control of procedure. That is why it is so important that the House can devise special sets of procedures for considering each major bill and adopt them by simple majority vote—and why it is so important that the Senate cannot do so.

More generally, the underlying characteristics of House and Senate procedures affect the tenor and the dynamics of the legislative process. Because of the emphasis in House rules on majority powers, the proponents of a bill need compromise only as much as is necessary to satisfy a majority of their colleagues. A bill's supporters may try to build a larger supporting coalition for strategic reasons—for example, to encourage Senate action or to discourage a presidential veto. But victory on the House floor requires support by only a dependable majority, however minimal.

The procedures in the Senate give an entirely different cast to policy decision-making. The possibility of filibusters renders support by a minimal majority insufficient for victory. More support than that is needed for cloture, and it is far preferable to avoid having to invoke cloture at all by attempting to satisfy all senators to the extent that no significant minority will resort to a filibuster. In short, the Senate's rules create impressive incentives for accommodating a more diverse array of preferences than do the procedures of the House, even if it means that the Senate devotes weeks to floor action on a bill that the House debates, amends, and passes in only a day.

For these reasons, proposals to "reform" seemingly technical or obscure provisions of House or Senate rules can provoke floor debates as heated and vituperative as those over the most contentious issues of national or international policy. Decisions on policy, however important they may be, affect only that policy and can be revisited and reversed on a

later day by the same procedures. Changes in the procedures themselves, however, can redistribute the balance of power within the House or Senate in fundamental and lasting ways. As a result, procedural changes can affect a wide array of policy choices not only for the present but for the unforeseeable future when the dominating majority of today may become the weakened minority of tomorrow.

BIBLIOGRAPHY

Basic Sources
The essential reference sources on congressional floor and conference procedures are the official compilations of House and Senate rules and precedents. The House publishes its rules every two years in its manual, *Constitution, Jefferson's Manual, and Rules of the House of Representatives.* The Senate also publishes its standing rules periodically as *Standing Rules of the Senate* and in a larger volume, the *Senate Manual,* which also contains the texts of related orders, resolutions, and laws.

Supplementing the rules are the voluminous bodies of precedents that have developed for interpreting and applying them. The House's eleven-volume set of *Hinds' and Cannon's Precedents of the House of Representatives,* published in 1907 and 1936, is out of print, as is *Cannon's Procedure in the House of Representatives* from 1963. More recent and accessible are the 1974 edition of *Procedure in the U.S. House of Representatives* and the 1985 and 1987 *Supplements.* Still being completed is the series of *Deschler's Precedents of the U.S. House of Representatives;* between 1977 and 1992, nine volumes were published and others were still to appear. The Senate's precedents, by contrast, are compiled in a single volume: *Riddick's Senate Procedure* (Washington, D.C., 1992).

Rules and Floor Procedures
The previously mentioned reference works are to be consulted, not read in search of a systematic description or coherent explanation of House or Senate floor procedures. For this pur-

pose, the single most useful volume is WALTER OLESZEK, *Congressional Procedures and the Policy Process,* 3d ed. (Washington, D.C., 1989). Three earlier books retain some value, but all of them must be read with caution because of the changes in formal procedures and informal practices that have occurred since their publication: LEWIS A. FROMAN, JR., *The Congressional Process: Strategies, Rules, and Procedures* (Boston, 1969); GEORGE B. GALLOWAY, *The Legislative Process in Congress* (New York, 1953); and FLOYD M. RIDDICK, *The United States Congress: Organization and Procedure* (Manassas, Va., 1949).

Understanding and exploring the consequences of legislative procedures have not been high priorities for contemporary scholars of Congress. Nonetheless, several recent monographs have addressed legislative rules in the House of Representatives as a necessary part of attempts to understand the political dynamics of congressional decision-making. See, for example, STANLEY BACH and STEVEN S. SMITH, *Managing Uncertainty in the House of Representatives: Adaptation and Innovation in Special Rules* (Washington, D.C., 1988); RONALD M. PETERS, JR., *The American Speakership: The Office in Historical Perspective* (Baltimore, 1990); and BARBARA SINCLAIR, *Majority Party Leadership in the U.S. House* (Baltimore, 1983).

The Senate has not received as much attention of this kind, but an important exception is BARBARA SINCLAIR, *The Transformation of the U.S. Senate* (Baltimore, 1989). On conference committees, the most complete study is LAWRENCE D. LONGLEY and WALTER J. OLESZEK,

Bicameral Politics: Conference Committees in Congress (New Haven, Conn., 1989); also of interest is DAVID J. VOGLER, *The Third House: Conference Committees in the United States Congress* (Evanston, Ill., 1971).

An ambitious and successful study of recent developments in and affecting congressional floor activity is STEVEN S. SMITH, *Call to Order: Floor Politics in the House and Senate* (Washington, D.C., 1989). KEITH KREHBIEL, *Information and Legislative Organization* (Ann Arbor, Mich., 1991), takes an approach that reflects and discusses recent developments in information theories and the formal or public-choice approach to the study of politics.

Congressional History

Finally, there remains available a remarkable series of books that were published early in the twentieth century and that continue to be invaluable today for their insights into how Congress has developed and changed over the long course of its history. Particularly noteworthy are DE ALVA STANWOOD ALEXANDER, *History and Procedure of the House of Representatives* (Boston and New York, 1916); CHANG-WEI CHIU, *The Speaker of the House of Representatives Since 1896* (New York, 1928); MARY PARKER FOLLETT, *The Speaker of the House of Representatives* (New York, 1896); PAUL DEWITT HASBROUCK, *Party Government in the House of Representatives* (New York, 1927); GEORGE H. HAYNES, *The Senate of the United States* (Boston, 1938); ROBERT LUCE, *Legislative Procedure* (Boston, 1922); SAMUEL W. MCCALL, *The Business of Congress* (New York, 1911); and ADA C. MCGOWN, *The Congressional Conference Committee* (New York, 1927).

SEE ALSO Constitutional and Political Constraints on Policy-Making: A Historical Perspective; The Role of Congressional Parties; AND The Rules Committee: The House Traffic Cop.

FLOOR PROCEDURES AND CONFERENCE COMMITTEES IN STATE LEGISLATURES

Wayne L. Francis

Efficiency is a central concern of most legislative bodies. The main reason for this is clear: a great volume of demands for official action flows into the system in the form of written proposals, and it is the challenge of each legislature to respond to these demands through a form of deliberation that is consistent with constitutional requirements for democratic procedure. Therein lies the puzzle. How do legislators organize themselves to do this job within the constraints of time, pay, and majority rule?

From an organizational perspective, the larger puzzle may be reduced to the following subpuzzles:

1. Can the legislative leadership or majority party create an efficient outcome by using an internal method of controlling the agenda?

2. Can the apportionment of duties and responsibilities among semi-autonomous standing committees and subcommittees produce economies of specialization and scale; that is, can increased efficiency arise from a topical division of legislative duties?

3. Can floor procedure be confined to productive decision-making?

4. Can the bicameral system be streamlined through innovative interchamber communications?

This essay deals explicitly with floor decision-making and interchamber communications, but the issue of leadership control raised in the first question must be taken into account to the extent that it may have an impact upon floor and interchamber activity.

The above questions seem to run contrary to Woodrow Wilson's argument in *Congressional Government* that the legislature should be an open forum of lengthy and thorough debate over the great issues. But as Alan Rosenthal and Rod Forth have illustrated, the state legislatures in modern times seem to be like "law production factories," with all the connotations of mass-production manufacturing. In a sense, the twentieth century has been a period of transition, from a time when legislative policy evolved in full forum heavily embedded in a tradition of oral argument, to the present practice of legislating through prepared written argument. Both arenas of debate are essential, but officeholders now have many other ways of attracting attention and promoting their popularity among constituents. This does not mean that debate and discussion are unimportant—only that they occur under more-controlled conditions and more often in committee than on the floor.

When considering the chamber floor procedures and interchamber communications that are adopted by legislators, it is important to keep in mind that legislators may have larger goals in mind. First, they have policy preferences and will wish to satisfy those preferences as much as possible. Second, they have a career perspective and may want to improve their career options, which can depend, in part, on their reputations as legislators. In other words, there is an obvious incentive for legislators to worry about the ability of the organization to process legislation, and it is clear that in many states the sheer volume of formal legislation makes the problem a serious one.

FLOOR OPERATIONS AND PROCEDURES IN THE STATES

The fifty state legislatures function within a common constitutional context, but they must carry out their work within extraordinarily diverse demographic settings. State populations vary from about a half million each in Alaska and Wyoming to almost thirty million in California. California has only eighty members in its house, whereas New Hampshire, with a population of only one million, boasts four hundred legislators in its lower chamber. In a small state, such as Rhode Island, legislators have a short drive to work, but in other states, such as Texas or Montana, legislators must travel great distances to the state capitol. States with rapidly increasing populations, such as Arizona and Florida, require major reapportionments of legislative seats. In other states, such as North Dakota and Nebraska, such changes are minor. These are but a few of the many differences in the work environment of legislators. Such differences should lead us to expect a variety of ways in which legislators have adapted.

In spite of these diversities, the states have all experienced an increase both in the size of state government and in the volume of demand for legislative action. The state legislatures have had a number of ways to respond that do not necessarily affect floor procedures. Almost all state legislatures have increased the amount of time they are in official session, by moving from biennial to annual sessions, by lengthening the session, or both. In addition, all states have had committee consolidation and reform, and in about two-thirds of the chambers, subcommittees have grown as the number of committees has declined. Finally, all states have had staff increases. These factors—more time in session, committee consolidation, and staff increases—can occur without affecting floor procedures one iota, however.

In current practice, the typical state legislature conducts its floor operations according to the appearance of bills in defined stages of completion and passage. These stages are characterized by whether the bills are up for first, second, or third reading. Normally, the first reading refers to the introduction of bills and signals their routine assignment to a standing committee. The second reading is held for bills that are reported out of committee to the floor through the appropriate chamber calendars. The second stage, which is marked by amendments and formal debate, is usually an important step. Party positions and differences are often made clear, and the extent to which the committee will get its way will be deter-

mined. In most states roll-call votes are not taken at this stage unless requested by one or more members. The presiding legislator normally will ask for a voice vote or show of hands to save time. The bills that are approved (and most are at this stage), with or without amendments, are then put into final form for the next stage.

At the third reading, or final-passage stage, bills are brought to the floor for a final up-or-down roll-call vote, but as in other stages, the procedure is not uniform across states. In about half of the chambers, amendments at third reading are allowed, and thus a number of amendment votes may occur prior to the vote on final passage. Not very many bills are defeated on the floor, for the committees and the calendar system are the primary screens for legislation. The time consumed on the floor after committee hearings will partly depend on the number of bills that the committees approve, the extent to which the committees have taken into account potential objections, and the degree to which debate is allowed by the rules.

While the above procedures are common to most chambers, the exceptions and modifications are numerous. Several chambers, for example, amend bills in the "committee of the whole," which is in essence a separate order of business. Arizona, Colorado, Idaho, Kansas, Minnesota, Montana, and Wyoming deal with legislation in this manner. By contrast, the Maine, South Dakota, and North Dakota legislatures do not have a third reading. Some state chambers allow amendments at any time beyond the first stage, such as in Nebraska, Colorado, or Iowa. In Oregon, however, amendments are allowed on the floor only by unanimous consent.

When each legislative chamber must prepare to act as a collective whole on all legislation reported out of committee, it is clear that floor procedures can be very time-consuming. Apart from processing legislation, floor time is also taken up by the introduction of resolutions, citations, and various ceremonious events that reflect the public nature of the institution. When time is scarce it is sensible and rational for legislative leaders and followers alike to press for more efficient floor behavior. Improvements have come mainly in three areas: 1) the introduction of computer-related technology; 2) the use of prefiling, work flow, and scheduling requirements; and 3) the implementation of procedures to improve the coordination between both houses.

Technology

One of the most timesaving steps has come with the advent of the electronic voting machine, now used in most state senates and in all but a few state houses. The lengthy call of the roll is avoided, and presiding officers do not need to worry as much about quickening the pace with voice or standing votes or other creative facsimiles for simplifying the counting. Most of the current electronic systems keep a running display of the total vote as it occurs, and a few of the systems offer an amendment display as well. Other conveniences that assist floor behavior include the computer printing of bills and the daily floor calendar, and the provision of television coverage outside the chamber. The entire technology package can have an impact on floor business by offering prompt and easy access to information.

The Flow of Legislative Work

While the implementation of computer technology perhaps receives the most publicity, a variety of "rule and procedure" innovations have been aimed at improving the flow of legislation. Those changes adopted most often by the state chambers are as follows:

1. Prefiling of bills. The filing of bills before the session convenes allows the legislative drafting office to "clean" (a check on legal grammar and correctness) and prepare the bills for formal consideration. Fewer technical problems are left to the session. In some states prefiling allows early interim-committee and staff preparation as well. Almost all states use prefiling.

2. Deadline for the introduction of bills. The deadline occurs during the session to prevent further floor time from being used up by bills that probably will not have time to follow the entire legislative route in any case. All but a few chambers have a deadline provision.

3. Prefiling of floor amendments. About 60 percent of the chambers require prefiling

of floor amendments. Usually this is by chamber rule, but often it is simply an adopted practice. Prefiling helps prevent confusion or even chaos on the floor.

4. Carryover bills from the first session. About half the chambers have adopted this procedure, which avoids the duplication of floor time on bills that are reintroduced.

5. Deadlines for committee and chamber action. Again, the purpose of these deadlines is in part to free up time for floor consideration of bills that have received early approval. About half the chambers have these deadlines.

6. Floor amendments confined to a single order of business. About three-fourths of the chambers attempt to confine amendments, usually to the second-reading stage, the committee of the whole, or possibly a third reading.

7. Committee bills. About two-fifths of the chambers allow standing committees to put forth a committee-sponsored bill, which often means that two or more related bills have been consolidated into one. Committee sponsorship also sends a positive signal to the rest of the chamber and such bills are perhaps less likely to elicit floor amendments.

8. Printed bill introduction. About one-third of the chambers do not introduce bills on the floor one by one. Instead, those chambers publish a list and approve the list with a simple motion, or they print the bills in the calendar, journal, or distribution sheet, whereupon the bills are considered introduced. The committee assignment is often printed as well.

A principal purpose of all of these innovations is to allow chamber floor procedures to maximize benefits while minimizing costs. The costs may be seen essentially as the time spent on the floor of the chamber during all orders of business. Members benefit by having their preferences legally confirmed in the passage of bills—almost all legislators have a bill agenda for which they seek passage. Because questions of quality of legislation are worked out at the committee and subcommittee stages, legislators will be impatient with a system that grinds to a halt in the chamber. The idea behind maximizing benefits is to have a system whereby floor proceedings focus upon the actual passage of legislation, including helpful amendments. The defeat of legislation is normally accomplished earlier in the process.

Logjams   One past concern of many legislative observers has been the seemingly inevitable logjam at the end of the annual session. A very high proportion of the bills that come to the floor for approval are scheduled to do so at the very end of the session. Consequently, many bills either do not come up for vote or are hastily considered. The most-thorough investigations of this subject have been completed by Harvey Tucker. As Tucker points out, logjams were seen as a major problem by the reform-minded Citizens Conference on State Legislatures (CCSL) as early as 1969. However, Tucker's investigation of thirty-seven states demonstrates that many of the recommended reforms, such as longer sessions, staff assistance, fiscal notes, or warning of budgetary impacts of bills, bill-introduction deadlines, and fewer committees, do not reduce logjams. There was some evidence, though, to suggest that bill prefiling and bill-carryover provisions do tend to reduce logjams.

Further inquiry reveals that the term *logjam* in many cases may be inaccurate or inappropriate. Many state legislatures have organized their work such that the latter part of the session is seen as the time when final actions are taken. This means that committee and amendment negotiations are completed earlier in the session, but that final actions on items requiring tax revenue or funding must wait until all estimates and requests are known. State legislative sessions like those in Texas, Florida, and many other states are designed to function in this manner. Bills can therefore be voted on very quickly because the necessary foundation is laid well before the end of the session. As a result a great proportion of these bills pass without difficulty. The logic is one of minimizing the amount of floor time early in the session to maximize available committee time (for example, attendance need not be required during the introduction of bills). Then, when bills are in their final stages, legislators are not burdened with "original" committee work. Only the budget-committee meetings, the conference-committee meetings, and possi-

bly committee meetings on bills sent over from the other chamber are necessary.

There is a third view on logjams that deserves further examination. John Pitney's study of the New York legislature suggests that what "editorials call sloppy timing is really a leadership ploy" (p. 495). Legislative leaders do not want to make a lot of concessions on bills until they have their own major agenda items under consideration by the chamber. The major item is usually the budget bill, or possibly a revenue-raising item. Persuasion works best when the leadership can withhold the pet legislation of pivotal members. When the calendars or rules committees are jammed with bills, the bills can serve as bargaining material. As Pitney suggests, "it takes a logjam to logroll."

Calendaring   All state legislatures utilize a calendaring process for bills reported out of committee. This system controls when bills will be admitted to the floor for consideration. A survey conducted by the American Society of Legislative Clerks and Secretaries (1988) reveals that there are three common ways to manage the main calendar of the legislative chamber: the bills are taken up in the order in which they are received, the presiding officer or other leader sets the order of business, or a rules or calendaring committee sets the schedule. About 40 percent of the chambers use the automatic first-in-first-up procedure, 25 percent leave it up to a presiding officer, and another 20 percent have a committee set the calendar. A number of other state chambers use a hybrid of the above, which allows the leadership to take special actions on important legislation. Others have a unique system, such as in New Hampshire, where bills are placed in alphabetical order according to committee names. North Dakota arranges the measures according to bill number assigned in order as bills are introduced. Almost all chambers have at least one additional calendar, often called a "consent" calendar, for separating out the many noncontroversial bills and resolutions that legislators inevitably introduce. This subset includes the many local bills that affect only the district(s) of the sponsors and resolutions, which can express the spirit and intention of the legislative body but which generally are of minor significance.

The calendar offers a way for the leadership to maintain control of the agenda, especially near the very end of the session when approval is needed on the major budget bills. The pet ideas and projects of many legislators may hinge on their support of the leadership agenda. The quid pro quo of mutual support can appear in many ways, but there are no guarantees. Conference committees can delete items in the budget and add others. The item veto in most states means that the governor can also cancel out the bargaining agreements reached earlier in the process. Nevertheless, from the point of view of the individual legislator, the first chamber is the major hurdle, and a place early in the calendar is crucial as the close of the session draws near. In some states, such as Florida, the rules committee is a prestigious assignment. Where it is appointed by the presiding officer, the supportive members are often considered the subleaders of the chamber, many of whom may chair or serve on another important committee, such as appropriations, or tax and finance.

In brief, while the expeditious processing of legislation is a major concern of floor management, political control of the outcomes can be the dominant factor in deciding what actually reaches the floor. Part of the so-called logjam is often the artifact of leadership preferences. Not all members can have what they want because there is not enough revenue, they have not shown sufficient cooperation on the leadership's pet legislation, or their preferences simply run contrary to those of the leadership. What is often palatable legislation in committee becomes indigestible later in the process, so that legislators often change their votes from committee to floor, even for unamended legislation. Some of this switching is caused by party or leadership needs, but where the rejection of a bill can be accomplished in the calendaring process, the floor vote does not need to occur.

Open Meetings, Information, and Debate
A discussion of new efficiencies and legislative calendars may give the impression that the legislative session is a highly managed experience. However, it is the floor of the chamber that most requires strict management, since every hour spent on floor business consumes an hour of time of each member. Quite possibly, mismanagement and confusion occur more often at the committee and subcommittee level, where dozens of subgroups may meet in overlapping and conflicting time slots. There are also many opportunities to engage in redundant work due to the overlapping subject-matter of committees and repetitive committee reviews of subcommittee decision-making. Still, the temptations to use up floor time are great. The floor of the chamber has always been open to the public and the news media. An articulate legislator can attract free coverage by becoming a visible actor and speaker on the issues. It is also a way of going on the record when it seems politically important for constituency support.

The "sunshine laws" opening up more legislative activity to public inspection have dramatically changed the tone of legislative business, however. All states now require public access to standing-committee meetings by rule, if not by statute. In an earlier period, committees had hearings, and then afterward met in closed executive sessions to discuss and vote on the legislative bills; now the meetings are open throughout. The interested public—mainly the press and interest-group leaders or supporters—are better informed by going to the committee meetings. These same interested participants then act as conveyors of information to the larger public. In a sense, the committees (or subcommittees, where appropriate) have become mini-legislatures—proposing and adopting amendments, hearing testimony, debating the pros and cons, and taking a public vote on the bills.

In 70 percent of state legislative chambers, when the members of the entire chamber receive the committee recommendations and reports, they also receive a copy of the amendments adopted in committee along with the committee recommendation. In about one-third of the chambers the total committee vote is included. Sixteen chambers also include the roll-call committee votes on the recommendations, on amendments, or both. In about half the chambers the majority-party caucus is fairly active; that is, it is active beyond the formal selection of chamber officers. One typical role for the active party caucus is to review the committee decisions and discuss the party position before legislation reaches the floor. In most of the states these strategic caucus meetings are closed. At this stage it is often decided, if the legislation is important, whether a partisan debate on the floor will take place. Partisanship shows up most often when the legislature meets in full forum, and one may presume that it is partly the intervention of the leadership or caucuses that stimulates partisan decisions. Whereas the committees are more task-oriented, the caucuses and leadership are more likely to consider overall political and ideological realities.

Interchamber Coordination and Conference Committees

Bicameral coordination is an important topic in all states except Nebraska (the only unicameral system among state legislatures). The main question that arises is one of redundancy. How do legislators in the two chambers avoid duplication of effort? The oldest formula requires a bill to begin in one house, and then if successful in clearing all of the hurdles, to be sent on to the second chamber for further processing. Original deliberations are held in each chamber in the interest of having full and diverse consideration. If the chambers disagree, the bill goes to conference committee, which contains appointed members of both chambers. The conference committee drafts a compromise bill that subsequently goes back to both chambers for approval. As wonderfully simple as this sounds, certain problems have developed.

First, with the avalanche of legislation inundating each session, it takes a very long time for legislation to traverse even one chamber. Many state houses and many senates now also have a subcommittee stage prior to committee hearings, and in addition, most state legislative sessions are relatively short. Second, if one chamber does not know what the other is doing, the chambers end up in endless conference committees. Alternatively, the legislation dies for lack of time to arrive at negotiated agreements.

In apparent response to the above dilemma, three innovations have gradually gained in popularity. First, as mentioned earlier, the carryover of bills from the first to the second session allows more time for coordina-

tion. Second, in about half the states companion bills, which are in effect the same bill, are introduced simultaneously into each chamber. No doubt this practice has occurred informally for a long time—legislators or lobbyists will surmise that the chance for passage might be greater if both chambers process a similar bill simultaneously. But explicit recognition of companion bills makes the coordination of committee chairs and the leadership much easier. Third, the use of the substitute-committee-bill provision, originally designed to allow committees to consolidate amendments and bills assigned to the same committee, has been expanded in some states by a rule that allows the companion bill of the other chamber to be substituted as the committee bill. This makes sense when the committee of the other chamber passed a bill that took into account the preferences of its sister committee. The use of companion bills and substitute provisions reduces the need for formal conference committees.

A small number of states seek bicameral coordination through the use of joint committees. Connecticut and Maine use standing joint committees exclusively, and Massachusetts uses them except for Ways and Means, Rules, and Ethics committees. Maryland and Rhode Island also use several joint committees. Another seven states utilize joint finance committees only (Arkansas, Colorado, Delaware, South Dakota, Utah, Wisconsin, and Wyoming). These joint committees apparently do not fulfill the role of a conference committee entirely. All of these states still use conference committees because they are normally small, with three to six members from each chamber. By contrast, standing joint committees are usually oversized, with twenty or more members.

A state-by-state tally of precisely how often conference committees are used is not available; clearly, practices vary widely. Delaware and New York are reported not to use them at all, while Minnesota uses more than 100 conference committees in each session. The Florida legislature typically uses a conference committee five or six times per session, even though it enacts more than five-hundred bills per session. Idaho employs conference committees perhaps once or twice per session. While the most common use appears to be for budget or appropriations negotiations, thirteen states reported that appropriations bills rarely or never go to conference.

Nevertheless, it may be said that where conference committees are employed, they are most likely to be employed for important legislation—legislation involving major policy decisions or the allocation of dollars. A large number of states have either open-meeting laws or chamber rules that apply to legislative committees. The conference committees are normally included under these requirements, although near the end of the session there is some flexibility in the amount of notice that must be given before the committee meets. Since conference committees are very small (usually three members from each chamber) yet face a potentially very large audience, there would seem to be a strong incentive to pre-negotiate. Very little is known about the preparation for conference committees, however.

A number of scholars have been interested in whether it is the senate or the house that "wins" in conference. On the surface this seems to be a trivial question since in all states the members from each chamber are elected from equally apportioned districts and there is not reason to assume that there are any consistent ideological differences distinguishing senators from representatives. So what is the point?

Gerald Strom and Barry Rundquist made this question more interesting by demonstrating for the U.S. Congress that the "second-acting" chamber seems to have the advantage. This was a theoretically more significant account of earlier observations that documented the ability of the U.S. Senate to win on a much higher percentage of the disagreements. Essentially, the first-acting chamber produces a bill that represents a compromise among the contending groups or factions, and the second-acting chamber, rather than make major or fundamental revisions, makes only marginal recommendations for change. The first chamber, unlikely to want the package undone, will tend to go along with most of the second-chamber demands. This produces the illusion that the second chamber wins more often, but in fact the first chamber is able to set the basic parameters of the legislation.

Confirmation of the empirically thin Strom and Rundquist explanation appeared in Donald Gross's 1980 study of appropriation bills of ten state legislatures. In four of the state legisla-

tures studied (Kansas, Minnesota, North Dakota, and Washington), the senate was not necessarily the second-acting chamber. In those states, the second-acting chamber on bills had a higher success rate than the upper chamber. The same pattern of upper-chamber and second-chamber dominance is illustrated in Thomas Lauth's ten-year study of thirty agencies and their appropriations. However, in the case of Georgia the governor has a strong role in the budget process. More often the conference-committee decision came out closer to the governor's request than to either the house or senate bills. Georgia is one of about twenty states in which the conference committee is not limited to the differences between the two chambers.

The above studies of conference decisions help highlight the importance of structure and procedure in the legislative process. However, conference committees must also be seen as an important political tool of the leadership since it is the presiding officer or majority leader who appoints the members to serve on these committees in all but three or four states. Usually three members are appointed from each chamber. By selecting particular legislators and excluding others, the leadership can influence the outcome of conference committee negotiations. The leadership may be very accommodating when making the original committee assignments at the beginning of the session, but conference committees are a different matter. The specific positions of legislators are made known in the regular meetings of the standing committees. With the help of the committee chair, the leadership from each chamber can select a cohesive group to go to conference. Legislators are aware of the implications of this influential tool, and in many chambers they have set down restrictive rules of appointment, as shown by these examples:

• Fifteen chambers require the chair of the standing committee to be a member.

• Twenty-eight chambers require at least one minority-party member.

• Twenty-four chambers require the bill sponsor or carrier to be a member.

• Sixteen chambers require a majority of appointees to be members who voted in favor of the bill.

When the chambers are controlled by different parties, as is often the case, the delegations sent by each chamber to conference are more likely to have severe disagreements. In a ten-state study of appropriations by Donald Gross, the level of interchamber disagreement in conference was found to be primarily the result of partisanship factors. The incentives can change, however, when the same party controls both chambers and the governor is of the other party. From a partisan perspective it then pays for the two chambers to cooperate in conference and to forge an agreement that is resistant to the success of gubernatorial vetoes. When the same party controls both chambers and the office of the governor, appointments to conference are not simplified by partisanship incentives. The differences in the policy preferences of the leadership may be less distinct and conference proceedings are more likely to reflect bargaining over very specific numbers on very specific items, or on whether minor items should be included in the package.

On broad omnibus legislation, usually involving a great number of items as well as the budget, it is not uncommon for members to anticipate compromises by including low-priority items or inflated dollar amounts. In addition, some items have been included to pacify potentially troublesome members or interest groups, but without much commitment to retain such items. In sum, one should not take at face value everything in the house or senate version of a bill. Thus, the uncertainties approaching conference decisions on major budget legislation are due not only to real disagreements, but also the varying degree of commitment by each house to the many items in its package.

In summary, floor procedures and interchamber communication are important parts of that primary puzzle that the legislators confront. Pressured by demands from all sides for official action on legislation, members across the country, bit by bit, have initiated new rules and new methods to utilize their time more efficiently and to prevent duplication of effort. The most scarce commodity is the real time of the legislator. This does not mean that legislators ignore rituals and public relations in promulgating their products. A promenade of events, the daily prayer, applause for classes of schoolchildren, and endless resolutions highlight the show. But to revise an old legislative pun, most of the work is for dough, not show.

BIBLIOGRAPHY

Reference Sources on Legislative Procedure
The following works report procedural information for all fifty state legislatures: COUNCIL OF STATE GOVERNMENTS, *The Book of the States, 1988–89* (Lexington, Ky., 1988, 2d ed. 1990), a biennial publication; TONY HUTCHISON and KATHY JAMES, *Legislative Budget Procedures in the 50 States: A Guide to Appropriation and Budget Processes.* (Denver, 1988); and REPORTS OF THE AMERICAN SOCIETY OF LEGISLATIVE CLERKS AND SECRETARIES, *Inside the Legislative Process.* (Denver: National Conference of State Legislatures).

An earlier influential study that focuses upon general procedural reform is CITIZENS CONFERENCE ON STATE LEGISLATURES, *The Sometimes Governments* (New York, 1971).

Committees and Floor Behavior
Several scholarly works analyze the relationship between committees and floor behavior. They include: WAYNE L. FRANCIS, *The Legislative Committee Game* (Columbus, 1989); KEITH E. HAMM, "Consistency Between Committee and Floor Voting in U.S. State Legislatures," *Legislative Studies Quarterly* 7 (1982): 473–490; RONALD D. HEDLUND and KEITH E. HAMM, "Institutional Innovation and Performance Effectiveness in Public Policy Making," in LEROY RIESELBACH, ed., *Legislative Reform: The Policy Impact* (Lexington, Mass., 1978), pp. 117–132; and RONALD D. HEDLUND and PATRICIA K. FREEMAN, "A Strategy for Measuring the Performance of Legislatures in Processing Decisions," *Legislative Studies Quarterly* 6 (1981): 87–113. The earliest

work criticizing the interference of committees with floor action is WOODROW WILSON, *Congressional Government* (Boston, 1885).

Conference Committees

Conference committees of state legislatures and Congress are evaluated in DONALD A. GROSS, "House-Senate Conference Committees: A Comparative State Perspective," *American Journal of Political Science* 24 (1980): 767–778; DONALD A. GROSS, "Conference Committees and Levels of Interchamber Disagreement: A Comparative State Perspective," *State and Local Government Review* 15 (1983): 130–133; THOMAS P. LAUTH, "The Governor and the Conference Committee in Georgia," *Legislative Studies Quarterly* 15 (1990): 441–453; PATRICK J. McCORMACK, "The Third House: The Role of Conference Committees in the Minnesota Legislature," (manuscript); GERALD S. STROM and BARRY S. RUNQUIST, "A Revised Theory of Win-

ning in House-Senate Conferences," *American Political Science Review* 71 (1977): 448–453; and DAVID J. VOGLER, "Patterns of One House Dominance in Congressional Conference Committees," *Midwest Journal of Political Science* 14 (1970): 303–320.

Bill Processing

For a study of the increase in bill processing and the phenomenon of logjams, see ALAN ROSENTHAL and ROD FORTH, "The Assembly Line: Law Production in the American States," *Legislative Studies Quarterly* 3 (1978): 265–291; JOHN J. PITNEY, JR., "Leaders and Rules in the New York State Senate," *Legislative Studies Quarterly* 7 (1982): 491–506; HARVEY J. TUCKER, "Legislative Workload Congestion in Texas," *Journal of Politics* 49 (1987): 565–580; and HARVEY J. TUCKER, "Legislative Logjams: A Comparative State Analysis," *Western Political Quarterly* 38 (1985): 432–446.

SEE ALSO Committees in State Legislatures.

THE CONGRESSIONAL BUDGET PROCESS

Walter Oleszek

Operation Deficit Storm, said Congressman Howard Coble (R.-N.C.) to his House colleagues on 14 March 1991, is what the Congress and country must focus on in the aftermath of Operation Desert Storm, the military operation in the Persian Gulf. Coble's comments refer to the huge escalation of the nation's debt. When the 1980s began, the federal government's national debt (the accumulation of each year's annual deficit) was a little less than $1 trillion. In 1991 it was estimated at $3.6 trillion—and growing—with the annual deficit for that year at about $300 billion. In short, the national government was awash in red ink. This flood tide of deficits occurred despite several consecutive years of record-breaking economic expansion.

The reasons for the deficits are complex and produce heated debates about "good debt" (for investment) and "bad debt" (for consumption). Analysts differ as to the causes and consequences of deficits and how a better balance can be achieved between revenues and expenditures. With a 1991 budget in excess of $1.4 trillion, citizens could rightly wonder why the budget and political processes regularly produce expenditures far in excess of the amount collected in taxes.

Many lawmakers recognize that the shortfall between revenues and expenditures is a fundamental national challenge. They perceive deficit control as essential to the nation's economic well-being. Yet, as of the early 1990s, Congress's budget-writing processes were unable to break the intractable deficit problem.

Political factors account for part of that intractability. Citizens want more government benefits than they are willing to pay for. They also believe that the government wastes taxpayers' dollars; voters seem more fearful of actions to cut the deficit than the deficit itself. No wonder lawmakers are reluctant to propose spending reductions or tax hikes.

A sluggish economy also contributes to the deficit. Absent economic growth rates of the post–World War II period (about 4 percent then to about 2 percent in 1992) and the relative decline of productivity, there are fewer financial resources flowing into the Treasury. There is no economic "fiscal dividend" to finance existing governmental programs adequately or to expand or establish new programs. Lawmakers often engage in cutback budgeting rather than the earlier and less conflict-laden incremental approach, whereby agencies and programs received modest increments in additional funding each year.

Procedural considerations, too, have a hand in large and persistent deficits. Rudolph Penner, former director of the Congressional Budget Office, stated in 1990 testimony before the House Budget Committee that Congress's budgetary procedures seemed chaotic in the late nineteenth and early twentieth centuries, but they produced good results. "Now we have a process that looks very elegant on paper," he said, "but it is leading to very dishonest and disorderly results." To achieve program cuts or meet deficit-reduction targets, lawmakers promote illusory spending reductions or employ devices that only appear to save money.

The national budget of the United States reflects numerous decisions made by Congress. It is a document of immense economic and political importance. The budget defines national priorities, the size and scope of federal activities, and future fiscal commitments. This essay, then, will focus on Congress's power of the purse by examining the legislature's contemporary budgeting system. More specifically, it will review legislative budgeting prior to passage of the landmark Congressional Budget and Impoundment Control Act of 1974. Then it will examine the 1974 act and how it altered Congress's fiscal landscape. The essay will then assess the escalation of annual deficits during the 1980s and Congress's response to them: the enactment in 1985 and 1987 of deficit-reduction plans informally called Gramm-Rudman-Hollings (after the sponsoring three senators) and the Budget Enforcement Act of 1990.

EVOLUTION OF CONGRESSIONAL BUDGETING

The development of legislative budgeting underscores Congress's responsiveness to internal pressures and external challenges. Internally, pressures typically emanate from rivalries among taxing, authorizing, and spending committees and lawmakers' frustrations with fiscal procedures. Externally, the challenges stem mainly from two quarters: the huge costs and economic difficulties associated with wars and presidential attempts to assert tighter control over fiscal affairs. Either or both of these forces have triggered changes in Congress's fiscal operations. This section discusses the character of early budgeting, the formation of the appropriations committees, and the establishment of an executive budget. Next follows a look at the fundamental features of the authorization-appropriations process.

Pre–Civil War Period

The framers of the U.S. Constitution granted the "power of the purse" to Congress. Under Article I, Section 7, the so-called origination clause, "all Bills for raising Revenue shall originate in the House of Representatives; but the Senate may propose or concur with Amendments as on other bills." The framers granted this exclusive right to the House because it was then the only chamber directly elected by the people. With two-year terms, representatives could be held accountable rather quickly at the polls for their revenue-raising decisions. Senators, with their six-year terms, were indirectly elected until the ratification of the Seventeenth Amendment in 1913.

Other constitutional provisions authorize Congress to lay and collect duties, imposts, and excises; to borrow money on the credit of the United States; and to coin money. Article I, Section 9, provides that "no Money shall be drawn from the Treasury, but in consequence

of Appropriations made by Law." (By custom, the House also initiates general appropriation bills.) Given the constitutional separation-of-powers system, replete with its checks and balances, national budget-making from the beginning involved both Congress and the White House.

President George Washington's Treasury secretary, Alexander Hamilton, was directed by Congress to provide it with estimates of how much money should be appropriated to run the government. The bicentennial history of the House tax-writing committee states,

> The House worked closely with Hamilton to prepare annual estimates of revenue and expenditure, the closest equivalent then to an annual federal budget. Each year the executive officers submitted estimates to Congress of recommended sums needed to operate their departments. The House then considered these estimates, submitted in the form of a letter to the Speaker, and either approved the figures or sent them back to the executive department for revision. Upon approval by a Committee of the Whole House, the estimates were referred to a House select drafting committee to prepare an appropriations bill that required the approval of both Houses of Congress and the signature of the President to become law.

Neither chamber during those early days had a system of permanent committees; each functioned with select or temporary, ad hoc panels.

Lawmakers soon began to criticize government departments' closeness to Hamilton and the executive branch. Their drumbeat of criticism contributed to Hamilton's resignation in 1795 as Treasury secretary. It was also in that year that the House created a tax-writing committee, which became a standing committee in 1802; the Senate created a Finance committee in 1816. Thereafter, the history of legislative budgeting is largely the history of the House Ways and Means Committee and the Senate Finance Committee. These two panels made recommendations for both revenues and appropriations. They recommended, in short, the ways to raise money and the means to spend it.

Several features of this early period seem gone forever. Congress had adequate funds, derived from custom revenues, to finance the modest needs of the national government. The consolidation of revenue and spending decisions in the tax committees permitted centralized control of legislative budgeting, but the Civil War would later force Congress to change.

Establishment of the Appropriations Committees

Extraordinary circumstances beget extraordinary actions. President Abraham Lincoln pushed executive power during the Civil War to its farthest reaches. In 1865, annual federal expenditures passed the billion-dollar mark for the first time ever. The need for money to finance the war prompted Congress to expand its revenue-raising devices, including the unprecedented imposition of an income tax (later repealed). And the House created two new committees, Appropriations and Banking, by reducing the jurisdiction of the Ways and Means Committee. Work load was a prime factor in the change. "No set of men," said Representative Schuyler Cox (D.-Ohio) on 2 March 1865 to his colleagues, "however enduring their patience, studious their habits, or gigantic their mental grasp, when overburdened with the labor incident to the existing monetary condition of the country growing out of this unparalleled civil strife, can do this labor as well as the people have a right to expect of their Representatives."

A few lawmakers opposed the jurisdictional split on the ground that it was imperative for financial authority to be centralized in one committee. Cox replied to these concerns by suggesting that Appropriations and Ways and Means would informally consult each other to ensure that revenue estimates matched estimates of government expenditures. He added that either Ways and Means or Appropriations "will be a veto on the other; and something of economy may be gained, and something of extravagance restrained." Two years later, the Senate followed the House's traditional lead on money issues by establishing a new Appropriations Committee. "The purpose," said Senator Henry Anthony (R.-R.I.) on 6 March 1867, "is to divide the onerous labors of the Finance Committee with another committee."

During the next two decades, the House and Senate Appropriations Committees assumed great influence over policy and fiscal matters. Lawmakers complained that the Appropriations Committees exercised their role as "watchdogs of the Treasury" too stringently. "It is not economy to take an estimate of $20,000,000, sent in by one of the Departments," said Congressman Charles Lore (D.-Del.) on 17 December 1885, "and pare it down $5,000,000, without any regard to the necessities of our Government." Lawmakers were also angry with the Appropriations Committees because those panels often added "riders" (extraneous policy provisions) to their bills, thereby undercutting the prerogatives of the other standing committees.

Antipathy toward the Appropriations Committees mounted. The House took the lead by adopting a series of rule changes that stripped the Appropriations Committee of its right to appropriate for different areas (agriculture, rivers and harbors, and consular and diplomatic matters, for instance). These topics were assigned to other standing committees with substantive jurisdiction for these issues. (Centralized control of appropriation bills was also sundered in the Senate at about the same time.) By the mid-1880s, authority to report appropriation bills was spread among eight different House panels. This "scatteration" weakened (as had the tax panel division twenty years earlier) Congress's facility for fiscal integration.

The Executive Budget

Legislators and presidents in subsequent decades became concerned about who was in control of public finances. Committees and commissions were created to recommend ways to bring coherency to a diffuse budgetary process. Things had simply gotten too complex and confusing in Congress and in the executive branch under a financial system that permitted department officials to submit their individual budget requests to numerous House and Senate committees without paying heed to what others were seeking. The 1919 report of the House Select Budget Committee notes,

> Practically everyone familiar with [the] workings [of executive-branch budgeting] agrees that its failure lies in the fact that no one is made responsible for the extravagance [of agency requests]. The estimates are a patchwork and not a structure. As a result, a great deal of the time of the committees of Congress is taken up in exploding the visionary schemes of bureau chiefs for which no admin-

istration would be willing to stand responsible. (H. Rept. 362, 66th Cong., 1st sess., p. 4)

World War I precipitated action on budget reform. Before the war, yearly federal spending was about $700 million. By 1918, federal expenditures exceeded $12 billion, with the national debt at more than $25 billion, compared to about $1 billion in 1916. Numbers of this magnitude focused the attention of national officeholders on fiscal change. The result was that in 1921, Congress passed the Budget and Accounting Act. This act represented a joint effort by Congress and the president to establish a comprehensive and coordinated national-budget preparation process. It also directed the president to prepare an annual national budget for submission to Congress, established the Bureau of the Budget (now the Office of Management and Budget) to assist the president in determining the revenue and expenditure needs of the government, and provided for an independent audit of government accounts by a new agency responsible to Congress, the General Accounting Office (GAO). Concomitant with these fiscal developments, the House in 1920 and the Senate in 1922 reconsolidated jurisdiction for all appropriation bills in their respective Appropriations committees.

Congress tried after World War II to draft a legislative budget of its own, but the effort failed, as did its experiment in 1950 with a consolidated appropriations bill (bundling twelve separate spending measures into one package). Interchamber, interparty, and intercommittee conflicts, among other factors, contributed to the demise of these initiatives. Lawmakers, it seemed, preferred to continue with the traditional authorization-appropriations process.

THE AUTHORIZATION-APPROPRIATIONS PROCESS

Fundamental to the congressional budget process is the distinction between authorizations and appropriations. This two-step, sequential procedure is intended to work as follows: Congress first passes an authorization bill that establishes or continues an agency or program and provides it with the legal authority to operate. Authorization legislation may also include recommended funding levels for programs. These bills are approved by the House and Senate and submitted to the president for his signature or veto. Before any money can be withdrawn from the Treasury, however, a separate appropriations law must be enacted. Actual funds, in short, are provided to agencies and programs by the appropriations statute; authorizations are somewhat akin to fishing licenses, the fish in this case being appropriations.

In practice it is hard to keep the two stages distinct. There are authorization bills that carry appropriations, and appropriation bills that contain authorizations (policy topics); and the order of their enactment may be reversed. Furthermore, either chamber may choose to ignore or circumvent this sequence of action.

Much of Congress's internal organization reflects the authorization-appropriation distinction. Each chamber has legislative, or authorizing, committees (Agriculture, Armed Services, Commerce, and so on), with responsibilities different from those of the House and Senate Appropriations Committees. Authorizing committees function as Congress's policy experts. They propose solutions to public problems and recommend levels of funding to resolve those problems.

The two Appropriations Committees and their thirteen virtually autonomous subcommittees have the responsibility to specify how much federal agencies and programs ought to receive in relation to available fiscal resources and economic conditions. The funding options of these spending panels are three: they can provide all the monies recommended in the authorization bills, propose reductions in the amounts authorized, or refuse to provide any funds. Worth noting is that less than half of all annual federal spending is subject to the authorization-appropriations process. The other spending occurs under laws, such as those concerning Medicare, that permit funds to be expended automatically to all eligible parties.

Budget Authority and Budget Outlays

Appropriation laws provide "budget authority" to executive entities; this means that an agency or department has the legal right to incur fiscal obligations, which the Department of the Treasury is required to pay for by check, cash, or electronic fund transfer. When Treasury issues the check to meet a financial commitment, this is called an "outlay." Budget outlays, then, are the actual expenditures made in any fiscal year (an accounting period that runs from 1 October to 30 September); budget authority is authority granted agencies to enter into obligations, such as contracts for the purchase of goods and services, that are subsequently liquidated, sometimes over the course of several years, through the disbursement of funds. House Armed Services chairman Les Aspin (D.-Wis.) explained the distinction on 2 November 1987 in floor remarks to his House colleagues:

> Budget authority is permission to spend; outlays are actual spending. . . . Congress appropriates all the budget authority needed to complete a weapon in advance, regardless of how long it will take to spend. To give an example, suppose the Department of Defense asks for $100 million to build a ship. The Navy will spend this money over the several years it takes to build the ship. . . . Congress will appropriate $100 million of budget authority for the ship this year. Outlays this year will be much less, on average only $6 million for ships. Next year outlays will be $20 million; the year after, $25 million; and so on. While budget authority is spent only slowly in shipbuilding, it is spent quickly in the military personnel accounts. For every $100 million in military personnel budget authority, $98 million is spent the first year.

Budget authority is a good predictor of an agency's growth or decline in fiscal resources. Outlays are important in determining the annual deficit. Lawmakers are sensitive to the outlay implications of budget-authority accounts (personnel, procurement, and research and development, for instance) and may even shift budget authority from accounts that expend money quickly to others with a slower "spend out" rate in order to keep deficits down for a specific fiscal year.

Origins

The authorization-appropriation dichotomy is not required by the Constitution. Rather, it is a process that is required by the rules of the House and Senate and, in a few cases, by statute. Of the two steps, the appropriations stage is on firmer legal ground because it is rooted in the Constitution. An appropriations bill may be approved even if the authorization has not been enacted.

Informally, Congress employed this division of labor from its beginning, as did the British Parliament and various colonial legislatures. Senator William Plumber (Fed.-N.H.) wrote in his 1806 diary, "Tis a good provision in the constitution of Maryland that prohibits their Legislature from adding anything to an appropriation law." Called "supply bills" in early Congresses, appropriation measures had a narrow purpose—to provide specific sums of money for fixed periods and stated objectives. These bills were not, by custom, to contain substantive policy proposals.

The conventional explanation for having two stages is that it provides a double check on the expenditure of funds. Moreover, it gives virtually every committee and lawmaker an opportunity to share in Congress's power of the purse. The historical explanation involves the need to combat the practice of adding riders or extraneous policy matter (a perennial complaint) to appropriation bills. This practice mushroomed in the 1830s and delayed enactment of the supply bills. "By 1835," wrote the scholar and lawmaker Robert Luce in his study of legislative problems, "delays caused by injecting legislation [extraneous policy riders] into these [appropriations] bills had become serious, and John Quincy Adams . . . suggested that they be stripped of everything save appropriations" (pp. 425–426). Two years later the House adopted a rule requiring authorizations to precede appropriations. The Senate later followed suit.

Bicameral Distinctions

The House and Senate have authorization-appropriation rules, but their operation in each chamber varies considerably. This variability reflects basic institutional differences: the smaller Senate operates more informally than the larger House. Unauthorized appropriations, for example, are technically not permitted in either chamber. However, the Senate permits such an array of exceptions to this general rule—the Appropriations Committee may even report authorizations—as to dilute the formal requirement. The Senate prohibits legislation (policy matter) in an appropriations bill unless it is germane to the House-passed bill. The

Senate's broad interpretative standards enable many issues to be defended as germane to House-passed measures.

Wide opportunities exist to consider unauthorized appropriations or to include legislation in an appropriations bill. Even the stricter House provides exceptions to its rules. Formally, the House forbids legislation in any general appropriations bill but explicitly permits such policy-making if it is a retrenchment (reduction) and if it is "germane to the subject matter of the bill." The purpose of this rule, which originated in 1876, is to encourage economy in government. Informally, lawmakers may offer "limitation" riders. Limitations are based on precedents that allow the House to restrict or limit the use of funds for any part of a program or activity. Always phrased negatively, limitations make policy, with abortion being a classic example: "None of the funds appropriated by this Act shall be used to pay for abortions or to promote or encourage abortions."

The double check inherent in the authorization-appropriations process informally reinforces the duality of the bicameral Congress. Traditionally, the House, on the recommendation of its Appropriations Committee, will agree to spending cuts from levels proposed in authorization bills or the president's budget. The Senate Appropriations Committee may then function as a court of appeals, hearing requests from agency officials to restore funds slashed by the House. (Agency "justification books," which contain detailed spending information, are provided to the Appropriations Committees in advance of the formal hearings on departmental spending requests.)

Types of Appropriations and Authorizations

When Congress enacts individual authorization or appropriation bills, it typically specifies the length of time (annual, multiyear, or permanent) that the legislation will remain in effect. Appropriation laws, unless otherwise noted, are enacted for only one fiscal year. (To be sure, annual appropriations enhance the political-policy clout of the two Appropriations Committees.) These annual enactments are called general, or regular, appropriations. Should Congress fail to enact one or more of the thirteen general appropriation bills that fund the three branches of government by the start of a fiscal year, it will enact continuing appropriations (also called continuing resolutions, or CRs) to provide stopgap funding for agencies. The budget submitted to Congress each year by the president represents his request for annual appropriations to fund the government and administration priorities.

The president may also ask Congress to provide additional funds to those specified in general appropriation bills to meet unexpected, unforeseen, or emergency contingencies or to fund high-priority items. These are called "supplemental appropriations." Sometimes these measures are titled "urgent," "emergency," or even "dire-emergency" supplementals. Supplemental authorizations commonly precede the enactment of supplemental appropriations. For example, in March 1991, Congress first passed legislation authorizing appropriations for Operation Desert Storm and then enacted a bill making dire-emergency supplemental appropriations to cover certain costs associated with the Persian Gulf conflict.

Multiyear appropriations make budget authority available to an agency for two or more fiscal years. There are very few multiyear appropriations. (Sometimes Congress enacts a "no-year" appropriation, which permits budget authority to remain available to an agency until it has been obligated.) Permanent appropriations, despite this appellation, are reported by the authorizing, not appropriating, committees. They provide funds automatically to various programs, such as Social Security, under laws enacted years or, in the case of Social Security, even decades earlier by the legislative branch. Today, permanent appropriations constitute the fastest growth area in federal expenditures and are the principal reason why the two Appropriations Committees, as noted earlier, have control over less than half of each year's new budget authority.

Authorizations, too, are assigned different durations. Until the 1950s, most federal programs and agencies were permanently authorized. The standard phraseology was, "There are authorized to be appropriated such sums as may be necessary to carry out this act." Permanent authorizations, which remain in effect until changed by Congress, provide continuing statutory authority for the operation of federal agencies; however, up through World War II, to get the money (budget authority) to carry out their legal mandates, agencies had to go before the appropriating committees and request funding. Needless to say, their control of the purse strings gave the appropriating committees more control over agency activities than that exercised by the authorizing committees. This situation began to change after World War II when the authorizing committees won enactment of laws that converted most permanent authorizations into annual or short-term authorizations and recommended dollar limits.

Several factors influenced the shift to short-term authorizations, but two are fundamental. First, the authorizing committees wanted to exercise greater control and oversight of executive activities. Senator Daniel Inouye (D.-Hawaii) explained on 27 April 1987 to his Senate colleagues, "Before 1981, the [Federal Communications Commission] had a [permanent] authorization. The Congress initiated a biennial authorization so that it could better oversee the many significant actions of the Commission." Second, annual and short-term authorizations put pressure on the appropriating panels to fund programs at levels recommended by the authorizing committees. If the two-stage process is being followed, an authorization may be enacted only a few weeks before Congress takes up the companion appropriation bill. The result is that the authorization will exert a direct influence on the amount recommended in the appropriations bill.

Needless to say, the authorization-appropriations procedure is a source of continuing intercommittee conflict. Predictably, the authorizing committees generally support high levels of spending for the programs and agencies under their jurisdiction. The appropriating panels generally believe that part of their job is to curtail or say no to some funding requests. Turf fights often erupt over such issues as unauthorized appropriations or legislation in appropriation bills. "You all on the Appropriations Committee are not a college of cardinals around here," declared a House member on 9 August 1988 in raising the "trespass" charge. Although cooperation is also a pervasive theme in the relationships between committees, intercommittee conflicts were among the factors that weakened Congress's budgetary controls and prompted the mid-1970s reorganization of its fiscal procedures.

PRELUDE TO CHANGE

Congress excels at sharing power among committees and members. That is its special institutional strength, for it permits broad participation in decision-making, multiple points of access to the legislative process, and consideration of competing viewpoints. Congress's excessive fragmentation in budget matters, however, was one of the significant criticisms of the pre-1974 period.

Excessive Fragmentation

The thirteen Appropriations subcommittees each proposed spending decisions independently of actions by the others. The tax committees considered revenues independently of the spending recommendations of the appropriating committees. Congress funded programs without adding up their total cost. No specific group or committee had responsibility for calculating the overall effect of individual tax or spending decisions on the national economy or to relate expenditures to revenues. Significantly, Congress approved "backdoor spending" techniques (the "frontdoor" route is the authorization-appropriations process), which bypassed the appropriations stage, weakened controls on budgeting, and escalated federal expenditures.

To sidestep the Appropriations Committees, the authorizing committees devised a variety of funding devices that gave agencies the right to obligate government funds without the necessity of an appropriation. Opponents of back doors suggested that these devices violated the constitutional mandate that money cannot be withdrawn from the Treasury except "in consequence of appropriations made by law." Senator Hubert Humphrey (D.-Minn.) rebutted this charge on 1 July 1959 when he told his Senate colleagues,

> It so happens that the two words "by law" have been somewhat excluded from this debate. The language does not say "appropriations made by Appropriations Acts." It does not say "appropriations made through the process of the Committee on Appropriations." It says "ap-

propriations made by law." For 75 years the country operated without an appropriations committee.... Money was appropriated by law.

The authorizing panels designed three main types of back doors to circumvent the anti-spending proclivities of the appropriating panels: borrowing authority, contract authority, and entitlements.

Borrowing authority provides legal authority to agencies via an authorization to borrow a specific amount of money from the Treasury to carry out specified objectives. Initiated in 1932, it has been used to finance farm price supports, student loans, and low-cost public housing. Between 1932 and 1975, Congress authorized agencies to borrow more than $160 billion from the Treasury.

Congress also authorized billions of dollars in contract authority. Under this arrangement, agencies are statutorily permitted to enter into contractual agreements (a dollar limit is provided in the law) with private firms to meet public commitments. The Appropriations Committees are involved after the fact in providing the funds required to liquidate the contracts. For example, the 1972 Water Pollution Control Act authorized $18 billion in contract authority for the 1973, 1974, and 1975 fiscal years. That act involved federal, state, and local governments in a massive program of sewage-treatment plant construction. The following year, Congress appropriated $600 million to liquidate some of the contractual obligations incurred under the 1972 act.

Entitlements, however, are the real force behind the escalation of federal spending. One of the fastest-growing parts of the budget, these statutes stipulate that eligible beneficiaries are "entitled" to receive payments from the government based on benefit levels established by law. Social Security and Medicare are the largest entitlement programs; others include Medicaid, veterans' pensions, and federal retirement programs. Entitlements are judicially enforceable by anyone who meets the eligibility criteria—age, income, and so on—and the government must spend whatever is necessary for all who qualify for the benefits.

Approximately half of the federal budget is for entitlements or transfer payments to individuals. Unlike defense or domestic discretionary programs for which the Appropriations Committees recommend annual amounts and on which all lawmakers may vote, entitlement spending occurs automatically under the terms outlined in the statute. There are some "appropriated entitlements," which means that budget authority is provided in annual appropriation acts rather than authorizations. Efforts are under way to move toward "means-testing" (establishing an income-eligibility level for the receipt of benefits) most entitlement programs in order to curb their costs. However, some officials argue that means-testing could erode national support for entitlements by transforming them into welfare programs.

The surge in entitlement spending began during the Great Society era under President Lyndon Johnson. Prior to that time, most federal funds were spent on government operations (personnel costs, travel, supplies, equipment, and so on). As Allen Schick declaimed in discussing the national government's capacity to budget, federal "spending is predominantly in the form of transfers to 'third' parties," especially entitlement recipients. The size and scope of the transfer payments, according to Schick, "recast the main domestic role of the government from a provider of public services into a stabilizer and redistributor of private incomes" (p. 18).

In short, the backdoor devices weakened Congress's capacity to control federal spending. Government spending was on "automatic pilot" and "uncontrollable" because of laws previously enacted by Congress. Uncontrollables include entitlements, interest on the national debt, and contract obligations. While Congress could change these laws, that could be electorally perilous. Entitlement beneficiaries, especially the elderly, constitute potent voting blocs.

Presidential Impoundments

During the 1966–1973 period, government spending outpaced revenue increases to fund the Vietnam War and Great Society programs. Mounting deficits, weak economic performance, and bitter conflict over the war combined to foster interbranch struggles for control of the purse strings. President Richard Nixon, in particular, clashed with Congress over spending priorities and frequently impounded (refused to spend) monies appropriated by Congress.

THE CONGRESSIONAL BUDGET PROCESS

Since Thomas Jefferson's time, presidents had impounded funds to effect program savings or to meet contingencies. Nixon, however, aggressively impounded to thwart the Democratically controlled Congress's policy objectives. Legislative-executive conflict was exacerbated by Nixon's charges during the 1972 presidential campaign that Congress was fiscally irresponsible and disorganized. As he told the citizenry on October 8 in a nationwide radio broadcast:

> But, let's face it, the Congress suffers from institutional faults when it comes to Federal spending.... Both the President and a family must consider total income and total out-go when they take a look at some new item which would involve spending additional money.... In the Congress, however, it is vastly different. Congress not only does not consider the total financial picture when it votes on a particular spending bill, it does not even contain a mechanism to do so if it wished.

Despite the partisan rhetoric and interbranch clashes over impoundments and spending limitations, lawmakers by this time recognized that their budgetary system required renovation. In October 1972, Congress created a Joint Study Committee on Budget Control to recommend improvements; this panel's report was revamped by appropriate House and Senate committees and then enacted into law as the Congressional Budget and Impoundment Control Act of 1974. This act did not fundamentally restructure the budget system. Such an effort would have produced struggles among the most powerful lawmakers and thereby jeopardize passage of any budgetary reorganization. Instead, the 1974 act added a new budget-resolution process on top of the old authorization-appropriations process. The goal was to join legislative fragmentation with budgetary integration and thus strengthen Congress's power of the purse.

THE CONGRESSIONAL BUDGET ACT OF 1974

The 1974 Budget and Impoundment Control Act made major institutional and procedural changes in Congress. Institutionally, the act created three new entities: the House Budget Committee, the Senate Budget Committee, and the Congressional Budget Office (CBO). The major function of the budget panels is to craft a concurrent budget resolution that addresses the federal budget as a whole and its effect on the economy. Broken into two main parts, the budget resolution (1) establishes budget totals (revenue, new budget authority, outlays, surplus or deficit, and public debt) for the fiscal year and then (2) divides all spending into twenty-one functional categories (defense, health, and so on). An objective of these features is to encourage Congress to make explicit trade-offs among different categories of spending.

The House and Senate Budget committees are constituted differently. The House panel is required to have a rotating membership. Representatives, with some exceptions, may not serve more than six years during the same decade. Further, the committee is composed of lawmakers drawn from the other standing committees (five each from Appropriations and Ways and Means and around thirty from the various authorizing panels), including a nonrotating leadership member from each party. By contrast, the Senate Budget Committee has no restriction on tenure, nor are its twenty-one members required under the 1974 act to come from other designated committees. A consequence of the membership difference is that the permanently assigned senators have greater opportunity to acquire in-depth understanding of budgetary matters than their short-term House counterparts and, therefore, are better equipped to shape conference-committee deliberations to their chamber's liking.

The third entity, the CBO, functions to provide budgetary, economic, and policy analysis in support of Congress's budgetary system. For example, it provides five-year budget and economic projections and identifies spending and revenue options for deficit reduction. Important, too, is its scorekeeping and baseline budget projections. "Scorekeeping" refers to monitoring the revenue and spending actions of the House and Senate by calculating the cost estimates of tax and entitlement legislation. (Scorekeeping aroused controversy in 1991. The House wanted the CBO to score its tax and entitlement bills, despite the requirement of the 1990 Budget Enforcement Act granting this function to the OMB. The House did not trust the OMB to make "unpolitical" estimates as to whether a proposed program expansion would cost relatively little or would be so expensive as to require tax hikes or cost offsets in other programs.) "Baselines" provide the Budget Committees with a benchmark against which they can measure changes in tax and spending laws. Generally, it means last year's spending plus inflation. Members often discuss projected government spending as above or below the baseline.

Procedurally, the 1974 act established a timetable for budgetary action. Committees, for example, are to submit by a certain date their "views and estimates" of the funding needed for programs under their jurisdiction to the House or Senate Budget Committee. This information assists the budget panels in drafting the concurrent budget resolution. The act stipulated other deadlines (timetables for the reporting of authorizations to prevent delays in considering appropriations, for instance), but Congress seldom meets these target dates. However, until Congress adopts its budget resolution for a fiscal year, it may not take up any spending, revenue, entitlement, or debt legislation affecting that year unless this prohibition is waived both by the House and Senate.

The 1974 act also tightened controls over the backdoor spending devices (largely by subjecting them to review by the Appropriations Committees) and defined two types of impoundments, rescissions and deferrals. "Rescissions" occur when the president chooses to rescind funding for programs, explaining the reasons in a special message to Congress. Unless both the House and Senate enact legislation approving the rescission within forty-five days of the message's receipt, the president must spend the appropriated funds. Inaction ensures the spending. The "deferral" (a temporary delay in the expenditure of funds) procedure, as originally stated, was that either chamber could overturn delays in spending by passing a resolution of disapproval. In 1983 this one-house veto was declared unconstitutional by the Supreme Court. Subsequent federal court decisions distinguished between policy deferrals (which negate Congress's will) and programmatic deferrals (which achieve budgetary savings). Presidents may propose the latter but not the former; Congress may overturn deferrals by passing a law, which the president may veto.

Originally, the 1974 act contemplated the enactment of two budget resolutions, one in

the spring and one in the fall. (Concurrent budget resolutions are not subject to presidential veto.) The latter resolution was soon dropped for two reasons: lack of time and the recognition that the first resolution sets the fiscal framework for Congress. In effect, the country now has two national budgets: a presidential budget and a congressional budget. With multiple budgets came difficulties for the public and press in holding either branch accountable for the federal budget.

With passage of the budget resolution, each House and Senate committee with jurisdiction over the twenty-one functional categories is allocated a "bank account" by the Budget Committees. Then, the committees subdivide their spending allocation among their subcommittees. Panels are expected to stay within their financial allocation or face parliamentary objections on the House or Senate floor. As the "top-down" shapers and monitors of fiscal policy, the Budget Committees gradually gained centralized direction over tax and spending issues. Party leaders, too, became heavily engaged in influencing budget resolutions, for these measures reflected partisan and policy priorities. Internal power, in short, gravitated from the other committees to the budget panels.

Further buttressing centralized budget-making was reconciliation. Intended by the 1974 act to be a modest exercise following action on the now-defunct second budget resolution, it has been included since 1980 in the first budget resolution and has the effect of making that resolution binding on House and Senate committees. In effect, this means that reconciliation is used to compel panels to reduce spending, primarily through entitlement savings, and to increase revenues.

The procedure has two steps. First, the budget resolution contains reconciliation instructions that require House and Senate committees to recommend budgetary savings by a certain date to the budget panels. These committees then package the proposals into an omnibus reconciliation bill, which, if enacted into law, will produce the spending cuts and revenue increases.

In 1981, reconciliation was used by President Reagan and his congressional allies to force almost every House and Senate committee to make unwanted cuts (about $130 billion over three years) in domestic programs under their jurisdiction. Never before had reconciliation been employed on such a grand scale. The irony is that Congress's budget process, which was designed to advance and assert the legislature's power of the purse, was captured by the White House and used to advance Reagan's goal of downsizing the national government's domestic role.

Another irony is that the revamped budget process, which produces whatever fiscal outcomes can attract majority support, failed to achieve either the balanced budgets or spending reductions that many lawmakers anticipated when they voted for the 1974 measure. Instead, spending continued to rise and revenues failed to keep pace. Deficits grew larger and larger. By the 1990s, interest payments trailed only defense and Social Security as the largest spending items in the federal budget. Few probably foresaw that the the 1980s would produce deficits so massive that they would trigger two other transformations in legislative budgeting: the mid-1980s deficit-reduction act informally called Gramm-Rudman-Hollings after the three Senate sponsors—Phil Gramm (R.-Tex.), Warren Rudman (R.-N.H.), and Ernest Hollings (D.-S.C.)—and the Budget Enforcement Act of 1990.

GRAMM-RUDMAN-HOLLINGS: AUTOMATIC SPENDING CUTS

Prior to the start of the 1980s, the nation was experiencing rampant inflation, productivity declines, oil price shocks, and economic challenges from Japan and Germany. The nation was ready for change and experimentation, and President Ronald Reagan provided both. He was elected on a platform that stressed defense increases (a spending pattern started in President Carter's last year), domestic spending cuts, tax reduction, and budgets that balanced. Reagan delivered on many, but not all, of these goals. Never, for example, did he submit a balanced budget to Congress. However, he did cut domestic spending, increase defense expenditures (over $2 trillion), and cut taxes. The centerpiece of Reagan's "supply side" agenda was the 1981 tax cut ($1 trillion over five years). Tax cuts were designed to stimulate savings, investment, higher economic growth, and thus generate more government revenue to offset the tax losses.

The experiment did not quite work as planned. Annual deficits in the $200–$300 billion range quickly became commonplace. Big peacetime deficits became accepted as part of national policy-making. The public debt, which took 192 years to accumulate to $1 trillion, more than doubled in eight years. The nation went from being the world's largest creditor in 1981 to its largest debtor nation. Interest payments on this pile of debt soared. "Borrow and spend" and "debt and consumption" became bywords of the decade. Analysts spoke of "structural" deficits—excess spending built into the fabric of laws but without the compensatory revenue to achieve some balance between the two. While the 1982 recession curbed inflation, the economic recovery that followed still saw an upsurge in deficit spending.

Deficits became an all-consuming issue for political parties and national elective branches, and gave rise to a politics of fiscal austerity, or "zero-sum" budgeting (increases for one program meant decreases for another or tax hikes). Policy debates focused primarily on the costs of programs and less on their substantive merits. The executive and legislative branches accelerated central control over budgetary issues, a development associated with tight spending and the need to ensure funding for high-priority programs. In the executive branch, power flowed from the departments and agencies to the OMB and the White House. In the legislative branch, party leaders and the Budget Committees asserted greater control over fiscal decision-making.

Despite fixation with the deficit, there was little consensus about how or even whether it ought to be addressed. The White House stuck to its antitax pledges and worked to enlarge defense expenditures. Democrats in Congress emphasized protection for domestic spending and essentially removed Social Security and other entitlements from the deficit-reduction bargaining table. Each branch tried to reduce the deficit, but by means unacceptable to the other.

There is no wonder that missed deadlines, bitter impasses, and sharp partisan disputes became standard fare. To discourage presidential vetoes, Congress resorted to massive bills ("packages" hundreds of pages in length) that combined Congress's priorities with some of the president's. Omnibus measures enabled congressional leaders to limit the number of unpopular votes on competing priorities, to acquire political leverage in dealing with the White House and committee leaders, and to expedite passage of these bills through an inherently fragmented institution. Because the partisan and policy stakes were so high, most major fiscal decisions in this period were hammered out in budget summits composed of congressional leaders, the OMB director, and top White House aides.

Disagreements surround the causes of soaring deficits. Some trace the roots of those increases to the "guns and butter" policy of the Vietnam War (paying for higher military expenditures without attempting to sacrifice domestic spending) and the creation and indexation of entitlement programs during the 1960s and 1970s. The latter produced automatic spending growth fueled by double-digit inflation and an aging population. Other commentators say the problem began with the 1981 tax cut and the accompanying increases in defense spending. This imbalance was compounded by a deep recession and failure to shrink domestic spending significantly. Republicans laid the blame on a generation of tax-and-spend Democrats; Democrats charged Republicans with economic mismanagement. Some asserted that the large deficits were part of a GOP plan to limit and reduce the national government's domestic role and to bludgeon Congress into giving the president greater fiscal powers.

Citizens, as noted earlier, hold inconsistent attitudes. They resent big government, but want the public services it provides in such areas as law enforcement, environmental protection, and health care. Politicians cannot reconcile public demands for more spending and lower taxes.

Some economists argue that deficits hardly matter so long as their percentage of gross national product remains stable or declines. The chief concern, these economists say, is to foster a healthy economy by spending more on productive investments (education, research, and infrastructure, for example). With the generation of new wealth from such investments, re-

ducing the deficit would be relatively easy to accomplish.

That President Reagan's policies were bold and controversial is an understatement. That they produced consternation in Congress is also an understatement. Both circumstances combined to provoke Congress in the mid-1980s to change its budgetary procedures again. In October 1985, Senate GOP leaders faced the politically unpleasant task of raising the statutory debt ceiling to over $2 trillion. Without the votes to enact the hike, the GOP leaders searched for a way out of the dilemma. The problem was compounded by growing public concern about the deficit, profound frustration at legislative-executive ineffectiveness in dealing with the deficit, and the reelection imperative. With the November elections only weeks away, senators of both parties desperately wanted to vote for some means of deficit reduction rather than simply for an extension of the government's authority to borrow more money. Enter Senators Gramm, Rudman, and Hollings. They offered the complex Gramm-Rudman-Hollings (GRH) amendment to the debt-ceiling legislation that passed the Senate and eventually became law.

The fundamental objective of GRH was to balance the federal budget within six years. The statute required that a set quantity of dollars be chopped yearly from the budget to achieve this goal. As the years passed, the amount of money annually appropriated would be reduced until it met the amount of money raised by taxes and other sources—thus achieving a balance between income and outgo. Although the Supreme Court declared a portion of the law unconstitutional in 1986, Congress quickly fixed the constitutional defect (the grant to a legislative agency of executive functions, in violation of the separation of powers) by passing GRH II the next year.

To ensure that Congress and the president met the successive installment payments on the deficit, GRH contained an automatic deficit-reduction mechanism known as sequestration. It was the core element of the whole proposal. Called a "bad idea whose time has come," sequestration stipulated that if Congress and the White House deadlock in making the required fiscal reductions, then the president is obligated to issue an order making permanent across-the-board cuts divided equally between defense and domestic programs. (Over two-thirds of total federal spending was exempt from sequestration, however.) The specter of sequestration was designed to force Congress and the president to negotiate responsibly to reduce the deficit.

The two branches remained at logger-heads. The president refused to discuss tax increases; Congress refused to cut domestic programs; and neither branch wanted to cut defense significantly. The October 1987 stock market crash produced some legislative-executive cooperation (e.g., all thirteen general appropriations bills were passed before the start of the fiscal year), but the threat of a planned fiscal train wreck failed to have its intended effect. Several factors account for this.

First, Congress and the White House devised ways to circumvent the sequestration procedure through artful budgetary gimmicks. Deficit-reduction targets were met on paper, but not in reality. For example, illusory spending cuts and overly optimistic economic scenarios produced billions in budgetary "savings." Or deficits were cut by placing some programs "off-budget." This meant that their costs are not reflected in official budgetary totals, even though they add to the government's total deficit. Lawmakers also took advantage of the reconciliation process to initiate or expand program spending.

Second, with most of the budget exempt from sequestration, especially the popular entitlement programs, significant reduction was difficult to achieve. Finally, GRH's stress on the short-term imperative of meeting the annual deficit-reduction target distorted fiscal policy-making. Tax legislation, for instance, was fashioned to maximize the quick infusion of money into a fiscal year, even if such measures produced significant revenue losses in later years.

GRH did produce important procedural changes in legislative budget-making. Members who proposed spending more for something had to identify offsetting receipts or cutbacks in other programs. A variety of congressional rules restrained budget-busting proposals. For instance, any senator could raise a point of order against floor amendments unrelated to the deficit-reduction purposes of reconciliation

legislation. A supermajority of sixty votes was imposed to inhibit waivers of this requirement. Spending was not significantly curbed by such procedures. The deficit persisted and triggered enactment of another budgetary change, the Budget Enforcement Act of 1990.

THE BUDGET ENFORCEMENT ACT OF 1990

In October 1990, Congress enacted the Budget Enforcement Act (BEA) and once again changed its fiscal procedures. The product of protracted negotiations among House, Senate, and White House leaders (facilitated by President Bush's earlier renunciation of his "no new taxes" pledge of the 1988 campaign), the BEA was enacted as Title XIII of the omnibus reconciliation bill. The legislation outlined a binding, multiyear deficit-reduction plan (almost $500 billion over five years) and established complex procedural controls to restrain federal spending. The BEA also sought to defuse legislative-executive conflict by deciding the big financial questions (spending for broad governmental categories) and to compel both branches to make tough choices about national priorities within each category. These goals are to be accomplished in several ways. First, the BEA shifted Congress's attention from deficit reduction to spending control. It set strict spending caps for three discretionary categories—domestic, defense, and international—and forbade any shifting of funds between the categories. No longer could Congress raid the defense category to fund domestic programs. This prohibition was designed to transform the traditional "guns versus butter" debate into "guns versus guns" or "butter versus butter." The segmentation of discretionary spending into categories was to last for three years; the president was obligated annually to adjust the caps to accommodate economic, technical, or other changes. During the last two years (1994 and 1995), governmental spending was to be lumped into a single pot; this was expected to again produce the guns-versus-butter clash. The BEA retained overall deficit targets and a general sequestration procedure, but the threat of an automatic fiscal guillotine was to be removed if conditions beyond Congress's control (inflation or emergency funding, for instance) pushed the deficit upward.

To ensure that the limits for each category of appropriations spending would be adhered to, any spending that exceeded the overall cap was to be subject to a "minisequester." On 25 April 1991, for example, the president ordered a minisequester because the spending cap for domestic programs was breached by $2.4 million when Congress enacted a supplemental appropriations bill. To make up for the $2.4 million, each account in the domestic category was reduced across the board by .0013 percent (or $13 for every $1 million).

Second, taxes and entitlement programs were to be subject to a new "pay as you go" (PAYGO) procedure. Spending increases for existing entitlements or funding for new entitlement spending had to be offset either by cuts in other mandatory spending programs or by revenue increases. Otherwise, a minisequester would occur that reduces spending for certain entitlement programs. The same principle was applied to tax cuts: they were to be accomplished in a deficit-neutral manner. Proposals for a middle-class tax cut, for instance, were to be offset by tax increases (such as a surtax on wealthy families) or spending reductions. It is worth noting that the 1990 reconciliation bill cut entitlements, especially Medicare. However, Medicare expenditures and interest payments on the debt continued to soar, and overall, it remains difficult to restrain entitlement spending. Entitlement spending that escalates for reasons beyond Congress's control (more people becoming eligible for these programs, for instance) would not trigger the PAYGO sequester.

Given spending caps and PAYGO requirements for entitlements and taxes, the place of reconciliation in legislative budgeting appears diminished. To be sure, there are other winners and losers. The Budget Committees seem to have lost some influence, because their role in drafting budget resolutions has been undercut by the budget summit's five-year fiscal blueprint. By contrast, the Appropriations Committees gained from the budget accord. They no longer had to worry that after having made spending cuts in compliance with budget resolution instructions, they would suffer a "double hit" under a GRH sequestration because other panels failed to make their required budgetary

savings. The OMB appears to have gained authority too. It would calculate ("score") the spending and tax decisions of Congress on a continuous basis to determine whether the spending caps had been breached or whether any tax breaks (also called "tax expenditures" because they result in revenue losses to the Treasury) had been offset with revenue increases. In January 1991 the Democratically controlled House, distrustful of the OMB, changed its rules and gave the CBO (and also the Joint Taxation Committee) authority to determine if spending or tax bills violated the budget agreement. The White House charged House Democrats with reneging on the budget deal, and the president threatened to veto legislation containing CBO cost estimates.

CONCLUSION

The national budget is a series of legislative enactments that reflect the priorities of the president and the public as expressed through its elected lawmakers. That the elective branches disagree over spending priorities is nothing new. They represent different interests and constituencies. Both want to spend, but often for different purposes. This clash is just one of the factors that contribute to the persistent gap between tax receipts and governmental expenditures.

Although Congress has several times revamped its budgetary processes, adding layer upon layer of complex refinements, procedural change alone cannot restore fiscal equilibrium. Ultimately, the citizenry must accept some fiscal discipline for the long-term collective good. The challenge ahead for policymakers appears at least threefold: persuade the electorate to accept some fiscal belt-tightening so as to minimize "passing the buck" to subsequent generations, determine what level of government that citizens are willing to support with taxes, and devise a program of economic growth that ensures the nation's future prosperity. However one views the deficit, it surely is symptomatic of larger issues affecting society. These include America's ability to compete with other nations, to achieve and maintain high standards of living for all segments of the populace, and to enhance the effectiveness of the governance process. As the nineteenth-century British prime minister William Gladstone said, "Budgets are not merely affairs of arithmetic, but in a thousand ways go to the root of prosperity of individuals, the relation of classes and the strength of kingdoms."

BIBLIOGRAPHY

The Federal Budget

Among the books that trace the evolution of federal budgeting and discuss its fundamental features and characteristics are LOUIS FISHER, *Presidential Spending Power* (Princeton, N.J., 1975); ARTHUR SMITHIES, *The Budgetary Process in the United States* (New York, 1955); LUCIUS WILMERDING, *The Spending Power* (New Haven, Conn., 1943); EVERETT SOMERVILLE BROWN, ed., *William Plumber's Memorandum of Proceedings in the United States Senate, 1803–1807* (New York, 1923); and ROBERT LUCE, *Legislative Problems* (Boston, 1935). Worth noting here are the annual discussions of the federal budget published since 1971 by the BROOKINGS INSTITUTION in Washington, D.C., and titled *Setting National Priorities* and AARON WILDAVSKY's classic *The Politics of the Budgetary Process*, 4th ed. (Boston, 1984). WILDAVSKY's study was first published in 1964 and analyzed, among other things, incrementalism as a fundamental budgetary norm. His *The New Politics of the Budgetary Process* (Glenview, Ill., 1988), examines the new features and demands of budgeting in a historical context. Another useful overview of federal budget politics is DENNIS S. IPPOLITO, *Uncertain Legacies: Federal Budget Policy from Roosevelt Through Reagan* (Charlottesville, Va., 1990).

Appropriations

Of various studies of the appropriations and revenue processes, several merit mention. The landmark study of the appropriations process, with a particular focus on the Appropriations Committees, is RICHARD F. FENNO, JR., *The Power of the Purse: Appropriations Politics in Congress* (Boston, 1966). His committee-based analysis spawned comparable studies of the revenue panels, including JOHN F. MANLEY, *The Politics of Finance* (Boston, 1970), and RANDALL STRAHAN, *New Ways and Means* (Chapel Hill, N.C., 1990). For a review of tax policy in the 1980s, see JOSEPH J. MINARIK, *Making America's Budget Policy* (Armonk, N.Y., 1990). A good analysis of the 1986 overhaul of the internal revenue code is TIMOTHY J. CONLAN, MARGARET T. WRIGHTSON, and DAVID R. BEAM, *Taxing Choices: The Politics of Tax Reform* (Washington, D.C., 1990). For a history of the House Committee on Ways and Means, see DONALD R. KENNON and REBECCA M. ROGERS, *The Committee on Ways and Means: A Bicentennial History, 1789–1989* (Washington, D.C., 1989).

The 1974 Budget Act

Several important studies provide assessments of the conditions that prompted passage of the 1974 Budget Act and review its implementation and effectiveness. The most thorough discussion can be found in ALLEN SCHICK, *Congress and Money* (Washington, D.C., 1980), and in his short treatise *Reconciliation and the Congressional Budget Process* (Washington, D.C., 1981). Other useful examinations include JOEL HAVEMANN, *Congress and the Budget* (Bloomington, Ind., 1978); DENNIS S. IPPOLITO, *Congressional Spending* (Ithaca, N.Y., 1981); LANCE T. LELOUP, *The Fiscal Congress* (Westport, Conn., 1980); and HOWARD E. SCHUMAN, *Politics and the Budget,* 2d ed. (Englewood Cliffs, N.J., 1988).

The 1990s

The most complete examination of the tumultuous 1980s, and a likely classic of budgeting, is JOSEPH WHITE and AARON WILDAVSKY, *The Deficit and the Public Interest: The Search for Responsible Budgeting in the 1980s* (Berkeley and Los Angeles, 1989). Another valuable analysis of the new budget order on Capitol Hill is JOHN B. GILMOUR, *Reconcilable Differences? Congress, the Budget Process, and the Deficit* (Berkeley and Los Angeles, 1990). A major discussion of the crisis in budgeting, which includes recommendations for reform, is ALLEN SCHICK, *The Capacity to Budget* (Washington, D.C., 1990). A readable account of the political circumstances that surrounded the 1990 budget summit meetings is LAWRENCE J. HAAS, *Running on Empty: Bush, Congress, and the Politics of a Bankrupt Government* (Homewood, Ill., 1990). On the Budget Enforcement Act, see the spring 1991 issue of *Public Budgeting and Finance,* which contains three articles that analyze the changes the BEA made in federal budgeting.

Other Works

A diverse range of studies focus on certain aspects of budgetary policy and politics. Several are provided for illustrative purposes. They include HERMAN B. LEONARD, *Checks Unbalanced: The Quiet Side of Public Spending* (New York, 1986), which looks at such topics as federal credit activities and federal tax expenditures; JAMES T. BENNETT and THOMAS J. DILORENZO, *Underground Government: The Off-Budget Public Sector* (Washington, D.C., 1983); PETER G. PETERSON and NEIL HOWE, *On Borrowed Times: How the Growth in Entitlement Spending Threatens America's Future* (San Francisco, 1988); R. KENT WEAVER, *Automatic Government: The Politics of Indexation* (Washington, D.C., 1988); and JAMES D. SAVAGE, *Balanced Budgets and American Politics* (Ithaca, N.Y., 1988).

SEE ALSO Congressional Appropriations Committees; The Fragmentation of Power Within Congressional Committees; The House Committee on Ways and Means; AND Legislatures and Political Rights.

CONGRESSIONAL OVERSIGHT

William F. West

Congress has become more conscious of its overseer's role as the bureaucracy has grown in size and power. Yet, although most scholars accept this proposition, they disagree considerably about the extent and viability of legislative review of agency performance. Scholars also offer very different assessments of the desirability of legislative involvement in the administrative process.

The following essay examines several key issues surrounding legislative oversight. Some of these issues reflect empirical disagreement concerning the nature of oversight and its impact on American government. Other issues reflect differing normative positions or value judgments, which are rooted in considerations of good policy and sound constitutional practice. This distinction is somewhat artificial, however, for as with most institutional analysis, normative and empirical premises are closely intertwined. The desirability of oversight is obviously contingent on the effects it has. By the same token, the effects of oversight are almost always judged on the basis of assumptions about the purposes it should serve.

Legislative oversight has often been portrayed as sporadic and ineffectual. This portrayal has been based, in part, on the assertion that Congress lacks the resources in either time or staff to review administrative performance. In addition, oversight has been alleged to be a low priority in light of the careerist ambitions that drive congressional behavior. If these characterizations were ever accurate, however, evidence suggests that Congress takes its role in the administrative process very seriously. In a related vein, scholars have questioned the assumptions about the nature of administration and its relationship to the legislature's systemic role that underlie traditional assessments of limited oversight resources and incentives.

The alleged ineffectiveness of oversight has often been viewed as a regrettable, if inevitable, neglect of an important legislative function. At the same time, however, growing congressional involvement in administration has often been greeted with sharp criticism. The same characteristics of Congress that have been cited as explanations for ineffective review are offered to explain undesirable effects when oversight does occur. Despite its popularity, the case against congressional oversight often reflects simplistic assumptions about institutional behavior and questionable ideas concerning systemic norms about the proper relationship between the legislative and administrative processes.

THE NATURE OF OVERSIGHT

Although the meaning of *oversight* is frequently taken for granted, a precise and widely accepted definition does not, in fact, exist. Individual scholars use the term in vague and contradictory ways, and conceptions of what oversight is vary significantly, even where clear definitions are offered. However conceived, oversight also takes place through a wide variety of formal and informal mechanisms. How one chooses to define oversight and the form it takes are crucial in assessing its effects and its desirability.

Definitional Issues

Review and Casework Definitions of oversight vary along several lines. One issue concerns the the kinds of agency decisions subject to legislative review. In many instances, the term is reserved for review of agency policy statements and the general direction and effectiveness of implementation. For example, this is true of Dennis Riley's suggestion that oversight can be categorized as legislative (determining whether programs work); fiscal (making sure that money is spent the way Congress wants it spent); or investigative (inquiring into government economy, efficiency, and effectiveness). Congress's interest in the administrative process is not limited to such considerations, however. As used by some, the term oversight may also refer to the review of agency decisions applying policy to individuals—what is commonly referred to as casework; for example, the assistance congressmen give to constituents who wish to reverse agency decisions that have affected them adversely.

Another distinction concerns the timing of legislative involvement. In an early and influential treatment of the subject, Joseph Harris has defined oversight as "review after the fact" (p. 9). For other scholars, oversight consists of congressional review during, as well as after, policy implementation. Some go even further, defining oversight as any type of legislative behavior that affects the administrative process. For instance, Lawrence C. Dodd and Richard L. Schott have discussed appropriations and enabling legislation—in essence, forward-looking actions—as means of performing oversight.

Passive and Active Involvement A broader issue is whether oversight should be confined to review or whether the term should encompass direct influence by Congress on the administrative process. Traditionally oversight was conceived of in terms of monitoring or passive supervision, since legislation was supposed to be the only appropriate means for Congress actively to address administrative deficiencies. One rationale for this position was that direct congressional influence over administration created what was, in effect, legislative policy outside the formal legislative process. Another rationale was that Congress simply lacked the expertise to participate intelligently in agencies' technical decisions. As a practical matter, however, Congress often exerts influence or control over bureaucratic decisions without resorting to new legislation. One might argue, in this regard, that if intervention in the administrative process naturally accompanies review, it makes sense to include it under the heading of oversight, especially for evaluative purposes.

The distinction between monitoring and active involvement is obviously related to the question of timing. Limiting the meaning of

oversight to review after the fact conforms with the notion of passive supervision, whereas review during implementation is obviously necessary if oversight is to include direct influence over agency actions. In a similar vein, the distinction between monitoring and influence has important implications for the classification of legislative tools. Formal means of congressional intervention, such as the legislative veto, obviously fall outside the realm of passive supervision but are compatible with definitions that include active involvement in administration. The argument that policy influence by way of oversight is functionally equivalent to legislation may also help account for definitions that include legislative actions before the fact. This reasoning lies behind Morris Ogul's definition of oversight as "behavior by legislators and their staffs, individually or collectively, which results in an impact, intended or not, on bureaucratic behavior" (1976, p. 11).

Political Content A final question has to do with the relationship between oversight and policy. Beyond confining Congress to a monitoring role, the traditional definition of oversight viewed the purpose of legislative review as ensuring that implementation achieved statutory goals. Although many still subscribe to this instrumental conception, others view oversight as a process that can be political; that is, it can involve the determination of policy objectives. This latter conception has been offered as a realistic description of congressional motives. Politically-based oversight has also been defended as legitimate on the grounds that administration itself often involves important choices among competing social objectives. The distinction between political and instrumental review is related to the question of whether casework and other types of reactive intervention that are motivated by constituent demands should be classified as oversight.

It is important to emphasize that definitions of oversight can reflect ideas either about Congress's actual or its proper role—this helps to explain the interrelationship between empirical and normative analysis alluded to earlier. The issues outlined here will reemerge throughout this essay, but Christopher H. Foreman's description of oversight as "two interlocking congressional processes" will serve as a broad working definition. Oversight is conceived of by Foreman as "efforts to *gather in-*

formation about what agencies are doing and to *dictate or signal* to agencies regarding the preferred behavior *or* policy" (p. 13). Beyond this, defining the term so broadly as to include legislative activities before the administrative process begins renders it practically meaningless by encompassing practically everything that the legislature does. One should bear in mind, nonetheless, the important relationship between oversight and Congress's authorization and appropriations powers; that is, its powers to sanction and fund agency work.

Resources and Techniques

The Committee System Definitional issues are closely related to the way oversight is performed. To the extent that oversight involves review of agency policy, it is conducted largely by congressional committees in their substantive areas of responsibility. Appropriations subcommittees from each house, and at least one set (and often several) of authorization committees or subcommittees typically review a given agency's activities. In addition, both the House and Senate's Government Operations committees have general oversight responsibilities pertaining to agency procedures and organization as well as to the overall "economy and efficiency" of the administrative process.

Dodd and Schott have observed that each committee has a unique mission, environment, and internal structure and culture that determine the way oversight is performed. For instance, standing subject-matter committees vary substantially in the character of their relationships with administrators and, relatedly, in terms of the oversight techniques they prefer to use. Joel Aberbach has observed, in this regard, that some committees view oversight primarily as a means of policy advocacy, whereas others have a more critical orientation. Some scholars have felt that the degree of centralization is an especially important consideration in determining the nature and extent of oversight. John Bibby has noted that, while some committees delegate much of their oversight responsibility to subcommittees, others are highly centralized, conducting most hearings at the full-committee level and giving the respective chair substantial control of the oversight agenda.

The review of agency programs frequently entails the collection and evaluation of considerable information. Committee staff are crucial in this regard. A great majority of the roughly 2,600 staffers in the House and Senate devote some portion of their energies to oversight. Beyond their own internal resources, committees can call for assistance on several organizations that lend general support to Congress. The most important of these is the General Accounting Office (GAO), which conducts financial audits and policy evaluations of agency programs. In addition, committees can rely on the Congressional Research Service for assistance in collecting and analyzing data, scholarly articles, and documents that are relevant to oversight. The Office of Technology Assessment and the Congressional Budget Office also provide expertise and staff assistance in performing various tasks.

Hearings, Reports, and Vetoes Congressional efforts to review and influence administrative actions occur in a variety of institutional settings. The most visible forum is the oversight hearing, while agency officials and other parties are called before committees or subcommittees to testify about administrative practices and program effects. Agencies are also frequently required to describe and assess their own activities. The GAO prepares scores of reports each year on program implementation. In addition, much oversight occurs as a by-product of other congressional functions such as hearings on new legislation. In some cases, Congress includes special provisions in enabling statutes that enhance its oversight capabilities beyond those it generally enjoys. A common example is the use of temporary authorizations, which requires the legislature periodically to reconsider and reapprove agencies or the programs they implement.

Until 1983, the legislative veto provided another convenient tool by which Congress could systematically monitor and assert itself in the administrative process. In the most common scenario, administrative proposals were submitted to Congress and could not go into effect until a mandatory waiting period had elapsed. One or both houses of Congress, or elements thereof, could disapprove agency actions during that time. The most popular forms of the veto were invalidated by the Supreme Court in *Immigration and Naturalization*

Service v. *Chadha*, 103 S. Ct. 2764 (1983). But analogous, though less effective, devices remain in use. These include "report-and-wait" provisions that allow Congress time to block or amend agency actions through the legislative process; requirements that both the Houses and the president affirm administrative proposals; and a variety of other mechanisms that bring agency policies to Congress's attention and provide opportunities for corrective action. Actual use of the legislative veto or failure to reauthorize a program may not be defined as oversight, per se, but such devices do facilitate and encourage oversight in the sense that they institutionalize systematic review.

Informal Contacts It is important to add that Congress does not rely exclusively—or perhaps even primarily—on formal devices in its efforts to review and correct administration. Legislators and their staff obtain information about agency performance or underperformance from the media, from agencies with overlapping or conflicting responsibilities, and from a variety of other sources. Complaints from constituents or interest groups are especially important here. Morris Ogul has observed that much of Congress's communication with bureaucracy is conducted through telephone conversations, private meetings, and other off-the-record contacts. Not all scholars have defined these informal actions as oversight, but most have agreed with Ogul that members of Congress and their staff often prefer such measures because of their expediency. In addition, private contacts enable legislators to avoid potentially damaging publicity associated with program failure or with efforts to change the course of administrative policy in directions that are unpopular with constituents.

The success of informal communication is obviously determined, in part, by the formal oversight tools Congress holds in reserve. In a similar way, the actual or threatened use of powers not directly related to oversight gives Congress leverage over bureaucratic activities. Foremost among these powers are legislative control over budgets and enabling statutes, which are the lifeblood of the administrative process. Congress can also influence bureaucracy through its traditional powers to reorganize and relocate agencies; through senatorial prerogatives to confirm political appointees; or through its powers otherwise to influence the numbers and types of personnel within agencies or to specify terms of access to agency decision-making by outside participants.

In brief, legislative oversight is a varied process to say the least, and the combination of different information-gathering techniques and different means of intervention yields countless permutations. Joel D. Aberbach's *Keeping a Watchful Eye: The Politics of Congressional Oversight* (1990) contains the most extensive effort to categorize and quantify different oversight activities. For instance, the book identifies twenty-one ways in which committees keep track of agency activities and points out fourteen formal and informal oversight techniques. Aberbach's interviews with committee staff also represent one of the few rigorous attempts to describe the frequency of different kinds of oversight. His findings indicate that Congress stocks a balanced arsenal of techniques but that informal conversations between committee staff and agency personnel are clearly its weapons of choice.

THE EFFECTIVENESS OF OVERSIGHT

The question most frequently asked about congressional oversight is "Does it work?" The answer most frequently given, at least through the 1970s was "Not very well."

The conventional assessment of oversight's limited effectiveness is outlined below. Though the outline may not correspond in its entirety with any particular work, it is accurate as a rough synthesis of common assumptions and arguments that once dominated the thinking on this subject. As such, it provides a point of departure for considering the impact of legislative review. A growing body of evidence suggests that oversight is not consistently weak, but that it is conditioned by various contextual factors. [Beyond this, the strength of the conventional view as a broad characterization has eroded under the weight of studies questioning its assumptions about congressional incentives and capabilities, and (relatedly) about the criteria that should define effective oversight.]

Limitations on Oversight: The Conventional View

Capabilities The conventional view is based, in part, on the observation that Congress cannot conduct a comprehensive review or even a systematic sampling of bureaucratic actions. A key premise is that the legislature simply lacks the wherewithal to monitor the administrative process. Notwithstanding committee staff and other institutional resources, the sheer size of bureaucracy and the diversity of its activities are alleged to render anything beyond haphazard oversight as an unrealistic expectation. The problem is compounded by Congress's lack of expertise in increasingly complex areas of policy implementation; by bureaucracy's well-known inclination to preserve its autonomy; and by competition from the president, interest groups, and others with a stake in the administrative process.

To the extent that Congress is able to monitor agency action, it has limited tools at hand to enforce statutory implementation. Terry Moe has observed that legislative and budgetary powers are unwieldy instruments that give congressional committees only limited bargaining power in their relations with the bureaucracy. The utility of these devices is discounted by the fact that they require bicameral (two-chamber) majorities and presidential approval as well as by the same asymmetries of information and expertise that hamper efforts to review bureaucratic performance. Moe has further contended that the Senate's confirmation power is a crude means of control, at best, and that in practice Congress defers strongly to the president in personnel matters.

Dodd and Schott have observed that the decentralized and overlapping structure of the committee system may also inhibit coherent oversight by allowing agencies to play off one set of legislators against another. Their analysis reveals frequent competition and conflict over administrative policy, both among authorization committees and between authorization and appropriations committees. The authors have added that matters have become worse as the devolution of authority from committees to subcommittees has further muddled the lines of accountability for oversight.

Incentives   The fact that legislators are not motivated to perform systematic oversight compounds the problems mentioned above. Morris Ogul, Seymour Scher, and John Bibby have discussed a number of these disincentives in their works. The subject matter of day-to-day oversight is often mundane and uninteresting to legislators. This is particularly true of congressmen assigned to committees responsible for dry areas, such as the District of Columbia or the Post Office. Moreover, the organizational structure of oversight may discourage critical review. Why? Because the same committees that draft legislative policy are responsible for assessing the effectiveness of programs as they are carried out. Politicians, needless to say, are reluctant to point out their own mistakes. Mutual respect and friendships, developed over years of interaction between bureaucrats and committee members, may further inhibit critical review. Finally, members of Congress who belong to the same party as the president may also be reluctant to uncover failures in policy implementation that embarrass the administration.

According to conventional wisdom, the most crucial disincentive for vigorous oversight amounts to this: review of policy implementation is simply not a cost-effective way for legislators to pursue their primary goal of being reelected. Most administrative actions are routine matters of low visibility, which do not command voter attention. In addition, legislators face a formidable challenge in attempting to master the details of policy-making in most areas. Given these facts, the investment of limited time and staff resources in other activities (such as attaching one's name to prominent legislation) yields far greater dividends in terms of credit claiming and building name-recognition. This assessment of oversight's low priority meshes with popular interpretations of congressional behavior, which emphasize careerist ambitions and the dominance of self-interest over broad policy concerns.

Contextual Factors
Affecting Oversight

Newsworthy Issues   It is important to add that few, if any, analyses assert that legislators are consistently uninterested and uninvolved in policy implementation. One of the most common themes in the studies of oversight is that various contextual factors can be more or less conducive to legislative review. Highly visible issues are a commonly cited exception to Congress's general pattern of neglect. Addressing well-publicized policy failures that result from bureaucratic wrongdoing or incompetence (for example, the National Aeronautics and Space Administration's disastrous approval of the 1986 flight of the space shuttle Challenger) can provide substantial opportunities for legislators to build name-recognition and project themselves as guardians of the public trust. In addition, even the most pessimistic assessments of oversight are likely to view intervention in matters highly salient to constituents as an important means by which members of congress pursue the reelection strategy of credit claiming. Morris Fiorina has used this hypothesis to argue that the expanded opportunities for casework, created by the growth of the administrative state, explain the overwhelming electoral advantage enjoyed by incumbents since World War II.

Political Climate Scholars have examined a variety of other factors affecting oversight. Based on his interviews with legislators and his observations of regulatory oversight between 1938 and 1961, Seymour Scher has found that although "committee review is a spasmodic affair marked by years in which the agencies are virtually ignored" (p. 530), it is encouraged by certain political conditions. He has suggested, for example, that oversight can occur as a by-product of widespread congressional interest in policy revision. He has also found that oversight is more likely when there is partisan conflict between the administration and congressional leaders. In addition, perceived threats of presidential interference in the affairs of independent regulatory commissions may precipitate reciprocal efforts by Congress to regain control of what it views as its rightful domain.

Aside from political climate, other factors explain variation in Congress's inclination to conduct review of a more programmatic nature. Aberbach's data on hearings suggest that oversight is taken less seriously in redistributive than other policy areas. This is consistent with Theodore Lowi's thesis that redistributive issues, such as welfare, are typically the domain of the president and key leaders in Congress rather than committee members. Scholars have also found that structural characteristics within the legislature affect the frequency and nature of oversight. Evidence suggests that, as one would predict, a large and capable committee staff and the existence of specialized oversight subcommittees are both conducive to review.

Committee Structure Subcommittee autonomy is perhaps a more interesting determinant of oversight. Analyses by Bibby and Aberbach indicate that decentralized committees, where control over hearing agendas and the allocation of staff are delegated to subcommittees, are more prone to review administration than those where authority is centralized. One plausible explanation for this is that because committee chairs have more pressing and rewarding concerns, oversight fares better in the relatively free hands of subcommittees. A related point is that the decentralization of authority within a committee makes it a more attractive place for members to further their individual careers. Decentralization may also be conducive to oversight in that it promotes membership stability and the development of expertise. Finally, it may influence the allocation of members' limited time among competing committee assignments.

Aberbach's analysis is especially valuable because of his efforts to explain different methods of oversight as a function of institutional design. Aberbach has found, for example, that special oversight committees or subcommittees are more likely to conduct critical, objective review than are other groups, which tend to view their role in the administrative process as one of program advocacy. From interviews with staffers, Aberbach concludes that the institutional structure of oversight has much to do with whether review occurs primarily in response to constituent complaints or whether it reflects active efforts by committee members to investigate agency performance. Thus Congress is likely to show initiative in examining administrative performance when oversight occurs in the context of reauthorization. The impressions of staffers also suggest that active oversight is much more prevalent in appropriations (budget) committees than in authorizing committees.

Reassessing Oversight

Investments of Both Time and Energy Variation in the nature and extent of congressional review undermines the generalization that oversight is consistently a low priority. The fact that committee arrangements, which account for much of this variation, are controlled by the Congress itself further contradicts the assertion that the legislature is powerless to perform effective review. Yet despite their recognition of variations in oversight, scholars have traditionally concluded that legislative review of administration is limited and therefore ineffective on the whole. Many still adhere to this appraisal.

At the same time, however, the popularity of the conventional view has eroded considerably under the weight of recent scholarship. The reassessment of the effectiveness of oversight centers around two interrelated challenges. A growing body of evidence suggests that Congress considers review of administration to be an important activity worthy of substantial organizational resources. Key institutional changes further evince an increased legislative interest and presence in the administrative process over the past three decades. A reinforcing observation has to do with the definition of effective oversight. Thus, perhaps a more fundamental challenge is that, by equating effectiveness with comprehensive or at least very extensive review, the conventional assessment reflects an unrealistic view of the relationship between policy implementation and Congress's institutional goals.

As mentioned earlier, analyses have often measured oversight in terms of hearings, reports, and the like. Yet many scholars have noted that such formal mechanisms account for only a fraction of the legislative review and influence that actually take place. Christopher H. Foreman's analysis of congressional involvement in the administration of social regulatory policy illustrates this well. He has observed that informal oversight occurs frequently and in a wide array of contexts. It may take the form of direct communications or indirect signals that are, nonetheless, effective in shaping agency decisions. Foreman has argued that focusing on "formal structure can be misleading in at least two respects. First, it encourages the nonsensical perception that oversight is something that happens entirely apart from the other two processes [authorization and appropriation]. Second, it probably biases discussion toward an underestimation of cumulative congressional influence" (p. 12). Whether informal communications are considered to be oversight is again a matter of definition. At any rate, they have often been ignored in assessing the extent and impact of legislative involvement in agency affairs.

Aberbach's 1990 work presents extensive evidence that oversight is generally taken very seriously by Congress. Based largely on interviews with committee staff, it indicates that various types of review collectively consume a large share of legislative attention and resources. In contrast to what the conventional view would predict, Aberbach's book suggests that authorization, appropriations, and oversight committees all engage in a significant amount of oversight. Data concerning such characteristics as education and employment history further reveal that the staff responsible for oversight are a talented and experienced group who possess considerable expertise in their substantive policy areas.

Scholars may have tended to underestimate the legislature's interest in, and influence over, policy implementation, especially when they confined their analyses to formal methods of oversight. At any rate, a variety of institutional developments suggest that Congress has become increasingly intent on reviewing administrative behavior since the 1970s. One indication of this is a dramatic increase in the number and days of oversight hearings, both in absolute terms and as a percentage of all hearing activity. This suggests a growing congressional will and capacity to perform oversight (at least assuming that the comparative attractiveness and incidence of informal review has not declined at the same time). Aberbach and others also observe that the staff devoted partly or primarily to oversight have expanded, both in absolute and relative terms.

The Resurrected Veto Other changes point to increased interest in oversight. Although the legislative veto existed since the early 1930s, about two-thirds of all vetoes were enacted after 1970. Joseph Cooper and Patricia Hurley have observed that these later vetoes, to a much greater extent than their predecessors, were designed to facilitate review and control of agency policy statements as opposed to casework. Although the most popular forms of the veto were declared unconstitutional in 1983, Congress has continued to enact analogous devices that institute more systematic review and that enhance Congress's power to shape bureaucratic policy. This trend indicates the legislature's increased desire to exercise effective review over administration as well as its frustration with more traditional methods.

Several other developments may account for Congress's expanded efforts to review and influence administrative performance. Increased interest in oversight may be attributable, in part, to basic changes in legislative structure. Given Bibby's observation that the extent of oversight corresponds to the level of committee decentralization, one would expect the devolution of power from committees to subcommittees, which culminated in the mid-1970s, to have had a substantial impact on the amount of oversight performed.

Aberbach has argued that constituent demands have also resulted in the growth of oversight. The simple explanation for this is that bureaucracy has come to affect more people in more ways as the administrative state has expanded dramatically. Yet the relationship between bureaucratic growth and demands for oversight may be exponential rather than linear. Hugh Heclo and others have observed that many of the programs in social regulation and other areas enacted in the 1960s and 1970s created new rights or otherwise legitimated and strengthened old interests. Because of this and because of fiscal concerns, born of changing economic conditions and the proliferation of federal programs, it has become more likely that implementation decisions in any one given area will evoke opposition from other agencies and other congressional constituencies. Legislators' efforts to extend their control over the bureaucracy may be plausibly explained as a reflection of demands generated by the increased conflict that has come to characterize bureaucratic politics.

In a far-reaching sense, one might explain Congress's growing emphasis on oversight as an organizational effort to adapt to a changing task environment. Joseph Cooper and others have argued that the ability to monitor and influence the administrative process has become an important way for Congress to sustain its traditional role of shaping policy, even as society's demands for government action have forced it to delegate increasing amounts of discretionary authority to the bureaucracy. This interpretation is consistent with explanations that stress the ambitions of individual legislators. An increasingly strong linkage between oversight and reelection can thus be explained in terms of Congress's representative function of making policy in accordance with constituent demands. Similarly, decentralization can be seen as both a cause of, and a response to, the

need for more oversight and for more policy specialization generally, as Congress's legislative and administrative work load has become larger, more varied, and more complex.

Effectiveness and Legislative Goals

Interest aside, whether the legislature is up to the task of effective oversight may be another matter. In evaluating congressional efforts to control bureaucracy, many scholars contend that review is destined to remain reactive and sporadic—and therefore ineffectual—under any feasible augmentation of powers and resources. Experts frequently argue that the further expansion of staff resources required for comprehensive oversight, would be so great as to create a congressional bureaucracy that would be almost as far removed as the executive branch from effective supervision by elected representatives.

Still, effectiveness is relative to one's choice of goals, and its equation with "continuous watchfulness" implicitly reflects the traditional belief that the purpose of legislative review is to ensure that the bureaucracy serves as an accurate and efficient transmission belt in carrying out substantive statutory intent. The most fundamental challenge to the conventional view from a theoretical standpoint is the argument that oversight is effective precisely because it is reactive. Two distinct hypotheses are possible in this regard, each of which reflects an alternative conception of delegated authority and its relationship to legislative interests. One assumes that reactive oversight is an effective way of ensuring compliance with the original political (rather than substantive) objectives behind statutes, while the other views it as a means by which Congress shapes policy implementation according to its changing preferences.

Reelection and Constituent Interests Rational-choice theorists have played a leading role in reassessing the effectiveness of oversight. In the first applications of this theory to Congress, Scher, David R. Mayhew, and Fiorina, merely echoed the conclusion that the electoral incentive dominating legislative behavior was conducive only to sporadic review, review that had little impact on the shape of administrative policy. Spurred, however, by evidence of growing legislative interest in oversight, proponents of this school of thought have altered their views. Since the 1980s, rational-school theorists have argued that self-interested members of Congress effectively monitor and control administrative policy for ends that extend beyond casework and the exploitation of occasional opportunities to generate favorable publicity. Committee members are motivated to do so because of their desire to ensure that the constituent interests represented by winning legislative coalitions are, in fact, transformed into policy as programs are implemented. In a 1983 statement and test of this thesis, Barry Weingast and Mark Moran have demonstrated a close correspondence between the Federal Trade Commission's (FTC's) policy and the membership turnover and policy orientation of the House and Senate Commerce committees.

As part of their argument, Weingast and Moran have noted that it is more cost-effective for legislators to focus limited-oversight resources on controversial decisions than on comprehensive review of the entire administrative process. The reason for this is that most agency actions do not evoke opposition from important constituents and are therefore of little consequence to legislators, who are motivated primarily by the desire to be reelected.

The Fire-Alarm Theory Matthew McCubbins and Thomas Schwartz have expanded this thesis by likening Congress's preferred strategy to a system of fire alarms as opposed to police patrols. McCubbins and Schwartz argue that fire alarms can be relied on to signal trouble thanks to legislatively imposed administrative procedures that provide opportunities for constituents to monitor agency decisions and to object to action that they find offensive. These include such devices as notice-and-comment rule-making procedures, freedom of information requirements, and statutory provisions that enhance the standing of certain interests to participate in agency policy making or to challenge administration actions in the courts.

As developed by McCubbins and Schwartz, the fire-alarm argument is based on an analogy to private-sector transactions known as principal-agent theory. Just as employers (principals) use contracts and salaries to ensure that employees (agents) carry out their goals, so members of Congress use the rewards and sanctions at their disposal to control bureau-

cratic policy. Although their original work is vague as to the exact purpose of such control, a pair of later articles by McCubbins, Roger Noll, and Weingast makes it clear that reactive oversight is a technique for ensuring that the interests of original winning legislative coalitions are served as programs are implemented. This later work asserts that the delegation of discretionary authority to bureaucracy results from Congress's lack of expertise or its inability to anticipate specific issues that will arise in administration. The legislator's fear, under this scenario, is that bureaucrats will pursue their own agendas to subvert the political goals that are reflected in the passage of statutes.

The purpose of fire alarms is thus to signal deviations from the original agreement in the distribution of costs and benefits to constituents. Congress employs administrative procedures to this end as well, not only as strategically-placed fire alarms, but as constitutional arrangements within the administrative process that "stack the deck" in favor of the interests represented by winning legislative coalitions. As it has evolved, then, the rational-choice perspective is like the traditional one in its assumption that oversight and other legislative controls bears an instrumental relationship to statutory goals. Where it differs is in its somewhat vague conceptualization of those goals in political as opposed to substantive terms.

The late-1980s theory of fire alarms is part of a thought-provoking effort to provide a common framework for understanding direct and indirect legislative controls over the administrative process. As noted by Jeffrey Hill and James Brazier, however, the assumption that Congress's relationship with the bureaucracy serves interests of winning coalitions is problematic as a basis for a general, empirical theory of oversight. The most obvious difficulty is that administrative discretion in statutes may reflect more than uncertainty about means-ends relationships; Delegation is often political, in the sense that it results from Congress's inability to resolve conflicting social interests. Legislative preferences obviously change, moreover, and oversight necessarily gives influence, not to original winning coalitions, but to whatever interests dominate Congress at the time that administrative issues are brought to its attention. (In this sense, the use of deck-stacking procedures is obviously inconsistent with the realities, if not with the theory, of fire-alarm oversight.) As mentioned above, the 1983 analysis of Weingast and Moran, undertaken outside the constraints of principal-agent logic, suggests that oversight reflecting changing committee preferences had a substantial effect in curtailing the Federal Trade Commission's efforts to "prevent unfair or deceptive practices"—a mandate notorious for the political discretion it confers.

In a more general sense, however, effective reactive oversight is not contingent on the conditions that Congress's political goals are clearly defined in the legislative process or that they remain stable over time. Groups and individuals with significant political resources tend to be well informed about government actions that might affect them. Furthermore, it is almost axiomatic that when these interests are dissatisfied with policy outcomes produced by one part of the system, they will turn elsewhere for satisfaction. Fire alarms exist, then, regardless of whether they have been instituted as such. And if they are not infallible, they do enable legislators to identify a large share of the agency policy decisions that are vital to key constituents. Cooper and I have argued that reactive oversight in this way provides a useful mechanism for Congress to respond to important political issues that arise in the administrative process. The fact that such demands have increased no doubt explains much of the legislature's effort to enlarge its capacity to perform oversight.

Students of Congress will not find this latter conception of reactive oversight to be particularly enlightening. Indeed, some have remarked that the original fire-alarm thesis (which does not address the strategy of protecting winning coalitions) is only an elaborate restatement of something that everyone already knew. This criticism misses the point in one respect, however. Although the legislature's tendency to intervene reactively was well known and often reported, it was seldom used to make the case that oversight was effective in terms of Congress's institutional goals: resolving conflicts of interest and performing representative functions, among others. This point has important normative as well as empirical implications. Again, comprehensive review, designed to ensure the attainment of substantive statutory objectives, has been and continues to be the most prevalent evaluative standard. Ogul has noted that legislators themselves often express regret that their involvement with bureaucracy tends to be haphazard and reactive and that systematic, comprehensive review is seldom attained even within isolated programs. As noted at the essay's outset, the issue of effectiveness ultimately cannot be divorced from value judgments about institutional responsibilities and prerogatives.

The Issue of Direct Influence

It remains to be asked whether legislative involvement in policy is constitutionally sound and otherwise desirable. Few question Congress's right to monitor agency performance. Rather, the key issue is whether the legislature should play an active role in directly influencing agency decisions. (This distinction between review and influence is often implicit, probably because the two are assumed to be natural companions.)

The preceding discussion provides a useful background for considering the normative issues surrounding oversight. Just as assumptions about the legitimate purpose of congressional review guide efforts to assess its impact, the determination of what types of intervention are desirable must be based, in part, on the consideration of institutional motives and capabilities. Aside from empirical premises, arguments as to the desirability of oversight can be traced to conflicting assumptions about the way policy should be made. The most important normative issues must be understood in the context of delegated authority, the problems it presents, and its implications for institutional roles and responsibilities. Prescriptive analysis (analysis based on what should be, rather than what is) of congressional oversight cannot be divorced in these respects from a consideration of judicial, presidential, and bureaucratic prerogatives.

Two basic questions arise in normative discussions of oversight. 1. Whether oversight results in good policy, and 2. Whether congressional involvement in administration is constitutional or otherwise legal. In both cases, but especially the latter, analyses often focus on particular institutional forms of review rather than on oversight in general. Having said this, it is important to add that policy and legal questions are closely interrelated. Constitutional principles are deeply embedded in our political culture and are obviously present in the criteria used to evaluate institutional arrangements on other than strictly legal grounds. By the same token, our notions of sound policy-practice may well influence how we construe the meaning of the Constitution's vague assignments of institutional roles.

If the old consensus on the limited impact of oversight is breaking apart, a new one is forming on congressional intrusiveness. Criticism has grow harsher as Congress has sought to exercise more control over the administrative process. Political pundits argue that legislative involvement exacerbates the problems of fragmentation and parochialism already inherent in American bureaucracy. Although less consistently, students of law contend that Congress's efforts directly to influence administrative actions go beyond constitutionally specified limits. In both these regards, scholars assert that a strong administrative presidency or judicial review is preferable to congressional control as a means of promoting bureaucratic accountability. Notwithstanding their popularity, however, normative and legal arguments against legislative oversight often misrepresent institutional behavior in important ways, and they typically neglect important systemic values.

The Traditional Model of Oversight

Doctrinal issues surrounding oversight were once much simpler than they are today. The so-called traditional model derived from the premise that "had to do with getting things done." As such, agency action was distinct from the legislative process of deciding what should be done. This clear division of labor, often referred to as the politics/administration dichotomy, dominated thinking about bureaucracy and its role in government from the late 1800s to the 1930s. It also produced a functional conception of institutional roles in the administrative process that fit neatly with the Constitution's separation of powers.

Because the traditional model conceived of administration in instrumental terms, the purpose of legislative, executive, and judicial oversight was to ensure that agencies effec-

tively achieved statutory goals. To this end, Congress should confine itself to the passive supervision of agencies, taking care to avoid involvement in the "details of administration." This precept was based, at least, in part on the belief that as politicians and generalists, legislators were neither motivated nor able to make competent administrative choices. Given its decentralized structure and limited expertise, the judiciary was also expected to defer to agencies on technical and policy matters. Judges should limit themselves to ensuring objectivity in individual-application decisions through the enforcement of procedural due process. In contrast, the traditional model envisioned an active role for the president in the administrative process. His mission as chief executive was conceived of, not in policy-making terms, but as a managerial function of promoting efficiency within, and coordination among, administrative programs.

These neat divisions predictably fail to jibe with reality.

The obvious problem with the traditional model is that agencies do more than administrate. Bureaucracy must frequently resolve conflicting social values as it implements statutory mandates, a fact that most have come to view as an inevitable feature of modern government. The realization that agencies make political choices has greatly complicated the task of reconciling bureaucracy with the tenets of representative democracy. It has also complicated the task of defining Congress's role. If the bureaucracy claims for itself the legislature's privilege of policy-making, the question can be asked: Should not the Congress be permitted to remake or reshape policy during the oversight process? Much of the confusion surrounding Congress's legitimate role in the administrative process can be traced to the breakdown of the politics/administration dichotomy as a viable foundation for institutional theory. Though some scholars envision oversight as properly consisting of active participation in agency policy-making, most have struggled to maintain the rule of passive review.

Policy Considerations

A coherent, widely accepted doctrine has not emerged to replace the traditional one. With this caveat, certain broad trends of thinking can be identified about bureaucratic discretion and its implications for legislative oversight. To an increasing extent, Congressional review and influence have come to be viewed as sources of fragmentation and inequity in policy implementation.

Many theorists were initially sanguine about administrative policy-making pluralists, who saw uninhibited group politics as the key to democracy and welcomed the growth of bureaucracy as something that enriched the medium in which competing interests could exert their demands. Agencies were viewed as additional access points for registering preferences. Theorists, such as Norton Long, seldom addressed the legitimacy of legislative influence in a direct way, but their logic implicitly endorsed a more active administrative role for Congress than the one prescribed by the traditional model. Given the pluralists' general blurring of distinctions among formal institutional roles (as well as their fusion of politics and administration), it followed that legislative involvement in agency affairs was a natural and healthy practice that facilitated the accommodation of interests.

The pluralist position, however, was never accepted uncritically by constitutional purists, and its strength has ebbed since the 1970s as the result of unflattering accounts of policy implementation. Lowi and others have identified bureaucratic discretion as a root cause of a fundamental pathology in American government—the appropriation of public authority for private ends. The same characteristics of Congress that have been cited as explanations for ineffective review are offered to explain undesirable effects when oversight does occur. Indeed, the idea that congressional involvement in administration has undesirable policy effects has probably gained wider acceptance than more general criticisms of delegated authority.

A common indictment of oversight is the assertion (discussed earlier) that Congress is simply not up to the task. Because of its small size and lack of expertise, it cannot approach comprehensive and therefore effective review. An appendix to this argument is that oversight leads to a false sense of security. Since legislators mistakenly believe that oversight will later be available as an effective check on bureaucracy, they may rationalize broad delegations of authority, especially in controversial areas. Crit-

ics charge that oversight in this way distracts Congress from its primary responsibility of enacting sound and specific legislation in the first place. Thus, it has the net effect to weaken rather than to strengthen legislative control over program implementation.

In addition to its ineffectiveness, critics have often claimed that to the extent oversight occurs, it frequently makes things worse rather than better. If the political content of administration has become more apparent, many continue to view implementation as essentially an instrumental process best left to bureaucratic experts. The problems presented by congressional oversight in this regard are allegedly reinforced by the institutional structure of legislative review. Because the committees that conduct oversight are not representative of Congress as a whole, congressional involvement is often informed by special interests or by other narrow policy concerns. Oversight is thus frequently portrayed as an element of subgovernment politics, a widely criticized phenomenon in which alliances of committees or subcommittees, agencies, and clientele groups manipulate policy to serve their own ends. In an enthusiastic version of this thesis, some scholars argue that committee members deliberately secure vague legislation—legislation ostensibly designed to serve the public interest—knowing that they can subsequently use their influence over administrators to pervert policy to serve narrow interests as it is carried out.

A related charge against oversight is that it provides a postlegislative round of opportunities for special interests to alter, delay, or block agency actions. Not all groups can sustain their influence throughout the policy-making process. It is usually only intense and well-organized interests that are able to monitor agency performance and lobby Congress to intervene on their behalf. Critics thus claim that reactive oversight often serves to dilute programs originally intended to serve the general public and other poorly represented interests. Many illustrations of this charge are drawn from areas of social regulation. For example, Congress has intervened at the behest of industry groups to block or modify agency initiatives dealing with cigarette labeling, seat belts in automobiles, and disclosures in the sale of used cars. More narrowly defined interests have been alleged to suffer, as well, as the result of reactive oversight. As one illustration, Harold Bruff and Ernest Gellhorn have argued that middle-class interests used their influence with Congress to secure more liberal eligibility criteria for student-loan programs, originally structured by the Office of Education to benefit lower-income families.

Executive and Judicial Oversight

Legislative oversight cannot be fully evaluated without considering its effects on the broader institutional system in which it occurs. Critics frequently say, in this regard, that congressional influence over administration is not only bad in itself; it is also inferior to unconstrained agency discretion or to other institutional controls over bureaucracy. This argument provides further justification for limiting Congress to a role of passive supervision, since one branch's power in the administrative process is necessarily served at the expense of the other branches.

The President's Role Many view presidential control as an antidote for administrative fragmentation that is reinforced by the decentralization of power in Congress. The administrative presidency has always had its supporters. As articulated in sources such as the Brownlow Report, drafted by leading New Deal intellectuals, the traditional model advocates a powerful, managerial chief executive who ensures faithful and rational implementation of the laws. The president's role has been necessarily redefined in political terms; the call for it is not less. If anything, the demand for executive control has grown stronger in recent years. Authorities such as James Sundquist have argued that the resources of executive office provides the president with the institutional capacity to perform much more through oversight that the Congress. Equally as important is the argument that the president is the only official with an electoral incentive to conduct coordinative review pursuant to broad political objectives endorsed by national constituencies. Not only is presidential control preferred to legislative oversight for these reasons; congressional involvement is criticized because it naturally interferes with executive prerogatives.

Administrative Due Process In addition to presidential control, many scholars have advocated an interlocking system of administrative procedures and judicial review as a means of ensuring bureaucratic accountability. What might be loosely described as formal due process has long constrained regulatory adjudication, but in recent decades it has been extended to individual application decisions in many nonregulatory areas. Moreover, both Congress and the courts have often required agencies formulating general policies to conduct quasi-judicial hearings and to base their rules on the "substantial evidence" contained in a record.

The popularity of administrative due process as a control on bureaucratic discretion is attributable in part to the perception that bureaucrats are often captured by special interests, or that they are otherwise motivated by narrow professional norms or program goals at the expense of broader social and economic considerations. First, it requires administrators to justify their decisions with sound reasoning and solid, comprehensive evidence, which has been tested through the adversary process. Second, administrative due process is designed to facilitate more searching judicial review based on the same criteria. In this regard, it reflects a much less deferential role for the courts in reviewing agency determinations than the one envisioned by the traditional model. Advocates of such procedures frequently criticize congressional oversight on the grounds that communications from legislators and their staff, which typically occur informally, undermine the integrity of agency records and thus the ability of the courts to ensure objective and reasoned administrative decisions.

Constitutional Theory

Judicial efforts to define institutional roles in the administrative process have generally conformed with the criticisms of active legislative oversight. As mentioned above, the Supreme Court struck down the leading forms of the legislative veto in its 1983 *Chadha* decision. In addition, the Court has invalidated delegations of administrative authority to congressional appointees as an infringement on the president's prerogative of choosing personnel. In contrast with these restrictions on legislative power, the courts have placed only marginal limitations on initiatives giving agents of the president authority to review decisions left by Congress to agency heads. One example of these initiatives is a program, instituted by Ronald Reagan's administration—and still in effect—that requires Office of Management and Budget (OMB) clearance of all executive-branch rules and other agency policies. (An executive rule is a general policy statement issued by an executive-branch agency as opposed to one of the independent commissions such as the FTC or SEC.)

A formalistic conception of separation of powers has provided the dominant constitutional rationale for limiting Congress's role within the administrative process. The courts have generally equated administration with the executive function and have accordingly reasoned that direct control over the bureaucracy should be solely a presidential prerogative. Yet if this formula has yielded appealing results, its assumption that even the broadest delegations of power are executive in a functional sense has proved unsatisfying to many as an intellectual foundation for constitutional theory. The inherent difficulty of this approach is evident in the *Chadha* opinion. In handing down this decision, Chief Justice Warren Burger implied that all administrative activities are executive by definition, but he also contended that congressional vetoes of specific decisions by the Immigration and Naturalization Service created what amounted to legislation unicamerally (by one body) and without the president's signature.

In short, separation-of-powers analysis has proved unconvincing as a basis for prescribing oversight roles in accordance with what most have come to view as sound practice. This dilemma has led some scholars to search for a theory of presidential dominance over Congress in the administrative process that does not rely on a resurrection of the old politics/administration dichotomy. A notable effort to this end has been made by Peter Strauss, who argues that the framers of the Constitution fully understood that administrators would make important policy decisions. Proceeding from the premise that ours is a system of shared (rather than separated) powers, Strauss contends that the framers's intent was to create a strong administrative presidency as a counterpoise to the policy-making power Congress enjoys by virtue of its control over the legislation. In this way, the president's ambitions and constituency ties

can serve as a check on congressional ambitions and constituency interests. Strauss's reasoning leads him to the unexpected conclusion that the president should be dominant in overseeing areas of administration that are functionally legislative, but that Congress should perhaps be permitted more direct influence in other areas.

The Case for Legislative Oversight

Despite its seeming reasonableness, the case against a strong legislative presence in the administrative process has not gone unchallenged. Nor have prescriptions for presidential and judicial control been accepted uncritically. Cooper and I have argued that indictments of congressional influence over agency policymaking are based on oversimplified assumptions about institutional behavior. We also maintain that critics of oversight often proceed from unrealistic premises concerning the nature of delegated authority and from illogical inferences concerning its constitutional implications.

For one thing, congressional involvement in the implementation of statutes is not as narrowly based as its critics claim. The distinction between general and special interests is, in itself, highly subjective. If Congress has occasionally intervened in administration at the behest of relatively small and intense groups, it has often stopped actions that would have benefited well-organized and politically powerful agency clientele at the expense of weaker interests. Although Congress is a decentralized institution, the allegation that legislators are free to pursue their own agenda without regard for the sentiments or interests of other members ignores a variety of formal and informal sanctions used by the whole to keep committees and subcommittees within acceptable bounds.

A counterpart to these arguments is that executive oversight is neither comprehensive nor is it always guided by broad considerations of the public interest. The literature on the Reagan administration's program of regulatory review provide many illustrations of this. Erik Olson, George Eads, and Michael Fix observe that the Office of Management and Budget (OMB) review of agency rules has been far from systematic, showing little concern for the type of managerial coordination envisioned by advocates of a strong administrative presidency. Rather, such review has often been precipitated by the same narrowly-based clientele interests said to influence reactive congressional oversight. The primary targets of OMB review have been health, safety, and environmental regulations—precisely the kinds of public-interest programs alleged to suffer as the result of legislative review.

Nor does judicial oversight appear to be all that its advocates claim. One common criticism is that, as generalists, judges frequently lack the expertise to participate intelligently in agencies' substantive policy decisions. Judges certainly fare worse in this regard than congressional committee members and their staff. Critics have also observed that the judiciary also falls short as a representative institution. Federal judges are unaccountable through the electoral process and typically drawn from elitist social backgrounds. In addition, judicial review, which requires affected interests to present their cases before the courts in formally structured arguments, imposes a bias in favor of well-organized and well-funded groups that can afford lawyers, and may well exceed the legislature's preference for special interests. Finally, the judicial process itself is alleged by many to stifle the kind of bargaining and compromise that are often appropriate for resolving broad administrative policy issues.

One should take care not to exaggerate these points. The presidency is obviously a more centralized institution than Congress, and it may well be more inclined to perform coordinative oversight in response to far-reaching programs endorsed by national majorities. Moreover, the courts have a very legitimate role in the administrative process. This is especially true in areas of agency adjudication, where objective standards should arguably govern decisions enforcing regulations or otherwise applying policy in individual cases. These concessions, however, are hardly damning for the case of congressional review. The underlying goal of the American constitutional system is not, after all, efficiency but that policy decisions should reflect the input of different institutions based on different constituency principles. Assuming that the administrative process involves substantial freedom to choose among

these values, perhaps the most compelling question that critics of congressional oversight have overlooked is why the legislature should be denied an active role in reviewing and influencing agency decisions.

One response to this question is that the administrative process need not entail broad discretion. Theodore Lowi has made the argument that Congress can reassert its control over policy simply by writing more-detailed legislation as an act of will. Yet most feel that this is an unrealistic prescription, if government is to respond within a decent time frame to society's demands. Assuming that Congress must cede broad grants of authority to the bureaucracy, the only logical way to salvage the case against legislative oversight is to argue, as Peter Strauss has, that presidential policy-making power in the administrative process is designed to counter-balance congressional power exercised elsewhere.

Cooper and I argue that Strauss has been correct in viewing control over the administrative process as a matter of striking the proper balance between institutionally shared powers. We maintain, however, that his application of this approach is ahistorical. Assume, for argument's sake, that the framers did intend executive dominance over agency policy-making to counterbalance Congress's legislative power. It remains nonetheless true that the bureaucracy of their day was much smaller and less powerful than ours and exercised a much smaller share of total government power. Given the massive expansion of bureaucracy, legislative review and influence over administration has become increasingly important if Congress is to retain a measure of control over its core function of policy-making.

Strauss's argument is also ahistorical in its failure to consider presidential gains in law-making power. The president's role in the legislative process was typically minimal in the nineteenth century. Today, in contrast, many of the most important statutes passed by Congress are initiated and guided by members of the administration, a development made possible by the institutionalization of a large "legislative presidency" (the president's institutionalized capabilities in the legislative process—a large White House staff, domestic counsel, etc.) in the Office of Management and Budget since the New Deal. Because some administrative and legislative policy-making powers are functionally equivalent (and to an extent, equivalent and interdependent as well), the growth of presidential prerogatives in the latter arena provides a further justification for Congress's involvement in agency rule-making as a legitimate means of preserving its basic institutional role.

CONCLUSION

My intent has been to present a general overview and assessment of some of the central empirical and normative issues surrounding legislative oversight. I have not sought to provide a comprehensive review of the literature on the subject and, indeed, have failed to mention many excellent studies. Most of the works cited demonstrate convincingly that the ability to supervise and influence policy implementation is important to Congress. Oversight consumes a growing proportion of that body's time and energies. Whether oversight is effective depends largely on how one defines the term. Although Congress shows interest in sound administration, the purpose of review is probably not to ensure that policy implementation is consistently faithful to statutory intent or that it is otherwise economical and efficient. Rather, oversight seems a useful way for Congress to further its own objectives of representation and policy-making. Legislators would hardly waste so much time and effort on the process if this were not the case. Constituent demands, among other cues, enable the legislature to respond to key issues without conducting systematic review.

To say that Congress has substantial oversight interests and capabilities is not to endorse a theory of congressional dominance, such as that developed by the rational-choice theorists during the 1980s. The three constitutional branches clearly share and compete for influence over administration, and the bureaucracy has its own power resources, as well. Congress would not struggle to defend such oversight-enhancing devices as the legislative veto if it enjoyed a position of unchallenged supremacy in the administrative process. Neither would it show so much concern with executive innova-

tions, such as OMB review of agency rule-making.

Perhaps the most important limitation of the empirical scholarship is its failure to pay more attention to contextual factors that affect legislative review. Some gains have been made in describing and assessing the significance of the environment and institutional structure of oversight. Nevertheless, even sophisticated analyses often speak of congressional motives and influences as if administration were a homogeneous whole, ignoring important variation in what agencies do. For example, little is known about oversight with respect to different types of agency action such as rule-making, agenda setting, and policy development. The extent, methods, and timing of review may vary substantially among these different areas of administration.

An examination of what might be termed the task environment of program implementation may also lead to a clearer understanding of oversight. Agencies' technical considerations may be more or less complex, for example, and may entail more or less uncertainty. Only limited attention has been paid to the effects of such factors, notwithstanding their importance for Congress's ability to monitor agency performance. As James Wilson and others have observed, task environments also vary substantially with regard to the level and type of political conflict agencies must confront. Yet here, too, there has been relatively little effort to categorize such factors and relate them to oversight incentives and effects. Considerations of the instrumental and political elements of agency discretion are obviously tied to questions of delegation and its relationship to legislative goals that inform competing empirical theories of oversight.

Contextual factors are highly relevant to normative and constitutional analysis, as well. The most difficult challenge facing prescriptive theory is to define the proper balance or tension of bureaucratic, executive, and legislative powers within the administrative process. Several legal scholars have argued that the procedural or functional characteristics of agency action should be important considerations in determining the oversight roles of the three constitutional branches. For instance, direct congressional influence over agency decisions is arguably more appropriate in the quasi-legislative area of rule-making than in the quasi-judicial area of adjudication or in quasi-executive area of internal management decision. It may also be more appropriate where the delegation of legislative authority results from a lack of consensus on political goals. The issues in this area are complex, and existing studies have only begun to explore the normative and legal implications of functional variation within the administrative process. Much remains to be done, both in terms of classifying agency actions and defining the responsibilities of the three constitutional branches as they relate to administration.

Broadly speaking, few would dispute the fact that agencies make important decisions in allocating scarce resources among competing interests. The most basic indictment of normative studies of oversight is that most scholars have refused to come to grips with this fact and its implications for Congress's role in American politics. Since oversight is frequently reactive and politically-motivated and since it often results in direct influence over agency decisions, legislative involvement in administration hardly conforms with the traditional model of passive monitoring. Yet this model was based on the premise that administration is inherently instrumental. To the extent that administration must entail important political choices, active legislative involvement in agency policy-making seems a sound adaptation to the realities of twentieth century American government. To deny this proposition is to assert that Congress can effectively control policy through the legislative process, to endorse unconstrained bureaucratic discretion in balancing competing social values, or to advocate legislative deference to judicial, or especially presidential, government.

BIBLIOGRAPHY

General Accounts

JOSEPH P. HARRIS's *Congressional Control of Administration* (Washington, D.C., 1964) is still a useful study of the institutional techniques and the motives that shape legislative oversight. *Congress and the Administrative State* (New York, 1979) by LAWRENCE C. DODD and RICHARD L. SCHOTT is also an excellent analysis based on observations from across a broad range of agencies, congressional committees, and policy areas. The most comprehensive general work on legislative oversight to date is JOEL ABERBACH's *Keeping a Watchful Eye* (Washington, D.C., 1991). Based in part on extensive interviews with committee staff and on a sensitive interpretation of longitudinal data, ABERBACH's book provides important insights concerning the determinants of oversight. It also lays to rest the argument that oversight is not important to legislators.

Case Studies

A number of studies provide accounts of congressional oversight in particular policy areas. MORRIS S. OGUL's *Congress Oversees the Bu-reaucracy* (Pittsburgh, 1976) examines efforts by the Senate Judiciary Committee to monitor and influence the enforcement of civil rights policy. *Signals From the Hill* (New Haven, Conn., 1988) by CHRISTOPHER H. FOREMAN is a somewhat broader study dealing with Congress's involvement in the implementation of social regulation. JOHN P. BRADLEY's "Shaping Administrative Policy with the Aid of Congressional Oversight," *Western Political Quarterly* 33 (December 1980) examines the impact of oversight in the implementation of Medicare. All of these works and a number of others yield important insights about the dynamics and effects of legislative-bureaucratic interaction that can only be attained through in-depth case studies.

Analyses of Variation in Oversight

Other scholars have focused on variation in oversight, both among agencies and policy areas and over time. In "Committee Characteristics and Legislative Oversight of Administration," *Midwest Journal of Political Science* 10 (February 1966), for example, JOHN F. BIBBY examines the relationship between oversight and committee structure. In "Congressional Committee Members as Independent Agency Overseers," *American Political Science Review* 54 (December 1960), SEYMOUR SCHER examines the effects of different political variables on the willingness of committees to perform oversight. ABERBACH's recent book (cited above) examines many of the same hypotheses about variation in oversight posited by BIBBY, SCHER, and others. ABERBACH also examines Congress's increased emphasis on oversight over time in his book and in a series of earlier articles. See, for example, ABERBACH's "Changes in Congressional Oversight," *American Behavioral Scientist* 22 (May/June 1979).

Normative and Legal Analyses

Most descriptive analyses of legislative oversight offer passing assessments of its desirability. In addition, there is a substantial literature, the primary aim of which is to judge the policy effects and the constitutionality of oversight. For a representative critical assessment of the effects of oversight, see HAROLD BRUFF and ERNEST GELLHORN's "Congressional Control of Administrative Regulation: A Study of Legislative Vetoes," *Harvard Law Review* 90 (May 1977). For a more sanguine view, see WILLIAM F. WEST and JOSEPH COOPER, "The Legislative Veto and Administrative Rulemaking," *Political Science Quarterly* 98 (Summer 1983). Most legal analyses of oversight focus on the constitutionality of devices that allow Congress directly to intervene in agency decision-making. In "The Role of Constitutional and Political Theory in Administrative Law," *Texas Law Review* 64 (November 1985), RICHARD J. PIERCE applies a strict separation-of-powers argument in arguing against the legislative veto and other means of direct control. HAROLD BRUFF makes a similar argument in "On the Constitutional Status of the Administrative Agencies," *American University Law Review* 36 (Winter 1987). For a defense of the legislative veto on constitutional grounds, see WILLIAM F. WEST and JOSEPH COOPER, "Legislative Influence v. Presidential Dominance: Competing Models of Bureaucratic Control," *Political Science Quarterly* 104 (Winter 1989–1990).

SEE ALSO Congress, Sectionalism, and Public-Policy Formation Since 1870; The Congressional Committee System; Congressional Staffs; Legislative-Executive Relations; Legislatures and the Judiciary; AND Pressure Groups and Lobbies.

BUDGET PROCEDURES AND EXECUTIVE REVIEW IN STATE LEGISLATURES

James J. Gosling

State general-fund budgets are significant substantively and politically. Their size represents a major commitment of private resources to public purposes, ranging from a fiscal 1992 high of $43 billion in California to $517 million in South Dakota. Yet beyond their size, state budgets serve as key vehicles for public policy-making. They establish policy priorities for the year or biennium to come, backed by budgetary appropriations. State budgets cut through political rhetoric, laying priorities bare.

This essay looks at the state budget as a policy-making tool that lies at the very heart of state politics. Yet, at the same time, social, cultural, religious, structural, and legal differences among the states influence the character of their budgetary politics. As with any comparative political analysis, this essay strives to generalize about budgetary politics at the state level, while offering caveats when appropriate. And amidst the considerable diversity that exists among the states, frequent qualification becomes a necessity.

The roles, resources, and influences of the executive are compared with those of the legislature in the development, enactment, and execution of the state budget. The resulting portrait draws on empirical political research, including multistate, aggregate data analyses and in-depth studies of the politics of budgeting in a single state. Collectively, this research suggests that the balance of executive-legislative influence has shifted since the early 1970s, with legislatures having become formidable competitors to the governor in shaping state budgets.

Just as executive and legislative influence in the state budgetary process can be compared over time, so can patterns of stability and change in state-policy agendas pursued

through the budget. At the same time, it is apparent that amid shifting policy agendas, several areas of the budget consistently comprise the state budget's policy and fiscal core, claiming the lion's share of budgetary resources from year to year. Assessing the demands and constraints placed on state budget makers, this essay concludes that state-budgetary systems have worked well. As will be shown, governors and legislators have not shrunk from the tough decisions required to balance the budget.

A PUBLIC POLICY–MAKING TOOL

Political executives and legislatures at all levels of government establish priorities by enacting appropriations. Public programs are treated differently; some get bigger shares of available resources, and some grow faster from year to year. Yet governors and state legislatures are best positioned among their counterparts to use the budget as a policy vehicle. Budget-makers in many states possess, along with appropriations, the constitutional or statutory discretion to include substantive language within the budget itself. That discretion, where it exists, can range from allowing provisions to be included in the budget that create, amend, or repeal state law, to those that place contingencies on the release of appropriated funds or specify how funds can be used.

As we shall see later, governors are motivated to include policy initiatives in the budget for several reasons: (1) to render any changes made by the legislature subject to the item veto; (2) to have their proposals considered in the more contained budgetary process, as compared to the regular single-bill legislative process; and (3) to include a number of major policy initiatives within the same legislative package, giving governors greater bargaining power in negotiating trade-offs. Legislative leaders may use their state's flexibility to include policy in the budget for similar reasons. The budgetary process narrows the scope of influence among legislative participants. The variously named appropriations, budget, or fiscal committees function as the committee of record, acting on executive recommendations and initiating recommendations of their own. The standing committees usually play no binding decision-making role in the process, although they may hold hearings on those parts of the budget that programmatically affect them most, offering recommendations to the appropriations committees.

Critics of liberal use of the budget as a vehicle for substantive policy initiatives argue that the budgetary process does not permit issues to be aired as fully as they could be in the regular legislative process, in which the substantive standing committees hold hearings on each major policy initiative, affording those interested in the legislation ample opportunity to register their support or opposition. They also suggest that the regular legislative process allows the media to follow the legislative debate more closely, thus being better positioned to inform the public about what is at issue, who the key supporters and proponents of the legislation are, and what compromises appear to be in the making. Critics see the budgetary process as truncating public debate, consigning highly important policy issues to subcommittee and partisan caucus forums, and compressing consideration of a broad range of substantively disparate initiatives within the budgetary process's tight timetable.

In comparison to the state policymakers, those at the federal level enjoy less flexibility. Although the House and Senate Appropriations Committees set maximum spending levels, substantive policy continues to be the province of the standing committees through the authorization process. Appropriations can only be granted for authorized programs, and changes to those authorizations characteristically come before the standing committees, not the Appropriations Committees. However, after meeting certain procedural requirements, Congress can attach nongermane riders to appropriations bills, a practice that is used sparingly and most often for controversial legislation that might not pass or would likely be vetoed if it had to go through the legislative process on its own.

Local chief executives and legislative bodies have the least flexibility to put policy in the budget. Budget bills at the municipal and county levels typically contain only appropriations. Expressions of intent, where they exist, tend to be confined to letters or other legally nonbinding documents.

EXECUTIVE-LEGISLATIVE COMPETITION

The states are diverse, and thus, generalizations about their politics must frequently be followed by caveats. States differ significantly in their social, cultural, religious, and partisan political heritages, not just in their legal frameworks. Aside from constitutional and statutory prescriptions and proscriptions about what can be included in the budget bill, key differences center on the relative formal authority of the governor and the legislature over budget development, execution, and control. States also differ in terms of the resources available to governors and legislatures, such as gubernatorial veto power, appointment authority, and the size and type of staff support.

The way in which the legislature organizes itself to conduct its budgetary business can also differ from state to state. Not only do the structure and size of budget committees vary among the states, but some states make use of joint committees (with membership drawn from both chambers of the legislature) and still others employ separate committees in each chamber. Some committees exercise responsibility for both revenue and spending matters; others have sole responsibility for one or the other.

Legislatures also differ in the number of budget bills that are introduced and considered during the budgetary process. Twenty state legislatures entertain only a single budget bill; the other thirty consider from 2 to 350 separate budget bills. The number of bills not only can affect legislative work load but can also influence legislative decision-making and executive-legislative relations. A large number of bills can further fragment an already highly decentralized legislative decision-making process.

Differences in staff support exist among the states, and they are of greatest significance on the legislative side. Governors can readily draw on the staff resources of cabinet agencies (where the agency head serves at the pleasure of the governor) to supplement those of the state budget office and the governor's own executive office staff. Legislatures do not enjoy that breadth of support. They have to rely on the assistance provided by their own staffs, whether centralized within a legislative fiscal office or assigned to budget committees. The ability of the legislature to secure adequate independent staff support can be an important factor in how the balance of influence between the legislature and the governor is achieved.

That relative balance has shifted since the early 1900s. State legislatures clearly dominated budgetary politics at the beginning of the century. In those days, state agencies sent their budgetary requests directly to the legislature, bypassing the governor. Frequently no common budgetary or accounting structures or formats existed across agencies within the same state. Budget requests tended to be presented as lump sums, and direct negotiations between the agencies and the appropriations committees determined the shares approved for each program.

Prompted by the notoriety associated with municipal budget reforms, the executive budget movement spread among the states between 1910 and 1930, receiving a boost by the federal Budget and Accounting Act of 1921. That legislation made the president responsible for developing and presenting the national budget to Congress, and it gave the president the tools to get the job done. It required federal departments to send their requests to the president, who in turn decided which requests, and at what level, to include within his recommendations to Congress. The act also created the Bureau of the Budget to assist the president in reviewing agency requests and preparing the administration's budget.

In the wave of reform, state legislation typically gave the governor the authority to issue budgetary guidelines to the executive-branch agencies; to review, modify, and include or not include agency requests in the executive budget; and to control the budget's execution at the hands of the agencies. At the state level, as at the federal level, legislation created executive budget offices to assist the governor in exercising these new responsibilities. Some state legislatures, as exceptions, enacted legislation that required the governor to share authority for budget development with other executive-branch officeholders and, in a few instances, with legislative leaders as well. Those early choices have shaped patterns of gubernatorial-legislative influence right down to the present.

Budget Development

Except in a few states, the governor is responsible for development of the executive budget. The governor, assisted by staff, crafts the fiscal and policy blueprint for the state. The executive budget establishes a policy agenda and recommends resource allocations consistent with its priorities. The governor's role as chief budget developer requires him to reconcile a vast array of competing demands within available revenues. Of course, the governor can elect to increase revenues by recommending tax or fee increases, but governors most often recommend major increases in response to economic difficulties or other exogenous forces, such as court orders. When revenues fall short of projected expenditures, the governor is forced to bring the budget into balance through budget cuts. In that environment, base budget reallocation becomes the means to finance any new initiatives. Existing programs must be pruned back in order to free up the necessary budget authority to cover new or expanded programs.

Although the governor sets the strategic direction for executive budget development, the majority of budget items appearing as gubernatorial recommendations come from other sources, including agency requests, the preferences of legislative leaders of the governor's political party, recommendations of task forces and commissions, innovations that have successfully been tried in other states, the advice of staff members, and, most important, the state budget office. State budget offices play a number of important roles in budget development. First, they provide instructions that guide agencies in preparing their budget requests. In twenty-three states, that role extends to giving agencies budget targets that limit the amounts to be requested. Cabinet agencies tend to observe these ceilings, but those independent of the governor feel less compunction about complying. Second, state budget office staff members analyze state agencies' requests and make recommendations to the governor. Third, budget analysts may also conduct policy studies, which can lead to budget recommendations apart from any agency request.

State budget offices vary in size, activity, and the composition of their staffs. The largest offices can be found in New York (218 professional staff members), California (65), New Jersey (57), and Florida (54). The smallest include North Dakota and West Virginia (5 each), and Mississippi, New Hampshire, and South Dakota (6 each). The size of a state budget office's professional staff largely reflects the roles it plays. The largest offices tend to be most active in policy development. Not only do they analyze agency requests and make budget recommendations to the governor, but they also take the lead in initiating policy proposals on their own. That leadership may be exercized in cooperation with cabinet agencies, or it may take place with little or no agency involvement or even in an environment of agency opposition, particularly when the agency head is a political rival of the governor. The smaller offices often emphasize their comptrollership responsibilities rather than their role in policy development.

Although development of the executive budget is widely viewed as a gubernatorial prerogative, the governor and his executive budget staff do not have a monopoly on budget development in all states. In five southern states, legislative leaders are intimately involved in crafting the executive budget. In North Carolina, a twelve-member commission consisting of four gubernatorial appointees, four state senators, and four state representatives decides what should go into the executive budget. The commission receives budget requests directly from state agencies, holds public hearings, and makes budget recommendations. That does not mean that the governor is without influence in the process, but his influence is weakened by institutionalized power-sharing. The fact that the state budget office provides staff support to the commission strengthens the governor's hand somewhat, although the legislative members frequently turn instead to their own fiscal aides for counsel. South Carolina institutionally

weakens the governor's position even further. Two independently elected officials, the state treasurer and the comptroller general, join the governor and legislative leaders on the Budget Control Board.

In Arkansas, Mississippi, and Texas, the governor's budget faces stiff competition from an alternative version shaped by the legislature. Although the governor's budget office in Arkansas receives agency requests and puts together an executive budget, it is referred to the legislative council, which, under the supervision of legislative leaders, prepares the official state budget for consideration by the legislature. In Mississippi and Texas, legislative committees formulate an alternative version to the governor's executive budget, and both go to the legislature for consideration. Not surprisingly, the legislature's version gets the lion's share of attention.

These cases serve as visible exceptions to the rule of gubernatorial dominance in executive-budget development. Governors see budget development as their domain; from their perspective, the legislature's turn comes after the executive budget is introduced into the legislature for review. That gubernatorial prerogative is most jealously guarded in the strong executive-budget states of Illinois, Michigan, Minnesota, New Jersey, New York, Pennsylvania, and Washington.

The Legislature's Turn

Just as the governor is positioned to dominate the budget development process, the legislature holds a privileged position in the process of budget review and enactment. Only the legislature can appropriate funding, subject to the governor's veto. But even if the governor exercises the veto, the legislature can still do what it wishes if it has the votes to override the governor's objection. As exceptions, the constitutions of Maryland and Nebraska limit the legislature's discretion somewhat. In Maryland, although the legislature can reduce the spending levels recommended by the governor, it cannot increase them. In Nebraska, it takes a three-fifths extraordinary majority for the legislature to increase spending beyond the governor's recommended level.

After its introduction, the budget is assigned to the appropriations committee (which may also be called a fiscal or budget committee) of the chamber into which it was introduced or to a joint committee, the latter being found in fifteen states. The committee then reports out the amended budget to the chamber of introduction. Committee deliberation usually takes place in two phases. The first involves a hearing of the full committee, in which the governor's representatives—usually from the state budget office—and state agency officials defend the executive budget's requests. However, it is not uncommon for noncabinet agency heads to use the hearing as a public forum to express the needs that they believe were not met by the governor's recommendations. Cabinet agency heads have to be a bit more subtle in expressing their "druthers."

The second and more significant forum is the subcommittee hearing. Appropriations committees in all but six states make use of subcommittees. The number of subcommittees found in the lower chamber ranges from none in Indiana to twenty-three in Texas. At the senate level, Florida and Indiana make use of only three subcommittees, but four or five can be found in most state senates. Subcommittees are typically organized along programmatic lines—such as education (with primary and secondary often considered apart from higher education), transportation, human services, and natural resources—frequently paralleling the structure of the appropriations bills themselves. Obviously, legislatures that employ hundreds of appropriations bills do not create a separate subcommittee to consider each. Instead, a subcommittee characteristically considers several programmatically related bills. Subcommittees are staffed by fiscal analysts assigned to each subcommittee or by staff members centralized within a legislative fiscal services office. In either case, legislative fiscal analysts brief members on the governor's recommendations, offer alternatives, and sometimes make recommendations. When analyst do not make formal recommendations, the way they frame issues and discuss alternatives can give members a good sense of their preferred alternatives. The growth in legislative fiscal staff support has outstripped that of state budget offices, nearly doubling between 1975 and 1988. The largest fiscal staffs can be found in New York and California, each employing more than one hundred professional staff members. Illinois, Michigan,

and Texas have more than fifty. In contrast, the Wyoming legislature employs only three fiscal analysts.

Upon completion of subcommittee deliberations, votes are taken on motions to amend the governor's executive budget. Successful motions then go to the full committee for consideration. Subcommittees prefer to go to the full committee with a solid consensus backing their recommended amendments. When that cannot be accomplished and the vote is fairly evenly split, ranking subcommittee members frequently lead the debate before the full committee. Overall, subcommittee motions usually carry the committee as a whole, with only a few or no objections. Reciprocity is the name of the game at the full committee stage. The unwritten expectation is that members of each subcommittee will support the motions of other subcommittees. Symbolically, it is the chairs of other subcommittees who second a subcommittee's motion for passage before the full committee. Discipline is maintained out of a shared recognition that a subcommittee cannot expect to receive the support of other subcommittees if it does not give its support in return. Exceptions to the norm of reciprocity do occur, most frequently involving matters of financial aid to local units of government. Each committee member, after all, represents at least one municipality, county, and school district and is therefore protective of its interests. The ready access to computer simulations gives members the quick ability to see how proposed formula changes affect their districts. This "politics of printouts" can often create strange political bedfellows, shaping coalitions that can cut across partisan political lines.

The governor's legislative aides and the state budget director may play active roles throughout the committee phase of the budgetary process, especially when the governor and legislative majority are of the same political party. Legislative leaders and committee chairs attempt to reach understandings with gubernatorial representatives about what changes might be sufficiently unobjectionable to escape the governor's veto pen. The governor's representatives press for desired accommodations and compromises. The governor may personally visit with legislative leaders in order to win concessions or shape compromises.

After all appropriations committees have

acted on the executive budget, the amended bills are forwarded to the legislature as a whole, commonly accompanied by a staff document highlighting the committee-endorsed changes. Upon receipt, legislative leaders schedule floor debate, usually allowing time for legislators to first meet in their respective party caucuses to discuss partisan strategy.

In the majority-party caucus, legislative leaders and chairs of the appropriations committees characteristically try to generate support for the amended budget that they nurtured through the committee phase. When the governor is of the same party as the majority, the state budget director or key gubernatorial aides may be invited into the caucus to represent the governor's interests. Sometimes the governor may attend personally. Of course, legislators are again interested in assessing how far they can go in amending the budget without incurring the governor's rancor and ultimately his veto. The caucus chair attempts to gauge the degree of support within the caucus for the budget. Often additional concessions are necessary to engender enough support to be able to pass the budget on the floor. When that is the case, the caucus proceedings take on the air of an auction, with legislative leaders assessing what further amendments are necessary to gain the required support for the budget's passage. Discontent legislators may join forces in ad hoc coalitions aimed at winning further concessions. If they are successful in attracting so many supporters that legislative leaders no longer possess the required level of caucus support for passage, they can hold the entire caucus hostage to their demands. Compromises can then be expected from both sides. When all is done, the majority party usually leaves the caucus room knowing whether it can pass the budget on its own; if not, it has at least a good sense of how much minority-party support is required.

The minority-party caucus is commonly less eventful, particularly in those legislatures in which the majority party holds a decided numerical advantage. In those cases, the majority party may be able to pass the budget without any assistance from minority-party members. Discussion in the minority caucus then often centers around how most effectively to take political shots at the majority party for both its exclusiveness and its budgetary choices. Where the majority party clearly needs minority-party support to pass the budget, the minority-party caucus proceedings more closely resemble those of the majority party.

Two features characterize the legislative process once debate shifts to the floor. First, the time constraints on it are the tightest of any phase of the budgetary process, which can be a problem if the two chambers find difficulty in reaching an agreement. Second, the agenda is less shaped by staff members than at any previous stage of the process. Legislators have brought their own distilled agendas to the caucus, and the commitments that emerge from caucus accommodations shape voting behavior on the floor. Staff members may prepare fiscal notes associated with proposed and adopted amendments, but their influence wanes when compared to their involvement in the committee phase of legislative deliberations. The emphasis at this stage of the process is more on the politics of coalition building and less on policy or fiscal analysis.

The Governor Gets Another Chance: The Veto

After the budget clears both chambers, the governor gets another opportunity to shape its final form. Governors in forty-three states possess item-veto authority over appropriations bills, including the budget bill. Recommendations for veto come from the state budget office, state agencies, the governor's aides, legislators, and interest groups. Although state budget officers identify candidates for veto, the state budget office plays a less-pronounced role in the veto-deliberation process than it does during budget development. The discussion becomes more political, and the advice of close aides and legislative allies becomes more salient. The governor and close aides focus considerable discussion on whether the veto can be sustained. In addition, unlike budget development, when the governor and budget staff members are inundated with requests and state budget office initiatives, prospective vetoes constitute a small but highly controversial portion of the budget, thus personally engaging the governor actively in the deliberations.

It is the legislature that gets the last voice, having the opportunity to override the governor's vetoes. With a two-thirds requirement for override common to most states, the governor needs only to secure the support of one-third plus one of either legislative chamber. Typically, that support can be found within the governor's own party. When the count is close, governors and their legislative liaisons can be found calling in political debts and promising future favors to those legislators straddling the fence. Here again, state budget office and legislative fiscal staff have little part in the politics of veto deliberation. They may prepare analyses of the effects of vetoes and their override, but political influence peddling falls to others.

Controlling Budget Execution

After the budget has been enacted into law, the execution phase of the budgetary process begins with the start of the new fiscal year. Controls on budget execution are necessary to ensure that spending does not exceed appropriated levels, is for authorized purposes, and is consistent with legislative intent. The state budget office plays the primary role in controlling budget execution. It does so by allotting funds approved in the budget for expenditure by state agencies and by approving requested budget transfers during the course of the fiscal year.

Allotments, which are employed in forty-two states, give agencies the authority to spend up to a certain amount, in designated budget categories, within a specified period of time. State budget offices may issue allotments covering the entire fiscal year, or they may apportion them quarterly or monthly. Quarterly or monthly apportionments become most significant toward the end of the fiscal year, when agencies have an incentive to spend down appropriations authority that would otherwise lapse into the state treasury if unspent at year's end.

Control over spending does not end when agencies receive their allotments of spending authority. Additionally, preauditing of expenditures provides another check on state spending. Preauditors compare actual spending requests to the agencies' allotted budgets to ensure that the proposed expenditures are authorized and that sufficient unspent appropriations authority remains. Typically the state budget office or the executive-branch agency having responsibility for state financial ac-

counting delegates preaudits to the state agencies themselves. The central office establishes operational guidelines and conducts sample audits to monitor whether those guidelines are being followed in practice.

State budget offices also possess the authority to approve agency requests to transfer budget funds during the course of the fiscal year, but often under strictures set by the legislature. In all but six states, the state budget office has the authority to approve transfers from one object of expenditure to another, such as from salaries to supplies. It also commonly possesses the authority to approve transfers from one program to another within the same agency, although state statutes may limit such transfers to a specified percentage of the appropriation. The legislature, in contrast, usually reserves to itself the authority to transfer funds from one state agency to another, although legislatures in Indiana, Iowa, and South Dakota delegate that authority to the governor (to be exercised by the state budget office).

In addition to selective transfers of the kind discussed above, other potentially more dramatic changes may be required during the course of the fiscal year. Revenues may fall short of projections, or expenditures may rise faster than expected. The two can occur simultaneously in recessionary times. When severe enough and when internal transfers cannot do the job, such circumstances can force the budget to be recast. And that may require the legislature to reconvene to deal with the revenue shortfall. In some states, the governor may unilaterally possess the constitutional or statutory authority to withhold funds from being spent, in order to keep the budget in balance.

Most states restrict the governor's ability to impound funds. Ten states require the governor to make reductions across the board; nine set limitations on the percentage that can be reduced; and seven require the governor to consult with the legislature before acting, presumably to give the legislature the option of enacting legislation if it does not find the governor's approach acceptable. As an alternative to gubernatorial action, the legislature, where empowered, can call itself into session, or where lacking the power, it can urge the governor to call a special session of the legislature. If that happens, the governor, assisted by the state-budget office, typically prepares a budget-adjustment package for the legislature's consideration. In following the legislative route, the governor is not likely to propose across-the-board reductions, but would come in with recommendations reflecting gubernatorial priorities. If the situation is bad enough, the governor's package might even include recommendations for tax increases.

Studies of Executive-Legislative Influence

Studies of executive-legislative influence in state budgeting commonly take one of two forms. The first utilizes multistate aggregate-data comparisons of agency requests, gubernatorial recommendations, and legislatively approved appropriations in an attempt to model budgetary decision-making and untangle the relative influence of budget participants. Such studies, because of their approach and limited data, offer only limited contextual insights into the institutions, processes, or patterns of interaction in the states included in the aggregate analysis. They may identify general rules of decision-making (such as the governor cutting back agency requests and legislatures appropriating about what the governor recommended), but they fail to penetrate much below the political surface. Little or nothing is learned about how the different types of budget items constituting the whole can affect choice (for example, their cost, their relative political significance, and whether they affect local levels of government). Also, one is given little or no appreciation of differences in political culture, institutional characteristics, the roles of staff, and patterns of participant interaction.

The second type of study focuses in depth on the politics of budgeting in a single state. It tends to be much richer contextually, filling the void described above. It may make use of quantitative analysis, but when it does, the variables employed tend to be tailored to the institutional, procedural, and political distinctiveness of the state in question. When more-interpretive assessments are followed, these studies benefit from their in-depth treatment of the influences of history, political culture, distinctive special interests, and patterns of participant interaction. Their major limitations are that they characterize budgetary politics within the confines of particulars, lack a com-

mon organizing framework, and are conducted at different points in time, making it difficult to generalize from their findings.

The following highlights those empirical studies which have contributed most to the understanding of the politics of state budgeting, recognizing their limitations, as discussed above. Ira Sharkansky's classic study of influence and budgetary decision-making in nineteen states has served as a model for subsequent research. In his 1968 study, Sharkansky found that legislatures generally followed the governor's recommendation instead of the agency's request. He also found that acquisitive agencies tended to do better budgetarily than those with modest aspirations. Agencies that requested the largest budget increases received proportionally the greatest cuts from governors but realized the largest relative gains over base-budget levels. Legislatures largely followed the governor's lead; governors trimmed agency requests by 14 percent on the average, while legislatures reduced them by 13 percent.

Two researchers, Gary Moncrief and Joel Thompson, replicated Sharkansky's model in 1980, but added an independent variable, the partisan balance between the governor and the legislature. Their study of thirteen states corroborated Sharkansky's earlier findings. But, controlling for partisanship, they found that agreement between the legislature and governor was highest when the governor was from the same political party as the legislative majority and lowest when they came from opposing parties, signaling to other researchers the importance of partisanship in executive-legislative budgetary relations.

Seven years later, Joel Thompson replicated the study again. He found that the overall patterns remained consistent: agencies requested increases, governors cut them back, and legislatures appropriated about what the governor had recommended, although unlike the earlier studies, Thompson's found that the legislatures upped the governor's ante a modest amount. In addition, the increases granted agencies were higher than found in the previous studies. Yet most of that growth could be attributed to higher rates of inflation occurring during the budget years included in Thompson's 1987 study.

Although the results of the many single-state studies are consistent with Sharkansky's general findings, they depict a more complex set of relationships than aggregate data suggest. These studies suggest that the state legislature does not merely rubber-stamp the governor's recommendations but actually exercises selective independence from the governor. Within apparent aggregate-level agreement, legislatures opt to modify gubernatorial recommendations on specific budget items, often in ways that get canceled out in the aggregated comparisons.

A study of Wisconsin state budgeting found the legislature's joint finance committee routinely going along with the governor's budget recommendation for the low-to-medium-cost budget items that affected state government operations. The legislature as a whole similarly followed the finance committee's recommendations for those items. However, the committee exerted considerable independence for the high-cost items, particularly those that affected local units of government. Again, in a similar vein, on the chamber floor the legislature tended to follow suit, feeling freer to make changes in the committee's recommendations for this high-cost, politically charged portion of the budget. A study of budgeting in New York State also supported the picture of selective legislative independence. The legislature made at least moderate changes in more than one-third of the budget items included for the nineteen state agencies over the six-year period studied. Another single-state study found the legislature in Ohio consistently adding to the governor's budget recommendation, increasing spending to reflect legislative priorities excluded or inadequately funded in the executive budget.

Studies of budgeting in Georgia and North Carolina provided interesting twists. Although the Georgia legislature was found pretty much to follow the governor's budget recommendation, it departed from the governor's lead in estimating the costs required to continue the current budget, regularly coming in lower than the governor's estimate. By minimizing the amounts needed to finance the cost-to-continue budget, the legislature gave itself additional fiscal room to finance new spending initiatives. The North Carolina study found the legislature following the governor's recommendation for 99 percent of the budget. But for that other 1 percent, the legislature went its own way, with the Democratic leadership distributing the roughly $37 million as if it were part of a designated pork barrel appropriation. These funds were directed at "special legislative needs," not following any gubernatorial priorities. Lacking an item veto (or any veto power, for that matter), the North Carolina governor was unable to strike any of the pork from the final budget. Perhaps he was willing to accept these highly selective departures as a trade-off for the legislature's otherwise high degree of support.

Finally, studies of budgeting in Mississippi and South Carolina found the legislatures dominating the budget-making process, a dominance that was found to begin with the legislatures' inroads into the traditionally executive-dominated process of budget development. In both states, the governor institutionally shares power in budget development with legislative leaders. Thus, in both states, the legislature not only gets the opportunity to review executive budget recommendations, but to shape them as well.

This picture of the importance of structure in shaping relative gubernatorial and legislative influence over budgeting is reinforced by the results of a survey administered to state executive-budget officers and legislative fiscal officers. An analysis of their responses suggests that legislative domination tends to be associated with line-item budgeting systems or executive-budgeting systems operating independently of the governor and with independent budget preparation by legislative staff members. However, legislative dominance was found to exist in only a relatively small minority of the states.

In an attempt to overcome the limitations inherent in single-state case studies, political scientists Edward Clynch and Thomas Lauth commissioned studies of budgeting in thirteen states, following a common framework and standard time frame. In doing so, contributors were asked to respond to several questions that probed formal organizational relationships and processes and to provide an assessment of actual practice. The editors imposed no standardized data elements—other than structural factors—to be used in answering the queries about participant influence; they relied instead on each author's own interpretation. The collection includes states from all areas of the country, providing a rich comparative laboratory. As the editors note, the states range from rural to highly urban, from resource-rich to resource-poor, from high- to low-population, from those with population growth to those with population decline, and from high-tech economies to work forces dominated by unskilled and semiskilled labor. They also differ in terms of the partisan balance between the governor and the legislature. Unfortunately, the absence of systematic empirical analysis of these factors and their effects on budgetary influence limits the comparative utility of these studies beyond their discussion of diffences in formal structure.

In interpreting what these studies say collectively, the editors suggested that state budgetary influence follows formal structural relationships to a certain extent. However, they noted that tight revenue constraints appear to advantage the governor at the expense of the legislature. Governors typically bear the onus of proposing new taxes (typically not a happy task for them) and expenditure reductions in difficult economic times. The editors also saw the "power equation" between the governor and legislature as changing over time, with the strengthening of one institution prompting the other to reevaluate what it needs to close the power gap. Moreover, the editors perceived public opinion as playing a role in influencing the balance of power, insofar as a popular desire for strong leadership prompts legislatures to make concessions to gubernatorial initiatives. Conversely, demands for greater pluralistic access open up executive-dominated budgetary systems, leading to greater legislative influence over budgetary choices. And so the dialectic was expected to continue.

LEGISLATIVE INROADS INTO EXECUTIVE PREROGATIVE

In addition to asserting itself in its budget-making relationship with the governor, the state legislature has made several inroads into other areas of traditional budget-related executive prerogative. Legislative incursions have been made into such areas as the receipt and allocation of federal funds, revenue estimating, budget-information systems and aid formula modeling, and program auditing.

Federal Funds

Since the early 1980s, legislatures have increasingly become involved in the review and receipt of federal funds, traditionally a right of the governor and his executive-branch agencies. As recently as 1979, most state legislatures did not appropriate or even review the federal funds coming into their states. The executive budget's appropriations schedule contained only an estimate of expenditures that would be financed by federal funds. The executive branch was free to accept and decide how to use whatever federal money might come into the state. By the mid-1980s the picture had changed significantly. In the 1981 legislative session alone, nearly half the state legislatures enacted provisions giving themselves the authority to appropriate federal funds. By the end of 1983, that number increased to thirty-seven, as state legislators felt the fiscal fallout of the 1981–1982 recession. With state resources becoming scarcer and the costs of recession-sensitive programs growing dramatically, legislative leaders continued to push for greater control over all resources supporting programs offered within their jurisdiction. By 1988, two more states were added to the list, bringing the total to thirty-nine.

State legislatures have also given themselves the authority to act on federal funds received by the state after the budget has been enacted into law. In thirteen states, the governor must consult with the legislature before receiving and allocating federal funding; in another eleven, the legislature has reserved that authority for itself. In both instances, the legislature typically delegates its authority to a fiscal or budget committee, which acts on behalf of the entire legislature when it is out of session.

Legislatures intruded themselves into federal-funds budgeting for four reasons: first, to gain control over all state spending; second, to advance their own priorities for the use of federal funds; third, to exercise discretion over the purposes to which state matching funds (where required) are committed; and, fourth, to limit future demands for state funds to pick up the costs of federally supported programs when federal funding ends. Faced with a perceived legislative intrusion, governors of several states have challenged the legislature's authority over federal funds in the courts, arguing that each state constitution gives the governor, as the state's chief executive officer, authority over intergovernmental funds. The first test case occurred in Pennsylvania, where in 1980 the legislature granted itself the authority to appropriate federal dollars on a line-item basis. Upon petition by the governor, a lower state court and, subsequently, the Pennsylvania Supreme Court ruled that the legislature's action was not in violation of the state constitution. Governor Milton Shapp appealed to the U.S. Supreme Court, which in turn refused to consider the case, thus in effect sustaining the state courts' decisions. Subsequent decisions in Kansas, Montana, and New York also supported the legislature's position, but state courts in Arizona, Colorado, Massachusetts, and New Mexico have ruled in favor of the governor's opposition.

The issue of interim legislative discretion over federal funds has also been litigated in the courts. Here the pattern is more clear-cut. State courts in Alaska, Missouri, Montana, North Carolina, and Oklahoma have ruled against legislative committees acting on behalf of the full legislature in appropriating federal funds. The courts have found that it is one thing for legislatures to assume control over federal funds and quite another for them to delegate that authority to a single committee.

Revenue Estimating

Revenue estimating can be both a technical and a political business. Technically, the challenge is to estimate revenues as accurately as possible so that policymakers will know how much revenue exists to finance spending in the budget. Overestimates result in revenue shortfalls, when actual revenues prove insufficient to finance budgeted expenditures. Underestimates can produce revenue balances, which, if inordinately large, can result in public cries of overtaxation. They can also create a tighter budgetary climate than is necessary, causing spending opportunities to go unused.

Revenue estimating can be used as a political tool in the budgetary process. A governor who wants to hold the line on spending can urge the revenue department or the state budget office—whichever has the responsibility for revenue estimating—to estimate revenues conservatively. And since legislatures have traditionally been dependent on executive-branch revenue projections, they have been wary about authorizing spending beyond what can be accommodated by the executive's revenue estimates, even though they may have suspected that greater revenue flexibility existed than the official forecasts suggested.

In response to their dilemma, state legislatures have increasingly developed their own revenue estimating capabilities. Legislatures have hired trained personnel, tied into the state's econometric model (where one exists), and have even acquired independent models of their own. Having access to econometric modeling, which contains assumptions about changes in employment, personal income, inflation, and interest rates, legislative staff can adjust national economic projections to the state level, accounting for the interactive effects of often several hundred variables on state revenues. Like governors, legislatures can use revenue estimating to their political advantage. After the governor's budget has been introduced into the legislature, several months after the administration's official revenue estimates have been made public, legislative revenue projections may "find" additional revenues that leaders can point to in support of increased spending on legislative priorities. The 1970s saw legislative revenue estimating spread rapidly among the states. By the early 1980s, thirty state legislatures had developed their own revenue-estimating capabilities. That number grew by another seven during the remainder of the decade.

Legislative Information Systems

The executive branch has traditionally controlled budget information, which includes data on past years' expenditures, agency requests, gubernatorial recommendations, committee actions, final legislative appropriations, and gubernatorial vetoes. In addition, it has maintained control over state-aid formulas, thus being able to restrict access to their use in simulation. Executive staff could model proposed formula changes and readily see their redistributive effects, providing the governor and his aides with the ammunition needed to develop coalitions in support of favored policy changes. Legislators could ask executive agencies for copies of the printouts, or they could even ask them to run a given aid model with their own proposed formula changes. In either case, legislators had to ask, wait for a response, and, in the process, perhaps telegraph their political intentions. For the legislature, independence would only come when legislators and their aides shared direct access to budget-information systems and aid formulas. Today, legislatures in most states enjoy that access. Several even have distinctive software packages that enable them to manipulate the data in ways not always available to the executive branch.

Program Auditing

Postauditing constitutes the final phase of budgeting. Its purpose is to check on whether budgeted funds were spent consistent with appropriations authority and legislative intent. The legislature appoints postauditors in most states, although ten states have both a legislatively appointed auditor and an elected state auditor. Where auditors serve at the pleasure of the legislature, they usually function under the oversight of a legislative committee. Legislative audit committees approve the auditor's agenda, often monitor the progress of controversial audits, accept or reject audit reports, and propose corrective legislative action.

In addition to the traditional financial postaudit, legislative auditors have increasingly turned their attention to program audits. Program auditing not only assesses the extent to which programs are in compliance with statutory authority and legislative intent but also looks at how well and efficiently programs are accomplishing their goals and objectives. It has largely become an activity of the legislative branch. Of the thirty-one state audit agencies that conduct program audits, twenty-six, or 84 percent, fall under the legislature's auspices.

An eight-year study of legislative program audits, involving nearly five hundred reports across the states, focused on the nature of their recommendations. About one-half proposed statutory changes, and about one-quarter recommended that the legislature pursue budgetary changes, illustrating program auditing's link to budget-making. With program auditing, the legislature possesses still another tool to compete with the executive branch in policy-making.

BUDGETARY SYSTEMS AND PARTICIPANT INFLUENCE

No one, uniform type of budgetary system is employed across the states. State budgetary systems variously reflect the inheritance of past budgetary reforms. The adoption and expansion of the planning-programming-budgeting system (PPBS) among federal agencies in the 1960s triggered experimentation at the state level. Program budgeting has its intellectual base in rational decision-making theory. Both are based on the proposition that goals and objectives should drive decision making. The bottom line becomes achievement of those goals and objectives, recognizing that alternative ways can get you there. The trick is to identify the best means, and for PPBS that is the most efficient means.

Program budgeting had its origins within the Department of Defense in 1961. Secretary of Defense Robert McNamara believed that all elements of the defense budget could be related to the department's overall objectives, regardless of organizational structure. Their respective contribution and costs could be assessed and compared, with budgetary support flowing to that combination which best realized national defense objectives at the lowest cost. The use of PPBS spread well beyond the Defense Department. In 1965 the Bureau of the Budget (BOB) imposed it on all executive departments. Goals, objectives, programs, subprograms, and program elements had to be identified for all agencies, and base budgets and new budget requests had to be restructured along these programmatic lines. The BOB developed formats and forms to structure requests. One such form was the program memorandum (PM), requiring analytical justification for each program element and showing how it contributed to programmatic objectives.

Although the use of analysis in budgeting was not in itself new, the attempt to incorporate it structurally within a prescribed system of budgeting was. In reality, program budgeting at the federal level became an exercise of form over substance. The program-budget structure never caught on with Congress. Appropriations committee members had long become comfortable with the agency-specific, line-item budget format. Executive agencies found it to be a lot of work with a questionable payoff. By 1969, only three federal agencies had made substantial progress toward implementing program budgeting as intended by PPBS. By 1971, the Office of Management and Budget (OMB, successor to the BOB) discontinued the requirement that federal agencies submit all of the special PPBS-related forms. By the end of the Nixon administration, PPBS had been allowed to die quietly. Nonetheless, the states got caught up in the fervor over program budgeting. A large Ford Foundation grant supported technical assistance to states wanting help in implementing program-budgeting systems. Other states initiated systems on their own; California, Hawaii, Michigan, New York, Pennsylvania, Vermont, and Wisconsin took the lead.

On the whole, the experience of the states closely paralleled that of the federal government. Program budgeting, as originally conceived, never became a reality. Several states continued to structure their budgets along so-called programmatic lines, but those lines typically coincided with organizational structure. For example, a state transportation department might identify the following programs: highways (with subprograms perhaps for new construction, reconstruction, and maintenance), mass-transit assistance, assistance to short-line rail operators, airport development assistance, the state patrol, and motor-vehicle regulation (with possible subprograms for vehicle registration and driver licensing). Organizationally, each program could be the administrative responsibility of a separate division or bureau. Thus, the program budget would look very much like an organizationally based budget; program-related numbers became organization-related numbers. Of all the states, Pennsylvania came closest to implementing a "pure," cross-organizational program-budgeting system. In program budgeting's short-lived experiment in Pennsylvania, the legislature required fiscal staff members to develop budgetary "crosswalks" relating the program budget back to the agencies' organizational structure. Today, only the trappings of the original program budgeting remain.

In addition to their desire for organizationally related numbers, legislators across the states tended to view program budgeting as a tool of executive centralization, in which agency heads and ultimately the governor, could set program objectives, control the budget structure, and decide what analytical methods to employ in weighing alternatives. The evidence, however, suggests that legislative concerns, where they existed, were probably exaggerated, since program budgeting never really functioned the way its designers intended.

Zero-Base Budgeting

As state budget-makers abandoned fledgling efforts at implementing program-budgeting systems, they turned their attention to another form of budgeting that was gaining popularity and notoriety in the state of Georgia. That form, which became popularly known as zero-base budgeting (ZBB), had its origins in the private sector. It allowed managers to adjust their operating budgets for different business scenarios. Alternative levels of market demand would generate different levels of revenues and costs. Executives could vary their assumptions from a continuation of existing demand to increases and decreases from the base level. Governor Jimmy Carter of Georgia, newly elected in 1972, believed that this budget technique could be altered and used effectively in state government.

ZBB asked agency administrators to show what their budget requests would look like at different funding levels. They would have to deal with what would remain if funding were to drop to specified percentages below their existing base level and what would be added if funding were available at specified increments above the base. Such alternative scenarios, Carter and other proponents of ZBB believed, would clearly flush out the agencies' priorities.

During his campaign for the Democratic presidential nomination, Carter frequently alluded to ZBB's success in Georgia. He pledged to apply it to federal budgeting if he were elected president. He claimed that ZBB's introduction would force federal agencies to scrutinize their entire budgets, not just show how additional resources would be used; budgets would have to be justified from scratch. In practice, ZBB did not work that way in the federal government, nor had it worked that way in Georgia.

At President Carter's direction, the OMB developed regulations requiring that ZBB be used by all federal departments in structuring their budget requests for Fiscal 1978 and beyond. The accompanying instructions required agencies to break their budget requests down into discrete decision units, the lowest level at which meaningful management decisions are made. The instructions left it up to each agency to determine what should constitute a decision unit. It could be a component corresponding to what had been program budgeting's categories (program, subprogram, or program element), or it could be something altogether different. Regardless of the budget level selected, agency managers had to identify and rank the decision units at four alternative levels: (1) the minimum level, below which the government enterprise would no longer be viable; (2) the maintenance level, or level that would be required to continue the existing level of operations or services without any policy change; (3) the intermediate level, at an agency-determined point between the first two; and (4) the improvement level, requiring additional resources to expand the current level. Four alternative budgets had to be prepared, one for each alternative level.

The response to ZBB was mixed. The OMB liked the approach because it forced agencies to set priorities. The agencies themselves found it to be a lot of extra work. In fact, agency budget officers spent most of their time trying to show the disastrous effects that all but level four would have on agency programs. Thus, the exercise became a guarded and defensive one. Nonetheless, the national attention given ZBB prompted state policymakers and budget officers to try it at the state level. Following Carter's lead, governors and legislative leaders, attempting to get some political mileage from it, held up ZBB as a means of controlling budget growth by scrutinizing the budget from top to bottom. That promise made for appalling political rhetoric.

The type of ZBB commonly used at the state level was not unlike that used within the federal government. In both cases, ZBB took the form of alternatives budgeting rather than budgeting from a base of zero. State budget agencies typically required agencies to submit requests corresponding to various target levels—at, below, and above the base. The operating presumption was that below-base levels would cull the lowest priority items from the budget. In practice, agencies could be found to include highly sensitive budget items within the lists of what would have to be cut at below-base levels of support, particularly those protected by strong constituent groups. Of course, this was done with the expectation that budget reviewers would find those cuts politically unacceptable and would restore them.

Unlike PPBS, ZBB did not challenge existing budgetary approaches; it could be used with line-item budgeting or within a program-budget structure. It did not centralize decision-making and benefit the executive in the eyes of legislators. Instead, it broadened participation down the management structure; lower-level managers assembled suggested decision packages, to be reviewed by progressively higher-level managers. In doing so, they used whatever criteria they deemed important.

ZBB, as it was formally employed within the federal government, is no longer used as such within the states; but vestiges of it remain in several states in the form of alternative target budgeting. Where used, governors and legislatures continue to be attracted to its priority-setting features, although top agency officials remain chary about having to lay out lower-priority items for executive and legislative budget reviewers to cut.

DISSECTING THE STATE BUDGET

The state budget can be viewed in different ways. First, it can be seen as a plan for spending all the revenues that come into the state's treasury, regardless of their source. This is the most inclusive way of looking at the state budget. It obviously yields the highest budget figures, and budget-makers refer to it as "the total state budget" or often "the all-funds budget."

Another variant, the general-fund budget, includes only appropriations financed from state general-purpose revenues, which are derived from state tax and fee instruments that are not legally pledged to any specific category of expenditure. Major sources of state general tax revenue include the personal and corporate income tax, the sales tax, death and gift taxes, and non-earmarked excise taxes (most commonly those placed on tobacco products and alcoholic beverages). Revenues from pari-mutuel gambling and lottery sales also usually end up in the general fund. These revenues collectively support most of the activities of state government. They finance the operation of universities and colleges, prisons, and mental health institutions. They support state agency operations, such as tax collection and processing, social services, and tourism promotion. They also aid local schools, provide property-tax relief, and finance the state's share of the Aid to Families with Dependent Children (AFDC) program and Medicaid. They usually do not support state-highway construction and repair, bridge replacement, the maintenance and operation of state parks, or the regulation of hunting and fishing; instead, earmarked revenues, referred to as "segregated revenues," finance these activities.

Segregated revenues most often come from state-imposed user fees and are dedicated to public purposes associated with that use. A motor-vehicle operator pays a fee to register his automobile or truck for on-road use. That same driver pays a tax on each gallon of motor fuel purchased. These revenues together go into a segregated highway or transportation fund to pay the costs of highway construction and repair. Similarly, revenues derived from the sale of hunting or fishing licenses are segregated to finance natural-resource protection. These revenues cannot legally be used interchangeably, nor can they, for example, be used to increase the salaries of public university professors. Any of these uses outside of the purposes for which the revenues are segregated would require statutory authorization. Where constitutions proscribe such transfers altogether, not even the legislature can authorize them.

Budget comparisons between the states usually employ general-fund budget figures, exclusive of support from federal funds. General funds also draw the most attention politically. Balanced-budget requirements apply to the general-fund budget, not to the more inclusive all-funds budget. In addition, projected revenue shortfalls in the general fund may require increases in the politically volatile state sales or personal income taxes. The general fund finances all of the state budget's big-ticket items, except highways.

Budget Policy and Fiscal Core

Several areas of the budget constitute its policy and fiscal core, from year to year and biennium to biennium. They claim the lion's share of state resources and are usually at the center of the state policy debate. These areas include school aid, state revenue sharing with local units of government, Medicaid, AFDC, community social service aid, colleges and universities, prisons and other state institutions, and property-tax credits. Together, they claim 70–85 percent of general-fund resources, depending on the state in question. Thus, everything else in the general-fund budget falls within the remaining 15–30 percent.

These areas of the budget compete with each other for state general-purpose revenues, and that competition can be especially keen in bad economic times. In recessionary economies, increased levels of unemployment can drive up the costs of public assistance. As more families qualify for AFDC, they also become eligible for Medicaid. Since recipients who qualify have been determined by the courts to have a property right to receive the benefits for which they are entitled, AFDC and Medicaid present a first claim on state revenues. Similarly, growing numbers of sentenced felons place pressures on state correctional systems. Crowded prison conditions create the need for enhanced security, requiring additional correctional officers. If prison crowding becomes too severe, governors and state legislatures may have to authorize the construction of additional correctional institutions, and new facilities require staffing, in reality constituting a nondiscretionary budget item. At the same time, budgeteers have to balance demands for increased direct property-tax relief, for higher university faculty salaries in an increasingly competitive marketplace, and for quality improvements in primary and secondary education in an environment of declining student achievement. In difficult economic times, merely the increased costs to continue these high-budget programs can absorb available marginal increases in state revenues. Deep recessions may even require program reductions, and with these major programs making up to 85 percent of the state budget, they cannot be held harmless form cuts.

Aid to Local Governments

States financially assist local governments to help them bear costs that would otherwise have to be covered by local revenues. Local assistance programs perennially get a great deal of political attention in the state budgetary process. Not only do they constitute significant claims on state resources, but they often precipitate political battles over the allocation of aid. All legislators have an interest in local-assistance programs. State aid to local governments has a tangible quality. As noted earlier, each legislator represents at least one municipality, county, or school district. Through computer modeling, legislators know how different formula changes will affect their districts.

State aid to local governments can take one of two forms—unrestricted or restricted. Unrestricted aid, commonly referred to as state general-revenue sharing, can be used for any local public purpose. Restricted aid, on the other hand, is appropriated for a designated purpose, such as for primary and secondary education, local highway repair, mass-transit operations, or solid-waste recycling.

On the average, about 35 percent of all state expenditures go to local assistance, but considerable variation exists among the states. At the high end can be found California (49.9 percent), Wisconsin (42.5 percent), Minnesota (41 percent), Wyoming (40.6 percent), and North Carolina (39.5 percent). At the bottom lie Hawaii (1.9 percent), New Hampshire (14.4 percent), Rhode Island (17.1 percent), Vermont (17.9 percent), and Delaware (19.3 percent).

Of all state aid to local governments, only about 10 percent, on the average, is provided as unrestricted assistance. However, in three states, Nevada, Wisconsin, and Massachusetts, unrestricted aid accounts for more than a quarter of all local assistance. Nearly two-thirds of restricted aid goes to primary and secondary education, followed by public welfare (12 percent) and highways (5 percent).

BUDGETARY RESPONSIBILITY AND FISCAL CHALLENGES

State-budgetary systems have worked well. Governors and legislatures have responded to fiscal and programmatic challenges and have made the tough decisions required to balance the budget. Their ability to cope with mounting claims on state resources during periods of revenue scarcity was sorely tested at times during the 1980s and early 1990s. Yet governors and legislatures have established a record of responsibility, doing what is necessary to make fiscal ends meet, while pursuing policy priorities. When economic times improved, they were not averse to reducing taxes that they had raised earlier.

The states' plight as a result of the 1981–1982 recession must be viewed in light of their experience toward the end of the preceding decade. The late-middle and end of that decade had been good to state treasuries. Sound economic growth, along with rising inflation, multiplied state revenues and produced surpluses in many states toward the end of the decade. In that climate, governors and legislatures in a number of states tried to outdo each other in proposing tax reductions. In fact, mounting state surpluses prompted political challengers in several states to assail incumbents for taking more of the taxpayers' money than was needed. The popular cry became "Give it back." And give it back they did. State legislatures, usually following or upping their governors' recommendations, reduced personal income taxes in thirty-five states and sales taxes in nineteen between 1978 and 1980.

The 1981–1982 recession and its immediate aftermath changed the rules of the budgetary game for all except the oil-producing states, where rising oil prices insulated their economies from the national recession. Rising unemployment depressed a revenue base that already had been pared back through tax cuts. It also pushed up the costs of recession-sensitive expenditures, most notably those for public-assistance programs. That combination created a fiscal environment in which state policymakers had little choice but to raise additional revenues and cut budgets. In fact, by the end of fiscal 1982, legislatures in twenty-three states had come back into session to pass budget-adjustment bills. The same thing happened again the following year, but this time legislatures in thirty-nine states enacted midyear budget reductions. During those two years, the personal income tax was increased in twenty-eight states and the sales tax in thirty—tough tasks that no politician relishes.

The middle of the decade saw a shift in the states' fortunes. Those industrial states that were hardest hit by the recession experienced the strongest recovery. Yet, in a twist of fate, the oil-producing states and, to a lesser extent, the heavily agricultural states faced a reversal of fortune, as declining oil and agricultural commodity and land prices created selective revenue shortfalls across the nation. As a result of this dichotomy, twenty-five states lowered general-purpose taxes between 1984 and 1986, and twenty-four others increased them.

The economic recovery in the Northeast and parts of the industrial Midwest proved to be short-lived. By the decade's end, a brewing national recession forced most state budget-makers into an increasingly conservative posture. Both governors and legislatures cut deeper into agency requests, with the result that fiscal 1991 brought near-record-low expenditure increases across the states. Even so, by the end of that year, state general-fund balances were at the lowest level since comparative records on fund balances had been collected and reported.

The economic outlook for fiscal 1992 held the promise that budget reductions alone would not be able to secure balanced budgets in many states. In response, state legislatures—typically responding to gubernatorial recommendations—collectively enacted for fiscal 1992 the largest dollar tax increase in state his-

tory. Two-thirds of the states enacted net tax increases. Yet, even with these increases, the strong likelihood existed that midyear-budget reductions would still become necessary in several states.

Amid this fiscal chaos, governors and legislators appeared to be setting substantive policy priorities. The largest-percentage budget increases among the major budget items in the early 1990s went to Medicaid and corrections. Higher education has felt the greatest pinch, followed by AFDC, although the latter can in part be attributed to policy changes involving tightened eligibility and cost controls. Primary and secondary education, which constitutes the single biggest spending component in state budgets, increased just 3.8 percent in Fiscal 1991, falling short of budgeted levels for that year—largely the result of spending deferrals. In addition, contrary to the experience of the mid-to-late 1980s, eleven states actually decreased general-fund spending on K-12 education in fiscal 1991.

In contrast to budget makers at the federal level, governors and legislatures have done what has been necessary to balance state budgets. They have done so largely through tax increases and budget cuts, not by using budget gimmicks. They also decreased taxes when presented with the opportunity. Their job of balancing the budget and setting policy priorities within that balance will likely continue to test their mettle. Medicaid, education, and property-tax relief programs will continue to exert strong claims on state revenues, as will higher education following several years of flagging state financial support. (On the other hand, prison capacity may have caught up with need.) The experience of the recent past suggests that governors and legislatures will be up to the challenges. The budgetary process has worked at the state level, and it can be expected to do so in the future.

BIBLIOGRAPHY

General Studies

No single book still in print provides a comprehensive treatment of state budgeting, from budget making to budget execution. ALLEN SCHICK, *Budget Innovation in the States* (Washington, D.C., 1970) and S. KENNETH HOWARD, *Changing State Budgeting* (Lexington, Ky., 1973), were written at a time when budget makers were experimenting with program budgeting in several states, drawing on the federal government's experience with PPBS. Both books concentrate on the implications of program-budgeting systems for the states, taking a sympathetic view of the prospects. Nonetheless, HOWARD's book provides insightful discussion of the substance and politics of state budgeting at the time.

ALAN P. BALUTIS and DARON K. BUTLER, eds., *The Political Pursestrings: The Role of the Legislature in the Budgetary Process* (Beverly Hills, Calif., 1975), covers the legislature's role in state budgeting. It tends to be highly descriptive, and since it was written at a time when legislatures in many states were only beginning to assert themselves in budgeting, it fails to capture a number of significant subsequent developments. EDWARD J. CLYNCH and THOMAS P. LAUTH coedited a collection of essays on budgetary politics in thirteen states. Their *Governors, Legislatures, and Budgets* (New York, 1991) imposes a common organizing framework and standard time frame on the single-state studies, thus increasing their comparative utility. JAMES J. GOSLING has authored chapters on state budgeting in two books: DENNIS L. DRESANG and JAMES J. GOSLING, *Politics, Policy, and Management in the American States* (New York, 1989) and JAMES J. GOSLING, *Budgetary Politics in American Governments* (New York, 1992). The latter is part of a broader assessment that also looks at budgetary politics at the national and local levels. A few books on budgeting, although they largely focus on federal budgeting, include allusions to the budgetary experience of the states. Prominent examples include IRENE S. RUBIN, *The Politics of Public Budgeting* (Chatham, N.J., 1990) and ROBERT D. LEE, JR., and RONALD W. JOHNSON, eds., *Public Budgeting Systems* (Baltimore, 1989). The former focuses on the politics of public budgeting, while the latter concentrates on budgetary systems.

Comparative Studies

A number of scholarly articles on state budgeting merit attention and can be divided into two categories: those which take a comparative approach and those which deal with single states. IRA SHARKANSKY, "Agency Requests, Gubernatorial Support, and Budget Success in State Legislatures," *American Political Science Review* 62 (1968), constitutes the classic analysis of relative executive-legislative influence and decision-making in state budgeting. It has served as the model for substantive comparative studies, including GARY MONCRIEF and JOEL A. THOMPSON, "Partisanship and Purse Strings: A Research Note on Sharkansky," *Western Political Science Quarterly* 33 (1980) and JOEL A. THOMPSON, "Agency Requests, Gubernatorial Support, and Budget Success in State Legislatures Revisited," *Journal of Politics* 49:3 (1987). Another important comparative analysis that focuses on the governor's use of the line-item veto can be found in GLENN ABNEY and THOMAS P. LAUTH, "The Line-Item Veto in the States: An Instrument for Fiscal Restraint or an Instrument of Partisanship?" *Public Administration Review* 45:3 (1985). It suggests that governors use the item veto more as a tool of partisanship than fiscal restraint.

For those looking for comparative data drawn from among the states, the following publications provide helpful references: NATIONAL CONFERENCE OF STATE LEGISLATURES, *Budgetary Procedures in the Fifty States* (Denver, 1988) and NATIONAL ASSOCIATION OF STATE BUDGET OFFICERS, *Budgetary Processes in the States* (Washington, D.C., 1989).

Single-State Case Studies

Noteworthy single-state case studies include NAOMI CAIDEN and JEFFREY CHAPMAN, "Budgeting in California," *Public Budgeting and Finance* 6 (1986); EDWARD J. CLYNCH, "Budgeting in Mississippi: Are Two Budgets Better Than One?" *State and Local Government Review* 18 (1986); EAGLETON INSTITUTE OF POLITICS, *The Role of the New York Legislature in the Budget Process* (New Brunswick, N.J., 1977); JAMES J. GOSLING, "Patterns of Influence and Choice in the Wisconsin Budgetary Process," *Legislative Studies Quarterly* 10 (1985); THOMAS J. LAUTH, "Exploring the Budgetary Base in Georgia,"

Public Budgeting and Finance 7 (1987); RICHARD SHERIDAN, *State Budgeting in Ohio* (Columbus, Ohio, 1978); JOEL A. THOMPSON, "Bringing Home the Bacon: The Politics of Pork Barrel in the North Carolina Legislature,"

Legislative Studies Quarterly 11 (1986); and MARCIA LYNN WHICKER, "Legislative Budgeting in South Carolina," *State and Local Government Review* 18 (1986).

CONGRESSIONAL STAFFS

Susan Webb Hammond

The United States Congress has the highest level of staffing of any legislature in the world. Although it is in this way unique, it is also typical of legislatures in that it operates within the demands and constraints of a wider political system, is linked to that system in numerous ways, and is responsive to it. As with other legislatures, Congress is characterized by *collegiality* among its members—that is, they are all equal—and by structural decentralization. And Congress, by its nature and in response to the external political environment, imposes constraints on internal operating bureaucracies. These characteristics have determined the development of staffing resources for the Congress, and they have continued to govern staffing patterns.

Sizeable staffs have become a permanent feature of the congressional landscape. Staff assist members of Congress in carrying out individual and institutional responsibilities. They help members achieve policy, power, and reelection goals; they also handle collective responsibilities of legislation, representation, and oversight of the executive branch and federal programs. Staff are organized to be responsive to individual members, as well as to groups and administrative support offices in Congress. Although senior legislative staff often have significant impact on the policy process, all staff operate in supporting roles for the principal actors: the elected senators and representatives.

This essay focuses on the development of staffing within Congress, the distribution and management of staff, as well as the characteristics, activities, and role of staff. Staffs directly attached to member, committee, and leadership offices are the primary focus; although other staff—administrative staff and those in the legislative support agencies—are also discussed.

AN OVERVIEW OF CONGRESSIONAL STAFFING

Neither the Constitution nor the First Congress anticipated the legislative support staff of the early 1990s. The 101st Congress, which convened two hundred years after the First Congress in 1789, employed slightly more than 23,000 staff aides in member, committee, party and leadership, and administrative offices, as well as legislative support agencies. These staff were employed by or worked directly for Congress. There were about 11,400 staff in members' offices, 3,500 committee staff (including staff on special, select, and joint committees), about 200 staff in leadership or party offices, and 5,500 employed by administrative support offices, such as those under the officers of each chamber. Another 2,700 staff worked in the legislative support agencies—the Congressional Research Service of the Library of Congress; the General Accounting Office (30 percent of its work is for Congress, so 30 percent of its total staff are reported as congressional support staff); the Congressional Budget Office; and the Office of Technology Assessment. Of the total employed, about 11,000 staff worked for House offices; nearly 6,000 worked for Senate offices. Slightly more than 100 aides served on joint committee staffs, and about 3,000 worked in joint support offices of the Architect of the Capitol, who oversees the renovation and maintenance of the Capitol and other nearby federal buildings, and the Capitol Police Force.

Congressional staff numbers are often reported as much higher, usually around 30,000. This figure includes the employees of a number of nonlegislative agencies which have by tradition been funded by the Legislative Branch Appropriations bill each year: the U.S. Tax Court, the Botanic Garden, and various commissions—like the National Commission on the Prevention of Infant Mortality. It is, however, more accurate to focus on staff who actually are appointed by or perform support work for Congress; that number, in the 101st Congress, was slightly more than 23,000.

Factors in the *polity*, or political society, the organizational characteristics of legislatures, and the goals and responsibilities of individual members determine congressional staffing patterns. Recent studies treat congressional staff as resources because staff assist members and groups of members (such as committees, subcommittees, and party offices) in reaching individual goals and carrying out institutional responsibilities. Staff are both the reward and the source of power.

THE INSTITUTIONAL CONTEXT

Institutional values and structures affect congressional staffing. The shared values of the polity, the demands to which Congress is expected to respond, and the constraints of Congress as a legislature set the parameters for the historical growth and the contemporary patterns of congressional staffing. The democratic values of the American public shape the role and responsibilities of the individual member of Congress, as well as the role of Congress within the American political system.

The individual member is elected by and accountable only to his or her constituency; Congress does not control who can join the organization. Each member remains closely linked to the external political environment. All members are formally equal. Each member has one vote and the same responsibilities of legislating, representation, and oversight.

The institutional environment is highly individualized and political. Member equality and autonomy are reflected in the organization and structure of the institution, which is characterized by structural decentralization with many autonomous subunits, an absence of hierarchy, and multiple points of access for the polity. The work of Congress—what Joseph Cooper in *The House at Work* (1981) refers to as the *productive system* of legislative, representation, oversight, constituent service, and educa-

tion outputs—is carried out by a decentralized system of committee, member, and leadership offices. Committees permit a division of the work load and specialization of labor, and although committee recommendations must be approved by the full membership of each chamber, committee work is a determinative element in final policy outcomes. Each member also has a personal office which supports the various legislative, representational, oversight, constituent service, and education duties associated with the productive system.

The absence of hierarchy is evident, both in the decentralized decision structure and in the role of the institution's leaders. Although elected as leaders, both of the parties represented in Congress and of the institution itself, they are in reality first among equals, with responsibility to coordinate but without power or authority to make final legislative decisions. Coordination of autonomous members of Congress and of decentralized committees is necessary for collective policy-making and oversight. However, these coordinating mechanisms must not conflict with established democratic values or institutional norms. Therefore, coordinating mechanisms are not allowed to encroach on the equal status of members, multiple points of access to the institution, or collegial operating processes.

Staffing patterns reflect these values and structures. Individual autonomy and equality govern the distribution of staff, so the staffing structure is decentralized. Staff are recruited by and attached to the autonomous *subunits* within Congress: member offices, committees, leadership and party organizations, and administrative support offices. Most staff are appointed by and accountable to individual members, not to the institution. In some instances, appointment of committee staff is formally approved by the full committee or the committee's Democratic or Republican members. Even so, most staff consider themselves responsible to one member—usually the committee or subcommittee chairman, or ranking minority member. In leadership offices, although staff are in an institutional office, they work for the Speaker or another leader and identify with that individual. Norms of loyalty to individual members and sensitivity to politics characterize the work environment.

Each member may appoint a personal office staff which assist in carrying out legislative, representative, and other responsibilities. All members of the House of Representatives receive the same staffing allowance, because each representative has about the same number of constituents (570,000 in 1990). Each representative may appoint the same number of personal staff, and gets the same salary allowance for them. In the Senate, each senator is allotted the same basic allowance for personal staff, with additional monies that vary according to the population of the state. Because allowances vary, there is no set limit on the number of staff in each office.

Egalitarian norms govern committee-staffing patterns also. For many years, the number of staff that could be appointed by each standing committee of both Senate and House was the same (with the exception of the Appropriations committees and the House Budget Committee). The Senate now approves a variable number of staff for each committee, but the House works under the old system. Additional staff for House committees are appointed only after additional monies have been authorized and approved by the chamber. Leadership and administrative offices appoint staff after justifying the need for them.

Also reflecting egalitarian norms, autonomy, and a decentralized structure, Congress has no central staff-recruiting mechanism and no congressional civil service system. Individual subunits set rules for their employees within broad parameters established by each chamber. Indeed, congressional scholars refer to the *enterprise* of the individual member—the aides on personal and committee staffs, and in some instances party staffs, which one member controls.

Staff duties reflect Congress's character as a political institution responsive to its environment. Each subunit's staff is a link to the political system, and is responsive to the demands of that system, which it helps process. Committee staff assist in committee hearings and draft legislation. Members' office staff listen to, and sometimes generate, constituent demands; they respond to policy concerns and to requests for help on individual problems with federal agencies, and they work with communities and constituent groups on federal programs. Staff are also involved in the highly political task of building legislative coalitions.

In sum, the distribution of staff, the accountability of staff, and the work of staff reflect the influence of democratic values and the unique characteristics of legislative organizations. These have also affected the growth of staff.

THE GROWTH OF STAFF

Controversy has surrounded the employment of congressional staff since the early days of Congress. In the early Congresses, members disagreed as to whether there should be any congressional staff. In the early twentieth century, there was divisive disagreement about making staff official employees of the institution. Disputes continue, particularly about staffing levels and the appropriate role of staff.

A number of themes have recurred over the years, many of them reflecting the values and constraints described above:

• Equal access by all members to staff resources, a concern regularly voiced by the *have-nots.* In the late nineteenth century, when committee chairs had staff, other members sought authority to appoint personal staff to help them on committee and noncommittee duties. In 1975, a coalition of junior senators obtained Senate approval for additional personal staff monies. This permitted senators who served on committees—but did not have the authority to appoint committee staff—to appoint personal legislative aides to assist them on committee work.

• The need for minority-party staffing on committees and subcommittees, also an equity issue. Throughout the late twentieth century, the minority party in Congress had regularly sought, and partially achieved, a share of committee staff appointments.

• House-Senate equity, in staff levels and staff salaries.

• Congressional equity with the executive branch in access to information and in policy-making, and the need for staff assistance to achieve this. These concerns were based on the independence of Congress in the separation-of-powers system.

• During the 1970s, when members came to believe that they could no longer rely on the executive branch for timely, accurate information on policy issues, they successfully argued for increased congressional staffing to help them.

• Sensitivity to constituent concern about increased congressional expenses, particularly when some of those expenses are attached to individual members.

• Arguments about how to achieve more efficiency in a notoriously inefficient institution, and disagreement as to whether additional staff will help or hinder that effort.

• The proper role of staff, and whether staff wrongly assume duties and responsibilities which rightly belong only to the elected members.

Staffing changes have generally been incremental, which is typical of legislative decision making. Change occurs in response to external changes in the polity; for example, Congress may assume a greater work load, and increase staff, because of increases in constituent demands for assistance. Or Congress may increase staff numbers to assist in handling the increase in the number and complexity of issues on the national agenda. Interinstitutional rivalry serves as a catalyst for staffing change, as occurred during the 1970s when Congress sought information parity with the executive branch by increasing staff. Shifts within the institution also result in staff changes; during the 1970s, changing norms with regard to fuller participation by junior members, along with increased constituent demands, resulted in a more equitable distribution of staff.

Although these examples are primarily of changes in staff numbers, the same pressures brought about other types of staff change. Staff have been deployed more widely and more equitably, and are more highly educated, more professional, and more specialized. As Congress has become institutionalized, staffing decisions have become more universal and automatic. Staffing records and regulations governing staffing have become more open. The first staff-salary records were kept by hand in ledgers and were not available outside Congress; by the late twentieth century the Clerk of the House and the Secretary of the Senate regularly published a listing of congressional employees and their salaries. For many years a staff salary was figured as a base salary (which was reported) and subsequent percentage increases (which were not reported) so it was nearly impossible to understand the actual salary. (In 1952, for example, a staffer receiving a base salary of $8,000 actually earned $11,646 per year.) Since 1970, actual amounts have been reported.

Finally, the distinction between committee and personal staff has become increasingly explicit. During the nineteenth century, committee chairs were expected to use committee staff to handle the work of their personal office also and, for much of the twentieth century, committee staff were expected to handle noncommittee-related work for committee members. The Legislative Reorganization Act of 1946 made explicit that committee staff could only work on committee business. For aides on members' personal staffs, the line is somewhat less clear. Personal staff aides, particularly in the offices of junior members, continue to handle committee-related work for their members; and associate committee staff—personal aides appointed to assist members with committee assignments—are based in member offices but have committee staff status. Thus, all aides on a personal staff—including those who are appointed as associate committee staff—work on material related to the individual member's duties and responsibilities; the distinction is that personal aides handle committee-related work for the member, and not for the committee.

Staffing has become more flexible within broadly established parameters. Early legislation providing staff was specific; committees authorized to employ staff were listed, and the number of clerks and the salary of each was specified. In the 103rd Congress, each member of Congress is allotted monies to hire personal staff, with the size of House staffs limited. House committees appoint a core staff of professionals and clerks, with additional staff authorized each year by House resolution. Senate committees are authorized monies for all staff and committee expenses biennially.

Some practices of earlier years have been changed. Nepotism is prohibited; staff must work in members' offices. Staff may no longer be employed by both Congress and an executive department.

Some legislation, which at the time of passage members believed authorized incremental staff change, in fact brought about major shifts. Important bills authorized first the employment of clerks by committees, then the employment of clerks by members who were not committee chairs (effectively authorizing personal staff); later, both chambers approved the employment of full-time, permanent clerks rather than per diem aides. Landmark legislation put House personal aides *on the rolls*, with salary paid directly to the aide rather than from a clerk-hire allowance paid to the member. The Legislative Reorganization Act of 1946 recognized the changed nature of the staffing job and explicitly provided for appointment of professional staff on congressional committees. After each major change, the debates shifted because Congress accepted the new staffing provisions as a baseline, and the debates on that baseline would not be reopened. Each change also contributed to the institutionalization of Congress, to a more complex congressional system with more policy actors, with increasing staff professionalization and specialization, and with less-personalized and more-automatic and universal procedures.

A Chronology of Staffing

The first staff in Congress were part-time committee staff. By the 1840s, as the system of permanent standing committees developed, Congress authorized the employment of per diem clerks for specific committees during the congressional session. In 1856, the House Ways and Means Committee and the Senate Finance Committee were authorized to employ full-time clerks. As committee staff became increasingly accepted, full-time staff were approved for other committees as well.

By the mid-1880s, senators who were not committee chairs, and therefore had no staff assistance, prevailed in their fight for staff aides. In the Senate, and a few years later in the House, have-not members argued that chairs could use their committee aides on personal business, while other committee members either used personal funds to hire secretaries or handled the work themselves, answering letters

in longhand—sometimes during floor debate. In 1885, the Senate approved legislation permitting senators who were not committee chairs to appoint personal clerks at six dollars per day during the congressional session. Eight years later, similar provisions were approved by the House for noncommittee chairs. By the late 1890s both chambers had approved year-round personal staff for all members.

By about 1920 staff aides in both houses were paid directly by the Congress. The bill to put House staff on the rolls was approved only after bitter debate and contributed directly to institutionalization of staffing and of Congress. Aides were, in effect, recognized as official congressional employees. Henceforth, procedures governing staffing would become less personalized and decision making more automatic.

Staff numbers increased gradually. By 1891, there were 41 committee aides in the Senate and 62 in the House. By 1930, the numbers had increased to 163 in the Senate and 112 in the House—still relatively small numbers by late-twentieth-century standards. Personal-staff numbers increased more rapidly in these years, reflecting the inclusion of have-not members, as well as the greater number of members' offices eligible for staff assistance. In 1891, there were 39 personal staff in the Senate; there were none in the House because the House had not yet authorized their appointment. By 1930, all senators and all representatives could appoint personal staff; there were 280 in the Senate and 870 in the House. During the Great Depression years, these numbers held fairly steady, but all staff and members took decreases in pay.

The 1946 Legislative Reorganization Act was watershed legislation. In this post–World War II era, committee and personal staffs continued to be relatively small. Somewhat more than two-hundred aides served Senate committees; slightly under two-hundred worked in the House. Few committees appointed expert staff. Representative Mike Monroney (D.-Okla.), vice chairman of the Joint Committee on the Organization of Congress, which drafted the act, estimated that only 4 of 76 committees had expert staff. The House authorized a maximum of five aides on personal staffs; each senator employed, on average, six personal staff aides. And yet work loads had increased. There were more issues, more casework, and increased constituent demands, and legislation was more complex. The provisions of the Legislative Reorganization Act sought to deal with these problems. Professional and permanent committee staff were explicitly authorized. Each standing committee—except Appropriations, which set its own personnel numbers—could employ four professional and six clerical staff on a permanent basis. And the committee personal staff distinction was made explicit: professional committee staff could work only on committee business, and they could not be assigned other duties. Although provisions with regard to personal staff were dropped from the final version, practice soon extended professionalization, and specialization, to personal staff also.

After 1946, staffing changes were influenced by pressures for the equitable distribution of staff, and the perceived need for both expert assistance and independent information and analysis. Gradually, staff numbers increased and staff became more specialized. A few committees appointed nonpartisan staffs, but most found experts who also identified with Democrats or Republicans. The 1970 Legislative Reorganization Act had two major committee staffing provisions: the number of permanent professional staff for standing committees was increased from four to six, and the minority party was authorized to appoint one-third of the professionals and one of the six clerical aides.

After 1970, the chambers independently made further changes in staffing, which continued to reflect a response to equity and increased work load issues. The House in 1974 tripled the size of permanent committee staffs, confirming reality and acknowledging the permanence of temporary investigative staff. A 1975 House rule authorized each subcommittee chair and ranking minority member to appoint one aide to work on subcommittee matters. Also in 1975, the Senate, continuing to respond to equity issues raised by junior senators, approved the appointment of additional personal staff to assist members on work for their committees if they did not appoint any committee staff. And the Senate Committee Amendments of 1977 required that a committee's majority-minority staff ratio reflect the majority-minority member ratio on the committee.

Two factors drove up a rapid increase in the size of both committee and personal staffs during the 1970s. Issues of equity and changing norms of member participation led to rule changes that distributed staff differently; as a consequence, subcommittee leaders and junior members in both chambers could appoint more staff. Confrontation with the president and the executive branch on a variety of issues, including the president's use of the impoundment authority and the scondal of Watergate, resulted in a Congress which wanted increased staff as a source of independent information and analysis.

In the 1980s, staff levels on committee, personal, and leadership staffs remained generally stable. Both the Senate and the House sought to streamline decisions on staffing, and more explicitly tied approval of committee staff levels to committee work load. In both chambers, the committees that handle committee funding specified percentage-increase guidelines for committees to follow in requesting funding. And both chambers developed procedures that enabled members to pass judgment on the funding requests of their colleagues; review of funding requests has become far more than a pro forma exercise, an interesting development in an institution which thrives on egalitarianism and *logrolling*, that is, the trading of favors.

Both the Senate and House gave attention to staffing levels and issues of equity. The number and percentage of committee staff which can be appointed by the minority party, the provision of personal staff for assistance with committee assignments, and issues of discrimination in appointment, retention, and pay have been significant issues in congressional staffing debates. These issues have been raised in the party caucuses, in committee, and at the floor level, and changes have been made at all three levels. Streamlined procedures which do not require a formal vote sometimes occur in committee, as, for example, a request for work load data. Staff changes are made in caucus rules—as occurred in 1973 when House Democrats approved the "Subcommittee Bill of Rights" guaranteeing staff to subcommittees—or through Senate or House rules. At the floor level, the annual Legislative Branch Appropriations bill typically serves as the vehicle for staffing changes, but on occasion other legislation, such as the 1991 Civil Rights bill, includes provisions which relate to staff.

STAFFING ARRANGEMENTS IN THE EARLY 1990S

In 1991, during the first session of the 102d Congress, there were 23,400 congressional staffers working within Congress and in legislative support agencies. Fifty-five hundred of these were administrative support staff attached to joint offices of Congress (the Capitol Police and the Architect of the Capitol) or to central offices within the House and Senate (such as the Clerk of the House or the Secretary of the Senate). Most staff deployment is decentralized, however. In accord with congressional norms of egalitarianism and individual accountability, aides are appointed by and work for individual autonomous subunits in each chamber. This section focuses on these staff aides, those who work for committees, on personal staffs of members, and for the leadership, with a briefer assessment of the role of the staff in the legislative support agencies.

Committee Staffing

Committee staff are based in Washington, D.C., on Capitol Hill. Staff are formally appointed by the full committee. However, Susan Webb Hammond and Harrison W. Fox, Jr., in their book *Congressional Staffs: The Invisible Force in American Lawmaking* (1977), report that most staffers feel responsible to one member, usually the committee or subcommittee chairman, or ranking minority member. Committee staffs are partisan; most aides serve on a majority or minority staff, and eighty percent of them hold a strong party preference. In the House, a few prestigious committees permit and fund associate committee staff, located in the member's office to assist on committee work, for rank-and-file members. All senators receive a member office allotment—not committee monies—to appoint staff based in their personal offices, but with the privileges of committee staff, to assist them on their committee assignments.

In 1989, the first year of the 101st Congress, standing committees employed 3,383 staff aides; 1,986 worked for the twenty-two standing committees of the House; and 1,013 for the sixteen standing committees of the Senate. House committee staffs varied in size, from eight on Standards of Official Conduct to 196 on Appropriations. Senate staffs ranged from twenty-two on Small Business to 127 on Judiciary. The ten select and special committees (five in each house) employed a staff of 205. Variation in staff size among committees is based primarily on differences in workload, whether it's the number of hearings, bills, nominations, and so forth or a short-term investigation, as occurred with the Watergate and Iran-Contra inquiries. Shift in party control also affects staff numbers; in 1981, after winning control of the Senate, Republicans carried out a 1980 election promise to cut committee staff somewhat.

Senate and House funding procedures for committee staff differ slightly. Senate committees, at the start of each Congress, submit a two-year budget request for committee operations and staff to the Senate Committee on Rules and Administration. After hearings, the committee reports an omnibus funding resolution which authorizes monies for staff and expenses of Senate committees for a two-year period; it is then debated and approved by the full Senate. Funds are appropriated through the Legislative Branch Appropriations bill, passed each year by Congress. Committees have generally carried over unexpended funds into the second year, or from one Congress to the next. Since 1988, Senate committees have been required to provide quarterly work load data on activities such as nominations, investigations, and hearings to the Senate Committee on Rules and Administration. Funding levels are based on guidelines set by the Committee; levels increased incrementally during the 1980s. Committees also request, and may be granted, a one-time major increase that does not become part of the funding base.

Staff pay is set by each committee, within parameters set by the *president pro tempore* of the Senate (the most senior senator of the majority party). In 1991, the top pay permitted was $122,415 for standing committee aides.

Monies for House committee staff are authorized in two ways. Permanent legislation authorizes salary funds for thirty professional and clerical staff for each standing committee (except Appropriations and Budget, which are not subject to the thirty-staff limit) and for the Permanent Select Committee on Intelligence. This is, in effect, a permanent authorization for these *statutory* committee employees. Funds for additional staff, the investigative staff, are authorized each year after committees submit a budget request, which is scrutinized and approved by the House Administration Committee, then debated and passed in an omnibus funding resolution by the full House. Monies for both permanent and investigative staff are appropriated in the Legislative Branch Appropriations measure each year. There is virtually no difference between statutory and investigative staff; investigative staff are not limited to investigations, and like statutory staff, keep their jobs from one Congress to the next.

House rules authorize staff for up to six subcommittees of each standing committee, with one aide to be appointed by the subcommittee chair and one by the ranking minority member. As in the Senate, staff salaries are determined by each committee, within the maximum-salary guidelines set by the Speaker of the House. In 1991, three aides on each committee could earn up to $115,092 per year, nine could earn up to $108,837, and others could earn up to $101,331. Maximum-salary levels never exceed the pay of senators and representatives.

Members' Offices

Personal staff work in Washington, D.C. and offices in the member's home state. Each senator and representative has at least one office in their state, or district, respectively; most have several. Much of the constituent service work, including casework, is handled by district offices. In some instances, the top-ranking aide works primarily in the district rather than in Washington, D.C.

Changing norms of increased participation in legislative action by junior members, a greater emphasis on egalitarianism, and distrust of the executive branch led to an increase in the number of personal staff during the 1970s. Senate staffs nearly doubled, from 2,426 in

1972 to 3,554 in 1977; House staffs increased from 5,280 to 6,942 in the same period. Many observers expected the increase to be in constituent-service and public relations positions—caseworkers, press aides and so forth—and the number of these positions has increased. But the increase also occurred in policy positions, as a 1977 study by the Commission on the Operation of the Senate reported. Between 1960 and 1976, the number of Senate aides with legislative duties increased from 73 aides in 53 offices to 718 aides in 95 offices. Even this may be underreported, because counsels, administrative assistants, and others who work on policy matters are not included.

As staffs increased in size, staffers became increasingly specialized. Titles are not uniform, but most offices appoint administrative assistants, sometimes executive assistants, caseworkers, legislative assistants, correspondents, and press aides. Some offices also appoint counsel and staff assistants. All offices handle similar matters: responding to constituent requests; casework, and assisting constituents with federal program applications; legislative work; answering mail; and press work.

Virtually all Senate offices, and many House offices, are organized in departments by function (press, legislative) or by issue area. The administrative assistant oversees and coordinates the work of the office. Even in member offices, staff jobs are increasingly specialized, and different aides handle different issues such as foreign policy, health and education, or transportation and energy. In comparison to the executive branch, however, congressional staff are generalists. Each office also establishes salary, benefits, and job descriptions independently, within parameters set by the Senate or the House.

In keeping with the egalitarian norms of the institution, each House member may employ the same number of personal staff: up to 18 full-time aides, and four part-time or temporary aides. During the first session of the 102d Congress (1991), House staffs averaged fifteen in number. The staff salary allowance for members was $475,000, and House personal staff could earn up to $101,331 per year.

The Senate does not set a ceiling on staff numbers; rather, all senators are given an allotment for staff salaries, which varies by state population. Senators from states with a larger population are allotted more monies for representational activities, such as answering constituent correspondence. In 1991, the allowance for staff varied from $847,410 for senators from states with fewer than one million constituents, to $1,836,990 for senators from states with twenty-eight million or more constituents. In addition, every senator received a Legislative Assistance Allowance ($280,887) to appoint aides to assist with committee work. Senators designate one aide for each of their committees, certifying that employee to the chair or ranking minority member of the committee. In 1991, Senate personal staffs averaged 38 in number; personal staffers could be paid up to $120,559.

Leadership Offices   The elected leaders of both House and Senate oversee leadership offices as well as personal offices. In the House, the Speaker's office, and in both chambers, offices of the majority and minority leaders and majority and minority whips assist leaders in carrying out leadership duties. In addition, the party caucuses of all Democrats or Republicans in each chamber, and party committees—such as the Senate Democratic Policy Committee, or the Republican Research Committee and the Democratic Steering and Policy Committee in the House—are also staffed by leadership aides.

Leaders are both institutional and party leaders, and leadership aides assist in both areas. Leadership offices have administrative and policy responsibilities, which include coordinating the work of Congress and gathering and disseminating information. Staff conduct research and assist in developing policy positions, shaping legislation, and building coalitions. Staff also assist leaders in managing floor debate.

Leadership staff in the House has decreased slightly during the 1980s, from a high of 162 in 1979 to 133 in 1989. During 1990, the Speaker employed 26 aides; the majority leader, 19, the minority leader, 25, the whips, 31, and the party conferences and committees, 51. In the Senate, staff levels increased between 1979 and 1981 (from 91 to 106) and have remained relatively stable since. The president pro tempore had a staff of 6; the majority leader employed 7; the minority leader, 19; the whips, 8; and the party conferences and committees employed 27. The vice president, who is also president of the Senate, had 36 Senate aides in 1990, accounting for much of the increase in Senate leadership staff since 1979.

Funds for leadership offices are based on demonstrated need, with rough parity between majority and minority offices. Usually the minority party, because it controls fewer committee staff, has more extensive research and analysis capabilities at the leadership level.

Legislative Support Agencies   The four legislative support agencies—the Congressional Research Service (CRS) of the Library of Congress, the General Accounting Office (GAO), the Congressional Budget Office (CBO), and the Office of Technology Assessment (OTA)—provide nonpartisan information and analysis. The agencies work primarily for congressional committees—for example, the Budget and Appropriations committees rely on the scorekeeping reports and economic forecasts which the CBO produces. But the agencies also conduct studies and respond to requests of individual senators and representatives. They vary in size: in 1991, the CRS employed 860 staffers; the CBO employed 226; the OTA employed 143; and the GAO employed 1,504 (30 percent of the total) who worked directly for Congress.

Agency staffs increased substantially during the period of congressional reform in the 1970s, as Congress sought sources of information and analysis independent of the executive branch. The CBO and the OTA were established during this decade; the GAO staff expanded by 17 percent, and the CRS staff more than doubled, from 323 in 1970 to 856 in 1979. Unlike the committee, personal office, and leadership staff who work directly for members, agency staff recruitment, pay, and conditions of employment follow that of a civil service, with a clear career path through established grade levels and salary schedules. On occasion, agency staff are lent on assignment to committees, or other congressional offices, to serve as staff members.

All Offices   Because each office operates as an autonomous unit, different offices may have different salary scales, vacation, and sick leave, although here too the trend toward automatic and universal decision making affects staff. Both chambers establish broad parameters for staff pay and benefits, and policies are becoming more uniform among subunits.

Offices are organized differently, although

there are fairly standard types of office organization. Usually, the work of an office is directed by a senior aide—the personal office administrative assistant, the committee staff director, or the leadership office chief of staff—to whom all staff report, either directly or through department heads or supervisory staff. Staff do not have job security; personal staff, leadership staff, and many committee staff lose their jobs when members shift committee or leadership posts, or leave office.

Congress has traditionally claimed exemption under the separation of powers and Speech and Debate provisions of the Constitution from major laws and regulations regarding employment discrimination. Both Senate and House rules now include provisions prohibiting job discrimination and providing equal pay for equal work. The provisions of various civil rights and employment discrimination laws have also been extended to employees. House employees are also covered by wage/hour and overtime provisions of the 1989 Fair Labor Standards Act, as amended. In the House, the House Fair Employment Practices Board, with representative and staff members, handles employee grievances. Under the 1991 Civil Rights Act, the Senate established a Senate Fair Employment Practices Board to handle employee grievances; decisions may be appealed to a federal appellate court.

STAFF CHARACTERISTICS AND RECRUITMENT*

Congressional staff are young. In 1990, the Congressional Management Foundation reports the average age of House personal staff was 34.8 years. (The average age of the federal civilian work force was 42.1 years.) The average age of administrative assistants was 38; of legislative directors, 32; of legislative assistants, 26;

---

*Until the 1970s, there was little published data on staff characteristics. This section is based primarily on four studies conducted since 1970: *Congressional Staffs* by H. W. Fox and S. W. Hammond (1977); the report of the House Commission on Administrative Review (1977); *The House at Work*, eds., Joseph Cooper and G. Calvin Mackenzie (1981); and the biennial studies of Senate and House *Employment Practices* in personal offices by the Congressional Management Foundation of Washington, D.C.

of press secretaries, 29.5; executive assistants and office managers were, on average, 36. Personal staff in the Senate are slightly older, according to the 1991 report of the Congressional Management Foundation. The average age of personal staff was 34.6; except for office managers, staff in the senior positions were, on average, four to six years older than in the House. The average age of Senate administrative assistants was 42; of legislative directors, 38; of legislative assistants, 33; of press secretaries, 36; of executive assistants, 36; of office managers, 40. Generally speaking, committee staff, as reported by Fox and Hammond, are somewhat older than personal staff; the average age of professionals was 40.

Women comprise about 60 percent of all personal staff in both House and Senate, but only 40 percent of the staff are professionals. (Secretarial, mail-room, and computer-operator positions are examples of nonprofessional services.) Only at the most junior professional position—that of legislative correspondent—is there gender parity. Fox and Hammond report that most committee professionals are men. CMF data indicate that about 13 percent of members' staffs are black, Latino, or from other minority groups.

Staff professionals are highly educated. Virtually all staff in senior professional positions on House and Senate personal staffs hold a graduate degree; 75 percent of all committee professionals hold graduate degrees. Lawyers predominate, particularly in staff positions which relate directly to legislating. 45 percent of *all* committee professionals, 52 of Senate legislative assistants, and 25 percent of House legislative assistants are lawyers. A majority of members are also trained as lawyers, with the skills of negotiating, bargaining, and compromise which characterize the legislative process; and lawyer-members appear to feel comfortable appointing lawyers as aides.

Professional staff often come to a Hill position from other government jobs as Fox and Hammond report. Thirty percent of committee aides held other congressional jobs just prior to their committee appointments; another 35 percent had most recently held jobs in the executive branch. In *The House at Work* (1981), Brady reports that about half the staff in member offices had no Hill experience prior to appointment. However, 73 percent of the press secretaries—a job for which local ties are useful—had no previous Hill experience. In contrast, most office managers and caseworkers did have previous Hill experience.

Many aides have ties to a state or district (Fox and Hammond). Nearly two-thirds of the staff on senators' personal staffs maintain their legal residence in the same state as the senator. Committee professionals are in sharp contrast: the District of Columbia, Maryland or Virginia is the state of legal residence of about two-thirds.

The lack of job security, in combination with no clear career path, contributes to high staff turnover. Moving from legislative correspondent to legislative assistant, or from legislative assistant to legislative director, is a promotion. But it is less clear that a move from administrative assistant in one office to the same position in another office, or from administrative assistant in a member office to counsel of a committee, is also a promotion. The autonomy of each office makes development of a hierarchy of positions between offices difficult.

STAFF ACTIVITY AND COMMUNICATION PATTERNS

Congressional aides help members carry out every kind of duty. They handle administrative and other support chores; answer mail; draft newsletters; gather, analyze, and evaluate information; draft legislation; work with constituents and nonconstituent interest groups; speak on behalf of members to constituents and the press; build legislative coalitions; and develop and help implement legislative strategy. Members rely especially on senior aides for judgment and advice. Aides often work out and negotiate the details of legislation or policy compromises on behalf of members, and within the parameters set by members. And, like White House presidential staffs, senior aides affect policy.

Staff in both member and committee offices are active in writing floor remarks and speeches, as Fox and Hammond's work shows. Committee staff regularly help members set up and prepare for committee hearings. Both committee and member personal office staff work on legislation, meet with lobbyists and interest groups, and conduct investigation and over-

sight. However, committee staff focus on legislation or oversight.

Data on staff communication reveal a similar pattern. Personal staff aides communicate much more frequently with the senator or representative for whom they work, reflecting the smaller size and less formal hierarchy of member offices. Personal staff also communicate more frequently with constituents. Both types of staff talk with the bureaucracy and the press with the same frequency. Committee staff work more frequently with other committees than do personal staff. But rather surprisingly, Senate personal staff talk more frequently with White House aides than committee staff do—perhaps because the White House contact personal staff when the roll-call voting stage is reached. Studies indicate that staff are engaged in all aspects of congressional work.

SCHOLARLY LITERATURE ON CONGRESSIONAL STAFF

Studies of congressional staffing have matured as the political science field has changed. The pre-1960 studies were primarily descriptive, and often evaluative. The literature is characterized by a variety of perspectives: scholars draw on role theory, organization theory, decision-making and policy-making constructs, and purposive behavior frameworks. Scholars use different kinds of data: systematic interviews or surveys, quantitative data derived from legislative documents, and participant observation. The level of analysis varies. Individual-level studies focus on the individual staff job and present data on staff characteristics, activity patterns, norms, and functions (within the member, committee, or leadership office, or within the institution). Subunit-level studies focus on the staff of legislative subunits—usually committee or member offices—and analyze their role, function, and effect on subunit output and relationships; a subunit focus permits comparison among subunits, and between different types of subunits. Studies also employ an institutional perspective, analyzing the impact of staffing patterns and activities on Congress as an institution.

In most studies, staff are the independent, causal variable affecting office or institutional output, norms, and function. Some studies focus on staff as the intervening variable—affected by, for example, member and subunit goals, but also affecting the subunit or the institution. In a few studies, staff are the dependent variable.

Several themes run through staffing studies: mapping the terrain of congressional jobs, staffing as a cause and consequence of congressional change, staff as processors and important actors in information networks, and the impact of staff on congressional policy-making and outputs. Although much of the staffing literature is non-evaluative, normative judgments also run through it; early studies argue the value of nonpartisan, committee staff; some later studies argue that too much staff interferes with the representative function of elected legislators by keeping them from face-to-face deliberation.

Scholars have demonstrated that staff recruitment, background, training, tenure, activities, and communication patterns vary with job position (see Fox and Hammond, and Cooper and Mackenzie). Context is important. In a 1970 study, Samuel C. Patterson concluded that committee context affects staff capabilities and constraints. Staff activities reflect the legislative goals of members. Staff norms of limited advocacy, loyalty to committee chairs, anonymity, and limited partisanship varied across committees, according to committee situation and leadership. In a 1971 study, David Price examined the effect of committee context on staff capability for innovation. Member goals and orientation determine the opportunities and constraints for staff innovation. Staff policy *entrepreneurs*—those who seek new policies for their congressional bosses—search more widely for information and are more innovative than nonpartisan professionals; their opportunities to be innovative vary with committee context. In 1988, Christine DeGregorio analyzed the working styles and influence of subcommittee staff directors and found that context—committee leadership styles, precedents, and the nature of the issues—affect these staff aides' partisanship, accessibility, and objectivity. Fox and Hammond, in a 1977 study of member and committee staffs, suggested that different types of office organization result in variation in office output.

Organization theory, and the context of the House as an institution, inform the 1977 studies of the House Commission on Administrative Review (the Obey Commission) and the essays in *The House at Work* (1981), edited by Joseph Cooper and G. Calvin MacKenzie, which draw on Commission data. Two of the essays—David W. Brady's "Personnel Management in the House" and Susan Webb Hammond's "The Management of Legislative Offices"—analyzed staff deployment and management in the context of the House as a collegial, representative institution.

A number of studies focus on staff as information processors, and as important actors in and coordinators of information networks. Richard F. Fenno, in *The Power of the Purse* (1966), found that Senate staff have wider information networks than House staff. In 1977, Fox and Hammond reported that committee-and-member-office communication patterns vary. One of the 1977 Obey Commission studies, as well as a 1981 article by Louis Sandy Maisel, reported that staff—whether committee or personal—are the major information source for members on legislation, public-policy issues, and district matters. In 1990, Joel D. Aberbach reported on staff search for oversight information and styles of processing that information. Michael J. Malbin, in his book *Unelected Representatives: Congressional Staff and the Future of Representative Government* (1980), demonstrates that different types of staff—entrepreneurs, nonpartisan and partisan bureaucrats—use similar information differently, thereby affecting policy outcomes.

A few studies focus on members' use of staff. In these studies, staff are viewed as resources, and their use can be affected by such things as members' ideology or seniority. Richard F. Fenno, Jr., in his book *Home Style: House Members in Their Districts* (1978), found that seniority, electoral margin, family residence, and distance from Washington do not make a difference in how members allocate their staff resources between the district and Washington. In 1979, Thomas Cavanagh studied staff distribution in the competing institutional (Washington) and electoral (district) arenas, drawing on data from the House Commission on Administrative Review. In a 1975 study, "Legislative Behavior and Legislative Structures," Norman J. Ornstein found that members who are northern Democrats, who are less senior, more liberal, and more active, use staff most heavily on legislative work. In 1983, Steven H. Schiff and Steven S. Smith suggested that larger staffs permit members to pursue multiple goals simultaneously.

Robert H. Salisbury and Kenneth A. Shepsle, in two 1981 articles, also offered a different perspective. They suggested that members and their current and former staff are a separate and autonomous subunit, an enterprise. This perspective cuts across traditional subunit and institutional boundaries. Enterprises affect both policy outputs and Congress as a whole. In a 1979 study on freshmen members of the House, Burdett A. Loomis used a similar perspective; he looked at member offices as small businesses which assist members in pursuing multiple goals.

The overriding question which scholars have sought to answer is the influence of congressional staff: the effect of staff on policy outcomes; which staff activities have influence; the points where staff influence is felt; and variations in influence, either by activity or by staff type. A corollary question is the impact of staff on the institution. Patterson concluded that staff innovation varies according to issues, leadership, and staff style. Price found that policy entrepreneurs are more innovative than other types of committee professionals. Malbin concluded that "personalized, entrepreneurial staff" has helped congressional innovation (*Unelected Representatives*, p. 240). Ornstein reported correlation between office size and staff function; senators' office staffs are "an integral part of the decision making process", in contrast to staff of the smaller House member offices. Fox and Hammond showed that committees with larger staffs are more active on a range of measures—hearings, writing bills, and frequency of communication. DeGregorio found that staff are important in establishing committee agendas. Most assume that policy innovation is an acceptable congressional, and staff, function.

A number of scholars have conducted research designed to assess staff influence. Donald F. Matthews, in a 1960 study, concluded that staff influence derives from staff position in communications and information. Patterson found that staff have influence through information gathering and processing, drafting legislation, and other activities of the policy process. Fox and Hammond reached similar conclusions after analyzing data on staff communications and activities. To analyze influence, DeGregorio distinguished between routine activities such as information gathering, and more significant policy activities such as bargaining and negotiation, and found that staff are most involved in routine activities, and least involved as surrogates for principals in policy deliberation activities. In early studies, Matthews, Fenno, and John F. Manley also concluded that staff are influential on routine matters—in fact, are primarily influential in this way. Studies also show that staff influence congressional activity and outcomes through their position in the policy-making structure and process, relying primarily on activity data to reach this conclusion. Other studies demonstrate member reliance on staff for information and assistance.

Some of the most interesting work seeks to assess the impact of staff on Congress as an institution. Several scholars have concluded that staff play a major role in Congress and in policy-making, contribute to subunit integration (committees, the member's enterprise), to integration of the institution, and integration between government branches and across issue areas. In *Unelected Representatives*, Malbin argued that staff undermine the representative function by impeding true deliberation by elected representatives. Salisbury and Shepsle, as well as Loomis, speculated that members' staff enterprises enable members to pursue multiple goals simultaneously. Scholars have agreed that staff have influence, although that influence is measured in different ways.

Those who believe that staff interfere with the deliberative function of members and the institution will continue to call for reducing staff numbers and changing staff roles. Others, who view staff as important to meeting member and institutional responsibilities, will focus on issues of diversifying staff expertise and better staff training, distribution, and management within the constraints of a legislative organization.

CONCLUSION

Understanding of congressional staff roles and functions has increased substantially in the last thirty years. A number of studies have described the distribution, characteristics, and activities of congressional staff. The institutional context—of Congress and of congressional subunits—affects staff operations, as do staff and member goals. Staff contribute to structural integration within the Congress and within the broader political system. Staff influence public policy and constituent representation. Staff enable members to pursue multiple goals simultaneously. Staff link the micro and the macro levels; in working for individuals, staff help Congress achieve collective, or institutional, goals. Staff are viewed as power resources by members, enabling them to achieve individual and collective goals, to affect policy, and to gain other resources in an exchange of assistance.

The studies of the late twentieth century have developed useful hypotheses and important conclusions. In future research, further careful definition of concepts, development and precise statement of hypotheses, and specificity of measurement are needed. Reconceptualization may be useful—a focus on staff as resources, for example, or theoretical constructs which link the micro and the macro levels. Research designs which distinguish among staff activities, or between different types of staff, or among staff groups will be useful, and will offer more precise answers to questions about staff effect on individual and collective goal achievement, or staff influence. Comparative study is needed—for example, of subunits, of the two chambers, or of Democratic and Republican staffing. A central question should always be: What are the consequences of these findings, particularly for Congress as an institution?

Congressional staff will continue to play an important role in the policy process and in representation. Increasingly, emerging democracies and institutionalizing legislatures in other countries seek information and counsel on legislative staffing from Congress. Although some observers view Congress as a model to be avoided rather than copied, it nevertheless behooves observers and researchers to seek to understand the organization, activities, and consequences of congressional staffing.

BIBLIOGRAPHY

Studies Describing and Analyzing All Types of Congressional Staff
DAVID W. BRADY, "Personnel Management in the House," in JOSEPH COOPER and G. CALVIN MACKENZIE, eds., *The House at Work* (Austin, Tex., 1981), analyzes characteristics of House staff, arguing that the organizational characteristics of the House affect the autonomy and working conditions of the personnel systems. SUSAN WEBB HAMMOND, "The Management of Legislative Offices," *The House at Work*, analyzes staffing and management patterns of House personnel, committees, and leadership offices. *The House at Work* also includes chapters on staff as information resources and in constituent service work, as well as extended essays analyzing the organizational context of the work environment. HARRISON W. FOX, JR., and SUSAN WEBB HAMMOND, *Congressional Staffs: The Invisible Force in American Lawmaking* (New York, 1977), is a comprehensive overview of staff characteristics, activities, and communication patterns, including a history of staffing and analysis of staff influence. MICHAEL J. MALBIN, *Unelected Representatives: Congressional Staff and the Future of Representative Government* (New York, 1980), using case studies of staff work at different stages of the legislative process, argues that staff undermine the deliberative function of the Congress. CONGRESS, U.S. HOUSE OF REPRESENTATIVES, Commission on Administrative Review (Obey Commission), 95th Congress, *Final Report*, H.Doc. 95–272, 2 vols. (Washington, D.C., 1977), includes sections on staff and information and work management, based, in part, on an extensive survey of representatives and staff.

Statistics on Congressional Staff
Three works, issued and updated biennially, present data on staff numbers. NORMAN J. ORNSTEIN, THOMAS E. MANN, and MICHAEL J. MALBIN, *Vital Statistics on Congress* (Washington, D.C., 1992), CONGRESSIONAL MANAGEMENT FOUNDATION,

U.S. House of Representatives Employment Practices (Washington, D.C., 1990), and CONGRESSIONAL MANAGEMENT FOUNDATION, *U.S. Senate Employment Practices* (Washington, D.C., 1991).

Studies of Staff in State Legislatures

Two studies, in particular, present and evaluate important hypotheses regarding legislative staffing: RANDY HUWA and ALAN ROSENTHAL, *Politicians and Professionals: Interactions Between Committee and Staff in State Legislatures* (New Brunswick, N.J., 1977); and ALAN ROSENTHAL, "Professional Staff and Legislative Influence in Wisconsin," in JAMES A. ROBINSON, ed., *State Legislative Innovation: Case Studies of Washington, Ohio, Florida, Illinois, Wisconsin, California* (New York, 1973).

Statistics on Congressional Staff

Three works, issued and updated biennially, present data on staff numbers. NORMAN J. ORNSTEIN, THOMAS E. MANN, and MICHAEL J. MALBIN, *Vital Statistics on Congress* (Washington, D.C., 1992), CONGRESSIONAL MANAGEMENT FOUNDATION, *U.S. House of Representatives Employment Practices* (Washington, D.C., 1990), and CONGRESSIONAL MANAGEMENT FOUNDATION, *U.S. Senate Employment Practices* (Washington, D.C., 1990).

Other Staffing Studies

JOEL D. ABERBACH, *Keeping a Watchful Eye: The Politics of Congressional Oversight* (Washington, D.C., 1990) includes material throughout on staff as information, analytical, and influence resources in congressional oversight. JOHN F. BIBBY, "Committee Characteristics and Legislative Oversight of Administration," *Midwest Journal of Political Science* 10 (February 1966): 78–98, is an early study that proposes that committee characteristics affect staff operations and influence. THOMAS E. CAVANAGH, "Rational Allocation of Congressional Resources: Member Time and Staff Use in the House," in DOUGLAS W. RAE and THEODORE J. EISMEIER, eds., *Public Policy and Public Choice* (Beverly Hills, 1979), assesses staff use in the "two arenas"—Washington, D.C., and the representative's district. CHRISTINE DeGREGORIO, "Professionals in the U.S. Congress: An Analysis of Working Styles," *Legislative Studies Quarterly* 13 (November 1988): 459–476, analyzes the style and influence of senior subcommittee aides. Two major studies by RICHARD F. FENNO, JR., *The Power of the Purse* (Boston, 1966) and *Home Style: House Members in Their Districts* (Boston, 1978), include insightful analysis of the role of staff and their work in committee and institutional integration, and as member resources. SUSAN WEBB HAMMOND, "The Operation of Senators' Offices," in U.S. Congress, Senate, Commission on the Operation of the Senate, 94th Congress, 2d Session, *Senators: Offices, Ethics, and Pressures*, Committee Print (Washington, D.C. 1977), analyzes member office staff and management. SUSAN WEBB HAMMOND, "Legislative Staffs," *Legislative Studies Quarterly* 9 (May 1984): 271–317, is a survey of congressional, state, and comparative studies on legislative staffing. BURDETT A. LOOMIS, "The Congressional Office as a Small (?) Business: New Members Set Up Shop," *Publius* 9 (Summer 1979): 35–55, suggests that autonomous member offices assist members in pursuing reelection, policy-making, and institutional goals simultaneously. LOUIS SANDY MAISEL, "Congressional Information Sources," *The House at Work*, includes discussion of staff as major information resources. JOHN F. MANLEY, "Congressional Staff and Public Policy-Making," *Journal of Politics* 30 (November 1968): 1046–1067, is an early study that suggests several variables, such as complexity of subject matter and staff organization, affect staff role. DONALD R. MATTHEWS, *U.S. Senators and Their World* (Chapel Hill, N.C., 1960), is a major Senate study that, in the discussion of staffing, proposes hypotheses about staff activity and suggests that staff influence the policy behavior of senators. NORMAN J. ORNSTEIN, "Legislative Behavior and Legislative Structures: A Comparative Look at House and Senate Resource Utilization," in JAMES J. HEAPHEY and ALAN P. BALUTIS, eds., *Legislative Staffing: A Comparative Perspective* (Beverly Hills, 1975), analyzes the factors which affect the utilization of policy staff in member offices. SAMUEL C. PATTERSON, "The Professional Staffs of Congressional Committees," *Administrative Science Quarterly* 15 (March 1970): 22–37, is a seminal article that suggests a theoretical construct and framework for analytic study of congressional staff, and explores the capabilities and constraints of staff. DAVID E. PRICE, "Professionals and 'Entrepreneurs': Staff Orientations and Policy Making on

Three Senate Committees," *Journal of Politics* 33 (May 1971): 316–336, focuses on staff capability for innovation, and identifies committee and staff factors which enable staff to operate as professionals or entrepreneurs. ROBERT H. SALISBURY and KENNETH A. SHEPSLE, "Congressional Staff Turnover and the Ties-That-Bind," *American Political Science Review* 75 (June 1981): 381–396, and "U.S. Congressman as Enterprise," *Legislative Studies Quarterly* 6 (November 1981): 559–576, propose a different perspective on staff: all staff—committee, office, and alumnae—of a member operate as an enterprise to further the policy, institutional power, and reelection goals of the member. STEVEN H. SCHIFF and STEVEN S. SMITH, "Generational Change and the Allocation of Staff in the U.S. Congress," *Legislative Studies Quarterly* 8 (August 1983): 457–467, analyzes staff utilization by different generations of members of Congress. JAMES A. THURBER, "The Evolving Role and Effectiveness of the Congressional Research Agencies," in *The House at Work*, is an analysis of the staff of legislative support agencies.

STATE LEGISLATIVE SUPPORT STAFFS AND ADMINISTRATION

Gregory S. Thielemann

Although the use of legislative staff has been an integral part of the legislative process in Congress for some time, the evolution of state legislative staff has been much slower. This is partially because state legislatures have not become highly professional policy organizations at the same pace as the national legislature. With the Legislative Reorganization Act of 1946, Congress set out to protect the specialization of its membership by limiting the members' committee assignments, thus creating greater opportunities for developing expertise. In addition, Congress had the forethought to increase the legislative staff support while also more evenly distributing—and, in many cases, reducing—the individual members' work loads. The continued evolution of congressional staff has led to the creation of the highly specialized, professional, policy-advising staff member common in Washington, D.C., today.

In spite of all the obvious advantages of employing such staff members at the national level, state legislatures, for the most part, have been slow to duplicate this practice. It is important to note at the outset that it is impossible to describe a generic state legislature. All legislative branches face unique policy-making environments and develop unique organizational responses to these environments. One of these adaptations is the use of staff, and although some commonality exists among states, there are usually structural variations. In order to explicate these commonalities and exceptions, three areas are explored here: the evolution of state legislatures, the general evolution of staff, and some of the contrasting models of state legislative staffing systems.

THE EVOLUTION OF STATE LEGISLATURES SINCE THE 1960s

In many ways, the staffs of the state legislatures reflect the bodies they serve. Prior to the 1960s, state legislatures were more similar to each other than they are today. These bodies were primarily rural-dominated, part-time institutions of questionable ability and professionalism. Although by today's standards such bodies would be, and in some cases still are, appalling, they in many ways reflected the times and usually respected the wishes of the populace. For example, the dominant feeling in Texas was that the citizens would benefit from the part-time legislature because "as long as they weren't in session they couldn't hurt anybody." In fact, this sentiment was common in most southern states, many of which were governed by constitutions written at the close of Reconstruction specifically to prevent government from becoming as extensive or corrupt as it had been when the region was occupied by Union forces. Such organizational patterns of limited government and weak executives were common outside the South as well, but for different reasons.

The nonprofessional status of state legislatures appears to be justified by two factors: the policy agenda at the time seemed simple enough to handle on a part-time basis, and there was an idealistic commitment to the citizen legislature, a notion that members could not make a living through legislating alone. The evolution of American society had not approached today's level at the onset of the 1960s. Organizationally, American society was evolving toward enhanced specialization and expertise in everything from business and industry to education. The evolution brought greater division of labor and hierarchical relationships. In the context of government, this trend led to an expansion of the federal bureaucracy as the government attempted to expand on the traditions of the New Deal and fulfill the promises of the New Frontier and the Great Society. In reality, the increased specialization and departmentalization of the bureaucracy posed serious problems for state governments that were not prepared to deal with the highly specialized federal bureaucrats charged with coordinating administration through the states. In order to avail themselves fully of the federal dollars available through the bureaucracy, state legislatures needed to understand the programs' guidelines and regulations. The fact was—and, in some cases, still is—that these legislatures were hopelessly overmatched. The less professional they were, the less likely they were to be in a position to take advantage of federal windfalls. The irony is that in many of the states with less professional legislatures, the need for the programs has been the greatest.

As state executive branches realized the need for specialists, they were quick to develop experts in policy areas and regulation who could aid in coping with the new federal bureaucracy. In states with a powerful executive branch, the challenge was met by providing experts from within the executive branch. In these states, the legislature was subservient to the executive branch anyway, making reliance on the executive branch acceptable. In states with constitutionally strong legislative branches, highly skilled executive staff members did little to enhance the ability of policymakers to cope with the more specialized environment that surrounded it. These state legislatures had two choices: to develop a more specialized membership that would require upgrades in both professionalism and staff support or to cling to the past and resist change. There are examples of each in this discussion.

In periods of political change, state legislatures also were faced with a changing political environment. Socially, the civil rights movement brought tensions and conflict to the legislative agendas and forced serious consideration of the responsibilities of state government. On the legal front, the Supreme Court held in *Baker* v. *Carr*, 369 U.S. 186 (1962), that representation systems that resulted in underrepresentation in local government were unconstitutional, and in *Reynolds* v. *Sims*, 377 U.S. 533 (1964), it held that the one-person, one-vote principle was universal; this ruling effectively ended rural control of state legislatures and state government.

As the membership of legislative bodies was being restructured to reflect the growing importance of urban society in the United States, reform in general received a boost. Reformism lost its taboo stigma as the new legislators who were more urban, professional, and in many cases, more representative of the changing face of society took their places in state legislatures. The general trend, with notable exceptions, was toward creating more-professional legislators who, even if not full-time legislators, would at least be more deliberative and able to expend more energy on the business of legislating. In general, this goal has been achieved; only a handful of smaller states and Texas continue to cling to the part-time legislature with part-time pay, high turnover, and questionable policy-making skills. Overall, salaries are much higher and lawmakers commonly consider lawmaking an occupation rather than an avocation. The session lengths have increased, as has the frequency of those sessions, thereby transforming policy-making—or at least policy consideration and contemplation—into a year-round task. Legislators make and take the time to study proposals carefully by employing advanced communication and computer technologies to aid them in their deliberations. Of course, along with the advanced technology comes the requirement for more technologically advanced personnel to run it.

THE EVOLUTION OF STATE LEGISLATIVE STAFF

In general, legislative staff has evolved parallel to the legislatures: the more professional and deliberative the legislatures as a whole became, the more advanced the staff support became. In legislatures, professionalization is associated with higher pay, longer sessions, and full-time legislators. In the area of staff support, professionalization is most often discussed in terms of increased staff size, clarified procedures, and higher levels of technical expertise.

One important trend in the professionalization of state legislative staff systems is the increase in the size of the staffs. As the numbers of legislators and committees vary across states, so do the sizes of the staffs that support them. This is illustrated by the fact that there are more than 25,000 full-time staffers and an additional 10,000 part-time staffers in state legislatures nationwide. Since the 1970s, staff size has grown significantly. In New York, for example, the legislative staff numbered fewer than 800 in 1979, but by 1990 it numbered more than 4,000. This trend has been repeated in smaller states: for example, in 1979, Vermont and Wyoming each employed fewer than 25 professional staff members, while in 1990 Wyoming employed 200 and Vermont employs 100. Obviously, the differences between these three states is tremendous. The overall trend toward increasing professional staff support, however, is visible in states of varied traditions in staff support.

Categorizing state legislative staffs by size is not without caveats, as is indicated by the significant variation in the total number of staff in the three states mentioned above. Obviously, variations in population, economic strength, state-run public-sector programs, and legislative environment have an impact on the numbers of professional staff being employed. It is also important to point out that in many states, the number of staff employed will vary significantly over the course of the year, depending on whether the legislature is in session. In such states as West Virginia, Hawaii, New Mexico, and Texas, permanent staff operate central agencies year-round, although additional agencies and much of the members' personal staffs are only employed during the sessions. The permanent staff tend to be shared by both houses of the legislatures and to take on technical duties, such as auditing, bill drafting, preparing fiscal notes, acquiring budgetary information, and researching specific issues.

Like increases in the size of staffs, the procedures have become more routinized. Although in Congress, members routinely involve their staff members in developing policy positions, the dominant function of state legislative staff is assistance with procedural questions. This was reflected at a conference for state legislative staff when staff members were asked to discuss their greatest contribution. Although the answers varied significantly, virtually every answer referred to a procedural contribution rather than citing how a staff member may have affected a substantive policy. In other words, state legislative staff is generally management-oriented rather than policy-oriented, in that they manage the flow of legislation rather than actively shape its content.

In some states, as the legislatures have become full-time bodies, staff have started operating on a full-time basis. As this trend has made legislative activity more routinized, and correspondingly less haphazard, staffs have instituted procedural changes designed to routinize and thus streamline the legislative process. In general, these changes are designed to enhance efficiency by altering or instituting a consent calendar, altering the rules pertaining to amendments and perhaps, most important, computerizing the process, thereby giving virtually any legislator or staff member access to both the legislation and its course. The variations in such streamlining techniques are necessarily as significant as the variations in staff size. This suggests that in regard to an overall trend, routinization can only be discussed as a generality.

The final component of staff professionalism is technical expertise. In some ways, this component overlaps with the previous one, in that higher levels of technical expertise are often associated with the technologies available to be exploited. To some extent, this is linked to the computerization of state legislatures. Some systems, such as the one in Texas, remain hopelessly outdated. In response to an open-ended question in a random survey of one hundred legislative staff members, 63 percent identified the outdated computer system as the biggest problem they faced in carrying out their work. Specifically, they cited speed and downtime as problems in tracking legislation and even in producing bill analyses in time for the members to study them before floor votes. In Texas, as in most states, the legislature now uses computers to carry out most, if not all, of the bill-distribution functions. With the growth in personal computers, it is now possible for members to access the mainframe's data and yet keep all internal office communications private. This means that politically neutral programmers are of less importance, as staff are more inclined to be computer-literate and to carry out these functions without needing additional technical expertise. For example, California, New Jersey, and North Carolina have all created sophisticated computer networking to aid legislators and their staffs. Budgetary considerations constitute the most common example of networking; New Jersey and North Carolina receive data on state agency budgets as it is put on-line, although many other states put the state budget on-line for the members.

Perhaps the most important trend in computerization and more technologically advanced staff support is visible in redistricting. Networks provide legislatures with the ability to access digital data directly from the U.S. Census Bureau as it becomes available. While this system cannot correct undercounts, it allows redistricting specialists to create technologically sophisticated maps using multiple data bases. The computerization of data has certainly opened up the process and moved redistricting from dark, smoke-filled rooms limited to the legislative leadership.

This enhanced access was particularly true in the 1991 reapportionment. Virtually anyone with a personal computer could create and offer redistricting plans in any number of states. In this round of reapportionment, it was possible for the staff agencies to compile and overlap information ranging from the census data to precinct-level electoral behavior in creating a master file. For example, in Texas this task is assigned to the redistricting division of the Legislative Council. As the data were assembled, training sessions were held for members and staff that enabled them to sit at their personal computers and literally draw new districts that came complete with demographic and electoral data. In retrospect, one might question whether this evolution helped or hurt the process, but it certainly created a more technically sophisticated information base.

MODELING STAFF SYSTEMS

Unfortunately, as is painfully obvious, even in the case of general trends in the evolution of state legislative staff, significant variations exist between the states. This is to be expected because the external, environmental pressures that face each state legislature are different, thus making staff responses similarly unique. It is virtually impossible to place all staff systems into a few categories without having forty-nine exceptions to the one rule on some element of importance. Nevertheless, it is possible to develop general models that the state legislative staffs resemble.

Even if one does not attempt to quantify the degree of professionalization in each staff system, one finds two variables that appear to be of some importance in developing models of staffing: the degree of partisanship and whether or not the staff is organized around a legislative council system. The variations in partisanship are usually reflections of the degrees of partisanship in the legislature as a whole. That is to say, if the leadership and committee structure are highly partisan and divisive, the staff will follow suit and reflect the same pattern. Similarly, if the leadership and committee system are not partisan-based, making parties weak in an institutional context, the staffing system will usually reflect those same nonpartisan values.

Whether or not a staff system is based on a legislative council model depends on the perceptions of the legislature itself as it was developing its system. If the body feels it can trust an independent staff that is usually not affiliated with either party or chamber, it will rely on a centralized legislative council rather than create separate staffs to perform essentially identical functions. Conversely, traditional staff systems were developed to afford expertise to smaller policy-making units. In that way, each chamber, and sometimes each party within each chamber, created its own source of expertise. There appear to be roughly four types of staffing systems: the traditional nonpartisan model, where the primary staff are nonpartisan and technocratic; the traditional partisan model, where staffing is linked to partisan divisions and the primary staff members are tied to the chamber's partisan leadership; the amalgam model, where there is no primary staff and in which various staffing entities all have different loyalties, thereby reducing cooperation; and the legislative council model, where a central staffing agency serves everyone. Most staff systems seem to fit into one of these categories, although as the discussions will indicate, these categories are not absolute.

The Traditional Nonpartisan Model

California is the most frequently discussed example of a highly professional, traditional nonpartisan staffing system. The California legislature has traditionally been ranked among the finest in the country with respect to staff. In regard to size, the California legislature ranks among the largest, with well over three thousand staffers. California is credited with creating many features of the desired model for modern legislative staff. The evolution of the California legislative staff was not an overnight phenomenon, although the modern California staff has evolved in order to meet the perceived organizational needs.

The California Assembly and the California Senate have found it prudent to share staff where their organizational needs overlap. Because budgetary concerns are a constant in state legislatures, California has created a staffing entity to evaluate and provide expertise on budgetary matters. In 1941 the state took the first step toward creating legislative-based expertise in fiscal and budgetary matters by creating an auditor's office to oversee executive agencies. By 1960 the agency was called the California Office of the Legislative Analyst; it was then staffed by more than forty budget analysts to provide internal expertise on the budget. In its modern form, the office is divided into seven groups, each charged with analysis in an exclusive subject area. In that way, any bill assigned to fiscal or budgetary committees is analyzed by the office for its costs and implications.

With the evolution of litigation as a means to influence policy, legislatures have found it increasingly important to have good legal advice in order to cope with this environmental pressure. As a result the California Assembly and Senate responded with the Legislative Council Bureau, which, although legally an independent agency, works exclusively for the legislative branch. This agency serves the legis-

lature by providing research, legal opinions, assistance with litigation, and reviews of the members' bills.

Although the Legislative Council Bureau and the office of Legislative Analyst are shining examples of cooperation between the chambers, significant numbers of staff serve one chamber or the other. In reality each chamber provides essentially the same types of services, although the senate generally provides less staff support than the assembly. Because the senate staff mirrors the assembly's in an organizational sense, this discussion will center on an in-depth look at the structure and functions of the assembly's system of staffing rather than simply restating the same pattern twice.

In the California Assembly, the most important staff member is the chief clerk. Although historically this office was filled on the basis of patronage and served few organizational purposes, the evolution of the California staff system has transformed it into an important position. The chief clerk in the modern California Assembly facilitates the day-to-day operations of the chamber. This means that he or she assists with the management of the calendar, the production of the journals, and generally handles administrative tasks, such as ensuring security, office space, and parking. In the California Senate, the senate secretary performs essentially the same functions. Although these positions are made with partisan considerations in mind, competence is required, and the membership of the majority party must confirm the appointments.

As is the case in many legislatures, an extensive committee system has evolved, resulting in significant divisions of labor. In the California Assembly, committee staff members are charged with implementing the responsibilities of the committees. Organizationally, California is second to none in terms of providing adequate committee staff. In California the committees select as many as sixteen staff members with professional credentials, and although the formal appointment of these members is not made by the committee's membership, in reality these committee members select their own staffers. This selection process is made by the entire committee and is distinctively nonpartisan. As a result, members from each party can rely on the information the committee staff provides, and technical information generally remains free of partisan overtones.

The assembly's Rules Committee performs many of the gatekeeping functions that its federal counterpart does, but in addition, it deals with bill assignments and performs administrative duties that cover the full range of office support. This committee oversees everything from providing support staff in the form of messengers, data processors, and word processors, to furnishing accountants who manage purchasing, district office accounts, and financing. Even in this area duplicative services between the assembly and the senate are dealt with by joint staffing, as each chamber assigns staff for on-site nursing care, security, and tour guides. Although these services are not uncommon in other state legislatures, the fact that they are handled by an important legislative committee is a rarity.

Yet another example of the excellence of the California staffing is found in the assembly's Office of Research staff. This staff is divided into substantive policy areas not unlike those found in the Office of the Legislative Analyst, although they tend to have narrower jurisdictions. This office was created in the 1950s to assure the assembly access to independent policy evaluations. It seems that some members felt that the Office of Legislative Analyst had been captured by the state agencies with which its staff worked so closely. In general, California's system is efficient, although on the surface, this duplicative function performed by the Office of Research staff seems an exception.

Although most state legislatures have experienced rapid growth in technological applications, few have coped with this advance as smoothly as has the California Assembly. In order to take full advantage of technological advancement, the assembly created its Office of Information Services not only to maintain the capital computer system, but also to facilitate the linkage of that system to the multiple networks that enhance the policy-making process. As a result, the offices of California Assembly members in Sacramento are linked to their district offices to aid in constituency service and information distribution.

In the assembly, the overall trend in its staffing system has been toward enhancing policy-making as efficiently as possible. Al-

though the Rules Committee sets the staffing limits for committees and capital offices, the members hire their own district staff. The assembly provides the leadership of each party in the chamber with staff to track bills and assess the proposals for partisan implications. Each party caucus selects its own staff in order to ensure responsiveness. In every case, staff support has grown over the years, and that has enabled the assembly to do more. Because the chamber has emphasized providing these functions efficiently, more staff has generally meant more policy analysis, as the increased numbers rarely perform duplicative functions. This is not to suggest that the California Assembly's staffing system operates free of conflict. Partisan interpretations and subsequent disagreements do emerge. Additionally, conflicts exist between technocratic staff (bill drafters) and policy-making staff (bill analyzers), but these are natural and occur in virtually every legislature. What is unique about the California Assembly is that so much of the staff is nonpartisan, and therefore these tensions are often not so great as in other assemblies, and a higher premium seems to be placed on nonpartisan, technocratic information.

The Traditional Partisan Model

Where partisan divisions are strong and constitute an inherent part of a state legislature's political tradition, staffing is more likely to take on partisan overtones. Northeastern states commonly exhibit such tendencies, and when models of partisan staffing are discussed, New York, Massachusetts, and Pennsylvania are most often mentioned. In this essay, the staffing system of New York—and particularly of its senate—is discussed as a representative example of this model. The principal difference between New York and California is the role of partisanship. Although California has developed an extensive staffing system that is designed to produce nonpartisan technocratic information, New York's system is based on accentuating the partisan divisions in the body. Party leaders divide the New York legislative branch through their extensive powers, and because staff members are appointed on the basis of partisanship, they reflect those same divisions. If cooperation is central in the California system, the adversarial relationship is central to the New York system.

STATE LEGISLATIVE SUPPORT STAFFS AND ADMINISTRATION

The New York Assembly and Senate are dominated by their leaders. The leaders exercise control over their jurisdictions and treat policy-support functions as fiefdoms for their administration. At a basic level, cooperation is not desired, for it would dilute their control. This is not to say that the New York staffers do not provide high-quality support; it is simply to point out that the support uniformly takes on partisan qualities as the leadership of each party defends its turf.

In spite of the pressures designed to enhance partisan power, some cooperation does take place in the context of the New York staffing system. Cooperation between the chambers does take place in two broad areas: providing technical expertise and providing administrative oversight. Although the staff divisions that perform these services are important, they do not approach their California counterparts. This distinction is made because, even though some of these divisions were established to act as nonpartisan support units, they are not free from party influence.

Cooperation between chambers in regard to technical expertise is probably the easiest to justify. Because the information produced is technical, and not substantive, the partisan influences that are so significant in New York should be less important in such technical matters. In New York, three staffing units shared by the assembly and the senate provide such technical expertise. The Legislative Library, like most legislative libraries, provides general information to all members and their staffs. The Assembly and the Senate share the Legislative Bill Drafting Committee, which handles the technical and legal aspects of creating legislation. As this service is essentially technical, its work is distinctively less partisan in nature. As in other legislatures, this work is critical in that it affords the membership information on the legal aspects of bills by considering them in the context of judicial interpretations of which members may be unaware. The Legislative Commission on Expenditure Review is the closest approximation to California's Office of Legislative Analyst, but partisan considerations dominate here to a degree uncommon in California. This means that the financial and expenditure reports it produces on state agencies are not free of partisan influences and therefore do not bring the same universal credibility commonly found in similar reports from its California counterpart. Although this agency was originally created to reflect nonpartisan qualities, partisan control makes it suspect.

Because agency oversight is a key part of the New York Assembly and Senate's responsibilities, the cooperation exhibited in the creation of the Administrative Regulations Review Commission is important. Although the Legislative Commission on Expenditure Review provides each chamber with financial information on the behavior of the agencies, the Administrative Regulations Review Commission provides each chamber with an analysis of each agency's legal authority and legislative intent. It does not treat an agency as merely the subject of a fiscal note, or cost estimate, but rather makes assessments as to the impacts of changes in agency policy on both the budget and intergovernmental relations.

In spite of these examples of cooperation, the bulk of staff in New York operate as facilitators of partisan influence and are exclusive to one chamber or the other. Reliance on this staff is more common than reliance on the cooperative staff, as it more closely reflects the political realities and partisan division in New York. As was the case in California, each chamber mirrors the other, making an in-depth analysis of only one chamber necessary.

In the New York Senate, the senate secretary's office is of critical importance and has significant influence. In comparison to the senate secretary's staffs of other states, New York's is one of the strongest, if not the strongest. It also reflects the partisanship of the chamber as it coordinates all majority-party appointments and committee assignments. Organizationally the senate secretary's staff is divided into subunits, each of which is generously staffed and maintains clear jurisdictions. The organizational clarity of the jurisdictions leads to a high degree of specialization and competence in selected areas. For example, the Senate Office Automation Project is charged with providing information services and networking capabilities. These services are not linked to members' district offices, as they are in California. In order to deal with tremendously important federal grants, the senate secretary's staff has a subunit in Washington, D.C., to provide a local liaison office. In addition, the Senate Research Service conducts research projects for the membership. This research can be requested by the majority leadership, standing committees, or individual members.

Given the importance of the majority leader in the New York Senate, it is not surprising that his staff is of considerable size and importance. Although these staff are technically assigned to the majority leader, the nature of the New York Senate is such that the senate secretary's staff is also under the control of the majority leadership, thus making the majority leadership very powerful with respect to policy-making and organizational control. As with the senate secretary's staff, the senate majority leader's staff is structured for organizational benefits and takes on specialized functions. The counsel for the majority staff manages the majority party's legislation. In addition to monitoring bills, it conducts research and performs a valuable, although rarely mentioned, function by negotiating with the Assembly leadership staff on bill content. In this way, potential pitfalls may be worked out before the two chambers become hopelessly deadlocked. Also under the direct control of the majority leadership is the Program Office, which provides linkage between the majority leadership and the Senate Research Service. This office coordinates research activity so that the research projects conducted by the Senate Research Service are compatible with the majority party's legislative objectives. In addition, the Communications Office provides media services for all senators.

Because the New York Senate is a partisan chamber, committee staffs reflect the partisan orientations of the chamber as a whole. Senate committee staff sizes range from two to ten professional members, plus clerical staff. Committee chairs receive staff allowances from the majority leadership, although it is worth noting that the Finance Committee receives special treatment and has a special budget of its own. From that allocation, the chair assigns funds to the committee's minority-party members for staffing. Unlike those of other states, New York state senators are not fiscally constrained in hiring staff. In the early 1990s the average member's staffing budget was around $140,000. Much of this allocation goes to district-office staff, but senators may receive additional staff on the basis of their committee assignments. Although one might debate the merits of the

New York model, it is certain that an attempt is made to provide the membership with high-quality information. The partisan nature of that information reflects the partisan nature of the institution, and although it may obviously influence the information, that is understood and accepted at the outset. In both California and New York, the emphasis has been on providing professional services for their professional legislatures, and either model is preferable to the third model, that of Texas.

The Amalgam Model

On the surface it is easy to compare Texas to other states, even California in some respects, but when one scratches below the surface, obvious differences appear. In many ways these differences reflect the Texas legislature as a whole and serve to illustrate the unprofessional nature of the institution. Texas is the largest state to maintain a part-time legislature; according to the state constitution, sessions last 140 days every other year and members earn $7,200 annually. Texas has stubbornly resisted the national trend toward creating more-professional, deliberative legislatures, and as a result, the state has a staffing system completely void of cooperation and unity of purpose. Unlike the staffing systems of other legislatures, in which conflicts may exist between partisan and non-partisan staff, the Texas staffing system is made up of separate staffs with loyalties to each leader, each committee, each member, and the nonpartisan Legislative Council. The Texas House has remained distinctively nonpartisan, with significant Republican representation as committee chairs, even though the speaker has always been Democratic and the chamber has always been dominated by the Democrats. In spite of the highly visible summit meetings between the speaker and the lieutenant governor, cooperation between the Texas House of Representatives and the Texas Senate is a rarity; the legislative structures of each chamber tend to follow dramatically different approaches, rendering cooperation difficult or in some cases impossible. With 150 members, the Texas House is one of the nation's largest lower chambers, but with 31 members, the Texas Senate is one of the smallest upper chambers. As a result, senators tend to be overworked, resolving salient issues in the Committee of the

Whole, while house members have widely varied work loads and rarely skip the committee process with substantive legislation. The committee systems reflect that same division: the senate has eleven committees, and the house, thirty-six. Because each chamber has endless jurisdictional overlap, legislation is assigned haphazardly in each chamber, thus making cooperation between committees unlikely. There is virtually no cooperation among the various staffs with respect to negotiating differences in bill content. The New York model, by contrast, affords the staff the mechanisms to iron out potential problems in wording before the members and their personalities take over. In Texas, where conference committees are typically places to kill bills rather than iron out differences, the failure to involve staff in reducing potential conflict is often apparent.

In many ways, Texas is a perfect setting for the nonpartisan cooperation in staffing found in California. Because the house operates as a nonpartisan entity and because parties play no formal role in either chamber, the idea of nonpartisan technical support staff is not far-fetched. In technical staffing, the Texas system has created what may be the perfect nonpartisan staffing entity in its Legislative Council. The council is governed by a joint legislative committee chaired by the lieutenant governor, vice-chaired by the speaker, and made up of the chairs of each chamber's administration committee and other delegate members from each chamber. This committee appoints an executive director to oversee the following six divisions: the Legal Division, which assists in statutory revisions and bill drafting; the Administration Division, which deals with staff management; the Research Division, which provides research on any subject any member wants studied; the Redistricting Project, which technically is a part of the Research Division, although it has taken on a life of its own with twice as large a staff as the Research Division; the Document Production Division, which produces all legislative documents, except the house and senate journals, which are produced by their respective chambers; and the Data Processing Division, which operates and maintains the computer networks in the capitol complex. Nonpartisanship is the rule in the Legislative Council, and it is taken seriously. Even on such touchy subjects as redistricting,

the council makes certain that it offers confidential technical expertise to any member, regardless of his or her rank and party.

A similar arrangement exists with respect to the Legislative Budget Board. Natural tensions between the executive and legislative branches made the Legislative Budget Board a necessary fixture of the Texas legislature. Although the governor has a line-item veto, the budget process in Texas is dominated by the legislative branch. Because Texas must constitutionally operate under a balanced budget, the Legislative Budget Board was created along the same lines as the Legislative Council, in order to provide nonpartisan, technical information on budgetary matters. The Budget Board attaches a fiscal note to every bill so that the members can gauge its fiscal impact.

What sets Texas apart from the previous two models is the role of leadership in the legislative process. In the Texas House, unlike in New York's, the leadership is nonpartisan, which often leads to a three-sided conflict between an individual member's partisan staff, committee staffs that reflect the partisan orientations of the chairs, and the speaker's staff, which is personally loyal to the speaker. This amalgamation of interest and loyalties presents even more problems when the nonpartisan staff is involved. In conflicts, the speaker is at a distinct advantage, in that his staff is much larger; the speaker has even been known to assign staff members to help with, and monitor, key committees. In addition to the fact that the speaker appoints a majority of all committees and the entirety of the procedural committees, including Appropriations, Ways and Means, and Calendars (the gatekeeper committee), he or she has enormous discretion over where bills are assigned. Because no single piece of legislation is exclusively within the jurisdiction of a single committee, the speaker can use his extensive staff to guide legislation to friendly or unfriendly committees. This means that although technical information may be of the highest quality, it is not uniformly accepted in the arena of the Texas House, where the speaker and key members have their own staffs to aid in creating legislation more in line with their political objectives. In the senate, enormous power rests in the office of the lieutenant governor. His staff is comparable to the speaker's and performs roughly the same functions.

One might argue that the size of the chamber allows the lieutenant governor even more control over the process because his formal powers are similar to the speaker's.

Although in some systems the administrative duties of staffing are handled by rules committees, the administrative duties of each chamber of the Texas legislature are handled by a separate administration committee. The secretary of the senate, the chief clerk in the house, the calendar clerks, messengers, and the sergeants-at-arms are all under the control of the administration committees. Because each of these committees is made up of members of each party, the outputs tend to be nonpartisan.

Committee staff are a separate breed altogether. In each chamber, the chair is given additional administrative funds to staff chair committees. Although these staff members technically service the entire committee and in some cases amount to little more than paperpushers, they are hired and fired by the chairs. The size and quality of staffing on these committees vary significantly. Because there is a high degree of turnover among committee chairs, there is a high degree of turnover among committee clerks. New chairs often bring in their own people, which yields little in the way of technical experience. Some house clerks have impressive credentials and appear to be legitimate experts in their respective policy areas, while others have no experience in the policy area. This is less true in the senate, where the committee clerks universally seem to possess expertise. In the senate, where staff generally receive higher salaries, it is common to find both more staff members and a higher quality of staff members with more-specialized duties. For example, a senate committee may have a chief clerk to expedite the legislative process and a legal expert to evaluate statutory questions. In the house, with the exception of the most powerful committees (such as Ways and Means, Appropriations, and Calendar), the committee staff is small, usually numbering fewer than two full-time employees. The senate's staff can be four to five times that size.

Although cooperation does exist in regard to technical information and staff support, no cooperation is visible between the house and senate committee staffs. There is no attempt made to track legislation through the other chamber, and partly as a result of the absence of jurisdictional clarity, no relationship exists between similar committees in each chamber. Cooperation is therefore limited to sharing bill analyses; that amounts to little more than placing a caption at the top of the proposed legislation.

There are also significant variations in personal staffs, which owe their loyalty to those who hire and fire them. At the beginning of each session, the house sets an operating budget for the members to hire staff. Traditionally, this figure is significantly smaller than the senate's allocation, and in each chamber the members routinely use funds out of their officeholder accounts to hire additional staff support, both during sessions and at home in their district offices. In the senate, staffing is significant, with every senator having several full-time staff members to provide clerical and legislative assistance, including constituency casework and bill tracking. In the house, the more powerful the member, the more likely he or she will have multiple legislative assistants. In regard to the capital staff, some members have several staff members to track legislation and perform constituency service in addition to office manager/receptionist/clerical worker types. Other members have no legislative assistants and rely exclusively on the general clerical helper. As expected, these members tend to be the least effective. The same can be said of the variations in district staff. Although these staff members are primarily used in constituency casework, their skills vary dramatically. This may in fact be a result of the emphasis the member places on constituency service. In Texas, members tend to raise large amounts of money from lobbyists outside of their districts, and that reduces the overall importance of constituency service, particularly when the state uses an antiquated reporting and disclosure system that makes such facts difficult to use in political campaigns to unseat incumbents.

The Texas staff system is chaotic at times because most of the staffing is in the hands of the individual members. These staff members' objectives are to satisfy their employers, who come to the legislature with predisposed political views. Often these staff members interact with the nonpartisan staff, and the inevitable conflicts over each group's goals appear. When this occurs, the partisan staff seem to win out, in part because the Legislative Council has no policy objectives and is designed to be completely nonpartisan. This problem is exacerbated further by the short sessions and high turnover among membership and staff.

The Legislative Council Model

The final model is the legislative council system. Unlike the system in Texas, which also has a legislative council, these staffing systems tend to rely on the legislative council as the primary staffing unit. Although there is significant variation among the various legislative council states, they do have much in common. These systems emerged in part as a solution to two perceived problems with traditional staffing models: too much control in the hands of a limited few (either partisan leaders or nonpartisan leaders) and a lack of continuity among staffs in traditionally fragmented systems. Legislative councils were to act as nonpartisan providers of technical and even substantive information. Later variations have produced some councils that account for partisan deviation, but the unifying and distinguishing element in these models is that the central information provider is the legislative council, which is shared by both chambers and charged with providing unbiased information. Although this model is most common in sparsely populated western states such as New Mexico and Wyoming, more-populous states such as Kentucky, North Carolina, South Dakota, and Vermont also have adopted variations of the legislative council model. The titles of the states' centralized nonpartisan agencies may vary, but the fact that each is a single agency under the shared control of both chambers of each state's legislature does not.

As was the case in the traditional models, the policy-making environment of each state shapes the organizational response. In Vermont the staff is centralized into one agency that performs all staffing duties from research to statutory revision. In New Mexico's council system, the council provides a similarly wide range of services by providing virtually all the information to the legislature. New Mexico's system specialized into three distinct agencies. The New Mexico Legislative Council's fiscal officer now has broken off to form the Legislative Finance Committee, and the Legislative School Study Committee allows policy specialization in education, which consumes 50 percent of the state's budget. This arrangement is simplified by a relatively small number of partisan splits in the body and by the fact that the council has a trusted reputation among virtually all members. In New Mexico, although the council has specialists the majority of staff are generalists. Other states, such as Vermont and Wyoming, have followed a similar trend toward breaking down staff into specialized subunits to meet environmental needs. These two states have created a separate staffing unit to cope with financial questions, which effectively serves as a centralized legislative accounting division and a separate generalist division to deal with policy and legal questions. In sharp contrast, Maine organizes its staff into distinct divisions. Each of these divisions corresponds to a staff function and includes fiscal review, policy and legal analysis, statutory revision, and general research.

In spite of these varied structural adaptations, these council-system states share many common features. As a result of the relatively higher levels of efficiency obtained by eliminating duplication of services, staffing systems based on the legislative council model have fewer staff members than do the other models. The largest numbers in council-system states are found in Kentucky and North Carolina where staff numbers under five hundred. Even in these states, the staff is only a small fraction of that found in the states that use the other models. In many ways, the small size is related to the relatively smaller state budgets. Efficiency is mandated in these states, with smaller and less dense populations. Party divisions are less common in these states as well. Of the states with legislative councils, only Nevada has a competitive party system at the state level, which makes reliance on a central nonpartisan staffing agency all the easier.

These systems have evolved in response to the environments facing the respective legislatures. In each case, one could easily argue that the council system is best suited to that state. In terms of efficiency, the council system obviously reduces duplication and, on a secondary level, increases coordination in the legislative process. The trade-off in this situation is that the staff tend to be generalists and therefore less likely to provide highly technical information. Of course, as the New Mexico model suggests, the council can create specialization if it is desired.

One can debate the merits of creating staffs that are politically neutral. These staff members do not have loyalty to any leader or party, and consequently, they should theoretically provide information that is less biased. However, these staff members may not understand the political consequences of policy-making. In response to these problems, some states with a council-type structure have attempted to create politically loyal staff within the council framework. Connecticut, New Jersey, and Ohio have attempted to mix council staff with partisan and committee staff. What differentiates these states from Texas is that in each the council has maintained its role as the central staff agency, in spite of the meshing of partisan and committee influences.

CONCLUSION

This discussion has centered on three overall trends in state legislative staffing and the various models of staffing systems that have evolved. The unifying element here is that each state or system has been forced to adapt to its own policy-making environment. In general, the trends toward larger numbers of staff, greater routinization of procedures, and more technologically advanced staff hold true across all states; the specific methods of employing the staff does not, though, and this is reflected in the various models.

Each of the models of staff development is related to the corresponding development of a state's legislative branch. As legislatures assume greater policy-making responsibilities and professionalism, the staff systems adapt to respond to those changes. Although the trend in the council systems has been toward more specialization and even, in some cases, departmentalization, the overall trend in state legislative staff has been toward more centralization. The reasons for this are many, but center on adaptation to changes in the policy-making environment. Perhaps most important is the fact that government in general has been faced with budget problems; in the late 1980s and early 1990s, most state governments found themselves on extremely tight budgets and were reluctant to increase taxes. From Connecticut to California, from New Jersey to Texas, budgetary problems have forced state governments to cut where they can, and staffing systems have provided a convenient outlet for legislators to cut duplicative services through consolidation in the name of efficiency. Although it is doubtful that states will deviate from their current models to any significant degree in the near future, it is much more likely that in those cases where change does occur, it will be toward centralization. Of course, as state legislatures vary structurally, so do their staffs, and unless state legislatures become structurally more similar, it is unlikely that staffing systems will become more easily categorizable than they are today.

BIBLIOGRAPHY

The following sources were used in this essay and provide useful information for continued reading on state legislative staffing: COUNCIL OF STATE GOVERNMENTS, *The Book of the States*, vol. 27 (Lexington, Ky., 1993); JAMES J. HEAPHY and ALAN BALUTIS, eds., *Legislative Staffing* (New York, 1975); JAMES J. HEAPHY, "Legislatures Political Organizations," *Public Administration Review* (September/October 1975); LYNN HELLEBUST, *State Legislative Sourcebook, 1990* (Topeka, Kans., 1989); DONALD HERZBERG and ALAN ROSENTHAL, eds., *Strengthening the States: Essays on Legislative Reform* (Garden City, N.Y., 1971); ALAN ROSENTHAL, *Legislative Performance in the States* (New York, 1974); ALAN ROSENTHAL, *Legislative Life: People, Process, and*

Performance in the States (New York, 1981); LUCINDA A. SIMON, *A Legislator's Guide to Staffing Patterns* (Denver, 1988); BRIAN WEBERG, "Changes in Legislative Staffing," *Journal of State Government* (November/December 1988); BRIAN WEBERG and BETH BAZAR, *Legislative Staff Service: Fifty State Profiles* (Denver, 1988); and JOHN A. WORTHLY, ed., *Comparative Legislative Information Systems: The Use of Computer Technology in the Public Policy Process* (Washington, D.C., 1976).

SEE ALSO Committees in State Legislatures; Floor Procedures and Conference Committees in State Legislatures; AND State Legislatures in the Twentieth Century.

CONGRESSIONAL REFORM

Leroy N. Rieselbach

Conventional wisdom holds that the U.S. Congress is a static institution. Nothing could be further from the truth. The national legislature is in a constant state of flux. At the turn of the century, the political parties dominated congressional politics. By the 1960s, in stark contrast, Congress was a committee-centered institution. Two decades later the parties had begun to show renewed strength. For the most part, change on Capitol Hill is evolutionary, not revolutionary; small shifts in the way Congress conducts its business, often unnoticed by all but the closest observers of the legislative scene, are commonplace as the members try to find a better way of operating.

On rare occasions, however, discontent with the capacity of Congress to perform adequately reaches a sufficient pitch to induce the lawmakers to make wholesale changes in the organization and procedures of the legislature. The year 1910 and the years thereafter were one such period; 1965–1977 another. These eras of reform saw concerted efforts to remedy perceived defects in Congress's ability to play its proper part in the national policy-making process. Ordinarily, perceived congressional shortcomings create little controversy; "business as usual" is the order of the day. But in times of severe economic dislocation or international crisis, they are more likely to inspire efforts to reform legislative practices to improve the quality of Congress's performance. The problem is that serious reform is hard to enact and its consequences difficult to foresee. What reformers want is not always what they get.

REFORM AND CHANGE: INCENTIVES AND PURPOSES

The disparity between reformers' intentions and their accomplishments occurs largely because *reform*—defined as intentional efforts to reshape institutional structures and processes—is only one, and perhaps not the most significant, source of organizational alteration. *Change*—conceived more broadly as any shift, intended or inadvertent, gradual or abrupt—takes place more randomly and unobtrusively. Of the two, change appears more pervasive and fundamental. In this light, reform is merely one type of change: a conscious, explicit attempt to bring about preferable results through specific structural or procedural shifts.

It is no easy task to separate the causes and consequences of reform from those that the broader forces of change induce. For one thing, events outside the legislature may impinge directly on it. Recession at home or war abroad may pose problems to which Congress must respond, even if it is ill-prepared to act effectively. Failure to meet such challenges may goad reformers to seek to restructure the legislature. Such external developments may raise new issues or induce a change in Congress's agenda, requiring new institutional forms. In addition, membership turnover brings new people, with different backgrounds, experiences, and perspectives, to the legislature, who may operate the existing machinery in ways at variance with old routines or try to rebuild the legislative engine to produce more efficient performance. Alternatively, events and new issues may compel incumbent legislators to reassess their views, leading to policy change, reform efforts, or both. In short, events, new issues, and new members, neither planned nor predictable, may contribute as much or more to legislative change than any self-conscious reform movement.

The reform impulse thus flows from internal and external imperatives. On the one hand, representatives and senators may recognize that their institution does not work well. They may sense that they have ceded their policy-making capacity to the executive, to the detriment of their ability to formulate programs to their liking. They may come to feel that the policy-making processes do not enable them to address items on the policy agenda effectively. Members may conclude that procedural defects preclude treating and resolving the issues that the voters in their states and districts sent them to Washington to handle. Thus, they may decide to undertake organizational reform.

On the other hand, pressures from the country at large may arouse the reform spirit. Their failure to satisfy public calls for legislative action may result in lawmakers not being reelected; an unhappy prospect for legislators who aspire to long-term careers in Washington. Discontent with legislators may also arise out of nonpolicy matters, such as a breach of ethics, that are no less threatening to reelection chances. Institutional restructuring of Congress may enable it to get and stay in touch with the electorate. The continued legitimacy of the legislature, in other words, may rest on its response to some perceived public outcry.

BROAD THEORIES OF REFORM

The challenge for would-be reformers is to construct a new set of organizational forms that implement their vision of the "better" legislature. Although a number of general portraits of the ideal Congress exist, none has energized the lawmakers themselves, who, in the last analysis, must enact whatever reforms seem desirable.

Executive Force Theory

At one extreme is the *executive force* theory. Proponents of this view are pessimistic about congressional capacity to govern. They stress the need to solve pressing policy problems yet despair over the ability of the legislature to contribute meaningfully to policy formulation. The executive, by contrast, is likely to be the catalyst for progress; Congress, a decentralized institution, representing multiple interests, can only impede innovation. Consequently, the president must be empowered to lead, unobstructed by a recalcitrant Congress. Reform should reduce legislative ability to frustrate presidential leadership. The executive suprem-

acy view, in sum, stresses presidential authority and reduces Congress's role to legitimation, perhaps modification, and review after the fact.

Responsible Party Theory

An alternative avenue to escape congressional obstructionism is to create a disciplined, cohesive *"responsible" party system*. A unified majority party in Congress could readily enact its proposals at all stages of the lawmaking process. If the majority was loyal to a president of its own party, it could pass the chief executive's proposals without risk of delay or defeat. Proponents of responsible parties would permit the party national committees to control nominations for Congress, giving them substantial leverage over rank and file legislators. Inside Congress, the rules should ensure that majorities could more easily carry the day. Here, too, Congress would eschew independent policy-making, act to confer legitimacy on presidential initiatives and to emphasize nonpolicy (e.g., representational) activities.

Literary Theory

What appear to adherents of the executive force and responsible parties models as Congress's vices are virtues to those who support the *"literary"* theory. The latter pay homage to the constitutional tradition of checks and balances and separation of powers. They read the Constitution literally and believe it requires Congress to restrain the power-seeking executive, during both policy formulation and execution. Policy departures should come slowly, after careful deliberation and after a national consensus emerges. Thus, a decentralized legislature that acts cautiously is desirable. These virtues have been lost, and reform is required to restore them. Literary theorists resist all centralizing mechanisms, preferring an election system that protects legislators' independence. They fear cohesive political parties that might centralize Congress, and they favor congressional procedures that protect the power of individual lawmakers to slow action and to oversee and control executive-branch administration of enacted programs. Overall, they want Congress to countervail the executive.

CONGRESSIONAL REFORM

Congressional Supremacy Theory

The literary view shades off into a vision that assigns even greater weight to the centrality of Congress, the *congressional supremacy (or "Whig") model.* Legislative supremacists see Congress as the prime mover in national politics. They favor all the reforms that the literary theorists endorse, as well as other changes intended to strip the president of most major bases of authority. This "Whig" view envisages a Congress that will both make policy—explicitly and on its own terms—and oversee its implementation.

Overall, then, broad visions of Congress exist, each with its own set of structural and procedural reforms. Each view could, theoretically, provide benchmarks against which to assess particular reform proposals. Central to such evaluation is a general question about what government is obligated to accomplish and a narrower question about what the role of Congress should be in policy-making. Proponents of both the executive force and responsible parties theories stress the need for action to solve policy problems. In contrast, the literary and congressional supremacy theories advocate focus on caution and consensus. Each theoretical emphasis entails a distinctive congressional organization. Those who desire active policy-making—the executive force and responsible parties theorists—seek to subordinate Congress in a set of centralized structural arrangements. Those who prefer inaction—the literary theory adherents and the Whigs—look favorably on a decentralized legislature that moves only after attending to many points of view and melding them into widely acceptable programs.

SOME NARROWER STANDARDS

These broad visions of the "good" legislature have inspired little action. They are hard to implement; each would in all likelihood require amending the Constitution, a difficult chore under any circumstances and more onerous still when it involves altering basic features of the political process. The divergent proexecutive and legislative supremacy positions offer little ground for compromise. Furthermore, in the "real world" of politics, few with the opportunity and authority to reform the way Congress operates—the members themselves—have the luxury to examine Congress and its policy-making role in philosophical terms. Rather, they tend to react pragmatically and to call for reform only if it seems unavoidable. Members seem to evaluate Congress's performance using three criteria: responsibility, responsiveness, and accountability. These standards relate to the broader visions but do not require the same levels of agreement or pose insuperable obstacles to adopting particular reforms.

Responsibility

The first standard, *responsibility,* focuses on problem solving. A responsible institution enacts successful policies that resolve the major issues confronting the country. The responsibility criterion emphasizes speed, efficiency, and success. Can Congress adopt programs that deal promptly and effectively with national problems? If not, reform to improve the product of the legislative process seems warranted. To the extent that Congress ratifies the president's program, it acts as the executive force or responsible party advocates prefer: it concurs with the executive, and policy independence is minimal. To the degree that Congress imposes its own priorities for legislative programs, it behaves consistently with the legislative supremacy positions: it will do what it thinks best, regardless of what executives, interest groups, or public opinion may favor. A policy-oriented legislature will spend more time and effort studying and debating legislation and less on other, representational and oversight, activities. In any event, the responsibility standard assesses Congress in terms of the legislature's ability to enact workable public policies with speed and efficiency.

Responsiveness

The second criterion, responsiveness, emphasizes process more than product. Concern with the substance of programs is secondary to attention to the process of policy formation. To be responsive, Congress must listen to, and take account of, the ideas of those whom its actions will affect, such as citizens, organized groups, local and state governments, and national executives. The lawmakers must provide open channels of communication for those whom their decisions will influence. Congress should not act until all with opinions have had the chance to voice them.

A responsive Congress will be a deliberate, slow-moving institution. Unless and until it gets unequivocal and forceful policy messages, an infrequent occurrence, it is likely to resist rapid, innovative policy-making. Congressional supremacists (literary theorists and Whigs) tend to appreciate responsiveness; they desire a legislature that restrains the executive, preferring one that listens, waits, and acts only when a true and enduring national consensus emerges. The responsiveness standard plays down the costs of inaction or inefficiency.

Accountability

A third criterion is *accountability*: citizens should hold Congress accountable for what it does or does not accomplish. If voters disapprove of Congress's policy choices or perceive that members have unethically placed self-interest above the public good, they can use the ballot box to send new, presumably wiser and more honest individuals to Washington. Thus, the lawmakers must calculate the popular reaction, real or potential, to their actions. Accountability operates after the fact; public disapproval may terminate legislative careers.

An accountable Congress is an institution on public display. Interested citizens can discover what their elected representatives are doing and saying in committee and on the House and Senate floors. Citizen scrutiny is likely to promote caution. To avoid alienating voters, members will take care not to make rash statements, to take up controversial causes, or to engage in activities of doubtful propriety. They may defer to the president or delegate authority to the bureaucracy, eschewing policy-making independence, thus pleasing the proponents of executive force notions. If, by contrast, Congress refuses to act, policy immobilism may ensue, to the pleasure of the congressional supremacists. In short, accountability inclines members to avoid risks even as it exposes their behavior and ethics to public examination.

These three criteria—responsibility, responsiveness, and accountability—are not mutually exclusive; they can be applied simultaneously. This is readily apparent in the case of accountability. Regardless of whether voters judge congressional performance in terms of product or process (responsibility or responsiveness), they remain capable, in theory, of discovering what their representatives are doing and of sending those whose performance they deem unworthy into early retirement. Similarly, in theory, decision-makers may act both responsibly and responsively; they can move rapidly on the basis of full consultation to adopt workable policies. In practice, however, responsibility and responsiveness are likely to conflict. The former requires speedy and efficient problem solving; the latter calls for careful attention to a wide variety of viewpoints. A problem may grow less manageable or effective solutions may become obsolete while Congress waits for the expression of numerous sentiments. It is unlikely that Congress can be fully responsible *and* entirely responsive; there will be tension between the two standards. Nonetheless, each criterion provides a benchmark—narrower than the broad philosophic visions—against which reformers assess Congress's performance.

REFORM IN PRACTICE

Congressional reform has reflected politics and pragmatism rather than commitment to any grand vision of the "ideal" legislature. It has dealt with individual matters without much reference to some grand design. It is unrealistic to expect otherwise. Members of Congress are the major reformers; they may respond, willingly or not, to outside, external pressures—from presidents, pressure groups, and public opinion—but unless and until they decide to institute changes, there is no reform. Not surprisingly, both the environment and the congressional way of operating—external and internal conditions, in varying proportions—incline Congress to enact reform. Members enact reforms in the same fashion as they legislate on other subjects.

Reform in the twentieth century has concentrated on the House of Representatives. The larger chamber represents more diverse constituencies, its members are more likely to specialize on one or two substantive topics (often those that serve the voters back home), and it relies more heavily on a division of labor that uses an elaborate system of standing committees. Personal relationships among its members tend to be formal and less intimate than those among senators. These diversities require more formal procedures to define an organizational structure that will permit the House to work its will. The rules, when they seem to thwart the purposes of a significant number of members, become the targets for reform.

The Senate, in sharp contrast, is more open and flexible. Its members represent broader, more homogeneous constituencies; senators have more opportunity to act as generalists, dealing with a range of substantive topics. Their personal relationships, while not necessarily intimate, are nonetheless closer than usually found among those serving in the House. They have less need for strong political parties to impose some central discipline and can handle the procedural requisites informally without the need for enforcing an elaborate set of formal rules. While such procedures exist, they are readily circumvented using unanimous-consent agreements, negotiated understandings to which all senators must subscribe, that expedite business and offer a way around strict written rules. The Senate, in short, has proven more adaptable than the House, and major reform efforts have focused on the latter.

1910–1911: The "Revolt" Against Cannon

The legislative legacy of the nineteenth century was a House of Representatives more responsible than responsive. The leaders, particularly the Speaker of the House, acting for partisan purposes and within partisan majorities, came to dominate House proceedings. Speaker Thomas B. Reed (R.-Me.), who served in that capacity from 1889–1891 and from 1895–1899, established the authority of the majority party. As presiding officer, he came to dominate floor proceedings; he established control over the Committee on Rules, which he used to define the terms under which legislation would be considered on the House floor. The Democratic minority fumed, but was powerless to overcome the Republican majority. The latter enacted its legislative program, or blocked the Democrats', at its pleasure.

Joseph G. Cannon (R.-Ill.), who served as House Speaker from 1903–1911, built on existing precedents to centralize House operations under his and his party's aegis. Cannon not only managed floor proceedings with an iron hand but also controlled the careers of the members. He took complete charge of the committee assignment process; members served on panels at the Speaker's discretion. Members opposed so powerful a party leader at their political peril; their careers depended on his goodwill. The House, for all practical purposes, was Cannon's fiefdom. It could act promptly and efficiently in conformity with the Speaker's wishes, but members, including more moderate elements of his own party, were unable to respond to their own and their constituents' policy preferences. It could act responsibly but was unresponsive. The period was one of "czar rule."

In the process of bending the House to his will, Cannon sowed the seeds of reform; a bipartisan majority emerged in 1910 to strip the Speaker of his powers and to undercut the ability of the majority party to have its way. New rules adopted by The Insurgents denied the Speaker the authority to appoint members to House committees, providing instead they should be "elected by the House, at the commencement of each Congress." Cannon was denied a seat on the Rules Committee, making it difficult for him to control the content of legislation or its movement to the House floor. His power as presiding officer was sharply curtailed and he could no longer arbitrarily decide who would make a speech or offer an amendment. The reformers set up a Consent Calendar, an agenda of noncontroversial bills to be considered by the floor, to provide for easy, automatic treatment of routine bills; they provided for a discharge petition procedure to permit majorities to extract legislation from committees that refused to report out bills for consideration by the House. The minority won the right to offer a recommittal motion prior to the final vote on the passage of legislation; the dissidents could propose to send the bill back to committee with instructions to substitute their proposals for those embodied in the committee's version. A year later additional rules changes provided for the election, rather than the appointment, of committee members and leaders. The reformers undermined the capacity of a centralized House to act with dispatch. The long-term result of their success was to create the capacity for individual members to respond to the interests of their constituents and to exercise authority independently.

The revolt against Cannon set in train an evolution that fundamentally altered the character of Congress. Hierarchical control of the House by a powerful Speaker, with the support of the majority party, gradually gave way to a fragmented, decentralized chamber where independent, individualistic members reached decisions through intricate processes of negotiation and compromise. In short, the House became "institutionalized." The emergence of an elaborate committee (and subcommittee) system with numerous positions of some influence developed, and helped make the organization of the House more complex. Committees and their chairs became the locus of the most important congressional decisions. The political parties were rendered suitors for their own members' affections rather than dispensers of authoritative instructions. Partisan cohesion, when the roll was called, declined over the years.

Congress adopted automatic procedures that served to award and preserve individual members' prerogatives. Seniority, years of consecutive service, defined legislators' standing on their committees. The most senior majority party member became panel chair. To accommodate members and external pressures, Congress continually created new committees; by 1945, there were 48 House and 33 Senate panels. The rules attempted to spell out the jurisdictions of the burgeoning number of committees. Norms, unwritten understandings that pre- and proscribed certain behaviors, came to characterize the conduct of congressional business. Lawmakers who failed to observe the folkways—who declined to specialize on a relatively narrow range of policy matters, to act to protect the reputation of the chamber, or to reciprocate favors their colleagues proffered, for instance—were denied the respect and influence that membership in the "club" conferred. By the onset of the World War II, Congress had become a decentralized institution where individual members shared power widely, if not altogether equally. Parties were weak, acting as brokers in an intricate dance of coalition formation, while committees and their chairs were strong, producing Congress's authoritative decisions relatively unchallenged. The legislature was responsive to multiple interests but was often hard pressed to integrate the views it heard into responsible solutions to pending and pressing policy problems.

The Legislative Reorganization Act of 1946

Efforts to cope with the Great Depression and World War II persuaded many observers that Congress was ill-equipped to cope with the complexities of modern government. Washington had assumed control of the economy, undertaken to manage an enormous federal bureaucracy, and been forced to conduct a massive war effort. Congress was not, in the view of its critics, institutionally capable of playing its part in dealing with these national obligations. Its protection of the vested interests of numerous, relatively autonomous, legislators meant that it could not formulate and enact meaningful public policies. Congress was hard-pressed to oversee executive-branch performance effectively and was forced to delegate too much authority to the bureaucratic apparatus.

These external criticisms were codified in a report of the American Political Science Association's Committee on Congress in 1945. The academic analysis suggested some fundamental reforms designed to permit the legislature to reassert its power vis-à-vis the executive and to reclaim its policy-making leadership. The message was not lost on Congress, which established a Joint Committee on the Organization of Congress in 1945. After extensive hearings it weighed in with a proposal advancing thirty-seven reform recommendations. Vested internal interests, mainly from Democrats holding committee chairs, forced abandonment of many of the Joint Committee's more radical ideas; the surviving changes were enacted as the Legislative Reorganization Act of 1946.

The most significant thrust of the 1946 act was an effort to rationalize the congressional committee system. The statute clarified the jurisdictions of vastly simplified committee arrangements and wrote them into the House and Senate rules. The thirty-three Senate committees were reduced to fifteen, while the forty-eight House panels were reshuffled into nineteen; only two House and a single Senate committee were actually abolished. A second impulse of the act was to expand legislative expertise. Committee staff resources were enhanced substantially; each committee could hire four professional and six clerical staff, although no limit was placed on the number that could be hired by the Appropriations Committee. In addition, the Legislative Reference Service of the Library of Congress, a research arm of Congress, was strengthened with a larger, more expert, better paid staff. The reformers hoped that these new information resources would enable Congress to establish its own capacity to develop innovative public policy proposals that could compete with those that the president initiated. Finally, and boldly, the Reorganization Act instituted a new budgetary process. Recognizing the incoherence of fiscal policy-making in a decentralized legislature, the act established a centralized procedure designed to produce a unified legislative budget specifying the nation's revenues and expenditures. The act directed the House Ways and Means and Senate Finance committees and the Appropriations committees of both chambers, acting as a Joint Budget Committee, to prepare each year a government-wide budget containing estimates of total receipts and expenditures.

There was, however, less to the act than met the eye. Congress subverted the committee restructuring by creating new committees which a legislative majority can do whenever it desires. After 1947, the House created four standing committees—Science and Astronautics (1958), Standards of Official Conduct (Ethics) (1967), Budget (1975), and Small Business (1975)—and abolished the Un-American Activities Committee in 1975. The Senate established three new panels—Veterans Affairs (1970), Budget (1975), and Small Business (1980)—but eliminated three others—Astronautical and Space Sciences, District of Columbia, and Post Office and Civil Service—in 1977. In addition, each chamber has had a varying number of special or select committees, allegedly temporary, to deal with specific topics not treated in the permanent standing committees. The House abolished its four such committees in 1993; the Senate continued to have four select committees as the 103rd Congress opened in 1993.

More important, the proliferation of subcommittees after 1946 enlarged the number of independent work units substantially. By 1973, the House had 132 subcommittees; in 1989, the number reached 152. Efforts to stem the tide managed to reduce the number to 121 in 1993. The Senate had 44 subcommittees in 1946, when the Reorganization Act took effect, 140 in 1976, and a more modest 87 in the 102d Congress. Fewer full committees did not mean fewer decision-making centers in Congress.

In the face of opposition from the dominant finance and spending committees, the omnibus legislative budget process was a dead letter by 1950. The leaders of these committees simply refused to implement its provisions, and the process quickly reverted to the fragmented procedures—independent consideration of tax and appropriations legislation and treatment of the latter in thirteen separate spending bills for various portions of the budget—that the 1946 act had sought to remedy. Enlarged and enhanced staffs endured, but in the hands of independent committees and subcommittees may have contributed more to the fragmentation of legislative authority than to the creation of an expert Congress poised to challenge a powerful president. While it recognized the Congress's irresponsibility, the 1946 act, in practice, failed to find ways to overcome legislative incapacity and immobilism.

Reformers concerned to make Congress more responsible launched one additional foray against the forces of fragmentation in 1961. Their target was the House Rules Committee, which they perceived as the graveyard for liberal legislation. An effective southern Democratic-Republican conservative coalition controlled the committee and scuttled desirable bills. After a bitter fight, that Speaker Sam Rayburn (D.-Tex.) led personally, the House voted narrowly, 217–212, to enlarge the committee from twelve to fifteen members. The new appointees, on the Democratic side at least, were expected to thwart the capacity of the conservative alliance to control the flow of legislation to the House floor. To further the same end, the reformers in 1965 reinstituted a 21-day rule (first adopted in 1949, and subsequently repealed) that permitted committee chairs to bring a bill directly to the floor if the Rules Committee refused to act within twenty-one days. The rule survived only for a single Congress and a House majority, preferring a strong and independent Rules Committee, struck the provision from the chamber rules in 1967. Along with the 1946 act, the assault on the Rules Committee clearly revealed a sense on the part of many, inside Congress and out, that if the legislature was to perform as a responsible maker of public policy, reform was essential.

Reform in the 1970s

The stimuli for the reforms that the revolt against Cannon engendered and for those that the Legislative Reorganization Act of 1946 embodied were relatively straightforward. The former reflected an internal dissatisfaction with the responsiveness of Congress; the latter a reaction to an external perception that the legislature was unable to act responsibly. In sharp contrast, the 1970s witnessed wholesale but piecemeal efforts to make Congress simultaneously more responsible, responsive, and accountable. The result was a series of major congressional reforms that transformed the legislature.

In the 1960s and 1970s, political considerations provided irresistible incentives for reform. Electoral concern and pledges to improve a Congress widely seen as ineffective led many newcomers to the legislature to push reform. The Watergate scandal, which increasingly consumed President Nixon's energies and weakened his standing with the public, gave them the opportunity to do so with minimal political risk. The increasingly difficult policy agenda—the Vietnam War and a faltering economy, for example—often proved intractable. The public, or a newly emerging "public interest" lobbying movement on its behalf, made louder and more forceful demands on the legislature and insisted that the lawmakers respond openly. Structural reform seemed to offer one route to repair policy-making deficiencies and to recapture public esteem. Such reform, however, ran up against vested interests in the old ways of doing business; members were disinclined to surrender their established prerogatives. Reform, when it came, was imposed according to standard congressional operating procedures, through the usual bargaining, compromising search for agreements typical of a fragmented, decentralized policy process. Members had neither time nor inclina-

tion to pursue some philosophical vision of the ideal Congress; instead they reacted to the difficulties of the moment with a process they found congenial.

But react they did, starting formally with the Legislative Reorganization Act of 1970, to promote two broad aims. The first was to reassert congressional power, particularly vis-à-vis the executive, to recapture influence unwisely abandoned, and to make Congress a more responsible policymaker. The second was to democratize the legislature, to diffuse influence more widely among members and citizens, and to give more of them a greater opportunity to participate meaningfully in congressional deliberations. These steps would make the institution more responsive and more accountable.

Reforms for Responsibility   The first set of reforms were reforms for responsibility, mostly aimed directly at the executive. Presidential assertiveness and congressional acquiescence had combined to create an imbalance between the two, in the executive's favor. Congress's difficulty in influencing the administration's Indochina policy and in holding Richard Nixon to account in the Watergate affair symbolized the idea of an "imperial presidency" and suggested that Congress had lost, or ceded, many of its traditional powers to declare war, to control the federal purse strings, and to oversee the bureaucracy. Reform would allow the legislature to reassert its rightful role in the policy process, imposing its preferences when it determined to do so.

To start, Congress moved against the president's military authority, enacting, over Richard Nixon's veto, the War Powers Resolution in 1973 to circumscribe the commander in chief's ability to commit the armed forces to combat. The legislation empowered Congress to compel the executive to withdraw troops sent into the field within sixty days (or ninety days under special circumstances). Second, acknowledging past failure to exercise effective control over federal expenditures, Congress passed the Budget and Impoundment Control Act of 1974. The new budget process offered, in principle, the opportunity for the legislature to produce a coherent, unified budget that compared revenue and expenditure totals, thus presenting a clear picture of the deficit (or surplus), according to a fixed timetable. The act sought to enable Congress to centralize and coordinate its consideration of the budget and to compete on even terms with the executive for fiscal primacy. Third, Congress moved to assert its ability to curb the president's power to impound—refuse to spend—duly authorized and appropriated funds.

In addition, to remedy disadvantages in information and analytic capacity, to generate independent expertise to countervail that available to the executive, Congress moved to enlarge its data resources. It established two new support agencies—the Congressional Budget Office (CBO) and the Office of Technology Assessment (OTA)—and it strengthened two old ones—the Congressional Research Service (CRS) of the Library of Congress and the General Accounting Office (GAO). It greatly enlarged committee staffs and members' personal staffs and sought to harness computers to its information needs. Finally, it began to assert more forcefully already established powers. Oversight of the bureaucracy received additional emphasis, and the legislature often enacted legislative veto provisions that enabled it, or its committees, to block or delay executive actions—reorganizations or regulations—within a specified time period.

A second strand in Congress's effort to enhance responsibility was to make the policy process more efficient. Decentralized decision-making impedes coherent policy formulation, and the reformers professed a desire to make it easier for Congress to act. The reforms, the most significant of which were in the House, sought to strengthen the political parties and their leaders and to reduce the possibilities for minority obstructionism. In consequence, the independent committees were brought to heel.

Specifically, the House Democratic Caucus, as the majority party, won the right to determine who would chair committees, breaching the seniority rule. In addition, Democrats created a Steering and Policy Committee that replaced the Democratic members of the Ways and Means Committee as the party's "committee on committees" to make committee assignments. Steering and Policy also advised on party policy positions. Finally the Caucus assumed the power to instruct the Rules Committee, to prevent that sometimes defiant committee from thwarting the party majority. The Speaker won new authority as well, including the personal power to nominate Rules Committee members, to bind that panel firmly to the leadership. The Speaker also gained a major voice in the Steering and Policy Committee. He secured new ability to regulate the flow of legislation to and from committee (through the prerogative to refer bills multiply to several panels) and to create ad hoc committees to facilitate systematic treatment of complex policy issues. On the Senate side, modest reform gave the leadership some controls over referring bills to particular committees for consideration and over bill referral and scheduling.

Congress also adopted other reforms for efficiency. The new budget process contained considerable potential for centralization. A series of rules changes, most notably alteration of the Senate rule of unlimited debate, the filibuster, so as to eliminate dilatory tactics, was designed to curtail the minority's ability to subvert the majority. Finally, both chambers sought to realign and rationalize their committee jurisdictions. Such efforts were more cosmetic than real in the House, but the Senate succeeded in adopting modest but meaningful changes that redefined committee jurisdictions somewhat and reduced the number of assignments that individual senators held. Senators were allowed to serve on no more than three committees and to chair only one committee and one subcommittee of a major panel. In consequence, senators went from on average of eighteen full or subcommittee assignments to eleven in the 102d Congress (1991–1992). All in all, parties and party leaders secured some new opportunities to move their legislative programs ahead more efficiently.

Reforms for Responsiveness Congress also put in place a significant series of reforms for responsiveness, reflecting dissatisfied lawmakers' unwillingness to forego the chance to improve their own positions. Many members, especially liberal and junior legislators, chafed under the restrictions on their participation and policy influence that the old committee-dominated regime imposed. The committee chairs, often in collaboration with the ranking minority members, dominated the panels. The disenchanted lawmakers quickly seized on the reform mood to introduce new rules and procedures. Particularly in the more hierarchical House, substantial pieces of committee power were reallocated to the rank and file. New rules reined in the full committee chairs, limited the number of committee and subcommittee chairs that individual members could hold, and established procedures that enabled more members to attain desirable subcommittee assignments.

Specifically, House Democrats empowered the party Caucus to vote, by secret ballot, to accept or reject the Steering and Policy Committee's recommendation for chair. In 1975, the Caucus put teeth in the new procedure, ousting three elderly, conservative southern panel chairs and replacing them with younger, more mainstream partisans. House Republicans and both parties in the Senate came to adopt similar procedures for electing committee chairs. In addition, House reforms sought to dilute the concentration of power: no member could chair more than one legislative subcommittee, serve on more than two full committees, or be a member of more than one important ("exclusive") committee.

More important, in the House, the reforms devolved much full committee power on the subcommittees. In 1973 the House Democratic Caucus adopted a "subcommittee bill of rights" to protect the independence of subcommittees, requiring that subcommittees have fixed jurisdictions and that legislation on these subjects be referred automatically to them. It permitted subcommittees to meet at the pleasure of their members, to write their own rules, and to control their own budgets and staffs. New procedures facilitated members' accession to positions of subcommittee authority; senior legislators could no longer monopolize desirable subcommittee assignments and leadership positions at the expense of their junior colleagues. In 1975 the Caucus mandated that all House committees with more than twenty members create a minimum of four subcommittees. These reforms, by "spreading the action," made possible wide participation in subcommittee activity.

These reforms democratized Congress. Both the House and Senate are decentralized. Committee chairs must, under threat of ouster, share their authority with full-committee majorities and subcommittee leaders. More lawmakers, operating from power bases within

committee and subcommittee, exercise some authority. More members are involved in finding solutions to pressing policy problems. More legislators, voicing different sentiments and articulating a broader range of constituent opinions, bring more points of view into legislative decision-making. Democratizing reforms, in sum, extend congressional responsiveness.

Reforms for Accountability The third dimension of the 1970s reform movement, reforms for accountability, sought to counter increasingly hostile public opinion. Policy failure, apparent conflicts of interest, and a highly publicized series of scandals combined to damage the prestige of Congress. To restore Congress's public standing, the Legislative Reorganization Act of 1970 and subsequent revisions of House and Senate rules, adopted between 1971 and 1975, sought to expose the legislature's operations to citizen scrutiny. First, members were to conduct the public's business in public. Legislators' votes, in committee and on the floor, were to be recorded and published. The committee process was also opened up. All sessions, including *markups*, where bills are revised on a section-by-section basis, and conference committee meetings between representatives of both houses to reconcile differences over a bill, were to be public unless a majority voted, in public, to close them. The 1970 act allowed televising, broadcasting, and photographing of committee meetings at the discretion of individual panels. In 1978, the House balked, fearing that television would encourage members to "grandstand" rather than to focus on legislative business. It relented, however, in 1986, and soon the C-Span cable television network brought committee and floor proceedings into millions of homes.

Second, both the House (1977) and Senate (1978) adopted codes of ethics, including financial disclosure provisions, intended to deter or expose conflicts of interest. Senators and representatives were required to report their earned income, income from dividends and interest, honoraria received from lectures and other activities, the value and donor of gifts tendered, holdings in property and/or securities, and their outstanding financial obligations. The outside income they could earn was limited. Such disclosures aimed to enable concerned citizens to discover to whom, if anyone, legislators were financially beholden and to assess whether members' personal interests impinged on matters about which they had to vote or otherwise act.

Third, the Federal Election Campaign Act of 1971, as amended by Congress and interpreted by the Supreme Court in *Buckley* v. *Valeo* (1976), established an election-finance system that limited contributors' donations but not candidates' expenditures. Candidates report in detail the sources of their funds—individuals and political action committees (PACs)—and the uses to which they put their money. Individuals can give candidates $1,000 per election (primary, general, and where necessary, runoff); PACs can donate $5,000 per candidate per election. The Federal Election Commission oversees the statute, receiving and disseminating the candidate spending reports. A variety of interest organizations and the media analyze the data and publicize the sources of funds flowing to members of particular committees and to lawmakers promoting particular policies. On their face, these *sunshine reforms*—open procedures, ethics codes, and campaign finance regulation—make it possible, though not easy, for interested citizens to satisfy themselves that members of Congress are acting on the basis of public-regarding, rather than self-serving, considerations.

The 1970s reforms—for responsibility, responsiveness, and accountability—were broad and deep. Each involved a reaction to an immediate need: the weakness of the policy process and confrontation with the executive, the restlessness of junior lawmakers, and a decline in Congress's public standing. Because each entailed a challenge to vested interests in Congress and to the conventional routines for conducting business, each required considerable bargaining and compromise before winning enactment. The reforms flowed in large part from broader changes in the environment—events outside Washington and an altered policy agenda—and from personnel changes the electoral process wrought. In pushing their programs, the reformers had little incentive to look beyond the short run. Like other forms of legislation, reform proceeded piecemeal, without detailed analysis of its compatibility with proexecutive or prolegislative visions of the "ideal" Congress. Rather, reform advanced pragmatically in reaction to ordinary political considerations. The character of the reform movement contributed to its consequences.

THE RESULTS OF REFORM

That reform changes Congress is incontrovertible. The Congress of the 1990s differs markedly from the legislature of the 1960s, which in turn was dramatically distinct from the assembly that Speaker Cannon dominated at the turn of the century. The issue is whether the reformed Congress is better than the one it replaced. This question is not easy to answer definitively, given that observers' views of what sort of Congress is desirable vary widely. Different visions will lead to differing assessments. In addition, an unequivocal answer may be impossible because it is difficult to attribute postreform behavior to the reforms themselves. Reform is, after all, part and parcel of broader change. Crises outside Congress, new issues, and new members may contribute as much or more than specific reforms to any altered patterns of congressional behavior.

From one perspective, the reformers of the 1970s achieved their purposes: Congress became more responsible, responsive, and accountable. The legislature is, potentially at least, more efficient. It is more capable of imposing its policy preferences on the executive when it opts to do so, and more centralization is possible. It is more democratic; more members and citizens participate in congressional deliberations. It is more visible; more of its operations, and its members' campaign and financial dealings, are matters of public record. In another sense, however, the reforms did not always produce the results that their proponents predicted. Over the longer haul, it has proven difficult to predict what impact reforms will have, and many have expressed reservations about one or another of the enacted reforms.

Responsibility

Foreign Policy   At best, Congress seems only marginally more responsible. The War Powers Resolution has not enabled the legislature to impose its will systematically on the executive. All presidents, from Nixon to Bush, have steadfastly denied the constitutionality of the law and have refused to acknowledge any formal compliance with it. In reality, Congress has the opportunity to participate in military policy-making only when troops remain in the field for extended periods. Most military adventures (e.g., Gerald Ford's rescue of the ship *Mayaguez*, seized by Cambodia in 1975, or George Bush's capture of General Manuel Antonio Noriega of Panama in 1990) were over before a decentralized Congress could formulate an official response. On two occasions, however, Congress played a visible part with respect to sending armed forces abroad. In 1983, it forced Ronald Reagan to acknowledge his obligations under the War Powers Resolution and in return authorized the dispatch of U.S. Marines to Lebanon for eighteen months. On the eve of the 1991 Persian Gulf War, the legislature voted grudgingly, by a narrow 52–47 margin in the Senate, to permit George Bush to use force to end Iraqi occupation of Kuwait. The War Powers Resolution may be more significant as a prior deterrent to dubious or precipitous armed intervention; never entirely certain that Congress will approve their actions, presidents may think twice before committing troops abroad.

On balance, however, in the international arena the president's position is likely to prevail. To be sure, Congress has flexed its institutional muscles frequently. The Senate refused to ratify the second Strategic Arms Limitation Treaty (SALT II) in 1979; the legislature has repeatedly blocked or delayed arms sales abroad, the export of nuclear materials, and numerous treaties with neighboring countries. During the Reagan administration, Congress regularly cut the defense budget below the president's request (but allowed it to rise dramatically above previous levels), imposed limits on production and deployment of the MX missile (but refused to eliminate the system entirely), and reallocated military and economic assistance to foreign nations. These decisions were at the margins; in general the president defined the broad contours of the nation's foreign policy.

Such assertiveness as Congress displayed may reflect basic, evolutionary change more than structural reform. Even without reform, new members, with new ideas on new issues, eager to secure the support of their constituents, may use basic legislative prerogatives to challenge the administration. As membership and situations alter, the pattern of congressional deference or contention is likely to ebb and flow. Members' policy preferences and political purposes more than institutional reforms may be the decisive determinants of congressional challenges to the executive.

The Budget Process Assessment of the new budget process yields a similar picture: reform intersects with other forms of change to produce unpredictable results. On the plus side, the Budget and Impoundment Control Act of 1974 clearly restored Congress's potential to assert legislative supremacy in financial affairs. When and if the legislators want to act decisively, they can use the new procedures to do so. Between 1975 and 1979, Congress observed the form of the new scheme and, for the most part, it formulated a coherent budget, specifying revenues, outlays, and the size of the deficit, although it deviated from the prescribed timetable. But the process did not fundamentally alter spending priorities (between military and domestic programs) or staunch the flow of red ink (the deficit and the national debt continued to grow inexorably).

By the end of the 1970s, political and economic circumstances had changed dramatically, and in consequence, so did the operation of the new budget process. Economic affluence gave way to fiscal scarcity, and there were no longer sufficient funds available to support the multitude of federal programs on the books, let alone undertake new initiatives. Political circumstances were different as well. Ronald Reagan came to office in 1981, committed to shrinking the size and scope of the federal government. His aims ran headlong into the preferences of a new breed of lawmaker: younger, eager to enact a new legislative agenda (which would shore up their electoral support in their constituencies), and ensconced in positions of power in a reformed legislature.

In 1981, Reagan carried the day; the more centralized budget process worked, at least in principle, to enable the president to win the taxation and spending programs he sought. Creative use of the new procedures—especially a device known as reconciliation that forced Congress to vote on omnibus bills that precluded votes on single programs in which members had vested interests—permitted the administration to lower taxes, to cut domestic spending, and to raise defense expenditures enormously. The centralized congressional process produced a budget efficiently and on time but it did not restore an independent congressional influence in financial matters. The legislature deferred to the president, as the executive force theorists would have it; the administration had, for once, the majorities in the Senate and House needed to use the procedures of the Budget and Impoundment Act of 1974 to push through a unified budget. The lawmakers were unwilling to make the hard political choices—to cut programs that their constituents desired to retain—needed to make the budget-process work. As a result the deficit ballooned to more than $200 billion for Fiscal Year 1985 (it had not exceeded $100 billion from 1975 through 1981).

In 1985, the legislature acted forcefully to revise the budget process to deal with the issue, passing the Balanced Budget and Emergency Deficit Control Act (popularly known as Gramm-Rudman-Hollings [GRH] after its Senate sponsors). The law constituted an effort to force Congress to use the 1974 budgetary procedures effectively. If the lawmakers could not adopt a budget, using the regular process, that met specified deficit targets, automatic cuts, a "sequester," would take effect. While many politically untouchable programs, like Social Security, were exempt, the remaining budget items, discretionary domestic programs and large portions of the defense budget, would be slashed to bring the deficit down to the prescribed level. The budget was to be in balance by 1991.

The Gramm-Rudman-Hollings law did not work. Congress complied formally with its terms, using accounting sleight of hand to pass budget resolutions that, on paper, appeared to reduce the deficit. In fact, the legislators were unable or unwilling to abide by their self-imposed limits and continued to appropriate funds in excess of the budget targets. In addition, events—the need to rescue the savings and loan industry and to fight a war in the Persian Gulf in 1991—intervened, and the deficit for that fiscal year topped the $300 billion mark. In that year, Congress abandoned the GRH deficit–limit scheme in favor of spending caps (fixed ceilings) for discretionary spending and "pay-as-you-go" financing (increased spending in one area must be offset by equivalent cuts elsewhere in the budget) for mandatory expenditures (entitlement programs such as Social Security and Medicare). The reformers intended to make it impossible for spending to exceed a fixed limit. In sum, efforts to control federal spending and hold down the deficit have not worked to make Congress a responsible budgeter.

The Information Revolution Similar uncertainties appear about the results of the "information revolution." On the one hand, members have greater access to more and better data than ever before. Increased staff resources, new agencies, more effective old support facilities, and improved computer technology have enormously expanded Congress's capacity to engage in analyses that can sustain legislative alternatives to executive initiatives. On the other hand, members may not have incentives to use these new opportunities. They are politicians, not objective policy analysts; they may search less for optimal policies than for programs that will serve their political purposes. Moreover, information that the reforms make available may distract lawmakers from programmatic activities. Overwhelmed by "information overload," legislators may be inclined to look to staff for guidance; conversely, staff may be prepared to be "entrepreneurs" rather than impartial "professionals." Dependence on staff may undercut members' ability to make independent judgments. Finally, there is an information-management problem: members may spend more time and energy administering their staffs than they do using data that the staff supplies. These problems, on the whole, may impede legislators' ability to delve into the substance of policy questions.

Political Parties Congressional reformers also sought to improve responsibility through strengthening the political parties. More cohesive, centralized parties would be better able to move a program through Congress efficiently and to overcome the opportunities for delay and defeat built into a pluralistic institution. In reality, the legislators were unwilling to cede more than a modicum of their individual independence to the party leaders, and the movement toward centralization has proved halting at best. The parties, on balance, remain weak, dependent on the willingness of their partisans to support the leadership.

There have, however, been some party successes in the House. In the Senate little effort was made to increase party power, and members' freedom of action continues unencumbered. By contrast, in the House the Democratic Caucus has assumed and exercised the right to hire and fire committee chairs and has occasionally insisted on a party policy position. Party leaders, through the Steering and Policy Committee, have had some influence over committee assignments and have gained some influence over the Rules Committee, and to a lesser extent, Ways and Means Committee. The Speaker's enlarged bill-referral power has been a mixed blessing. While he can refer a bill to several committees at once and impose time limits on its consideration, multiple referral greatly exacerbates the difficulty of coordinating congressional activity, requiring more individual members to reach agreement before legislation is enacted. In short, House leaders' new powers have proven inadequate to overcome the decentralizing forces that dominate Congress.

Leadership rests on the talents of those who rise to the top party positions. Leaders have few sanctions with which to compel their nominal followers to vote the party line. Party power remains more psychological—members want to back their party when and if they can—than tangible. Party loyalty is voluntary; leaders cannot easily enforce it. But in the 1990s, an age of austerity and divided government, some members have come to recognize the difficulties inherent in legislative decentralization and have reluctantly deferred to party leadership, especially with respect to budgetary policy. Party leaders, augmented by the chairs and ranking members of the important fiscal committees, have negotiated budgets at "summit" meetings with the administration. On other matters, to achieve their personal, political, and policy purposes, House members have seen greater benefits in strong party leadership and have urged their leaders to take advantage of the party-enhancing reforms of the 1970s. Even so, centralization—reflecting reform or member acquiescence—remains elusive, and without it, policy-making responsibility remains a will-o'-the-wisp.

Finally, revising the rules has produced only minimal effects. Dilatory tactics seem somewhat more difficult to use, and legislation is less likely to get enmeshed in parliamentiary thickets in the House. Less-demanding quorum requirements (making it easier to get the necessary number of members to conduct business to the floor), quorum call requirements, voting by machine, clustering votes, and permitting committees to meet more readily have expedited the flow of business, but these reforms have had little impact on the substance of congressional policymaking. Neither has the revised Senate cloture rule, designed to prevent unlimited debate, facilitated the more rapid processing of legislation. Sixty votes (rather than two-thirds of those present and voting) is sufficient to end a filibuster, and debate after invocation of cloture is limited to thirty hours. Simultaneously, however, Senate norms limiting the use of "extended debate" to major issues have lost their hold; there have been more filibusters, on more mundane matters, in the modern Senate. While cloture is invoked more frequently, more than half of such motions have failed in the recent period. Thus, the filibuster, conducted or merely threatened, continues to shape Senate floor action on much legislation.

Responsiveness

Committees   If reform and change have made Congress marginally more responsible, these forces have increased the legislature's capacity for responsiveness considerably. Congress is surely a more democratic body than it was before 1970. The reformers' chief targets were the full committees that powerful, sometimes tyrannical, conservative chairs dominated. By lessening the power of committee oligarchs, they hoped to make Congress more responsive. Thus, the reformers modified the seniority rule for choosing chairs, limited the number of committee positions any individual could hold, altered the committee assignment process, and devolved much committee power to subcommittees. Viewed narrowly, these changes may have accomplished their purpose, but from a long run perspective, their proponents may have won the battle but lost the war.

Increased responsiveness may have slowed the legislative process, requiring more elaborate bargaining among more participants to reach agreement, but it may also have made congressional decision making more arduous.

With respect to seniority, the old order has been altered. Although only the House has deviated from the seniority rule, election in both chambers has put House and Senate committee chairs on notice that they retain their positions only at the pleasure of their committee and party colleagues. Similarly, in the reformed Congress, individual members have increased opportunities to compete for preferred committee assignments. The new rules in both parties in both chambers guarantee all members a major committee post. Yet members do not always succeed in winning the places they covet, especially on the most desirable panels. There are not always enough seats to go around. Party leaders may intervene when seats on particularly important committees are at stake. Thus, members have greater opportunity to find congenial places in committees, but there is no certainty that they will succeed in doing so.

The major thrust of the committee reform was to create and sustain independent subcommittees, and here the reformers have succeeded admirably. The House moved a long way toward subcommittee government when it adopted the subcommittee bill of rights in 1973 and passed new rules granting more members significant subcommittee positions. But power has not increased uniformly across all subcommittees, nor is it clear that subcommittee influence exceeds that of the full committees. Subcommittees have assumed greater significance in the House, but they are not automatically the prime movers in congressional policy-making.

Still, the subcommittee reforms did enable junior members to advance rapidly to assume subcommittee chairs. The new chairs are more liberal, more "typical" Democrats, thus making committee leadership more representative of the entire party. More important, many subcommittees are independent and active. They hold more hearings and initiate consideration of more legislation, and their leaders manage more bills on the floor. They are often expert (with their own staffs) and they are protected from outside interference by guarantees of jurisdiction, control over their own rules, and ad-

equate budgets. Party leaders seldom intervene in subcommittee affairs.

But subcommittee independence is not autonomy. Subcommittee control of the conduct of legislative business is restricted. They remain subordinate to the full committees, which ultimately report legislation to the floor. The full committees may challenge and reverse their more adventurous subcommittees. In addition, subcommittees—particularly, those that deal with pork barrel, constituency matters—are open to external, group influences and may find it necessary to defer to clientele interests. The broader range of policy-making participation that democratization has fostered has led nonmembers to take a greater interest in committee and subcommittee operations, enlarging the range of opinions that subcommittees need to consider. In short, full committees, ordinary members of Congress, and outside groups constrain subcommittees.

On balance, democratization has increased members' opportunity to participate in congressional deliberations at the expense of the full committees, but it has not done so uniformly or with consistent effects on legislative policymaking. Nowhere is the variation in the impact clearer than with respect to bicameralism, or the constitutional division of Congress into two legislative chambers. Reform and change moved the House some distance toward subcommittee government. The Senate, in sharp contrast, changed very little. New members, pursuing a new agenda with a new spirit of independence, promoted individualism in the House; in the Senate personal freedom of action had long been the rule. With numerous and desirable committee assignments, senators had less need to use\subcommittees as a forum for influencing policy and little incentive to increase the authority of the subcommittees. The full committees continue to make the major decisions. Hard-pressed senators, short of time but not of influence in full committee and on the floor, have less need to strengthen and use subcommittees.

Staff Assistance   A final feature of the move toward responsiveness was to give members more staff assistance. Here reformers have accomplished much of what they set out to do. Members' personal staffs have grown enormously, and so have committee payrolls. In the Senate, each member is entitled to a staff aide for each committee assignment. These resources, coupled with research assistance from the enhanced congressional support agencies, give individual members access to substantial data that they can use to support their policy preferences. Presumably, these enlarged staff resources have improved congressional responsiveness.

Results of Democratization The move toward democratization has spread authority, especially in the House, more widely among the lawmakers. The reforms have made the House more like the Senate. Committee chairs must share their power with full committee majorities and more active and independent subcommittee leaders. More individuals have influence, at least on some small piece of the legislative turf. From these bastions, they can shape public policy. Electorally secure, fully staffed, and more assertive vis-à-vis the president, members are in position to respond to a wide variety of viewpoints. In this sense, the reformers have attained their purposes.

The reformers, however, have paid a price for enhanced responsiveness. Diffusion of power has damaged Congress's capacity to make policy effectively and efficiently; that is, to be responsible. In the House, the increased dependence on subcommittees has expanded members' work load, and even with more staff help they may have difficulty coping with the new demands on their time and energy. Specialization and expertise in the House seem to have declined; only those representatives on any given subcommittee may be well-enough informed to deal decisively, as specialists, with particular policy issues. Fewer individuals take the lead in narrower policy domains, and as they leave Congress or move to other full or subcommittee positions, "institutional memory," the ability to relate current problems to past performance, may be damaged.

In addition, more subcommittees may make members more vulnerable to interest-group representatives. Lawmakers with responsibility for particular programs are less numerous and thus more easily identifiable. Lobbyists know whom to approach, and members may have incentives to enter into mutually beneficial, in a narrow sense, relationships with group representatives. The broader, national interest may get less attention in such circum-

stances. Finally, independent subcommittees add a new layer to an already decentralized decision-making process. To pass, programs must now clear subcommittee and full committee hurdles. Committee and party leaders must consult more members, particularly because subcommittee jurisdictions are not always clearly defined, and several panels may insist on considering the same piece of legislation. To deal with this organizational complexity takes time, and legislation may be slowed if not sidetracked by the need to consider compromise and to construct coalitions among so many participants.

In the Senate the story is different, but the result is the same. Individualism has long been the hallmark of senatorial behavior, and reform has not undercut individual members' freedom of action. Senators, like representatives, are able to pursue their policy predilections relatively unencumbered. For Congress as a whole, reform has enlarged the potential for responsiveness but at a cost in responsibility. By multiplying the number of power centers, reform and change have increased the need for elaborate bargaining and compromise to reach agreement and move congressional business ahead.

Accountability

The third focus of the 1970s reformers was on congressional accountability. Legislative deliberations and lawmakers' finances were to be matters of public record. The more the public knows about lawmakers' legislative activity and connections to pressure groups, economic interests, individual campaign contributors, and political action committees, the greater its opportunity to hold members to account. In principle, sunshine laws, permitting the public to observe much more of Congress's activity, Federal Election Campaign Act disclosures of campaign financing, and congressional codes of conduct have put legislators' accounts and activity on public display.

Congressional Visibility In practice, the reformers seem to have succeeded again. Congressional meetings are open, and roll-call votes, in committee and on the floor, are part of the record. Voluminous data on members' personal and campaign finances are available, and the media and various public interest groups publicize them. But beneath the seeming success may lie a different, less sanguine, reality. For one thing, there is little persuasive evidence that citizens pay greater attention to Congress than they did in the prereform era. Polls reveal that the electorate is not better informed about legislative action. Incumbents continue to win reelection with relative ease (though in 1990 and 1992, in the wake of difficulties in passing budgets, the televised Clarence Thomas–Anita Hill hearings, and the House Post Office and Bank scandals, a number survived with reduced pluralities).

Second, with committee proceedings and voting matters of public record, lawmakers can no longer hide behind closed doors and unrecorded votes but must act in the open. With media, citizens, and campaign contributors watching, they must take care to protect their political futures. The presence of lobbyists and administrative officials at public sessions—where they can monitor members' behavior, offer texts of amendments, and notify their employers when and where to apply pressure—may make it more difficult for committees to act decisively and to be responsible. Increasingly, they have resorted to "executive" or "informal" sessions, held prior to official meetings, where members can talk freely and develop compromises without the intrusive presence of outsiders. Formal meetings may do little more than ratify agreements reached in private.

Financial Disclosure   Mandated by the House and Senate ethics codes, financial disclosure has had limited visible effect. There has been little if any diminution in the frequency of ethical problems, as the travails of the "Keating Five" senators—found in 1991 to have used poor judgment or worse in attempting to influence regulators' treatment of a troubled savings and loan institution—amply illustrate. The future, however, may be more promising. Voters have not been particularly sympathetic to legislators exposed as unethical. Members tarred in some way by scandal or conflict of interest have been prominent in the ranks of the few incumbents defeated for reelection.

Finally, campaign-finance reform has led to paradoxical results. On the one hand, the new election system—with its full disclosure provisions and its limits on contributions but not on expenditures—has seemingly helped to entrench incumbents, especially in the House. Private groups, particularly the PACs, have preferred contributing to incumbents, who potentially hold powerful committee or party positions in Congress, to the riskier strategy of funding challengers who might someday hold prominent posts. Contribution limits appear to have hindered hard-pressed House challengers. Senate contests, by contrast, are more competitive. Challengers are more visible and attractive, better able to solicit the funds they need and to unseat the incumbent. To whatever degree incumbent electoral safety reduces personnel turnover, accountability, however plausible in principle, will be inhibited. Old members espousing old points of view will continue to serve—even if they are out of touch, in policy terms, with their constituents—because they can fend off serious challenges.

At the same time, campaign finance and personal disclosure requirements have made life difficult for members of Congress. During the 1970s, record numbers of legislators—many relatively young, with substantial seniority and positions of prominence and power—chose to retire rather than to risk the relentless exposure of their daily routines, and those of their families, to public scrutiny. Many found the rewards of legislative service not worth the long hours and the loss of privacy. The exodus, however, slowed appreciably in the 1980s, and members now seem prepared to endure the attention that their positions in Congress attract.

In sum, the potential for citizen-enforced accountability is real but unrealized. While congressional activity is more accessible to citizens, the evidence suggests that sunshine reforms have had limited effects. In fact, visibility may contribute to legislative inertia. Ever aware that they are on display, members may conclude that inaction is the better part of valor. Rather than alienate constituents and groups whose electoral support is vital, they may avoid controversy and decline to act. By increasing the participation of external actors in congressional politics, the accountability reforms may have made Congress not only more democratic but also more permeable—more open to outside pressures that reduce the institution's capacity to make effective public policy. Steps to increase accountability, like those to promote responsiveness, may have undercut congressional responsibility.

CONCLUSION

While Congress changes constantly, members' perceptions of powerlessness, public disapproval, and electoral needs periodically lead the legislature to undertake more or less systematic reform to improve its responsibility, responsiveness, and/or accountability. At the turn of the century, the thrust was toward responsiveness; in the post–World War II period, it was toward responsibility; and in the 1970s, the focus was on all three goals. Eschewing broad, philosophical visions of the ideal Congress, reform comes in incremental fashion, pragmatically in reaction to political needs and pressures; and it comes differently in the House and Senate. Because it consists of incompatible elements that intersect with broader changes inside and outside the legislature, reform produces an uneven record of anticipated and unanticipated results.

The reformed Congress of the 1970s illustrates the point. Certainly Congress increased its potential to act responsibly and to make policy effectively, even in the face of presidential opposition. The War Powers Act of 1973, the 1974 budget law, and increased analytic capacity allowed the legislature, on occasion, to act as a more responsible decision-maker; at other times, however, it lacked the will to assert itself. Centralizing reforms—new party and leadership authority in the House, and reduced ability for the minority to obstruct in both chambers—were put in place but were seldom employed decisively. In the absence of centralization, Congress was hard-pressed to act responsibly. The early 1990s saw a growing push for increased centralization and enhanced leadership, but the fate of such reforms remains uncertain.

On the other hand, reforms have made Congress more responsive. The attack on the full committees dispersed political influence more widely in the House, where subcommittees have become more significant forces in policy-making. More senators and representatives, with more ties to more interests, possess the potential to affect policy. Junior members have secured advantageous legislative terrain but have cultivated it differently, in different committees and subcommittees and on different policy questions.

In addition, since the passage of campaign spending, financial disclosure, and sunshine reforms, it is easier to hold Congress accountable. More can be known about congressional performance, but there is little evidence that ordinary citizens actually do know more. The legislature is more accessible, but that very permeability has increased legislators' vulnerability to organized external influences and constrained an already fragile centralized leadership. Congress is unquestionably more democratic than it was in the prereform period but at a price: it is less able to exert institutional power and to enact innovative programs. It has, in effect, traded some responsibility for enhanced responsiveness and accountability.

Reform is no panacea. Part and parcel of broad currents of change, congressional reform reflects a welter of societal and institutional forces. Altered circumstances undercut expectations and produce unforeseen outcomes; short-run success evolves into long-term disappointment. Reform prompted by mixed motives produces mixed results. Given the myriad of influences shaping legislative performance—new personnel with different values and aims; new economic, social, or political conditions; and the organizational character of Congress itself—reformers find that their best-laid plans may often go astray.

BIBLIOGRAPHY

General Works
A few studies assess Congress generally and offer broad philosophical visions of a reformed legislature. JAMES M. BURNS, *The Deadlock of Democracy* (Englewood Cliffs, N.J., 1963) and JOSEPH S. CLARK, *Congress: The Sapless Branch*

(New York, 1964) lay out the executive-force theory. AMERICAN POLITICAL SCIENCE ASSOCIATION, COMMITTEE ON POLITICAL PARTIES, *Toward a More Responsible Two-Party System* (New York, 1950) and RICHARD BOLLING, *House Out of Order* (New York, 1965) advance the responsible party perspective. JAMES BURNHAM, *Congress and the American Tradition* (Chicago, 1959) is the classic exposition of the literary theory and ALFRED DE GRAZIA, "Toward a New Model of Congress," ALFRED DE GRAZIA, coord., *Congress: The First Branch of Government* (Washington, D.C., 1966) sets forth the congressional supremacy position.

A second set of studies focuses on congressional reform more narrowly. These include CENTER FOR RESPONSIVE POLITICS, *"Not for the Short Winded": Congressional Reform, 1961–1986* (Washington, D.C., 1986); ROGER H. DAVIDSON, DAVID M. KOVENOCK, and MICHAEL K. O'LEARY, *Congress in Crisis: Politics and Congressional Reform* (Belmont, Calif., 1966); LAWRENCE C. DODD, "The Rise of the Technocratic Congress: Congressional Reform in the 1970s," in RICHARD A. HARRIS and SIDNEY M. MILKIS, eds., *Remaking American Politics* (Boulder, Colo., 1989); CHARLES O. JONES, "Will Reform Change Congress?" in LAWRENCE C. DODD and BRUCE I. OPPENHEIMER, eds., *Congress Reconsidered* (New York, 1977); NORMAN J. ORNSTEIN, ed., *Congress in Change: Evolution and Reform* (New York, 1975); LEROY N. RIESELBACH, *Congressional Reform: The Changing Modern Congress* (Washington, D.C., 1993); BURTON D. SHEPPARD, *Rethinking Congressional Reform: The Reform Roots of the Special Interest Congress* (Cambridge, Mass., 1985); SUSAN WELCH and JOHN G. PETERS, eds., *Legislative Reform and Public Policy* (New York, 1981); and PAUL J. QUIRK, "Structures and Performance: An Evaluation," in ROGER H. DAVIDSON, ed., *The Postreform Congress* (New York, 1992). Other papers in Davidson's book offer a comprehensive view of the postreform Congress of the 1990s.

Theoretical Perspectives

A handful of works offer explicit, narrower, and more pragmatic ways to think about congressional change and reform. See JOSEPH COOPER, "Organization and Innovation in the House of Representatives," in JOSEPH COOPER and G. CALVIN MACKENZIE, eds., *The House at Work* (Austin, Tex., 1981); LAWRENCE C. DODD, "A Theory of Congressional Cycles: Solving the Puzzle of Change," in GERALD C. WRIGHT, LEROY N. RIESELBACH, and LAWRENCE C. DODD, eds., *Policy Change in Congress* (New York, 1986); LAWRENCE C. DODD, "Woodrow Wilson's *Congressional Government* and the Modern Congress: The 'Universal Principle' of Change," *Congress & the Presidency* 14 (1987); ROGER H. DAVIDSON and WALTER J. OLESZEK, "Adaptation and Consolidation: Structural Innovation in the House of Representatives," *Legislative Studies Quarterly* 1 (1976); CHARLES O. JONES, *The United States Congress: People, Place, and Policy* (Homewood, Ill., 1982), 413–417; WALTER J. OLESZEK, "Integration and Fragmentation: Key Themes of Congressional Change," *Annals* 466 (1983); and DAVID W. ROHDE and KENNETH A. SHEPSLE, "Thinking About Legislative Reform," in LEROY N. RIESELBACH, ed., *Legislative Reform: The Policy Impact* (Lexington, Mass., 1978).

Historical Studies

Historical background on congressional reform and change can be found in GEORGE GALLOWAY and SIDNEY WISE, *History of the House of Representatives*, 2d ed. (New York, 1976); ROGER H. DAVIDSON, "The Advent of the Modern Congress: The Legislative Reorganization Act of 1946," *Legislative Studies Quarterly* 15 (1990); SAMUEL P. HUNTINGTON, "Congressional Responses to the Twentieth Century," in DAVID B. TRUMAN, ed., *The Congress and America's Future*, 2d ed. (Englewood Cliffs, N.J., 1973); and WALTER KRAVITZ, "The Advent of the Modern Congress: The Legislative Reorganization Act of 1970," *Legislative Studies Quarterly* 15 (1990). ROGER H. DAVIDSON and WALTER J. OLESZEK, *Congress Against Itself* (Bloomington, Ind., 1977) presents a thorough analysis of Congress's treatment of the Bolling Committee's 1970s reform proposals.

Empirical Studies

Considerable research assesses the impact of reform and change on particular aspects of the congressional system. On committee reform, see ROGER H. DAVIDSON, "Two Avenues of Change: House and Senate Committee Reorganization," in LAWRENCE C. DODD and BRUCE I. OPPENHEIMER, eds., *Congress Reconsidered*, 2d ed. (Washington, D.C., 1981); CHRISTOPHER J. DEERING, "Subcommittee Government in the U.S. House: An Analysis of Bill Management,"

Legislative Studies Quarterly 7 (1982); CHRISTOPHER J. DEERING and STEVEN S. SMITH, "Subcommittees in Congress," in LAWRENCE C. DODD and BRUCE I. OPPENHEIMER, eds., *Congress Reconsidered*, 4th ed. (Washington, D.C., 1989); RICHARD L. HALL, "Committee Decision Making in the Postreform Congress," ibid.; RICHARD L. HALL and C. LAWRENCE EVANS, "The Power of Subcommittees," *Journal of Politics* 52 (1990); LEROY N. RIESELBACH and JOSEPH K. UNEKIS, "Ousting the Oligarchs: Assessing the Consequences of Reform and Change on Four House Committees," *Congress & the Presidency* 9 (1981–1982); STEVEN S. SMITH and CHRISTOPHER J. DEERING, *Committees in Congress*, 2d ed. (Washington, D.C., 1990); STEVEN S. SMITH and BRUCE A. RAY, "The Impact of Congressional Reform: House Democratic Committee Assignments," *Congress & the Presidency* 10 (1983); and RANDALL STRAHAN, *New Ways and Means: Reform and Change in a Congressional Committee* (Chapel Hill, N.C., 1990). SUSAN W. HAMMOND, "Congressional Change and Reform: Staffing the Congress," in LEROY N. RIESELBACH, ed., *Legislative Reform: The Policy Impact* (Lexington, Mass., 1978) and MICHAEL J. MALBIN, *Unelected Representatives: Congressional Staff and the Future of Representative Government* (New York, 1980) examine the changing role of enlarged congressional staffs.

On the changing fortunes of the political parties and their leaders, see JOSEPH COOPER and DAVID W. BRADY, "Institutional Context and Leadership Style: The House from Cannon to Rayburn," *American Political Science Review* 75 (1981); SARA B. CROOK and JOHN R. HIBBING, "Congressional Reform and Party Discipline: The Effects of Change in the Seniority System on Party Loyalty in the U.S. House of Representatives," *British Journal of Political Science* 15 (1985); ROGER H. DAVIDSON, "New Centralization on Capitol Hill," *Review of Politics* 50 (1988); LAWRENCE C. DODD and BRUCE I. OPPENHEIMER, "Consolidating Power in the House: The Rise of a New Oligarchy," in LAWRENCE C. DODD and BRUCE I. OPPENHEIMER, eds., *Congress Reconsidered*, 4th ed. (Washington, D.C., 1989); BRUCE I. OPPENHEIMER, "The Changing Relationship between House Leadership and the Committee on Rules," in FRANK W. MACKAMAN, ed., *Understanding Congressional Leadership* (Washington, D.C., 1981); DAVID W. ROHDE, *Parties and Leaders in the Postreform House* (Chicago, 1991); BARBARA SINCLAIR, "The Emergence of Strong Leadership in the 1980s House of Representatives," *Journal of Politics* 54 (1992); and GARRY YOUNG and JOSEPH COOPER, "Multiple Referral and the Transformation of House Decision Making," in LAWRENCE C. DODD and BRUCE I. OPPENHEIMER, eds., *Congress Reconsidered*, 5th ed. (Washington, D.C., 1993).

Legislative efforts to reclaim authority from the executive have produced considerable analysis. On the War Powers Resolution, see LOUIS FISHER, "War Powers: The Need for Collective Judgment," in JAMES A. THURBER, ed., *Divided Democracy: Cooperation and Conflict Between the President and Congress* (Washington, D.C., 1991); DANIEL P. FRANKLIN, "War Powers in Modern Context," *Congress & the Presidency* 14 (1987); ROBERT A. KATZMAN, "War Powers: Toward a New Accommodation," in THOMAS E. MANN, ed., *A Question of Balance: The President, the Congress, and Foreign Policy* (Washington, D.C., 1990); and JOHN H. SULLIVAN, "The Impact of the War Powers Resolution," in MICHAEL BARNHART, ed., *Congress and United States Foreign Policy: Controlling the Use of Force in the Nuclear Age* (Albany, N.Y., 1987).

HOWARD E. SHUMAN, *Politics and the Budget: The Struggle between the President and the Congress*, 2d ed. (Englewood Cliffs, N.J., 1988); JOHN B. GILMOUR, *Reconcilable Differences? Congress, the Budget Process, and the Deficit* (Berkeley, Calif., 1990); ALLEN SCHICK, *The Capacity to Budget* (Washington, D.C., 1990); JOSEPH WHITE and AARON WILDAVSKY, *The Deficit and the Public Interest: The Search for Responsible Budgeting in the 1980s* (Berkeley, Calif., 1989); SUNG DEUK HAHM, MARK S. KAMLET, DAVID C. MOWERY, and TSAI-TSU SU, "The Influence of the Gramm-Rudman-Hollings Act on Federal Budgetary Outcomes, 1986–1989," *Journal of Policy Analysis and Management* 11 (1992); and JAMES A. THURBER, "New Rules for an Old Game: Zero-Sum Budgeting in the Postreform Congress," in ROGER H. DAVIDSON, ed., *The Postreform Congress* (New York, 1992) chart the course of congressional efforts to reassert control of the federal budget and reduce the deficit.

On Congress's efforts to use aggressive oversight generally and the legislative veto more particularly to manage the executive branch, see JOEL D. ABERBACH, *Keeping a Watchful Eye: The Politics of Congressional Oversight* (Washington, D.C., 1990); CHARLES H. FOREMAN, JR., *Signals from the Hill: Congressional Oversight and the Challenge of Social Regulation* (New Haven, Conn., 1988); DANIEL P. FRANKLIN, "Why the Legislative Veto Isn't Dead," *Presidential Studies Quarterly* 14 (1987); and FREDERICK M. KAISER, "Congressional Control of Legislative Actions in the Aftermath of the *Chadha* Decision," *Administrative Law Review* 36 (1984).

For assessment of the effects of reforms to increase congressional accountability, consult CONGRESSIONAL QUARTERLY, *Congressional Ethics: History, Facts, and Controversy* (Washington, D.C., 1992); VERA VOGELSANG-COOMBS and LARRY A. BAKKEN, "The Conduct of Legislators," in JAMES S. BOWMAN and F. A. ELLISTON, eds., *Ethics, Government, and Public Policy* (Westport, Conn., 1988); DAVID B. MAGLEBY and CANDICE J. NELSON, *The Money Chase: Congressional Campaign Finance Reform* (Washington, D.C., 1990); and MARGARET L. NUGENT and JOHN R. JOHANNES, eds., *Money, Elections, and Democracy: Reforming Congressional Campaign Finance* (Boulder, Colo., 1990). On the term-limit movement, see GERALD BENJAMIN and MICHAEL J. MALBIN, eds., *Limiting Legislative Terms* (Washington, D.C., 1992).

Reform affects Congress's ability to enact public policy, as demonstrated in SUSAN W. HAMMOND and LAURA I. LANGBEIN, "The Impact of Complexity and Reform on Congressional Committee Out-put," *Political Behavior* 4 (1982); BRUCE I. OPPENHEIMER, "Policy Effects of U.S. House Reform: Decentralization and the Capacity to Resolve Energy Issues," *Legislative Studies Quarterly* 5 (1980); NORMAN J. ORNSTEIN and DAVID W. ROHDE, "Shifting Forces, Changing Rules, and Political Outcomes: The Impact of Congressional Change on Four House Committees," in ROBERT L. PEABODY and NELSON W. POLSBY, eds., *New Perspectives on the House of Representatives*, 3d ed. (Chicago, 1977); and KENNETH A. SHEPSLE, "Representation and Governance: The Legislative Trade-off," *Political Science Quarterly* 103 (1989).

REFORM IN STATE LEGISLATURES

Alan Rosenthal

American state legislatures, like other political institutions, are continuously undergoing change. Through membership turnover, new leadership emerges and rules are revised. Over time, the legislature may be transformed as a result. Nelson Polsby's examination of the institutionalization of the U.S. House of Representatives is a model analysis of long-term change in a legislature.* But change and reform are not necessarily synonomous. Legislative reform is one category of change, which involves the intentional reshaping of the institution, its processes, structure, personnel, facilities, operations, and functions.

In popular as well as professional discourse, "reform" connotes improvement. Not all reform is necessarily for the better, however. Just how it turns out is an empirical question, and one's assessment depends in part on one's values and interests.

During the period from 1965 to 1980, substantial legislative reform swept across the states of the nation. In these years, legislatures practically everywhere underwent significant institutional restructuring and modernization. This era, which can appropriately be termed that of "the rise of the legislative institution," saw the modernization of traditional assemblies. Earlier, during the years from 1950 to 1965, legislatures operated under relatively primitive conditions, with few resources and with only a limited ability to function effectively. Alexander Heard described legislatures at that time as poorly organized; technically ill-equipped; lacking time, staff, and space; and with outmoded procedures and committee systems. "State legislatures," he summed up in a

clarion call for reform, "may be our most extreme example of institutional lag" (p. 3).

Even in the prereform era, however, change had been taking place, with some states ahead of the pack. In the early 1900s, state legislative reference services were created to help draft and provide information on bills. In the 1930s, legislative councils, the precursors of centralized staff agencies, were established. Wisconsin, for example, pioneered in the creation of a legislative reference bureau and then a legislative council, and its legislature was far better equipped than most other legislatures by the 1960s. California was also out in front, for it had begun to expand staff and provide offices for members as early as the 1950s.

The postreform period can be said to have begun roughly in 1980. Reform is still taking place in the 1990s, though on a more episodic basis. For example, in regular or special sessions in 1992 and 1993, proposals focusing on legislative ethics and campaign finance were important items in Kentucky, New Mexico, and New Jersey, and were on the agendas of other states. Somewhat earlier, Virginia explored authorizing the legislature to make revenue projections, a capacity already developed by other legislatures, in order to match the executive in the budgeting arena. Legislatures continue to refashion and re-equip themselves.

Acknowledging the continuity of legislative reform and the variation from state to state, it is still possible to characterize the fifteen-year period from 1965 to 1980 as one of legislative modernization. Each legislature experienced these years somewhat differently, depending on its culture and politics, the people and personalities in office, and the circumstances of the time. In California, for instance, reform started in the assembly, and was taken up by the senate some years later when assembly members moved over to the other body.

*"The Institutionalization of the U.S. House of Representatives," *American Political Science Review* 62 (March 1968): 144–168.

New Jersey, for example, went through a "traditional" period of little institutional change, then a "transitional" period that showed the beginnings of change, and finally, from 1968 to 1975, a "developmental" period of significant change.

It is risky to generalize about the states, but it can be done, so long as allowance is made for exceptions. In generalizing, this essay shall examine the *conditions and causes* of the reform that was undertaken, specify the *characteristics* of the reforms adopted, and analyze the *consequences* of reform for state legislatures.

CONDITIONS AND CAUSES

Legislative reforms can come about in response to pressures from the external environment or in response to internal demands. In the case of the former, reforms are designed to facilitate an organization's adaptation to the outside. In the case of the latter, an organization attempts to relieve internal stresses and tensions. Reforms may be imposed by groups outside or initiated by members themselves. Adoption and implementation depend, in large part, on support from within the institution. In the case of the reform era of 1965–1980, the principal impetus in most states came from legislators themselves, although the activities of citizens and other groups played an important role, too.

While it is difficult to generalize about patterns of change within a single state or differences from one state to the next, it is relatively easy to identify the conditions and causes that affected legislative reform overall. In some states, such as Minnesota, the political culture was conducive to legislative reform, although it could not be said to have caused it. Change and experimentation had already become a norm of California politics when the reform movement started in the California Assembly. But for the most part, change in political institutions occurred slowly. Legislative reform needed further impetus.

In Wisconsin, a major stimulus to modernization was a shift in party control of the executive and legislative branches. The state had traditionally been dominated by Republicans. But in the late 1950s, politics became highly competitive in partisan terms, and the subsequent confrontation in 1961–1964 between a Democratic governor and Republican legislature prompted a drive for a stronger legislature.

If there was a single precondition to the modernization movement, however, it was the turnover in legislative membership caused by the reapportionment of the 1960s. In 1962 the U.S. Supreme Court, in *Baker* v. *Carr*, 369 U.S. 186, decided that the issue of legislative apportionment was justiciable—that is, under the courts' purview. And in 1964, in *Reynolds* v. *Sims*, 377 U.S. 533, it ruled that both branches of a state legislature must consist of districts that are "as nearly of equal population as is practicable." Within a few years of this decision every state legislature had been redistricted. Entrenched patterns of representation were undermined, a new generation of legislators assumed office, and legislative outlooks took on a different shape.

The resurgence of most state legislatures had roots in the reapportionment revolution. With redistricting that accurately reflected urban and suburban populations, a new generation of members took seats in the senates and houses of legislative assemblies and fewer members from rural districts, who had shaped the legislature's earlier norms and cultures, returned to office. Many of the new arrivals were professionals, particularly attorneys. They were appalled by the conditions that confronted legislators—no offices, few facilities, low salaries, inadequate staff, outmoded procedures, narrow participation, inactive committees, a scarcity of information on proposed bills and alternative policies, and a tendency on the part of the legislative branch to bow to the executive. Members of the reapportionment generation were not only open to institutional change, but they were also principal leaders in the modernization movement.

Florida exemplifies the impact of reapportionment on the legislature. Although the Florida legislature managed to redistrict itself after the early judicial rulings, the U.S. Supreme Court in *Swann* v. *Adams* (1964) declared that it was still malapportioned and ordered another election based on a new formula. As a consequence, Republicans gained seats in what had been a traditionally Democratic legislature. But, more important, the Florida legislature swung away from rural control by the so-called porkchoppers. When the legislature convened, many of the members were new, with about one-third of the senate and over half the house first elected in the special elections two or five months before.

These newcomers, who entered an old institution, were without ties—unbeholden to legislative leaders, to lobbyists, or to old cabinet officers who had reigned in Tallahassee for ages. Having arrived so recently on the scene, they could take a completely fresh look at government. They soon acquired power, learned how to use it, and succeeded in modernizing not only the legislature but the executive and judicial branches as well. The quality of the individuals who emerged was so high that this period became known as the golden age of the Florida legislature.

Even in a favorable climate and with the loosening of traditional bonds, legislative modernization would not have occurred—at least not to the same extent and at the same pace—without leadership from within the legislature. A number of legislators spearheaded efforts within their own institutions. Moreover, they fashioned a national network that helped to spread the modernization agenda from state to state.

Without doubt, the single most influential leader of the reform movement was Jesse Unruh, a Democrat, who assumed the speakership of the California Assembly in 1961 and held it until 1970. Unruh did not originate legislative reform in the California Assembly, but he crystallized and organized member feelings, accelerated change, and launched a public crusade. By the mid-1970s the California legislature was acknowledged to be the finest state legislative body in the nation. Leaders in other states were working simultaneously along the same lines. In Illinois, the president pro tem of the senate, Russell Arrington, devoted himself to the strengthening of the legislative branch, pushed the development of a permanent legislative staff, and advocated longer legislative sessions. Robert Knowles, as president pro tem of the Wisconsin Senate, had similar ends in mind. These individuals were principally motivated by an abiding belief in the legislative branch.

A number of national organizations also had legislative reform high on their agendas. As early as 1945, the Council of State Govern-

ments (CSG), which represented legislators as well as other state governmental officials, established a committee on legislative processes and procedures. The CSG committee made recommendations on sessions, compensation, terms, staff, the organization and procedures of committees, and rules. The National Legislative Conference (NLC), composed of legislators and legislative staff, in 1961 issued a report titled *American State Legislatures in Mid-Twentieth Century*, and in 1963 one titled *Mr. President . . . Mr. Speaker*. These reports made the same types of general recommendations regarding legislative reform. By the late 1960s and into the 1970s, the three organizations representing legislatures—NLC, the National Society of State Legislators (NSSL), and the National Conference of State Legislative Leaders (NCSLL)—were all involved in a nationwide movement designed to improve legislatures. At annual meetings and other sessions of these associations, members would discuss with one another the prescriptions for and the progress of legislative reform.

The national reform movement was nurtured by the legislative organizations, sustained by the experiences of states like California, and led by Unruh and other legislative leaders. It was also able to count on strategic support from agencies outside of the legislature. Of enormous importance was funding for the enterprise from the Ford Foundation and the Carnegie Corporation of New York. The Ford Foundation financed the American Political Science Association's activities in this field as well as an American Assembly meeting and volumes of papers on the subject. It also made grants to the National Municipal League for a study of constitutional barriers to legislative reform, the Citizens Conference on State Legislatures (CCSL) for an evaluation of legislatures in the fifty states, and to the activities of individual states. In Wisconsin, for instance, the Ford Foundation paid half the costs of a six-year program that began in 1960 and helped the legislature develop new techniques of budget review and fiscal analysis, fashion procedures to inform legislators better about legislation, and conduct demonstration projects to determine the value of staff services.

The role of Unruh and funding from Ford and Carnegie were instrumental in establishing the Eagleton Institute of Politics at Rutgers

University as an academic center focusing on state legislatures and institutional reform. In 1963 a concurrent resolution of the New Jersey legislature—initiated by Ray Bateman, the speaker of the assembly—requested Eagleton to conduct a study and make recommendations for its improvement. The institute submitted its report later that year. Meanwhile, Unruh began spending time at Eagleton as politician-in-residence, joined the faculty as a visiting professor, and with the institute's director, Donald G. Herzberg, secured funding for several legislative improvement ventures. Under the leadership of Unruh and Herzberg and with funding from the Carnegie Corporation, the institute during 1966–1975 held annual week-long conferences in Florida for outstanding legislators from the fifty states. Over the decade, a total of 432 legislators—most of whom were in their second or third terms—participated. Inspired by a number of legislative leaders who participated, and by one another, many of these legislators returned to their states and advocated and accomplished significant change. Conferences such as these facilitated the transmission of ideas about reform, furnished evidence that change could be accomplished, offered examples of leadership, and provided a network of mutual support for participants. Their effects were felt in Alaska, Alabama, Colorado, Florida, Idaho, Kansas, Louisiana, Maine, Nebraska, North Carolina, Tennessee, and Virginia.

The movement extended beyond the legislatures themselves to groups of citizens within the states and citizens' groups organized nationally. In some places a citizens' group campaigned, contrary to the desires of many legislators, to restructure the institution in a radical way. In Massachusetts, for instance, the League of Women Voters led a long struggle for a reduction in the size of the house, which was adopted by referendum in 1974. One of the influential efforts by citizens was the 1967 report on legislative improvement issued by the Committee for Economic Development (CED). Because of the prestige of CED member companies, its recommendations received widespread publicity, further fueling reform fires. Probably the most effective work in stimulating citizen involvement in the legislative reform movement was that conducted by the Citizens Conference on State Legislatures (CCSL). Formed in 1965, CCSL was headquartered first in Kansas City, Missouri, and later in Denver; after some years its name was changed to Legis 50, and a while after that the organization was dissolved. CCSL was headed by Larry Margolis, who earlier had been Unruh's principal aide. Supported mainly by corporate contributors, the conference helped organize, and then collaborated with, state citizen commissions; ran seminars for legislative leaders, legislators, and the press; conducted a program to increase public awareness of the need for legislative improvement; and engaged in a large-scale study evaluating the fifty state legislatures.

Because of the efforts of legislators, legislative organizations, CCSL, and Eagleton, in the 1960s alone at least thirty states undertook studies concerned with the organization, staffing, and/or procedures of their legislatures. Additional states launched studies in the 1970s. These endeavors pursued either an outside strategy, an inside strategy, or some combination of the two. Outside strategies were those orchestrated primarily by CCSL. Sometimes they were designed to exert pressure on legislatures that were reluctant to change their ways. In a number of cases, CCSL was invited into a state by the legislature's leadership or an invitation was extended by a local group. Occasionally, however, the initiative came from outside. During this period, citizens' campaigns took place in Georgia, Idaho, Iowa, Kentucky, Minnesota, Montana, and West Virginia, with varying degrees of success. Inside strategies were those launched from within the legislature itself, even though citizens might have been appointed to serve on the study committees that were established. The Illinois Commission on the Organization of the General Assembly—the so-called Katz Commission, named after its chairman, Representative Harold Katz—was largely an inside endeavor. Katz, a freshman Democrat, in the 1965 session won bipartisan support for a bill to create a commission to study the processes and operations of the legislature. Legislative leaders thereupon appointed both legislators and citizens to serve as members. The commission reported eighty-seven recommendations to the general assembly at its 1967 session, and bills incorporating its recommendations were introduced by legislator members. Within four years, seventy-two of the recommendations had been achieved in full or in part, with legislative leaders supporting many of them, particularly those that did not adversely affect their leadership interests.

Rhode Island (1967), Wisconsin (1968), Florida (1969), Mississippi (1969), and Arkansas (1972) were other states where the initiative for reform came from within. Each of these legislatures commissioned the Eagleton Institute to undertake a comprehensive study over the course of a year. Legislative leaders were mainly responsible for the efforts in Rhode Island, Wisconsin, and Mississippi. Lawton Chiles returned to Tallahassee from the Carnegie-funded conference for outstanding legislators that he attended and sponsored the study in Florida. Cal Ledbetter and a few other legislators from Arkansas, who had also participated in one of the Carnegie conferences, returned to Little Rock and persuaded their legislature to embark on a study. The Arkansas legislature authorized the project and established a special committee that included legislators and public members.

In a number of states, including Maine, Oregon, and Utah, legislators and citizens collaborated on special legislative-study committees. In other places, legislators and citizens went their separate ways, but tended to reinforce rather than undermine one another's endeavors. In Maryland a committee of Young Democrats was organized by a particularly entrepreneurial individual, and began to advocate reform of the general assembly. Marvin Mandel, the speaker of the House of Delegates, did not relish the possibility that a legislative-reform agenda might be imposed on the institution by outsiders. So, Mandel and the senate president announced a study of their own and called upon Eagleton to do it and make recommendations to the Maryland General Assembly. Thus, legislative leadership committed itself to an improvement program, and one was subsequently implemented. In Connecticut, also, a two-pronged drive took place—one by the leadership, with Eagleton assisting, and the other by a state citizens' commission that endorsed changes suggested by the institute and adopted by the general assembly.

Reformers like Margolis of CCSL, who looked to the experience of California, felt that they knew what legislatures needed. Discovery was not the primary purpose of a legislative or citizens' study; the primary purpose was to persuade legislative leaders and carry the press and public opinion along in support of recommendations. One vehicle that CCSL used in a campaign to achieve legislative reform was its Legislative Evaluation Study, which was funded by a million-dollar grant from the Ford Foundation. Begun in early 1969, the study's specific intentions were to (1) focus attention on the disabilities of legislatures; (2) give guidance to lay and legislative endeavors to accomplish improvement; (3) provide documentation that would allow for the measurement of progress over time; and (4) generate discussion of what constituted legislative effectiveness. In the CCSL study, legislatures were assessed and ranked from one to fifty on the basis of six dimensions—their functionality, accountability, information-handling capacity, independence, representativeness, and overall performance. The legislatures that ranked highest overall were California, New York, Illinois, and Florida. Those ranking lowest overall were North Carolina, Delaware, Wyoming, and Alabama. Although the rankings were considered by many to be justified, others were critical of the evaluation study's methodology and the CCSL's assumptions that certain features were essential to legislative performance.

The forces lined up on the side of reform were impressive—new legislators, legislative leaders, national legislative organizations and other groups, the Citizens Conference and Eagleton Institute, many influential citizens in states across the country, and even a sympathetic press in a number of states. But there were obstacles that had to be overcome. Those who wanted to maintain citizen legislatures opposed change, arguing that longer sessions would lead to full-time legislatures and, hence, further government and bureaucracy. Also, there were the "good old boys" who opposed any change and had no desire to see reforms adopted. Furthermore, partisanship in a legislature from time to time created divisions, even on supposedly nonpartisan proposals. And senates and houses, although controlled by the same party, sometimes could not agree between themselves on a reform agenda. A number of critical changes, moreover, required amendment of the state's constitution, and this entailed public education and turning out an affirmative vote. The responsibility for elements of legislative reform, thus, rested with the electorate; its approval at the polls seldom came easily.

In a number of states, governors were important obstacles to legislative reform. Generally, the executive did not welcome a stronger legislative branch of government, one with which to share power on a more equal basis. Some governors stood aside, however, lending no encouragement to the reformers; some quietly opposed measures, hoping that they would not reach the governor's desk for signature or veto; and some stated their opposition vocally and even exercised their veto after a legislative bill arrived in their office for signature. Ironically, hostile governors might have done more to solidify legislatures than legislatures could have done to solidify themselves.

Florida offers an example of a legislative-gubernatorial clash. The election in 1966 of the state's first Republican governor in about one hundred years set the stage for the confrontation. The legislature, in response to a recommendation in a study it had commissioned, decided to raise its members' pay from $1,200 to $12,000 per year. The pay raise had been signed off on by both houses and by the majority and minority parties. Without warning, however, Governor Claude Kirk vetoed the bill, breaching an agreement he had with the Republican minority leader of the Florida House. After the Republican leader took the floor to apologize to his colleagues for the governor's action, the legislature easily overrode the veto. The Republicans continued to be estranged from their governor and the Florida legislature went on to build substantial institutional strength.

Connecticut offers another example of confrontation. Here, Democratic governor John Dempsey had had little difficulty dominating the Democratic-controlled General Assembly. However, on the basis of recommendations made in a study it had commissioned, the legislature in 1969 passed a reform package that was acknowledged to be its declaration of independence. Governor Dempsey took exception and vetoed the act; but his veto was overridden by unanimous votes in both houses. The veto and its override served to unite both legislative parties in support of a program of legislative improvement, a rare display of bipartisanship in a very partisan state. Several years later, the Connecticut General Assembly overrode a Republican governor's veto, this time on a bill

that created a legislative-oversight agency and staff.

CHARACTERISTICS

Legislators and their allies joined in a loosely articulated movement to reshape their institutions. Although they had no explicit plan or strategy, the models they had in mind were the U.S. Congress and the California legislature. These legislatures had developed considerable capacity and professionalization—more frequent and longer sessions, additional staffing, more time spent on their jobs by members, and usually greater compensation—that appeared to improve their performance and confer benefits upon members. As legislative reform agendas swept through the states, the particulars varied but the programs were balanced so that their appeal was widespread.

Recommendations for reform ran the gamut from those that had profound implications, such as reducing the size of the house, to those that were mainly administrative in nature, such as eliminating the time lag between introducing or amending bills and having them available in printed form. The recommendations, however, were plentiful. There was something for everyone and everything. In its evaluation report, which was published in 1971 as *The Sometime Governments*, the Citizens Conference on State Legislatures made a total of 73 general recommendations, as well as specific recommendations for each of the fifty states (as many as 35 for Wyoming and 33 for Alabama, which ranked at the bottom in the CCSL evaluation, and 17 for California and 23 for New York, which ranked at the top). In the comprehensive studies it conducted, the Eagleton Institute offered the following number of recommendations: Rhode Island, 59; Maryland, 92; Wisconsin, 183; Connecticut, 108; Florida, 79; Mississippi, 103; and Arkansas, 116. Many of them were minor indeed.

A number of the more important recommendations made by CCSL, Eagleton, and other groups were adopted, in some form or fashion by various states. The Eagleton studies had considerable impact. Within a few years, Rhode Island adopted the most important suggestions for reform. Modernization also proceeded apace in Maryland and Connecticut. Florida acted quickly, adopting changes even before a report had been drafted. Arkansas made considerable change. The results were less tangible in Wisconsin, both because the legislature there already had undergone development and because reform proposals became embroiled in ideological and partisan controversy on other issues. Generally, when legislatures were ready to move, they needed only support, not prodding, from outside. Fifteen years after its report was issued, CCSL's recommendations were reviewed by the Advisory Commission on Intergovernmental Relations (ACIR), which concluded that virtually all of the states had participated in the adoption of recommended reforms. Of the seventy-three recommendations that CCSL advanced, legislatures changed considerably in response to thirty-eight and made little or no change with respect to five. The other thirty recommendations could not be assessed by ACIR because of a lack of information. Overall, the record of adoption was extremely positive.

The characteristics of the legislative-reform agenda can be specified more precisely by examining the major CCSL recommendations that were proposed to the states (with the figure in parentheses denoting the number of states to which such recommendations were made) and the later ACIR assessment of adoption. Variously phrased and differently stressed, depending on time and place, the legislative-reform agenda ran as follows:

1. *Increase in the frequency and length of legislative sessions*, without limitation of time or subject. This recommendation meant the removal of constitutional limitations that restricted the length of regular sessions or the time that the legislature could spend in the interim (twenty-seven states) and the amendment of the constitution so that the legislature could convene itself in special session (twenty-six states). Reformers had in mind more frequent and longer sessions. According to ACIR, considerable progress was made along these lines. In 1969, annual sessions were the practice in twenty-six states; in 1985, legislatures met annually in thirty-seven states. Some progress was also made with respect to the legislature's power to call itself into special session. All told, legislatures wound up spending more time convened, both during regular and special sessions and in the periods between sessions. During the 1964–1965 biennium twenty-four

legislatures spent one hundred or more legislative days in regular and special sessions. By the 1979–1980 biennium, forty were in session for at least one hundred days, with twenty close to or exceeding two hundred actual legislative days.

2. *Reduction of the size of legislative bodies*, so that they are no larger than fair representation requires. In CCSL's view, constitutions had to be amended so that houses would be no larger than 100 members and both bodies combined would have between 100 and 150 members (thirteen states). Some of the larger houses, such as those in Illinois and Massachusetts, were reduced because of pressure from outside, but in several places legislative bodies have grown slightly, mainly to ameliorate the effects of reapportionment. Overall, there has not been much change here.

3. *Increase in compensation and related benefits*, with the expenses of legislative service fully reimbursed. An increase in salaries was proposed by CCSL for nearly all the legislatures (forty-two states). For legislator salaries to have a chance of being raised, it would be necessary that they be determined by statute, subject to change by legislation, and not specified in the constitution, which could only be changed by the electorate (twenty-four states). Considerable progress has been made on the matter of compensation. By 1985 only nine states still set legislator compensation in their constitutions, while a number of others had established special legislative compensation commissions that provided legislators with some political cover when salaries were raised. Increases in compensation occurred practically everywhere. The 1965 average annual salary of $3,900 had grown by 1979 to $14,000.

4. *The adoption of more rigorous standards of conduct*, by means of codes of ethics and conflict-of-interest, disclosure, and lobbying legislation, as well as the establishment of ethics committees or commissions with some enforcement powers. Among the CCSL recommendations were conflict-of-interest laws (fifteen states), prohibiting practice by lawyer-legislators before state agencies (twenty-five states), barring legislators from doing business with the state (twenty-two states), and disqualifying members of a legislator's family from employment by the legislature (twenty-three states). By the time of ACIR's review, many states had taken action along these lines.

5. *Adequate space and facilities for committees and individual members*, including electronic data processing and roll-call voting equipment. Expansions of legislative space and facilities were among the principal objectives of reformers. CCSL advocated individual offices for members (thirty-six states), support of district offices for members (twenty states), additional facilities for committees (twenty-eight states), and the improvement of press facilities (thirty-nine states). In the 1960s, offices for rank-and-file legislators were rare; by 1980 a majority of legislatures provided them. Renovated capitols, new legislative office buildings, district offices, and facilities of all types were far more common by the mid-1980s than they had been two decades earlier.

6. *Improvement of legislative operations*, to ensure efficiency in the consideration of bills and the widespread dissemination of procedural and substantive information. Many reform suggestions for proposals to streamline the legislative process were advanced. Among the most important was that each house, or the two houses jointly, should have a management committee, composed of legislative leaders and other members, as was recommended by CCSL (twenty-five states). Also recommended were bill deadlines to ensure the orderly flow of work (twenty-six states), a consent calendar for expeditious consideration of bills (nineteen states), and an automatic calendar for bills favorably reported by standing committees (nineteen states). In addition, there were recommendations to reprint amended bills (twenty-five states), include a statement of the sponsor's intent (twenty-four states), and provide a bill summary (twenty states). Progress has been made on most of these proposals, with leadership taking increased responsibility for legislative management, deadlines and cutoff dates for bill drafts, their introduction, and consideration in committee and on the floor, and consent calendars and automatic calendaring of favorably reported bills.

7. *Strengthening of standing committees*, by reducing their number, defining their jurisdictions, and improving their procedures. CCSL emphasized the importance of reducing the number of standing committees (twenty-seven states) and the number of committee assignments for members (twenty-nine states), so that each committee had serious jurisdictional responsibility and each member could focus his or her attention. Also recommended were uniform committee rules (twenty-four states), official jurisdictions (thirty-one states), open meetings (twenty-seven states), advance notice of meetings (twenty-three states), the requirement that committees act on all bills (twenty-one states), issuance of bill reports (twenty-seven states), the publication of record votes (twenty-nine states), and interim work by standing committees (thirty-five states). Recommendations related to committees were widely adopted, according to the ACIR review. House committees were reduced in number in three-quarters of the states, and senate committees were reduced in number in four-fifths of the states. There was also some decrease in committee assignments. By the mid-1980s, two out of three states had uniform committee rules, all had open committee meetings, and most provided advance notice of meetings. There has been little change in the requirement that all bills be reported out by committees, and although many legislative bodies now issue committee reports, the nature of these documents varies considerably. Three-fifths of the states, by 1985, were making use of standing committees during the interim period.

8. *Increasing the number and competence of legislative staff*, including staff for the leadership, committees, and rank-and-file members. Staffing was certainly one of the principal concerns of reformers, if not *the* principal concern. CCSL advocated the strengthening of staff support (thirty-eight states), committee staffing (thirty states), staff for leaders (thirty states) and for the rank and file (thirty-three states), and a Washington office for the legislature (twenty-three states). Since the 1960s, legislatures have made tremendous gains in the variety and number of professional staff. By 1980, forty-three states had permanent legislative-research councils, as compared with only thirteen two decades earlier, and forty states provided staff for all committees, as compared with only eleven two decades earlier. And by 1980, thirty senates and twenty houses provided members with personal staff, a significant increase over the earlier period.

9. *Enhancing the effectiveness of legislative leadership*. In order to focus on leadership within the legislature, CCSL advocated a diminution of the legislative role of lieutenant governor (sixteen states). It also called for the discontinuance of the practice of limiting pre-

siding officers to a single, two-year term (nine states), the strengthening of the minority leadership role (nineteen states), and giving the minority some representation on the rules committee (ten states) and responsibility for the appointment of its members to standing committees (twenty states). Since these proposals were advanced, the role of the lieutenant governor has been diminished in several states, the rotation of leadership has been abandoned in a few places, and minority parties have grown somewhat stronger.

10. *Establishing legislative responsibility for oversight of programs and administration.* CCSL touched lightly on the post audit of state government, which examined the legality of agency expenditures, recommending that the function be transferred to the legislature and conducted by an office of legislative auditor. Meanwhile, the Eagleton Institute was engaged in several programs demonstrating the value of performance auditing and program evaluation, and other groups were promoting additional mechanisms related to legislative oversight. By the time of ACIR's review, forty legislatures had taken a responsibility for the post audit and an increasing number were reviewing administrative regulations, overseeing the appropriation of federal funds, evaluating ongoing programs in one way or another, and performing sunset reviews.**

CONSEQUENCES

Legislatures in the mid-1990s bear little resemblance to their predecessors of earlier years. Today's legislatures are more capable, more effective, and more responsive. But although there is general agreement by observers and participants that legislatures as political institutions have been transformed, there is little hard evidence to that effect.

Case studies of the effects of reform in California, Florida, Illinois, Ohio, Washington, and Wisconsin show a checkered pattern, leading one political scientist to conclude that the more things change, the more they may appear

to remain the same. Yet, these cases indicate some changes of major magnitude and other smaller adjustments. For example, examination of staffing in Wisconsin distinguished among types of staff—fiscal staff, caucus staff, and legislative interns. It also conceptualized the effects of staff in terms of (1) individual legislators and their adjustment to legislative life; (2) legislative structures to make decisions and how power is distributed; (3) integration or disintegration, within the legislative parties and between the houses; and (4) performance, or the sharing in the formulation of state policies and the control of administration. In the short term, measurement before and after the development of fiscal and caucus staffs demonstrated noticeable effects as a result of the reforms.

Such analysis demonstrated some of the effects of staff in the short run; longer-term effects might have been different. The time period over which effects are tracked is thus important. Effects are most discernable not immediately but within a relatively brief period of time. They are less measurable as time passes; but over time the effects are more enduring and, thus, likely to be more significant.

Despite the difficulty in generalizing across the states, it is useful to specify the consequences of legislative reform, not only for individual legislatures, but also for legislatures generally. Many of the consequences, as they have evolved, were not intended or anticipated by the proponents of legislative reform. For example, one of the intentions legislative leaders had in staffing was to lighten the work load of legislators. Quite the contrary happened, however. Staff generated information, uncovered problems, and proposed solutions, thereby adding to the work load of members.

One can conceive of consequences to individual legislators and how they adjust to legislative life, to legislative organizations, including structures for decision and distributions of influence, and to the balance of power with the executive branch of government. Or one can conceive of consequences with respect to leadership, the internal division of labor, linkage to the environment, and alteration in policies. Or one might explore the functions served (such as adaptation or consolidation), or the institutional effects realized (such as legislative supremacy, executive force, or party responsibility), by the changes accomplished through

---

**Reviews of agencies and programs that will expire unless the legislature reauthorizes them. Sunset reviews determine whether they should be reauthorized, and with what changes.

legislative reform. For present purposes, consequences are conceived of in terms of (1) public policy; (2) institutional capacity; (3) governmental power; (4) functional performance; and (5) institution and process.

While it is possible to isolate various consequences of reform at a conceptual level, it is extremely difficult to separate out effects—one from another and from other phenomena—at the empirical level. Aspects of institutional capacity, such as staffing and information, are intertwined with functional performance and the nature of the institution and process. Moreover, what are posited as consequences of legislative reform usually cannot be linked to specific changes, such as the strengthening of standing committees or giving the legislature authority to call itself into special session. Nor can broad-gauged consequences be attributed solely to even a general package of reforms. Other factors, such as changes in the political-party system, in the political culture, and in federalism, undoubtedly played a part in shaping today's legislatures. Nor are the linkages direct; instead they are mediated by multiple changes that have ripple effects.

Thus in any single state, legislative reforms may have been small in magnitude and absorbed by an adaptive institution. "Accordingly," as Samuel Patterson has observed, "such changes become part of the legislature's characteristic structure, so that they have little in the way of consequences in measurable terms except to maintain the existing structure" (*Legislative Reform*). But one reform engenders another reform, and substantial change tends to take place. Over the longer haul, therefore, conditions and practices shift and the effects cumulate. The institution is transformed, and the reforms themselves, as well as the new ways of thinking and behaving that reform engenders, bear a measure of responsibility.

Public Policy

In much of the research inquiring into the impact of reform, effects have been conceptualized in terms of public policy. That is because, for a period of time, political scientists focused their attention on the inputs, such as member salaries or the size of the professional staff, and outputs of the legislative process. It was their view that

if policy, as a significant output, was not affected, then change was of little consequence.

Earlier research on the effects of the legislative reapportionment of the late 1960s and early 1970s found little relationship between districting and alterations in policies. Such linkage could not reasonably have been expected. Reapportionment did have consequences for personnel and process, and in the longer term may have indirectly helped shape the agendas of state legislatures and the policies produced. But at an early point, statistical analysis of available operational indicators of district and policy found little connection between reapportionment and public policy.

Measurement of the relationship between legislative reform and public policy has similarly generated few definitive results. One reason is that frequently the data examined are neither meaningful nor useful. Another is that the reforms undertaken could not be expected to affect policy in any observable way. One study, for instance, tried to test whether "reformed" and "unreformed" legislatures, as measured in the Citizens Conference evaluation, differed significantly in policy outputs. Another study employed expenditure data in the areas of welfare, and concluded that reform's effects were policy-specific. That conclusion was unpersuasive, for most researchers discover no relationships whatsoever. After examining the CCSL ranking of legislatures and expenditure data, and controlling for wealth, one political scientist uncovered few correlations and concluded that structural reforms had little impact on public policy. Two other investigators came to a similar conclusion, unable to distinguish more- from less-reformed legislatures according to the fiscal nature of public policy. Studies that examined the effects of reforms within specific states, rather than by comparative analysis of all fifty states, produced similar results. One political scientist compared urban legislation in a prereform session with that of a postreform session of the Illinois legislature and discovered no change, concluding that legislative reform did not have an identifiable impact on policy in that state. Another, who inquired into whether legislative reforms in Indiana had any discernible role in the formulation of public policy, found that the effects were negligible.

Whatever the particular findings of a series of studies, there is no reason to believe that changes in organization, structure, or procedures of a state legislature will produce changes in policy—not in the overall shape of policy, and certainly not in the budget increments allocated to a policy area. If reapportionment's linkage to policy is tenuous, indirect, and distant, then the linkage of legislative reforms is even more so. Professional staffing is one reform that virtually everyone believes is significant. But why would increases in staffing produce policies in the aggregate different from those that otherwise would be produced? The effects of staff, at the very least, would depend on just where staff additions occurred. Caucus staffs, fiscal staffs, committee staffs, and member staffs relate quite differently to policy. The effects would also depend on how policy was operationalized. Levels of expenditures, or changes in levels, or alterations in policy cannot be expected to be affected by any legislative reforms. Too many other factors—such as gubernatorial leadership, the mobilization of interest groups, the composition of the legislature, and economic conditions—have more to do with policy outcomes than does the level or pattern of staffing in a legislature. Staffing may contribute to or facilitate the process by which policy is made, by increasing information and analysis and encouraging deliberation, but a more direct relationship is not to be expected. Nor does it exist, except in unusual cases.

If the linkage between staffing and policy is loose, that between other reforms—the reduction of the number of committees, the increase in the frequency and length of sessions, higher legislator salaries—is even looser. What reason is there to believe that policies will undergo change as legislative compensation rises? Under the assumptions that party affiliation and ideological orientation help shape policy preferences and that preferences affect policy, there may be an indirect linkage, if higher salaries result in the election of more Democrats and more liberals. Over the course of time, and along with other factors, this may indeed have happened, but it would be difficult to prove. Higher salaries may have other, more direct effects on the incentives and careers of legislators and thereby on the nature of the institution.

The fact is that contemporary legislatures are generating policies different from those of their predecessors of the 1960s. But these differences cannot be attributed to the reform movement. There are no direct linkages, and the indirect ties have been mediated by numerous other factors and conditions.

Institutional Capacity

Probably the clearest and most immediate consequence of the reform movement was the strengthening of the institutional capacity of the state legislatures. Many of the measures that had been adopted, in fact, related directly to capacity, that is, the legislature's wherewithal to do its job. As was noted above, nearly all of the nation's legislatures during the 1970s and 1980s acquired additional resources, ones that were requisite or at least useful if legislatures were to share power with the executive and perform the functions expected of them.

The improvement of legislative facilities, with the renovation of capitol buildings and the construction of legislative office buildings, provided space for standing committees, rank-and-file members, and staff. This tended to attract members to their capital offices to work, even when the legislature was not in session, and legislators were thus apt to be more available for tasks associated with lawmaking. One of the most recent developments, the Legislative Office Building across from the State Capitol in Hartford, stands as a monument to the modernization of the Connecticut General Assembly (LOB). Dedicated in April 1988, the LOB furnished members such attractive quarters that they began spending additional time in the capital, thus moving closer to the status of full-time legislators.

Institutional capacity depends on time as well as space. Legislators are spending many more days in session than previously. California, Pennsylvania, Illinois, Massachusetts, Ohio, and Wisconsin meet ten months per year; Michigan, nine; and New York, seven. Those that have shorter sessions meet three or four days per month on interim projects conducted by standing or special committees or commissions. Even though not all of the additional time is translated into enhanced legislative capability, some of it is. Extra time enables the legislature to deal more thoroughly and deliberatively with policy matters, to become more involved in the formulation and review of the budget, and to challenge the gubernatorial administration on the conduct of government itself. Unlike in earlier years, the legislature is a constant presence in more than half the states today. It cannot be ignored—by the governor, administrative agencies, interest groups, or lobbyists.

Undoubtedly, the single greatest boost to legislative capacity came as an outgrowth of professional staffing. The staffs in many state legislatures have increased tremendously since the reform movement began. On average, legislative staffs grew by a quarter between 1979 and 1988, by which time the number of full-time professionals exceeded fifty in all but twelve legislatures. As the decade of the 1980s drew to a close, the ratio of staff per member was 23.9 in California, 17.0 in New York, 9.9 in Florida, 8.7 in Michigan, 8.1 in Texas, 7.8 in Pennsylvania, 6.5 in New Jersey, and 6.0 in Illinois. However, the ratio continued to be low in Idaho, New Hampshire, New Mexico, North Dakota, Vermont, and Wyoming, where one staffer on average served three, four, or five members.

As important as sheer numbers was the distribution of staff within legislatures, so that the benefits of staffing tended to be widespread. Leaders acquired greater support, and their ability to challenge executive proposals was strengthened. Standing committees, whose authority was on the rise, received the assistance necessary for them to delve deeply into policy areas and formulate initiatives of their own. Fiscal staffs developed special competence, thus affording the appropriations and finance committees the opportunity to play a larger role in the budget process. Caucus and partisan staff buttressed the legislative parties, legislatively and electorally. Audit and evaluation staffs enabled the legislature to engage in oversight, reviewing the effectiveness of ongoing programs and inquiring into the efficiency of governmental agencies. Finally, and most recently, staff for individual members helped the rank and file generate their own proposals, expand their entrepreneurial activities, and provide better service to their constituents—and also enhance their prospects for reelection.

Although facilities, time, and personnel constituted the major elements in the legislature's capacity-building enterprise, other factors were also at work. Revisions in the bill process, computerized information systems, and the unification of national membership organizations were among them. But probably the principal gain by legislatures organizationally was in the improvement of committee systems. Before the legislative-reform movement, standing committees, with few exceptions, did little to review and revise bills referred to them. As a result of consolidation, staffing, and the desire on the part of legislators to make committees meaningful, standing committees became the workhorses of the legislature. Today, they provide for a division of labor, opportunities for members to have an impact, a degree of specialization, more-intensive scrutiny of substantive matters, and a broader distribution of influence within the legislature. The significance of committees is shown in a survey of two thousand legislators, who were asked to rank, from the eight alternatives offered, the three most important decision-making arenas in the legislature. Almost two-thirds of the respondents ranked regular committee meetings just below the presiding officers and majority leaders.

Thus, legislative reform resulted first and foremost in capacity building by many of the nation's legislatures. Some of them developed far greater capacity than others, but almost all of them shared in the gains to some degree. Greater capacity, in turn, led, along with other factors, to additional effects. One of the most important was that legislatures achieved, and began to wield, greater governmental power.

Governmental Power

During the Nixon, Carter, and Reagan administrations, relations between the states and the federal government changed markedly. Washington devolved itself of a measure of power that it had accrued since the New Deal era and reduced its financial-aid commitments to the states considerably. State governments, therefore, were left with greater power to make policy and to regulate economic activity and also with greater responsibility for paying the bills. In earlier years, such power and responsibility at the state level would have been shouldered mainly by the executive branch. But as a consequence of legislative reform, and the new capacity that resulted, legislatures insisted on sharing power with the executive and took on the responsibility for shaping budgets that would provide the resources needed to make up the gap left by the flight of federal dollars.

The assertion of legislative power vis-à-vis

the executive was nourished by a new sense of legislative independence. One of the principles, and also one of the goals, of the reform movement was the coequality of the legislative branch of government. Just as the rhetoric of reform instilled that idea in many legislative bodies, the activity of reform reinforced the separation of legislative from gubernatorial power. The provision of additional legislative capacity fed the sense of efficacy in institutions whose self-images were on the rise; it also afforded them the wherewithal to assert their independence. As legislatures developed professionally, legislators began to feel that their institutions should be independent of the governor and the executive branch. They began to take to heart the legislative articles of their state constitutions and checks-and-balances theory. They became protective of what they deemed to be their rightful prerogatives and evidenced concern that the executive was encroaching on the legislature.

In some states the emergence of the spirit of legislative independence was facilitated by governors themselves, especially governors who happened to be in the party opposite to that in control of the legislature. In those states—such as Florida, Kentucky, and Virginia—traditionally dominated by the Democratic party, the advent of Republican governors galvanized the legislature. In other states—Connecticut is an example—governors tried to block their legislature's modernization and wound up stoking the fires of independence.

Legislative reform accounts only in part for the resurgence of state legislatures, and their growing assertiveness vis-à-vis the executive. While tensions between the two branches are inherent in the constitutional structure of government, legislatures acquired the resources needed to assert their independence and to exercise power. Not only have they shared with governors in making policy, determining the budget, and even running government, but they also continue to challenge the executive over matters of authority. Legislative reform has been among the forces contributing to a balance of governmental power in the states. In some places—Arizona, Colorado, Mississippi, and South Carolina—the legislature traditionally had been the dominant branch. In many more places, governors traditionally had dominated. But with enhanced capacity, a spirit of independence, and a newly acquired assertive-

ness, legislatures have narrowed the gap in power. Therefore, in most states today, although the governor may have some advantage, the two branches are in rough balance. Just as the balance tends toward equilibrium, it varies from place to place, from time to time, and is partially dependent on personalities and circumstances of the moment.

Legislative reform has also played a role, albeit indirectly and as one of a number of factors, in encouraging conflict between the executive and legislative branches. Although conflict is deeply rooted in the nature and history of the institutions and in the struggle between the parties, what is new about the bases of conflict is the independence and assertiveness of legislatures nowadays, and the defensive posture assumed by governors. Legislatures repeatedly breach the boundary between the two branches, while governors try to draw the constitutional line and repel legislative incursions. Such conflict frequently invites the judiciary to serve as a referee between the executive and legislative branches. It also leads to stalemate and would appear to erode public confidence in government generally, but especially in the legislature.

Functional Performance

As far as policy is concerned, legislatures are no longer at the mercy of governors. The governor's priorities loom large in a legislative session. His or her program commands attention, and the press and legislators take it seriously. Moreover, governors achieve considerable success with their proposals. But they are very selective, limiting themselves to not more than half a dozen or so major initiatives per year. Nor are all of these initiatives strictly gubernatorial in origin; some have been drafted in collaboration with legislative leaders and so involve the legislature from the outset of the policy-formulation process. In all but a few cases, legislatures leave their imprint on gubernatorial initiatives, with little emerging from the legislative process unscathed and without modification. On some issues, especially tax proposals, it is not unusual for governors to go down to defeat, either because they refuse to accommodate their legislatures, fail to anticipate the strength of the opposition, or insist that a certain course of action is necessary no matter what its political feasibility. The legislature also pursues its own agenda, which includes many items that are not on the governor's agenda. Legislative items usually command less public attention but can be quite important nonetheless. Divided government encourages legislative activity, but whatever the partisan split in the two branches the trend since legislative reform has been for greater initiation of policy by the legislature, just as it has been for greater legislative involvement in policy initiated by the executive.

As far as the budget is concerned, the governor has advantages because at the start of the process he formulates the budget (except in the case of a few states such as Arkansas, North Carolina, and Texas) and at the end of the process he can wield an item veto (except in the case of seven states). But the legislature, thanks in large part to the fiscal staff that was one element of legislative reform, is heavily involved in review and modification—adding, subtracting, or eliminating funds, programs, and projects.

Fiscal staffs vary in how they are organized, mainly whether the appropriations committee has its own staff, as in Florida, or draws on assistance from a central staff agency, as in the majority of states. They also vary in their size, with the largest staffs being in California, New York, Michigan, Illinois, and Texas. But whatever the organizational pattern or size, fiscal staff has made an enormous difference to the legislature's performance on the budget. The governor's budget can be taken apart for analysis, understood in its details, and then reconstructed to reflect legislative as well as gubernatorial preferences. There is no question, therefore, that legislatures have more and better fiscal information than in earlier years. Furthermore, as a result of reform, legislatures now receive the budget requests made by the agencies of the governor. Probably the most important advance in the intelligence capability of legislatures has been the undertaking of revenue projections and forecasts, a critical part of the budgetary process that was formerly the prerogative of the executive.

A macroscopic view of the budget would suggest that the legislature gives the governor most of what the governor wants. The budget base remains intact, and the legislature's net impact on discretionary funds is seldom large. If one takes a microscopic view, however, the legislative role in shaping the budget appears far more influential. The legislature amends the governor's proposal considerably, cutting here and adding there. This is shown, for example, in a study that examined 538 decisions for fourteen major state agencies in Wisconsin's 1977–1979 biennial budget. It found that 90 percent of the joint finance committee's proposals were incorporated into the budget, as were 85 percent of the proposals made by amendments on the floor of the legislature. Of the approved decision items of major policy significance and relatively high cost, 38 percent were contributed by the joint finance committee and 18 percent arose from floor amendments.

Finally, there is the administration of state government, which according to the conventional wisdom is beyond the legislature's legitimate scope. Yet, legislatures have come to involve themselves in the running of government, exercising a measure of control over executive departments and agencies by means of both their budget and oversight authority. One reason for the legislature's involvement in administration stems from the legislative reform movement and its legacies of staff, independence, and the belief that among the legislature's principal functions is oversight.

Legislatures intrude in administration by trying to control spending. They attempt to get around line-item vetoes and overcome transfers of funds. They have the capacity to insert conditional language into the appropriations act and in accompanying documents and letters of intent. Another area in which legislatures have become active is that of reviewing proposed regulations, which is done in four-fifths of the states. In twenty-nine of these states, legislatures have given themselves the power to veto, suspend, or otherwise prevent regulations from going into effect. In conducting oversight, legislatures are also intruding on the executive. Oversight practices vary greatly, ranging from members and their staffs doing casework for constituents to committee hearings, committee investigations, statutory sunset reviews, performance audits, and program evaluations.

Many of the performance audits, program evaluations, and other studies are intended, among other things, to recommend to top administrators how their agencies should be organized and run. They afford legislatures an additional measure of control. Little of this would have been achieved without the new legislative orientation, legislative authority for post auditors and post audit functions, and additional specialized staff.

Institution and Process

The legislative institution and legislative process are considerably different today from what they were before legislative reform. Not all of the differences are attributable to the reforms of the late 1960s and 1970s, nor are any of the differences solely attributable to these reforms. Many other factors were at work. Yet, along with the significant social and political changes that took place in the United States from the 1960s on, the more limited tinkering with legislatures led to the following contemporary trends: careerism, politicization, and fragmentation. Not every state has undergone these trends or undergone them to the same extent. The larger states, with the most developed and modernized legislatures, have been most affected. California, Illinois, Massachusetts, Michigan, New York, Pennsylvania, and Wisconsin are in that category. Other states such as Colorado, Connecticut, Florida, Kansas, Minnesota, Missouri, Nebraska, Ohio, and Washington are less affected, but are subject to these trends as well. Still other states such as Montana, New Hampshire, Utah, and Wyoming are being touched only lightly, if at all.

The latest generations of members are quite unlike their predecessors. The increase of women representatives—from 4 percent of the nation's total in 1969 to 20 percent in 1993—stands as testimony to the success of the feminist revolution. The increase of African Americans, from 2.2 percent in 1970 to about 6 percent currently, and of Hispanics in California, Florida, and New Mexico stands as testimony to reapportionment, the civil rights acts, and the mobilization of American minorities. But the change in the occupational composition of legislatures, and in particular the decline in representation by farmers, business persons, and practitioners of various private professions, is largely a consequence of legislative reform. Attorneys, and especially those in larger firms, cannot afford to spend the amount of time required of legislators today. Furthermore, they do not want to sacrifice their legal practices by disclosing the names of clients, as required by conflict-of-interest laws and regulations. Nationally, the proportion of attorneys

serving as legislators declined from 30 percent in 1980 to 20 percent in 1979, and was down to about 16 percent by 1986.

The old breed of citizen legislator, the part-time member whose primary career was elsewhere, is being replaced by the career politician. Careerists are people who are willing to put in the time that legislative, constituent, and political work now demand. In most states the pressures are great for legislatures and legislators to move toward full-time status. Because of the rise in salaries, another reform of the recent past, serving a lengthy stint in a state legislature has become more appealing. Current salaries exceed $40,000 in California, Michigan, New York, and Pennsylvania, and exceed $35,000 in Illinois, Massachusetts, New Jersey, Ohio, and Wisconsin. In a number of states, salaries and related compensation doubled over a decade; in other states, where salaries were low at the outset, increases were even more marked.

The new breed of legislator tends to include teachers, unseasoned lawyers, spouses of professionals, single people who can live on legislative salaries, and former members of the legislative staff. What distinguishes those in the ranks of the new breed is that they have either more disposable time or little in the way of outside pursuits. They are attracted to careers in government and politics and want to remain in public office for the long haul. At least two-thirds of the members in Michigan and Pennsylvania now are career politicians. Half or more of those in Illinois, Massachusetts, New York, and Wisconsin are full-time or practically so. Slightly fewer in Arizona, Iowa, Missouri, and Ohio and about one-quarter in Connecticut, Florida, and Minnesota are full-time legislators. Whether essentially full-time or still part-time, more members today identify their principal occupation as "legislator," and not farmer, insurance agent, or attorney, as in the past.

In large part because of the rise in salaries, better facilities, and expanded opportunities for influence in the legislative process, members have tended to remain in the legislature for eight, ten, twelve years or longer, or until they can run for higher office. On average, only one out of ten departs voluntarily each biennium. And since only about 10 percent of incumbents lose races for reelection, legislative turnover has declined substantially since the 1960s—in the case of lower houses from 33 percent to about 20 percent by 1992. All of this is likely to change, however, in the fifteen states—including California, Colorado, Michigan, and Ohio—where the electorates in 1990 and 1992 voted to limit the terms of legislators.

Since members wish to hold on to legislative office as long as they can, politics and elections have become one of their principal concerns. Generally, the more full-time the service and the higher the salaries, the greater the stake in reelection. In many places, campaigns never end. Fund-raising has come to be one of the major tasks of legislators, and energies are redirected from other activities to that of campaign finance. Not only are legislators from marginal or targeted districts preoccupied with reelection, but even those from relatively safe districts attend diligently to their campaigns. All of them have seen lightning strike someone, and to be forewarned is to be forearmed.

The impact of elections on the legislative process extends beyond the activities of individual members. Most states currently are competitive at the legislative level, even though within a state typically 75–80 percent of districts are reasonably safe for one party or the other. The legislative parties seek to maintain their majority or gain a majority, and thus enjoy positions of chamber and committee leadership and principal control. Thus, legislative leaders and/or legislative parties in approximately two-thirds of the states have taken on the job of raising funds and allocating them to members and challengers alike. While the legislative party and legislative party leadership used to have governing as their primary focus, they have now displaced party organizations at state and local levels, taking over the electoral function as well.

With the rise in the cost of campaigns everywhere and the increased fund-raising activities of legislative leaders and legislative members, ethical issues have come to the fore in many places. For lobbyists, interest groups, and political action committees, there seems to be no end of requests for campaign contributions; they feel that they are being shaken down by legislators. At the same time, the press and the public are calling into question the integrity of an institution and process that are so dependent on special-interest money. Moreover, there are more than enough cases of corruption and abuse by legislators—as re-

vealed by stings in California, South Carolina, Arizona, and Kentucky—to feed the popular belief that government is for sale to the highest bidders. The irony of all this is that while reform has succeeded in making legislative office more desirable, heightening the competition for control of legislatures, and helping to restore the role of political parties in the legislature, the results appear to the press and the public to be mainly negative. The costs of campaigns in a competitive system keep rising, the race to acquire campaign funds intensifies, the advantages of incumbents (many of whom are in relatively safe districts) grow, and abuses inevitably occur.

By its very nature as a representative body, the legislature is permeable to outside influences and subject to a dispersal of power within. In recent years, outside influence has grown and the legislature as an institution has become more fragmented than previously. Along with reform, but not necessarily as a result, more and more interest groups have organized and mobilized in state capitals. Lobbying activity has increased and the pressures on legislatures have become both diverse and intense. Meanwhile, reforms that democratized the process have succeeded in dispersing power to an even greater extent within the body. Standing committees, which had been strengthened significantly, now rule over their own turf, with substantial power delegated to them. The organization of caucuses of women and minority members and local delegations in some places spread power further.

The distribution of staff resources has also helped disperse power broadly. As legislators on committees, in caucuses, or as individuals acquired their own staff, they also acquired information, and thereby their own power in the process. In any legislative body, however, probably the greatest impetus toward institutional fragmentation is the constituency basis of representation. And one reform of the 1970s and 1980s has been to move away from multi-member districts and toward single-member ones, thus encouraging greater parochialism on the parts of members. Add to this the district offices and district-office staffs that are available to legislators in about one-quarter of the states, and the centrifugal forces become even stronger.

All of these fragmenting tendencies reinforce the individualism of members, particularly of the new breed. Because of the candidate-centered nature of political campaigns, the opportunities afforded by television and other media, and the legislative resources at their disposal, the individualism of legislators has undergone a marked rise in recent years. Concurrently, the power of legislative leadership has undergone a decline, dramatically in a few states and gradually in others. In Connecticut, for example, in the distant past "the word"—the decision of the leadership, the governor, and the party chairman—reigned supreme. Not anymore; now the word is more diffuse; it comes from constituents, from influential groups, and from elsewhere. Putting together a majority in the legislature—for a major policy or a state budget—has become an increasingly difficult task for both governors and legislative leaders. A potential outcome of legislative fragmentation and legislator individualism, therefore, is the greater likelihood of deadlock on some of the controversial issues facing the state.

THE COURSE OF LEGISLATIVE REFORM

The legislative-reform movement clearly succeeded. Legislatures modernized; their capacity grew. Their performance in policy-making, budgeting, and oversight of administration improved. Their power vis-à-vis the executive expanded. Individual members began to reap benefits from legislative life, incentives for political careers increased, and the appeal of legislative office intensified. Not all of these consequences were intended by the reformers and none of them stemmed exclusively from legislative reform. Yet the movement of 1965–1980 had a substantial impact nonetheless. Over the years, the first-, second-, and third-order effects of reform, along with other factors, have served to make state legislatures more like the U.S. Congress. The professionalized legislatures in California, Pennsylvania, New York, Michigan, Illinois, Massachusetts, Ohio, Wisconsin, Florida, and New Jersey have moved furthest along these lines, while the less-developed legislatures in New Mexico, Wyoming, New Hampshire, North Dakota, Idaho, South Dakota, and West Virginia have moved least. But throughout the nation, the congressionalization of legislatures has been proceeding apace. When the reform movement got under way in the 1960s, Congress was held up as a model for legislative development. Congress continues as a model for state legislatures today, one to which they may not consciously aspire, but whose path they seem to be following.

BIBLIOGRAPHY

Pre-Reform Legislatures

Belle Zeller, ed., *American State Legislature* (New York, 1954), is the report of the Committee on American Legislatures of the American Politics Science Association. Terry Sanford, *Storm Over the States* (New York, 1967), describes the problems of state governments prior to reform. Alexander Heard, ed., *State Legislatures in American Politics* (Englewood Cliffs, N.J., 1966), includes essays by Herbert Jacob, William J. Keefe, Malcolm E. Jewell, Duane Lockard, and John C. Wahlke that lay the groundwork for reform proposals.

Reform Proposals

The Citizens Conference on State Legislatures, *The Sometime Governments* (New York, 1971),

evaluates and ranks the fifty state legislatures along several dimensions and offers a large menu of reforms. The Citizens Conference on State Legislatures, *State Legislatures: An Evaluation of Their Effectiveness* (New York, 1971), includes the design, methodology, and technical details for the evaluation study. Donald G. Herzberg and Alan Rosenthal, eds., *Strengthening the States: Essays on Legislative Reform* (Garden City, N.Y., 1971), includes essays by practitioners and political scientists on the scope, strategy, and tactics of reform. Donald G. Herzberg and Jesse Unruh, *Essays on the State Legislative Process* (New York, 1970), is a call for reform by two of the leaders in the movement. The Advisory Commission on Intergovernmental Relations, *The Question of*

State Government Capability (Washington, D.C., 1985), provides data and assessments on the adoption and implementation of reforms in state legislatures.

Input-Output Analysis of Reform

ALBERT K. KARNIG and LEE SIGELMAN, "State Legislative Reform and Public Policy: Another Look," *Western Political Quarterly* 28 (September 1975): 548–552, correlates CCSL's rankings of states with revenues, expenditures, and other factors to see whether reform matters. LEONARD G. RITT, "State Legislative Reform: Does It Matter?" *American Politics Quarterly* 1 (October 1973): 499–510, correlates CCSL's rankings of states with expenditure data and discovers minimal impact of reform. PHILLIP W. ROEDER, "State Legislative Reform: Determinants and Policy Consequences," *American Politics Quarterly* 7 (January 1979): 51–69, examines the effects of legislative professionalism and capability on policy, using CCSL's rankings on welfare spending. JOEL A. THOMPSON, "State Legislative Reform: Another Look, One More Time, Again," *Polity* 19 (Fall 1986): 27–41, uses CCSL's rankings to examine the effects of reform on legislative processes rather than policy outputs. SUSAN WELCH and JOHN G. PETERS, eds., *Legislative Reform and Public Policy* (New York, 1977), include analyses of state legislative reform by ROBERT F. SITTIG, RICHARD WINTERS, ALAN P. BALUTIS, LOUIS C. GAWTHROP, JAMES L. McDOWELL, SAMUEL K. GOVE, LEONARD RITT, JOHN GRUMAN, and SAMUEL C. PATTERSON.

Case Study Analysis of Reform

RICHARD E. BROWN, *The Effectiveness of Legislative Program Review* (New Brunswick, N.J., 1979), examines the establishment of auditing and evaluation capacity in state legislatures and early results. JAMES J. GOSLING, "Patterns of Influence and Choice in the Wisconsin Budgetary Process," *Legislative Studies Quarterly* 10 (November 1985): 457–482, documents legislative influence over the budget. TIMOTHY O'ROURKE, *The Impact of Reapportionment* (New Brunswick, N.J., 1980), provides a thorough study of effects on representation, parties, legislative leadership and procedure, conflict, and policies. GARY MONCRIEF and MALCOLM E. JEWELL, "Legislators' Perceptions of Reform in Three States," *American Politics Quarterly* 8 (January 1980): 106–127, looks at members' perceptions of the goals of reforms. JAMES A. ROBINSON, ed., *State Legislative Innovation* (New York, 1973), includes case studies of the effects of reform in California, Florida, Illinois, Ohio, Washington, and Wisconsin. MALCOLM E. JEWELL and PENNY M. MILLER, *The Kentucky Legislature: Two Decades of Change* (Lexington, Ky., 1988), shows the effects of the reform movement in a single state.

Consequences of Reform

WAYNE L. FRANCIS and JAMES W. RIDDLESPERGER, "U.S. State Legislative Committees: Structure, Procedural Efficiency, and Party Control," *Legislative Studies Quarterly* 7 (November 1982): 453–471, examines the distribution of power within senates and houses of the fifty legislatures. KARL T. KURTZ, "The Changing Legislatures (Lobbyists Beware)," WESLEY PEDERSEN, ed., *Leveraging State Government Relations* (Washington, D.C., 1990), categorizes legislatures in terms of session length, compensation, staff, and turnover. ALAN ROSENTHAL, *Governors and Legislatures: Contending Powers* (Washington, D.C., 1990), analyzes the legislature's power vis-à-vis that of governors in making policy, determining the budget, and running government. ALAN ROSENTHAL, "The Legislative Institution—In Transition and at Risk," CARL E. VAN HORN, ed., *The State of the States*, 2d ed. (Washington, D.C., 1993), discusses the most recent trends in state legislatures.

SEE ALSO Budget Procedures and Executive Review in State Legislatures; Floor Procedures and Conference Committees in State Legislatures; Political Parties in State Legislatures; AND State Legislators and Policy Innovators

LEGISLATIVE RECORDS AND PUBLICATIONS

M. Philip Lucas

Since the adoption of the Constitution, Congress and state legislatures have generated a mountain of records. The enormous amount of published and unpublished documented material is significant both for its diversity and the effect such records have had on politics and society. These records also afford scholars a better sense of the influences on lawmakers and, as a whole, reflect the changing concerns of the country at the national and state levels and the evolution of the American legislative process.

There are many examples of how the diversity and impact of legislative records have had a lasting influence on our understanding of the legislature in general and also of how the Congress began to implement the new Constitution (*Annals of Congress* by Joseph Gales and William Seaton). Sometimes the value of legislative journals has been more immediate and local such as when a Mississippi state senator in 1818 requested the secretary of state to send him the journal of the Mississippi Senate without delay so that he could refute misrepresentations by his election opponent. Historians are well acquainted with the few antislavery petitions which initiated a contentious debate on the floor of the U.S. House of Representatives in 1836. Opposition to the resulting 'Gag Rule' served as a rallying point for abolitionists and others concerned with the preservation of the constitutional right to petition. The petitions and reports of Dorothea Dix shocked and shamed one state legislature after another into improving the condition of asylums and prisons in the mid-nineteenth century.

Congressional hearings have occasionally shaken the entire nation and provoked significant executive actions. It was as a result of the Ku Klux Klan hearings in 1871 that legislation supporting President Ulysses S. Grant's actions to break the back of the Ku Klux Klan in the postwar South was enacted. Part of the reason for President Richard Nixon's resignation was as a result of information which emerged during the Senate Select Committee on Presidential Campaign Activities.

Scholars have often noted that the way in which legislatures are organized and function reflects the concerns and nature of the larger society. Certainly this has affected the amount and diversity of legislative records at both the national and state levels. However, the changing function of these legislative materials is reflected in the way certain types of records have been arranged and preserved in state and national archives. As will be seen, since 1789 congressional and state legislative records have retained a multifarious nature, but there were shifts in the relative importance, or even existence, of specific types of records over time. Another pattern that should not be too surprising is that despite the inevitable loss of records throughout history, the latter half of the twentieth century has witnessed a significant expansion in the materials to and created by the legislative branch.

Neither Congress nor state legislatures have been close to perfect in retaining their records. Nevertheless, there has been a more consistent and systematic effort to collect congressional rather than state legislative records. Because of this and because of their different constituencies and constitutional responsibilities, Congress and the state legislatures deserve separate consideration. No causal relationship is implied by this organization, especially since Congress and the state legislatures responded independently to the larger social, economic, and political forces outside their chambers.

RECORDS OF THE UNITED STATES CONGRESS

Perhaps the most frequently consulted records of the Congress are the published floor proceedings. The Constitution requires that "each

House shall keep a journal of its proceedings and from time to time publish the same" (Article I, section 5). This explains the publication of the House *Journal,* the *Senate Legislative Journal,* and the *Senate Executive Journal* since 1789. These volumes record the referral of petitions, the receipt of executive messages, and roll-call votes. The National Archives retains the manuscript version of the House *Journal* and the *Senate Legislative Journal.* The original manuscripts of the *Senate Executive Journal* have been routinely destroyed since 1898.

Interested citizens and scholars have been aided by several private organizations in their efforts to gain access to congressional roll-call votes. The Inter-University Consortium for Political and Social Research has gathered all roll-call votes between 1789 and 1987 on computer. The *Congressional Quarterly Almanac* (published since 1945) also details how every member of Congress voted during the previous session and summarizes the major legislative issues.

The membership and organization of the House and Senate can be found in their respective journals as well as in a couple of supplementary official publications. The *Biographical Directory of the U.S. Congress, 1774–1989* ably summarizes who has served in Congress since the Revolution. This Senate publication lists the members and officers of both houses of Congress by session and has brief biographies of every member and delegate to Congress. The Inter-University Consortium for Political and Social Research maintains a similar database. Members of the current Congress, their biographies, committee assignments, and election margins are published in the sessional *Official Congressional Directory.* It also lists the personnel of the Executive Department, independent agencies, the government of the District of Columbia, international organizations, and the officially approved press. The *Directory* has increased in size since its first publication in 1809; this reflects the growing complexity of the federal government and the widening scope of congressional activities.

How Records Have Evolved

Records of congressional debates have slowly evolved since the First Congress. Beginning in

1832 Gales and Seaton began a thirty-year project to reconstruct the debates of the first eighteen Congresses from numerous newspaper and other reports. Their efforts resulted in *The Debates and Proceedings in the Congress of the United States,* more commonly known as the *Annals of Congress* (1789–1824). Although far from perfect it is still the best and most accessible account available. Where the *Annals* cease the *Register of Debates in Congress* begins. Gales and Seaton published their own abstracts of the floor debates in both houses from 1824 until 1837. In 1833 the editors of the *Washington Globe* received official authorization for printing congressional debates. Francis P. Blair and John C. Rives and their successors published and edited the *Congressional Globe* until 1873. The *Globe* initially offered third-person abstracts, but later printed near-verbatim transcriptions. From 1873 to the present, the *Congressional Record* has contained what seem to be verbatim transcripts, but the debates were subject to editing by the individual members of Congress. Yet another publication, the *Daily Digest,* published since 1947, records floor and committee proceedings on a daily basis. In deference to the twentieth century, Congress finally introduced video to record floor debates. Tapes of the House exist since 1983 and the Senate since 1986.

The publication of successful legislation has a far more stable history. The *United States Statutes at Large* is available and covers the First Congress to the present, while bills and resolutions in their earlier stages can be found in a variety of places. The original enrolled and engrossed bills reside in the National Archives and the Library of Congress. However, while original House bills are available from 1808 to the present and original Senate bills from 1813 onward, many of the earliest original bills that were dropped into the Senate and House hoppers did not survive.

By and large it is possible to trace the amendments to original bills, but where the researcher looks depends on the Congress and in which house the bill originated. By the turn of the nineteenth century the Senate and House had devised a fairly systematic procedure for preserving committee records. However, records revealing the evolution of bills and resolutions in the 1700s and 1800s are somewhat erratic. A major development in the institutionalization of the Congress was the creation of permanent standing committees with broad policy responsibilities in the early 1800s. In the House of Representatives many nineteenth-century standing committees kept drafts and copies of the bills. The committees on Military Affairs, Foreign Affairs, and Ways and Means, for example, preserved many of the bills that came before them. Most standing committees have at least some record of how their legislation evolved but there is a wide variation. The files of the more temporary and usually more narrowly focused select committees, which did the vast bulk of the work in the House during the first ten Congresses, contain many drafts of bills pertaining to a variety of subjects.

The Senate's records of this type tend to be much less extensive. Only the standing committees on Military Affairs, Judiciary, Finance, and Post Office preserved pre–Civil War bills and resolutions. Dozens of standing committees did so after the war. In the Senate there are few select-committee records which include bills.

The House in 1865 and the Senate in 1887 created separate bill files to record privately sponsored legislation. These files usually contain petitions, correspondence, reports, and bills. As far as committee records were concerned, in 1903 the House required all committees to maintain bill files for all bills and resolutions. The Senate began this practice in 1901 but unlike the House, it collected all the so-called legislative case files at the conclusion of each session from each committee. This practice ended in 1946, and now as in the House of Representatives, the bill files remain with each individual committee's records. This offers a better sense of the work load as well as the pace of business within a specific committee.

Executive Influence in Policy-making

Crucial to many congressional committee decisions is information supplied by the executive branch. Evidence of this practice increases over time and appears in many places. *American State Papers* and the *Congressional Serial Set,* published from 1815 onward, offer the most accessible published version of key executive messages, reports, and documents. During the period from 1832 to 1861, Gales and Seaton constructed the *American State Papers* series

from what they considered to be the most important executive and congressional documents. The *Congressional Serial Set* is a bigger and more inclusive publication that gives a better sense of the legislators' activities and the evidence that contributed to their decisions. The growing sophistication and responsibility of the federal government are reflected in the number of documents the Congress requested of the executive branch and subsequently ordered to be printed in the *Congressional Serial Set.*

To some extent the influence of material supplied by the executive branch on the decision-making process of congressional committees is underestimated by the *Congressional Serial Set.* Messages and correspondence from the presidents, and particularly from the executive departments and independent agencies, are located in the records of practically every Senate and House committee. Not surprisingly, the House and Senate committees on Agriculture or Naval Affairs received extensive information from their counterparts in the executive branch. Some lesser-known and now-obsolete committees depended heavily on various executive offices for information. The Commissioner of Patents sent annual reports and answered queries for the House and Senate committees on patents (now subcommittees in the House and Senate Judiciary committees). Before the House Committee on Expenditures in the Executive Departments, which existed between 1927 and 1952, and the present Committee on Government Operations, which came into being in 1953, the House employed numerous narrowly focused committees such as the committees on expenditures in the Post Office Department, in existence between 1816 and 1927, and the Expenditures in the Interior Department, which operated during the period 1860–1927. These standing committees regularly conducted investigations, examined account books, and received correspondence from the executive branch in order to advise on legislation. Many of these documents are to be found in the files of these now-defunct committees.

There is less material of this sort among the records of select committees. However, it does increase in volume through the nineteenth century, with the House select committees' records being more extensive than the Senate's. After

World War I the number of select committees in both houses decreased, and they tended to be investigatory in purpose. Because of the switch in focus from decision-making to investigation the amount of documentation from various federal agencies and executive departments to the individual committees clearly expanded. The House Select Committee of Inquiry into the Operation of the United States Air Service, which existed between 1924 and 1925, not only held hearings and investigated European air services, it also sent extensive questionnaires to the Navy, War, and Post Office departments demanding information about personnel, facilities, accidents, and procurement guidelines. The Senate Select Committee on National Water Resources, which existed between 1959 and 1961, depended on testimony from public hearings as well as reports from state governments and several federal agencies to produce its final report.

The Growth in Reports to Committees

Since World War II a few changes have occurred in the flow of information from the executive to the congressional standing committees. First, the Legislative Reorganization Act of 1946 reduced the number of House and Senate standing committees. This enabled the remaining committees to more effectively collect executive department and independent agency correspondence. This has led to a significant augmentation in the paper flow from the executive, some of it mandated by law, to the point that not all of it is printed in the *Congressional Serial Set.* For the researcher, such information can often only be found in the committee or subcommittee records.

The flood of executive documents to Congress in the twentieth century represents the changing responsibilities of the legislative branch and the growing abundance of committee prints—official committee publications that generally serve as internal background information—substantiate this trend. The reports come from federal agencies, outside consultants or, more recently, the Congressional Research Service of the Library of Congress. According to the *CIS U.S. Congressional Committee Prints Index,* between 1829 and 1865 committees published just eight prints. Between 1866 and 1899, seventy-eight prints were

ordered by all congressional committees however, after the turn of the century, each session of Congress commissioned anywhere from thirty to seventy prints. By the mid-1930s more than two-hundred prints per session were common. Nevertheless, the clear majority of committee prints have their origin after World War II. Six hundred or more were ordered in each session for the fourteen years after the war, and by the 1960s more than one-thousand per session were published. Their number and diversity illustrate the relatively recent expansion of congressional committee duties.

Since 1789 maps have informed the committee decisions of both houses. Congress has transferred more than two thousand maps to the Cartographic and Architectural Records Branch of the National Archives; dozens more still reside among some committee records. Together, the Army Corps of Engineers and General Land Office prepared many of the maps, some of which have been published while others remain only in manuscript form. Photographs, also used in decision-making, are generally kept in the records of individual House and Senate committees.

A lot of nineteenth-century legislation originated with the receipt of petitions and memorials from individuals, organizations, and states. These requests for congressional action, often accompanied by supporting evidence, such as correspondence from private citizens, affidavits, maps, and engineer's reports, range over a wide variety of topics. According to Charles Schamel (*Guide to the Records of the U.S. House of Representatives*), "a great many petitions" sent to the House burned during the British occupation of Washington in 1814 (p. 3). Congress never referred them to committee. Among the fifty-seven linear feet of petitions that the House ignored between 1789 and 1871 are the antislavery petitions—victims of the infamous Gag Rule—as well as appeals for the rechartering of the Bank of the United States and the elimination of the Fugitive Slave Act of 1850. Between 1815 and 1966 the Senate tabled more than 250 feet of petitions and memorials after their presentation including some dealing with the annexation of Texas, dueling, bankruptcy legislation, prohibition, and a canal in Nicaragua.

The House and Senate referred the vast majority of petitions and memorials to standing and select committees. Practically every standing committee of the House and Senate received petitions. For some committees, petitions form a substantial portion of the surviving records. One-third of all the records for the House Committee on Territories, during the period 1825–1946, are made up of these petitions that usually contain requests by citizens for the organization of their territories and admission into the Union; or concerns about the extension of slavery; the morality of polygamy in the Utah Territory; or the limits of Native American rights. Other committees with less connection to the general population received only a few petitions. The Senate Committee on Printing, for example, in over one hundred years of existence between 1841 and 1944 accumulated only one foot of petitions in its files.

Before select committees became investigatory in nature in the twentieth century, petitions usually stimulated the creation of such committees in both houses to explore a wide variety of issues and constituent problems.

It is difficult to calculate the number of petitions received by each and every Congress, or more importantly, how significant these documents were in generating legislation. What is clear, however, is that by the early twentieth century, with the expansion of federal agencies and the quantity of their reports and studies, there were more sources of legislation available to congressmen than just memorials and petitions. For example, the House Foreign Affairs Committee received twenty feet of petitions between 1810 and 1897, 22 feet between 1897 and the end of World War II, and twenty-seven feet between 1946 and 1968. Over the same one hundred fifty years presidents and their secretaries of state conveyed information to the committee, but after World War II, however, there is considerably more correspondence, testimony, and additional records from the executive branch. Committee staff reports and memoranda help to broaden the representative's knowledge about what issues have to be dealt with before sitting in committee. At most, there is 73 feet of committee papers between 1810 and 1945, but between 1946 and 1968 there are 254 feet, more than three times as much material in the twenty-two years after World War II than in the one hundred thirty-five years before it.

Personal Claims and Committees

Individual petitions or claims which demanded government compensation for personal loss or injury occasionally occupied substantial amounts of time in certain committees if not the entire Congress. However, the history of these requests is distinct from the petitions and memorials that drew attention to broader social problems. A limited number of standing committees in the House have handled the wide variety of claims. Land claims, for example, went to the committees on Private Land Claims or Public Lands, while seven different standing committees and numerous select committees dealt with pension requests. On a more personal note, while Eli Whitney's petition regarding the protection of patent rights for the cotton gin received consideration from a select committee between 1811 and 1813, the victims of sectional violence in Bleeding Kansas submitted more than 300 claims for damages to the Committee on the Territories. The Senate generally received fewer claims petitions and dealt with them in relatively few standing committees.

Claims of all types consumed much energy. The Committee on Claims established in 1794 was one of the oldest standing committees in the House. As early as 1810 the House set aside particular days to deal exclusively with these petitions. One study calculates that approximately 40 percent of all bills introduced in the 1888 House were pension requests. During the Fifty-ninth Congress, between 1905 and 1907, 89 percent of the legislation enacted by Congress derived from claims of all sorts. More than 6,200 private bills passed during that session alone.

Congress has since successfully passed several laws to reduce the amount of time spent considering these requests. In 1917, legislation was passed which created a fundamental shift as the perception of veterans' pensions switched from being a gratuitous reward to a full-fledged pension. This meant case-by-case examinations were unnecessary, and the federal government established several veterans' programs that automatically satisfied the vast majority of individuals. Similarly the Federal Tort Claims Act of 1946 provided for the settlement of certain claims by executive agencies. Although the House Judiciary Committee still considers a fair number of private claims that exceed a certain dollar amount, their number is greatly reduced when compared to the situation before World War I.

Petitions, claims, drafts of bills, floor debates, and correspondence from the executive branch and private citizens reveal much about how Congress dealt with legislation. Standing committees also occasionally maintained docket books which listed all matters referred to the committee and the actions taken on them. The House committees on Military Affairs, Claims, Revolutionary Pensions, Manufactures, District of Columbia, Public Lands, Post Office and Post Roads, and Foreign Affairs have significant quantities of docket books dating from before the Civil War. Most of the surviving docket books from the House date from the nineteenth century and particularly the years between the Civil War and World War I. House committees since World War II have maintained legislative calendars. The Senate standing committees generated far fewer records of this type. Only three committees—Military Affairs, Indian Affairs, and Judiciary—kept docket books before the Civil War. The majority were produced between the 1890s and the end of World War II. Legislative calendars appear in only a few of the Senate committees' files after World War II.

Committee Minute Books   The earliest minutes chronicle the actions of several House select committees in the 1790s and 1820s. Committee minute books are more valuable than the dockets for understanding how committees worked. Again, the House produced more of these than the Senate. Before the Civil War only a few standing committees in the House kept substantial minutes such as the committees on Claims, Elections, Accounts, and Ways and Means. Senate committee minutes from this era are even rarer and less complete.

Most House standing committees kept minutes after the Civil War but there are frequent and frustrating gaps in these records. The Committee on Banking and Currency files contain minutes between 1867 and 1919, but there are no such records during the period 1920–1945 when the minutes resume. By contrast, the minutes from the House Committee on the Judiciary, which begin in 1857 and continue to 1968, are among the most complete

and thorough of any committee in Congress. In the Senate committee minutes are far less common and have even more discontinuities. Unlike the House, which preserved a significant number of volumes from the nineteenth century, minutes of Senate committees come largely from the twentieth century.

The reorganization after 1946 of congressional standing committees produced three changes in the records of minutes in both houses. First, almost all committees have kept minutes continuously since 1946, with only a small number of gaps in the records. Second, verbatim transcripts of committee meetings in both houses become more frequent in the years after 1946. This parallels events at the state level. Third, minutes and transcripts of subcommittee sessions are more common, but less so than for the full committees.

Public Hearings   In the late nineteenth century the public hearing became an increasingly popular device for congressional committees to gather information. Transcriptions of congressional hearings were often published, but even if not, these records became part of the official record and guided committees and the full house to decisions about appropriate legislative action. Although it was not until the passage of the Legislative Reorganization Act of 1946 that required committees to transcribe their hearings systematically, hundreds of earlier hearing records can be found throughout House and Senate committee files.

The Senate Committee on the Judiciary created records of the earliest hearings in May 1824 and March 1826. On these occasions the committee heard from witnesses regarding the nominations of Benjamin Ames for United States Marshall of Maine and Charles J. Ingersoll for United States Attorney of the Eastern District of Pennsylvania. In the House, the Committee on Public Lands held the first recorded hearings between 1832 and 1833 for their investigation into the official conduct of Elijah Hayward as commissioner of the General Land Office. A total of six witnesses appeared before the committee. Only fourteen hearing transcripts exist from before the Civil War—seven in each house. During the Civil War period between 1861 and 1865, Congress held sixteen different hearings for which we have records. Thereafter hearings became more common events.

From the late 1860s through the 1880s there were, on average, twenty-three hearings per session in the House and ten per session in the Senate but many more hearings were held in Congress after the turn of the century. Committees in the Fifty-ninth Congress (1905 and 1907) recorded 478 hearings, ten years later the Sixty-fourth Congress (1915 and 1917) convened over one thousand, and during the late 1920s and the 1930s two thousand per session were common. The rapid increase in hearings continued after World War II as evidenced by the 2,825 held during the Seventy-ninth Congress, the 3,800 hearings during the Eighty-fourth Congress, and the 5,530 hearings during the Eighty-ninth Congress. After the committee reorganization of 1946, subcommittee-hearing records begin to appear with increasing frequency. The *Congressional Serial Set* contains many but certainly not all of the hearings. Many unpublished transcripts, which influenced congressional decision-making, are located only among the committee records.

A wide range of committees held hearings in the late nineteenth and twentieth centuries. Beginning in the mid-1880s, the House Committee on Education, in particular, scheduled large numbers of hearings until 1916, when it was merged with the Committee on Labor. The newly combined committee, not surprisingly, continued to depend upon frequent hearings. On the other hand, the Senate Committee on Foreign Relations apparently held only scattered hearings before World War II. After that, the number of hearings increased, as did the number of transcripts.

A committee's labors culminated in the report to the entire house, which recommended acting on or rejecting a particular measure. Its decisions were rooted in the published and unpublished records previously discussed, although some decisions followed simply from the petition or claim possibly supported by information from the executive branch. By the twentieth century the report was more likely to be based upon more extensive information from executive agencies and departments, committee staff reports, public hearings, and so forth.

Where Records Are Kept

The preservation and publication of committee reports has a tangled history. Before 1861, reports from the House select and standing committees were kept in the committees' files. The clerk of the House usually made copies for his records. Gales and Seaton included the most important reports, in their opinion, in the *American State Papers.* Beginning with the Sixteenth Congress, 1819–1821, the House published all the committee reports in the *Congressional Serial Set.* From that Congress 167 reports were printed in two volumes. Drafts of reports—some with printers' corrections as well as the manuscript originals—are maintained in the individual committee's records. The committees on Naval Affairs, Public Lands, Indian Affairs, Rivers and Harbors, and Ways and Means have particularly complete records of their reports. Other committees have gaps; some are rather extensive. After 1819, the *Congressional Serial Set* has by far been the best source of House committee reports.

The Senate handled its committees' reports in a slightly different fashion. *American State Papers* contains some of the most important from the earliest Congresses. Until 1847, Senate committee reports are usually found among the records of the individual committees. However, from 1847 onwards reports were separated from the committee files and, for the first time, published in the *Congressional Serial Set.* More than 330 Senate committee reports from the Thirtieth Congress were published in two volumes.

The number of committee reports published in the *Congressional Serial Set* does not follow a simple pattern over time. Usually the House of Representatives printed more reports than the Senate. This has been the case since the Forty-third Congress. The Thirty-ninth to Forty-second Congress was the longest period of time during which Senate committee reports outnumbered those from the House. However, during periods of war there was a reduction in the amount of committee reports. Before the Civil War there were approximately 1,000 reports per Congress, but while the war lasted during the years 1861 and 1869, the number of reports dropped to between three and four hundred. Likewise there was a 25-percent drop in the number of reports issued by Congress during the World War I era between 1917 and 1921 than in either of the immediately preceding or succeeding Congresses. Similarly the committees of the Seventy-seventh and Seventy-eighth

Congresses during World War II produced 17-percent fewer reports than the Congresses before and after. No significant change is apparent during the Spanish-American, Korean, or Vietnam wars.

Throughout the nineteenth and twentieth centuries this fluctuating pattern continued. Before the Civil War, there was a steady increase in the number of committee reports from 167 in the Sixteenth Congress (1819–1821) to 1,400 in the Twenty-seventh (1841–1843). After the unprecedented lows during the Civil War the House and Senate committees reached new degrees of activity in the 1870s and 1880s. Between the Forty-third and Fifty-first Congresses (1873–1875, 1889–1891, respectively) the number of House reports rose from 1,188 to 4,058 and Senate reports from 693 to 2,627. Following a 50-percent reduction in the early 1890s, the quantity of congressional committee reports expanded enormously by the turn of the century. The Fifty-fourth Congress (1897–1899) printed more than 4,600 reports in twenty-three volumes, the Fifty-sixth Congress (1899–1901) printed nearly 5,500; the Fifty-seventh Congress (1901–1903) almost 7,300; and the Fifty-eight Congress (1903–1905) more than 9,300 reports. The peak came in the Fifty-ninth Congress (1905–1907) when congressional committees churned out approximately 15,510 reports which necessitated thirty-seven volumes in the *Serial Set.*

Much of the dramatic increase came from the resolution of private claims and pensions originating from the Civil War and Reconstruction eras. In 1907 the fifth and final law reducing Congress's role in the settlement of Civil War pensions passed. This greatly reduced the number of reports so that the House and Senate committees submitted only 3,400 reports to the Sixtieth Congress (1907–1909). With the exception of the two world war periods, the number of congressional committee reports remained relatively stable until recently. In the 1950s the number temporarily swelled to more than 5,000 per Congress, but since the Eighty-ninth Congress (1965–1967) there has been a steady decline to the point that the Ninety-seventh, Ninety-eighth, and Ninety-ninth Congresses (1981–1983, 1983–1985, 1985–1987, respectively) have averaged only 1,700 committee reports per session. Regardless of the changes in the nature of the reports made to the House and Senate over the years, these documents have always been fundamental in determining the course of congressional business. Apart from this integral function, other legislators, judicial officials, and scholars can see from the dockets, minutes, and drafts of bills which supplement these reports exactly how legislative proposals were arrived at.

While the quantity of committee reports has alternately ebbed and flowed and the number of petitions and memorials has remained stable or decreased in the twentieth century, other congressional records have seen dramatic increases. In recent times committee hearings have become increasingly common as has the dependence on committee prints and executive and staff documents. The Legislative Reorganization acts of 1946 and 1970 authorized House and Senate committees to employ professional staff to assist them. This has greatly increased the number of records since the end of World War II. The following table clearly demonstrates this growth.

TABLE 1
GROSS CHANGES IN CONGRESSIONAL
RECORD-KEEPING

	House records in cubic feet	Senate records in cubic feet
1789–1946	9,100	6,600
1947–1968	5,900	7,000
1969–1988	17,900	7,000

Sources: House—Schamel et al., *Guide to the Records of the United States House of Representatives,* pp. xv, 355, and passim. Senate—Coren et al., *Guide to the Records of the United States Senate,* p. 259 and passim.

Not all of the records kept by House and Senate committees since 1947 have been transferred to the National Archives, and there is limited access to those received after 1969. Clearly, the quantity of records between 1968 and 1988 will increase dramatically. It is rather startling that the Senate from the Ninety-first to the Ninety-ninth Congress (1969–1971, 1985–1987, respectively) accumulated about the same amount of records as it did in the first seventy-nine. Equally dramatic is the fact that the House of Representatives preserved more records between 1969 and 1988 than the first ninety Congresses. These developments reflect not only vast improvements in record keeping, but also the rapidly growing sophistication in the national government, especially in the latter half of the twentieth century, and specifically Congress's role in government and society. The diversity of responsibilities facing members of Congress in committees and subcommittees necessitates the additional staffing and the increase in research and supporting materials. All of these records are likely to be kept because of demands by the National Archives, jurists, scholars, and other constituencies.

RECORDS OF STATE LEGISLATURES

It is less than surprising that the fifty state legislatures have also generated, preserved, and published a great diversity of records over two centuries and as each state has been free to decide its own policies, there is considerable individualism in their respective records and publications. Although independent, state legislatures also share common features one of which is the publication of a journal documenting each chamber's actions. Despite the fact that in several states journals from a very small number of sessions have been lost, all fifty states have an extensive record of what occurred in their legislatures after statehood. States that had a territorial phase often have fairly complete descriptions of the territorial legislative process.

These publications chronicle the presentation of petitions and bills, how such proposals are referred to committees, and the ultimate fate of many such measures. Roll-call votes are important in pinpointing the degree of controversy as well as who supported or opposed a particular measure. This is because legislatures seldom recorded the reports of committees in the journals except for very important measures facing the state. Some state journals contain far more of these reports than other state journals, but even individual state legislatures were not consistent from decade to decade in presenting much detail about their committees' deliberations. Trying to establish the views of minority positions is difficult because reports were seldom published to accompany the majority decision.

There is nothing comparable on the state level to the *Congressional Record* or *Congressional Globe* and thus debates in the state legislatures have been lost to scholars. Newspapers have sometimes reported the discussions on highly controversial matters, and for the nine-

teenth century this is the best, albeit enormously incomplete source for speeches and debates in the state legislatures.

On a far more limited scale, a few legislatures in the nineteenth century authorized publication of segments of debate and individual speeches on controversial topics. The heated debate in the Alabama legislature on apportionment was printed in 1854, as were speeches by Illinois lawmakers on the revenue system in 1881. The advent of the war between the U.S. and Great Britain in 1812 resulted in the publication of speeches delivered in the Massachusetts legislature against the conflict. During the Civil War, New Jersey printed one legislator's oration against the enlistment of African American troops and later a full-fledged debate over the ratification of the Thirteenth Amendment. One of the most famous debates, cited frequently by historians, was the fateful contest in the Virginia legislature over the future of slavery in that state, published in 1832.

Although the absence of published legislative debates is clearly the norm, Pennsylvania, Indiana, and Maine are three notable exceptions. The journals of the Pennsylvania legislature from 1789 to the present have occasionally reported portions of debates on some crucial matters. In Indiana a private service recorded the debates in that legislature between 1858 and 1887, and the Maine *Legislative Record*, published from 1897 onward, contained a verbatim record of the proceedings in both houses of the legislature.

Audiovisual Records Recently an increasing number of state legislatures have allowed the audiotape recording of the floor debates. Tennessee began this practice in 1955, followed by Utah's lower house in 1959. Utah's Senate followed suit in 1967. Nevada initiated the taping of floor sessions in 1961 and Delaware in 1963. Oregon's House of Representatives began taping its floor discussions in 1963. Its Senate did so in 1973 and in 1987 it began to videotape the legislative sessions. Only Oregon, along with the Massachusetts House since 1987, and California since 1990, currently permit video recordings of their legislative proceedings.

Obviously these audiovisual records, along with the other records, afford scholars, jurists, and future legislative officials the best opportunity to ascertain legislative intent in conjunction with other records. However, still over half of the states say that this recording method is too expensive and lacking in privacy to justify the benefits from such documentation. Montana officials adamantly refuse to record legislative discussions because they believe this will encourage more open debate while at the same time protecting legislators.

Like the Congress, every state publishes session laws (a volume containing all the laws enacted at the last legislative session) several months following adjournment. Since their entrance into the Union all states have carefully preserved these documents as well as volumes of revised statutes. However, each state decides its own timetable for the publication of revised statutes.

In the nineteenth century, the legislature and executive sometimes issued laws in separate publications before their appearance in the state's session laws. How widespread a distribution these publications received is difficult to ascertain—given their republication by newspapers. Most of these laws related to issues that affected a broad segment of the state's population such as the militia, public schools, revenue and taxation, and railroad rates. In 1891, 1889, and 1893, respectively, Ohio, Pennsylvania, and Kansas published secret Australian ballot laws soon after they were enacted. Bank laws frequently were printed in the years before the Civil War. However, the frequency of such publications decreased dramatically by the early twentieth century, probably because the popular press started to report on the legislature.

Bills on File   State legislatures, like the Congress, retain all submitted bills on their records whether they are passed or not, although the extent of these records varies considerably from state to state. Vermont only began collecting all bills and resolutions submitted to the legislature in 1985. Idaho began in 1963 and South Carolina in 1969 but the records for the other states go back further. Twenty-four states, among them Massachusetts, Rhode Island, Tennessee, Florida, Texas, Iowa, Nebraska, Oklahoma, New Mexico, and Alaska, have records of original bills that begin at statehood. Fire destroyed fifty-five years of such records in Oregon, and haphazard record-keeping in New Hampshire and Mississippi has left significant gaps in their files. These days better archival management, twentieth-century legislative councils, and a general awareness of the value of these records has led to their preservation. To some degree these collections of original bills reveal legislative intent and the broad concerns of society.

The creation of bill files in several states has expanded the influence of these records. Bill files document the amendments attached to proposed legislation as the measures progress through the committees and on the floors of each chamber. Since 1775, Massachusetts has created a file for each bill that contains the original bill, petitions, committee notes, relevant correspondence, and amendments. It does not hold committee reports or hearings. Illinois adopted a similar system in 1929, but its bill files are composed of the original bill, the final act (if it got that far), committee reports and recommendations, and the roll-call votes. About one dozen states have similar systems, most of which were initiated or greatly expanded in the twentieth century. Since 1849, California has kept a record of the progress of bills through the legislature as well as textual changes. This has occurred in a number of different ways. Around 1950 the legislature encouraged the creation of authors' bill files, wherein legislators who proposed the original bills would voluntarily donate to the archives the petitions, correspondence, rationale, other background information, and their floor remarks. In 1960 California expanded this and passed a law which required the maintenance of Committee Bill Files in order to preserve the text, executive agency opinion, testimony, correspondence, Legislative Counsel opinions, committee minutes, and press releases for every bill submitted to any committee. Many states preserve similar materials but in different ways.

Recording the Governor's State Address

One of the first tasks in a state's legislative session has been receiving and evaluating the governor's message to the legislature and then delegating the various issues suggested by the governor to the appropriate standing or select committee. Almost all state legislatures have preserved and published these seminal documents in one of two forms. Some legislatures published their respective governor's message as well as other key reports from the executive branch in the journals of both houses. Other state legislatures recorded them in a separate publication. The earliest example of this is New York, which began doing so in 1777. Having included these documents in the House and Senate *Journals* for ten years, Iowa published a new volume entitled *Legislative Documents* in 1856. Maryland separated legislative documents from its journals in 1824, Massachusetts in 1827, Maine and Kentucky in 1833, North Carolina and Indiana in 1835, and Michigan in 1838. Not all of these have survived to the present day. Indiana and Kentucky ended publication in 1912 and 1943, respectively; Nevada's series entitled *Appendix to Journals of the Senate and Assembly* runs between 1875 and 1977. These documents were either reincorporated in the legislative journals or published by the executive agency or department that authored them.

Petitions at the State Level

As with Congress, petitions and memorials often instigated legislative action at the state level. These documents, which seem to parallel the pattern of petitions and memorials to Congress, were more important or at least more prevalent in the nineteenth century than in the twentieth. Records of petitions suffer from probably being the least systematically maintained of all major legislative documents, and only six states—Pennsylvania, Massachusetts, North Carolina, Texas, Wisconsin, and Kansas—have continuous runs from statehood to the present. In all other states, records of petitions fade at various points from not long after statehood, as with Minnesota and Florida, to various points in the nineteenth century. At least eighteen states for all practical purposes retained no petitions.

A handful of petitions encompassing a variety of social and economic issues were published in the nineteenth century at the direction of several state legislatures. Mississippi printed Dorothea Dix's petition for immediate improvements in that state's insane asylums and prisons; in 1869, 1879–1881, and 1852, respectively, the legislators of Connecticut, New Jersey and North Carolina authorized the printing of petitions in favor of temperance; and in 1847 and 1853, respectively, Alabama and Kentucky printed railroad companies' requests for state assistance. Despite these examples of petitions reflecting popular and corporate economic and social concerns, literally hundreds of them have been lost over the past two centuries.

Because of this it is ultimately impossible to determine the volume of petitions for any decade, especially where records are often poorly organized or not preserved at all. While the available sketchy evidence suggests petitions were far more commonplace in the nineteenth century than in more recent times, how significant a force they were or how well they would cast light on the legislators' intent is largely lost to history. Perhaps studies of individual state legislatures that preserved these records would provide some clues as to their impact on the lawmaking process.

State Committee Records

About thirty states currently preserve committee reports. Although these records have been common and vital at the congressional level, they are much less important at the state level despite the fact that all states legislatures have a committee system. This is reflected in the fact that each state legislature has pursued its own way of writing and preserving committee reports. Moreover, at least twelve states have kept no reports at all. This has happened in Alabama, where, because there were no rules governing the recording of committees, no records were kept. In Massachusetts the committees of the General Court have traditionally issued recommendations on whether bills should pass or not pass or pass with an amendment but these reports are not written. Only New York, Michigan, Wisconsin, Minnesota, Kansas, Nebraska, and Hawaii have runs of committee reports since statehood, but even these states have lost some of their nineteenth-century records, and their collections are only substantial from the 1960s onwards. In New York, for example, if a report was not published in the *Legislative Document* series it has probably been destroyed. It was not until the mid-1970s that the state initiated a systematic collection of all committee reports. Michigan's records were greatly expanded in the late 1960s.

The nineteenth-century collections of committee reports are erratic. Approximately seventeen states have preserved no more than a handful of committee reports each between 1860 and 1900 and even fewer of them did so systematically. Tennessee has none of these records from 1862 to the early 1970s while fire destroyed more than fifty years of committee records in Oregon. Florida has no legislative committee reports from the mid-1870s to the 1950s.

However, compared to debates, bills, and petitions, committee reports have usually reached print more often because they have tended to be more controversial in nature. In states where volumes of public documents were published, committee reports were sometimes included with executive documents. Each state established its own policy and did not necessarily stay consistent from decade to decade. In the nineteenth century, state legislatures did publish committee reports separately when the members felt the issues were of interest to a significant portion of that state's population. Reports on issues such as penitentiaries, asylums, banks, public education, railroads, and taxes were very common in many states. Other reports reflected the states' special interests or concerns. In the late 1860s and early 1870s committees from Louisiana, Arkansas, and Mississippi independently published their findings on Mississippi River levees. Three separate committees in North Carolina in the 1850s issued reports on the status of Cherokee tribal lands within the state. The Ohio legislature published its committee report on the Standard Oil Company in 1857. The causes of the "coal famine" was the subject of a joint committee's investigation in Kansas in 1903. Sometimes state legislative committees even debated national issues. In 1812 and 1813 Connecticut published two reports on the war of 1812; in 1832 Louisiana evaluated the nullification of a federal tariff by South Carolina; and in 1852 Wisconsin published a report on the Fugitive Slave Law.

The early twentieth century witnessed a decline in these publications and the maintenance of only a few substantial collections of reports. Vermont has an extensive collection beginning in 1917 and Connecticut in the 1930s, but they are the exceptions. Only fourteen state legislatures preserved the committee reports they wrote in the sessions immediately after World War II. It was not until the 1960s

that there was a statewide increase in the number and volume of a committee reports being preserved. As mentioned before, New York's records expanded greatly in the mid-1970s, North Dakota's after 1959; Michigan's after 1965; and Florida after 1969. California does not have any reports until 1960, Idaho until 1970, Washington until 1971, Colorado until 1973, Maryland until 1975, and South Dakota until 1980. Investigations into legislative intent will find committee reports valuable, but such records are scattered before the 1960's and completely absent in some states.

Although records of congressional committee hearings began to appear in significant numbers at about the turn of the century, it was not until the 1960s that verbatim accounts become relatively common at the state level. Only eight states have hearing transcripts before 1950 and only thirteen before 1960. Some exceptions include Connecticut, where the general assembly has preserved transcripts of hearings as far back as 1900, and Louisiana, which has preserved sporadic copies of hearings during the period 1880–1908. New York published the testimony from a few hearings in its legislative documents series throughout this century.

Currently about twenty-three state legislatures consistently preserve committee hearings which are documented in a variety of ways. New Jersey's hearing records consist of a few scattered publications. In Massachusetts the only hearing transcripts are recorded by a private news service. Committees in the Maine legislature hold hearings, but very seldom are they recorded. In Oregon careful summaries of testimony are kept rather than exact transcriptions. The improvement in technology in the 1960s and 1970s has led to the recording of hearings on audiotape in twelve states. Texas introduced taping as early as 1962, and Florida adopted the practice in the house in 1965 and the senate in 1968. However, for the researcher, technology has brought mixed blessing. In West Virginia and Nevada regulations dictate that records of hearings are destroyed after ten and two years, respectively. The vast majority of recordings that are available come from the early 1970s to the present.

State legislative committees have generated a wide assortment of miscellaneous records much like their congressional counterparts. There is, again, a wide diversity in what individual states have preserved. Furthermore, these materials originated largely in the years after World War II, which parallels the records of Congress.

Correspondence to and from state legislative committees reside in many state repositories. Florida and Massachusetts organize correspondence in their bill files, while other states employ other systems. A variety of financial accounts survive in several states; in Delaware there are records of this sort between 1789 and 1850. The Mississippi legislature has preserved assorted materials related to investigations it carried out during separate periods between the 1870s and 1922. Nevada, Utah, and Minnesota maintain collections of exhibits used during committee work.

Recently available in a number of states, nonpartisan advisory reports significantly contribute to understanding the legislative process and to the understanding of scholars trying to determine intent. Oregon, Kentucky, Illinois, Ohio, and Minnesota, in particular, have a substantial amount of this and other research material. The California Legislative Counsel submits legal opinions on many bills, which are then stored with the Committee Bill Files. In Maine, the Office of Policy and Legal Analysis issues study reports to assist legislative committees. Nebraska's unique unicameral legislature demands a more formalized process. Created in 1937, the Legislative Council, which is a crucial advisory body to Nebraska's legislature, considers policies between sessions and presents a program accompanied with research reports and other data to the legislature and its committees. Wyoming and Utah also have substantial amounts of records—correspondence, exhibits, and memoranda—from their interim committees.

Because of the sparsity of other state legislative committee records, committee minutes take on more significance at the state level than the congressional level. Currently twenty-six state legislatures keep fairly complete minutes of their standing committees. However, few state legislatures consistently took and preserved minutes before 1950, so most of these records are of fairly recent origin. There are exceptions of course. Minnesota has preserved committee minutes since 1878, and in Wisconsin the house committees began keeping minutes in 1857 while the senate began the practice in 1907. Vermont's records are very complete and extend back to 1917. New Hampshire and Oregon have also maintained committee minutes since before World War II. These records offer valuable insights into which bills received extensive consideration, which topics were discussed, the lists of experts and other witnesses, the committee's recommendation, and the members' vote on each item.

The quality of such records has been greatly enhanced in nine states which now tape-record committees' proceedings. Florida was the first to do this in 1965; Alaska followed in 1969, Texas in 1972, Minnesota in 1973, Colorado in 1973, Tennessee in 1975, Kentucky in 1976, North Dakota in 1981, and Washington in 1983.

Additional Records In addition to session laws, legislative journals, and volumes of legislative and public documents, state legislatures have published other materials separately. A few bills, debates, petitions, and committee reports were printed in the nineteenth century. The listings in the *Monthly Checklist of State Publications* published from 1910 onward show an interesting shift in legislative publications in the twentieth century. In the 1910s many state legislatures continued to print more than journals and volumes of public documents, particularly individual bills, resolutions, governors' messages, and calendars of bills. These actions resemble the nineteenth-century pattern. Only a few committee reports were included. In terms of quantity, the number of individual publications in the 1910s has only been exceeded in recent years. In the 1920s and 1930s the types of publications remained the same, but there was a 50- to 60-percent reduction in the number of authorized printings. The decline in the publication of these types of documents came around 1940, the same time as the current emphasis on committee reports, studies by state legislative councils or research departments, and occasionally legislative committee hearings, began to take over.

A rough accounting from the *Monthly Checklist* suggests that the number of state legislative publications doubled between 1940 and 1950, followed by a more gradual increase until the 1980s. In more recent times, there has been another upsurge in publications. The first three months of 1990 saw a four-fold increase in the number of publications over a comparable period in 1970. Although the publications also came from a broader range of states, the issues raised in the publications have remained remarkably consistent since the 1940s. Through these printed documents the public and press are informed about legislative decisions on highways, taxes, public education, labor laws and policies, public utilities, welfare, and agriculture. Recently, there has been an increase in the frequency of legislative publications on the drug problem and environmental issues, the purpose of which is to keep the public acquainted with issues of broad social concern. The increase in the number of state publications resembles the growth of the *Congressional Serial Set.*

The Organization of State Records

A lack of resources has prevented most state archives from organizing their legislative records as well as the National Archives. It is therefore impossible to quantify the amount of records from state legislatures or determine with any precision how legislator's attitudes have changed. This is further complicated by the fact that each state legislature creates and preserves different types of records and documents. Wyoming's legislative records are consistently sparse, and an Arizona legislative official has warned that the dearth of anything but very recent records makes "legislative intent very difficult to find." Missouri, Oregon, and West Virginia experienced tragic fires that destroyed significant amounts of legislative records.

Within state legislative-record collections, subtle changes occur over time which are difficult to measure. In Vermont, for example, petitions from the late eighteenth and early nineteenth centuries are well maintained and catalogued. However, there are no committee records from those centuries, other than brief mentions in the House and Senate *Journals.* In 1917, the state legislature began to maintain a rather extensive collection of standing-committee reports and minutes. The records of the Tennessee legislature show a similar trans-

formation. According to a 1990s archivist there, "The miscellaneous descriptive reports and individual petitions of the early nineteenth century give way to the official bills and documents required to be kept by the Secretary of State in the twentieth century." The transitions in these two states and others is probably a reflection of not only changing record-keeping practices, but also the growing sophistication of government and the expansion of its responsibilities in the twentieth century. In this general way the pattern of state legislative records and publications parallels that of Congress.

The increase in state legislative records since World War II, and particularly since 1960, may, in fact, exceed that of congressional records, although again this varies from state to state. While the publication of session laws and legislative journals and the preservation of original bills have been constant for every state, empirical evidence points to a significant growth in records such as debate transcripts, official publications, committee reports, committee hearings, committee minutes, and miscellaneous legislative documents. A comparison of Connecticut's legislative records from the 1930s and 1970s reveals that not only did the legislature meet every year instead of every other year in the 1930s, but the quantity of records per year increases dramatically. The increasing business of the Connecticut legislatures of the 1970s, compared to their counterparts forty years earlier, can be clearly seen from the increase in the committee records. In Missouri the archives preserved one box of miscellaneous House committee reports from 1937. By the 1972 session there were bulging files from sixty-four separate house and senate committees.

It appears that the 1960s were years of significant change in most state legislative records. In 1969 the Florida legislature established a new system for permanent standing committees. Since that time, it has amassed at least 3,700 cubic feet of records, compared to ten cubic feet of records from the nineteenth century. The turning point in Montana came as a result of this its constitution in 1971, while in Oregon a 1961 law required the recording of committee minutes. In 1971, Washington State passed the Legislative Records Act which required the preservation of committee files, minutes, reports, and other materials. This pattern has been repeated throughout the states.

Present and Future Practices

The type of congressional records located in the National Archives can also be found in the archives of state legislatures. State lawmakers have always recorded their actions like their federal counterparts. They have kept the testimony of witnesses at public hearings, heeded both the petitions of their constituents and the studies of their staffs or outside agencies, and written reports to justify their committees' recommendations. Each state legislature, however,

has placed different priorities on what records to maintain or even create. The congressional records are far more consistent, although there are differences in the types of records obtained or kept by congressional committees. Finally, both Congress and the state legislatures are responsible for a dramatic increase in the amount of records in the latter half of the twentieth century. The addition of professional staffs and the increasingly sophisticated responses to more-complex social and economic issues are reflected in the amount and nature of congressional and state legislative records. This pattern is not likely to change in the near or distant future.

BIBLIOGRAPHY

Congressional Records

ROBERT W. COREN et al., *Guide to the Records of the United States Senate at the National Archives, 1789–1989* (Washington, D.C., 1989) and CHARLES E. SCHAMEL et al., *Guide to the Records of the United States House of Representatives at the National Archives, 1789–1989* (Washington, D.C., 1989) are well-written, well-organized, and indispensable descriptions of the surviving records of Congress; HOWARD E. HUFFORD and WATSON G. CAUDILL, *Preliminary Inventory of the Records of the U.S. Senate* (Washington, D.C., 1950) and BUFORD ROWLAND, et al., *Preliminary Inventory Number 113: Records of the United States House of Representatives, 1789–1946* (1959), are the outdated and occasionally inaccurate predecessors to COREN and SCHAMEL, respectively. Their abstracts, however, are sometimes useful supplements to the more recent guides.

The *Biographical Directory of the U.S. Congress, 1774–1989* (Washington, D.C., 1989) and U.S. CONGRESS, *Official Congressional Directory* (Washington, D.C., 1809–present), are official publications which list congressional members by session and provide brief biographies.

Congressional Information Service, *CIS Cumulative Indexes and Abstracts* (Washington, D.C., 1970), detail the multitude of congressional publications since 1969 and thereby continue the individual indexes begun for earlier Congresses. *CIS Index to Unpublished U.S. House of Representatives Committee Hearings, 1833–1936*, 2 vols. (Washington, D.C., 1988) and *CIS Index to Unpublished U.S. House of Representatives Committee Hearings, 1937–1946*, 2 vols. (1990), are careful accountings of hearings not contained in the *Congressional Serial Set* and only found among the committee records of the House; *CIS Index to Unpublished U.S. Senate Hearings, 1823–1964*, 5 vols. (Washington, D.C., 1986), surveys the Senate committee records. *CIS U.S. Congressional Hearings Index, 1833–1969*, 42 vols. (Washington, D.C., 1983), lists House and Senate hearings that were published; *CIS Congressional Committee Prints Index*, 5 vols. (Washington, D.C., 1980), offers year-by-year listings of these committee reference documents; *CIS U.S. Serial Set Index, 1789–1969*, 36 vols. (Washington, D.C., 1975), provides valuable access to the multitude of official documents published under congressional authority; *Congressional Quarterly Almanac* (Washington, D.C., 1945–present), provides roll-call data and summaries of legislation by session; INTER-UNIVERSITY CONSORTIUM FOR POLITICAL AND SOCIAL RESEARCH, *Guide to Resources and Services, 1990–1991* (Ann Arbor, Mich., 1991), describes several valuable databases for congressional membership and roll calls.

LEGISLATIVE STRUCTURES AND PROCESSES

RICHARD ROGERS BOWKER, *State Publications: A Provisional List of the Official Publications of the Several States,* 4 vols. (1899), although outdated, is still the most accessible survey of the wide variety of nineteenth-century state-government publications; ROBERT ALLAN CARTER, *Legislative Intent in New York State* (Washington, D.C., 1981), combines a description of New York's legislative records with how that state's courts have interpreted those records to ascertain legislative intent. Unpublished, and sometimes difficult to obtain, finding aids for state-archives collections of legislative records exist for most states; DAVID W. HASTINGS (comp.), *Guide to the Records of Washington State's Legislative Archives* (Olympia, Wash., 1990), was published and is one of the best; *Monthly Checklist of State Publications,* 81 vols. (Washington, D.C., 1910), demonstrates quite clearly the yearly expansion in the official publications of each state government; JUSTIN E. WALSH, *The Centennial History of the Indiana General Assembly, 1816–1978* (Indianapolis, 1987), is one of the few thorough, well-documented studies of a state legislature.

GERALD N. GROB, "The Political System and Social Policy in the Nineteenth Century: Legacy of the Revolution," *Mid-America* 58:1 (1976) and MARGARET SUSAN THOMPSON and JOEL H. SILBEY, "Research on 19th Century Legislatures: Present Contours and Future Directions," *Legislative Studies Quarterly* 9:2 (1984), link legislative record-keeping to legislative institutionalization. ROBERT ZEMSKY, "American Legislative Behavior," *American Behavioral Scientist* 16:5 (1973), argues the vast array of legislative data reflect larger societal forces.

Part IV

LEGISLATIVE BEHAVIOR

CONSTITUTIONAL AND POLITICAL CONSTRAINTS ON CONGRESSIONAL POLICY-MAKING
A Historical Perspective

David W. Brady

America's Founding Fathers created a constitutional system designed to keep popular majorities from hastily enacting broad and decisive public policy. Recognizing the importance of the popular will, they created the House of Representatives as *the* democratic legislative body. In Alexander Hamilton's words, "Here, sir, the people govern. Here they act by their immediate representatives." But the authors of the Constitution feared that the House, as the people's branch, would tend to act too quickly and chaotically. Therefore, they created an indirectly elected upper house, the Senate, which they expected would use reason and judgment to temper the lower house's expected haste and extremism.

Now, some two hundred years later, the Founding Fathers might be pleased to see how well they succeeded: not only is Congress unable to enact public policies hastily, it seems to exhibit a persistent inability to legislate any major policy changes at all. The Founding Fathers, however, would be puzzled by the roles of the House of Representatives and the Senate in the policy process. They would find that after two centuries the Senate does not need to temper passions in the other house at all. The Senate as well as the modern House both are characterized by continuity, stability, and incremental policy development, not rapid and sweeping change. As a result, Congress as a whole hardly ever can be counted on to take any major policy initiatives, even when they are needed. It cannot do so.

This policy incrementalism and failure to meet broad policy challenges have regularly provoked a great deal of criticism of Congress.

In a famous speech in 1925, the Ohio Republican Nicholas Longworth, then Speaker of the House, said, "I find that we [the House] did not start being unpopular when I became a Congressman. We were unpopular before that time. We were unpopular when Lincoln was a Congressman. We were unpopular even when John Quincy Adams was a congressman. We were unpopular even when Henry Clay was a Congressman. We have always been unpopular." The political scientist Samuel Huntington argued that the intensity of criticism of Congress has varied inversely with the degree and dispatch with which Congress approves the President's legislative proposals. The House's power, he suggests, is the power to obstruct legislation. And certainly since the 1930s, when the era of dominant executive government began, Congress has retained greater obstructionist power than have other Western parliaments—indeed, it seems that its major power, simply put, is obstruction.

To account for the inability of Congress to legislate major policy changes, or its ability to obstruct broadly purposeful legislation, requires understanding how the American constitutional system has constrained the political system in particular ways. A key point is the inability of American political parties to build broad, purposeful, national majorities that can act in a sweeping manner within Congress.

THE CONSTITUTIONAL CONTEXT

The Founding Fathers gathered in Philadelphia in 1787 to amend what they considered to be

873

significant weaknesses of the Articles of Confederation, which had proved unable to pull together the nation's very diverse and contentious state and sectional interests. Since the 1770s, there had been debilitating internal conflict and constant uproar in the country, most recently in Shay's Rebellion (an uprising in western Massachusetts under the leadership of Daniel Shays, a veteran of the Revolution). But the Founding Fathers faced an extremely awkward problem: creating a more effective centralized government, but one not so centralized that it would be repudiated by those representing varying and potent sectional interests. There was never any serious thought given to creating a uniform national government. Not only would the idea have been repugnant to many of those gathered in Philadelphia, but there was no practical political possibility of creating such a government. Delegates to the Constitutional Convention were selected by each state; voting was by state; the various governmental proposals (such as the Virginia and New Jersey plans), were proposed by and named after states; and ratification was by state. Before, during, and after the Constitutional Convention, the importance of state interests was an accepted fact of political life.

The federal nature of the resulting constitutional system reflected the social, economic, and religious differences between states and sections. The Constitution itself recognizes in government organization these differences between states—it demonstrates a "numerous and diverse population." The father of the Constitution, James Madison, argued that such a population constituted a real check on the formation of a majority capable of acting in haste. As a focal point for those differences, Congress not only has had to deal with issues in a political sense, but also to temper sectional demands by integrating sectional divisiveness into its deliberations. From Alexander Hamilton's use of the Treasury Department to boost industrial and monied interests, to the present sunbelt/snowbelt controversy, different sectional interests have pressured Congress to pass legislation viewed as beneficial to one and inimical to others. The Civil War, the 1896 electoral realignment, and countless other events in American history all testify to the effects of sectional diversity on the American system of government. And, of course, as James Madison anticipated in

1787, such divisiveness made it difficult to form "hasty" majorities—that is, majorities capable of enacting significant policy changes.

Sectional diversity has been the root cause of much policy disagreement in American political history, and political parties have been based in individual states, thus assuring the representation of sectional differences both in party systems and in governmental institutions. But that was not the only limit on Congress's ability to establish broad national policies. The drafters of the Constitution did not feel that a federal government was a sufficient constraint against what they expected to be repeated attempts to override the nation's diversity. In short, ensuring that sectional and state differences were represented in Congress—such as the large- versus small-state controversy—did not convince the drafters of the Constitution that Congress would check itself.

Because diversity in itself was not a sufficient roadblock to potentially tyrannical majorities, and assuming that concentration of legislative, executive, and judicial powers in the same hands would invite tyranny, the Founding Fathers wrote into the Constitution two doctrines: that of separation of powers and that of checks and balances. These doctrines have resulted in the American system of government, characterized by "separate powers sharing functions," in contradistinction to other Western democracies, where power is centralized and functions are more specific. Thus, one distinguishing feature of Congress is that, unlike the British House of Commons, it shares power with the President, the courts, and the bureaucracy.

The most immediate effect of the separation of powers and of checks and balances is that even when Congress can build internal majorities for innovative policies, the president or the courts can thwart them. In the American system, having a majority in favor of a policy in Congress does not readily translate into significant policy change. Those who seek to preserve the status quo always have a decided advantage. This contrasts with the way majorities are built in most other Western democracies. Policymakers in either house are likely to compromise or water down strong policy proposals made by the other branches of government. Such compromises, whether anticipated or forced, are readily associated with incremental public policy.

The way legislators are elected also contributes to their inability to enact laws in a broad, purposeful, and "national" manner. The only popularly and directly elected body established by the Constitution is the U.S. House of Representatives. Each member of the House represents an approximately equal number of people, and more importantly, each representative is responsible to his or her constituents. There is no national party to supervise or control nominations. There is no mechanism to purge members who did not follow party principles. The electoral method of single-member plurality winner districts has enhanced and nourished localized elections. Members elected on local issues by localized and limited constituencies owe little to House leaders and can behave as they choose as long as their constituency is happy. After the passage of the Seventeenth Amendment in 1913, senators elected on state issues were in a similar situation. They owed little to Senate leaders.

An important consequence of localized elections is that local interests are intensely represented throughout Congress, especially the House, across a broad range of issues. Once elected, representatives and senators choose to serve on committees that will enhance their reelection chances. Members from agricultural districts serve on agricultural committees and subcommittees; members from other types of district serve on committees and subcommittees relevant to their constituencies. Thus, committees and policy activity are dominated by local interests. This phenomenon has been called policy-making or control by "little government," "the iron triangles" of (1) interest group liberals who seek to push one particular favored issue above all others; (2) pork-barrel manipulation, wherein congressmen seek to bring financial or other benefits to their own districts; and (3) the process of policy reciprocity, in which trading occurs between individual congressmen seeking support for their own interests and which they vote for each other's particular desires. What counts in all of this is that localized interests are congealed within the structure of the Congress's policy-making process by the constitutional arrangements that frame elections and by the distribution of power. Against a backdrop of institutionally localized interests and constitutional constraints, forming majorities capable of enacting major policy changes is difficult at best, impossible at worst.

POLITICAL PARTIES IN CONTEXT

Although many parameters of the doctrines of federalism, separation of powers, and checks and balances have changed over time to make the governmental system more democratic and much more centralized, the American system of government still remains fragmented and cumbersome. Shortly after the Constitution took effect, difficulties inherent in governing within its framework became apparent. In response, from his post in the president's cabinet, Alexander Hamilton crossed executive boundaries to organize and lead pro-national factions in the Congress. Over time these factions developed into political parties. Even though American parties were founded because without them the system was too diverse and cumbersome, that same system also inhibited full development of the parties as national integrators and promoters of national legislation.

Perhaps the most distinguishing characteristic of American political parties is that their roles—in the electorate, as organizations, and in the government—are disjointed and not coherently united to achieve one main goal. Federalism, separation of powers, checks and balances, and single-member plurality districts are in no small way responsible for the fragmented nature of the American party system.

The most basic effect of a federal form of government on the American party system is that rather than having a two-party system, we have a fifty-state party system. Each state's party system has its own demographic, ideological, structural, and electoral peculiarities. Thus the Democratic party in the electorate and as an organization in New York is distinct from the Democratic party in the electorate and as an organization in Georgia. The same applies to the components of the Republican party in these states. The heterogeneity of the state party systems means that at the national level, not like-minded, but "*unlike*-minded" people bearing the same party label will come together in the U.S. Congress. Put another way, the federal system brings to Congress inherent differences between states and regions even under similar party labels. Although this may be useful in maintaining equilibrium in the system, it most often has been an extremely poor basis for building coherent congressional parties. American political history abounds with examples of successful electoral coalitions that cannot make major policy changes because of their own internal ideological differences.

It is not difficult to surmise how such coalitions lead to static or incremental policy. The New Deal coalition of rural Southern and agricultural interests on one hand, and urban Northern industrial interests on the other, is a case in point. Long after this coalition had achieved its major policy objectives, it continued to serve as an electoral base for the Democratic party. Such successful electoral coalitions, however, often are divided on major policy issues. In fact, on a number of them, such as civil rights and social welfare, the components of the New Deal coalition were always poles apart.

The principles of separation of powers and of checks and balances also enhance the fragmentary, disjointed status of American parties. Parties formed out of numerous and diverse state party systems will emphasize electoral success and minimize policy cohesion (and thus policy success). When formed on a sectional, coalition basis, and when given the opportunity to support candidates for numerous offices (both appointive and electoral) in the various branches, national parties will be further fractionalized. Thus, for example, one faction of the party may be dominant in presidential politics, another in congressional politics, and, because both government branches have powers over the courts, an equal division of court appointments may result. The Democratic party from 1876 to at least 1976 was characterized by such an arrangement. The northern wing dominated presidential politics and elections, the southern wing dominated congressional leadership posts, and both wings influenced court appointments. Such a system may enhance the representation of the nation's many differences, but it does little to elect congressional majorities capable of legislating change in public policy.

The constitutional arrangement of single-member district plurality elections also contributes to fragmenting the American party system. House members elected on local issues by a localized party in the electorate build local party (or personal) organizations. Once elected, owing little to national party leaders, representatives can behave in nonpartisan ways with little consequence for themselves. As a result, throughout most of congressional history, party leaders have had to persuade members to vote "correctly" because they did not have the ability to force them to do so. But party leadership without even the threat of sanctions is likely to be unsuccessful in building consistent partisan majorities. Representatives elected by local majorities can work and vote on behalf of those interests when it suits them, regardless of the national party position. It should not be surprising that the highest levels of voting along party lines in the history of the Congress occurred at a time when sanctions over members available to the Speaker were most powerful and when the Senate was run by a hierarchy that also had powerful sanctions over members.

The ways local and state diversity are institutionalized in the American system of government allow diversity to work its way up almost unchanged from party affiliation in the electorate, through the party organizations, to the national congressional parties. Thus, at the top, as at the bottom, the American party system reflects the cumbersome and fractional nature of the American system of government. Whatever policies parties are able to enact under these conditions are bound to be incremental in nature, and changes in the status quo will be hard to come by.

Congressional Organization

Like all organizations, the Senate and the House of Representatives adapt to social change by creating internal structures designed to meet the pressures (or demands) from their various constituencies and to perform their own policy-making functions. In order to respond to the pressures generated by the enormous range of interests in the United States, each house established a division of labor. The result is a highly complicated committee system. When the country was in its infancy and government was limited, the House of Representatives, for example, formed temporary, unspecialized, ad-hoc committees; by the Jackson era, however, a standing-committee system was in place. As the country grew more industrial, the House responded by expanding and enlarging the committee system.

Early in this process, committees were established to deal with policy areas such as war, post offices, roads, and ways and means to raise revenues to support the government. These committees were organized around governmental policy functions; they were—and still are—decentralized decision-making structures. The creation of Reconstruction policy after the Civil War as well as Woodrow Wilson's claim that "congressional government is committee government" testify to the power of committees before the twentieth century. Having power decentralized in committees was a necessary response to pressures for government action in certain policy areas; it meant, however, that to the extent the committees decided policy, party leaders remained limited in their ability to direct policy-making. As noted, being mechanisms for decentralized decision-making, committees are dominated by members elected to represent local interests. Within limits members can choose the committees on which they serve, which determines to a large extent the direction the committees' policy choices will take.

The decentralized committee system that allows members to represent local interests has become a powerful force for policy stability. In the modern House of Representatives, committees have become entities unto themselves: they are stable, with little membership turnover, and when new members do join, they are quickly socialized to committee norms that affect policy decisions. Because turnover is slow and decision norms remain stable, committee leaders often are able to prevent majorities from enacting major changes in policy. Norms of specialization and expertise as bases of power take years for new members to acquire, thus enhancing both the committees' power and stability in the policies they advance. For example, since the late 1930s, majorities of both the American people and the Congress favored policies such as medical aid for the aged and federal aid to schools, yet House committee leaders were able to obstruct enactment of relevant legislation until the mid-1960s. Almost thirty years of obstructing the will of majorities

is proof of both the independence and the power of the committee system. It is reasonable to conclude that the decentralized House committee system constitutes an effective deterrent to building majorities capable of enacting major policy changes.

What the division of labor pulls apart in organizations, some form of integrative mechanism pulls together. In the House the major integrative mechanism is the majority congressional party. And as we have seen, congressional parties are limited by the governmental structure established by the Constitution and by members being elected by local groups on the basis of local issues. Members responsible to and punishable only by local electorates tend to be responsive to constituents, not parties. Under such conditions, party strength tends to be quite low. Even when party voting was at its peak in the House, parties were less united than was common in other Western democracies. Even under ideal conditions the congressional parties have a limited ability to become integrated. This means that under normal conditions, policy decisions are likely to reflect localized committee interests, thereby limiting attempts by leaders of the national party to guide majorities toward decisive policy solutions to pressing problems. Congressional voting patterns show different coalitions active on different policy issues. Coalitions cut across regional party and social and economic lines, making party leaders' jobs a ceaseless maneuvering to find coalitions capable of governing in specific policy areas.

Along with governmental structure and localization, a third, internal factor affects Congress's ability to legislate quickly: as a collegial body each house has a limited ability to organize itself hierarchically. The American constitutional and cultural emphasis on equality has affected the overall operation of Congress. In the House of Representatives, for example, because each member represents a separate and equal constituency, members receive the same pay, have the same right to introduce bills, to serve on committees, and so on. Equality in this sense limits the House's ability to organize itself on a hierarchical basis, and because hierarchy is limited, the House has established elaborate procedural rules and precedents to control the passage of legislation from Speaker to committee to floor. This elaboration of procedure emphasizes the right of individual members to affect legislation at various decision points in the formation of policy. The result is slower policy-making and a fostering of compromise to avoid parliamentary snafus. Slowness and compromise both favor incremental solutions to policy problems.

The House then, is a relatively nonhierarchical body, with power decentralized in committees with elaborate rules and procedures for passing legislation. The weakness of the congressional parties is partly the result of factors external to the House (local elections, cultural stress on equality, separation of powers, etc.), and partly the result of the way the House is organized (members' preference for decentralized power and the lack of leadership sanctions). Over time the relationship between committee power and party strength has waxed and waned, but the general rule has been that committees are strong while congressional parties are weak, and House leaders thus become middlemen, not drivers. And the policy choices emanating from this system have been normally incremental in nature.

In general, the U.S. Senate's organization has the same features as the House's organization: The Senate is a nonhierarchial body with power decentralized to committees with elaborate rules and procedures. As in the House, the weakness of parties in the Senate is partly the result of external factors (local elections, etc.) and partly the result of the way the Senate is organized. In short, committees are "normally" strong, and parties are weak and divided. The Senate has developed a complex committee system that parallels the House's. Senators from farm states serve on committees that deal with agriculture, and senators from energy states serve on committees that deal with energy matters; senators representing local interests on decentralized committees are a force for stability in exactly the same way as shown above for the House. Political parties in the U.S. Senate are as constrained as are House parties. Senate party leaders have few sanctions to use to keep senators in line, and, as long as senators please their constituents, party leaders have little ability to forge party majorities for policy change. Senators' voting patterns show different coalitions active on different issues.

As in the House, Senate coalitions cut across regional, social, and economic lines.

Like the House, the Senate has a limited ability to organize itself hierarchically. In fact, given its tradition as an exclusive club, the Senate is even less likely to be hierarchical than the House. The rules and precedents of the Senate governing procedure, like those of the House, primarily are concerned with how legislation moves from committees to the floor and emphasize each member's rights to affect legislation. However, the rules are more open than those of the House and allow greater levels of individual discretion.

In sum, major public policy changes occur rarely in the Congress of the United States for the following reasons: (1) members are normally elected by local interests on local issues; (2) once elected, members choose committee assignments (within limits) based on those local interests and issues, thus localizing and congealing rather than nationalizing policy alternatives; (3) the committee system is powerful, in part, because it is stable; (4) the congressional parties are normally weak and divided because members' preferences are heterogeneous and conflicting, and thus members cannot assemble coalitions to override the localism of committee decisions; and (5) the organization, rules, and procedures of the Congress serve those who wish to preserve the status quo.

Federalism, separation of powers, and checks and balances all have shaped the development of congressional parties, which are an aggregate of the different preferences and interests found in congressional districts, states, and regions. Thus both parties are characterized by heterogeneous membership. There are liberal and conservative Democrats and liberal and conservative Republicans who differ across issues ranging from gun control to military preparedness. These inherent differences are exacerbated when the president and Congress are controlled by different parties, in a so-called "divided government." From 1945 to 1992 we have had 28 of 46 years when the president was a Republican and at least one house of Congress was Democratic, and for twenty years since 1968. Divided government is possible only under a system that has separate powers elected via different constituencies. (The

French and Korean governments also have systems where divided government is possible, and within the last decade both have had short periods where the government was divided.) Under these conditions truly responsible party government is impossible. That is, unlike parliamentary systems, the U.S. system does not establish a majority government to make party policy public policy, and then within a specified period put itself up for reelection based on its record.

By repeatedly choosing Republican presidents and Democratic Congresses, the U.S. electorate apparently desires centrist policies. In some sense the electorate must *want* conservative presidents fighting a liberal congress over public policy on education, taxing and spending levels, and so on, although the election of a Democratic president, Bill Clinton, in 1992 might have signaled a change in this pattern. State legislative parties do not have a federal constraint, but all fifty states have forms of separation of powers and checks-and-balances constraints. It is possible in the states to have divided government: a governor of one party, a legislature of the other. In 1991 thirteen states had Democratic legislatures and Republican governors; three states had Republican legislatures and Democratic governors; and thirteen other states had divided control of the state legislature. In short, a majority of states had the ultimate result of a system of separation of powers—divided government.

State legislative parties, like their federal counterparts, are characterized by (1) members elected by local constituencies on local issues; (2) members choosing committees based on their interests; (3) weak legislative parties; and (4) rules and procedures that serve those wishing to preserve the status quo. Of course, given the number of states, the variance around these issues is greater in the states than it is in the U.S. Congress. Legislative parties in Massachusetts, for example, are stronger than they are in the U.S. Congress. Nevertheless, Massachusetts has divided government. Legislative committees in Texas have more power than do U.S. House and Senate committees, given the weak governor system found in Texas, yet for 8 of the last 13 years Texas also has had divided government. The point is that despite the variance across states, all state political parties have

been constrained by constitutions featuring separation of powers and checks and balances. State legislative parties share the basic characteristics of federal congressional parties because they, too, are constrained by the rules governing elections and the policy process. No American state has a legislative party system that resembles a European strong party system, which is a conscious result of choosing constitutions featuring separation of powers and checks and balances to constrain and shape the development of state parties.

POLICY CHANGE UNDER CONDITIONS OF DIVERSITY, FEDERALISM, AND WEAK PARTIES

Constitutional developments in America have shaped American parties so that policy incrementalism or status-quo politics is the norm. Yet as political analysts often note, political systems must over time adjust to majority pressure for change or face extreme, even violent, destabilizing pressures. How is this accomplished in the U.S. Congress? The answer lies in what happened during the three electoral realignments in American history—in 1854–1860, 1894–1896, and 1932–1936. These popular voter revolutions had a significant impact on the American governing process.

Studying their effects in the House of Representatives, the only legislative body with a continuous two-hundred-year history of popular elections, illuminates the process. Most House elections normally are determined by local factors, thereby assuring the dominance of localism in House politics; in each of the realignments, however, elections were dominated by overriding national issues, which we will look at in turn. Prior to each realignment, powerful issues there arose that did not readily fit within the framework of the existing two-party system. Ultimately, the parties took positions on these issues and offered clear-cut alternatives to voters. (In the Civil War realignment, however, the Republicans replaced the Whigs before the choice was clear.) When the realigning election or elections occur, the result is a new congressional majority party elected largely on its positions on national matters, not local issues.

The effect of these elections in the House was to reduce the major drawbacks to party-line voting by representatives. As we have seen, elections decided on a localized basis make the congressional parties amalgams of different interests. During realignments, representatives are elected on the basis of party positions on the national issues. The majority party is united on the issues of the realignment, local factors are not involved in policy choices, and a unified majority party votes major policy changes into law. In addition, the influx of new members during realignments strongly reduces committee stability, and new leaders emerge who support the party position in favor of major policy innovations. In sum, the influx of new members during realignments reduces the impact of localism and committee stability in the House. The result is increased party-line voting, especially on the issues that prompted the realignment in the first place.

In each of the major electoral realignments that have occurred in American history, a principal cross-cutting issue dominated the elections. In the first realignment, the second American party system was broken up by the battle over the extension of slavery, and, ultimately, the secession issue. The two dominant parties of the 1832–1856 period were the Whigs and the Democrats. Each party had Northern and Southern wings that ultimately could not accommodate the slavery issue. The Missouri Compromise and the Compromise of 1850 were valiant efforts to patch over differences of opinion, but the introduction of the Kansas-Nebraska Act led to the Whigs' demise. The Republican party replaced the Whigs as the second major party in the 1856 elections, and by 1860 the Democrats were seen as the proslavery party, while the Republicans battled against any further extension of slavery into new territories. Thus, the electorate was offered a clear policy choice between the parties.

The cross-cutting issue of the 1890s realignment was whether America's future was to be industrial or agricultural. The rise of industrialization in the aftermath of the Civil War generated the displacement of farmers and a change from a society of local, self-sufficient communities to a highly interrelated industrial society. The result was the displacement of agricultural interests and the end of a way of life. The overarching issues were specifically fo-cused on questions of gold and silver policies, the protective tariff, and American expansionism. Being debtors, agricultural interests favored the inflationary coinage of silver, free tariffs, and antiexpansionism. Industrial interests favored exactly the opposite. The rise of the pro-farmer Populist party testifies to the cross-cutting issues in the 1896 realignment. The Democrats, under William Jennings Bryan, adopted the Populist position while the Republicans adopted a proposition on gold, protective tariffs, and expansionism.

The cross-cutting issue during the New Deal realignment was the result of a single event—the Great Depression. The question was, Would the government adopt policies to combat the effects of the depression? The Republican incumbent, Herbert Hoover, would not adopt policies to aid farmers, workers, cities, and the unemployed. By 1932 the Democratic party answered by proposing relief funds and programs to aid those most affected by the depression. Once again, voters were offered clear-cut choices between candidates and parties. Table 1 shows the party differences on these issues in the party platforms for each of the realignments. The higher the numerical value, the greater the policy disagreement the parties expressed in their national platforms in presidential election years.

Table 1 clearly shows that the Civil War and the 1890s realignments were characterized by deepening party differences regarding the cross-cutting issues leading up to the critical elections. For the New Deal realignment, the pattern is somewhat different. The parties differed in 1924, but it was not until 1932 that the Democrats could convince the electorate to send a new majority party to Congress. In addition, the magnitude of these figures suggests that the parties were less polarized in the positions they took during the New Deal than they were during the Civil War and 1890s realignments. Clearly, however, in each of the realignment eras, the major political parties took opposing positions on the issues of major concern. Thus, when voters went to the polls in the elections of 1860, 1896, and 1932, they were offered "a choice, not an echo."

Table 2 suggests that realigning elections are characterized by higher turnover in membership and on committees, and that realignment brings the new majority party into control

Table 1
PARTISAN PLATFORM DIFFERENCES ON MAJOR ISSUES IN THREE REALIGNMENT ERAS

Era	Slavery	Capitalism	Depression
Civil War			
1848	0		
1852	.10		
1856	.24		
1860	.71		
1890s			
1884		.08	
1888		.04	
1892		.44	
1896		.55	
New Deal			
1920			.02
1924			.30
1928			.19
1932			.26

of the government for at least fourteen years. It also suggests that under electoral conditions where parties take distinct stands on national issues, the new members in the House will vote along party lines because they have a mandate to act. Party voting in the House will increase because members are not pressured by local interests differing from national party positions. Thus, one should expect to see party voting increase during the realignment relative to the period of politics preceding it.

Table 3 shows the average percentage of party votes in the five house sessions preceding the realignment and the percentage of party

votes in the realignment houses. Party votes are defined in two ways. First, the percentage of votes that pitted a majority of one party against a majority of the other party (50 vs. 50) is presented. Second, a more stringent criterion is used, defining party votes as those where 90 percent of one party opposed 90 percent of the other (90 vs. 90).

The results clearly indicate a rise in partisan voting during each of the realignments. While these results help to corroborate this interpretation of the events, they do not provide information on whether party voting increases dramatically on the cross-cutting issues associated with realignments. To help isolate this information, a set of scales was created for each of the following realignments and issues: the Civil War, with the issues of slavery, secession, and civil rights; the 1890s, with the issue of monetary policy; and the New Deal, with the issue of social welfare (for a fuller discussion, see Brady and Stewart, 1982). The hypothesis is that on each of these dimensions in the prerealignment era, party will be highly correlated with voting. We measure the extent of the relationship by correlating a representative's party identification (0–2 = Democrat, 1 = Republican) with his voting score. The higher the correlation (+1.0 = the highest) the stronger the relationship, and the greater the party structuring of the vote.

Table 4 presents the results, which support the hypothesis. In each of the realignments, the correlation between party and support for, or opposition to, the dominant issue increases during the realignment. During the Civil War realignment the Republicans became more an-

Table 2
HOUSE MEMBER AND COMMITTEE TURNOVER AND LENGTH OF UNDIVIDED PARTISAN CONTROL OF GOVERNMENT FOR THREE REALIGNMENTS

Eras	% Member Turnover	% Turnover on Ways and Means	Years of Undivided Party Control
Pre Civil War	49.6	38.5	2 years since 1840
Realignment	56.4	67.9	14 years (1860–1874)
Pre-1890s	38.7	26.5	2 years since 1876
Realignment	43.4	76.5	14 years (1896–1910)
Pre-New Deal	19.5	15.0	10 years since 1912
Realignment	27.8	80.0	14 years (1932–1946)

Table 3

PERCENTAGE OF PARTY VOTES IN PRE-REALIGNMENT AND REALIGNMENT ERAS

Era	50 vs. 50		90 vs. 90	
	Pre-Realignment	Realignment	Pre-Realignment	Realignment
Civil War	66.4	74.7	8.9	20.9
1890s	53.8	75.4	21.1	50.1
New Deal	48.7	69.4	7.9	16.4

tislavery, and during the 1890s realignment more pro-gold. In the 1930s realignment, the Democrats became more pro–social welfare. In short, during each realignment, party affiliation predicted the voting structure in the House, especially on the realignment issues.

During each of these realignments, clusters of major policy changes occurred. The Civil War realignment ultimately resulted in the end of slavery, the passage of the Thirteenth, Fourteenth, and Fifteenth amendments, and an increased governmental role in modernizing the economy. The 1890s realignment resulted in noninflationary money policies, protective tariffs, the annexation of Hawaii, and the Spanish-American War. In short, the 1896 realignment assured America's industrial future. The New Deal introduced the welfare state to Amer-

ica: Social Security, unemployment assistance, pro-labor legislation, agricultural assistance, and government management of the economy are but a few of its legacies. In sum, in each of these realignments, election results were transformed into major public policy changes. Elections did matter.

As we have seen, electoral realignments at the congressional level are determined more by national issues than by local factors. The electoral turnover generated by the realigning elections results in a congressional majority party that behaves in a partisan fashion to achieve major policy changes. Electoral turnover generated by the realignment results in an American form of party government. The reduction of pressuring by constituents and party across issues and the sense of mandate from

Table 4

CORRELATION (R) BETWEEN PARTY VOTING AND THE CROSS-CUTTING ISSUE IN THREE REALIGNMENT ERAS

Civil War
Issue: Slavery/Secession/Civil Rights

Year	1853	1855	1857	1859	1861	
Congress	33d	34th	35th	36th	37th	
r	.551	.41	.89	.87	.88	

1890s
Issue: Currency

Year	1891	1893	1895	1897	1899	
Congress	52d	53rd	54th	55th	56th	
r	.02	.42	.71	.96	.96	

New Deal
Issue: Social Welfare

Year	1925	1927	1929	1931	1933	1935
Congress	69th	70th	71st	72d	73rd	74th
r	0	0	0	.72	.89	.94

CONSTRAINTS ON POLICY-MAKING

the results creates a new majority party capable of legislating major shifts in American public policy.

CONCLUSION

It should be mentioned that in the post–World War II period, the likelihood of critical elections again occurring has significantly decreased in the United States. Since 1946, the number of safe congressional seats has risen dramatically and, conversely, the number of seats for which the parties complete has dropped sharply. Moreover, since 1946 the safety of House seats has become personalized; that is, a good share of an incumbent representative's vote totals is based on his or her own appeal to voters, not on his or her party. As long as the personal vote for incumbents is the dominant factor in House elections, presidents will not have coattails and House members will owe little to either the president or to their party.

Given these conditions—divided governments, members owing little to presidents and parties—there is little chance that the realigning conditions necessary for major policy change will occur. Thus, the primary mechanism able to bring about change in and out of legislatures has become severely constrained. As a result, the predominance of localism and policy incrementalism as Congress's normal condition seems assured.

BIBLIOGRAPHY

Constitutional and Political Constraints
Extended discussion of constitutional and political constraints on policy-making can be found in DAVID W. BRADY, *Critical Elections and Congressional Policy Making* (Stanford, Calif., 1988) and WILLIAM H. RIKER, *Liberalism Against Populism: A Confrontation Between the Theory of Democracy and the Theory of Social Choice* (San Francisco, 1988).

Committee Structure
On how committee structure affects policy development, see JOHN FEREJOHN, *Pork Barrel Politics: Rivers and Harbors Legislation, 1947–1968* (Stanford, Calif., 1974); KENNETH SHEPSLE, *The Giant Jigsaw Puzzle: Democratic Committee Assignments in the Modern House* (Chicago, 1978); CHARLES O. JONES, "Representation in Congress: The Case of the House Agricultural Committee," *American Political Science Review* 55 (June 1961): pp. 358–367; and RICHARD F. FENNO, *Congressmen in Committees* (Boston, 1973).

Realignment
The realignment process is discussed in JEROME M. CLUBB, WILLIAM H. FLANIGAN, and NANCY H. ZINGALE, *Partisan Realignment: Voters, Parties, and Government in American History* (Beverly Hills, Calif., 1980). The nationalizing of party appeals is discussed in BENJAMIN GINSBERG, "Critical Elections and the Substance of Party Conflict, 1844–1968," *Midwest Journal of Political Science,* 16 (1972): 603–625. On congressional elections, see GARY C. JACOBSON, *The Politics of Congressional Elections* (Boston, 1983) and BARBARA SINCLAIR, *Congressional Realignment, 1925–1978* (Austin, Tex., 1982). The impact of realignment on policy-making is the theme of DAVID BRADY and JOSEPH STEWART, JR., "Congressional Party Realignment and the Transformation of Public Policy in Three Realignment Eras," *American Journal of Political Science* 26 (May 1982): 333–360.

SEE ALSO Agenda Setting, Actors, and Alignments in Congressional Committees; Congress, Sectionalism, and Public-Policy Formation Since 1870; The Congressional Committee System; Electoral Realignments; AND The Role of Congressional Parties.

PARTIES, ELECTIONS, MOODS, AND LAWMAKING SURGES

David R. Mayhew

Four times since the 1790s, lawmaking in the American national government has followed a striking surge pattern. In each case, unusually large numbers of major laws kept getting enacted year after year, Congress after Congress, for half a decade or more. These spans of activity had beginnings and ends (although the boundaries are not crystal-clear); it is as if the system's "volume" could somehow be turned up, stay high for a while, and then be lowered again.

As it happens, there were also similarities in each era's legislative content, with a notable thrust toward enhancing the powers, activities, or reach of the national state. Approaches to these ends included increased public spending and taxation, new federal programs, direct coercion, government planning, regulation of the economy, and restructuring of the polity or society through such means as guaranteed citizen rights.

Not all the enactments of these eras worked. Many had unanticipated negative consequences or simply fizzled out—that is often the way with laws. But in each surge there was considerable policy impact nonetheless, even if it did not live up to the extraordinary level of legislative ambition of the times.

The subject of this essay is the four "legislative surges" in U.S. history. The first section characterizes each era's statutory product—not law by law, but in enough detail to demonstrate the existence of "surges." Actual statutes are emphasized, not catchphrases such as "the New Deal" or various statistics that are often taken to be indicators of legislative action. The second section speculates about what might have caused or correlated with such surges, by considering the roles of parties, elections, the economy, and public moods.

LEGISLATIVE SURGES IN HISTORY

The four eras of legislative surges—the Civil War and Reconstruction era, the Progressive Era, the New Deal era, and the 1960s and 1970s—are discussed in chronological order below.

The Civil War and the Reconstruction Era: 1861 Through 1875

Drives against slavery and for civil rights were this era's obvious focuses, but according to many interpretations, powerful impulses were also aimed at building a centralized national state and nourishing corporate capitalism. The laws of the time reflect these multiple or compound aims.

Occurring early in a sequence of unprecedently ambitious lawmaking that stretched through eight Congresses were moves enacting an updated version, more or less, of the previous Whig blueprint for an "American system." In early 1861, once the South had seceded, a lame-duck Congress passed the Morrill Tariff Act. That began a Republican high-tariff regime that lasted, with interruptions during the Democratic Cleveland and Wilson administrations, until the 1930s. In 1862 came the Homestead Act (offering federal land to homesteaders for a nominal fee), the Morrill Land-Grant College Act (giving federal land to construct colleges), and the Pacific Railroad Act (giving land subsidies to build a transcontinental railroad). Financing the war required banking measures that had a Whiggish motif of central control: the Legal Tender Act of 1862 (fostering a national currency) and the National Banking Act of 1863 (creating a national, though short of tightly centralized, banking system).

Once the Civil War was under way, Congress passed some antislavery measures that had had no chance until then—for example, bans on that practice in the territories and the District of Columbia. But in 1863, Lincoln preempted the legislative process with his Emancipation Proclamation. Lawmaking gained the initiative in 1865. Early that year, Congress approved the Thirteenth Amendment outlawing slavery and established the Freedmen's Bureau to serve the liberated black population of the South. Under President Andrew Johnson, the Thirty-ninth Congress enacted the Civil Rights Act of 1866 (which prefigured the content of the Fourteenth Amendment), approved that amendment later in the same year, and passed the First Reconstruction Act over a presidential veto in March 1867. That act provided for military rule in the South and restructured southern state politics through enfranchisement of blacks and disfranchisement of many ex-rebel whites. Three more Reconstruction acts followed in 1867 and 1868, as well as the Fifteenth Amendment, guaranteeing black suffrage, in February 1869.

That amendment is sometimes taken to be the era's last signal measure. In fact, however, during the two ensuing Congresses, great energy, commitment, and public attention were devoted to enacting the five Enforcement acts of 1870 through 1872. These were implementation instruments, giving mandates to the Attorney General, that particularly tried to make the Fifteenth Amendment actually work in the South. The third of these acts is sometimes called, because it in effect outlawed that body, the Ku Klux Klan Act. By the mid-1870s these measures had failed, though some have been redeployed for use since World War II. The era's last measure of note was the Civil Rights Act of 1875, the late-career project of Senator Charles Sumner (R.-Mass.), which won enactment during the lame-duck session of the Republican Congress elected in 1872.

The Progressive Era: 1906 Through 1916

Efforts to regulate the economy, polity, and society keynoted lawmaking drives during the Progressive Era. That much is generally agreed upon, despite scholarly disagreement about the aims of the era. Railroad regulation figured prominently during the era's early years; labor measures, during the later ones; and the regulation of parties and elections, throughout. Government institutions and programs were initiated and funded. To determine the period's beginning and end dates, it helps to take account of events at the state level, where much of the notable reform action occurred. The years 1905 through 1914 are often cited as the approximate time of accelerated state lawmaking. Progressive programs were continually being enacted somewhere during those years, notably in Wisconsin in 1903 (an early outlier) and 1905; Minnesota in 1905 and 1907; New York in 1907; Georgia in 1907–1909; California, New Jersey, and North Dakota in 1911; Massachusetts in 1911–1914; New York again in 1913; and Ohio in 1913–1914.

At the national level, President Theodore Roosevelt made the era's dramatic opening move by winning congressional approval of the Hepburn Act of 1906. A plan to regulate railroad rates, that measure, according to Jeffrey K. Tulis's assessment, gave birth to the modern administrative state. Its passage required an eighteen-month campaign of mobilizing public opinion and maneuvering on Capitol Hill. Also enacted in 1906 were the Pure Food and Drug Act and the Meat Inspection Act. Roosevelt's last Congress of 1907–1909, which did little legislating, is a gap in the sequence. That may be because the White House supplied the national legislative agenda during these early Progressive years, and because presidents rarely are successful in getting domestic programs through Congress after six years in office (these were Roosevelt's seventh and eighth years).

Lawmaking came alive again in 1909 under President William Howard Taft. Prodded by Democrats and by Republican insurgents, the Republican Congress of 1909–1911 passed the Mann-Elkins Act (another notable attempt at railroad regulation), created a postal-savings system (an idea that had brewed for four decades), and approved the Sixteenth Amendment authorizing a federal income tax. The Congress of 1911–1913, split between a Republican Senate and a Democratic House, approved the Seventeenth Amendment requiring direct election of U.S. senators, voted an eight-hour day for workers on federal contracts, established a federal Children's Bureau and the Department of

Labor, and enacted the third and most ambitious of a 1907, 1910, and 1911 sequence of campaign-finance reforms. These reforms banned corporate contributions in federal elections, required disclosure of monetary transactions by congressional candidates, and placed a ceiling on candidate spending. The inspiration for these measures was rather like that behind enactments later in the 1970s, although the Progressive Era instruments, by comparison, lacked teeth of enforcement.

Woodrow Wilson's first Congress of 1913–1915 produced the Underwood Tariff Act (which lowered duties and initiated, following the ratification of the Sixteenth Amendment, the general income tax that has been with us ever since), the Federal Reserve Act, the Clayton Antitrust Act, a measure establishing the Federal Trade Commission (FTC), and the La Follette Seaman's Act (regulating maritime working conditions). A second drive under Wilson in 1916 generated the Federal Farm Loan Act, workers' compensation for federal employees, a ban on interstate sale of goods produced by child labor (later struck down by the Supreme Court), the Adamson Act mandating an eight-hour day for railroad workers, and the Revenue Act of 1916, which transformed the income tax into the federal government's chief revenue instrument. That year's was the last energetic program of the era. Some congressional moves came later—the Eighteenth Amendment (Prohibition of alcohol) in 1917 and the Nineteenth Amendment (woman suffrage) in 1919. But in general, the Progressive lawmaking impulse faded away during World War I.

The New Deal Era: 1932 Through 1938

If approached as a sequence of lawmaking aimed at either recovery or reform, the New Deal era can be said to have spanned four consecutive Congresses, of which the two during Franklin Roosevelt's first term unquestionably stand out. The celebrated "first hundred days" of 1933 produced the quasi-corporatist National Industry Recovery Act, the Agricultural Adjustment Act (which inaugurated the modern regime of crop subsidies), the Emergency Banking Act, the Federal Emergency Relief Act, the Home Owners' Loan Act, the Securities Act, and measures creating the Civilian

Conservation Corps (CCC), the Federal Deposit Insurance Corporation (FIDC), and the Tennessee Valley Authority (TVA). The 1934 session brought the Reciprocal Trade Agreements Act (which lowered tariff rates but arguably improved the government's planning capacity), the Taylor Grazing Act, the Indian Reorganization Act, and measures setting up the Securities and Exchange Commission (SEC), the Federal Communications Commission (FCC), and the Federal Housing Administration (FHA).

The strenuous "second hundred days" of 1935 featured the Social Security Act (setting up that social-insurance system), the National Labor Relations Act (establishing federal regulation of collective bargaining), the Public Utilities Holding Company Act, the Wealth Tax Act, the Banking Act of 1935 (centralizing monetary authority), and the Guffey-Snyder Coal Act (regulating that industry). The Emergency Relief Appropriation Act of 1935 served as a charter for the Works Progress Administration (WPA), the relief agency administered by Harry Hopkins. Measures during the 1936 session included the Soil Conservation and Domestic Allotment Act and an act authorizing the Rural Electrification Administration (REA) as an independent agency.

The Congress of 1937–1938 greatly disappointed New Dealers, considering its immense Democratic majorities (Republican seats fell to record lows of seventeen in the Senate and eighty-nine in the House). Many initiatives foundered, including Roosevelt's plans to pack the Supreme Court with additional justices sympathetic to his domestic agenda and to reorganize the executive branch. But at least five notable measures passed. These were the Wagner-Steagall Housing Act (a commitment to low-income public housing), the Farm Tenancy Act (a commitment to sharecroppers and tenant farmers that was never fulfilled), the Fair Labor Standards Act (the first federal minimum-wage law), the Agricultural Adjustment Act of 1938 (an important move consolidating farm legislation enacted earlier during the New Deal), and an expensive antirecession pump-priming measure in 1938 that set a Keynesian precedent. These enactments closed out the era. New Deal reform ideas kept germinating during Roosevelt's remaining years, but few got very far on Capitol Hill.

But it remains to discuss the start of the era, which occurred in 1932 (although that choice of date is unconventional) at a time when Herbert Hoover faced a Republican Senate and a Democratic House. The extension of the period backward to the Hoover administration can be explained by focusing on ambitious laws that were passed during the depression of the 1930s, rather than by, as is customary, what Roosevelt asked for and received starting in March 1933. Five measures passed in 1932 deserve mention. Hoover's Reconstruction Finance Corporation (RFC), authorized that year, became the first of the Depression-era's "alphabet agencies." The Glass-Steagall Act allowed a more expansionary monetary policy. The Emergency Relief and Construction Act committed the government for the first time to public-works and relief spending designed to counteract the effects of the economy's contraction. The Norris–La Guardia Act, one of the century's key measures regulating labor-management relations, outlawed yellow-dog contracts (that is, contracts prohibiting employees from joining unions) and curbed the use of antiunion injunctions by courts. Finally, the Revenue Act of 1932, which raised taxes substantially and made their incidence more progressive by way of corporate, estate, and high-bracket-income levies, came to serve as the federal government's basic revenue instrument of the 1930s. It took a Capitol Hill coalitional reshuffle during the spring of 1932 for that tax measure to pass: rank-and-file Democrats and progressive Republicans revolted against the leaderships of both parties to defeat a proposed national sales tax. As a generator of recovery and reform measures, as those causes were understood then, the Congress of 1931–1933 arguably ranks with that of 1937–1938 discussed above. (Note that Congress traditionally held lame-duck postelection sessions—as in early 1933—until the Twentieth Amendment abolished them starting in 1935.)

The Johnson/Nixon/Ford Era: 1963 Through 1975–1976

Whether one looks at gross indicators of congressional work load or at particular statutes enacted during the time, the early or mid-1960s through the mid-1970s stands out as the period of the most exceptional legislative productivity since World War II. The Great Society's burst of lawmaking under President Lyndon Johnson is well-known. Hardly less striking in retrospect—although Vietnam, Nixon's "social issues," and Watergate overshadowed it at the time—is the record of enactments under Presidents Richard Nixon and Gerald Ford. The ideological direction was largely the same under all three administrations. In general, the entire era amounted to one long successful drive to enact a liberal agenda of new federal programs, increased spending, and increased regulation of society and the economy.

The boundary dates are not clear-cut. President John F. Kennedy had won some legislative victories earlier in 1961–1963, but in general his New Frontier domestic program stalled; hence, 1963 is chosen as the era's opening date. Soon after Kennedy's assassination later that year, legislative output ratcheted upward. Within a year, the results included the controversial Keynes-inspired tax cut that Kennedy had requested but not received, the Economic Opportunity Act (Johnson's ambitious antipoverty program), and the Civil Rights Act of 1964 (the most far-reaching such measure since the 1870s), as well as, for example, the Higher Education Facilities Act of 1963, the Wilderness Act of 1964, and the Food Stamp Act of 1964. Following the 1964 election, the hyperactive congressional session of 1965 produced the Elementary and Secondary Education Act (the first broad-based federal funding of local schools), Medicare, and the Voting Rights Act, as well as many other measures aimed at, for example, highway beautification, Appalachian development, higher education, and subsidized housing.

There customary historical accounts often end or become cloudy. But in fact, these moves were just the beginning. In social-welfare spending, for example, the country's striking postwar surge in actual outlays started in 1965 and lasted through 1976, peaking under Ford. Contributing to that surge were many statutes enacted during the Johnson years (including major housing acts in 1966 and 1968), but also many passed after 1968 under Nixon and Ford. These include the Food Stamp Act of 1970 (greatly increasing that program's funding); Supplementary Security Income in 1972 (establishing a federal income floor for the aged, blind, and disabled); the Comprehensive Employment and Training Act of 1973 (creating CETA jobs); expansions of unemployment insurance in 1970 and 1976; the Housing and Community Development Act of 1974 (inaugurating housing block grants); the Higher Education Act of 1972 (creating Pell grants for lower-income students); and Social Security hikes in 1969, 1971, and 1972 that raised benefits 23 percent, controlling for inflation. According to Robert X. Browning's count, 77 new social programs were started under Johnson, but also 44 under Nixon and Ford. Other spending during Nixon's time included much-increased funding authorizations for mass transit and water-pollution control.

On the regulatory front, most of the era's initiatives occurred after Johnson left the presidency. The "new social regulation" of American industry, according to David Vogel, came about during roughly 1964 through 1977; the peak reform years were 1969 through 1974. Two new federal regulatory agencies came into existence under Johnson plus seven under Nixon and Ford. In the area of consumer protection, enactments began with the Traffic Safety Act of 1966 (inspired by consumer advocate Ralph Nader) and the Fair Packaging and Labeling Act of 1966 and continued with, for example, the Truth-in-Lending Act of 1968, the Consumer Product Safety Act of 1972, and the Magnuson-Moss Act of 1974 (empowering the Federal Trade Commission to set industry-wide rules barring unfair practices). Key environmental measures included the National Environmental Policy Act (NEPA) of 1969 calling for the preparation of "environmental-impact statements" to precede federal construction projects, the Clean Air Act of 1970, and the Water Pollution Control Act of 1972. Workplace conditions were addressed in the Coal Mine Health and Safety Act of 1969 and the cross-industry Occupational Safety and Health Act (OSHA) of 1970. Private pensions came under strict regulation for the first time in the Employee Retirement Income Security Act (ERISA) of 1974.

Otherwise, federal regulation of state and local governments set new records under Nixon and Ford—as through, for example, statutory requirements for nondiscrimination in public employment and clear air and water, and the National Health Planning and Resources Development Act of 1974, which prodded the government into new planning tasks. Confronted by economic troubles in the early 1970s, Congress reached for planning, not market, remedies. Instances are the Economic Stabilization Act of 1970, which authorized wage and price controls that Nixon later used, and the Emergency Petroleum Allocation Act of 1973, which called for distribution of petroleum products by government formula. The financing of political campaigns received strict, comprehensive regulation for the first time through the Federal Election Campaign Act of 1974. Westerners who launched the "sagebrush rebellion" of the late 1970s—an angry response to federal moves impinging on the economies of the western states—were reacting to, among other things, two ambitious land-planning measures enacted under Ford—the National Forest Management Act (NFMA) of 1976 and the Federal Land Policy Management Act (FLPMA) of 1976. In the area of rights, the civil rights instruments of 1964 and 1965 were followed by the important Open Housing Act of 1968 and, among other items, an unprecedented set of women's-rights measures during the period 1971–1972 that included the Equal Rights Amendment (ERA)—though not enough states would ratify it for its inclusion in the Constitution—and provisions of the Equal Employment Opportunity Act of 1972.

That summarizes the era's lawmaking drive. The end of the surge did not come abruptly. A 1977 act regulating strip mining, for example, continued the impulse. But, in general, further plans for spending and regulation fared badly under Carter in 1977–1980. Proposals for national health insurance and a consumer protection agency, for example, came to nothing despite sizable Democratic majorities in the House and Senate. Legislative production in general, particularly of major laws, fell off. The content shifted; deregulation of industry became a prominent theme. The program-building dynamism of the 1960s and early 1970s was gone.

ANALYSIS OF THE LAWMAKING SURGES

That completes the presentation of the four "legislative surges." Obviously, they do not exhaust U.S. legislative history. Virtually any Congress enacts at least some notable laws. Smaller, briefer bursts of lawmaking have occurred that one can categorize as expanding the reach of the national state. That was true of Alexander Hamilton's program as Secretary of the Treasury in 1789–1791. Some historians point to the Republican "billion-dollar Congress" (1889–1891) under President Benjamin Harrison, which passed the Sherman Antitrust Act (to curb corporate monopolies), the Sherman Silver Purchase Act (giving silver a status as backing for currency), the McKinley Tariff Act (raising duties), the Naval Act of 1890 (inaugurating the modern navy), and the Dependent Pension Act of 1890 (greatly expanding the Civil War pension system). Government size and scope also mushroomed by way of war-mobilization enactments under Wilson between 1917 and 1918 and Roosevelt between 1942 and 1945.

Furthermore, not all important legislation aims to expand the reach of the national state. Sometimes disengagement of the state from the society or economy requires major legislative action. That was true of Reagan's tax and domestic expenditure cuts in 1981; Jefferson's measures to cut taxes, defense, and the national debt after 1800; and Jackson's veto of the bill rechartering the Bank of the United States in 1832. (The latter may be the leading instance of a major policy change—not just preserving the status quo—that derived from using the legislative process to block a bill rather than to pass one.)

Still, the four legislative surges of 1861 through 1875, 1906 through 1916, 1932 through 1938, and 1963 through 1975–1976 stand out for their ambition, length, and volume of major enactments. And it is probably no coincidence that all four featured drives to expand the reach of the national state. That, after all, is a kind of enterprise that is likely to require a great deal of strenuous legislative action.

CAUSES OF LEGISLATIVE SURGES

What can be said about the causes—or at least correlates—of legislative surges such as the ones described above? There does not exist any one clinching answer. It is therefore probably best to consider that question under a number of rubrics, as below.

Political Parties

To what degree can the enactments of any legislative surge be attributed to one political party that seizes and monopolizes the legislative initiative and thereby shapes an era? If party government always functioned unambiguously in the United States, the answer would be obvious: such surges would always be entirely traceable to one party. But the reality is more complicated and varied.

Without much doubt, the leading exhibit of a surge driven by one party was that between 1861 and 1875. To be sure, significant disagreement occurred within the ruling Republican party's ranks. Also, because the South abandoned Capitol Hill in 1861, what happened afterward has the flavor of a Northern, not just a Republican party, surge. The absence of the Southerners permitted not only the antislavery achievements, but also the tariff and transcontinental-railroad acts, for example. Still, the Republicans carried the laws. Of the era's enactments itemized above, every one bore a clear Republican stamp.

Much more complex was the record of the Progressive Era. The parties had lawmaking roles, but those varied over time and were sometimes complex. Through 1908, a reform-oriented executive branch of the Republican party provided most of the period's programmatic initiative. Instances are Theodore Roosevelt as president and Governors Robert La Follette, Sr., in Wisconsin and Charles Evans Hughes in New York. But the chief opposition came from that same Republican party's conservative ranks in the legislatures. Between 1909 and 1912, notable reforms were typically ushered through by cross-party coalitions of Democrats and Progressive Republicans. That phenomenon happened in Congress as well as, for example, in Massachusetts, New Jersey, and North Dakota. After 1912, the Democrats took over as the successful proposers and carriers of legislative programs—in the national capital under Wilson, but also in such states as New York and Ohio.

The Democratic party obviously engineered the New Deal, which consisted largely of enactments initiated by Franklin Roosevelt or allied Democrats—Senator Robert F. Wagner, for example, in the cases of the National Labor Relations Act of 1935 and the public housing measure of 1937—and passed by Democratic Congresses. Still, although the Democrats earned a reputation as the era's prime movers, the reality at the actual lawmaking level was a bit more muddled. In fact, the 1930 election and the Depression revived the cross-party coalition of Democrats and progressive Republicans that had operated under Taft and Wilson. That coalition carried, for example, the Revenue Act of 1932. Progressive Republicans (or former Republicans) took the lead on some measures that year and also afterward. An example is Senator George Norris's role in both passing the Norris–La Guardia Act of 1932 (La Guardia was also an insurgent Republican) and creating the Tennessee Valley Authority in 1933. The role of progressive Republicans became less significant as the decade went on, but it is important to realize that after 1934, Roosevelt's policy initiatives increasingly divided his own party. By the 1937–1938 period, Capitol Hill Democrats provided the president's chief Washington, D.C., opposition as well as his chief support. The opposing faction included more than just southerners: its leader in the struggle against court-packing was, for example, Senator Burton Wheeler of Montana who had excellent progressive credentials. This was a strange kind of "party government."

The Democratic party carried Johnson's Great Society in the 1964–1966 period. The civil rights measures were an exception of a sort: the roll-call pattern for them was North against South, not Democrats against Republicans. Still, in general, the Great Society unquestionably offers one of U.S. history's best instances of party-based lawmaking. As the era's lawmaking thrust continued beyond 1968, the simplicity of party rule gave way. In general, the legislative initiative stayed with the Democrats—but now with that party's congressional branch. Thus, passage of the National Environmental Policy Act of 1969 owed largely to Senator Henry Jackson (D.-Wash.), the Clean Air Act of 1970 to Senator Edmund Muskie (D.-Maine) and the 20-percent Social Security hike of 1972 to Representative Wilbur Mills (D.-Ark.). One Democratic legislative

drive after another succeeded. But the Nixon administration played a part in the surge too. Many spending and regulatory measures owed to the White House's inspiration—for instance, the great expansion of food stamps—or, at least, its collaboration or acquiescence. Ostensibly at each other's throats, Nixon and congressional Democrats shared a surprising joint responsibility for the era's legislative product.

The clearest case, then, for a one-party lawmaking model is that of 1861–1875. The New Deal, on balance, is a fine case. In the 1960s and 1970s, the record is clear under Johnson but muddled under Nixon. In the Progressive Era, even though one party or the other animated many legislative enterprises, the overall pattern is exceptionally muddled.

To take a slightly different approach to the question about parties, to what extent have legislative surges come about during times of unified party control—that is, when one party formally controlled the Senate, House, and presidency? This is worth asking, since it is conventional wisdom in political science that major lawmaking requires such unified control. Otherwise, it has been believed, "deadlock" or "stalemate" between parties will set in.

The surge of 1861–1875 presents an almost pure case. Republicans had control of all three elective federal branches during that time, and they used it to pass the laws. (The "almost" derives from taking account of President Andrew Johnson, who had a shaky commitment to the Republican party and whose vetoes had to be overridden in 1865–1869 for the party's program to prevail.) Also, the 1861–1875 period was preceded and followed by times of divided party control, and during those earlier and later years, major enactments were sparser and some important initiatives did indeed lose out to party conflict.

The New Deal era also presents an almost pure case for a unified-party-control model. Formally unified control by the Democrats underpinned all the legislative action beginning with the "first hundred days" in 1933. The "almost" here owes to the record in 1932, which featured the era's initial burst of lawmaking under Hoover, who blocked some important initiatives but championed or at least signed others.

The 1960s and 1970s present a split case. Unified Democratic control underpinned Johnson's Great Society and prevailed until the 1968 election. But major initiatives kept on passing under Nixon and even Ford, despite the switch in 1968 to divided control (the Democrats kept winning majorities of the House and Senate).

Once again, the Progressive Era presents disorder. Some major legislative programs were enacted by way of unified-control party government. That was famously true of Woodrow Wilson's presidential program in 1913–1916: as party leader, he operated through Democratic party caucuses on Capitol Hill. At the state level, Democrats in control of governorships and legislatures put through ambitious programs during those same years in, for example, New York and Ohio. Theodore Roosevelt won support for his program from a Republican Congress in 1905–1906 (though in fact he needed some Democratic help), as did Governor Hughes from a Republican legislature in New York in 1907. Wisconsin had a formally all-Republican government when Governor La Follette's program was enacted in 1903 and 1905, as did California when Governor Hiram Johnson's program passed in 1911. But here we are descending into part-truths. The chief opposition to reform in those states, vanquished through defeats in nominating processes, also came from Republicans. And many notable programmatic successes at the state level—including those mentioned above in North Dakota, Minnesota, Massachusetts, and New Jersey (with Woodrow Wilson as governor)—took place in circumstances of formally divided party control. Nationally, that was also the background under Taft in 1911–1913, when lawmaking proceeded at a rather fast pace anyway. During the Progressive Era, major legislative programs were carried out in an impressive variety of formal party circumstances.

Are parties, then, the engenderers of legislative surges? The reality is obviously mixed and complicated. For the 1861–1875 and New Deal eras, it seems safe enough to answer affirmatively. For the opposite extreme, the Progressive Era, one has the sense that hyperlawmaking would have somehow come about anyway—that the parties' roles, though evident, were derivative of a greater phenomenon. In the 1960s and 1970s, the Democratic party sup-

plied most of the legislative dynamism, though there remains the ample role of the Nixon administration and the fact of divided party control after 1968. There is no clear trend between the 1860s and the 1970s: the New Deal, for example, ranks higher for single-party achievement than does the Progressive Era. Still, the particulars of the four surges are compatible, at least, with the idea that parties were more central to government functioning in the nineteenth century than they have become in the twentieth. Perhaps they were. Beyond that, although the evidence is slim, it seems plausible that conditions that might detach hyperlawmaking from single-party control have become particularly prominent since World War II. It is during these recent decades that electoral politics has taken a turn toward candidate-specific (as opposed to party) appeals, and that both Congress and the presidency have adopted legislative routines that in a sense transcend parties. These include the annual presentation of "the president's program," and Congress's staff-rich, committee-based legislative mills that grind on year after year regardless of all else. Ambitious cross-party lawmaking of the sort witnessed under Nixon may yet come to seem normal.

Another question might be asked about parties. Does congressional party voting, as political scientists define the concept, rise during times of legislative surges? Is that kind of party-versus-party square-off needed to carry major laws? A party-voting score, for the House or Senate during any one Congress, reflects the proportion of roll calls on which a majority of Democrats opposed a majority of Republicans. (In principle, the measure may vary from zero, for a Congress when no roll calls exhibit such a party-versus-party alignment, to 100, for a Congress when all roll calls show most Democrats voting against most Republicans.) The overall answer is close to a flat no. For the House, for example, between 1861 and 1984, the mean party-voting score for Congresses during legislative surges was 60; that for other Congresses was 57. There is a long-term decline in the statistic, of course, that makes simple averaging dubious. The best pieces of evidence for a positive relation are that 1861–1875 scored about four points higher, on average, than 1875–1891 (perhaps a fair choice of years to compare); and that 1931–1938 scored about nine points higher than the preceding Republican decade (1921–1930). Those results accommodate a view associating high party voting with surges, at least modestly. But party voting was unremarkable during the Progressive Era, and it bottomed out during Nixon's years, reaching an all-time low score of 29 in 1969–1970. What we may be seeing here is that party voting rises slightly during legislative surges that heavily implicate one party as the progenitor of laws, but that it will not rise—it may fall—during other surges. That would not be surprising. The general relation, therefore, is weak or even nonexistent. Confronted by just a time series on congressional party voting in either chamber from 1861 to the present, one would have great difficulty guessing when or if legislative surges took place.

Elections

Can legislative surges be traced to election outcomes? That query raises, for one thing, the issue of electoral realignments—the major shakeups in U.S. voting patterns that are said to have occurred roughly in 1800, 1828, 1860, 1896, and 1932. These are seen as boundary points between successive party systems. Such realignments certainly helped to bring on the lawmaking surges of 1861–1875 and 1932–1938. It is difficult to imagine the former without the Republicans' rise to power in 1854–1860 or the latter without the Democrats' great congressional gains in 1930 and 1932 combined with Roosevelt's landslide victory in 1932. The analogy between the 1960s and the 1930s is perhaps the most attractive feature of realignment theory.

But beyond those two supporting examples, electoral realignments fail badly as an explanation of "legislative surges." Consider U.S. history since the 1870s. The surges of the Progressive Era and the 1960s–1970s did not owe to any electoral shakeups that appear in the realignment canon listed above. And the realignment of 1896—historic though that may have been for its reordering of popular voting patterns, its staving off of William Jennings Bryan's Populist-flavored candidacy, and its elevation of a new ruling Republican coalition—did not set off any legislative surge. Perhaps it is surprising that the Republicans, who enjoyed solid congressional majorities under McKinley,

did not repeat their lawmaking dynamism of a decade earlier under Benjamin Harrison. But they did not; they chalked up, at best, an ordinary legislative record in 1897–1901. Evidently the leading enactments were the Gold Standard Act of 1900, which confirmed the gold standard that Grover Cleveland's Democratic administration had so tenaciously protected during 1893–1897, and the Dingley Tariff Act of 1897, which, after Cleveland's reductions, returned rates to Republican levels (higher ones for dutiable imports, but lower ones for all imports, than in the party's previous instrument of 1890). So far as the parties were concerned, the 1896 election was realigning; but from the standpoint of the U.S. politico-economic system it was merely maintaining. No doubt that goes far to explain the quiet legislative period that followed.

But a less ambitious question can be asked about elections. Are there particular ones—besides the realigning ones already mentioned—that have seemed to help authorize or deauthorize legislative surges? There are obvious candidates for those roles. On the authorizing side, the post–Civil War 1866 midterm election is sometimes seen as a particularly important showdown victory for pro-Reconstruction forces. The 1910 election produced not only a generally pro-Progressive Democratic tide, but also a decisive defeat for the Republicans' conservative wing in state and district primaries. Wilson and the Democrats claimed a mandate after the 1912 election. More recently, the 1964 election greatly helped the Great Society cause by generating a rare two-to-one Democratic edge in the House; the energetic legislative session of 1965 followed.

On the deauthorizing side, the Republicans' disastrous defeat in the 1874 midterm election is certainly part of the reason why Reconstruction lawmaking ended. And the 1918 and 1938 midterms, both bringing Democratic losses, are often associated with the flagging reform impulses of Progressivism and the New Deal, although that argument should not be carried too far, in that World War I is more often cited as the extinguisher of national Progressivism. And the sagging of the New Deal was already abundantly evident in 1937–1938, before the 1938 election.

Particular elections help explain the level of lawmaking, but they do not illuminate everything. There remains the national inauguration of Progressivism by Theodore Roosevelt in 1905–1906, which is not ordinarily ascribed to an electoral mandate, although it is possible that the unprecedented presidential landslide of 1904 has been underinterpreted. Likewise, the downswing in government activism under Carter does not seem to have derived from any deauthorizing election (although the 1980 election may be said to have ratified it).

Of course, the subject of electoral relations is not exhausted by pointing to particular elections and their alleged verdicts. Alert incumbent parties or politicians can accommodate major changes in public opinion by changing along with it. Government policy reversals can thus occur without the prod of any party's election gains or losses—though those often help. In 1977–1978, for example, incumbent Senate and House members seem to have responded to a perceived swell of public opinion against government spending and regulation. Many simply changed their positions: in 1975, Republican Representative John B. Anderson of Illinois had supported the controversial proposal to create a consumer-protection agency; in 1977, in response to new constituency grumbling, he turned against it. During those same years, Senator Edward Kennedy (D.-Mass.) embraced deregulation of industry as a new personal cause. Broad policy change can come about that way too.

The Economy

There are at least two ways in which the state of the economy might be hypothesized to underpin legislative surges. In a static model, basic underlying conditions might have distinctive effects. Thus it is sometimes argued that the lawmaking surge under Johnson and Nixon needed a booming economy as a base. That provided the necessary slack for spending commitments and regulatory experiments. Take away the growth rate, bring on budgetary pressure, and the lawmaking would sag as it did in the mid-1970s. A similar prosperity-based argument could be made about the Progressive Era. Unfortunately, the New Deal era presents an exactly opposite scenario: the uniquely bad economy of the 1930s accommodated both spending and regulatory drives. So much for

any single relation between prosperity and activist lawmaking.

Quick economic downturns offer another possibility for explaining surges. They might operate by triggering election upheavals, or, without that, by inciting public opinion which, in turn, impinges on elected officials. The depression of 1929 obviously spurred Democratic election gains and the legislative surge of the 1930s. Economic slumps seem to have helped close out at least two of the surge eras. The depression of 1873 was evidently a major cause of the Republicans' loss of Congress in 1874. The precipitous recession of 1937–1938 seems to have helped turn public opinion against further New Deal experiments; that, in turn, weighed heavily against lawmaking even before the 1938 election.

Yet not all economic downturns have any such lawmaking effects, and even when they do, there is no one determinate policy direction in which they push. Note that economic downturns helped to begin but also end the New Deal: that of 1929 spurred governmental activism, while that of 1937–1938 had the opposite effect. What seems to happen is that a serious economic downturn can delegitimize any governing party along with its economic policies, while the opposition starts to look appealing regardless of its agenda.

Moods and Movements

Another approach to explaining the causes of lawmaking surges emphasizes public moods. Arthur M. Schlesinger, Jr., has argued that the U.S. citizenry, now and then, gets caught up in moods of public purpose—a kind of secular revivalism. Large numbers of people throw themselves into public affairs for periods as long as a decade with the aim of reforming politics and society. Schlesinger cites the Progressive Era, the New Deal era, and the 1960s–1970s as the twentieth-century instances of such public moods, which obviously correspond with the century's three legislative surges.

Public moods are much more elusive than economic indicators or election results, but, in fact, historians or other witnesses have often pointed exactly to mood changes as the reasons why legislative surges began or ended. All four surges' endings have received that interpretation: in each case, after years of reform exertion, there occurred a rather swift onset of activism fatigue that brought lawmaking and other activities to a halt. In the mid-1870s, it is said, the North lost its faith that Reconstruction could work and hence its activist drive. Under Wilson, World War I is credited with draining away every last ounce of public purpose, for domestic as well as foreign causes; a mood change thus took place that had its own effects. A pronounced anti–New Deal mood shift is evident in 1937–1938; the economy's new plummet at that time joined with other events to sow pessimism about the New Deal enterprise in general. And the activism of the 1960s and 1970s is said to have lost out to a mood shift under Carter: the idea that society could be made over through government action gave way to pessimism, deregulation drives, and the low-taxism of California's Proposition 13.

As for the beginnings of legislative surges, analysts give prominence to a mood change in only the case of the Progressive Era, whose onset of lawmaking surges at both state and federal levels is conventionally credited to a mood shift toward reform activism occurring in 1905—or more broadly, 1904 through 1906. Journalistic muckraking starting in 1902 had paved the way for it. Neither an election result nor a turning point in the economy seems to have played any comparable role.

Much of the dynamism of public-purpose moods seems to be provided by what we ordinarily call political movements. The Progressive Era exhibited one long-term, all-embracing movement or else a set of more-discrete interlocking ones, depending on how it is viewed. In some instances, that era's lawmaking can be directly traced to movement activity—as with the women's movement and the creation of the Children's Bureau in 1912. The 1960s and 1970s presented a welter of interrelated movements—civil rights, consumer, antiwar, labor, student, women's liberation, environmental, and public-interest campaigns. Again, causal arrows to specific laws can be drawn. To cite some examples, the civil rights movement, through demonstrations in Birmingham and Selma, Alabama, helped to bring

about the Civil Rights Acts of 1964 and 1965; the consumer movement, the Fair Packaging and Labeling Act of 1966; the environmental movement, the air-and water-pollution measures of 1970 and 1972; the women's movement, Congress's approval of the ERA in 1972; and Common Cause, the Federal Election Campaign Act of 1974. In the case of the 1860s and 1870s, Eric Foner's interpretation of Reconstruction gives it a movement, activist cast that took shape as early as 1863. Interpretations that the New Deal era was movement-driven are least convincing, in that there does not seem to have been much of a movement underpinning for the lawmaking of the "first hundred days" in 1933. The depression emergency was enough of a spur. Still, rolling movement activity by Townsendites, share-the-wealth Longites, labor union organizers, and the Communist party provided a lively setting for the "second hundred days" of 1935. Some analysts credit that session's Social Security Act and National Labor Relations Act at least partly to the pressure of background movements.

These four accounts of legislative surges—addressing parties, elections, the economy, and moods and movements—obviously overlap. An economic downturn, for example, can motor an electoral upheaval or a mood shift, a mood shift may help along an electoral shift, and an election shift may be taken by contemporaries as evidence of a mood shift. Movement activism may nest inside a party and lend that party a degree of dynamism, as evidently occurred during Reconstruction. However, there does not exist any one neat set of causal or correlative relations that applies to all four legislative surges of the last century and a half. As shown, lawmaking through party government keynotes some eras but not others. Elections, whether realigning or not, illuminate some junctures but not others. Likewise, the economy speaks loudly at some times but is silent at others. Moods and movements seem to be the most reliable factor; they ordinarily come into play but, going by the elusive evidence, not always. With such ambiguity, therefore, there is no substitute for being sensitive to varying causal structures as one goes from one lawmaking era to another.

BIBLIOGRAPHY

Legislation

Lawmaking during the Civil War and the Reconstruction era is discussed in LEONARD P. CURRY, *Blueprint for Modern America: Nonmilitary Legislation of the First Civil War Congress* (Nashville, Tenn., 1968); ERIC FONER, *Reconstruction: America's Unfinished Revolution, 1863–1877* (New York, 1988); WILLIAM GILLETTE, *Retreat from Reconstruction, 1869–1879* (Baton Rouge, La., 1979); and J. G. RANDALL and DAVID DONALD, *The Civil War and Reconstruction* (Lexington, Mass., 1967). RICHARD L. McCORMICK, "The Discovery That Business Corrupts Politics: A Reappraisal of the Origins of Progressivism," *American Historical Review* 86 (Fall 1986): 245–262, reflects on the absence of major lawmaking following the election of 1896.

Three standard sources on legislating during the Progressive Era are JOHN MILTON COOPER, JR., *Pivotal Decades: The United States, 1900–1920* (New York, 1990); JAMES HOLT, *Congressional Insurgents and the Party System, 1909–1916* (Cambridge, Mass., 1967); and DAVID SARASOHN, *The Party of Reform: Democrats in the Progressive Era* (Jackson, Miss., 1989). JEFFREY K. TULIS, *The Rhetorical Presidency* (Princeton, N.J., 1987), emphasizes the precedent-setting character of Theodore Roosevelt's program of 1905–1906.

For the 1930s, JORDAN A. SCHWARZ, *The Interregnum of Despair: Hoover, Congress, and the Depression* (Urbana, Ill., 1970), is authoritative on legislating during the late Hoover administration. WILLIAM E. LEUCHTENBERG, *Franklin D. Roosevelt and the New Deal, 1932–1940* (New York, 1963), covers Franklin Roosevelt's first term. JAMES T. PATTERSON, *Congressional Conservatism and the New Deal: The Growth of the Conservative Coalition in Congress, 1933–1939* (Lexington, Ky., 1967), addresses the coalitional difficulties that the New Deal encountered on Capitol Hill after the mid-1930s.

JAMES L. SUNDQUIST, *Politics and Policy: The Eisenhower, Kennedy, and Johnson Years* (Washington, D.C., 1968), is the best guide to legislating during the Kennedy and Johnson years. ROBERT J. LAMPMAN, *Social Welfare Spending: Accounting for Changes from 1950 to 1978* (Orlando, Fla., 1984), documents the increase in domestic spending under Johnson and Nixon. ROBERT X. BROWNING, *Politics and Social Welfare Policy in the United States* (Knoxville, Tenn., 1986), tracks domestic welfare programs during those administrations. Good sources on policy in particular areas during Nixon's years are TIMOTHY CONLAN, *New Federalism: Intergovernmental Reform from Nixon to Reagan* (Washington, D.C., 1985); and DAVID VOGEL, "The 'New' Social Regulation in Historical and Comparative Perspective," THOMAS K. McGRAW, ed., *Regulation in Perspective: Historical Essays* (Cambridge, Mass., 1981). ROGER H. DAVIDSON, "The New Centralization on Capitol Hill," *Review of Politics* 50 (Summer 1988): 345–364, provides a useful summary of congressional politics and policymaking during the activist era under Johnson and Nixon. DAVID R. MAYHEW, *Divided We Govern: Party Control, Lawmaking, and Investigations, 1946–1990* (New Haven, Conn., 1991), documents major federal laws enacted in those years, giving emphasis to the productivity under Johnson and Nixon, and also addresses the Progressive and New Deal eras.

To track, respectively, revenue policy, tariff policy, and overall government growth since 1860, see JOHN F. WITTE, *The Politics and Development of the Federal Income Tax* (Madison, Wis., 1985); JOHN MARK HANSEN, "Taxation and the Political Economy of the Tariff," *International Organization* 44 (Autumn 1990): 527–551; and ROBERT HIGGS, *Crisis and Leviathan: Critical Episodes in the Growth of American Government* (New York, 1987).

Party Voting

Standard sources on party voting since the 1860s are PATRICIA A. HURLEY and RICK K. WILSON, "Partisan Voting Patterns in the U.S. Senate, 1877–1886," in JOHN R. HIBBING and JOHN G. PETERS, eds., *The Changing World of the U.S. Senate* (Berkeley, Calif., 1990); and JEROME M. CLUBB and SANTA M. TRAUGOTT, "Partisan Cleavage and Cohesion in the House of Representatives, 1861–1974," *Journal of Interdisciplinary History* 7 (Winter 1977). DAVID W. BRADY, *Critical Elections and Congressional Policy Making* (Stanford, Calif., 1988), explores the historical relationship between electoral realignments and innovative lawmaking. The authoritative source on good or bad economic times and the electoral fortunes of parties in power is GERALD H. KRAMER, "Short-Term Fluctuations in U.S. Voting Behavior, 1896–1964," *American Political Science Review* 65 (March 1971): 131–143.

Public Moods as Spurs to Activist Policy-Making
See SAMUEL P. HUNTINGTON, *American Politics:* *The Promise of Disharmony* (Cambridge, Mass., 1981); and ARTHUR M. SCHLESINGER, JR., "The Cycles of American Politics," in SCHLESINGER, *The Cycles of American History* (Boston, 1986). A more recent work exploring the nature of such moods is JAMES A. STIMSON, *Public Opinion in America: Moods, Cycles, and Swings* (Boulder, Colo., 1991).

SEE ALSO Congress, Sectionalism, and Public-Policy Formation Since 1870; The Contemporary Congress; Electoral Realignments; The Modernizing Congress, 1870–1930; The Role of Congressional Parties; AND The U.S. Congress: The Era of Party Patronage and Sectional Stress, 1829–1881.

THE ROLE OF CONGRESSIONAL PARTIES

Joseph Cooper
Rick K. Wilson

Whereas the study of political parties has a long and rich history in the United States, specialized concern with the role of congressional parties is a far more recent phenomenon. Analysis of the operations and impacts of congressional parties did not become a major interest of students of Congress or of political parties until the early 1940s, when dissatisfaction over the state of party responsibility sparked a major debate within the political science profession over reform. Detailed and rigorous analysis of the role of congressional parties began only in the late 1940s and 1950s, when the heightened interest in congressional parties was pursued in the context of new canons of scientific inquiry advanced by proponents of the behavioral revolution in political science. That period, however, did witness the publication of several landmark works that defined many of the basic contours of subsequent research and, for perhaps the first time, provided the foundation for a continuing and cumulative research enterprise.

Since the 1950s, the literature on congressional parties has become extensive and sophisticated. This body of literature derives both from research that focuses generally on American parties and politics and from research that focuses more specifically on congressional behavior, structures, and outcomes. These different strands, combined with the increase in the volume and sophistication of work, have produced a rich and multifaceted set of claims and findings regarding the role of congressional parties. Nonetheless, the current literature is not without serious issues and anomalies. Indeed, many would argue that knowledge and understanding regarding the role of American parties generally is now in crisis, despite all the advances made over the past half-century. This "crisis"—if the term fairly describes the sub-stantial increase in uncertainty and disagreement among researchers in this field—has another source as far as the role of congressional parties is concerned. It derives, on the one hand, from the effects that varied events associated with the decline of party have had in challenging traditional ways of understanding American parties and politics; and on the other, from new definitions of what constitutes a good or sound explanation—hence knowledge—in terms of political analysis. It is this combination of problems and the serious issues they raise for understanding the role of congressional parties that prompts this essay.

CONTEMPORARY RESEARCH

To delineate these issues in greater detail, we must first survey the contemporary research that bears on the role of congressional parties. For the purposes of this essay, such research can be divided into two very broad categories: traditional and nontraditional.

Traditional research designates research whose defining perspective on parties is shaped by what Leon Epstein has called (in *Political Parties in the American Mold*, 1986) the "scholarly commitment to parties"—that is, research that explicitly or implicitly sees party as a key unit in, and agent of, a representative system of government. This research centers either on empirical analysis of aspects of party operations within the boundaries set by representative institutions in the United States, or on normative assessment of the success or failure of such operations in terms of standards set by the needs or demands of representative government in the United States.

Nontraditional research means research whose perspective is defined by a commitment to a certain form of explanation rather than a concern with how representative government works, or should work, in the United States. Most characteristic of this approach is research guided by the assumptions of rational choice analysis, which insist that explanation to be sound must be rooted at the individual or micro level of human behavior and rely on conceptions of "utility maximization."

It should be noted from the outset that these two categories are not watertight. Nor are researchers working within them united on a variety of important issues regarding both substance and method. In traditional research the topics of research, the levels of analysis, the conceptual frameworks and measurement techniques, the character of empirical findings, and the assessments of success or failure all can vary widely. In nontraditional research as well the understandings of "utility," the definitions of conditions or parameters, the levels of analysis, the topics of research, and the degree of formalization all can vary widely. Moreover, analysts may or may not address the problem of representative government and may differ significantly on the impact of party and the need to take it into account in explaining congressional politics. Nonetheless, despite these caveats, the distinction between traditional and nontraditional research provides a broadly accurate and serviceable guideline for organizing an analysis of the multifaceted patterns of contemporary research that bear on the role of congressional parties.

Traditional Research

Traditional research that addresses the role of congressional parties includes general theoretical approaches as well as more particular empirical or behavioral approaches. Research guided by general theory involves systemic levels of analysis and treats congressional parties as part of a broader and integrated framework of analysis. Empirically or behaviorally framed research focuses directly on varied aspects of linkage among members, the electorate, and the executive establishment, or on varied aspects of behavior, structure, and outcomes within Congress. Traditional research, then, is not integrated or organized in any overall sense; nor is it shaped or guided to any large degree by some shared set of concepts and

methods. As a result, some findings can be inconsistent and disjointed while others can be reinforcing and cumulative.

At broad systemic levels of analysis, a number of researchers have used the concept of "realignment"—that is, massive and consistent shifts in the electoral composition of the two major parties—to develop a general theory capable of explaining basic patterns in electoral and policy outcomes over time. At the electoral level, realignment theory has been based on claims regarding both change and stability. It has assumed not only that realignments occur periodically in American history, but also that they involve changes in patterns of party allegiance that structure voter attitudes and behavior in a stable and comprehensive fashion for decades thereafter. In this regard, realignment theory has drawn support and inspiration from the work of students of voting behavior, particularly those who developed and now seek to refine the strand of research that emphasizes party identification. However, the goals and concerns of realignment theory are not and have never been confined to the electoral level.

Realignment theorists have shared the traditional assumptions of students of party in the United States that party provides the primary link between electorates and governors, and therefore plays an indispensable role in maintaining representative government in the United States. From this perspective, one of the most critical roles of party is to integrate leadership and policy making across all the components and levels of national government. Hence, the ability of a party to establish enduring, unified control of the legislative and executive branches becomes a prime hallmark of a realignment. More specifically, a number of realignment theorists have sought to explain the linkage between elections and policy outcomes. These students have devoted considerable attention to the precise mechanism by which realignments produce significant policy change. With varying degrees of emphasis, the explanation generally involves changes in divisions on policy issues and coalitional patterns at the electoral level, ties between electoral voting patterns and party voting in Congress, and shifts in policy outcomes linked to increased party voting in Congress.

Since the 1970s, realignment theory in all its various dimensions has been subject to criticism and increasing skepticism. At the electoral level, criticism stems from a variety of sources. On the one hand, there is little convincing evidence for the emergence of the kind of extensive, consistent, and enduring shift in the balance of party forces which occurred in the New Deal realignment of the 1930s, despite the time that has elapsed since then. In addition, the changes in party composition that have occurred in recent decades have not been accompanied by an increased concordance between policy views among party voters in the electorate and partisan policy positions in the Congress. On the other hand, a large number of authors have found strong evidence of the erosion of both the strength of party allegiance and the links between party allegiance and voting behavior. Some have also questioned the basic claim that party allegiance merits treatment as a stable causal factor even in the short run, and in so doing have undermined the very notion of realignment as a conceptual foundation for analysis. Such findings have led to extensive discussions of the "decline of party" and theories of "dealignment" rather than realignment. Nonetheless, some researchers maintain the realignment approach, and not all who have rejected it accept the theory of dealignment. Rather, the extent of party decomposition and the impact it has had on linkage remain disputed.

At the institutional level, evidence of party strength has combined with evidence of party weakness to contribute to the critique of realignment theory. One component of the decline of party at the electoral level has been the increase in split-ticket voting, in relation both to congressional and presidential candidates and to House and Senate candidates. As a consequence, the 1970s and 1980s have witnessed various forms of divided government; and such patterns of split control appear to be as typical of modern American politics as the traditional pattern of unified control was of past eras. Indeed, this development as much as any other makes it difficult to resist the argument that realignment theory is obsolete. In contrast, levels of party voting in the House and Senate have risen in the 1980s. This result provides an intriguing anomaly for party theory. Theoretically, such voting should not increase if party decline and decomposition are as strong and

pervasive as many critics of past research on party identification contend. The fact that it has testifies not only to serious problems in approaching electoral-legislative linkages too narrowly in terms of realignment theory, but also to the complex web of factors that party as a linkage mechanism involves.

Normative Approaches   In addition to realignment theory, one other type of general theory that bears on the role of congressional parties deserves mention. The traditional perspective on the role of party reflected in realignment theory has generated an even more historic, enduring, and broadly defined approach to the role of party in the United States. This approach focuses far more openly and directly on normative issues concerning the role of party in American politics. While it is compatible with realignment theory, it emphasizes analysis of the proper role of party in a representative democracy and the demands of that role. It therefore can be and often has been pursued independent of realignment theory.

This approach has prompted a continuing debate between those theorists who emphasize the desirability and possibility of highly disciplined and responsible parties and those who emphasize the empirical limits to "reform" and the benefits of weakly disciplined parties and shifting majorities. Much of the debate concerns the role of party and party organizations in linking citizens to governors through elections; however, a related and important feature concerns the proper role of the president in the legislative process. In the first regard, the case for strong parties assumes that programmatic and disciplined parties are vital to majority rule and to ensuring the triumph of the public interest over special interests. In the second, the case for strong parties is often tied to the case for strong presidential leadership of the legislative process, both on the basis of the president's position in the party system and because of assumptions made about the president's superior ability to represent the public interest. At this level, realignment theory and theories of presidential leadership can easily be combined, given the centrality of the president in realigning elections and in defining and implementing new party programs.

Critics of strong parties often proceed on the basis of a very different normative perspective, one that adopts a Madisonian view and emphasizes the beneficial aspects of conflict among the diverse constituencies that the House, Senate, and president represent. This school of thought does accept party as performing a primary linkage role; but it rejects rigidifying or exaggerating party beyond its aggregative abilities, emphasizes the advantages of flexible adjustment through bargaining and deliberation in specific policy areas, and identifies the furtherance of the public interest with a process rather than the superior qualities of a single office or person.

The decline of party and the emergence of divided government have created serious anomalies for normative theorists of the role of party as well as for realignment theorists. These anomalies are more difficult to resolve for strong-party theorists than for weak-party theorists. Nonetheless, since both schools of thought accept the importance of party as a linkage mechanism in representative democracy, these developments have perplexed researchers in both camps.

External Relationships   So much, then, for general approaches to party that operate at systemic levels of analysis. An even larger body of contemporary research that qualifies as traditional is far less broadly framed. As suggested earlier, such research is oriented toward causal explanation of specific facets of congressional operations and performance at both individual and organizational levels of analysis. It focuses both on aspects of linkage between Congress and its two primary environmental arenas—the electorate and the executive establishment—and on aspects of behavior, structure, and outcomes within Congress.

The empirical literature that deals with relationships among electorates or constituencies and members of Congress has a variety of facets. A large amount of work on congressional elections emphasizes such topics as the rise of incumbency, the decline in presidential "coattails," the consequences of campaign finance, the emergence of candidate-centered media campaigns, the impact of economic voting, and so forth. On the whole, this literature has fueled discussion of the decline-of-party thesis that figures so prominently in more general theoretical disputes. In addition, there is a great deal of research that concentrates directly on the character of policy linkages between

members of Congress and their electorates or constituencies.

Implicitly, most of this research has sought to understand how representation in the United States operates at the national level, but only a restricted portion of this literature is explicitly formulated in this way. The most outstanding exception is Richard F. Fenno's *Home Style* (1978), though more qualitative than most work in his area. Noteworthy work has also been done by others interested in whether representation should be approached "dyadically," in terms of member-constituent relations, or "collectively," in terms of relations among aggregates of members and voters. In general, however, research on electoral policy linkage focuses simply on the relationship between substantive and/or political facets of constituencies and policy outcomes in Congress. Typically, substantive variables that are treated as independent or causal are conceptualized in terms of interests, ideological orientations, or policy attitudes and political ones in terms of safeness, homogeneity, degrees of partisanship, and so on. The dependent variables, or effects to be explained, are typically defined in terms of member ideological orientations, policy positions, or voting behavior. In some cases, however, the dependent variable is the level of party voting in the Congress. Such work is primarily interested in exploring the electoral bases of party voting in Congress, but it assumes that differences in levels of party voting have policy consequences.

As far as questions of linkage generally or the role of party more specifically are concerned, the findings of this research are not conclusive. The sheer amount of research, combined with differences in underlying theoretical perspectives, multiple options in choosing and relating variables, and problems of measurement, have produced a large number of contradictory results as well as significant methodological controversies over even classic studies of constituency influence (for example, the Miller-Stokes [1963] findings regarding the varying influence of constituency opinion in different policy arenas). Moreover, much of this research has proceeded and continues to proceed either by ignoring the impact of party at the electoral level or by understanding it in ways that attribute much of its impact to other factors. In recent years, however, more attention has been paid to the role of party, and the way in which partisan impact or influence has been conceptualized has improved. As a result, a number of researchers have found positive evidence regarding the partisan connection on the interchanges between congressional and constituent policy views, especially insofar as these effects are mediated by such factors as shared ideological orientations, the role of party activists, and the safeness of districts.

Attention to linkages between Congress and the electorate has been complemented by attention to linkages between Congress and the executive establishment. The 1970s and 1980s gave rise to many empirical studies of the character and determinants of presidential influence in Congress. In particular, researchers have explored the relationship between presidential influence or success and a variety of factors, ranging from matters of strategy and personal skill to public standing and partisan size and/or cohesion. Disagreement over how much weight should be given to each of these factors persists, as well as to whether and how to incorporate more general aspects of political or economic climate into the analysis. Further complications have been introduced by the realization that unified government, and with it presidential command of party policy and party forces, could threaten congressional autonomy as well as by the emergence of divided government. These phenomena have revealed that the relationships among presidential influence or success, unified party control, and effective congressional performance are far less straightforward than have previously been assumed.

The 1970s and 1980s have also witnessed an increase in sophisticated, empirically oriented studies of congressional oversight. This work has substantially improved our understanding of the determinants, consequences, and limitations of congressional control of administrative decision-making. However, there are still disagreements and confusion over how to define oversight and measure its influence, and how to assess the proper roles of the branches in an era in which the growth of administrative discretion has greatly complicated old standards and distinctions. Conflict thus prevails over the proper role and effectiveness of congressional oversight vis-à-vis control by the president or the courts. But there is general agreement that party is a factor of only limited importance.

Internal Operations The traditional research that focuses on internal congressional operations and performance constitutes the largest body of work that bears on the role of congressional parties. In particular, there is an abiding interest in the character and causes of party voting within the Congress. Considerable attention has been given to charting the aggregate levels of party voting over time and weighing the relative influence of external electoral and internal organizational determinants. There has also been growing attention given to the role of ideology as a factor that structures congressional voting in general and party voting in particular. However, whatever the determinants of party voting, scholars agree that it reached its high points around the turn of the century, and that party voting has declined in the twentieth century, albeit with significant upturns in the 1930s and the 1980s. In addition, a good deal of work examines congressional voting at the individual level from a perspective that focuses on the voting decision per se, rather than exploring the character of constituency linkages. Among other determinants, this type of work analyzes the impact of party on voting at the individual level and assesses the historic claim that party represents the single most important factor in voting choices. Not surprisingly, the claim has been supported, rejected, and qualified.

This interest in the character and strength of party voting reflects a broader interest in the relation between party voting and policy outcomes. A few scholars have sought to differentiate policy areas schematically, in terms of each area's salient or defining characteristics and determinants. In part, their object in doing so has been to account for the varying impact of party as a basis for majority coalitions in different policy areas. Others have applied such schema in largely qualitative analyses of coalition building and policy outcomes. But the majority of scholars have tried to understand the relationship between party voting and policy outcomes quantitatively. This research has taken a variety of forms, including analysis of aggregate levels of party strength and policy outcome, analysis of the impacts of major intraparty divisions, and analysis of the growth and causes of universalism, that is, outcomes that distribute benefits to members generally rather than selectively. In contrast, some students of congressional voting have rejected the analysis of policy outcomes in terms of aggregate levels of party voting and argued that policy outcomes can best be understood in terms of issue dimensions that are established statistically; still others have relied on dimensional analysis simply to clarify the relationship between aggregate levels of party strength and policy outcomes.

A final focus of research bearing on the role of congressional parties concerns questions of structure and leadership. Research of this type has clear links to the past and is often sensitive to contextual as well as internal determinants. It has sought to analyze a variety of fundamental, albeit highly interwoven aspects of the relationships among party, structure, and leadership. One major topic it addresses has been the causes or determinants of structure and structural change in both the formal organizational and congressional party systems, with special attention paid to the relative roles of party strength, work load, size, complexity, and so on. Another major topic has been the impact of structure and structural change in the formal and party systems on patterns of operation and performance, with attention to the relative roles and power of committee units, party units, and members on the floor. A third major topic has been the character and determinants of leadership roles and styles.

The literature on these topics is immense. It has drawn on the past as well as the present to further understanding of congressional operations and performance, generally and the role of congressional parties more specifically. Such work has broadened the theoretical foundations and reach of research by combining existing and familiar political science conceptions regarding power, the pursuit of self-interest as a primary but not exclusive goal, and bargaining, with new conceptions drawn in an eclectic manner from a variety of disciplines and interdisciplinary approaches (for example, social theory, social psychology, and organization theory). It has continued to be open to various combinations of qualitative and quantitative research techniques, but current research no longer pressures a world of static, mechanistic relationships. Rather, it has accepted a dynamic orientation toward explanation and become highly concerned with explaining the causes and consequences of institutional change.

Among the topics that have been investigated are the basic processes of institutionalization in the Congress; the origins and development of the committee system; the rise and fall of centralized power in the House of the early twentieth century; changes in procedures for bill introduction and referral in the past and present; changes in the mechanisms for bringing business to the floor; the evolving role of the Rules Committee in the House and Unanimous Consent Agreements in the Senate; the decline of committee power on the floor; changing patterns of norms in the House and Senate (especially those pertaining to seniority and apprenticeship); the growth and increased roles of party organizational mechanisms (such as the whip systems, steering committees, and caucuses); the current roles of party leaders in committee assignments, agenda control, and majority building; the changing styles of party leaders; patterns of leadership, motivation, and decision making within and among congressional committees; changing patterns of work load and productivity; and congressional reform.

In general, scholars agree that the Congress of the 1990s is an institution very different from its mid-twentieth-century predecessor. In the House, the proliferation of subcommittees and staffs, as well as the enhanced role of party units in committee appointments, has served to undercut and disperse the power formerly concentrated in committee chairs and committee units. At the same time the role and power of the party leadership has grown, because of a variety of political and structural changes—among them, the increase in party cohesion and voting, the emergence of divided government, and changes in formal and party mechanisms that have enhanced both the leverage of party leaders and reliance on their initiatives at the committee level and on the floor. In the Senate as well, the role of party leaders, as opposed to committee leaders, has increased. The old Senate was run by informal networks of committee leaders from both parties and tightly regulated by a set of norms that supported such oligarchic rule. The "new" Senate is far more individualistic and decentralized. In it, committees are accorded far less deference and party leaders are relied on far more to coordinate action at all levels of decision making, and especially on the floor. However, for a variety of reasons they are denied the kinds of organizational leverage they enjoy in the House. As a result, though the wider dispersion of power in both bodies has made coordination and action more difficult, the Senate has become a perceptibly more turbulent and chaotic body than the House.

Nontraditional Research

A far smaller proportion of nontraditional research bears on the role of congressional parties. Moreover, though the nontraditional literature embodies several different stances on whether and how to treat party as a factor in legislative politics, its thrust thus far in the case of Congress is clearly to ignore or heavily discount the importance of party.

This literature can also be divided into broadly framed systemic approaches and more restricted treatments of particular aspects of linkage, operations, and performance. Nontraditional research, framed in general systemic terms, has little in common with either theories of party government or realignment theory. This is not because it ignores party or the issues of representative government, but rather because it refuses to assume any fundamental linkage between them.

General Approaches One strand of nontraditional research refuses to operate, implicitly or explicitly, within a framework that involves concern for representative government. Rather, rejecting the "functionalism" it sees in the traditional perspective, it seeks to put research on a basis that is wholly empirical and rooted in the concrete motivations of individual actors. Thus, it proceeds on the basis of rational choice assumptions about the centrality of utility maximization as an explanatory factor. So oriented, it emphasizes the pursuit of individual self-interest and focuses analyses on the desire of candidates and officeholders to win electoral victories. In contrast to traditional systemic approaches, which can be seen as mass-oriented because of their emphasis on linking voters to governmental outcomes, this approach can be seen as elite-oriented because it

views policy as an instrument of politicians and treats voters as noncritical, exogenous factors in any adequate approach to party.

Party, as a result, is not ignored but highlighted: it is treated as a unit or construct that derives from the desire of politicians to secure collective electoral advantages or benefits. In Anthony Downs's version of this approach in *An Economic Theory of Democracy* (1957), party politicians define and promote broad ideological stances as a means of mobilizing electoral support in the face of the large costs, in terms of time and effort, voters must pay to acquire information about candidates and policies. In Joseph A. Schlesinger's version (see the three articles listed in the bibliography), party is a product of the combination and coordination of individual campaign units, or nuclei, into various organizational mechanisms for the purpose of gaining common or shared electoral benefits.

A second strand manifests a similar distaste for the "functionalism" it also perceives in the traditional perspective on party, and a similar desire to place research on what it considers to be an empirical basis. It nonetheless directs analysis toward issues in representative government by defining the problem of representative government as a problem of combining individual preferences (assumed to be of equal worth and validity) into collective decisions that serve the desires or welfare of all involved. Representative government thus becomes a collective action problem that one approaches by assuming that individuals will act rationally to maximize their preferences, and that one solves by showing how individual desires or preferences can be combined into collective decisions in a manner that is not arbitrary either procedurally or substantively. Here again, then, utility maximization at the individual level serves as the central explanatory factor. However, since collective action is approached in purely individualistic terms, this strand diverges from the first by providing no basis for party while still focusing attention on representative government.

In one variant of this strand, illustrated by the work of William Riker, Arrow's paradox and the problems of cycling or arbitrary voting results provide the fulcrum of the analysis. Riker concludes that such difficulties are endemic to democracies, which means in turn that representative government must lie essentially in popular control of governors, not policies. Interestingly enough, this is precisely what theorists of strong parties deny, both empirically and normatively. A second variant is illustrated by the work of James Buchanan and Gordon Tullock. Here the basic problem consists in the various difficulties of combining individual preferences into collective decisions in a manner that truly maximizes the satisfaction of the self-interested desires of the citizens involved. Their analysis explores the impact of decision rules generally and the effects of majority voting systems in direct and representative democracies. Although the analysis is insightful, what emerges is an approach to political decision making whose individualistic orientations make representative government a flawed and unwieldy mechanism of collective choice, justified primarily by the prohibitive inefficiencies of direct democracy in large polities. Once again this is a perspective that is highly at variance with the perspectives of normative party theory and largely because of the different assumptions it makes regarding the role of particular interests in constituting the common good or public interest.

Both these strands have strengths and weaknesses. The first strand, represented by Downs and Schlesinger, is suggestive as to how parties may solve their collective action problems and in so doing contribute to solving the larger system's collective action problems. Ideological cues and incentives as well as organizational mechanisms and incentives potentially have much to contribute to such explanation. Still, both authors tend to emphasize party as an instrument for securing mutual benefits far more than they explain how intraparty and intrasystem problems of self-interest can be overcome. In contrast, Riker, Buchanan, and Tullock are far more sensitive to the difficulties of solving collective action problems; yet their analyses are so atomistic that the mediating role of an organization like party, left with little room for theoretical development, is dismissed as a secondary concern at best. Even so, their work is important and suggestive. The very difficulty of solving cycling and collective action problems in starkly individualistic terms suggests that party may indeed be one reason that

they are so much better solved in practice than they have been thus far in rational choice theory. As we shall find later in this section, this is an intuition that some rational choice theorists have very recently begun to consider and to elaborate.

Linkage Research   The more restricted portions of nontraditional literature that bear on the role of congressional parties have also been marked by a distributive and particularistic view of politics. In Theodore J. Lowi's "American Business, Public Policy" (1964) and James Q. Wilson's *Political Organization* (1973), a politics, based on the distribution of particularistic benefits to constituency interests, provides only one of several policy types and associated political processes. However, the rational choice approach as applied in the 1970s and 1980s to the study of Congress as an institution has brought distributive politics to the forefront.

At the risk of being slightly arbitrary, we shall again simplify our discussion by distinguishing research that focuses on linkage from that focusing on institutional behavior, structure, and outcomes. As for the former, the growth of incumbency after 1964 sparked several influential studies of congressional operations and performance which viewed congressional politics in distributive terms and members as utility maximizers whose primary motivation was to gain reelection. These studies advanced several arguments: that reelection is best served by the delivery of particularistic benefits and services to constituents; that party is a weak, if not irrelevant factor in determining congressional voting and policy outcomes; that substantive policy concerns had declined in importance; and that the desire for reelection explains a whole gamut of congressional practices and outcomes, including such matters as staff growth, committee organization, an emphasis on advertising and credit-seeking, and expanded delegation to executive officers. Such claims have not gone unnoticed nor uncontested. Rather, they have been subject to critique on the basis of perspectives that see congressional politics as more than distributive politics, members as more than seekers of reelection, and constituents as more than seekers of particularistic benefits and services. In other words, critics have asserted the continuing importance of party and policy concerns among members and constituents.

The rational choice research that has been criticized in this way is far more qualitative than quantitative, and it is concerned much more with linkages to the electorate than to the executive establishment. However, there is a more quantitative strain of research into constituency linkages which proceeds on rational choice assumptions; and over the past five years, rational choice theorists have also begun to devote considerable attention to legislative-executive relations.

In the first regard, a number of researchers have analyzed the linkage between constituencies and congressional voting in terms of utility maximization. Such work assumes that members, as seekers of reelection, are strictly governed by the economic interests of their constituents, who in turn are thought to vote in ways that will maximize their own utility. The analytical techniques applied are quite sophisticated empirically, but here again there are contradictory findings. For example, some studies have found that ideology is more important than economic interests. In addition, because politics is viewed primarily as distributive, very few of these studies pay any heed to party effects.

In the second regard, rational choice theorists have applied utility maximization assumptions and conceptions drawn from principal-agent analysis to examine congressional control of administrative behavior. Among the topics studied have been the bases of congressional power; existing oversight patterns and their effectiveness; causes and consequences of delegation; and the use of administrative procedure as a weapon of congressional control. Though this research, like traditional research, has ignored party, work by Kiewiet and McCubbins has highlighted the role of party in a principal-agent approach to analyzing the appropriations process. This body of literature is largely qualitative in character and its claims regarding congressional power and behavior have evoked substantial criticism from those who find its explanations exaggerated or erroneous on contextual, institutional, empirical, and even motivational grounds. Furthermore, some rational choice theorists have turned their attention to divided government and

begun to analyze bargaining between the branches in broad game-theoretic terms. This work, of necessity, recognizes party, but primarily only as a salient or defining characteristic of the participants.

Institutional Research If we turn now to those portions of nontraditional research that focus on internal behavior, structure, or outcomes, this work, in contrast to the research on linkage, is largely formal. Questions regarding congressional voting and outcomes have provided a major topic of inquiry among formal theorists. They too have approached these topics from the perspective of distributive politics by assuming that decision making in Congress is essentially a matter of "dividing up a pie" of particularistic benefits. Hence, they have focused their efforts on explaining coalition building in distributive terms and sought to account for deviations from minimal winning coalitions and for pork-barrel outcomes in which costs exceed benefits. Others have explored the impact of sophisticated voting and strategic agenda manipulation. In addition, a small group of formal theorists have begun to explore communication and information effects on coalition building.

This body of research is substantial and theoretically enlightening, but it has paid little heed to the role of party or party leaders. Here, as elsewhere, rational choice analysis has been framed in terms of the maximization of gains or utility by individual decision makers and premised on a distributive view of politics. Its principal contribution has been to explore how various structural forms yield equilibrium results that the distribution of preferences could not on their own sustain, and to a lesser extent, how structural forms and changes in these forms are rooted in utility maximization at the individual level.

However, not all of the nontraditional literature on congressional structure is formal. In one area, especially, the analysis of committee composition, research has been quantitatively oriented. In contrast to the formal literature, such research has not completely ignored party; but it has dismissed party as a factor of much significance. Nonetheless, analyses of committee composition remain highly disputed, even among rational choice theorists. The gains-in-trade version of distributive politics leads to the view that committees are self-selected and composed of "outliers"—that is, dominated by special interests. This conventional view has been challenged by Keith Krehbiel. While retaining individualistic and distributive perspectives that marginalize party, he emphasizes information needs as a basis of committee power and presumes that majorities will seek to maximize their preferences. He therefore argues, with substantial supporting empirical evidence, that committees will be composed so that they will reflect and be responsive to floor majorities.

Despite the highly individualistic and distributive thrust of the rational choice literature in the 1970s and 1980s, it would be a mistake to conclude that this literature or the rational choice approach has no relevance for understanding the relationships that exist among party, structure, and leadership. First, the basic "institutional" concerns and topics that rational choice theorists have addressed parallel, in several ways, those of traditional theorists. The primary exception thus far has been the topic of leadership, which in the 1970s and 1980s received only scant attention in rational choice research. Aside from leadership, however, rational choice analysts have dealt with fundamental and broadly shared questions of institutional analysis: the origins and bases of committee power; the impact of order or sequence in agenda power; the impact of debate limitations on voting outcomes; the determinants of various kinds of agenda control; and the role of specialization.

This work is important for traditional students of institutions as well as proponents of a rational choice approach. At basic theoretical levels, it uncovers determinants and relationships that students of party cannot ignore and will have either to discount or integrate into their own explanations of structure and leadership. Equally important, this work suggests propositions regarding actual operations, which bear on the validity of conflicting perspectives on congressional politics and which are subject to empirical tests. Good examples are the current disputes over the relative roles of congressional parties, majorities, and particularistic interests in the selection and composition of congressional committees.

Second, the boundaries between rational choice analysis and nonrational choice analysis

of structure and leadership are not so rigid or absolute as one might imagine. On the one hand, as Keith Krehbiel's work illustrates, rational choice analysis is open to relaxing key assumptions about political actors, the basis of their decisions, and the contexts of their interaction. This in turn can lead to adaptations and extensions of the findings and insights of the more traditional behavioral and organizational literatures. On the other hand, both rational choice and nonrational choice analysts can blend rational choice and broader contextual and/or behavioral perspectives at qualitative levels of analysis. Thus, for example, traditionally oriented students of Congress, such as Richard J. Fenno, Lawrence C. Dodd, David W. Brady, Mark Morgan, and Barbara Sinclair have incorporated notions of utility maximization into their analyses, whereas nontraditional ones, such as Morris P. Fiorina, John Ferejohn, Kenneth A. Shepsle, and Keith Krehbiel, have introduced contextual, organizational, and even traditional normative considerations into their work.

Third, and related to the preceding point about flexibility, rational choice analysis is dynamic, not static. It is not preordained that rational choice analysis cannot encompass party at institutional levels of analysis, and it need not view politics in a narrowly distributive or highly particularistic way. Thus, it is worth noting that several scholars of Congress have recently begun to apply the rational choice approach to explaining and analyzing congressional parties, and these efforts include questions of structure and leadership as well as voting. Such work has been both formal—for example, Aldrich's (see the three articles listed in the bibliography) and nonformal (Gary W. Cox and Matthew D. McCubbins). Both variants, however, challenge conventional rational choice approaches and findings—first, by assuming that party can and should be seen as a collective action problem, and second, by seeking to demonstrate the importance of party for voting, structure, and outcomes while still adhering to a broad utility maximization perspective. It is true, of course, that disagreement persists in the ranks of nontraditional researchers over whether and how to treat the role of party in Congress, but is very unlikely that the rational choice approach will be as indifferent to this issue in the future as it has been in the past.

THE ROLE OF CONGRESSIONAL PARTIES

THE NEED FOR THEORY

This review of the research bearing on the role of congressional parties reveals a sophisticated, multifaceted, and extensive body of work, but one that is divided in its perspectives and findings, and uncertain regarding the implications for both change and reform. What is largely absent in this work is any extensive analysis of the concept of party or the issues involved in understanding it. While there is a good deal of discussion about party reform and speculation about the future of parties, few have tried to conceptualize party, its operations, and its impacts in terms of a coherent and comprehensive framework. Rather, party has largely been taken as a given. In the traditional literature it is viewed in an abbreviated and matter-of-fact manner as a fixed entity that performs functional roles within the political system. In the nontraditional literature, party has usually been ignored—but when it is recognized, it has also largely been taken as a given. The consequences for understanding and explaining congressional politics in both cases have been very deleterious: party has been too superficially equated with labels or identifications and too quickly pressed into service in the analysis of linkage, voting, structure, and outcomes. As a result, understanding of the role of party has been marred by confusion, conflict, and in some quarters, even skepticism about the use of party as an explanatory factor.

Problems in Traditional Studies

In the traditional literature party has been both treated as a given and analyzed segmentally—that is, inquiry has typically proceeded by categorizing various aspects of party operation and then organizing analysis in those terms. Thus, party in the electorate, party in the government, and party as an organization have been distinguished from one another and from party in an overall sense; and the particular characteristics of each segment have usually defined the contours of the analysis carried on by individual researchers.

The reasons party has been treated this way in traditional research are easy to understand. While the reality of party in any overall sense seems quite ephemeral, the reality of party as an organization, as a factor in elec-

tions, and as a component of governmental operations seems hard and clear. Still there is another, perhaps even more important, reason—the plain fact that the task of conceptualizing party is difficult and frustrating. Defining a view of parties as they interweave the various levels of government is a very difficult task. Combining this task with tying the role of party to the heart of the representative relationship, explaining how party serves to organize and coordinate decision making within the Congress, and understanding the effects of change over time renders the problem a seemingly intractable one.

Given the complexity of the standards, conditions, and relationships involved, attempts to develop general theories of parties have produced so much disagreement that most students of American politics have accepted V. O. Key's judgment that it is best to get on with the job of studying American parties and to defer more elaborate conceptualization until understanding of their operation improved. There is wisdom in Key's strategy, but it has been followed for almost half a century. If this long period of research has enriched our understanding of many aspects of American parties, it is also true that postponing the task of developing a concept of party that provides more than a set of categories cripples any effort to address wide gaps in our understanding that cannot be filled by incremental and disjointed additions to our knowledge. It therefore can well be argued that taking party as a given now involves far greater costs than benefits, and that it poses a substantial barrier to significant increase in our understanding.

Promoting Confusion   Ironically enough, the present divided and uncertain state of research is related to the high degree of agreement on taking a party as a given. In truth, party cannot be taken as a given in any pure or absolute way; some perspective, broad or narrow, for conceptualizing and analyzing party must be adopted. As we have seen, taking party as a given masks great differences in the character and mix of assumptions that guide and constrain an inquiry and, consequently, its results; very different phenomena are treated as the defining features of a common general concept, and over time the likelihood of conflict and confusion increases, even as the volume and sophistication of research grows.

The point applies at both broad and restricted levels of analysis. Both normative theory and realignment theory—the former explicitly, the latter implicitly—see party in terms of its role in linking electoral and institutional behavior and outcomes. The normative approach explicitly directs attention toward the needs or demands of representative government; its analysis centers on assessing these needs relative to the normative standards and empirical conditions presumed to govern them. The realignment approach, on the other hand, focuses on comprehensive change in the composition of the major parties and its impact at institutional levels in overcoming barriers to inaction. Analysis centers on the factors that determine change and stability in electoral patterns and the mechanisms of impact at institutional levels. Moreover, added complexity is provided by divisions within the broad approaches themselves—for example, conflict between strong and weak party theorists, on both normative and empirical grounds, as well as different versions of the defining features of a realignment. Such differences in basic orientation and view lead to differences, not only in patterns of inquiry and dispute, but also in what evidence is seen as relevant and what it means. To see strong parties as critical instruments for attaining the "public interest" and to condemn interest-group politics set standards for normative assessment and empirical inquiry quite different from when one sees parties simply as instruments for aggregating and accommodating interests. Indeed, weak party theorists may even reject the notion of a public interest and see politics simply as a clash of interests in which the role of government is to provide access, fairness, and order. These illustrations do not exhaust the patterns of disagreement that exist. To see parties as stable webs of allegiance, which involve a policy dimension but also are the products of historical circumstances and psychological forces, is to impose far stronger constraints on political engineering than to see parties in terms of policy principles or programs that provide voter choice and accountability. It is not surprising, then, that realignment theorists typically do not join in cries for party reform, even though they believe, as strong party advocates do, that to be representative the processes by which policy

outputs emerge at institutional levels in response to voter opinion must be tightly organized by party and led by the president. Nor is it surprising, given the differences within realignment theory, that there is disagreement among realignment theorists over the meaning or significance of particular elections and shifts in voting patterns.

Similar problems can be found at more restricted levels of analysis, often in more extreme form. Empirically oriented research that takes party as a given may avoid, but cannot escape, the complexity and fragility in the phenomena it wishes to capture by analyzing party effects. Treating party as something so hard and fast that it can be posited and measured with little concern for the consequences of the way it is conceived leads easily to substantial differences in assessing both the strength of party at electoral and institutional levels and its role in linking the various levels. It is true, of course, that there are several empirically oriented theories or frameworks which provide guidance at electoral and institutional levels—for example, the Michigan model, theories of ideological constraint, and various typologies of policy-making. However, these theories or frameworks are partial and disjointed, and they themselves reflect more general assumptions that are disputed. Equally if not more important, while change is constant, the ways we conceive and measure it are not advanced enough to prevent disagreement and uncertainty as to whether our findings reveal actual change or mere deficiencies in conceptualization and measurement. Given all this, it is not hard to understand why there is so much controversy over the decline of party at the electoral level, so many contradictory findings about the electoral determinants of congressional voting, and so much uncertainty about the patterns of cause and effect that govern relations among structure, party voting, and policy outcomes in Congress.

Promoting Rigidity   There is, in addition, a flip side to the confusion and divisiveness that taking party as a given promotes. Researchers themselves are rarely aware of the limitations they introduce by the assumptions they make when they take party as given. The inevitable result is nonetheless to rigidify and constrict analysis in unforeseen ways. To illustrate, consider the treatment of the following two topics in the traditional literature.

The first concerns the way in which time is incorporated as an element of party analysis. Taking party as a given leads scholars to view parties either as entities that are fixed and stable in congressional politics or as entities that are gradually fragmenting. However, *both* positions ignore the fact that congressional parties are continually in flux. Shifts over time in Congress's work load and institutional structure alter the effectiveness with which parties organize within it; consequently, parties are unlikely to be static units that are immune to internal changes. At the same time, conditions external to Congress will affect the unity and organizational strength of the parties. Hence, while treating party as a "black box" may uncover interesting relationships in a particular cross-section of time, it inevitably ignores the ways in which congressional parties are continually reshaped by their members and buffeted by external forces. Similarly, although realignment theorists are correct in arguing that upheavals in the electorate will produce policy change, they do not adequately explain how parties adapt to their environments continually, not periodically, or why policy change is not limited to isolated time periods. It is crucial, then, to study how internal and external conditions affect parties, as well as what this means both for politics in Congress and for policy change. What is needed is a broader understanding of the ebb and flow over time of party strength in Congress over time and the conditions and determinants of policy change.

The second concerns the treatment of the representative relationship between electorates and governors. Here, too, accepting party as a given leads to rigidities in analysis that need to be recognized and examined. Those scholars who take the responsible party view claim that parties ought to be national entities bound to clearly stated policy programs. Given the focus on national parties, the president is regarded as the leader of the party and, consequently, the party's agenda setter. For a theory of congressional parties, the implicit corollaries are that the party should be united in its support of a party president, and that the legislature should have no agenda beyond that delivered by the president. However, this all stems from a view of party which uncritically equates the president's party with the nation and has little regard for the representative role of Congress or the value of a separation of powers.

At the opposite end of the spectrum are those scholars, largely taking an empirical tack, who hold that the key to the representative relationship is the direct linkage between constituents and the congressman. Party, in most of this research, is treated as a separate and residual factor that helps to explain what a simple model of constituency linkage cannot. However, doing so denies party a role as a component of a congressman's constituency: it assumes that party and district interests are dichotomous and conflicting. Missing is any acknowledgment of the fact that congressional parties are rooted in a member's district and, overall, are defined by commonalities in interest and view across districts. Trying to isolate the independent effects of constituency and party is difficult if not impossible without a solid conceptual understanding of congressional parties.

Thus, positions on the role of party in representation often are determined by constraining normative assumptions or very stark empirical assumptions about the linkage between congressmen and their constituents. Such assumptions define a starting point that takes a particular view of party for granted and treats party uncritically thereafter as a given. Yet, when fixed and stable stances are taken with respect to party without probing the complex issues involved, is it surprising that analysis should be rigid and constricted?

Problems in the Nontraditional Literature

There are problems with the ways congressional parties are treated in the nontraditional research as well, despite its broad agreement on how explanation should be approached. Three distinct groups of rational choice analysts may be identified in terms of their stance on congressional parties: those who recognize congressional parties but dismiss their importance; those who simply ignore congressional parties; and those who have begun to develop a theory of congressional parties within a utility maximization framework.

Downgrading Party   The first group views politics in a very distributive and particularistic manner and emphasizes reelection as the primary goal members seek to maximize. This group of analysts recognizes party as a factor, but treats it, much as the traditional literature does, as a given. Hence, though these analysts proceed within a broad theory of politics, they neither develop nor rely on a broad theory of party. The results are withering for the role of party and party leaders. When reelection is emphasized and made contingent on an understanding of politics defined in distributive and particularistic terms, parties are reduced to being mere "furniture" on Capitol Hill, and party leaders to security guards patrolling the boundaries of acceptable behavior.

Such a view has serious problems. To combine a traditional approach to party with a distributive and highly particularistic approach to politics is to produce findings that are mere artifacts of such a combination. This is true both for those who apply a rational choice framework qualitatively and for those who do so with an emphasis on testing propositions about causal relationships. Taking party as a given involves assumptions of scope and stability that make assessments of its influence quite vulnerable to evidence of variation or fragility. At the same time, it often leads to modes of operationalizing party that separate party from its effects. Equally, if not more important, when rational choice analysts take party for granted, they can too easily ignore its connections to a broader view of politics than is recognized in their highly distributive and particularistic approach. As a result, assessments of the significance of party are isolated from the empirical and normative claims about politics upon which they depend. The inevitable result is to render the role of party quite vulnerable to challenges on distributive grounds by arguments that assume what they need to prove.

We may conclude, then, that this first group of rational choice theorists has not yet made a convincing case for marginalizing party in the Congress. To dismiss party, they—like those who wish to emphasize its importance—must first place their analysis of congressional parties on a firmer theoretical basis.

Ignoring Party   The second group of rational choice analysts simply refuses to take party into account in their treatments of congressional politics. This has been particularly true of formal theorists, whether they have focused on voting and coalition formation, the impacts of structure on the stability and distributive effects of outcomes, or the role of congressional leaders. The reasons such analysts ignore party are theoretical and they are powerful enough to bridge their differences over the version of distributive politics to be applied. As noted earlier, the exchange of favors or "gains-in-trade" view has recently been challenged by researchers who treat outcomes as a function of majority preferences, informational asymmetries, and uncertainty in decision making. Nonetheless, proponents of both positions agree that party should not figure permanently in their explanations because they see it as a façade—as something that, because it merely mirrors more basic forces, need not be treated as anything more than a secondary or residual factor.

This viewpoint has been elaborated and powerfully stated by Keith Krehbiel, who argues that simplified median voter models are sufficient to explain the effects that others traditionally attribute to party. His conclusion is based on two seemingly undeniable postulates: that when called upon to vote members will vote their preferences, and that when votes are taken majorities will rule. If party has an impact, it thus must take the form of inducing members to vote against their preferences. However, not only is such behavior exceedingly difficult to demonstrate, it is also very unlikely on its face. Similarly, Krehbiel finds little evidence of party impact on congressional procedures and processes—notably in committee appointments, rules-committee actions, and conference behavior. In general, he concludes that a theory framed by preference aggregation with emphasis on the decisive position of the median voter provides far better explanations than do theories based on party divisions and conflicts.

Nonetheless, an approach to congressional politics that discounts party is once again subject to skepticism. Compelling reasons exist for believing that the apparent importance of party in the everyday operations of Congress is no myth, and that congressional politics cannot be understood without taking party into account. Substantial aspects of politics do not proceed on the basis of the distribution of particularistic benefits but rather on the basis of the collective pursuit of shared benefits. In this regard ideological orientations do constrain and organize preferences, and in so doing provide incentives, along with electoral benefits, for collective action through party. Similarly, it appears unlikely that procedural mechanisms would be so consistently staffed and controlled by party leaders if they had little or no impact on partisan policy goals. Party, then, to the degree that it is successful in shaping issues and choices—through aggregating preferences and through controlling structure—can help to explain how and why members of the Congress act in stable and organized ways to secure collective benefits, despite the difficulties the coordination of action pose and the endemic threat of vote cycling multidimensional issues involve.

In sum, then, there is an organizational dimension to congressional parties that cannot be adequately captured by treatments that base analysis on atomistic individuals and freely forming majorities. Despite Krehbiel's contentions, majorities in Congress appear to be highly ordered by partisan commitments, cues, and incentives, as well as by the various forms of organizational leverage that party leaders possess. Indeed, it is difficult to see how shifting and freely forming majorities that aggregate preferences on an individual basis can provide a basis for either the ordered patterns of voting that occur or the sizeable distributions of leverage that many organizational structures involve. Moreover, if party's contribution toward facilitating majority construction and providing a fulcrum for organizing distributions of power and task does in fact help Congress to solve the generic problems of cooperation that all organizations confront, why should the impact of party be judged in terms of its ability to induce members to vote against their preferences? Once we recognize that organization is problematic, not automatic, party's significance lies, rather, in facilitating the ability of members to derive benefits from shared or compatible aspects of their preferences. Thus, it is far more likely that one can explain congressional politics with a theory of party than without one.

Emphasizing Party   A third group of rational choice theorists recognizes both the importance of congressional parties and the need for firmer theoretical grounding. These analysts believe there is ample room as well as justification for including party within a rational choice framework. They see congressional parties as crucial to solving one or more of three generic dilemmas that all organized decision making bodies confront, and which are particularly severe in Congress because of the equality and autonomy of its members.

The first of these dilemmas can be characterized as the coordination problem. It stems from the inability of individual actors, who share common concerns or goals, but act independently, unable to achieve orderly and effective patterns of cooperation. Understood narrowly, this problem is tractable and can be solved through reliance on informal norms, formal procedures, leaders, and various other means. The second dilemma is far more difficult and so primary that it is usually characterized in rational choice theory as the collective action problem. It stems from the fact that independent actors can make individually rational decisions, and yet produce an overall result that is to everyone's disadvantage. The dilemma is thus how to devise strategies and mechanisms for inducing individuals to act collectively in a manner that will secure the full benefits of cooperation, while still assuming that they will behave as rational actors, that is, as utility maximizers. The final dilemma, generally characterized in rational choice theory as the collective choice problem, is difficult as well. It is particularly severe in organizations that, like Congress, rely primarily on collective choice mechanisms for decision making. The crux of the problem is that unless actors have unique and limited arrays of preferences, any coalition of those actors can be formed and broken apart when decision making involves multidimensional issues. As a result, there will be little coherence or stability to collective decisions, and even shared concerns will quickly disintegrate.

These organizational dilemmas are commonly posed in rational choice literature. But what makes this third group of rational choice theorists distinctive is that they have brought congressional parties to the forefront by emphasizing their impact and seeking to explain how they play critical roles in helping Congress to solve its coordination, collective action, and/or collective choice problems. Nonetheless, this group of theorists are far from solving these problems within a rational choice framework, and there is good reason to believe they will encounter substantial barriers to success.

First, whereas this group of rational choice theorists does see party as providing a crucial basis for solving fundamental organizational dilemmas, there is no consensus as to what the "glue" that holds congressional parties together might be. Some have emphasized the electoral benefits members gain from cooperative party strategies, postures, and operations. However, it is doubtful that these advantages are substantial enough in the American political system to explain the character and range of collective action on the basis of party that does occur. Others have emphasized the impact of broad policy principles, but this line of thought has received only sketchy development thus far and will ultimately require a very different theory of politics than the narrowly particularistic and distributive one now dominant among rational choice analysts.

Second, any adequate theory will have to explain party strengths and weaknesses in inducing or providing a basis for cooperative action in Congress at particular points in time as well as variation in these patterns over time. Rational choice theory has much to contribute on the basis of the theoretical work proponents have done regarding the impact of the size of core groups in bargaining situations. Still, explanation will remain severely restricted if the impacts of contextual variables as well as conditions outside Congress and of organizational constraints and commitments within Congress are not taken into account. Yet, such theorizing will be difficult for the rational choice approach to accomplish. It has made progress by treating such factors as "unknowns" outside the model and typically meets great difficulty when it tries to include them as matters to be explained and assessed.

In conclusion, the work of this third group of rational choice theorists is quite appealing. Unlike most analysts in both traditional and nontraditional camps, they recognize the need for a theory of party, understand many of the dimensions of such a theory, and have begun to try to supply one. However, these theorists too have their limitations, and their theorizing

about party needs substantial development and modification if it is to succeed.

ISSUES IN THEORY CONSTRUCTION

This criticism of current approaches to explaining the nature and role of congressional parties does not imply that we are ready or able to provide a full-blown theory of congressional parties—or even that it is necessary or likely that only one such theory can be formulated. The issues are so fundamental and complex that we can envision the emergence of a number of theories. However, any such theory, if it is to be taken seriously, will have to confront and deal with the three basic organizational dilemmas outlined above.

To accomplish this goal, party theorists will have to be sensitive to macro- *and* micro-level factors and seek to balance and blend them appropriately. The new group of rational choice theorists has provided a good deal of understanding about how parties successfully organize themselves in order to solve a variety of collective choice and collective action problems simultaneously. Yet such an approach ignores how external and internal contexts affect the behavior of party members, how such micro behavior leads to macro outcomes, and how those outcomes then have micro consequences. On the other hand, traditional theorists have provided a great deal of understanding about how shifting party strength is related to external context, typically by focusing on aggregate levels of party cohesion over time. Yet this latter approach has avoided questions about how and why legislative party coalitions, composed of individual partisans, can be mobilized, stabilized, and deployed effectively without disintegrating due to collective choice or action problems. Thus, both general approaches have missed important aspects of party politics, and both could be improved by increased attention to the ties that exist between micro and macro levels of analysis.

What is required, then, is a way of conceptualizing congressional parties and their effects which accords appropriate recognition to macro or contextual factors as well as micro or motivational factors. Obviously, this is no easy task—it requires blending research perspectives and agendas that have been quite independent—but it is a strategy with great potential. Instead of taking party simply as a given, it frames the problem in contingency terms from the very start and in so doing provides leeway for handling the large amounts of variance and fragility that party operations actually involve. Equally important, it provides a way to theorize about party which is sensitive to the interaction among external context, internal organizational constraints, and individual motivation.

As useful as this approach may be, it will not easily or quickly lead to a general theory of party. The final section of this essay identifies and discusses four sets of issues that must be confronted if such a theory is to be provided. While these different categories of issues do not exhaust the problems of building a theory of congressional parties, they do represent areas that are both crucial to that endeavor and ripe for further theorizing and research.

Conceptualizing Congressional Parties

The first set of issues concerns the varied and perplexing problems involved in articulating the nature and basis of congressional parties. If, as suggested, congressional parties should be approached as systems of cooperative action, they must be seen as associational in nature. What then is the basis of association? What is the glue that holds congressional parties together? In short, a rationale for party allegiance, voting, and organization must be established at the individual level that can serve as a basis for explaining how the barriers to organization posed by the dilemmas of coordination, collective action, and collective choice can be overcome, and why patterns of party cohesion, structure, and leadership style vary.

Gary W. Cox and Mathew D. McCubbins have proposed to solve the problem by emphasizing the reelection benefits of membership in congressional parties. There is merit in this argument; the ceaseless maneuvering in Congress by party leaders for political advantage in the eyes of the public lends intuitive support for this claim, as do the partisan (as opposed to the individual) bases of incumbency advantage. Both factors reinforce the empirical evidence that Cox and McCubbins bring to bear.

However, party voting patterns would not have attained their historically high levels of strength and stability if they were not substan-

tively rooted in policy desires or preferences as well. Indeed, an argument based on reelection motives implicitly rests on the positive effects of the party label—and such effects cannot be entirely devoid of policy content. Given the high degree to which partisanship structures and stabilizes voting patterns, the claim that it is rooted in substance as well as politics raises a very basic, traditional question: Are congressional parties aggregations of interests, formed purely and simply through the trading of advantage, or are they aggregations of interests whose formation has been disciplined and shaped by ideological orientations that combine beliefs and values into broad stances on public policy?

The former alternative should, however, be distinguished from the position of those who treat congressional politics as narrowly particularistic and distributive. That position equates the representation of interests with the representation of local and isolated district interests, and leads quite easily to the conclusion that parties are a façade. Yet viable conceptions of party rest instead on the recognition that American politics involves the conflict and reconciliation of interests and/or views that crisscross individual districts. Whether combined with theories of exchange or with theories of the constraining impact of shared value and belief systems, such a perspective provides a basis for party in the policy preferences or goals that unite members across districts. Members who share a set of policy goals might plausibly decide to cooperate to further those goals by organizing parties, using them to structure and stabilize coalition building, and creating organizational units and leaders with special powers and responsibilities to aid in those endeavors. This view, then, accomplishes something that a narrowly distributive and particularistic view cannot. Though one alternative remains broadly distributive, both provide a "glue" for party in the shared policy preferences or goals of members. In so doing, they also provide a framework for explaining variation in levels of party cohesion, the role and powers of party units, and the role and style of party leaders over time.

The Basis of Action The plausibility of forming and acting through parties presupposes the necessity and utility of organized action as an instrument for achieving member goals, and thus our argument still begs an important question. If preferences are shared, why would members organize parties rather than simply acting to implement their preferences?

Interestingly enough, once members share goals or preferences to some significant degree, the very dilemmas of coordination, collective action, and collective choice, which pose barriers to organized cooperation also provide incentives for overcoming them. This is especially true in legislatures, such as the House and Senate, where members are very autonomous. In such contexts, the endemic multidimensionality of issues threatens the stability of coalitions, even when an important set of preferences is shared. There is a need to translate policy desires into specific programs of action, to establish trust and confidence in the belief that cooperation will involve more benefits than costs, and to keep extraneous issues from dividing what would otherwise be a majority coalition. Organized action on the basis of party, its units, and its leaders serves all these ends.

This is not to suggest that these kinds of incentives easily or automatically resolve the three basic organizational dilemmas that exist at the individual level. Rather, the degree to which they do will depend on their strength—and their strength, in turn, will depend on the commonalities of interest and/or view that unite partisans. Even then, side payments or rewards drawn from extraneous sources will be a useful, if not essential, factor, and both sources of cohesion will be influenced by the state of external variables as well as internal organizational variables. The same is true of the incentives provided by reelection motivation. All of this testifies to the necessity, here as elsewhere, to blend micro and macro factors when seeking to construct a theory of party.

Unresolved Questions In concluding this section, a number of issues critical to understanding the nature and basis of congressional parties should be highlighted. Though we have taken general positions on several of these issues, all are difficult, and fundamental questions remain. What is the relative influence of political and policy motivations in providing the glue that unites party? To what degree do these motivations reinforce each other, and to what degree do they conflict? If they do conflict, how are these conflicts resolved or han-

dled? Substantively, how should one conceptualize the policy basis of party, and what connections exist to broader views of the character of American politics? What portion of American politics is narrowly particularistic and distributive, and how does this pattern of politics coexist with party politics? Must party politics in whole or in large part be viewed as essentially distributive, albeit in a broad, nonparticularistic sense? If so, how can this view be further developed, and what role should be give to ideological constraints in the form of shared value and belief systems? Or if not, can a valid view of American politics and parties be premised on on and developed wholly or largely in terms of the shared beliefs and values of the American people? And finally, what role, if any, do side payments play, and how should their role be identified and integrated with the primary explanation?

Linkage Issues

A second set of issues concerns the role of congressional parties in linking congressional behavior and outcomes to the two major external arenas with which the Congress interacts—the electorate and the executive branch. Congress is, of course, rooted at the electoral level, and the relationship between members and constituents lies at the heart of the representative process. At the same time, congressional operations and performance are profoundly affected by the president and his key staff and agency lieutenants, all of whom have partisan allegiances and connections. Nor should it be forgotten that intense and continuing interaction between members and political echelons of the executive branch takes place both in the initial processes of making law and in the subsequent processes of administering or implementing it.

These various modes of interaction are not rigidly compartmentalized from one another, rather, they overlap. Interaction among the various actors in the legislative and executive branches, as well as with the electorate, is dynamic and multidimensional, both in terms of time and of the decision making level or process. Moreover, party does not provide the sole mechanism of linkage either in legislative-electoral relations or legislative-executive relations; and the congressional party is only a component of a wider party entity. All these factors complicate the problem of specifying the linkage role of congressional parties. Nonetheless, given the close and continuing forms of interaction that occur and their impacts on congressional operations and performance, it is a task that congressional party theorists must address.

Legislative-Electoral Interaction If we turn first to legislative-electoral interaction, traditional literature accords party generally, and the congressional party specifically, a critical linkage role in tying policy outcomes in Congress to the electorate. However, nontraditional research has been less inclined to do so, and has for the most part treated representation on an individualistic, distributive, and particularistic basis. Thus, both the existence and dimensions of the linkage role of congressional parties remain open to dispute, and there are a number of serious problems that party theorists must confront and resolve.

To start, the specific mechanisms by which party establishes a policy tie between members and constituents need to be identified more clearly. This is a key problem for any theory of congressional party which approaches party as associational in nature and based on interests and/or views that crosscut constituencies. Given existing levels of voter information and apathy, as well as the bluntness of electoral decision making in plurality elections, it is not at all obvious how meaningful voters' choices can be, nor how party serves as an effective mechanism for aggregating voter opinions or preferences. Some progress in this regard has been made by those who see broadly defined ideological orientations as integral and defining components of party coalitions. The argument that the organization of policy options in terms of broadly defined systems of belief and value serves to facilitate both voter choice and preference aggregation on the basis of party has considerable appeal as well as support in the empirical literature. Yet such results may well be contingent on the presentation and character of policy issues. It is therefore not surprising that the strength of ideological factors in American politics remains disputed. Claims for the role of party based on the effects of ideology thus remain open to challenge and in need of further analysis and substantiation.

A related problem concerns the importance of linkage through partisan processes of aggregation. Strong party theorists and realignment theorists agree that meaningful choice and accountability occur only when the party as a whole is united on a policy program and the congressional party behaves in a highly cohesive and disciplined manner. The linkage role of the congressional party, then, is crucial and closely tied to its ability to operate as an important component of a broader national party. In contrast, those who view American politics from a Madisonian perspective do not equate representative government and party government. Rather, they take a far more limited position on the role of party in linking Congress to the electorate. While they do acknowledge that party plays an important linkage role, they emphasize freely forming congressional majorities. As a consequence, they embrace coalition building on the basis of party only insofar as the resulting majorities are neither artificial nor coerced. And by extension, they do not believe that such majorities must or should be stable; nor do they object to bipartisan majorities. Opponents of party government thus take a far more contingent view of the linkage role of congressional parties, and they are far more tolerant than strong party proponents of other forms of linkage. Yet, if the strong party view can be criticized for making party a factor that exhausts the processes of linkage and representation, it is equally true that the Madisonian view leaves the roles both of party and of other units or mechanisms too ambiguous. Hence, both approaches leave the problem far too unresolved; as a consequence, they add to rather than ease the burdens of constructing an adequate theory of congressional parties.

Finally, positions on the role of congressional parties in linking members and constituents are often based on unexamined and needlessly exclusive assumptions about questions of autonomy and dependence. Many students of Congress, both traditional and nontraditional, assume that dependence is the condition to be explained and maximized. The reasons are varied, and they relate to views of representation as well as to ease of measurement. Yet it is undeniable that elections are very blunt instruments of voter choice, and that members attempt both to frame issues for constituents and to explain or justify actions that are not closely tied to electoral outcomes. Still, other students of Congress, again in both traditional and nontraditional camps, assume that autonomy, not dependence, is the governing condition. Some value it because of its alleged contributions to representation and deliberation; others stigmatize it because they see it as a facet of the self-serving manipulation of constituents by members. Yet, members in quite fundamental ways do remain dependant on serving, and winning the favor of, their constituents. It is therefore difficult to accept "either-or" choices on questions of autonomy and dependence. Balanced treatments that focus on patterns of autonomy and dependence are preferable—and some exist. However, this problem has not been addressed at length or in depth, despite its fundamental importance to understanding the linkage role of congressional parties.

Legislative-Executive Interaction The issues regarding legislative-executive relations are broadly similar in character and equally difficult to resolve. Once again, there are problems in establishing the linkage role of congressional parties per se. Although such a role is generally acknowledged in the lawmaking process, it is ignored or denied in the case of the administrative process: both traditional and nontraditional students of congressional oversight treat party as having little or no importance. This assumption needs to be reexamined. On the one hand, the majority party organizes the structures and processes of Congress through which oversight activities are conducted; on the other hand, huge delegations of policy discretion have been accorded to executive officers in areas of policy where stark partisan differences exist. It is worth asking, then, whether partisan policy goals and partisan maneuvering for political advantage play a larger role in congressional oversight of administrative decision making than analysts have recognized. Recent work by Roderick Kiewiet and Mathew D. McCubbins (*The Logic of Delegation* [1991]) suggests that this is indeed the case. It may well be that the effects of partisan concerns vary under different conditions of cohesion and control—for example, divided government versus unified government, or the division of the president's party in Congress into opposing blocs. But in any event the role of party in oversight under different conditions needs to be more fully explored.

Second, though the linkage role of congressional parties is widely acknowledged in the lawmaking process, serious problems continue to confront party theorists. Various aspects of this linkage have been explored, largely by empirically oriented students of presidential power who treat party as one of several factors that determine presidential success. Their analysis, however, has been too static and conventional to contribute much to any theory of the role of congressional parties. In contrast, students of Congress have been stymied by the president's ambiguous status as a member of the congressional party. They have, as a result, either ignored or sidestepped the task of pinning down the character and contours of the linkage role of congressional parties in a theoretically adequate manner.

Yet, if the problem is reformulated, it can be addressed. The fact that the president is not a member of Congress does not mean that he does not participate in the legislative process, so the part that the congressional party plays in linking party members in the two branches remains a fundamental question. Still, it is clear that the institutional differences separating the president and Congress do impede linkage through the congressional party. Given different constituency bases, different powers and responsibilities, and different internal decision-making structures, divergences in policy views and political fortunes between partisans in Congress and a party president are inevitable.

It follows that the ability of party to link a president and his fellow partisans in Congress is a highly contingent matter. The fact that the president is not formally a member of the congressional party should not bar inquiry; rather, it defines a key parameter. What requires further examination and elaboration as part and parcel of any theory of congressional parties are the conditions and factors that determine the degree of cooperation in the linkage that party establishes between fellow partisans in the legislative and executive branches.

A related problem concerns the importance attributed to party in linking the legislative and executive branches. Once again, strong party theorists and realignment theorists have no viable alternative to linkage on the basis of party: they see the congressional party as an integral component of a wider party with a designated role to play if valid representation and effective action are to be secured. Both suffer if a president cannot mobilize stable and cohesive partisan majorities to support his programs. Weak party cohesion as well as the emergence of bipartisan majorities frustrate presidential leadership and in so doing promote the triumph of special interests. And divided government is inherently flawed and regarded simply as a recipe for unrepresentative and ineffective government.

In contrast, those with a Madisonian perspective take a different view. Their tolerance for loosely coupled relations between the congressional party and the wider party, and their belief that party deserves no more force or legitimacy than its ability to aggregate preferences, join with their regard for the separation of powers and rational deliberation to cast party in the role of an important, but not exclusive or dominant, linkage mechanism. Indeed, in the Madisonian view, linkage on the basis of party poses a danger if it serves to subordinate Congress to the president. Students of Congress with a Madisonian perspective thus have a far more qualified view of presidential leadership than do strong party theorists or realignment theorists. Their understanding that there are beneficial effects of a clash of institutions based on different constituency principles and that rational deliberation can contribute refinements to lawmaking leads them to accept presidential leadership only in the form of presidential initiative and persuasion, not control.

Such a position, it should be noted, is not necessarily adverse to divided government. This fact has not been apparent because, in the past, weak party theorists have accepted the proposition that unity is necessary to representative and effective government, even if responsible party government is not. However, this acceptance is not theoretically rooted and yet another case in which the Madisonian view has not been sufficiently spelled out under different conditions of party strength.

Obviously, this is a need that should be addressed. Understanding the consequences of divided government for representation and effectiveness is crucial to an adequate theory of congressional parties. Moreover, for those with a Madisonian perspective, this problem depends on the actual contours and impacts of linkage on the basis of party. It is thus a question whose examination both involves and transcends the role congressional parties play in executive-legislative linkage when the president and the congressional majority share the same partisan allegiance.

Finally, as with treatments of legislative-electoral relations, there has been a distinct tendency in treating legislative-executive relations to assume that questions of autonomy and dependence pose exclusive alternatives. Theorists, both of strong party and of realignment, have emphasized dependence and treated congressional autonomy in the lawmaking process as a problem to be corrected; in contrast, Madisonians have emphasized autonomy and sought to preserve it in the face of a secular growth in presidential power. Yet what prevails, in fact, are not autonomy or dependence per se, but changing patterns of autonomy and dependence in lawmaking. A similar situation exists in treatments of congressional oversight of the executive. Analysts have tended either to assume dependence and emphasize congressional power or to assume autonomy and emphasize congressional ineffectiveness. Thus, both areas need, as an integral part of a theory of congressional parties, a more balanced treatment of the actual patterns, change in their character over time, and the factors that determine such change.

Unresolved Questions To summarize, there are a number of important linkage issues that any theory of congressional parties must address if it is to be adequate. For legislative-electoral relations the most important questions are: What role does party—as opposed to nonpartisan modes or mechanisms—play in linking members and constituents, and how and why does its role vary? Given the obstacles that exist, how does party succeed in providing meaningful choices to voters and aggregating preferences across constituencies? Can reliance on ideological factors to explain party-based linkage be further extended and confirmed? How important is the linkage that party establishes between members and constituents for representative government? And finally, can one establish decline in the role of party as a linkage mechanism and translate findings on linkage into findings on representation?

In analyzing legislative-executive relations, the most important questions are: In the lawmaking process, what are the contours and determinants of the linkage party establishes between members and top political echelons of the executive branch? What other modes or mechanisms of linkage exist, and what determines their role and strength? Is linkage on the basis of party crucial to representative and effective government, or should it be judged in relation to changing conditions of party strength and institutional control? How does one determine and assess performance given the conflicts that exist between effectiveness and representativeness? Should party theorists continue to ignore or discount the role of party as a linkage mechanism in the administrative process, despite the presence of many of the same structures of power and incentive that exist in the lawmaking process?

And a final question bears on both fields: In analyzing relations or interaction with both the electorate and the executive, how can patterns or mixtures of congressional autonomy and dependence be identified so as to permit these factors to be treated in a balanced, rather than dichotomous, fashion?

Operational Issues

A third set of issues concern the role of congressional parties in the operations of Congress. Despite the prominence of party leaders and partisan factors in the day-to-day operations of the Congress, the impact of party on congressional structures, processes, and outcomes remains theoretically murky. This stems from both the high degree to which party has been treated as a given in the traditional literature and the challenges to conventional wisdom about party posed by the nontraditional literature as well.

The Role of Party   We have argued in this essay that rational choice approaches which seek to explain legislative operations solely in individualistic and atomistic terms, with little or no regard for the role of party, are deficient. Indeed, this is a view that even some rational choice theorists have acknowledged. It is one thing to believe that explanation must have a basis in individual motivation, but quite another to seek to account for cooperation in organized settings in an entirely individualistic and atomistic manner. Thus, the gains-in-trade and median voter models, despite their sensitivity to fundamental theoretical issues, cannot adequately explain how Congress handles or

resolves the basic organizational dilemmas that confront it. They cannot explain the high degree of patterning in roll-call voting or the stability of outcomes. Nor, given the wide-ranging impact fixed structural arrangements have across issue areas and the differential distributions of power and authority they involve, can these models explain why structural change typically occurs only incrementally over time, why structure divides into formal and party components, why it has become so elaborate and complex in Congress, or why key positions in the formal structure are allocated by party mechanisms according to partisan criteria and filled by party leaders. This is not to say that congressional structure and process can be explained entirely by the force of party—but rather that party stabilizes majority formation in ways that permit structural elaboration, require the design of structure to be subject to partisan considerations, and make it rational to confer advantages on party leaders in the use or manipulation of structural arrangements.

Contrary to the dominant thrust of rational choice theory, congressional parties are far more than a façade; they do play an important role in helping Congress handle its basic organizational dilemmas. To be sure, Congress's success in mastering these dilemmas is far from complete. However, all organizations experience some degree of failure in this regard, and the struggle is necessarily a continuing one in all organizational settings. It is also true that party's ability to contribute to congressional effectiveness varies, depending on its ability to handle or resolve the problems of coordination, collective action, and collective choice that it confronts as an organization. Nonetheless, the degree to which congressional parties—especially the majority party—successfully manage such problems is the degree to which they contribute to Congress's ability to overcome these same barriers to effective decision making at institutional levels of operation.

Consider the distinctive parameters that frame coordination, collective action, and collective choice problems in the Congress and the role party can play in overcoming them. In an organization that must make its key decisions by continuously aggregating highly autonomous members into majorities, party provides a framework in terms of shared goals and beliefs for building such majorities on specific policy programs across diverse issue areas. In an organization that cannot rely on hierarchy or technical knowledge either to restrain the clash of opinion or to control the divisive effects of the divisions of labor needed to provide specialized information, party provides crucial inducements for the creation of integrating mechanisms in the formal structure as well as party leaders and units to do the work and bear the costs of coordinating decision making in both the formal and party structures. In an organization in which decision making issues are open to member choice or definition and multidimensional in character, and in which institutional restrictions on self-serving behavior are very lax, party provides policy incentives to focus attention and effort on selected goals, political incentives to pursue career goals in collective and cooperative fashion, and opportunities for party leaders to build feelings of trust and comity that reduce the inclination of members to act in risk adverse and narrowly self-serving ways.

The Limits of Party   These claims on behalf of party are valid, but they are also quite general. As such, they necessarily gloss over a number of serious issues that party theorists cannot ignore. First, we need to understand better the determinants of party's ability to solve its internal organizational dilemmas, and thereby contribute to Congress's ability to handle or resolve the broader coordination, collective action, and collective choice problems it confronts as an institution. Given the electoral roots of party, much of the answer undoubtedly lies in the factors and conditions at the electoral level that promote party cohesion at the legislative level. These factors and conditions are complex. They include not only geographic configurations of interests and/or views across the nation, but also historical circumstances, career interests, and the connections between congressional and presidential elections. Yet, despite the importance of electoral determinants, it would be a mistake to ignore the role of other external and internal determinants. Certainly, the political leverage provided by a party president is an important factor, as are the roles played by congressional party leaders and party mechanisms. Nonetheless, the degree to which party cohesion is based on electoral factors and determines, rather than reflects, the character and impact of these factors is not

clear. The historical record indicates that it takes very high levels of party cohesion to sustain strong and effective party organizational mechanisms, and that such mechanisms atrophy as party cohesion declines. However, the terms of this relationship remain quite hazy. Finally, the impact of party leaders and mechanisms on party cohesion is affected by the degree of elaboration and centralization in the formal structure. Party leaders use their positions and resources in the formal structure to reinforce their influence in the party structure and vice versa. Here as elsewhere, then, the relationships we wish to examine are not linear but interactive, and thus in need of careful disentanglement. This is no easy task—especially since great care must be taken not to confound causes and effects in relying on measures of party strength derived from floor votes.

Second, although it is true that party's ability to assist Congress in handling its organizational dilemmas depends on the party's ability to master these same problems internally, it does not follow that Congress's ability to operate effectively as a decision making entity depends entirely on the role of party. It is important not to ignore or downgrade the role of party, but it is equally important not to exaggerate it. Yet, delineating the terms of the relationship between various levels of party success in handling its organizational dilemmas, on the one hand, and institutional effectiveness, on the other, presents the most formidable theoretical problem of all.

The roots of this difficulty are deeply grounded in basic patterns of politics and linkage in the United States. The terms of this relationship are far less complex in those legislatures where coalition building, structural elaboration, and structural use respond for the most part to partisan considerations and are controlled by party leaders. Conversely, they would also be far less complex in legislatures where these three key aspects of legislative operations respond directly and immediately to atomistic and shifting majorities, aggregated on the basis of kaleidoscopic configurations of preferences in different policy areas. However, the institutional and political parameters that shape the Congress define a legislature that is neither the British Parliament nor the marketlike arena of rational choice theorists. It is, rather, something between these two extremes. Moreover, its position between these extremes varies, depending on the ability of party to order preferences in terms of broad policy orientations and to stabilize them around a set of party policy programs.

Thus, while party produces the most stable, comprehensive framework for coalition building available in the Congress, it does not exclude other modes or bases of coalition building. Floor majorities, even when they involve party splits of substantial proportions, are rarely purely partisan, and there are always policy areas in which majorities are not partisan but bipartisan or even virtually unanimous. There are, in short, other bases for aggregating preferences that reinforce as well as replace party. What is more, the average levels of these different types of majorities vary over time, as does their overall configuration in relation to each other. It is facts such as these that render simple condemnation of divided government erroneous and complicate the task of assessing its impact.

Similarly, although partisan considerations affect the leeway for and design of structural arrangements, these arrangements usually respond far more to balanced judgments of what is needed to allow majorities to rule as opposed to what is needed to protect the interests of minorities and individual members. Thus, partisan considerations do not bar structural arrangements for handling coordination, collective action, and collective choice problems that can be controlled and used by other majorities, minorities, and individuals apart from, and even against, the majority party—for example, committee systems, amendment procedures, special calendars, dilatory procedures, and so on. As a result, structural arrangements overall do not vary as much in relation to levels of party strength as they do in relation to many other external and internal factors that have far more impact in determining the balances that the rules establish among the competing needs identified above. Note, for example, that House structure has continually grown more complex and elaborate over time despite great variation in party cohesion, and that current House and Senate structures differ markedly despite similar levels of party cohesion.

Finally, although structural arrangements by nature confer disproportionate advantage on certain members, the factors that control a procedural mechanism's scope and design neither establish nor guarantee party dominance. As noted above, structural arrangements can be used apart from, and even against, party leaders and party majorities. What is critical, then, to party's ability to use or manipulate structure is the breadth and depth of its internal cohesion, though negative or obstructive exercises of power are more easily sustained than are positive exercises that seek to advance policy programs. It is true that party derives substantial advantages in its ability to use or manipulate existing structure from its status as the stablest, most comprehensive form of majority and from the presence of its own internal decision making mechanisms. Still, when party cohesion declines, party's control over structural arrangements and the advantages it derives from such control erode. Indeed, depending on the aspect of structure involved and the character of the decline, party control can become a mere façade, as the role of southern Democratic chairs in the 1940s and 1950s well demonstrates.

It should be clear, then, that the institutional effectiveness of Congress is not a simple function of the role of party. The instincts of rational choice theory are quite sound, even if their manifestations in analysis have been highly procrustean. To understand Congress's ability to handle or resolve its basic organizational dilemmas, one must understand the determinants of coalition building and structure more generally, and not merely the determinants of party strength and effectiveness. The manner in which all these factors interact and affect congressional structure, process, and outcomes is obviously complex—and, to complicate matters further, patterns and results vary with party strength.

The Role of Party Leaders   In seeking to disentangle the components and terms of such an involved pattern of interaction, party theorists need to address a third aspect of the puzzle whose successful treatment in all probability is essential to further theoretical progress —namely, the role of party leaders.

Party leaders in Congress are the key actors in the formal and party arenas as well as in the linkage between the two. They therefore play a crucial role in bringing the force of party to assist Congress in successfully managing its coordination, collective action, and collective-choice problems. This is true not simply because their relationship to the president and their positions in the formal and party structures endow them with leverage in building majorities and manipulating structural arrangements on their behalf, or because they can be induced by the rewards and responsibilities of office to bear most of the personal costs involved. It is also true because so much in both the formal and party arenas depends on their talents for harmonizing differences, for manipulating incentives and sources of structural advantage, for framing the discussion of issues and controlling the agenda, and for developing reputations for competence, trustworthiness, and fair judgment. Moreover, since they are formal leaders as well as party leaders, they play a critical role in the processes of coalition building and structural use or manipulation that reinforce and even replace reliance on party. Party majorities often need assistance from minority elements to succeed, and party leaders play a pivotal role in providing it. Similarly, bipartisan and unanimous majorities often require their involvement—and almost always their favor or acquiescence—in some important aspect of voting or procedure.

Thus, if congressional effectiveness depends on interaction between the role of party and other more general factors or conditions that affect coalition building and structural design, then it is party leaders who must be relied on to mobilize the force of party and to bridge the gap when this force proves inadequate or irrelevant. Yet our understanding of the role, style, and effectiveness of party leaders is quite primitive. It is clear that great variations occur over time, as well as between the House and Senate, and that contextual factors and personal skills are involved. Indeed, rational choice theory, with its treatment of factors such as trust, reputation, and so on, has opened up analysis of the personal dimension, while organization theory has much to contribute on the contextual side. Combining these approaches to explain variations in the behavior and impact of party leaders, and to tie such explanation to a more general theory of the role of party in legislative operations holds great promise, but it is a task that remains to be done.

Unresolved Questions In summary, then, party is neither irrelevant to institutional effectiveness in the Congress nor the only factor of consequence. To elaborate this proposition into a theory capable of explaining the complex relationship between the role of party and Congress's ability to resolve its basic organizational dilemmas, a number of difficult questions must be answered. These include many of the above-mentioned questions concerning the concept of party and linkage, because positions on these issues provide necessary foundations for addressing operational issues. With that understood, the key questions that need to be posed directly with respect to operations are as follows: What factors determine variation in party cohesion or strength, and how should the relationship between various external and internal determinants be understood? How does party, at various levels of cohesion or strength, interact with more general factors to affect Congress's ability to handle its coordination, collective action, and collective choice problems? Does the solution of this problem require a general theory of congressional structure and process? If so, how can the roles of individual preferences, contextual parameters, and organizational constraints be integrated? Finally, how should we understand the work of party leaders and its relation to party as a determinant of institutional effectiveness?

Normative and Empirical Issues

A fourth and final set of issues concerns how the unavoidable overlaps between normative and empirical aspects of research on congressional parties should be handled or treated.

Reasons for Overlap When the role of parties is directly and openly approached in a normative fashion, beliefs about existing conditions and the potential for constructive change are integral parts of the positions that emerge regarding the needs or demands of representative government. It is not surprising, then, that empirical claims about the power of special interests, the responsiveness and accountability of legislators, and the consequences of change are usually among the most disputed topics when advocates and opponents of more responsible parties clash over issues of reform. The same point applies even more strongly when normative analysis focuses on issues of government performance instead of the needs or demands of representative government. The presumption here is that the standard is hard and objective because it centers on the effectiveness and efficiency with which policy outputs are produced. This approach, however, involves considerable self-deception; short of manifest paralysis or breakdown, it cannot be pursued without subscribing to representative ideals that prize action over consent and the resolution of dispute over conflict—far more than would a Madisonian view of how these choices should be evaluated. Ineffectiveness per se, then, is quite a hazy standard. Despite appearances of objectivity, a performance-based approach necessarily rests on claims about empirical reality to an even higher degree than do overtly moral ideal normative approaches.

When the role of parties is approached in an empirical fashion, overlaps with normative concerns are equally unavoidable. Choices of empirical frameworks involve choices about how to view reality, and in politics such choices have normative content because politics itself does. This is particularly clear when traditional approaches, such as realignment theory, take stances that implicitly view American politics as an effort to achieve the public interest through representative government and treat party as a crucial means of achieving such results. However, the point also applies to those broad approaches which see American politics more starkly, as an effort to control the assertion of interests (both individual and group) so as to resolve conflict or to secure maximum collective benefits in some utilitarian sense. In fact, the point extends even to narrowly defined empirical work, because this type of research also accepts and operates within key parameters set by such basic features of representative government as elections and majority rule. Thus, in politics as opposed to physics a seamless blend of normative and empirical assumptions are involved in the frameworks with which analysts view and question reality.

For these very reasons, the findings of empirical research have normative implications. To be sure, these implications are more obvious and significant to the degree that the normative content implicit in the framework is deep and pervasive—for example, the normative implications of realignment theory are clearer and more comprehensive than those of research on party identification or the determinants of committee appointments. Nonethe-

less, research on all these topics has normative significance because it has clear implications for the validity of the web of empirical and normative assumptions that the framework of inquiry accepts as correct. In sum, then, evidence about empirical reality is always important for normative judgments, even if it cannot dictate them, because such judgments involve beliefs about the empirical world and the possibilities of ordering it.

This is not to argue that there is no basis for rational argument about normative questions apart from empirical evidence, nor that empirical evidence is worthless when basic views of empirical reality conflict. Shared moral or ideal commitments provide a basis for rational argument about the content of these commitments and how they should be balanced or prioritized. Similarly, the claim that theory interpenetrates fact to such an extent that the world becomes totally subjective or interpretive is false. The world is not entirely subject to intellectual construction, and evidence does apply across paradigms. It is *certainty* that is the victim of a more sophisticated understanding of science, not the existence of objective reality or our ability to attain knowledge regarding it. Nonetheless, it is true that the problems created for research by the overlaps of empirical and normative factors make rational analysis based on evidence even more complex in politics than in physics. Thus, it is critically important that researchers recognize these difficulties and devise ways to handle them.

Reactions to Overlaps These needs have received little attention in the study of congressional parties. The very character of normative approaches involves the danger that facts will be identified and chosen primarily to serve as instruments of the framework's normative assumptions rather than as a basis for testing the empirical beliefs supporting these assumptions. Still, in the case of congressional parties these difficulties have become almost completely intractable because many analysts refuse to question or even to recognize their normative assumptions—either per se or when new evidence challenges the empirical claims or beliefs these assumptions involve.

The situation with respect to empirical approaches is also troubled. Many analysts simply ignore the normative content or implications of their work, claiming that, as research scientists, normative concerns are not their responsibilities. Yet, even if empirical results do not challenge the web of normative and empirical assumptions underlying a particular framework, these results nevertheless inevitably have normative implications, and they may well be significant—for example, that representative government is impeded more than served by the barriers to action that typify nonrealignment periods, that politicians have gained substantial ability to manipulate electoral control to benefit their own careers, or that majority outcomes in Congress are subject to manipulation through agenda power, strategies of voting and presentation, and/or information control.

Other empirical analysts do confront the normative implications of their findings. This occurs most often when results or findings starkly challenge the blend of normative and empirical assumptions that their frameworks of inquiry involve. The efforts of realignment theorists to cope with divided government and the decline of party are a case in point. At times, these confrontations also occur because empirical results contradict the very general normative standards an analyst holds, even though these standards are only loosely tied to the analyst's framework of inquiry and may well not be entirely compatible with it. Morris P. Fiorina's critique of his own findings in *Congress: Keystone of the Washington Establishment* (1977) on the basis of their deleterious consequences for the public interest and effective policy making provide a good illustration. Whatever the reasons, however, confrontations are typically haphazard, partial, and nonproductive. When analysts respond to the serious contradictions between their findings and their frameworks of inquiry, they are often so imprisoned by their assumptions that they contribute little more than confusion and dismay. For reasons they do not fully understand, the world does not work as postulated—but they are not hesitant to conclude that the results are clearly bad. Similarly, when analysts respond to their findings with critiques that are only ambiguously tied to their frameworks of inquiry, their responses suffer from lack of grounding in normative theory or even in the analysts' own empirical findings.

Further Directions   Still, there are some encouraging developments as well. The emergence of divided government in the 1980s has prompted an extensive and critical reexamination of traditional views of the causes and consequences of both unified and divided government. Moreover, contemporary analyses of the roles played by congressional parties and committees have involved trenchant and extensive reassessments of prior research. Thus, work on congressional parties in the late 1980s and 1990s manifests a new willingness to question existing explanations and assumptions, both normative and empirical, on the basis of challenging evidence drawn from the current operation of the American political system. Such openness is welcome. It needs to be combined with heightened sensitivity to the inevitability of overlaps between the empirical and the normative in politics, as well as with more sophisticated theorizing about patterns of interdependence between these two realms, and strategies for dealing with the problems that result. There are, of course, no quick and easy solutions to these problems; indeed, what is at issue here are basic questions of epistemology that are critical to the social sciences generally. Nor is it at all likely that scholars of congressional parties will agree on how to deal with the problems that result from these overlaps, if or when the issue is widely confronted. Nonetheless, there is far more to gain by addressing these problems than by continuing to treat them as if they were nonexistent or unimportant. Benign neglect can only produce more confusion and discord.

CONCLUSION

Congressional parties, as is so often the case in political science, are a moving target. The roles they play are the products of a complex set of internal and external determinants whose identities we sense only broadly, and whose patterns of interaction we understand only in limited ways. This is not to deny that the time and effort we have spent studying them has given us a great deal of knowledge about them. Nonetheless, our knowledge is vulnerable to changes in basic parameters and patterns of interaction among determinants. To our surprise and distress, such changes transform congressional parties into entities that behave and are structured in ways we do not anticipate and have considerable difficulty explaining.

As a result, much of what we accept as certain about congressional parties in one period or era seems no longer to be true in a succeeding period or era. Indeed, there is considerable irony in the fact that the scholarship of a succeeding era typically regards its understanding as superior to that of a prior era, yet the knowledge of each is highly dependant on the existing state of underlying parameters or conditions and their immediate effects on the mix of determinants that govern the role of parties. All this highlights one of the prime themes of this essay—the need to fill the theoretical gaps that exist with respect to the role of congressional parties. We have taken too much for granted while arguing about empirical and normative issues of great importance. The inevitable result is that events continually outdistance our knowledge and our arguments.

As is generally true, the problem of understanding basic parameters and determinants in the case of congressional parties is a problem that will continually redefine itself as theory grows more sophisticated. Moreover, a great deal of indeterminacy will have to be accommodated theoretically, because we are dealing with human actors who define the meaning of events. Nonetheless, we can do better than we have done by confronting the time-bound character of our knowledge and the challenges posed by nontraditional analysts.

This essay has argued that the best path to constructing a theory of congressional parties lies in addressing the issues posed here and seeking to resolve them by examining and mixing the micro- and macrofoundations of congressional politics and parties. Some may disagree, but what remains above dispute is that there is no more fundamental issue in the social sciences than the bases and consequences of cooperative action in organized settings, and that the legislative and party components of American democracy provide an appropriate and useful context in which to address it.

BIBLIOGRAPHY

Early General Work on Parties

A number of texts are particularly useful for establishing the broad parameters of analysis and concern that have shaped the study and understanding of congressional parties. Some works of consequence did appear in the late nineteenth and early twentieth centuries. The most noteworthy are WOODROW WILSON, *Congressional Government* (New York, 1956 [1885]); JAMES BRYCE, *The American Commonwealth* (New York, 1973 [1889]); ARTHUR N. HOLCOMBE, *The Political Parties of To-day: A Study in Republican and Democratic Politics* (New York, 1924); and PAUL D. HASBROUCK, *Party Government in the House of Representatives* (New York, 1927). Landmark studies of the 1940s and 1950s include E. E. SCHATTSCHNEIDER, *Party Government* (New York, 1942); V. O. KEY, *Politics, Parties, and Pressure Groups*, 2d ed. (New York, 1942); JAMES M. BURNS, *Congress on Trial: The Legislative Process and the Administrative State* (New York, 1949); JULIUS TURNER, *Party and Constituency: Pressures on Congress* (Baltimore, 1951); BERTRAM M. GROSS, *The Legislative Struggle: A Study in Social Combat* (New York, 1953); and DAVID TRUMAN, *The Congressional Party: A Case Study* (New York, 1959). A handful of authors before 1940 focused on sources of leadership in Congress and in so doing also devoted attention to the place of party. They are as follows: MARY P. FOLLETT, *The Speaker of the House of Representatives* (New York, 1904 [1896]); GEORGE R. BROWN, *The Leadership of Congress* (Indianapolis, 1922); CHANG-WEI CHIU, *The Speaker of the House of Representatives Since 1896* (New York, 1928); and PENDLETON HERRING, *Presidential Leadership: The Political Relations of Congress and the Chief Executive* (New York, 1940).

Traditional Systemic Approaches

A number of essays have generally tackled the question of political parties and their relationship to governance. A useful starting point for gaining a normative perspective representing a great deal of the traditional party literature is AUSTEN RANNEY, *The Doctrine of Responsible Party Government* (Urbana, Ill., 1962). Especially important for specifying the systemic place of parties from a traditional perspective are these works: LEON D. EPSTEIN, *Political Parties in the American Mold* (Madison, Wis., 1986); JAMES L. SUNDQUIST, *Dynamics of the Party System: Alignment and Realignment of Political Parties in the United States* (Washington, D.C., 1973); GIOVANNI SARTORI, *Parties and Party Systems: A Framework for Analysis* (Cambridge, Eng., 1976); SAMUEL J. ELDERSVELD, *Political Parties in American Society* (New York, 1982); ARTHUR A. MAASS, *Congress and the Common Good* (New York, 1983); DENISE L. BAER and DAVID A. BOSITIS, *Elite Cadres and Party Coalitions: Representing the Public in Party Politics* (New York, 1988); and FRANK J. SORAUF and PAUL A. BECK, *Party Politics in America*, 6th ed. (Glenview, Ill., 1988). For a good general survey of these positions (and others), see LEON D. EPSTEIN, "The Scholarly Commitment to Parties," in ADA W. FINIFTER, ed., *Political Science: The State of the Discipline* (Washington, D.C., 1983).

A second type of work, on realignments, is profuse, and the positions taken by scholars are many. For a summary and extension of this literature see DAVID W. BRADY, *Critical Elections and Congressional Policy Making* (Stanford, Calif., 1988). For other discussions, on realignments in American politics and related concerns with the decline of parties, see WALTER DEAN BURNHAM, *Critical Elections and the Mainspring of American Politics* (New York, 1970) and *The Current Crisis in American Politics* (New York, 1982); EVERETT C. LADD and CHARLES D. HADLEY, *Transformations of the American Party System: Political Coalitions from the New Deal to the 1970's* (New York, 1975); NELSON W. POLSBY, *Consequences of Party Reform* (New York, 1983); WILLIAM J. CROTTY, *The Decline of American Political Parties, 1952–1980* (Cambridge, Mass., 1984); and MARTIN P. WATTENBERG, *The Decline of American Political Parties, 1952–1988* (Cambridge, Mass., 1990).

Other Traditional Approaches

Separate from the traditional systemic overviews of congressional parties is a large body of empirical work. One stream of this research has focused on linkages with constituents via electoral mechanisms. In particular, see the surveys by HERBERT B. ASHER, "Voting Behavior Research in the 1980s: An Examination of Some Old and New Problem Areas," in ADA

FINIFTER, ed., *Political Science: The State of the Discipline,* (Washington, D.C., 1983), and PAUL A. BECK, "Choice, Context, and Consequence: Beaten and Unbeaten Paths Toward a Science of Electoral Behavior," in HERBERT F. WEISBERG, ed., *Political Science: The Science of Politics* (New York, 1986). Other work includes WARREN E. MILLER and DONALD E. STOKES, "Constituency Influence in Congress," *American Political Science Review* 57:7 (1963); RICHARD F. FENNO, *Home Style: House Members in Their Districts* (Boston, 1978); MALCOLM E. JEWELL, "Legislators and Constituents in the Representative Process," in GERHARD LOEWENBERG, SAMUEL C. PATTERSON, and JEWELL, eds., *Handbook of Legislative Research* (Cambridge, Mass., 1983); GERALD C. WRIGHT, "Elections and the Potential for Policy Change in Congress," in GERALD C. WRIGHT, LEROY N. RIESELBACH, and LAWRENCE C. DODD, eds., *Congress and Policy Change* (New York, 1986); GARY C. JACOBSON, *The Politics of Congressional Elections*, 3d ed. (New York, 1992); CATHERINE SHAPIRO, DAVID W. BRADY, RICHARD A. BRODY, and JOHN A. FEREJOHN, "Linking Constituency Opinion and Senate Voting Scores: A Hybrid Explanation," *Legislative Studies Quarterly* 15:2 (1990); and WARREN E. MILLER, "Party Identification, Realignment, and Party Voting: Back to the Basics," *American Political Science Review* 85 (1991).

A second branch of this empirical work concerns voting within the legislature. A useful starting point for this literature is MELISSA P. COLLIE, "Voting Behavior in Legislatures," in GERHARD LOEWENBERG, SAMUEL CHARLES PATTERSON, and MALCOLM EDWIN JEWELL *Handbook of Legislative Research* (Cambridge, Mass., 1985); and JOHN W. KINGDON, *Congressmen's Voting Decisions*, 2d ed. (New York, 1981). Another branch of this literature focuses on historical trends related to party voting. For instance, see DAVID W. BRADY, JOSEPH COOPER, and PATRICIA A. HURLEY, "The Decline of Party in the U.S. House of Representatives, 1887–1968," *Legislative Studies Quarterly* 4:3 (1979); JEROME M. CLUBB, WILLIAM H. FLANIGAN, and NANCY H. ZINGALE, *Partisan Realignment: Voters, Parties, and Government in American History* (Beverly Hills, Calif., 1980); STUART ELAINE MACDONALD and GEORGE RABINOWITZ, "The Dynamics of Structural Realignment," *American Political Science Review* 81:3 (1987); SAMUEL C. PATTERSON and GREGORY A. CALDEIRA, "Party

Voting in the United States Congress," *British Journal of Political Science* 18 (1988); and PATRICIA A. HURLEY and RICK K. WILSON, "Partisan Voting Patterns in the U.S. Senate, 1877–1986," *Legislative Studies Quarterly* 14:2 (1989). Among other noteworthy articles bearing on the determinants of party voting in Congress are JOSEPH COOPER, DAVID BRADY, and PATRICIA HURLEY, "The Electoral Basis of Party Voting," in L. MAISEL and J. COOPER, eds., *The Impact of the Electoral Process* (Beverly Hills, Ca., 1977); KEITH POOLE and R. S. DANIELS, "Ideology, Party, and Voting in the U.S. Congress, 1959–1980," *American Political Science Review* 79: 2 (1985); and GERALD C. WRIGHT, "Policy Voting in the U.S. Senate: Who Is Represented," *Legislative Studies Quarterly* 14:4 (1989).

A third branch of this work looks at the internal operation of Congress, linkages with the executive branch, and policy outputs. For overviews of internal operation empirically tied with party, see ROBERT L. PEABODY, *Leadership in Congress: Stability, Succession, and Change* (Boston, 1976); BARBARA SINCLAIR, *Majority Leadership in the U.S. House* (Baltimore, 1983); and STEVEN S. SMITH, *Call to Order: Floor Politics in the House and Senate* (Washington, D.C., 1989). A number of works have recently appeared on the role of party in the balance between the legislature and the executive. In particular, see JAMES L. SUNDQUIST, *The Decline and Resurgence of Congress* (Washington, D.C., 1981); JON R. BOND and RICHARD FLEISHER, *The President in the Legislative Arena* (Chicago, 1990); and JOEL D. ABERBACH, *Keeping a Watchful Eye: The Politics of Congressional Oversight* (Washington, D.C., 1990). In addition, a number of empirical pieces have focused on policy outputs, detailing the role that congressional parties play in the process. For instance, see MARTHA DERTHICK and PAUL J. QUIRK, *The Politics of Deregulation* (Washington, D.C., 1985); and DOUGLAS R. ARNOLD, *The Logic of Congressional Action* (New Haven, Conn., 1990).

Finally, the traditional literature includes attempts to apply organization theory to extend theoretical understanding. Though focused on Congress as an institution, this work also deals with the role of congressional parties. Its theoretical concerns in many cases mirror those of recent authors in the nontraditional literature, but the analysis emphasizes contextual and organizational factors, not individual motivation. See JOSEPH COOPER, "Congress in Organizational Perspective," in LAWRENCE C. DODD and BRUCE IAN OPPENHEIMER, eds., *Congress Reconsidered* (New York, 1977); and JOSEPH COOPER, "Organization and Innovation in the House of Representatives," in JOSEPH COOPER and G. CALVIN MACKENZIE, eds., *The House at Work* (Austin, Tex., 1981).

Nontraditional Literature

The nontraditional literature, as used here, is primarily taken from the arena of rational-choice theory. General applications can be found in ANTHONY DOWNS, *An Economic Theory of Democracy* (New York, 1957); DAVID R. MAYHEW, *Congress: The Electoral Connection* (New Haven, Conn., 1974); MORRIS P. FIORINA, *Congress: Keystone of the Washington Establishment* (New Haven, Conn., 1977); CHARLES HAINES STEWART, *Budget Reform Politics* (Cambridge, Eng., 1989); D. RODERICK KIEWIET and MATTHEW D. MCCUBBINS, *The Logic of Delegation: Congressional Parties and the Appropriations Process* (Chicago, 1991); KEITH KREHBIEL, *Information and Legislative Organization* (Ann Arbor, Mich., 1991); and DAVID W. ROHDE, *Parties and Leaders in the Postreform House* (Chicago, 1991). For a critique of general applications pertaining to congressional oversight see JERRY L. MASHAW, "Explaining Administrative Process: Normative, Positive, and Critical Stories of Legal Development," *Journal of Law, Economics, and Organization* 6 (1990).

In the area of rational-choice theory, three general clusters of research predominate for those interested in congressional parties. Work examining Congress from the perspective of "gains-in-trade" focuses on what drives a congressman's reelection incentives and how allocations of goods are split among members. A good deal of this literature takes its cue from JAMES BUCHANAN and GORDON TULLOCK, *The Calculus of Consent: Logical Foundations of Constitutional Democracy* (Ann Arbor, 1962), and WILLIAM H. RIKER, *The Theory of Political Coalitions* (Westport, Conn., 1962), of which both point to the problems with sustaining coalitions in the face of divisible goods. Included in the current work on such problems is BARRY R. WEINGAST, "A Rational Choice Perspective on Congressional Norms," *American Journal of*

Political Science 23:2 (1979); DAVID P. BARON, "Distributive Politics and the Persistence of Amtrak," *Journal of Politics* 52:2 (1990); DAVID AUSTEN-SMITH and JEFFREY BANKS, "Elections, Coalitions and Legislative Outcomes," *American Political Science Review* 82:2 (1988); JOHN FEREJOHN, "Logrolling in an Institutional Context: A Case Study of Food Stamp Legislation," in GERALD C. WRIGHT, LEROY N. RIESELBACH, and LAWRENCE C. DODD, eds., *Congress and Policy Change* (New York, 1986). Other elements of this work point to the importance of institutional structure for solving the problem of sustaining stable majorities. In particular see WILLIAM H. RIKER, "Implications from the Disequilibrium of Majority Rule for the Study of Institutions," *American Political Science Review* 74:2 (1980); WILLIAM H. RIKER, *Liberalism Against Populism: A Confrontation Between the Theory of Democracy and the Theory of Choice* (San Francisco, 1982); KENNETH A. SHEPSLE, "Institutional Equilibrium and Equilibrium Institutions," in HERBERT F. WEISBERG, ed., *Political Science: The Science of Politics* (New York, 1986); and KEITH KREHBIEL, "Spatial Models of Legislative Choice," *Legislative Studies Quarterly* 8 (1988). Nonrational choice approaches to the discussion of distributive goods include THEODORE J. LOWI, "American Business, Public Policy, Core Studies, and Political Theory," *World Politics* 16 (New Haven, Conn., 1964), and JAMES Q. WILSON, *Political Organizations* (New York, 1973).

A second branch of this literature denies the need for parties and treats legislative outcomes as little more than the natural outcome of the preferences of actors. A set of papers by KEITH KREHBIEL—"Are Congressional Committees Composed of Preference Outliers?" *American Political Science Review* 84:1 (1990), and "Where's the Party?" unpublished manuscript, Stanford University (1991)—most carefully delineates this position.

A third branch of this nontraditional work has begun to tackle the problem of party seriously. JOSEPH A. SCHLESINGER has a number of papers seeking to handle the problem, including "The Primary Goals of Political Parties: A Clarification of Positive Theory," *American Political Science Review* 69:3 (1975); "On the Theory of Party Organization," *Journal of Politics* 46 (1984); and "The New American Political Party," *American Political Science Review*

79: 4 (1985). JOHN ALDRICH has a number of unpublished papers that seek to establish a role for party from this perspective, including "Modeling the Party-in-the-Legislature," a paper presented at the annual meeting of the American Political Science Association (1988); "On the Origins of the American Political Party: The Endogeneity of the Party in the Legislature," a paper presented at the annual meeting of the Public Choice Society, Orlando, Florida, (1989); and "An Institutional Theory of a Legislature with Two Parties and a Committee System," *Duke University Papers in American Politics,* Working Paper no. 111, (1990). Finally, the work by GARY W. COX and MATHEW D. MCCUBBINS, *Parties and Committees in the House of Representatives* (1991), is insightful and challenging on the question of congressional parties.

As noted in the text, there are a number of authors who bridge the traditional and nontraditional literature, including work by RICHARD F. FENNO, Jr., *Congressmen in Committees* (Boston, 1973); LAWRENCE C. DODD, "The Cycles of Legislative Change: Building a Dynamic Theory," in HERBERT F. WEISBERG, ed., *Political Science: The Science of Politics* (New York, 1986); DAVID W. BRADY and MARK MORGAN, "Reforming the Structure of the House Appropriations Process," in Mathew McCubbins and Terry Sullivan, eds., *Congress: Structure and Policy* (New York, 1987); BARBARA SINCLAIR, *The Transformation of the U.S. Senate* (Baltimore, 1989); MORRIS P. FIORINA, "The Decline of Collective Responsibility in American Politics," *Daedalus* 109 (1980); and KENNETH A. SHEPSLE, "The Changing Textbook Congress," in JOHN E. CHUBB and PAUL E. PETERSON, eds., *Can the Government Govern?* (Washington, D.C., 1989).

Issues in Party Theory

Many of the items cited thus far bear significantly on the issues party theory must address. Readings on several specialized topics, however, may also be suggested. On the topic of divided government see JAMES L. SUNDQUIST, "Needed: A Political Theory for the New Era of Coalition Government in the United States," *Political Science Quarterly* 103 (1988–1989), and MORRIS P. FIORINA, "An Era of Divided Government," in BRUCE E. CAIN and GILLIAN PEELE, eds., *Developments in American Politics* (New

York, 1990). For an analysis of performances as a standard see JOSEPH COOPER, "Assessing Legislative Performance: A Reply to the Critics of Congress," *Congress and the Presidency* 13 (1986). For an insightful and suggestive treatment of party leadership from a rational choice perspective see RANDALL CALVERT, "Coordination and Power: The Foundation of Leadership Among Rational Legislators," a paper presented at the annual meeting of the American Political Science Association (1987). Finally, on the normative dimensions of politics, see JACK L. WALKER, "A Critique of the Elitist Theory of Democracy," *American Political Science Review* 60:2 (1966); TERRANCE BALL, "The Ontological Presuppositions and Political Consequences of a Social Science," in D. SABIA and J. WALLULIS, eds., *Changing Social Science: Critical Theory and Other Critical Perspectives* (Albany, 1983); and BENJAMIN BARBER, *The Conquest of Politics: Liberal Philosophy in Democratic Times* (Princeton, N.J., 1988).

PARTY COHERENCE ON ROLL-CALL VOTES IN THE U.S. HOUSE OF REPRESENTATIVES

Gary W. Cox
Mathew D. McCubbins

Students of legislatures, particularly in the United States, have long argued that the institutions can and should be studied by analyzing the observable behavior of legislators—in particular, their voting patterns. Indeed, roll-call voting is one of the most intensely studied congressional activities. (For recent surveys, see Collie, 1984; Thompson and Silbey, 1984). A recurrent theme in many of these studies has been that members of Congress have become increasingly individualistic in their voting behavior; i.e., that the characteristics of individual members or their constituencies have become increasingly important determinants of their voting decisions, relative to the impact of party membership. Whereas most studies of roll-call voting find that party is the single best predictor of congressional voting behavior (Marwell, 1967; Matthews, 1960; Truman, 1959; Turner, 1951; Turner and Schneier, 1970), the importance of party voting in Congress is seen to have declined over time (Brady, Cooper and Hurley, 1979; Clubb and Traugott, 1977; Collie, 1988; Collie and Brady, 1985; Cooper, Brady, and Hurley, 1977). The major finding of this recent literature, Collie summarizes, is "an erratic but overall decline in the levels of both intraparty cohesion and interparty conflict since the turn of the century" (1984, p. 8).

These results on the decline in party voting fit together with other arguments regarding the salience of parties in the U.S. Congress, most importantly the emergence of the conservative coalition, whose rise and eventual decline has, more or less, been coterminous with the decline and (more recently) the resurgence of party voting in Congress. The apparent decline in party voting has been used as evidence of the emergence of nonpartisan or bipartisan coalitions, universalism, and the implantation of a "new textbook Congress" founded on the principal of maximizing each member's independence of action and ability to intervene on policy decisions. (A succinct discussion of the "textbook Congress" perspective can be found in Shepsle, 1989.)

The major components of the new textbook Congress that emerged in the literature on Congress in the 1970s, Shepsle argues, are the development of an incumbency advantage, the rise of professional staff and other resources to maintain and increase that advantage, and the decline of congressional norms supporting both cooperation between members and committees and supporting the committee division of labor/issue specialization system. The old textbook Congress—"committee politics"—which Shepsle argues prevailed during the 1940s and the 1950s, rested on three foundations: weak central party organs and a strong seniority system (i.e., "parties at best coordinated legislative activity rather than coerced it"); a set of largely orthogonal committee jurisdictions; and a set of "norms and folkways" that reinforced and rewarded committee activity (Shepsle, 1989, p. 246).

Our purpose in this essay is threefold: first, to discuss some recent work dealing with trends in party voting in the 1980s, a period not included in the literature cited above; second, to review and critique the methods used and results found in the literature on the pre-1980 period; and third, to provide a new perspective on historical trends in party voting since the New Deal. The new perspective for which we argue centers on the activity of party leaders rather than party majorities. Parties, we contend, need not be disciplined and coherent on every issue and every vote in order to structure some voting. Indeed, a party needs to be concerned only with those issues important to its reputation; it is on these issues that the leadership will take measures to structure, or to get the party whips to "whip," member votes. Our argument is grounded in a theory of the electoral connection between voters and individual members of Congress that is informed by the social-choice literature of the past three decades, arising out of the work of Kenneth Arrow (1951), much of which has been highly pessimistic about the prospects for democratic theory (see, e.g., Riker, 1980, 1981; Fiorina, 1977, 1980). We draw fundamentally differenct conclusions about the "collective responsibility" (Fiorina, 1980) of party members than do many of these authors, however. (For a general discussion of the electoral connection and the motivation of party leaders, see Cox and McCubbins, 1993).

Thus, for example, instead of focusing on such standard measures as the number of party votes—or roll calls in which a majority of Republicans oppose a majority of Democrats—we look at *party leadership votes*—defined as roll calls in which the Republican and Democratic leaderships oppose each other. If one seeks to assess the importance of parties as organizations, the usual measures are less-appropriate foci than are measures of first, the cohesion of each party in support of its leadership on those roll calls for which the leadership takes a clear stand; and second, the number and importance of the roll calls on which the leadership takes a clear stand. When we reexamine the data from this perspective, little indication is found of a secular (i.e., long-term) decline in the importance of party-voting cues in the period after the New Deal—at least for the majority party.[1]

In the following section, we examine the theory and evidence offered in previous research purporting a decline in party voting, focusing, in particular, on one exemplar of the "decline" literature that is offered by Joseph Cooper, David Brady and Patricia Hurley. Our reading of that evidence suggests that congressional parties were not markedly less important

in the 1940s, 1950s, and 1960s than they were in the 1930s. We then evaluate the evidence on intraparty cohesion, suggesting that the base over which cohesion is measured is too broad in previous studies—that the base should be over *whipped* votes only.

The section concludes by suggesting two new measures of party strength—the size of the party's agenda and the party's cohesion in support of its leadership on the party agenda, which we then examine in the third section. We find little evidence of a secular decline in party cohesion; however, we do find that the Republican party agenda has shrunk mildly over time and the Democratic party agenda took a dip in the Eighty-ninth through Ninety-fifth Congresses. Later in this essay, rather than examining globally the size of the party agendas, and party cohesion overall, we look instead at these two measures for a particular issue area—fiscal policy. We find that in this important area, there has been no decline in either measure.

REEVALUATION OF THE EVIDENCE FOR PARTY VOTING

Some Current Research

Systematic study of historical trends in congressional party voting first became feasible in the mid-1970s, with the compilation of machine-readable roll-call votes by the Inter-University Consortium on Political and Social Research. Soon thereafter, the first entries into the field appeared in print, providing and analyzing lengthy time series of data on party voting (Clubb and Traugott, 1977; Cooper, Brady, and Hurley, 1977). Obviously, these works could not cover the late 1970s and 1980s. Most of the subsequent literature also has not looked beyond the 1970s.

The chief exceptions to this characterization are a series of recent papers by David Rohde (1988, 1989, 1990) and Joseph Schlesinger (1985). Using essentially the same methodology as previous researchers, Rohde has extended the time series to the late 1980s. His findings are important. First, they show an increase in the frequency of *party votes* (recorded votes in which a majority of nonab-

---

1. We use the term "secular" to mean "extending over . . . a long period of time," as per *Webster's*. The only further connotation we attach is that of steadiness: we think of secular trends as those which take a long time to unravel and which, during the period of unraveling, are more or less continuously in evidence.

staining Republicans oppose a majority of nonabstaining Democrats [with pairs counted as nonabstaining]) as a percentage of all roll calls from the mid-1970s to 1988; and, second, a strong increase in cohesion on these party votes. (Party-unity scores are computed below as follows: First, the number of times a member supported his or her party in a party vote is divided by the number of times that member participated in party votes. Second, the average across all members of this party-unity score is calculated.)

> Democratic party unity, which had stabilized at a low point between 70 and 72 percent during the first Nixon term (1969–1972), began increasing sharply in the 1980s.... The average for the 100th Congress (1987–88) was 88 percent, and to find a Congress in which that level was exceeded one has to go back to the 61st (1909–11). (Rohde, 1990, p. 6)

The importance of Rohde's findings, for present purposes, is not what they show—a significant increase in party voting in the 1980s—but also in what they suggest about the causation of previous trends. Rohde notes that most previous researchers gave no indication that they expected long-term decline in party voting to end, much less reverse itself (although some may, of course, have had this possibility in mind). In the general literature on party, the view developed that party decline in the legislative arena was linked to party decline in the electoral arena. Both seemed to have had a considerable inertia behind them, owing to the cumulative and long-term effects of a host of party-weakening forces (starting with Progressive Era reforms and ending with the rise of candidate-centered elections). As Rohde points out, however, "the apparent immutability of partisan decline that was explicit or implicit in earlier research has to be taken as disproved" (Rohde, 1990, p. 32).

Even if not irreversible, the decline in party voting up to 1980 may nonetheless have been substantial and steady; yet, was it? To answer this question, we shall consider the evidence in greater detail. We will concentrate in particular on the two variables that have received the most attention in the literature: the relative frequency of party votes, and average levels of party cohesion.

The Evidence on Party Votes

Consider first the relative frequency of party votes (here, measured relative to the total number of votes). Cooper, Brady, and Hurley (1977) provide the appropriate figures for the Fiftieth (1886–1887) through Ninetieth (1966–1967) Congresses. Using regression analysis, they find that party votes as a percentage of all roll calls fell, on average, by about half a percentage point per Congress.[2] If the time series is extended forward ten Congresses and the same regression is performed for the Sixtieth through One-hundredth Congresses, the result is a slope of −.45, only slightly smaller (and still statistically significant).

What do these results mean? The answer depends on what constitutes evidence that parties are important in structuring floor voting. Cooper, Brady, and Hurley stake out a clear position on this issue, arguing that both intraparty cohesion and interparty conflict must exist before one can say that parties are important.[3] They clearly state that high internal cohesion alone is not evidence of party strength: "in a context of low divisiveness [internal cohesion] does not testify to the strength of party as a

---

2. They found a slope of −.52, measuring "time" by Congress number, as do we in the regression reported next in the text. Regression analysis concerns the problem of describing and evaluating the relationship between a given *dependent* variable and a set of *independent* or *explanatory* variables. In the case of ordinary least squares (OLS) regression of a dependent variable on a single independent variable, it involves finding the equation of a straight line that "best" describes the relationship between the two variables—say, x and y, where we are estimating y as a function of the xs—where "best" is defined as minimizing the sum of the squared differences between the observed ys and the ys predicted by the regression line. In this paper, we use regression analysis to investigate trends over time in leadership-support scores. For more on regression analysis and the use of statistics in the study of politics, see, e.g., Kennedy, 1985; King, 1989; Maddala, 1977; Wonnacott and Wonnacott, 1980.

3. Indeed, they measure the importance of party in structuring floor votes by multiplying intraparty cohesion (measured by Rice's coefficient) and interparty conflict (measured by party-vote percentages). Rice's coefficient of cohesion is computed for a single roll call and party by taking the absolute value of the difference between the percentage of a party's membership voting "aye" in the roll call and the percentage voting "no." Averages are then computed over a set of roll calls in the usual (unweighted) fashion.

determinant of voting" (Cooper, Brady, and Hurley, 1977, pp. 35–36).

Given this view of party strength, it follows that the decline in the relative frequency of party votes is straightforward evidence that "party strength" is declining. We do not share Cooper, Brady, and Hurley's view of party strength, however, because we do not think that interparty conflict is a necessary condition of party strength.

To see why this is so, consider a hypothetically cohesive majority party that succeeds in passing its program against an opposition so divided (or coopted) that the relative frequency of party votes is very low (Collie, "Universalism and the Parties"). By Cooper, Brady, and Hurley's measure, party strength for the majority party in this example would be low because, although the party's cohesion is high, the level of interparty conflict (measured by the party-vote percentage) is very low. But, is the majority party really not very strong in this situation? It is *ex hypothesi* both internally cohesive and successful in passing its program. It is only the minority party that seems unimportant.

The point of this example is not to deny the broader point that Cooper, Brady, and Hurley may have been pointing to: that party strength is a function both of the frequency with which a party springs into action and of its cohesion, when it does. Indeed, this entire essay is structured around this notion. But, if this is what Cooper, Brady, and Hurley had in mind, we certainly disagree with their next step: measuring the frequency with which a party acts by the frequency with which it disagrees with the other party. If one were trying to measure how frequently a gang acted as a gang, would one count only the instances in which they fought another gang, or would one also include the cases where they acted against an unorganized opponent or no opponent at all? The Cooper, Brady, and Hurley measure is better suited to measuring the overall state of the party system than in measuring the strength of individual parties. Here, because of our interest specifically in the latter, we attempt a different tack in measurement. Nonetheless, as we will show, both of the measures suggested below also rely to some extent on interparty conflict as a clue to the existence of party action.

In light of the foregoing discussion, what

should one make of the trend in party votes? Recent work by Collie (1988) fills in some more pieces of the puzzle by tracking not just party votes but also two other categories: roll calls on which at least 90 percent of the voting members vote in the same direction, which can be called universal votes; and a residual category of roll calls, those that are neither party votes nor universal votes. At least for the period that Collie studies (1933–1980) the decline in party votes as a percentage of all roll calls is not accompanied by a mirroring incline in the residual category of votes. Collie finds that the trend over time in the residual category is essentially nil. The bulk of the action is in party votes and universal votes, with the latter increasing as the former declines. Thus the relative decrease in party votes reflects not so much the increasing activity of shifting cross-party coalitions as the increasing activity of universal coalitions. The *chief* question is not, why have moderately sized bipartisan coalitions become more prevalent but, instead, why have nearly unanimous coalitions become more prevalent?

It seems quite possible to answer this question in a way that does not do much damage to one's image of how important parties are in determining floor votes. The increasing frequency of nearly unanimous votes might be explained, for example, in terms of increased incentives to record votes on "motherhood and apple pie" issues or, perhaps, in terms of increased incentives for small minorities to push things to a vote. Neither of these explanations would entail less powerful or important parties. As an example of the second case, nineteenth-century British politics is edifying. In the early 1880s in Great Britain, Irish obstructionists forced a huge number of divisions on the issue of Home Rule. Both major English parties opposed these initiatives overwhelmingly, and consequently, the party-vote percentages for these years are much lower than for either preceding or succeeding years. Yet no one argues that any significant decline in the strength or opposition of the parties occurred.

Put another way, suppose one excluded the nearly unanimous votes from analysis, as is often done in the computation of internal cohesion. Would there still be any substantial trend? The answer is less clear than when dealing with all roll calls. If one regresses party votes (as a percentage of nonuniversal votes) on time for the period examined by Collie, there is still a significant negative declivity. The slope is no longer significant, however, if one deletes the Seventy-third Congress (1933–1934). Moreover, the decline is far from steady. The average party-vote percentages by decade for the 1930s through 1970s are: 73.1, 60.3, 65.5, 62.1, and 57.0. The decline from the 1930s to the 1940s seems relatively large, but not much happens from the 1940s to the 1960s.

How much should one make of the eight to thirteen percentage points that separate the House of the 1930s from that of the succeeding three decades? It should be noted that this decline is not always clearly interpretable as party decline. Suppose, for example, that the Republicans stopped opposing core New Deal programs in the later decades, after their popularity became obvious. Then votes on such programs should have been passed by bipartisan majorities, where previously they had been passed by the Democrats alone. Such a change is the minority party throwing in the towel, not that "party"—the majority party in particular—is less important in understanding what policy is passed and what is not. *On the basis of the party-vote evidence alone,* it would be hard to argue that the congressional parties were markedly less important in the 1940s, 1950s, and 1960s than they were in the 1930s.

Evidence on Intraparty Cohesion

Findings on intraparty cohesion can be divided into two subcategories, depending on whether cohesion is averaged over all roll calls or just over party votes. The first type of evidence, cohesion on all roll calls, is presented by both Cooper, Brady, and Hurley (1977) and Clubb and Traugott (1977). In both works, little trend is found over the periods they examine (1887–1969 and 1861–1974, respectively). As Clubb and Traugott report, based on an investigation of the longer period: "The average index of cohesion for the Republicans is effectively uncorrelated" with time, while the correlation for the Democrats is "at best only moderately higher" (Clubb and Traugott, 1977, pp. 394–395). They conclude:

Taken in total, it appears that declining trends in party voting in the House can best be characterized as involving diminution of differences between the parties [as reflected in the decline in the relative frequency of party votes] rather than generalized and increasing partisan disunity. (Clubb and Traugott, 1977, p. 397)

Nonetheless, the cohesion figures in certain subperiods do show a decline. In particular, Clubb and Traugott report regressions on time for the period 1897–1933 and find large and significantly negative slopes for both parties.

Clubb and Traugott also examine party cohesion just on party votes, rather than on all roll calls. These data corroborate the negative slope for both parties in the 1897–1933 period and show a continuing decline in the 1933–1974 period. Collie in a 1988 report finds similar results for the period 1933–1980; she finds that the average percentage of party members voting with a majority of their party falls from the high 80s in 1933–1934 to the low 70s in the Ninety-first and Ninety-second Congresses, recovering thereafter.

Although the trends in cohesion on party votes are fairly clear, what this reveals about parties is less clear. It is conventional to note that some roll calls concern minor issues on which the parties do not oppose one another. Those who discard universal votes before computing average cohesion are usually attempting to get rid of some of the more obvious of such votes. Moreover, the rationale for looking at cohesion only on party votes is often the same, the reasoning being that roll calls on which party majorities oppose one another are particularly likely to involve important partisan issues.

Even roll calls on which party majorities oppose each other, however, may not be party votes in the sense that some party leader wished to bring them on, was active in organizing support behind one side or the other, or held out the possibility of punishment or reward to party followers. Yet if one is interested in the strength of parties as organizations, then the attitude of party leaders is crucial.

The point can be made clearer by referring to a distinction made in British politics between "whip" votes and "open" votes. *Whip votes* are those on which a party's whip organization is active—and this activity is tantamount to a declaration that the party leadership is united in favor of the position that the whips are urging. *Open votes,* in contrast, are those on which the party leadership—hence the whip organization—is silent. No one would think to measure the strength of the leadership of British parties by the levels of party cohesion on open votes. We think a similar restriction should apply in the United States.

It is true, of course, that the power of party leaders is vastly less in the United States than in the United Kingdom, but that is beside the point. There is a detectable variation both in the degree to which an American party's leadership is united and in the degree to which they communicate their united intent to their followers. The importance of party leaders as voting cues should be measured by the frequency with which they give a fairly clear cue and the cohesion of their followers when party leaders do.

Following this line of thought, we shall adopt the following definitions: for a given party, the *party agenda* is the set of all roll calls on which its top leadership is active and unified, whereas a *party agenda vote* is a roll call in the party agenda. A *party leadership vote* is a roll call on which the top leadership of one party is unified in opposition to the top leadership of the other. (Operational definitions of both these terms are given in the next section.)

Cohesion on party leadership votes and on party agenda votes seem more readily interpretable statistics than cohesion on conventionally defined party votes. On party leadership votes, for example, the parties clearly confront one another in a meaningful sense. On party votes as usually defined, however, this is not clear: issues devoid of organized partisan conflict may very well find majorities of the parties opposed, simply because of the like-mindedness of members of the same party. If like-mindedness is of interest, then perhaps such roll calls should be included. But if the issue is the strength of the parties as organizations, then presumably one would want to isolate those roll calls on which the organizations are indeed active. The appropriate measures of a party's strength then are (1) the size of the party's agenda and (2) the party's cohesion in support of its leadership on the party agenda. In the next section, we pursue this approach.

PARTY AGENDAS AND PARTY LEADERSHIP VOTES

One might identify roll calls on which the leadership of a given party was active in any of a number of ways. One method would be to include only those roll calls prior to which the party's whip organization had polled the membership and made clear the leadership's position. Another method would be to include roll calls only on issues that the party leaders had identified publicly as of concern to them as leaders of the party.

These methods would produce fairly small subsets of votes in most postwar Congresses that would be reasonably close analogs of the British whip vote. The problem is that getting information on the relevant actions is difficult: we simply do not know the issues on which the parties' whip organizations have been active, except for a few Congresses (Froman and Ripley, 1965); and there is no single forum in which party leaders have announced their agendas, so that one could be assured of cross-time comparability in identifying "litmus test" votes or the like.

The method that we have therefore had recourse to in identifying party agendas relies on more readily observable actions: the voting decisions of the majority and minority leaders and whips. On each roll call, we have ascertained how the floor leader and whip for each party voted. If a party's leader and whip both voted on the same side, then that side was taken to be the party leadership's position (which, henceforth, we shall also refer to as the party's position).

The *party agenda* can then be defined in either of two ways. One way is to include all roll calls on which the party has a position. In practice, however, this definition yields party agendas that are probably too large. Roll calls on which both leader and whip vote on the same side constitute about 70–75 percent of all roll calls in the typical Congress (at least in the period 1933–1989). Moreover, on many votes both parties' leaders are on the same side of the issue, indicating that it is not a matter of partisan division. A second definition of the party agenda—the one that we shall use in what follows—excludes these votes. (This is where we borrow from the approach taken by Cooper, Brady, and Hurley, by using interparty disagreement as evidence of what really is a party stand.) Thus, the party agenda is the set of all roll calls in which the party has a position and in which the other party either takes no position or these positions are opposed. Then the roll call is considered a party leadership vote.

These operational definitions obviously do not perfectly capture our original conceptions of party agendas and party-leadership votes. On the one hand, the operational definitions are likely to be too inclusive. The floor leader and whip of a party may both vote on the same side of a roll call without taking any stand or exerting any effort as party leaders. Their votes may both be cast in a purely private capacity. On the other hand, the operational definitions may also be too exclusive on occasion. Illness or unavoidable commitments may prevent a leader from voting, even on an issue to which he and the other top leaders have devoted considerable attention.

Nonetheless, our definitions have the considerable advantage of being systematically implementable for a large number of Congresses. Party floor leaders and whips are both identifiable by the opening decade of the twentieth century. There are several gaps in the lists of Democratic whips in the first three decades of the century, but by the 1930s the lists were complete and the offices were well established.

We have chosen to begin our analysis with the New Deal, conforming to one of the conventional cutting points in the literature (cf. Clubb and Traugott, 1977; Collie, 1988). Data exists through the One-hundredth Congress, but it concentrates on that portion of the time series that ends in the Ninety-sixth Congress, in order to make our results comparable to earlier studies. Thus, *all the regression results reported below refer, unless otherwise noted, to the period from the Seventy-third to Ninety-sixth Congresses.* All of the graphs, however, include the data from the Ninety-seventh through One-hundredth Congresses, so that the interested reader can see what has happened in the 1980s.

Party Agendas

The first questions to be answered concern the size of party agendas, the levels of support that leaders got on these agendas, and trends in these two variables. The measure of size used is simply the number of roll calls in the party agenda as a percentage of all roll calls. The relevant figures for both parties are presented in Table 1. For the Democrats, the relative size of the party agenda ranges from a low of 23.6 percent of all roll calls to a high of 67.7 percent, with a median of 45.4 percent. The Republican figures are similar but generally lower. Over the period stretching from the Seventy-third to Ninety-sixth Congresses, regressions on time reveal a decline in the size of the agenda for both parties. However, the decline is statistically discernible from zero only for the Republicans.

Support for the party agenda is measured by the percentage of times a legislator voted with his party leaders or paired in their favor on agenda items (the denominator for the percentage being the total number of agenda roll calls in which the legislator did participate, either voting or pairing). (This measure of party loyalty or leadership support is essentially the same as that used by Mayhew, 1966.) The average of these leadership scores for each party and Congress is reported graphically in Figures 1 (Democrats) and 2 (Republicans). Regressions on time of these averages show a large (−.66) and significant (t=7.1) decline for the Republicans, and a small (−.09) and insignificant (t=4) decline for the Democrats. These results merit some consideration. Previous investigators have found that cohesion declines significantly for both parties, when averaged over all party votes (see the party-unity scores presented in Table 2). Our results show a significant decline only for the Republicans. What explains the difference in conclusions regarding the Democrats?

It is not the use of average support scores rather than average cohesion coefficients. These correlate at a very high level, when averaged over the same roll-call base. Indeed, if every legislator votes in every roll call, then the average across legislators of party support scores must equal the average across roll calls of cohesion coefficients.

So the difference in results must be traced to the difference in roll calls used: the set of votes on which a party's leadership takes a united stand (and is not joined by the other party's leaders) is not coextensive with the set

Table 1
THE SIZE OF PARTY AGENDAS, SEVENTY-THIRD TO ONE-HUNDREDTH CONGRESSES

Congress	Total No. of Roll-Call Votes	Democratic Party Agenda as % of All Roll Calls**	Republican Party Agenda as % of All Roll Calls**	Party Leadership Votes as % of All Roll Calls***
73	143	65.7	56.6	40.6
74	212	23.6	55.2	10.4
75	158	67.7	48.7	35.4
76	227	52.0	53.3	33.0
77	152	65.1	32.9	30.2
78	156	44.2	54.5	32.1
79	231	57.1	45.9	35.1
80	163	42.3	59.5	33.7
81	275	46.5	39.3	23.6
82	181	62.4	47.0	35.9
83	147	27.9	50.3	23.8
84	149	41.6	34.9	26.2
85	193	39.9	44.0	21.8
86	180	52.2	43.9	35.6
87	240	52.9	38.8	24.2
88	232	52.2	41.8	32.2
89	394	41.9	43.9	26.4
90	478	40.2	34.9	19.7
91	443	26.2	25.1	13.1
92	649	33.1	37.6	17.1
93	1078	42.1	32.8	18.7
94	1273	49.4	36.2	22.5
95	1540	41.4	32.9	16.3
96	1276	45.4	34.4	18.9
97	812	40.3	38.2	21.8
98	896	45.3	45.6	27.3
99	890	52.9	49.6	33.9
100*	488	63.5	53.7	42.4

Notes:
(*) First session only.
(**) The Democratic party agenda is defined as the set of all recorded votes on which (a) both the Democratic floor leader and the Democratic chief whip voted on the same side; and (b) it was not the case that both the Republican Leader and whip agreed with the Democratic leaders. The Republican party agenda is defined similarly.
(***) The set of party leadership votes consists of all recorded votes such that the Democratic floor leader and whip oppose the Republican floor leader and whip. It is the intersection of the two party agendas, as defined in note 2.

of party votes as conventionally defined. This can be illustrated by considering some figures for the Eighty-fourth through Eighty-sixth Congresses. There were 255 party votes in these three Congresses, only 177 of which were in the Democratic party agenda. The other 78 (or 31 percent) divide into three classes: (1) 10 votes on which the Democratic leader and whip voted against one another; (2) 36 votes on which either the leader or the whip abstained; and (3) 32 votes on which the Democratic leadership and the Republican leadership

agreed. Clearly, there were enough party votes not in the Democratic agenda—and, for that matter, agenda votes that were not party votes (there were fifty-six such votes in the Eighty-fourth through Eighty-sixth Congresses)—so that cohesion figures calculated over party votes and cohesion figures calculated over party agenda votes need not be the same in any given Congress. This difference opens up the possibility that trends, over time, in the two measures may differ, and indeed we found that they do: although Democratic cohesion on

PARTY COHERENCE ON ROLL-CALL VOTES

Figure 1

AVERAGE LEADERSHIP SUPPORT SCORES ON THE DEMOCRATIC PARTY AGENDA, SEVENTY-THIRD TO ONE-HUNDREDTH CONGRESSES

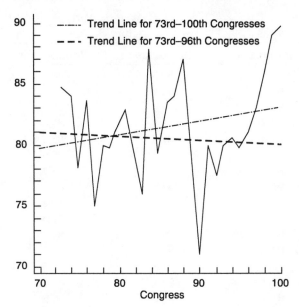

party votes declined over time, it did not decline on agenda votes.

This difference should probably have been expected. The regional split in the Democratic party between the North and the South is well known and well represented among party votes (Rohde 1988, 1989, 1990, 1991; Poole and Rosenthal, 1991). Thus, as the North/South split in the Democratic party worsened over time (with the onset of civil rights), it automatically appeared in the cohesion figures for party votes, producing a decline. But there are two reasons why this split is probably underrepresented on the Democratic party agenda. First, what goes into the agenda is a matter of choice. If the top leaders of the majority party seek to avoid being drubbed on the floor, they may choose to abstain on certain issues. But abstention by either leader or whip removes the roll call from the party agenda. Second, on issues that split the Democratic party, the floor leader and whip may themselves have been split. This also would remove the roll call from the party agenda.

The primary effect of the North/South split, therefore, should not have been to lower cohesion on the party agenda but rather to diminish the size of the party agenda. Assuming that the leadership got neither better nor worse

over time at anticipating defeats and avoiding them, one would expect no particular trend in cohesion but a decline in the size of the agenda. Similarly, if the floor leader and whip became neither better nor worse as barometers of splits in the party, then one would again expect a decline in the size of the agenda but no decline in cohesion.

Therefore, there is no significant trend in Democratic cohesion, but there is a decline in the size of the agenda. Nonetheless, the decline is not significant, and one might wonder why. If the North/South split was large enough to produce a significant declivity in cohesion on party votes, but cohesion on the party agenda shows no significant trend, does this not suggest that increasingly many party votes must have been excluded from the agenda, which should thus have shrunk significantly? There are two points to consider in this regard.

First, if one looks at the size of the majority party's agenda, rather than at the size of the Democrats' agenda—which entails substituting the Republican figures for the Eightieth and Eighty-third Congresses—one finds a significant decline. Two of the smallest Democratic agendas occur in these Congresses, when the Democrats were in the minority. An investigation of both Congresses in the first half of the

Figure 2

AVERAGE LEADERSHIP SUPPORT SCORES ON THE REPUBLICAN PARTY AGENDA, SEVENTY-THIRD TO ONE-HUNDREDTH CONGRESSES

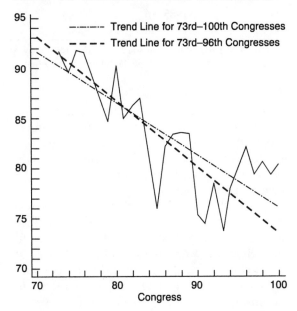

939

Table 2
AVERAGE LEADERSHIP SUPPORT SCORES ON PARTY LEADERSHIP VOTES, SEVENTY-THIRD TO ONE-HUNDREDTH CONGRESSES

Congress	Years	Average Leadership Support Scores on Party Leadership Votes		Average Party Unity Scores	
		Democrats	Republicans	Democrats	Republicans
73	1933–34	85.5	93.3	85.5	88.5
74	1935–36	86.8	90.0	83.5	85.8
75	1937–38	76.7	93.6	80.4	87.0
76	1939–40	85.6	92.4	83.1	87.6
77	1941–42	75.8	89.5	81.5	85.4
78	1943–44	79.2	90.3	79.6	85.9
79	1945–46	77.9	84.6	79.5	84.7
80	1947–48	79.3	91.5	82.6	89.6
81	1949–50	81.5	84.1	80.1	81.2
82	1951–52	76.5	85.6	75.4	79.0
83	1953–54	77.2	86.5	76.7	83.7
84	1955–56	86.1	82.7	80.1	77.7
85	1957–58	79.7	76.7	77.8	74.5
86	1959–60	83.6	82.7	80.1	80.8
87	1961–62	82.1	84.6	83.0	80.8
88	1963–64	84.2	85.1	83.1	81.9
89	1965–66	78.1	83.5	80.3	80.7
90	1967–68	72.2	77.5	75.3	78.7
91	1969–70	78.5	71.6	71.0	71.5
92	1971–72	72.6	77.7	71.2	76.0
93	1973–74	78.9	71.4	73.8	72.8
94	1975–76	77.2	76.1	75.0	76.7
95	1977–78	74.0	79.4	72.7	77.0
96	1979–80	78.3	81.6	76.3	79.0
97	1981–82	81.9	77.4	76.0	78.0
98	1983–84	83.8	80.7	81.5	78.6
99	1985–86	88.3	78.0	86.0	78.1
100	1987–88	88.8	78.8	88.0	79.4

Sources: The party unity scores are from Cooper, Brady, and Hurley 1977, p. 138 (for the Seventy-third to Ninetieth Congresses) and Rohde, 1990, Table 1 (for the Ninety-first to One-hundredth Congresses).

period reveals that they tend to flatten the slope of decline. In contrast, two of the largest Republican agendas occur in these Congresses, so substituting the Republican figures strengthens the downward trend in the size of the majority-party's agenda.

Second, the Seventy-fourth Congress was an unusual one for the Democrats. Their floor leader, William B. Bankhead, was seriously ill throughout the first session and did not vote at all. This poor attendance record translates into the smallest party agenda for the Democrats in the entire period: 23.6 percent. If the Seventy-fourth Congress is omitted as an outlier, then the decline is strengthened and becomes significant.

Either or both of the latter two explanations point to an average decline of .73 to 1.09 percentage points per Congress in the size of the majority-party's agenda, this decline being statistically discernible from zero. Over the span of about twenty Congresses, this translates into an estimated decline in the percentage of all roll calls that are in the majority-party's agenda from the mid-sixties in the early 1930s to the mid-forties in the late 1970s. As can be seen in Table

1, the majority party's agenda grew substantially in the 1980s, reaching 63.5 percent in the One-hundredth Congress.

Party Leadership Votes

A set of questions similar to those just asked about party agendas also can be asked for party leadership votes (i.e., for those roll calls in the intersection of the two parties' agendas). How many party leadership votes have there been, relative to all roll calls? How much support from their followers have the top leaders received? How have these two variables changed over time?

Taking first the question of how many party leadership votes there have been, one can see in the last column of Table 1 that as a percentage of all roll calls such votes have declined significantly. This decline was to be expected given that (1) the size of both parties' agendas declined and (2) the set of all party leadership votes is the intersection of the two party agendas.

One might at this point ask which set—the set of party agenda votes or the set of party leadership votes—is a better approximation of our original conceptual variable of "votes on which the party leaders are active and united". The answer is that neither is fully satisfactory, with one too inclusive and the other too exclusive. The set of party agenda votes is too inclusive because it excludes only those votes on which the top leaders were either obviously inactive (in the sense that one or both did not vote) or clearly disunited (in the sense that they voted against one another). Thus, party agenda votes are simply those in which the party leaders pass a weak test of activity and unity: they are active and unified enough to give a consistent voting cue. And while the set of all votes on which the top leaders give a consistent voting cue, and the level of support they get when they do, are interesting in their own right, they do not tally precisely to the question of party voting per se. Indeed, the party agenda vote may be hard to interpret as a measure of party activity for reasons similar to those we used to criticize party votes: there is too high a chance that party leaders are not really active as such, but only involved in a private capacity on a par with every other member of the House.

One can be more sure that the party leaders were acting as such on party leadership votes, because one has the extra clue of interparty conflict. But using interparty conflict as a clue to party activity runs a risk: the relative frequency of votes in which the two-party leaderships oppose one another seems a good measure of interparty conflict, but it is problematic as a measure of the activity of a single party. To confine the analysis to just these roll calls and use party opposition as a defining condition of party activity, ignores the possibility of roll calls on which one party alone is active.

Thus, there is a trade-off in using these two measures. Our own view is that the "real" party agenda lies somewhere between the two operational versions on offer. Since both operational measures show a decline, we can be fairly confident that the "real" party agenda declined as well.

Turning now to the second question, average levels of support for the leadership on party leadership votes decline for both parties (as can be seen in Table 2 and Figures 3 and 4). The decline for the Republicans, however,

Figure 3

AVERAGE DEMOCRATIC LEADERSHIP SUPPORT SCORES ON PARTY LEADERSHIP VOTES, SEVENTY-THIRD TO ONE-HUNDREDTH CONGRESSES

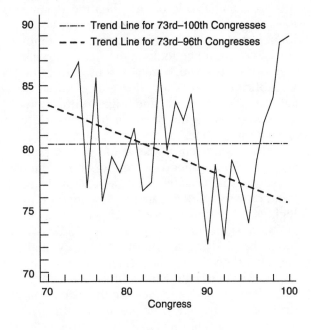

Figure 4

AVERAGE REPUBLICAN LEADERSHIP SUPPORT
SCORES ON PARTY LEADERSHIP VOTES,
SEVENTY-THIRD TO ONE-HUNDREDTH
CONGRESSES

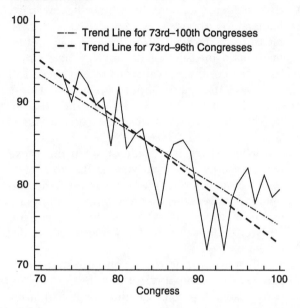

is much larger and much steadier. The decline
for the Democrats, although statistically discernible from zero, needs to be hedged about
by caveats similar to those we noted above
when discussing the size of the party agenda.
First, if one excludes the Seventy-fourth Congress (in which the Democrats' floor leader
was absent unusually often), then the decline
in average leadership-support scores is no
longer statistically significant for the Democrats. Second, if one looks at the figures for the
majority party—which entails substituting the
Republican averages for the Democratic averages in the Eightieth and Eighty-third Congresses—then, again, there is no statistically
significant decline.

Moreover, if one looks at the plot of average leadership-support scores for the Democrats over time (Figure 3), one sees virtually no
trend over the period from the Seventy-third to
Eighty-eighth Congresses (confirmed by a regression slope of .003 for this period), followed by: a sharp decline in the Eighty-ninth
and Ninetieth Congresses; fluctuations in the
Ninety-first through Ninety-fifth Congresses;
and a large, monotonic increase thereafter. The
story one would tell to go along with this pattern is not one of secular party decline.

Rather, it would seem that when civil
rights and the Great Society came to dominate
the Democratic agenda, southern Democrats
abruptly became more disloyal to the leadership. This conjecture is confirmed by Figure 5,
which plots separately the average leadership-
support scores for northern and southern Democrats. As can be seen, there is essentially no
trend over time in the loyalty of northern Democrats. The drop-off in the overall figures in the
Eighty-ninth through Ninety-fifth Congresses is
produced primarily by the large drop in southern loyalty. Similarly, the marked recovery in
overall loyalty in the late 1970s and 1980s is
primarily due to the return of southern loyalty
to pre–civil rights movement levels.

Table 2 also presents party-unity scores for
both parties, in order to facilitate comparison
between our figures and those used in the previous literature. The correlation between our
loyalty scores and the party-unity scores in the
last two columns is quite high for the Republicans (.95), somewhat lower for the Democrats
(.77). The primary differences between the
Democratic trend depicted by the loyalty
scores and that depicted by the party-unity
scores are as follows: the trend in party-unity
scores over the period from the Seventy-third

Figure 5

AVERAGE LEADERSHIP SUPPORT SCORES ON
PARTY LEADERSHIP VOTES, FOR NORTHERN
AND SOUTHERN DEMOCRATS, SEVENTY-
THIRD TO ONE-HUNDREDTH CONGRESSES

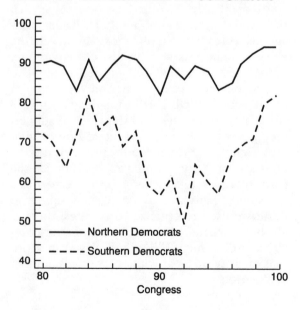

942

to Eighty-eighth Congresses is slightly downward (−.20) and approaching significance at the .10 level (t=1.4); the decline thereafter continues into the Ninety-first Congress and is somewhat steeper. There is little in the way of fluctuation in the period from the Ninety-first through Ninety-fifth Congresses, and the recovery thereafter is not monotonic, although it is basically the same in both size and timing. Our interpretation of events—wherein there is little trend in party cohesion until the civil rights movement hit the national agenda—is not supported by the party-unity data as much as by the loyalty-score data; but it is nonetheless possible to argue a similar position with these data (cf. Rohde 1988, 1989, 1990, 1991).

PARTY ACTIVITY AND COHESION ON REVENUE AND EXPENDITURE VOTES

A natural question to ask regarding our results is whether they would differ were we to look at different issue areas, such as defense, social welfare, and so on. We have not investigated the full range of issues but can report here on one important issue area encompassing the raising and spending of money. Because who pays for what and who gets what are questions central to partisan politics, we expect that there should be even less indication of a decline in party activity and cohesion when attention is confined to such matters.

This expectation is borne out by the data that we can marshal here. Using Rohde's detailed classification of roll calls for the Eighty-third through Ninety-sixth Congresses (Rohde, 1991), we identified all roll calls pertaining to taxes, appropriations, and budget resolutions. For this subset of roll calls, we repeated the analyses conducted above for all roll calls.

The results show no statistically significant decline in any of our measures; that is, the relative frequencies of party agenda votes and party leadership votes (within the subset of budgetary roll calls) do not decline, nor do average leadership-support scores on (budgetary) party agenda votes or party leadership votes. This, of course, contrasts with the findings presented above for all roll calls, which showed that most of these measures did decline significantly. Part of the explanation

for this contrast is that the analyses reported in previous sections all pertained to the period from the Seventy-third to the Ninety-sixth Congresses, whereas the analysis of budgetary roll calls pertains only to the Eighty-third to Ninety-sixth Congresses. If one repeats the previous analyses for the shorter time period, the results would be weaker for all roll calls as well. Nonetheless, there is still a significant decline in the relative frequency of both Republican party agenda votes and party leadership votes, when looking at all roll calls. So there is some difference attributable to the issue domain as well. In particular, the Republicans have kept up a steadier presence on budgetary matters than they did on the entire range of issues. The decline in their overall agenda must be due to decreased leadership activity on other issues.

CONCLUSION

Previous research has suggested that there has been a downward trend in partisan behavior in Congress throughout most of the twentieth century (1910–1980). This body of work argues that there have been relatively fewer and fewer party votes (votes in which a majority of Republicans oppose a majority of Democrats) over time. At the same time, it also argues that intra-party cohesion on party votes has declined. Political scientists have widely inferred from these findings that there was a secular decline in the importance of party throughout most of the twentieth century.

Reexamining these two measures of the importance of party voting, we argue that they lack a sufficiently clear connection to the activity of parties as organizations. Party votes are counted even when the two parties' leaders have neither taken a stand nor otherwise acted to structure the outcome of the vote. The frequency with which party majorities oppose each other on such votes, and the internal cohesion of parties on such votes, are surely more important questions in the United States than in Britain. But these questions fail to get at the strength or importance of the party organizations in the United States any more than they would in Britain.

Another feature of the party-vote percentage that we have emphasized here is that it is not well suited to measuring the activity of individual parties, because it requires both parties to be active. This criticism can be leveled at any measure that identifies party activity with interparty conflict (such as our "party-leadership-vote percentage"). For example, a hypothetical majority party that was active (and perfectly cohesive) on every roll call, but faced an opposition that never opposed it, would be judged inactive by both the party vote and the party-leadership-vote percentages.

We have argued that the appropriate way to measure the importance of a party organization in structuring the vote is first to identify votes on which the top leadership of the party is active and united (the analog of whip votes in the United Kingdom) and then to answer two questions: How many such votes (collectively referred to as the party agenda) are there, relative to all votes? How cohesive is the party on such votes? The first question attempts to answer how often leaders take a stand, and the second asks whether they are supported when they do.

The method we have used to identify votes on which a given party's leaders are "active and united" begins by verifying whether or not the party's floor leader and whip both voted on the same side of the issue at stake. This gives a very weak operational sense to "active and united"; it merely excludes those votes on which the top leaders were either inactive (in the sense that one or both did not vote) or clearly disunited (in the sense that they voted against one another). The result is to divide the set of all roll calls into two groups: those in which there is some indication that the leaders are inactive or disunited, and those in which they are at least active and united enough to give a consistent voting cue. Interparty conflict is then used as a further clue, excluding those votes on which the leaders of both parties were in agreement. Finally, we ask how many votes there were in which both a party's floor leader and whip gave a consistent cue (not offered by the other party's leaders), and what the level of support they received was, when they did.

Following this procedure, we find that the roll-call evidence does not suggest a secular decline for both parties in the post–New Deal era. The decline for the Republicans can accurately be characterized in this way: both the

size of their party agenda and their cohesion on this agenda diminished considerably, and fairly steadily, from Franklin D. Roosevelt to Ronald Reagan. But the story is different for the Democrats. Their party agenda does shrink (growing again in the 1980s), but there is no evidence of a long-term erosion of party cohesion on the party agenda. Rather, there is a sharp dip in the Eighty-ninth through Ninety-fifth Congresses, produced mainly by the reaction of southern Democrats to the civil rights movement and the Vietnam War, with a substantial recovery thereafter.

Measures that depend on the actions of both parties—such as the widely-used party-vote percentage—tend to hide the difference between the Republican and Democratic experiences. It is important to note, however, that the evidence for secular decline is substantially weaker for the majority than for the minority party.

A final way to underscore this point is to look directly at the majority-party leadership's "batting average"—the percentage of all party leadership votes that it wins. In the Seventy-third through Seventy-ninth Congresses (1933–1946), the majority-party leadership won, on average, 75 percent of the time; in the Eightieth through Eighty-eighth (1947–1964), 77 percent of the time; in the Eighty-ninth through Ninety-fifth (1965–1978), 74 percent of the time; and in the Ninety-Sixth through One Hundredth (1979–1988), 81 percent of the time.[4] There is little support for any notion of secular decline in the strength of the majority party in these figures.

---

4. These figures were obtained as follows: first, within each period, the total number of party leadership votes was counted, excluding votes that pertained to suspension of the rules or to attempts to override a presidential veto. These votes were excluded because they involved a two-thirds rather than a simple majority vote. Second, within each period, the number of leadership-opposition votes, not involving suspensions or veto overrides, that the majority party won was counted. Third, this latter number was divided by the former to yield the majority-party leadership's batting average on "ordinary" votes—those not requiring a two-thirds vote to pass. The cut points were chosen to correspond to the periods "through the war," "early post-war textbook Congress," "Civil Rights transition," and "the 1980s."

BIBLIOGRAPHY

Relevant works include KENNETH ARROW, *Social Choice and Individual Values* (New York, 1951); DAVID W. BRADY, JOSEPH COOPER, and PATRICIA A. HURLEY, "The Decline of Party in the U.S. House of Representatives, 1887–1968," *Legislative Studies Quarterly* 4 (1979): 381–407; JEROME M. CLUBB and SANDRA TRAUGOTT, "Partisan Cleavage and Cohesion in the House of Representatives, 1861–1974," *Journal of Interdisciplinary History* 7 (1977): 375–402; MELISSA P. COLLIE, "Legislative Voting Behavior," *Legislative Studies Quarterly* 9 (1984): 3–50; COLLIE, "The Rise of Coalition Politics: Voting in the U.S. House, 1933–1980," *Legislative Studies Quarterly* 13 (1988): 321–342; COLLIE, "Universalism and the Parties in the U.S. House of Representatives, 1921–1980," *American Journal of Political Science* 32 (1988): 865–883; COLLIE and DAVID W. BRADY, "The Decline of Partisan Voting Coalitions in the House of Representatives," in LAWRENCE C. DODD and BRUCE I. OPPENHEIMER, eds., *Congress Reconsidered* (Washington, D.C., 1985); JOSEPH COOPER, DAVID W. BRADY, and PATRICIA A. HURLEY, "The Electoral Basis of Party Voting: Patterns and Trends in the U.S. House of Representatives," in LOUIS MAISEL and JOSEPH COOPER, eds., *The Impact of the Electoral Process* (Beverly Hills, Calif., 1977).

Also see GARY W. COX and MATHEW D. McCUBBINS, *Legislative Leviathan: Party Government in the House* (Berkeley, Calif., 1993); MORRIS P. FIORINA, *Congress: Keystone of the Washington Establishment* (New Haven, Conn., 1977); LEWIS A. FROMAN, JR., and RANDALL B. RIPLEY, "Conditions for Party Leadership: The Case of the House Democrats," *American Political Science Review* 59 (1965): 52–63; PETER KENNEDY, *A Guide to Econometrics*, 2d ed. (Cambridge, Mass., 1985); GARY KING, *Unifying Political Methodology* (New York, 1989); G. S. MADDALA, *Introduction to Econometrics* (New York, 1988); *Gerald Marwell,* "Party, Region and the Dimensions of Conflict in the House of Representatives, 1949–1954," *American Political Science Review* 61 (1967): 380–399; DONALD R. MATTHEWS, *U.S. Senators and Their World* (New York, 1960); DAVID MAYHEW, *Party Loyalty Among Congressmen* (Cambridge, Mass., 1966); KEITH T. POOLE and HOWARD ROSENTHAL, "Patterns of Congressional Voting," *American Journal of Political Science* 35 (1991): 228–278; WILLIAM RIKER, "Implications from the Disequilibrium of Majority Rule for the Study of Institutions," *American Political Science Review* 74 (1980): 432–446; RIKER, *Liberalism Against Populism* (San Francisco, 1982); DAVID W. ROHDE, "Variations in Partisanship in the House of Representatives, 1953–1988: Southern Democrats, Realignment and Agenda Change," presented at the annual meeting of the American Political Science Association, Washington, D.C., 1988; ROHDE, "Democratic Party Leadership, Agenda Control and the Resurgence of Partisanship in the House," presented at the annual meeting of the American Political Science Association, Atlanta, 1989; ROHDE, "'The Reports of My Death Are Greatly Exaggerated': Parties and Party Voting in the House of Representatives," in GLENN R. PARKER, ed., *Changing Perspectives on Congress* (Knoxville, Tenn., 1990); ROHDE, *Parties and Leaders in the Postreform House* (East Lansing, Mich., 1991); JOSEPH SCHLESINGER, "The New American Political Party," *American Political Science Review* 79: 1152–1169; KENNETH SHEPSLE, "The Changing Textbook Congress," in JOHN E. CHUBB and PAUL E. PETERSON, eds., *Can the Government Govern?* (Washington, D.C., 1989); MARGARET SUSAN THOMPSON and JOEL H. SILBEY, "Research on Nineteenth-Century Legislatures: Present Contours and Future Directions," *Legislative Studies Quarterly* 9 (1984): 319–350; DAVID B. TRUMAN, *The Congressional Party* (New York, 1959); JULIUS TURNER, *Party and Constituency: Pressures on Congress* (Baltimore, 1951); TURNER and EDWARD V. SCHNEIER, *Party and Constituency: Pressures on Congress,* rev. ed. (Baltimore, 1970); and THOMAS H. WONNACOTT and RONALD J. WONNACOTT, *Regression: A Second Course in Statistics* (New York, 1980).

This research was supported by the NSF under grant SES-8811022.

SEE ALSO Legislative Norms; Measuring Legislative Behavior; Modern Legislative Careers; AND The Motivations of Legislators.

POLITICAL PARTIES IN STATE LEGISLATURES

Keith E. Hamm
Ronald D. Hedlund
R. Bruce Anderson

The most enduring and pervasive feature of the organization of American state legislative bodies is political parties. As organizations, political parties emerged shortly after the adoption of the U.S. Constitution as outgrowths of the divisions between different political leaders and have evolved into potent forces that structure debate, deliberation, and decision-making in contemporary state legislatures. Only one state, Nebraska, currently has a nonpartisan state legislature, and only one other, Minnesota, had a nonpartisan legislature in the past (1913–1974) (Epstein, p. 126). Thus, political parties and partisanship are common characteristics of American state legislatures and their effects can be seen throughout the legislative process. For example, in the ninety-eight state legislative chambers using political parties, legislators seek election through a party-based election system. In all but a handful of these chambers, the selection of legislative chamber leaders is organized through political parties, the work-assignment process via committees reflects the partisan character of the body, and the decision-making process through voting underscores the party balance. Consequently, any understanding of state legislatures and legislators must include close attention to political parties.

In order to provide insights regarding political parties and their effects in state legislatures, this essay provides a brief historical overview of the emergence of political parties and their development. The primary concern here is with the evolution of parties in state legislatures from the agrarian-oriented, elitist society that existed after the American Revolution to the urban-based, ethnically and racially diverse society of the 1990s. This will facilitate a discussion of the roles of political parties in electing legislators; organizing legislative bodies (especially leadership selection); structuring legislative decision-making via legislative leadership, caucuses, and committees; and legislative voting on matters of public policy. By focusing on these topics, this essay provides an overview of how political parties have affected the development of state legislatures during the nation's two centuries of unprecedented political growth and turmoil and of how political parties structure the activities of contemporary state legislators and legislatures. Throughout, we apply existing and new data to questions about political parties and their operations at the state legislative level.

HISTORICAL OVERVIEW

Political parties have existed in state legislatures since colonial times, but their roles have varied considerably. This section divides the history of political parties into five time periods, corresponding to those generally used by historians: (1) the formative years (late 1780s–1820s); (2) the second party period (1830–1865); (3) the post–Civil War era to the 1890s; (4) the early twentieth century; and (5) the post–World War II period.

The Formative Years: Late 1780s–1820s

An example of the pattern of party development during the nation's early period can be found in the Virginia General Assembly from 1780 to 1800. The Virginia legislature was at first unorganized, with factional groups, representing less than half of the membership, forming around prominent individuals. With the passage of time, regional and economic coalitions emerged and replaced the early rallying role of single individuals (Risjord and DenBoer, pp. 963–970). Consequently, the largely personalized nature of political parties tended to fade as a new basis for organization was laid. By the election of 1800, the first nonpersonalized party system had emerged, at least in terms of the selection process.

With this development, party loyalty became a major criterion for the appointment of individuals to both executive and legislative offices. Nearly all members of the legislature and all candidates for the electoral college were identified by party (Risjord and DenBoer, p. 984). However, party does not appear to have been a key factor in organizing the legislature. James H. Broussard's study of the Virginia, North Carolina, and South Carolina legislatures from 1800 to 1812 highlights the lack of party importance in decision-making. The study cites numerous indicators of weak party organizations:

> no ceremonial party clash over the speakership, no systematic allocation of committee seats by party, no high degree of party cohesion in voting on state issues, no regular use of the caucus . . . [and] the willingness of the Republican majority to allow an occasional Federalist to be speaker and the unconcern about minority-party control of important committees . . . reinforce this impression. (p. 52)

To what extent did the parties divide over questions of policy in the state legislatures? Unfortunately, there are few systematic studies of party voting in this period; however, Harry Marlin Tinkcom's study of the Pennsylvania legislature from 1795 to 1799 provides two tantalizing findings. First, when analyzing record votes, one finds that party splits on national issues—such as the Virginia Resolutions, concerning constitutional changes, the manner of electing presidential electors, and opposing war by the national government in any guise—were noticeable throughout this period. Second, party-line voting was at best infrequent when the vote did not deal with issues that had national importance (p. 211). The collapse of the first party system grew out of several factors. The Federalists had formed as a resistance movement "against" certain initiatives, and had no coherent proactive program of their own; for this reason, the organization had little to offer new members. Several of the leaders of the party retired or turned their hand to other work—this meant that those attracted by particular personalities in the party looked elsewhere for political guidance. In any case, by the 1820s, the Federalists had lost both membership and momentum, and disappeared as a political force.

The Second Party System

State legislative political parties underwent several changes during the 1830s to 1890s. Probably the dominant theme relative to party strength is that described by Joel H. Silbey: "In the era from the 1830s to the 1890s, they [political parties] were strong, stronger than at any other time in our history" (p. 55). Further, Silbey noted that "party unity was remarkably high at both national and state levels. This unity had content to it. Voting positions tended to square with rhetorical stances found in the party campaign literature" (p. 66).

It is certain that the rise of the second party system was not an unplanned, unforeseen event but rather a conscious channeling of interests and conflicts into a party framework. The collapse of the Federalist party had led, in part, to disunity and lack of cohesion in the Jeffersonian Republican party. It seems that once the conflict with an opposing party had been removed, the raison d'être for party organization became obscure. The founding of the New York political organization known as the Albany Regency was a clear and unequivocal response to this disarray—a conscious effort on the part of state politicians to reinvigorate the party system. Martin Van Buren's revitalization of the Jeffersonians in the 1820s and 1830s led to the formation of the Regency, the first true state organization that can properly be called a "machine," in the sense that the state leadership came to be identified with dispensing political favors to its friends and punishing its enemies. The federal system enhanced and nurtured the party system. The national parties were flimsy structures, coming together every four years to elect a president, while the state parties formed the rugged core of voter support—support predicated on the actions in statehouses and governors' offices, not in Washington.

Although the reestablishment of the national two-party system would not be formally recognized until 1834, the factions that eventually merged to form the Whig party were in evidence both in the assembly and on the ballot at the state level in New York as early as 1827. By the election of 1832, the two parties had sorted themselves out, in New York at least, into a relatively stable, cohesive, and measurable pair of entities (Benson, pp. 28–31). The 1820s had begun with the Jacksonians in complete domination of the state legislature, but by decade's end, an opposition had been molded around financial issues strongly associated with the dominant party's control of political favors.

Given the emergence of strong, united political parties with differing ideological positions, one expects to see the emergence of internal mechanisms to facilitate the establishment and maintenance of party control. Accounts of parties beginning in the Jacksonian era show the emergence of one such important force—partisan caucuses. For example, as Peter D. Levine found, in New Jersey, the selection of legislative leadership became the undisputed responsibility of party caucuses, with straight party voting on the floor occurring when the minority party decided to offer a candidate.

Levine's analysis of party behavior in the New Jersey legislature reveals a number of important observations about how parties operated and how the legislature as a body channeled conflict at the state level. New Jersey selected, in a Joint Meeting of members of the two houses, the state's U.S. senators; governor; secretary of state; attorney general; the state treasurer; general and field militia officers; reporter, clerk, and justices of the state supreme court; functionaries of the prison system; and representative on the board of New Jersey's largest transportation company. Numerous local officials were also selected (p. 92). More than 6,700 of the 7,146 appointments made from 1829 to 1844 did not require roll-call votes; the majority party's choices were simply acknowledged without opposition. Most of these appointments were prearranged in a party caucus; the mean number of 447 appointments took (on average) less than four days to finalize in the joint meeting (p. 94). Thus, caucuses in New Jersey during the mid-nineteenth century not only gave legislative party members the ability to overcome interpersonal differences and other internal problems but also operated as cohesive forces in the legislative process (pp. 38–46).

These caucuses did not necessarily operate independent of party leaders from outside (including governors). In fact, Levine notes that

"in some instances these individuals [nonlegislative party leaders] were responsible for drawing up the [legislative] agenda of the party conclaves" (p. 38). Therefore, while party caucuses emerged as an important control mechanism within some state legislatures during this period, they did not operate in such a fashion as to exclude nonlegislative party leaders either from the legislative organization or from involvement in day-to-day legislative operations.

A quite different pattern was found in other states during this period. For example, Donald A. DeBats's analysis of Georgia's lower house between 1806 and 1861 shows that parties emerged as an important factor in state legislative operations, only to recede after a few decades. In Georgia, parties replaced a factional system of organization in the early 1830s, but disappeared within twenty years. During the height of partisanship, "Georgia experienced a system of intense party competition between two well-balanced and well-organized party machines. Party regularity became the watchword in the wider electorate" (p. 441). At the same time, political parties within the legislature were not necessarily as consistently important as noted in New Jersey. In fact, majority-party control of standing committees as well as chairs was absent for some key committees.

Studies of roll-call voting in the state legislatures reveals just how deep the conflict was between the parties. The range of issues around which party voting emerged varies considerably by state during this period. In several state legislatures, members of political parties coalesced when voting to organize the legislature or to make patronage appointments, including those in New Jersey and North Carolina. For example, high party unity emerged over issues that affected the political party in New Jersey as an independent institution with its own concerns. Included were resolutions on national political issues, gerrymandering proposals, election laws, contested election outcomes, and printing contracts (Levine, pp. 222, 230).

Aside from these votes on party issues, there is a broader question: Did party cleavages exist across a wide range of substantive issues? The answer appears to be no, not in all states. Several studies indicate that state legislative political parties evidenced a fair amount of cohesion on national issues, including those in the Illinois General Assembly (cf. Davis) and the North Carolina legislature (cf. Kruman). In some cases, this cohesion even affected state policies (Kruman, p. 53).

In a study of six state legislatures in the years 1833–1842, Herbert Ershkowitz and William G. Shade argued that the Whigs and Democrats divided over several major policy issues: corporations, paper currency, banks, and social and economic reform. They stated that "the patterns are consistent enough to warrant the conclusion that the Whig and Democratic parties were more than national combinations of ambitious politicians united to promote a common presidential aspirant and to divide the spoils of office" (p. 613).

From a different perspective, DeBats noted that in Georgia during the period 1834–1859 "nearly 70 percent of the bills on which the parties of Georgia disagreed during the antebellum period related to political rather than to social or economic issues" (p. 447). Indeed, there is not a single substantive policy issue on the list of bills with the highest level of disagreement during the whole antebellum period. This, according to DeBats, "reinforces the observation that the parties of Georgia found it much easier to unite around abstract political issues than around the more difficult questions of state policy" (p. 446).

Finally, Levine, in his thorough study of the New Jersey legislature, offered some very interesting results for the period 1833–1844. The extent of party cleavages varied significantly, ranging between 25 percent and 100 percent for various policy areas. A majority of each party was likely to oppose the other at least 75 percent of the time on issues of surplus revenue, constitutional reform, banking, national resolutions, elections, joint companies, election disputes, taxation, and government involvement in business. Partisan conflict was generated on less than one-half of the roll-call votes on enclosures, insurance, mining, religion, and "special privileges to communities" policies (calculated from Tables A.3 and A.4 in Levine, pp. 241–242). Levine observed that "conscious partisan attempts to shape legislation, however, remained confined primarily to questions that in some manner concerned competitive party organizations as interests" (p. 233).

In the decade immediately preceding the Civil War, conflict between the two parties dissipated in many northern state legislatures. State-to-state variations existed, but in general the trend appears to have been that interparty conflict on roll-call voting had decreased by the early 1850s from earlier levels (Holt, pp. 113–114). By 1853, the party system was still nominally in existence largely because no formal challenger had arisen to dislodge the hapless Whigs from their positions. In the South, the second party system in Georgia, Mississippi, and Alabama collapsed after the Compromise of 1850 (Holt, p. 92). In North Carolina, the bitter battles of early years gave way to a political consensus by the 1850s (Kruman, p. 269).

Civil War to the 1890s

Following the Civil War, the Republican party was ascendant everywhere, but nowhere is the evidence of the changes wrought on state legislative activity, institutional makeup, and policy orientation more evident than in the Reconstruction South. Eric Foner (1990) noted that the institutional aspects (the barring of "unreconstructed" Confederate sympathizers from voting, enfranchisement of African Americans, the dole of federal patronage, and so on) were critical to the transformation of southern legislatures. In all, more than six hundred blacks served as legislators during the period (p. 151). This influence, coupled with that of the white Republicans who maintained much of the political control, led to major changes in southern legislatures.

The issues that faced the southern state legislatures were overwhelming. State policy had, in many areas, favored the plantation classes for so long as to raise class antagonisms to the boiling point. Thus, in addition to issues of black enfranchisement, there were issues regarding voting restrictions on poor whites, the inadequacy of schools and roads in the hinterland, and debt relief for mortgaged farmers. The newly elected legislatures of the late 1860s were swamped with measures often utopian in their language and their expectations. They responded with an outpouring of reform legislation. South Carolina provided medical care to the aged, Louisiana paved roads and drained swamps, Alabama provided free legal service to the poor, and North Carolina provided internal improvements of a social reform nature.

Party voting in these legislatures was often quite impressive, given the diverse composition of the Republican party. For example, in North Carolina's lower house, of the 126 members who served from 1868 to 1870, there were 39 Democrats and 87 Republicans, with the latter consisting of 18 African Americans, 11 northerners ("carpetbaggers"), 52 native whites, and 6 whites of unknown extraction (Trelease, p. 320). When 190 roll-call votes were scaled for the sessions between 1868 and 1870, "there was almost no overlap between members of the two parties. The top two-thirds of the list consisted entirely of Republicans except for two Democrats near the bottom of that segment. The lowest third was solidly Democratic except for a single Republican" (Trelease, p. 341).

As political parties continued to evolve across the states, party caucuses came to dominate the state legislative process in the years immediately following the Civil War. During the late 1890s, at least in several midwestern states, party caucuses were activated in every legislative session, with the frequency of meetings varying according to the nature of the issues and the balance of party strength in the legislature. What functions did these caucuses have? Ballard Campbell provided a concise evaluation:

> The scant surviving records of these caucus meetings indicate that they served as occasions for mutual discussion, not as command performances in which leaders dictate instructions to the rank and file. Unanimity was not universal, for walkouts, absenteeism, and complaints were recorded. The important point, however, is not how much leaders may have attempted to twist members' arms at these gatherings, but rather that caucus meetings actually occurred. They offered yet another way in which the institutionalized presence of party was manifested. Caucuses facilitated intraparty communication, reminded lawmakers of their partisan attachments, and further elevated the visibility of party as a set of symbols and a collectivity of specific people. In this regard, no comparable rival existed in these forums. Given its omnipresence, the wonder is not that party cued some voting responses but that its impact was not greater. (pp. 189–190)

To what extent did party members vote along party lines during this period? Those who have studied this topic, including political scientists and historians, utilize different yardsticks in judging whether party voting occurred. For example, A. Lawrence Lowell, in his study of voting in England and the United States at the end of the nineteenth century, settled on the most restrictive definition: When 90 percent or more of one party voted against 90 percent or more of the main opposition party, partisan voting had occurred (p. 323). Lowell concluded that party voting was significant in the New York Senate (25 percent to 30 percent) and Assembly (45 percent to 50 percent), but minuscule in other chambers of legislatures in Massachusetts, Pennsylvania, Ohio, and Illinois. A different picture emerges for this period when the party voting criteria are relaxed. When a party vote is defined as one where the opposition is 80 percent or is a simple majority, the average percent of contested roll calls over the same five sessions in the 1880s and 1890s increases from 15 percent to 34 percent to 72 percent in Illinois, from 9 percent to 29 percent to 62 percent in Iowa, and from 9 percent to 30 percent to 64 percent in Wisconsin (calculated from Ballard Campbell, Figure 1, p. 82). Campbell noted that "regardless of measurement criteria, party had no comparable rival among policy determinants in midwestern lower houses" (p. 199), and in these states, "the most pronounced partisan disagreements occurred over definitions of social behavior" (p. 97).

Early Twentieth Century

While the party was the major organizing device in nonsouthern legislatures, it was perceived to be somewhat inadequate in certain spheres. During the 1890s through the 1920s "parties dominated government more thoroughly than they ever had before or would again, but many people considered the parties' policies and governmental methods inadequate. Charges of corruption, which so pervaded the [era], added to the awareness of the parties' limitations" (McCormick, p. 229).

Much of the antiparty rhetoric could be traced back to Madison and beyond. Parties, the reformers wrote, prevented the election of the most-qualified to office, because they required the dedication of an individual's life to ladder-climbing and manipulation rather than to an education that could be applied to problems best addressed by experts. Parties developed positions on policy for reasons of election advantage and the "party line" rather than formulating any "objective" and possibly unpopular solutions to pressing problems. Consequently, party-based elections and their attendant hoopla came in for the most virulent criticisms by the press and reformers.

Until the 1890s, the two-party system (one-party in the South) was in its golden age, and little in the way of third parties or reform movements made any impact. By the 1890s, reform movements, often tied to party as well as to policy entrepreneurs of various ideologies, were making serious headway under a variety of banners. At the heart of the motivation of the reformers was the "spoils system." Although the flow of federal patronage—as well as the protected bailiwicks of the national parties in Congress—was easily identified, influence over state appointments was much more difficult to determine. Certainly "bosses" like Roscoe Conkling of New York had patronage appointments and positions at the federal level (such as the two hundred employees of the New York customhouse) that were theirs by right of electoral aid to the administration (Dobson, pp. 64–66); however, the pervasiveness of state party influence on state appointments is more difficult to assess.

One-party domination was the rule in the South during the period following the ascendancy of the reformers, but it was not confined to the South. Republican Simon Cameron had built a significant organization in Pennsylvania, and but for a few isolated positions in the state's lower house, the Republicans ruled. The Democrats practically went into hiding in New Hampshire, where factionalism in the Republican party replaced two-party rule. In Iowa a state machine maintained by Senator William B. Allison was in control, and the Republicans could win any office for which they could find a nominee (Dobson, p. 29).

By the turn of the century, the influence of the party machines in many state legislatures had begun to wane. Lobbyists who had once felt confidence bordering on arrogance in dictating party positions in the legislature became circumspect and then fearful. The number of states that passed legislation regulating lobbying for the period went from none in 1903–1904 to ten in 1907–1908; no states had passed legislation prohibiting campaign contributions by corporations by 1903, but by 1908, twenty-two had done so. The mandatory direct primary had been implemented in thirty-one states by 1908, and by that year the regulation of railroads by commission had been instituted in forty-one states, where no such legislation had even been introduced prior to 1903–1904 (McCormick, p. 343).

While passage of direct-primary legislation was intended to weaken parties, in effect it more firmly entrenched them in election law than before. The measures passed to enact direct primaries also gave the parties formal status as nominating bodies, and, as McCormick observed, "regulated their practices, and converted them into durable, official, bureaucracies" (McCormick, 347).

During this period, significant differences and similarities appear to have existed among the state legislatures in terms of the role that political parties played. On the one hand, political parties appear to have been fairly consistent in organizing the legislature. As Robert Luce noted, "in Massachusetts as in all other States, the majority control of committees goes to the dominant party, carrying out the theory that one party or the other should in general be responsible for the aggregate product of the session." Luce stated further, "Chairmen in American assemblies are almost invariably members of the dominant party. Once in a great while a minority chairmanship may be given to an unusually popular member of the minority who can be trusted to make no trouble" (pp. 119, 123). On the other hand, the role of partisanship in decision making was much more variable: "We shall find a wide range of methods and conditions, with adjacent states at the two extremes—New York, where partisanship is magnified to the highest degree, and Massachusetts, where it is in legislative practice insignificant. Between these two extremes, the other forty-six states show every shade of political habit" (p. 491).

A brief look into the Wisconsin experience with progressivism reveals that the parties remained quite active, albeit transformed. The Republican party remained dominant from

1900 to 1925, holding between fifty-seven and ninety-two of the hundred seats in the state assembly (Brye, p. 226). In 1914 the Republicans held sixty-two of the hundred seats in the assembly and twenty-one of thirty-three in the senate; by 1918, they had gained seven seats in the assembly and six in the senate; and by 1920, the Republicans held ninety-two of the seats in the assembly and retained twenty-seven in the senate (Brye, p. 375). But this numerical dominance is somewhat illusory, for most of the conflict in Wisconsin's state legislature took place, not between Democrats and Republicans, but among the "Stalwarts," led by Emanuel Philipp, and the Progressives, led by Robert M. La Follette. By 1925, the split became formal, with the old-guard Stalwarts forming the Republican party of Wisconsin, a new entity, in contrast to the Republican party, whose machinery was by then controlled by the Progressives, who would leave in 1934 to form their own party. The Progressives would not reach their high-water mark as a separate party until 1936, when they held forty-six seats in the assembly (the Republicans, inheritors of the Stalwart banner, held twenty-one; the Democrats, thirty-one; and the Socialists, two). While the Democrats experienced a brief surge from 1912 to 1914, they faded almost from sight after World War I, trailing even the Socialists from 1918 to 1928. (In 1928 the Democrats were down to one seat in the state assembly and no senate seats at all.)

The New Deal period brought about several changes. The revolution inspired by Franklin D. Roosevelt at the national level has often functioned as a screen through which political scientists view the realignment in the states. As James L. Sundquist pointed out, this is a misconception. Ticket splitting, now taken for granted as a feature of the political process, made its first substantial appearance during this period. While in many areas the vote for Roosevelt immediately translated into overwhelming Democratic majorities at the state level, the phenomenon was not universal. Even Sundquist, a major theorist of realignment, noted that unlike "the major realignments of the nineteenth century . . . the realignment of the 1930s has been drawn out over an extraordinarily long period" (p. 229). It may be that conversion of voters played a relatively minor role—or at least a coequal role only—in the swing to the Democrats. Kristi Andersen has conducted empirical work that suggests that a great many of the new Democratic voters were just that—new voters (p. 232). Whatever the source, Sundquist made the point that New Deal voting patterns, which at first favored Democrats at the state level, underwent a recession over time, so that the Republicans regained positions of dominance in the areas where they had held sway before the elections of 1932–1934.

In North Dakota, the Nonpartisan League, an artifact of progressivism, had held on far longer than in most western states, albeit as a "party within a party"—an organized faction of the Republicans (conservative Republicans also organized a faction, the Independent Voters Association; cf. Sundquist, p. 242). While North Dakota voters went for Roosevelt in 1932, they threw their support at the state level, not to Democrats, who had until then been only a minor force in North Dakota politics, but rather to the slate of candidates put forward by the Nonpartisan League; as a result, the League gained control of the legislature for the first time since 1919. Disappointed with the few policy initiatives of successive League-controlled legislatures, whose members seemed only concerned with maintaining themselves in office, North Dakotans returned the conservative Republicans to office shortly after the end of World War II. By 1956, a new organization (including a revitalized Nonpartisan League), through a series of complex and shifting alliances among the factions in the Republican party, left the party altogether and joined the Democrats, who then took control of the legislature.

State Legislatures After World War II

In his ground-breaking study of party political conflict in state legislatures in 1955, Malcolm Jewell was able to identify twenty-three states as one-party entities—that is, states in which "partisan factors *can have* no significant influence over legislative voting habits" (p. 674; emphasis added). The eleven southern states had remained Democratic since the period of the so-called "redeemers" and the collapse of Reconstruction Republicanism. In addition, Jewell identified five other states as dominated by the Democrats; seven as Republican one-party entities; and two as nonpartisan. He also found that Wisconsin, because of its unique progressive and Republican factional orientation, did not fit the general trend of party conflict (see the discussion of Wisconsin above). This left twenty-two states, in which some partisan basis for legislative voting could be identified. These findings suggest a basic dichotomy of partisan behavior present in the states during the 1940s and 1950s: about half of the states were dominated by one party, with conflict restricted to intraparty factionalization, and the other half displayed varying levels of interparty conflict.

In 1954, Belle Zeller reported that majority-party caucuses existed in roughly two-thirds of state senates and state assemblies, but were of significance in only about one-half of all legislatures. In fact, Zeller noted that among all of the two-party states, only in California was the party caucus completely unimportant (p. 194, n. 9). Yet, these findings tend to overstate the importance of the caucuses, for "in only thirteen states do majority caucuses meet frequently and exert or attempt to exert any significant control over their members or the program of the legislature" (p. 194). At the same time, minority-party caucuses existed in about one-half of the states, but were only of some importance in those fifteen legislatures in which the strength of the minority party was substantial.

Zeller's mixed findings regarding party caucuses and Jewell's findings regarding party voting in the 1950s are worth noting because they provide a good indication of the range of partisan division that was possible in states with two competitive parties. The first important observation made by Jewell is that "among those states with two strong parties, those with the most intense party competition are not necessarily those with the highest level of party voting" (1955, p. 791). For example, Colorado, a state with one of the closest balances of parties in its legislature, had one of the lowest scores for party cohesion and interparty conflict, while in New York the level of party unity was high in both houses of the legislature, despite a large Republican majority in 1947.

The second significant finding for this period was that "the degree of party voting appears to be significantly higher in those two-party states which [were] larger and more urban" (Jewell, 1955, p. 791). Jewell suggested that urban states have their Democratic base in the larger cities and metropolitan areas, whereas the Republican party drew its members from rural areas and small towns. Thus, an urban-rural split is associated with Democratic-Republican competition. While the membership of neither party in large urban states fitted this description perfectly, the existence of relatively different constituency bases provides an explanation for the higher levels of cohesion.

Finally, Jewell's analysis helps to explain the types of issues on which the parties divided during the 1940s. He noted, "The most partisan issues in the legislatures of all states, and particularly the large, urban states, involve narrow party interests, the prestige and fiscal program of the administration, and economic and social issues" (1955, p. 791). Yet party voting was low on a variety of issues: legal and judicial affairs, civil service, state and local administration, and business regulation (1955, p. 790). Parties differed on some, but not all, issues.

Summary

This brief historical review of political parties in American state legislatures provides several themes for analyzing their roles in contemporary political activity. Parties appeared initially as groupings of legislators around strong and widely admired heroes of the American Revolution. Their primary purpose seemed to be to provide some electoral advantage to the individuals because of their association with a well-recognized person. Gradually, these groupings tended to adopt differing positions on issues and to vote together on at least an occasional basis; however, the issues that divided members along group (party) lines were highly idiosyncratic and tended to be politically oriented rather than ideological.

As these leaders disappeared from the political scene, groupings based on election advantage and broader issue congruence began to emerge. Such more-generalized groups began to act more like political parties, but remained fragile and susceptible to disappearance. Through merging, dissolution, and consolidation, new, more-durable party entities began to appear during the antebellum and Civil War periods. The consequence was a golden age of party strength and dominance of state political activity. Interests found that alliances with political parties provided the best strategy for advancing their positions at the state and national level.

The appearance of abuses in the form of political machines and widespread political corruption and patronage based on the parties led to challenges of this new status quo from reformers, disillusioned citizens, and disaffected leaders. These challenges, at times, resulted in new political parties forming to compete during elections and in controlling government and at other times in reform via one of the established parties. Regardless, the consequence was change in the political system to remove the factors that permitted abuses by either party. Gradually, new alignments of voters and changes in party dominance saw the emergence of greater party competition and the evolution of new party organizations in many states. In addition, partisan differences became more pronounced in issue positions, including fiscal and economic programs as well as social issues. The setting for political parties in the 1960s, then, was one of pressure toward responsiveness to citizens, representation of traditional interest sectors, and the maintenance of electoral advantage.

THE ELECTION PROCESS

Perhaps the most critical role political parties play is in the election process. As noted above, state legislative candidates have run without formal party labels in only two cases—Minnesota from 1913 through 1974 and Nebraska beginning in 1935. Thus, party identification and partisan activities are prevalent in the selection process for state legislators. In fact, by the 1990s, party leaders in many state legislatures had become especially active in recruiting persons to run, in providing campaign resources (money and services as well as advice), and in coordinating partisan activities directed toward electing party majorities. This increasing attention by legislative leaders to party election efforts developed because many party organizations had overlooked these efforts and concentrated on national and gubernatorial races. Without a firm majority in state legislatures, however, many party efforts toward maintaining and building an electoral base via reapportionment, as well as in policy-making, would be ineffective at best. Consequently,

electoral activities are critical in maintaining a political party and its policy-making in a state legislature.

The understanding of state legislative elections, while not as complete as for the U.S. Congress, has increased dramatically in recent years. The relative importance of incumbency, money, district characteristics, national and state economic performance, and presidential and gubernatorial coattails have all been examined by James E. Campbell; Laura R. Winsky; Gregory Caldeira and James C. Patterson; and Malcolm Jewell and David Breaux.

Perhaps the most unanticipated finding is that the very high rate of incumbency success is not simply a phenomenon of the 1980s; rather, in states that have used single-member districts from the late 1960s through the 1980s, incumbents experienced a high level of success, regardless of the time period. The reason for the impact of incumbency is still unclear, since state legislators do not enjoy all of the re-election perks available to members of Congress (e.g., franking). The best explanation may be found in the resource-acquisition capabilities of incumbents; in the ability of incumbents to gain greater name recognition, provide constituent services, and perform in a satisfactory manner; or in some combination of these factors.

The understanding of the trends in two-party competition has also increased. Those elections in which a Democrat faced off against a Republican and the winning candidate obtained less than 60 percent of the two-party vote decreased in most of the twenty state lower houses studied during the period from 1950 to 1986. The decreases in different dimensions of competition are best explained by greater levels of legislative resources, use of multimember districts, and, on a more limited basis, the frequency of incumbents seeking re-election (Weber, Tucker, and Brace, p. 45).

This essay expands on Weber, Tucker, and Brace's research by examining general-election results in forty-six senates and houses. Three dimensions of legislative elections were examined. The first dimension is the level of contestation. Single-party contestation was measured as the percentage of legislative-district general elections in which a political party fielded a candidate. Separate calculations were made for Democrats and Republicans. Next, a measure of two-party contestation was calculated as the percentage of constituency-level general elections in which both major parties were represented. The second dimension, competitiveness, taps the percentage of district-level races in which the party's nominee had a creditable showing, thus eliminating those token candidates who occupy a slot but do not have more than a minuscule chance of emerging with a victory. The authors operationalized single-party competitiveness as the percentage of the total races in which the party's candidate received 40 percent or more of the total general-election vote. Two-party competitiveness occurred when both parties received at least 40 percent of the total general-election vote. The third dimension is the level of party success. It was defined simply as the percentage of the general-election races in which the party's candidate had the greatest number of votes.

In constructing these measures, three major problems had to be addressed. First, some candidates were listed as running on a combined party ticket (e.g., Republican-Democrat). In instances where this happened (New Hampshire and Pennsylvania), a determination was made as to the party identification of the candidate. Second, viable third parties existed in some of these states at different times throughout the twenty-year period (e.g., the Liberal and Conservative parties in New York). In those cases where candidates ran under more than one of the two major political parties' banners, the winning party was listed as being Democrat or Republican unless a check of the incumbency records indicated otherwise. Finally, the existence of third-party votes had the potential for confounding the competitiveness vote. While most scholars prefer to exclude third-party totals when discussing competition, the authors opted for the percentage of the total vote as a better measure of the actual competitiveness of a party.

A major difficulty in comparing results across different states is the variation in type of electoral system utilized. No problems were posed if single-member districts or multi-member districts with individual races for specific positions were used by the state. Analytical difficulties arise in free-for-all multimember district races. Here, the authors decided to follow Richard G. Niemi, Simon Jackman, and Laura R. Winsky's approach and created pseudo–single-member districts. The Niemi, Jackman, and Winsky logic is simple: pair the highest Democratic vote-getter with the lowest Republican vote-getter, and continue the rank/order in a descending/ascending pairing. Not only does this protocol match the election outcomes properly (and probably reflects voter preference), but it also provides the best measure of competitiveness.

Given the historically significant variation in the extent of party competition in different regions of the country, data were divided into subsets of South and non-South categories. The South consisted of the eleven original Confederate states, minus Louisiana, which was excluded because it had an election system in which the general election could be contested by two members from the same party. The non-South group comprised the remaining states, with the exclusion of Nebraska, Vermont, and Minnesota. Minnesota was excluded because it did not start holding partisan elections until 1974, and Vermont, because data were provided only for 1986.

Analysis of the political parties in state legislative elections has been immensely aided by the availability of the state legislative election data for the period 1968–1987 from the Interuniversity Consortium for Political and Social Research (ICPSR) at the University of Michigan. In order to facilitate comparison, the election data for the twenty-year span are aggregated into two ten-year periods, 1968–1977 and 1978–1987. To see if significant differences exist between the two time periods, the authors performed simple OLS (ordinary least squares) regression analysis—used to measure variance—in which time was treated as a dummy variable (i.e., 0=1968–1977, 1=1978–1987).

Contestation

As illustrated in Table 1, the mean level of two-party contestation during the 1968–1977 period was roughly 72 percent. The variation in two-party contestation spanned almost the entire range of possibilities, from a low of 1 percent in the Alabama Senate elections to a high of 100 percent in elections for both the New Jersey Senate and Assembly and the Connecticut Senate. Democrats and Republicans were more than twice as likely to face off in the non-South

POLITICAL PARTIES IN STATE LEGISLATURES

Table 1

POLITICAL-PARTY CONTESTING, COMPETITION, AND SUCCESS IN STATE LEGISLATIVE ELECTIONS
1968–1977 and 1978–1987 (in percentages)

	State Senates		State Houses	
	1968–1977	1978–1987	1968–1977	1978–1987
Contestation				
All States				
Both parties	72.0	67.1	70.1	63.6
Democrats	94.1	91.7	93.6	89.9[c]
Republicans	77.5	75.3	76.3	73.4
Non-South[a]				
Both parties	82.1	75.1	79.5	71.5
Democrats	94.1	90.8[c]	93.0	89.3
Republicans	87.9	84.2	86.3	81.8
South[b]				
Both parties	35.5	38.0	36.5	35.4
Democrats	94.0	94.7	96.0	92.1
Republicans	40.0	43.3	40.2	43.1
Competition				
All States				
Both parties	36.5	31.3	36.0	28.0[c]
Democrats	79.7	75.7	78.0	71.9[c]
Republicans	54.7	54.7	54.2	52.6
Non-South				
Both parties	42.4	34.6[c]	41.2	31.1[d]
Democrats	77.4	72.0	75.7	68.7[d]
Republicans	63.7	61.8	62.4	59.0
South				
Both parties	15.2	19.2	17.4	16.7
Democrats	87.6	89.0	86.6	83.1
Republicans	22.1	28.8	24.8	29.8
Success				
Non-South				
Democrats	55.7	54.2	55.9	54.6
Republicans	44.2	45.6	43.9	45.1
South				
Democrats	84.2	83.9	84.8	79.6
Republicans	14.3	16.1	14.9	20.2

a. "Non-South" consists of states not captured by "South" with Minnesota (nonpartisan during first of study); Nebraska (unicameral) and Vermont (data not available) are excluded. $N = 36$.

b. "South" consists of Tennessee, Georgia, North and South Carolina, Texas, Arkansas, Mississippi, Florida, Alabama, and Virginia. Louisiana is excluded for lack of appropriate data. $N = 10$.

c. Significant difference at .05.

d. Significant difference at .01.

states as in the southern states. Democrats contested at least 90 percent of the seats in elections for thirty-eight of forty-six state senates and houses, and fielded candidates for at least 63 percent of the seats in the remaining states. Republicans fielded candidates for 90 percent or more of the seats in elections for twenty-two state senates and twenty state houses. Not surprisingly, Republicans were weakest in the South, where in six of the ten states they did not challenge the Democrats in even a majority of the legislative districts.

During the ensuing decade, the overall level of contestation decreased, with the decrease being greater for the lower houses. This analysis of a larger number of states tends to confirm Ronald E. Weber, Harvey J. Tucker, and Paul Brace's thesis that contestation decreased with time. As expected, the level of two-party contestation in 1968–1977 was negatively related to the magnitude and direction of the change between the two time periods (Pearson correlation = −.493), indicating that typically, the higher the initial level of two-party contestation, the more likely a larger decrease in the rate of two-party contestation during the late 1970s and 1980s. For example, twenty-two of the twenty-three party systems with more than 90 percent two-party contestation rates in 1968–1977 experienced a decrease in two-party contesting during 1978–1987.

A relatively large decrease occurred in the rate at which the two major political parties contested elections for both chambers in the non-South states. For the thirty-six non-South states, two-party contestation decreased in elections for thirty-four state houses and twenty-eight state senates. In the majority of these states, this decrease was less than 10 percent; however, in a few states contestation levels fell more than 20 percent (both chambers in Delaware and the lower chambers in Idaho and Rhode Island). While the decrease in any particular state may be mainly attributable to one party's inability to offer candidates at the same rate as in the past (e.g., Republicans in the Delaware state senate elections), neither party is solely responsible for this overall decline. Rather, single-party contestation rates fell in more than three-fourths of the non-South senates and houses for both the Democrats and the Republicans during the late 1970s and 1980s.

The results for the ten southern states are more puzzling. It was anticipated that given the rise of the Republican party in the South during the 1980s, a greater mobilization of Republican candidates would occur and, therefore, two-party contestation levels would increase significantly. Yet, the percent of races in which the two parties contended against each other increased, on average, a mere 2.5 percent in the state senate elections, while actually decreasing for elections to the state lower houses. In line with expectations, significant increases (i.e., greater than 10 percent) occurred in the elections for both houses of Alabama and for the Virginia Senate. However, two-party contestation actually decreased significantly in elections for the Arkansas Senate and the lower houses of South Carolina and Tennessee.

A closer analysis provides answers for these disparate patterns. As expected, in seven of the ten states, Republicans offered candidates for a greater percentage of seats in 1978–1987. At the same time, the percentage of candidates running under the Democratic banner decreased in all the state lower houses and all but two state senates. When these two changes in the level of single-party contestation are combined, a wide range of outcomes is perceived: (1) both parties increased their levels of contestation in one chamber; (2) both parties decreased their levels of contestation in five chambers; (3) the Democrats' decreases were sufficiently large to produce a negative rate of change, even though the Republicans increased their level of contesting in six chambers; and (4) an increase in two-party contests due to one party, typically the Republicans, occurred, registering an increase larger than the decrease for the other party in eight chambers.

Competitiveness

When the analysis shifts from contestation to competition, two contrasting trends become evident. Among non-South states there was a significant decrease in two-party competitiveness, slipping, on average, from slightly more than 42 percent in 1968–1977 to less than 35 percent in 1978–1987. This decrease in two-party competitiveness occurred in almost all of the thirty-six non-South states with an increase registered in only four state lower houses and five state senates. While in some states this decrease was relatively small, the decrease exceeded 10 percent for eleven senates and eighteen lower houses. A major decrement in two-party competition, exceeding 20 percent, occurred in elections for six state senates (Indiana, South Dakota, Wyoming, Illinois, Colorado, and Hawaii) and four lower houses (South Dakota, Indiana, Montana, and Wyoming). Interestingly, among the non-South states, the relationship between the original level of two-party competition and the change in competitiveness between the two periods was negative (Pearson correlation = −.585), indicating that the higher the initial level of competition, the greater the decrease in competition across time.

A focus on the competitiveness of individual parties outside the South uncovers three key trends. First, Democrats experienced a decrease in the number of competitive districts in two-thirds of the state senates and 80 percent of the state lower houses, while for the Republicans, the figures were only 58 percent and 75 percent, respectively. Second, for the Democrats, major decreases in competitiveness (i.e., more than 10 percent) occurred in elections for five state senates (Illinois, Utah, Colorado, South Dakota, and Wyoming), while the same fate befell the Republicans only in elections for the Hawaii Senate. Third, while there is an inverse relationship between the amount of change in the competitiveness of the Democrats and Republicans, it is not very strong (Pearson correlation = −.325 and −.361 for the upper and lower houses, respectively). Cases can be cited where a big loss for one party had relatively little impact on the other. For example, in the South Dakota state senate elections, Democrats saw the percentage of seats in which they were competitive fall from 78 to 55. However, this Democratic decrease did not translate automatically into an increase in competitiveness for the Republicans. Rather, the Republican level of competitiveness only increased from 85 to 86 percent of the races. To further complicate matters, in twenty-three of the thirty-six state lower-house elections, both parties suffered a decrease in the level of competitiveness, while the same pattern occurred in ten state senates. In a few states the reduction was large for both parties (e.g., Illinois Senate).

Changes in the levels of competitiveness in the southern states were more uniform. Republicans increased the number of seats in which they garnered 40 percent or more of the vote in eight out of ten state senates and lower houses. By contrast, Democrats experienced a decrease in the percentage of competitive seats in seven senates and eight lower houses. Somewhat surprisingly, both parties increased their share of competitive seats in the elections to five of these chambers, while both parties suffered a decrease in another four.

Two general conclusions can be drawn from this discussion of contestation and competitiveness. First, partial confirmation exists for Weber, Tucker, and Brace's thesis that contestation and competitiveness have decreased over time. When comparisons are made using all forty-six states, there is an unmistakable movement toward less two-party contestation and competition. Second, while significant South/non-South differences exist for both time periods, there is a trend toward a narrowing of these differences, save for Democratic contestation and competitiveness.

Party Success

While political parties may be concerned about contesting elections and being competitive, a more general concern is with the number and the percentage of races that their party nominees win. As shown in Table 1, during this twenty-year period the Democrats were able to win a greater percentage of seats overall. Even if the overwhelming Democratic advantage in the South is excluded, the Democrats still won, on average, about 54 or 55 percent of the seats in the non-South senates and lower houses during 1968–1987.

Republican success varied markedly among the states. During 1968–1977, Republicans captured at least 40 percent of the seats in forty-eight of ninety-two chambers included in the analysis, twenty-four state senates and twenty-four state lower houses. They were the majority party during this period in twenty-five chambers: both houses of the Kansas, Arizona, Indiana, New Hampshire, Idaho, Colorado, Wyoming, Iowa, South Dakota, and North Dakota legislatures; the senates in New York, Maine, and Michigan; and the lower houses in Delaware and Utah. At the other end of the spectrum, they secured less than 10 percent of the seats in the South Carolina Senate and in both houses of the Alabama, Mississippi, Arkansas, and Texas legislatures.

In 1977–1987, Republicans registered victories, on average, in 40 percent of the races in twenty-three state senates and twenty-five lower houses. They controlled a majority of the seats during this period in twenty-six chambers, including twenty-one that had had a Republican majority in the earlier period. The only additions were the Pennsylvania, Alaska, and Utah senates; the Montana House; and the New Jersey Assembly. They no longer controlled a majority in either chamber in Iowa and in the Maine and Michigan senates.

However, it would be incorrect to see the change in Republican fortunes as increasing only incrementally across all the states. While this may be true for the majority of cases, Republicans experienced a significant change in the rate of success in thirteen chambers. Their share of seats won dropped by 10 percent or more in six state senates: Hawaii, Maine, Michigan, Virginia, Iowa, and California. At the same time, they saw their share of seats increase by 10 percent or more in seven chambers. Interestingly, the most significant growth occurred in only one southern chamber, the Virginia House of Delegates. The other six were all in the western part of the United States: both chambers in Utah; the Idaho House of Representatives; and the senates in New Mexico, Kansas, and Nevada.

Summary

Overshadowing the effects of political parties in state legislative elections were the effects of incumbency: as in Congress, incumbents in state legislatures had an enormous electoral advantage when seeking reelection, regardless of political party. The advantage seems to stem from the name recognition, constituent service, and identification with policy-making activities that accrue to incumbents.

A look at just the indicators of competition between the two major parties in state legislative elections for 1968–1987 shows great interstate variation in the level of two-party contestation. In the North, Democratic and Republican candidates were twice as likely to face one another as in the South. Also, Democrats were more likely to field a candidate in a state legislative race than were Republicans; however, by the 1990s, contestation levels had decreased, especially outside the South.

Regarding the competitiveness of elections (i.e., elections in which the minority party received at least 40 percent of the votes), in non-South states there was a significant decrease in two-party competitiveness in the 1980s. Democrats, for example, saw the number of state legislative races in which they were "competitive" decrease. Further, the higher the original level of competitiveness, the greater its decrease in the years studied. Democrats thus were more "victimized" by decreases in competitiveness than were Republicans. Within the South, Republicans became more competitive in state electoral races as seen in the increased number of seats for which they received at least 40 percent of the popular vote. Democrats have generally experienced a decrease in the percentage of competitive seats that they contested. Contestation and competitiveness in state legislative election contests decreased, indicating a reduction in the degree of two-party competition.

Finally, in spite of changes in contestation and competitiveness, Democratic candidates held a decided advantage in the number of state legislative seats they won: 54 or 55 percent of the legislative seats outside of the South were Democratic. Republican fortunes at the state legislative level advanced most in the western portion of the United States.

ORGANIZATION OF THE LEGISLATURE

After state legislators have been selected via the district election process, the legislative chamber must be organized in order to conduct its business. In a legislative chamber with overlapping terms of election (the staggered election of one-half a senate every two election years), a certain amount of stability in organization is probable; yet, even here the electoral fortunes of the parties in a particular election may result in a change of party control and consequently a change in the legislative chamber's organization. In most lower chambers, the election of all members at each election offers the possibility of a complete change in membership. Consequently, the organization of a legislative chamber—leadership selection—is a critical task for every legislative chamber. By tradition, political parties are responsible for this activity.

After the elections, the task of organizing the legislature awaits the members of the political parties. Before the commencement of a new legislative session, legislators of each political party caucus to choose their leaders in most, but not all, state legislatures. This intraparty procedure has two components: selection of those to hold key positions within the legislature and selection of leaders of the political party within the legislature. While the tasks overlap to some extent, they are treated as separate for ease of presentation.

Choosing Chamber Leaders

The presiding officer in the forty-nine lower houses is the Speaker, who is elected by the membership. The situation in the state senates is somewhat more complicated in that the presiding officer in twenty-seven senates is the constitutionally elected lieutenant governor.

While in a handful of states the majority-party caucus either does not exist or has not taken a formal role in the selection of the Speaker (e.g., Texas, Louisiana, Mississippi, and Alabama), in most chambers the majority-party caucuses do determine which of its members will be chosen as the presiding officer of the chamber. The majority-party caucus decision is tantamount to election by the entire membership, because in most states, the members of the majority party vote as a bloc when the vote on the presiding officer is taken to the floor. However, a cross-party coalition sometimes forms to thwart the wishes of the majority caucus. Two examples highlight this trend. In the strong-party state of Connecticut in 1989, the incumbent Speaker, who was seeking a third term, lost when thirty-one of eighty-eight members of the Democratic majority teamed with all sixty-three members of the minority party to install a more conservative Democrat (Jacklin, pp. 13–15). Also in 1989, the powerful North Carolina Speaker Liston Ramsey was ousted after being in the post for eight years when forty-five of forty-six Republicans and twenty of the seventy-four Democrats opted for another Democrat (Christensen, pp. 16–19).

A Speaker pro tempore or president pro tempore office exists in thirty-three state lower houses and 43 upper houses. The powers and duties of this person vary. In some state senates where the lieutenant governor presides, the power over committee appointments is lodged in the president pro tempore (e.g., Connecticut, Delaware, New York). In other state senates the position is really only honorary in nature (e.g., Texas). In most of those chambers where the position exists, the entire membership is responsible for choosing the person, although the presiding speaker or president is given that duty in nine chambers. Otherwise, as a rule, the majority-party caucus choice prevails in those states in which the caucus was instrumental in electing the presiding officer.

Choosing Legislative Party Leaders

The formal legislative party organization varies among the chambers, but in general, the main positions are those described below.

Majority or Minority Leader Typically, in the lower houses the majority leader is the floor leader, with responsibilities for leading debate on the floor, helping to develop the calendar, and assisting the Speaker. The minority leader is key to developing a minority-party position, interacting with the majority leadership, and leading debates on the chamber floor. Majority and minority leader positions exist in eighty-seven of the ninety-nine state legislative chambers. They are absent in some southern state legislatures and Nebraska's unicameral legislature, which is a nonpartisan body.

In thirty-four lower houses the majority leader is elected by the majority caucus, while in eight states (i.e., California, Florida, Illinois, Massachusetts, New Hampshire, New York, Oklahoma, and West Virginia), the Speaker makes the appointment. In North Carolina the majority leader is elected by the entire lower house, with the majority leader also being the Speaker pro tempore. By agreement of the lower house in Arkansas, the outgoing Speaker is the majority leader. In thirty-four states, the senate majority leader is elected by just the majority-party caucus, and in six states (Connecticut, Indiana, Maryland, Massachusetts, New Hampshire, and Wisconsin) is appointed by the president or president pro tempore. In the Ohio Senate and House, the rules dictate that all party officers are to be selected by the entire chamber. The minority leader position is chosen by formal rules in all but two states: New Hampshire, where the presiding officer in each chamber appoints the individual, and Ohio.

Assistant Majority or Minority Leader
The assistant majority or minority leader position is sometimes a stepping-stone to that of majority or minority leader. Specific duties vary, but the main task is to assist the majority or minority leader. The position of assistant majority leader exists in roughly one-half of the lower chambers and in slightly more than one-half of the state senates. The assistant majority leader is chosen by the caucus in about two-thirds of the lower houses and in about three-fourths of the state senates.

The assistant minority leader position exists in twenty-four lower houses and twenty-seven upper houses. The minority caucus elects individuals to the position in all but five state lower houses and seven state senates. In a minority of chambers, the presiding officer appoints the assistant leader.

Majority or Minority Caucus Chair
In those states with active caucuses, a caucus chair often presides over the caucus, develops the caucus agenda, and sees that it is adhered to. The formal position of caucus chair exists in nineteen lower houses and eighteen upper houses. These leaders are elected by the caucus membership in all but the Illinois and West Virginia lower houses and the Illinois and New York senates. A specially designated minority caucus chair position exists in nineteen lower houses and seventeen upper houses. The minority caucus elects the caucus chair in all but two state lower houses (i.e., Florida and Illinois) and two senates (i.e., Illinois and New York).

Majority Whip
The majority whip has several duties, including ensuring that party members attend floor debate, counting the number of votes for various proposals, and generally trying to lobby for the position taken by the legislative party. Majority whips exist in thirty lower houses, with the caucus making the selection, except in six chambers in which the leadership makes the appointment and in Ohio, where the entire chamber votes on the position. In slightly more than one-half of the state senates, the majority whip position exists, with the caucus making the selection in all but nine cases, eight of which are by the leadership and one by the entire senate membership.

One-half of the state senates have a minority whip position, the holder of which is chosen by the legislative party leader in Indiana, Massachusetts, New Hampshire, and New York. Thirty-two lower chambers have a minority whip position; party leaders make the selection in Connecticut, Florida, Illinois, New Hampshire, New York, and West Virginia, but in the remaining chambers, the caucus membership is given responsibility for making the choice.

As suggested by the above analysis, considerable variation exists among the chambers in terms of the configuration of legislative party organization. In fact, one can construct a continuum based on the number of unique party positions that exist, and each chamber can be arrayed along it. At the one end are eleven chambers in which no formal party leaders are selected, although this is somewhat misleading. In the Texas House, for example, majority and minority caucuses exist and leaders are chosen; however, the legislature itself is not organized formally by party. Thus, these leaders are excluded in any analysis.

Among the chambers in which party leaders are selected, the most basic arrangement is that in which there are only a majority leader and a minority leader, a setup that occurs only in the Alaska Senate and House. One of the two parties adds a whip position in another three chambers. More complexity is offered in fourteen chambers in which both parties have two leadership positions: the majority or minority leader and either a whip or an assistant majority leader. Thus, a relatively simple leadership structure exists in nineteen chambers.

The party leadership structure is much more complex in the remaining sixty-nine chambers. The least-complex arrangement among these has three leadership positions for each party. At the other end of the continuum is the New York Assembly, in which both parties have numerous official positions. To give some idea of the complex nature of this organizational structure, the list of party positions for the 1991–1992 session is listed in Table 2, along with the positions for three chambers varying in degree of complexity.

POLITICAL PARTIES IN STATE LEGISLATURES

Table 2

VARIETIES OF LEGISLATIVE PARTY ORGANIZATION

Majority Party		Minority Party
Alaska Senate (most simple)		
	President	
Majority leader		Minority leader
Nevada House		
	Speaker	
Floor leader	Speaker pro tem	Floor leader
Assistant floor leader		Assistant floor leader
Whip		Whip
Pennsylvania House		
	Speaker	
Floor leader		Floor leader
Whip		Whip
Caucus chair		Caucus chair
Caucus secretary		Caucus secretary
Policy chair		Policy chair
Caucus administrator		Caucus administrator
Majority Appropriations Committee chair		Minority Appropropriations Committee chair
New York Assembly (most complex)		
	Speaker	
	Speaker pro tem	
	Asst. Speaker pro tem	
	Deputy Speaker	
Majority leader	Asst. Speaker	Minority leader
Deputy leader		Leader pro tem
Asst. majority leader		Deputy leader
Whip		Asst. leaders (2)
Deputy whip		Asst. leader pro tem
Asst. whip		Whip
Majority Conference chair		Deputy whip
Majority Conference vice-chair		Asst. whip
Majority Conference secretary		Steering Committee chair
Steering Committee chair		Steering Committee vice-chair
Steering Committee vice-chair		Program Committee chair
Program Committee chair		Rep. Conference chair
Ways and Means Committee chair		Rep. Conference vice-chair
		Rep. Conference secretary
		Joint Conference Committee chair
		Joint Conference Committee vice-chair

The complexity of the party organizational structure can also be defined by the number of members occupying party positions. If those chambers in which political parties had no organizational structure in the late 1980s are excluded, then a mean of 5.1 majority-party members had party organizational positions, with the range between 1 and 25. In eleven chambers, 10 or more legislators had officially designated positions. If the presiding officer and Speaker pro tempore are included as members of the majority party, then the mean number rises to 6.8, with the range now being between 2 and 29. The largest number was found in the Michigan House, where the breakdown was as follows: Speaker (1), Speaker pro tempore (1), associate Speaker pro tempore (1), assistant associate Speaker pro tempore (1), majority floor leader (1), assistant floor leaders (13), and majority whips (11). For the minority party, 4.7 legislators had party positions, with the range being between 1 and 17. In seven chambers, 10 or more members of the minority party had party positions.

To obtain a better understanding of the extent of party organization, the authors divided the number of members with party positions, including presiding officer and pro tempore, by the number of legislative party members. The results indicate that the proportion of members who had these positions exceeded 25 percent for both parties in eleven state senates (i.e., Connecticut, Hawaii, Illinois, Indiana, Michigan, New Hampshire, New Jersey, New York, Rhode Island, Tennessee, and Washington) and just two lower houses (i.e., Michigan and New Jersey). This sizable proportion of members holding "leadership" positions indicates the scope and inclusiveness of members in leadership ranks.

Contrary to expectations, the majority party does not always have a greater number of legislators with party-designated positions than does the minority party. In fact, if the chamber officers are excluded, then the two parties have the same number of members in forty-seven chambers; in eighteen chambers the majority has more, but in twenty-two chambers the minority has a more complex organization. If the chamber officers are included, then this imbalance in favor of the minority party drops to just six chambers.

Summary

Legislative party organization, in terms of the leadership hierarchy, exists in a variety of forms in the ninety-nine state legislative chambers. All except Nebraska share the partisan basis for determining how this leadership hierarchy will be configured within each political party. Some legislative leadership hierarchies are very simple, with a single leader controlling the organization, while others exhibit a fairly complex leadership structure, with an extensive division of labor and numerous leadership positions. While each pattern has its advantages, evidence suggests that a more complex pattern prevails in approximately two-thirds of state-legislative chambers.

THE STRUCTURING OF LEGISLATIVE DECISION-MAKING

In addition to organizing a legislative session through leadership selection, political parties also serve to structure the reviewing, deliberative, and decision-making activities of a state legislature. Such structuring takes place through discussions and positions agreed on in party caucuses; through committee review of, deliberations on, and shaping of legislation; and through the division of parties on the chamber floor. Each of these party-based organizational features contributes to the molding and crafting of the choices available in the final policy-making of a legislative body.

Party-Leadership Style

Party-leadership style is defined as the type of relationship and degree of direction a leader uses in going about his or her leadership duties vis-à-vis rank-and-file members. In other words, leadership style describes how legislative leadership works in bringing about group activity. While legislative leadership is generally conceded to be an important factor in how each political party works during a legislative session, comparatively little systematic and across-state attention has been given to leadership style, with the exception of case studies of individual leaders—an approach that has not provided useful across-time or across-state comparisons (cf. Whicker and Jewell). In a survey questionnaire developed by the authors and mailed to all members of eighteen state legislatures covering the period 1977–1986, each legislator was asked a number of questions about the leadership style used by legislative leaders of each political party in his or her chamber. Responses permitted the authors to develop a five-session profile of leadership style as used by leaders for both political parties in thirty-six legislative chambers. Here the authors will focus on two statements—"Leaders ruled with an iron hand" and "Leaders punished and rewarded members"—that probed leadership style as perceived by legislators of each political party. The legislators' perceptions of these two leadership measures are shown in Tables 3 and 4.

Individuals were able to respond to each statement by using a 1–5 scale: 1 = very false, 2 = false, 3 = true/false, 4 = true, and 5 = very true. Mean session scores greater than 3.0 indicate that members of that party agreed that the statement was more true than false.

Three general findings emerge from these tables. First, legislators do not typically see their party leaders as having an operating style that emphasizes rewards and punishments or using an iron-hand approach. The characterization of the old-style ironhanded leader was perceived to be more false than true in 79 percent of the total sessions/party combinations, while party members saw the reward-punishment characterization as more false than true in 63 percent of the total session/party combinations.

Second, as expected, a relationship exists between the two variables. The greater the perception that leaders punish and reward members, the greater the likelihood that they agree that they rule with an iron hand. However, the strength of the relationship varies by political party, with the Pearson correlation between the two values being .678 for senate Democrats and .696 for house Democrats, but only .361 for senate Republicans and .363 for house Republicans. (The reason for the party differences will be discussed at the end of this section.)

Third, the results shown in Tables 3 and 4 indicate that substantial differences exist among the thirty-six chambers, even among members of the same party. Overall, support

for the old-style leader who punished and rewarded party members and tried to keep a very tight control on the operations of the legislature appears to best fit in the Ohio House, where Vern Riffe, a strong leader, managed majority Democrats for all ten years of this study, and in the Massachusetts House, where Thomas McGee, also known as a strong leader, presided. The large contingent of Democrats in the Pennsylvania House also rated their leadership highly on these two variables, but at slightly lower levels than were found in the other two lower houses.

Why the substantial difference between the Democrats and Republicans on these two issues? The answer is tied to which political party is in the majority. During 1977–1986, Democrats had majority control of the chamber in a greater number of states and for a greater number of sessions than did Republicans. The importance of this can be ascertained if one compares the scores between the majority and minority parties. For both questions, in only slightly more than one-quarter of the senate and one-sixth of the house comparisons did the minority-party mean evaluation exceed the majority-party mean. By and large, majority-party members are more likely to rate their leaders as tending to use rewards and punishments and to be more dictatorial in their behavior than do minority-party members. While the differences in some cases are relatively small, they nonetheless point out the importance of viewing legislative leadership from the perspectives of majority and minority status.

Party Caucuses

A potentially important mechanism for enhancing the role played by political parties as seen in the historical section of this essay is the legislative party caucus. What roles do these organizations play in the contemporary state-legislative process? Several studies in the 1980s addressed this question (National Conference of State Legislatures; Harmel; Francis; Jewell, 1986; Jewell and Olson; American Society of Legislative Clerks and Secretaries; and Euchner and Jewell). A key finding in these studies is that political party caucuses perform a multiplicity of functions. One perspective is that party caucuses may be hierarchically ordered, from

(continued on p. 968)

Table 3
EVALUATION OF THE EXTENT TO WHICH LEADERS RULED WITH AN IRON HAND
Five Legislative Sessions by Political Party (1977–1986)[d]

State	Chamber	Democrats			Republicans		
		Mean	Range	No. of Sessions with Score >3.0	Mean	Range	No. of Sessions with Score >3.0
Ariz.	S	1.69	1.0–2.5	0	1.75	1.6–1.9	0
	H	1.65	1.3–2.0	0	3.05	2.4–4.0	2
Calif.	S	2.33	1.2–4.0	1	1.67[b]	1.0–3.0	0
	A	2.61	2.1–3.0	0	2.56	1.0–3.3	1
Fla.	S	2.75[a]	2.0–4.0	0	1.00[a]	1.0–1.0	0
	H	2.88	2.6–3.3	1	1.74	1.5–2.1	0
Ga.	S	2.54	1.8–3.1	1	1.33[b]	1.0–2.0	0
	H	2.76	2.2–3.1	1	1.66	1.1–2.7	0
Iowa	S	2.44	1.6–3.1	1	2.47	1.8–2.9	0
	H	2.51	1.8–3.1	1	2.26	1.8–2.9	0
Maine	S	1.88	1.3–2.9	0	2.00	1.1–2.8	0
	H	2.78	2.2–3.3	1	1.85	1.6–2.2	0
Mass.	S	3.58	3.0–4.0	4	1.38[a]	1.0–2.0	0
	H	3.39	2.2–3.9	4	2.02	1.6–2.5	0
Nev.	S	1.95	1.4–2.5	0	2.18[b]	1.7–3.0	0
	A	2.24	1.7–3.2	1	2.11	1.2–3.4	1
N.C.	S	2.66	1.7–3.4	2	1.25[a]	1.0–1.7	0
	H	2.51	2.1–3.1	1	1.53	1.0–2.2	0
N.Dak.	S	1.92	1.2–2.5	0	2.11	1.9–2.3	0
	H	1.74	1.4–2.1	0	2.40	1.8–2.7	0
Ohio	S	2.84	2.6–3.0	0	1.78[a]	1.4–2.4	0
	H	3.55	3.2–4.1	5	1.90	1.3–3.0	0
Pa.	S	2.72	2.3–3.3	0	2.21	1.6–2.5	0
	H	3.01	2.6–3.3	3	2.41	1.8–3.0	0
S.Dak.	S	1.44	1.0–2.0	0	2.23	1.8–2.8	0
	H	1.84	1.3–2.3	0	2.83	2.2–3.3	2
Tenn.	S	1.59	1.3–2.0	0	1.63	1.2–2.0	0
	H	3.30	2.4–4.5	2	1.45	1.2–1.7	0
Tex.	S	1.67[a]	1.0–2.3	0	1.07[b]	1.0–1.2	0
	H	1.67	1.5–2.0	0	1.11	1.0–1.4	0
Wash.	S	2.32[a]	1.9–2.6	0	1.95	1.5–2.4	0
	A	2.05	1.6–2.8	0	2.71	2.3–3.4	2
W.Va.	S	2.31	1.8–3.0	0	1.50[c]	1.5–1.5	0
	H	2.72	2.2–3.2	1	2.08[a]	1.8–2.4	0
Wis.	S	1.79	1.2–2.4	0	1.57	1.1–2.0	0
	H	2.20	1.9–2.7	0	2.02	1.9–2.1	0

a. Indicates data are available for only 4 two-year sessions.
b. Indicates data are available for only 3 two-year sessions.
c. Indicates data are available for only 2 two-year sessions.
d. Scores can range from 1 (very false) to 5 (very true).

Table 4

EVALUATION OF THE EXTENT TO WHICH LEADERS PUNISHED AND REWARDED MEMBERS
Five Legislative Sessions by Political Party (1977–1986)[d]

State	Chamber	Democrats			Republicans		
		Mean	Range	No. of Sessions with Score >3.0	Mean	Range	No. of Sessions with Score >3.0
Ariz.	S	1.57	1.0–2.5	0	2.55	2.3–2.9	0
	H	2.46	1.7–3.2	1	2.63	2.4–3.3	1
Calif.	S	3.10	2.5–4.0	1	2.50[b]	2.0–3.0	0
	A	3.14	2.0–4.2	2	3.38	2.0–4.8	4
Fla.	S	3.59[a]	2.9–4.5	2	1.66[a]	1.0–2.0	0
	H	2.85	2.2–3.8	1	2.87	2.3–3.5	2
Ga.	S	2.96	2.4–3.1	3	1.33[b]	1.0–2.0	0
	H	2.61	2.2–3.1	1	1.87	1.3–2.3	0
Iowa	S	2.80	2.1–3.6	1	2.38	1.9–2.9	0
	H	2.70	2.3–3.1	2	2.27	1.8–2.9	0
Maine	S	2.82	1.8–3.2	2	2.13	1.7–2.6	0
	H	3.06	2.6–3.3	3	2.15	1.8–2.4	0
Mass.	S	3.40	2.8–4.2	2	1.79[a]	1.0–3.0	0
	H	3.26	2.2–3.9	4	2.70	1.7–3.7	1
Nev.	S	1.98	1.0–3.0	0	2.25[c]	2.0–2.5	0
	A	2.76	1.8–4.1	2	2.20	1.2–3.9	1
N.C.	S	2.78	2.2–3.3	0	1.33[a]	1.0–2.0	0
	H	2.93	2.7–3.3	2	1.69	1.0–2.4	0
N.Dak.	S	2.22	1.8–2.7	0	2.71	2.3–3.1	1
	H	1.69	1.4–2.1	0	2.18	1.9–2.4	0
Ohio	S	3.62[a]	3.0–4.1	3	2.02[a]	1.8–2.6	0
	H	3.63	3.1–4.0	5	2.69	2.3–3.0	0
Pa.	S	2.69	2.3–3.0	0	2.06	1.0–2.7	0
	H	3.14	2.9–3.5	3	2.03	1.9–2.2	0
S.Dak.	S	1.78	1.0–2.3	0	2.03	1.5–2.5	0
	H	1.69	1.4–2.0	0	1.86	1.8–2.0	0
Tenn.	S	2.51	1.4–3.3	2	1.49	1.0–2.0	0
	H	2.95	2.6–4.0	1	2.40	2.1–2.6	0
Tex.	S	1.85[a]	1.2–2.2	0	1.40[b]	1.0–2.0	0
	H	2.23	1.8–2.9	0	1.37	1.0–1.6	0
Wash.	S	3.02[a]	2.8–3.5	1	1.78	1.3–2.1	0
	A	2.66	2.2–3.1	1	2.75	2.3–3.2	1
W.Va.	S	2.62	2.0–3.0	0	3.00[c]	3.0–3.0	0
	H	3.16	3.0–3.4	4	2.49[a]	2.3–2.7	0
Wis.	S	2.46	1.6–2.8	0	2.30	1.7–2.7	0
	H	2.96	2.7–3.7	1	2.49	2.2–3.3	1

a. Indicates data are available for only 4 two-year sessions.
b. Indicates data are available for only 3 two-year sessions.
c. Indicates data are available for only 2 two-year sessions.
d. Scores can run from 1 (very false) to 5 (very true).

those which have the greatest to the least impact on public policy. Under this conceptualization, the ranking includes (1) caucuses with binding votes on members (e.g., Wisconsin on budget bills); (2) caucuses used by strong leaders to affect policy (e.g., Pennsylvania); (3) caucuses that contribute significantly to party cohesion (e.g., Iowa); (4) caucuses that contribute significantly to policy-making (e.g., Maine); (5) caucuses that serve primarily to keep the membership informed (e.g., North Dakota); and (6) caucuses that are designed to control leaders (e.g., Massachusetts; Jewell and Olson, pp. 235–244). In a few states, caucuses are used simply to choose the party leadership at the beginning of the session and play no other role.

A second key finding is that party caucuses, at least at the beginning of the 1980s, were considered to be centers of decision-making in about 50 percent of the chambers (Francis, p. 44). It is instructive to compare these chambers to those deemed to have a strong majority-party caucus in the early 1950s (Zeller, p. 196). While it has to be acknowledged that different criteria exist in the two studies for the assignment to the "important" or "strong" category, significant differences still exist between the two time periods. Clearly one-fourth of the chambers deemed to have strong party caucuses in the 1950s were not judged to be at all important as decision-making loci in the 1980s (e.g., Nevada Senate, Rhode Island House). In fact, none of the remaining strong-party caucuses in the 1950s were judged to exercise decision-making powers exclusively in the early 1980s; rather, decision-making was shared with the leadership, the committees, or both. Furthermore, the Michigan Senate, the only chamber judged in the 1980s to have the caucus as the key decision-making center, was not even listed in the 1950s as having a strong caucus, let alone the strongest.

Additional data may shed some light on the changing role played by caucuses over time. In the eighteen-state questionnaire study, members were asked to indicate where the most significant decisions were made for the two-year session under study. Six alternatives were provided: party caucus, floor, regular committee meetings, prelegislative sessions, governor's office, and policy committee. Given their frequency of write-ins, two additional responses were coded—Speaker and leadership. Respondents were asked to list their top three choices. These data provide a basis for across-session as well as across-state comparisons regarding the locus of significant legislative decision-making activity. Table 5 illustrates the percentage of respondents who indicated that their chamber party caucus was one of their three choices, along with the rankings of the caucus percentages among the eight possibilities for two time periods, 1971–1980 and 1981–1986.

To the extent that member perceptions are accurate reflections of how a legislative chamber works, these data suggest that party caucuses are an important decision-making mechanism in a number of chambers. Sixty-seven percent of state/chamber/session combinations (174 of 258) rank party caucus among the top three loci of significant decision-making. An impressive number of respondents chose the caucus as a place where significant legislative decisions are made. While some across-session variation is noted, sizable across-time consistency exists in the importance given to party caucuses: sixteen of thirty-six chambers report that caucuses are significant decision-making locations for all eight sessions, compared with ten in which it is consistently ranked low. Three across-time patterns emerge: (1) chambers in which party caucus is consistently chosen as a significant locus of decision making by large numbers of respondents (both chambers in Arizona, Iowa, Maine, North Dakota, Pennsylvania, South Dakota, Washington, and Wisconsin, as well as the Ohio Senate); (2) chambers in which the caucus is sometimes chosen as an important decision-making location by a large proportion of respondents and sometimes not (both chambers in California—however, generalizing about the California Senate is difficult, given the low response rate in many sessions—Tennessee, and West Virginia, as well as the Ohio House, the Nevada Assembly, and the North Carolina House); and (3) chambers in which party caucus is consistently low in the proportion of respondents choosing it as a place for significant decision-making (both chambers in Florida, Georgia, Massachusetts, and Texas, as well as the North Carolina and Nevada senates).

Another important finding illustrated in

Table 5

SELECTION OF PARTY CAUCUS (1ST, 2ND, OR 3RD CHOICES) AS PLACE "WHERE MOST IMPORTANT LEGISLATIVE DECISIONS ARE MADE"

By Session, Chamber, and State, by Percentage[a] of Respondents Selecting Caucus and Rank of This Percentage, 1–8.

State	Chamber	1971–1980					1981–1986				
		Percent		Rank		No. of Sessions (top 3)	Percent		Rank		No. of Sessions (Top 3)
		Mean	Range	Mean	Range		Mean	Range	Mean	Range	
Ariz.	S	100	100	1	1	4[b]	89	71–100	1.3	1–2	3
	H	92	82–100	1	1	5	85	79–96	1.3	1–2	3
Calif.	S	53	0–100	4	1–8	2[c]	64	50–74	2.0	1–3	3
	A	82	47–100	2	1–4	2[c]	86	70–100	1.0	1	3
Fla.	S	50	0–100	4.5	1–8	2[b]	35	0–80	5.3	2–8	1
	H	23	11–43	5.2	3–7	1	33	18–44	4.7	3–7	1
Ga.	S	25	0–91	6.3	3–8	1[b]	25	24–27	5.7	5–6	0
	H	16	3–25	5.8	3–7	0	20	15–28	6.0	5–7	0
Iowa	S	NA	NA	NA	NA	NA	83	74–91	1.0	1	1
	H	NA	NA	NA	NA	NA	90	79–96	1.0	1	1
Mass.	S	64	0–100	5.3	1–8	3	27	10–50	4.3	3–6	1
	H	40	26–52	3.4	2–5	3	23	15–32	5.0	4–7	0
Maine	S	93	84–100	1.4	1–2	5	76	51–100	2.0	1–3	5
	H	82	62–96	2.2	1–3	5	60	56–65	3.3	3–4	2
Nev.	S	40	0–99	4.3	2–8	2[b]	21	0–38	5.3	4–8	0
	A	46	0–67	4.0	2–8	3	57	0–92	3.3	1–8	2
N.C.	S	7	0–35	7.2	4–8	0	47	12–83	4.0	1–7	1
	H	50	6–100	3.4	1–7	3	47	31–64	2.5	2–4	1
N.Dak.	S	98	90–100	1.2	1–2	5	96	93–100	1.3	1–2	3
	H	91	80–100	1.6	1–3	5	90	79–100	1.3	1–2	3
Ohio	S	99	94–100	1.0	1	4[b]	100	100	1.0	1	3
	H	68	38–100	2.6	1–4	3	53	39–65	2.7	2–4	2
Pa.	S	100	100	1.0	1	5	96	89–100	1.0	1	3
	H	88	76–100	1.0	1	5	66	50–75	0.7	1–3	3
S.Dak.	S	95	87–100	1.0	1	5	90	81–95	1.0	1	3
	H	91	84–100	1.4	1–3	5	82	77–90	1.3	1–2	3
Tenn.	S	66	10–100	2.6	1–5	4	33	9–51	4.0	4	0
	H	84	73–100	1.4	1–2	5	56	25–81	3.0	2–5	2
Tex.	S	33	0–100	5.7	1–8	1[c]	29	26–34	4.7	4–5	0
	H	25	11–33	4.4	3–7	1	10	2–22	6.7	5–8	0
Wash.	S	99	95–100	1.0	1	4[b]	96	93–100	1.0	1	3
	A	88	81–100	1.0	1	5	92	80–100	1.0	1	3
W.Va.	S	86	63–100	1.6	1–3	5	34	0–90	5.0	2–8	1
	H	42	0–71	3.8	1–8	3	50	23–73	3.0	2–5	2
Wis.	S	NA	NA	NA	NA	NA	94	89–100	1.0	1	3
	H	NA	NA	NA	NA	NA	91	85–95	1.0	1	3

a. Percentages are from a weighted analysis to assure proper party balance in responses.
b. Indicates data are available for only 4 two-year sessions.
c. Indicates data are available for only 3 two-year sessions.
NA   Question not asked for this set of respondents

Table 5 is the degree to which both chambers in a state share a similar pattern in the perceived significance of party caucuses for decision making. Although traditionally senates and lower houses pride themselves on their differences from the other chamber, in these data one finds fairly consistent perceptions regarding the importance of party caucuses in twelve of the eighteen states (only California, Nevada, North Carolina, Ohio, Tennessee, and West Virginia seem to have differing perceptions about caucus roles in decision-making across upper and lower house members). This suggests that both chambers in a state tend to exhibit similar patterns regarding the importance of a partisan factor—caucuses—in their decision-making roles.

Previous empirical analyses indicate that caucuses are perceived to be more important in several well-defined situations: in smaller chambers; in chambers with greater levels of competition between the two-parties; in those chambers with more extensive outside party organizations; when caucuses are concerned primarily with policy-related activities; when caucuses are an extensive of relatively cohesive parties; and, finally, when caucuses hold frequent meetings (list compiled from Harmel and Francis).

An analysis of the eighteen-state questionnaire data revealed two major factors related to the basic trends—party competition and leadership preferences. Traditional, one-party southern states tended not to have influential caucuses emerge until party competition became a real possibility (Florida, Georgia, and Texas). The political mores in these states seem to be against using party mechanisms for decision making. Conversely, two-party states where both parties have substantial numbers seem to have fostered use of caucuses for decision making (Iowa, Maine, North Dakota, Pennsylvania, Washington, and Wisconsin). In these states, the caucus has become an important decision-making tool for both parties.

The second factor seems to be the nature and predispositions of leaders: strong leaders sometimes choose to avoid using caucuses for decision-making (Massachusetts, West Virginia, and Ohio lower houses in the late 1970s and early 1980s). In these cases, the members' expectations for decision making in caucuses have been weak enough to allow leaders to avoid caucuses.

Committees

Although party caucuses may be important in the legislative process, this does not mean that legislators are satisfied with the decisions reached in those bodies. Analysis of data supplied by legislators in fifty state-legislative chambers where the caucus was deemed to be important indicates that members of the majority party are more satisfied with the decisions made by standing committees than those made by the caucus, while the members of the minority party preferred caucus decisions over those of the committees (Francis, pp. 49–50). The reason for the variations in response between members of the two parties is not readily apparent. A general argument could be made that members of both parties would prefer that decisions be made in the smaller, less party-dominated settings. Majority-party members equate this with standing legislative committees, while minority members, being outmatched by the majority on standing committees, equate this with caucuses (cf. Francis).

Theoretically, political parties, either through the political caucus or through the party leadership, have the opportunity to control the composition of various standing and ad hoc committees formed in a legislative chamber. What levels or configurations of control would one expect to find if both political parties are organizationally strong? Malcolm Jewell indicated that some array of four conditions will be met:

1. each party controlling their appointments to committees;
2. party leaders appointing and removing committee members without taking seniority into account;
3. party ratios on each committee reflecting the party ratios in the chamber; and
4. the chairperson of each committee being a member of the majority party. (1986, p. 2)

At present, significant variation exists in terms of these four conditions. First, the minority leader is given responsibility, either formally or informally, but not absolute control for appointing minority committee members in forty-seven legislative chambers (American Society of Legislative Clerks and Secretaries, p. 60). If southern state-legislative chambers, where political party has traditionally been less important, are eliminated, minority leaders have the power to appoint committee members in about 60 percent of the remaining state-legislative chambers (including such traditionally strong two-party states as Illinois, Indiana, Connecticut, New York, New Jersey, and Pennsylvania).

As to the second criterion—the absence of a seniority criteria—no definitive statement may be made for all state-legislative bodies. In the South Carolina Senate, for example, the leadership plays no role in the assignment process; members simply pick their committees, subject to a few limitations, based on their time spent in the chamber. In the majority of cases, however, the leadership does not have to adhere to a stringent seniority rule.

If the majority-party leadership is to organize the legislature, then the least it can do is make sure that the chair of each committee is a member of the majority party. While it may be obvious that this condition should prevail, no one has undertaken a systematic, cross-state verification of the extent to which this behavior is practiced. Using data obtained from *Book of the States,* the authors examined two legislative sessions, 1975–1976 and 1989–1990. This analysis revealed that in both time periods, the chairperson of every committee was a member of the majority party in sixty-eight of the ninety-six legislative chambers (nonpartisan Nebraska was excluded, as were the two chambers that experienced a tie in terms of party strength, the Wyoming Senate in 1975 and the Indiana House in 1989). In seven chambers for both sessions, the minority party was able to place at least one of their own in the position of chair. A significantly greater number of chambers had exceptions to the majority-control rule in 1989 than in 1975 (twenty-four and twelve, respectively). Clearly, the bulk of this increase resulted because minority-party Republicans in southern legislatures in the late 1980s were being appointed to chair committees, whereas in the mid-1970s there were few, if any, Republicans elected in the South, let alone serving as committee chairs. In fact, the majority party controlled all the chairs in only eight of the twenty-two southern chambers in

1989. In the remaining chambers, this primarily meant that Republicans were given control over one or two committees at most. In three chambers, however, the extent of Republican influence was much greater. In the Florida Senate, where a bipartisan coalition of Republicans and conservative Democrats had elected the senate president, the minority-party Republicans were chosen to chair nine of the twenty-two standing committees, including two potentially influential ones, as well as two of the five joint committees.

In the Texas House, where the Speaker is elected via a pledge-card system, the Republicans with more than one-third of the chamber membership were named to chair nine of thirty-six committees (Harmel and Hamm). Finally, in the Tennessee Senate, long accustomed to two-party competition, the president appointed the minority party to chair four of twelve standing committees and the only joint committee.

This tendency to have the minority party control some committees via the chair position is not a phenomenon limited to the South. Similar deviations occur in another fourteen chambers, with two-thirds of these being state senates. What is somewhat surprising is the extent to which this sharing of committee power is found, albeit in only a few committees, in state legislative chambers that are typically considered to be "strong" in terms of party organization (e.g., Connecticut Senate and House, New Jersey Senate, Illinois Senate, and Michigan Senate). Extremely unusual circumstances also existed in the Vermont House for both sessions studied; specifically, while the majority of legislators were Republicans, the Speaker was a Democrat, and more than a majority of committee chairs were from the minority Democratic party (82 percent in 1989). This situation appears to deviate most from the expected pattern.

Jewell's contention that proportional representation would be expected in strong-party states is supported by the findings in a study by the Society of American Legislative Clerks and Secretaries (pp. 67–68). Proportional representation is practiced in roughly two-thirds of the legislative chambers where it is possible (some chambers have rules that prevent political parties from playing this role), guaranteed by legislative rules or statute in twenty-four chambers, and an unwritten norm in the other chambers.

Further analysis of thirty-two chambers over a sixteen-year period indicates that variation exists in the extent to which majority and minority parties are represented on committees. Specifically, overrepresentation of the majority party is more likely to exist if three conditions are met: (1) the majority party has only a slim lead in terms of chamber ratios; (2) the political party caucuses are deemed to be important; and (3) the committee deals with control (e.g., rules), as opposed to substantive matters (e.g., transportation; cf. Hedlund and Hamm).

Seating Arrangements

When American state legislators gather in their chamber for debate and voting, they are seated in either semicircular patterns or in rectangular arrangements, with the desks of all members facing the front of the chamber. In no state legislature do members of the two political parties sit on benches that directly face each other across a narrow aisle, as in many parliaments. What may be learned about political parties from seating patterns? Samuel C. Patterson suggested that

> where legislative party oppositions are relatively unimportant, we would expect to find legislators scattered about the legislative chamber regardless of their party affiliation. In a highly developed partisan legislature, we would anticipate a high degree of clustering, or aggregation of legislators with the legislatures in one party clustered together in one part of the chamber and members of the other party seated together in another. (1972, p. 349)

In the late 1960s, in about one-half of forty-three lower houses and 58 percent of thirty-eight state senates, legislators were seated by political party (Patterson, 1972, p. 349). Results from Alan Rosenthal's study of seating patterns in eighty-seven state legislative chambers in the early 1980s indicate that there has been no significant change in the aggregate percentages. In about 45 percent of the forty-four state senates and 54 percent of the forty-three state lower houses surveyed, members were seated together (clustered) by party.

Stated differently, in nineteen states, in both chambers members are seated by political party, while in another nineteen states, party is not the determining criteria in either chamber. Typically, "where the two political parties are relatively competitive, Democrats sit on one side of the chamber and Republicans on the other. But not everywhere" (p. 22).

What impact does chamber seating have on legislative behavior? Patterson theorized that a chain of reinforcing factors may develop:

> Political party consciousness produces intraparty spatial proximity, or clustering in the legislative chamber by party. Intraparty personal friendships appear to develop largely out of spatial proximity, although certainly some members may choose in advance to sit by their friends.... Friendship among legislators presumably reinforces similarities of attitudes about public policy.... To the extent that these acquaintanceship voting cues tend to be homogeneous within the legislative parties, cohesive party voting will naturally be high. (1972, p. 365)

What evidence is there for this argument? Patterson (1972) demonstrated that party voting tended to parallel the level of party seating in the Iowa House during the period 1945–1967. An examination of the consequences of an increase in the number of minority-party Republican legislators in the Texas House indicates that both the degree of party voting and the level of party seating have increased, even though seating is based on seniority considerations, not on party. This provides further evidence that as party competition increases, parties tend to cluster together in the seating patterns used in the chamber.

Adding another perspective, Rosenthal reported that 84 percent of the forty-three chambers in which members are seated by political party are classified by him as partisan, with fourteen very partisan and twenty-two somewhat partisan. However, the lack of partisan seating does not automatically translate into a nonpartisan environment. To the contrary, almost two-thirds of the forty-four chambers with nonparty seating are classified as partisan, with eleven being very partisan and eighteen somewhat partisan (p. 24). How does one account for this unanticipated finding? One possible explanation is reliance on constituency criteria for seating purposes, which tends to mask the importance of party. In the Connecticut Senate, for example, seating is in a semicircle composed of seats numbered from 1 to 36 to correspond to the thirty-six senate districts. Each member takes the seat number that corresponds to his district number (p. 22).

Summary

When structuring decision-making within a political party, legislative leaders adopt differing styles and approaches for interacting with and among rank-and-file members. Legislative lore of strong-willed, heavy-handed leaders who ruled via commands with rewards and punishments seems out-of-place in many state-level chambers. While considerable variety exists across states and between majority and minority parties, consultative leadership styles have become more common at the state level since the early 1980s.

The role played by the party caucus in contemporary state legislatures is much different from that seen seventy-five or one hundred years ago. During this earlier period, the legislative caucus was an important partisan device for achieving and enforcing a party position on pending legislation and organizational issues. While the overall potency of caucuses seems to have waned in states legislatures, during the 1980s caucuses were considered by the legislative membership to be a key center of decision making in about half of the chambers. Caucuses play an important role in structuring decision-making, but not in all legislative chambers and not on all issues.

Perhaps the most important partisan-based organizational device that legislative bodies use in decision making is the committee system. Every state legislative body in the United States uses the committee as a critical element in decision making, and partisan influence on committees and via committees cannot be ignored or minimized. The majority party controls committee composition via the appointment process in almost every legislative chamber. Similarly, the minority party formally or informally determines its members' committee assignments in the vast majority of upper and lower chambers. Further, the convention in most states is that the committee leadership—embodied in the chairperson—rests with the majority party. When the minority party does

hold a chair position, it is typically for a minor committee rather than a fiscal, organization, or major substantive committee. Partisan representation on committees tends not to be proportional unless so mandated by statute or rule.

One interesting aspect of partisan structuring in legislative chambers relates to the seating patterns used among members. About half of the state-legislative chambers seat members according to political party, with Democrats on one side and Republicans on the other, while the other half permit members to be assigned seats anywhere in the chamber, regardless of party identification, or assign seats based on district. Presumably, a pattern that groups party members together reflects and reinforces partisan divisions.

Taken together, these examples of party influence on differing legislative features indicate the extensive and intensive effects of party on the decision-making process at the state level. Parties play a role in determining chamber seating patterns in half the states. A purely partisan organization—the legislative party caucus—selects leaders, fosters position-taking on bills, and sometimes enforces party discipline on its members' voting. Chamber leadership is party-selected and party-based, while legislative work groups—legislative committees—are selected by the party and reflect party organization. Virtually no part of the legislature involved in structuring the decision-making process escapes the influence of parties; however, the degree of domination and single-minded partisanship in how these factors work varies from state to state.

PARTIES AND VOTING BEHAVIOR

Perhaps the most enduring question posed about political parties concerns their effect on member behavior and consequently on legislative outcomes. This section considers the impact of party on committee decision-making and on legislative chamber policy-making.

Committee Voting

What effects do political parties, either as organizations or as cue-giving agencies, have on the level of conflict in committees? Do members divest themselves of their partisanship at the committee door, opting instead for a more technical, problem-solving approach to the business of the committee? The expectation, based on studies from national assemblies in several countries, is that partisanship is more likely to be a factor in floor debate than in committee deliberations (Lees and Shaw, p. 424; Francis, p. 40). Evidence of the variable effect of party across state legislatures is demonstrated by examining change in each individual member's voting between the committee and the floor in seven state legislative chambers. In those chambers in which party considerations are most important, members of the minority party are more likely than members of the majority party to shift their vote between the committee and floor, coming more in line with the positions of a majority of their party colleagues (Hamm, "Consistency Between Committee and Floor Voting").

Political parties and leadership also appear to have some impact on the level of overall cohesion within committees. In those systems in which party caucuses or leadership have greater control over the day-to-day actions of the committee system or in which committee decisions can be reversed easily, the tendency to resolve differences on a nonpartisan basis is lessened and lower levels of committee voting cohesion are produced. In addition, bipolar voting, with majority-party members aligned against minority-party members, was more likely to occur in strong two-party states, and intraparty voting (i.e., bipartisan) was highest in weak-party legislatures. However, regardless of the legislative chamber, party voting in committees is most noticeable on election issues (Hamm, "Cohesion and Structure").

Chamber Voting

Another important issue regarding how political parties organize the legislature pertains to their part in structuring legislative conflict at the debate stage and in serving as a cue for legislators when roll-call decisions are being made. If political parties in fact influence the outcome of the political process, one would expect parties to take different positions on issues and "convince" other members to provide at least some modicum of support to the party.

The extent to which members of the same party vote together, and in opposition to members of the other party, varies across all the states (excluding Nebraska which is nonpartisan). In order for party voting to occur, two parties must exist in the legislature; however, increased party voting is most closely associated with the following:

Strong statewide party competition for a long time
More-urbanized and -industrialized states
Representing different distinctive interests
Strong state and local party organizations
The election of a minority-party governor
The operation of single-member districts
Close balance between the two parties in the legislature
The nature of the issues, being greater on major economic and social issues (Jewell and Patterson, pp. 222–224; Jewell and Olson, pp. 246–249)

Greater understanding of the extent of party voting and cohesion has emerged from studies of the legislatures over several sessions. In these cases, conclusions are less likely to be subject to short-term political fluctuations. For example, drawing on a study of the Vermont legislature from 1955 to 1978, Frank M. Bryan concluded that "a 'morning-glory' party system [emerged] in the legislature that opened with the coming of the first Democratic governor in a century and closed just as quickly when he left office" (p. 258). In contrast, Jonathan Euchner found that both party voting (when a majority of one party opposes a majority of the opposition party) and party cohesion (the extent to which members of the same party vote together) increased between 1945 and 1989 in the Iowa legislature, although a simple monotonically increasing pattern was not produced after party voting reached its apex in 1965; at the same time, while some issues (e.g., labor, legislative organization and procedure, elections, constitutional amendments, and certain national issues) divided the parties across the entire time span, other issues (e.g., appropriations and conservation) were apparent only in the later years of the study (pp. 13, 18).

Generally, in one-party legislatures, voting patterns are unstructured, with legislators clustered into numerous groupings, often changing as the character of the issue changes (cf.

Broach; Patterson, 1962; Bernick; Kirkpatrick). What happens when formerly one-party systems are transformed by the addition of a significant number of minority-party members? In speaking of the Texas House, Harmel and Hamm concluded that "when it comes to voting behavior ... the party label does mean something!" (p. 7). In the Texas House, both party voting and the development of identifiable party clusters increased as the size of the Republican minority increased from 8 out of 150 members in 1969 to 57 in 1989. Is this pattern typical of the various one-party southern states undergoing transformation to a more competitive two-party system? At this point, no answer can be given, because the necessary studies have not been completed. However, evidence from South Carolina, where Republicans had not reached the critical one-third threshold as of 1987, suggests that party voting did not increase there as the size of the Republican contingent increased (Graham and Whitby).

Even if legislators divide in such a way as to make it seem that party voting has taken place, there is no guarantee that party-related actors entered into the decision. To what extent do legislators rely upon intralegislative party sources (e.g., party leadership) or party agents external to the legislature (e.g., state party chairpersons or local party officials) when they are deciding how to vote on a bill? Three findings stand out in the literature regarding these factors. First, when responses from a sample of legislators from all fifty states were considered, legislative party leaders in general were not perceived to be major sources of cues on legislation. Greater importance was attached to personal friends in the legislature or legislative specialists in a policy area (Uslaner and Weber, p. 429). Thus, cue-giving and cue-taking from nonparty sources frequently appear to take place in state legislatures.

Second, on specific issues, party leadership may be a key source of cues in particular states, such as Massachusetts, because the leadership is able to dispense substantial monetary benefits to those who hold positions of power, such as committee chairpersons (Ray). Consequently, state-specific factors may affect partisan cue-giving and cue-taking.

Third, in some state legislatures, party leadership is a variable cue-giver, being important for only a very narrow band of issues (particularly, organizational, procedural, and redistricting issues) and relatively unimportant for other issues (Songer et al.; Hurwitz). Variation in partisan influence based on differing issues is also observed.

What decisions do legislators make when confronted by conflicting pressures? The 1985–1986 version of the eighteen-state questionnaire study of legislator perceptions contained a section that provides some insights regarding this concern. Respondents were asked to indicate, through a paired-comparison rating technique, which group among seven possible groups (district, state, legislator's own conscience, governor, party, interest groups, and legislative leaders) their legislative chamber members would favor when making decisions about the content of legislative bills. While somewhat cumbersome, the questionnaire's twenty-one-question format permits precise positioning of each of the seven groups along a continuum. Table 6 summarizes the results of the six questions in which political parties was one of the possible responses, including the percentage of times the party was selected and the rank of this percentage.

As illustrated in Table 6, legislators believe that party is a very low-priority force in the decision-making hierarchy; this response has the lowest rank (seventh or tied for sixth) eleven times and the second lowest (sixth or tied for fifth) thirteen times out of thirty-six. Stated differently, two-thirds of the time, political party is ranked last or next to last out of seven groups that might be favored whenever conflicting pressures are present. In terms of percentages, party was selected as the group being followed in a relatively modest number of cases, usually in fewer than 10 percent of the choice situations.

A different pattern is found for leadership preferences as a priority in the legislature. Leaders were more frequently selected than political party as the group being followed by members when determining the content of bills. Leadership was the most frequently chosen factor in three chambers (the Massachusetts Senate, the North Carolina House, and the Ohio House), the second most frequently cho-

Table 6
SELECTION OF PARTIES AND LEADERSHIP AS
GROUP ACTUALLY FAVORED BY LEGISLATORS
WHEN DETERMINING BILL CONTENT
By Percentage[a] of Respondents Selecting Parties
and Leaders and Rank of Percentage, 1–7

State	Chamber	Session			
		Parties 1985–1986		Leaders 1985–1986	
		%	Rank	%	Rank
Ariz.	S	9	6	20	3
	H	9	6	18	3
Calif.	S	5	6	19	3
	H	10	5	20	2
Fla.	S	4	6[b]	10	5
	H	6	6	22	2
Ga.	S	6	7	14	3
	H	6	7	19	3
Iowa	S	10	5	17	3
	H	13	4	20	3
Mass.	S	3	7	29	1
	H	8	6	19	3
Maine	S	13	5	14	4
	H	14	4	17	3
Nev.	S	4	7	24	2
	A	11	6	11	5
N.C.	S	16	4	19	2
	H	16	3	22	1
N.Dak.	S	14	5	15	3
	H	14	5	15	4
Ohio	S	6	7	10	5
	H	13	4	22	1
Pa.	S	14	5	15	4
	H	11	5	18	3
S.Dak.	S	10	6	11	5
	H	9	6	13	5
Tenn.	S	8	7	10	5
	H	10	5[b]	15	3
Tex.	S	5	6	21	2
	H	7	6	19	3
Wash.	S	7	6	18	3
	H	7	7	17	3
W.Va.	S	0	7	14	4
	H	12	6	15	3
Wis.	S	6	7	16	3
	A	8	7	17	3

a. Percentages are from a weighted analysis to assure proper party balance in responses.
b. Indicates a tie in rank among choices that includes parties or leadership choice.

sen in five chambers, and the third most frequently chosen in eighteen chambers. Consequently, leadership preferences regarding the content of legislation was seen, in terms of its use by state legislators, as being a much more important factor than party; however, the fact that partisan preferences and orientations are frequently interpreted through and by leadership means that partisan predispositions may yet be an important criterion used by legislators in decision making. Party cues frequently find their way into decision-making through leadership rather than directly through other partisan message-giving mechanisms.

A longitudinal analysis between 1965 and 1989 in Iowa confirms the general low priority attached to political party. Most important, "in none of the conflict situations (norms or loyalty) has attachment to party increased since 1965. However, there have been significant increases in the willingness of legislators to admit that the question of being partisan in any given conflict situation is not always easy to decide" (Euchner, p. 23).

Summary

Just as political parties structure decision-making, so parties affect the outcome of decisions in the voting patterns seen among party members. Political parties do affect committee decisions. For example, in highly partisan chambers, minority-party committee members are more likely to shift their votes on the floor away from the position they took in committee than are majority-party members. Further, higher levels of partisanship in the legislative chamber are likely to result in more bipolar partisan voting behavior. Levels of general partisanship in a chamber are thus related to partisanship in voting on the floor.

While the amount of party voting varies by state, some degree of partisanship is evident in virtually every state legislature's voting record. Party-based divisions are more evident on certain issues. Partisan impact is most noticeable on chamber organizational issues, on matters related to the electoral success of the party, and on a series of party-based issues (e.g., economic and labor issues). Party is a potentially potent voting cue for large numbers of state legislators.

CONCLUSION

Having surveyed the history of political parties in American state legislatures and analyzed their contemporary role in electing, organizing, and structuring legislators and legislative activities, the authors must confront one nagging question: How important are a legislator's political party and partisan considerations in legislative decision-making? A review of the evidence may offer an answer.

Groupings of members into party-like organizations have existed from the beginnings of state legislatures. While the early manifestations of these groupings were quite different in structure and purpose from current political parties, one can identify organizations that sought to select and elect similarly oriented members in pre-1800 state-legislative bodies. Subsequent events and issues witnessed both a rearranging of individuals around differing principles (e.g., Republican versus Federalists, Democratic Republicans versus the National Republicans, Democrats versus Whigs, Republicans versus Democrats), as well as a waxing and waning of political party strength; but political parties have remained as enduring organizations in forty-nine of the fifty state legislatures. (Some critics have even suggested that the nonpartisan Nebraska unicameral legislature has its partisan moments.) Consequently, political parties have not been static organizations; rather, they have endured in part because they have evolved and changed.

Much of the nineteenth century was devoted to the growth and strengthening of political parties as organizing and cue-giving mechanisms. As a result, by the start of the twentieth century, most of the modern features of political parties in state legislatures were in place. By 1900, political parties were important factors in recruiting persons to seek legislative office, in electing persons with a similar partisan identification to office, in organizing state legislative bodies to conduct their business, and in orienting members for and during the decision-making process. Thus, for almost one hundred years political parties have played a relatively constant and critical role in American state legislatures.

From their beginnings, political parties have been a vital force in recruiting and selecting state legislators. This is testified to by the fact that only a handful of nonpartisan legislators are elected to serve at any one time in the fifty state legislatures. In obtaining a position in a legislative body, then, one is forced to consider how one can relate to existing political parties. Even if someone decides to run without a party label and party support, that person must evaluate the considerable consequences of running *outside* the party system. *A nonpartisan candidate for any state-legislative position must surmount these additional obstacles to success.*

Political parties play a considerable role in organizing the activities and conduct of business in state legislatures. The selection of leadership and committees appointments reflects partisan considerations in the overwhelming number of state legislative chambers. While the handful of cases in which political parties *do not* play this role suggests that other factors can substitute and play an orienting role, *the dominating position of parties in this suggests that party is a convenient, acceptable, and reasonably effective organizing factor in state legislatures.*

Throughout the twentieth century, political parties have provided a key to understanding state legislative activities in addition to their organizing role. For example, virtually every study of member voting in any state legislative body—except Nebraska and Minnesota when it was nonpartisan and those legislatures in which all members belonged to one party (e.g., some southern legislatures in the 1950s) —begins with an analysis by party identification. *Political parties are assumed to affect voting in state legislatures.* A finding that party makes no difference leads inevitably to further analysis and explanation of why member decisions—individually or in aggregate—fail to conform to a partisan interpretation. While individual case studies of policy-making conclude that a variety of forces affect decisions, the role of political parties is always examined. Thus, expectations have been established, based on considerable persuasive evidence, that lead observers and analysts of state legislative decision-making to examine the role of political parties.

Regarding the future, the authors see no evidence to suggest the relinquishment by parties of their electoral and organizing roles in state legislatures; however, evidence does suggest that parties need to become more adaptable in their legislative strategies. For example, the increasing proportion of the electorate identify themselves as independents, together with the decreasing numbers of voters identifying strongly with either party, suggests that the electoral base is changing. Efforts by parties to stem this change have not been successful; therefore, some other coping strategy seems inevitable, lest political parties become minority players on the electoral scene.

Further, there is increasing evidence that while most legislators run with a party label, they do so with less financial support from their respective parties with each passing election. Lower levels of party financial support for state legislative candidates constitute an increasingly important factor, since considerable fund-raising efforts are needed for a successful state legislative campaign. While many state legislative leaders now engage in campaign fund-raising for state legislative elections, these efforts offer no substitute for party support in a members' campaigns. The consequence of greater independence in the electoral activities of a legislator translates into weakened ties to the political party, stronger ties to contributors (usually groups with vested interests), and a more piecemeal approach to decision making (e.g., support for one group on this policy and for another group on that one due to their contributions). Such trends are directly related to the emergence of special interest–dominated legislative bodies and legislation oriented toward a series of narrow constituencies. The outlook for changing this situation by increased funding via parties appears bleak, since special interests now realize the success of efforts directed toward individual legislators rather than parties.

Consequently, while the authors expect parties to retain their importance in state legislative activities, they do not expect parties to become the dominant factor in policy decision-making that they once were. Further, without some basic adjustment in how political parties formulate their issue positions, represent citizens in decision making, and develop relationships with their elected officials, political parties will continue either to erode or at best maintain their current position as cue-giving mechanisms for policy formulation. Thus, while parties may continue in their electoral and organizing roles, their position in the policy-making process is becoming increasingly perilous.

BIBLIOGRAPHY

The sources used in this chapter fall roughly into two general categories—historical and empirical. Historians have, it seems, taken a greater interest in the early party period in state legislatures than have empirical political scientists, though one must be aware of the special problems presented in conducting quantitative research in this area. Continuing study of the early Congress and an increasing interest in state legislatures across the field of American political science bode well for future research.

Empirical Studies
KRISTI ANDERSEN, *Creation of a Democratic Majority: 1928–1936* (Chicago, 1966), sheds light on the origins and dynamics of Democratic dominance during the New Deal era; E. LEE BERNICK, "The Impact of U.S. Governors on Party Voting in the One-Party-Dominated Legislatures," *Legislative Studies Quarterley* 3 (August 1978), is a study of the impact of the executive in states without a two-party system in the legislature; GLEN T. BROACH, "A Comparative Dimensional Analysis of Partisan and Urban-Rural Voting in the State Legislatures," *Journal of Politics* 34 (1972): 905–921, examines the cleavages between representatives from these differing backgrounds in diverse state legislatures; DAVID L. BRYE, *Wisconsin Voting Patterns in the Twentieth Century, 1900–1950* (New York, 1979), is an excellent empirical study examining the third-party movements, national party divisions, and the La Follette phenomenon in Wisconsin.

POLITICAL PARTIES IN STATE LEGISLATURES

GREGORY CALDEIRA and SAMUEL C. PATTERSON, "Bringing Home the Votes: Electoral Outcomes in State-Legislative Races," *Political Behavior* 4 (1982): 33–67, explores electioneering at the state legislative level with an eye to differentiating these races from congressional races; JAMES E. CAMPBELL, "Presidential Coattails and Midterm Losses in State Legislative Elections," *American Political Science Review* 80 (March 1986), documents presidential party vulnerability during off-year elections, here examining the phenomenon at the level of state legislative elections; RODNEY O. DAVIS, "Partisanship in Jacksonian State Politics: Party Divisions in the Illinois Legislature, 1834–1841," in ROBERT SWIERENGA, ed., *Quantification in American History: Theory and Research* (New York, 1970) is one of the few truly empirical pieces on the Jacksonian party period that looks at the state level; DONALD A. DEBATS, "An Uncertain Arena: The Georgia House of Representatives, 1808–1861," *Journal of Southern History* 56 (August 1990), makes excellent use of a sparse data in teasing out trends and patterns of political activity in a southern state legislature in an almost unstudied period; JONATHAN EUCHNER, "Partisanship in the Iowa Legislature: 1945–1989," a paper presented at the 1990 annual meeting of the Midwest Political Science Association, presents empirical evidence of changing patterns of partisanship in this state; JONATHAN EUCHNER and MALCOLM E. JEWELL, "Party Caucus Influence in the Iowa Legislature," a paper presented at the 1990 annual meeting of the American Political Science Association, examines the role of the party caucus in structuring the legislature.

WAYNE L. FRANCIS, *The Legislative Committee Game: A Comparative Analysis of Fifty States* (Columbus, Ohio, 1989), investigates the structure and outputs of committee systems across state legislatures; COLE BLEASE GRAHAM, JR., and KENNY J. WHITBY, "Party-based Voting in a Southern State Legislature," *American Politics Quarterly* 17, no. 2 (April 1989), explores the changing one-party system in South Carolina; KEITH E. HAMM, "Consistency Between Committee and Floor Voting in the U.S. State Legislatures," *Legislative Studies Quarterly* 7 (1982): 473–490, seeks to answer a persistent question on congruity between committee and floor behavior; and HAMM, "Cohesion and Structure in Committee Voting: Evidence from State Legis-

latures," a paper delivered at the 1982 annual meeting of the Midwest Political Science Association, examines the degree of partisan voting in state legislative committees. ROBERT HARMEL and KEITH E. HAMM, "Political Party Development in State Legislatures: The Case of the Texas House of Representatives," a paper presented at the 1991 annual meeting of the Midwest Political Science Association, traces the development of party politics in a formerly one-party legislative body; RONALD D. HEDLUND and HAMM, "The Representation of Political Parties on State Legislative Committees," a paper presented at the 1990 annual meeting of the Midwest Political Science Association, finds that despite assumptions to the contrary, the committee system at the state legislative level is not always structured along strict party lines; JON HURWITZ, "Determinants of Legislative Cue Selection," *Social Science Quarterly* 69:1 (1988) surveys sources of cue-taking in state legislatures; MALCOLM E. JEWELL, like SAMUEL PATTERSON, his frequent collaborator, deserves a special place in state legislative scholarship, and it should come as no surprise that much of the material in this chapter relies on JEWELL's research. JEWELL collaborated with DAVID BREAUX on "The Effect of Incumbency on State Legislative Elections," *Legislative Studies Quarterly* 13:4 (1988), which seeks to discover whether phenomena observed in connection with incumbency in congressional races obtains in the state legislative arena; JEWELL and PATTERSON, *The Legislative Process in the United States,* 4th ed. (New York, 1986), is basic for the study of American state legislatures.

MARC W. KRUMAN, *Parties and Politics in North Carolina, 1836–1865* (Baton Rouge, La., 1983), explores the dynamics of party politics in a southern state during the Jacksonian era and its subsequent transformation from the decline of the Whigs to the Civil War; PETER D. LEVINE, *The Behavior of State Legislative Parties in the Jacksonian Era: New Jersey, 1829–1844* (Rutherford, N.J., 1977), is a quantitative analysis of legislative party behavior in the second party system; NATIONAL CONFERENCE OF STATE LEGISLATURES, "Legislative Caucus Procedure: Policy and Practice," *State Legislative Report,* (January 1981), provides a concise overview of the roles played by legislative party caucuses; RICHARD G. NIEMI, SIMON JACKMAN, and LAURA R. WINSKY, "Candidacies and Competitiveness in

Multimember Districts," *Legislative Studies Quarterly* 16 (February 1991), suggests a parsimonious and elegant methodology for resolving the problem of multimember districts in analysis.

SAMUEL C. PATTERSON, "Dimensions of Voting in a One-Party State Legislature," *Public Opinion Quarterly* 26 (1962), examines the differences between one-party and two-party dynamics, and his "Party Opposition in the Legislature: The Ecology of Legislative Institutionalization," *Polity* 4 (1972): 345–366, provides a multistate model of legislative party development; DAVID RAY, "The Sources of Voting Cues in Three State Legislatures," *Journal of Politics* 44 (November 1982), surveys the cues to legislative behavior using John Kingdon's model; ALAN ROSENTHAL, "Where Do You Sit?" *State Legislatures* 10:3 (March 1984), provides a concise summary of state legislative seating patterns and their relationship to levels of partisanship; DONALD R. SONGER, JAMES M. UNDERWOOD, SONJA G. DILLON, PATRICIA E. JAMESON, and DARLA W. KITE, "Voting Cues in Two State Legislatures: A Further Application of the Kingdon Mode," *Social Science Quarterly* 66 (December 1985), applies Kingdon's voting-cue model to state legislative environments.

CHARLES M. TIDMARCH, EDWARD LONGERGAN, and JOHN SCIORTINO, "Interparty Competition in the U.S. States: Legislative Elections, 1970–1978," *Legislative Studies Quarterly* 11 (1978): 353–374, is an empirical examination of legislative electoral behavior and variation. ALLEN TREALEASE, "Republican Reconstruction in North Carolina: A Roll-Call Analysis of the State House of Representatives, 1868–1870," *Journal of Southern History* 17 (August 1976), is an exploration of the issues and divisions in the state legislature of North Carolina during the transformatory period between Reconstruction and the rise of the Redeemer movement.

ERIC M. USLANER and RONALD E. WEBER, *Patterns of Decision Making in State Legislatures* (New York, 1977), investigates decision-making in state legislatures using survey data; MARCIA LYNN WHICKER and MALCOLM E. JEWELL, "State Legislative Leadership: An Overview" a paper presented at the 1990 annual Midwest Political Science Association, explores the variation of leadership types and processes across the states; LAURA R. WINSKY, "The Role of District, State, and National Factors in State Legislative

Elections," a paper presented at the 1990 Conference on State Legislative Elections, Lexington, Kentucky, investigates the linkages between these factors and their effects on the electoral process in the states; and BELLE ZELLER, *American State Legislatures* (New York, 1954), contains a relatively comprehensive survey of the state legislative process in all fifty states during the early 1950s.

Historical Studies

LEE BENSON, *The Concept of Jacksonian Democracy* (Princeton, N.J., 1961), is still one of the best works on the Jacksonian era, despite its age; JAMES H. BROUSSARD, "Party and Partisanship in the American Legislatures: The South Atlantic States, 1800–1812," *Journal of Southern History* 43 (February 1972), describes components of the early party system in that region and suggests that this transitional period set the pattern for later party activity; FRANK M. BRYAN, *Politics in the Rural States: People, Parties, and Processes* (Boulder, Colo., 1981), examines the interplay of individuals, the parties, and policy in the rural states of Montana, Mississippi, and Vermont; BALLARD CAMPBELL, *Representative Democracy: Public Policy and Midwestern Legislatures in the Late Nineteenth Century* (Cambridge, Mass., 1980), is a good source of material from this period, particularly on the issue dimensions; ROB CHRISTENSEN, "Growing Republican Ranks Help Topple Speaker," *State Legislatures* 16 (April 1989), reports the fall of the house speaker in North Carolina and the role of the changing partisan composition of that chamber in his demise; JOHN M. DOBSON, *Politics in the Gilded Age: A New Perspective on Reform* (New York, 1972), is still one of the best investigations of the intentions and outputs of the early progressive movements; LEON EPSTEIN, *Political Parties in the American Mold* (Madison, Wisc., 1986), is an insightful examination of the broad sweep of party politics; HERBERT ERSHKOWITZ and WILLIAM G. SHADE, "Consensus or Conflict? Political Behavior in the State Legislatures During the Jacksonian Era," *Journal of American History* 58 (1971): 591–621, examines the claim that the Jacksonian political system was a golden age of consensus, offering convincing evidence that it was not; ERIC FONER, *Reconstruction: America's Unfinished Revolution, 1863–1877* (New York, 1988, rev. ed., 1990), remains the seminal work on this period; L. RAY GUNN, "The New York State Legislatures: A Developmental Perspective: 1777–1846," *Social Science History* 4 (August 1980), investigates the early party period quantitatively in New York; MICHAEL F. HOLT, *The Political Crisis of the 1850s* (New York, 1978), is a rich source of material on party maneuvering in an atmosphere of increasing hostility over the issue of slavery; JOHN HURWITZ, "Determinants of Legislative Cure Selection," *Social Science Quarterly* 69:1 (1988), surveys sources of cue-taking in state legislatures; THOMAS E. JEFFREY, *State Parties and National Politics: North Carolina, 1815–1861* (Athens, Ga., 1989), traces the linkage between national issues (such as slavery) and the state legislature, which seems to run, counterintuitively, from state to national politics.

SAMUEL A. KIRKPATRICK, *The Legislative Process in Oklahoma, Policy Making, People, and Politics* (Norman, Okla., 1978), provides a broad review of the many facets of legislative life and activity in Oklahoma; MARK W. KRUMAN, *Parties and Politics in North Carolina, 1836–1865* (Baton Rouge, La., 1983), explores the dynamics of party politics in a southern state during the Jacksonian era and its subsequent transformation from the decline of the Whigs to the Civil War; A. LAWRENCE LOWELL, "The Influence of Party upon Legislation in England and America," in *American Historical Association Annual Report for the Year 1901,* vol. 1, is an old but important study that examines comparatively the effect of party; ROBERT LUCE, *Legislative Procedure: Parliamentary Practices and the Course of Business in the Framing of Statutes* (Boston, 1922), is an excellent source

on the theory of legislative organization in a dynamic setting; RICHARD PATRICK MCCORMICK, *The Second American Party System: Party Formation in the Jacksonian Era* (Chapel Hill, N.C., 1966), is an excellent overview of the economic and social forces leading to the formation of the second party system; and DAVID M. POTTER, *The Impending Crisis, 1948–1861* (New York, 1963), argues that despite evidence of consensus in some quarters during the 1850s, the issue of slavery continued to have a divisive effect in the polity. NORMAN K. RISJORD and GORDON DENBOER, "The Evolution of Political Parties in Virginia, 1782–1800," *Journal of American History* 60:3 (March 1974), is a helpful study of the early party system in Virginia; JOEL H. SILBEY, *The Partisan Imperative: The Dynamics of American Politics Before the Civil War* (New York, 1985), is the definitive modern treatment of pre–Civil War parties in the United States; JAMES L. SUNDQUIST, *The Dynamics of the Party System* (rev. ed., Washington, D.C., 1983), examines party politics from the view of realignment theory and contains a wealth of information on parties at all levels of government and historical data rarely brought together in one place; HARRY MARLIN TINKCOM, *The Republican and the Federalists in Pennsylvania, 1790–1801: A Study in National Stimulus and Local Response* (Harrisburg, Pa., 1950), is an investigation of the first party system at the state level; and W. F. WILLOUGHBY, *Principles of Legislative Organization and Administration* (Washington, D.C., 1934), is a somewhat dated but still informative study of the structural aspects of state legislatures.

SEE ALSO Committees in State Legislatures; Elections to the State Legislatures; Executive Leadership and Party Organization in State Legislatures; AND The Origins and Early Development of State Legislatures.

COMMITTEE SELECTION IN CONGRESS

Charles S. Bullock, III

The identities of most members of Congress, particularly those in the House, are linked to their committee assignments. It is through these assignments, coupled with growing seniority, that legislators secure power, subject-matter expertise, and benefits for their districts; establish information networks; and promote their own reelection. Given the potential significance of committee assignments, it is hardly surprising that identifying and obtaining a useful appointment is a top priority for freshmen. Those who fail to attain an optimal assignment may make persistent efforts to transfer. Committee changes are also sought by members who redefine the dominant concerns of their careers.

The politics of committee selection involves several considerations. The availability of desirable assignments is determined by fluctuations in committee size. A separate assignment procedure operates for each party in the Senate and House to allocate the available slots among freshmen and sitting members who have requested transfers or additional assignments. The four committees on committees respond to member preferences, which may reflect one or more basic career motivations. While most assignment activity involves freshmen, each Congress sees some sitting members attempt to improve their committee holdings through transfers. Analyses of transfers permit the development of rankings of general committee desirability. A potential consequence of the weight accorded member requests in making assignments is that committees will not represent the personal characteristics or policy preferences of the chamber.

COMMITTEE SIZE

It has become traditional for the number of seats per committee allocated to each party to be negotiated by leaders of the two parties. The ratio of Democrats to Republicans on most committees approximates the partisan ratio in the chamber. The three House committees that have traditionally been most desirable and whose members are generally prevented from serving on other committees are exceptions to this rule. The majority party has historically enjoyed a two-to-one majority on the Rules Committee, regardless of party ratios in the chamber. The majority-party advantage on Appropriations and Ways and Means has been smaller, with the majority party holding about 60 percent of the seats.

When the modern committee structure was instituted in 1947, the 435 House members held 482 seats so that only some 10 percent of the members had a second assignment. The reformers of the mid-1940s wanted to promote expertise by limiting most members to a single assignment. For a number of years thereafter, rules, which were frequently waived, cited the ideal of one assignment per member. Despite the goal of the reformers, the total number of seats has risen constantly, augmented by the creation of additional standing committees. By 1989 there were 812 House committee seats for an average of almost 1.9 seats per member. From 1947 to 1989, the number of Senate seats rose less dramatically from 201 to 311. While the number of House committee seats has yet to reach the prereform level of more than nine hundred, the objectives of the Legislative Reorganization Act of 1946 have been thwarted.

Several factors have been identified as potential explanations for the rise in dual assignments. Writing in the mid-1970s, Louis P. Westefield suggested the presence of an exchange system allowing leaders of the majority party to honor requests from their members for good assignments. Adding seats to desired committees permits past loyalty to the party to be repaid more rapidly than if the leadership awaits vacancies occurring through natural turnover due to death, retirement, electoral defeats, and committee transfers. Westefield suggested that recipients of good assignments would be more loyal to the leadership in the future.

Enlarging highly prized committees is not cost-free, since increasing the number of seats depreciates the value of assignments, which has prompted current committee members to oppose expansion. The majority-party leadership operates within a tension created by demands from nonmembers for good assignments and opposition from those who already have coveted posts. Further, more committee participants may make it harder for the leadership to assemble coalitions needed to pass legislation. Westefield speculated that the leadership would react to the conflicting pressures by expanding committees in the middle and upper ranges of attractiveness in order to meet demands for more committee posts, but at the same time it would be hesitant to enlarge the most desirable committees, thereby not blunting its most valuable leverage tools.

Westefield reported that the largest increases in size occurred not on the premier committees but in the middle range. From 1927 to 1945, committee increases were concentrated in the upper-third range of desirability, while from 1947 to 1971, increases spanned much of a broad middle range of committee attractiveness. The least desirable committees were rarely enlarged.

Kenneth A. Shepsle offered more complex explanatory models to account for increases in the number of Democratic committee seats. He suggested that a major factor would be changes in party-committee ratios derived from fluctuations in the partisan makeup of the chamber. Thus, when Democrats picked up additional seats in an election, they would be entitled to more committee slots, and when they suffered electoral setbacks, their entitlement would decline. If changes in party ratios operated within a fixed number of committee seats, then it would be necessary to remove some returning legislators from their committees, unless shifts in chamber partisan ratios were reflected across each committee. For illustrative purposes consider the following: In one Congress, Democrats hold 55 percent of the seats and have a similar presence on the Energy and Commerce Committee, with twenty-four of forty-three seats. In the next Congress, Democrats have a 60 percent majority, entitling them to twenty-six of forty-three Energy and Commerce seats. If, however, all nineteen Republicans on the committee in the previous Congress are reelected and want to retain their assignments, the two least senior Republicans must be bumped. Alternatively, the nineteen returning Republicans could be accommodated by enlarging the committee to forty-eight, allowing the Democrats twenty-nine members. Committee expansion has been the preferred reaction to changes in chamber partisan ratios.

Shepsle included a variable for the seats needed to accommodate the minority party along with several elements suggested by Westefield. A model that incorporated a number of factors found changes in the chamber ratio, minority-party needs, turnover in the majority party due to election, first preferences by freshmen, and requests from nonfreshmen to be significantly linked to changes in committee size. Also related was a countermeasure for time, meaning that there has been a tendency for committees to get bigger even when the previously mentioned factors are taken into consideration.

David Whiteman went beyond Westefield and Shepsle to give greater emphasis to the minority party. Like Shepsle, Whiteman argued that committees are often enlarged as a result of (1) changed party ratios in the chamber and (2) a reluctance to remove a sitting member in order to bring a committee in line with the chamber ratio. Whiteman suggested that party ratios on less desirable committees could usually be met without expansion, since their members often moved to better assignments. It is on the most prestigious committees from which members rarely transfer voluntarily that shifting party ratios due to elections might necessitate removing a sitting member. Whiteman hypothesized that expanding desirable committees to avoid removing existing personnel created pressures for second seats by other members. Democratic party rules limit dual assignments to members who hold at least one nonmajor committee. Members who see advantages to a second assignment, since it may allow them to do more for their constituency or to become involved in a wider range of legislative activities, will find virtually any second assignment preferable to a single one. As the Democratic party relaxed its rule against second assignments, the basis for rejecting calls for expanding relatively less desirable committees evaporated, thereby explaining the growth in less coveted committees.

Chairs of major committees as well as members of Appropriations, Rules, and Ways and Means are generally restricted to a single assignment. Consequently, once members not subject to that restriction have two appointments, demands for committee expansion should abate in the absence of a moderation of the rule limiting members to two nontemporary appointments. (In order to complete rosters, it is sometimes necessary to allow members to take a third, temporary appointment. This appointment does not accrue seniority, and a person with a third assignment can be bumped by a member who wants the appointment as a legitimate first or second assignment.)

Bruce A. Ray and Steven S. Smith challenged Westefield's conclusion that committees are expanded to give majority-party leaders influence over rank-and-file members seeking good appointments. They showed that changes in the partisan composition of the House are always a strong predictor of change in committee size. Competition for vacancies was significantly linked to increases in committee size during the speakership of Carl Albert (D.-Okla.), but not during the speakerships of Sam Rayburn (D.-Tex.), John McCormack (D.-Mass.), or Thomas P. "Tip" O'Neill (D.-Mass.). Committee prestige proved not to be a factor except when combined with change in the House ratios, and even then it was a useful additional predictor only during the Rayburn years. Time independent of other factors had no effect on changes in committee size.

Ray and Smith challenged Westefield by noting that it was relatively low-prestige committees that grew more and that additional seats on these committees were unlikely to secure compliant behavior from recipients. Ray and Smith seemed to agree with Whiteman that committees were enlarged, at least during the Albert speakership, to promote harmony within the Democratic party by reducing the jealousies of members holding single assignments to nonprestigious committees. By the O'Neill era, committee requests outnumbered vacancies relatively infrequently. Reduction in potential conflict stemmed from near saturation of dual assignments (that is, almost every member eligible for two assignments had two) and the receipt of a good assignment by most members.

Expansion in the number of Senate committee seats has attracted little attention. Steven S. Smith and Christopher J. Deering suggested that there is less pressure to expand Senate committees because of that chamber's greater openness, which allows senators to influence policies shaped by committees on which they do not serve. Nonetheless, figures presented earlier show a 55-percent increase in committee seats since 1947, indicating an eagerness among senators to shoulder additional responsibilities. Barbara Sinclair suggested that since 1947 the increases, particularly expansion of the most prestigious committees, were accomplished to satisfy demands of large influxes of liberal Democrats into the chamber.

THE ASSIGNMENT PROCESS

Democrats and Republicans in each chamber have their own assignment processes that, except for individuals elected to Congress as replacements during the course of a term, are played out at the beginning of each new Congress. While there are similarities in the processing of requests, there are also distinctions. As will become apparent shortly, far more is known about the Democratic than the Republican approach. House Democrats have allowed scholars greater access to the documents pertinent to their process for filling committee vacancies, and in recent years, political scientists have occasionally attended sessions at which assignments were made. Scholars have not, however, had access to the paper records accompanying appointment decisions for Republicans, and legislators involved in the decisions have been reluctant to speak about them in detail.

House Democrats

For more than a half century, House Democrats received their assignments from the Democratic contingent on the Ways and Means Committee. Prior to 1974, each Ways and Means Democrat served as the geographic-zone representative of one or more delegations, including his or her own. The committee-assignment responsibility augmented the Ways and Means Committee's control of issues such as the tariff, Social Security, and the Internal Revenue Code, a control that made the committee among the most powerful in the chamber. Membership on this august body was disproportionately southern and conservative. Ways and Means Democrats were accused of favoring members of their states and staffing important committees with those who shared their beliefs.

Until 1973 when the Speaker, majority leader, and chair of the Democratic Caucus were permitted to participate in deliberations on committee assignments, the party leadership was excluded altogether. Ways and Means Democrats had gatekeeping authority, since a committee aspirant had little hope of success without the support of his or her zone representative on the committee. Indeed, before 1971 one could be nominated only by the zone representative; thereafter state party delegations could recommend names. During much of this era, freshmen achieved the more desirable committees only infrequently, so that a two-step process was often necessary to reach the better committees; this increased the influence of Ways and Means.

Beginning with the Ninety-fourth Congress (1975–1976), the Democratic Steering and Policy Committee made committee assignments. This committee is chaired by the Speaker (at least so long as Democrats have a majority in the House; presumably should there be a Republican majority, the Steering and Policy Committee would be chaired by the minority leader). The Speaker is joined by other Democratic leaders such as the majority leader, majority whip, chief deputy whip, chair and vice chair of the caucus, and chair of the Democratic Congressional Campaign Committee. In addition, eight members are named by the Speaker, although in the 102d Congress, Speaker Thomas Foley (D.-Wash.) was allowed to pick nine, since Vic Fazio (D.-Calif.) doubled as caucus vice chair and chair of the Congressional Campaign Committee. Among these eight appointees, it is customary to include a representatives of the Black Caucus, Hispanic Caucus, and Women's Caucus. The Speaker may also choose individuals to ensure repre-

sentation of some of the junior representatives. Other leaders guaranteed places at the Steering and Policy table are the chairs of the Appropriations, Budget, Rules, and Ways and Means committees.

As is shown in Table 1, Steering and Policy contains twelve elected regional representatives, the heirs of the zone representatives found on Ways and Means. Elected members, like those who are appointed, are limited to a pair of two-year terms. The rules are designed to ensure that the elected membership not be exclusively from the ranks of the senior representatives, as was the tendency on Ways and Means. If a region's representative has had twelve years or more of House service, the successor must have fewer than six terms. Most regional representatives, as seen in Table 1, represent multiple states, although three represent a single state.

At meetings of the Steering and Policy Committee, nominations for committee vacancies can be made by any member. The voting rules provide that to secure a slot, a person must have a majority of the votes cast, and only one slot is filled per ballot. Filling vacancies one seat at a time allows for the continual reappraisal of the balance of regional, ideological, and other elements on committees as their rosters are being fleshed out.

The Democratic contingents of all standing committees are assigned in this fashion save for Rules. The centrality of this committee to the party leadership is such, due to its control over scheduling, that the Speaker unilaterally names all Democrats on Rules and selects the chair. This is the one instance in which the seniority norm does not guarantee maintenance of an individual's assignment from Congress to Congress.

House Republicans

Republicans have a Committee on Committees, but the real work is done by an executive committee of that body. Every state with a Republican in the House has one representative on the full committee, while the executive committee is dominated by state delegations having at least five GOP members in the House, each of which has a member on the executive committee. In addition, the executive committee has a

COMMITTEE SELECTION IN CONGRESS

Table 1

COMPOSITION OF THE HOUSE DEMOCRATIC STEERING AND POLICY COMMITTEE IN
1991 AND THE BASIS OF SELECTION OF MEMBERS

Ex Officio

Thomas Foley (Wash).	Speaker
Richard Gephardt (Mo.)	Majority Leader
William Gray (Pa.)	Whip
David Bonior (Mich.)	Chief Deputy Whip
Steny Hoyer (Md.)	Caucus Chair
Vic Fazio (Cal).	Caucus Vice Chair and Congressional Campaign Committee Chair
Jamie Whitten (Miss.)	Appropriations Chair
Leon Panetta (Cal.)	Budget Chair
Joe Moakley (Mass.)	Rules Chair
Dan Rostenkowski (Ill.)	Ways and Means Chair

Appointed by Speaker

Ray Thornton (Ark.)	Freshman Class
Barbara Kennelly (Conn.)	Women's Caucus
Marty Russo (Ill.)	
John Lewis (Ga.)	Black Caucus
Albert Bustamante (Tex.)	Hispanic Caucus
Al Swift (Wash.)	
Dan Glickman (Kan.)	
Matthew McHugh (N.Y.)	
Butler Derrick (S.C.)	

Elected by Region

I.	Robert Matsui (Calif.)	Calif.
II.	Pat Williams (Mont.)	Ariz., Colo., Hawaii, Idaho, Mont., Nev., N.Mex., Ore., Utah, Wash.
III.	Gerald Kleczka (Wis.)	Mich., Minn., Wis.
IV.	Romano Mazzoli (Ky.)	Ill., Ind., Ky.,
V.	Mike Synar (Okla.)	Ark., Iowa, Kans., Mo., Nebr., N.Dak., Okla., S.Dak.
VI.	Martin Frost (Tex.)	Tex.
VII.	W. J. "Billy" Tauzin (La.)	Ala., Fla., La., Miss.
VIII.	Roy Rowland (Ga.)	Ga., N.C., S.C., Tenn.
IX.	Norman Sisisky (Va.)	Del., Md., N.J., Va., W.Va.
X.	Dennis Eckart (Ohio)	Ohio, Pa.
XI.	Thomas Manton (N.Y.)	N.Y.
XII.	Sam Gejdenson (Conn.)	Conn., Maine, Mass., N.H., R.I.

single representative for those delegations having four Republicans. Another person represents delegations having three Republicans, a third person represents delegations having two Republicans, and another member from delegations having a single Republican sits on the executive committee. Typically the representative on the Committee on Committees is the dean (most senior Republican) of the state party delegation; however it is the perogative of the delegation to choose its representative.

Each member of the committee has as many votes as there are Republicans in his or her state delegation. The executive committee is presided over by the party leader who, since the 101st Congress, casts twelve votes. The party whip, who also serves on the committee, casts six votes. Awarding weighted votes to the leader and whip is an attempt to strengthen the leadership's influence. Since the delegation representatives are chosen by the rank and file of their state, awarding weighted votes to the leadership does not put them in so strong a position as that enjoyed by the Speaker among Democrats, who names eight members of the Steering Committee and is accompanied by a number of party leaders.

As with House Democrats, vacancies are filled one by one, even when there are multiple slots available on a committee. To be named to a committee, a person must receive the support of members casting at least half of the weighted votes. Bargains are reportedly struck between deans of large delegations that link the filling of multiple vacancies.

Given the use of weighted voting on the committee, representatives of the larger delegations can, if united, dominate the process. In the past when Congress generally was more hierarchical, larger delegations were reported to run roughshod over the small ones, capturing an inordinate share of the more desirable vacancies. The unchecked power of the large delegations was first restricted by assigning positions on the executive committee to representatives of smaller state delegations. Subsequently there have been instances in which the small-state representatives have united and, with the support of some of the more sympathetic representatives of the larger delegations, dominated the process. In some instances there has been a split between the minority leader and the whip, with the whip joining forces with the small-state insurgents and prevailing.

Senate Democrats

The Democratic party leader chairs the Steering Committee, which serves as the Committee on Committees and names its members. This committee, which has grown over the years, included twenty-five of the fifty-six Senate Democrats in the 102d Congress.

Newly elected Democrats as well as the more senior senators who seek reassignment apply to the Committee on Committees. Judging from the availability of materials in the papers of Democratic leaders, it appears that over time, the request process has changed from being largely oral to one in which there often is a written request. This request, a letter setting forth the desired assignment and the reasons for it, may be a backup to an initial face-to-face discussion. Lyndon B. Johnson of Texas took a very active role in the assignment process as Senate Democratic leader from 1953 to 1960, presenting the Steering Committee with a set of nominees that was usually accepted. Since then the Steering Committee has been more involved in the selection process.

In matching senators' requests with vacancies, there are limits to how many committees of various levels of quality an individual can have. Within the broad categories of "A" and "B" committees, a senator can have no more than two assignments to "A" committees (that is, the more desirable committees). A further restriction limits senators to a single exclusive committee on the "A" list, as designated in Table 2. Senators are allowed as many as three "B" committees. Democrats permit waivers to these general rules, allowing senators three class "A" committees if the individual did not receive his or her first preference, lacks an exclusive committee assignment, or is up for re-election. Waivers apply for a single Congress, after which a senator must decide which two "A" assignments to retain.

Table 2

SENATE COMMITTEES GROUPED BY QUALITY OF THE ASSIGNMENT

Class A Exclusive

Appropriations
Armed Services
Finance
Foreign Relations

Class A

Agriculture
Banking
Commerce
Energy
Environment
Governmental Affairs
Judiciary
Labor

Class B

Budget
Rules and Administration
Small Business
Veterans' Affairs

Senate Republicans

In the 102d Congress, the Senate Republican Committee on Committees had four members and was chaired by the Minority Whip, Trent Lott of Mississippi. Requests for new or additional committees must be made in writing. Senators list separately their priorities for "A" and "B" committees, and appointments are made within the following constraints: one exclusive committee, two class "A" slots, or three class "B" seats per individual.

While seniority is a significant factor for all committees on committees, it has been widely reported that the seniority of the claimants will invariably determine the outcome in contests for committee seats among Senate Republicans. Adherence to such a rule reduces conflict and simplifies the task of the Committee on Committees, which may explain its small size.

MEMBERS' PREFERENCES

Until recently only the favored few could count on receiving their desired committee assignments, and even for these it was necessary to pay one's dues before attaining a position on a highly sought committee. When the apprenticeship norm was still fully operable, first-term members often received appointments that were of little interest or utility for them.

Change came first in the Senate when Lyndon Johnson became the Democratic party leader. To win the loyalty of junior members, he instituted what came to be known as the Johnson Rule, which provides that before any Democratic senator obtains a second prized assignment, all members of the party must have at least one good appointment. In time the practice was also adopted by Senate Republicans and is most visible in the restriction of members to one exclusive committee each.

Committees on committees solicit assignment preferences from their party members. House Democrats once provided a single rank ordering of preferences. Subsequently they submitted two rankings, one for nonmajor committees (see Table 3) and the other for major and exclusive committees. Currently two lists are offered but with no ordering of preferences. Sitting members seeking transfers or an additional assignment usually make a single request, while freshmen may turn in lengthy lists, although three per category has become the norm for first-termers. Most applicants provide rationales for their committee preferences, some of which are discussed below.

In addition to providing lists of preferences, it is common to make personal requests of committee-on-committees members, with party leaders particularly likely to be approached. Requests may be made by the applicant or by the dean (senior member) of the applicant's delegation. Candidates for a highly sought assignment may seek an endorsement of their candidacy from the chair of the committee in question. Some aspirants line up letters from interest groups that frequently appear before the committee on which a seat is being sought.

The assignment process has evolved to the point where member preferences are the chief criteria for assignments. Each Senate Democrat is assigned to an "A" exclusive committee. Each Republican senator is entitled to two major and one minor appointment. House Democrats are guaranteed a seat on either an exclusive or a major committee as listed in Table 3 and almost always get at least one of the appointments they sought. We turn now to an examination of the factors underlying committee preferences.

A Classificatory Scheme for Committee Motivations

Richard F. Fenno, Jr., observed that committee assignments fit into the broader concerns of legislators. Members of Congress seek assignments that will allow them to pursue their dominant political objectives. In his seminal *Congressmen in Committees* (1973), Fenno identified four basic motivations: (1) to promote reelection, now increasingly referred to more broadly as advancing constituency interests; (2) to make good public policy; (3) to achieve prestige or power within the institution; and (4) to attain higher office. Some committees fulfill multiple needs for particular individuals and not everyone currently on a committee or those who desire to be on a committee will act on the same motivation. Examinations of committee motivations by Smith and Deering concluded that multiple motivations

Table 3
PARTISAN CLASSIFICATIONS OF HOUSE COMMITTEES

Democrats	Republicans
Exclusive	Red
Appropriations	Appropriations
Rules	Rules
Ways and Means	Ways and Means
	Energy and Commerce
Major	White
Agriculture	Agriculture
Armed Services	Armed Services
Banking	Banking
Education and Labor	Education and Labor
Judiciary	Judiciary
Public Works	Public Works
Energy and Commerce	
Nonmajor	Blue
Budget	Budget
District of Columbia	District of Columbia
Government Operations	Government Operations
House Administration	House Administration
Interior	Interior
Merchant Marine	Merchant Marine
Post Office	Post Office
Science and Technology	Science and Technology
Small Business	Small Business
Standards of Official Conduct	Standards of Official Conduct
Veterans' Affairs	Veterans' Affairs

Source: Steven S. Smith and Christopher J. Deering, *Committees in Congress*, 2d edition (Washington, D.C., 1990), pp. 116–117.

are becoming increasingly common. Following Fenno's lead, Charles S. Bullock III developed a classificatory scheme for all House committees based on the reasons cited by freshmen for their preferences. An updated version of the classificatory scheme for both chambers appears in Table 4.

Legislators drawn to an assignment to advance their relations with their constituents often emphasize committee work that they hope will make them more electorally secure. A constituency concern is especially likely among those who perceive themselves to be in trouble with the electorate, particularly freshmen elected by narrow margins. Legislators motivated by constituency concerns are likely to see electoral rewards flowing from committees involved with a facet of the economy important in the district. Thus a legislator from a rural area might be attracted to the Agriculture Committee; westerners representing large districts often seek assignment to the Interior Committee. Urban legislators looking for money for rapid transit or for subsidized housing may gravitate toward the Banking, Finance, and Urban Affairs Committee, while those from coastal areas may go on the Merchant Marine and Fisheries Committee. The Public Works Committee offers opportunities to snare federal construction dollars for almost any district. The Armed Services Committee is helpful to legislators who have military bases or prime military contractors in their districts. Since the death in 1964 of Clarence Cannon (D.-Mo.), the chair of the Appropriations Committee who sought to keep representatives away from assignments that would allow them to channel money into their districts, this committee has

Table 4

COMMITTEES CLASSIFIED BY MOTIVATIONS EXPRESSED BY MEMBERS
OF CONGRESS SEEKING TO SERVE ON THEM

House	Senate
Prestige	**Policy**
Appropriations	Budget
Budget	Foreign Relations
Rules	Governmental Affairs
Ways and Means	Judiciary
	Labor
Policy	**Policy/Constituency**
Banking	Armed Services
Education and Labor	Banking
Energy and Commerce	Finance
Foreign Affairs	Small Business
Government Operations	
Judiciary	
Constituency	**Constituency**
Agriculture	Agriculture
Armed Services	Appropriations
Interior	Commerce
Merchant Marine	Energy
Public Works	Environment
Science	
Small Business	**Unrequested**
Veterans' Affairs	Rules and Administration
	Veterans' Affairs
Duty/Unrequested	
District of Columbia	
House Administration	
Post Office	
Standards of Official Conduct	

Source: Steven S. Smith and Christopher J. Deering, *Committees in Congress*, 2d ed. (Washington, D.C., 1990), pp. 87, 101.

come to offer opportunities for solidifying constituency ties.

A second common motivation is interest in a committee's policy domain. Fenno identified Education and Labor and Foreign Affairs as committees that attracted individuals chiefly because of their concern about the subject matter. The Energy and Commerce Committee, with its wide-ranging responsibilities for health care, transportation, the financial markets, energy, and consumer protection, has been one of the most prized committees in recent Congresses. Government Operations, which is authorized to investigate the entire array of

governmental activities, has taken on new luster in an era of increasingly tight budgets. With many of today's legislators having entered politics in order to influence policy, committees that handle the hot topics are often oversubscribed.

While Energy and Commerce was previously sought chiefly for its wide array of policy responsibilities, it has recently been seen as offering an electoral bonus. Not only can one expect to work on legislation likely to win press coverage and to develop substantive knowledge that will impress constituents, but the centrality of the issues confronted by Commerce may also facilitate campaign fundraising. Issues high on the national policy agenda often catch the eye of major interest groups that contribute to the campaign coffers of those in a position to help and who are not inflexibly hostile to the contributor's position.

Contrast the popular Commerce Committee with Judiciary, another policy committee. Judiciary handles interesting but politically charged questions such as abortion and school busing. These topics inflame passions among large segments of the electorate, and Judiciary members may have to select a no-win position. While some of Judiciary's topics generate marches, rallies, and prime-time television footage, they do not inspire generous campaign contributions. Despite interest in Judiciary's policy agenda, its reelection liabilities have contributed to the committee's declining attractiveness and hence to difficulties in filling its ranks.

Table 4 identifies the Rules Committee plus the three money committees as prestige committees in the House. These committees are the ones most likely to have an impact on the ambitions of all chamber members. Direct input into questions of spending and taxing allows committee members to help or hurt legislators concerned about obtaining benefits for their districts or putting policy decisions in place. Some members of prestige committees enjoy the deference accorded them by their colleagues. Others recognize the opportunity afforded by Appropriations and Budget to bring to fruition projects begun when they served on constituency or policy committees. The ongoing budgetary crisis made money committees even more central in the 1980s and 1990s than they had been.

The Rules Committee is infrequently requested because Democratic members are named by the Speaker and not appointed through the regular Committee on Committees route. Nonetheless the committee has historically been prized for its location at the key juncture on the legislative trail. Bills reported by substantive committees typically do not reach the floor until passing through Rules, where decisions are made as to the length of time for debate and whether amendments will be permitted. Rules continues to exercise those functions, but its desirability waned after it became an arm of the House leadership and lost much of its independence.

Fenno's fourth motivation was the desire to use a committee to help achieve higher office. Fenno did not elaborate on this motivation as he did the other three, and it has received little attention from others. Perhaps the best example of this motivation at work is in the Senate, where presidential aspirants have often requested the Foreign Relations Committee to enhance their credentials for a key aspect of the presidency.

At the bottom of Table 4 are committees that have had few suitors. These unrequested or duty committees are ones that are rarely prized. They do not handle policy questions that attract widespread concern, nor do they provide legislators with access to bountiful political action committees. By their very inability to attract applicants, they betray their low standing in the eyes of members. In the 1940s and 1950s, large contingents of first-termers passed through these committees and, later on, moved up to better assignments. Now, since freshmen get at least one desired appointment, these committees serve as second assignments for individuals whose primary interest lies elsewhere.

The most onerous House assignment is to Standards of Official Conduct, which evaluates allegations of ethical lapses by colleagues. Here are found individuals who bowed to entreaties from their party leaders and will flee at the first opportunity. So as to avoid any appearance of partisan bias, Standards of Official Conduct has equal numbers of Democrats and Republicans.

Table 4 shows that in the Senate, only constituency and policy interests play much of a role in member requests. To the extent that interest in achieving prestige and power in the upper chamber comes into play, it tends to be in connection with two of the money committees, Appropriations and Finance. Even on these committees, however, policy and constituency concerns are more frequently voiced. Senate committees sought chiefly for their policy opportunities are, with the exception of Budget, also among the committees for which policy interests are mentioned in the House. The Senate's constituency committees include Agriculture, Environment (the Senate analogue for Public Works in the House), and Energy (the analogue for Interior in the House).

There is a third category of Senate committees for which members offer policy and constituency rationales with roughly equal frequency. These include two committees classified as constituency committees in the House (Armed Services and Small Business), one classified as policy (Banking), and one as prestige (Finance).

The Senate's Rules and Administration Committee, which falls into the unrequested category, is a far different creature from the House Rules Committee. In the Senate there is unlimited debate and thus no opportunity for a committee to set time parameters. Also the Senate is open to riders as amendments to its legislation, while in the House, even germane amendments can be precluded by the Rules Committee. The Senate Rules and Administration Committee has only housekeeping chores along the lines of those handled by the House Administration Committee.

Legislator Backgrounds

Legislators motivated chiefly by public-policy interests may derive those concerns from vocational or political experiences. The strongest vocational connection allows only lawyers to serve on the Judiciary Committee. This practice is emulated, albeit less rigidly, elsewhere with bankers gravitating toward the banking committees, farmers to Agriculture, and teachers to Education and Labor. Chester Bowles (D.-Conn.), who had been ambassador to India, sought and served on the Foreign Affairs Committee.

Some legislators attempt to pursue the same interest in Congress that they had followed in the state legislature. For these the cost of mastering a new subject matter is a disincentive for taking on new issues while simultaneously learning a new job. For others the inability to resolve problems with which they dealt as state legislators entice them to pursue the problem in Congress in the hope that the political and financial muscle of the federal government will enable them to achieve goals they could not attain as state legislators.

Delegation Concerns

Sometimes the pursuit of the constituency benefit applies to more than a single legislator's district. Many state delegations strive to maintain a presence on committees of critical concern for the entire state or a large segment of it. This concern may derive from any of the possible motivations that drive the behavior of individual legislators. Thus delegations seek a presence on the financial committees, since these can promote the economic well-being of the state. Furthermore, midwestern and southern delegations are eager to have one of their own on the Agriculture Committee to look after the various crops cultivated by their farmers. Similarly a state with numerous military installations wants a representative on Armed Services.

At times, interest in maintaining a seat is more localized than a state party delegation and may go to a particular district. For example, representatives of Georgia's Tenth Congressional District served continuously on the Banking Committee for more than seventy years. Similarly, in recent decades the Georgian who represents the district with military installations at Warner Robins and Fort Benning was always on the Armed Services Committee.

Once a state party delegation has served continuously—or almost continuously—for a length of time on a committee, this fact may become an argument for retaining a seat. While such claims are often honored by the committees on committees, their acceptance is not guaranteed. Between 1947 and 1988, 119 of the House seats were held by a single delegation for at least thirty-six years. On the Senate side, delegations have only two members, and it is more difficult for the state to have personnel available to maintain a continuous presence. Nonetheless, 40 of the seats have been held by a single delegation for at least thirty-six of the forty-two years. In each chamber almost twice as many seats were held by a single delegation for at least eighteen years from 1969 to 1988 as were held for at least thirty-six out of the forty-two years.

Considerations in Making Assignments

While an attempt is made to honor at least one request for each legislator, the oversubscription of the more attractive committees necessitates an allocation procedure. Senior members more often achieve their requested assignments than freshmen when the two are in competition.

A factor that comes into play for Democratic nonfreshmen is their partisan reliability. Speaker Tip O'Neill began the practice of reporting on the reliability of sitting Democrats who sought to transfer committees. It has since become sufficiently institutionalized so that when the Speaker fails to report how often a member stood with the party on close roll calls, Steering and Policy Committee members request the information. It should be noted that this information is not the same as *Congressional Quarterly's* Party Unity and Party Opposition scores. In contrast with *Congressional Quarterly*, which reports the number of times that a legislator voted with the party on votes that pitted most Democrats against most Republicans, the party loyalty measure used by Democratic Speakers focuses on those instances in which a special plea to stand with the party was made.

While the choicest assignments may be denied to party rebels, the practice of giving all members at least one desirable committee circumscribes the power of the leadership. In the House, freshmen no longer start out with the worst assignments and the need to demonstrate competence or loyalty before earning a promotion. Senators automatically get one of the top four appointments (that is, on Appropriations, Armed Services, Finance, or Foreign Relations).

Another consideration limits most House party delegations to one seat per committee, which permits wider dissemination of the benefits produced by an attractive committee. Large delegations, such as Democrats from Texas, New York, or California or Republicans from Ohio, New York, or California frequently have multiple members on most committees, since it would be impossible for large delegations to be limited to a single slot per committee. In the Senate both senators from a state will not be assigned to the same committee, although there are occasional exceptions when a state's senators represent opposing parties.

When multiple members of a state party delegation aspire to a committee and the delegation is entitled to only one appointment, the delegation's dean may seek to rechannel the ambitions of some members. The dean can meet with junior colleagues from the delegation and suggest alternatives. Should all of those interested in a particular assignment—say, several Iowa freshmen wanting a seat on Agriculture—continue to pursue it, their competition might keep all of them from obtaining the appointment. However, if the delegation

rallies behind one nominee for Agriculture while another seeks Public Works, the chances of both will be enhanced.

In pursuing competitive assignments, applicants may stress their electoral needs. Members recently elected with a narrow margin or freshmen who defeated an incumbent of the other party may feel entitled to special consideration. Smith and Deering reported that among House Democrats in 1981, the most frequently mentioned rationale for committee requests was an electoral linkage. Second most frequently cited was a prescriptive claim that the seat belonged to the delegation because the previous occupant was from their state. Only these two reasons were mentioned at least ten times.

The popularity of claims based on electoral needs is long-standing. But are these claims honored when assignments are distributed? Early work on committee assignments, which was heavily anecdotal, emphasized the importance of promoting reelection as a goal in making assignments. Later, more systematic studies failed to find evidence that the committees on committees consistently reward members who were narrowly elected.

Growth in the number of committee seats has reduced competition for appointments. Most assignments are now uncontested, with a pattern of more requests than vacancies common only for exclusive committees and a few top major committees, such as Commerce. Party leaders and those serving on the committees on committees exercise extensive control over committee composition only on the exclusive committees. This is a significant change from the 1950s and 1960s, when competition was more widespread and involved a broader array of committees. More slots and less competition combine to reduce legislator dissatisfaction with the output of the committees on committees. There is still no guarantee that an individual will receive his or her top choice, but there is now a near certainty of appointment to one of the committees on the legislator's preference schedule.

Some risk takers pursue a strategy of indicating a single preference, and even these brash individuals are not always disappointed. Democrats have ceased asking for rank-ordered preferences, concluding that the information provided was imprecise and could not reflect changes that result from the one-at-a-time process by which vacancies are filled.

In the most sophisticated effort to understand the process of committee assignments, Kenneth Shepsle identified factors associated with successful campaigns for committee appointments among House Democrats from the late 1950s until the assignment process was turned over to the Steering and Policy Committee in 1974. Attaining a committee request was strongly related to a lack of competition for the slot from others representing districts in the same region. Among nonfreshmen seeking to transfer to another committee, success was associated with making fewer requests.

Efforts to explain committee assignments in the Senate have been less successful than in the House. Regarding Senate Democrats, Bullock reviewed factors similar to those considered by Shepsle in his House analysis and found that only the relative seniority of the senator making the request was important: senators were more successful when they had greater seniority than those who were competing for the assignment.

COMMITTEE TRANSFERS

Not all freshmen obtain their top preferences, and some of the disappointed ones seek transfers as vacancies become available on more preferred committees. By transferring, members can pursue their basic goals, but transfers sacrifice seniority accrued on the existing committee, and the transferee begins at the bottom of the seniority roster on the new committee.

Bullock's research on House committees from 1949 to 1969 found that in both parties, more than 40 percent of all transfers occurred at the beginning of members' sophomore terms. After two terms approximately two-thirds of all transfers had occurred, and after a third term, almost 80 percent of the transfers had occurred. A replication by Gary W. Copeland covering the Ninety-sixth through Ninety-eighth Congresses found only a slight increase in the proportion of transfers coming at the end of the first term. However, by the end of two terms, 80 percent of all transfers had occurred, and more than 90 percent of transfers took place within the first three terms. An explanation for transfers coming somewhat earlier in

members' careers is that they now often achieve desirable committees at the outset and consequently have less incentive to move. Virtually all first-termers get at least one of their committee requests, and while it is still rare, a greater number of freshmen are assigned even to exclusive (or red) committees.

Bruce A. Ray compared the percentages of vacancies filled by freshmen for the Eighty-eighth through Ninety-second Congresses with the Ninety-third through Ninety-seventh Congresses. The proportion of vacancies filled by freshmen on Foreign Affairs increased by 27 percent over the two time periods, and there were increases of more than 20 percentage points for Ways and Means and Judiciary. Other desirable committees did not show comparable increases because even in the earlier period more than 70 percent of their openings went to freshmen. Only three committees experienced a more than one-percent drop in the share of the vacancies going to freshmen. Ray's data conform to expectations that with the erosion of the apprenticeship norm, freshmen fare better in bidding for committees. Further evidence is that by the 1970s, only on exclusive committees were fewer than two-thirds of the vacancies filled by first-termers.

A comparison of figures from Bullock and Copeland shows that the share of transfers to committees desired for their prestige has risen, so that in the Ninety-sixth through Ninety-eighth Congresses, these committees attracted 47 percent of all transferees, up from the 37 percent observed by Bullock. Transfers are increasingly made to prestigious committees, and for Appropriations, Rules, and Ways and Means, Ray found that fewer than one in four vacancies went to freshmen. There was a decline of 10 percentage points in the share of all transfers that came from undesired committees, or committees that do not prompt prestige, policy, or constituency motivations. Members now leave undesired committees less often, holding onto these slots as second assignments and building seniority there even as they seek appointment to better committees.

Beginning with Donald R. Matthews's work on the Senate, transfer patterns have been used to rank committees. Matthews's approach placed at the top those committees that attracted members from virtually every other committee and lost members to none, while placing at the bottom those committees that lost members to most committees and rarely attracted any members from committees with a higher ranking. Thus Foreign Relations added sixteen transferees from the Eightieth through the Eighty-fourth Congresses and attracted members from every committee except Government Operations and District of Columbia; it lost transfers to no committee. Appropriations, which ranked second, attracted a net of fifteen members from other committees and had transfers from all but three committees. At the bottom Post Office had a net loss of nineteen members to other committees; those departing went to all but three other committees. There were, not surprisingly, a few instances in which transfers were not in the expected pattern.

Charles S. Bullock, III and John Sprague took another approach to assessing committee desirability based upon transfer patterns. They devised a transfer ratio that divides the number of transfers to a committee by the total transfer action to and from the committee. They argued that the patterns are not the same for the three major groupings (northern Democrats, southern Democrats, and Republicans), and Bullock later presented separate rankings for each of the three groups. At the upper reaches, as shown in Table 5, there was little variation across the top seven committees, with the exclusive committees invariably ranking in the top three and with Foreign Affairs, Armed Services, Commerce, and Judiciary always within the top ten. At the other extreme, Veterans' Affairs and Post Office invariably had far more

Table 5

RANKINGS OF HOUSE COMMITTEES BASED ON TRANSFER PATTERNS

	80th–91st[a]				88th–92d[b]		93d–97th[c]	95th–99th[d]	
House	ND	SD	GOP	Dom[d]	Drwg	Hldg	Drwg	Transfer	Dom
Ways and Means									
1	1.5	2	1	1.5	1	3	2	1.5	1
Appropriations									
2	3	2	2	1.5	3	1.5	1	1.5	2
Rules									
3	1.5	2	3	3	2	1.5	3	3	3
Foreign Affairs									
4	4	6	5	6	4	4	4	6	6
Armed Services									
5	6	4	4	5	5	5	5	5	5
Commerce									
6	5	7	8	4	6	7	6	4	4
Judiciary									
7	7	5	7	7	7	6	13.5	17	13
Agriculture									
8	8	10	11	11	9	18	9	10	18
Public Works									
9	9.5	8.5	12	8	19	13.5	16	19	14
Education and Labor									
10	17	13	6	13	10	8	15	11	19
Science									
11	11	11.5	13.5	10	11	19	11.5	14	16
Banking									
12	14	11.5	10	12	12	11	17	9	11
Internal Security									
13	20	16	9	NA	16	12	–	–	–
District of Columbia									
14	15.5	14	13.5	NA	17	10	13.5	NA	NA

(*continued*)

Table 5 (*continued*)

House	80th–91st[a]				88th–92d[b]		93d–97th[c]	95th–99th[d]	
	ND	SD	GOP	Dom[d]	Drwg	Hldg	Drwg	Transfer	Dom
House Administration									
15	12	17	15	NA	15	20	18	NA	NA
Interior									
16	15.5	8.5	16	9	18	16	7	8	10
Merchant Marine									
17	13	18	19	16	13	13.5	19	15	8
Government Operations									
18	9.5	15	20	14	8	15	8	12	12
Post Office									
19	18.5	20	18	15	20	17	11.5	16	9
Veterans' Affairs									
20	18.5	19	17	17	14	9	20	18	17
Small Business									
—	—	—	—	—	—	—	10	13	15
Budget									
—	—	—	—	—	—	—	—	7	7

ND = Northern Democrats
SD = Southern Democrats
GOP = Republicans
NA = Not available
Dom = dominance ranking
Drwg = ranking based on drawing power
Hldg = ranking based on holding power

Sources:

[a] Charles S., Bullock, III, "Committee Transfers in the United States House of Representatives," *Journal of Politics* 35 (February 1973): 94.

[b] Malcolm E. Jewell, and Chu Chi-Hung, "Membership Movement and Committee Attractiveness in the U.S. House of Representatives, 1963–1971," *American Journal of Political Science* 18 (May 1974): 438.

[c] Bruce A. Ray, "Committee Attractiveness in the U.S. House, 1963–1981," *American Journal of Political Science* 26 (August 1982): 610.

[d] Michael C. Munger, "Allocation of Desirable Committee Assignments: Extended Queues Versus Committee Expansion," *American Journal of Political Science* 32 (May 1988): 325.

members leaving than coming to them from other committees.

Efforts to rank committees based on transfer patterns require data from multiple Congresses, since committee exchanges in any single Congress are too few to establish an ordering. A difficulty with using multiple Congresses is that the relative desirability of committees changes over time.

Malcolm E. Jewell and Chu Chi-Hung provided a visual presentation of patterns for House committees for the Eighty-eighth through Ninety-second Congresses. They sorted committees into eight levels, with each higher level attracting members from below and rarely losing members downward. The exclusive committees constituted the top level and lost only one individual across the three commit-

tees. At the next level were Armed Services and Foreign Affairs, which lost members to the exclusive committees while drawing members from below. At the bottom were District of Columbia and Veterans' Affairs, which exchanged some members but did not attract members from other committees.

In addition to the categorical ranking based on whether a committee attracted or lost members to other committees, Jewell and Chi-Hung offered two quantitative measures based on transfers. The first of these, the index of drawing power, weights the transfers to a committee in terms of the seniority of the transferees on the committees from which they came. The greater the seniority given up, the higher the index of drawing power. As shown in Table 5, the exclusive committees rank in the top three, with the attractive policy committees of Foreign Affairs, Commerce, and Judiciary coming close behind. Armed Services and Agriculture are two constituency committees with relatively high drawing power, while Post Office and District of Columbia fall towards the bottom.

The other measure, the turnover rate, is the number of departures divided by committee membership. Here, departures, both as transfers to other committees and as leaving a committee without obtaining a replacement, are considered. On this index, variation in the ranking of the top seven committees is modest. There are a surprising number of scores in the lower ranks, particularly the relatively higher standing of Veterans' Affairs and the lower-than-usual score for the Science Committee.

Bruce A. Ray updated the drawing-power index for five congresses, and his figures for the 1970s were quite similar to those reported by Jewell and Chi-Hung. Among the notable exceptions were the fall in the attractiveness of the Judiciary, Merchant Marine, Banking, and Education and Labor committees; note that three of these are policy committees. Moving in the opposite direction, Interior, a constituency committee, and Post Office, demonstrated heightened attractiveness.

Building on the earlier works is the net transfer dominance score of Michael C. Munger. Munger looked for intercommittee exchange patterns and ranked one committee higher than another if the first committee had at least two more individuals transfer to it from the second committee than moved in the opposite direction. Where no clear dominance was visible, Munger used the transfer ratio to order committees. He calculated dominance scores for the Eightieth through Ninety-first Congresses using Bullock's data and then developed scores for the Ninety-fifth through Ninety-ninth Congresses. For the earlier period, there is little difference in the ranking of the top seven committees, with the exclusive committees occupying the first three places. The greatest difference, as shown in Table 5, is Interior, which has a dominance ranking of nine but a transfer-ratio ranking of sixteen. Munger's dominance scores exclude three duty, or undesired, committees.

His replication for the period 1977 through 1985 produced little change in the top six committees, but Judiciary, which had placed seventh on the dominance ranking in the earlier period, fell to thirteenth place. Agriculture, Public Works, Education and Labor, and Science lost stature. The new Budget Committee came in with a respectable ranking of seventh.

Munger offered several possible explanations for the decline in desirability of some committees. Leadership decentralization makes some policy committees less desirable for members having policy goals, since they need strong leadership. The replacement of Emanuel Celler (D.-N.Y.) by Peter Rodino (D.-N.J.) brought a weaker chair to the Judiciary Committee, which may account in part for its fall in desirability. Education and Labor, a policy committee that suffered from the disruptive leadership of Adam Clayton Powell (D.-N.Y.), also became less attractive. A second explanation for changes in committee desirability is the increase in seats. Munger found support for the warning issued by others that as committees are enlarged, their value to legislators declines. Thus there is a fairly strong relationship (correlation of $-.57$) between change in the number of seats and change in the committee's ranking once the exclusive committees are left out. A third possibility—that taking on divisive new issues may make a committee less attractive—shows promise only for the Judiciary Committee.

Table 5, which includes different perspectives on transfers over forty years, shows some continuities, such as the invariably high ranking accorded exclusive committees and the relatively high ranking for Armed Services, Commerce, and Foreign Affairs. Interior is probably the best example of a committee that has become more attractive, and its rise in stature may be due to growing public concern for environmental protection and energy matters. Going in the opposite direction is the Judiciary Committee, which has fallen out of the top third and now has difficulty filling its ranks.

Seniority is frequently essential for appointment to the most desirable committees. This has sometimes been expressed in terms of a queuing procedure. Aspirants must wait in line for an opportunity to get on desired committees, with the party leadership controlling access. Some writers, like Westefield, have seen the leadership's control of access as providing it with leverage, while others, like Munger, have acknowledged that there is little here which party leaders can use to enforce discipline.

Anecdotal evidence suggests that members acknowledge a queue. Interviews with people close to the assignment process indicate that a request may be made for a committee even when there is little potential for success, simply to get in line for future vacancies. This notion of queuing is apparent in letters written by legislators to Committee on Committee members. Some senators have, vulture-like, written to renew their requests upon receiving word that a senior colleague on the desired committee has been hospitalized. Length of time in the queue, while a factor in obtaining an assignment, is not always determinative, as some members have bitterly pointed out after being disappointed time after time.

Another factor to consider is change in the driving motivation of individual members. Some individuals who as freshmen were chiefly concerned about reelection may be emboldened to transfer to exclusive committees once they have expanded their reelection coalition. Moreover, members with seniority may come to realize that they enjoy greater latitude in how they invest their time so that case workers, district staff, and perhaps symbolic gestures on their own part along with the appropriate home style can allow them to pursue objectives other than serving constituents, such as policymaking or obtaining power within the chamber.

In distributing requests across committees, it appears that those making the appointments are sensitive to concerns of race and gender. Women and minorities have been appointed to a wide range of committees so that their sparse numbers can provide leaven to the white male dominance of committees.

OUTLIERS

With self-selection the norm in committee assignments, it has been suggested that committee rosters poorly reflect overall chamber membership. With members gravitating toward committees that will meet the needs of their constituencies or match their policy interests, one could expect that each committee would overrepresent legislators with personal agendas to pursue. Those outside of Congress interested in shaping legislation are well aware of the critical role played by committees. Such a state of affairs accords with the widespread notion of policy triangles in which specialists from the committee, the bureaucracy, and the private sector work with little oversight to fashion public policy to meet the needs of all three. It has been suggested that constituency committees would be most unrepresentative of the chamber, since these committees' members are chiefly concerned about providing benefits to their districts, and where benefits are concentrated, oversight tends to be less. Committees whose members share relevant characteristics may also more often be policy outliers whose preferences are more extreme or even different from those of most members of Congress. As has been noted previously, constituency committees attract members from similar constituencies (for example, rural westerners going onto Interior), again suggesting that such committees are more likely to be peopled by preference outliers who will aggressively seek benefits distributed by their committees for their constituents. Nonmembers may be more sensitive to the costs of providing those benefits. In contrast it is expected that policy and, particularly, prestige committees, which make decisions of concern to a wider range of legislators, must operate more in accord with the expectations of the party or the chamber.

Conclusions about the outlier proposition differ, depending on how preferences are assessed. Based on an analysis of general liberal-conservative dimensions (using the support scores developed by the Americans for Democratic Action) as well as indices developed by interest groups whose concerns are handled by specific committees, Keith Krehbiel concluded that committee members' preferences did not differ from those of the chamber. He found committee members in both chambers to be heterogeneous and the mean scores for committee members to be similar to those of nonmembers.

Krehbiel's critics claim that there are deficiencies in the roll-call voting measures used. They note that interest-group indices include votes on bills that did not come before the committee. Moreover, even issues before a committee tap varying levels of interest from members. Using a more precise measure of committee interests—namely, specific legislation handled by the committee—Richard L. Hall and Bernard Grofman reported that (1) the membership of committees, particularly of constituency committees, is homogeneous; (2) committee preferences are statistically different from those of the full chamber; and (3) Democrats on these committees vote differently on the issues that had been dealt with by their committees than did Democrats not on the committees. While the voting behavior of committee members and nonmembers differ statistically, the bulk of both sets generally support legislation coming out of the committee.

Congruence with the full chamber tends to be greater for nonconstituency committees. It is not clear whether this is because the influence of these committees evokes more chamber support or because committee members modify their positions so as to avoid rebuke on the floor.

SUMMARY

The committee assignment process in Congress is handled by four separate committees on committees, one for each party in each chamber. The committees on committees vary greatly in size and in the degree to which they are designed for representativeness. In carrying out their functions, they operate within constraints that fix the number of assignments allowed per legislator as well as limitations on the permissible combinations of assignments. In each chamber, legislators who receive assignment to one of the most desirable committees are precluded from certain other appointments.

Legislators' preferences carry great weight in the assignment process, with members typically receiving at least one of their top preferences. In both chambers interest in influencing the policy process and a desire for an appointment important to the economy of a legislator's constituency are major motivations for member requests. In the House, but not the Senate, a third major determinant of committee preferences is the desire for power and recognition within the chamber. Since members can usually achieve their preferences for committee assignments, there has been concern that committees are peopled by individuals who are not representative of the membership of the larger body. Researchers disagree over whether committees constitute pools of preference outliers.

While members increasingly obtain their top preferences as freshmen, a number of transfers to more preferred committees occur later in legislators' careers. Analyses of transfer patterns permit a rank ordering of overall committee desirability.

BIBLIOGRAPHY

General Works
KENNETH A. SHEPLSE, *The Giant Jigsaw Puzzle: Democratic Committee Assignments in the Modern House* (Chicago, 1978), provides a most extensive analysis of committee assignments by House Democrats in the later years when the function was performed by the party contingent of the Ways and Means Committee. Sheplse was carrying out his research at the time that the function was shifted to the Steering and Policy Committee and devotes a final chapter to an analysis of the initial consequences of that change. More recent but briefer overviews of the assignment process appear in STEVEN S. SMITH and CHRISTOPHER J. DEERING, *Committees in Congress* (Washington, D.C., 1984 and 1990). The second edition updates and expands on the discussion of the assignment process contained in the first edition. Smith and Deering present their own analyses as well as drawing upon the work of others. GEORGE GOODWIN, JR., *The Little Legislatures: Committees of Congress* (Amherst, Mass., 1970), provides an earlier overview of the assignment process that is more descriptive than analytic.

The intensive study of committee assignments begins with NICHOLAS A. MASTERS, "Committee Assignments in the House of Representatives," *American Political Science Review* 55 (June 1961): 345–357. Masters focuses chiefly on the Democrats. More-extensive analyses of the process that consider both parties are found in CHARLES S. BULLOCK, III, "Apprenticeship and Committee Assignments in the House of Representatives," *Journal of Politics* 32 (August 1970): 717–720; "Freshman Committee Assignments and Reelection in the United States House of Representatives," *American Political Science Review* 66 (September 1972): 996–1007; "Committee Transfers in the United States House of Representatives," *Journal of Politics* 35 (February 1973): 85–120; and BULLOCK and JOHN SPRAGUE, "A Research Note on the Committee Reassignments of Southern Democratic Congressmen," *Journal of Politics* 31 (May 1969): 493–512. Others who have contributed to this literature include LINDA L. FOWLER, SCOTT R. DOUGLASS, and WESLEY D. CLARK, "The Electoral Effects of House Committee Assignments," *Journal of Politics* 42 (February 1980): 307–319; DAVID W. ROHDE and KENNETH A. SHEPLSE, "Democratic Committee Assignments in the House of Representatives: Strategic Aspects of a Social Choice Process," *American Political Science Review* 67 (September 1973): 889–905; and GARY W. COPELAND, "Seniority and Committee Transfers: Career Planning in the Contemporary House of Representatives," *Journal of Politics* 49 (May 1987): 553–564.

Motivations for Requests

RICHARD F. FENNO, JR., *Congressmen in Committees* (Boston, 1973), sets out basic motivations for committee requests based on analysis of six committees. CHARLES S. BULLOCK, III, "Motivations for U.S. Congressional Committee Preferences: Freshmen of the 92nd Congress," *Legislative Studies Quarterly* 1 (February 1976): 201–212, applies the Fenno categories to the full range of House committees. Bullock provides a classification of Senate committee motivations in "U.S. Senate Committee Assignments: Preferences, Motivations, and Success," *American Journal of Political Science* 29 (November 1985): 789–808.

Committee Size

A number of articles have examined the growth in committee size, beginning with LOUIS C. GRAWTHROP, "Changing Membership Patterns in House Committees," *American Political Science Review* 60 (June 1966): 366–373. More-

extensive efforts to explain the growth in committee size have been offered by LOUIS P. WESTEFIELD, "Majority Party Leadership and the Committee System in the House of Representatives," *American Political Science Review* 68 (December 1974): 1593–1604; DAVID WHITEMAN, "A Theory of Congressional Organizations: Committee Size in the U.S. House of Representatives," *American Politics Quarterly* 11 (January 1983): 49–70; and BRUCE A. RAY and STEVEN S. SMITH, "Committee Size in the U.S. Congress," *Legislative Studies Quarterly* 9 (November 1984): 679–695. BARBARA SINCLAIR, "The Distribution of Committee Positions in the U.S. Senate: Explaining Institutional Change," *American Journal of Political Science* 32 (May 1988): 276–301, explores the growth in committees in the upper chamber.

Transfer Patterns

The initial work on committee-transfer patterns in the Senate appears in DONALD R. MATTHEWS, *U.S. Senators and Their World* (Chapel Hill, N.C., 1960). Research into House-committee attractiveness based on transfer patterns is found in the works on committee transfers by BULLOCK listed above. Others who have done work in this area include MALCOLM E. JEWELL and CHU CHI-HUNG, "Membership Movement and Committee Attractiveness in the U.S. House of Representatives, 1963–1971," *American Journal of Political Science* 18 (May 1974): 433–441, and MICHAEL C. MUNGER, "Allocation of Desirable Committee Assignments: Extended Queues Versus Committee Expansion," *American Journal of Political Science* 32 (May 1988): 317–344. BRUCE A. RAY updates the JEWELL and CHI-HUNG article in "Committee Attractiveness in the U.S. House, 1963–1981," *American Journal of Political Science* 26 (August 1982): 609–613.

Outliers

On the question of whether standing committees are outliers with homogeneous membership that differs from the membership of the chamber or the party from which it is chosen, KEITH KREHBIEL, "Are Congressional Committees Composed of Preference Outliers?" *American Political Science Review* 84 (March 1990): 149–163, argues that committee memberships are not significantly different from the chamber membership. Using roll calls more closely related to the work of the committees, RICHARD L. HALL and BERNARD GROFMAN, "The Committee Assignment Process and the Conditional Nature of Committee Bias," *American Political Science Review* 84 (December 1990): 1149–1166, reach the opposite conclusion.

Bibliographical Work

For an exhaustive review of the literature on committee assignments through 1984, see HEINZ EULAU, "Committee Selection," in GERHARD LOEWENBERG, SAMUEL C. PATTERSON, and MALCOLM E. JEWELL, eds., *Handbook of Legislative Research* (Cambridge, Mass., 1985).

SEE ALSO The Congressional Committee System; The House Committee on Ways and Means; and The Motivations of Legislators.

AGENDA SETTING, ACTORS, AND ALIGNMENTS IN CONGRESSIONAL COMMITTEES

Richard L. Hall
Gary McKissick

Unlike most parliamentary systems, the United States Congress has considerable discretion in developing significant initiatives of its own, independent of the plans and policies of the executive branch. As several generations of scholars have emphasized, congressional committees are the prime institutions in setting the legislative agendas of both the House and the Senate. Despite their crucial importance in the agenda-setting process, however, too little is known about how committees make the specific agenda decisions that they do, or why they take one set of specific initiatives as against another. Nevertheless, several themes run through the research that has been done about these questions, providing some understanding of the complex world of committee behavior in the contemporary Congress.

AGENDA SETTING IN COMMITTEES

The point of departure for most discussions of committee agendas is the definition of formal committee jurisdictions laid out in the standing rules of the House and Senate. These rules have been described as the legislative equivalent of the formal "division of labor" that characterizes the allocation of specific tasks to workers in private firms. Ratified by the parent chamber at the beginning of each congress, the rules identify the general topics, specific statutes, and particular agencies to which a committee's legislative actions might be addressed. When legislation is formally introduced, such guidelines govern its referral to committee and form the basis for resolving disputes should a committee attempt to take up an issue beyond its traditional jurisdictional boundaries.

Important though such institutional arrangements are to the shape of committee agendas, however, they are not determinative. Two points bear emphasis. The first follows from David C. King's recent work on committee jurisdiction and institutional change which argues that committee jurisdictions are not simply static institutional facts, subject to alteration only during extraordinary moments of procedural reform (such as the 1946 Legislative Reorganization Act). Rather, there are "statutory" and "common law" dimensions of committee jurisdictions. The former refers to the specific issues delegated to a committee, issues that are codified in the House rules; this is what students of legislative institutions normally have in mind when they speak of committee jurisdictions. An equally important but largely ignored dimension of a committee's legislative domain is its common law jurisdiction—the set of issues it comes to routinely handle not as a result of some formal delegation of authority, but as a result of entrepreneurial activity on the part of committee members responding to new issues emerging in a changing political environment. Statutory jurisdictions, in turn, are largely codifications of the cumulative changes in committee common law jurisdictions. According to this view, then, committee jurisdictions are best thought of not solely as institutional constraints on the agenda decisions of committee actors, but as products of those decisions, at least in part. At the same time, the practice of referring large or complex bills to more than one committee in the House has grown in recent years. This practice has diminished the monopoly committees formerly held over specific issues, thereby weakening the extent to which statutory jurisdictions delimit a committee's theater of operations.

To emphasize the discretionary nature of committee jurisdiction in the long run, however, is not to suggest that jurisdictional definitions do not roughly circumscribe the range of topics with which a panel might deal at any given moment. Such boundaries remain particularly important for understanding what issues a committee will not oversee, what bills it cannot legitimately take up. But within somewhat fluid boundaries, it remains a matter for the collective choice of legislators which among the dozens of particular problems or issues competing for agenda space will ultimately get addressed. This point lies at the heart of the distinction, first advanced by Walker (1977) in his study of Senate agendas, between fixed and discretionary agenda items. The fixed, or nondiscretionary, agenda is a set of concerns a committee (within its statutory jurisdiction) takes up that is so clearly determined by procedural requirements and the expectations of interested outsiders that there is little room to accommodate the agenda preferences of determined members. By dint of say, budgetary cycles, the option of neglecting some issues is so burdened with costs to the committees and their members that action is forced upon them. At the same time, the judgment as against the requirement that committees set legislative priorities within their policy domains is increasingly at issue. Thus, several generations of textbooks have emphasized the proposal power of committees or, more recently, of congressional subcommittees—that is, their ability to set and control the legislative agenda repeatedly, regardless of strict formal sanction or authority. How does this happen? What drives the decisions that are made in this discretionary area? Why do committees decide to take up some issues and not others?

Committee Leaders and the Discretionary Agenda

Most scholarly studies of discretionary agenda-setting have focused on the behavior of committee chairs. The agenda powers of these individuals are substantial indeed. They enjoy formal authority to hold hearings and schedule markups of legislation from which derives an ability both to initiate and to block consideration of particular matters that might be referred to their panel. Equally important is the chair's authority to hire, fire, and thereby control, the committee's professional staff. Even if particular members have a strong desire to push issues on or off the committee agenda, to do so requires the commitment of substantial time and energy and the development of policy-specific expertise. In the contemporary Congress, such ambitions are limited by the organizational capacity of what analysts Robert Salisbury and Kenneth Shepsle call the individual member's "enterprise"—the office, staff, and other resources upon which the member can draw. Committee chairs, by contrast, command large staffs that allow them to develop the political and technical intelligence to engage in the labor-intensive politics of agenda setting.

Since the congressional reforms of the 1970s, however, the procedural authority to schedule meetings and call witnesses, the right to receive and act on bills within one's jurisdiction, and the right to at least a modest professional staff have devolved to the subcommittee chairs as well. The potential for agenda-setting activity is thus more widely distributed among senior members of the committee majority. Such developments have led some to worry that the simultaneous expansion and fragmentation of the power over committee agendas has increased the opportunities for interest groups to force their way into committee deliberations and has diminished the capacity of Congress to develop coherent and timely responses to public problems.

While research supports the view that committee agenda development turns heavily on the entrepreneurial and obstructionist behavior of formal leaders, however, systematic attempts to explain that behavior are relatively few. David E. Price, who conducted the most comprehensive work in this area, found that the legislative agendas of Senate committees were driven in large part by the political interests and ambitions of the committee chairs—that the understanding of agenda formation required attention to the "creative and purposive character of 'policy entrepreneurship'" (1972; p. 292). For instance, the decisions by Senate Commerce Committee chair Warren Magnuson (D.-Wash.) to markup consumer protection and cigarette labeling bills in the 1960s reflected his desire, first, to improve his visibility as a consumer-minded legislator at a time when he anticipated a strong electoral challenge, and second, to protect his committee's jurisdiction and thus his political reputation within the chamber.

More generally, Price suggests that the pursuit of expansive or aggressive agenda strategies (or relatively reactive ones) in Senate committees is related to four characteristics of activist committee members: (1) ideology, or the extent to which a member believes in the potential of federal governmental action to address social ills; (2) legislative orientation, or the extent to which the member feels comfortable with a high level of activism and public visibility; (3) the member's ties to electoral constituencies or interest groups with a stake in committee agenda change; and (4) the skills, expertise, and experience of members institutionally situated to push matters onto or keep matters off of the committee agenda. Such themes are echoed in the conservative inclinations of House Education and Labor Committee chair Graham Barden (D.-N.C.) in the 1960s, which predisposed him to block or delay President Lyndon Johnson's initiatives on minimum wage and federal aid to education, while Barden's liberal successor, Adam Clayton Powell (D.-N.Y.), expanded the committee staff and pushed a number of liberal initiatives onto the committee's agenda, even as he blocked others that he found insufficiently attentive to the needs of his constituents (Fenno 1973, pp. 128–131).

If the interests and prerogatives of committee leaders figure prominently in the agenda-setting process, however, various research stresses the constraints on committee leaders' discretion imposed by the agenda preferences of the committee majority. This general observation lies at the heart of Richard Fenno's attention to the patterns of member goals on different committees. Indeed, Fenno points out that Powell's obstructionist tactics with respect to important labor and antipoverty bills in the mid-1960s were so at odds with the policy preferences of the committee majority that the committee stripped him of several prerogatives and ultimately deposed him as chair—this in the prereform House, when committee chairs were considerably more powerful than they are today. Likewise, Fenno describes how the strong constituency orientations evident among members of the House Interior committee gave rise to the universalist decision rule that the committee would take up all member-sponsored, constituency-supported bills. Other works, in turn, reinforce the important point that, chair prerogatives to the contrary, agenda setting in committees is still a form of collective action. Committee leaders (like all leaders) must be, in part, followers; they must make decisions about the committee (or subcommittee) agenda with an eye to the interests and preferences of the committee majority.

The Impact of Environmental Factors

A final theme that runs through the research that has been conducted on agenda setting in committees is the importance of factors in their political environment. Legislative entrepreneurs have serious problems in developing rational agenda strategies in a complex political environment with numerous actors and points of access. The agenda process has been characterized by John Kingdon as consisting of three "streams"—those of problems, policies, and politics. Each stream exists relatively independent of the others, but their "coupling" greatly enhances the chance that an issue will achieve viability on the political agenda. A committee entrepreneur is one actor in the political stream, but he or she must act with an eye to what is going on in the other streams. At any given moment, members with the institutional position and resources to act may have several candidates for inclusion on the committee agenda. But they pursue some and not others on the basis of their expectations about whether factors in the other streams are likely to conspire in their favor. The expected payoff of entrepreneurial activity, in short, turns on the likelihood of an individual committee member's agenda-setting success, and such estimates depend on various factors in the political environment.

The impact of specific environmental factors on committee agenda decisions has been noted in research focused more squarely on congressional committees. Even as he elaborated the importance of member goals and purposive behavior, for instance, Fenno (1973) emphasized the importance of environmental "constraints" on committee action. Education and Labor Committee bills increased both in number and strength as committee liberals responded to the Great Society agenda of a Democratic president working with a large Democratic majority in the House. The agenda of the House Foreign Affairs Committee, likewise, was influenced heavily by proposals handed down from the executive branch, which themselves are often driven by the occurrence of an international crisis and/or some other crystallizing event. Similarly, the publicity garnered by consumer advocate Ralph Nader's automobile-safety campaign was instrumental in helping the Senate Commerce Committee move successfully into the area of traffic safety legislation. The number of new committee initiatives has been curtailed in the last decades of the twentieth century by the press of budget constraints and the more centralized congressional budget process. Similarly, changes in committee agendas are sometimes engineered by such environmental factors as party, chamber, or interest group pressures; although the specific conditions under which various external factors will matter have not been clearly determined.

In research that constitutes one of the most important works on committee agenda-setting, David E. Price suggested a more abstract conceptualization of a committee's political environment (1978). Specifically, he conceived of two dimensions along which a committee's political environment might vary, issue by issue. The first is the issue's political salience—the extent to which it is visible and important to some substantial segment of the public. The second is the level of conflict in the relevant policy community—the extent to which an issue evokes divisive and intractable cleavages among constituents, interest groups, or other actors with a stake in the outcome. Price argues that committee actors have especially strong incentives to push high-salience, low-conflict issues while avoiding low-salience, high-conflict issues. The former provide a good opportunity for publicity on an issue where there is a high probability of success; the latter are more likely to alienate as much as ingratiate, and will be less likely to reach a happy conclusion in any case. By pinning variation in the environment to the characteristics of particular issues, then, Price's salience-conflict model provides substantial leverage in answering questions about how rational committee actors choose to pursue some issues (within or near their jurisdiction) and not others. By mod-

ifying or extending Price's categories, in turn, subsequent scholars have improved our understanding of the way in which agenda attention varies according to the nature and definition of particular issues and the interests that they evoke.

PARTICIPATION IN CONGRESSIONAL COMMITTEES

In committees as in other legislative contexts, there are essentially two decisions that each member must make for every issue that comes before him or her: what position to take and how active to be. The former matter has been a preoccupation of both empirical and theoretical scholars, subsuming work on the determinants of committee voting and several related issues, such as committee integration, fragmentation, and coalition building. But as Richard L. Hall (1987; 1994) has shown, members' issue-by-issue participation decisions are especially important for understanding the politics of collective choice in congressional committees. The patterns of participation that arise from individual members' choices regarding their personal priorities are important in several specific ways. First, these patterns have a direct bearing on the representativeness of committee deliberations. Who participates at this crucial stage of the process can affect the terms of democratic debate. A second and related point is that members' participation decisions have a direct bearing on the distribution of influence within the committee. While the decision to commit one's time and legislative resources to a particular issue does not guarantee that a member's views will influence the collective outcome (some participants win, some ultimately lose), it tends to be a precondition for influence.

While seldom a central theme, the selective nature of members' participation in committee decisions has been noted by several generations of congressional scholars. Indeed, scattered evidence indicates that members' tendency to selectively participate in decisions holds true across committees of very different jurisdictions and across committees of both the Senate and the House. As early as the 1960s, for instance, Charles L. Clapp concluded that "from one third to one half of a committee's membership constitute the hard core that can be depended on in nearly every activity, other members injecting themselves when they are interested in the subject under discussion" (1963, p. 265). Such tendencies toward selective participation have only grown more striking as the size of the federal establishment and the work load of Congress have expanded and the number of congressional panels has multiplied.

Participation Norms in the Prereform Congress

In attempting to account for these patterns, congressional scholars have employed two types of behavioral theory. Much of the research prior to the 1970s drew on the sociology of small groups and emphasized the group norms that were learned by newcomers and that subsequently structured their behavior. One of the most important works of this genre was Richard Fenno's study of the House Appropriations Committee. Crucial to the functioning of the group, Fenno argued, was "a fairly consistent set of norms, widely agreed upon and widely followed by the members," along with "control mechanisms (i.e., socialization and sanctioning mechanisms) capable of maintaining reasonable conformity to norms" (1962, p. 310). Most of these norms dealt specifically with committee participation. For instance, members were expected to practice an ethic of "hard work" and "specialization"; that is, to concentrate on a narrow range of the committee's complex subject matter and master the details. A related norm was that newcomers were to endure a period of apprenticeship, during which they were to be seen more than heard by their senior colleagues. Likewise, a norm of reciprocity dictated that members not get involved in matters outside their own subcommittees, for example, by offering amendments or challenging subcommittee decisions during full committee markup.

By the time that Fenno produced his classic study of committees, however, evidence was growing that group norms were increasingly limited in their ability to explain member participation. While Fenno devoted some attention to the "participation-specialization norms" of House committees in his book *Congressmen in Committees,* for instance, the comparative nature of his research design highlighted the fact that Appropriations was somewhat unusual among committees in the behavioral weight attached to the norms of hard work, specialization, and apprenticeship. Other scholars subsequently argued that the institution was simply changing. The group norms that had governed member participation in the past were giving way.

Participation, Purpose, and Institutional Structure

With these traditional norms now considered all but dead, explaining member participation has become more difficult. If we cannot use group norms to understand members' participation decisions, how are they to be explained? Several scholars have emphasized the growing "decentralization" of the institution, suggesting that the increasingly widespread and differentiated subcommittee system determines participation in the contemporary Congress. Fenno's description of participation and specialization focused almost exclusively on the importance of subcommittees, as have other studies since. Recent research has adopted a different theoretical tack, however, one that emphasizes the interests and calculations of individual members as well as the organizational structure of the chamber. In particular, Hall (1987; 1994) takes issue with the heavy emphasis placed on an institutionalized division of labor, suggesting that subcommittee position is only one of several constraints that shape participation in committee, and he notes that that constraint is largely self-imposed. Building directly on the purposive side of Fenno's study, Hall argues that committee members invest their time, staff, and other legislative resources in such a way as to advance any of several goals or interests, such as serving one's constituency, making good public policy, and prosecuting the president's agenda. Even on a single committee or subcommittee, particular issues will arise that simultaneously evoke several of a member's goals while other issues may evoke none at all, with the level of participation affected accordingly. From the parent chamber's point of view, in turn, this is an efficient means of achieving policy-relevant information. As Keith Krehbiel has argued, the parent chamber has a strong interest in assigning members with expertise and interest in particular committees' jurisdictions. Such members become "low-cost specialists" for the chamber (1991).

At the same time, however, members are not equally endowed with the resources necessary to pursue their interests. Subcommittee membership and, more importantly, committee and subcommittee leadership positions do not impose responsibilities so much as they provide opportunities for and constraints on the participation of purposive individuals. More specifically, they (1) diminish barriers to entry into the negotiations over particular legislative issues; (2) provide greater access to staff and other resources, thereby subsidizing the time and information costs associated with participation; and (3) provide procedural advantages that increase the expectation that one's efforts will prove efficacious. According to this account, finally, the concept of legislative apprenticeship, that is, the expected reticent behavior of new members, takes a different cast. While no group pressures or sanctions may threaten the otherwise ambitious newcomer, he or she is less likely to have expertise and political experience in committee matters and less likely to have lines of communication with other relevant actors.

Applying this theory to the study of deliberations in House committees, Hall (1994) draws several conclusions. First, widespread nonparticipation is evident for most issues taken up in House committees, even within the more specialized and highly self-selected subcommittees, and the patterns of legislators' involvement are systematically related to the several issue-specific interests that members bring to their committee work. Even on a highly constituency-oriented committee such as House Agriculture, for instance, members' ideological commitments and personal policy interests often affect their legislative priorities; likewise, even on an ideologically charged "policy" committee such as Education and Labor, constituency interests prove important for understanding who participates and who abdicates on particular questions. Second, while the procedural prerogatives and informational resources associated with subcommittee membership are important, much of the structuring effect attributed to these institutionalized divisions by participant-observers is actually due to the higher level of interest that self-selected subcommittee members bring to

issues within their panels' jurisdictions. Third, the negative effect of freshman status on committee participation is a robust behavioral regularity, the demise of apprenticeship as a prescriptive norm notwithstanding. In the contemporary Congress, it still takes considerable time before a newcomer is able to match his or her senior colleagues in legislative output.

Studies conducted on Senate committees, in turn, emphasize these same themes. (Evans 1991a,b; Hall 1989; Sinclair 1989). In the Senate as in the House, assignment to the panel of jurisdiction diminishes the costs of serious participation on an issue, but the self-selective nature of Senate assignments also produces subcommittees composed of "interest outliers," legislators actively interested in or determined to shape the subcommittee's actions. In both the House and Senate, subcommittee membership and leadership position provide only a point of departure for understanding the patterns of participation that drive committee decision-making. Unlike more formal organizations, the legislative labors of Congress are not explicitly divided and assigned; rather, they arise from the largely discretionary decisions of individual members about how to spend their time and allocate their staff.

Committee Participants and the Influence of Other Institutional Actors

While systematic studies of participation in committee decision-making remain relatively rare, research suggests that the study of participation may be important to several larger questions regarding the influence that other institutional actors have on committee decision-making. For instance, one of the principal themes of David Price's study of Senate committees (1972) is that the power of Congress vis-à-vis the executive turns directly on the incentives, resources, and opportunities that shape committee activism. Writing at a time when other scholars were lamenting the growth of an "imperial presidency," Price suggested that the role of Congress in policy innovation and modification could be enhanced by increasing committee staff capacity and expanding the incentives for members to adopt more active legislative roles.

Looking at the same behavior from a different angle, however, other scholars have emphasized the strategies that executive-branch actors adopt in order to enlist committee members as their legislative agents. For instance, R. Douglas Arnold (1979) found that the coalition-building strategies of agency bureaucrats are developed with an eye to mobilizing committee members sympathetic to the agency's programs; specifically, Arnold found that program bureaucrats allocate district and state benefits in such a way as to give important committee actors a strong stake in their programs, thereby encouraging them to serve as coalition leaders on the program's behalf. In a similar vein, the Reagan White House sought out sympathetic members on the relevant House committees to "carry water for the administration," often in the form of proposing administration substitutes or amendments or engaging in dilatory action during committee markup of a particular bill. Sympathy with the administration's agenda, as a result, turned out to be an important predictor of Republican participation in committee decision-making (Hall, 1987).

Finally, there is some evidence that the legislative priorities of individual committee members are an important focus of interest group strategists as well. Hall and Wayman (1990) found that the principal purpose of political action committee (PAC) allocation strategies is not so much to win over converts to the group's position nor affect the outcomes of congressional campaigns. Rather, group contributions are intended to mobilize individual members who sit on the committees important to the group's interests and who are already predisposed to support the group's point of view. In short, committee deliberations often may be distorted in important ways not only by the self-selection process that tends to govern committee assignments, but by the selective participation of individual members in post-assignment decision-making.

COALITION BUILDING IN COMMITTEES

Coalition Leaders and Informal Bargaining

In general, the preferences and strategic calculations of committee leaders have a major impact on what issues will become the focus of a competition for votes, how those issues will be framed, and hence the shape of the alignments within committee that might ultimately appear. As one might infer from the previous two sections, the building of a majority coalition in a committee typically takes shape around a small subset of individual actors who reveal the most intense interest in the particular matter at hand. On routine or otherwise minor bills, the central players almost always include the subcommittee chairs and ranking members; for more salient issues, such responsibilities usually extend to their full committee counterparts as well. For instance, it is not unusual for almost all of the preferences expressed by formal leaders and most of the preferences expressed by informal entrepreneurs to be incorporated into the committee's final bill.

Besides the principal coalition leaders, other members variously perceive that they have an interest at stake in a bill that comes before the committee and thus enter the informal bargaining game. While subcommittee leaders are central to the bargaining process, Barry Rundquist and Gerald Strom also found that about half of the preferences expressed by backbenchers during committee hearings are ultimately incorporated in the final reports. Since the 1970s, in fact, the members of the reporting subcommittees have typically formed the core of the winning coalitions. For instance, one study of House committees found that more than 80 percent of the members who played a major role in bargaining over the original drafts of committee bills were members of the reporting subcommittee. The same study found that of the issues that became the subject of a contested committee roll call, a majority of the reporting subcommittee was on the losing side in only one out of six. In short, when divisions at the subcommittee level appear, those divisions tend to structure the alignments at the committee stage.

Of course, many important issues are resolved by means of a formal roll call in full committee. But even in these cases, it is easy to exaggerate the majoritarian nature of the process. Unlike either chamber floor, House and Senate committees permit members to vote in absentia; that is, individual members can designate a colleague to cast their proxy for any or all matters that might come to a vote during a particular committee markup. In theory, members might inform themselves in advance about the specific issues likely to come up during markup and give specific voting instructions to the colleague holding their proxy. In practice, however, such instructions are seldom given; indeed, typically a member who relinquishes his proxy to a committee colleague is largely indifferent with respect to the matter at hand, and thus has little sense of what his preferences are over the various alternative proposals that might be considered. Neither is there strong evidence that a member always chooses a colleague to cast his proxy according to whether the colleague's general policy views are similar to his; regardless of a member's ideology, seniority, or region, the clear tendency is for members to give uninstructed proxies to the committee or, more often, to the subcommittee leaders of the member's party. Indeed, it is not uncommon for some decisions to be won by a "majority" of one or two members who, endowed with their colleagues' proxies, outvote a more numerous group of members who are present and voting. Still, it remains something of a puzzle how it is that a minority subset of a committee is able to dominate committee decisions when any disgruntled individual can, in open committee markup, propose an alternative that a majority of members might prefer.

Committee Coalition-building in a Multistage Process

Such tendencies to the contrary, none of this is to suggest that coalition leaders and other interested members in the committee bargaining process are uninhibited in their ability to create informal majorities and thus dominate policy decisions within their panel's jurisdiction. While on routine issues, most members of the committee may abdicate (or trade away) much of their legislative authority, even on these issues coalition leaders exercise their own enhanced authority within the boundaries of what the silent committee majority will tolerate. On more salient matters, in turn, the preferences of the committee majority are likely to be even more constraining. Moreover, this principle holds true as individual entrepreneurs attempt to build support for a bill in which actors beyond the committee are likely to be interested. Indeed, one of the most important things one

must understand about committee coalition-building has to do with the place it holds in a multistage, sequential process. In the enterprise of bargaining and compromise necessary to build majority support, as in the business of developing an agenda, committee leaders must operate with an eye to the reactions that other actors will have to the committee's action at subsequent points in the policy process.

Again, this lesson is evident from what remain the best books on committee decision-making in Congress. Beginning with *The Power of the Purse,* Fenno emphasized the importance of other institutional actors in shaping the coalitional patterns within committee. The principal reference group for House Appropriations was the parent chamber. In fact, the committee exhibited a remarkable commonality of purpose or "integration," in part because of a deep-seated consensus regarding the committee's role as the legislature's guardian of the federal treasury. Hence, partisan cleavages were typically submerged during Appropriations deliberations during the period of Fenno's study, with the consequence that committee recommendations enjoyed high levels of floor success.

Different forces in the political environment of tax, trade, and social security policies, on the other hand, produce cleavages within the Committee on Ways and Means that are less unidimensional. While the policy proposals that structure decision-making on this committee typically come from the executive branch, the principal issues within the committee's jurisdiction are matters on which there are fundamental party disagreements. For both committees, however, the salient nature of their jurisdictions provide a strong incentive to build coalitions within committee that reflect the larger concerns of the House. Typically this has required that the committee push as much as possible toward a consensus position (or at least a larger than minimal winning coalition), so that the committee's bills would not be defeated on the floor. For instance, John Manley found that both the consensual leadership style of Ways and Means Chair Wilbur Mills and the committee's general tendency to seek bipartisan majorities were driven in large part by the fact that the major issues within the committee's jurisdiction were important to most committee nonmembers. This pattern of "restrained" or "moderate" partisanship in dealing with potentially divisive issues has, with brief but important lapses, characterized Ways and Means deliberations in the post-Mills era as well (Strahan; Ward).

The theme of environmental influences on committee coalition-building is extended and generalized in Fenno's *Congressmen in Committees*. Fenno characterizes the coalitional patterns that form in different committees according to the particular institutional actors that are prominent in their political environment and thus stand to challenge the committee's work at subsequent stages. He described four distinct patterns of coalition leadership in House and Senate committees: those that tend to be House-led, executive-led, clientele-led, or party-led. Fenno's comparative committee focus, that is, revealed that not all committees exhibit the broad scope/high salience jurisdiction of the appropriations or tax committees. Other committees are subjected to the attentions and pressures of very different actors. In the case of Education and Labor, for instance, Fenno concludes that "the parties have provided a rubric under which all other environmental elements have organized to influence the committee" (p. 32), while concern with the parent chamber is submerged. Likewise, Fenno found that committees such as Interior and Post Office dealt with few issues that evoked partisan divisions or fell high on the list of administration priorities. Instead, most members were attracted to these committees because of their jurisdictions' relevance to district constituencies. On such committees, then, policy coalitions tended to be driven by the particular clientele groups (mining interests or forestry interests, postal workers or federal employees) that stood to benefit from sympathetic committee action and stood to help or harm the reelection chances of committee members.

Subsequent systematic analyses of voting alignments in committees have generally reinforced the value of Fenno's categories and, more generally, the importance of the observation that committees differ in the nature of the issues they address and hence in the political alignments they evoke. An analysis of House committees over an eight-year period concluded that committees can be categorized according to the influences that structure the voting patterns in committee roll calls (Parker and Parker, 1985; see also Unekis and Rieselbach). Party-line and ideologically polarized voting appears most prominently in committees such as Budget and Commerce. The influence of the administration can be detected in the voting patterns of Appropriations and Foreign Affairs. The influence of constituencies or clients appear prominent in the alignments observed on committees such as Agriculture and Banking, Finance, and Urban Affairs. More generally, research by Daniel Ward (1990) has uncovered a clear trade-off between the frequency with which a committee deals with clientele-centered programs and the loyalty that members display to their party in committee voting decisions.

However, such analysis has also given rise to three additional generalizations about the nature of committee voting alignments. First, if political parties in the United States Congress do not have the organizational force that they do in most parliamentary systems, party loyalties and the ideological affinities that underlie them are nonetheless important for understanding voting behavior across committees of very different types. Fenno's observation about the relative importance of party divisions on Ways and Means and Education and Labor, in short, reflect differences of degree, not of kind. For every committee in the House, there is evidence of strong party alignments. Ward's longitudinal analysis, in turn, shows that partisan defections in committee roll calls have declined over the last two decades, regardless of the committee one studies and despite the conventional wisdom that American politics is going through a period of party dissolution. In sum, party is the point of departure for coalition building in congressional committees, even if other environmental actors matter, more or less, in the politics of different committees.

Second, if all panels are to some degree "party-led," all panels are to some degree "chamber-led" as well. This is especially true in the Senate, where committees are less autonomous and floor decision-making is less constrained. But whatever the nature and size of the successful coalitions that form in House and Senate committees, their bills are subject to review, amendment, and perhaps rejection on the chamber floor. While committees do have certain procedural devices by which they can protect their bills at subsequent stages, these devices are not insurmountable (Krehbiel, 1991). In fact, the incidence of successful amendment to committee bills has grown over the last two decades, suggesting that coalition leaders in committee who fail to anticipate the reactions of interested nonmembers do so at some risk. For instance, even a relatively well-integrated, clientele-led committee such as House Agriculture has given favorable treatment to federal nutrition programs (which benefit urban more than rural districts) in an effort to preempt opposition to omnibus farm legislation on the floor (Ferejohn, 1986).

Third, the nature of the cleavages that emerge on particular committees varies with the issue and thus varies in the aggregate as committee agendas change over time. If the House and Senate committees on the interior were largely clientele-led at the time of Fenno's study, the growing importance of environmental issues and the proliferation of public interest lobbies has changed the array of forces to which these panels must respond; it has also changed the policy motives of the members attracted to these panels, with more individuals harboring strong environmentalist beliefs seeking assignment. Likewise, the available research suggests that constituency and client considerations are increasingly prominent in the coalitional patterns of the House and Senate appropriations committees, where exponents of fiscal restraint have given way to claimants for budgetary resources. Still, the

general lesson remains the same: powerful though committee actors tend to be, they operate in a complex political environment in which other actors have both the opportunities and resources to affect what committees do. Successful coalition-building on committee, then, must reflect the larger forces at work in the relevant policy communities.

CONCLUSION

In 1885 Woodrow Wilson observed that the principal purpose of Congress was not to deliberate but to ratify the conclusions of its committees as rapidly as possible (Wilson, 1981 [1885]). While Wilson is often quoted, his simple generalization was probably not true at the time that he wrote it, and it is certainly not true now. The legislative process in Congress *is* committee-centered; one cannot fully understand the factors that shape the congressional agenda and the policies that ultimately get enacted without examining the purposes and strategies of committee participants. But if committee actors often drive the legislative action, they rarely act with impunity. Their actions are subject to a number of institutional constraints and are influenced by a number of important institutional actors, among them the parent chamber, the president and the executive agencies, political parties, and a diverse range of clientele and constituency interests.

BIBLIOGRAPHY

Valuable research on decision making in congressional committees dates back to the late nineteenth century. Of special historical significance is the treatment of committees by Professor (later to become President) WOODROW WILSON in *Congressional Government* (Baltimore, 1981 [1885]). The most important and comprehensive study of committee decision-making in the twentieth century, however, is RICHARD F. FENNO, JR., *Congressmen in Committees* (Boston, 1973), a classic book that has been updated and extended by STEVEN S. SMITH

and CHRISTOPHER J. DEERING, *Committees in Congress* (Washington, D.C., 1984).

On the topics of committee agenda-setting and jurisdictions, book-length treatments include DAVID E. PRICE, *Who Makes the Laws? Creativity and Power in Senate Committees* (Cambridge, Mass., 1972) and DAVID C. KING, *Border Wars: Committee Jurisdictions and Institutional Change in Congress,* forthcoming. On the topics of participation and specialization in committees, see RICHARD L. HALL, *Participation in Congress* (New Haven, Conn., 1994); KEITH

KREHBIEL, *Information and Legislative Organization* (Ann Arbor, Mich., 1991); and the Price work listed above. The most comprehensive works on committee leaders, coalitions, and voting alignments are C. LAWRENCE EVANS, *Leadership in Senate Committees* (Ann Arbor, Mich., 1991); GLENN R. PARKER and SUZANNE L. PARKER, *Factions in House Committees* (Knoxville, Tenn., 1985); and JOSEPH K. UNEKIS and LEROY N. RIESELBACH, *Congressional Committee Politics: Continuity and Change* (Chicago, 1984).

Other important works on these and other topics related to committee decision-making include R. DOUGLAS ARNOLD, *Congress and the Bureaucracy: A Theory of Influence* (New Haven, Conn., 1979); R. DOUGLAS ARNOLD, *The Logic of Congressional Action* (New Haven, Conn., 1990); HERBERT ASHER, "The Changing Status of the Freshman Representative," in NORMAN J. ORNSTEIN, ed., *Congress and Change: Evolution and Reform* (New York, 1975); DAVID P. BARON and JOHN A. FEREJOHN, "Bargaining in Legislatures," *American Political Science Review* 83 (December 1989); DAVID W. BRADY, *Critical Elections and Congressional Policy Making* (Stanford, Calif., 1988); CHARLES L. CLAPP, *The Congressman: His Work as He Sees It* (Westport, Conn., 1963); MELISSA P. COLLIE and JOSEPH COOPER, "Multiple Referral and the 'New' Committee System in the House of Representatives," in LAWRENCE C. DODD and BRUCE I. OPPENHEIMER, eds., *Congress Reconsidered,* 4th ed. (Washington, D.C., 1989); ROGER H. DAVIDSON, "Subcommittee Government: New Channels for Policymaking," in THOMAS E. MANN and NORMAN ORNSTEIN, eds., *The New Congress* (Washington, D.C., 1981); and C. LAWRENCE EVANS, "Participation and Policy Making in Senate Committees," *Political Science Quarterly* 106 (Fall 1991).

Still other important works on committee decision-making include two other classics by RICHARD F. FENNO, JR., "The House Appropriations Committee as a Political System," *American Political Science Review* 56 (June 1962), and *The Power of the Purse: Appropriations Politics in Congress* (Boston, 1966); JOHN FEREJOHN, "Logrolling in an Institutional Context: A Case Study of Food Stamp Legislation," in GERALD C. WRIGHT, LEROY N. RIESELBACH, and LAWRENCE C. DODD, eds., *Congress and Policy Change* (Boston, 1986); MORRIS P. FIORINA, "Universalism, Reciprocity, and Distributive Policy Making in Majority Rule Institutions," in *Research in Public Policy Analysis and Management,* vol. 1 (Greenwich, Conn., 1981); RICHARD L. HALL, "Participation and Purpose in Committee Decision Making," *American Political Science Review* 81 (March 1987); RICHARD L. HALL, "Participation, Abdication, and Representation in Congressional Committees," in LAWRENCE C. DODD and BRUCE I. OPPENHEIMER, eds., *Congress Reconsidered,* 5th ed. (Washington, D.C., 1993); RICHARD L. HALL and C. LAWRENCE EVANS, "The Power of Subcommittees," *Journal of Politics* 52 (May 1990); RICHARD L. HALL and FRANK W. WAYMAN, "Buying Time: Moneyed Interests and the Mobilization of Bias in Congressional Committees," *American Political Science Review* 84 (September 1990); BARBARA HINCKLEY, "Policy Content, Committee Membership, and Behavior," *American Journal of Political Science* 19 (1975); MICHAEL J. MALBIN, *Unelected Representatives: Congressional Staff and the Future of Representative Government* (New York, 1980); JOHN F. MANLEY, *The Politics of Finance: The House Committee on Ways and Means* (Boston, 1970); DONALD R. MATTHEWS, *U.S. Senators and Their World* (New York, 1960); and DAVID MAYHEW, *Congress: The Electoral Connection* (New Haven, Conn., 1974).

See also LYNETTE P. PERKINS, "Influences of Members' Goals on Their Committee Behavior: The U.S. House Judiciary Committee," *Legislative Studies Quarterly* 5 (August 1980); DAVID E. PRICE, "Policy Making in Congressional Committees: The Impact of 'Environmental' Factors," *American Political Science Review* 72 (June 1978); CATHERINE E. RUDDER, "Fiscal Responsibility, Fairness, and the Revenue Committees," in LAWRENCE C. DODD and BRUCE I. OPPENHEIMER, eds., *Congress Reconsidered,* 4th ed. (Washington, D.C., 1989); BARRY S. RUNDQUIST and GERALD S. STROM, "Bill Construction in Legislative Committees: A Study of the U.S. House," *Legislative Studies Quarterly* 12 (February 1987); ROBERT H. SALISBURY and KENNETH A. SHEPSLE, "U.S. Congressman as Enterprise," *Legislative Studies Quarterly* 6 (November 1981); KENNETH A. SHEPSLE, *The Giant Jigsaw Puzzle: Democratic Committee Assignments in the Modern House* (Chicago, 1978); BARBARA

SINCLAIR, *The Transformation of the U.S. Senate* (Baltimore, 1989); STEVEN S. SMITH and CHRISTOPHER J. DEERING, *Committees in Congress,* 2d ed. (Washington, D.C., 1990); RANDALL STRAHAN, *New Ways and Means* (Chapel Hill, N.C., 1990); DANIEL S. WARD, "Explaining the Decline in Partisan Defection in House Committees," paper presented at the annual meeting of the Midwest Political Science Association (1990); BARRY R. WEINGAST, "A Rational Choice Perspective on Congressional Norms," *American Journal of Political Science* 23 (May 1979); and BARRY R. WEINGAST and WILLIAM J. MARSHALL, "The Industrial Organization of Congress; or, Why Legislatures, like Firms, Are Not Organized as Markets," *Journal of Political Economy* 96 (February 1988).

SEE ALSO Congress, Sectionalism, and Public-Policy Formation Since 1870; The Congressional Committee System; Legislative Norms; AND Legislatures and Bureaucracy.

THE APPROPRIATIONS COMMITTEES

Charles Stewart III

This power over the purse may, in fact, be regarded as the most complete and effectual weapon with which any constitution can arm the immediate representatives of the people, for obtaining a redress of every grievance, and for carrying into effect every just and salutary measure. (James Madison, *The Federalist,* no. 58)

HOW THESE COMMITTEES FUNCTION

The "power over the purse" has often been called the fundamental legislative power, the key to the legislative control of the executive. Congress has many instruments through which to control the behavior of the president and the executive branch, but the constitutional provision that "no money shall be drawn from the Treasury, but in consequence of appropriation made by law" often provides it with the most direct route from legislative will to executive action.

The annual appropriations passed by Congress (and signed into law by the president) obviously affect how authorizing legislation will be carried out; a new federal agency in pursuit of lofty goals will be a paper tiger if it receives a paltry appropriation. Less obviously, the requirement that federal agencies annually justify their past behavior and future plans to agents of the two chambers of Congress—its appropriations committees—provides a degree of scrutiny over programs unmatched on a regular basis elsewhere in the legislative process.

Finally, the power of the purse serves as the ultimate legislative check against the usurpation of executive power. Through provisos to appropriations bills, such as the "Hyde amendment" and the "Boland amendment," majorities in the House and the Senate may be able to get the president to capitulate to their legislative demands when the normal legislative route is blocked through threat of the presidential veto.

As with other important matters in Congress, the rank-and-file of the two chambers do not administer this most basic of legislative powers directly. Instead, a division-of-labor system in Congress assigns much of the routine implementation of the power of the purse to two appropriations committees, one in each chamber. Given the committees' jurisdictions, it is not surprising that they have been centers of congressional power ever since they were created in the 1860s. The purpose of this article is to examine the behavior of these committees in light of the centrality of the power of the purse to legislative life.

The prominence of the House and Senate appropriations committees in exercising the power of the purse, especially the House committee, can deceive us into focusing too much attention on the committees themselves. The committees are charged with overseeing on a continuing basis federal spending and the appropriations process. Still, the appropriations committees are not the only mechanisms the two houses have erected to oversee federal spending. And, since the creation of the two committees, their powers have waxed and waned with the unfolding of political events. Hence, one focus of this essay will be on understanding the control function the committees perform in light of the other mechanisms Congress has erected to control appropriations, and in light of the events that have led to the expansion and contraction of the committees' authority over the past century.

Because the appropriations committees serve as the most conspicuous symbols of appropriations control, they have frequently been the targets of attack from supporters of a larger role for the federal government in general and from supporters of expanded spending for particular federal projects. The House created its Appropriations Committee to critically evaluate the spending designs of agencies and constituents. But, in turn, majorities of Congress prefer that some programs be received more skeptically than others. This desire on the part of congressional majorities to see some types of federal spending be more closely scrutinized than others has resulted in some spending being exempt from the jurisdiction of the appropriations committees. Most of the money that is permanently authorized for expenditure is not overseen by the two appropriations committees. This type of spending includes the largest appropriations account, the federal old-age and survivors insurance program (Social Security), which is overseen by the two taxing committees. Spending for other significant federal programs also falls outside the purview of the appropriations committees.

HOW MONEY IS ALLOCATED

Precise estimates vary, but only about half of federal spending is subject to formal annual scrutiny by the appropriations committees, the remainder being permanently authorized. This type of spending is sometimes called "uncontrollable spending," since it is not controlled through the normal annual appropriations process. Some budgetary scholars have argued that "uncontrollable spending" is a misnomer, since all spending is ultimately subject to legislative review of some sort—Congress could presumably "control" spending in areas such as Social Security, veterans benefits, and Medicare if it wanted to. And, even permanently authorized programs are usually administered through agencies that receive annual appropriations. The old age and survivors insurance program is administered through the Social Security Administration, which received an appropriation of $47 million in fiscal year 1991, for instance.

Still, the exclusion of certain politically important programs from the annual appropriations process has two implications. First, the implementation of these programs is given

wider berth, since they are not subject to annual scrutiny via appropriations hearings.

Second, these programs are harder to cut, since any delay in legislation to cut spending for one of these programs means that spending continues as it has in the past. The 1974 Budget Act was designed in part to address this problem with permanent spending authorizations and entitlements. It was only in the budget battles of 1981 that the Budget Act actually lived up to its advance billing in this regard. Still, the fact that congressional reformers had to find a way to bring entitlements under some sort of annual discipline—and have had such a difficult time actually effecting this discipline—speaks to the ability of the designers of some spending programs to insulate them from shifting political winds.

"Permanent," "backdoor," or "uncontrollable spending" contrasts with spending for programs contained in the annual appropriations bills. Because appropriations bills are "must pass" pieces of legislation, items considered within them are subject to political compromise. That legislation to continue spending in "uncontrollable" areas need not pass each year diminishes the opportunities to change spending directions in light of shifting political circumstances.

The fact that Congress has created an abundance of ways to circumvent the annual spending review by the appropriations process—and most practically by the appropriations committees—is another clue that alerts us to the dangers of considering the functions of the appropriations committees in isolation from other spending control mechanisms. The appropriations committees may be the most important congressional mechanisms for the control of federal spending, but they are not the only mechanisms, nor are they impenetrable.

The remainder of this essay proceeds as follows. First, we discuss what it means for Congress to "control" spending and some of the ways Congress could choose to exert that control. Second, we discuss the historical development of the House and Senate appropriations committees in light of the congressional desire to exert control over federal appropriations. Third, we examine in more detail the behavior of the two appropriations committees in the post–World War II era, paying particular attention to changes in the committees following the passage of the 1974 Congressional Budget and Impoundment Control Act (CBICA).

CONGRESSIONAL CONTROL OVER FEDERAL SPENDING

The appropriations committees exist ultimately to allow members of the House and Senate to control federal spending. Control over federal spending takes two forms: *fiscal* control and *policy* control. Fiscal control is concerned with keeping spending totals within acceptable aggregate limits. Before the 1974 Budget Act, the taxing and spending committees were responsible for affecting fiscal control within Congress. A major purpose of the 1974 Budget Act was to transform the setting of fiscal policy so that its major constituents, spending and taxing, could be considered simultaneously rather than sequentially in the traditional committees. Yet, it remains controversial whether the appropriations committees have, in fact, lost the lion's share of their fiscal policy power as a consequence of the budget act.

Policy control refers to the use of the power of the purse to achieve more particular substantive goals. It is a more subtle form of control whose significance is often overlooked by academicians, journalists, and politicians. Given a set fiscal policy, different specific policy aims can be met through the precise channeling of funds, as money is directed to some objects and away from others. The budget for the Federal Trade Commission (FTC) could be changed, for instance, to allocate more money to enforce garment labeling regulations and to withhold funds to process antitrust enforcement actions. The appropriations committees, by virtue of their agenda control, have a tremendous say in these sort of allocational decisions, and thus they may have as much say over the implementation of federal programs as the legislative committees that oversee the creation of federal programs and their reauthorization.

Fiscal Appropriations Control

Whenever members of Congress (MCs) talk about the role of the appropriations commit-

tees, the idea that they help Congress control spending is always prominent. Control, in this context, frequently is defined as reducing spending. In *Power of the Purse,* Richard Fenno's classic study of the House Appropriations Committee (HAC), the role of the HAC in keeping down spending was expressed this way:

> The workaday jargon of the Committee is replete with negative verbs, undesirable objects of attention, and effective instruments of action. Agency budgets are said to be filled with "fat," "padding," "grease," "pork," "oleaginous substance," "water," "oil," "cushions," "avoirdupois," "waste tissue," and "soft spots." The action verbs most commonly used are "cut," "carve," "slice," "prune," "whittle," "squeeze," "wring," "trim," "lop off," "chop," "slash," "pare," "shave," "fry," and "whack." According to their regional backgrounds, members speak of "doing a little woodshedding," "picking the sour apples out of the barrel," "doing some selective logging," or "thinning out the herd." The tools of the trade are appropriately referred to as "knife," "blade," "meat axe," "scalpel," "meat cleaver," "hatchet," "shears," "wringer," and "fine-tooth comb." Members are hailed by their fellows as being "pretty sharp with the knife." Agencies may "have the meat axe thrown at them." Executives are urged to put their agencies "on a fat boy's diet." Budgets are praised when they are "cut to the bone." And members agree that "you can always get a little more fat out of a piece of pork if you fry it a little longer and a little harder."

This orientation toward spending requests is a conscious part of both the HAC's design and the recruitment of new committee members. The HAC is an "exclusive" committee, meaning that its members are forbidden from serving on any other House committee. (The only exception is the delegation of HAC members who also serve terms on the House Budget Committee.) Thus, the HAC's members are not tempted to defend program spending based on their ties to agencies through other committee memberships. Second, members recruited to the HAC are also "responsible legislators." Members are frequently appointed to help maintain regional and ideological balance between their party contingents and the committee. Congressional neophytes are rarely appointed to the HAC; thus, party leaders usually can predict the behavior of even new committee members.

Before the wave of committee reform that swept the House in the 1960s and 1970s, the process of assigning committee members to subcommittees was also a mechanism that tended to undermine the "interest-leniency-sympathy" syndrome. In the years when Clarence Cannon (D.-Mo.) and his sidekick John Taber (N.Y.) ran the committee, they regularly assigned subcommittee members in ways that undercut the relationship between a member's constituency interests and his work on the committee. (Cannon served as the ranking Democrat on the HAC, either as its chair or a ranking minority member, from 1941 to 1964. Taber was the top-ranked Republican from 1933 to 1962.)

The story Fenno used to illustrate this pattern was the "socialization of Fred Santangelo." Santangelo (D.-N.Y.), who represented East Harlem, entered the HAC in 1958. Because of his urban background, he was promptly appointed to the subcommittee on agriculture. But, by being a responsible member of the subcommittee—he became an expert on food stamps, which the subcommittee oversaw—Santangelo was first given a second unimportant appointment, followed by a subcommittee appointment to the more important Labor-HEW subcommittee. As the socialization of Santangelo suggests, Cannon and Taber were cognizant of their followers' constituency interests when they made committee assignments—Santangelo eventually received an appointment to his liking. But, before then, he had to be socialized to the committee's ethos and prove himself reliable.

Following the subcommittee reforms of the 1970s, this mechanism for undercutting the interest-leniency-sympathy syndrome was vitiated, since the locus of the subcommittee assignment process migrated from the committee chair and the ranking minority member to the committee members themselves. Changes in how subcommittee members were assigned to House committees were prefigured in the HAC. When George Mahon (D.-Tex.) became HAC chair in 1965, he instituted a variant of the Johnson Rule, in which all Democrats were guaranteed at least one good subcommittee assignment. The subcommittee reforms of 1974 gave committee members throughout the House the right to choose subcommittee assignments in order of their committee seniority and then vested them with seniority rights in the subcommittee assignments that they hold.

The results of these changes have been mixed. On the one hand, committee members have continued to be more conservative than the rest of the House. Hence, the subcommittees themselves have tended to be comprised of members whose inclinations to spend are below the House as a whole. Therefore, the subcommittees are still less lenient toward agencies than they would have been if they had been simple random samples of the House. On the other hand, Kiewiet and McCubbins show in the *Logic of Delegation* that during the Cannon-Taber era, new subcommittee assignments were made with a *systematic* design to balance existing ideological makeups: A subcommittee left with "too many" liberal members, owing to electoral turnover, could count on receiving an infusion of conservative members, and vice versa. Since 1966, however, new subcommittee assignments have not been made systematically to overcome ideological imbalances. Thus, the subcommittees have remained relatively conservative since the mid-1960s largely by the chance assignment of members who belong to a committee that is already more conservative than the House as a whole. Whether the change in the mechanism for assigning members to appropriations subcommittees has made a difference to the nature of appropriations decisions remains a topic for future research.

The fiscal conservatism of the HAC, which has been emphasized by modern students of appropriations politics, is nothing new. Frugality is a virtue that was frequently extolled in nineteenth-century discussions of budget reform, and it has led to a pattern of spending cuts by the HAC that has endured a century. HAC has always cut agency requests; evidence of this long tradition of budget cutting extends from the most aggregated to the most disaggregated spending measures. Considering together all the regular annual appropriations bills, between fiscal years 1889 to 1991, the House Appropriations Committee has cut an average of 5.6 percent off of agency appropriations requests. (These figures are taken from *Appropriations, New Offices, Etc.,* an annual publication, produced variously by either the House or the Senate appropriations committees staffs.) At a more disaggregated level of analysis, Stewart, in *Budget Reform Politics,* reported that 78 percent of the appropriations bills reported from committee to the House floor between fiscal years 1871 and 1922 contained a net cut of the agency's total request. Fenno reported that 74 percent of the budgets submitted by 36 federal bureaus between 1947 and 1962 were cut by the Appropriations Committee. In Kiewiet and McCubbins's follow-up to Fenno's study, their data show that 64 percent of the budgets submitted by sixty-six federal bureaus between fiscal years 1963 and 1985 were cut with changes in estimates amounting to an average 3.8-percent reduction each year. Thus, for the past century, the House Appropriations Committee has cut agency budgets approximately three-quarters of the time, making cuts that have averaged about 5 percent of requests.

The Senate Appropriations Committee (SAC) has served a different role from its House counterpart, at least on the surface. Fenno noted that the SAC functioned as an "appeals court," in which items cut by the House were scrutinized and spending increases—compared to the amount passed by the House—were the order of the day. In *The New Politics of the Budgetary Process,* Wildavsky noted that the "responsible legislator" on the SAC

> sees to it that the irrepressible lower House does not do too much damage either to constituency or to national interests. And though members of the House Appropriations Committee tend to view their opposite members in the Senate as frivolous spendthrifts of the public purse, senators reverse the compliment by regarding their brethren in the other chamber as niggardly and jealous types who do not care what happens to 'essential' programs so long as they can show that they have made cuts.

Of the 575 spending decisions examined by Fenno from 1947 to 1962, 56.2 percent of the time an agency emerged from the Senate Appropriations Committee with a higher spending recommendation than the House had passed. During this time, SAC recommendations averaged 4.2 percent greater than the HAC recommendation and 3.9 percent larger

than those passed by the House. During the period from 1962 to 1980 (fiscal years 1963–1981) the SAC continued to serve as an appeals court and to augment slightly agency budgets compared to the House; Senate Appropriations Committee recommendations averaged 2.7 percent greater than House-passed appropriations during this period.

The traditional appeals court role of the SAC has been explained by two structural factors: appropriations sequence and committee size. Coming to the Senate after facing the House, it is natural that agencies would emphasize in Senate hearings what they perceived to be unfair cuts made by the lower chamber.

The smaller size of the SAC forces its members to use rules of thumb to focus their attention on appropriations matters. In the 102d Congress, the HAC consisted of fifty-nine members while the Senate Appropriations Committee consisted of twenty-nine. Each committee maintained thirteen subcommittees, one for each annual bill. The subcommittees in each chamber are virtually the same size on average: ten in the House and eleven in the Senate. The real difference between the two committees, as far as specialization is concerned, is the average number of subcommittees each committee member serves on: two in the House and five in the Senate. Thus, the emphasis by the agencies on the cuts made by the House, combined with the smaller size of the Senate committee and with the divided attention of its members, produces Senate committee recommendations that are more favorable to the agencies.

The budgetary battles of the early 1980s upset the established patterns of the appropriations committee's behavior. The Senate Appropriations Committee, reflecting the fact that it was controlled by a Republican party that was pledged to reorienting federal spending, hardly served as an appeals court happy to please agencies by restoring cuts made by the House. And, the House committee, controlled by a Democratic party that was associated with many of the programs that were targeted by the Republicans for reduction or elimination, was fully capable of bolstering agency requests that were deemed too low.

The Reagan administration came into office in 1981 asking for a 4.6 percent overall reduction in federal spending. Reflecting the platform on which he ran, President Ronald Reagan distributed most of these cuts among domestic programs, asking for a net increase for defense. Most of the domestic spending reductions involved changing the statutes that determined eligibility standards and payment formulas for entitlement legislation and other social programs. Hence, the domestic budget cutting involved the legislative committees as much as it involved the appropriations committees.

In the short term, the reorientation of spending priorities effected in 1981 was dramatic in many program areas; compared to the fiscal 1980 budget and using inflation-adjusted figures, total outlays were 6.7 percent greater in fiscal year 1982, national defense outlays were 19.5 percent greater, human resources outlays (education, health, Social Security, etc.) were 4.8 percent greater, physical resources outlays (energy, environment, transportation, etc.) were 20.9 percent less, and outlays for all other functions of government, except interest payments, were 4.1 percent less.

The appropriations committees had a role in this reprioritization, although the funds contained in the annual appropriations bills amounted to only a fraction of total spending. On the surface, the two appropriations committees acted according to past patterns; the HAC cut an aggregate of 1.4 percent from agency requests and the SAC added an aggregate of 1.6 percent back onto the House-passed bills. At a more detailed level, however, the transformation of these two committees into agents of the parties that controlled them is apparent. For instance, after the HAC had recommended a cut in military personnel, defense research and development, and military construction by $12.9 billion (19.4 percent of requests for these items), the SAC increased them by $7.6 billion, or 12.0 percent more than the amount passed by the House. (Because the House increased these items by $10.1 billion, the difference between the HAC- and SAC-recommended amounts was even greater: $17.1 billion, a 33.1 percent difference.) Likewise, after the HAC and the House had left the requests for the Departments of Housing and Urban Development, Labor, and Transportation virtually unchanged, the SAC recommended cutting housing by 8.2 percent ($2.1 billion), labor by 9.5 percent ($839 million), and transportation by 6.6 percent ($683 million).

During the rest of the 1980s, appropriations politics was not nearly so dramatic, nor were the traditional roles of the two appropriations committees so reversed. However, the combined effects of a decade of divided government in Washington, the fiscal constraints imposed by chronic budget deficits, and various "budget deals" meant that extricating the federal government from those deficits severely diminished the degree to which either committee was able to change appropriations bills. With conservative presidents in the White House, most appropriations requests already erred on the conservative side; neither of the appropriations committees was in much position to change agency estimates all that much.

Together, the two appropriations committees aid Congress in keeping spending down in normal budgetary times. Changes in committee and budgetary politics of the past two decades have altered the ways in which the committees serve as guardians of the Treasury. The two committees were more overtly partisan in the 1980s than they were in the 1950s and 1960s. Much of the focus of spending control within Congress has now shifted to special ad hoc agreements that are hammered out through informal negotiations between the president and congressional leaders—leaders who of course include the chairs of the appropriations committees. But without the appropriations committees, even the ad hoc agreements that became common in the late 1980s would have been toothless tigers in the face of the complexity that characterizes federal spending.

Programmatic Appropriations Control

Less closely followed than fiscal control, but no less important, is control over spending that is undertaken for programmatic reasons. Although popular discussion of appropriations politics often ignores this aspect of spending control, and congressional opponents often deride it as "micromanagement," the power of the purse remains the key to legislative power because it can be so effective in changing agency behavior at almost any level.

On an ongoing basis, the annual appropriations process is the most immediate way that Congress exercises formal oversight over federal agencies. Each appropriations bill is considered by subcommittees of each appropriations committee. Hearings on the budgets occupy many days that stretch across several weeks, at which times agency officials justify their requests to the committees, committee members send signals to agencies about what constitutes proper behavior in the future, and clientele groups testify about the performance of the agencies overseen by the subcommittee.

Hearings for the fiscal year 1990 budget, which were held in the spring and summer of 1989, illustrate the degree of oversight provided through appropriations hearings. In 1989, almost 2,400 people addressed House subcommittees and about 1,100 addressed Senate subcommittees about proposed agency appropriations. These hearings produced enough information to fill fifteen feet of bookshelves and more than 110,000 pages of formal testimony and material.

A good number of the witnesses in both the House and Senate were supplicants from localities arguing the merits of federal construction projects in their districts, hence the large number of outside witnesses addressing the energy, interior, and transportation subcommittees. But, even in these hearings, important policy questions were also addressed, such as the safety of commuter airlines.

After appropriations hearings are over, the degree of formal oversight does not stop. Indeed, the large staff contingents assigned to the various subcommittees ensure that the committees are in continual contact with the agencies throughout the year.

Programmatic control of the agencies manifests itself not only in the informal signals and information that are exchanged during hearings and informal conversations, but in provisos that appear in appropriations bills. To give one example, the fiscal year 1989 appropriation for the Interior Department (Public Law 100–446) contained almost one hundred provisions that either directly contravened established federal statutes or somehow restricted the expenditure of funds. The Bureau of Land Management (BLM), a medium-sized bureau within the Interior Department, was restricted from killing "healthy, unadopted, wild horses and burros" under its care. One provision of the appropriations bill established restrictions on procedures for appealing BLM grazing allotments on public rangelands. And finally, the bill allowed BLM employees to receive reimbursements of up to $400 per year for uniforms, contrary to the standard federal restriction of $125 per annum.

The annual appropriations process gives Congress, through its agents the appropriations committees, a degree of ongoing oversight that is unmatched elsewhere in Congress. Because the committees are constructed to afford a faithful mapping of chamber views onto committee deliberations, and the committees are afforded significant staff resources to execute their responsibilities, this degree of oversight is substantial in the long run.

The staffs of the two appropriations committees tend to be the largest committee staffs on Capitol Hill. For instance, in the 102d Congress, the *1992 Congressional Staff Directory* listed two hundred professional staff working for the HAC and eighty-five working for the SAC.

Although the committees are equipped to engage in continuing oversight of executive agencies, even this annual oversight has its limits. And, the control the appropriations committees exercise over agency behavior and federal programs comes at a cost to members of Congress not privileged to serve on either committee.

Committees' Power of Control

Students of the appropriations process have long noted the limits to programmatic oversight as exercised through the appropriations process. One limit, which will not be explored in detail here, is frequently made by economists who argue that oversight rarely considers the indirect social costs of federal programs.

The first major shortcoming in using the appropriations process as a mode of oversight that is emphasized by political scientists is that the congressional power of the purse is ill-proportioned; Congress can restrain agencies from future activities by withholding funds, but this is of little relief if the problem with the agency is the underperformance of its labors. Congress passed the 1974 Impoundment Control Act, in part, to deal with the peculiar problem of forcing agencies to spend money appropriated to them. But, experience with the early Reagan years demonstrated that agencies could vary in their programmatic zeal even when they were spending their allotted funds.

In the second place, control over the substance of programs through appropriations mechanisms is limited because there is a fundamental ambivalence about how effective Congress wants this type of oversight to be. Even in the 1950s and 1960s, when the HAC was at the peak of its power, Fenno could comment on the sanctions the House periodically imposed on the committee when it overstepped its authority.

This ambivalence regularly surfaces in the steady stream of floor amendments to appropriations bills, each successful one of which is testimony to the contingent nature of the appropriations committees' powers. As discussed by Smith in *Call to Order,* amendments to appropriations bills, along with amendments to other major legislation, increased dramatically from the 1960s to the 1980s. There is controversy over whether the rise in amendments to appropriations bills constitutes a fundamental weakening of the appropriations committees' institutional position, especially of the House committee. Barry R. Weingast, for instance, has argued that part of the rise of floor amendments is due to the right of committees to make counteramendments; this strategy of fighting fire with fire may increase the shear number of amendments while preserving most of the HAC's authority to set the appropriations agenda.

At the root of the difficulty that the appropriations committees face in maintaining their positions as "control committees" is the fact that appropriations control is a public good that is subject to the problems of free riding discussed by Olson in *The Logic of Collective Action.* While most members of Congress would prefer all of federal spending to be controlled, they each would most prefer control to be achieved excepting his or her own pet projects. On aggregate, this temptation to defect from a regime of budget control is a problem that party leaders spend a good deal of their time trying to overcome.

Yet another, but related, difficulty that arises in the programmatic oversight of agencies is the degree to which agencies adapt their behavior to changing expectations of the appropriations committees rather than to their authorizing committees or to the chambers themselves. Once legislation is passed, bureaus typically have significant leeway in determining how legislation will be implemented, a problem political scientists have been tackling through the application of microeconomics' "principal-agent theory." The problem of ensuring that the coalitions that favored a piece of successful legislation get what they wanted when it is implemented is one that has attracted considerable academic attention. Although the appropriations committees are charged with overseeing agencies on behalf of their chambers, there is no automatic mechanism to ensure that the floor, in fact, will be assisted through this oversight. With the committees possessing vastly superior knowledge about the implementation of legislation than the rank and file, there are temptations for the committees to take advantage of this informational asymmetry and "extract rents" by influencing details of policy implementation.

While such rent-seeking temptations are acknowledged to exist in theory, and many anecdotes exist to suggest that this is a problem, the systematic evidence on this score is only suggestive, at best. For instance, Arnold, in *Congress and the Bureaucracy,* studied the closure of major army and air force bases from 1952 to 1974. He found that bases located in districts not represented on one of the military subcommittees of the HAC were thirty-five to forty times more likely to be closed than bases that were located in districts with members on these subcommittees. (The subcommittees were on defense and on military construction. In the analysis the size of military installations was taken into account.) The strength of the appropriations subcommittees was shown by the fact that bases located in districts represented in the House Armed Services Committee were twice as likely to be closed as those represented on one of the appropriations subcommittees.

Foreman, in *Signals from the Hill,* discussed the importance of Senator Jake Garn (R.-Utah), the chair of the appropriations subcommittee on housing and urban development in the early 1980s, in influencing how the Consumer Product Safety Commission (CPSC) developed regulatory priorities. Working with Commissioner Stuart Statler, the conservative Garn first made the CPSC identify its top-ten priorities; then Garn threw his support behind shifting funds to the limited number of items the commission wished to pursue. The critical position of an appropriations subcommittee chair was used, first, to overcome political opposition within the commission to a focusing of its program, and then to bolster political support for the commission's work within the administration. All of this happened without recourse to changes in statute.

HISTORY AND DEVELOPMENT OF THE APPROPRIATIONS COMMITTEES

Congress has used committees to help it control spending from the beginning of the Republic, although the appropriations committees themselves are only about a century old: the HAC was created in 1865, the SAC in 1867. Although both houses of Congress have always relied one way or the other on committees to help them control spending, this does not mean that the appropriations committees have been equally powerful throughout time, with equal jurisdictions or authority. Because appropriations control exists in tension with other political goals, the chambers have periodically restricted the committees when majorities believed that control had gone too far.

In the first days of the Republic, Congress initially vested much of the authority over appropriations in the newly created Treasury Department and its first secretary, Alexander Hamilton. Conflicts between Hamilton's supporters, who believed in a strong role for the central government in economic development, and the supporters of Thomas Jefferson, who believed in a circumscribed role, prompted the House to develop a capacity to consider fiscal matters independent of the executive branch. Towards this end, the Ways and Means Committee began operating as an ongoing enterprise in December 1795. It was made a standing committee of the House in 1802. Ways and Means was responsible in these early days for all financial legislation, including taxing, banking, and appropriations.

Consistent with the Senate's often passive role in legislating during these early years, the upper chamber allowed the House to take the initiative in fiscal matters. Until 1816, appropriations were considered in the Senate in temporary, special committees. In 1816, eleven standing committees were created in the Senate, including the Finance Committee, which handled appropriations bills for the next half century.

Concern about the ability to control the executive branch's use of the power of the purse was a common refrain in the early years of the Republic. Even as early as 1806, John Randolph, chair of Ways and Means, decried the lack of fiscal control in Congress, declaring that appropriations were "a matter of form, or less than a shadow of a shade, a mere cobweb against expenditures."

A good example of looseness of spending control was pensions. Even before the Civil War, pension legislation for veterans and their survivors was very popular. Prior to 1865, Congress had passed legislation extending revolutionary war pensions fourteen times; the last revolutionary war pension was not paid out until 1906. Military pensions constituted a major portion of federal spending in the years following the War of 1812 and the Mexican War, making up 11 percent of spending by 1840. And yet, actual control over this spending lay not with the committees empowered to report appropriations, but with the pension committees. The job of Ways and Means and of Finance was to predict each year how much money would be spent under the various pension acts and to provide for it.

Prior to the Civil War, reform proposals were discussed which would split the jurisdiction of the Ways and Means Committee, to allow greater attention to both spending and taxing. However, nothing came of these proposals until after the war. The Civil War, in addition to embodying a constitutional crisis, produced one of the greatest fiscal crises in American history. Virtually overnight the scope of the federal government grew by orders of magnitude, from $67 million in fiscal year 1861 to $1.3 billion in fiscal year 1865. (In real (1982) dollars, spending rose from $586 million to $6.7 billion between fiscal year 1861 and fiscal year 1865. After the war, spending dropped until it attained a range of $250–$300 million, about $2.4 billion in 1982 dollars.) This sea change in federal government finance was accompanied by uncertainty about how this financing activity would take place and whether corruption would affect its implementation.

Stirred by the desire to get its fiscal house in order, the House in 1865 acceded to the entreaties of reformers and split Ways and Means into three parts, giving banking to a new Banking and Currency Committee, allocating appropriations to the new Appropriations Committee, and retaining taxing oversight within Ways and Means.

Not long after the HAC had been established, its authority began to be undermined. In the decade between 1875 and 1885, the committee endured a half dozen serious attacks on its jurisdiction. At first it was successful in beating back these challenges, losing only the right to report appropriations for rivers and harbors in 1877 and Agriculture Department appropriations in 1880.

In 1885, the dam burst. In the devolution of 1885, the House voted to remove from the HAC the right to report appropriations for the army, the military academy, consular affairs, the navy, and the post office. In its place, the House authorized the appropriate legislative committees to report these annual spending bills. The House also continued to allow the Agriculture Committee to report agriculture spending and the Rivers and Harbors Committee to report water-project spending. The HAC retained the right to report appropriations for the Washington bureaucracy, pensions, fortifications, and supplemental appropriations, leaving it with only about half of federal spending to oversee.

The HAC Before 1885

Numerous explanations have been offered to interpret the events that led up to the devolution of 1885. The most common of them center on the behavior of the chair of the Appropriations Committee, Samuel Randall. Randall, a Democrat from Pennsylvania, had served as the House Speaker between 1876 to 1881 (Forty-fourth to Forty-sixth Congresses). The Democrats lost control of the House in the Forty-seventh Congress. When they regained control in the Forty-eighth Congress, Randall was dumped as the Democratic leader and replaced by John Carlisle, from Indiana, who was elected Speaker. Randall's primary "sin" for

which he was deposed was his stand on the tariff—he was a protectionist in a party of free traders.

Although Randall stood outside the Democratic mainstream on the issue of free trade, he was not entirely alone, and led a sizable minority faction of free-trade Democrats. Thus, to ensure peace within the party, Randall's wishes had to be accommodated somehow; Randall was then appointed to chair of the HAC.

In the nineteenth century, Speakers made committee assignments themselves, unlike the current practice in which committee assignments are made by party committees. Speakers' committee assignments reflected many criteria, some of which are still used, but many of which seem alien to current practice. For instance, no House member had a right to hold a committee seat or to chair a committee by dint of seniority. Speakers frequently used their right to assign members unilaterally to committees—and to depose committee chairs if necessary—not only to sustain committee expertise, but also to shore up political support within their party caucuses. Thus, by assigning Randall to chair the HAC—a committee on which Randall had not served for three Congresses—Carlisle was following an established practice of placing rivals in important positions, thereby placating party factions.

Carlisle's appointment of Randall to chair appropriations was controversial among his closest supporters. And, his estimate that this appointment would buy him peace proved to be mistaken. Randall continued to obstruct free-trade efforts, this time using the special privileges of the HAC to his advantage.

The committee, then as in our time, has the right to report appropriations bills any time it wishes. Randall used this right strategically. He would roam the House floor with appropriations bills in his pockets. Whenever a piece of legislation of which he disapproved was ready to come to the House floor, Randall would demand to be recognized and report an appropriations bill, thus tying up the House floor. This tactic was especially effective at the end of a session, since it simultaneously kept unwanted legislation off the floor and reduced the scrutiny the floor could give to the appropriations bills that were being considered. Thus, the most common explanation for why the House decided to strip the HAC of most of its power in 1885 is that a majority of the House—and especially the majority Democrats—wanted to take a slap at Randall for his anti-tariff and obstructionist ways.

Related to the charge of obstruction was the plaint that the committee was unnecessarily frugal in guarding the treasury, and that the needs of particular regions, notably the West, were ignored. The HAC's credentials as budget cutters were well-established; before 1885, the average appropriations bill was cut 17 percent by the HAC before being reported to the floor, with Randall-era cuts averaging closer to 25 percent. There is very little data or systematic analysis to judge the charges about the decline of spending. By looking at the overall membership of the committee, it is difficult to discern the source of such a regional bias, since its membership before 1885 was a fair sample of the nation's regions as reflected in House membership. The statement of one westerner expressed, however, a common feeling among many supporters of the devolution:

> While the center of population of the United States has passed a thousand miles westward from the Atlantic coast, the center of appropriations and expenditures of public money will be found on a line drawn from this Capitol through the city of Philadelphia to Boston by way of New York.
>
> To my mind the despotism of the Committee on Appropriations, as constituted in the last Congress, is in keeping with the domination which the East has exercised over the West, since there has been a West. (James Laird, quoted in Stewart, *Budget Reform Politics,* pp. 123–124)

The distributional consequences of a devolution were probably apparent to House members, however, since the committees that were receiving the right to report appropriations were not fair samples of the chamber, embodying in their memberships the sorts of regional biases one would expect. (For instance, the Naval Affairs Committee had an overabundance of members from the eastern seaboard, while the Indian Affairs Committee was overrepresented with westerners.)

Although press reports at the time stressed the centrality of Randall and the committee's frugality in explaining the devolution, and although modern scholarship has frequently repeated these points, reflection upon these events in light of modern scholarship and theory cast doubts upon explanations that rely too heavily on Randall's role as a villain. If the target had been Randall himself, there were many other options that could have sanctioned him directly without gutting one of the two most important committees in the House. Other House rules could have been changed to limit the committee's obstructionism, or Randall could have been deposed as HAC chair.

One alternative explanation for why the HAC lost half of its authority in 1885 can be gleaned from the modern literature on congressional oversight of the executive. During the period spanning the 1870s to the 1890s, the Democrats found themselves capable of winning control of the House quite regularly, but unable to win control of the Senate or the presidency. Thus, Democrats began casting about for ways to influence executive-branch behavior, given that both the Republican Senate and presidency could jointly veto Democratic efforts to change organic acts and could jointly act independently of the House to appoint executive-branch officials. Democrats in the House had already hit upon a device, the Holman Rule, that allowed provisos to be easily slipped onto appropriations bills.

Another way to think about the devolution of 1885, then, is through the lens of congressional control of the executive. By farming out appropriations oversight to legislative committees, the House Democrats might have a better chance to influence the behavior of a federal government that was otherwise dominated by Republicans.

The one detail that would have gotten in the way of using devolution as a method of greater congressional oversight was the fact that the legislative committees, before 1885, were stacked with supporters of the agencies—we would now call them "high demanders" for agency services. Thus, the committees might be expected to oversee the agencies with the interests of specific clienteles in mind, not with the interest of the House floor in mind. Indeed, this point was the core of Randall's attack on the rules change. The solution to this problem was provided by Speaker Carlisle, who after the devolution passed, remade his committee assignments to mute policy biases on the legislative committees that gained appropriations power.

After the devolution, then, these committees— Agriculture, Rivers and Harbors, Military Affairs, Naval Affairs, Foreign Affairs, and Post Office—were less inclined to serve particular clienteles and more inclined to serve as agents of the House. Further, Speakers constituted the chairs of all these committees as a "College of Cardinals" which periodically met to coordinate spending, both the aggregate sums and their distribution.

In addition to being often used as the prime example of how an appropriations committee can have sanctions applied to it for straying too far from chamber expectations, the devolution of 1885 has also been adduced as evidence for how the decentralization of appropriations oversight leads directly to spending profligacy. The most obvious reason for this conclusion is that the devolution marks a break in eras of American appropriations history: before 1885 was a period of retrenchment; afterward was a period of sustained appropriations growth. Between fiscal years 1871 and 1886, spending in all the annual appropriations bills grew by less than 1 percent per year; during the fiscal years 1887–1922 they grew at an annual rate of 9 percent.

Recent studies of spending decisions during this period cast doubts on using the devolution of 1885 as an object lesson against the decentralization of appropriations. In general, the difference in spending levels before and after the devolution can be accounted for by growth in the economy, prices, wars, and the addition of new federal programs. Once these factors are taken into account, there is little difference in the types of spending decisions made by the HAC and the legislative committees such as Agriculture and Foreign Affairs.

The reason for so little difference in the quality of decisions made by committees before and after 1885 was mentioned previously: House majorities had no interest in allowing particular interests to dominate spending policy around the turn of the century—the committees were agents of the House, not of societal interests or of the bureaus. It was the job of Speakers to maintain this agency arrangement. Thus, Speakers acted to counteract the interest-leniency-sympathy syndrome through their committee appointments, much the way that Clarence Cannon and John Taber used subcommittee assignments to control agencies in the postwar HAC.

Formation of the SAC

True to historical pattern, the Senate lagged behind the House in virtually every institutional innovation relating to appropriations. The SAC was not created until 1867. It managed to escape the turbulent attacks on its jurisdiction that the HAC endured during the 1870s and 1880s (although the Senate Commerce Committee did receive the authority to report the rivers and harbors bill). After four years of debate, however, the Senate in 1899 voted to mimic the House's 1885 devolution, with slight modifications. In the Senate, the river and harbor bill continued to be referred to the Commerce Committee, and the agriculture, army, military academy, Indian affairs, navy, pensions, and post office bills were given to the appropriate legislative committees. This left the SAC with deficiencies; consular and diplomatic; District of Columbia; fortifications; legislative, executive, and judicial; and fortifications appropriations.

Although we now know that the devolutions of 1885 and 1899 were not major contributions to the expansion of federal spending around the turn of the twentieth century, they did, at the time, serve as a symbol for reformers interested in retrenchment and the importation of "business methods" to government. The fact that agencies submitted their budget requests directly to Congress, with no oversight from the president, and that a dozen committees considered these requests on Capitol Hill was labeled the epitome of irresponsibility.

While reformers and some presidents, such as William Howard Taft, pushed on the outside for reform, Congress itself considered the recentralization of appropriations authority during the period 1900–1910. The problem was that while most members acknowledged the need for some sort of formal coordination of appropriations bills, there was disagreement about how to achieve it. Two proposals were the most prominent in the House: either to restore the HAC's former jurisdiction encompassing all appropriations; or to establish a new Budget Committee, which would consist of representatives of all the "money" committees.

Many supporters of the status quo saw either proposal as a threat, and thus occasionally joined with supporters of one proposal to defeat the supporters of the other.

The election of 1918 broke the logjam of reform. That election turned the Democrats out of the Congress, restoring Republican control there for the first time in eight years. Republicans had campaigned on a platform that scathingly attacked the Democrats for the mismanagement of World War I and demanded the centralization of fiscal policy-making, both in Congress and in the executive branch. Thus, the new Republican majority in both houses had the motive and the opportunity to redeem its campaign pledges to both recentralize appropriations authority in Congress and to pass the Accounting Act, which centralized appropriations authority within the executive branch.

President Woodrow Wilson vetoed the Accounting Act, and Congress failed to override it. The point of contention was over who had the right to remove the Comptroller General and who would head the General Accounting Office. Following the 1920 election, Congress repassed this law as the Budget and Accounting Act, which president Warren Harding signed in 1921.

The Budget and Accounting Act (BAA) was coupled with a restoration of the HAC's full jurisdiction in 1920 and the SAC's in 1922. Together, these reforms formed the foundation of the appropriations process in the modern Congress. The most important change in that process came with the passage of the 1974 Congressional Budget and Impoundment Control Act (CBICA), which is discussed later in this essay, but even that act did not alter the most fundamental aspects of the appropriations process spelled out at that time.

The BAA authorized the creation of a presidential budget. Prior to the BAA, agencies submitted their appropriations requests directly to Congress. The only executive action was when the Treasury secretary took the requests and bound them together for formal transmission to Congress; the president and Treasury secretary were prohibited by law from changing the requests. The BAA not only authorized the president to change the requests as he thought prudent, but it also created two important agencies to oversee appropriations on an ongoing basis. The Budget Bureau (now the Office of Management and Budget) was created to assist the president in constructing his budget and in overseeing spending in the various agencies. The General Accounting Office was created to provide a capacity within Congress to audit executive agencies.

Although the reforms between 1919 and 1922 represented a significant increase in the power of the two appropriations committees, proposals to further centralize the fiscal power in Congress continued into the future. A significant provision of the 1946 Legislative Reorganization Act (LRA) was the creation of the Joint Congressional Committee on the Legislative Committee. The Joint Budget Committee was a "committee of the whole" which consisted of all the members of the House and Senate appropriations committees, the House Ways and Means Committee, and the Senate Finance Committee. The task of the committee was to estimate revenues and to set a limit on the amount that could be appropriated in the following fiscal year.

The experiment with the Joint Budget Committee failed; revenue and expenditure estimates were inaccurate, the method of setting spending ceilings was inflexible, the Joint Budget Committee was too large (more than one hundred members) to be workable, and the House and Senate continually disagreed. As a countermeasure, Clarence Cannon tried to establish centralized spending control by incorporating all spending measures into an omnibus appropriations bill for 1950. A combination of the need for large supplemental appropriations to fund the Korean War and an incipient revolt by the subcommittee chairs of the HAC led Cannon to abandon this strategy in 1951. There were no more major, formal changes to the appropriations committees' power until the 1974 CBICA.

A significant informal change in the process was the acceleration of spending not subject to annual review by the appropriations committees, which accompanied the passage of the Great Society programs of President Lyndon Johnson in the 1960s. In fiscal year 1963, the amount of money contained in the thirteen annual appropriations bills equaled 82 percent of federal outlays. By fiscal year 1976, the annual bills were the equivalent of 63 percent of federal outlays. (Excluding from consideration interest payments on the public debt, the annual bills dropped from 89 percent of outlays to 67 percent.)

This shift in authority over spending from appropriations to the legislative committees (and to Ways and Means and to Finance) catalyzed members of the two committees into support for some sort of reform which would allow them to reestablish control over these sums. The 1974 CBICA, in fact, contained provisions to bolster the authority of the appropriations committees over "backdoor spending." For instance, most new borrowing authority was made dependent on prior appropriations; the appropriations committees were given the right to review new entitlements if the legislation called for spending in excess of the budget-resolution figures allocated for that function.

THE APPROPRIATIONS COMMITTEES IN AN ERA OF BUDGETARY POLITICS

The 1974 Budget Act represented the most significant formal change to the budgetary process in more than a half century. It established a series of budget resolutions to set broad spending targets and fiscal policy, established limits on the expansion of backdoor spending mechanisms, and established two sets of institutions—budget committees in each chamber and a joint Congressional Budget Office—to oversee the whole process. Whether the process has "worked" is a large, complex topic beyond the scope of this essay. The focus of this section will be on discussing the degree to which the operation of the act—and budgetary politics in general—served to change the two appropriations committees after 1974.

At the time of its passage, there was little consensus about how the Budget Act's implementation would affect the power of the appropriations committees, especially that of the House committee. In *Congress and Money,* Allen Schick summarized the ultimate effect on the appropriations committees this way:

> The benefits [of the Act] were not equally distributed among the various participants. The authorizing committees which had risked the least also gained the least. The Appropria-

tions Committees, however, had put their jurisdiction over federal spending on the line and they were rewarded with expanded jurisdiction. (p. 79)

In addition to simply gaining greater jurisdiction over new borrowing and contract authority and some review of entitlements, the appropriations committees were also put in a position to play a significant role in the budgetary process, along with the taxing committees, once it began operation. In the House, the twenty-three member Budget Committee was created so that five members had to be drawn from the HAC, five from Ways and Means, and the remaining thirteen drawn from the other nineteen House standing committees. In the Senate, where committees were less dominant to begin with, there was no requirement that Senate Budget Committee members be drawn from either the SAC or Finance. Still, the SAC has tended to provide the most members to the Senate Budget Committee over the years.

Thus, the combination of an expanded jurisdiction for the appropriations committees and an important role for the committees within the budget committees boded well for a revitalization of centralized spending control. At the same time, however, the creation of two new budget committees to stand between committee (i.e., constituency) wishes and the Treasury raised some fears that the HAC would relinquish its role as guardian of the Treasury. This is how Schick expressed it:

> The Budget Act also redefined the roles of the Appropriations Committees. No longer are these committees regarded solely as the protectors of the purse; they are now seen as claimants whose spending inclinations must be policed by the budget process.... The actions of the Appropriations Committees are monitored by controllers from the Budget Committees to assure that the budget targets and ceilings are protected. When an appropriations bill is debated in the House or Senate, the chairman of the Budget Committee usually takes the floor to announce whether the Appropriations Committee has complied with or violated the budget controls....
>
> These procedures are built on the expectation that the Appropriations Committees cannot be trusted to abide by the congressional budget unless their actions are watched and controlled. To put the matter bluntly, the budget process exists to prevent "budget bust-

ing" by the Appropriations Committees (as well as other congressional spenders). This casting of the former guardians as claimants is the logical culmination of the transformation of the Appropriations Committees during the decade preceding the Budget Act. (pp. 441–442)

Schick's account of the implementation of the Budget Act was written during the process's infancy—before it had been subjected to the strains of the 1981 budget battles or to the uncertainties of the deficit politics of the 1980s that followed. In the ensuing decade, the budget act was further transformed, with the relationship of the appropriations committees to the entire budgetary process changed even further. Over the decade, attempts to impose some semblance of centralized coordination over budgetary decisions deviated more and more from the formal outlines of the Budget Act. In its place were put ad hoc arrangements, arrived at through informal bargaining between congressional leaders and Republican administrations. The best-known of these arrangements were the Gramm-Rudman-Hollings amendments of 1985, which established a mechanism for balancing the federal budget over a five-year period, and the budget deal of 1989 which barred transfers among three broad budgetary categories for at least three years.

While congressional leaders and administration officials have been bogged down in informal negotiations over general budgetary parameters, the appropriations committees have gone ahead, attempting to assert control over the details of budgetary politics. For instance, during the period 1983–1984, while the budgetary process was mired in indecision, the HAC decided to move ahead with the annual appropriations bills in order to demonstrate that it could assert control over budgeting using its traditional incrementalist strategy.

Another factor leading to the revitalization of the appropriations committees in the 1980s was the expanded use of continuing resolutions to fund federal agencies. Generally speaking, a continuing resolution is a temporary appropriations measure that funds federal agencies if an appropriations bill is not passed at the beginning of a fiscal year. Because of their urgency, continuing resolutions frequently attract riders—legislation that might not pass on its own. Historically, continuing resolutions have been stopgap, keeping agencies from closing down while Congress and the president haggle over the details of appropriations bills at the start of a fiscal year.

In the 1980s, as negotiations over appropriations became virtually intractable, few appropriations bills had been passed by the beginning of each fiscal year. In 1986 and 1987 (fiscal years 1987 and 1988), congressional leaders chose to fund all object in the thirteen annual appropriations bills through a single continuing resolution which was effective for the entire fiscal year. These continuing resolutions were known as omnibus appropriations bills. Because of their size—the fiscal year 1987 bill weighed thirty pounds—and the rush to enact them, only a few of the members of the appropriations committees adequately understood the details of these measures. One of the best-known and controversial provisions that was slipped into the fiscal year 1988 continuing resolution was a provision sponsored by Senator Daniel Inouye (D.-Hawaii), chair of the foreign operations subcommittee of SAC, to provide $8 million for the education of North African Jews in Paris, which was later repealed.

As the highly visible politics of budgetary aggregates has grown intractable and immutable to significant change—a problem attributable to divided government in the 1980s—the benefits of exerting budgetary control through a less visible, "incremental" process have been evident to both members of Congress and to political analysts. First, with major budgetary aggregates hammered out through intra-institutional bargaining, attempts to set gross spending priorities through the normal budgetary process and its resolutions have become nearly worthless. Second, budgetary coordination within the normal appropriations process has become routinized through face-to-face meetings of the chairs of the HAC subcommittees—the "College of Cardinals." "Discretionary spending"—roughly two-fifths of all spending—is divided among subcommittees before subcommittee deliberations begin. Within aggregates set through intercommittee negotiation, the subcommittees in turn apply their expertise garnered through direct contact with agencies to produce final appropriations recommendations.

Thus, the appropriations process that has emerged nearly two decades after the passage of the 1974 Budget Act is not much different from the process that emerged in the decade after the 1885 devolution: spending aggregates are set through informal negotiations involving congressional leaders and top administration officials; a major allocation of spending authority takes place in negotiation among a "College of Cardinals"; and appropriations subcommittees—authorizing committees between 1885 and 1921—implement this allocation.

CONCLUSION

The appropriations committees serve as the first line of control over agency behavior. It is not the only method of control, nor always the best, but it does provide both chambers of Congress with the most direct and ongoing procedures for oversight that exist. Because the services the committees provide to their chambers are so fundamental to the achievement of legislators' goals, the appropriations committees will always be among the most valuable assignments in Congress. This does not mean that the value will be unchanged nor that the power of the committees will be constant over time. Rather, it does mean that time has demonstrated the value to the members of Congress of close supervision of federal agencies using the lifeblood of agency action: money. Through the 1980s, as negotiations over budgetary matters were often mired in deadlock; the piecemeal manner in which the appropriations committees dealt with agency funding often provided the only opening for acting at all on fiscal matters.

BIBLIOGRAPHY

Historical and General Studies

DAVID BRADY and MARK A. MORGAN, "Reforming the Structure of the House Appropriations Process," in MATHEW D. McCUBBINS and TERRY SULLIVAN, eds., *Congress: Structure and Policy* (New York, 1987), examines the effects that the devolution of 1885 had on subsequent federal spending in the areas of agriculture and legislative appropriations. LOUIS FISHER, *Presidential Spending Power* (Princeton, N.J., 1975), examines the rise of presidential appropriations power—and the ensuing battles with Congress—since the first days of the Republic. DALMAS H. NELSON, "The Omnibus Appropriations Act of 1950," *Journal of Politics* 15 (1953), analyzes the attempt to pass an omnibus appropriations bill in the early 1950s; MANCUR OLSON, *The Logic of Collective Action* (Cambridge, Mass., 1965), though not about the appropriations committees directly, is the classic discussion of the problems of providing public goods through collective action. ALLEN SCHICK, *Congress and Money* (Washington, D.C., 1980), is the definitive accounting of the passage of the 1974 Congressional Budget and Impoundment Appropriations Act and the effects the act had on the appropriations committees during the early years of its implementation. STEPHEN S. SMITH, *Call to Order* (Washington, D.C., 1989), discusses the causes and consequences of the loosening of committee grips over the legislative process in the House since the mid-1960s. CHARLES STEWART III, *Budget Reform Politics* (New York, 1989), analyzes the creation and reform of the House Appropriations Committee from 1865 to 1921 and the effects that the devolution of 1885 had on spending in the late nineteenth century. U.S. SENATE, *Committee on Appropriations* (Sen. doc. 21, Ninetieth Congress), is an official history of the Senate Appropriations Committee on the occasion of its centennial.

Congress, Committees, and Agencies

R. DOUGLAS ARNOLD, *Congress and the Bureaucracy* (New Haven, Conn., 1979), examines how bureaucratic decisions are tailored in order to gain support within Congress and its committees for agency programs. D. RODERICK KIEWIET and MATHEW D. McCUBBINS, *The Logic of Delegation* (Chicago, 1991), utilizes economic and management theory to demonstrate how the congressional parties employ the appropriations committees, along with other mechanisms, to control appropriations policy. AVERY LEISERSON, "Coordination of Federal

Budgetary and Appropriations Procedures under the Legislative Reorganization Act," *National Tax Journal* 1 (1948), provides a contemporary scholarly account of the politics of the Joint Budget Committee. MATHEW D. MCCUBBINS and THOMAS SCHWARTZ, "Oversight Overlooked: Police Patrols vs. Fire Alarms," *American Journal of Political Science* 28 (1984), discusses how congressional control over executive agencies can be effected without much overt oversight activity. TERRY M. MOE, "An Assessment of the Positive Theory of 'Congressional Dominance,'" *Legislative Studies Quarterly* 12 (November 1987), provdes an important critique of the extant congressional-dominance literature and of the limits of informal control over agencies exerted by congressional committees. WILLIAM NISKANEN, *Bureaucracy and Representative Government* (Chicago, 1971), presents a controversial account of how agencies dominate congressional committees in the appropriations process. BARRY R. WEINGAST, "Floor Behavior in the U.S. Congress: Committee Power under the Open Rule," *American Political Science Review* 83 (1989), argues that an increase in amending activity, such as was experienced with appropriations bills beginning in the 1960s, need not indicate a lessening of committee power to affect policy outcomes.

Sociological and Behavioral Studies

RICHARD F. FENNO, *The Power of the Purse* (Boston, 1966), is the classic treatment of the appropriations committees, utilizing sociological theory to examine committee politics in the postwar era. His *Congressmen in Committees* (Boston, 1974), examines how variations in congressional goals and committee environments create predictable variations in committee behavior, including detailed discussion of the appropriations committees. CHRISTOPHER H. FOREMAN, JR., *Signals from the Hill* (New York, 1988), explores how Congress, through its committees, influences agency behavior without passing legislation. DAVID R. MAYHEW, *Congress: The Electoral Connection* (New Haven, Conn., 1974), discusses the electoral logic of congressional behavior, with particular attention to how "control committees" such as Appropriations mitigate many of the negative consequences of this logic. STEPHEN S. SMITH and CHRISTOPHER J. DEERING, *Committees in Congress* (Washington, D.C., 1984; 2d ed., 1990), compares and contrasts behavior within the congressional committee system, with an eye toward understanding changes since Fenno's *Congressmen in Committees*. AARON WILDAVSKY, *The Politics of the Budgetary Process* (Boston, 1964; 4th ed., 1984), analyzes the strategies that budgetary actors employ in the face of limited information and established modes of behavior in the appropriations process. *The New Politics of the Budgetary Process* (Glenview, Ill., 1988), is a major revision of Wildavsky's earlier argument, taking into account the political and economic changes of the previous two decades.

The 1980s Budget Process

JOHN B. GILMOUR, *Reconcilable Differences?* (Berkeley, Calif., 1990), argues that the 1974 Budget Act served to rationalize budgetary decision-making in Congress and to infuse the process with a majoritarian vitality; the failures of the 1980s to balance budgets were not due to the failures of the Budget Act, but due to the failures of Congress and the president to reach a consensus on proper budgetary policy. MATHEW D. MCCUBBINS, "Party Governance and U.S. Budget Deficits," in ALBERTO ALESINA and GEOFFREY CARLINER, eds., *Politics and Economics in the Eighties* (Chicago, 1991), argues that imbalanced budgets in the 1980s were due to the effects of a bilateral veto game played between two parties with divergent spending preferences. RUDOLPH G. PENNER and ALAN J. ABRAMSON, *Broken Purse Strings: Congressional Budgeting* (Washington, D.C., 1988), gives an accounting of the breakdown of budgetary control during the 1980s from the perspective of a former director of the Congressional Budget Office.

Periodicals

CONGRESSIONAL QUARTERLY, *Almanac* (Washington, D.C., annual), *Congress and the Nation* (Washington, D.C., quadrennial), and *Weekly Report* (Washington, D.C., weekly), provide indispensable detail in following appropriations politics throughout the postwar era. OFFICE OF MANAGEMENT AND BUDGET, *Budget of the United States Government* (Washington, D.C., annual), is the definitive record of past appropriations decisions and current administration goals.

THE HOUSE COMMITTEE ON WAYS AND MEANS

Catherine E. Rudder

Of all the committees in the U.S. House of Representatives, there is no better vantage point from which to understand Congress than the Committee on Ways and Means. Throughout the House's two-hundred-year history few committees have rivaled the power of this legislative and political behemoth.

The primary responsibility of this panel has been that of raising revenues, a matter of utmost importance to the nation's founders. Article I, Section 7, of the Constitution requires that all bills for raising revenue originate in the House of Representatives. Only in the area of taxes did the founders establish such a requirement. The delicate subject matter entailed by taxation was explicitly spelled out by James Madison in *The Federalist,* no. 10. He admonished, "The apportionment of taxes . . . is an act which seems to require the most exact impartiality; yet there is, perhaps, no legislative act in which greater opportunity and temptation are given to a predominant party to trample on the rules of justice." This prescient warning is as relevant today as when Madison penned it.

DEVELOPMENT OF THE COMMITTEE

Given standing-committee status in 1802, the capacious jurisdiction of the Ways and Means Committee covered appropriations and banking as well as revenue matters. Without a doubt the Ways and Means Committee was the leading committee of the House throughout the antebellum period. Its chair, Virginian John Randolph (1801–1807), served as de facto majority floor leader, a precedent followed by his successors throughout the nineteenth and early twentieth centuries.

By 1865 the work load of the committee had become so vast and the power of the irascible chair (and leader of the majority party)

Thaddeus Stevens (R.-Pa.) so resented, that the House voted to divide the jurisdiction of the committee among three panels: Banking and Currency, Appropriations, and, for revenues, Ways and Means. As reformer Samuel S. Cox (D.-Ohio) explained on the House floor on 2 March 1865, "powerful as the committee is constituted, even their powers of endurance, physical and mental, are not adequate to the great duty which has been imposed by the emergencies of this historic time."

This theme was to resound in the twentieth century as the jurisdiction and power of the Ways and Means Committee steadily expanded in response to new conceptions of the role of the federal government in American life and the need for revenues to finance those ideas. In fact, by the 1970s, Ways and Means was responsible for not only the raising of all revenues for the federal government but also the authorizing and appropriating of 40 percent of all spending—a situation not entirely dissimilar to the antebellum period, when Ways and Means carried the lion's share of legislative work.

After the tripartite division of Ways and Means' jurisdiction at the close of the Civil War, the committee, nevertheless, remained central in the House and, because of congressional dominance during the second half of the nineteenth century, in the government generally. The panel's chairs continued in their party leadership roles. That position was fortified in 1885 when Speaker John G. Carlisle (D.-Ky.) appointed the chairs of the Ways and Means Committee and the Appropriations Committee to form with him a three-person majority on the Rules Committee, which was beginning to take on increasing importance in the management of the legislative business of the House.

The power of the Ways and Means chair in this collegial leadership position culminated during the Speakership of Thomas Brackett Reed (R.-Maine) when the Republicans took the majority in 1889. Reed, with the aid of Appropriations chair Joseph G. Cannon (R.-Ill.) and Ways and Means chair and future president William McKinley (R.-Ohio), successfully fought to change the method of counting quorums, which had obstructed the flow of legislation on the House floor. Increasing the power of the Rules Committee, and thus that of McKinley, Reed also made use of special orders through which the committee set the time and method of consideration of legislation on the floor.

The legislative predominance of the Ways and Means Committee, and especially its chair, did not go unchallenged during this period, as the Finance Committee, Ways and Means' counterpart in the Senate, flexed its muscle both by amending House revenue bills, a well-established practice, and by attaching its own tax legislation to other House-passed bills. Complaints that such action violated Article I, Section 7, of the Constitution notwithstanding, the Senate continues this practice today, sometimes with explicit acquiescence of the House. In 1982, for example, the House voted to go to conference on a tax bill that had been written by the Senate Finance Committee and approved by the Senate, as the House decided not to bring a bill of its own to the negotiating table.

HOUSE REVOLT

By the turn of the twentieth century, signs of professionalization of the House and, by implication, the Committee on Ways and Means, were manifest. Three-fourths of the committee chairs held their posts by virtue of seniority; the average tenure of House members was increasing; subcommittees were more regularly being employed to hold hearings and consider legislation; and House rules had become more articulated. Still, the Speaker of the House used his considerable power to hold sway in a manner unacceptable to a majority of House members. Speaker Joseph Cannon's powers included selecting committees, choosing chairs of those committees, naming the majority leader (and Ways and Means chair), and dominating activities on the House floor. Just as the reforms instigated by Speaker Reed in 1890 had strengthened the position of the Ways and Means Committee and its chair, the revolt of 1910 and the reforms in Democratic party rules the following year redounded to the decided benefit of this panel to an even greater extent.

In 1910, House Democrats and a group of insurgent Republicans were able to form the necessary majority to strip the Speaker of his position on the Rules Committee and his authority to appoint its members. The following year the new Democratic majority handed the power to make committee assignments for their side of the aisle to Democrats on the House Committee on Ways and Means. This group became the Democratic party's Committee on Committees, giving Ways and Means a new dimension of influence and prestige in the House of Representatives that was to last for the next sixty years.

Coupled with the fact that the chair of Ways and Means also served as majority leader, this new charge created a unique committee in the House, one with a very important legislative jurisdiction and with an even more significant party leadership role in running the House. It would not be inaccurate to conclude that from 1911 to 1915, as chair of the Democrats' Committee on Committees and of the Committee on Ways and Means, Oscar Underwood (D.-Ala.) was in a better position to influence the work of the House than anyone else, including Speaker Champ Clark (D.-N.Y.).

The Republicans, too, altered their rules. In 1917 the Republican caucus created a Republican Committee on Committees—unconnected with Ways and Means—and separated the floor leader's position from the chairmanship of Ways and Means. By the 1920s both parties had designated Ways and Means, along with Rules and Appropriations, as exclusive committees—meaning that a House member can serve only on that one committee. Thus, while the Democratic chairs of Ways and Means no longer functioned as floor leaders or served on the Rules Committee, the net gain for Democratic members of the Ways and Means Committee was considerable with the addition of the committee-assignment duty. For the Republicans, committee membership was valuable primarily for its significant jurisdiction.

THE HOUSE COMMITTEE ON WAYS AND MEANS

FUNCTIONING OF THE COMMITTEE

These rules changes set the parameters for the functioning of the committee for the next half century. The Ways and Means Committee, moreover, had begun to develop structures and traditions that were to affect not only its own work but also that of the House as a whole. And, while the formal jurisdiction of the committee did not change, its legislative responsibilities were vastly enlarged with the development of the income tax, the creation of entitlement programs such as Social Security, and new demands for revenues.

Although the size of the committee expanded somewhat in response to the growth in the number of House members, by the 1920s the pattern was set with only twenty-five members assigned to Ways and Means and with a party ratio of fifteen in the majority and ten in the minority (with only four exceptions: 1921–1923, with seventeen Republicans and eight Democrats; 1935–1937 and 1937–1939, with eighteen Democrats and seven Republicans; and 1965–1967, with seventeen Democrats and eight Republicans). This division, not representative of the actual overall party ratio in the House, provides another illustration of the specialness of the Ways and Means Committee.

Criteria for Ways and Means Committee service also became set by the early twentieth century. Aspirants were expected to have served in the House and to have been party loyalists. Most new members had served at least one term and often several terms before being assigned to Ways and Means. By the 1920s, turnover had become the exception, with 88 percent of the members continuing on the committee from one Congress to the next.

A concomitant of longer tenure for members and the selection of committee chairs by seniority was that chairs—absent majority-party turnover—served for longer periods of time. Robert L. Doughton (D.-N.C.), for example, began his chairmanship in 1933. He led Ways and Means for eighteen years (interrupted by the Republican Eightieth Congress), longer than any other chair. Since then, whole tax eras are best summed up by referring to the Ways and Means chair of the period: Wilbur D. Mills (D.-Ark., 1958–1974), Albert C. Ullman (D.-

Oreg., 1975–1981), and Daniel D. Rostenkowski (D.-Ill., beginning in 1981).

Other patterns were apparent by the turn of the century as well. As the work load of the committee expanded, temporary and then permanent subcommittees were brought into use. The holding of public hearings became a common practice to allow various interests to express their positions on tax issues.

Legislation, however, was marked up in private, and often the minority party was effectively cut out of the negotiations entirely. In the writing of the Underwood Tariff of 1913 (which provided for an income tax), for example, the Democrats of the committee were divided into seventeen subcommittees that then reported back to the Democratic majority of the committee. Similarly, the Smoot-Hawley Tariff of 1930 was written by the Republicans of the committee who divided themselves into fifteen subcommittees. After the Republican majority assembled the legislation, they presented it to their party caucus for alterations and approval before bringing it up on the House floor.

This extremely partisan modus operandi, however, was to ebb temporarily as the Great Depression brought on an atmosphere of crisis and a sense among committee members of the need to cooperate. Still, by 1934 the Democrats did not bother to consult committee Republicans on legislation following the lopsided Democratic victory in the midterm elections. Democratic losses in 1938 and the emergence of the conservative coalition of southern Democrats and Republicans dampened partisanship (but not conflict), as did the crisis created by World War II and, a decade later, President Dwight D. Eisenhower's opposition to large tax reductions.

Staffing of the committee was much more sparse in the first two decades of the twentieth century than subsequently, but was to expand to a lesser degree than that of the other major House committees. At the turn of the century there was only one committee clerk who, in effect, was a personal assistant to the chair. By 1946 the committee staff had grown only to ten in number. This group, however, was not the only source of expertise available to the committee.

In fact, it was the Ways and Means Committee that pioneered the use of a legislative counsel to help draft bills. The committee's Revenue Act of 1918 authorized the creation of a Legislative Drafting Service for use by any committee desiring help in drafting legislation. In 1924 the name of the service was changed to the Office of Legislative Counsel, its current name.

Two years later another unique office was set up to provide tax expertise, that of the Joint Committee on Internal Revenue Taxation. (Its name was changed in 1976 to the Joint Committee on Taxation.) Formally composed of five senior members of the House Committee on Ways and Means and five from the Senate Finance Committee, its purpose has been to provide objective, bipartisan expertise on tax issues for the two committees.

This staffing arrangement created a bridge between Ways and Means and Senate Finance unparalleled in any other legislative area except, since 1974, that of the budget, where the Congressional Budget Office serves both the House and the Senate budget committees. The combination of the House Legislative Counsel and the Joint Committee on Taxation created a highly expert source of help for the tax committees. A major difference between the two, however, was that the expertise of Joint Tax was available only to members of the two tax committees and primarily to their chairs, a source of great resentment on the part of reform-minded House members by the 1970s.

In addition to providing an informational and communications link between Ways and Means and Senate Finance, the joint committee staff developed the practice of working closely with the Department of the Treasury and the Internal Revenue Service to share information and estimates of the political feasibility of specific proposals. The connective tissue across chambers and institutions also extended to the public, as the staff of the joint committee, and especially its staff director, began to deal directly with interest groups.

Little over a decade after the establishment of the joint committee, its chief of staff assumed a role perhaps as important as that of the committee chair. Colin F. Stam served as staff chief from 1938 to 1964. His successor, Laurence N. Woodworth, held that position until newly elected President Jimmy Carter brought him into the administration to lead Treasury's tax staff. While still an important position, no one since Woodworth has served as long or been as seemingly indispensable as he or Stam.

A final source of official expertise for the Ways and Means Committee lay in the executive branch. By the turn of the twentieth century it was standard practice for Treasury officials to provide expert advice and to sit in on closed markup sessions. Moreover, staff from the Tariff Commission helped write tariff bills and the Social Security Board helped draft the Social Security Act in 1935.

THE WORK OF THE COMMITTEE

Prior to World War I the major sources of federal revenues were tariffs and excise taxes. During the Civil War an income tax was instituted to fund that conflict but was phased out by the 1870s, as revenues were sufficient to fund the obligations of the national government. Debates on the appropriate levels of duties on imported goods, in fact, focused less on revenue needs than on protectionist sentiment at least until the financial panic of 1893, which created a need for new revenue.

An income tax was enacted in 1894 but was overturned by the Supreme Court the subsequent year as unconstitutional in *Pollock* v. *Farmers' Loan and Trust Co.*, 158 U.S. 601 (1895). Popular sentiment from the South and West for the institution of a national income tax, coupled with bipartisan congressional and presidential leadership, was sufficient to overcome the opposition of Speaker Cannon to this innovation. In 1909, Congress passed the Sixteenth Amendment to allow an income tax and enacted a tax on corporate profits. By the time the thirty-sixth state ratified the amendment in 1913, the income tax as a fixture in the American revenue structure had become a virtual fait accompli.

Although the tax initially affected fewer than 2 percent of American earners, revenue needs, stemming primarily from World Wars I and II and from the Great Depression, led to the use of an income tax as the primary source of federal revenues. Adjustments to that tax—taking into account revenue needs, equity (variously defined), popular sentiment, interest-group demands, and fiscal effects—became the central work of the House Committee on Ways and Means in the twentieth century.

The jurisdiction of the committee gradually expanded—first with Franklin Roosevelt's New Deal and then with Lyndon Johnson's Great Society—with the enactment of social-welfare programs tied to the tax system. These include Social Security and unemployment compensation, enacted in 1935, as well as the earned income tax credit for the working poor and Medicare for the elderly, legislated three decades later. The combination of the entitlement programs under the jurisdiction of the Committee on Ways and Means totals almost 50 percent of all federal spending.

THE MILLS ERA

When Wilbur D. Mills assumed the chairmanship of the House Committee on Ways and Means in 1958, its jurisdiction, traditions, and patterns of operating were well set. Having served on the committee for sixteen years already, Mills was amply prepared for this leadership role, which he quickly mastered. Ironically, he was to witness the undermining of the power of his committee and of his own position, leading to his resignation as chair in 1974, in a wave of reform that engulfed the House. Fortunately for Ways and Means, although the reforms were initially devastating, they were not irremediable nor, significantly, was the jurisdiction of the committee substantially altered, despite attempts to carve it up.

To understand what happened and the consequences, it is useful to review the Mills committee during its heyday, as uncovered by John F. Manley in his *The Politics of Finance: The House Committee on Ways and Means* (1970). According to Manley, recruitment to the committee, leadership style and methods, committee norms, the committee's modus operandi, House expectations of the committee, the quality of committee performance, rules, party balance in the House, and the committee's relationship with the Senate Finance Committee and the administration are all important pieces in explaining the puzzle of legislative outcomes and especially the enormous success of Ways and Means bills passing intact on the House floor. Between 1933 and 1964 the committee won on the floor 93 percent of

the time, losing only 18 out of 248 roll calls. By anybody's reckoning, this was a record of power and success.

Ways and Means was successful on the House floor largely because it was granted privileges that enhanced its ability to keep tight control over its legislation and because the committee produced bills that satisfied a majority of the members. The House seems to have appreciated Madison's argument that tax legislation requires a special vigilance. Individual members may, for example, want to provide particular benefits for interests. Cutting taxes has always been more popular than raising them and thus difficult to resist without special structures. Altering one part of a tax package can unravel a carefully crafted compromise necessary for passage and can have an inadvertent deleterious impact on other parts of the tax code. Tax decisions can have an important impact on the functioning of the overall economy. Trade decisions affect not only revenues but also the relationship of the United States to the rest of the world and could, as in the case of the Smoot-Hawley Tariff, help precipitate a worldwide depression.

In short, the jurisdiction of Ways and Means was considered to be much different from that of other committees, requiring protection from frivolous short-term political maneuvering. A committee was needed that could take into account, in Madison's words, the long-term interests of the community and that could take the resulting political heat. At the same time, potentially momentous decisions emanating from the committee needed to be attuned to contemporary politics. It was on the shoals of the need for responsiveness that the Mills ship eventually foundered.

The protection given Ways and Means to do its work without damaging interference fell into three areas: House rules governing the committee, recruitment practices, and internal methods of operating. The most significant House practice regarding the Ways and Means Committee involved the use of the closed rule for legislation issuing from the committee. Bills brought to the House under the closed rule are permitted no amendments, only an up or down vote on passage and on a motion to recommit or send the bill back to the committee for further consideration.

Manley reported that of the ninety-six Ways

and Means bills debated under a rule from 1947 to 1966, only sixteen of the rules were open, eight were modified closed rules allowing specific amendments, and seventy-two were closed. This pattern had been in place since the 1930s for tax legislation and was applied more broadly to all Ways and Means bills in the postwar period. In return for the closed rule, said committee ranking minority member Robert L. Doughton in 1947, "tax bills were reported only after the fullest, fairest, and politically impartial consideration by the members of the committee" (as quoted in *The Politics of Finance,* p. 223). House members could explain to interest groups that it was impossible to offer any amendments on the floor, thus funneling pressure back to the committee and freeing other members of any blame for politically problematic provisions in the legislation.

In addition to the closed rule, the House kept the Ways and Means Committee small, with only twenty-five members, and maintained a party ratio that overrepresented the majority party (fifteen to ten in the Mills period, except for 1965–1967, when the Democrats increased their representation to seventeen). The small size of the committee limited access to it, while the party ratio helped the majority within the Democratic party work its will, although the existence of the conservative coalition had the opposite effect. Finally, as an "exclusive" committee, along with Rules and Appropriations, Ways and Means members did not have conflicting demands from other committee assignments.

The recruitment process provided the committee additional leeway to work its will and yet be responsive to party sentiment to some degree. The Republicans and Democrats followed remarkably similar criteria in selecting their partisans for the committee, although their procedures differed somewhat. Democrats selected Ways and Means members using a party caucus, whereas Republicans operated through their Committee on Committees. In both cases party leaders played a key role, as did large state delegations, as vacancies left by members representing populous states were typically filled by members from the same state. Because Ways and Means Democrats served as the selection committee for all the other committee assignments, Democratic leaders had a special stake

in who was named to Ways and Means. The committee on committees' function also lent logic to the Democrats' decision to divide the committee into regions to ensure geographic representation.

Both Republicans and Democrats chose members for Ways and Means who had already served in the House for several terms. For Democrats the average tenure of a new Ways and Means Committee member was 7.4 years, while that of a new Republican committee member was 4.7. Most committee members won their congressional seats with ample margins, a fact which meant that committee membership was highly stable and that members could afford to withstand interest-group pressure without the fear of losing their next election.

Party loyalty was an important criterion as well. Democrats on the committee had higher party-unity scores—that is, voted with their fellow partisans on votes that divided the parties—than did House Democrats as a whole. Similarly, committee Republicans scored higher on party unity than did House Republicans. Both parties emphasized philosophy in their Ways and Means selections, with the committee Republicans more conservative than House Republicans (and against Medicare) and with committee Democrats usually holding the following specific positions: in favor of Medicare (after 1960), of retaining the oil-depletion allowance (especially prior to 1960, thanks to the insistence of Speaker Sam Rayburn from the oil-producing state of Texas), and of free trade. Democrats were further expected to support the administration. As for philosophy, the existence of southern Democrats who were willing to join the Republicans on some votes lessened the liberalism of committee legislation.

The final set of criteria applied by both Republicans and Democrats pertained to the temperament of candidates. Members of the Ways and Means Committee were expected to be pragmatic and moderate in their approach to legislation and tolerant toward other committee members. Crusaders for particular causes were blackballed. As Manley emphasized in his study, "responsible, regular guys" were sought for assignment to this committee.

These criteria helped ensure that the committee would be representative of party and region, would in general be acceptable to party leadership and be able to help work the will of both leadership and each party caucus, would produce legislation that was careful in its approach to tax policy, and would be able to protect the House from excessive interest-group and popular pressure.

The committee members themselves would be willing to withstand such pressure because serving on the committee was highly prestigious and lent considerable power to committee members, especially the Democrats. Such service was also very helpful in attracting campaign contributions.

Ways and Means was considered to be one of the best if not the best committee assignment. Once on the committee, virtually no one moved off in preference of another assignment. Those attracted to the committee were less interested in pursuing specific public-policy interests or in using the committee to serve constituents than they were in the power such an assignment afforded them. This fact itself reinforced the tendency of the committee to produce legislation that would maintain the unique position of the House Ways and Means Committee, as the committee strived to live up to the implicit bargain of producing acceptable legislation that protected the House and the tax code in exchange for the privileged treatment the committee received.

A third layer of protection, after House rules and recruitment practices, stemmed from the committee's modus operandi, especially under Mills's chairmanship, which insulated not only the House from blame for individual provisions but also the committee members themselves. These methods included operating in secret, tightly controlling information and expertise, centralizing tax deliberations in a committee of the whole rather than using subcommittees, and zealously guarding their jurisdiction.

Other practices—such as working very slowly to develop consensus within the committee and approaching markups in a relatively bipartisan manner by fully including the minority in deliberations—contributed to a more widely acceptable legislative product. However, these techniques, which had worked to the advantage of the committee for many years, were to become the incriminating evidence in the case against Ways and Means brought successfully by reform Democrats in the early 1970s.

At the center of the committee stood Mills, who was widely regarded as the most knowledgeable member of Congress on tax matters and as a master legislative tactician. Mills became the keystone of the committee arch, the central conduit for interest-group and member demands. He held all markups in executive session, closed to the public and inclusive only of members of the committee, selected tax staff, and one or more Treasury experts. The sessions were long and grueling, and although all committee members were invited to participate, in practice a subgroup did the vast majority of the work. Tax bills typically started as concepts that were discussed in arduous detail and then drafted line by line.

Upon reporting the legislation, Mills would shepherd it through the House and then lead the House delegation in conference with senior members of the Senate Finance Committee, which typically loosened provisions and added tax breaks to House-passed bills. Thanks to the negotiating skill of Mills and to his willingness to provide cover for the Senate, many of those provisions would be dropped in conference.

Mills's reputation stemmed not only from his expertise and hard work, but also from his ability to develop consensus within his committee. Rather than express his position at the outset, he would listen carefully to the concerns of the participants and nudge the group toward an acceptable solution. He made a point to include the Republicans and to accede to their interests where possible. Mills's goal was to report a bill from his committee with the widest support possible. Failing that, he would develop a majority primarily composed of Democrats, but sometimes the conservative coalition would hold sway.

Because the committee usually was representative of the House, legislation acceptable to the committee was likely to be enacted by the larger body. Mills's method of building support within his committee meant that even when Republicans ended up voting against the committee's final product, much of it bore the stamp of Republican participation. Still, political scientists John Manley and Richard Fenno, Jr., both maintain that Ways and Means bills were enacted because members of the House approved of them rather than because members lacked the expertise, willingness to risk reprisals (such as not getting a desired committee assignment), or procedures to defeat tax legislation.

To elicit support for legislation, Mills did more than listen and create artful compromises. Committee members were often willing to cast their votes with Mills because they were grateful to him for the help he gave them. This help ranged from visiting a member's district to writing campaign letters for committee members to facilitating passage of so-called members' bills, which presumably affected very minor parts of the tax code but were of great help to a constituent or an organized interest. Mills worked closely with his committee members on making committee assignments for the House as well.

Moreover, cooperation by individuals was made as painless as possible. No one was required to attend the lengthy markups, as Mills and a rotating subgroup (depending on the subject matter) were willing to do all the work. Because the sessions were held in secret no individual member had to take the blame for politically difficult provisions. As Manley put it, service on Ways and Means entailed "high prestige at a low cost" (p. 75). Individual members were expected to act according to the norms of the committee, including serving an apprenticeship at first, deferring to more senior members, and protecting the position of the committee vis-à-vis the House.

In return, they reaped the benefits of being members of the prestigious and important Committee on Ways and Means. Member Democrats, as the party's Committee on Committees, were rewarded with the power of shaping the fundamental structure of the House. All committee members had the satisfaction of writing the tax law, molding the country's most important social-welfare policies, and overseeing trade policy. The jurisdiction of the committee grew appreciably in the 1960s—not without considerable disagreement within the committee—with President John F. Kennedy's explicit use of the tax code to affect economic performance, the enactment of Medicare, the expansion of aid to the poor, and the increasing use of tax expenditures, or breaks, in place of spending programs.

THE SEEDS OF CHANGE

Only a year after Mills assumed the chairmanship of the Committee on Ways and Means, a group of liberal Democrats dissatisfied with the status quo formed the Democratic Study Group (DSG) to force committees to be more responsive to the Democratic majority. The DSG was behind the successful move to expand the Rules Committee from twelve to fifteen members in 1961. In 1965 this group succeeded in affecting a group of reforms that included reestablishing the use of the Democratic caucus to approve committee assignments made by Ways and Means Democrats, bypassing the Rules Committee if it was obstructionist, changing party ratios on committees, creating a joint committee to study congressional organization, and removing the seniority of two Democrats who supported Senator Barry Goldwater of Arizona, the Republican nominee for president. By the end of the decade this liberal group had successfully pressed to reinvigorate the Democratic caucus and to have it hold regular meetings.

In 1970, Republican reformers teamed up with liberal Democrats to make public the work of committees and of the House as a whole. The Legislative Reorganization Act of 1970 increased the accountability of individual members by recording members' votes on amendments on the House floor. The reform also improved the ability of individual members to have a say in legislative matters by providing for time to deliberate on bills reported out of committee and by increasing the number of congressional staff.

At the same time that these inroads were being made, the complexion of the House was beginning to change. Southern Democrats, who were in line with the mainstream of the party, such as Charles Weltner (1963–1967) of Georgia were being elected to Congress. This trend accelerated as the 1965 Voting Rights Act began to take effect. Republicans were beginning to capture formerly Democratic seats in the House, thus lessening southern and conservative representation in the Democratic caucus. The elections of 1970, 1972, and especially 1974 helped bring in a new generation of Democratic members who had not been a party to the implicit bargain concerning Ways and Means. In fact, most of the seventy-five freshman Democrats elected in 1974 were elected as reformers intent on opening up and democratizing Congress. The changes in the makeup of Congress reflected attitudinal changes in the American public, especially in the attentive public who, through groups such as Common Cause and Public Citizen, exhorted Congress to alter its way of doing business.

If these indications were insufficient to alert the old guard that a fresh wind was blowing through the House, difficulties within the Ways and Means Committee itself might have served as a signal. Partisan conflict, exacerbated by the retirement of ranking Republican John W. Byrnes in 1973, increased markedly between the Ninety-second (1971–1973) and Ninety-third (1973–1975) Congresses. A new type of member was being assigned to Ways and Means. On the Democratic side were James C. Corman of California, William J. Green of Pennsylvania, Sam Gibbons of Florida, and Joseph E. Karth of Minnesota, and on the Republican side was Bill Archer of Texas, all appointed between 1969 and 1973 and all pursuing policy goals and eschewing norms such as apprenticeship and cooperation.

Mills himself was beginning to wear out. Disappointed in his failed run for the presidency in 1972, in pain from a back ailment that kept him away from the committee in much of 1973 and early 1974, drinking heavily since 1969, and suffering two important and previously unthinkable defeats on the House floor in 1970 and 1973, Mills must have sensed that the world in which he operated was shifting. Yet rather than respond as the master politician that he had been, he reacted defensively, fighting the establishment of subcommittees, failing to report tax reform (that is, removing special tax breaks) and national health insurance as desired by the Democratic majority, dodging instructions from the Democratic caucus, and asserting his authority as it slipped away.

REFORMS

Unlike the Revolt of 1910, in which a coalition of Republicans and Democrats attacked the prerogatives of the Speaker, the reforms of the 1970s were engineered by dissidents within the Democratic party and were effected via the Democratic caucus. For all practical purposes, the Republicans were not involved.

The unbridled wielding of power by committee chairs, the operating behind closed doors, the muffling of participation by junior members, and the thwarting of the will of the Democratic majority were all losing legitimacy by the 1960s and collapsed in the 1970s. The implicit bargain between the House and its Committee on Ways and Means was no longer tenable. In fact, Ways and Means became the symbol of illegitimate power and the focus of reform efforts of the Democratic Study Group (DSG) working through the Democratic caucus.

During the Ninety-third Congress the caucus put in place several procedural reforms that were to set the stage for frontal challenges to Ways and Means when Democrats organized for the Ninety-fourth. First, the caucus mandated that all committee markups were to be held in public unless a majority of committee members with a quorum present agreed in a roll-call vote to close the meeting. This change was aimed directly at Ways and Means, which still held 30 percent of its meetings in executive session. As a spokesperson for Common Cause commented after the vote, "We're going to try very hard to keep Ways and Means open. They're perhaps the worst offender, except possibly for Armed Services."

Second, in 1973 the caucus created a procedure that would make removal of committee chairs easier. There was now to be a secret-ballot vote in the caucus on each chair. Under a change in 1971 the newly created Democratic Steering and Policy Committee would nominate each chair and the caucus would approve each nomination. These changes created the possibility that someone other than the most senior member of the committee might be selected committee chair. As a result, committee chairs became more responsive to the Democratic caucus and to party leadership. Those chairs who were recalcitrant could be removed.

Third, the procedure by which major legislation would go to the floor under the closed rule—the most powerful weapon in Ways and Means' arsenal—was altered. Rather than leave the decision to grant a closed rule to the Rules Committee, the caucus decided that fifty Democrats would be able to propose to the caucus an amendment to a bill. If a majority of the caucus approved, then the Democratic members of the Rules Committee would be instructed to report a rule to allow that specific amendment to be voted upon by the entire House. This change signaled that the closed rule itself had lost legitimacy and was to be used more sparingly on Ways and Means legislation during the remainder of the 1970s.

Fourth, three party leaders (the Speaker, the majority leader, and the caucus chair) were officially added to the Democrats' committee on committees, heretofore composed only of Ways and Means Democrats. Party leaders, of course, had traditionally enjoyed substantial influence in the selection process, but their role had been informal.

Although Ways and Means was the primary target of these reforms, the caucus decided against substantially reducing the vast jurisdiction of the committee, the one change that could have hurt it the most in the long run. Many people thought that the committee was overworked and produced bills too slowly. Richard Bolling (D.-Mo.), who headed a House Committee on Committees which recommended in 1974 that work be shifted away from the Ways and Means Committee, commented that its jurisdiction was "so vast that it can't possibly be handled by a committee that doesn't even have subcommittees," echoing the words of Representative Cox over a century before (quoted in Strahan, p. 41). Fortunately for Ways and Means, the changes recommended by the Bolling committee had a broad and unacceptable impact on a number of committees.

Instead of approving the Bolling recommendations, the caucus adopted a rule, aimed specifically at Ways and Means, that required all committees with twenty or more members to have at least four subcommittees to improve the rate of production and to spread the power within the committee. (The requirement of five subcommittees was added subsequently. While Ways and Means complied by establishing the required subcommittees, including one on oversight, it decided not to establish a separate panel to consider major tax bills but to keep that work within the full committee.)

If senior members of the Ways and Means Committee thought these reforms were sufficient admonishment, they were mistaken. Mills's erratic personal behavior involving a striptease dancer, his frequent absences from the committee, and his defiance of the caucus undermined his position. The seventy-five freshmen Democrats strengthened the hand of the reformers. When the Democratic Caucus of the Ninety-fourth Congress met from 2 December to 5 December 1974, they were prepared to strike the final blows to Ways and Means.

Going to the heart of the committee's uniqueness, the caucus stripped the power of Democratic members to make committee appointments for the party and shifted that duty to the Steering and Policy Committee. This change lessened the prestige of serving on the committee, as did the caucus decision to enlarge the committee from twenty-five to thirty-seven members and to change the previously permanent party ratio of three to two to reflect the Democratic margin of two to one. A loss of prestige, however, was only one of the effects of such changes. The very nature of the committee was altered, at least at first.

As these caucus-mandated changes were being adopted, Mills was hospitalized and shortly thereafter resigned as chair. Had he not resigned, Mills would have had to face nomination by the Steering and Policy Committee and secret-ballot election by the restive caucus. Al Ullman of Oregon, the next senior Democrat on the committee, was elected to replace Mills.

The committee was now in a position to be more fully responsive to party majorities. National health insurance and tax reform could now be enacted. Individual provisions such as the oil-depletion allowance could be extirpated from the tax code. Power was now democratized within the committee, and with a larger committee, a wider variety of views could be expressed. Subcommittees would have staff, would work under the aegis of their own chairs, and would not be stacked by the full-committee chair. It would be much more difficult for the chair to be unilaterally obstructionist. Legislation emanating from Ways and Means would not have to be considered in a take-it-or-leave-it manner. All members would be accountable to the public and to the party for the positions they took both in committee and on the floor of the House. Democratic members who voted against Ways and Means positions would not have to worry about retribution through the committee-assignment process.

Underlying these reformist expectations, however, were a series of assumptions stemming largely from a disregard for the need for mechanisms to enforce responsibility, especially, as Madison made clear, in the tax area. Like people who are determined not to make the same mistakes that their parents had made in raising children, the reformers overlooked the strengths of the old system and the important functions served by centralization, secrecy, binding rules, and strong leadership. They further assumed that Democratic majorities on issues existed apparently a priori and that positions would hold firm. They seemed unaware of the phenomenon of cyclical majorities. In removing the layers of insulation from the committee, reformers forced a responsiveness to short-term political considerations, to an escalating multitude of interest-group demands, and to popular sentiment, to paraphrase Madison negatively, unrefined and unenlarged by thoughtful distillation of the legislative process.

ASSESSING CHANGE

Assessing the effects of reforms in a natural environment that is itself changing is no easy task. Not only does the environment change, but leaders change as well. One must consider the possibility that Ullman's approach, for example, was quite different from that of Mills. Further, because there is no way to control variables under these circumstances, it is impossible to trace the effects of each reform positively. Still, assessments, while less than conclusive, can be made. This task is eased by the fact that by 1983, Dan Rostenkowski's second term as chair, committee operations were in many ways recentralized so that three periods can be compared: the Mills era, the postreform years of 1975–1982 (Ullman and the first two years under Rostenkowski), and the period since 1983, when authority was reasserted.

Such a comparison leads to the inescapable conclusion that rules that allow agreements to be made and kept, that limit choice, and that give leaders the ability to lead are at least as important in a representative system of government as are widespread participation, decentralization, extensive responsiveness to multiple claims, and constant accountability for positions taken. These two sets of values must be balanced against one another in order for representatives to be both responsive and able to govern. Second, leadership style and ability can matter and should not be treated as an idiosyncratic factor. Third, the external environment has a large impact on legislative outcomes in a representative democracy. For the tax area, key aspects of the environment include election results, the state of the economy, consensus or lack of it in the American public, party control of institutions, presidential leadership, and perceptions of fiscal realities.

AFTERMATH: THE POSTREFORM YEARS

The immediate democratizing effects of the changes met the reformers' expectations, but there were some apparently unintended outcomes as well, owing in part to the changing political environment. The reforms did not make reaching consensus easier, in part because the environment in which Congress was operating was shifting. Specifically, there was no obvious Democratic majority on many issues as the 1970s came to be dominated by the politics of energy, which divided the House by region instead of by party. Furthermore, the intransigence of stagflation, a stagnant inflationary economy, was leading to a shift in public philosophy, particularly concerning fiscal policy, that left the Democrats divided and uncertain. Both energy issues and stagflation created a new sense of limits that had been absent in the 1960s and early 1970s. Finally, the new Democratic president, Jimmy Carter (1977–1981), was unable to provide the leadership necessary to create Democratic consensus. It is in this context that the reforms must be evaluated.

The enlargement of the committee and the formation of six subcommittees (Social Security, Trade, Public Assistance and Unemployment Compensation, Health, Oversight and Select Revenues—the current designations—with the full committee responsible for major tax issues) had the effect, as one member expressed it in an interview in 1975, of "spreading the cookies around." Subcommittee chairs could select and control their own staffs. Information, as a consequence, was more widely available. On nontax legislation the existence of subcommittees allowed the committee to act more quickly, to work on more than one subject at a time, and to hold hearings on and report out legislation that it might not otherwise have had time to complete or to consider in detail.

In the full committee where tax matters are taken up, legislative markup was very slow going after the reforms. As one veteran Democrat observed, "The difference in trying to get a consensus of 35 members as opposed to 25 is tremendous, and it's more than the numbers would indicate." This difference can be traced to the change in the composition of the committee, an effect desired by reformers. For instance, for the first time in the twentieth century an African American, Charles Rangel (D.-N.Y.), and for the first time ever a woman, Martha Keys (D.-Kans.), were selected to serve on the committee. In addition, previous recruitment criteria that had helped produce consensus were discarded. New members were now more likely to be outspoken and to participate immediately. Four freshmen Democrats, two of whom had served in the House previously, were assigned to the committee. Prior House service dropped from an average of 8.0 years in the Ninety-second Congress to 4.5 years in the Ninety-fourth. Thus, the committee after the reforms was intentionally more diverse, less legislatively experienced, and less insulated from electoral demands.

Open meetings, as well, had their intended impact, with virtually no closed sessions through the remainder of the 1970s. In general, aides from the Department of the Treasury and the Joint Taxation Committee had less exclusive control over the information members received. However, open meetings made members more accountable to whoever cared to pay attention, especially lobbyists. For freshmen and members with unsafe seats—products of the change in the recruitment process—interest groups could affect reelection prospects, thereby making their demands difficult to ignore, especially with the development of grass-roots lobbying techniques. One member evaluated open markups this way: "The open meeting is not as fruitful as I thought it would be. . . . The public's not there, but the interests are. . . . Open meetings put special interests into the process and gave them an active input." Moreover, negotiating in public made it harder to make trade-offs. This

reform's strength was its weakness: making deals publicly made such necessary bargaining much more difficult to conclude.

Another reform, the creation of an appeal process within the caucus to force a vote on the House floor on individual provisions within a tax bill, was used sparingly and to good effect in the 1970s. It permitted separate consideration of the oil-depletion allowance—a thorn in the sides of liberals for many years and a symbol of backroom politics—in the 1975 Tax Reduction Act.

In contrast to the new "appeal" procedure, the gradual use of modified-open and open rules was less salutary. For example, the energy tax bill of 1975, reported under an ironically entitled "orderly open rule," was gutted on the floor of the House. One view is that the open rule prevented the House from producing a coherent and tough bill. However, the House's performance on energy legislation may have simply reflected the possibility that the House and the country were not politically ready for a strong energy policy. There is some truth in both of these positions, but it is also clear that a restrictive rule helps hold together agreements and permits members to vote for provisions that they could not afford to vote for if separate votes were required. In any case, this reform had its intended effect of giving individual House members more say on tax legislation and reducing the committee's exclusive claim on tax bills in the House. Half of the major tax bills considered by the House between 1975 and 1986 were either substantially amended or rejected, according to Randall Strahan (1990).

A final procedural reform, the loss of the Democratic committee assignment duty, is probably best evaluated by borrowing from Richard Fenno's work on the importance of members' goals in understanding the work of congressional committees. According to Manley, the main value of controlling committee assignments was to lend prestige and power to Ways and Means Democrats, and this role was seen by them as very important. Prior to the reforms, members whose primary goal was to achieve influence in the House (as opposed to constituent service or public policy) were thus attracted to the Ways and Means Committee. One likely result of the loss of the assignment duty was that a different kind of member, one with different goals, would be attracted to the committee.

To test this proposition, Strahan interviewed fourteen Democrats and seven Republicans who joined the committee between 1975 and 1986 and asked them their reasons for having wanted a seat on the committee. While he did not separate the Republican and Democratic responses, his data do provide an indication that postreform members' goals differed from their predecessors'. As many members cited either policy goals or a combination of policy and constituency goals as those who cited prestige or influence goals. This finding suggests a more mixed set of goals than during the Mills era, more policy-oriented and more willing to use the committee to serve constituency interests.

Taken together, the reforms reduced the autonomy, control, and prestige of Ways and Means and of its chair. The establishment of subcommittees and increased staff improved the ability of the committee to handle its vast jurisdiction and spread power among committee members. Increasing its size improved the committee's diversity on several dimensions. The changes in the use of the closed rule gave House members, and especially Democrats, access to the individual provisions in tax bills. Open meetings and recorded roll calls made the actions of each committee member visible. Democratization of the legislative process was served by these reforms.

Some other effects expected by reformers, such as the passage of more liberal legislation including national health insurance, did not materialize, not because reforms thwarted them but because the legislative environment changed. In fact, by 1978 the House passed a Revenue Act reported by Ways and Means that from a tax-reform standpoint had exactly the opposite effect that liberal Democrats of the early 1970s would have desired.

Still other effects—stemming from reforms and environmental shifts—were apparently not anticipated. Committee members became more responsive to constituency-based interest groups than to the committee chair, the ranking minority member, or their party. Since many members, even those winning their elections by wide margins, feel electorally insecure, the absence of committee constraints had an adverse impact on the entire membership, not only on those who had experienced close elections.

By the end of the 1970s, tax scholars' verdict on the reforms was decidedly negative. In an article in *Tax Notes* on 2 February 1981, Stanley S. Surrey concluded that "the consideration of tax legislation by the Congress has completely disintegrated. The picture has been one of almost utter chaos without responsible control residing anywhere." A primary culprit, according to Surrey, was congressional reform, in particular the increased size of the Ways and Means Committee and the proliferation of subcommittees and staff. Former reform advocate Thomas J. Reese in *National Tax Journal* (September 1979) came to a similar conclusion but fingered open sessions as well as other reforms for decreasing influence of professional centers of expertise, such as the tax staffs of the Treasury Department and the Joint Committee on Taxation, and for increasing the influence of lobbyists on tax policy.

LEADERSHIP

At first some observers blamed the new chair, Al Ullman, for the difficulties Ways and Means was experiencing. It should be clear, however, that the situations that Mills and Ullman faced were entirely different, and style is circumscribed by opportunity. One member of the committee, for example, commented in an interview in 1975, "The chairman must react differently from the way he reacted in the past. He's not protected by seniority. This causes a tremendous change in the way the committee operates."

Ullman was challenged in the committee, on the floor, and in conference to a much greater extent than Mills ever was, and he could not count on his committee partisans to support him either on the floor or in conference. While the new chair was admittedly less forceful than his predecessor, he also lacked the tools to enforce his will or to create a committee consensus. Renewing a technique practiced in earlier periods, Ullman tried to forge agreement by making use of the Democratic caucus on the committee. He set up task forces composed of Democrats who met behind closed doors to develop legislation. It was a technique, among others, that his successor, Dan Rostenkowski, was to adopt in order to re-establish authority within the committee.

When Rostenkowski first assumed the chairmanship after Ullman's defeat in the 1980 election, he was no more successful than Ullman had been in controlling his committee and tax policy-making. If anything, the two major tax bills of 1981 and 1982 could be considered case studies in legislative disarray.

Rostenkowski inherited a fractious, undisciplined committee. The political environment was one of divided party government, with the Republicans holding the White House and, to the dismay and surprise of Democrats, the Senate as well. Republican gains in the House, coupled with votes of southern Democrats, were sufficient to give the Republican president, Ronald Reagan, an operative majority on key legislation.

By 1983, however, with Democratic gains in the 1982 elections, Rostenkowski brought some semblance of order over tax policy-making. By 1986 he and the committee had passed major tax-reform legislation over the opposition of a great variety of interest groups and to the amazement of virtually everyone. He accomplished this feat by harkening back to the techniques of the Mills era and utilizing some new ones. Overall he got the individual members of the committee to start thinking of themselves as a committee with a stake in its performance and its consequent prestige. Moreover, he turned the fact of divided government to his, and the country's advantage. Rostenkowski did what Ullman could temperamentally never have done, but success required undoing many of the democratic reforms of the 1970s.

THE REASSERTION OF AUTHORITY

There was more than one surprising defeat in the 1980 congressional elections. Along with Ullman, House Democratic whip John Brademas of Indiana lost his seat as well, opening the third highest Democratic leadership post in the House and one which promised to be a sure step on the ladder to the speakership. Dan Rostenkowski seriously considered accepting the appointment but chose to assume the chairmanship of Ways and Means instead. This decision is an important indicator that Rostenkowski, a savvy politician who was desirous of power, judged the Ways and Means Committee to be a more suitable vehicle for his ambitions than the whip position would have been. This committee, even in its reformed state, remained at the top of the hierarchy in Rostenkowski's judgment.

It was not until the third year of his chairmanship, however, that Rostenkowski began to gain control of his committee and experience legislative success. In 1981 he and House Democrats engaged in a devastating legislative battle with Ronald Reagan over tax cuts, with each side vying to provide the most tax advantages to as many interest groups as possible. The result exceeded the worst fears of Madison. The lack of discipline, cautious leadership, or procedural controls led to the largest tax cut in the nation's history, one that the country could ill afford. The actual bill enacted was the administration's, thanks to the help of southern Democrats and in particular Democratic Ways and Means Committee member Kent Hance of Texas. Thus, Rostenkowski was defeated on his first major piece of legislation, with the help of one of his own committee partisans, and he himself contributed to the decimation of the tax code and the revenue base, responding only to short-term political advantage.

In 1982 the Ways and Means Committee fared no better. When it became clear that the unprecedented tax cuts of 1981, coupled with other revenue-depressing factors such as an economic recession, would require large tax increases, it was Republican Senate Finance Committee Chair Robert Dole of Kansas, not Rostenkowski, who took the lead in a remarkable performance that included writing the bill in closed caucuses involving only the committee's Republicans. On the Senate floor, using the provisions of the Budget Act of 1974 that limit debate and amendments on bills of this type, Dole enforced sufficient discipline to achieve a 50–47 majority. In contrast, Rostenkowski was unable to unite the Democrats on his committee. He offered his own tax package, one that was rejected by Ways and Means Democrats who, with the assent of the House, agreed to go to conference without a House bill, an admission of impotence unthinkable in the Mills era.

By 1983, however, Rostenkowski was beginning to take control of his committee and the tax-writing process. While he could never recapture the spirit of the implicit bargain between the House and the committee that characterized the early Mills era, he could reassert authority, control excesses, and exercise responsibility. To accomplish this task, Rostenkowski used a number of techniques in developing a deficit-reduction package in 1983 and 1984 that have come to characterize his chairmanship.

First, he closed committee markups, even on uncontroversial bills. Second, he made frequent use of Democratic caucuses in the committee, just as Dole did with the Republicans on Senate Finance, to develop partisan majorities in the committee. Third, like Mills before him, he worked to develop legislation that met the major concerns of his Democratic committee members. Fourth, he worked for a package of tax increases that would be acceptable to both the House and the president. Fifth, like Dole, he floated deficit-reduction packages to assess the strength of interest-group opposition and the likelihood of passage.

Rostenkowski also used the closed rule so that the package could not be picked apart on the House floor, and he added "sweeteners" (like Mills's members' bills)—benefits to particular interests that members care about—so that the legislation could win a majority even though many specific provisions might not pass if voted on separately. Rostenkowski used these same techniques in enacting the most remarkable piece of legislation in his career, the Tax Reform Act of 1986, a model of responsible, careful, controlled policy-making.

More broadly, in working to reshape his committee (especially the Democrats) into a cooperative group with a stake in the reputation and welfare of the committee, Rostenkowski implemented a series of changes, identified by Strahan in *New Ways and Means*. In contrast to Ullman, Rostenkowski became directly involved in committee recruitment. Throughout the 1980s, no freshmen Democrats were appointed to the committee, nor was anyone from a marginal district. Rostenkowski worked to encourage group solidarity and identity in a variety of ways, including holding issue-oriented retreats outside of Washington and hosting a gala celebration of the two-hundredth anniversary of the committee in 1989. Members have felt they have been a part of the committee, in part, because Rostenkowski has consulted widely with committee members to include their concerns in legislation and to secure a firm commitment for their votes.

Rostenkowski has used more forceful techniques as well. He is willing to punish dissidents and defectors, as Kent Hance found out when his committee-paid trip to China was cancelled and he found he had lost the ear of the chair. This kind of treatment leads members to cooperate with the chair. Also, Rostenkowski has taken control of staff resources. He hires subcommittee as well as committee staff with the exception of one clerical and one professional appointment allowed subcommittee chairs under House rules.

Combined with these methods have been external developments that have helped recentralize leadership. Divided government and the seemingly unending budgetary crisis led to the need for the key actors in the House, Senate, and the administration to meet and negotiate on behalf of their bodies. The rules related to the Budget Act of 1974, as amended to require budget reductions and spending limits, also contributed to recentralization and control, especially in the Ways and Means Committee, with its crucial jurisdiction over taxes and many entitlements.

Despite the recentralization, reassertion of control, and backsliding on reforms such as open markups, the Rostenkowski era is distinct from that of Mills. The House Committee on Ways and Means is less insulated from the House and the country than it once was, and it is more immediately responsive to the wishes of the majority party, but it has recovered from its state of chaos of the postreform years. House Democrats continue to want to keep a close eye on the committee. In 1991, for example, the caucus voted to require that subcommittee chairs of the Ways and Means Committee be approved by the caucus.

Perhaps Rostenkowski accomplished what the reformers had in mind but could not themselves immediately effect: a responsive committee, sensitive to short-term political forces but with concern for the enduring interests of the national community. Achieving this balance lies at the heart of the founders' idea of representative government.

BIBLIOGRAPHY

History

In 1989 the House Committee on Ways and Means celebrated its 200th anniversary with the publication of the best single work on the history of the committee. In writing *The Committee on Ways and Means: A Bicentennial History, 1789–1989* (Washington, D.C., 1989), authors DONALD R. KENNON and REBECCA M. ROGERS took their assignment seriously. Despite the fact that it is an official document, the work is nonpartisan and evenhanded in its approach, but it is not particularly critical of the committee nor is it especially analytical. Still, by unearthing original sources, Kennon and Rogers have produced an outstanding piece of historical scholarship. Moreover, the book is beautifully printed and is well worth having.

Also historical but with a more analytical thrust is JOHN F. WITTE's superb *The Politics and the Development of the Federal Income Tax* (Madison, 1985). This book provides an important base from which to understand tax policy and politics. Economist JOSEPH A. PECHMAN's classic work *Federal Tax Policy,* 5th ed. (Washington, D.C., 1987), also offers a penetrating examination of tax policy and its distributional effects—subjects vital to understanding the Ways and Means Committee.

Political Science

As one moves from history and political economy to political science, one ground-breaking work of the behavioral revolution is JOHN F. MANLEY, *The Politics of Finance* (Boston, 1970), along with his classic article, "Wilbur D. Mills: A Study in Congressional Influence," *American Political Science Review* 63 (1969): 442–464. It could be argued that Manley got too close to his subject, but until Manley's study scholars knew little about the functioning of the Committee on Ways and Means or Senate Finance. His most important contribution was his understanding of the sources of Mills's power. To have read Manley in 1970, however, would not have alerted readers that the rumblings of a legislative earthquake could already be heard, that Mills's power was threatened, and that the committee, as a special target of the congressional reformers, was soon to be under siege.

RANDALL STRAHAN, *New Ways and Means: Reform and Change in a Congressional Committee* (Chapel Hill, N.C., 1990), ably covers the post-Mills period from the 1970s through the mid-1980s. He examines the effects of institutional reforms on the committee and on the parent chamber, and he wrestles with the puzzling question of how the committee was able to report comprehensive tax-reform legislation in 1985, contrary to the predictions of lobbyists and scholars alike.

For an outstanding journalistic recounting of the tax-reform bill and the political maneuvering it entailed, see JEFFREY H. BIRNBAUM and ALAN S. MURRAY, *Showdown at Gucci Gulch* (New York, 1987). TIMOTHY J. CONLAN, DAVID R. BEAM, and MARGARET T. WRIGHTSON, *Taxing Choices: The Politics of Tax Reform* (Washington, D.C., 1989), offers a more analytical approach.

In addition to monographs, a plethora of useful articles about the contemporary committee is available. Citations for many of the best of these articles can be found in Strahan's *New Ways and Means,* cited above.

THE RULES COMMITTEE:
THE HOUSE TRAFFIC COP

Bruce I. Oppenheimer

The Committee on Rules, which had been a select committee since 1789, was created as a standing committee of the U.S. House of Representatives on 2 March 1880. In a major revision of its rules and structure committees, the House provided the Committee on Rules with jurisdiction over "all proposed action touching on the rules and joint rules" (*Journal of the House of Representatives,* Forty-sixth Congress, 2d Session, 2 March 1880, p. 1543). This general charge left the Rules Committee's role for others to define. Little attention was given to its movement from select to standing committee. Within a short time, however, the Rules Committee became a crucial element in the operation of the House of Representatives. (A *rule* is a resolution providing the terms for consideration of a bill on the floor.) Although the committee's role has shifted during over a century of its existence, it has remained a powerful vehicle in the structure of national legislative processes.

In 1880 the House was in a state of chaos, a situation not alleviated by revisions in its rules and committee organization. The minority party had the means to obstruct majority rule. The legislative calendar of the House was growing rapidly, and the leadership was unable to manage the work load. In bringing order to the House, in giving priority to legislation awaiting consideration on the House floor, and in serving as a key vehicle for the majority party and its leadership to control the House, the Committee on Rules established itself as a center of power.

Although there have been ebbs and flows in the Rules Committee's power since 1880, its unique position and functioning within the House (the Senate has no equivalent committee) make it critical for understanding the operation of Congress and how changes within the institution and in the broader political and social context of American government affect the policy influence of America's national legislature.

There are five areas that have served as the focus of scholarly attention on the Rules Committee. First has been the use of the Rules Committee as a vehicle of the majority party in the House of Representatives. By studying the committee we learn much about the majority's success in managing the House. Except for the period 1937–1972, the link between majority party control of the House and the Rules Committee, although varied, has been close. (Ironically, it is the interlude when the committee operated as an independent power base for a cross-party coalition that has received most attention.) The Rules Committee has been the "traffic cop" in the House but has not always been responsive to the same authority.

Second, although its role in the day-to-day workings of the House has seemed to be primarily procedural, the Rules Committee has had important substantive policy impact throughout its history. It is easily assumed that in controlling the flow of legislation to the floor and in setting forth the terms for floor debate that the Rules Committee is a procedural "traffic cop" or gatekeeper. Alterations in this role have carried with them important policy implications. Sometimes this has meant negating the work of authorizing committees, sometimes expediting it, sometimes requiring changes, and sometimes even removing bills from their control. In doing so, the committee has affected the amount, substantive content, timing, and conditions of legislative floor activities.

Third, the Rules Committee has always been important. Yet because of its importance and the central and critical nature of its function, the committee has often been the focus of controversy. Because it sets the terms for House debate and can propose changes in the rules of the institution, it has been the locus of tension between majority rule and minority rights in legislative decision-making. In addition, it has been at the heart of the tension over the role of political parties in the Congress. How much should the Rules Committee reflect the will of the majority party? Should members of the committee be agents representing the constituents who elected them or agents of their parties? Beyond that, the Rules Committee has been at the center of tension between the goals of individual House members and the goals of an institution. How much freedom can a democratic institution allow its members in the process of debate and amendment without undermining its operations?

Fourth, the Rules Committee has reflected the political and social environment of the House. For example, as the policy demands on the national government have increased, so has the work load of the House. It has been the Rules Committee that often has devised methods for the House to adjust. At times, when the committee has not been responsive to changes in the environment, it has come under attack and found its authority threatened. Thus, in 1910 the revolt against Speaker Joseph G. Cannon cost him the chair and membership of the Rules Committee but not of the Speakership. And in the 1960s the Rules Committee became the focus of the liberal Democrats' attack on disproportionate conservative control of the House.

Finally, throughout its history the membership of the Rules Committee has been an important feature in understanding its workings. Although its size has varied, the Rules Committee has always been a small committee that has not always represented the diversity of the House. Small shifts in its membership have sometimes had major consequences for committee decisions. During most of its history, it has been closely linked to the majority-party leadership and the Speaker. When this has not been the case, the composition and method of appointment of its membership have been major concerns. In the 1970s, as we shall see, membership turnover and a change in the method of appointment as well as the ideology of new members reestablished the Rules

Committee as an arm of the majority-party leadership.

This essay will focus on these five approaches to analyzing the impact of the Rules Committee on the House. Its principal concern will be to understand how the Committee has changed so that in the late twentieth century it operates to allow the majority party to legislate in the House. Primarily, this will involve the examination of the three most recent periods in the Committee's history as a traffic cop in the House: (1) 1937–1960, when the Committee operated largely independently of the majority party and was instead the power base of the conservative coalition of Republicans and southern Democrats; (2) 1961–1972, when conservative coalition control of the Committee declined and it entered a period of tenuous cooperation with the majority-party leadership; and (3) 1973–1990, when it was reestablished as an arm of the majority-party leadership and developed mechanisms for centralization of House decision-making. To provide the proper context for understanding the struggle for control of the Rules Committee that began in 1937, it will be valuable first to examine the committee's during the first fifty-seven years of its existence as a standing committee. It was during that time that the basic "traffic cop" role and powers of the committee were established.

THE SPEAKER DOMINATES, 1880–1910

The full potential of the new standing Committee on Rules was not immediately realized. But Speaker Samuel J. Randall (D.-Pa.), its first chair, who served from 1876–1881, wasted little time in investing it with special procedural powers. He ruled that all future revisions in the rules must be referred to that committee and that it could report at any time to the House on issues related to rules (*A History of the Committee on Rules,* p. 60). This gave the committee privileged status during floor proceedings. Because the Speaker not only was a member and chair of the Rules Committee but, in addition, appointed its four other members, powers given to the Rules Committee were effectively powers given to the Speaker.

From Randall's elevation of the committee's status until the revolt against Speaker Cannon in 1910, two aspects of the committee's role were established and maintained. First, the Rules Committee was the major vehicle in the effort of Speakers to develop orderly control of the House and to process the majority party's program as the Speaker envisioned it. And second, the minority-party members played little beyond a cameo role in the workings of the committee. Because Speakers only appointed the most loyal members of their party to the other two seats on the Rules Committee, the support, votes, and imput of the two minority-party members were rarely needed, sought, or offered.

The Rules Committee helped to establish order in the chaotic environment of the House that continued after the 1880 reforms. Three specific problems received its attention: the use of dilatory (or delaying) motions, the flow of legislation from calendars, and the disappearing quorum. Dilatory motions and the disappearing quorum pitted the advocates of minority rights against the advocates of majority rule. To prevent passage of legislation they opposed, members of the minority party would offer countless motions to delay consideration and votes on it. In addition, they could often prevent passage of legislation by refusing to vote even though they were present on the floor. This latter tactic, known as the disappearing quorum, was effective because inevitably with some members of the majority party unavoidably absent and the minority present but refusing to vote, the number of members voting would fall short of a *quorum*. (A quorum is the number of members required under the rules to conduct business. For the House a majority of members constitute a quorum.) These two tactics could effectively stalemate the House.

It was the Rules Committee and Thomas B. Reed (R.-Maine.), first as a member of the Committee and later as its chair and Speaker of the House, who pushed the necessary reforms for the majority party to assert control. Reed's assault began in 1882 when he used a contested-elections bill to amend the rules and stop dilatory motions on matters under the Constitution. Reed argued that existing House rules were infringing on the constitutional right of Congress to judge elections, returns, and qualification for membership. And if the House did not change its rules, then the Speaker had the right to rule dilatory motions out of order.

The problem of an obstructing minority received broader treatment from Reed and the Rules Committee when he was elected Speaker at the start of the Fifty-first Congress in 1889. In the Rules Committee, Reed discussed strategy for dealing with the disappearing quorum. Again using an elections case, before the House adopted its rules formally for the new Congress, Reed had the clerks record the members who were present and not voting for the purpose of establishing a quorum on the vote. After initial uproar and several days of debate, the minority Democrats yielded. In addition, the old House rules were substantially rewritten allowing the Speaker to refer legislation to committee without debate, making it easier for committees to report, and reducing the size of a quorum to one hundred in the Committee of The Whole House under the State of the Union, or the house itself operating under another name to expedite business. Thus, ten years after its creation as a standing committee the Rules Committee became the vehicle for a strong Speaker to alter the way the House would conduct business.

One other change added greatly to the Rules Committee's arsenal. This was its use of "special orders" to control the flow of legislation to the floor. Prior to the development of "special orders," legislation had to wait its turn on the appropriate calendar to reach the floor. Thus, a mundane matter might have priority over an important bill simply because it was placed on the calendar first. This made it difficult to manage a legislative program in the House. The little control that existed was in the hands of the Appropriations Committee. The special status of Appropriations bills meant that they served as instruments for grafting on substantive legislation, especially when the substantive matter was caught in a calendar backlog.

A special order became a means whereby a bill could be brought to the floor, regardless of its position in a committee or on a calendar, and taken up for consideration. It was first used by the Rules Committee in the Forty-seventh Congress, Second Session, to save a tariff bill, but not firmly accepted as procedure until several years later. Asher Hinds notes in the fourth volume of *Precedents of the House of Represen-*

tatives that this power of the Rules Committee was rarely used to report legislation while John G. Carlisle (D.-Ky.) was Speaker from 1883 to 1889 and was "in 1887 . . . still regarded as a proceeding of doubtful validity." (p. 192). However, special orders became the core of the committee's power. Although most legislation still came to the floor in order of its position on legislative calendars, special orders gave the Rules Committee the means to manage a chaotic House. The committee could use this power to report a resolution that set the time and manner for consideration of a given bill on the floor, and the committee needed only a majority vote to adopt and implement such a resolution. Eventually these special orders would be commonplace for the flow of most legislation not otherwise privileged, and the term "rule" would replace "special order" to denote the function of these Rules Committee resolutions.

Taken together, the changes meant that by 1890 the House had been transformed from a body in which the minority party or even a few members could bring activity to a standstill to one in which the Speaker, working through the vehicle of the Rules Committee, kept the majority in tight control. DeAlva Stanwood Alexander in his *History and Procedures of the House of Representatives,* commenting on the importance of the special order power, noted that "the Committee on Rules, after the adoption of this procedure, began to fill the public eye. Like Pandora's box it seemed to conceal surprising possibilities" (p. 204). The Rules Committee's role as the traffic cop, with responsibility for access to the House floor, was established. The committee's interpretation of that role would, however, be subject to change.

Through a number of strong speakers of both parties, Republicans Reed and Joseph G. Cannon (Ill.) and Charles F. Crisp (Ga.), a Democrat, the Rules Committee's power and the Speaker's control of the majority party were institutionalized. In the 1890s some members of the minority party made efforts to limit the committee's power by increasing its size, providing each state with a member, and making all committee chairs members. But in an era of strong, cohesive congressional parties, and with a memory of the disorder of earlier days, such proposals did not receive serious consideration.

Change did not occur as long as the majority party was united and as long as the Speaker and the Rules Committee remained within the bounds of what the House judged acceptable. By the time Cannon became Speaker in 1903, the political context had changed. Most members had not been around during the deadlocks of the 1880s and earlier, and were less willing to accept centralized leadership. As important, the Republican party was becoming less unified both in the country and in the House. Insurgent Republicans had their causes buoyed by the presidency of Theodore Roosevelt (1900–1908). Yet their legislative goals were largely incomplete when he left office, and they faced frustration in the House, which continued in the hands of the epitome of regular Republicanism, Speaker Joseph Cannon. Cannon stood for party regularity as well as regular Republicanism. He used the speakership, the Rules Committee, and their resources against insurgent Republicans who represented the progressive wing of the party.

Because the Rules Committee was a primary source of Cannon control, it became the object of attack by the Insurgents. The Rules Committee, with Cannon as its chair and with its other members appointed by Cannon, not surprisingly, had no Insurgents among its members and prevented Progressive legislation reported from other committees from being considered on the House floor. In 1908, Insurgent Victor Murdock (R.-Kans.), proposed simplifying House rule, election of the Rules Committee by the House, and open Rules Committee meetings. His proposals, like similar ones before and after, were referred by the Speaker to the Rules Committee, never to reach the floor (*History of the Committee on Rules,* p. 85).

A year later Cannon was willing to compromise by allowing the adoption of a Calendar Wednesday procedure which established an alternate method to bring legislation to the floor. But by then the Insurgents had forged an alliance with progressive Democrats. The revolt against Cannon and the strong speakership could not be averted.

The details of the revolt are less important than its outcome. The Rules Committee membership was upped from five to ten, and the Speaker was precluded from serving as a member. Thus, the Speaker's domination of the

Rules Committee ceased. In most respects the immediate impact on the Rules Committee was more symbolic than substantive. True, the enlarged committee was more representative than its predecessor, and the following year the Speaker lost the power to appoint committees. But insurgents were not among the Republican members of the new committee. Except for Cannon, the other members of the old committee were made members of the new one. John Dalzell (R.-Pa.), a close associate of Cannon, who had served on the Rules Committee since 1895, was appointed chair. Most important, the role of the Committee remained unchanged. The power of the majority party through its Rules Committee traffic cop to control the order of House business and to prevent the chaos of earlier years remained. The attack had been on the powers of the Speaker, not on the role of the Rules Committee. Although the seeds for a more independent Rules Committee may have been planted, especially once the Speaker lost the power to appoint its members, it continued as an arm of the majority party.

PARTY VEHICLE AND POTENTIAL FOR INDEPENDENT POWER, 1911–1936

The "traffic cop" function of the Rules Committee remained intact following the 1910 revolt, but membership on the committee carried less prestige, especially after Democrats won control of the House in the 1910 elections. During the eight years of Democratic majorities, power in the House moved from the Speaker to the Democratic caucus and the majority-party leader.

The Democrats made the caucus, the organization of all House Democrats, central to the operation of the party's legislative program. House Democrats were accountable to the caucus, not to the Speaker. It had the power with a two-thirds vote to bind its members to decisions or to subject them to loss of membership in the caucus. (There were circumstances under which members were exempted from caucus positions, such as when they had made commitments during their respective campaigns for office.) Accordingly, Rules Committee Democrats needed to respond to the caucus.

In addition, the Democrats removed committee assignment powers from the Speaker and gave them to a new Committee on Committees, to be composed of the Democratic members of the Ways and Means Committee. This new party committee became responsible for the assignment of Democratic House members to standing committees. The majority leader served as chair of the Ways and Means Committee, with jurisdiction over tax and other revenue legislation, and as chair of the Democratic Committee on Committees. As floor leader, chair of Ways and Means, and of the Committee on Committees, Oscar W. Underwood (D.-Ala.) became the most influential member of the House.

None of the Democrats appointed to the Rules Committee in 1911 at the start of the Sixty-second Congress had previously served on it. They owed their positions to Underwood and to the Democrats on Ways and Means. Not surprisingly, Underwood used the Rules Committee in helping to schedule the legislative program of the caucus and, following the election of Woodrow Wilson in 1912, the legislative program of the first Democratic president in sixteen years. Although inexperience led these new Democratic Rules members to overstep their bounds on occasion, they did not often exercise independent judgment. When the committee produced a special order that would have prevented the Republicans from offering a motion to recommit on a court injunctions bill, Speaker Champ Clark (D.-Mo.), who served from 1911–1919, supported the objections of the Republican floor leader, James Mann (Ill.). This, however, was the exception.

Normally, the Rules Committee and the Democratic leadership worked in close harmony. With only a small Democratic majority in the Senate in the Sixty-third Congress, the Rules Committee's role was particularly valuable in managing Wilson's program. By expediting consideration of key bills in the House, the Rules Committee kept pressure on the Senate. And in the following Congress, with a reduced Democratic majority in the House and with controversy surrounding Wilson's actions after the sinking of the British passenger ship the *Lusitania* by a German submarine, in which 128 Americans died, the Rules Committee worked with Wilson to prevent House debate on a resolution that might demonstrate the disunity of the American position (*A History of the Committee on Rules,* p. 105).

Another indication that the changes of 1910 did not affect the general traffic-cop role of the committee can be seen in the reaction of the Republicans. In the minority, they were no more pleased with the actions of the Rules Committee in this eight-year period than the Democrats had been previously. When Mann complained of a "gag rule" on bills in the Sixty-second Congress, Robert Henry (D.-Tex.), chair of the Rules Committee, expressed little sympathy in answering: "It grieves me to see my distinguished friend . . . gag when we administer to him a sugar-coated dose of his own medicine" (*Congressional Record,* vol. 48, 8 July 1912, p. 8719).

The Republicans had another turn at controlling the flow of legislation to the floor and the terms of floor debate with the start of the Sixty-sixth Congress in 1919. During the next twelve, uninterrupted years as the majority party, the Republicans renewed the status of Rules Committee membership by recognizing the chair as a formal member of the party leadership and by granting the committee additional procedural powers. Ironically, while renewing the formal linkage between the Rules Committee and the leadership, the Republicans also allowed it to be perceived as a somewhat more independent traffic cop.

Three primary factors were responsible for the changes in the committee. First, the chair of the Rules Committee was formally designated as part of the Republican House leadership. As part of a five-member party steering committee, the Rules chair shared responsibility for the party's program with the Speaker and the majority leader, giving the position a standing that had not existed since the revolt against Cannon.

Second, Philip Campbell (R.-Kans.), the new Rules chair, evolved the powers available to him in ways not envisioned previously (at least since 1910). This was partly tolerated because of his designated leadership position, and partly because Campbell was far more senior than any of his Republican colleagues on the committee. He realized that the chair had the prerogatives to advance or retard legislation. Often Campbell would conduct Rules Committee business without the presence of a quorum. In 1921 Democrats charged that Re-

publican Rules members rarely attended meetings and that decisions were made without a quorum present. Campbell admitted that meetings were called suddenly at times, and that the minority did not raise the quorum issue because it recognized the duty of the majority to order House business (*Congressional Record,* vol. 61, 3 May 1921, pp. 976–980). Because Campbell called the meetings, this effectively meant that he was in charge of what bills were considered and given rules.

When the majority of the committee made decisions with which Campbell and/or the Republican leadership disagreed he was even more inventive. As chair, Campbell had the responsibility to report Rules decisions to the House. By refusing to do so, he could veto committee decisions. For example, in 1922 when the committee voted to grant a rule providing for consideration of the Woodruff-Johnson Resolution, calling for an investigation of the Justice Department, Campbell simply refused to communicate that decision. In reporting this event in his book *The United States Congress: Organization and Procedures,* Floyd Riddick quotes Campbell's response to his critics on the Rules Committee: ". . . it makes no difference what a majority of you decide, if it meets with my disapproval, it shall not be done; I am the Committee, in me reposes absolute obstructive powers."

Campbell's behavior on Woodruff-Johnson and in other instances was most likely done with the tacit approval of the other House Republican leaders. It may have been the first time but was certainly not the last when the Rules Committee or its chair would be called upon "to take the heat" for the majority party leadership. More importantly, it offered a brief glimpse of how an independent Rules chair or a independent Rules Committee might operate. In this case, Campbell largely affected the role of a rogue traffic cop. By the late 1930s, however, this role would become common.

Parliamentary rulings by Speaker Frederick Gillett (R.-Mass.) provided a third avenue of renewed influence and attractiveness of the Rules Committee. Gillett, who served from 1919 to 1925, allowed that the Rules Committee could legitimately report a special order or rule on legislation that had not yet been referred to it. The implication of this ruling was that it was within the power of the Rules Committee to grant a rule on a bill that was pending before another House committee, effectively discharging that committee and allowing for the bill to be taken up on the House floor. Although rarely used, the power established in this ruling heightened the Rules Committee's standing, and the mere suggestion of its use could be a catalyst for moving legislation. In a separate and less significant ruling, Gillett gave the Rules Committee the ability to suspend indirectly the Calendar Wednesday procedure.

The end of Campbell's tenure in the House and a major revision of House rules adopted in 1924 tempered the resurgent traffic cop of the House. Under the rules changes, the committee had to report its decisions to the House within three legislative days; it became more difficult for a rule reported by the committee to be considered on the House floor on the same day; and the Rules Committee became liable to a discharge petition on legislation, whereby 150 members could force a bill bottled up in committee onto the floor. The impact of these changes was small. In the case of the discharge petition, it was not until 1932 that a petition to discharge the Rules Committee from consideration of a bill received the necessary support (145 members had to sign at that time) to be taken up on the floor. And then the House voted against discharging the committee.

The Rules Committee's return to prominence was evidenced by the House leaders who were recruited from its members in the 1920s. William Bankhead (D.-Ala.), Speaker from 1936 to 1940, and Joseph Martin (R.-Mass.), Speaker from 1947 to 1949 and 1953 to 1955, ascended to that position from party floor leadership, and Bertrand Snell (R.-N.Y.) and Finis Garrett (D.-Tenn.) became party floor leaders. The link between the House traffic cop and the party leadership, although not severed in 1910, was firmly reestablished in the 1920s.

Following the 1930 elections, the Democrats returned to majority status in the House. For three Congresses, the Seventy-second to the Seventy-fourth, the Rules Committee continued to work as an arm of the majority party. In the Seventy-third Congress it played an especially important role in expediting Franklin Roosevelt's New Deal legislative program. The membership composition of the Committee

was of little concern during much of this period. As was the case through Wilson's presidency, at least half of the Democratic members came from southern or border states. But in the early New Deal period, as during the Wilson administration, the regional distinction between Democrats was not critical. If anything, southern House Democrats were more supportive of their presidents' legislative programs than were northern Democrats, a number of whom were conservative machine politicians. The fact that five of the eight Rules Committee Democrats in the Seventy-second and Seventy-third Congresses and five of ten in the Seventy-fourth Congress were southerners was not worthy of concern.

The Rules Committee proved most helpful to the majority party during the last session of the Seventy-third Congress. The committee provided eight New Deal measures with closed rules, under which no floor amendments were allowed. This served to protect the legislation from efforts to weaken it and made for expeditious consideration on the floor. Never before had so many closed rules been granted in a single session. Among the New Deal programs protected with closed rules were the Agricultural Adjustment Act, Tennessee Valley Authority Act, Securities Act, and National Industrial Recovery Act. Republicans complained about the restrictions. Even on the most controversial bill, the National Industrial Recovery Act, the rule was adopted, albeit by a narrow 209–187 vote. Of the Rules Democrats, only Eugene Cox (Ga.) voted against the rule.

Some foreshadowing of the problems an independent Rules Committee could create for the majority party became apparent in the Seventy-fourth Congress. As the scope of the New Deal extended, some conservative Rules Democrats began to resist. The leadership of the resistance came from a New Yorker, the committee's chair, John J. O'Connor. It surfaced most clearly in 1935 on the Holding Company Act. The Roosevelt administration working with then Commerce Committee chairman Sam Rayburn (D.-Tex.), sought a rule providing for a recorded vote on a key amendment. O'Connor successfully urged the Committee's members to deny the request. Such behavior on the Rules Committee's part was still, however, the exception. It continued most of the time as a traffic cop, working for the majority party in managing the House. But when regional and ideological differences led to a division in the Democratic party in 1937, an independent Rules Committee, quite different than the one that had existed for more than a half century, arose.

TRAFFIC COP FOR THE CONSERVATIVE COALITION, 1937–1960

With the exception of the Eightieth and Eighty-third Congresses, 1947–1948 and 1953–1954 respectively, when Republicans controlled the House, the Rules Committee ceased to be a reliable vehicle of the majority party after 1936. The small fissures that were evident by the end of Franklin Roosevelt's first term in 1936 grew to a major split in 1937. James Patterson in his book *Congressional Conservatism and the New Deal* carefully documents the split between northern and southern Democrats and the development of the conservative coalition of Republicans and southern Democrats. Southern resistance to a larger role for the national government in regulating the economy, to social-welfare and labor legislation, and to the growing civil rights component of the national Democratic party fueled this bipartisan alliance. Nowhere was the strength of this cross-party coalition more visible than on the Rules Committee. Throughout the remainder of the New Deal and into the 1960s, the Rules Committee, acting as the vehicle for the policy goals of the conservative coalition, created problems for liberal Democratic policy goals. Although it no longer served the interests of the majority party, its powers, so well established over more than fifty years, were unaltered.

Several factors explain the establishment and maintenance of conservative-coalition sway in the Rules Committee. First, the turnover of Rules southern Democrats, who were usually conservative, was low. The Democratic leadership, therefore, did not have many opportunities to alter the membership composition in a way more favorable to party programs. Eugene Cox stayed on the Committee from 1931 until his death in late 1952. Howard Smith (D.-Va.), the most skilled and influential southern conservative, was a member of the Rules Committee from 1933 to 1966 and its chair for the last twelve of those years. And William Colmer (D.-Miss.), appointed as a New Dealer in 1939 but who within a few years joined the conservative bloc, remained on the committee until his retirement in 1972.

Second, this low turnover was exacerbated by the small size of the committee. During the early part of this period the committee had fourteen members (nine Democrats and five Republicans) but that decreased to twelve (eight Democrats and four Republicans) in the Seventy-ninth Congress. The longevity and the small number of seats meant that even after Cox's death, Smith and Colmer could join with the four Rules Republicans to block legislation in the committee. And that assumes that the Democratic leadership could count on the consistent support of the six other Democrats, a situation that was rarely the case.

The third ingredient to this extended period of conservative-coalition control was the institutionalization of the seniority system. When the speaker was stripped of the power to make committee assignments and appoint committee chairs, after the revolt against Cannon in 1910, this responsibility moved to party committees. Gradually, committee chairs were selected on the basis of seniority, as measured in years of consecutive service on a committee, and members once placed on a committee were not removed, except when adjustments for party balance required it. Unlike Reed or Crisp or Cannon, Speaker Rayburn could not threaten Howard Smith with removal from his Rules chairmanship.

The effect of seniority principles are best illustrated in the case of William Colmer's reappointment to the Rules Committee in 1949. Because the Republicans were the House majority in the Eightieth Congress (1947–1948), the Rules Committee switched from 8 to 4 Democratic control to 8 to 4 Republican control. In the process, Colmer was bumped from the committee. There was some discussion of denying Colmer a seat on Rules when the Democrats returned to control in the Eighty-first Congress. Instead, seniority-related rules were adhered to, and Colmer was reappointed.

Finally, even when vacancies did occur among Rules Democrats, filling them was in the hands of the Democrats on the Ways and Means Committee, who might or might not be

THE RULES COMMITTEE: THE HOUSE TRAFFIC COP

responsive to requests from the party leadership. Southern Democrats were well represented among the Ways and Means Democrats.

The influence of conservative-coalition control on the Rules Committee after 1936 was marked. The Committee remained the traffic cop for the House, but that role was considerably altered. Instead of assisting the flow of its party's and its president's legislation, the Rules Committee became a major roadblock. Among its tactics were delaying or defeating rule requests on liberal legislation, granting rules on such legislation but not the desired ones, requiring that a committee requesting a rule amend the bill before a rule would be granted, and, at times, using the committee's power to push conservative initiatives to the floor against the wishes of the Democratic party leadership.

Conservative coalition control of the Rules Committee impacted a broad range of legislation from the New Deal of the 1930s to the Great Society of the 1960s. Major legislative initiatives in civil rights, housing, health care, education, and labor among others were delayed, defeated, or watered down by the Rules Committee. James Sundquist in his book *Politics and Policy* documents the effectiveness of the conservative coalition, on the Rules Committee and elsewhere, in stopping liberal Democratic proposals.

The policy impact of the Rules Committee in this era of cross-party coalition control was not uniform throughout. A number of factors led to ebbs and flows in its influence. Conservative-coalition strength on the committee and in the House varied somewhat during the period. From the Seventy-sixth to the Seventy-ninth and the Eighty-first to the Eighty-second Congresses, Adolph Sabath (D.-Ill.) chaired the committee. A liberal Democrat of limited legislative skill, Sabath nevertheless was sometimes able to use the resources of his position to stifle the conservative coalition. He would use his prerogatives as chair to delay reporting a rule desired by the conservatives or to control floor debate on such rules and argue against them. More frequently, he was overrun by the committee's conservative majority in efforts to get rules for New Deal and Fair Deal legislation.

By comparison, when Howard Smith (D.-Va.) was chair the resources of the position were fully exercised on behalf of the coalition.

This went far beyond Sabath's futile efforts to manage rules on the floor. Lacking a written set of rules for its own operations, the Rules Committee worked largely at the chair's discretion. If a bill that Smith opposed had enough support among Rules members to obtain a rule, he would simply refuse to call a meeting of the committee, refuse to place the bill on its agenda, or adjourn a meeting should a quorum of members momentarily be lacking. In the Eighty-fourth Congress, for example, an areas redevelopment bill that had passed the Senate and been reported out by the Banking and Currency Committee in the House did not receive a rule because Smith went back to his congressional district and would not call a meeting. Just the threat of such tactics would frequently bring substantive concessions from bill sponsors.

Under Smith's leadership, Speaker Rayburn found it necessary to bargain over the Rules Committee agenda. Richard Bolling (D.-Mo.), who was the prime Democratic leadership representative on the Rules Committee from 1955 to 1982, wrote in his book *House Out of Order* that Rayburn met with Smith at the start of the Eighty-fifth Congress and obtained a commitment from him to report three designated bills. In exchange, Rayburn had to guarantee that Bolling would help prevent other rules from being granted. Whereas a skilled and independently powerful chair such as Philip Campbell, who supported his party's goals, could make the House's traffic cop an expediter of a legislative program, Howard Smith developed that same position to create insurmountable roadblocks.

Other political features affected the level of success of the Rules Committee's cross-party coalition. The party composition of the House, for example, had a strong impact. Because the South was solidly Democratic, changes in Democratic House membership meant changes in the number of northern Democrats. In the Seventy-eighth Congress with the Democrats reduced to 218 members, the Rules coalition could be particularly bold. It frequently reported rules on administration bills but provided waivers so that nongermane amendments for conservative legislative causes could be considered. For example, a debt-ceiling bill was used to get consideration of a bill repealing a war-ordered limit on salaries. By contrast, in the Eighty-first Congress, there were enough

Democrats in the House to enact the "21-Day Rule." This change in the House rules gave House committee chairs a way of bringing legislation to the floor that had been pending before the Rules Committee for twenty-one days and on which the Rules Committee had either defeated the request for a rule or had not acted. Actual or threatened use of the 21-Day Rule was successful in bringing a number of key pieces of the Truman domestic legislative program to the floor including a housing bill, an anti–poll tax bill, and a bill authorizing the National Science Foundation. When the Democrats lost twenty-eight seats in the 1950 elections, the conservative coalition had sufficient votes to repeal the 21-Day Rule.

The policy impact of the conservative coalition majority on the Rules Committee was not uniform on all issues. In certain legislative matters, such as those involving agriculture and public works, the Rules Committee still acted as a vehicle of the majority party. But even these issues became the currency of exchange for legislation on which the committee and the leadership were at odds. And on civil rights legislation, the southern Democrats could not always depend on the active backing of the committee's Republicans. In the 1950s Smith relied on the powers of the chair to block civil rights bills from committee consideration. In 1957 the Democratic House leadership pushed for a special meeting of the Rules Committee to consider the civil rights bill when Smith would not call a meeting. Six Democrats and one Republican, Hugh Scott (Pa.), provided the majority necessary to call a special meeting of the committee (the other Committee Republicans were committed to not opposing Smith on procedural matters) to consider a rule on the civil rights bill. Without this unusual effort, it is doubtful that the first civil rights bill since 1875 would have become law.

In only two Congresses between 1937 and 1960 did the Rules Committee perform like the committee of old in working with the majority party leadership. Both instances occurred when Republicans were in the majority in the House. The Eightieth and Eighty-third Congresses were reminders of how useful the Rules Committee could be as a traffic cop working for the majority party. In the Eightieth Congress, the Committee granted nine closed rules, one short of the record set during the

Seventy-third Congress. In addition, on six appropriations bills the Republicans produced rules waiving points of order against authorizing legislation within each. In these cases the purpose of the authorizing language was to disband programs or restrict agencies. This allowed the Republicans to bypass the authorizing committees in undoing certain New Deal programs. During the Eighty-third Congress, Eisenhower's first, the Republican leadership and the administration used the Rules Committee to pressure other committees. Knowing that Ways and Means Committee Republicans were not sympathetic to an extension of an excess-profits tax bill, the Rules Committee reported a rule for its consideration upon the request of the Republican House leadership. This was done despite the fact that the bill had been referred to Ways and Means only two days previously.

These two congresses offer a marked contrast with the Rules Committee during Democratic congresses. The Rules Committee and the Republican leadership were of one mind in the Eightieth and Eighty-third Congresses, and the committee was a reliable vehicle for managing the party's legislative program. The leadership did not have to bargain with the committee's chair. Traffic-cop powers were used to alleviate obstructions, not to create them.

As the stronghold of the conservative coalition, the Rules Committee was a source of frustration for the Roosevelt and Truman administrations as well as for a growing contingent of liberal Democrats during the Eisenhower years. By the Eighty-sixth Congress pressure to make changes took on new urgency. The Democrats had made large gains in the 1958 election, but the eight Rules Democrats remained the same. Howard Worth Smith and William Colmer joined the committee's four Republicans to block legislation that liberal Democrats had the votes to report from authorizing committees. Despite the efforts by Speaker Rayburn, Smith refused to compromise. As long as there was a Republican president, the claim could be made that the Democratic agenda would be subjected to presidential vetoes, and a confrontation with the Rules Committee would be fruitless. But the election of John Kennedy to the presidency in 1960 removed that argument, and the Rules Committee necessarily became the focus of attention.

THE RULES COMMITTEE: THE HOUSE TRAFFIC COP

CONFRONTATION TO COOPERATION, 1961–1972

Pressured by the Democratic Study Group, a newly organized group of liberal House Democrats, and unable to gain concessions from Chair Howard Smith during the Eighty-sixth Congress, Speaker Rayburn agreed to confront the blocking power of the committee. After considering several alternative approaches including changing the party ratio 8–4 to 9–3, adopting a new 21-Day Rule, and removing Colmer (who had opposed Kennedy during the 1960 general election campaign), Rayburn decided to fight for enlarging the committee from twelve to fifteen members for the Eighty-seventh Congress. Many rules requests were being defeated by 6–6 tie votes in the committee, with Smith and Colmer joining the committee's four Republicans in opposition. By adding two Democrats and one Republican to the membership, it was anticipated that the Democratic leadership could produce an 8–7 majority for reporting bills in the Kennedy legislative program.

The intensity of this fight over expansion is somewhat deceptive when the impact of the change is evaluated. Both party organizations took positions on the expansion—the Democrats in favor and the Republicans opposed. According to Milton Cummings and Robert Peabody in their article "The Decision to Enlarge the Committee on Rules," attempts at compromise proved unsuccessful. The Kennedy administration sought a guarantee from Smith that he not block the administration's legislation, and Smith responded by agreeing to do so for only five pieces of the administration's program. Following floor debate on the proposed change that included a rare speech by Rayburn, the House passed the expansion on a vote of 217–212.

Although the two Democrats added to the Rules Committee, B. F. Sisk (Calif.) and Carl Elliot (Ala.) were both viewed as national Democrats, supportive of the Kennedy administration, the impact of expansion was smaller than either its supporters or opponents expected. In the Eighty-seventh Congress only, fewer rule requests were either denied or unheard by the committee than in the Eighty-sixth. But Smith continued to use his powers as

chair to frustrate the Democratic leadership. At times it was necessary to force him to call meetings. In other instances Smith placed bills on the committee's agenda to which the leadership was opposed. Bargaining and threats of using discharge petitions and Calendar Wednesday to bring legislation to the floor still had to be applied in dealing with Smith. Most importantly, the expectation that instead of 6–6 ties the expansion would produce 8–7 votes in favor of reporting legislation proved incorrect. As Richard Bolling pointed out in a 1975 interview as reported by Bruce Oppenheimer in "The Rules Committee: New Arm of Leadership in a Decentralized House":

> There was never anytime when we had the eight that I didn't leave with a nervous stomach. There was always the opportunity for a pick off and make an 8–7 win an 8–7 loss. Smith and Colmer together or separately were capable of figuring out who to approach and how; be it in terms of district or personal preference or a trade-off or whatever. They had eight targets sitting there. If they get one, it turns from a majority to a minority.

In the Eighty-seventh Congress, these "pick offs" meant that key Kennedy bills on aid to education, mine safety, and job training among others were denied rules.

The same scenario was typical in the Eighty-eighth Congress when the enlargement of the Rules Committee was made permanent. Only after threatening a discharge (to remove from its control through a discharge petition) of the Rules Committee did Smith agree to hold hearings on the 1964 Civil Rights Bill. He kept these going for nine days before allowing a vote on the rule request. Often, special efforts had to be made to ensure that Smith would call a meeting.

In an effort to counter Smith's capacity to create a roadblock in the Rules Committee, a new 21-Day Rule was adopted in the Eighty-ninth Congress. It differed slightly from the 21-Day Rule of the Eighty-first in that the Speaker was given greater discretion in recognizing a member of the authorizing committee to call up a bill. Of the eight bills brought to the floor under the 21-Day Rule, seven passed the House and five became law during the Eighty-ninth Congress. These included civil rights legislation, a housing bill, and a school construction bill. Most importantly, the actual or threatened use of the 21-Day Rule undercut Smith's ability to delay legislation.

In addition the Eighty-ninth Congress saw the Rules Committee stripped of its capacity to report a resolution sending a bill to conference, that is, to a special joint conference committee appointed to reconcile differences when a bill passes the two house of Congress in different forms. Under existing House rules, if a unanimous-consent request to send a bill to conference was objected to, a resolution from the Rules Committee was required. The change enabled the Speaker to recognize the floor bill manager (normally a committee chair) to offer the motion. Thus, another weapon in Smith's and the conservative coalition's arsenal was removed.

By neutralizing the Rules Committee, the huge Democratic majorities in the House and Senate made the Eighty-ninth Congress the most productive ever in terms of legislative accomplishment. The 1966 election reduced the Democratic House majority substantially, making it inevitable that the 21-Day Rule would be repealed. Other events offset this loss of the Speaker's countervailing power in dealing with the Rules Committee. Howard Smith's congressional seat had been redistricted, and after twenty-three terms in the House he was defeated in the Democratic primary. Not only did this remove a conservative southern Democrat from the committee, but it opened the way for a new chair.

Speaker John McCormack (D.-Mass.), who served in that position from 1962 to 1971, did not leave the task of filling the seats left vacant by Smith and by a defeat of a moderate, James Trimble (D.-Ark.), to the Ways and Means Democrats. He ensured that his preferences, William Anderson (Tenn.) and Spark Matsunaga (Hawaii), both with records of strong party support, were selected to fill the Democratic vacancies. This made the Democratic leadership margin on the committee somewhat more favorable than what had been under the best of circumstances only an 8–7 split.

Of greater consequence was the decision over the chairmanship. Liberals, wanting to deny Colmer the position, first proposed adding the House majority and minority leaders to the committee, making the former its chair.

The Democratic Study Group also proposed removing Colmer. Whether as a result of these threats or not, Colmer was willing to accept a written set of rules for the committee, and no formal effort to violate seniority and deny him the chair was made. The rules required regular, weekly meetings of the committee and allowed for calling of meetings by a majority of its members. The chair retained responsibility for the agenda and for the staff, but his capacity for arbitrary control was diminished.

As chair, Colmer was generally far more cooperative than Smith with the requests of the Democratic leadership. Part of the change may have been due to the personal friendship between Colmer and Speaker McCormack. McCormack had been largely responsible for protecting Colmer's reappointment to the Rules Committee after the 1948 election. More important, the onset of the Nixon administration meant that the committee no longer was faced with managing the legislative program of an activist Democratic president. It became only the occasional focus of controversy, as when it denied rule requests favored by the majority party leadership. Yet in a changing House this somewhat passive Rules Committee, although no longer a source of obstruction, was not very useful in helping the leadership to manage the expanding work load of an increasingly decentralized institution.

RENEWED ARM OF THE LEADERSHIP, 1973–1990

Three factors were critical in turning the Rules Committee from its passive, cooperative state into a strong, working arm of the majority party leadership: membership turnover, effective committee leadership, and the changing House environment. Not only did the Rules Committee reestablish its close links with the leadership during this period, it became a key vehicle in the development of the strongest period of party control of the House since early in the Wilson administration.

The first ingredient in this change was the replacement of departing Rules Democratic members. Changes in both the type of members chosen to fill vacancies and the method of their selection cemented the relationship between the Speaker and the Rules Committee's majority members. Throughout Colmer's six years as chair the membership of the Rules Committee consisted of the same fifteen people. At the start of the Ninety-third Congress, there were three Democratic vacancies to fill (and one Republican). Although not formally empowered to do so, Speaker Carl Albert (Okla.), 1971–1977, ensured that his choices filled the Rules seats. Albert asserted his authority in a demonstrable fashion. One seat was given to Clem McSpadden (Okla.). Not only was he from Albert's home state, but he was a newly elected House member, the first to serve on the Rules Committee since 1917. In filling the seat opened by Colmer's retirement, Albert rejected the recommendation of a caucus of conservative Democrats and instead appointed Gillis Long (La.), a moderate, to the position.

These appointments clearly established informally the Speaker's authority to name Rules Democrats. In 1975, as the Ninety-fourth Congress began, Richard Bolling offered a resolution at a meeting of the Democratic Caucus giving the Speaker power to nominate all Rules Committee Democrats at the start of each Congress. Although the nominations required caucus approval, the implications of this change were quite clear. Not only did the Speaker have the authority to name new members, but continuation as a Rules member was also within his authority. No Democrat has been denied reappointment by Speakers Albert, O'Neill, Wright, or Foley, although in one instance, at least, O'Neill reminded some Rules Committee Democrats who were reluctant to support a rule he favored that they could find themselves on the District of Columbia Committee in the next Congress.

The Speaker may not dictate to the Rules Democrats, but it is clear that they are chosen, in part, because of their willingness to support the position of the majority party and that they serve at the pleasure of the Speaker. The members see themselves as part of the party leadership with responsibility for assisting the advancement of the party's program. It is no longer a matter of merely cooperating or bargaining or resisting as in the period 1937–1972.

The change in Rules Committee leadership provided the committee with the impetus to develop its capacities much more fully than previously envisioned. Colmer was replaced as chair by a liberal Democrat, Ray Madden (Ind.), who was in harmony with the goals of the Democratic Party and gladly did what the Speaker requested. Much the same was true of his successor, James Delaney (N.Y.). Both came to the chairmanship in their later years. Critically, however, without Colmer as chair, Richard Bolling assumed a more effective role in leading the committee. Until he became chair in 1979, Bolling's vision of the Rules Committee's role could not fully blossom. Recognized as one of the great legislative students and tacticians in the history of the House, an advocate of strong parties and a strong speakership, and the architect of numerous reforms, Bolling realized the potential of the Rules Committee to assist the Speaker in centralizing decision making in an increasingly decentralized House. It was Bolling who understood that the committee, once it no longer had to struggle over the decision to grant a rule, could devote more of its efforts to designing rules that fitted the special needs of individual bills, providing greater focus for floor debate and reducing the opportunities for floor obstruction. In addition, he realized that the committee was not making serious use of its original jurisdiction to modernize the institution's rules, procedures, and processes. By the time he left the House in 1982 at the end of the Ninety-seventh Congress, the traffic-cop role had been redesigned.

Lastly, the changing political environment allowed the Rules Committee to play a more active role. In the 1880s the Rules Committee became influential because the chaos of House proceedings resulted in a level of obstruction that eventually proved unacceptable to a majority of House members. Neither the personal goals of the members nor the policy goals of the institution were being met. The situation in the early 1970s was in some ways analogous. The democratization of the House and the development of subcommittee government had created its own kind of chaos. As more members felt free to speak and to offer numerous amendments to committee bills under open rules, scheduling a legislative program became a nightmare for the leadership, and individual members could not plan their own schedules. Debate was as likely to focus on piecemeal amendments as on a bill and its major alternatives.

The growth in floor amendments combined with another effect of subcommittee government to exacerbate the flow of legislation on the floor. Increasingly, the responsibility for managing legislation fell on relatively inexperienced subcommittee chairmen. With fewer bill-management opportunities, they generally proved less skilled than the full committee chairs who had previously monopolized floor-management duties. Often bills would unravel, or be watered down, on the floor because bill managers were unprepared to respond to an outpouring of surprise amendments.

The growing number of jurisdictional disputes added to these problems. Efforts to significantly reorganize committee jurisdictions in the 1970s to reflect the changing mix of issues was unsuccessful. Many key bills cut across existing committee and subcommittee jurisdictions, including legislation dealing with energy, the environment, health, transportation, and the economy. Committee and subcommittee chairs were strongly motivated to protect their policy turf and to make claims on any legislation that fell within their defined boundaries. To deal with this, in 1974 the Speaker was given the power to refer legislation to more than one committee. But when committees reported out competing versions of the same bill, or when claims that committee jurisdictions had been violated arose, jurisdiction disputes often delayed the progress of legislation more than substantive opposition. Of course, substantive opponents found such disputes as useful vehicles to camouflage their opposition.

In this environment the Rules Committee, closely linked to the majority party leadership and with someone of Richard Bolling's knowledge and understanding of the committee's potential able to operate with few restrictions, developed mechanisms through the rule writing process to bring order to a chaotic floor. The procedural arrangements it instituted, beginning in the mid-1970s, carried with them major substantive policy implications.

Instead of writing either simple open or closed rules for the consideration of bills on the floor, the Rules Committee experimented with a variety of complex rules. In the beginning the complexities added were relatively

modest. To settle jurisdictional problems, the Rules Committee divided control of floor debate time between managers from the competing committees and set up a procedure whereby the alternative versions would receive consideration. To make floor management more predictable, the committee specified in the rule that amendments to be offered had to be printed in the *Congressional Record* by a certain date. This enabled inexperienced bill managers, and experienced ones as well, to better prepare their tactics and responses to potential amendments. To focus debate on the major alternatives and prevent a "bits and pieces" amending process, rules were written that specified that a particular amendment or substitute was in order, or that limited the amendment process to a specific number of particular amendments. Sometimes a rule included more than one of these complexities.

In the Ninety-fourth and Ninety-fifth Congresses, complex rules were used somewhat sparingly. In almost every case, they were used to protect the consideration of major legislation. In the Ninety-fourth Congress this included an emergency natural gas bill, campaign finance amendments, a lobbying regulation bill, unemployment compensation amendments, revenue sharing amendments, military aid to Turkey, and domestic use of naval petroleum reserves.

In the democratized House the use of these complex rules, especially the more restrictive ones, was controversial. Republicans frequently argued that limitations on the amending process were antidemocratic and unfairly denied the minority party the chance to present its full range of alternatives. Some Democrats also objected, primarily when amendments they wished to offer were not made in order.

At no time did the policy implications of complex rules receive greater attention during the experimental period than in the consideration of the energy package proposed by the administration of President Jimmy Carter in 1977. The package was first broken into pieces and referred to a range of appropriate committees and then brought together again by the Ad Hoc Committee on Energy in a single bill. The Rules Committee designed a rule that made in order twelve specific amendments (in addition to those offered by the Ad Hoc Committee), a Republican-sponsored substitute, and a recommital motion. The amendments covered major issues in disagreement. Under this procedure, the House floor was able to complete action on the energy package in five days. With such assistance the Carter energy program was able to become law in the Ninety-fifth Congress. Without the work of the Rules Committee, the package would have been the victim of the obstructionism that had derailed energy legislation for the previous six years.

In developing these complex rules, Bolling and other Rules Democrats worked closely with their party's leaders. In part, this involved persuading Speakers Albert and O'Neill to support the use of such rules. To some degree, especially in the crafting of the specific language of a given rule, the committee worked independently. Because the committee's Democrats were, in effect, part of the leadership, they could be trusted to carry out this work. The traffic cop that developed during this period identified with and shared the goals of the leadership and was allowed a fair amount of independence.

In addition to the leadership's growing appreciation of complex rules, resistance to them among rank-and-file House Democrats was breaking down. In August 1979, forty-two Democratic House members signed a letter to the Speaker and the Rules chair asking that reasonable limits on floor amendments and debate time on those amendments be undertaken to move the legislative program more efficiently. As Steven Smith observes in his book *Call to Order,* "These Democrats were expressing their willingness to take steps to restrain amending activity, even if it meant that their own opportunities to offer amendments sometimes would be restricted" (p. 41).

If the use of complex rules had been an experiment previously, in the Ninety-sixth Congress, with broader membership backing and with Bolling as Rules Chair, it became accepted practice. In *Managing Uncertainty in the House of Representatives,* Stanley Bach and Steven Smith present data demonstrating an increase in the use of various forms of complex and restrictive rules and the corresponding decline in the use of simple open rules beginning in the Ninety-sixth Congress. In addi-

tion, they note that the level of complexity increased.

The innovations in the development and use of complex rules continued in the 1980s. Two primary areas of innovation have been alternative substitutes and self-executing provisions. When multiple committees produce different versions of the same bill, the Rules Committee on occasion requires them to work out their differences before it will grant a rule. This may involve the participation of the leadership and may result in a bill very different than those reported by the committees. This "alternate substitute" will then be made in order in the rule. Because it is usually the product of sensitive compromises or a leadership-designed bill, the rule will often also limit the amendments that can be offered to the substitute. The committee does not want to chance that amendments may unravel the compromise. The use of alternative substitutes has substantially increased the Speaker's power of multiple referral, the power of the Speaker since 1975 to refer a bill to more than one committee.

Self-executing rules provide for some additional action to be taken when the House adopts the rule. It may allow the vote in favor of the rule to make modifications in the bill without having a separate vote on the amendment in the Committee of the Whole.

It is hardly surprising that some complex rules are the subject of controversy on the floor. After all, the substantive outcomes often hinge on these procedural decisions. For example, the struggle over budget matters in Ronald Reagan's first year as president in 1980 were effectively won or lost over votes on the rules providing for consideration of the three key pieces of legislation—the budget resolution, the reconciliation bill, and the tax-cut bill. In these cases the Democratic leadership and its Rules Committee were unsuccessful.

Through the crafting of complex rules, the Rules Committee also has enabled the Democratic party leadership to unite its members. When the leadership knows what amendments will be offered, it can more effectively lobby the party members for their support. It can use carefully crafted rules to ensure that its members do not have to vote on amendments that divide the party. Similarly, amendments that

Republicans might offer to create embarrassments for Democrats in their home districts can be avoided. This makes it easier for Democratic members to side with their party against constituency pressures on those substantively important votes on which the leadership really needs them.

By the late 1980s, House Republicans became increasingly disenchanted with the more restrictive nature of complex rules. In addition, Speaker Wright was taking a far more intrusive role in the rule-writing process than O'Neill or Albert. Under Speaker Tom Foley (Wash.) there has been some recognition that the forces of majority rule may have pushed marginally too far. In addition, Foley has been more willing to let the committee's Democrats write the rules. But these are modest adjustments in the way the traffic cop performs its role since it returned to being an arm of the majority party.

Outside its rule-writing responsibilities, the Committee has engaged in other activities to assist the majority party leadership manage the House. The committee's hearings since the early-1970s have become a "dress rehearsal." Bill managers use their appearances before the committee to present their bills in a trial run before this leadership-oriented cross section of Democrats and Republicans. Because legislation is often developed in the relative isolation of a subcommittee, Rules Committee hearings become a first test in a broader environment. The Rules Committee members, in addition to providing feedback to the bill's managers, can communicate with their respective party leadership and policy committees about strengths, weaknesses, and anticipated areas of controversy when the bill reaches the floor.

Finally, because the committee no longer devotes nearly all its time to struggling over whether to grant a rule, it has been able to devote more attention to areas of original jurisdiction that are important in the management of the House. The development and subsequent alterations of the budget process, the television broadcasting of the House floor, and adjusting the permanent rules of the House are some of the areas that have received the attention of the committee. Under Bolling's leadership two Rules subcommittees were established to deal with matters of original jurisdiction (bills and resolutions coming to it directly as opposed to coming from another committee).

CONCLUSION

The Rules Committee continues to be a traffic cop for the House of Representatives just as it has been since shortly after its establishment as a standing committee. For most of that time it has been in the employ of the majority party in the House. Only in the 1937–1972 period did it divorce itself from that arrangement, working instead as the hub of the conservative coalition for most of that period. And for most of the panel's history, the traffic cop role has focused on expediting the legislative program of the majority party. To the degree that the majority party has been unified, this task has not engendered extensive controversy. The majority has willingly supported this vehicle of majority rule. The minority party and its members on the committee have consistently complained when the committee has undercut their opportunities.

When unity is lacking in the majority party, as during the revolt against Cannon and the fissure between northern and southern Democrats, the Rules Committee has been the subject of controversy. Struggle for party and House control has often occurred within the committee's deliberations.

As with other traffic cops, the Rules Committee's authority has varied with the broader environment within which it operates. When House operations have become disorderly to the point of chaos, the members have been willing to give the institution's leadership greater authority to reestablish order. Under those circumstances, Rules Committee influence rose. At other times the members have sought to free themselves from restrictions imposed from above.

Importantly, the Rules Committee does not perform the traffic cop role today the same way it did a century ago. The work load of the House is far heavier and more complex. It operates year-round, not just for a few months. Subcommittee government involves extensive specialization and a division of labor unimaginable in the 1880s. Floor time is a scarce commodity and must be rationed with care. The job of the Rules Committee involves far more than deciding in what order legislation should proceed from a calendar to the floor for deliberation by the House membership. It involves more than just deciding whether to grant an open or closed rule.

THE RULES COMMITTEE: THE HOUSE TRAFFIC COP

Although its decisions are procedural in nature, the policy impact of the Rules Committee is substantial. This was most clear when the conservative coalition used the committee to block legislation from reaching the House floor. The skill with which the Rules Committee helps the leadership manage and expedite its legislative program has equally important, if not greater, policy consequences.

BIBLIOGRAPHY

DeAlva Stanwood Alexander, *History and Procedure of the House of Representatives* (Boston, 1916), is the best of the early histories of the House. It is particularly useful in explaining rules and procedures of the House in the nineteenth century and in the overview it offers. Stanley Bach and Steven S. Smith, *Managing Uncertainty in the House of Representatives: Adoption and Innovation in Special Rules* (Washington, D.C., 1988), traces the development of the use of complex rules by the House Rules Committee. It presents the reasons why these rules were needed, the growth in their use, and the impact they have had. Richard Bolling, *House Out of Order* (New York, 1965), provides a perceptive insider's account of the struggle for the liberal policy agenda in the 1950s and 1960s. The material on the 1957 civil rights bill is especially instructive in understanding the conflict with Chairman Howard Smith. Milton C. Cummings, Jr., and Robert L. Peabody, "The Decision to Enlarge the Committee on Rules," Robert L. Peabody and Nelson W. Polsby, eds., *New Perspectives on the House of Representatives,* 2d ed. (Chicago, 1969), offers the best analysis of the 1961 fight to add three members to the committee. In addition to analyzing the floor vote and the politics leading up to it, they discuss the impact of the change. Bruce I. Oppenheimer, "The Rules Committee: New Arm of Leadership in a Decentralized House," in Lawrence C. Dodd and Bruce I. Oppenheimer, eds., *Congress Reconsidered* (New York, 1977), demonstrates how the Rules Committee's roles changed in reaction to House reforms of the 1970s. These roles include as new traffic cop, dress rehearsal, and field commander and are used to assist the leadership in managing the House. Bruce I. Oppenheimer, "Policy Implications of Rules Committee Reforms," in Leroy N. Rieselbach, ed., *Legislative Reform: The Policy Impact* (Lexington, Mass., 1978), extends the analysis of the committee's changing roles in the 1970s and examines the policy impact of these changes. James T. Patterson, *Congressional Conservatism and the New Deal: The Growth of the Conservative Coalition in Congress, 1933–1939* (Lexington, Ky., 1967), is the outstanding historical study of the development of the conservative coalition in Congress. The discussion of the critical role of the Wage and Hour Act in cementing the split in the Democratic party is most persuasive. Floyd M. Riddick, *The United States Congress: Organization and Procedures* (Manassas, Va., 1948), is a useful study from an individual known for his expertise on rules and procedures and for his accuracy. James A. Robinson, *The House Rules Committee* (Indianapolis, 1963), is the major book of political-science research on the Rules Committee and is particularly strong in documenting the period of conservative coalition dominance of the Committee. Steven S. Smith, *Call to Order: Floor Politics in the House and Senate* (Washington, D.C., 1989), presents material on efforts of leaders to develop better control of floor proceedings in the House and Senate in the 1970s and 1980s. It integrates the use of complex rules with other tactics that leaders have used in the House. James L. Sundquist, *Politics and Policy: The Eisenhower, Kennedy, and Johnson Years* (Washington, D.C., 1968), is the definitive study of domestic legislative struggles during the Eisenhower, Kennedy, and Johnson years. The case studies of a range of policies are filled with material on the critical role of the Rules Committee and the ongoing contest between Howard Smith and liberal Democrats. U.S. Congress, *A History of the Committee on Rules,* was prepared for the 100-year anniversary of the committee. The research it contains was executed by staff or the Congressional Research Service and several outside scholars. It thoroughly documents the development of the committee and changes in it from the First Congress until 1980. It integrates the changing role of the committee with changes in the House and with conflicting democratic values. In addition, the book contains information and data about the committee's members as well as an excellent listing of source material.

SEE ALSO The Congressional Committee System; Congressional Reform; Legislating: Floor and Conference Procedures in Congress; AND Legislatures and Civil Rights.

THE FRAGMENTATION OF POWER WITHIN CONGRESSIONAL COMMITTEES

Glenn R. Parker

Congressional committees are natural channels for societal and political pressures. Congressional hearings, for example, provide opportunities for those interested in a committee's policy decisions to have their voices heard and, in rare instances, their suggestions followed; other legislative actors, such as executive agencies, press their claims on committees at earlier stages in the formulation of public policies. The "permeability," or accessibility, of congressional committees to organized pressure may even encourage individuals and groups to press their demands on committee members. Congressional committees are usually treated as cohesive units wherein committee members act in concert to realize shared goals, and committee decisions are thus perceived as reflecting the pursuit of collective benefits. While this characterization of congressional committees is accurate to some degree, it tends to ignore the myriad of ways in which committees are fragmented. If divisions, or factions, exist within committees, the benefits of collective action may not outweigh the costs; hence, committee decisions may mirror conflict-reduction processes more than the realization of collective benefits. In short, viewing committees as singular units in pursuit of collective benefits overshadows the ways in which power is fragmented within congressional committees. Moreover, an examination of divisions within committees leads to a search for decision-making processes that reflect the give-and-take associated with the formation of coalitions. For these reasons, then, the study of the fragmentation of committees assumes considerable importance in yielding information about the operations of committees and the nature of committee decision-making.

This essay examines the sources of committee fragmentation and how they affect the formation of coalitions within congressional committees, especially in the House of Representatives. Its objective is to identify the divisions that exist within the House committee system and to suggest how these divisions affect coalition formation. The first section describes such sources of fragmentation as the election of committee leaders, the expansion of subcommittee rule, and the formation of committee voting blocs. The second section discusses how cleavages arise within committees and why factions form, especially cleavages within the House committee system over the eight-year period 1973–1980. The third section presents a classification schema for describing committees in terms of the overlap in factional loyalties within congressional committees and shows how it can be used to explain the size of successful coalitions in House committees. The concluding section discusses some of the implications for majority-party coalition-building.

SOURCES OF FRAGMENTATION

Prior to the 1970s, congressional committee chairs possessed both power and job security. Committee leaders were selected on the basis of committee seniority, and while some violations of the seniority system occurred, seniority remained the guiding rule for determining those who would lead the committees. Since committee chairs could not be removed from their positions of power without violating unwritten—but compelling—rules, they exercised almost autocratic control over their committees. They often decided if, and when, issues would be debated and committee meetings held. Their control over the internal operations of the committee and its agenda provided committee leaders with critical opportunities to influence the course and substance of legislation. Such powers made committee leaders a centralizing influence, if not an authoritarian one, in committee decision-making and made congressional committees autonomous centers of power—a cause as well as a consequence of the decline in party leadership in the House.

If congressional reforms enacted during the 1970s failed to make these powerful "whales" of Congress extinct, the revolt by House Democrats against three committee leaders in the Ninety-third Congress (1973–1975) assured them a place on the endangered-species list. The reforms of the 1970s gradually stripped House committee chairs of many of their powers and prerogatives and established procedures for their appointment. These procedures required incumbent committee leaders to gain membership approval with each new Congress. At first, this requirement seemed to have little effect on the selection of committee leaders in the House, since all committee leaders were approved following the implementation of this new procedure in the Ninety-third Congress. The effects of this selection procedure were far more dramatic two years later in the Ninety-fourth Congress: an unusually large influx of Democratic House members led the movement to unseat three of the most powerful and autocratic committee leaders—F. Edward Hebert (D.-La.) of Armed Services, W. R. Poage (D.-Tex.) of Agriculture, and Wright Patman (D.-Tex.) of Banking, Finance, and Urban Affairs.

On the surface, the leadership-selection procedures adopted seem a useful way to exercise party control over committee leaders, especially since the Speaker is allowed to select a large proportion of the membership of the Democratic Policy and Steering Committee, which is empowered to make nominations for committee leadership positions. Could House party leaders regain some of the influence they had lost as a result of the growth of the seniority system and the routinization of committee assignments? Such was not the case. Committee leaders became responsive, but not to the dictates and demands of party leaders. Now, committee leaders needed to court a broader following; as a consequence, committee chairs became more concerned with pleasing committee colleagues, but not necessarily party leaders. Rather than serve the designs of party leaders, the election of committee leaders actually strengthened the hold of committee members on their own committees.

By removing the most autocratic committee leaders in the Ninety-fourth Congress, the Democratic Caucus succeeded in sending a warning to all committee chairs to use their powers fairly, but the message did not include demands for party fidelity. While the three defeated committee leaders were frequently at odds with party leaders, other chairs who were equally distant from the policy preferences of their party's leaders and liberal majority retained their positions. The main difference between the party mavericks who were defeated and those who retained their committee leadership positions was that the defeated leaders used their positions of power to impose their minority policy views on the committee and the party's majority. Thus, the centralizing power of committee leaders became subject to periodic review and approval; leaders now had to pay greater attention to the interests of other committee members. Autocratic rule was replaced by democratic rule, but party leaders gained little additional leverage over committee power. Clearly, party leaders in the House gained in the sense that another center of power had been restrained; nevertheless, they found themselves in the unenviable position of having to deal with a further decentralized power structure as subcommittees moved to fill the void in committee power that committee leaders had relinquished.

In the Senate the story is somewhat different: the election of committee leaders appears to have done little to reduce their influence. Fear of offending a committee leader by voting against him or her keeps most members cautious about joining campaigns against even the most disliked chairs. The greater diffusion of power in the Senate and the greater degree of individual power resulting from the rules regarding unlimited debate and nongermane amendments may restrain most senators from conspiring to defeat a committee leader. Thus, committee chairs are relatively less powerful in the Senate than in the House, and the looseness of floor procedures grants senators (even those not on the committee considering the legislation) a greater influence on the formulation of policy. These factors largely account for the more volatile impact of present committee leadership-selection practices in the House than the Senate.

Another example of committee fragmentation is the growth of subcommittee rule. This trend has been promoted by several factors: the complexities of societal problems requiring policy specialization, the demands of interest groups for access, and the desire of members for greater involvement in policy-making. To these factors can be added the reforms within Congress that have guaranteed certain "rights" to subcommittees, especially those in the House. These rights have given House subcommittees greater control over the policy agenda by stipulating jurisdictions, budgets, and staffs. Rather than deal with a small subset of leaders, party leaders now have to dig deeper within the committee if they intend to influence committee decisions.

This shift to subcommittee decision-making has been most pronounced in the House of Representatives because of reforms that have accentuated subcommittee power. The "Subcommittee Bill of Rights" and other reforms adopted in the 1970s created a relatively secure and independent collection of subcommittee leaders. Instead of allowing full committee chairs the authority to appoint subcommittee leaders, Democratic committee members bid, in order of seniority, for the position of subcommittee chair, and the caucus of Democratic committee members must approve these bids. In addition, reforms have limited members to serving as either a committee or subcommittee chair, thereby significantly increasing the number of members who hold positions of authority within Congress.

The rise in subcommittee rule has resulted in the shifting of basic legislative responsibility from approximately 20 House committees to more than 170 committees and subcommittees. Subcommittees, like committees, jealously guard their jurisdictions and develop mutually beneficial relationships with agencies and clientele groups. As a result, the power of chairs no longer rests on their abilities to balance diverse, conflicting interests, but on their attention to a few particularized policy areas and the actors with interests in these areas. Subcommittee leaders are also less concerned with aggregating a broad range of interests than with serving the narrow interests of a few. Just as committees are frequently "captured" by groups and agencies, the shift of policy responsibility to congressional subcommittees makes them susceptible to similar processes of entrapment, producing a further fragmentation of committee power.

Congressional committees are also fragmented by the external pressures that operate in the political environments of these committees. The environment of a congressional committee can be viewed as the political context in which decisions are made. It is a milieu composed of the major forces that shape legislative behavior: parties, ideologies, constituencies, presidents, agencies, policies, and interest groups. Simply put, the environment represents all factors (and actors) that are external to the committee but impinge on the behavior of individual members. Committee decisions occur, therefore, within a political setting where environmental influences compete to shape the responses of committee members to the policy choices deliberated within the committee.

The most salient environmental influences create cleavages by generating support among committee members for certain positions on legislation within the committee's jurisdiction; the alignment of committee members into voting blocs, or factions, is a response to these cleavages. These influences push and pull committee members in different policy directions, thereby creating discernible factions within the committee and cross-pressures on committee members. As a consequence, committee factions are not themselves cohesive groups; members have varying commitments to other factions within a committee while in most cases maintaining a primary allegiance to a single committee faction. For instance, ideology and party may result in separate factions within a committee, but Democrats and Republicans can be expected to align with both ideological (liberal and conservative) factions to some degree. When the overlap of factional loyalties or commitments forms a consistent pattern, factional polarization may materialize within a committee. This phenomenon is evident in the ideological polarization that frequently pits Democratic liberals against Republican conservatives in many committees.

The formation of coalitions occurs among

factions with similar attitudes, policy orientations, or loyalties; that is, factions that represent mutually accommodative interests tend to coalesce. As the cleavages created by environmental forces become evident during committee deliberations, factions coalesce among those who find themselves pushed in the same policy directions by the interplay of these forces. Committee decisions can be viewed as the result of a majority faction having its own way or as the merging of several factions representing mutually accommodative interests around a specific policy position.

SOURCES OF COMMITTEE CLEAVAGES AND FACTIONS

The sources of the major types of cleavages and factions found in congressional committees are several, as shown below.

The most obvious cleavage within Congress is a consequence of the two-party system that assures conflict between Democrats and Republicans. History and events divide the parties, and only in the areas of foreign and military affairs are these cleavages somewhat muted. Political parties operate in several ways to create divisions within congressional committees. Party leaders, for instance, pressure committee members to follow the party's position on legislation before the committee, and in fact, certain committees are expected to function as an arm of the party's congressional leadership.

Party leaders can also influence the level of partisanship within a committee through assignment practices. The partisan environment of the House Committee on Education and Labor is at least partially a response to the practice of assigning Democratic liberals and Republican conservatives to the committee. Richard Fenno thus noted that "members of the House committee come from among those in their respective parties who already are in the widest disagreement" (Fenno, 1963, p. 201). He makes the same observation about the House Committee on Ways and Means:

> When party leaders make appointments to Ways and Means, they make policy orthodoxy

a test of membership. Candidates from both parties are checked to make sure they adhere to the party position on such matters as trade and medicare and to ascertain whether they will follow the party leaders, especially the one in the White House. (1973, p. 25)

Partisanship may also influence committee members in a less explicit fashion. Since members tend to consult exclusively with those of the same party, the communications network that disseminates information among House members contains a partisan bias. "If congressmen turn to informants with whom they agree," John Kingdon observed, "it is only natural that they turn to those within their own party" (p. 78). Party may also supply voting cues by serving as a reference group within Congress (cf. Matthews and Stimson, p. 97), especially since feelings of compatriotism are a natural by-product of common electoral opposition.

Committee jurisdictions also exacerbate partisanship within committees; the work of some committees yields distinct partisan political advantage. For example, congressional committees involved in investigations, such as the House Government Operations Committee and the Senate Governmental Affairs Committee, concentrate on errors in the administration of laws, regulations, and programs. The findings of these investigations can provide the opposition to the president with ammunition to embarrass the administration:

> When the congressional majority and the President hold different party allegiances, the opportunity for partisan advantage is vastly increased. In such a situation the minority party in Congress is much more likely to be highly sensitive to criticisms of their President. The majority party, on the other hand, is in such circumstances given an ideal opportunity to carry out investigations under the guise of oversight which embarrass the current Administration. (Henderson, p. 42)

In this way, partisan interest may serve as an impetus to committee activities. The possibility of partisan gain or advantage means that committee members will pay sharp attention to the political complexion of the committee's work. Under these conditions, committee decision-making is likely to proceed along partisan lines. For example, House committees with jurisdictional responsibilities that yield partisan advantages—Budget, Government Operations,

House Administration, and Rules—tend to exhibit partisan factions. The Budget Committee establishes expenditure limits that reflect the policy preferences and priorities of the majority party and its leaders. The major task of Government Operations is to oversee the functioning of the executive branch; errors in agency administration, once detected, can provide useful ammunition for political attacks on the president's party. Finally, majority-party control of the House Administration and Rules Committees provides the party with influence over internal procedures and the perquisites of party control.

Finally, there are some political issues for which party positions are matters of historical record; such issues increase the saliency of partisan considerations in committee decision-making. The topics of labor, education, and poverty have traditionally divided the parties and exacerbated the level of partisanship exhibited within the House Education and Labor Committee (Fenno, 1973, p. 31). In a similar vein, party stands on trade, social security, taxation, and Medicare produce cleavages among Democrats and Republicans on the House Ways and Means Committee (Fenno, 1973, p. 24). Partisan disagreement among House Public Works and Transportation Committee members also occurs on issues that have historically divided the parties, such as "whether private or public power should be supported; whether the federal government or the state governments should assume responsibility for treating water pollution; how the financial burden of the Interstate and Defense Highway system should be distributed; and finally, whether or not new construction in the District of Columbia should be undertaken" (Murphy, p. 169).

In some cases, issues handled by a committee may change from obscure, nonpartisan matters to salient partisan concerns, thereby introducing greater partisanship into the committee's deliberations. This seems to be the case in the House Interior and Insular Affairs Committee where issues such as land-use policy and surface-mining regulations have attained national saliency and divided the parties in significant ways (cf. Parker and Parker). As a consequence of these diverse partisan elements, Democratic and Republican factions can be found within most House and Senate committees.

Ideological Cleavages

The composition of Congress leaves its imprint on the committee system in the form of cleavages reflecting ideological divisions in the House and Senate, notably differences arising from the historic North-South split within the Democratic party and differences in ideological outlook between the parties. Ideology is one of the most divisive factors within the Democratic party, evidenced by the fact that conservative Democrats, particularly those from southern states, tend to vote less frequently with the Democratic majority than do their more liberal colleagues. This ideological cleavage among Democrats has led to the formation of a conservative coalition on the floors of the House and Senate. If Republicans and southern Democrats vote together on the floor, they can be expected to do the same within committees.

An ideological gulf also separates the two parties. Norman Ornstein and David Rohde (1977) reported that the ideological differences between Democrats and Republicans have intensified as a consequence of turnover in congressional membership. This has strengthened the ideological-partisan polarization within congressional committees. While committee-assignment practices, committee vacancies, and member preferences and characteristics may mediate this ideological conflict, whenever the same conditions existing on the floor of the House and Senate arise within a committee—that is, a substantial number of southern Democrats or sharp ideological differences among committee members, along with issues that incite ideological feelings—ideological cleavages will probably become evident.

Although scholars continue to disagree about the effects of ideology on floor voting (Clausen; Matthews and Stimson; Schneider), a strong argument can be made for ideological voting within congressional committees. One major explanation for the lack of ideological voting on the floor, for instance, is that members are unable to identify the ideological content of most legislation (Matthews and Stimson, pp. 32–37). This occurs as a result of the volume of issues that members must vote on and the lack of a manifest ideological content to most legislative votes. The characteristics of the congressional committee system alleviate many of these impediments to ideological voting. While members may lack a detailed understanding of most of the issues they are called on to consider, the norm of specialization assures that members will be better informed about those issues that arise within the committees on which they serve. As a result, members are better able to discern the ideological positions on issues within their committee's jurisdiction; hence, cue voting of an ideological nature may be even easier to accomplish within committees than on the floor of the House or the Senate. Further, committee members have access to staff that can alert them to the underlying issues and nuances, and appraise them of the ideological impact of individual amendments. For these reasons, ideological voting appears to be salient within committees.

Clearly, the ideological nature of committee factions is relative to the levels of liberalism and conservatism within the committee. For instance, the conservative Republicans on Judiciary are considerably less conservative than those on Standards or Public Works. The same ideological cleavage is present in both cases, but the divisions occur at different places along the liberal-conservative continuum in the three committees. Thus, the most "liberal" bloc of committee members may still be "conservative," but less so than other factions in the committee.

In some committees, like the House Interior and Commerce Committees, partisan and ideological elements polarize the sympathies of committee members. Two factors account for this ideological-partisan polarization. First, the jurisdictions of these committees stir both ideological and partisan conflict; hence, partisan and ideological attitudes move committee members in the same direction. The major policy dimension in Interior, for instance, relates to land and surface mining and is strongly correlated with measures of ideology and partisanship. Second, the ideological differences between Democrats and Republicans reinforce their partisan attachments. For example, in the House Interior Committee the influences of party and ideology are virtually impossible to disentangle. As a consequence, many committees exhibit factional structures that are polarized along both partisan and ideological lines (cf. Parker and Parker).

The Executive Branch

The nature of committee jurisdictions explains the differential interest of the executive branch in committee decision-making. When the executive branch has a strong interest in issues falling within a committee's jurisdiction, cleavages between executive-branch supporters and adversaries are apt to form. Those committees which have jurisdictional responsibilities impinging on important executive functions—such as the maintenance of national defense (Armed Services), the development of foreign policy (Foreign Affairs and Foreign Relations), and the level of governmental spending and revenue (Appropriations, Finance, and Ways and Means)—are the most likely targets of executive influence. The area of foreign policy is a good example of this relationship because it has constitutionally and historically been an area of executive responsibility; not surprisingly, the cleavages within the House Foreign Affairs Committee reflect this historic tug-of-war between the president and Congress over foreign-policy matters.

In those cases where there is disagreement within the administration, cleavages within a committee are also likely to reflect the influence of agencies within the executive branch. While the president may have many powerful allies both inside and outside the committee, an obstinate agency may wield equal or greater influence within the committee. The mutually supportive relationships between agencies, groups, and congressional committees—"cozy triangles" (see Parker, 1989, pp. 199–215)—assure that some members are unusually attentive to agency demands. Since agency expenditures often favor particular congressional districts, many members of Congress have good reason to support agency positions. "Bureaucrats allocate expenditures both in gratitude for past support and in hopes of future congressional support; and congressmen support agencies both because they owe them for past allocations and because they desire future allocations" (Arnold, p. 36).

The influence of the executive branch on committee decision-making can also appear as a mixture of presidential persuasion and partisanship. In fact, partisanship may obscure the impact of presidential power on committee decisions. Party loyalty is, after all, an appeal that presidents invoke in trying to influence members within their own party. Still, party and administration loyalties often differ, even among members of Congress in the president's own party. Neither are all members of the president's party successfully courted, nor are all party members susceptible to pleas for loyalty. Further, the chief executive is normally not averse to crossing the aisle to form a successful bipartisan coalition of administration supporters, as in the House Foreign Affairs Committee (Fenno, 1973, p. 90).

Constituent and Group Interests

Interest groups are ubiquitous features of the legislative process and an additional source of committee factionalism. They create cleavages within committees in the natural pursuit of their legislative objectives. Normally, groups restrict their lobbying efforts to those who are sympathetic to their causes, avoiding those in opposition to their positions for fear of mobilizing them. As a result, committee members supportive of the group's interests coalesce around the group's position, and those opposed to that same interest, because of attitudes, ideology, or loyalty to other groups, also close ranks. In addition, the common practice by interest groups of rewarding friends and punishing enemies is likely to create differing group attachments. The AFL-CIO, for example, "devotes enormous resources of manpower, money, and organization to help elect liberal Democratic Presidents and Congressmen—including members of the Education and Labor Committee" (Fenno, 1973, p. 34). Such differential treatment serves to solidify group attachments.

Constituency interests may enter into the calculus of committee decision-making, especially where policies distribute benefits relevant to individual constituencies. In many cases, committee assignments are determined on the basis of a member's desire to serve constituent needs (Masters, p. 354; Price, p. 6). Those members who serve similar constituent interests may find it strategically beneficial to organize as a bloc in order to assure that these interests are accommodated within the framework of any policy decision; this seems to be the case among House Agriculture Committee members who represent specific commodity interests (Jones). This sensitivity to constituent or district interests could result from the recruitment mechanism and/or district electoral competitiveness.

While it is possible to find independent cleavages representing constituency interests and the influence of organized groups, a hybrid of the two frequently appears. Interest groups are most effective and influential where they have linkages to congressional constituencies. As John Kingdon (pp. 143–146) notes, interest groups have little effect on committee votes when they lack this constituency connection. Further, members seek to accommodate the demands of their "strongest supporters" in their "reelection constituency" because these contributors provide the financial aid and campaign assistance that help incumbents to stave off electoral defeat (Fenno, 1978, p. 19). When such support comes from interest groups within the member's constituency, the effect of interest groups and constituency influences are collinear and impossible to separate theoretically or empirically.

Interest groups and constituents are the least salient environmental influences on House committees. Aside from the obvious conclusion that such influences have little impact on congressional committees, there are at least two explanations for the lack of saliency. First, cleavages created by the impact of constituency concerns and interest-group demands may be obscured by the influence of party and ideology. The intertwining of constituency and group interests with the pervasive, ubiquitous effects of party and ideology may obscure these interests. For example, the absence of cleavages created by the conflicts between environmentalists and commercial interests on the House Interior Committee, noted by Fenno in 1973, may be the result of the collinearity of positions on land use and ideological and partisan sympathies; liberal Democrats support the demands of environmentalists, and conservative Republicans promote the interests of commercial users. Second, the influence of such interests may be absent because a consensus has developed over the distribution of particularistic benefits for constituencies or groups. For instance, the House Public Works Committee has developed a consensus over the requirements for the funding of constituency projects (Murphy). Such a consensus may take the form of agreement on formulas for the distribution of constituency benefits, as in the Public Works Committee (cf. Murphy), or the resolution of conflict through some sort of partisan mutual adjustment process (such as bargaining or compromise).

In sum, committees operate within a milieu composed of the major forces that shape legislative behavior: parties, ideologies, constituencies, presidents, agencies, and interest groups. The competition among these forces to influence the policy preferences of committee members forms the backdrop against which committee decisions are formulated. In the process of influencing committee members, these forces create cleavages within the committee that appear as factions of committee members. Members coalesce into factions in

order to gain more influence within the committee and to promote policies that they favor. The rationale behind such action is the simple adage of power in numbers; blocs of members can wield more influence than individual members acting on their own. Most committee cleavages exhibit little change, in large part because of the stability of committee jurisdictions and responsibilities.

In Table 1 the types of cleavages in the House committees from 1973 through 1980 are described. Partisan cleavages occurred in most House committees, the notable exceptions being the bipartisan factions that characterize the Foreign Affairs, Armed Services, and Standards of Official Conduct committees. Ideological cleavages were even more pervasive than partisan ones, appearing in every House

Table 1

SUMMARY OF THE SALIENT CLEAVAGES WITHIN HOUSE COMMITTEES, 1973–1980

Committee	Party		Ideology		Executive		Constituency Interests	
	1973–1976	1977–1980	1973–1976	1977–1980	1973–1976	1977–1980	1973–1976	1977–1980
Agriculture	X	X	X	X			X	X
Appropriations	X	X	X	X	X	X		
Armed Services			X	X	X	X		
Banking, Finance, and Urban Affairs	X	X	X	X			X	X
Budget	X	X	X	X				
Education and Labor	X	X	X	X			X	X
Foreign Affairs			X		X			
Government Operations	X	X	X	X				
House Administration	X	X	X	X				
Interior and Insular Affairs	X	X	X	X				X*
Interstate and Foreign Commerce	X	X	X	X				
Judiciary	X	X	X	X				
Merchant Marine and Fisheries		X		X				X
Post Office and Civil Service	X	X	X	X	X	X		X*
Public Works and Transportation	X	X	X	X				
Rules	X	X	X	X				
Science and Technology	X	X	X	X				
Standards of Official Conduct			X					
Ways and Means	X	X	X	X	X	X		

*New cleavages

committee. Four committees displayed constituency cleavages in addition to partisan and ideological cleavages—Agriculture, Banking, Education and Labor, and Merchant Marine and Fisheries. In the Banking and Agriculture committees, there were identifiable divisions within the Democratic ranks that were the result of constituency-group pressures. In these two committees, members who supported constituency interests aligned with separate factions; supporters of commodity interests in Agriculture and supporters of financial institutions and urban constituencies in Banking aligned with separate factions and divided the Democratic membership. By contrast, in the Education and Merchant Marine committees, constituency interests coincided with partisan interests and polarized members rather than dividing them. This strengthened partisanship on these latter two committees, whereas in Agriculture and Banking constituency interests weakened partisanship. Finally, five House committees exhibited administration cleavages—Appropriations, Armed Services, Foreign Affairs, Post Office, and Ways and Means. Because the jurisdictional responsibilities of these committees touch on important executive functions, administration pressures and cleavages were virtually assured. Republican presidents tended to divide Democrats on these committees, while a Democratic president tended to reinforce committee partisanship.

These cleavage patterns were quite stable over the eight-year period of study. Despite this resiliency, the cohesion of Democratic coalitions within these committees tended to increase during the Democratic presidency of Jimmy Carter; conservative Democrats, especially southern Democrats, voted more frequently with their liberal colleagues than during the years 1973–1976. The only significant changes in committee cleavages occurred in the Interior and the Post Office committees. In both of these committees, constituency cleavages emerged in the second time period (1977–1980) to increase the number of cleavages present in these committees. The "conservationist-user" conflict over the exploitation of western lands in Interior was appended to the already existing partisan and ideological divisions within the committee. In Post Office, disagreement over the rights of federal employees added a constituency cleav-

age to existing administration, partisan, and ideological cleavages. These were the only exceptions to the stability displayed by committee cleavages.

EFFECTS OF CLEAVAGES ON COALITION SIZE

The factions that form as a result of committee cleavages are central to the formation of committee coalitions, because they provide the basic ingredients for the emergence of successful coalitions: factions that represent mutually accommodative interests tend to coalesce into committee coalitions. When committee cleavages reinforce one another, a polarization of committee members occurs. When committee cleavages intersect or are more independent of one another, there is a greater fragmentation in the loyalties of committee members. In these latter instances, committee cleavages will exercise contradictory pressures on members, resulting in committee members being cross-pressured in the same way that voters are cross-pressured by inconsistent identifications. Southern Democrats probably epitomize such a cross-pressured subset of Congress, since their ideological and partisan attachments frequently push and pull them in opposite directions.

When attachments and loyalties to the party are reinforced by other committee cleavages, the successful coalition needs to accommodate few interests other than those associated with the majority party's positions. This occurs because alternatives that satisfy party interests also tend to satisfy other interests in the committee. Frequently, this pattern of reinforcing cleavages results in a highly polarized committee where cleavages divide the members in the same way. Since fewer "independent" interests need to be accommodated within a successful coalition in polarized committees, the size of a winning coalition tends toward the minimum necessary for victory.

When the cleavages within a committee intersect rather than covary with party, greater numbers of independent factions need to be accommodated within a successful coalition. This often leads to the expansion of the coalition in order to accommodate these divergent views. Simply put, when partisan loyalty is insufficient to produce winning coalitions consistently, party leaders find it necessary to broaden their appeal in order to gain coalition support. This results in winning coalitions that are beyond the minimal size necessary for victory.

Finally, in committees where partisanship is minimal, an emphasis is placed on promoting consensus because of the collective nature of the policies that the committee handles. The distinguishing characteristic of these committees is the presence of bipartisan committee factions. These committees display unusually large winning coalitions. In sum, the more cleavages within a committee and the less the congruence between these cleavages and partisan attachments, the broader (larger) the coali-

tions that form. This occurs because a greater number of factions need to be accommodated in order to form a winning coalition. As a result, coalitions of minimum size are expected to occur more frequently in "polarized-partisan" committees than in either "mixed-partisan" or "nonpartisan" committees. In contrast, nonpartisan committees will have a greater frequency of unusually large coalitions. Mixed-partisan committees will have a greater likelihood of coalitions that are larger than the minimum, but smaller than those which frequently arise in nonpartisan committees.

The theoretical relationships between cleavage patterns and the size of committee coalitions are summarized in Table 2. An em-

Table 2

THE RELATIONSHIP BETWEEN CLEAVAGE PATTERNS AND THE SIZE OF WINNING COALITIONS IN HOUSE COMMITTEES

Types of Cleavage Pattern	Committees with Specified Cleavage Pattern	Hypothesized Skew in Size of Winning Committee Coalitions
Polarized-partisan	Budget Education and Labor Energy and Commerce Interior and Insular Affairs Ways and Means	Toward minimum size
Mixed-partisan Ideological	House Administration Public Works and Transportation Rules Science and Technology	Minimum to large majorities
Administration	Appropriations Government Operations Judiciary Post Office and Civil Service	Toward minimum size under conditions of unified party control (presidency and House controlled by same party)
Constituency	Agriculture Banking, Finance, and Urban Affairs	
Nonpartisan	Armed Services Foreign Affairs Standards of Official Conduct	Consensus

pirical test of this theoretical classification of committees can be executed by examining the skew in the size of winning coalitions within House committees under both Democratic and Republican presidents. By pooling a committee's votes over a long period of time—here an eight-year period—one expects that the size of winning coalitions will vary over the entire spectrum (i.e., from minimum to universal coalitions). In order to test the empirical validity and predictability of this classification schema, one must examine the frequency (probability) with which coalitions of a certain size arise; hence, the predictions pertain to the shape of the distribution of successful committee coalitions—that is, whether a committee's distribution of coalition outcomes is skewed toward minimum or maximum size. As committee cleavages crosscut majority-party attachments, the size of winning committee coalitions should expand.

Polarized-Partisan Cleavage Patterns

Five House committees can be classified as having polarized-partisan cleavage patterns: Education and Labor, Interior and Insular Affairs, Energy and Commerce, Budget, and Ways and Means. In these five committees, partisan and ideological cleavages are closely intertwined; unlike other committees with partisan and ideological cleavages, these five committees have ideological differences that reinforce existing partisan divisions. This coincidence between partisan and ideological attachments polarizes these committees' membership.

In addition to the partisan and ideological cleavages that characterize polarized-partisan committees, cleavages in Education, Interior (1977–1980), and Ways and Means include other sources of committee conflict that also reinforce existing partisan cleavages. In the Ways and Means Committee, there is some evidence that administration cleavages divide committee members into supporters and opponents of the president's policy initiatives. While pressures from the president constitute an additional source of committee conflict, the cleavages within Ways and Means remain polarized and reinforce existing partisan loyalties. That is, there is a strong collinearity between partisan, ideological, and administration loyalties among Ways and Means Committee mem-

bers (Fenno, pp. 23–25; Parker and Parker, pp. 142–151).

The Interior Committee was also characterized by three committee cleavages in the 1977–1980 period. In addition to the partisan and ideological cleavages, members also divided over constituent interests related to environmental issues. The members from western states favored exploitation of the mineral, wilderness, and water resources of their states, while members from eastern states sought to restrict such usage. This constituency cleavage did not disrupt the polarized-partisan cleavage pattern within the committee because the cleavage was collinear with partisan and ideological attachments. Simply put, ideology, party, and constituency influences pushed committee members in identical directions. As a result, liberal Democrats supported conservation policies, while conservative Republicans favored the development of western lands.

In Education and Labor, there was an unusual degree of overlap between partisan, ideological, and group attachments. Committee Democrats were generally supportive of liberal causes and the interests of organized labor, while committee Republicans were more conservative and supportive of the interests of the employer. Consequently, a more polarized-partisan cleavage pattern existed in the Education and Labor Committee than might be expected of a committee with ideological, partisan, and constituency-group cleavages.

As anticipated, successful coalitions in polarized-partisan committees tended to be skewed toward the minimum end of the distribution of successful coalitions—Interior, Commerce, Budget, and Ways and Means (see Figure 1). In these four committees, more than 50 percent of the successful coalitions could be considered as minimum winning coalitions (containing between 51 percent and 60 percent of the membership). The Budget Committee had the highest number of minimum winning coalitions; 47 percent of the coalitions contained between 51 percent and 55 percent of the members, and 63 percent of the successful coalitions contained between 51 percent and 60 percent of those voting in the first time period; during the Ninety-fifth and Ninety-sixth Congresses, one-quarter of the successful coalitions in Budget contained between 51 percent and 55 percent of the members voting.

Figure 1
DISTRIBUTIONS OF THE SIZE OF SUCCESSFUL COALITIONS IN POLARIZED-PARTISAN
COMMITTEES: 1973–1980

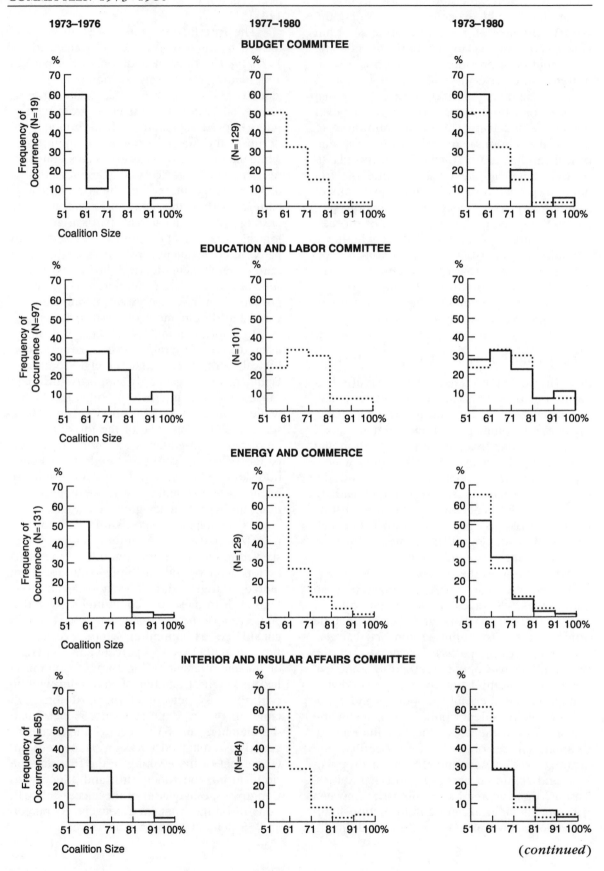

(*continued*)

THE FRAGMENTATION OF POWER WITHIN COMMITTEES

Figure 1 (*continued*)

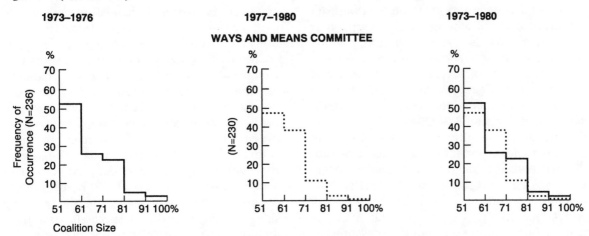

Source: Committee roll-call votes, U.S. House of Representatives, 1973–1980.

Generally, between one-quarter and one-third of the successful coalitions in these four committees contained less than 56 percent of the members voting. In short, the distribution of successful coalitions in polarized-partisan committees was skewed toward the minimum size (51 percent to 60 percent of the voting membership). Thus, it appears that the reinforcement of partisan cleavages in committees promotes minimum-sized winning coalitions.

The one exception to this generalization was the Education and Labor Committee. Although the committee was fragmented by ideological and constituency-group cleavages, the cleavages tended to reinforce partisanship. Such a polarized cleavage pattern should have produced a greater proportion of minimum winning coalitions. Successful coalitions in the Education and Labor Committee, however, did not exhibit such a pattern. The pattern in Education resembled the pattern in mixed-partisan committees more than the pattern in polarized-partisan committees—a greater concentration of coalitions that extend beyond the minimum size (greater than 60 percent of those voting) necessary to assure success.

This anomaly cannot be explained in terms of the desire of committee members to improve their chances of floor passage by building larger coalitions: "Education and Labor members' policy goals do not lead them to place a special value on floor success; they do not feel constrained by the institutional prescription of the House; and they do not adopt consensus-building, influence-preserving proc-

esses" (Fenno, 1973, p. 235). The greater participation of committee liberals, however, can explain the creation of larger coalitions. This greater involvement by liberals could promote larger coalitions by discouraging the participation of conservatives. Conservative Republicans on the committee may have felt they could have a greater impact on committee legislation once it reached the floor of the House. There, at least, they could subject the committee's legislation to amendment with greater prospects for success, especially in light of the committee's liberal image.

Mixed-Partisan Cleavage Patterns

A large subset of House committees have cleavages that are not mutually reinforcing. In these committees, partisanship is fragmented by the existence of ideological, administration, and constituency-group cleavages; since these cleavages crosscut one another, there is a fragmentation of member loyalties. Unlike partisanship in polarized-partisan committees, partisanship in mixed-partisan committees is not uniformly reinforced by other cleavages. Instead, these cleavages crosscut partisan loyalties and therefore reduce the cohesion of partisan groupings. Committee factions, therefore, tend to reflect the influence of each committee cleavage. Mixed-partisan committees can be further classified according to the types of cleavages that tend to disrupt the partisanship of committee members, especially those from the majority party.

While all committees exhibit ideological cleavages, ideology appears to be the dominant source of division among Democrats on four committees: House Administration, Public Works and Transportation, Rules, and Science and Technology. In several other committees, administration cleavages divide majority-party members—Appropriations, Government Operations, Judiciary, and Post Office and Civil Service. In these committees, pressures from the president and/or executive agencies create additional divisions among committee members that crosscut partisan loyalties. Finally, two committees, Agriculture, and Banking, Finance, and Urban Affairs, exhibit cleavage patterns that include constituency-group pressures in addition to existing partisan and ideological cleavages within the committee. Partisanship in these committees is diluted by the interests of certain types of constituents, or groups associated with these constituencies, that do not normally follow existing partisan and ideological lines.

The major ideological divisions in House Administration, Public Works, Rules, and Science and Technology are between conservative and liberal Democrats. In contrast, the ideological loyalties of Republican committee members are less divisive of their partisan loyalties. These committees are similar to those that have been classified as polarized-partisan with respect to the limited number of cleavages within the committees and the partisan and ideological nature of the cleavages. The difference between the two types of committees is that ideology reinforces partisan loyalties among committee Democrats in polarized committees, whereas in mixed-partisan committees ideology is divisive of Democratic partisanship.

This division among committee Democrats in these four committees produces some coalitions that are of minimum size, but most of the successful coalitions with crosscutting ideological cleavages contain majorities larger than minimum size (see Figure 2): successful coalitions normally contain more than 60 percent of the voting members. This contrasts with polarized-partisan committees where a majority of the successful coalitions contain less than 60 percent of the voting members. Thus, the additional source of committee conflict among Democrats forces successful coalitions to expand beyond the minimum size in order to ac-

commodate the interests of dissident Democrats. (It is assumed that compromises and negotiations between various Democratic factions are involved in broadening majority-party coalitions.) Since liberal and conservative Democrats frequently form partisan coalitions in these committees, minimum winning coalitions arise with some frequency; about 30 percent of the successful coalitions contain between 51 percent and 60 percent of those voting. Nevertheless, the modal category of successful coalitions is usually composed of coalitions with 61 percent to 70 percent of the committee members voting on the winning side, and the majority of successful coalitions include more than 60 percent of the voting members.

The constituency-group interests that create cleavages in the Agriculture Committee are related to specific commodities. In Banking, the interests of commercial banking and savings-and-loan institutions and the constituency concerns of urban members create constituency and group cleavages within the committee. Some of these constituency-group cleavages exhibit a degree of convergence with party, but factionalism within the Democratic party normally prevents party-line voting from dominating committee decisions. For instance, while supporters of commodity interests are predominantly Democratic on the Agriculture Committee, ideology usually prevents the overlap of partisan and constituency cleavages from promoting a polarized-partisan cleavage pattern. The ideological gap between northern and southern Democrats on Agriculture reached an extreme level between 1973 and 1976. During this period, southern Democrats had more in common with Republican committee members (presidential support, conservative ideological support, degree of support for Democratic policies) than they did with other committee Democrats! This frequently led to successful coalitions of Republicans and southern Democrats. This polarization of ideological, partisan, and constituency interests dissipated during the Carter administration as the areas of agreement between Republicans and southern Democrats narrowed. However, even in this period (1977–1980) differences between northern and southern Democrats on the Agriculture Committee forced partisan coalitions to broaden their appeal. Similarly, urban

Figure 2
DISTRIBUTIONS OF THE SIZE OF SUCCESSFUL COALITIONS IN MIXED-PARTISAN COMMITTEES:
1973–1980

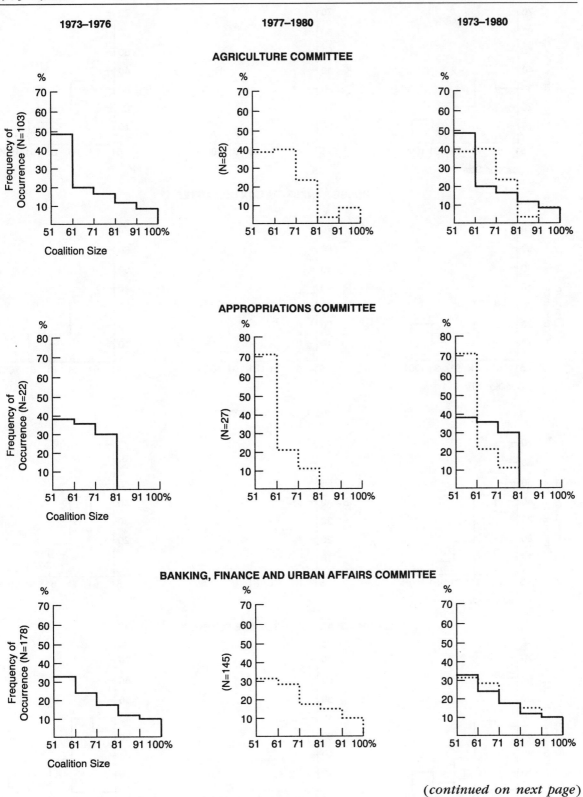

(*continued on next page*)

Figure 2 (*continued*)

1973–1976   **1977–1980**   **1973–1980**

GOVERNMENT OPERATIONS COMMITTEE

Coalition Size

HOUSE ADMINISTRATION COMMITTEE

Coalition Size

JUDICIARY COMMITTEE

Coalition Size

POST OFFICE AND CIVIL SERVICE COMMITTEE

Coalition Size

(continued)

Figure 2 (*continued*)

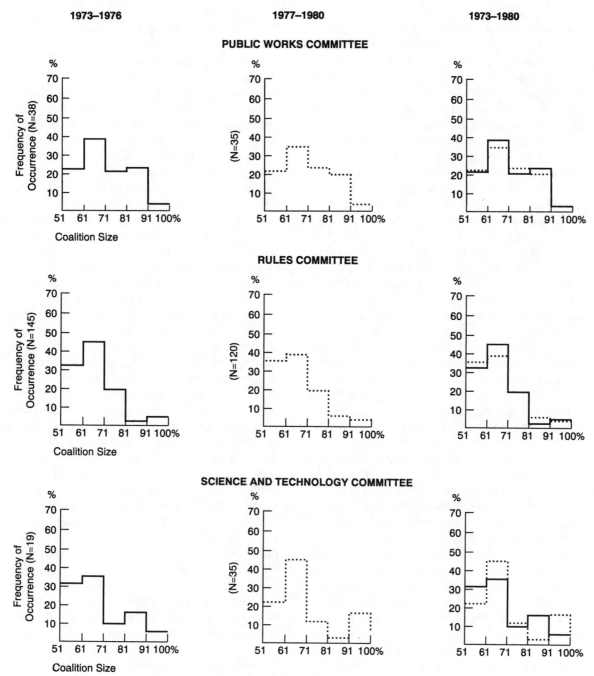

Source: Committee roll-call votes, U.S. House of Representatives, 1973–1980.

interests did not receive the same support among southern Democrats on the Banking Committee as they received from northern Democratic members.

The addition of constituency conflicts to those created by ideology and party necessitates the formation of coalitions larger than the minimum necessary to assure victory, especially where there is divergence between these cleavages. When committee cleavages are not mutually reinforcing, members are cross-pressured and successful coalitions expand beyond minimum size. This situation arises from the need of the majority party to formulate policies capable of satisfying a wider range of interests and a broader band of ideological and partisan attitudes. This expands the number of factions that can be incorporated into the successful coalition and increases its size.

Successful coalitions among this subset of

1083

mixed-partisan committees also tend to have a greater number of successful coalitions beyond the minimum size needed for success (Figure 2). The skew toward minimum-sized coalitions in Agriculture during the years 1973–1976 could be anticipated in light of the unusual polarization between partisan, ideological, and constituency cleavages during this period; such a polarized cleavage pattern produces more minimum-sized coalitions.

Coalitions in the Appropriations and Post Office and Civil Service committees have been described by Fenno (1973) as "executive-led," and administration cleavages can be found in both of these committees; administration cleavages coexist with partisan and ideological differences among members. Two other committees can be added to this subset of mixed-partisan committees with administration cleavages, Government Operations and Judiciary. The jurisdictions of these two committees—oversight of the operations of the executive agencies by Government Operations, and the Judiciary Committee's formulation of federal codes for criminal offenses and illegal practices—attract executive interest. Generally, administration cleavages are readily detected in committees with jurisdictions that touch on executive functions and responsibilities, but this is not the case with Government Operations and Judiciary (Table 1). The reason administration cleavages are obscured in these two committees may be the pervasive effects of party and ideology in these committees (Parker and Parker, pp. 74–80; 102–104). Other research suggests that the executive branch is an important influence in Judiciary (Perkins) and Government Operations (Henderson); therefore, these two committees can be included in the list of mixed-partisan committees with administration cleavages.

Administration cleavages are likely to crosscut partisan loyalties to some degree when a minority-party president finds it necessary to seek majority-party support for administration policies. That is, when the Democrats control Congress, a Republican president quickly recognizes the value of bipartisanship in securing sufficient support for the passage of his policies, but a Democratic president reinforces committee partisanship because of the coincidence between partisan and administration pressures on these committees; both pressures uniformly push committee Democrats

and Republicans in opposite directions. Democratic presidents can focus all of their persuasive skills on committee Democrats and ignore the interests of committee Republicans without endangering the prospects for a successful coalition of supporters. Hence, under Democratic presidents, with Democratic control of Congress, administration cleavages reinforce partisan attachments. Under Republican presidents, with Democratic control of Congress, these cleavages are less collinear with party. When administration cleavages reinforce partisan divisions, one can expect a greater concentration of successful coalitions at the minimum level (as in 1977–1980); when these cleavages are not mutually reinforcing (as in 1973–1976), successful coalitions tend to be larger.

In three of these four committees, Appropriations, Government Operations, and Judiciary, coalition outcomes became skewed toward the minimum size during the Democratic Carter administration (Figure 2). For example, during the Nixon and Ford presidencies only about one-third of the successful coalitions in the Appropriations and Judiciary committees contained less than 61 percent of those voting, but during the Carter administration more than one-half of the successful coalitions fell into this range (Figure 2). The reinforcement of partisanship when the majority party exercises united control of government produces a pattern of coalition outcomes that resembles the distribution of successful coalitions seen in polarized-partisan committees. When administration and partisan cleavages are not mutually reinforcing, as under divided control of government, coalition outcomes extend over a broader range and the skew toward minimum-sized coalitions is reduced.

The Post Office Committee did not exhibit this pattern of skew toward minimum-sized coalitions during the Carter administration. The emergence of a constituency cleavage in the committee divided the loyalties of committee Democrats and prevented minimum-sized coalitions from arising very frequently. This constituency cleavage reflected the divergent interests of federal workers and President Carter over the rights of federal employees. Such issues as civil service reform and the political rights of federal workers occupied the committee's agenda during 1977–1980. This division among committee Democrats served to offset the pressures that would normally reinforce committee partisanship during a Democratic administration. Thus, the pattern of successful coalitions in Post Office is the same under both Democratic and Republican administrations: successful coalitions are most likely to contain more than 60 percent of those voting (Figure 2).

Nonpartisan Cleavage Patterns

Nonpartisan cleavage patterns are found in committees that place a premium on achieving committee consensus by minimizing partisanship. The policy-making responsibilities of these committees tend to deal with collective goods, such as foreign policy (Foreign Affairs Committee), national defense (Armed Services Committee), and congressional ethics (Standards of Official Conduct Committee). While ideological cleavages are evident in these committees, there is barely a trace of partisanship. In the Armed Services Committee, for example, Democrats and Republicans frequently form bipartisan factions that are supportive of defense spending. When factions appear in Armed Services, the differences normally center on the degree of agreement with administration procurement and spending and allocation policies. In foreign policy, as in defense policy, presidents seek to promote consensual support for their positions: "Executive officials place great emphasis on nonpartisanship in day-to-day dealings with the [Foreign Affairs] Committee on the theory that procedural nonpartisanship will stimulate substantive bipartisanship" (Fenno, 1973, p. 29).

The policy responsibilities of the Standards Committee force its members to seek unusual levels of committee consensus because the committee is charged with investigating the ethics violations of House members. These investigations have the potential for embarrassing not only the individuals involved but also the political parties and the House in general. In order to minimize the pervasive fear of politically motivated retribution, attempts are made to achieve bipartisan support for committee decisions and to assure that any decision is based on fact rather than political rancor. In order to promote objective investigations, the Standards Committee, unlike others in the House, maintains an equal ratio of Democratic and Republican members.

The drive for bipartisanship in these committees reduces the influence of party as a vehicle for organizing committee majorities. The result is a skew in the size of successful coalitions toward consensus (universalism); that is, a large proportion of the successful coalitions contain more than 70 percent of those voting (Figure 3). In Armed Services, for instance, almost one-half (47 percent) of the successful coalitions between 1973 and 1976 contained more than 80 percent of those voting. During the same period, three-fifths of the winning coalitions in the Standards Committee contained more than 90 percent of the voting members. Finally, in the least consensus-oriented committee of this subset, Foreign Affairs, about one-fifth of the successful coalitions (21 percent) contained between 71 percent and 75 percent of the committee members.

CONCLUSION

The findings suggest that coalition size varies according to the structure of conflict within committees. Members of a committee are differentially influenced by forces in the committee's environment—party, ideology, administration, and constituency influences. The influences of these forces create cleavages within committees. Categorization of committees according to their cleavage structures enables one to predict the size of the coalitions that tend to predominate within committees.

An important predictor of coalition outcomes is the degree to which the partisanship of committee members is reinforced or disrupted by other influences operating in the committee; the more partisanship is crosscut by other cleavages, the larger the size of the coalitions that predominate in the committee. The most extreme case occurs when partisanship is relatively unimportant in committee decision-making. In these committees, coalitions that contain all or most members are likely to form with a high degree of frequency. At the other extreme, when partisanship is reinforced by its overlap with other committee cleavages, minimum winning coalitions are most likely to occur.

Figure 3

DISTRIBUTION OF THE SIZE OF SUCCESSFUL COALITIONS IN NONPARTISAN COMMITTEES

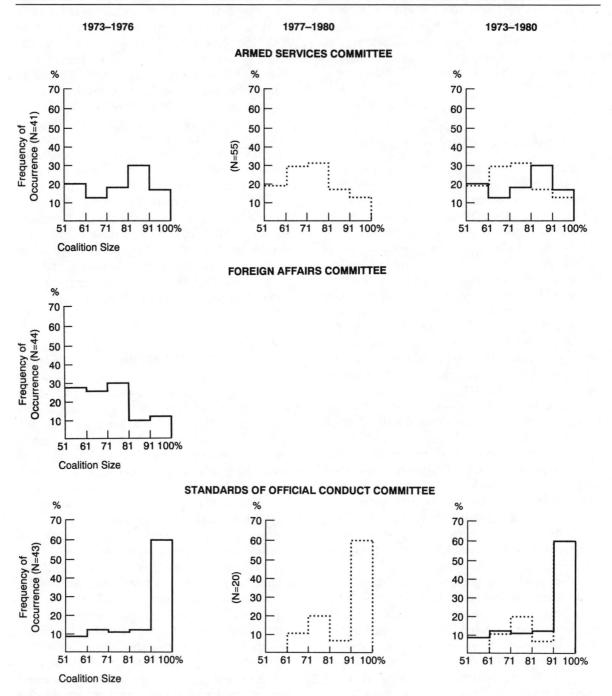

Source: Committee roll-call votes, U.S. House of Representatives, 1973–1980.

While most committees exhibited a significant degree of stability in the distributions of coalition size over the eight-year period 1973–1980, several potential sources of change exist. Committees in which party loyalties are cross-cut by administration influences are most likely to exhibit change because they are most sensitive to partisan control of the executive branch. When the majority party in the House controls the executive branch, partisanship is emphasized. The distribution of committee coalitions under these circumstances tends to skew toward minimum winning size. Divided control of the government promotes broader coalitions as the president seeks opposition support.

A second potential source of change in coalition outcomes is the emergence of new issues. In Post Office, for example, the issue of civil service reform resulted in the emergence of a constituency cleavage during the Carter administration. This cleavage divided partisan loyalties and resulted in larger-than-minimum coalitions, despite the fact that Democratic control of the presidency made partisan and administration cleavages more collinear. It is important to note that in order for a new issue to create new coalition outcomes, it must change the existing cleavage pattern in the committee. For instance, in the Interior Committee a new constituency cleavage appeared in the 1977–1980 period, but since it reinforced existing cleavages in the committee, it failed to alter the pattern in coalition outcomes significantly. The stability in committee jurisdictions tends to mitigate against such changes. Since the same categorical types of issues are deliberated within committees as a result of committee jurisdictions, cleavage patterns are infrequently disrupted. Therefore, coalition distributions display stability as well.

A third factor that has the potential for changing both cleavage and coalition patterns is membership change. There are three ways in which a change in membership could alter the cleavage and coalition patterns in committee. A change in the attractiveness of the committee could result in members with divergent goals joining the committee. As Fenno noted in 1973, similarity of members' goals leads to agreement on the strategic premises employed in committee decision-making. An influx of members with different goals could disrupt such agreement and lead to new divisions within the committee.

Once again, however, there are conditions that limit such changes. A member's goals in large part determine the type of committee he or she will choose. Since certain committees offer greater opportunities to satisfy certain goals, the types of members who gravitate to specific committees are relatively constant. In addition, changes in the House have made it easier for a member to receive at least one committee assignment of his or her choice. Finally, membership stability is also promoted by the practice of screening the membership of exclusive committees. New members selected for Appropriations or for Ways and Means must display a cooperative legislative style; an additional standard of party loyalty is applied to Ways and Means members. All these factors tend to promote stability in the types of members found on committees.

Changes in the ideological or partisan nature of a committee's membership can also introduce new cleavages or exacerbate older lines of cleavage. The Democratic leadership's efforts to liberalize the Democratic membership on the Budget Committee in the early 1970s served to strengthen the partisan-ideological cleavages in the committee. In this instance, coalition patterns did not change, because the membership changes strengthened, rather than disrupted, the cleavage patterns already present in the committee. Introducing more ideological divergence into a polarized committee might alter the lines of cleavage and change coalition outcomes. Similarly, introducing more partisanship into committees like Foreign Affairs and Armed Services by means of membership changes could significantly alter decision-making in those committees.

A major change in the electoral fortunes of one of the parties could also alter the coalition patterns in the committees. The addition of a large number of new party members could lead to new cleavage patterns and hence different coalition patterns. Even if cleavage patterns did not change, a lopsided majority by virtue of its numerical advantage could lead to larger coalitions. In this case, while one would expect the mean size of coalitions to become larger, one would not necessarily expect the skew of the coalition distributions to change.

What are the effects of committee fragmentation on coalition-building in committees? Clearly, party is a basic component of committee coalitions, but party is only one of several factions in most House committees; hence, majority-party coalitions will of necessity include legislators who have loyalties and commitments to other committee factions. When these loyalties are independent of party, committee leaders of the majority party will have to include a wide range of divergent views, producing unusually large coalitions and many policy compromises. Chairs benefit when the loyalties of committee members overlap partisan identifications; then, policy outcomes will be more constrained, since fewer views will diverge from party positions. Committee leaders exercise far greater control over these policy decisions and will be able to fashion policies that are more to the liking of their party leaders.

If committee leaders incur costs in transacting agreements to fashion winning coalitions, then polarized committees are the least costly, and mixed-partisan committees the most costly, to operate from the perspective of committee leaders. Moreover, the necessity of transacting more agreements in mixed-partisan committees makes coalition bonds weaker and more subject to "postcontractual opportunism" on the part of those cross-pressured by loyalties to other committee factions. The oversized nature of mixed-partisan committee coalitions may be a necessity because of the tenuous nature of the bonds linking members to committee coalitions; since the risk is so great, chairs build unusually large coalitions in expectation of coalition defections. In sum, majority-party coalition-building is destined to be an arduous and time-consuming task engulfed in risk in all but a few congressional committees. And even when committee leaders are successful in forming a winning coalition, the policy compromises may be so broad as to preclude party victories.

BIBLIOGRAPHY

Decision Making on the Floor
The study of floor voting in Congress has occupied a central position in empirical analyses of legislative decision-making. This emphasis has been a response to at least two basic points about roll-call voting; such votes are an essential component in congressional decisions, and they can be acquired and analyzed with relative ease. As a result, we have a good understanding of the factors influencing voting decisions on the floors of the House and Senate. Among the most important works on floor voting are R. DOUGLAS ARNOLD, *Congress and the Bureaucracy* (New Haven, Conn., 1979); DAVID W. BRADY and CHARLES S. BULLOCK III, "Is There a Conservative Coalition in the House?" *Journal of Politics* 42 (May 1980): 549–559; AAGE R. CLAUSEN, *How Congressmen Decide* (New York, 1973); BARBARA HINCKLEY, "Coalitions in Congress," *American Journal of Political Science* 16 (May 1972): 197–207; JOHN W. KINGDON, *Congressmen's Voting Decisions* (New York, 1973); DONALD R. MATTHEWS and JAMES A. STIMSON, *Yeas and Nays* (New York, 1975); and JERROLD E. SCHNEIDER, *Ideological Coalitions in Congress* (Westport, Conn., 1978).

Studies of Committees
Most of the studies of committee decision-making have focused on individual committees. Studies of individual committees include THOMAS A. HENDERSON, *Congressional Oversight of Executive Agencies* (Gainesville, Fla., 1970); ROBERT L. PEABODY, "The Enlarged Rules Committee," in ROBERT L. PEABODY and NELSON W. POLSBY, eds., *New Perspectives on the House of Representatives* (Chicago, 1963); RICHARD F. FENNO, JR., "The House of Representatives and Federal Aid to Education," in ROBERT L. PEABODY and NELSON W. POLSBY, eds., *New Perspectives on the House of Representatives* (Chicago, 1963); CHARLES O. JONES, "Representation in Congress: The Case of the House Agriculture Committee," *American Political Science Review* 55 (June 1961): 358–367; JAMES T. MURPHY, "Political Parties and the Porkbarrel: Party Conflict and Cooperation in House Public Works Committee Decision Making," *American Political Science Review* 68 (March 1974): 169–185; LYNETTE P. PERKINS, "Influence of Member Goals on Their Committee Behavior: The U.S. House Judiciary Committee," *Legislative Studies Quarterly* 5 (August 1980): 373–392; and DAVID E. PRICE, *The Commerce Committees* (New York, 1975).

A smaller subset of committee studies have attempted to compare decision making among several committees. Some of the major comparative studies of congressional committees include RICHARD F. FENNO, JR., *Congressmen in*

Committees (Boston, 1973); NORMAN J. ORNSTEIN and DAVID W. RHODE, "Shifting Forces, Changing Rules and Political Outcomes: The Impact of Congressional Change on Four House Committees," in ROBERT L. PEABODY and NELSON W. POLSBY, eds., *New Perspectives on the House of Representatives* (Chicago, 1977); and GLENN R. PARKER and SUZANNE L. PARKER, *Factions in House Committees* (Knoxville, Tenn., 1985).

Another important focus of studies of congressional committees is committee assignments. Two of the most important studies of committee assignment practices describe the criteria for assigning legislators to committees and how long it takes legislators to obtain their preferred assignments: NICHOLAS MASTERS, "Committee Assignments in the House of Representatives," *American Political Science Review* 55 (June 1961): 345–357; and IRWIN N. GERTZOG, "Routinization of Committee Assignments in the U.S. House of Representatives," *American Journal of Political Science* 20 (November 1976): 693–712.

A final area of committee research is the study of committee leadership and its selection. Among the studies in this area are GLENN R. PARKER, "The Selection of Committee Leaders in the House of Representatives," *American Politics Quarterly* 7 (January 1979): 71–93; and NELSON W. POLSBY, MIRIAM GALLAGHER, and BARRY S. RUNDQUIST, "The Growth of the Seniority System in the U.S. House of Representatives," *American Political Science Review* 63 (September 1969): 787–807.

Congressional Change

Congressional committees have undergone considerable change in their organization and operation in past decades. Two important articles exploring the impact of changes in committees are JOSEPH COOPER and DAVID BRADY, "Institutional Context and Leadership Style: The House from Cannon to Rayburn," *American Political Science Review* 75 (June 1981): 411–425; and NORMAN J. ORNSTEIN and DAVID W. RHODE, "Political Parties and Congressional Reform," in ROBERT L. PEABODY and NELSON W. POLSBY, eds., *New Perspectives on the House of Representatives* (Chicago, 1963).

Constituency Behavior

While there has been a heavy emphasis on the behavior of legislators in Washington, recent studies of Congress have drawn attention to the behavior of members in their constituencies and its impact on congressional decision-making. Some important studies of this topic include RICHARD F. FENNO, JR., *Home Style* (Boston, 1978); GLENN R. PARKER, *Homeward Bound: Explaining Changes in Congressional Behavior* (Pittsburgh, 1986); and GLENN R. PARKER, *The Characteristics of Congress* (Englewood Cliffs, N.J., 1989).

SEE ALSO The Congressional Committee System; Constituencies; AND The Role of Congressional Parties.

PACS AND CONGRESSIONAL DECISIONS

Daniel S. Ward

The stability of the U.S. political system has allowed journalists, scholars, and other observers to examine its institutions over long historical periods. As a result, political change is normally associated with incremental alterations in the structure or behavior of Congress, the presidency, federal courts, the political parties, voters, or other key political organizations or actors. Rarely does a new political institution emerge swiftly to play a critical role in American politics. Between 1971 and 1991, however, following major reform efforts, political action committees (PACs) became principal players in congressional campaign financing by contributing millions of dollars directly and indirectly to candidates for the U.S. House and Senate. Perhaps more troubling, some would argue, is that PACs have become a significant force in congressional policy-making.

The lack of historical perspective on PACs has produced a series of stylized assumptions about their conduct and their impact on congressional politics. In both the political and journalistic arenas, PACs have become a target of scorn and reform, with PACs portrayed as entities seeking to buy legislative votes. Because PACs emerged coincident with elaborate record keeping by the Federal Election Commission (FEC), their opponents have been supplied an arsenal of data, often forged into persuasive arguments about PAC influence. Titles such as *The Best Congress Money Can Buy* (by Philip M. Stern) and *Politics and Money: The New Road to Corruption* (by Elizabeth Drew) have become commonplace among critiques of the relationship between PACs and members of Congress. And yet, little evidence has been offered that inevitably leads to the conclusion that PACs buy votes rather than simply provide electoral backing after the fact for supportive legislators. Unfortunately, many of the most critical studies, including those by the public-interest group Common Cause, lack the rigorous analytical techniques required to disentangle the complex issues posed by PAC contributions. Less common and more ambiguous in their conclusions have been careful and systematic scholarly studies of this relationship.

Before exploring the conventional wisdom and empirical evidence regarding PACs and congressional decisions, this essay will place these organizations in the broader framework of interest-group politics, define the term *political action committee* formally and describe the standard categorization utilized legally and analytically, and briefly review the history of PACs and their patterns of behavior over time. This will make assessing the role of PACs in the legislative process an easier task.

PACs IN THE POLITICAL PROCESS

Although PACs have only recently become an institutionalized part of the American political process, they are, in fact, simply a specific type of interest group. Since the nation's founding, interest groups have been a source of concern or solace for political observers and analysts. Factions were at the center of Madisonian thought (see especially *The Federalist*, no. 10), and so astute an observer of American government as Alexis de Tocqueville noted the propensity of U.S. citizens to join in associations for a multitude of reasons (*Democracy in America*, Pt. 1, no. 12). For much of the twentieth century the pluralist paradigm structured debate about American politics. One disagreement between pluralists and their critics has centered on the potential for interest groups as representative institutions. Whether interest groups are viewed positively, as organizations that provide opportunities for political participation (cf. Truman), or negatively, as economically debilitating (cf. Lowi), most students of

American politics acknowledge the influence of organized interests.

To the degree that PACs resemble other organized interest groups, their emergence should not be cause for alarm. Like the AFL-CIO, the Business Roundtable, the NAACP, the AARP, or Greenpeace, any single political action committee is a collection of individuals (in most cases) with shared interests who have decided to unite in an effort to effect desirable political outcomes. But what is particularly interesting about PACs—and troubling to some—is the precise nature of their efforts to achieve their goals. Whereas lobbyists are increasingly limited in what they can provide for legislators in an attempt to influence the policy-making process, the essence of PACs is to provide financial resources to aid election campaigns. The direct provision of money to lawmakers conjures up images of influence peddling, vote buying, and power brokering, all of which are anathema to representative government. Thus, although PACs fall under the general rubric "interest groups," it is the financial nature of their relationship to members of Congress that makes them subject to close scrutiny.

PAC directors are not, of course, the first individuals to provide financial contributions to candidates for political office. With the exception of recent presidential elections, American campaigns have always been privately financed. A significant portion of this financing has now been institutionalized in the form of PAC contributions as a result of the reform efforts detailed below. The fact that PACs normally have specific and identifiable legislative interests has conspired with public-disclosure requirements to highlight the question of undue legislative influence. While the interests of a few wealthy benefactors, who were common prior to campaign-finance reform, may have been less apparent than those of a labor or business PAC, there is little reason to believe that the impact of the former would be any less pernicious. This is not to argue for or against PAC contributions, but simply to stress the broader historical context of interest-group politics and campaign finance in which PACs operate. In other words, PACs are relatively new to the American political process, but the work they engage in has a much longer tradition.

DEFINING AND CLASSIFYING PACs

PACs are regulated primarily by the federal election campaign laws, deriving from the Federal Election Campaign Act (FECA) of 1972 and its amendments (contained largely in titles 2 and 26 of the U.S. Code). The term *political action committee*, however, appears nowhere in the laws of the United States. The legal term applied to such organizations is simply *political committee*, which is defined specifically as

> (A) any committee, club, association, or other group of persons which receives contributions aggregating in excess of $1,000 during a calendar year or which makes expenditures aggregating in excess of $1,000 during a calendar year; or (B) any separate segregated fund established under the provisions of section 441b(b) of this title. (2 U.S.C. Sect. 431[4])

The statutory definition encompasses a broader spectrum of organizations than is normally associated with PACs, including local party committees. Though the same laws may govern these organizations, the Federal Election Commission (FEC), in its reporting of campaign contributions and expenditures, provides a separate accounting of party activity. "Political committees" are distinguished by statute from "principal campaign committees" and "authorized committees" affiliated with specific candidates for office. Political committees must register with, and report financial activities to, the FEC on a regular basis.

Another significant statutory definition that is relevant to the study of PACs is the "multicandidate committee," which refers to any political committee registered with the FEC for a least six months that has received contributions from more than fifty persons and has made contributions to five or more federal candidates (2 U.S.C. Sect. 441a[a][4]). Different contribution limits apply to organizations that succeed or fail to meet these criteria. Specifically, multicandidate committees may contribute up to $5,000 per election (primary, general, and runoff) to a single candidate; those that fail to qualify as multicandidate are termed "other committees" and may contribute only $1,000. Most analyses of PAC activity focus on multicandidate committees. The requirements and limitations imposed on multicandidate committees apply as well to party committees. Individuals, like "other committees," are limited to $1,000 contributions.

It is important to understand the classification scheme devised by the FEC to report on PAC contributions, in addition to the statutory definition of PACs. This categorization serves as the basis of most analyses (and criticisms) of PAC activity in legislative elections and policy-making. The FEC places PACs in one of six categories, depending on their parent organizations. The two most prominent are "labor" and "corporate." Labor organizations and businesses, barred from using their general treasury funds to make political contributions, are permitted to establish separate, segregated funds to contribute to campaigns for federal office. A third category of PACs comprises trade, membership, and health organizations that are sponsored by parent organizations (the term *trade* will be used throughout) and that, like corporate and labor PACs, must establish separate units to disburse contributions. Two smaller, less influential groups are corporations without stock and cooperatives. These two contribute less than 5 percent of all PAC expenditures in an average election cycle and will be combined as "other" in the discussion that follows.

The final PAC type, and one that has received a disproportionate amount of attention in the media, is the "nonconnected" committee. These PACs operate independently of sponsoring labor or incorporated organizations and exist almost solely for the purpose of contributing to political campaigns. In contrast to PACs in the first five categories, nonconnected committees have no parent organization to pay administrative and solicitation costs. Likewise, they have no natural population of potential contributors from which to seek contributions. As a result, nonconnected PACs have received considerable attention for their direct-mail solicitation procedures and frequent appeals to single-issue or ideological causes. In fact, the term *ideological PAC* is often used interchangeably with *nonconnected PAC*, though this frequently is a misnomer because many nonconnecteds have no specific ideological leaning.

The FEC's classification of PACs has become shorthand for analysts and critics of campaign finance and congressional behavior. The utility of the categorization is that the FEC provides elaborate reporting of activity in an easily digestible form. This naturally leads to characterizations. The number of business and nonconnected PACs are shown to have increased dramatically. Labor PACs are said to lean toward Democrats and business PACs toward incumbents. The popular association of nonconnected PACs with ideological causes has already been noted. The problem of painting with such broad strokes is that they mask a good deal of diversity that exists within categories, especially in the catchall nonconnected group. In addition, the significant financial role played by sponsoring organizations, which is reported separately, makes comparisons of financial activity across categories problematic. As a result, the data reported in the FEC classification scheme should be viewed as illustrative rather than definitive.

A SHORT HISTORY OF PACS

The close association between campaign-finance reform in the 1970s and the contemporary manifestation of PACs belies the actual origin of these committees in American politics. As early as the 1940s, organized labor was forming separate entities to influence the campaign process. First to do so was the Congress of Industrial Organizations (CIO), which created CIO-PAC in 1943 to collect voluntary contributions from its members and to disburse those donations to political campaigns. During the following year CIO-PAC expended more than one million dollars (Sabato, p. 5). Not coincidentally, at roughly the same time Congress began to take significant steps to control campaign contributions and spending.

The Hatch Act of 1939 and its amendments throughout the next decade not only established campaign-contribution limits but also prohibited political participation by federal employees and limited campaign contributions by individuals or businesses under contract with the national government. These limitations were later extended to labor unions (Sorauf, pp. 30–31). Furthermore, the Taft-Hartley Act of 1947 placed restrictions on the use of treasury funds for political purposes by labor unions and corporations. Organized labor continued to perfect the idea of a separate institution designed to engage in political activity.

The model for most modern PACs remains the Committee on Political Education (COPE), created after the merger of the American Federation of Labor and the CIO in 1955. Its successful strategy of solicitation and mobilization made practical use of labor's natural strengths, size, and unity. Lacking these organizational components, it was not until the mid-1960s that corporations and trade associations began to match the efforts of labor in the development of PACs. Ironically, the two most active business-related PACs, those associated with the National Association of Manufacturers (the Business-Industry Political Action Committee, or BIPAC) and the American Medical Association (AMPAC), combined virtually to equal the efforts of COPE with $1.2 million in expenditures for the 1968 campaign cycle. In the years prior to full implementation of the FECA, the number of business-oriented PACs increased dramatically, from just 11 in 1964 to more than 400 in 1976 (Sabato, pp. 6, 12). Thus, although the FECA is often presented as the spearhead of a new form of political financing, in reality it was a reaction to the already burgeoning business of PACs.

The Federal Election Campaign Act

The FECA began the legislative march toward campaign-finance reform in the 1970s. The system for financing presidential elections was completely overhauled, and congressional elections would be affected by contribution limits and the proliferation of PACs that was encouraged by the reforms. The primary purpose of the initial legislation was to place tighter controls on the reporting of campaign contributions and expenditures. Congress for the first time explicitly authorized corporations and labor unions to establish separate, segregated funds using their own treasury funds. Another provision of the legislation was the initiation of a presidential-campaign fund from federal tax revenue. The major flaw in the FECA was the omission of strong enforcement mechanisms. The responsibility for monitoring and enforcing campaign finance was dispersed among the clerk of the House, the secretary of the Senate, the comptroller general, and the Justice Department. Despite evidence of widespread corruption during the 1972 campaign, few cases were litigated.

The FECA amendments of 1974 had a more dramatic impact on the shape of campaign finance and on PAC activity than did the original legislation. First, the amendments established the FEC as an independent body to oversee all administrative functions of the campaign-finance system and to pursue legal remedies against violators. All PACs, campaigns, and party committees from then on had to file complete financial reports with the FEC as a result of the 1974 amendments. Another set of provisions with significant implications for PACs placed restrictions on the dollar amount of contributions by individuals, parties, committees, and candidates. Finally, the amendments established limitations on overall expenditures by campaigns.

Contribution limits were seen as a boost to PACs because they limited the sources of campaign money and provided a higher limit for PAC donations ($5,000) than for individuals ($1,000). The FECA amendments also placed a total $25,000 limit on the amount that any individual could contribute to all federal candidates combined in a given election cycle. No such limit was placed on PACs. As a result, PACs became a much more attractive source of campaign contributions. Any influence that would accrue to PACs as a result of contribution restrictions would be limited by the cap placed on campaign spending. In other words, as the overall need for financing is constrained by a spending ceiling, the relative advantage of PACs is reduced. The role of the Supreme Court in removing this impediment to PAC influence is discussed below.

A final important provision of the 1974 FECA amendments relevant to PACs was the removal of prohibitions on campaign contributions by corporations and labor unions under contract with the U.S. government. The new law allowed these organizations to establish separate, segregated funds as do all other businesses and unions. Combined with contribution limitations and subsequent Supreme Court action, this provision of the legislation helped promote the substantial growth of business-oriented PACs over the next decade, as the final barrier to full corporate participation in the election process was removed.

The High Court and PAC Development

A critical event in the development of the contemporary PAC system was the Supreme Court's decision in *Buckley* v. *Valeo*, 424 U.S. 1 (1976). The suit, brought by the independent-minded politicians Senator James Buckley (Cons.-N.Y.) and former Senator Eugene McCarthy (D.-Minn.), challenged all of the key provisions of the 1974 FECA amendments. The Court ruled that a number of principal portions of the law were unconstitutional. First, the appointment method for FEC commissioners was found to violate the principle of separation of powers, because four of the members of the commission were appointed by Congress, despite the body's executive powers. (Shortly after the Court's decision, Congress revised the appointment method in accordance with the ruling.) The Court also found limits on candidates' spending of personal funds to be unconstitutional. Of more relevance to the question of PAC influence was the Court's handling of contribution and expenditure limitations, the latter ruled unconstitutional.

The Court's reasoning on contributions and expenditures in *Buckley* v. *Valeo* rests on finely drawn distinctions, but the implications of the finding are profound. With regard to contributions, while recognizing the effect of limitations on First Amendment freedoms, the Court argued that there is a compelling government interest "to limit the actuality and appearance of corruption resulting from large individual financial contributions." So although money is linked to speech, the amount of money contributed is not equated with pure expression. It is easy to see that the Court could have applied the same logic to expenditure limitations. While it is clear that the ability to expend money during a political campaign is necessary for free expression, a reasonable limitation that accounts for the costs of modern campaigning could serve a compelling government interest to curtail the costs of campaigns and eliminate corruption, according to the same logic. The Court ruled otherwise.

In rejecting each of the arguments presented by the appellees in favor of expenditure limitations (alleviating corruption, equalizing the financial resources of candidates, reducing campaign costs), the Court argued that "the First Amendment denies government the power to determine that spending to promote one's political views is wasteful, excessive, or unwise." Using similar reasoning, the Court invalidated limits on personal spending for one's own candidacy and independent expenditure ceilings. The latter point is particularly significant for PACs, providing an alternative approach to affecting election outcomes. This finding would lead to the category of "uncoordinated" spending, whereby individuals or groups can advocate the election or defeat of a candidate without financial limits, so long as the spending is completely independent of the campaign itself.

Given the significance of these legislative and legal events for PAC development, it may be useful to reiterate the combined effect of the 1974 FECA amendments and the *Buckley* v. *Valeo* decision on PACs. First, corporations and labor unions under contract with the U.S. government could establish PACs, thus encouraging growth in the overall number of PACs; second, PACs were limited to $5,000 contributions to campaigns, compared to $1,000 for individuals, making PACs an attractive and efficient source of funding; third, independent expenditures by committees or individuals were allowed, providing an alternative means for spending on behalf of a candidate once direct contributions were exhausted; and finally, campaign-expenditure limitations were invalidated, meaning that there would be an unrestricted need for campaign finance. Another development that had a less obvious impact on PAC growth was the establishment of a federally financed presidential-election system. With matching funds available in the primary process and full government financing of the general election, fund-raising at the presidential level tapered off. Frank Sorauf likened the resulting process to a hydraulic system: "Available money seeks an outlet, and if some outlets are narrowed or closed off, money flows with increased pressure to the outlets still open" (p. 74). The outlets that were still open were PACs and congressional campaigns.

PAC Growth

The relationship between PACs and congressional decisions is only partially uncovered by looking at raw numerical counts of PACs and levels of contributions. Though a more elaborate analysis will follow, exploring the trend of PAC growth is a worthy initial endeavor. Figure 1 shows the rate of PAC growth between 1974 and 1990 by indicating the percent change in the number of PACs from each election year to the next. The rate of change between 1972 and 1974, following the original FECA, is not shown because it would distort the chart. The number of registered PACs increased from 113 to 608, a change of 438 percent. Between 1974 and 1976, the period of the 1974 FECA amendments and the *Buckley* v. *Valeo* decision, the number of PACs almost doubled to 1,146. The rate of growth steadily declined thereafter and has been below 10 percent since 1986, declining in real numbers for the first time in 1990. It is clear that after an initial surge, PACs reached a kind of threshold. Although group theory holds that there is an infinite number of potential interest groups in society, clearly a finite number has the incentive or resources to form a PAC.

The breakdown of PACs by category is presented in Figure 2 (1978 was the first year in which the FEC used the current classification). Corporate PACs dominate overall and have seen substantial growth, while labor and trade PACs have been relatively stable in number. Nonconnected PACs have had the greatest relative increase in numbers and now are the second most abundant category. In 1978, nonconnecteds accounted for just 10 percent of all PACs, but by 1990, 29 percent of PACs were

FIGURE 2

PAC GROWTH BY FEC CATEGORY, 1978–1990

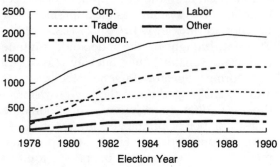

Source: Federal Election Commission.

nonconnected. Absolute numbers, of course, can be deceptive. Many nonconnected PACs are small and ephemeral, whereas corporate and labor PACs tend to be more enduring and active. For instance, during the 1990 election cycle less than 50 percent of registered nonconnected PACs made any contributions to federal candidates, but the rate was 80 percent for corporate, 78 percent for other, 75 percent for trade, and 64 percent for labor. This suggests that half of the nonconnected PACs are out of business, at least temporarily.

The importance of PACs lies not in their mere existence but in their activity, particularly the distribution of campaign contributions. It is here, as much as in PAC growth, that the increasing significance of PACs becomes apparent. Figure 3 shows inflation-adjusted contributions from all PACs to federal candidates from 1972 to 1990, as well as percent change figures for each year. Even controlling for inflation, the

FIGURE 1

PERCENT CHANGE IN NUMBERS OF PACs, 1974–1990

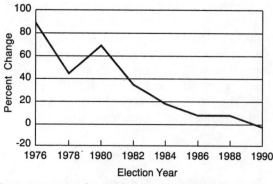

Sources: Larry J. Sabato, *PAC Power: Inside the World of Political Action Committees* (New York, 1989), pp. 12–13, and the Federal Election Commission.

FIGURE 3

PAC CONTRIBUTIONS TO FEDERAL CANDIDATES, 1972–1990

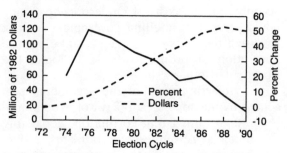

Source: Federal Election Commission.

increase in PAC giving is impressive. It is important to note, however, that the rate of change has decreased steadily and that overall contributions were down from the previous cycle for the first time in 1990. Clearly, the notion of unabated growth in PAC activity is disputed by the first three graphs.

Although PAC spending has increased substantially, so, too, has the overall level of spending on congressional campaigns. In order to argue that PACs have become more influential in the legislative process, it is necessary to show that PAC spending has more than kept pace with campaign spending generally. Figure 4 shows PAC contributions to federal candidates as a percentage of all congressional-campaign spending in each election cycle, all figures adjusted for inflation. Perhaps more than any other piece of information, Figure 4 shows the effect of campaign-finance reform and Supreme Court rulings. As the cost of campaigning continued to increase and alternative sources of financing were constrained, PACs stepped forward to fill a void, now providing over one-third of all campaign expenditures. In 1990, individuals contributed about 57 percent; candidates, 2 percent; and the party, 1 percent. Loans accounted for roughly 4 percent of expenditures. It is worth noting the stability of the PAC percentage figure since 1984, which is in line with the previous discussion.

Just as overall PAC growth rates masked important and distinctive trends among the various types of PACs, so do raw contribution figures. A disaggregation of contribution patterns

FIGURE 4
PAC CONTRIBUTIONS AS A PERCENT OF TOTAL CAMPAIGN EXPENDITURES

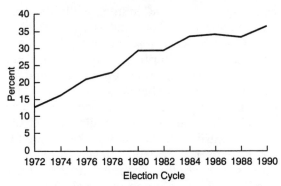

Source: Federal Election Commission.

FIGURE 5
CONTRIBUTIONS BY PAC TYPE, 1978–1990

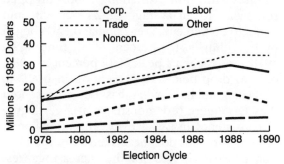

Source: Federal Election Commission.

takes one further toward an understanding of PAC behavior. Figure 5 shows the inflation-adjusted contribution figures for each category since 1978. Except for the first year, corporate PACs have been dominant, while trade and labor committees consistently rank second and third, respectively. Despite their current position as the second most numerous type of committee, nonconnected PACs have never been able to do better than fourth in contribution levels.

Finally, Figure 6 is an interesting representation of contributions by PAC category. It shows the percentage of all contributions attributable to each type of committee. In the first year of the period, corporate (28 percent), labor (29 percent), and trade (32 percent) contribution rates were very close. In the next six

FIGURE 6
SOURCES OF PAC CONTRIBUTIONS, 1978–1990

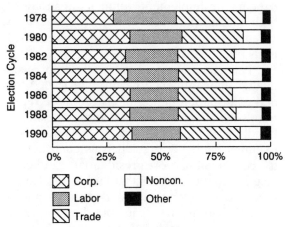

Source: Federal Election Commission.

election cycles, however, corporate contributions increased to an average 35 percent of the whole, with little variation. Labor dropped somewhat to an average of 23 percent, and trade, to 26 percent. Nonconnected PACs began by providing just 8 percent of all funding in 1978 and reached a peak of 14 percent in 1986, only to drop below 10 percent again in 1990.

Like much of what has been presented thus far, Figure 6 demonstrates a large degree of consistency in PAC activity. All notions of an onslaught of PAC dollars, a takeover of the election process by PACs or the increasing presence of ideologically motivated PACs, must surely be disputed by Figures 1–6. Instead, it appears that the PAC system has reached a state of near equilibrium. The rate of increase in the number of PACs and their contributions was sharply reduced by the early 1990s, and within the various categories of PACs, a stability in relative numbers and contributions to congressional candidates was achieved. "Stability" is not meant to imply a lack of influence or significance. To the contrary, the stability of the PAC system may be a tribute to its continuing relevance in the electoral process. From an analytical standpoint, stability in the system should provide confidence in research findings, alleviating concerns about time-bound results.

Any threat to the existing stability of the PAC system is not likely to come from growth in numbers or relative contributions but from legal reform or an adaptation of PAC contribution patterns. Most congressional sessions are replete with proposals for campaign reform, a substantial portion of which are aimed at PACs. Unless Congress is able to institute federal financing or implement voluntary restrictions, both remote prospects at best, the *Buckley* v. *Valeo* decision will continue to protect PACs from effective control.

PACs continue to seek methods of maximizing their influence beyond the $5,000 federal contribution limit. Among the more recent trends are the provision of soft money and the bundling of individual gifts. *Soft money* refers to funds explicitly precluded as contributions to congressional or presidential candidates (e.g., amounts over $5,000 and funds from a corporate or union treasury) that are channeled through state parties, "party-building" organizations, or voter mobilization efforts. Because many states have constructed no barriers to

such contributions, they are viewed by PAC critics as "backdoor" offerings to federal candidates when the organizations in question are linked to congressional or presidential campaigns (Drew; Sorauf, pp. 317–323). The most significant cause for concern is that there is no method to record and account for soft money, thus limiting the oversight capacity of the FEC.

The bundling of gifts is another strategy that takes on several different forms in the PAC system. Federal law permits organizations to aggregate individual contributions and transmit them to campaigns. As a result, contributions are recorded by the FEC in the name of the individual, but credit may be given by the candidate to the organization that solicited and delivered the funds. Another form of bundling involves the collective decision of multiple PACs to concentrate their contributions, thus maximizing the influence of their shared interests. These and other creative tactics (or "loopholes" to PAC critics) suggest that PACs, like other political institutions, are adaptive and may find ways to circumvent regulatory efforts in the future.

PAC STRATEGIES OF INFLUENCE

The previous section has provided a framework from which to consider the ways that PACs, individually or collectively, can use their primary resource, money, to influence legislative decisions. The two obvious methods, as noted in the introduction, are to help elect candidates who are likely to support the committee's positions or to make contributions to sitting members in order to influence their voting behavior on specific issues. The first strategy fits a sanguine view of the PAC system, while the latter represents a more conspiratorial tone.

If, as many PAC leaders claim, the primary purpose of PAC contributions is to protect like-minded legislators, then unopposed and extremely safe incumbents would receive few donations. And even in close races, which tend to be highly funded, the marginal effect of a single contribution is likely to be negligible. Yet, as empirical evidence presented below indicates, contributions continue to flow to incumbents, both safe and marginal.

Opponents of the PAC system paint a bleak

picture of vote buying and selling. Given the myriad influences on legislative voting, it would be surprising to find members of Congress selling their votes for contributions that, on average, equal about 0.25 percent of their entire war chests (Sorauf, p. 316). Further, a vote-buying strategy by PACs would lead to a pattern of widely dispersed contributions throughout the legislative session as committees seek to influence particular votes. Instead, there is strong evidence that PACs tend to make their contributions toward the end of the election cycle, with more than half their funds coming after 1 July of the election year (Malbin and Skladony, pp. 308–310). Naturally, the pure electoral strategy and overt vote-buying are rather simple and crude approaches, and neither is likely to provide a PAC with its desired return. As such, they are easily disputed empirically. The following discussion is designed to show that PACs employ a combination of these and other tactics to construct more-elaborate strategies of influence.

THE CONTEXT OF PAC GIVING

PACs operate in a complex matrix of individuals and groups seeking to influence congressional decisions. Moreover, individual PACs often are only part of a larger lobbying effort of a parent organization. Larry Sabato reported that roughly two-thirds of the corporations, labor organizations, and trade associations that operate PACs also have lobbying efforts in Washington, D.C. (p. 124). Whereas a corporation's PAC may distribute campaign funds to friendly members, paid lobbyists work at the same time to provide information, exert pressure in the home district, and otherwise seek to sway the same legislators. At times these organizations may work at cross-purposes, with a lobbyist seeking support from a key member on a piece of legislation while the PAC is contributing to his or her opponent. Alternatively, some lobbyists report frustration with PAC operators who continue to provide campaign support for "lost causes" (cf. Sabato, pp. 125–126, for enlightening quotes from participants).

The decision about whether to provide a campaign contribution is complex, and no two PACs are likely to utilize precisely the same

decision-making rules. There are a number of key questions that a PAC must consider if it is to make efficient use of limited resources. Figure 7 offers one possible decision-making model, highlighting some of the key elements derived from anecdotal accounts of PAC decision-making and aggregate-data analysis. Darkened arrows represent the most likely paths toward financial support, while hollow arrows depict possible but less certain paths. Straight lines suggest that a contribution is unlikely.

Incumbency is presented as the foremost consideration for most PACs. Given the extraordinary rates of reelection since the 1960s, this seems to be a distinctly rational form of behavior. In 1990, 78 percent of PAC contributions to Senate candidates went to incumbents (excluding open-seat races), and 92 percent of House contributions went to current officeholders. The incumbent strategy can be viewed as a form of insurance. While PACs may not know precisely what they can expect in return for

FIGURE 7
A SIMPLE MODEL OF PAC DECISION MAKING

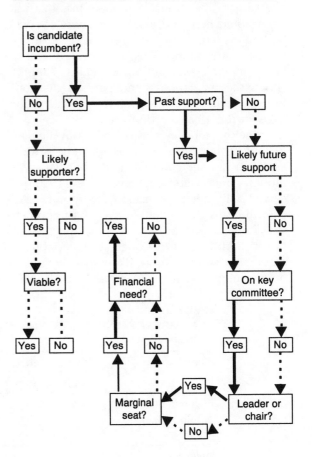

their contributions, they are fairly certain that the incumbent is more likely to be in a position to help. Even if the incumbent has not been particularly supportive of the PAC's position in the past, contributing to an opponent may only serve to alienate the member further. What may be lost is a fundamental resource that PACs and their parent organizations treasure: access.

Ideology, represented here as past or potential support, is another principal concern for PACs. If a candidate is not an incumbent, then the best hope for gaining financial support is to solicit help from PACs aligned with his or her own policy positions. But such support is likely to come only if the candidate can demonstrate electoral viability. Even in the case of a viable challenger who professes support for a committee's positions, there is uncertainty. Incumbents have a past history to serve as a guide to future behavior. As such, among incumbents, past support or promises of future support are pictured as primary questions in the model of PAC decision-making. In other words, not all incumbents are equally attractive to PACs.

Despite the strong incumbent bias that has been noted here and elsewhere, there is compelling evidence that ideology (i.e., past or potential issue support) is a critical deciding factor in PAC contribution strategies. Table 1 shows the incumbency and partisan distribution patterns of corporate, trade, and labor PACs in the 1990 election cycle.

The incumbency bias is clear from the data in Table 1, but partisan bias is apparent as well, especially among corporate and labor PACs. Although Democratic incumbents in 1990 received a higher percentage of corporate PAC contributions than Republicans, it is important to acknowledge the large Democratic majorities in both houses of Congress. A Republican incumbent is much more likely to receive corporate support than is a Democratic colleague.

Corporate contribution strategies in nonincumbent races are particularly telling. Less than 1 percent of all corporate gifts go to Democrats challenging incumbent Republicans, whereas Republican challengers, and particularly Republicans in open-seat races, receive substantial support. Labor PACs demonstrate an overwhelming Democratic bias in their distribution of campaign funds, among both incumbents and challengers. These data combine to show that incumbency is a significant though not controlling factor in PAC contribution decision-making.

PACs are likely to consider the institutional position of potential recipients, as well as incumbency and ideology. Those who serve on committees with jurisdiction over policies of particular concern to a PAC may be targeted for contributions. In addition, party leaders and committee chairs, because of their unique powers, may be attractive candidates for PACs. If access is valued by PAC leaders, then access to committee chairs and party leaders is especially appealing. Kay Schlozman and John Tierney (p. 232) showed that party leaders received more than twice as much, and committee chairs more than 50 percent more, in PAC contributions than the average incumbent.

A final set of considerations involves the nature of the campaign itself. Is the incumbent electorally marginal and/or in need of financial support? Schlozman and Tierney (p. 232) showed that the closeness of a race is a strong determinant of the level of PAC support. In fact, marginal losers receive, on average, more PAC dollars than do decisive winners. Marginal winners receive the most of all, and decisive losers, the least. Taking the decision-making model in Figure 7 to its logical extreme, the most likely recipient of PAC support would be an incumbent with a strong record of support for the PAC who sits on a relevant committee (ideally as chair) and is electorally vulnerable.

TABLE 1
INCUMBENCY AND PARTY BIAS IN 1990 PAC CONTRIBUTIONS, IN PERCENTAGES

Status	Corporate		Trade		Labor	
	Dem.	Rep.	Dem.	Rep.	Dem.	Rep.
Incumbent	43	38	48	34	65	6
Nonincumbent	3	15	7	11	29	1
Total	46	53	55	45	94	7

Source: Federal Election Commission.

There are many other factors that may help PACs determine which candidates will receive their support, but Figure 7 appears to capture the most important concerns. John R. Wright (1985) combined most of these elements in a statistical analysis of five active PACs, finding past support and electoral need to be more closely related to PAC support for incumbents than institutional status. PACs apparently invoke a more rational decision-making process than many critics claim. Financial assistance is provided to those who are most likely to be in a position to help (i.e., incumbents) and who have been supportive in the past. Those most in need of help are more likely recipients. The empirical realities of incumbency bias and contributions to unopposed or safe candidates, phenomena frequently criticized in the popular media, may be a simple function of a noncompetitive electoral system rather than a pathology in the PAC system.

PACs AND CONGRESSIONAL VOTING BEHAVIOR

Presumably PACs take much care in their contribution decisions, expecting to derive a specific positive effect. Helping to elect sympathetic legislators may be one goal, but in the end, PACs want support on key pieces of legislation. Access is often portrayed as the real benefit of financial support. What legislator could deny a hearing to a group that has contributed thousands of dollars to his or her campaign effort? But access is only a means to the ultimate end—legislative support. Both the popular and scholarly literature on Congress are replete with anecdotes about bold attempts to buy votes, some quite successful. Another common piece of evidence for untoward behavior is the overloading of contributions to members of influential committees, particularly their chairs. But without consistent, systematic verification of such events, the effects of PAC contributions must be relegated to isolated accounts and speculation. Moreover, anecdotal accounts do not provide an answer to the "simultaneity" problem. That is, are contributions a reward to members who have exhibited past support or an attempt to alter voting behavior? As a final effort to understand the relationship between PACs and congressional de-

cisions, a review of the best scholarly work on the question will be useful.

Empirical Tests of PAC Influence

In order to claim that a PAC contribution has had an impact on a congressional decision, there must be systematic evidence that the outcome would have been different in the absence of that contribution. Students of congressional behavior have taken up this difficult analytical task in a number of ways. One common method is to examine a single or limited number of policy areas, congressional committees, or votes in a case-study approach, using sophisticated statistical methods. Though results from such studies may not be generalizable to other policies, committees, or votes, identifying PAC influence in a limited arena is a first step toward understanding the possible paths of influence.

The combined results from research of this type are mixed at best. In one of the first attempts to explore fully the effect of PAC contributions on voting behavior, Harry Chappell (1981) examined votes on a single maritime bill in the U.S. House in 1977. In a simple voting model, where a member's vote was viewed as a function of an interest-group contribution, initial propensity to support the group's position, and a series of exogenous variables representing constituency characteristics and attributes of the member, contributions were found to exert a statistically significant effect on the vote. But when the vote was modeled more appropriately in a simultaneous equation, meaning that contributions themselves were considered a function of initial preferences and constituent characteristics, the effect of the contribution virtually disappeared. Chappell (1982) went on to test this model on an expanded sample of votes, achieving essentially the same results. The author's conclusion that the results are "unavoidably ambiguous" (1981, p. 309) is appropriate for much of the succeeding research in this area.

W. P. Welch examined campaign contributions from the dairy lobby and voting on milk price supports. Like Chappell, he found minimal effects for contributions and concluded that "they were the least important determinant of legislative voting" (p. 493). Instead, members who voted in favor of higher price supports were more influenced by constituents, ideology, and party. Likewise, D. E. Yiannakis found little influence of PAC contributions on Chrysler loan and windfall-profit-tax votes. In one of the most comprehensive efforts to address this issue, Janet Grenzke studied 120 PACs over a ten-year period, both statistically and through elite interviews, and concluded that contributions "generally do not maintain or change House members' voting patterns" (p. 19).

To contend that PAC contributions have no effect on voting behavior on the basis of these findings would be inappropriate. Allen Wilhite and John Theilmann found a significant effect of labor contributions on the propensity to support labor positions, even after controlling for the simultaneity problem discussed above. Kimberly Sims confirmed these findings. The utility of these studies is that they explore behavior on a series of votes relevant to organized labor and consider the overall effect of total labor contributions. As a result, they capture one important reality of the PAC system—the propensity of like-minded committees to contribute collectively, or to "bundle" contributions, thus maximizing their collective impact.

Several other studies added to the ambiguity of findings. Woodrow Jones and K. Robert Keiser found that the relative impact of PAC contributions depends on the visibility of the issue. In other words, when the constituency is attentive and interested, members are less likely to be swayed by campaign contributions. This finding is both intuitively plausible and consistent with existing process-oriented models of legislative decision-making (cf. especially Kingdon). John Frendreis and Richard Waterman found significant effects of American Trucking Association contributions on trucking-deregulation votes. Their failure to account for a simultaneity effect may bias these results, however.

As noted above, most studies of PAC influence on voting behavior have been limited in scope. As a result, the most conclusive statement one can make is that contributions have little impact overall but may influence voting in specific policy areas (labor policy, for instance) and nonsalient issues. Naturally, this is unsatisfactory as a general statement on the question of concern. Though such ambiguity may be an accurate reflection of the true impact of PAC contributions, the task of social scientists is to hold such important questions up to further rigorous testing. Among the more promising avenues for future exploration are studies of committee behavior and formal approaches to incorporating contributions in decision-making models.

A number of researchers have turned their attention to committee activity, arguing that these lower-visibility settings may afford an opportunity to specify more carefully the effects of exogenous factors, including campaign contributions, on congressional decisions. For instance, Wright (1990) found that direct contributions have limited impact on voting in the House Ways and Means and Agriculture committees once the level of lobbying is controlled. Richard Hall and Frank Wayman, alternatively, found that "moneyed interests are able to mobilize legislators already predisposed to support the group's position" through contributions (p. 814). Their emphasis on participation in committee activity rather than voting is a useful corollary to roll-call studies, recognizing that votes are only one manifestation of congressional influence. Clearly, these studies cannot wipe away the ambivalence of previous scholarly work, but they point toward fruitful areas for new research.

Finally, attempts have been made to incorporate interest-group activity and campaign contributions into formal theories of congressional behavior (e.g., Austen-Smith; Coggins; and Denzau and Munger). The utility of starting from a coherent theoretical system is that it allows for the deduction of interesting and testable hypotheses. For example, the Denzau and Munger model predicted that "interest groups will, in general, seek out legislators whose voters are indifferent to the policy the interest group seeks" (p. 89). This, then, offers a theoretical explanation for findings that members are most affected by contributions on nonsalient votes.

CONCLUSION

Whether PACs influence congressional decisions is of considerable concern for adherents of representative government. Representation is owed to constituents in a defined geographical area, and the notion of "one person, one vote" assumes equality among those constituents. PACs, like all interest groups, provide representation to the organized and resourceful. As such, if they direct voting behavior in Congress, the concern for representative government is real. Students of congressional behavior, applying the most comprehensive data and sophisticated analytical methods, have been unable to establish that a significant direct link between contributions and voting exists. This probably serves as no solace to opponents of PACs, who view their growth and wealth with alarm.

Though research findings on PACs and congressional voting are inconclusive, there are several indisputable trends that can be noted. PACs have become principal players in the area of electoral finance. But their growth in numbers, wealth, and influence has been met with a number of ironies. For instance, despite the initial belief that organized labor would dominate the PAC field because of its inherent strength in numbers, business-oriented PACs, corporate and trade, have eclipsed labor PACs in numbers and dollars. A second paradox derives from the expected influence of business PACs. Their opponents feared that already better-financed Republicans would be the primary beneficiaries of business-PAC influence. Instead, the incumbency orientation of these committees has worked to the benefit of many Democrats. Conventional wisdom has seldom prevailed in the world of PACs.

A significant finding of the present analysis is the considerable stability of the PAC system. The growth of PACs in numbers and campaign contributions slowed in the 1980s and was reversed in the 1990 election cycle. Further, the PAC system, in terms of the FEC categorization, has reached an impressive level of stability as well. Essentially, PACs are no longer a moving target. They are a significant part of, and contribute considerably to, the current electoral system. Recalling that the authors of the FECA did not envision the impending growth of PACs, reformers of the existing system should consider potential unintended consequences of their efforts.

The abolition of PACs may eliminate whatever influence they have in the legislative process (though most evidence suggests greater influence by lobbyists), but it could also leave the electoral system underfinanced. Despite the incumbency bias of most PACs, they also serve as one of the few sources of financing for serious challengers. Although it would be virtually impossible to increase existing reelection rates, there is no evidence that competition would be enhanced by the elimination of PACs. This is not to argue that PACs are a necessary part of the American political system, but simply that no major player should be eliminated without considerable thought about the state of affairs that will ensue.

BIBLIOGRAPHY

Data used throughout this essay are from Federal Election Commission publications, unless otherwise noted. The FEC publishes annual reports as well as special publications and periodic press releases. Computerized versions of extensive Commission records are also available to the public.

Overview and History
HERBERT ALEXANDER began an important series of quadrennial books with *Financing the 1964 Election* (Princeton, N.J., 1966), covering the source and use of campaign funds in presidential and congressional elections. ELIZABETH DREW, *Politics and Money: The New Road to Corruption* (New York, 1983), is a journalist's account of money in politics that carries a strong anti-PAC message. JOHN KINGDON, *Congressmen's Voting Decisions* (New York, 1973), provides an integrative model of legislator decision making, focusing on endogenous and exogenous influences on decisions. THEODORE J. LOWI, *The End of Liberalism: The Second Republic of the United States*, 2d ed. (New York, 1979), is a contemporary classic critique of interest groups in American politics. Lowi makes the provocative argument that "interest-group liberalism" is the pathological result of pluralism. MICHAEL J. MALBIN and THOMAS W. SKLADONY, "Appendix: Selected Cam-

paign Finance Data, 1974–82," in MICHAEL J. MALBIN, ed., *Money and Politics in the United States: Financing Elections in the 1980s* (Chatham, N.J., 1984), provides a wealth of useful information about the distribution of campaign dollars. Malbin's collection includes essays by some of the most noted experts on money and elections, including Herbert E. Alexander and Gary C. Jacobson.

LARRY J. SABATO, *PAC Power: Inside the World of Political Action Committees* (New York, 1984), is the most comprehensive study to date of the origins and operation of PACs. KAY LEHMAN SCHLOZMAN and JOHN T. TIERNEY, *Organized Interests and American Democracy* (New York, 1986), provides a detailed textbook account of interest groups, including theoretical and empirical issues. FRANK J. SORAUF, *Money in American Elections* (Glenview, Ill., 1988), is a balanced and thoughtful consideration of the major debates surrounding campaign finance. PHILIP M. STERN, *The Best Congress Money Can Buy* (New York, 1988), is a stark missive about the pernicious influence of money in Congress by an anti-PAC activist. DAVID TRUMAN, *The Governmental Process* (New York, 1951), is a classic text of American government grounded in pluralist theory.

Research

The following research articles are detailed in the text of the essay: DAVID AUSTEN-SMITH, "Interest Groups, Campaign Contributions, and Probabilistic Voting," *Public Choice* 54:2 (1987); HARRY W. CHAPPELL, JR., "Campaign Contributions and Voting on the Cargo Preference Bill: A Comparison of Simultaneous Models," *Public Choice* 36:3 (1981), and "Campaign Contributions and Congressional Voting: A Simultaneous Probit-Tobit Model," *Review of Economics and Statistics* 64:1 (1982); JAY S. COGGINS, "Political Triage and Interest-Group Behavior," paper presented at the Annual Meeting of the Midwest Political Science Associa-

tion, 1991; ARTHUR T. DENZAU and MICHAEL C. MUNGER, "Legislators and Interest Groups: How Unorganized Interests Get Represented," *American Political Science Review* 80:1 (1986); JOHN P. FRENDREIS and RICHARD W. WATERMAN, "PAC Contributions and Legislative Behavior: Senate Voting on Trucking Deregulation," *Social Science Quarterly* 66:2 (1985); JANET M. GRENZKE, "PACs and the Congressional Supermarket: The Currency Is Complex," *American Journal of Political Science*, 33:1 (1989); RICHARD L. HALL and FRANK W. WAYMAN, "Buying Time: Moneyed Interests and the Mobilization of Bias in Congressional Committees," *American Political Science Review* 84:3 (1990); WOODROW JONES, JR., and K. ROBERT KEISER, "Issue Visibility and the Effects of PAC Money," *Social Science Quarterly* 68:1 (1987); KIMBERLY A. SIMS, "PAC Contributions and Roll Calls: The Case of Labor," paper presented at the annual meeting of the Midwest Political Science Association, 1991; DANIEL S. WARD, "Policy and Party in Congressional Committee Decision Making," paper presented at the annual meeting of the Southern Political Science Association, 1990; W. P. WELCH, "Campaign Contributions and Legislative Voting: Milk Money and Dairy Price Supports," *Western Political Quarterly* 35:4 (1982); ALLEN WILHITE and JOHN THEILMANN, "Labor PAC Contributions and Labor Legislation: A Simultaneous Logit Approach," *Public Choice* 53:3 (1987); JOHN R. WRIGHT, "Contributions, Lobbying, and Committee Voting in the U.S. House of Representatives," *American Political Science Review* 84:2 (1990), and "PACs, Contributions, and Roll Calls: An Organizational Perspective," *American Political Science Review* 79:2 (1985); and D. E. YIANNAKIS, "PAC Contributions and House Voting on Conflictual and Consensual Issues: The Windfall Profits Tax and the Chrysler Loan Guarantee," paper presented at the annual meeting of the American Political Science Association.

SEE ALSO Legislative Ethics; Legislatures and American Economic Development; Legislatures and Corruption From Colonial Times to the Present; Pressure Groups and Lobbies; AND The Responsibility of the Representative.

PRESSURE GROUPS AND LOBBIES

John T. Tierney

Observers of American democracy have long been concerned that legislatures are especially vulnerable among U.S. representative institutions to the potentially pernicious influences of organized special interests. The periodically elected representative assembly is the most profound institutional expression of American democracy. But it is an institution pervasively open to the influences of particular interests, partly because of the way it was originally designed and partly because of the forces of gradual institutional developments that have shaped it. This openness is worrisome to many people. Lobbyists representing organized interests operate at the very heart of the legislative process, forging mutually beneficial relationships with legislators and their staffs. Each participant has resources of various kinds—information, access to scarce dollars, strategically placed allies, political support, and the like—that creates a mutually dependent need. This in turn binds legislators and lobbyists and draws them together in almost every facet of legislative life.

There is nothing new about the nervousness among observers that this engenders. From the Founding Fathers through the muckrakers to reform-minded observers today, a steady refrain in American political commentary—and a core element in the American political ethos—has been distrust of special interests' political power. It is no wonder that the central role of organized interests in legislative politics—both in Congress and in the state legislatures—raises so many concerns about democratic governance. After all, organized interest politics is the realm of American political life that most readily accommodates the conversion of private or market resources into political ones. This yields potentially great inequalities among groups in terms of access and influence and produces political circumstances in which the public interest is most vulnerable to subjugation by special interests.

The link between legislators and lobbyists is richly varied and complex. There are many continuities in the long history of this part of American political life, but there are also many changes that reflect developments across the entire governmental landscape. At the national level the activity of interest groups has been affected by the decentralization of power in Congress and the multiplication of political action committees (PACs). At the state level the increasing professionalization of many legislatures has influenced the political process. And at both the federal and the state levels, the relationships between legislatures and lobbyists have been shaped by such changes as the increasing scope of the governmental agenda and the tremendous explosion in the number and variety of organized groups seeking to influence governmental policy.

In addition to taking stock of these developments, this essay will discuss the activities and efforts of organized interests to influence American legislators and examine the sorts of circumstances under which their efforts are most likely to bear fruit. Finally, it is worth considering some of the larger consequences of this political pressure, both for legislative politics and for the political system in general.

THE MULTIPLICATION OF ORGANIZED INTERESTS

When one examines organized-interest politics over time, perhaps its most noticeable feature is the tremendous growth that occurred in the number of organized interests active in American politics in the 1960s and 1970s. One study analyzing this trend shows that of the 2,800 organizations with their own lobbying offices in Washington, D.C., as of 1982, 40 percent of them had been founded since 1960, and 25 percent since 1970. One could populate a small city with the more than 10,000 Washington professionals who spend their time attempting to influence governmental policy decisions on behalf of an incredible array of corporations, trade associations, labor unions, professional societies, single-issue cause groups, social-welfare and civil rights organizations.

Not only are there more lobbying organizations in Washington now than ever before, they are also more active than they used to be. There has been an explosion in organized-interest activity across all kinds of lobbying techniques—classic forms such as testifying at hearings and planning legislative strategy, and newer forms of high-tech lobbying such as orchestrating computer-based direct-mail campaigns to stimulate grass-roots pressure.

Some of this growth in the size and activity of the lobbying community in Washington has occurred because of the increasing size and scope of governmental activity. The federal government octopus has its tentacles into everything, and organized interests feel compelled to protect their interests and to keep from being surprised by governmental actions or policy initiatives that may affect them. Some of the increased activity by organized interests in Washington stems from important changes in the institutional environment (discussed below), which altered the environment of legislative lobbying and opened up some new avenues for potential influence. These changes have multiplied the number of persons on Capitol Hill who can influence policy matters, leaving organized interests that are intent on influencing legislative outcomes with little choice but to escalate the range and volume of their political activities.

Some of the growth reflects the emergence of entirely new interests—resulting from the growth of new technologies, new industries, new professions, and new ways of producing or providing goods and services—represented by organizations such as the National Computer Graphics Association, the American Academy of Physician Assistants, and Satellite Business Systems.

A similar expansion in the realm of organized interests has occurred at the state level, although the proportions of that growth are somewhat more difficult to assess than that in Washington. The reasons for the increase are much the same, however. Chief among them is the growing size and scope of the governmental agenda in most states. As the spending and regulatory decisions of state governments affect more segments of the economy and society, more interest groups are impelled to protect or advance the matters of concern to them.

INTERESTS IN POLITICS: A LOOK AT SOME PROMINENT KINDS

From the Academy for Implants and Transplants to Zero Population Growth, organized interests range from a to z. Similarly, from the American College of Nurse Midwives to the Casket Manufacturers Association of America, they embrace the human experience from the cradle to the grave. They include corporations, trade associations, labor unions, professional societies, social-welfare and civil rights organizations, and single-issue cause groups. Their diversity is so rich that there is no easy way (especially for an essay of this brevity) to categorize and analyze all of them, nor it is possible to note all of the dimensions on which they vary. However, it is worthwhile to mention a few prominent kinds of organizations that are conspicuous in contemporary interest-group politics either because of tremendous growth in their numbers or because of other characteristics that enhance their visibility.

Business and Other Economic Interests

It is not at all surprising that in the U.S. capitalistic economy the overwhelming majority of organizations actively engaged in representing their interests to the government are business organizations of one sort or another—corporations, trade associations, business alliances, and the like. Recent surveys of lobbying activity at the state level make it clear that the majority of groups lobbying in state capitals also are business groups, especially those representing businesses subject to extensive regulation by state governments: banks, truckers, railroads, insurance companies, and utilities. Even hospitals, although not usually considered business interests, per se, are also increasingly formidable political forces in the politics of most states.

At the federal level, the political prominence of the business community is even more noticeable. According to one study conducted in the early 1980s, a full 70 percent of all the interests then having some form of Washington representation were business interests, especially trade associations and corporations. Given how deeply the federal government penetrates the economy, it is only natural for business interests to mobilize politically to prevent unpleasant surprises arising from governmental actions and to try to shape public policies to their liking. After all, federal policies dictate virtually every aspect of business practices from the hiring of employees to the handling of industrial wastes, and from the physical characteristics of the individual workplace to the structure of competition in whole industries.

To deal with this, the business community has incredibly broad corporate representation in Washington, ranging from relatively small companies like Hershey Foods to huge conglomerates like General Electric. But the real backbone of political activity in Washington on behalf of business is the trade association. Trade associations are organizations that unite companies that are ordinarily competitors in the marketplace but share mutual interests in politics. Trade associations vary enormously in size and political weight. At one extreme are giants like the American Bankers Association with over 13,000 members and the National Association of Home Builders with almost ten times as many; at the other are dwarves like the Bow Tie Manufacturers Association and the Post Card Manufacturers Association, each having fewer than ten member-companies.

While the corporate and industrial segments of the business community maintain heavy representation at both the state and the federal level, certain professional and service groups (such as nurses, chiropractors, architects, surveyors, and funeral home operators) focus their lobbying activities at the state level, because typically state governments regulate or license the activities of their membership. Often this regulation is at the behest of the professionals themselves. For example, therapists who use massage techniques in physical therapy want state licensing to differentiate them from persons who perform massages in sleazy parlors. Some professional groups are politically active at both the state and the federal level and manage (as in the case of doctors) to maintain a significant political presence at both levels.

Citizens' Groups, Advocacy Groups, and Cause Groups

Although the political activity of business and occupational groups is conspicuous across the board, perhaps more noticeable are the efforts of citizens' groups, advocacy groups, and cause groups. Unlike unions, trade associations, and other membership organizations founded on common concerns of an economic or occupational nature, *citizens' groups* (often called public interest groups) do not try to pursue selective benefits on behalf of their own members; rather, they try to advance government policies and procedures that will benefit the public at large. These groups pursue a wide variety of goals in politics. Environmental groups like the Sierra Club push for policies that will result in clean air and water and the preservation of wilderness areas. Taxpayers' groups, such as the National Taxpayers' Union, promote reduced government spending and lower taxes.

Advocacy groups seek selective benefits on behalf of groups of persons who are in some way incapacitated or are otherwise unable to represent their own interests. Organizations that promote the welfare of children—for example, the Children's Defense Fund and the Child Welfare League of America—fall into this category, as do organizations that press for the rights of prisoners, the retarded, and persons in nursing homes.

Cause groups (sometimes called single-issue groups) are organizations of persons who care intensely about a single issue or a small group of issues, ordinarily of a noneconomic character. The various organizations battling over abortion (such as the National Right to Life Committee and the National Abortion Rights Action League) are cause groups, as are organizations such as Mothers Against Drunk Driving and groups mobilized on issues such as gun-control and bottle-deposit laws.

Although the number of politically active organizations representing the interests of broad publics and of traditionally disadvantaged or underrepresented constituencies has increased markedly over the past quarter century, such groups still constitute only a tiny fraction of the overall lobbying community. The kinds of high-profile, high-visibility political tactics that many cause and advocacy groups adopt (including protests and demonstrations, advertising campaigns, and direct-mail solicitation) creates the misleading impression that lobbying is now dominated by citizens' groups, but this is clearly not the case. Business interests overwhelmingly dominate the lobbying process.

The Intergovernmental Lobby

Increasingly active at both the federal and the state levels are organizations that represent assorted American governments—states, counties, cities, townships, and the like. This "intergovernmental lobby" includes such groups as the Council of State Governments, the National Association of Counties, the National League of Cities, the U.S. Conference of Mayors, and (especially at the state level) assorted municipal leagues, representing individual towns or municipalities.

Another component of the intergovernmental lobby is the growing array of organizations devoted to the concerns of particular kinds of functional specialists in government, especially at the state and local levels—such as highway engineers, county welfare directors, housing and development officials, and parks and recreation administrators. Also very important politically are the many organizations representing government workers, such as teachers, firefighters, and police officers, that watch out for the interests of their members on issues such as compensation, benefits, and work rules.

This brief overview does not begin to capture the heterogeneity and the rich texture of the interest-group community. Rather the objective has been to identify some of the prominent kinds of organizations active in legislatures at the national and state levels. However, in addition to having some sense of the different kinds of interests these organizations represent, it is worthwhile to note briefly some of the other ways in which these organizations vary.

SIZE OF AGENDA

As the reader may have noted from the above discussion, organizations vary substantially in the scope of their agendas. Some organizations pursue a single narrow objective; others are concerned with hundreds of issues at once. Cause groups—organizations composed of individuals with a singular commitment to one or a few concerns, usually a social issue—would fall into this first category. The political strength of many of these single-issue groups is enhanced by the intensity of their members' commitment. This intensity factor accounts for such seemingly paradoxical policy outcomes as the long-standing absence of any genuine handgun-control legislation in the United States despite the overwhelming support the American people have long articulated for such laws. Legislators know that the roughly 80 percent of the American people who say they want handgun control do not care intensely about that issue, whereas those who oppose handgun control—typically members of organizations such as the National Rifle Association—do care intensely about the issue and are willing to cast their votes for legislative candidates on the basis of their stance on that issue, and that issue alone. This sort of recognized intensity confers substantial clout on an organization in its dealings with a legislature.

Some organizations deal with a broad set of issues. A huge corporate conglomerate such as R. J. Reynolds Industries has to be attentive to policies in a number of areas including tobacco, food and beverages, energy, and transportation—all matters of concern to its subsidiaries. Even further along the continuum are multi-issue groups—organizations with lengthy and diverse agendas. Perhaps the most obvious of such organizations are the top business associations (such as the U.S. Chamber of Commerce) and labor unions. These are organizations that tend to be highly active on a wide variety of fronts simultaneously, monitoring and taking positions on issues ranging from pollution-control laws to Social Security and from tax incentives to housing subsidies.

It is worth noting, however, that the size of a group's agenda does not seem to have much impact on its bearing in politics. There are no discernible and predictable differences between single-issue groups and multiissue groups in terms of their political strategies or their effectiveness.

ORGANIZATIONAL RESOURCES

A factor more directly related to political activity is the degree of organizational resources that interest groups are able to mobilize in an effort to influence political outcomes in the legislative arena. There are many different kinds of politically relevant organizational resources, and these resources have differential utility to various kinds of organized interests.

The primary political resource that organized interests command is, of course, money. What makes money important in pressure group politics is its convertibility—the fact that it can easily be transformed into other valued political resources. Money buys things such as technically expert staff members; politically well-connected lobbyists; access to consultants; the technology such as computers and high-speed printers necessary for mounting grass-roots lobbying campaigns, and, not least, the capacity to forage for still more funds.

A politically important resource for some political organizations is membership, an asset that has some special characteristics as a political resource. Whereas it is surely true that the more money the better, with respect to membership the situation is more complicated. A large membership can be an important organizational resource in legislative politics in several ways. First large numbers of people can pool their time, energy, information, money, and political contacts, thereby transforming otherwise meager individual resources into significant collective ones. In addition, a large membership confers greater legitimacy on the demands an organization makes of public officials. On an issue such as wildlife conservation, members of Congress are more likely to listen seriously to an organization like the National Audubon Society, which has over half a million members nationwide, than to the Boone and Crockett Club, the nation's oldest society devoted to wildlife conservation, whose membership is limited to one hundred. Furthermore, if a group's members are distributed across many legislative districts (as in the case, say, of the National Association of Letter Carriers, or a state teachers' association), it will be able to make legitimate demands on a broad range of public officials and, therefore, increase its influence.

However, a small membership may be preferable to a large one under certain circumstances. For one thing, large organizations have special problems finding the right mix of inducements to attract and keep their members over time because of what economist Mancur Olson has called the free-rider problem—the tendency of individuals to withhold their time, effort, and money to the cause of a large organization under the rational calculation that the reduction of their effort will not in itself diminish the collective benefit that they will enjoy nonetheless.

Moreover, a large membership is more likely to be heterogeneous, with members having divergent preferences and even different interests on particular issues. Huge trade associations such as the American Bankers Association often find their political effectiveness compromised because their many members' irreconcilable positions on key issues muddle their lobbying efforts. By contrast, a small organization such as the Fertilizer Institute, representing a small assortment of chemical firms and agricultural companies, is effective because it focuses on rather narrow interests and pursues them relentlessly.

For effectiveness in legislative politics, it is certainly preferable for an organization to have a united, cohesive membership rather than a factious membership beset by quarrels and squabbles. A cohesive membership frees an organization from having to devote time and other resources to the resolution of disputes. Moreover, having a cohesive membership places an organization in a strengthened position in the eyes of legislators: cohesion provides a cloak of legitimacy that is lacking when an organization's members are conspicuously at odds with one another over public-policy issues.

One final characteristic of an organization's membership that affects its usefulness as a political resource is its *density*—that is, the proportion of its potential constituency that is mobilized. It is clear that enhanced density confers political legitimacy and thus increases political effectiveness. Legislators are more likely to be persuaded by a group that represents a substantial portion of its potential membership than one that mobilizes a smaller share of its possible supporters. For example, although the National Organization for Women is a large group with over 150,000 members nationwide, its political effectiveness on many policy issues is hampered by the fact that its membership constitutes a small percentage of American women.

It is vital for an organization to have a credible and trustworthy reputation, especially for groups whose representatives have direct contact with legislators. Insofar as an interest group ordinarily buttresses its case with facts on which legislators and their staffs rely when formulating policy, it is vital to an organization that policymakers believe its recommendations and supporting evidence. It is a commonly held belief among lobbyists that few things will damage a group's cause so much as a reputation for playing fast and loose with the facts.

THE PRINCIPAL TECHNIQUES OF INFLUENCE

Contemporary organized interests have many well-established political strategies and tactics that have been refined over the years for applying their resources in an effort to shape legislative outcomes. Most of the academic literature on interest-group politics offers complete discussions of the techniques of influence. Here it is possible only to take stock of the principal ways in which organized interests approach the task of shaping political outcomes in the legislative arena.

Engaging in Electoral Politics

Nothing about the political activity of organized interests in recent years has generated more controversy or handwringing than their increasingly prominent role in financing legislative campaigns, particularly through political action committees (PACs). Of course, there is nothing particularly new about interest groups giving money to candidates for legislative office; this has been going on for decades. But since the mid-1970s there has been explosive growth in both PAC formation and total PAC contributions, causing many observers to believe that the U.S. now has, in the view of some observers, "the best Congress money can buy."

Political scientists' efforts to examine the relationship between PAC contributions and congressional voting have failed to provide clear answers as to whether the quid pro quo of a campaign contribution is a policy favor. Some studies find a relationship between campaign contributions and legislative behavior, while others do not. Where a relationship has been detected, it appears that PAC influence is enhanced on issues of low visibility that generate no strong partisan conflict, constituency opinion, or ideological feeling on the part of the legislator. PAC influence seems to be less important on more visible issues and on votes where partisan interests, constituency concerns and ideological leanings are greater.

Most legislators and lobbyists insist—and some scholarly research confirms—that if anything is being purchased with a PAC contribution, it is not influence over legislators' votes, but rather access allowing interest groups to present their cases. Even if this is true, it is of little comfort to those who fear that interest-group politics reflects many of the inequalities built into the larger political system. It is clear that the business community accounts for the dominant share of PACs, while the interests of the disadvantaged (especially racial minorities and the poor) and other groups (especially environmentalists and consumers) are paid only marginal attention by PACs. Thus, while it may be important in the abstract to distinguish between access and influence, in practice, access begets influence and unequal access begets unequal influence.

Widespread cynicism and concern about PAC financing of congressional campaigns is also exacerbated by some of the persistent and stark patterns in the flow of PAC money: the increasing amount of PAC money collected by incumbents running without opposition, the tendency of PAC money to gravitate toward legislators in positions of power, and the custom of some PACs of contributing to both candidates in a race to ensure them of being in the good graces of the winner.

Were it not for two facts—that the demon dollar is at the center of all this, and that dollars are at least as unequally distributed in politics as they are in any other realm of life—patterns in PAC-giving would raise few eyebrows since they are in fact reflections of perfectly reasonable political calculations. When organized interests get involved in electoral politics, they may be pursuing one or both of two objectives. One of these is to influence the outcome of elections and, by affecting who wins or loses, elect ideologically sympathetic officials and defeat hostile ones. This strategy dictates that contributions and campaign assistance be directed to ideologically sympathetic candidates who need help and who seem to have a reasonable chance of winning.

Another objective is to demonstrate enough political muscle or create a sufficient sense of indebtedness on the part of winners so that they will be responsive to the organization's political needs. To achieve this, organizations will try to help incumbents who are on key committees (especially powerful ones with positions of institutional leadership in policy areas of concern) and to concentrate on races in geographically critical districts, such as where an association has many members or a corporation has a branch plant. Since the goal is to ensure that officeholders feel compelled to be responsive, organizations active in electoral politics frequently aid sure winners, even some candidates running unopposed.

Besides giving money to candidates, another way some organized interests (especially those with large memberships) seek to influence electoral outcomes is by trying to shape voters' perceptions of the candidates. One tactic common to this strategy is the issuing of a legislative scorecard—a summary put out by an interest group of selected roll-call votes designed to show the level of support by each incumbent for measures of importance to the group. Many organizations across the political spectrum employ this tactic—from organizations like the Veterans of Foreign Wars and the National Council of Senior Citizens to broad ideological organizations such as the Americans for Democratic Action and the American Conservative Union.

The underside of this tactic is to target certain candidates for opposition—that is, to construct a "hit list" of candidates, usually incumbents with low scorecard ratings, to be defeated. The practice of targeting candidates has been used by organizations as different as Environmental Action (which in the early 1970s selected twelve powerful incumbent legislators, all of them with poor records on environmental issues, and dubbed them the Dirty Dozen) and the National Conservative Political Action Committee, which in 1980 used the targeting tactic as part of its massive direct-mail campaigns to raise large amounts of money to defeat liberal congressional incumbents.

Organized interests also assist candidates in various ways in their campaigns. Some organizations provide services of a technical nature—assisting candidates with campaign organization, media relations, and polling. Another service, highly valued by candidates, is help with fund-raising. A lobbyist might sponsor a fund-raiser for a candidate, make phone calls to encourage friends in other organizations to attend a fund-raising event, or provide the candidate with the group's membership list if it would be a promising source of contributors. But the most common kind of nonfinancial campaign aid is to provide workers. Many organizations mobilize members to volunteer help with various election-related tasks and of necessity, such efforts must have a strong local component. Therefore, only organizations with local infrastructures and fairly substantial memberships, especially labor unions and citizens' groups, can engage in such activities.

At the state and local level, organized interests sometimes get involved in electoral politics not to elect certain candidates to the legislature but to dictate policy outcomes directly through the initiative process, whereby citizens propose specific legislation or constitutional amendments that then appear on the ballot in popular elections. Found in about half the states, the initiative process is used most often in the western states of California, Washington, Colorado, Oregon, Oklahoma, and Arizona. Success with the initiative process requires that a citizens' group have a formidable mix of political resources: sufficient organizational strength to secure the specified number of signatures to get the initiative on the ballot (often 5 to 10 percent of the number of ballots cast in the most recent general election); effective public-relations skills for making the necessary case to the public at large in an effective media campaign; and not least, an appealing cause or one that can somehow be cast in an appealing light.

Neither conservative nor liberal political interests seem to have an edge in the initiative process; it is a political tool that has been about equally useful to groups on both the Right and the Left and for a wide variety of purposes. Among the more dramatic uses of the initiative process were the taxing and spending limitations in the late 1970s such as Proposition 13 in California and Proposition 2.5 in Massachusetts. Perhaps signifying a growing dissatisfaction and frustration with getting policy measures through the legislatures, citizens' groups served up 70 ballot issues across the country in 1990, approaching the record of 90 set in 1914 at the height of the Progressive Era when initiatives first were introduced as a means of enabling citizens to circumvent corporate control of state legislatures.

Mobilizing Grass-roots Pressure

Ballot-issue campaigns mounted by interest groups have much in common with the sort of high-profile tactics that organized interests have been employing for decades in an effort to influence policy decisions in legislatures: mobilizing political pressure from the public at the "grass roots." Interest groups understand that when politicians are considering a policy issue before them, what often matters to them is not an amorphous perception of how the general public feels about the issue; rather, they pay attention to whether there is a narrower group of citizens who care intensely about the issue and are likely to act politically on their views. (This is the intensity factor cited above in noting the political advantage of the gun lobby.) Understanding this, organized interests have honed their techniques for preying on legislators' electoral insecurity and their sensitivity to their constituents' expressed preferences.

One way organized interests mobilize an attentive public is by using provocative advertisements or, increasingly, direct-mail appeals to inspire deluges of cards, letters, telegrams, and phone calls to legislative offices. With recent developments in data-processing and direct-mail technologies, such communications these days can be highly individualized, informing recipients across the country how their individual legislators stand on an issue and why the need to contact them is so urgent.

Some of these campaigns are stunningly successful. In the 1970s the soft drink industry used a brilliant advertising campaign to generate a tidal wave of popular resistance to a proposed ban by the Food and Drug Administration on the artificial sweetener saccharin. A few years later the American Bankers Association and the U.S. League of Savings Institutions undertook a multimillion dollar, multifaceted public-relations campaign to get Congress to repeal a provision in the 1982 tax bill that would have required commercial banks and savings and loan associations to withhold 10 percent of the interest and dividends paid to depositors. And in 1989 a blitzkrieg grass-roots repeal drive orchestrated by the National Committee to Preserve Social Security and Medicare successfully pushed Congress to repeal the Medicare Catastrophic Coverage Act, passed only the previous year.

Another grass-roots lobbying technique common to groups that have big budgets and large, easily mobilized memberships involves establishing a network of activists within the organization who can be relied on to contact lawmakers in response to an "action alert" issued by organizational headquarters. This is especially effective for (but is by no means limited to) organizations fortunate enough to have members in virtually every legislative district. The National Association of Letter Carriers' network is a good example. In each congressional district a union activist is appointed by top union leaders in the state to serve as the local liaison responsible for forming special committees of letter carriers, retirees, and spouses who can be contacted by union headquarters in Washington and counted on to stimulate a flood of letters and phone calls to members of Congress.

Legislators recognize that on many issues the seemingly spontaneous mail pouring into their offices has been inspired by some lobbying organization in the capital. But just because they are not fooled by this contrivance does not mean they feel free to ignore it. In fact, electorally insecure legislators are increasingly responsive to these campaigns, fearing that the organizational apparatus capable of producing a sophisticated outpouring of grass-roots pressure may also be able to affect the behavior of large numbers of voters at the polls.

Classic Direct Lobbying

Advertising and grass-roots lobbying campaigns can be effective in informing and mobilizing the public, but they also have an element of unpredictability. The message may get muddled, the expected response may never materialize, or the campaign may simply backfire, succeeding only in mobilizing the opposition without winning new converts. Thus, lobbyists find that to present their arguments in a more refined, focused, and controlled way, they must approach legislators more directly.

Lawmakers' greatest need is for information. They are confronted with a staggering number of complex issues about which they are expected to make informed judgments. In the face of these complexities, they need all the help they can get in trying to sort through difficult economic or technical problems and in determining the consequences of their assorted legislative decisions —who will be affected, in what ways, to what extent, and with what political reaction. Organized interests are especially well situated to provide this information.

Direct lobbying offers organized interests the clearest opportunity for presenting the substantive and political merits of their positions. By cultivating direct relationships with staff aides and lawmakers, especially those associated with key committees and subcommittees, lobbyists can position themselves to help draft legislation, plan legislative strategy, provide technical information, and demonstrate the political and policy consequences of assorted statutory alternatives.

In direct lobbying, as in grass-roots lobbying, organized interests find that among the most productive ways to command a legislator's attention is through his or her constituents, so they bring influential constituents to the capital to lobby their representatives. The notion underlying this approach is that in this era of legislative hypersensitivity to constituent concerns, an organized interest—say, for example, the American Hospital Association—has a better chance of making a persuasive case to a member of Congress on an issue it cares about if it brings in influential hospital trustees or administrators from the member's district than if it simply sends in one of the association's Washington lobbyists.

Playing the home-district card is not the only way of commanding a legislator's attention. Many groups try to increase their access by employing persons of high political status as lobbyists. Washington and the state capitals are full of political notables who have hung out their shingles as lobbyists and earn huge incomes serving as hired guns for the various interests that retain them. Former legislators constitute a growing portion of this lobbying community as they stay on in the capital and use their contacts and access to buttonhole their former colleagues on behalf of clients.

Corporate chief executive officers constitute another category of elites who have taken on the task of directly lobbying legislators. In Washington, members of Congress reluctant to make time in their busy schedules to meet privately with an obscure lobbyist for the automobile industry will make time when the head of General Motors requests an appointment. This is the main principle behind the Business Roundtable—an organization consisting of the chief executive officers from some two hundred of the nation's largest industrial, financial, and commercial institutions. But whereas the Roundtable was distinctive in its approach in the mid-1970s, the practice is now so widespread that "lobbyist" would seem to have become an unwritten part of most corporate chief executives' job descriptions.

Lobbying directly on Capitol Hill is a very different enterprise today from what it was in the mid-1960s when Congress was still a rather oligarchical institution, with power concentrated in a handful of committee chairs who stood astride the policy process. In those days, the lobbying task was rather straightforward, for the number of legislators who had much of a say in how things progressed was relatively small.

Today the situation for those who want to make their case directly on the Hill is much more complicated. Since 1970 there have been a number of changes in Congress that have rendered the institution still more accessible and more open to organized interests. At the same time, these changes have recast Congress's institutional character, making it more individualistic and unpredictable—and thus harder for organized interests to deal with—than in the past. These changes have altered the environment of legislative lobbying, opening up some new avenues for potential influence but also multiplying the number of persons on Capitol Hill who may have a say on policy matters. Thus, groups intent on trying to influence legislative outcomes have little choice but to escalate the range and volume of their political activities.

In the aftermath of congressional reforms, especially in the House, that weakened committee chairs and decentralized power to subcommittee heads and to rank-and-file legislators, it is no longer possible for an interest group to make its case effectively by contacting only a few powerful legislators. Lobbyists now must cultivate a broader range of contacts not only because there are more subcommittees whose jurisdictions touch each group's interests, but also because single committees and subcommittees no longer exercise as much control over legislation as they once did. With the growing tendency to refer bills to multiple committees, and with the general relaxation of legislative norms that once inhibited floor challenges to committee decisions, threats to a group's legislative interests may come from anywhere in the chamber and at many more points during a bill's progress through the legislative labyrinth. This necessitates greatly increased attentiveness on the part of organized interests and a lot more effort from them.

A similar consequence stems from the adoption by both chambers of so-called sunshine rules that liberalized public access to once-secret markup sessions (where bills are put into final form) and conference committee meetings. Lobbyists serious about watching out for their organizations' interests can scarcely afford to be absent at such crucial stages of the legislative process.

The tremendous expansion and professionalization of congressional staff in recent years have also complicated the direct lobbying tasks of organized interests by multiplying still further the number of people with whom lobbyists need to establish contacts. Staffers often play the principal part in briefing legislators before votes on bills or amendments, so it is important for lobbyists to make their case effectively to these aides. Moreover, when lobbyists are able to arrange one-on-one meetings with people on the Hill, they are more likely to be with congressional staff than with the legislators themselves. This is especially true on the Senate side, where the legislators are stretched thin and tend to be less conversant with the details of legislation and where the staffs are given considerable authority by their bosses to negotiate and are thus a policy-making force in their own right.

Although the institutional circumstances at the state legislative level vary widely and are generally a world apart from what one finds in Washington, some of the broad patterns are similar with respect to the ways institutional changes affect the relationships linking legislators and lobbyists. Consider, for example, the slow movement toward professionalism in the state legislatures, characterized by, among other things: lower turnover in membership; higher pay for members; longer legislative sessions; the creation in many states of full-time, year-round professional staffs for standing committees and personal staffs for each legislator; and the assumption of legislative tasks as a full-time job (though still the case in only a small handful of states). All this has fragmented power in these legislatures, increasing the number of persons in the legislative arena whom lobbyists have to try to contact, and making it harder to have influence on the legislators. Interest groups are likely to find it harder to have influence in professionalized state legislatures because the information which is their stock-in-trade carries less weight when legislators have their own staff resources to generate, sift, and evaluate information.

"Social" Lobbying

Information is obviously not the only coin of the realm. Organized interests have various other resources at their disposal that are used to influence legislators and their staffs. The dean of nineteenth-century Washington lobbyists, Samuel Ward, once held that "the way to a man's 'aye' is through his stomach." Although the arts of influence have changed considerably from the days when Ward regaled congressmen at nightly banquets of ham boiled in champagne and paid off the gambling debts of debt-ridden legislators, contemporary organized interests still do a lot of social lobbying, nurturing relationships with legislators by providing them relaxation and entertainment with cocktail parties, lavish dinners at expensive restaurants, tickets to the theater or sporting events, hunting trips, golf vacations, and the like. A lobbyist who provides such pleasures has a chance to cultivate a legislator's friendship and trust. The idea is to provide a relaxed setting in which legislators and lobbyists can get to know one another better and discuss matters of mutual concern. Most such meetings are quite low-key and involve no direct lobbying by the interests' representatives; if they need to ask for a legislative favor, they make the request at another time. To outsiders, however, these informal social contacts merely reinforce the editorial cartoonists' stereotyped caricature of the fat cat lobbyist living opulently and spending lavishly in an effort to subvert the common good in favor of special interests.

That stereotype is reinforced these days by the commercial media, which tend to sensationalize the problems in the lobbyist-legislator nexus. News stories that describe hardworking public officials and interest-group representatives collaborating in the pursuit of enlightened public policy are hard to make interesting and thus do not appear very frequently. By contrast, stories that link lobbyists to legislators in conflicts of interest, unsavory cash exchanges, or apparent sellouts of the public interest combine the two essential elements of popular journalism—celebrity and the whiff of scandal—and are thus irresistible to many reporters, editors, and publishers.

While all too many of these stories turn out to have more basis in fact than one might prefer, it is probably the case that organized interests have so many legitimate ways of exerting influence that outright illegal activity such as bribery is probably quite rare. There are, after all, many things that organized interests can do well within the boundaries of the law to heighten legislators' sense of obligation to them. The varied forms of social lobbying and the ubiquitous PAC donations—though they may be institutional bribery in the view of critics—are nevertheless on the fair side of the law.

There is, of course, no way to know for sure how much bribery and illegal activity goes on in the varied connections between legislators and lobbyists (what little is uncovered and prosecuted may be a tiny fraction of what actually occurs), but the general consensus among political scientists and journalists seems to be that lobbying in state capitals may be somewhat more coarse and unrefined—if not actually more crooked—than lobbying in Washington. Again, there is no way of documenting this, but it seems reasonable that state legislators may be more subject to the pressures and appeals of organized interests than are members of Congress. Despite the movement toward professionalism in many state legislatures, ethics codes governing legislators' behavior are not so well developed in the states as in Washington. Moreover, for many state legislators, their legislative careers are a secondary aspect of their lives. Compared to members of Congress, they meet less often and for shorter periods of time and earn less money, which may leave them more vulnerable to the financial inducements and blandishments of interest groups. Finally, although staff support is more and more common in state legislatures, it pales by comparison to that available in Congress, leaving state lawmakers still in the position of having to look to the lobbyists for much of the data and information they need in making legislative decisions.

REGULATING LOBBYING

Prompted by disclosures of bribery and corruption or by concern over the sheer volume of lobbying, Congress has intermittently investigated lobbying activity and has considered ways to regulate it. Even if the sorts of illegal dealings that we associate with lobbying in the days of the robber barons are not widespread today, everyone recognizes that there are many subtler forms of payment (perhaps favors is a less loaded term), which seem to border on bribery inasmuch as they involve payments of cash or the provision of goods and services for which policymakers would ordinarily have to expend personal funds.

In recent years, perhaps the best known of the regularized channels for funneling cash directly to the pockets of members of Congress—not to their campaign war chests via PAC contributions—has been the honorarium, a payment (usually of $2,000) for giving a speech at a group's convention or making brief remarks at a breakfast meeting. Through the 1980s, congressional rules permitted members of the House to accept honoraria totaling up to

30 percent of their salary; for senators, the ceiling was 40 percent. Thus, millions of dollars each year had been going directly into the pockets of legislators for their personal use.

Under pressure from reformers and from the glare of widespread media exposure of the honorarium racket, Congress in late 1989 passed the Ethics Reform Act in which House members agreed to forgo honoraria after December 1990 in exchange for a hefty pay raise; senators agreed to phase out honoraria more gradually, while accepting a series of smaller raises. But, as is so often the case with political reforms, this new ethics law left plenty of loopholes for legislators and lobbyists to exploit.

In considering broader measures to regulate lobbying, Congress has always had to balance its desire to protect itself from corrupting influences against the constitutional protections of the First Amendment, which requires that "Congress shall make no law . . . abridging the . . . rights of the people . . . to petition the Government for a redress of grievances." Furthermore, legislators have shown a marked reluctance to deny themselves the perks they enjoy. Hence, for the most part, the efforts of reformers over the years have done little to restrict the activities of lobbyists.

In 1946, Congress enacted the Federal Regulation of Lobbying Act and so took one small symbolic step in the direction of regulating lobbying by imposing registration and disclosure requirements on lobbyists. Specifically, the law requires any person hired for the principal purpose of influencing legislation to register with the Secretary of the Senate and the Clerk of the House, and to file certain quarterly financial reports disclosing the amount of money received and spent for lobbying. But the legislation is generally considered ineffective and limp, in large part because of its dramatically limited scope.

Widespread dissatisfaction with the 1946 act has prompted many efforts to revise the law, but Congress has been repeatedly unsuccessful at enacting a meaningful substitute. A number of proposals to regulate lobbying more vigorously have won the support of various congressional subcommittees or full committees but have failed to win enactment.

The states have been no more robust in their efforts to regulate lobbying activity. Many states emulate the federal government's model in requiring lobbyists who contact legislators to register and to reveal whom they represent and how much money they spend in the effort. But just as at the national level, these state laws are hard to enforce because the word *lobbyist* is hard to define and the activity itself is difficult to distinguish from the constitutionally protected efforts of individual citizens to communicate with legislators. Thus, in the states as in Washington, many hundreds of lobbyists never register under the pretext that they are not really lobbyists at all.

DO ORGANIZED INTERESTS DICTATE?

If one were to pay attention only to what the national newsweeklies, the network news programs, and the other media have to say about the varied links connecting legislators and lobbyists, one could easily come to the view that organized interests have become sovereign in American legislative arenas, with the lawmakers capitulating in their responsibilities to protect the public interest, and that the legislatures have simply become political anemometers registering the force of the prevailing interest-group winds. The stories come in a steady stream, fostering the impression that the integrity of the most democratic institutions are gradually being compromised or undermined by the pernicious influence of special interests.

Even the more detached and objective scholarly community has long held to an only slightly more benign variant of this theme, regarding the ties that link legislators and lobbyists as close and mutually beneficial. For the better part of a quarter century, scholars who studied the relationship between legislatures and interest groups were guided by the concept of policy subgovernments. The fundamental proposition of the subgovernment model is that routine policy-making within individual substantive policy areas (especially low visibility programs with distributive tangible benefits, such as subsidies to cattle ranchers) is dominated by relatively narrow, circumscribed, and autonomous sets of actors that operate virtually without interference by the chief executive or the majority of legislators. The form of subgovernment most commonly invoked by analysts is the "iron triangle" or the "triple alliance" —a subgovernment consisting of an agency or bureau within the executive branch, a committee within Congress, and an organized interest group—all united by their concern with a given policy area and all motivated by a consensual desire to maintain a mutually beneficial arrangement in which policies are formulated in ways meeting the needs of all partners to the triad. Iron triangles have been said to prevail at one time or another in many policy areas characterized by the distribution of benefits—for example, weapons contracts, veterans' benefits, agricultural subsidies, biomedical research grants, merchant shipping rates, and water resources.

Political analysis of these sorts of distributive policies suggests that when the benefits of a policy or program are concentrated on an identifiable interest in society (for example, sugar farmers, inland waterways operators, or veterans) but the costs are to be borne by everybody—or at least by a substantial portion of society—the lobbying activity surrounding the issue is likely to be imbalanced in favor of the interest. Organizations representing the beneficiaries will be vigorous in their support of the proposal, but since the costs are distributed at a low per capita rate over a large number of people (through price increases or generally higher taxes), the public has little incentive to organize in opposition. Such policies tend to produce symbiotic relationships between the legislators who authorize and appropriate money for these programs, the agency officials who administer them, and the beneficiaries or clients, who work hard to maintain and expand their benefits. To the extent that these programs encounter any organized opposition at all, it is likely to come from politically disadvantaged consumer and taxpayer groups.

The political logic here is hard to dispute, but in fact the cozy relationships between legislators, bureaucrats, and lobbyists who promote and sustain these programs are beset on all sides by changes in governmental institutions, political processes, and the larger political environment. One can point to many diverse factors that appear to be contributing to the decline of the iron triangle as an autonomous force in public policy-making: the rise of large numbers of new citizens' groups and advocacy groups, new patterns of investigative reporting and the enlarged role of the media in politics, the greater policy-making role of the

federal and state courts, the growing tendency among legislators toward an entrepreneurial style of policy activism, and the increasing aggressiveness of presidents and governors intent on controlling the agencies under their charge.

For these and many other reasons, there is diminishing reason to believe that organized interests are able to dictate public-policy benefits for themselves by virtue of their position in close relationships with policymakers. Most policy areas now are characterized not by such mutual self-help arrangements, but by complex webs of policy activists from both inside and outside the government who are in a position to bring formidable political resources to bear in pursuit of their policy preferences, providing counterweights to the expressed wishes of organized interests. Among these other important political forces are the following: presidents, governors, and their advisers; cabinet and subcabinet officers, program administrators, and policy analysts in executive agencies; legislative staffers; outside experts from think tanks, universities, and foundations; and the general citizenry. In other words, when it comes to voting on the issues before them, legislators are subject not merely to the claims and importuning of attentive organized interests but also to multiple other pressures as well.

Furthermore, at the national level, one need only look at many of the big policy battles that have raged in Washington in the past quarter century—consumer safety, environmental protection, occupational safety, transportation deregulation, and tax reform—to see that the so-called powerful interests (in most of these cases, organized business interests) were unable to dictate outcomes completely to their liking. Of course, business's relative losses in these battles were partly a consequence of the activities of other organized interests and of the efforts of policy entrepreneurs. But many analysts have suggested that such outcomes reflect something more profound—a gradual supplementing, if not a complete supplanting, of the politics of interests with a politics of ideas, in which the power of a good idea or a symbolically appealing cause can be just as persuasive or forceful in the policy-making process as a vested interest.

To the extent that there is such a new style of politics in Washington, it is no longer one in which organized interests, bureaucrats, and legislative leaders hold firm control over governmental action, but rather a much more open and fluid system in which power is extremely fragmented, policy entrepreneurialism abounds, and the ideas of experts, publicized and promoted through the media, may transcend group interests in politics.

Organized interests may not call all the shots in the legislatures these days, but they obviously still have considerable influence. Exactly how much is difficult to specify. Casual observations and conclusions (such as those made above about the influence of business interests) are hazardous: looking at what groups are involved in an issue and whether they seem to have won or lost tells us relatively little. After all, sometimes an apparent defeat masks the degree to which the outcome would have been worse for a group if it had not gotten involved at all. Similarly, a victory might offer false evidence of lobbying effectiveness, for the outcome might have been determined more by other factors (such as the unsolicited intervention of the president or of key legislators) than by a group's lobbying activity. In short, it is not always apparent who or what has made a difference in the outcome of a particular conflict and why.

WHEN ORGANIZED INTERESTS DO MAKE A DIFFERENCE

Still, it is possible to set forth some generalizations about the circumstances under which organized interests are most likely to have an impact on legislative policy-making. First, an organized interest has a greater chance of influencing legislative outcomes when legislators feel pressured to publicly support the position of the interest group (even though privately they may disagree with the position) because they do not see how they might explain any public disagreement with the group. Such situations are likely to occur where the group is the legislator's most attentive audience on a particular issue (and legislators thus have reason to fear the electoral consequences of not supporting the group) or where the group's position is strongly supported by party leaders

whom legislators do not wish to alienate or antagonize.

Following this line of argument, it is clear that the probability of success for an organized interest also depends on the structure of conflict in a particular controversy. Organized pressure on legislators is less likely to bear results if it is met, as it often is, by opposing pressure. Especially if this opposition is visible and involves a sizable threshold of attentive constituents, members will not feel as pressured to support the position of a more dominant group or of party leaders: they can point to a countervailing constituency interest.

Lobbying success is also likely to vary with the nature of the demand. It is an old chestnut in American politics that organized interests in a defensive posture—that is, organized interests that are resisting some proposed change—are at an advantage over their opponents who seek political change. The complexity of the legislative-policy process is such that any legislative-policy measure must clear multiple hurdles, thus providing organized interests with many opportunities to delay or kill it. So, an organization that is seeking to stymie a threatening measure is at a strategic advantage over one seeking to get a measure passed.

Moreover, organizations can ordinarily have greater influence on single, discrete amendments to bills than on entire pieces of legislation. Amendments are typically quite specific and sometimes technical (thus increasing the influence of the information provided by the group), and because they are generally narrower in impact, they do not usually attract broad opposition. Obviously, to say that it is easier for an organized interest to affect the details of a policy than its broad outlines is not to trivialize this form of influence. On the contrary, the best case studies of policy formulation and implementation demonstrate a central axiom of policy analysis: to know what a policy measure actually does, it is important to look beyond its broad purposes to the particulars. The details are what specify such critical matters as whom the measure covers, how much is to be spent, who has the authority to implement it, and under what constraints. How such particulars are defined determines whether a measure will be a mere symbolic gesture or a potentially effective policy.

PRESSURE GROUPS AND LOBBIES

THE BURDEN IS ON LEGISLATORS

What does all this add up to? Unfortunately, there is no ready answer to the question of how much influence organized interests now wield on Capitol Hill or in the state capitols. The evidence does not support a conclusion that organized interests call the shots. So, it is a mistake merely to accept wholesale the media's portrait of organized interests determining legislative politics. Yet it is also overly simplistic to dismiss lobbying influence as negligible, as did many political scientists in the early 1960s. It seems clear from the preceding discussion that there are certain circumstances in which the involvement of an organized interest is likely to make a difference to political outcomes.

Perhaps the important question is not whether organized interests are influential with legislators (surely they are), but whether the links connecting these political actors pose serious threats to the integrity and effectiveness of political processes and institutions. Again, there is no definitive answer, but there are reasons for concern.

The problem is not that organized interests have developed insidious new ways of trying to affect legislative outcomes. In fact, although there may be a new level of sophistication to their efforts, they mostly are doing more of what they have been doing for years. But it does not take a Cassandra to see that in politics as in oil spills, more of the same is not simply the same: where before there was potential for what Madison termed factional mischief, there now is potential for long-term harm.

The swarm of lobbyists in the halls of the federal and state capitols are crowding the public agenda with demands that tend to divert the attention of policymakers from the long run to the short run, from the substantively meritorious to the politically exigent. And by and large, when interests are well organized and politically involved, narrow interests prevail over broad ones in policy-making. The consequences of all this are far from benign, because such organizations are able to extract governmental concessions—such as agricultural price supports or a bailout of the savings and loan industry—that benefit their narrowly based constituencies in the short run but produce widely shared costs to be borne over a long time. Moreover, narrow interests are often able to stymie policies designed to confront problems having broad implications for society when those policies would impose disproportionate costs on their narrowly based but politically active constituencies. It is no wonder that Americans view with suspicion the connections between legislators and lobbyists.

Still, it is not clear what can—or should—be done to change this realm of political life. Any reforms would have to be introduced with great care lest, as Madison warned, the cure be more pernicious than the disease. Even to urge greater self-restraint on the part of clamorous and insistent interest groups is probably to place the burden on the wrong shoulders. The right to petition government collectively is so constitutionally protected that it is the obligation of those who presume to govern to watch out for the general public. Legislators have a special responsibility: To bear in mind that the expressions of opinion transmitted by organized interests are selective and that such communications overrepresent the views of narrow, intense publics at the expense of broad, diffuse ones and the views of the affluent at the expense of the less advantaged. Moreover, legislators have a responsibility in their policy deliberations to take note that the inducements, information, and expressions of preference on which they rely emanate more readily from some interests than from others. Heeding these responsibilities constitutes the core of legislative statesmanship.

BIBLIOGRAPHY

JEFFREY M. BERRY, *Lobbying for the People* (Princeton, N.J., 1977), is an insightful study of "public interest" citizens' lobbying groups; another work by BERRY, *The Interest Group Society*, 2d ed. (Boston, 1989), is a useful overview of contemporary interest-group politics in

America. RAYMOND A. BAUER, ITHIEL DE SOLA POOL, and LEWIS A. DEXTER, *American Business and Public Policy*, 2d ed. (Chicago, 1972), is a general analysis of business groups lobbying Congress on foreign-trade legislation. In a more general vein, the authors argue that the extent of interest-group activity and influence had been overstated by earlier students of the process; ALLAN J. CIGLER and BURDETT A. LOOMIS, eds., *Interest Group Politics*, 3d ed. (Washington, D.C., 1991), like the earlier edited volumes by these authors, is a highly useful collection of research by contemporary scholars looking at various aspects of organized-interest politics.

TIMOTHY J. CONLAN, MARGARET T. WRIGHTSON, and DAVID R. BEAM, *Taxing Choices: The Politics of Tax Reform* (Washington, D.C., 1990), is an instructive account of how the 1986 tax-reform bill passed despite the objections of many different lobbying organizations. The book also includes one of the most useful elaborations of the argument that the "politics of ideas" is becoming as important as the politics of interests. THOMAS CRONIN, *Direct Democracy: The Politics of Initiative, Referendum and Recall* (Cambridge, Mass., 1989), is a balanced summary and evaluation of the initative process and other instruments of direct democracy in the states. THOMAS L. GAIS, MARK A. PETERSON, and JACK L. WALKER, "Interest Groups, Iron Triangles, and Representative Institutions in American National Government," *British Journal of Political Science* 14 (1984): 161–185, presents a challenge to the notion that iron triangles govern the policy-making process. JANET HOOK, "New Law Leaves Loopholes for Benefits to Members," *Congressional Quarterly Weekly Report*, December 16, 1989, 3420–3424, provides a good journalist's account of the various ways members of Congress manage to get around reform measures, in this case the 1989 Ethics Reform Act. RONALD HREBENAR and CLIVE S. THOMAS, *Interest Group Politics in the American West* (Salt Lake City, 1987), compiles old and new research on interest-group politics in the western states. The editors are producing similar books on other regions of the country.

THEODORE J. LOWI, *The End of Liberalism*, 2d ed. (New York, 1979), is a critique of the excessive deference to interest groups in American politics. ANDREW MCFARLAND, *Common Cause* (Chatham, N.J., 1984), is a thoughtful case study of one of the nation's leading citizens' lobbies. DAVID B. MAGLEBY and CANDICE J. NELSON, *The Money Chase* (Washington, D.C., 1990), is a useful overview of the politics of congressional campaign-finance reform. LESTER MILBRATH, *The Washington Lobbyists* (Chicago, 1963), is a systematic survey of lobbyists, conducted during the late 1950s, which concludes that interest groups had less of a determinative role in governing than earlier group theorists had believed. TERRY N. MOE, *The Organization of Interests* (Chicago, 1980), is an analysis of economic interest groups and their incentive structures. MANCUR OLSON, *The Logic of Collective Action* (Cambridge, Mass., 1965), develops an economic theory of interest groups, showing how the free-rider problem makes some interests more fully and easily organized than others. RANDALL B. RIPLEY and GRACE A. FRANKLIN, *Congress, the Bureaucracy, and Public Policy* (Homewood, Ill., 1980), is a thorough synthesis of the literature on subgovernments and iron triangles and an instructive guide to the politics of different policy areas. LARRY SABATO, *PAC Power* (New York, 1984), is a complete discussion of the nature and activities of political action committees. E. E. SCHATTSCHNEIDER, *The Semi-Sovereign People* (New York, 1960), is a critique of pluralist democracy and, more specifically, an analysis of the problem of bias in the interest-group system.

KAY LEHMAN SCHLOZMAN and JOHN T. TIERNEY, *Organized Interests and American Democracy* (New York, 1986), is a comprehensive portrait of Washington interest groups and their political activities. KARL SCHRIFTGIESSER, *The Lobbyists* (Boston, 1951), provides a highly readable, historical look at lobbyists in American politics. CLIVE S. THOMAS and RONALD J. HREBENAR, "Interest Groups in the States," in VIRGINIA GRAY, HERBERT JACOB, and KENNETH N. VINES, eds., *Politics in the American States*, 5th ed. (Boston, 1990), present some of the broad outlines of ongoing research into the types of interest groups and lobbies active in the states and how they pursue their goals. DAVID TRUMAN, *The Governmental Process*, 2d ed. (New York, 1971), a classic work on American interest-group politics, is a sturdy defense of interest-group pluralism. JACK WALKER, "The Origins and Maintenance of Interest Groups in America,"

American Political Science Review 77 (1983): 390–406, presents systematic evidence showing that most current interest groups have come into existence since World War II and that group formation accelerated substantially after the early 1960s. JAMES Q. WILSON, *Political Organizations* (New York, 1974), lays out a theory of interest groups, emphasizing the incentives that they use to attract and retain members. The book also lays out a theoretical framework for understanding that the structure of political conflict and the nature of interest-group activity surrounding a particular policy issue will be determined by the degree to which the costs being imposed and the benefits being conferred are widely distributed or narrowly concentrated. BRUCE C. WOLPE, *Lobbying Congress: How the System Works* (Washington, D.C., 1990), is a useful guide to lobbying Congress, with case studies.

SEE ALSO Congressional Reform; Elections to the U.S. House of Representatives; Elections to the U.S. Senate; Legislative Ethics; Legislatures and Bureaucracy; AND Legislatures and the Media.

INSURGENCY AND THIRD PARTIES IN THE U.S. CONGRESS

Howard W. Allen

During most of its history the United States Congress has functioned with a two-party system. Congressional parties have appeared and disappeared, but only in a very brief period since the 1790s has Congress been without two vigorous, contending political parties. Even so, third, or minor, parties and insurgencies against party leadership have also been important to the history of Congress.

Minor parties and insurgent movements have in common an interest and/or an ideology not shared by the leaders of the major parties, but third parties and insurgencies also differ significantly. An insurgent movement does not involve a complete separation from the major party, while a third party exists and functions as an entirely separate political entity. This essay discusses five third-party movements and two insurgencies that had an impact on Congress. The insurgencies examined are: the Old Republican or "Tertium Quid" revolt against the Jefferson and Madison administrations, and the insurgent uprising in the Republican party during the Progressive Era. The third parties discussed are the Anti-Masonic party, the American or Know-Nothing party, the Free-Soil party, the Greenback party, and the People's or Populist party.

Identification of significant third-party and insurgent movements is somewhat arbitrary. In virtually every Congress before World War II at least a few members affiliated with a third party, failed to identify themselves with either of the two major organizations, or defied party leadership while maintaining party membership. Each of the third parties or insurgent movements included in this discussion held a relatively large number of seats in Congress and had substantial influence on the legislative process.

THIRD PARTIES: AN OVERVIEW

The members of Congress who did not affiliate with a major party divided themselves into two groups: those who identified with a minor party and those who did not identify with any party. The largest percentage of members of the House of Representatives who were in these two groups occurred in the first half of the nineteenth century. (See Table 1.) Partisan identification of members of Congress in the early decades is, at best, an educated guess. From the First Congress in 1789 to the late 1830s, Congress functioned informally, dominated by factionalism and personality. *Niles' Weekly Register* first published the partisan identification of congressional members-elect in 1826, and it was not until the Twenty-fourth Congress (1835–1837) that all members of the House of Representatives could be identified with a political party. In general it was not until the late 1830s that the parties in Congress began to assume some of the characteristics associated with modern legislatures.

The highest proportion of minor-party or unaffiliated House members appeared in the early days of the Republic, when political parties were new and relatively unorganized. In two Congresses of Thomas Jefferson's administration (the Seventh and Eighth Congresses), the percentage of House members who belonged to minor parties or were unaffiliated was 34.6 percent and 31.7 percent respectively. The average in the First to the Twenty-second Congresses (1789–1833) was 16.3 percent.

After the formation of the Democratic and Whig parties during the years sometimes referred to as the Age of Jackson, a much larger proportion of House members identified with one of the two major parties. Only an average

Table 1
MEMBERS OF THE HOUSE OF
REPRESENTATIVES IDENTIFIED WITH
A MINOR PARTY OR NOT AFFILIATED
WITH A MAJOR PARTY
Average Percentage

Congress Number	Dates	% Minor Party or Unaffiliated
1–22	1789–1833	16.3
23–33	1833–1855	6.6
34–40	1855–1869	15.1
41–55	1869–1899	2.4
56–72	1899–1933	0.7
73–79	1933–1946	1.5
80–99	1947–1986	0.0

Source: Adapted from Erik W. Austin, with the assistance of Jerome M. Clubb, *Political Facts of the United States Since 1789* (New York, 1986), 53–56, Table 1.21.

of 6.6 percent of the representatives in the Twenty-third to Thirty-third Congresses (1833–1855) belonged to a minor party or could not be identified with a political party. In the 1850s the Whig party disintegrated, primarily over the slavery issue, and was replaced by the Republican party. The American, or Know-Nothing, party experienced a flash of success in the mid-1850s and then disappeared.

The breakdown of the political system in the 1850s was accompanied by a substantial increase in the number of House members who belonged to a minor party or professed no partisan identification. The average percentage of representatives who did not identify with one of the major parties increased to 15.1 percent in the Thirty-fourth through the Fortieth Congresses (1855–1869). The largest share of seats held by members who did not identify with one of the major parties reached a high of 37.6 percent in the Thirty-fourth Congress (1855–1857) and gradually declined to a low of 4.5 percent in the Fortieth (1867–1869).

In the late nineteenth century, the presence of third-party or unaffiliated members of the House declined substantially, even during the years of the Populist movement and the depression in the 1890s. The average percentage of House members in the Forty-first through the Fifty-fifth Congresses (1869–1899) who identified with a minor party or were not affiliated with a party was only 2.4 percent. The

highest proportion of third-party members in this category occurred in the Fifty-fifth Congress (1897–1899) at 6.7 percent, but in most of the congresses in this period the percentage was much lower. In the twentieth century, the share of seats held by members who did not affiliate with a major party declined even more. Unaffiliated or third-party members occupied only one House seat in each of six Congresses between 1945 and 1987 (the Seventy–ninth to the Ninety–ninth). In the remaining fifteen Congresses the two major parties controlled every seat in the House.

The pattern of increase and decline in minor party members of Congress in the nineteenth century corresponded roughly with the occurrence of realignment eras—years when permanent change in voting behavior results in change in the relative strength of political parties. These occurred in the late 1820s, the late 1850s and early 1860s, and the 1890s. After 1900, few third-party members served in Congress, and the number of third-party members during the realignment of the 1930s differed little from the number in Congress in the 1920s.

The use of the single-member district, in which the candidate with the largest plurality wins the seat, made it very difficult from the very earliest days of the Republic for a minor party to succeed. A third-party candidate who received a relatively high percentage of the vote gained nothing unless the candidate received more votes than any other—a very unlikely prospect. With the probability of victory so low, voters tended to avoid supporting third parties, and candidates hesitated to run on third-party tickets for the same reason.

The decline in strength of third parties in Congress after the Civil War resulted in part from the development of very intense partisan identification due to the controversies over the war and Reconstruction. In the late nineteenth and early twentieth centuries, significant constitutional and legal barriers contributed to the decline in the number of third-party representatives. Upper-class political reformers, commonly known as Mugwumps, and after 1900, the Progressives, endeavored to free the political system of alleged corruption and dishonest elections through election reform. This legislation included the secret ballot, the introduction of an official ballot prepared by the state, and other complex legislation regulating election procedures.

These new regulations made it increasingly difficult for minor-party candidates to get elected. Since the electoral process was regulated by the states, filing deadlines and other requirements differed in each state. Thus it became increasingly more difficult for third parties to mount national campaigns.

In addition, historically third parties were never successful in raising campaign funds, even in the mid-nineteenth century. For example, the major parties spent much more money campaigning than the Liberty party in 1840, more than the Free-Soil party in 1848, and more than the Populist party in the 1890s. In the twentieth century, minor-party candidates have found fundraising even more difficult, and their inability to attract or to afford mass-media attention has presented additional problems.

Changes in the organization of both the House and Senate after the Civil War, and the development of the seniority system, raised formidable hurdles for minor-party members of Congress who aspired to a career in national politics. Even before the Civil War, major-party leaders exercised substantial authority over committee assignments and the selection of committee chairs. In the early days of Congress, seniority and party loyalty apparently played an insignificant role in these important decisions. The Speaker of the House appointed John Randolph of Virginia chair of the Ways and Means Committee early in Jefferson's administration, despite the fact that Randolph was only twenty-eight years old and had served in the House only one term. Likewise, the House elected Henry Clay of Kentucky Speaker in 1811, in his first term as a member.

By the middle of the nineteenth century, however, newcomers, insurgents and members of third parties found it increasingly difficult to obtain desirable appointments in both the House and the Senate. Congressmen increasingly found it imperative to have the confidence of the Speaker, who by then appointed committees and committee chairs and in general dominated House business. As Woodrow Wilson noted in 1884, the Speaker used his appointive powers to promote his partisan interests and usually relied upon the seniority of members of his own party in appointing chairs of the most influential committees. Thus, long

before the end of the nineteenth century, a third-party member or an insurgent usually could expect few desirable committee appointments, little likelihood of chairing an important committee, and difficulty in both gaining recognition during floor debates and finding support from the leadership for legislative proposals.

Major-party leadership could also severely punish members who strayed from the party fold. During the election campaign of 1912, Senator Miles Poindexter of Washington became the only member of the insurgent Republican band in the Senate to affiliate officially with the Progressive party. As a Progressive, Poindexter frequently voted with the Democrats, and they made him chair of a minor committee; but facing reelection in 1916, he returned to the Republican party. When Senator Henry Cabot Lodge (R.-Mass.) informed him that the Republican leaders had removed him as chair of his committee, Poindexter protested and asked Lodge for appointment to the committees on Foreign Relations, Judiciary, and Interstate Commerce—all important committees. The Republican leaders refused to appoint Poindexter to any of the three committees he requested, and he was made chair of the Committee on Additional Accommodations for the Library of Congress, one of the most insignificant committees in the Senate.

The relatively small number of third-party members in congressional history seriously understates the strength of support for the issues and policies that those parties represented. Major parties often moved quickly to absorb third parties by adopting some of their objectives and policies; often the ideological distinctions between minor- and major-party candidates from the same regions were small. For example, in New York State in the 1830s, Thurlow Weed and William Seward, who began their political careers in the anti-Masonic movement, played a major role in forming the Whig party. This effort successfully incorporated many of the values and the supporters of the anti-Masonic movement into a much broader-based political coalition with the potential to challenge the Democratic party. Similarly, in Nebraska in the 1890s, a Populist-Democratic coalition enjoyed great popular support, but George W. Norris remained loyal to the Republican party. After his election to the House of Representatives in 1902, however, Norris vigorously promoted many of the measures that had appeared earlier in Populist platforms.

THE OLD REPUBLICANS

The first political system evolved in the debate over Alexander Hamilton's proposal to secure the financial stability of the new Republic by funding the national debt, assuming state debts, and establishing a national bank. Thomas Jefferson and James Madison organized political opposition to Hamilton's program in Congress and throughout the country; by the end of John Adams's administration, the first American political system had taken shape. The differences between Hamilton's Federalist party and Jefferson's Republican party intensified in response to the events of the French Revolution and the subsequent outbreak of war between France and Britain in the 1790s.

Upon his assumption of the presidency in 1801, Jefferson adopted a policy of moderation, structuring his policy to appeal to a national constituency. His inaugural address called for reconciliation: "We are all republicans: we are all federalists." Under his leadership, the substantial Republican majority in Congress eliminated the most detested elements of the Federalist era. He substantially reduced the federalist debt, deeply slashed military expenditures, reduced taxes, pardoned political supporters who had been convicted under the hated Alien and Sedition Acts, and replaced the regal style of the Washington and Adams administrations with "republican simplicity." However, Jefferson did not call for the abolition of the National Bank; he appointed two New Englanders to his cabinet, and he revealed a willingness to expand national power for projects he deemed significant. He engineered the acquisition of Louisiana from the French despite his constitutional scruples; he proposed a plan for the construction of a national road system; and he authorized a naval campaign against the Barbary Coast pirates.

From the beginning, Jefferson's middle-of-the-road policies disturbed some southern Republicans in Congress. They expected a more rigid adherence to party principles that had been laid down when the party was in the minority. These differences created a loosely or-

ganized opposition within the Republican party known as either the "Tertium Quids" (because they claimed to be a "third something" between the other two parties), or the Old Republicans. The split dated from the very first days of the Jefferson administration. John Taylor of Virginia, one of the dissidents, later recalled in a letter to James Madison that "Mr. Jefferson did many good things, but neglected some better things." His critics, Taylor went on, "now view his policy as very like a compromise with Mr. Hamilton's ... Federalism, [which,] having been defeated, has gained a new footing by being taken into partnership with republicanism" (Risjord, p. 25).

In 1803 the Old Republicans, few in number, maneuvered to secure the election of James Monroe of Virginia as Jefferson's successor. They believed that Monroe was more committed to the principles of Republicanism than James Madison, who was perceived as Jefferson's heir apparent. They also took their fight to preserve the purity of Republicanism to Congress. When the Republicans assumed control of the House of Representatives in 1801 (the Seventh Congress), political parties were only informally organized, and many members had no partisan commitments. Thus, within the Jeffersonian coalition, an insurgent movement against the policies of the president took shape. It emerged under the leadership of John Randolph of Virginia. Eloquent and unpredictable, Randolph worked in relative harmony with the Jefferson administration, despite his private misgivings about some of Jefferson's policies, until two controversies caused him to break openly with the president.

The first was the Yazoo land question. Members of the Georgia legislature had accepted bribes to sell millions of acres of land, in what is now Alabama and Mississippi, to private land companies. Before the scandal became public, the land companies had sold some of the land to unsuspecting customers. Afterward, the buyers claimed rights to the land, even though in 1796 a subsequent Georgia legislature abrogated the land sales.

In 1802 a commission was appointed to resolve the question. It consisted of three representatives from the state of Georgia and, representing the United States government, Secretary of State Madison, Secretary of the Treasury Albert Gallatin and Attorney General Levi

Lincoln. The commission recommended that Georgia cede her western lands to the United States, with provision for an accommodation of those holding the Yazoo claims who were innocent victims of the fraud.

To John Randolph and the Old Republicans, this proposal smacked of speculation and commercialism, which they associated with Hamilton's debt-funding program. When the commission's report was submitted to the House, Randolph greeted it with a list of resolutions rejecting the report. He claimed that its recommendations violated states' rights, since it infringed upon the powers of the state of Georgia to rescind a fraudulent contract. He also charged that the report sanctioned corruption by yielding to the demands of land speculators. Randolph's speeches were personal and venomous. He pictured the compromise as a betrayal of Republican virtue and an indication that the moral decline that began under the Federalist party would continue if the commission's report were accepted. The House approved the report in spite of Randolph, but the Yazoo land-claims issue remained unresolved until 1814.

Randolph's uncompromising conduct during the debate over the Yazoo land claims alienated the president and most members of the Republican majority, but it attracted to him a small group of southern, mainly Virginian agrarians who shared his concern that the Jefferson administration had abandoned Republican principles. They shared as well a growing concern that the South was losing control of the Republican party, which was gradually increasing its following in northern states and becoming a truly national party. These apprehensions grew as the president attempted to grapple with delicate foreign policy matters and the European war which had erupted once again.

A foreign policy issue that concerned Jefferson involved the American claim to West Florida, a territory claimed by Spain that stretched along the southern boundary of the United States and the Gulf of Mexico, from the Perdido River west to the Mississippi. The American government maintained that West Florida was part of Louisiana, and in his annual message to Congress in 1805, Jefferson suggested the possibility of the use of force against Spain. In private, however, he asked party leaders for an appropriation of two million dollars to purchase West Florida. Randolph rejected the administration's efforts to win his support for the appropriation, and conducted another rancorous attack directed mainly at Madison, charging that the secret efforts to purchase territory—which some believed had already been paid for in the purchase of Louisiana—involved a dangerous expansion of the powers of the executive and a disgraceful exercise in bribery.

The House approved Jefferson's request to purchase West Florida early in 1806 by a vote of seventy-six to fifty-four. Randolph and twenty-seven Republicans, including over half of the Virginia delegation, joined the Federalists in opposition. The Senate also supported Jefferson's request, but four Republicans voted with the Federalists against Jefferson's request.

Events in Europe, plus Spanish unwillingness to negotiate, postponed the acquisition of West Florida to a later date and also forced Jefferson to direct his attentions to more pressing matters. The British victory at Trafalgar and Napoleon's triumph at Austerlitz in 1805 led to a war of attrition, in which the British used naval control of the Atlantic to obstruct the flow of trade to French-dominated Europe from the West Indies and North America, much of which was carried in American ships. A new British policy adopted in 1805 led to a substantial increase in the number of seizures of American ships and the impressment of their seamen. Jefferson strongly favored an American response; but, sensitive to Quid charges that his exercise of presidential initiative threatened to undermine the constitutional powers of the Congress, he held back while leaders of his party took the lead in writing the legislation. After much delay, partly because of the obstructive tactics of Randolph and some of the Quids, in early 1806 Congress passed the Non-Importation Act barring the importation of a list of British goods. The president then sent a special envoy—a prominent Federalist—to assist the American minister to Great Britain James Monroe in negotiating with the British government.

Randolph saw the Non-Importation Act as one more effort by the administration to expand executive power. He perceived "an invisible, inscrutable, unconstitutional cabinet.... I speak of backstairs influence—of men who bring messages to this House, which . . . govern its decisions" (Risjord, p. 55). He charged that the act endangered the economy of the nation for the interests of a small group of merchants, that the administration had abandoned its commitment to agrarian Republican principles, and that this policy might cause the United States to fall under the influence of Napoleon.

Randolph's obstructive behavior and personal vituperation, much of it directed at Madison, alienated even the more conservative Republicans who shared many of his values; after 1806, he was left nearly alone with little political influence. The values and interests that Randolph articulated reflected the position of a substantial group of southern agrarians, but by his actions Randolph alienated most of his followers and ultimately lost an opportunity to exercise a more significant impact upon the policies of the Jefferson administration.

On the other hand, the growth of support for Jefferson's party in the northern states created a party more national in perspective with more diversified economic concerns. From the perspective of the moderate, more practical Republican leaders like Jefferson and Madison, the Republican party could no longer afford to represent primarily the values and interests of Virginia planters.

THE ANTI-MASONIC PARTY

By the early 1820s the first two-party system had disappeared, and partisan considerations played a negligible role in Congress. This began to change late in the decade with the election of Andrew Jackson to the presidency. Partisan intensity in Congress centered upon Jackson's personality and policies, and one of the most vehement anti-Jackson groups was the small, very cohesive anti-Mason contingent.

The anti-Masonic movement erupted in the late 1820s in upstate New York and spread rapidly into other northeastern states. It was organized first in the so-called "Burned-over" district of western New York after a stonemason named William Morgan was abducted and probably killed in 1826 by members of the Masonic Lodge. Morgan had threatened to publish the Lodge's secret rituals. The very light sentences handed down by the courts to members of the Masonic Lodge who were convicted of involvement in the abduction inflamed many non-Masons. Critics of the Lodge maintained that it was a citadel of privilege and anti-democratic tendencies, hostile to traditional religion and morality.

The anti-Masonic movement developed within a year into a dynamic moral crusade which attracted substantial political support in the northeast. Prominent political leaders such as Thurlow Weed and William Seward in New York, John Quincy Adams in Massachusetts, and Thaddeus Stevens in Pennsylvania joined the movement. The Anti-Masonic party held the first national political convention in American history in 1831, when it nominated William Wirt for president. In 1832 Wirt won only 7.8 percent of the popular vote, and most of that was cast in northeastern states. After the election of 1832, Weed and Seward led a successful effort to unite the Anti-Masonic party with Henry Clay's followers and other groups opposed to Andrew Jackson and the Democratic party to form the Whig party, an effort which brought a quick demise to the significance of the Anti-Masonic party.

The Anti-Masonic party elected few representatives to Congress. Only one senator was a party member, and only 52 anti-Masons sat in the House of Representatives during the party's existence. (See Table 2.)

Anti-Masons strongly opposed the policies of the Jackson administration and voted consistently with those elements with whom they would coalesce in the Whig party by the end of the decade. Probably the most significant contribution of the anti-Masonic movement in and out of Congress was the role it played in shaping the northern Whig party. Several northern Whig political leaders began their careers in the anti-Masonic movement, and the moralistic spirit in the northern Whig party seemed to originate, at least in part, in the evangelical fervor of the anti-Masons.

THE FREE-SOIL PARTY

Until the late 1840s the antislavery movement in the United States was restricted to a relatively small group of abolitionists concentrated in the northeastern states. A faction of abolitionists organized the Liberty party in 1839 and nomi-

Table 2

MEMBERS OF THE ANTI-MASONIC PARTY IN THE HOUSE
OF REPRESENTATIVES

By State and Congress

Congress	Dates	N.Y.	Vt.	Pa.	Mass.	Ohio	N.H.	Tenn.	Total
21st	1829–1831	1	1	–	–	–	–	–	2
22d	1831–1833	10	–	3	–	11	–	2	26
23d	1833–1835	6	2	8	2	1	–	–	19
24th	1835–1837	–	2	–	–	–	3	–	5
25th	1837–1839	–	–	–	–	–	–	–	0

Source: Adapted from Alvin W. Lynn, "Party Formation and Operation in the House of Representatives, 1824–1837," Ph.D. diss., Rutgers University (1972), pp. 159, 170, 175, 183, and 189; Tables IV, VI, VIII, X, and XI.

nated James G. Birney for president. Abolition—the complete eradication of slavery—was a remedy far too drastic for the great majority of the American electorate; Birney received a mere handful of votes, and the Liberty party failed to elect any candidates to Congress.

The antislavery movement gained momentum after the outbreak of the Mexican War in 1846 and the controversy over the expansion of slavery into the territory seized from Mexico. Debate over the expansion of slavery into new territories dominated Congress until the Compromise of 1850 temporarily settled the issue. The Compromise of 1850 admitted California as a free state and organized the territories of New Mexico and Utah with or without slavery, thus leaving open the possibility that slavery could expand to the southwest. It also abolished the slave trade in Washington, D.C., and included a Fugitive Slave Act authorizing the use of federal officials to stop northern efforts to aid runaway slaves. The threat of slavery's expansion clearly evoked a much wider popular response than did abolition, and the Free-Soil party emerged as an expression of the northern opposition to the expansion of slavery into the West.

In 1848 the Free-Soil party nominated Martin Van Buren for president on a platform which opposed slavery's expansion. Van Buren received 10.1 percent of the popular vote concentrated in the northern states. Five members of the Free-Soil party won seats in the House of Representatives in the Thirty-first Congress (1849–1851). They represented the states of Connecticut, Indiana, Massachusetts, Pennsylvania, and Wisconsin. Salmon P. Chase of Ohio became the only Senator representing the Free-Soil party in the Thirty-first Congress.

In the Thirty-second Congress (1851–1853) two Free-Soilers from Massachusetts and Wisconsin, plus two Free-Soil Whigs from Massachusetts and Pennsylvania, served in the House. In the Thirty-second Congress, Chase was joined in the Senate by two additional members of the Free-Soil party, John P. Hale from New Hampshire and Charles Sumner from Massachusetts. No members of the Free-Soil party appeared in subsequent Congresses.

Voting patterns in Congress between 1841 and 1852 indicated that, in the House, the small band of Free-Soil party members voted consistently with the antislavery forces. In the Thirty-first Congress they voted solidly against the Compromise of 1850, which was designed to end the sectional controversy over the expansion of slavery, as well as proposals to outlaw slavery in Washington, D.C., and to adopt a more stringent fugitive-slave bill. Resolutely opposed to compromise, the Free-Soilers aligned themselves with the most consistent supporters of the extreme northern position. In the Thirty-second Congress the majority in the House voted in ways that indicated a strong commitment to support the Compromise and end the slavery controversy, but the two Free-Soilers and one of the Free-Soil Whigs voted with the majority of northern representatives of both major parties for measures designed to continue opposing compromise on the slave issue.

In the Thirty-first Congress, Senator Salmon P. Chase also stood firmly against the Compromise of 1850 with most northern Whigs. In the Thirty-second Congress Chase, Hale, and Sumner continued to support measures intended to agitate the slave question. In the voting on motions related to the Fugitive

Slave Act, all three aligned themselves in the most extreme position against the Act; a position taken in the Senate by only six senators, the three members of the Free-Soil party, two Democrats, and one Whig, all from northern states. The overwhelming majority of Whigs and Democrats, both northern and southern, opposed further agitation of the slave controversy.

On other matters, such as the question of the extension of land grants to veterans of the Mexican War and internal improvements in both the House and the Senate, the Free-Soil cohort did not vote as a bloc. Instead it divided in the same manner as did members of the two major parties, responding mainly to state and local interests. The issue of slavery and its expansion was the tie that bound the Free-Soil elements together.

THE AMERICAN (KNOW-NOTHING) PARTY

Despite the best efforts of those who supported the Compromise of 1850, the conflict over the spread of slavery into the West would not die. By the mid-1850s the political system formed in the Jacksonian era disintegrated. The Whig party crumbled; a new Republican party emerged almost spontaneously as a major party in the election of 1856, and for a few brief years, the American party flourished. The American party's official name was the Order of the Star Spangled Banner, but it was often referred to as the Know-Nothing party because its members were sworn to secrecy and were ad-

vised to deny any knowledge of the organization.

The American party was first organized in New York City in 1849 to resist the growing presence of Catholics and immigrants in American society. Bigotry seemed the central reason for its existence. But at the same time, the Know-Nothings in the northern states were solidly committed to the antislavery cause. In Massachusetts, the failure of the major parties to respond to the social problems associated with industrialization—the movement of rural people to factory towns, poor and crowded housing, and the constant threat of unemployment—also contributed substantially to the vitality of the Know-Nothing movement. The American party experienced extraordinary expansion across the nation after 1853, and in the elections of 1854 and 1855 it recorded dramatic victories in both northern and southern states.

The party found support in the South, where many strongly opposed unlimited foreign—particularly Catholic—immigration. Most of the adherents to the southern Know-Nothing movement were former Whigs who saw the American party as the only meaningful way to oppose the Democrats after the Whig party's demise. Furthermore, most members of the American party in the South were Unionists who hoped to use the party to overcome sectional differences over slavery.

In the Thirty-fourth Congress (1855–1857) forty-six House members identified themselves with the Know-Nothing party, but the real strength of the movement was much greater than this figure suggests (see Table 3). Approx-

Table 3
DISTRIBUTION OF MEMBERS OF THE AMERICAN PARTY IN THE HOUSE
OF REPRESENTATIVES, 1845–1863

Section	Congress Number								
	29th	30th	31st	32d	33d	34th	35th	36th	37th
New England	0	0	0	0	1	17	4	2	0
Mid-Atlantic	4	1	1	0	0	7	0	1	0
Border	0	0	0	0	0	14	7	7	0
South	0	0	0	0	0	8	3	5	0
Total	4	1	1	0	1	46	14	15	0

Source: Compiled from Inter-University Consortium for Political and Social Research and Carroll R. McKibben, "Roster of Congressional Office Holders and Biographical Characteristics of Members of the United States Congress, 1789–1991," Study #7803.

imately 120 members of the House were elected with Know-Nothing backing, and another large block of more than 100 House members were elected on antislavery platforms. In *The Impending Crisis: 1848–1861* (1976), David Potter and Don E. Fehrenbacher concluded that "this situation meant that most of the nativists were antislavery and most of the antislavery members were in some degree nativists" (p. 251).

However, the unity of the Know-Nothing coalition had been seriously breached prior to the meeting of the Thirty-fourth Congress, at a national meeting in Philadelphia in 1855. Here, the southern delegates won the adoption of a resolution that endorsed the Kansas-Nebraska Act, a law reopening the West to the possible spread of slavery. A majority of free-states delegates then walked out of the meeting. After this confrontation, the American party rapidly lost support in the North while it grew in strength in the South.

Thus, when the Thirty-fourth Congress met, the Democrats constituted the largest group, with eighty-five members, but fell short of a majority and were unable to elect a Speaker. The deadlock held up the Speaker's election for two months. Ultimately a coalition of northern antislavery and nativist elements elected as Speaker Nathaniel P. Banks, who had been a Democrat, a Know-Nothing, and by 1855 a Republican. The prolonged negotiations involved in the election of the Speaker required that the various elements in the antislavery movement come together in the House to form a majority. This coalition of antislavery and nativist groups marked a major step in the formation of the Republican party.

A few months later the Republicans were able to convince the northern wing of the American party to support John C. Frémont, the Republican candidate for president in 1856, and within a very short time the northern American party virtually disappeared. Its candidate for president in 1856, Millard Fillmore, ran well in the South, but in the North—where the American party had been strong in 1854—the Republican party prevailed. In the Thirty-fifth Congress (1857–1859), House members who identified themselves with the American party dropped from forty-six to fourteen. The party lost in all sections of the nation: from

twenty-four seats in the North to four, and from twenty-two seats in the border and southern states to only ten. Fifteen party members appeared in the Thirty-sixth Congress: four from the northern states, and eleven from the border and southern states. In the following Congress no member identified with the American party. The Republican party prevailed in the North by skillfully absorbing nativists who held antislavery sentiments similar to those held by most Republicans.

THE GREENBACK AND POPULIST PARTIES

The late nineteenth century was characterized by rapid economic changes which, by 1900, transformed the United States into one of the world's leading industrial nations. With the introduction of new technology and the cultivation of new land in the Great Plains and Pacific Coast states agricultural productivity increased. The South, the poorest and most agrarian region of the United States, experienced similar developments as the production of cotton, tobacco, and sugar grew enormously. Increased productivity depressed the price of farm products; farm prices generally declined between 1870 and 1897, and economic discontent could be found in many agricultural states.

Other factors contributed to late-nineteenth-century farm distress. Angry farmers and farm-town leaders accused railroads and grain-elevator operators of rate discrimination and other arbitrary and unfair practices that denied farm communities a reasonable profit and retarded the economic development of entire regions. Agrarian dissidents also complained that lack of capital and high interest rates robbed farmers and farm communities of their rightful share of economic growth and prosperity. Finally, they bitterly criticized the deflationary monetary policies of the United States government, which they believed had caused the long-term decline in farm prices.

In the post–Civil War years, the disruptive changes in the economy triggered two waves of protest that found representation in Congress. The first, the Greenback party, was primarily a protest against an 1878 act of Congress that required the federal government in 1879 to deflate the currency by withdrawing paper money, or greenbacks, from circulation and restoring the gold standard. The greenbacks had originally been issued by the government during the Civil War to help finance the war and were not backed by gold or silver.

Critics of the return to the gold standard organized third parties in many states to work for the restoration of the greenback and an inflationary monetary policy that they believed was more favorable to farmers and debtors. The Greenback movement elected congressmen under a variety of names—Greenback, National Greenback, Democrat and Greenback, and so forth—but it had only minimal impact as a third party in Congress. In the Forty-sixth Congress (1879–1881), there were six representatives who identified themselves as members of the Greenback party; eight in the Forty-seventh Congress (1881–1883); and one, then two, in the next two Congresses. The distribution of Greenback members in the House followed no clear sectional pattern, some representing urban states and some representing agricultural states. No member of the Greenback party sat in the Senate.

A second effort to promote an inflationary monetary policy and many other unorthodox measures emerged in the late 1880s as the People's or Populist movement. Populists held seats in the House and the Senate throughout the 1890s, and their strength was concentrated almost entirely in the agrarian South and West. The Populist party proposed a complex platform more comparable to a major-party platform than had most of the single-issue parties earlier in the nineteenth century.

The platform of the People's party was drawn up in Omaha in 1892, when the party nominated James B. Weaver of Iowa for president. It called for the adoption of a subtreasury plan. This was a proposal to transfer federal funds from private banks to county subtreasuries, where the funds would be used for loans to farmers who would store their surplus crops as collateral in government warehouses. The Omaha platform also called for inflation by the free coinage of silver; the nationalization of railroads, the telephone and the telegraph; reduction of the protective tariff; and a graduated income tax. The platform also endorsed a list of political reforms intended to restore the control of the government to the people: the secret ballot, the popular election of United States senators, the initiative and referendum, and the limitation of the president to one term.

As the national economy slipped into the worst depression in history after 1890, the strength of Populism spread. In most states in the South and West, Populist candidates competed for state and national offices. However, few of the candidates who used some variation on the Populist label—People's, Fusionist, Democrat and Populist, or Farmers' Alliance—won seats in the House and Senate. In the Fifty-second Congress (1891–1893), seven members of the House of Representatives were Populists; in the Senate, William A. Peffer of Kansas was the lone Populist. In 1892 the party elected ten of its members to the House (Fifty-third Congress, 1893–1895) and two to the Senate, Peffer of Kansas and William V. Allen of Nebraska.

In 1894, the worst year of the depression, the Democratic party suffered a disastrous loss of seats in the House, but the Populist party failed to profit from the debacle. Republicans captured most of the seats lost by the Democrats, and just seven Populists appeared in the House in the Fifty-fourth Congress (1895–1897), two less than in the previous Congress. Three Populists—Allen, Marion Butler from North Carolina and Peffer—sat in the Senate in the Fifty-fourth Congress.

In the 1896 election, the Democratic candidate William Jennings Bryan—who was also nominated by the Populist party—focused prominently on the free coinage of silver as the solution to the depression. Bryan lost to Republican William McKinley, and the Republicans attained majorities in both houses of Congress.

Populist candidates for the House ran better in 1896 than ever before. Twenty Populists were elected to the House in the Fifty-fifth Congress (1897–1899). In the Senate there were three Populists and one Fusionist, George Turner of Washington. However, Populist strength declined rapidly afterward. In the Fifty-sixth Congress (1899–1901), three Populists sat in the House and three, plus the Fusionist, in the Senate; in the Fifty-seventh Congress (1901–1903) five Populists appeared in the House, and one, plus the Fusionist, in the Senate. No Populists appeared in subsequent Congresses.

INSURGENCY AND THIRD PARTIES IN THE U.S. CONGRESS

The personal characteristics of Populist members of the House of Representatives in the Fifty-fifth and Fifty-sixth Congresses differed only slightly from Republicans and Democrats. Like them, the Populists were far better educated than the general population, although fewer Populists had attended college or a law or professional school than had Republicans and Democrats. A greater percentage of Populists were farmers than were Republicans and Democrats; a smaller proportion of Populists had been lawyers and judges; and a greater percentage had no previous political, executive, or judicial experience. Still, these third-party members belonged to a privileged class in American society: 61 percent had attended college or a professional school; 54 percent were lawyers and judges; and 81 percent had previous political, executive, or judicial experience.

Populists experienced the same obstacles that have bedeviled third-party members throughout the history of Congress. One of the two major parties controlled the organization of Congress, and the Populists had to depend on them for committee assignments and committee chairs, for allotments of time to speak on the floor of the House, and so on. For example, in 1891, Peffer of Kansas entered the Fifty-second Congress pledged not to join either the Republican or Democratic caucuses. He and Senator James H. Kyle of South Dakota, who called himself an Independent, asked for major-party recognition of their right to sit on committees as representatives of minor parties. Both major parties encouraged Peffer to vote with them, but when it became clear that he insisted upon retaining minor-party status, his requests for committee assignments were ignored. He asked for assignment to the committees on Finance, Agriculture, and Interstate Commerce; the Republicans assigned him a seat on Claims, the Census, Railroads, and Civil Service.

Like Peffer, the five Populist House members from Kansas also refused to join with either of the two major parties. They arrived in Washington with hope that others with Populist sympathies would join them in a party caucus, but these hopes were soon dashed. Southern Populists argued that the best strategy for securing help for farmers was to join the Democratic caucus. Except for Tom Watson of Georgia, the southerners did so, and voted for the Democratic candidate for Speaker—a conservative from Georgia who opposed the subtreasury plan and most other Populist reforms. In the course of the Congress, Populist congressmen proposed legislation designed to advance their goals, but without success. After the election of 1894 neither major party in the Senate controlled a majority of the seats, and the three Populists in the Senate attempted to build a majority by calling a meeting of senators who favored free coinage of silver. Fifty-two senators were invited to the meeting, but only four attended—three silver Republicans and one Democrat. The four stayed only long enough to indicate they would not break with their parties, and ultimately the Republicans organized the Senate. In subsequent debate it became clear that most Republicans and Democrats who favored monetary reform rejected most of the Populist platform. The Populists in this Congress were never able to establish themselves as an effective third element in the conduct of House business.

In the election of 1896, Populists won twenty seats in the House—more than in any other election in the 1890s—and held on to three seats in the Senate. But decisive Republican majorities meant that little could be done to further the Populist cause. The Republican majority in the Fifty-fifth Congress passed the Gold Standard Act and the Dingley tariff, a major victory for the advocates of both the gold standard and higher protective tariffs for eastern industry. Moreover, during President McKinley's first term, the economy improved dramatically. Populism had run its course, and the roster of legislators elected in 1902 to the Fifty-sixth Congress included no members of the People's party.

THE PROGRESSIVE INSURGENCY

The Populist party represented the last third party to claim more than ten seats in the House of Representatives. In the twentieth century, third-party candidates have run for president with some success, but they have enjoyed little success at the congressional level. Theodore Roosevelt ran a very successful campaign on a Progressive party ticket in 1912, polling over 27 percent of the popular vote, but few members of the Progressive party sat in Congress between 1910 and 1920. The Socialist party also did comparatively well during the Progressive years—Eugene V. Debs won almost 6 percent of the vote in 1912—but it recorded even fewer successes in congressional elections. However, a major Republican insurgency erupted in the Progressive Era which divided the Republican party for over five years, and may have made possible the election of Woodrow Wilson in 1912 and 1916.

Divisions within the congressional Republican party after 1900 were essentially sectional in nature. Northeastern Republicans dominated the leadership positions; In general, they favored eastern corporations and financial institutions, and exhibited indifference or downright hostility to western concerns. The western bloc members—who came to be labeled the Insurgents, or progressive Republicans—represented primarily Wisconsin and states west of the Mississippi River, where commercial agriculture was the major economic activity. With some exceptions these were the states that supported the Populist party in the 1890s and backed Bryan in 1896.

While prosperity returned to the Farm Belt after 1900, many of the problems that had so aroused the Populists remained. These included the protective tariff that favored eastern industry, the arbitrary and discriminatory practices of railroads controlled by eastern capitalists, high and allegedly unfair interest rates, and a general shortage of capital that western leaders continued to blame on Wall Street bankers.

In fact, most of those in Congress who actively participated in the insurgency had not been Populists, and several had campaigned against the agrarian movement in their states. For example, Miles Poindexter was elected to the House in 1908 from eastern Washington, a hotbed of Populism. Poindexter, a transplanted southern Democrat, claimed he had converted to the Republican party in the 1890s because the Populists controlled the Democratic party, but in the House—and, after 1910, in the Senate—Poindexter supported agrarian causes with no less commitment than that displayed by eastern Washington Populists in the 1890s.

If there were serious differences within the Republican party in Congress during the McKinley and early Roosevelt administrations, they were not reflected in the congressional voting record. In these Congresses, Republicans voted with high cohesion until Theodore Roosevelt's second term, and serious divisions did not emerge until William Howard Taft's administration. In Roosevelt's second administration the Republican leaders in Congress, and members from the northeastern and Pacific Coast states, frequently resisted Roosevelt's recommendations to increase government regulation of railroads and other corporations, and to enact new social and economic legislation and political reforms. On the other hand, congressmen and senators from the West and Midwest usually voted to support the president's vigorous efforts to pass his progressive program.

Committed to carrying on with a progressive agenda, William Howard Taft succeeded Roosevelt in 1909. In the 1908 campaign he insisted that the Republican platform include a pledge to revise the tariff. Taft also let it be known that he favored a reform of the House rules to reduce the power of the Speaker and replace Speaker of the House Joseph G. Cannon of Illinois.

Speaker Cannon, nearly seventy-three when the Sixty-first Congress convened in 1909, held traditional Republican views. He professed an unquestioned faith in the protective tariff and an instinctive suspicion of change. This led him to react negatively to bills that furthered western economic interests—what westerners liked to describe as progressive legislation. In effect, Cannon was a major obstacle to the progressive agenda, which was designed in part to free the West and South from northeastern economic domination. Using his appointive powers and his control of the powerful Rules Committee that he chaired, by 1909 Cannon had become, in the eyes of the progressive Republicans, a symbol of northeastern corporate control of the nation's economic and political system.

When Taft called the Sixty-first Congress into special session to revise the tariff, hostility against Cannon immediately surfaced. Thirty Republicans refused to attend the Republican caucus that endorsed Cannon for reelection as Speaker. The Republican insurgents, led by George W. Norris of Nebraska, thinking the president was behind them, prepared a proposal to change the House rules, which they anticipated would be supported by the Democratic minority. Meanwhile, Cannon and other

Republican leaders informed Taft that if he failed to defeat the Insurgents in the fight over rules reform, they could not guarantee passage of Taft's bill to reduce the tariff. Taft capitulated. To save his program, he did not oppose Cannon's reelection as Speaker.

Without the president's backing, and after the defection of some Tammany Hall Democrats from New York City who won promised tariff concessions, the Democratic–insurgent Republican coalition failed in its first effort to reform the House rules. In the vote for Cannon's reelection as Speaker, twelve Republicans voted for other Republicans—they would not vote for the Democratic leader, Champ Clark. More than twenty-five Republicans voted with most of the Democrats for rules reform, a motion that failed to win a majority. One year later, at the beginning of a new session of Congress, Norris again moved to reform the House rules. After thirty-six hours of debate, the Democratic–insurgent Republican coalition adopted Norris's proposals. The new rules removed the Speaker from the Rules Committee and enlarged it from five to fifteen members. The Rules Committee would henceforth be elected by the majority of the House, not appointed by the Speaker.

An equally turbulent wrangle erupted in the Senate over the tariff. The House passed the Payne tariff bill, which met the relatively modest expectations of President Taft and most of the House insurgent Republicans. But the Senate Finance Committee was chaired by Senate Majority Leader Nelson W. Aldrich of Rhode Island, a powerful advocate of eastern manufacturing and finance. The Aldrich committee added approximately eight hundred amendments to the Payne bill. Most of them increased rates on manufactured products, while several raw materials appeared on the free list.

The Payne-Aldrich bill seemed outrageously unfair to insurgent senators from the West and Midwest; led by Senator Robert M. La Follette of Wisconsin and Albert Beveridge of Indiana, they launched a lengthy and well-orchestrated attack on the bill. They claimed the high rates were unfair to their Farm Belt constituents and to consumers generally because the protective tariff was a tax on imports that increased the price of foreign goods and provided an opportunity for manufacturers in the northeastern states to increase domestic prices. Thus, the Insurgents charged that the regular Republicans, who represented mainly northeastern states, were reactionaries and tools of corporations.

Taft attempted at first to work with both factions in the party; but eventually Senator Aldrich, whom Taft respected, persuaded the president that he could achieve his tariff objectives in the Conference Committee, where the differences between the House and Senate bills were compromised. Taft secured some reductions in the final version of the bill, signed it into law and then delivered a speech in Winona, Minnesota where he praised the new measure as the best tariff act Congress had ever passed. It seemed to many of the insurgents that Taft had betrayed the 1908 party platform and Roosevelt's policies.

A third issue arose in 1910 to further exacerbate the divisions within the congressional Republican party. It concerned Taft's handling of the conservation issue. Roosevelt had made the conservation of natural resources one of the highest priorities of his administration and had worked with Chief Forester Gifford Pinchot, in the Department of Agriculture, to promote the preservation of the national forests. Pinchot and Secretary of the Interior James R. Garfield, who had legal responsibility for the administration of public lands and the national forest reserves and parks, cooperated closely in the execution of Roosevelt's policy. The three vigorously enforced conservation regulations, increased the size of the national forests, and extended their concern to oil and mineral reserves and water-power sites. These policies excited the vigorous opposition of powerful corporations, lumbermen, and ranchers, and other business interests in the western states.

President Taft appointed Richard A. Ballinger, a Seattle lawyer, to replace Garfield in the Interior Department; and while Taft retained Pinchot as Chief Forester in Agriculture, Pinchot lost the special status he had enjoyed under Roosevelt. Ballinger, who shared reservations about conservation with many western interests, convinced Taft that Pinchot and Roosevelt had exceeded their authority. He won the president's authorization to restore to the public domain some land that Roosevelt and Pinchot had set aside.

When Pinchot received accusations from an investigator in the General Land Office that

Ballinger had cooperated with a business venture organized in 1906 to develop Alaskan mineral resources, the "Morgan-Guggenheim syndicate," to illegally gain control of valuable coal deposits in Alaska, he submitted the charges to the president. Taft had them investigated, concluded that they were unfounded, and rejected them. Not convinced, Pinchot wrote a letter charging that Ballinger opposed Roosevelt's conservation policies to one of the insurgent Republican senators, who then read it on the Senate floor. A congressional investigation dominated by administration supporters cleared Ballinger of all wrongdoing, but he soon resigned from the cabinet. Republicans in Congress generally divided on the Ballinger-Pinchot controversy, much as they had over the reform of the House rules and the Payne-Aldrich tariff.

By early 1910 the Republican party was in shambles. In many states, especially in the West, insurgent or progressive Republicans seized control of the party from regulars whom Taft supported vigorously in nearly every instance. Forty-one incumbent Republican House members, all but one classified as regulars, failed to win renomination. In the Senate, all those identified with the insurgency won renomination; and in California, North Dakota, and Washington new faces identified with the insurgent cause were nominated. Roosevelt, who returned from Africa in June, tried to act as a moderator between the factions; but his relationship with Taft had become severely strained, and Roosevelt found it very difficult to resist the overwhelming evidence of his popularity among progressive Republicans.

Results of the fall elections revealed the calamity that internal divisions had brought upon the Republican party. Throughout the northeastern and border states, the Democratic party swept away Republican majorities, and only in the states west of the Mississippi River—where progressive Republicans ran— did the party hold its own.

In the Sixty-second Congress (1911–1913), the conflict between the regular Republicans and the progressive Republicans continued. These divisions culminated in 1912 in a convention fight between Taft and Roosevelt for the Republican presidential nomination. When Taft won the nomination, Roosevelt bolted the party, ran on the Progressive party ticket and, by dividing Republican voters between Taft and himself, made it possible for the Democratic nominee Woodrow Wilson to win the election. Similar divisions in congressional races in most of the nation also worked to the advantage of Democratic candidates. During the Sixty-third and Sixty-fourth Congresses (1913–1917), Democratic majorities in the House and the Senate provided Wilson with the votes to enact most of the major legislation of the Progressive Era.

In the early Wilson Congresses, the insurgent Republicans continued to vote at times with the Democratic majority for Wilson's program of tariff reform, business regulation, and other progressive measures. But by 1916 Republicans had plastered over their differences in the common desire to defeat the Democrats in the forthcoming election. Party cohesion returned, and virtually all congressional Republicans supported the Republican nominee, Charles Evans Hughes, in his losing effort to defeat Wilson. The president's conduct of foreign policy and World War I, and the strong personal dislike of Wilson among Republicans of all persuasions, provided the basis for a restoration of relative party harmony during the last two Wilson Congresses.

The progressive insurgency was colorful and dramatic. It tended, however, to obscure the major role of the Democrats in the passage of progressive legislation in these years. Of course the work of insurgents like Robert M. La Follette and George W. Norris was important, but in fact the Democrats provided most of the votes for progressive measures in the Roosevelt and Taft years—and, during the Wilson administration, most of the leadership as well. The insurgent Republicans did not vote consistently with the Democrats during the Taft and Wilson administrations. In fact, some of them voted over one-half of the time against the Republican majority in only one Congress during this period. That was in the first Taft Congress, during the fight over the Payne-Aldrich tariff and the autocratic tactics of Senator Aldrich and the Republican majority. Most of the time, most Republicans opposed progressive reform measures, and the cohesion of the congressional Republican party suffered only a brief decline during the Taft and early Wilson Congresses.

The Democratic–insurgent Republican coalition, which provided the support for progressive legislation, revealed the significance of sectional and local influence upon the national political process. Most Democrats represented the South and the West, and southern and western congressmen dominated the leadership positions in the Democratic party. The insurgent Republicans consisted mainly of representatives and senators from Wisconsin, the states of the Great Plains and, after 1910, the Pacific Coast. While supporters of progressive legislation represented all sections of the nation, the spokesmen of agrarian districts and states dominated the coalition. The Republicans who voted most like Democrats came mainly from the West; conversely, the Republicans who voted least like Democrats represented northeastern, urban, and industrial states.

Much of the progressive program—reduction of the protective tariff, regulation of railroads and other corporations, banking and currency reform, and the progressive income tax—consisted mainly of reforms that had in general been put forth by the Populist party in the 1890s. John D. Hicks was not far off the mark when he concluded, in his book *The Populist Revolt: A History of the Farmer's Alliance and the People's Party* (1931), "that many of the reforms that the Populists demanded . . . won triumphantly in the end" (p. 404).

THE 1920s AND 1930s

In the decade following World War I, sectional divisions within the Republican party in Congress persevered; but the public mood was decidedly more conservative, and the western Republicans less militant, than before 1917. Businessmen and the corporations had been instrumental in winning the war, and many radicals, including some progressive Republicans like La Follette and Norris, had opposed the war or supported it only halfheartedly. Reform and change were decidedly out of fashion, and the election of Warren G. Harding in 1920, with substantial Republican majorities in both the House and the Senate, signaled the beginning of a new political era.

Nonetheless, demands for additional federal assistance for commercial agriculture became one of the central themes in Congress in the 1920s. Agricultural demands for assistance grew strident in 1919 as the world prices for major commodities fell precipitously, and the American farm economy fell into a deep recession from which it never fully recovered until the 1940s. Congressional response took the form of a very loosely organized coalition of western and southern representatives and senators, which came to be known as the Farm Bloc. The coalition represented the same agrarian states that had produced the Populist movement in the 1890s and the progressive coalition in Congress after 1900. Southern Democrats provided substantial votes for successful Farm Bloc measures, although studies of the 1920s have focused more on the activities of a few Republicans and a handful of third-party members.

Third-party membership in the House remained a very small percentage of total membership throughout the 1920s. The largest number of members of third parties occurred in the Sixty-ninth Congress (1925–1927). This Congress was elected in 1924, when Robert M. La Follette of Wisconsin ran for president on the Progressive ticket. The third-party contingent in the House included one progressive Republican, one Democrat-Republican, one Socialist, and three members of the Farmer-Labor party. Clearly most members of the House in the 1920s had no stomach either for third-party activities or an outright break with party leaders.

In the Senate, the votes to support Farm Bloc measures also came primarily from Republicans and Democrats who declined to involve themselves in third parties. The largest number of third-party senators in any one Congress between 1921 and 1929 never exceeded three; a total of five third-party senators served between 1921 and 1929. The states represented were Iowa, North Dakota, Minnesota, and Wisconsin, and there were three third parties: Farmer-Labor, Progressive Republican, and Republican and Non-Partisan.

Members of the Farm Bloc found little sympathy for their cause in the White House during the presidencies of Warren G. Harding and Calvin Coolidge, or from eastern Republican leaders in Congress. Even so, when the western Republicans and southern Democrats found common cause, they could command a majority in both houses of Congress, just as they had during the Taft and Wilson administrations. During the 1920s the Farm Bloc secured passage of an impressive list of agricultural measures. It also played a major role in preventing the Harding and Coolidge administrations from turning over a wartime water-power project at Muscle Shoals, on the Tennessee River, to Henry Ford for far less money than it cost the federal government. At no time, however, did Republican members of the Farm Bloc defy party leadership as had the insurgent Republicans in the pre-war years, and it would be inappropriate to call these mostly western Republicans insurgents.

The stock market crash in 1929 marked the beginning of the economic depression that did not end until the beginning of World War II. Bank failures, the collapse of industrial production, and the highest unemployment levels in American history ended Republican domination of the federal government. Democrats gained control of the House of Representatives in 1930; in 1932 Franklin D. Roosevelt won the presidency; and in 1932, 1934, and 1936 landslide victories gave Democrats unprecedented majorities in both the House and the Senate. In the 1930s, under Roosevelt's leadership, the Democratic majorities in Congress enacted the most comprehensive program of legislation in American history up to that time. The more significant New Deal measures included farm legislation, emergency relief and work for the unemployed, creation of the National Recovery Administration, the Social Security Act, the National Labor Relations Act, and the Fair Labor Standards Act.

Democratic majorities in Congress in the 1930s were overwhelming, and despite the extent of the crisis, few members of third parties won election to Congress. This failure to win a substantial number of seats, at a time when economic discontent was especially acute, seemed a striking indication of the difficulty third parties faced in the twentieth century. In the first Roosevelt Congress, the Seventy-third (1933–1935), only five third-party members sat in the House, and between 1933 and 1941 the largest group of third-party members— twelve—appeared in the Seventy-fifth Congress (1937–1939). Third-party members in the House represented primarily two groups: the Farmer-Labor party from Minnesota, and the Wisconsin Progressive party. In all four Congresses between 1933 and 1941, the American-Labor party had

one representative from New York, the Non-Partisan party had one from North Dakota, and one member from California registered as a Republican-Democrat.

Few third-party members appeared in the Senate during these same Congresses. They represented the same agricultural section that produced most of the third-party members in the House. Between 1933 and 1941 the largest group of third-party members was four, in the Seventy-fifth and Seventy-sixth Congresses. The only states that elected third-party members to the Senate in these four Congresses were Minnesota (Farmer-Labor), Nebraska (Independent Republican), and Wisconsin (Progressive). In sum, most third-party members in Congress in the 1930s represented approximately the same agricultural states as the insurgent Republicans and most third parties had since the 1890s.

CONCLUSION

Third parties and insurgencies in the United States Congress had a significant, if not major, influence on congressional history. Third parties appeared most frequently in presidential politics, and few third parties have managed to win a significant block of seats in either the House of Representatives or the Senate. At times, however, third parties played an important role in Congress, especially in the nineteenth century. The Anti-Masonic party, while small, was very cohesive and provided a reliable block of votes in the fight against the policies of Andrew Jackson's administration. The Anti-Masons also contributed a firm ideological foundation to the organization of the northern Whig party. After the Mexican War, the Free-Soil party provided determined opposition to compromise on the slavery issue in Congress. Both it and the northern wing of the American party represented significant elements that coalesced in the formation of a second Republican party in the late 1850s. While the Populist party found it impossible to secure the legislation it sought during the agricultural depression of the 1890s, many Populist objectives were at least partially achieved during the Progressive Era.

Two significant insurgencies against major-party leadership in Congress can readily be identified. The first emerged early in the

Jefferson administration under the leadership of John Randolph of Virginia. The "Tertium Quids" challenged the party leadership of Jefferson and James Madison and created a great deal of consternation in the Jefferson administration. However, this was early in the history of Congress, long before the development of a modern party system and a tradition of party loyalty. The Quids attracted much attention, but their behavior seemed based upon personalities and very fine distinctions in principle, and the few who followed Randolph's lead seemed not to have suffered serious political costs for their disloyalty.

By the end of the nineteenth century, however, deviation from the two-party system extracted more serious penalties. During the 1890s, when a number of Populists held seats in the House and the Senate, they depended upon the major party that controlled the organization of Congress for committee assignments, committee chairs, for time to speak on the floor of the House, and so on. Twenty years later, nearly all of the Republican congressmen and senators who participated in the progressive insurgency refused to risk their political careers in Theodore Roosevelt's third-party adventure. While their revolt against Taft, Aldrich, Cannon, and the party majority in Congress contributed substantially to the division of the Republican party in 1912, very few insurgents joined the Progressive party. Apparently it had become obvious to the insurgents that, no matter how disenchanted they were with party leadership, their political careers, constituency interests, and legislative programs were best served under the umbrella of the Republican party. Such professional considerations help explain why there were few significant insurgencies and why the number of third-party members in Congress was small, even in the nineteenth century.

Several factors contributed to the difficulties faced by third-party members. One of the most serious obstacles minor-party candidates faced was the use of the single-member district, in which the candidate with the largest plurality won the election. Because third parties had a low probability of victory, voters avoided supporting them, and candidates hesitated to run on third-party tickets. Moreover, states regulated the election process; eligibility requirements, deadlines, and other requirements for prospective candidates differed from state to state. These regulations increased in complexity and number in the late nineteenth and early twentieth centuries, as mugwumps and Progressives endeavored to enact reform legislation to free elections of alleged corruption and dishonesty.

Once elected, third-party members who aspired to a successful congressional career faced major disadvantages. By the end of the nineteenth century, members increasingly looked to Congress as a lifetime career; and for most, third-party affiliation provided an unstable base for long and successful service in the national legislature. Usually the party in the majority assigned third-party members to committees, and rarely did the majority-party leadership assign chairs of important committees to a member of a third party. Similarly, third-party members had to look to the leadership of the majority party for office space assignments, for patronage for their supporters, and for a variety of other perks that were important to a successful congressional career. Likewise, a member of Congress who abandoned a major party to join forces with a minor-party movement faced a loss of seniority and probably a committee chair assignment, as well. Consequently, only the most dedicated dissidents committed themselves to third-party movements even in the nineteenth century, and by the middle of the twentieth century, the political costs had risen to the point where very few members of Congress were willing to pay the price.

BIBLIOGRAPHY

General Sources
ERIK W. AUSTIN, with the assistance of JEROME M. CLUBB, *Political Facts of the United States Since 1789* (New York, 1986), prints a valuable table on the partisan distribution of seats in the U.S. Congress. ALLAN G. BOGUE, JEROME M.

CLUBB, CARROLL R. MCKIBBIN, and SANTA A. TRAUGOTT, "Members of the House of Representatives and the Processes of Modernization, 1789–1960," *Journal of American History* 63 (1976): 275–302, is a very helpful analysis of biographical data on members of Congress and the institutionalization of Congress.

Two publications by the federal government are extremely valuable to the study of the United States Congress: *Biographical Directory of the American Congress, 1774–1961* (Washington, D.C., 1961); and CONGRESSIONAL QUARTERLY, INC., *Guide to U.S. Elections* (Washington, D.C., 1975).

The best analysis of the realignment process in American politics since the Civil War is JEROME M. CLUBB, WILLIAM H. FLANIGAN, and NANCY H. ZINGALE, *Partisan Realignment: Voters, Parties, and Government in American History* (Boulder, Colo., 1990). INTER-UNIVERSITY CONSORTIUM FOR POLITICAL AND SOCIAL RESEARCH and CARROLL R. MCKIBBEN, "Roster of Congressional Office Holders and Biographical Characteristics of Members of the United States Congress, 1789–1991," Study #7803, 8th ed. (Ann Arbor, Mich., 1991), provides party identification and other valuable biographical information of members of Congress in quantitative form. V. O. KEY, JR., *Politics, Parties & Pressure Groups* (New York, 1952), is a classic study in American politics. STEVEN J. ROSENSTONE, ROY L. BEHR, and EDWARD H. LAZARUS, *Third Parties in America: Citizen Response to Major Party Failure* (Princeton, N.J., 1984), is a useful discussion of the difficulties faced by third parties in American politics.

Early Nineteenth Century

WILLIAM N. CHAMBERS, "Party Development and the American Mainstream," in WILLIAM NISBET CHAMBERS and WALTER DEAN BURNHAM, eds., *The American Party Systems: Stages of Political Development* (New York, 1967), is a thoughtful essay on the history of the American party system. NOBLE E. CUNNINGHAM, JR., *In Pursuit of Reason: The Life of Thomas Jefferson,* Southern Biography Series (Baton Rouge, La., 1987), includes a thorough discussion of the "Tertium Quid" revolt. ALVIN W. LYNN, "Party Formation and Operation in the House of Representatives, 1824–1837," Ph.D. diss., Rutgers University (1972), is a valuable study of Congress during the era of the Anti-Masonic party. It provides

probably the most reliable partisan identification of party members available during the formation of the second party system and an analysis of voting patterns of minor as well as major party members. The most complete study of Thomas Jefferson's second administration is DUMAS MALONE, *Jefferson and His Time.* Vol. 5, *Jefferson the President: Second Term, 1805–1809* (Boston, 1974).

JOHN R. MULKERN, *The Know-Nothing Party in Massachusetts: The Rise and Fall of a People's Movement,* New England Studies (Boston, 1990), is a thorough study of the American party in Massachusetts state politics, and W. DARRELL OVERDYKE, *The Know-Nothing Party in the South* (Baton Rouge, La., 1950), provides information on the same party in southern politics. An excellent general treatment of the politics of the immediate pre–Civil War years is DAVID M. POTTER and DON E. FEHRENBACHER, *The Impending Crisis, 1848–1861,* The New American Nation Series (New York, 1976). NORMAN K. RISJORD, *The Old Republicans: Southern Conservatism in the Age of Jefferson* (New York, 1965), focuses on the insurgent movement in the Jefferson administration. JOEL H. SILBEY, *The Shrine of Party: Congressional Voting Behavior, 1841–1852* (Pittsburgh, 1967), concentrates on the major parties but publishes roll-call scales that include the scale scores of minor-party members in both the House and the Senate.

Late Nineteenth Century

PETER H. ARGERSINGER, *Populism and Politics: William Alfred Peffer and the People's Party* (Lexington, Ky., 1974), concentrates on Peffer's political career in state and national politics but includes useful information on the Populist party in Congress. See also ARGERSINGER's perceptive essay on the frustrations of Populist congressmen who found themselves rendered virtually powerless by the institutional rules and norms that had come to govern the Congress by the 1890s: "No Rights on This Floor: Third Parties and the Institutionalization of Congress," *Journal of Interdisciplinary History* 42 (1992): 655–690. DAVID W. BRADY, *Congressional Voting in a Partisan Era: A Study of the McKinley Houses and a Comparison to the Modern House of Representatives* (Lawrence, Kans., 1973), focuses on the major congressional parties but includes useful information on minor parties as well. JOHN D. HICKS, *The Popu-*

list Revolt: A History of the Farmer's Alliance and the People's Party, repr. ed. (Lincoln, Nebr., 1961), is a classic study of the Populist movement. For a perceptive study of late-nineteenth-century politics, see MORTON KELLER, *Affairs of State: Public Life in Late Nineteenth Century America* (Cambridge, Mass., 1977). NELSON W. POLSBY, "The Institutionalization of the U.S. House of Representatives," *American Political Science Review* 62 (1968): 144–168; and NELSON W. POLSBY, MIRIAM GALLAHER, and BARRY SPENCER RUNDQUIST, "The Growth of the Seniority System in the U.S. House of Representatives," *American Political Science Quarterly* 63 (1969): 787–807, together present a definitive analysis of the institutionalization of the House. An excellent study of politics and the money question in the mid-nineteenth century is IRWIN UNGER, *The Greenback Era: A Social and Political History of American Finance, 1865–1879* (Princeton, N.J., 1964).

Twentieth Century

HOWARD W. ALLEN, *Poindexter of Washington: A Study in Progressive Politics* (Carbondale, Ill., 1981), examines the career of the only insurgent Republican senator who joined the Progressive party in 1912, and it includes quantitative analysis of congressional voting during the Republican insurgency of William H. Taft's administration. JEROME M. CLUBB, "Congressional Opponents of Reform, 1901–1913," Ph.D. diss., University of Washington (1963), presents a quantitative analysis of the Congress during the administrations of Theodore Roosevelt and William H. Taft. For a good, brief synthesis of the Progressive Era emphasizing "sectional economic conflict," see SAMUEL P. HAYS, *The Response to Industrialism, 1885–1914,* The Chicago History of American Civilization (Chicago, 1957). JAMES HOLT, *Congressional Insurgents and the Party System, 1909–1916,* Harvard Historical Monographs, vol. 60 (Cambridge, Mass., 1967), is a useful study of the insurgent Republican revolt in the William H. Taft administration. The best general history of the Roosevelt and Taft administrations is GEORGE MOWRY, *The Era of Theodore Roosevelt, 1900–1912,* The New American Nation Series (New York, 1958); DAVID SARASOHN, *The Party of Reform: Democrats in the Progressive Era,* Twentieth Century America Series (Jackson, Miss., 1989), stresses the Democratic contribution to the enactment of progressive legislation in Woodrow Wilson's administration and examines the insurgent Republican and Democratic coalition. JULIUS TURNER and EDWARD V. SCHNEIER, JR., *Party and Constituency: Pressures on Congress* (Baltimore, Md., 1970), uses roll-call data to analyze party responses to issues and the formation of sectional coalitions in selected Congresses convened between 1921 and 1964.

SEE ALSO The Congressional Committee System; Electoral Realignments; Executive Leadership and Party Organization in Congress; Parties, Elections, Moods, and Lawmaking Surges; The Role of Congressional Parties; AND The U.S. Congress: The Era of Party Patronage and Sectional Stress, 1829–1881.

LEGISLATIVE WORK LOAD

L. Sandy Maisel

In 1960, former Republican leader of the House of Representatives Joseph W. Martin (Mass.) wrote,

> The great difference between life in Congress a generation ago and life there now was the absence then of the immense pressures that came with the Depression, World War II, Korea, and the cold war. . . . From one end of the session to another, Congress would scarcely have three or four issues of consequence beside appropriation bills. And the issues themselves were fundamentally simpler than those that surge in upon us today in such a torrent that the individual member cannot analyze all of them adequately before he is compelled to vote. (p. 49)

And few would deny that contemporary issues are far more complex than those about which Martin wrote. During the 101st Congress (1989–1991), legislators were asked to vote on literally hundreds of issues covering an all but unimaginable range of human activity, the complexity of which staggered experts whose careers were dedicated to just one specific issue—the bailout of the savings-and-loan industry, funds for AZT for AIDS patients, asylum for political refugees, restrictions on "Dial-a-Porn" telephone calls, SDI and the B-2 Stealth bomber, sanctions against South Africa and China, research on predicting earthquakes, legislation to combat acid rain, and campaign-finance reforms. The list could expand nearly without end, for even if legislation was not presented on a particular subject, constituents expected their legislators to be conversant with problem area after problem area and potential solution after potential solution. And the world was changing faster than the most astute observer could comprehend.

This essay on legislative work load will for the most part concentrate on the U.S. Congress. As the twenty-first century approaches, Congress faces a paradox. Congress must deal with more issues of more complexity, with graver consequences, in response to greater constituent demands than ever before, yet the Congress that is handling these matters is held in increasingly low regard by the very public that makes demands on it and that has reelected its members in greater and greater numbers. This essay will deal with that paradox, demonstrating how the work load has increased and raising questions about the meaning of that increase as Congress seeks to define the governmental role it plays—and that individual members play—in an age of divided government and furthermore, to have that role accepted. How representatives and senators have adapted to these increased demands will also be examined. The increase in congressional work load has carried over to state legislatures. While data are not so well developed for state legislatures, the discussion of Congress will be followed by a brief examination of how the shifting of programs from the federal to the state level has produced a concomitant increase in state legislative work load.

INCREASE IN THE CONGRESSIONAL WORK LOAD

What is meant by legislative (or congressional) work load? Many indicators of work load can be explored, but there remains the basic question of what each of these indicators measures. Consider Table 1. What do those numbers mean? Do they indicate a lot of work or not very much? If a laborer works 8 hours per day, 5 days per week, and has a two-week vacation, she or he works 250 days and 2,000 hours per year. The first two columns represent times the two houses are in session; of course, these are for a two-year period. But everyone knows that much more of the real work of Congress takes

Table 1

MEASURES OF CONGRESSIONAL WORK LOAD FOR SELECTED CONGRESSES

Measure of Work Load	Congress							
	85th (1957–1959)		90th (1967–1969)		95th (1977–1979)		100th (1987–1989)	
	House	Senate	House	Senate	House	Senate	House	Senate
Days in session	276	271	328	358	323	337	298	307
Hours in session	1,147	1,876	1,595	1,961	1,898	2,510	1,659	2,342
Recorded votes	193	313	478	595	1,540	1,151	939	799
Committee/subcommittee meetings	3,750	2,748	4,386	2,892	7,896	3,960	5,388	2,493

Source: Adapted from Ornstein, Mann, and Malbin, *Vital Statistics on Congress, 1989–1990,* Tables 6-1, 6-2, and 6-3.

place off the floor than on it. Compounding the difficulties of analysis is the recognition that even when the houses are in session, few members are in their seats.

What these data do reveal clearly is that the Congress is a year-round legislature. As recently as the 1930s, the first session of the average Congress adjourned early in the summer, and the second session ended before the political conventions, typically in June. Thus, legislators were expected to be in Washington only about six months a year. During World War II, Congress stayed in session virtually twelve months a year, a pattern continued throughout the rest of the 1940s. In the 1950s the pattern reverted to that of the prewar years, though typically each session ran about a month longer. Since the early 1960s, the pattern has been for the first session of Congress to run almost a full year (typically with a month's recess in August) and the the second session to recess for the conventions, but to reconvene in the autumn, not adjourning until about a month before the general election in November (cf. Maisel, Appendix 1).

The remaining two columns in Table 1 give other indications of congressional work load. One of the interesting points to note is the jump in recorded votes that occurred in the 1970s. The House changed its rules at this time to allow for recorded teller votes, making it easier to require members to express their views on amendments as well as final passage. Thus, the large increase in the number of recorded votes in the House between the Ninetieth Congress (1967–1969) and the Ninety-fifth Congress (1977–1979) is readily explainable. It is not so easy to account for the jump in Senate

votes, because Senate procedures did not change. If one were to look at all the data on recorded votes, one would see that the change actually occurred in 1971 in both houses, with peaks reached late in the 1970s and then a leveling off at about the current rate (cf. Ornstein, Mann, and Malbin, p. 158, Table 6-3). At least two factors seem to be at work here—the procedural changes in the House, which may have led the Senate to record more votes in order not to appear secretive, and the trend toward decentralization in both houses of Congress, leading more junior members to require votes on issues of concern to them. In either case, legislators are now required to record their votes approximately four hundred times a year, with each vote obviously reflecting considerable effort on the part of that member and/or his or her staff in order to become familiar with the issues and to know how to vote.

The last column in Table 1 provides an important clue about actual work in Congress. Woodrow Wilson's oft-quoted dictum that "it is not far from the truth to say that Congress in session is Congress on public exhibition, whilst Congress in its committee-rooms is Congress at work" was never totally accurate—but as he said, it was never far from the truth either. The history of committee work in Congress has been uneven. The number of Senate committee and subcommittee meetings began to rise sharply in the late 1960s, as that body dealt with President Lyndon Johnson's Great Society domestic agenda. The number of Senate meetings reached a peak in the mid-1970s, declining after the committee reforms passed the Senate in 1975. The current level of activity is not far different from that of the 1950s, with the important difference being that only slightly fewer meetings are being held by a significantly smaller number of committees and subcommittees.

In the House the number of committee and subcommittee meetings rose gradually in the late 1960s, but increased precipitously in the mid-1970s, a clear reflection of the decentralization of power to subcommittees and to more junior members of Congress. Since then, the number of meetings has declined, but still remains almost twice that of the 1950s. One of the continuing problems facing members of both houses is the necessity of balancing conflicting demands on their time. The large number of committee and subcommittee meetings, combined with multiple committee memberships, exacerbates this problem.

The measures of work load presented to this point deal only with how time is spent. Another approach is to examine the output of Congress. Table 2 presents some data on this point. The data in this table are interesting because they demonstrate that the number of bills enacted by Congress has declined, while the complexity of those bills (as indicated by their average length) has increased. And, of course, the increase in the complexity of legislation has led to a concomitant increase in the need for regulations promulgated by the executive branch, reflected in the third row of the table. The decline in the 1980s reflects the efforts at deregulation by the Reagan administration. The proportion of bills introduced that were enacted into law has ranged from more than half in the 1950s to less than a quarter in the early Reagan administration years. House percentages have consistently been much lower than Senate percentages. The rules of the two houses, as much as the intended output, affect these numbers; thus they are not deemed as

important as the amount of legislation passed and its complexity (cf. Ornstein, Mann, and Malbin, chap. 6).

But even these data do not reach all or even most of the interesting questions concerning legislative work load in Congress. As obvious as it may seem, one has to note that legislatures do more than legislate and that the job of the legislator is more than merely to pass laws. Increasingly, members of Congress are becoming involved with overseeing the federal bureaucracy, with managing their own staffs to handle their work load, and most important, with dealing with their constituents. The extent to which these tasks have overtaken Congress is difficult to measure, but once again some indicators point to obvious conclusions.

Since the reforms of the mid-1970s, House committees have had one subcommittee assigned the oversight role of investigating the programs under its jurisdiction. But, as commentator after commentator has observed, legislators are not inclined to invest much of their own psychic energy in oversight. That activity simply does not pay off in ways legislators value (Jones, pp. 384–387, has a detailed discussion of this point). But oversight still goes on. Much of the work performed by committee staff members involves overseeing existing programs so that new or revised legislation can be proposed.

Of course, much of the oversight in Congress—as well as much of the preparation for legislative work and much of the constituent service—is performed by staff members. One measure of the work-load increase in Congress is the increase in the size of the staff that aids members in performing their various duties. Table 3 gives various measures of staff growth. Clearly, the size of the staff has expanded. The increase in the size of the per-

Table 2

MEASURES OF CONGRESSIONAL OUTPUT FOR SELECTED CONGRESSES

Measure of Output	Congress			
	85th (1957–1959)	90th (1967–1969)	95th (1977–1979)	100th (1987–1989)
Public bills enacted	936	640	633	713
Pages of statutes	2,435	2,304	5,403	4,839
Pages in *Federal Register*	c. 20,000	c. 40,000	c. 125,000	c. 105,000

Source: Adapted from Ornstein, Mann, and Malbin, *Vital Statistics on Congress, 1989–1990,* Tables 6-4 and 6-5.

Table 3
GROWTH IN CONGRESSIONAL STAFF FOR SELECTED YEARS

Measure of Staff	Congress			
	85th (1957–1959)	90th (1967–1969)	95th (1977–1979)	100th (1987–1989)
House of Representatives				
Personal staff	2,441	4,055	6,942	7,584
Committee staff	348	566	1,776	2,024
Senate				
Personal staff	1,115	1,749	3,554	4,075
Committee staff	386	509	1,028	1,074
Support agencies				
Library of Congress	2,459	3,390	5,075	4,824
Congressional Research Service only	166	231	789	860
General Accounting Office	5,776	4,278	5,315	5,016
Congressional Budget Office			201	226
Office of Technology Assessment			139	143

Source: Adapted from Ornstein, Mann, and Malbin, *Vital Statistics on Congress, 1989–1990,* Tables 5-1, 5-2, 5-5, and 5-8.

sonal staffs for representatives and senators and of committee staffs was extremely rapid from the time of the Legislative Reorganization Act of 1946 until the late 1970s, when Congress began to be criticized for spending too much serving its own needs. Congress fell victim to charges of being the "billion-dollar Congress" and conspicuously slowed, though did not stop, the expansion of its staff resources. The staff increase—in support agencies as well as personal and committee staffs—reflects the congressional perception that its work load has increased. This increased work load has various components, including the ability to work on legislation and to oversee programs without having to rely on executive-branch sources for data and analysis, the need to compete with the executive in an era of divided government, and the need to communicate effectively on behalf of, and with, constituents, who have greater and greater expectations of response from Congress.

Measures of increased work load generated by constituency demands are difficult to come by. Two surrogates seem appropriate. First, since the early 1970s it has been possible to determine what percentage of representatives' and senators' personal staffs are physically located in district or state offices. Those numbers have risen steadily, from approximately two of nine in the House in 1972 to ap-

proximately 40 percent in the One-hundredth Congress and from only one in eight in Senate offices in 1972 to more than one-third in the One-hundredth Congress (Ornstein, Mann, and Malbin, Tables 5-3 and 5-4). Clearly, the staff in these offices deal mostly with constituents.

Table 4 provides some information on congressional communication with constituents. No data are available on telephone usage, WATTS lines, or FAX communication. Further, it is not possible to differentiate mail to constituents from mail to others, but the assumption that a vast majority of the congressional mail is to and from constituents seems warranted. The conclusion is clear: while data are not available for earlier Congresses, more mail is coming into the Congress from constituents. But even more evident is the fact that congressional offices are generating more and more mail. The jump—not to mention the concomitant cost increase—has been truly astronomical. Congressional offices are not just responding to incoming mail. Rather, using sophisticated computer technology, they are communicating with constituents on matters of concern to those constituents and generating correspondence between Capitol Hill and the districts. This is an obvious case of technology leading to an increase in work load that congressional offices see as beneficial to representatives' and senators' relations with their constituents. This

Table 4
CONGRESSIONAL MAIL FOR SELECTED CONGRESSES

Measures of Mail (in millions of pieces)	Congress			
	85th (1957–1959)	90th (1967–1969)	95th (1977–1979)	100th (1987–1989)
Incoming letters to House	n.a.	n.a.	54.8	70.3
Incoming "flats" to House	n.a.	n.a.	25.9	55.4
Incoming mail to Senate	n.a.	n.a.	52.5	86.0
Incoming "flats" to Senate	n.a.	n.a.	16.4	10.2
Congressional mailings	120.0	318.4	723.5	1200.3

Source: For 85th, 90th, and 95th Congresses, Ornstein, Mann, and Malbin, *Vital Statistics on Congress, 1989–1990,* Tables 6-8 and 6-9; for 100th Congress, House *Hearings Before a Subcommittee of the Committee on Appropriations on the Legislative Branch Appropriations for 1990,* pp. 77–78, and *Hearings Before a Subcommittee of the Committee on Appropriations on the Legislative Branch Appropriations for 1991,* pp. 96–97; for the 100th Congress, Senate, conversation with Gale Corey, Senate Post Office.

relationship has implications both for the representative function (a positive relationship) and for reelection chances (an incumbency-protection function).

The conclusion that the congressional work load is increasing seems clear. Members of Congress cope with these increases in a number of ways. First, they express concern that they are making decisions without the kinds of information they would like. Second, they have responded institutionally by increasing the resources available to them to perform their tasks. They hire more staff for their offices and for their committees; they have created new support agencies and increased their staffing as needs arise. They have employed new technologies, particularly computer technologies, to aid in their efforts to keep informed, to analyze data, and to communicate with their constituents. Third, they seem to work more and more hours.

COPING WITH THE INCREASED WORK LOAD

The conclusion that most representatives and senators would reach is that even with these efforts it is more and more difficult to keep up with their task. During the Ninety-fifth Congress (1977–1979), the House of Representatives Commission on Administrative Review (the Obey Commission) undertook a detailed study of how representatives spent their time. In addition to finding that representatives

worked an average of more than eleven hours a day while they were in Washington (no data were gathered on time spent in districts), the study demonstrated that over 55 percent of all representatives had at least one meeting conflict (i.e., they were scheduled to be in more than one place at the same time) on Tuesdays, Wednesdays, and Thursdays and that over 70 percent had such conflicts during the heaviest legislative months. The commission concluded that "legislators are under tremendous pressures to be at more places than is humanly possible. Members must decide which meetings to attend and how long to spend at each. Representatives must apportion their limited and valuable time to insure that they keep abreast of committee business" (Commission on Administrative Review, pp. 642–643).

While the Obey Commission proposed some steps to alleviate this situation and while the leadership of both the House and Senate have taken steps to ease the amount of conflict between committee and floor responsibilities, the increased demands for legislative action, oversight, and attention to constituents have made decisions on how to use one's time most efficiently more, not less, difficult. During the week of 15 April 1991, for example, representatives and senators faced competing demands for their time. As is typical, few committees and subcommittees met on Monday, but the Tuesday–Thursday period was particularly busy. On Tuesday, 16 April, 31 House and 17 Senate committees and/or subcommittees had hearings or markup sessions; on Wednesday the schedule listed 33 House and 19 Senate meetings, and on Thursday, 35 and 13. The week in committees wound down with a relatively light Friday schedule. Further, the House and the Senate met each day, with the House concentrating its efforts on the budget resolution and the Senate moving to passage of the reauthorization of the Commodity Futures Trading Commission. Legislators were also following the beginnings of American relief efforts for the Kurds in northern Iraq; they were hearing President Violetta Chamorro of Nicaragua talk of progress since her election and the exiled spiritual and secular leader of Tibet, the Dalai Lama, discuss Chinese occupation of his homeland; they were responding to a massive base-closing plan announced by the Department of Defense and to a controversial new education plan unveiled by the president. And they were undertaking all of these activities during one of the weeks in which Washington is visited by an unusually large number of tourists—and thus of constituents seeking appointments with their legislators.

A brief look at one member's schedule is instructive. In 1991, Thomas H. Andrews (D.-Maine) was a first-year representative from Portland. Elected leader of his class in Congress, Andrews served on the Armed Services Committee and the Committee on Small Business. His schedule for the week of 15 April, as prepared by his staff, listed not only the meetings he attended but also those he was scheduled to attend but could not, thus revealing his resolution of conflicting obligations. Monday was a relatively light day on Andrews's schedule. His day did not begin until nine in the morning. He had time for extended staff meetings, for working on coming speeches, and even for reading, and he had no apparent conflicts. That luxury did not recur until much later in the week. From Tuesday morning through Thursday afternoon, Andrews was constantly on the go. Each day began with eight o'clock breakfast meetings; on Wednesday and Thursday he had competing breakfast meetings, each of which he attended for brief periods. Andrews's subcommittee of the Armed Services Committee held three hearings, one of which conflicted with a hearing of the Small Business Committee on women's issues of concern to Andrews and a meeting on campaign-finance reform that he also wanted to attend.

Staff members covered the meetings when Andrews was not in attendance. Andrews also was present at the House sessions for the speeches by President Chamorro and the Dalai Lama and parts of other sessions. He had seventeen separate meetings with constituents or groups of constituents, with the topics ranging from pediatric health care to state libraries, from the closing of the Loring Air Force Base to pollution control and the retraining and employment of those over fifty-five years of age. Andrews attended meetings of the freshman class and of the Maine delegation; he spoke with those concerned about the civil rights bill and about freedom in Central America. He had conflicting luncheon engagements each day and attempted at least to "show his face" at each. On Tuesday and Wednesday nights he was invited to a total of sixteen receptions, many of which were hosted by members of Congress whom Andrews did not want to offend. Each night he made a number of obligatory stops, not finishing his day's work until after nine o'clock.

On Thursday afternoon, Andrews left the Capitol to fly back to Portland and then to drive another hour and a half for a reception in Waterville. Friday, Saturday, and Sunday were filled with a series of meetings and appearances in his district, some clearly impacting on his legislative work and some more for personal political reasons. His only scheduled free time was Sunday morning. Each day he traveled to a different part of the district, which is over 125 miles long and about 60 miles wide. His printed schedule included his mobile phone number, so that no time was wasted. His last appearance in Portland ended at 2:30 on Sunday afternoon; his plane back to Washington departed at 2:55. No representative's schedule is typical, but Andrews's certainly did not vary much from the norm. He was busy, involved, conflicted. He had little time to himself. He was a public servant in the truest sense of the term—his schedule was determined by the public, not by his own wishes. And there is no question that his workweek was full and demanding.

The conclusion one reaches in examining congressional work load is that the job of representatives and senators, individually and as members of a coequal branch of government, is an exceedingly difficult one. In many ways the difficulty was compounded between 1969 and 1993 by the emerging pattern of a legislature dominated by the Democrats and a White House controlled by the Republicans. What was once typically a pattern of cooperation was replaced by one of competition, as Congress strove to define its role and the Democrats sought to propose alternative solutions to pressing problems.

Representatives and senators work long hours on complex, controversial matters. As the issues facing the nation have become more complicated, the role of the federal government in dealing with these issues has increased and become more complex. As the role of the federal government has expanded, more and more organized interests have sought to have their views heard on Capitol Hill, and oversight of the administration has become both more essential and more time-consuming. As the population of the nation has grown, legislators in Washington have come to represent more people, and these constituents—spurred on by changes in technology that eases communication and by congressional efforts to encourage correspondence and exchanges of views—have demanded more and more of their representatives' time.

Legislators' time tends to be fragmented, disjointed. They are torn between competing committee schedules, running in and out of meetings and never having time to capture the richness of any one discussion. They are called off the floor to meet with constituents and out of staff meetings to answer roll calls. They rarely have time to reflect about the implications of policy matters and to focus on the future, much less to read or to see their families. They are expected to be in Washington to do their legislative duties, and they are expected to be back in their districts and states to hear the views of their constituents. They are dedicated men and women who are genuinely concerned about the future of the country; they are also politicians who care about their own careers. As Senator Henry Jackson (D.-Wash.) so aptly put it, "I have to be a senator before I can be a statesman."

This description helps to explain the paradox raised earlier in this essay. The work of the Congress frequently deals with questions to which no definitive answers are possible. Further, the very visible battles between those with differing views detract from the image of an institution wrestling with unsolvable problems. Frequently these disputes seem partisan, but at other times a reflection of institutional jealousy. And Congress as an institution, with internal squabbles, is incapable of competing with the president and the White House as a positive symbol in the national media. Individual representatives and senators, instead, deal with local or statewide media. They deal with constituents on a one-to-one basis. They create their own image. Thus, despite increased work load and efforts to cope with nearly overwhelming demands, Congress as a whole is not viewed positively, while individual legislators, unless they self-destruct through publicized scandals, have been able to maintain their own reputations.

STATE LEGISLATIVE WORK LOAD

Far fewer data are available on the work load in state legislatures than on that in Congress. However, some inferences can still be drawn. During the Reagan administration—as indeed during the Nixon administration—a concerted effort was made to return to the states significant policy choices that had gravitated to Washington because money was coming from the federal government. This shift led to an increased role for state legislatures. One would imagine, therefore, that the state legislative work load has increased.

In addition, anecdotal evidence from studies of congressional-candidate emergence reveal that an increasing number of state legislators opt to remain in office rather than to seek the seemingly higher office of representative in Congress. To some extent, these choices reflect strategic judgments that "a bird in the hand is worth two in the bush"—that is, continuing to hold an office is better than giving it up on the slight chance that one can advance. But these decisions equally reflect increased job satisfaction. State legislators more and more view their role as that of a professional public servant. They are working hard on important policy matters. These jobs, once part-time avocations for those who could benefit from public exposure (e.g., insurance agents or young lawyers) or those who had the freedom to take off significant amounts of time (e.g., seasonal farmers or retirees), have increasingly become full-time vocations. Annual compensation has risen, as have prestige and the number of legislators returning for multiple terms.

Perhaps the best data on work load to reflect this emerging professionalism among state legislators is a compilation of the amount of time spent in legislative session. Table 5 presents these data for the state legislative bienniums that parallel the Congresses discussed above. Some explanation is required. First, the fifty state legislatures are very different from each other. Increased professionalism in one is not necessarily an indicator of similar changes in another. The legislatures change at different rates and in different ways. Second, these differences are indicative of differences in state governments and state political cultures. No analysis of what is happening to state legislatures can ignore these differences. Third, different states present information on their governing processes in different ways. Some state laws restrict legislative sessions to a specified number of "legislative days." These legislative days are at times extended over more than one calendar day so that the legislature can complete its work without violating its own rules. Thus, the data presented in Table 5 are somewhat misleading in that they mix legislative days and calendar days. However, the intent of the table is to demonstrate a pattern over time, not to look at absolute number of days. Thus, increases, whether they be increases in legislative days or calendar days, reflect increased work load, at least by this measure.

Table 5 does show a clear pattern. Fewer states have extremely short legislative sessions with fewer than 75 or even fewer than 150 days in a biennium. The largest increase is in states that have between 150 and 250 meeting days in a two-year session. Typically a state legislature will meet for more days in the first year after an election and fewer in the second. One common pattern for a legislature meeting 200 days in a biennium might be for it to meet for most of the first six months of the year after its election and for perhaps two or three months during the next year. While this certainly would not make being a legislator a full-time job, the commitment necessary to serve is significantly greater than was the typical case decades ago, when about three-quarters of the legislatures met fewer than 150 days and the typical monthly commitment might be half of what it is now. Relatively few state legislators define their job as full-time, but it is clear that working expectations have risen substantially.

Another surrogate for measuring work-load expectations for state legislators is the number of staff allocated to serve them. The theory of allocating staff to individual members is that the amount of work they are expected to do—the amount of information they have to process, the number of bills they have to consider, the amount of contact with constituents they are expected to maintain—is more than an individual can do alone. For some time, legislatures have assigned staffs to committees. But few individual legislators were allocated staff until the late 1970s. No records are available for earlier legislative sessions, but Table 6 does demonstrate a clear pattern of change between 1977 and 1988.

In the 1977–1978 legislative session, only

Table 5
LENGTH OF STATE LEGISLATIVE SESSIONS

Number of Days in Session in Biennium[a]	Number of States			
	1957–1958[b]	1967–1968	1977–1978	1987–1988
<75	18	10	10	6
76–150	22	25	26	18
151–250	6	12	10	20
>251	2	3	4	6

[a] Some states report calendar days, and others report legislative days; some changed their reporting during this period. The reported numbers ignore these differences, presenting data for all states; a parallel pattern was found when state counting schemes were analyzed separately.
[b] Alaska and Hawaii were not yet states.

Source: Book of the States, 1958–1959; 1960–1961; 1968–1969; 1970–1971; 1978–1979; 1980–1981; 1988–1989; 1990–1991.

Table 6
GROWTH IN STAFF FOR STATE LEGISLATORS[a]

	1977–1978			1987–1988		
	Year-Round	Session Only	None[b]	Year-Round	Session Only	None[b]
Lower House						
Personal	11	7	32	19	7	24
District	9	1	40	15	0	35
Upper House[c]						
Personal	19	8	22	25	7	17
District	13	0	36	15	0	34

[a] Cell entries reflect the number of states with each staffing pattern.

[b] "None" means no personal staff assigned to individual legislators. Various staffing patterns (e.g., shared or pooled staff, interim staffs) exist in different states.

[c] Nebraska's unicameral legislature was counted as a lower house.

Source: Book of the States, 1978–1979; 1988–1989.

eighteen states' lower houses and twenty-seven states' upper houses allocated staff to individual legislators. By 1987–1988, those numbers had risen to twenty-six and thirty-two, respectively. Staff are allocated according to a number of staffing patterns. For present purposes, the most significant category comprises those states that allocate staff for the entire year, as opposed to the legislative session only or shorter periods of time. Again, the implication is that legislators have enough work to do to warrant staff assistance. The number of states allocating staff year-round grew by eight for lower houses (to nineteen) and by six for upper house (to twenty-five) between the two legislative sessions examined. This increase in staffing is a clear indication of an increase in work load.

A few states specify that staff allocated to legislators can be assigned to district offices. (Other states' regulations are silent on this issue, but the norm is for staff to serve in the state capital.) The number of states specifying district staff has also increased since the late 1970s, though it still remains quite small (fifteen of the fifty). However, again the logical conclusion is that legislators in these states are expected to be doing a significant enough amount of work in their districts to require staff; such expectations were very rare even in the 1970s.

One cannot underestimate the difficulty in generalizing about state legislatures. They vary from the extremely large and nonprofessional legislature in New Hampshire—a legislature

that is, by design, a citizen legislature, not one to be dominated by professional politicians—to smaller legislatures that meet nearly full-time and whose members are paid significant salaries, such as the California legislature, in which state senate districts are larger than state congressional districts. But trends can be identified, and one clear trend is for more significant policies to be debated at the state level, for the legislatures to deal with those, and thus for expectations and work load to increase.

CONCLUSION

As the United States continues its third century, the tasks facing the federal and state governments loom ever larger. One ongoing concern is the ability of this polity to attract talented, dedicated individuals to public service. The National Academy of Public Administration has undertaken a major research effort to examine the ways in which young executives can be drawn into service in the executive branch of the federal government. That study cites a relative decline in family standard of living and concern with lack of personal privacy as two deterrents of the willingness of some of the "best and the brightest" to leave the private sector for government service.

If that is true for appointed officials, it is even more true for elected officeholders. Concerned citizens seek public office because they want to make a difference in the lives of those around them in their community, their state, and their nation. The chance to effect significant change in public policy has long been an important stimulus toward entering public life. However, rigorous and expensive campaigns, intense media and public scrutiny, and strict limitations on income all make seeking elective office less attractive. The nearly impossible demands on the time of public service have also become a deterrent. Certainly this has been true in the Congress, in which representatives and senators complain that they have no time to think deeply about public problems and no time that is truly their own. Increasingly, this seems to be the case in state legislatures as well.

The work-load problem is compounded by the need to master complex and technical policy matters, by the knowledge that the problems presented for solution are the most trying and critical facing the nation, and by the competing demands for legislators' time. No easy solution is at hand. The role of Congress as an important competitor for national power has gained in prominence in the age of divided government. Much the same can be said at the state level in a number of states. And the response to this has been to continue to increase the amount of time legislators spend at their jobs and the amount of work they are expected to perform. The costs in terms of their needs as individuals and in terms of the attractiveness of the position to the next generation of elected leaders is rarely acknowledged and seemingly never a factor as the legislative job evolves.

One returns then to the paradox raised at the beginning of this essay. Perhaps that paradox is best symbolized by battles over the budget at the federal and state levels. President Reagan was elected on a platform that called for balancing the budget, President Bush shared that goal, and Congress has adopted plan after plan to bring the budget deficit under control. The struggle has continued into the administration of President Bill Clinton with no solution at hand.

At the state level, as fiscal year 1992 began, state government was shut down in Connecticut and Maine, because no budgets had been passed. Four other states began their fiscal year without annual budgets in place, despite constitutional demands that the budgets be passed.

State legislators face the same problems members of Congress face: they must bring budgets into balance, but the public demands that they do so without cutting programs and without raising taxes. No other alternatives exist.

As a result, legislators work harder and harder and become more and more frustrated. Legislators have clearly learned the political lessons of how to deal with this. They build relationships with their constituents. They take credit for what the government does well and displace blame for governmental problems. They guarantee their own reelection. But they also have begun to see the fallout from public dissatisfaction with the job that the government is doing. Incumbents won in overwhelming numbers in the 1990 elections, but margins of victory fell as voters began to express an anti-incumbent reaction. And the legislators themselves are feeling that dissatisfaction. As prominent a figure as William Gray (D.-Pa.), the majority whip in the House of Representatives, left Congress for the private sector, to serve as president of the United Negro College Fund, claiming that he could serve the interests he cared about more effectively outside the government.

State legislators, quite well protected from electoral repercussions, give more thought to leaving office voluntarily. If the public is dissatisfied with their efforts, let someone else try. The gains do not seem worth the costs. The pace and the demands of life in the legislature have increased, but the satisfaction of seeing the benefits of their service and feeling the gratitude of their constituents is no longer easily gained.

The need, of course, is for a new brand of political leadership, capable of attracting public esteem and of making difficult decisions. The trick is to find a politician who can succeed while preaching harsh lessons to the voters. And perhaps the solution will be found in leaders who understand what the government needs to do, who are willing to work toward that goal, but who are not so personally invested in their jobs that they are afraid of public reaction to unpopular programs. Not only has the task become more complex and onerous, but the qualities necessary to succeed have become even more difficult to identify.

BIBLIOGRAPHY

The COMMISSION ON ADMINISTRATIVE REVIEW OF THE UNITED STATES CONGRESS, HOUSE OF REPRESENTATIVES, *Final Report*, House Document No. 95–272 (Washington, D.C., 1977), contains detailed information on congressional work load and the uses of members' time; it is an invaluable source of data. ROGER H. DAVIDSON and WALTER J. OLESZEK, *Congress and Its Members*, 3d ed. (Washington, D.C., 1990), and CHARLES O. JONES, *The United States Congress: People, Place, and Policy* (Homewood, Ill., 1982), are the two most impressive texts on the Congress; they each discuss work load at appropriate points. L. SANDY MAISEL, ed., *Political Parties and Elections in the United States: An Encyclopedia* (New York, 1991), contains a series of articles that look at the impact of electoral politics on legislative work load at the state and national levels. JOSEPH W. MARTIN, *My First Fifty Years in Politics* (New York, 1960), provides interesting contrasts to congressional work load of an earlier era. NORMAN J. ORNSTEIN, THOMAS E. MANN, and MICHAEL J. MALBIN, *Vital Statistics on Congress, 1989–1990* (Washington, D.C., 1990), is the best single source of data on the modern Congress. ALAN ROSENTHAL, *Legislative Life: People, Process, and Performance in the States* (New York, 1981), remains one of the best sources on work load in the state legislatures.

SEE ALSO Congressional Oversight AND Congressional Staffs.

LEGISLATIVE ETHICS

Michael J. Malbin

The history of legislative ethics in the United States can be understood as a long period during which informal procedures were irregularly and infrequently applied, followed by formal codification in the 1960s and 1970s, and then by an increase in the numbers of members subjected to official investigations and sanctions. In the public's mind, the increase in formal activity has sometimes been equated with a deterioration of congressional ethics. However, any fair review will show that our attention level and standards are what have been heightened—not the level of corruption.

Not surprisingly, the tendency toward formal regulation at both the national and state levels has been intertwined with the growth of government and the professionalization of the legislature. A larger government means an increase in the potential for conflicts of interest. At the same time, a full- or nearly full-time legislature can pay well enough to permit members to think about limiting outside income. Hence the need, and the opportunity, for more formal codes.

Need and opportunity do not by themselves determine events. Government growth and professionalized legislatures may be enabling conditions that make formal ethics codes more likely; however, they are not sufficient either to bring about change by themselves, or to dictate the content of the changes that do occur. On several crucial occasions, well-publicized scandals were the essential catalysts for institutional change.

Whatever the origin, the new rules almost always go beyond the facts of the catalyzing scandal to make a broader range of behavior subject to official review. In this way, the new standards themselves have become catalysts for bringing attention to situations that once might have been accepted without question. This attention, in turn, creates pressure for still more changes in the formal rules and informal standards.

This essay will trace the development of ethics codes, and major ethics cases, in Congress. State legislative codes have had a more complicated history. There will be allusions to this history in this essay but, for reasons to be explained in an appendix, state codes will not receive the same attention as those of Congress.

CONSTITUTIONAL THEORY AND TEXT

Governmental corruption is often defined in contemporary discussions as the use of public office for private gain. Conflicts of interest are just as often described in terms of the conflict between a public official's self-interest and his or her public responsibilities. But the Constitution did not assume a sharp distinction between public and private interests. To the contrary, *The Federalist* explained the Constitution as an attempt to create institutions that would give officeholders self-interested reasons for serving the public's long-term good. However, "self-interest" in the framers' understanding was broader than "material self-interest," which tends to dominate current discussions.

The framers' basic ideas about containing corruption focused on the powers of the legislative office and the size of congressional districts. Offices were to be made powerful enough to attract capable people motivated by a nonmaterial ambition for power and honor. It was hoped that such people would either crowd out, or control the greed of, those whose dominant interests were materialistic or petty. Ambitious officeholders thus would serve the cause of public integrity because they would feel a personal stake—a selfish interest—in preserving the reputation and power of their own offices.

At the same time, the framers favored large districts, because they thought sizable constituencies would be less open to election fraud and corruption. They also thought large districts would be more likely to choose representatives with the scale of ambition needed to care about their institution's reputation. Thus, creating a self-interest for members to serve the public interest had both an institutional and an electoral—an inside and an outside—component.

This line of theoretical argument parallels the Constitution's two distinct approaches toward enforcing legislative ethics. For the sake of simplicity, these may be referred to as electoral control and internal discipline. For most of American history, internal controls—to the extent they were exercised—were largely informal. For both theoretical and practical reasons, members tended to leave formal judgments in the hands of the voters.

The reliance on external controls was not just a smokescreen for winking at corruption. One of the fundamental principles of representative government is that the representative serves as the agent of the people. We tend to take that idea for granted. However, as historian Morton Keller has observed, the notion of the representative as agent makes for a profoundly different kind of political community than one in which offices are personal property to be passed on to one's heirs or sold. In the latter case, the sovereign did not appoint the office-holder to a public trust, but granted the equivalent of a private charter. In such a situation, the line between fee payment and bribe, or between impartial judgment and special favor, sometimes was hard to draw.

In a representative government, however—whether the representative is a delegate or trustee—the idea of agency is that the office belongs to the people. That is what makes it possible to talk about a distinction between a representative's personal interests and his or her public obligations. However, this same principle also leads to a reticence about questioning the people's decisions regarding who should represent them. Under most conditions, the people's decision is to be accepted and respected. And so it has been for most of Ameri-

can history. Even today, the reliance on disclosure ultimately is a decision to rely on the public's choice of its own representatives.

Of course, the Constitution did not rely solely on voters to enforce appropriate standards within Congress. According to Article I, Section 5: "Each House shall be the Judge of the Elections, Returns and Qualifications of its own Members." In addition, "Each House may determine the Rules of its Proceedings, punish its Members for disorderly Behaviour, and, with the Concurrence of two thirds, expel a Member." These clauses do two things. First, they protect Congress by keeping the power of discipline in its own hands instead of turning it over to the executive. Second, at the same time as they protect Congress from the executive, they also create an obligation on Congress to keep its own houses in order.

However, the obligations are neither self-defining nor self-executing. For a long time, the main standard embodied in the rules of the House and Senate was based on an 1801 provision that Vice President Thomas Jefferson included in the *Manual* he compiled as the Senate's presiding officer. The basic idea was that members should refrain from speaking or voting on issues in which they had a private interest. "Private interests" were interpreted to refer to all "direct personal or pecuniary interests." Later, in an 1874 ruling, the definition was narrowed to permit members to vote on bills affecting their own interests, as long as the private interests were not exclusively their own, but were shared by a larger group—for example, all cotton producers rather than a specific farm. In other words, the rules have changed over time. So too have the interpretations, applications, and underlying customs or mores.

EXCLUSIONS, EXPULSIONS, AND CENSURES

One way to discover how rules are applied and interpreted is to look at actual cases. The language of the Constitution suggests three different classes of disciplinary actions open to Congress. The House or Senate can *exclude* a member-elect for failing to satisfy the qualifications for office, it can *expel* a sitting member (with a two-thirds vote), or it can mete out *another punishment,* such as *censure* or a lesser form of public criticism. A brief summary of the situations in which the three kinds of penalties have been invoked will show the infrequency of sanctions before 1968, when formal codes were adopted, and the greater frequency since then.

Exclusion

Since 1789, the Senate has excluded three senators-elect and the House has excluded 9 members-elect. (One of the nine, Socialist Victor L. Berger, was excluded twice, in 1919 and 1920.) All of the Senate exclusions and 6 of the House exclusions turned on qualifications for office specified in the Constitution. The primary ones specified are: age (Article I), citizenship (Article I), residency (Article I), loyalty to the Constitution (Article IV), or rebellion (Fourteenth Amendment).

However, the House also excluded Brigham H. Roberts (D.-Utah) for polygamy in 1900 and two—Benjamin Whittemore (R.-S.C.) and Adam Clayton Powell (D.-N.Y.)—for official malfeasance (that is, misconduct in, or misuse of, their public office). Whittemore was censured in 1870 for selling appointments to the U.S. Military Academy. He resigned, was re-elected, and then, excluded. Whittemore's and Roberts's cases raised essentially the same constitutional issue as the Adam Clayton Powell case of 1968, to be discussed later: whether Congress may look beyond the few grounds explicitly mentioned in the Constitution for exclusion. However, the Supreme Court ruled in 1969 that the Powell exclusion exceeded the House's authority. As of late 1992, that was the last time either chamber excluded a member-elect.

Expulsion

Unlike exclusion or censure, expulsion requires a two-thirds vote for adoption. Expulsion has been sought many times for corruption or other charges, without success. In fact, there is no legal or technical limit on the grounds for expulsion. However, all but one of Congress's successful expulsions before 1980 (14 senators and three House members) came during 1861–

1862 for rebellion. The sole exception was the 1797 Senate expulsion of William Blount of Tennessee, after the House impeached Blount for his involvement in a conspiracy to shift Florida from the control of Spain to Great Britain. Since 1980, however, one member has been expelled and five others have resigned under the threat of imminent expulsion.[1] All of these members had previously been convicted of crimes that fit our more normal understanding of corruption.

Censure and Other Penalties

The third category of potential congressional action includes the full range of disciplinary actions short of expulsion or exclusion. Congress has used an array of penalties, ranging from relatively mild letters of reprimand to formal denunciations and motions of censure adopted on the House or Senate floor. Since 1976 four House members have been censured,[2] two senators have been formally denounced,[3] seven House members have been reprimanded,[4] one House member received a "letter of reproval,"[5] and five other members resigned before formal House action was taken.[6] These five are in addition to the six who resigned under threat of expulsion.

Before 1976, Congress limited its formal actions to censure motions. Perhaps because this was the only penalty, it was rarely invoked. Between 1789 and 1975, seven senators[7] and eighteen representatives[8] were censured. Five of the Senate cases[9] and nine of the House censures[10] were for offenses against the deliberative character of the House or Senate: physical assaults by one member against another, insults against the House, and so forth. The most recent such case was the 1954 condemnation of Senator Joseph McCarthy (R.-Wis.) for abusing the processes and the honor of the Senate.

The first senator ever disciplined for financial misconduct was Thomas J. Dodd (D.-Conn.) in 1967. However, five of the pre-1976 House censures were for corruption.[11] Comparing these five censure cases (all during the 1970s) with ones Congress did not punish will give a fair portrait of the state of legislative ethics in the long period before there were formal codes.

NINETEENTH-CENTURY PRACTICES AND RULES

Three of the five nineteenth-century censure cases involved bribery, which is an easy case to handle conceptually. Short of direct vote-buying, however, lies a broad range of possibilities. The history of legislative ethics largely has involved sorting out conflicts of interest in that broad, uncharted range of behavior short of the bribe.

Daniel Webster

One instructive way to begin is with an example that most nineteenth-century contemporaries saw as falling well within permissible bounds. In the 1830s, Senator Daniel Webster (Fed.-Mass.) often acted as a private attorney before the Supreme Court. According to Senate historian Richard Allan Baker, forty-one of Webster's successful Supreme Court arguments were made on behalf of the Bank of the United States. The bank was a private company with a congressional charter. It paid Webster a regular fee as a retainer.

Some observers, long after the fact, might raise their eyebrows at this behavior. For these observers, at least two points are worth noting. First, Webster was not accused of basing his decisions as a senator on the legal fees he received from his private legal practice. Second, members of Congress at the time were part-time legislators expected to have some other source of livelihood. In fact, that is precisely why Webster's example was normal for much of Congress's history, and why it raises questions that still arise regularly in state legislatures today. Part-time legislators are expected to earn private incomes; the problem is to define what kinds of income are acceptable.

Webster's relationship with the bank raises two conflict-of-interest issues. First, should sitting members of Congress represent private parties before federal courts or executive branch commissions? John Quincy Adams (Fed.-Mass.) said no in 1845, when he served in the House and was asked to argue a case before the Supreme Court. A century-and-a-half later, when congressional service was considered a full-time career, most members of Congress would have agreed with Adams. However, most of Webster's own contemporaries took Webster's position, as do many state legislators today.

The second issue arising out of Webster's practice was whether private companies with public charters should be allowed to pay legal fees to the public officials upon whom their charters depend. This was an occasional issue at the federal level, but a constant one for state legislatures. There, the frequently corrupt relationships between legislators and corporations made Congress appear practically antiseptic. For example, railroad magnate Jay Gould distributed more than $500,000 in "legal fees" to New York State legislators in 1868 alone.

There were more possibilities for corruption at the state and local level than at the national level, because state and local legislators dealt more frequently with particularized benefits than did the Congress. The bank represented by Webster had a federal charter. That made it a rarity. Most corporations held state charters. Moreover, for much of the first half of the nineteenth century, there were no general laws of incorporation. Every private company that wanted to incorporate needed a special charter from the state legislature. In the absence of automatic, general rules, the opportunities for special favors—and therefore corruption—are obvious. By the 1840s, states had begun passing general laws of incorporation. Over the next three decades, the use of special charters faded.

Early Conflict-of-Interest Law

Of course, a charter was only one among many opportunities for special favors available to state legislators of the period. According to historian Ari Hoogenboom:

> The absence of a general incorporation law and the prevalence of special and local legislation made corruption easy. Legislators sold their votes to grant corporations privileges and then blackmailed these corporations by threatening to pass strike bills that would rescind their privileges. Out of 9,230 acts passed [by the Pennsylvania legislature] between 1866 and 1873, 8,700 were special and local acts, passed with little study or debate. (p. 128)

Thus, there is a direct connection between the character of the public agenda and the opportunity for corruption or conflicts of interest. To the extent that a legislature must pass a special act for every routine governmental benefit, potential beneficiaries have an interest in hiring legislators, for a fee, to serve their interests.

At the federal level, the parallel problem existed not so much with charters as with claims. As Robert N. Roberts has written:

> At the close of the revolutionary war, Congress established itself as the branch of government responsible for hearing and resolving claims against the federal government. After 1830, those who had suffered damage to property during the revolutionary war or the Mexican War of 1846, or who believed they were entitled to pensions because of the military service, flooded Congress with claims for monetary relief. Although Congress delegated some jurisdiction over claims to the Treasury Department and other federal agencies, not until the creation of the court of claims in 1865 did Congress attempt to bring some order to the system.
>
> Because of the time and distances involved in traveling to the nation's capital, few claimants could go to Washington to prosecute their own claims. Instead, they typically obtained the assistance of an influential friend or hired an agent.... Members of Congress and former government officials set up offices to prosecute claims before Congress, the Treasury, and other departments, openly advertising that they had the contacts to help expedite claims. (p. 9)

In response to the flood of claims that followed the Mexican and Civil wars, Congress passed its first ethics laws. The trigger for the first such law was an 1852 fraud. Thomas Corwin, then a senator from Ohio, served as the attorney for a Dr. Gardiner, who submitted a $500,000 claim to the Mexican Claims Commission. The claim, for a silver mine supposedly destroyed in the Mexican War, was discovered to be a fiction. Corwin himself was cleared but, in 1853, Congress passed a law forbidding members of Congress and other governmental officials from accepting fees for prosecuting claims before federal agencies.

The next major conflict-of-interest statute also passed in the wake of a scandal. On 2 July 1862, a motion was laid before the Senate to expel Senator James F. Simmons (Whig-R.I.) who had accepted a share of the potential prof-

its in return for helping two Rhode Island rifle manufacturers obtain war contracts. The expulsion motion became moot when Simmons resigned in August. Later that same year, however, the 1853 prohibition against accepting fees was extended to government contracts, and then in 1864 to all kinds of departmental proceedings.

Of course, the payment of fees for representation was only one of a large number of issues to arise after the Civil War. The three congressional censure cases of 1870 were straightforward examples of payment for service: Representatives B. F. Whittemore (R.-S.C.), John Deweese (D.-N.C.), and Roderick Butler (R.-Tenn.) all were censured for selling appointments to the military academy.

Crédit Mobilier

The remaining financial-conflict cases grew out of the Crédit Mobilier scandal. In 1862, Congress chartered the Union Pacific Railroad, with a partial federal subsidy, to build a transcontinental railroad. To reduce the financial risk for shareholders, a separate corporation was formed to contract for the railroad's construction—Crédit Mobilier of America. The company made enormous profits in an arrangement that was only one step removed from the federal treasury.

What made the relationship a matter of legislative ethics was that Representative Oakes Ames (R.-Mass.) was a major shareholder of Crédit Mobilier. As early as 1868, Ames had been lending money to colleagues in Congress to help them buy Crédit Mobilier stock at par, which was about half the price of the current market value. By the time he was finished, Ames had distributed stock to at least fifteen House members, including several major committee chairmen; six senators; and Vice President Schuyler Colfax. Ames's purpose was straightforward: he wrote to one of his partners that he "used this [stock] where it will produce [the] most good to us."

The Crédit Mobilier story was broken in the newspapers during the election campaign of 1872. In the lame-duck session after the election, Congress decided to investigate the situation. A House committee recommended that Ames be expelled, but the full House rejected expulsion in favor of censure. It should be stressed that Ames was not censured for owning a stock that placed him in a potential conflict, but for actively attempting to bribe his colleagues.

In addition to Ames, three other members were brought before the House or Senate on formal charges. For Representative James Brooks (D.-N.Y.), as with Ames, a recommendation of expulsion was reduced to censure. In addition to buying the stock when offered, Brooks made efforts to buy more stock later and tried to hide what he was doing. Senator James Patterson (R.-N.H.) was brought before the Senate for expulsion but escaped punishment. Finally, House Speaker James G. Blaine (R.-Maine) was brought up for censure in 1876. He beat the censure charge, but he lost the 1876 presidential nomination because of the publicity. Blaine did finally become the Republican nominee in 1884, but lost a close race to Grover Cleveland in which the old scandal was still an issue.

Most other members who bought stock through Ames were not disciplined for buying it at below-market value. That created an interesting anomaly. Ames's offerings of below-market prices and loans were considered to be gifts that were akin to bribes. In contrast, accepting the same goods in the same transaction was not treated as the receipt of a gift or bribe.

The distinction between Congress's treatment of the givers and the receivers paralleled what George Washington Plunkitt of Tammany Hall, the New York political machine, playfully described as the one between honest and dishonest graft. Dishonest graft is theft or bribery. Plunkitt's example of honest graft was the city council member who took advantage of inside information—"I seen my opportunities and took 'em." What Crédit Mobilier shows is that Plunkitt's well-known distinction was not made up for the laughs. It came fairly close to the operational definition of what was acceptable—or at least what was not punishable—in the late nineteenth-century Congress.

Despite the considerable embarrassment caused by Crédit Mobilier, there was no attempt to codify what kinds of gifts were permissible, require disclosure, or define a conflict of interest. The brief Civil War flurry of codification thus was at an end. Congress decided to leave this arena to ad hoc judgments for the better part of the next century.

FROM CRÉDIT MOBILIER TO THE 1960S

In the ninety-five years between 1873 (Crédit Mobilier) and 1968 (Adam Clayton Powell and Thomas Dodd), the Congress voted only once to discipline a member for behavior that in any way related to conflicts of interest. In 1929, the Senate censured Hiram Bingham (R.-Conn.) for bringing the Senate into disrepute. Bingham had put a lobbyist on the Senate payroll. For that, he was criticized for taking an action that was "contrary to good morals and senatorial ethics." The resolution specifically stated, however, that Bingham's action's were "not the result of corrupt motives."

During the same period, there were numerous times when Congress did *not* discipline a sitting member, when the same facts today almost surely would have produced formal proceedings. Several examples from the House of Representatives were collected in a 1951 book by H. H. Wilson, *Congress: Corruption and Compromise.*

- *James McDermott (1913).* In the course of a broad select committee investigation of lobbying, McDermott (D.-Ill.) was found to have "borrowed" large sums from local businesses without any evidence of repayment or intention to repay. Moreover, the two lenders were found to have had legislative business pending before Congress. The select committee referred the case to the Judiciary Committee, which recommended condemnation, but not expulsion. McDermott resigned rather than face a decision, and then was reelected. After reelection, the House let the case die without a decision.

- *John Main Coffee (1943).* Coffee (D.-Wash.) was alleged to have received $2,500 from a local contractor after helping the contractor on a pending bid. Coffee claimed that he helped the contractor as he would any constituent and that the contribution was intended for his campaign, to retire campaign debts. The allegations were investigated by the Senate Special Committee Investigating the National Defense, presumably because the contract was for war matériel. It was interesting, however, that the investigating committee was from the Senate. No House committee took up the case. The Senate committee issued no report, but Coffee was defeated for reelection. (It is worth comparing this with the 1990–1991 case of the Keating Five, below.)

• *Andrew Jackson May (1946)*. May (D.-Ky.) found himself in a similar situation. He was found to have undertaken extraordinary efforts on behalf of one contractor. No payments from that contractor were discovered, but some members of the contractor's board of directors were directors of a company that May also owned. Once again, the only investigation was done by the Senate Special Committee Investigating the National Defense, which technically had no jurisdiction over May's personal conduct. Again, the committee issued no report and May was defeated for reelection.

• *James Michael Curley (1943–1947)*. Curley (D.-Mass.), who was also the long-time mayor of Boston (1914–1918, 1922–1928, 1930–1934, and 1946–1950), was indicted for mail fraud in 1943 and convicted three years later. "It is noteworthy," Wilson wrote, "that throughout [the] period, after his first indictment in September 1943, to the end of his second term in January 1947, there is no evidence that the subject was ever discussed in the House of Representatives" (p. 72) Nor did it seem to bother his constituents, who reelected him as mayor after Curley had served a five-month term in prison without giving up his office.

BOBBY BAKER AND THOMAS DODD: TWO UNWILLING CATALYSTS

In the two decades after Curley's conviction, eleven other members of the House were the subjects of criminal indictments. Five were convicted, one pleaded guilty, one pleaded no contest, three were acquitted, and one case was dismissed. Like Curley, however, none of the indicted members were disciplined by the House. Congress seemed to have settled into a pattern in which it equated formal discipline with criminal proceedings initiated by the executive. It left the last word on all other cases of legislative ethics to the voters. However, Congress did not require public disclosure of the information that might have made such a review by the voters meaningful.

Bobby Baker

Congress's hands-off attitude began to change with the 1963 investigation of Bobby Baker, who was Secretary of the Senate. After allegations that Baker was engaged in influence peddling, the full Senate asked its standing Committee on Rules and Administration to investigate. The committee concluded in 1964 and 1965 that Baker was guilty of "gross improprieties." Baker's personal fate was settled ultimately in the federal courts, where he was found guilty of income tax evasion and fraud. However, the Baker case also provoked a larger institutional response from the Senate.

There was some public pressure at the time for an investigation of senators alleged to have been implicated in Baker's affairs. However, the chairman of the Rules and Administration Committee opposed using his committee to review the conduct of senators. Instead, the committee recommended that the Senate establish a separate ethics committee and adopt a formal code of behavior. In 1964, the full Senate created a Select Committee on Standards and Conduct to draw up formal rules of conduct and to hear cases involving senators or their staffs.

Despite its formal action, the Senate clearly was not enthusiastic about the new committee's responsibilities. For most of 1965, the ethics committee had no members. The first organizational meeting was not held until the year was almost over. It was not long, however, before the committee was busy.

Thomas J. Dodd

On 24 January 1966, columnists Drew Pearson and Jack Anderson began a series of what were to be dozens of columns about Sen. Thomas J. Dodd (D.-Conn.). Armed with thousands of documents supplied by former Dodd staff members, the columns alleged (1) that Dodd had improperly accepted contributions from and done favors for a registered foreign lobbyist, Julius Klein; (2) that a great deal of the money Dodd raised at "campaign events" was spent for personal use; and (3) that he frequently double-billed the Senate for travel expenses that had already been paid for by others.

The steady publicity produced a major response. After two sets of hearings, the committee said that it lacked the necessary evidence to make a judgment about Klein, but recommended that the Senate censure Dodd for misusing campaign contributions and for double-billing his travel expenses. The full Senate rejected the double-billing charge, but voted 92–5 on 23 June 1967 to censure Dodd on the contributions charge. That was literally the first time the Senate had ever taken formal action against a senator for financial misconduct. After his censure, Dodd remained in the Senate until he was defeated for reelection in 1970.

ADAM CLAYTON POWELL

As the Dodd case was going into its final months, the House was reviewing the status of Representative Adam Clayton Powell (D.-N.Y.). Powell was elected to Congress in 1944 and for his entire congressional career was the second most senior African American member of the House. In 1961, he became chairman of the Committee on Education and Labor.

Powell's chairmanship was soon rocked by controversy. By September 1966, committee members, distressed by his use of the chairman's prerogatives and the committee's funds, voted to curb some of his powers. When Powell attacked one of the revolt's leaders as a racist, that member retaliated by asking the Committee on House Administration to investigate Powell's expenditures from committee funds.[12] On January 3, the House Administration Committee reported that Powell's wife was drawing a full-time salary from the Education and Labor Committee at the same time as she was living in Puerto Rico and apparently doing no work for the Congress. (Powell himself had lived in the Bahamas for two years to avoid being jailed in his congressional district for contempt of court in a different case.) Other irregularities included the use of assumed names for purchases charged to an official credit card, and

the use of official funds for domestic help and for the expenses of traveling companions.

When the new Congress convened on 10 January 1967, Powell was asked to step aside without taking the oath until a select committee, chaired by Judiciary Committee chairman Emanuel Celler (D.-N.Y.), reported back to the House. On 23 February, the committee recommended that Powell be censured.

The committee's report made some sort of punishment a foregone conclusion. The question was whether the House would censure Powell, as the committee had urged, or seek a harsher penalty. House Democrats had stripped him of his chairmanship before the start of the Congress and there was sentiment for expulsion or exclusion before the committee was even appointed. The select committee said that because Powell "possesses the requisite qualifications of age, citizenship, and inhabitancy . . . and holds a certificate of election," he should not be excluded. Nevertheless, the full House voted 202–222 against Celler on a key procedural question and then proceeded to exclude Powell on 1 March by a vote of 307–166.

Powell immediately filed a lawsuit claiming that Congress had overstepped its authority. The Court of Appeals rejected Powell's claim in February 1968. In November of that same year, Powell was reelected to Congress. Then on 16 June 1969, the Supreme Court reversed the Court of Appeals, deciding by a 7–1 margin in *Powell* v. *McCormack,* 395 U.S. 486, that the House could not exclude someone from membership who satisfied the constitutional requirements for office.[13] With the principle thus settled that Powell's membership in Congress would be left up to his constituents, the twenty-six-year veteran was defeated by Charles Rangel in the Democratic primary election of 1970.

FROM POWELL THROUGH WATERGATE

When Powell was excluded from the House in 1967, many commentators expressed the thought that the harshness of the punishment had something to do with the color of Powell's skin. Whether racial motives were directly important for most members—and they probably were not—their importance for the general public cannot be discounted. There was a lot of constituency opinion expressed about this case. Responding to pressure is normal enough in a legislative environment, but many of the members were uncomfortable with feeling such pressures in a situation in which they were expected to play quasi-judicial roles.

There can be no doubt that the lack of formal rules made the process even more vulnerable to public pressure than it otherwise would have been. Representative Andy Jacobs (D.-Ind.) a member of the select committee that heard Powell's case, subsequently wrote that he was disturbed during the proceedings that "no objective rules of procedure and hardly any substantive rules of conduct" existed (p. 100). By the end of the year, this point of view became widely shared. Powell, Dodd, and Baker thus put Congress at a crucial turning point. In 1967, the House followed the Senate's lead by establishing a bipartisan Committee on Standards of Official Conduct. Then, in 1968, both chambers adopted formal codes of conduct.

However, the codes the House and Senate did adopt in 1968 were short, vague, and relatively easy to evade.[14] Over time, even some of the codes' early supporters began to question what purpose they were serving. Between 1969 and 1975, neither chamber's ethics committee conducted formal investigations into any member's conduct. Over the same half-dozen years, six House members were convicted of crimes.

By the mid-1970s, however, the atmosphere became conducive to more stringent regulation. In 1974, Richard M. Nixon became the first president in American history to resign from office. He did so after the House Judiciary had recommended that the full House vote to impeach him for, among other things, obstructing justice by helping to cover up a burglary of the Democratic National Committee's headquarters at the Watergate office complex in Washington, D.C. The burglars were hired by employees of the president's 1972 reelection campaign committee and were paid by funds ultimately traceable to the Committee to Reelect the President. For obvious reasons, this activity—and other questionable activies paid out of reelection funds, as well as the means the committee's finance director used to raise many large contributions, in excess of $100,000, from corporate donors—heightened both the public's and the press's sensitivity toward ethics in government. Moreover, this new sensitivity came as members were altering the legislative process at a historically feverish pace. Committees and subcommittees, party leaders, the budget process, war powers, and the rules for financing presidential and congressional elections all underwent major changes during this period. Congress clearly was predisposed to think about institutional reform.

THE 1977 CODES

In 1976—two years after a presidential scandal produced campaign-finance reform—the House had its own scandals to investigate and, once again, scandal led directly to procedural change. In the first of the 1976 cases, Common Cause—a self-described public interest lobby that has played a key role in campaign finance and ethics regulation—filed an official complaint with the ethics committee alleging that Robert L. F. Sikes (D.-Fla.) used his office to benefit companies in which he held stock. The committee voted 10–2 to reprimand Sikes, and the House accepted that recommendation by a vote of 381–3. Later that year, Elizabeth Ray, an employee of the House Administration Committee, told the *Washington Post* that she had been put on the committee's payroll by its chairman, Wayne Hays (D.-Ohio), solely because she was Hays's mistress. The committee voted 11–0 on August 30 to hold public hearings, but Hays resigned from Congress the next day.

Koreagate

The case with the potential for causing the most damage, however, was the one that became known as "Koreagate." On 24 October 1976, the *Washington Post* reported that the Justice Department was investigating reports that members of Congress were receiving more than $500,000 per year in gifts and illegal contributions from Tongsun Park and other South Korean agents. As many as 115 members were named in one way or another in connection with the scandal, including House Democratic whip John McFall (D.-Calif.) and Majority Leader Thomas P. ("Tip") O'Neill (D.-Mass.).

McFall, Edward Roybal (D.-Calif.), and Charles H. Wilson (D.-Calif.) were reprimanded by the House in 1978. Richard T. Hanna (D.-Calif.) was indicted and pleaded guilty and Otto E. Passman (D.-La.) was indicted and acquitted. All other members were cleared by the House and Senate ethics committees, including O'Neill, whose own connection to the scandal was tangential. However, the fact that the House's and Senate's reputations were under a cloud at this precise moment had important institutional consequences.

In late 1976, the quadrennial Commission on Executive, Legislative, and Judicial Salaries proposed that pay increases for Congress should be granted only if Congress were to adopt stricter codes of ethics, including a limit on outside income and gifts. By proposing such a limit, the commission was saying that Congress had become a full-time job and should therefore be a member's main source of income. These recommendations were endorsed by outgoing President Gerald R. Ford and President-elect Jimmy Carter.

When the new Congress convened on 3 January 1977, both chambers had new leaders. O'Neill was the new Speaker of the House and Robert C. Byrd (D.-W. Va.) was the new majority leader of the Senate. Management of the pay raise was going to be their first major leadership test. The new leaders turned the potential risks into benefits by using the members' desire for a pay raise, and their concern for the bad press Congress was getting, into support for new ethics codes.

The Obey Commission

O'Neill took the first step. Late in 1976, the House had appointed a Commission on Administrative Review chaired by David Obey (D.-Wis.). The main work of the commission was to continue the process of institutional reform that had begun in 1969. However, Koreagate and the pay raise changed the priorities. Bypassing the Committee on Standards of Official Conduct, O'Neill asked the commission to recommend a new ethics code as soon as possible, before moving to other subjects.

The Obey commission proposed a new code on 7 February, the House adopted it on 2 March, and the Senate passed a parallel code, with modifications, on 1 April. The new rules significantly strengthened the requirements for disclosing a member's and spouse's financial interests; limited honoraria and other earned income to 15 percent of a member's salary; and abolished office accounts funded by private contributions. Together with the campaign finance law, the new rules substantially reduced the avenues through which interested parties legally could give hidden money to benefit members of Congress. The disclosure provisions were codified in law and extended to upper-level executive branch employees in the 1978 Ethics in Government Act.

However, the 1977 honorarium limit proved to be only one middle point in a long and continuing battle. From 1974 through the 1980s, honorarium limits went up and down on a seesaw. Finally, in 1989, as part of a protracted fight over a pay raise, the House decided to raise its members' salaries from $89,500 to approximately $125,000 in 1991 and then let salaries keep pace with the cost of living. In return for the salary increase, the House prohibited all honoraria and limited other outside earned income to a total of 15 percent of the member's salary. For a House member who had been earning the maximum in honoraria, net income stayed constant. However, the public now would foot the whole bill, thus reducing potential conflicts of interest.

The Senate refused to take this step in 1989, deciding instead to take a smaller raise in pay and to give up only part of their honoraria. Then on 17 July 1991, the Senate added an amendment to the Legislative Branch Appropriations Act that raised Senate salaries to the same as the House's, in return for an immediate ban on honoraria. Despite the pay raise, however, the average senator's income would remain about the same. The new Senate salary of $125,100 was to be only $132 higher than the old salary ($101,900) plus the now defunct honorarium allowance ($23,068). As with the House, therefore, the fundamental effect would be to reduce conflicts of interest and not to increase income.

THE 1980s AND 1990s

After the ethics codes were approved in 1977 and the Ethics in Government Act was passed in 1978, there was an explosion of detailed interpretative regulations and advisory opinions issued by the two ethics committees. There also was a historically unprecedented flow of disciplinary proceedings. Some raised familiar issues; others focused on behavior that previously would have been overlooked. Most of these cases were identified earlier. A few raise questions that deserve to be singled out.

Abscam

In 1980 and 1981, six House members and one Senator[15] were convicted of accepting bribes after being caught in a Federal Bureau of Investigation sting operation known as *Abscam*. (An FBI agent, posing as an Arab sheik, offered each of the members bribes and videotaped the proceedings.) Carefully conducted sting operations are legitimate law enforcement tools, distinguishable from entrapment. However, executive agencies have to be sensitive as to the potential charges of partisan or other political motivations that could be raised if investigators appear to be on a fishing expedition. (Similar sting operations in the late 1980s targeted state legislators in California, Arizona, and South Carolina.)

Sexual Conduct

Seven other cases during the 1980s involved sexual conduct. In no case was a member disciplined simply for sexual activity. All seven either had been indicted, or else were engaged in, activities that involved the member's official duties.[16] However, none of the seven violated explicit regulations. Instead, they were all charged with having violated the first clause of the House's code of conduct: "A Member, officer, or employee of the House of Representatives shall conduct himself at all times in a manner which shall reflect creditably on the House of Representatives."

The use of this provision points out that no matter how detailed its regulations, Congress continues to feel the need for a broad catch-all provision that can be used to address its major concern in all ethics cases—preserving its institutional reputation. It should be noted, however, that codes based on honor and reputation are inherently subject to change. What is frowned upon today may be accepted tomorrow. Ironically, the press—and through it, the public—seemed to take greater notice of the personal conduct of public officials at roughly the same time as the public's own private standards seemed to become more permissive.

Speaker Jim Wright

On 6 June 1989, Jim Wright (D.-Tex.) became the first Speaker of the House ever to resign from Congress under a cloud. After a year of investigation, the House ethics committee found "reason to believe" that Wright had violated the House's rules in sixty-nine instances. A finding of "reason to believe" is the House's equivalent of an indictment. Wright's resignation stopped the proceedings after the first formal step.

The sixty-nine counts actually boiled down to two broad areas of concern: a book deal and a business partnership. Wright received 55 percent of the retail price as the author's royalties for his book, *Reflections of a Public Man*. (Normal royalties are 10 to 15 percent.) The committee report named seven occasions on which Wright made speeches to an organization and the organization purchased large numbers of copies of the book in lieu of an honorarium. The rules specifically exempt royalties from the definition of "earned income." However, the arrangement looked to committee members more like disguised honoraria than legitimate royalties.

In 1980, Wright and his wife formed a partnership, Mallightco, Inc., with a long time friend from Fort Worth, developer George Mallick, and Mallick's wife. The committee found three different ways in which Mallick, or Mallightco, made gifts to the Wrights: the Mallicks made apartments available to the Wrights free of cost from 1979–1984 and at reduced cost from 1985–1988; Mallightco paid Mrs. Wright a salary of $18,000 per year for four years (1981–1984), but the committee was not able to identify services performed by Mrs. Wright in return for the money; and Mallightco also gave the Wrights free use of a four-year-old Cadillac automobile from 1983 through 1988.

The committee's report raises important issues that go beyond the facts of Wright's specific case. It has always been permissible for members to receive gifts from friends, as long as the gifts are reported and the friends have no *direct* interest in legislation. However, the committee described Mallick as "an individual the Committee has reason to believe had a direct interest in legislation." Despite this, the facts suggest that Mallick's interests were not specific to him or his company. Thus, the committee implicitly seems to have expanded the definition of "direct interest" to include interests one has as a member of a class. That represented a break—with potentially far-reaching implications—from the narrower 1874 interpretation Congress put on this phrase taken from Jefferson's 1801 Manual (see above).

The Keating Five

The case of the so-called Keating Five was one in which there was no doubt about Keating's direct interest. Charles H. Keating, Jr., was the chairman and controlling shareholder of American Continental Corporation (ACC), a land development company chartered in Ohio and based in Phoenix, Arizona. ACC, in turn, owned the Lincoln Savings and Loan Association, which was based in California. (Lincoln eventually collapsed in the savings and loan crisis of 1989.) Keating, his associates, and his friends also were substantial contributors to the campaigns of several United States senators. Moreover, Keating consistently seems to have asked the recipients of his contributions to support legislation, oppose regulations, or pressure regulators in ways designed to benefit his companies specifically and directly.

The difficult part of the Keating case was to interpret the behavior of the five senators investigated: Alan Cranston (D.-Calif.), who was the majority whip; Dennis DeConcini (D.-Ariz.); John McCain (R.-Ariz.); John Glenn (D.-Ohio); and Donald Riegle (D.-Mich.), chairman of the Committee on Banking, Housing, and Urban Affairs. All five senators represented states in which Keating's companies had a substantial economic presence. All of them said that Keating's contributions were irrelevant to their actions, insisting that whatever efforts they undertook were because of his companies' importance to the economies of their states.

After a fourteen-month investigation, the Senate Ethics Committee on 27 February 1991 divided its recommendations into three groups. Proceeding from less to more severe, they were as follows:

1. McCain and Glenn were said to have exercised poor judgment, but essentially were cleared.

2. For Riegle and DeConcini, the committee used almost identical language: "While the Committee concludes that Senator [Riegle/DeConcini] has violated no law of the United States or specific Rule of the United States Senate, it emphasizes that it does not condone his conduct. The Committee has concluded that the totality of the evidence shows that Senator [Riegle's/DeConcini's] conduct gave *the appearance of being improper* and was certainly attended with insensitivity and poor judgment. The Committee concludes that no further action is warranted with respect to Senator [Riegle/DeConcini]."

3. Finally, the committee concluded that there is "substantial credible evidence" to conclude that Senator Cranston engaged in "an impermissible pattern of conduct in which fund raising and official activities were substantially linked." The committee therefore urged that the process move forward to the next stage.

The report triggered months of negotiations between the committee and Cranston. Cranston, who was being treated for prostate cancer and had already announced that he would not seek reelection in 1992, was determined to defend his reputation. While some committee members were inclined toward a compromise, others wanted the full Senate to issue a formal, public censure of Cranston's behavior, complete with a roll-call vote. In the end, the committee and Cranston agreed to have an official committee "reprimand" read on the Senate floor with all senators present, but without a roll-call vote or other formal action. As part of the agreement, senators agreed not to engage in a full debate of the issue. As a result, when Cranston himself took the floor, after the reprimand, to say that he was unfairly singled out, and that his "behavior did not violate established norms," no one replied formally to his assertions. One senator critical of the compromise later told reporters that "the committee whitewashed him and he tarred us." But the committee's vice-chairman, Warren Rudman (R.-N.H.)—also speaking to reporters—defended the result by pointing to the strong condemnation contained in the reprimand as well as to Cranston's "horrible physical condition" (*Congressional Quarterly Weekly Report,* 23 November 1991, p. 3433).

In addition to the novel sanction levied against Cranston, the committee's report on the Keating Five case broke new ground in at least two other respects. First, the official finding of an impermissible linkage between any member's fundraising and his or her official activities was unprecedented. Second, and at least as far-reaching, was the committee's controversial use of an "appearance" standard for Senators Riegle and DeConcini. Appearance standards are familiar parts of the canons used by bar associations, but they are new to Congress. The strength of such a standard lies in its flexibility; however, that is also its major weakness: what appears unethical may depend as much on the observer, and the surrounding publicity, as it does on the underlying action. In that respect, the standard shares some features with the more traditional requirement that House members and senators must not bring their institutions into disrepute. Both are more akin to common law than statute law. In its language the "appearance of a conflict" standard seems to put more emphasis on the way actions look, while the traditional rule's phrasing stresses the importance of actions actually taken to bring Congress into disrepute.

CONCLUSION

There has been a persistent relationship between scandal and reform since a contract fraud led to the statute of 1853. More recently, investigations involving Bobby Baker, Thomas Dodd, and Adam Clayton Powell led to the first ethics committees. The existence of the ethics committees created new institutional levers for hearing cases that broke in the mid-1970s. When some of those cases touched the House leadership, the leadership pushed for tougher codes in the late 1970s. The new codes meant more new cases. And then, in the late 1980s, new cases once again touched the leadership—this time leading to the resignation of a Speaker of the House, the resignation of a House majority whip, and the formal reprimand of a Senate majority whip.

In the wake of Speaker Wright's resigna-

tion, the House adopted still more formal regulations in 1989. As in 1977, reforming the code was linked to a pay raise. In addition to the pay-raise and honoraria limits mentioned earlier, the new rules for the first time applied one-year, post-employment lobbying restrictions to members of Congress and their staffs. Meanwhile, the Senate's first reactions to the Keating Five case included Senate passage of a (subsequently vetoed) campaign finance bill and the appointment of a committee to recommend guidelines for constituency service.

Legislative ethics is an evolving subject. That new cases will arise is merely a truism of human nature. What is more interesting is that the standards themselves seem to be changing.

APPENDIX: STATE LEGISLATIVE ETHICS

There have been several allusions during this essay to ethics and ethics codes in state legislative arenas. Unfortunately, we cannot present a thorough summary of legislative ethics at the state level until new primary source research is done. We can say, however, that we see some of the same kinds of provisions being enacted since the 1970s in some states as we do at the federal level. For example, at least thirty-three states required some form of personal financial disclosure for legislators in 1990. In addition, twenty-eight of the fifty states have statutes (and at least four additional state legislatures have rules) that (a) urge legislators not to accept an economic benefit that is designed to influence a vote, and/or (b) require legislators to abstain from voting or disclose their potential conflicts when they stand to gain a direct economic benefit, and/or (c) prohibit all public officers from using their positions to gain special privilege or financial advantage.

However, as even this cursory summary makes clear, there is also a great deal of variation from state to state. For example, when the New York State Senate asked its own research service to describe the law in the fifty states on one specific point—the use of legislative staff for campaign purposes—the resulting report filled 203 pages. And it took more than forty law review pages with 152 lengthy footnotes to lay out some of the rules for lawyers who serve in the fifty state legislatures.

Both the commonality across states, and the variation, are to be expected. One reason we see similar statutes in different states is simply that legislators and their staffs ask each other for ideas. Another is the old phenomenon of the solution in search of a problem. Two of the three states experiencing sting operations in the early 1990s were Arizona and South Carolina. In the May/June 1991 issue of *Common Cause Magazine,* the organization's Arizona director said that as scandals unravel, "many in the political arena will turn to [Common Cause] for models and solutions.... It's important to have a legislative agenda outlined ahead of time." And the South Carolina director said: "You have to hit right away and be creative in linking your issues to the cause of the sting."

The persistence of variation comes from more deep-seated sources. Some of these are cultural; others grow out of the structure of political power within a party caucus, or across institutional branches. One difference is very basic, however: only a few state legislatures are full-time, year-round operations. As long as legislators are expected to have nonlegislative sources of income, many of the congressional responses to financial conflicts would not be appropriate or even workable.

NOTES

1. The expelled member was Michael "Ozzie" Myers (D.-Pa.), 1980. Members who resigned under a clear threat of expulsion included Representative John W. Jenrette, Jr. (D.-S.C.), 1980; Representative Raymond Lederer (D.-Pa.), 1981; Senator Harrison Williams (D.-N.J.), 1982; Representative Mario Biaggi (D.-N.Y.), 1988; Representative Robert Garcia (D.-N.Y.), 1990; and Representative Donald Lukens (R.-Ohio), 1990.

2. Charles Diggs (D.-Mich.), 1979; Charles Wilson (D.-Calif.), 1980; Gerry Studds (D.-Mass.) and Daniel Crane (R.-Ind.), 1983.

3. Herman Talmadge (D.-Ga.), in 1979; and David Durenberger (R.-Minn.) in 1990.

4. Robert L.F. Sikes (D.-Fla.), in 1976; John McFall (D.-Calif.), Charles Wilson (D.-Calif.), and Edward Roybal (D.-Calif.) in 1978; George Hansen (R.-Idaho) in 1984; Austin Murphy (D.-Pa.) in 1987; and Barney Frank (D.-Mass.) in 1990.

5. Representative Jim Bates (D.-Calif.) was reproved for sexual harassment in 1989 and defeated for reelection in 1990.

6. Wayne Hays (D.-Ohio) in 1976; Daniel Flood (D.-Pa.) in 1979; Fred Richmond (D.-N.Y.) in 1982; Speaker Jim Wright (D.-Tex.) and Majority Whip Tony Coelho (D.-Calif.) in 1989.

7. Timothy Pickering (Fed.-Mass), in 1811; Benjamin Tappan (D.-Ohio), 1844; John L. McLaurin (D.-S.C.), 1902; Benjamin R. Tillman (D.-S.C.), 1902; Hiram Bingham (R.-Conn.), 1929; Joseph R. McCarthy (R.-Wisc.), 1954; and Thomas J. Dodd (D.-Conn.), 1967. Bingham and McCarthy officially were "condemned," but the judgments are generally considered to have been equivalent to censures.

8. William Stanbery (D.-Ohio), 1832; Joshua R. Giddings (Whig-Ohio), 1842; Laurance M. Keitt (D.-S.C.), 1856; Alexander Long (D.-Ohio), 1864; Benjamin G. Harris (D.-Md.), 1864; John Chanler (D.-N.Y.), 1866; Lovell H. Rousseau (R.-Ky.), 1866; John W. Hunter (Ind.-N.Y.), 1867;

Fernando Wood (D.-N.Y.), 1868; E. D. Holbrook (D.-Idaho), 1868; Benjamin F. Whittemore (R.-S.C.), 1870; Roderick R. Butler (R.-Tenn.), 1870; John T. Deweese (D.-N.C.), 1870; Oakes Ames (R.-Mass.), 1873; James Brooks (D.-N.Y.), 1873; John Y. Brown (D.-Ky.), 1875; William D. Bynum (D.-Ind.), 1890; and Thomas L. Blanton (D.-Tex.), 1921.

9. Pickering, Tappan, McLaurin, Tillman, and McCarthy.

10. Stanbery, Keitt, Chanler, Rousseau, Hunter, Wood, Holbrook, Brown, and Bynum.

11. Whittemore, Butler, Deweese, Ames, and Brooks. Whittemore's censure preceded his resignation, reelection, and exclusion (mentioned above).

12. The member was Sam Gibbons (D.-Fla.), who was one of the few Southerners to support the Civil Rights Act of 1964, at considerable political risk.

13. No one questioned the House's legal authority to *expel* Powell with a two-thirds vote after admitting him. However, *exclusion* raises different legal issues from expulsion. Each chamber has the absolute authority to *expel* a member for any reason by a two-thirds vote. In contrast, *exclusion* before swearing in requires only a simple majority. Therefore, it makes sense for the grounds to be limited. Interestingly, almost three-quarters voted yes on exclusion—more than enough for expulsion.

14. Both chambers (a) required limited financial disclosure, with additional financial information to be placed in a sealed file and (b) specified the purposes for which campaign contributions might be spent. The House also prohibited members from using their official positions improperly to receive compensation, prohibited the acceptance of gifts from groups or individuals with a direct interest in legislation, and prohibited honorariums beyond "the usual and customary value" for speeches and articles. The Senate's code was less detailed than the House's—as it has been after every subsequent revision.

15. Representatives John W. Jenrette, Jr. (D.-S.C.), Richard

Kelly (R.-Fla.), Raymond Lederer (D.-Pa.), John Murphy (D.-N.Y.), Michael Myers (D.-Pa.), and Frank Thompson (D.-N.J.); Senator Harrison Williams (D.-N.J.).

16. The three members indicted were as follows: Robert Bauman's (R.-Md.) 1980 indictment for solicitation was dropped after he agreed to seek alcohol treatment. Jon Hinson (R.-Miss.), was arrested in 1981 in a men's room in the U.S. Capitol. He pleaded no contest and resigned from the House. Donald Lukens (R.-Ohio) was indicted in February 1989 and convicted in May 1989 for having had sex in November with a minor. Neither Bauman or Hinson was a subject of formal House action for their behavior. (The disposition of Lukens's case is described below.)

The four whose cases did not involve indictments were as follows: Gerry Studds (D.-Mass.) was censured in 1983 for soliciting and engaging in sex with a male congressional page. Daniel Crane (R.-Ill.) was also censured in 1983 for soliciting and engaging in sex with a female congressional page. Barney Frank (D.-Mass.) was reprimanded in 1990 for using his office improperly to help a male prostitute with whom he had a relationship. Jim Bates (D.-Calif.) received a letter of reproval from the ethics committee in 1990 for harassing female employees.

Of the above seven: Hinson resigned and the others sought reelection. Bauman, Crane, and Bates were defeated for reelection; Studds and Frank were reelected. Lukens's fate involved both an election defeat and resignation. He was defeated for reelection in a May 1990 primary. Meanwhile, the ethics committee was still officially considering imposing formal sanctions as a result of the offense that had led to Lukens's conviction, when the committee received a second complaint against him on 17 October 1990. Lukens resigned from Congress on 24 October, the day he was scheduled to testify before the committee about the second allegation. This resignation occurred after his election defeat, but before his term had expired.

BIBLIOGRAPHY

History

As is often the case in congressional studies, *Congressional Quarterly* is a good place to start for an overview of the history of ethics cases and codes in Congress. Particularly useful are *CQ's Guide to Congress,* 4th ed. (Washington, 1991) and the annual *Congressional Quarterly Almanac.*

More-detailed, original scholarship may be found in RICHARD ALLAN BAKER, "The History of Congressional Ethics," in BRUCE JENNINGS and DANIEL CALLAHAN, eds., *Representation and Responsibility: Exploring Legislative Ethics,* The Hastings Center Series in Ethics (New York, 1985), as well as in virtually the entire collection edited by ABRAHAM S. EISENSTADT, ARI HOOGENBOOM, and HANS L. TREFOUSSE, *Before Watergate: Problems of Corruption in American Society,* Studies on Society in Change no. 4 (Brooklyn, 1978). Of particular interest in that volume are HOOGENBOOM's "Did Gilded Age Scandals Bring Reform?"; MORTON KELLER's "Corruption in America: Continuity and Change"; and JEROME L. STERNSTEIN's "The Problem of Corruption in the Gilded Age: The Case of Nelson W. Aldrich and the Sugar Trust."

MICHAEL J. MALBIN, "Congress During the Convention and Ratification," in LEONARD W. LEVY and DENNIS J. MAHONEY, eds., *The Framing and Ratification of the Constitution* (New York, 1987), contains an analysis of the Federalist understanding of the relationship between self-interest, institutional incentives, and the public good. JOHN T. NOONAN, JR., *Bribes* (New York, 1984), is a massive cross-cultural history that begins with Hammurabi and has a useful chapter on Crédit Mobilier. ROBERT N. ROBERTS, *White House Ethics: The History of the Politics of Conflict of Interest Regulation,* Contributions in Political Science no. 204 (New York, 1988), focuses on the executive branch, but has a good chapter on the Civil War conflict-of-interest statutes. WILLIAM RIORDAN, *Plunkitt of Tammany Hall* (New York, 1963), is a classic, turn-of-the-century rendering of Riordan's interviews of Plunkitt.

For the period leading up to the major changes of 1968 see PAUL DOUGLAS's *Ethics in Government* (Cambridge, Mass., 1953), which was written by a senator who influenced colleagues by his example. ROBERT S. GETZ, *Congressional Ethics: The Conflict of Interest Issue* (Princeton, N.J., 1966), gives a picture of the rules immediately before the Dodd and Powell cases. H. H. WILSON, *Congress: Corruption and Compromise* (New York, 1951), does a similar job for the 1920s through 1940s.

Important Cases

There are at least three valuable treatments of

the Adam Clayton Powell case. P. A. DIONISO-POULOS, *Rebellion, Racism, and Representation: The Adam Clayton Powell Case and Its Antecedents* (De Kalb, Ill., 1970), is good on legal issues. ANDY JACOBS, *The Powell Affair: Freedom Minus One* (Indianapolis, 1973), is a fascinating account by a member of the select investigating committee. KENT M. WEEKS, *Adam Clayton Powell and the Supreme Court* (New York, 1971), is sympathetic to Powell without papering over his actions.

For other important cases, JOHN M. BARRY, *The Ambition and the Power* (New York, 1989), is a sympathetic, but full portrait of Jim Wright's speakership by a journalist who spent a year in Wright's office. JAMES BOYD, *Above the Law* (New York, 1968), was written by the staff person who was responsible for exposing Dodd by getting documents from Dodd's office to Drew Pearson and Jack Anderson. PEARSON and ANDERSON's own *The Case Against Congress: A Compelling Indictment of Corruption on Capitol Hill* (New York, 1968), is an impassioned book with a chapter on the same case.

State Legislative Ethics

SUSAN BIEMESDERFER, "Making Laws, Breaking Laws," *State Legislatures* 17 (April 1991): 12–18, describes sting operations involving state legislators. GEORGE F. CARPINELLO, "Should Practicing Lawyers Be Legislators?" *Hastings Law Journal* 41 (1989): 87–129, is a carefully researched piece of scholarship. The COUNCIL ON GOVERNMENTAL ETHICS LAWS (COGEL) is a part of the Council of State Governments. Its *COGEL Blue Book: Campaign Finance, Ethics and Lobby Law,* 8th ed. (Lexington, Ky., 1990), is sketchy, but the only compendium in print. Also valuable are PATRICK J. DELLAY, "Curbing Influence Peddling in Albany: The 1987 Ethics in Government Act," *Brooklyn Law Review* 53 (1988): 1051–1085; KARL T. KURTZ, "The Changing State Legislatures (Lobbyists Beware)," in the PUBLIC AFFAIRS COUNCIL's *Leveraging State Government Relations* (Washington, D.C., 1990); MARK W. LAWRENCE, "Legislative Ethics: Improper Influence by a Lawmaker on an Administrative Agency," *Maine Law Review* 42 (1990): 423–452; NEW YORK STATE SENATE RESEARCH SERVICE, *Political Campaign Activity—The Use of Legislative Staff and Resources* (Albany, N.Y., 1988); and ROBERT REEVES, "Legislators as Private Attorneys: The Need for Legislative Reform," *UCLA Law Review* 30 (1983): 1052–1077. AMY YOUNG's brief column, "In The States," *Common Cause Magazine* 17 (May/June 1991): 41, is the source of quotations from Common Cause state offices.

MEASURING LEGISLATIVE BEHAVIOR

Aage R. Clausen

The measurement of legislative behavior is of a piece with the measurement of all social behavior. Measurement is one of the most important tools available to the scholar for inquiry, whether the discipline be social science, history, geography, anthropology, economics, political science, or humanism.

The humanists may initially, perhaps persistently, reject the key role of the measurement tool. The rejection is often due to connotations of counting, quantification, and statistics. These procedures may be viewed as productive of statistical summaries that do not further an understanding of the rich texture of human personality and social context.

To the extent that these criticisms are valid, and sometimes they are, measurement has not been properly conducted and its results appropriately interpreted. Yet if students of social and human behavior do not engage in measurement, or fail to realize that it is one of their tools, they also miss the mark.

The premise of this essay is that an understanding of human and social behavior requires *observation*; it cannot be achieved by the thoughtful hermit in the isolated mountain cabin. Once that premise has been accepted, measurement cannot be avoided, because it is inherent in observation. The measurement operation may not be explicated, as when the biographer portrays the subject, but measurement is taking place. The subject is being placed on a continuum as to any number of qualities and properties—intelligence, compassion, courage, skills, wealth, nationality, social status, political proclivities—and these continuums could not exist if variation among other human beings had not been observed. Day has no meaning without night. Just because a specific number has not been assigned to the subject's position on any of these continuums does not mean that measurement has not taken place.

This is perhaps too broad a definition of measurement for some. A narrower definition would be one that accepts only those observations that can be numerically ordered and statistically manipulated. One could perhaps distinguish between observations that lead to impressions and those that allow for precise quantification.

Indeed, there is a strong temptation in the observation of human and social behavior to rely on impressions and eschew the difficult demands of measurement. These demands include the following: (1) defining the concept or property (e.g., social class) to be measured and securing the agreement of colleagues; (2) devising a procedure for measurement of that concept or property that can be replicated by others or be repeated by a single researcher with exactly the same results; (3) deciding on the proper level of classification precision, varying from broad groupings to assignments of numerical magnitude to individuals; and (4) obtaining access to the subject, one of the difficulties that probably frustrates most the efforts of the scholar of human and social behavior.

These measurement difficulties will continue to present themselves as we study legislative behavior, with a focus on the large variety of methods used in the observation-measurement of it. Our review of the variety of measurement attempts will utilize the broad definition of measurement, which allows for the consideration of the large variety of observational techniques, maximizing the potential for understanding legislative behavior. This potential motivates the author of this essay as it must have motivated the editors' commission of it.

INTRODUCTION

The variety of measurement techniques used in the study of legislative behavior is exemplified by the major areas of active research. These include the patterns of collective behavior that denote the legislature as an institution with a separable identity and particular functions in the political system. These patterns of collective behavior are complex, changing, and generally a very strong challenge to measurement.

Within the context of the institutional arrangements, legislative scholarship has ranged from analysis of member characteristics and career patterns to the role of the legislative institution in its oversight of the bureaucracy. Between the member and the institution resides the legislative committee, whose great influence and centrality in the legislative process, particularly in the U.S. Congress, has invited intensive and extensive research. Here measurement is challenged by the difficulty of determining influence (the observation of attitudinal or behavioral changes in A that can be attributed to the actions of B), a difficulty widely shared in studies of human behavior. Also, systematic observation of the complex interrelationships of member, committee, institution, and external agents is frustrated by the difficulties of obtaining access to the relevant actors.

Focusing on individual members in the legislative setting, and taking into account their needs to serve constituents, obtain reelection, and achieve influence within the legislature, researchers have pursued the elusive systematic observation of the norms governing member behavior, the roles members assume, and the objectives and goals that motivate them. Researchers have attempted to map the topology of the patterns of individual decisions, particularly at the roll-call stage, and sought to understand the subterranean forces productive of this topology, the mix of constituency interests, interest-group pressures, partisan loyalties, personal attitudes, and interinstitutional relationships with the bureaucracy, the executive, and sometimes even the courts.

As this broad overview of research topics indicates, measurement as systematic observation is an inescapable component of legislative research. It is essential to recognize that careful measurement is not possible without the development of abstract representations of these very complex real-world phenomena. Measurement both requires and facilitates this abstraction. For example, the behavior of legislators in their interactions with one another and with their environment is initially represented by such abstract concepts as roles, representation, norms, ideology, legislative effectiveness, and committee influence. As we try to make sense of behavior by categorizing and naming, however, it is the relationships among the measurements of these concepts that demonstrate the linkage between these abstractions. These linkages are the stuff of the generalizations made from bits and pieces of factual observation that are needed to achieve communicable understanding, possibly even reaching the heights of theory.

Although the valid measurement of concepts is essential in moving from observations of, to generalization about, human behavior, the validity is always in question: does the measurement truly correspond to the concept, for example, IQ versus intelligence?

The correspondence of measurement and concept in legislative behavior research is more often than not a marriage of convenience. Measurement is performed in an ad hoc fashion, tailored to the immediate research context, and draws upon methods fashioned in a variety of settings of which the legislative is but one.

This is consistent with the characteristics of legislative research. It is variegated, as are the phenomena encompassed by any given subdiscipline. Limited success has attended efforts to define the research mission clearly and delineate priorities. Lacking is agreement on a limited range of concepts, and for individual concepts there is variation in measurements. In the field of legislative research, no methodology of observation and analysis has been developed; an organized, coherent set of rules, principles, and applications of measurement of legislative behavior does not exist.

This apparent indictment is softened by a recognition of the difficulty of the task and of its applicability to numerous fields of study in the humanities and social sciences. While our failures of measurement are in part our own, they are also in the nature of the phenomena under study: human beings in a social context. The object of study is normally not subject to the manipulation, control, and experimental isolation available to studies of lower forms of life and physical phenomena. Also keenly felt is the difficulty of assuring the replicability of observations given the constant of change. Thus, while physical processes are repeated in both time and space, legislative institutions, personnel, and processes change by whim and by design across space and through time.

Given the diversity of the legislative field and the lack of attention to coordinated conceptualization and measurement, the motivation of this review is to provide a sampler of legislative measurement. This is not a treatise on methodology or technique but a review of a large variety of measurement applications. While this review places the measurements in their substantive contexts, given our commitment to encompass the variety, we can seldom indulge the urge to discuss or illustrate *specific* substantive research applications. We review what researchers have tried to measure, and indicate how they have tried to do it, at varying levels of specificity. From this work the reader unfamiliar with legislative research can obtain a quick reading on measurement activities in areas of legislative research. Perhaps even legislative scholars may be made more aware of the measurement prowess of their peers.

We have selected measurement techniques for review in terms of conceptual importance, innovativeness, inherent interest, utility, potential, and usage. Our attention to various measurements is roughly approximated as a parabolic function of the related properties of complexity and difficulty: attention to easy or simple measurements is low, it increases as difficulty and complexity increases, but then diminishes as complexity and difficulty requires an immersion in methodological considerations beyond the depth that can be sustained by this essay. Thus, the party affiliation of a legislator, although theoretically important, receives no attention here because its measurement is straightforward. Measurements of a member's legislative effectiveness are less straightforward, involving multiple indicators, but their methodology is quite comprehensible. Toward the extreme of complexity and difficulty we encounter such concepts as the power of a member or a committee or the location of legislators in a multidimensional policy space, and so the attention paid in this essay diminishes.

Some Characteristics of Measurement

Measurement can vary from the nominal level of categorical, nonordered classifications to the ratio level, in which absolute magnitudes and absolute zero are recorded. For example, it may vary from merely classifying legislators ideologically as conservative or liberal, to ordering them using relative degrees of liberalness or conservativeness and filling in the continuum with moderates, and even to quantifying the relative distances between legislators along the liberal/conservative continuum.

However, the ratio scale, with its recording of absolute magnitudes, is usually beyond our capacity or lacking in substantive value. For example, one can count the number of times a legislator is successful in getting legislation adopted and thereby satisfy the statistical requirements for a ratio scale. However, this is little beyond a naked enumeration. There it stands, shivering and quaking in anticipation of the cold blast from a gleeful critic of quantitative and statistical techniques who launches the well-worn aphorism that "if you can count it, it doesn't count." To achieve significance this count needs to be clothed in the raiments of reason, justification, and measurement methodology, all interwoven with the threads of experience and good sense.

Indeed, in the practice of social-science measurement the attention to experience and good sense is clearly appropriate, because we rely on them as supplements to replicable measurements and substitutes for controlled testing. Thus, an aspect of the changing scenes of legislative behavior is commonly studied but once, less commonly revisited a number of times, and never subject to the relentless repetition of measurement and analysis found in the physical sciences and some other social sciences.

Given the fleeting opportunity for observation and the limited opportunity for replication, what is left but experience, good sense, and the rare flash of insight that borrows from the former and surprises the latter?

Our measurement review is organized in four segments, beginning with the measurement of the legislature as an institution of standing in the polity. An important cog in the institutional machinery is the committee; measurement relating to its function is the second topic. The focus then shifts to the more intangible norms, roles, objectives, and goals that govern and motivate the behavior of the individual legislators; these also lubricate the legislative machinery and diminish the damage of friction. The last stage in the legislative process, voting on the floor, is not least in this review, both because it is the subject of much measurement activity and because it applies the last formative stamp on the legislative product.

THE LEGISLATIVE INSTITUTION

Discussion of the measurement of the legislature as an institution begins with the concept of institutionalization, defined and elaborated below. At the level of individual members, we consider research on their social characteristics, legislative careers, and activities. Our review returns to the institutional level, considering research efforts to understand the relationship between the legislature and the bureaucracy in terms of legislative oversight.

There are difficult measurement problems in the study of institutionalization and in the research on legislative oversight. Thus, at a very early stage we exemplify both the difficulties of measurement and our unwillingness to restrict unduly our review of measurement to those phenomena most amenable to systematic observation.

Institutionalization

The central concern of the study of institutionalization is the degree to which an institution has an independent power position. For example, is the legislature really more than a rubber stamp for the executive, do its members have a degree of legislative independence from their political parties, is their influence within the legislature accorded them by the institution rather than by outside forces, and is their support of and pride in their institution marked by a desire for reelection and a professionalization of performance?

Principal ingredients of the definition of institutionalization are regular patterns of behavior of an institution's members; autonomy in its relationships to other elements of the social, political, and economic system; and a recognition of its boundaries. However, the concept of institutionalization is much more complex than can be summarized so briefly.

We expand on this definition by considering several of its facets.

One facet of institutionalization is the degree of professionalism. Measures of professionalization include level of staffing, capacity to generate information independently, existence of bill-drafting services, remuneration, days in session, legislative work load, and legislators' self concepts as full-time legislators. While this measurement has been used principally on state legislatures, it is reasonable to assume that Congress is the model.

The boundedness of an institution is reflected in part by a stable and identifiable membership, with controlled entry. Stability of membership is measured by (1) the average number of terms served by members in a sitting legislature; (2) the number of terms served by terminating members; (3) the percentage of members serving in each decade who began service in that decade; and (4) the percentage of members in each legislature who are new. The last measurement has been questioned in historical analysis because the number of seats can change, and a fifth measurement, that of percentage replacements, has been suggested instead, which may be distinguished from a sixth, the percentage of incumbents who are replaced.

The importance of measurement choices is exemplified in the latter part of the twentieth century when much notice has been taken of the 95 percent or greater reelection success of incumbents in the House. This has drawn attention from the level of turnover, which is better represented by the figure of 85 percent.

There is the additional issue of whether to treat a newly elected member as a new member if prior service was performed in that body. If institutionalization is the issue, one might argue that a reelected former member supports stability, or counter that a body in which members often serve several non-consecutive terms lacks properties of institutionalization.

However change in membership is measured, attention to its sources is important because it reflects the worth and stability of the institution. It is especially important to know whether departure is voluntary or not. Involuntary departure, such as through death or defeat, suggests support for the institution by its members' desire to remain to the very end, whereas voluntary departure may imply a questioning of the value of the institution by its very own members.

Another set of indicators of the institutionalization of a legislative body involves the selection and tenure of members in stable, responsible leadership positions. An institutionalized leadership is recruited from within, serves an apprenticeship, has substantial tenure in office, and the upper leadership positions tend to be recruited from the lower.

One measurement of recruitment of leadership from within is the seniority of the persons attaining leadership positions. This affirms boundedness and autonomy, as lateral movement from other public institutional settings is diminished.

Further indication of professional institutionalized leadership is the absence of a career after holding a legislative leadership position. An example is a Speaker of the House who retires without a subsequent major career move. The archetypal representation of noninstitutionalized leadership is the nineteenth-century career of Henry Clay, who held a number of public offices, including three separate hitches as Speaker. In comparison to twentieth-century House leaders, he appears downright fickle in his political career moves. The study of the pattern of leadership change and stability has been extended beyond the more formal party leadership positions to include important committee chairs within particular historical periods.

Institutionalization is also denoted by internal complexity and the division of labor. The number of committees and/or subcommittees is found wanting as a measure and deservedly so. However, the members' perceptions of the influence and authority of committees and committee chairs can be used to verify the meaningfulness of the committees as responsible participants in the policy-making process.

Attesting to the autonomy and importance of committees and subcommittees is the use of party *committee* seniority in determining the rank of the member on the committee or subcommittee, including the selections of chairs of committees and subcommittees. A principal alternative more often observed in state legislatures than in Congress is the appointment of chairs by party leaders or party committees.

Observations may also be made of the use of chamber party seniority to choose between competitors for a committee seat, again as opposed to choices made at the chamber party level.

In the assessment of the influence of the seniority rule in the selection of committee chairs, care has been taken to account for exceptions to the seniority rules. Thus, the measurement of the frequency with which seniority determines committee chairmanships has been refined to discount compensated violations of this rule. Compensated violations include such things as chairmanship of an equal or better committee, assignment to a better committee, and movement to a leadership position.

Implicit in these uses of the seniority rule are tests for another property of institutionalization: the relative absence of particularistic and discretionary decision-making (e.g., choices of chairs by party leaders) and the presence of universalistic and automated decision-making. A less central measure of the concepts of universalistic nondiscretionary decision-making is the nonpartisanship of decisions regarding contested elections to a legislative chamber. A more institutionalized legislature is expected to decide these cases on the merits according to universally applied standards rather than along party lines.

Although we do not usually refer to the sites of measurement, particularly as between Congress and state legislatures, because most are applicable in both settings, we want to note that the availability of measurements to assess institutionalization bodes well for comparative state analysis. This is illustrated by excellent studies in the professionalization of state legislatures; the degree to which state legislatures select, elevate, and retain leaders in accordance with the terms of an institutionalized legislature; and the use of seniority as an "automatic" or nondiscretionary criterion for committee appointments.

Legislative Careers and Member Activities

Interest in the legislative institution in a society with the individualistic bias of the United States quite understandably leads to an interest in the properties of its members. Related to institutionalization are measurements bearing upon the legislative career, or life cycle, and upon the activities of the legislator.

Career advancement is observed relative to member occupancy of positions ranked from least desirable committee memberships to top leadership positions. Another aspect of life cycle is the change in attentiveness to the constituency. Interest in this phenomenon derives from the basic norm of constituency responsiveness generalized beyond policy representation to include services and symbolic representation.

In addition to participant observation or close observation of the constituency habits of members of a legislature, quantitative measures of constituency attentiveness have been constructed: number of trips to district, length of stay, days in district, mailings to constituents, authorship of columns, district radio programs, resources allocated to district offices, staff assigned to district, and number of staff assigned as caseworkers. In contrast, an argument has been made for a measurement based solely on number of days in the constituency. A major argument is that it involves the use of a scarce resource, the personal time of the member.

Also related to the life cycle, as well as career patterns and legislative goals, are the activities of the legislator within the body, particularly as they indicate the legislative effectiveness of the member. Measures of wide application include number of bills sponsored, floor speeches given, and number of amendments offered. More direct measures of effectiveness have also been employed. These are scored as success in getting bills—of some significance and for which the member has major responsibility—out of committee and passed; or within committees, ability to move legislation from subcommittee to full-committee consideration.

Possibly preceding the concern with legislator life cycles and career patterns was the interest in the social characteristics of the members. In focus are such concerns as the representational character of the institution.

Social Characteristics

The representational character of the legislature can be measured by the social characteristics of its members. Results of studies of occupational representation have been a bit predetermined because of the persistent predominance of lawyers, although trends toward other occupations, such as that of educator, have been noted. Also of interest is the movement away from the farm in an increasingly urbanized society, as well as the staying power of the rural constituency as the origin of legislative leaders. Education and income levels, along with occupation, form the three sides of the ubiquitous socioeconomic triangle that inevitably receives attention.

Gender and race have drawn little attention, with some exceptions, because variation has been lacking, particularly in Congress. However, there has been considerable interest in the change in the age of the typical legislator as an indicator of institutionalization (noted more specifically in the age at retirement).

Studies conducted mainly by historians have been quite interesting in their efforts to measure and use social characteristics. In addition to representativeness, there has been a concern with the level of democratization, as indicated by family status, evidence on prior and succeeding generations' political experience, ratio of commissioned officers to enlisted personnel, and generation in the United States.

In considering the legislature as an institution, it seems appropriate to conclude with the topic of legislative oversight of the executive/bureaucracy. Here we have the legislature exercising constitutional institutional prerogatives as it reviews the implementation of its laws, the spending of its appropriations, and checks on the capacity of the bureaucracy to serve the citizenry.

Oversight of the Bureaucracy

Legislative oversight of the bureaucracy occurs in many guises, from the investigation of constituent complaints to the frequent interactions of legislative and administrative staff to the full-blown investigation and hearing process involving special budgets and extra personnel. Following from this description, and given the size of even the state governments, legislative oversight of the bureaucracy would not appear to lend itself to systematic measurement without the commitment of great resources. Even then, study through the analysis of documents suffers from incompleteness; and interview and questionnaire surveys of the relevant actors are costly, time-consuming, and inevitably subject to the frustrations caused by the inaccessibility of legislators and top administrators.

This discussion of the task of measuring oversight underscores the introductory remarks concerning the difficulties in quantifying observations of legislative behavior, particularly as regards the necessary supplementary roles of inference and common sense. Thus, one compensation for limited access and quantifiability is to stop short of direct measurement and assess the potential for oversight by considering the conditions that cause the degree and/or type of oversight to vary. This can also be used, along with available observations, to make some assessment of the quality and quantity of oversight. In addition, the conditions may provide criteria for selecting particular committees for more intensive study.

Conditions affecting oversight are legal authority, staff resources, competence of the staff assessed in absolute terms or in comparison with the competence of the administrative counterparts, the priority attached to oversight by individual members, and the organization of committees to enhance oversight. Other conditions expected to increase oversight are the amount of public interest in a topic and the lack of trust between legislators and administrators. Trust is predictably at a premium when different parties control the executive and legislative branches.

The committees chosen for intensive study can be observed with respect to frequency of informal discussions between top staffers and administrators, committee sources of information on agency activities (media, hearings, complaints, interest groups, reports), development of informational networks, and the number of information sources and how well they are used. Additional indirect measures of oversight activity are the assessment (perhaps through interviews or observation) of the priorities of members regarding the role of overseer. Also used has been the type of monitoring, along a continuum from active at all times to selectively reactive.

This review of some of the measurements of oversight activity alters a first impression of a phenomenon of great complexity not subject to measurement. The potential for measurement derives from the large number of available indicators, from which may be drawn a subset whose cross-validating properties reduce the need for additional information. As is true for other areas of legislative research, the problem of the objectification of measurement is partly a function of a failure to establish research priorities and to allocate existing resources, primarily human labor. This is certainly also true of the next topic of this essay, the legislative committees.

LEGISLATIVE COMMITTEES

If not for his presidency, Woodrow Wilson's main claim to fame among legislative scholars might well be his widely accepted late-nineteenth-century observation on the dominant role of committees in Congress. The importance of committees in state legislatures is also indicated by legislator perceptions of the committee as the locus of significant decisions, relative to leadership offices, party caucuses, governors' offices, the floor, and informal legislative activity.

The central role of committees derives from the need for members to share the legislative work, principally at the formulation stage, in a manner that will ensure some level of subject-matter expertise among those most responsible for the legislative product. This also assists the legislature in being independent of the executive and powerful external interests.

With the assignment of policy-formulation responsibilities comes the potential for influence, to both good and bad ends. Consequently, considerable attention has been given to the exercise of influence: how committees may act as units to increase their influence; how individual members behave within the committee context to increase their own as well as the committee's influence; to what extent committee influence compromises representation; which are the most influential committees—the list goes on. However, many studies relating to committees are not focused directly on influence; rather, their influence is a given, and studies about them are concerned with how they and their members go about their work.

Committee Success

As a surrogate for the measurement of the influence or power of committees, researchers have used indicators of the success of the committee in working its will on the floor. Tabulated is the proportion of roll calls on which the committee position is supported. More general categorization of action taken on reported bills—favorable, unfavorable, and none—have also been undertaken. Other measures are aimed at different aspects of the process, measuring the ability of the committees to get bills reported to the floor, to obtain action on bills reported, to avoid procedural challenges, and to fend off rules or agreements that increase the possibility of changes on the floor.

However, these are not direct measures of influence and some may actually be determinants of success. Thus, committees may have differential success rates because they are subject to different rules governing the decision process on the floor. And others may appear more successful because their legislation has precedence on the floor.

Now if committee influence is not at issue, but one is concerned only with description at the level of outcome, it does not matter that some committees are successful because they are favored by the rules. This description becomes part of an overall understanding of how the legislative process works. However, many scholars find the more interesting question to be, after controlling for all other factors, which committees are the most effective, influential, and powerful, and why?

Committee Influence

The influence or power of the committee may be defined as the ability of the committee to get what it wants independent of the chamber's preference. Given that scholars have generally found it difficult to measure the exercise of power, it should not be surprising that committee power has also been an elusive phenomenon.

If committee power, or influence, is to be established, it is argued that measurement of the personal policy preferences of committee members must be compared with the final legislative product. The simple presentation of this requirement challenges many measurements of committee influence or power.

Consider a committee ordering on a power continuum according to the infrequency with which committee legislation is amended on the floor. This may be misleading. A weak committee may get a high score because it is very successful in anticipating the response of the chamber, suffers few amendments, but sacrifices its members' own policy preferences. Similarly, the stronger committee may get a lower score because it is willing to risk the incursion of amendments, even to accept some, but still gets legislation that approximates its own preferences more than that of the parent chamber. Here, as in other measurements of committee influence, the key difficulty would appear to be that of distinguishing between committee strategies that are based on anticipated reactions and those based on personal preferences.

Efforts to solve this problem have been creative, and as usual, not conclusive. They are also too complex to describe here. A taste (less accurate than illustrative) of the effort is offered. Imagine an analysis of roll-call voting of committee members undertaken to establish their personal preferences. These preferences are then related to preferences of full-chamber members in an analysis that asks the question: Was the final version of the legislation closer to the preferences of the committee members than to the preferences of the full chamber? Whatever the answer, we may anticipate a critic of the analysis questioning the assumptions underlying the validity of the roll-call-based procedure for establishing personal preferences.

Short of establishing personal preferences of committee members by direct questioning, there is the possibility of using knowledgeable observers such as personal and committee staff. However, the personal preference is still measured indirectly. Even were it possible to interview legislators about their personal preferences, doubts would arise about the willingness of the legislators to reveal their preferences; absent that concern, there would be questions about the competence of the researchers in measuring preferences openly expressed.

Indeed, the difficulties of measurement seen here are quite generalized and one might do well to accept something akin to a law of approximating measurements: no single measurement will be satisfactory for any but the simplest construct and the desired goal is several imperfect converging measurements. Time and effort expended in the search for the one true measurement would be better expended on reasonable approximations, and on the application of the common sense and experience referred to in the introduction of this essay.

Indirect Measures of Committee Influence

We take leave of the pure measurement of committee influence or power by taking note of some indirect measures of the influence of committees at a more general level. One such measure is the prestige or attractiveness of legislative committees.

Fairly convincing quantitative measurements come in several forms but essentially involve comparisons of transfers to and from committees. For example, a committee that no one leaves voluntarily would get a top rating while a committee to which no one transfers would get a bottom rating. A committee with higher turnover, either in absolute but preferably in proportional terms, gets a lower prestige ranking. More attractive committees are those for which members give up seniority on other committees to begin at the bottom of the seniority ladder. Less prestigious committees will have more freshmen members and will be characterized by a lower average full-chamber party seniority.

Most of these measurements are very good. However, it is recognized that the ordering on prestige or attractiveness is not fully unidimensional across the membership. Individual members order the committees differently according to their needs or goals with respect to the exercise of influence, the service of constituencies, and commitment to good policy.

Another indirect measurement of the influence of a committee is its standing as a source of legislation. The following indicators, drawn from a committee's structure and internal operations, suggest the presence of serious policy-making activity: (1) the number of subcommittee meetings relative to those of the full committee, thereby discounting the formation of committees just to give members assignments to report to their constituents and spouses; (2) the ratio of standing to special subcommittees, the former likely to have a continuing specified jurisdiction of policy-making, and the latter a temporary status; (3) the ratio of named subcommittees to numbered ones, assuming the difference is between a defined and an undefined jurisdiction, or between a continuing responsibility and a temporary task; and (4) the amount of legislation reported to the full committee.

Aside from the concern with their influence, or tangential to the given condition of influence, researchers have examined the internal process of committees and tried to understand better the sources and effects of committee-member behavior. The following section deals with internal functioning and member behavior.

Committee Integration

The effectiveness and influence of a committee is often thought to be determined by its internal integration. Most simply put, at issue is the viability of the committee as a working unit.

Committee integration is a concept of such complexity, and of difficulty in precise conceptualization, that both conceptual and operational definitions will be varied. Loosely speaking, the integration of a committee implies the ability of its members to establish procedures for settling their differences, respecting each others roles, and producing a legislative product. An integrated committee is one that has the ability to repair stretched and frayed seams after centrifugal forces of disintegration have been subdued.

One of the difficulties of measuring committee integration is the likelihood of noncomparability of its manifestation across committees. For example, some committees may appear to have solved the problem of partisan division, presumably a force for disintegration, by subscribing to a norm against partisanship. Another committee may explicitly provide for limited partisanship as a necessary working condition. Yet another committee may find the absence of strongly held partisan views to be dysfunctional to committee decision-making (damn the consensus and full partisanship instead!).

One approach to the measurement of integration is on-site observation and interviews with the principals. This may also be the best given the need for observing the complex, dynamic interpersonal relationships and formal and informal social structures that reveal the degree of integration. However, the costs of replications across committees and time are great.

Alternative measurements that do not bear such high costs have been suggested. One is the degree to which committee members vote together on the floor on legislation originating in their committee. An alternative approach is to measure committee-member voting cohesion across all bills reported by all committees, on the grounds that integration implies agreement on fundamental values that needs to be assessed on a wide range of legislative issues. Yet another approach is to measure agreement within a committee relative to that observed on a set of members with similar vote-disposing characteristics.

Clearly there is the potential for disagreement in both conceptualization and measurement noted earlier. In particular, integration defined as the persistence of a system of relationships, which might for example accommodate fairly unrestrained partisanship, is getting at quite a different phenomenon than does a definition of integration as agreement on fundamentals as revealed in voting on a wide range of policy questions.

Committee Process and Member Activity

Given the important role of committees in American legislatures, the understanding of the legislative process requires good observations on the behaviors of committee members and their staffs. Investigators have the usual difficulty of access to the legislators, forcing them to depend in part on well-connected observers such as journalists or lobbyists for the outside interests. However, it is preferable to rely more on the committee or legislator office staffs, and on the documentary record, the latter being much more extensive for Congress than state legislatures.

A number of inventive studies have tried to use these resources in the committee context to study such difficult topics as the influence of interest groups, the relation of the legislators' purposive roles to their actual behavior, the role of staff, and the more general considerations of the paths and substance of the flow of information to legislators. The more convincing studies are those that focus on particular pieces of legislation and are very systematic and comprehensive in the gathering of data on its legislative processing. For example, with respect to information flow, an informative study is one that can identify the particular sources and the specific content of the information on which members rely, in order to observe its flow and influence on key actors. However, these focused studies involve a major investment, particularly in view of the need for replication to avoid the stigma of the "case study" from which it is difficult to generalize.

More readily available measurements reflect the opportunities for participation and influence: seniority or leadership position within the committees, minority- or majority-party status, participation in conference committees to settle differences between the two legislative chambers—except in the unicameral Nebraska legislature—and responsible roles in floor management of, and debate on, committee-sponsored legislation. Access to staff through interviews can provide mutually reinforcing information about the legislative influence of members, or call into question the findings from the more public record.

Participation of members in legislative activity on particular legislative issues, which can be used as an indicator of the effort to exercise influence, is measured from documentary records of attendance, speaking, voting, and offering amendments at markup sessions of committees and subcommittees. Gradations of each of these forms of activities increase the sensitivity of the measurements, for example, whether proposed amendments are major, minor, or technical changes.

Other Committee Characteristics

A number of other characteristics of committees have been measured for particular purposes. Examples are partisanship, measured by comparing the level of party cohesion within a committee to that of similar members not on the committee; committee heterogeneity, captured as variation in the safeness of seats or as partisanship of members' districts; and representativeness of committees, for which a number of measurements may be used, such as geographic distribution, ideological balance, urban-rural composition, and industry representation.

Supporting the operation of committees, and of the institution more generally, is a complex of legislator norms, roles, and objectives or goals.

NORMS, ROLES, OBJECTIVES, AND GOALS

The legislature is an institution particularly needful of rules and norms because of the disparate constituencies to which the members must respond. This requirement augments dispositions toward individual independence that already need little encouragement. Thus, the effective legislature is governed by rules that assign different functions to the members, create a division of labor, provide for orderly procedures, determine the membership, and specify the means by which decisions are made.

These formal rules, although recognized as being important, were slighted somewhat as the scholars of Congress became more behavioral and less historical, legalistic, and prescriptive in their studies. There arose a fascination with the unwritten rules of behavior, the norms of the institution. Since these were not codified or formally documented, they had to be inferred from various sources of evidence; from our perspective, they had to be measured.

The interest in norms was accompanied by an interest in the legislators' conceptions of the roles they played in the legislature. Role analysis was a means toward understanding what motivates legislative behavior. This is exemplified by the representational roles to which so much attention has been given. Whom do legislators represent: their constituents, their parties, or their personal attitudes? How do they see their relationship to interest groups? How do they relate to the policy-making process?

Related phenomena are the goals and objectives of legislators. Presumably if these can be measured, we can get other useful perspectives on the behavior of individual members.

The examination of roles, norms, objectives, and goals may be viewed as the most direct attempt to find out what makes legislators tick as human beings in this sociopolitical context. Who are they, what are they doing, why, and how are they constrained by the norms of the institution?

Norms

Norms that are most closely reviewed here are those of specialization, reciprocity, seniority, apprenticeship, and institutional loyalty. The apparent importance of norms, and the usual problem of legislator access, has resulted in measurement that is often impressionistic and unsystematic. The immutability and importance of some of these norms, as well as the quality of the measurement, have been challenged in certain studies. Measurements of the presence and effects of the different norms have been made through interviews with legislators, staff, and others with frequent legislator contact. Or they have been based on public documents.

This essay pays more attention to the document-based measurement of norms than might appear to be warranted by a reading of general works on the legislature where the emphasis is more likely to be on interview-derived measures. This approach has been undertaken because of the substantial variety and availability of documentary evidence. Also, this evidence has the advantage of reflecting behavior, as opposed to the attitudinal and perceptual measures whose linkage to behavior may be tenuous. The latter argument partially offsets the entirely appropriate criticism that the documentary measures are indirect, and all that one can claim is that the results are consistent with the existence of the norms.

The first norm to be considered in some detail, specialization, involves an expectation shared by legislators that members will develop areas of expertise and confine their activities thereto. This expectation can be measured by interviewing members and staff.

In the absence of interview data, specialization is indicated by the number of committee and subcommittee assignments per member. The offering of amendments on the floor by committee members, as opposed to committee nonmembers, constitutes other evidence. The accounting may involve the number of committee member versus noncommittee member amendments to legislation on the floor, or the ratio of the number of committee and noncommittee members so involved. Also relevant is the tolerance of the legislative body for nonspecialized behavior. This is reflected in the relative success of amendments proposed by committee and noncommittee members and can be measured for individual members as well as for the body.

Other indicators of specialization involve the substantive range of individual member bills and amendments, with the assumption being that the more specialized members are, the narrower will be the range of their substantive policy interests. One measurement considers the diversity of committee origins of legislation in which the legislator is involved. Another measurement depends on content coding of the amendments and bills. The latter may be preferred, especially in bodies where individual committee assignments are numerous or committee jurisdictions are heterogeneous.

Overlapping the norm of specialization is that of reciprocity, as when committee members stay on their own turf in offering legislation. Other aspects of reciprocity are abundantly in evidence but difficult to measure. Illustrative are common courtesy (sometimes treated as a separate norm) and the implicit logroll (a silent agreement made by legislators to support each other's legislation).

A norm not reviewed here, because it was discussed in relation to institutionalization, concerns the iron ladder of seniority to which the member has to cling and climb to gain preference and attain power. When combined with reciprocity, specialization in policy involvement, and the division of labor, the operation of seniority provides evidence of committees as powerful, independent policy-making entities.

Another norm with many ties to other legislative behaviors is that of apprenticeship. It relates to institutionalization, for it is a means toward acceptance within a bounded institution which, when abetted by the norm of seniority, is potentially a dominating component of the role of freshman legislator. Its meaning is commonly recognized in the dictums to listen, learn, and speak when asked—briefly. However, disagreement about its universality exists. Some of this disagreement may be a function of the many indicators used.

Apprenticeship has been measured through interviews and by using indicators drawn from documentary sources. The latter measures include the following: tenure when making maiden speech, offering first amendment, managing first bill, or getting first bill passed; and staff allocations and other perquisites. Collectively, there are measurements based on the seniority of members making amendments, procedural motions, debating legislation, and being assigned to conference committees. These behavioral indicators certainly deserve consideration along with interview-based measures.

The last norm to be discussed, that of institutional loyalty or patriotism, is one whose health is uncertain. If it is measured as an unwillingness to speak ill of the institution, it is either in decline or has long been overrated. If it is a willingness to assert congressional prerogatives in the face of executive, judicial, and bureaucratic challenges, the signs of life are there but systematic measurement is not.

Legislatures in the United States have been so consistently the source of pejorative humor that institutional loyalty suffers the condition of the bastard child of sickly demeanor known only to its parents. Its public display is not approached with alacrity. Given the importance of this norm to the effective functioning of an institution, legislative scholars may perform a public service by giving more attention to its measurement, and by doing so, support its legitimacy.

At the same time that legislative scholars developed a behavioral interest in norms, a comparable investigation of roles occurred. This investigation delved into the legislators' views of the roles they played on the crowded and busy legislative stage. More recently, attention was given to the related objectives, or goals of legislators.

Legislative Roles, Objectives, and Goals

Role theory in the study of American legislatures has had many applications. Most salient is the definition of the alternative representational roles of delegate, trustee, and politico. Given the centrality of the concept of representation in legislative politics, the attention to these roles is understandable.

The measurement of these roles usually involves a direct request to the legislator to respond as to which of the characterizations most applies to him or her: one who votes according to the wishes of the constituency or as a trustee whose primary responsibility is to exercise independent judgment, or who feels that one or the other applies at different times. Representational areal focuses—district or national—have been studied as well and tend to overlap with representational responsibilities, particularly in the trustee/national and delegate/district combinations.

The utility of the representational role definitions has been criticized, beginning with complaints that they have not been used in explaining or predicting behavior. Other complaints have been that member behavior is not consistent with subjective role definitions or it is consistent only under certain conditions. These criticisms reflect the difficulty and question the utility of measuring global role constructs.

Different techniques have been used to measure a tremendous variety of legislator roles or role orientations. In addition to classifying themselves, legislators have been categorized by researchers coding their responses to questions, and others have presented legislators with series of questions or statements used to order them on role continuums, such as from delegate at one extreme to trustee at another. Among the roles that have been measured are tribune (spokesperson for the people), ritualist (legislative professional), inventor (creative thinker, problem solver), broker (reconciler of divergent interests), and opportunist (candidate for reelection). There are more. On the basis of questions regarding attitudes toward party and toward interest groups, the party roles of superloyalists, loyalists, neutrals, and mavericks were defined while the roles of facilitators, resistors, and neutrals have been defined in relation to interest groups.

A characteristic of legislative studies using role theory is the dependence on the legislator to define his or her roles. Generally not used is the power of role theory to predict individual

behavior given a measurement of the role expectations of others (teachers lecture; students take notes). With rare exception such measures have not been taken. Consequently, we do not know to what extent role definitions derive from highly individualized, internally generated adaptations to a particular and unfamiliar environment as opposed to role-oriented perceptions of the expectations of others.

Related to norms and roles with respect to the motivations and behaviors of legislators are the objectives or goals of legislators, which have been put forth and quite widely accepted as useful characterizations of motivations and behaviors. Examples are the goals of reelection, good policy, internal institutional influence, and personal betterment. The validity of these well-accepted characterizations has rarely been challenged by enlisting more demanding measurement tests. These involve an observation of the match between verbal responses reflecting the different goals and the legislators' allocation of time to different goal-relevant tasks.

This essay on the measurement of legislative behavior quite appropriately concludes with the measurement of voting behavior. For this is the last stage of the legislative process, and it is most amenable to measurement.

LEGISLATIVE VOTING BEHAVIOR

Measurement of voting in legislatures has been used for a variety of purposes, varying from the analysis of legislator positions in a specific policy area to the testing of general propositions about legislator voting behavior. Four general areas of interest account for much of the voting research. One is the degree to which members vote along party lines, implicitly demonstrating the influence of party. The influence of constituency, of ideology, and the degree of presidential support are the others. These may be analyzed separately or put into a competitive context. Much of this analysis is furthered by the presence of data on the voting record over time. With respect to Congress, there is the ready availability of all roll-call votes since 1789, along with descriptions of the issues involved. State legislative voting records are much less accessible to analysis.

Our coverage is biased toward measurement based on large numbers of voting divisions in plenary sessions of legislative bodies. We will not review here the research concerned with strategies of voting.

Voting divisions are recorded in several ways, listed here in order of the declining likelihood of error and/or willful misrepresentation by the presiding official: voice votes, standing votes, teller votes in which the members pass by tellers of those for and against, roll calls on which the voiced yeas and nays of individual members are recorded, and roll-call votes recorded by electronic means.

For the most part, analysis is restricted to roll-call (RC) divisions that provide information on the individual member's vote. A common further restriction is the exclusion of the unanimous and near-unanimous RCs. The proportion of members required to be in the minority in this case is often 10 percent, but it may be 20 percent or less than 10.

The decision to exclude certain RCs in a study depends on one's purpose. Used as indicators of underlying dimensions, for instance of liberal-conservative voting, lopsided RCs run a risk of being uninformative. Thus the appearance of a small number of members in the minority may be due to a variety of idiosyncratic reasons rather than to a shared minority dissent from a majority position. Also, near-unanimous and unanimous RCs are often on procedural motions or involve noncontroversial votes for mother, home, and national sovereignty.

Unanimous and Near-Unanimous Voting

Given the academic penchant for noting the omissions or deficiencies of common practice, it is not surprising that some scholars would suggest the need to give more attention to these unanimous or near-unanimous RCs. Attention to the low-dissension RC is defensible on the general grounds that any unstudied phenomenon may represent a lost opportunity. For example, why do overwhelming majorities form in contradiction of the logic of the minimum winning coalition? If fewer members can agree on more, why broaden the coalition unnecessarily? Also, more study of consensus in a legislature might serve to counterbalance the appearance of conflict that rarely enhances its public image. An extension of this logic is to study motions passed by unanimous consent and the full set of divisions—voice, standing, teller—that for some reason were not subjected to a roll call.

Conflictual Voting

Returning to the "normal" analysis of roll-call voting that attends to the more conflictual RCs, we begin with a basic consideration in most of these measurements. While individual voting divisions may be studied as important distinct phenomena, there is a natural drive to include multiple RCs in an analysis. This is in accordance with an axiom of measurement that the more indicators, the better. Thus, the common occurrence of two or more RCs on various aspects of one piece of legislation, or of multiple RCs on particular substantive categories of legislation, holds the promise of more valid and more reliable measurements than can be achieved by confining the analysis to a single RC.

Party Voting Given the importance of political parties in legislatures, a number of measures have been used to represent different aspects of party voting. The level of party voting in the legislative body has been measured variously. One category of these measures requires different levels of oppositional majorities, appropriate to a country whose legislatures consist primarily of Democrats and Republicans. Most commonly a party vote is defined either as at least 90 percent of each party opposing the other, or as a majority of Democrats voting against a majority of Republicans.

Although the 90-percent opposition level was the first used, the simple-majority opposition requirement has become the preferred measure. Especially as regards the heavily studied Congress, the latter, lesser requirement appears to be more useful because of the scarcity of the higher levels of opposition. In addition, there is a reasonable argument for the simple-majority measure.

In a polity where majority rule has substantial credibility and legitimacy, a majority of the members of any group agreeing upon a position is reasonable to construe as an indication of a group position. This is affirmed by the additional requirement of opposing groups. Although seldom done, it would be desirable to require that there be evidence that members of a party have sought to establish a party position, thereby reducing the possibility that the division may have arisen for nonpartisan reasons.

Having designated a party vote, the measurement of party loyalty can be applied to individual members. This is usually the proportion of the party votes on which a member votes with his or her party majority.

A different category of party-voting measures, not dependent on an oppositional criterion, assesses the degree of difference between the parties on individual roll calls. One measurement of party difference, or its complement, party likeness, is simplicity itself: the difference in the percentages of two parties voting yea (or nay), irrespective of their majority positions.

Relative to the oppositional measure, its advantages are that: (1) variation in degrees of party difference are measured instead of the simple observation of opposition; and (2) there is no need for an arbitrary definition of a party vote. However, these gains are at the expense of a potentially valuable qualitative difference between legislative motions that have engendered bipolarized partisan voting and those that have not. On the other hand, the flexibility of quantification allows the observance of a large party difference ignored by the oppositional measure; for example, when a bare 51 percent of Republicans vote with 99 percent of the Democrats.

Included within the "party difference" category of measures are a large number of coefficients of correlations of party with vote. Although varying in their particulars, these coefficients share a common attention to the degree to which the yeas and nays are distributed differently within the two parties. Maximum values occur when all the yeas are cast by one party and all the nays by the other. In addition to being highly related to measures of party difference, these coefficients are also indifferent to the qualitative distinction between bipolarity and unipolarity of partisanship.

Correlational measures can also be used to assess the level of party voting with respect to indexes of voting based on subsets of individual roll calls with demonstrated substantive coherence. This is preferred on the ground that these indexes are representations of definable voting patterns on which the level of party voting is more meaningful than that achieved by a grand summary measure based on all RCs taken in a one-year session or two-year Congress.

Party Cohesion The level of party voting involves a comparison of the behavior of the two parties. Also of interest is the level of party cohesion within individual parties. This is calculated simply as the difference in the percentages of the party members voting yea and nay. Cohesion is minimal when the intraparty division is 50–50 and maximum under the condition of 100-percent agreement. Although seldom done, the two percentages could be converted into proportions, multiplied, and presented as the variance in a set of 0, 1 scores (e.g., 0 = yea, 1 = nay). This has the advantage of comparability to a host of measures using variance as a measure of heterogeneity (lack of cohesion).

It is also important to recognize that a different meaning may attach to cohesion when it occurs along with substantial party differences than when parties are in substantial agreement. This is most clearly illustrated by the "hurrah" vote of total consensus, where the impetus for party cohesion is not party-based.

A measure that attacks this problem combines the intraparty cohesion with the interparty difference by multiplication, producing a measurement of party strength for each party. An alternative is to restrict the measurement of cohesion to oppositional party votes.

The time spent on measuring and analyzing party voting is consistent with the importance of parties as the principal organizers of political activists and elites. There is also, however, the concept of bipartisanship, which may be defined as more than 50 percent of both parties voting in the same direction. Bipartisanship has attracted relatively little attention, in part due to its rigid complementarity to party voting.

However, attention has been given to the concept of universalistic voting. By one definition, this is 90 percent or more of the members of a body voting in the same direction. Although it is also negatively related to party voting, it does not have the same rigid complementarity to party voting. The slippage resides in the bipartisan roll calls on which more than 50 percent of each party agree but the agreement does not rise to the level of 90 percent of all members. Roll calls in this residual category have been designated as cross-cutting, in that the resulting divisions do not follow party lines.

The meaning of universalistic voting is yet to be established. One source of occurrence, beyond the "hurrah" vote, is legislation that distributes largesse to all members in a massive logroll of advantage to all constituencies.

Coalitions   A natural and common alternative to party voting in the legislative setting is the coalition, which crosses party lines. The coalition that has received the most attention, the Conservative Coalition, emerged in the U.S. Congress during the New Deal of the 1930s. It was originally defined as a coalition of a majority of northern Republicans allied with a majority of southern Democrats against a majority of northern Democrats. The number of southern Republicans was very small. Their increase has been accompanied by a conservatism more than equal to their northern brethren, so the sectional cast of the coalition has been somewhat diminished as all Republicans now form one component.

The sectional bases of the coalitional opponents represents a historically persistent theme in congressional politics. Measures of sectional voting have been several and important. The Conservative Coalition is used as our example because of its dominance among coalitions in the last half of the twentieth century, its repeated measurements, its visibility due to coverage by the *Congressional Quarterly,* and its additional use as a measurement of liberal-conservative ideology.

Coalitions may also be induced from voting patterns, without prior prescription as to membership. In this context, a potentially intersecting companion to the coalition is the voting bloc.

Cluster Bloc Analysis

The voting bloc embodies a principal concern with agreement among a set of members (e.g., the farm bloc). Voting blocs, or cluster blocs, are statistically derived from paired inter-

member similarity tabulations. While different measurements of similarities in voting behavior are available, the percentage agreement observed on pairings of legislators across a set of yea/nay votes represents what is being measured by most scholars.

Although not a requirement, cluster A of legislators may be accorded more validity as a bloc if its members disagree with legislators in cluster B, who themselves are in high agreement with one another. Invoked here is the principle that similarities are brought into sharper relief in juxtaposition with dissimilarities. This helps solve the measurement "altitude" problem of how high the agreement among members must be to infer a cluster bloc: higher than the agreement of members drawn from different cluster blocs.

One difficulty with the interperson-similarity measures is that their observation, across all pairs of legislators, may be daunting even with advanced methodology and computer assistance. The number of pairings is only slightly fewer than the number of legislators squared divided by two; for example, the current Senate membership of one hundred produces 4,950 pairs.

A major methodological problem, not restricted to studies of large memberships but seldom lessened in that condition, is that clusters of similar legislators do not form in neat array. It becomes truly problematic as to how many clusters there are and into which one each legislator fits.

The cluster-bloc procedure has been used for a variety of analytic purposes such as the testing of impressionistic views of existing groups, the settlement of historical controversies, and the analysis of issue-based voting behavior. Some of the same issues may be addressed by a methodology that bears many formal similarities but is launched from a different measurement platform. This is the method of dimensional analysis.

Dimensional Analysis

Dimensional analysis became an integral part of roll-call voting studies with the application of Guttman scalogram analysis. Guttman scaling held the promise of using several roll calls to measure legislator attitudes or policy positions, instead of relying on single indicators.

The central assumptions are that: (1) a single dimension—liberal/conservative, antislavery/proslavery, prolife/prochoice—accounts for voting on two or more roll calls; (2) both legislators and legislative motions are ordered on this dimension (e.g., in terms of their liberalness); and (3) this ordering manifested by a particular pattern of voting on a unidimensional set of roll calls.

The Guttman scaling model is very demanding with respect to the pattern of voting that must be observed to demonstrate the case for unidimensionality. Comparable techniques have been developed that substitute other measurement assumptions and make competing claims to validity.

Alternatives to the Guttman model involve pairings of divisions on roll calls. The roll-call pairings are treated very similarly to the cluster bloc pairings of legislators. The search for clusters of roll calls that measure a dimension replaces the search for clusters of legislators. Similarly, the validity of the dimensional interpretation is enhanced by observing a second cluster of roll calls that do not correlate highly with the first but do with each other.

There are a large number of dimensional-analysis techniques available including factor analysis, multidimensional scaling, and many varieties of cluster analysis. However, to the extent that there is a strong voting structure, the different techniques tend to converge on the same interpretation.

Shared by most of the dimensional techniques is the assumption that a legislator will accept legislation that is less strongly in support of a policy than the legislator would prefer. For example, liberals must not ally with the conservatives against the moderates in rejecting legislation, just because the legislation is not liberal enough. If this occured frequently, it would be necessary to enlist a proximity model that is more sensitive to the difference between the legislation offered and the legislators' ideal of the proper legislation.

If the proximity model were to fit legislative voting, it would not be possible to use the correlational or similarities approach of most dimensional-analysis techniques. The fact that these techniques work extremely well, at least statistically speaking, suggests that the extremes seldom join forces against the middle.

Another method of dimensional analysis, spatial analysis, locates the yea and nay positions on the roll calls along with the positions of the legislators in a space subject to dimensional analysis. Although not used by many researchers, it has demonstrated great statistical power in analyzing large numbers of roll calls over time. For this reason and because its application has suggested the dominance of a single dimension in congressional voting for most of the life of the Republic, it has received much attention.

Roll-Call Content in Dimensional Analysis

Most of the methods described thus far allow the statistical analysis a major role in defining the content of a yea or nay vote. An alternative is for the researcher to categorize each vote, as for example liberal or conservative, and score legislators on the number of liberal and conservative votes. This requires substantial knowledge of the legislative setting in order to be certain of the intent of a motion and the reasons for support and rejection. Still, it may avoid the imputation of meaning solely on the basis of statistical consistency.

Policy content has also been used to categorize legislation before subjecting it to dimensional analysis. This is commonly referred to as policy-dimensional analysis. One argument in its favor is that the resulting measures of voting are characterized by substantive coherence, for such was the categorization of the RCs prior to the analysis. Otherwise, it is quite possible for substantively disparate roll calls to form a dimension, in statistical terms, since techniques examine only the voting alignments and are blind as to content.

Arguments against this approach are well represented by the charge that the policy dimensions are an artifact of the initial content categorizations. Thus, the RCs found in multiple dimensions would have fit on many fewer dimensions, absent the categorizations. Somewhat predictably, multiple dimensions do tend to be found by those who use the policy-dimension approach, whereas one or two dimensions are more likely to be found by those who rely on statistical procedures without prior content differentiation. Results are often dependent on procedure.

We now turn to analyses of congressional

voting in which the researcher selects subsets of votes for particular purposes.

Presidential-Support Measures

Presidential-support measures receive attention because of their wide usage in the analysis of the influence of the single most powerful actor in the national legislative arena. Most common are the presidential-support scores, computed as the number of times a member takes the same position on a roll call as the president. These scores are less likely to be used for pre-1953 Congresses, when they were not provided by *Congressional Quarterly,* because of the substantial difficulty of determining the president's position on particular roll calls without temporally proximate access.

Criticisms of these measures are that: (1) even when divided into foreign- and domestic-policy measures they are highly aggregative with respect to policy; (2) they do not measure support so much as they measure agreement with the president's position; (3) equal weight is given to issues in the absence of knowledge regarding the priorities of the president; and (4) presidents may manipulate support scores by taking positions on measures likely to be supported by large majorities. Access to information on these matters is limited and normally is subject to substantial historical lag.

In an effort to separate support of the president from existing agreement with the president, to get at executive influence, the presidential-support positions of members have been compared to their "general policy" positions. To the extent that there is a difference, it is possible that presidential influence is being measured.

Presidential-support measures have also been constructed at the institutional level. Examples are frequency of attempts to override presidential vetoes; success in overriding (measured as either success or failure, or numbers of votes supporting override); and the presidential box score, which records congressional dispositions of presidential requests. The latter has the distinct advantage in that its scoring is not limited to requests that make it to the roll-call stage. Similar in this respect is a measurement that compares presidential requests in the State of the Union message with passage, or not, of legislation consistent with those requests.

Congressional support for the president at the bipartisan level is often discussed in the area of foreign policy. This is reasonably measured as the majorities of both parties voting with the president, either measured within each chamber or across both.

Not to be neglected in this discussion of purpose-driven subselections of roll calls are the numerous measurements of the policy positions produced by interest groups and publications. Interest groups have been particularly active for a number of years in assessing the performance of legislators relative to their policy preferences. This is typically accomplished by selecting a subset of roll calls dealing with topics of interest to the group and scoring members according to how often they took the group's preferred position.

One of these group ratings is of particular interest given its use in academic research to measure the liberalness of individual members of Congress, and by implication, their conservativeness. This is the rating provided by the Americans for Democratic Action (ADA). A conservative complement, sometimes used instead of or in combination with the ADA rating, is the ACA rating of the Americans for Constitutional Action.

Ideology in Congressional Voting

Attention to the measurement of ideology in congressional roll-call voting is warranted by the widespread use of the liberal and conservative labels in American legislative politics, and in American politics generally. In addition, it involves major issues in the interpretation and analysis of legislative voting behavior.

Measurements of legislators' ideological placement are undertaken for two general purposes. One is descriptive, enabling the depiction of the current Congress as more liberal than its predecessor or one senator as more conservative than another. The other is causal, allowing for the attribution of a representative's voting behavior to a liberal or conservative ideology.

The two different purposes can be illustrated in very familiar terms. The Americans for Democratic Action (ADA) rate members of

Congress as to their liberalness. It produces a valid description of the degree of liberalness of legislators, according to this organization, whose judgment must then be evaluated.

However, dispute ensues when these ADA ratings are converted into a measure of liberal/ conservative ideology, used to explain roll-call voting behavior. Implicit in the support for this measurement is the assumption that if the member acts as a liberal, he or she must be one. In the eyes of the critic, this assumption errs in making the outcome the predicate of the cause.

The critics also point out that the behavior characterized by the ADA may have its roots in the many familiar determinants of legislative voting behavior: constituency, region, party, and interest groups. Accordingly, at best, the ADA rating measures an unknown degree of influence exerted by member location on an ideological dimension. At worst, ideology may have nothing to do with it. And predicting other voting from ADA ratings may succeed because both the predictor and the predicted are caused by the same nonideological determinants.

In efforts to isolate the ideological component, attempts have been made to remove the impact of the other factors that cause the behavior reflected in the ADA ratings. This sometimes produces residual orderings on the ideological dimension that fly in the face of accepted characterizations of different legislators. Nor should it be too surprising that when the effects of determinants of voting correlated with ideology are removed, so is the ideology.

The classification of members as liberal, conservative, or moderate based on their ordering on the ADA index, without the added burden of measuring liberal-conservative ideology, is of a piece with a large number of classifications of legislators used over the years. This includes Progressives, radicals, boll weevils, isolationists, states' righters, and so on. These classifications include members who commonly vote together on specified issues and share predisposing characteristics. They are useful groupings for analytic purposes because they highlight differences, underscore similarities, and support generalizations about complex phenomena.

Notably lacking in the studies of roll-call voting has been the distribution and use of voting measures constructed by academic researchers. However, there has been wide distribution of indexes constructed by the *Congressional Quarterly,* or published by it but originating with interest-group rating services. Following is a subject listing of Congressional Quarterly index publications and their dates up through 1990: party voting (1946–1990), conservative coalition (1959–1990), presidential support–general (1953–1990), presidential support–foreign policy, domestic policy (1955–1971), bipartisan voting (1947–1978), limit federal spending (1957–1959), large federal role (1959–1968), group ratings–ADA, ACA, COPE (1959–1990), NFU (1961–1978), and voting attendance (1946–1990).

Although not strictly within the realm of this essay, it seems necessary to note at least that there has been significant work focusing on the process by which legislators decide how to vote. This includes the content of the precipitating factors and has highlighted a very important question: How do legislators manage to cast hundreds of votes on a diverse array of topics in a reasonably efficient and sensible manner? This question is particularly appropriate for the legislatures in which party discipline is lax and the party position is but one cue. These studies have used simulation techniques, dimensional and cluster-bloc analyses, and interview data.

CONCLUSION

The measurement of legislative behavior is widely practiced in the United States. This reflects the strong preference for descriptive and explanatory research as opposed to normative prescriptive treatises. However, measurement takes place without a corresponding effort to develop and refine techniques, and without soul-searching consideration of the correspondence between the conceptual construct and its measurement. Even in the area of roll-call voting behavior, where measurement methodology has been a greater concern than in any other area of legislative behavior, attention to measurement techniques has waned since the 1950s and 1960s. This lack of attention is only slightly exaggerated by the example of the ADA ratings of members of Congress: a small band of ideological liberals, using a small number of roll calls, measuring liberal/conservative ideology.

The measurement practices of legislative scholars reflect their wide-ranging efforts to comprehend the internal structure and processes of a complex institution, and the relationship of it and its constituent components with the rest of the political system. Advantage has been taken of available data, sometimes quite ingeniously. Unfortunately, this advantage has usually been limited to the resources commanded by individual scholars, working alone or in pairs.

The more effective measurement of legislative behavior requires two developments. The first is the formation of coteries of specialists on different aspects of legislative structure and process. Such specialization is required to provide the intellectual intercourse so essential for the clarification and measurement of concepts. It is also needed to ensure the second development, that of adequate data bases. This requires the pooling of resources and concerted efforts to obtain support from government and private foundations, and from the more limited coffers of academic institutions.

Not to be neglected in these efforts is the inclusion of the studies of state legislatures. This is an important if not essential means toward the comparative analysis that is crucial to the development of concepts and refinements of measurement. While Congress has not been overstudied, the state legislatures have been understudied.

To close, the importance of measurement, systematic replicable observation, derives from its public availability. The insightful legislative scholar, dependent on impressionistic soundings, carries to the grave his or her working assumptions and ways of cognizing and perceiving legislative behavior, leaving no legacy of method and measurement for others to use in the quest for knowledge. Indeed, the successful search for knowledge that does not leave a map has only partly fulfilled its mission.

BIBLIOGRAPHY

A bibliographic guide to legislative measurement is foreshortened by, and even inconsistent with, the practice of measurement in legislative research, though certainly there are occasional works on methods and measurement that offer critiques, alternative approaches, thoughtful reviews of efforts in a specialized area, or some combination thereof. A work of the latter variety is DUNCAN MACRAE, *Issues and Parties in Legislative Voting: Methods of Statistical Analysis* (New York, 1970). Here the author notes a concern consistent with our general point that measurement in legislative research is not subject to comprehensive treatment: "Unlike a general textbook on research methods, this book deals with methods of measurement and classification related to *particular* concepts." However, even this more specialized instructional treatment is not generally available.

The status of the issue of measurement in legislative scholarship is reflected in our inability to cite a chapter on measurement in a well-regarded, comprehensive review of the legislative research field. GERHARD LOEWENBERG, SAMUEL C. PATTERSON, and MALCOLM E. JEWELL, eds., *Handbook of Legislative Research* (Cambridge, Mass., 1985), may be consulted, however, for reviews of major components of legislative analysis, typically involving references to issues of methodology. These may be perused for citation of major publications that may exemplify the measurement methodologies in the various subfields. A review of legislative research by LEROY RIESELBACH, "The Forest for the Trees: Blazing Trails for Congressional Research," in ADA FINIFTER, ed., *Political Science: The State of the Discipline,* (Washington, D.C., 1983), provides an abbreviated guide to the discipline.

The absence of general works on measurement is quite understandable. Legislative scholars do not offer measurements in vacuo; rather, they are imbedded in applications and designed to serve an immediate need. Also, the fact that legislative research does not constitute a distinct discipline means that people coming to this field bring along the measurement techniques learned in their more general disciplines or borrowed from others.

Bibliographic reference to selected works could not approach anything resembling a representative indication. Indeed, it would be a flat contradiction of the witness of this essay to the variety and innovativeness of the measurement efforts of legislative research scholars, and might imply that which does not exist—a stock of measurements, evaluated for their validity and reliability, upon which to draw.

SEE ALSO Agenda Setting, Actors, and Alignments in Congressional Committees; The Congressional Committee System; Congressional Oversight; Modern Legislative Careers; AND The Motivations of Legislators.